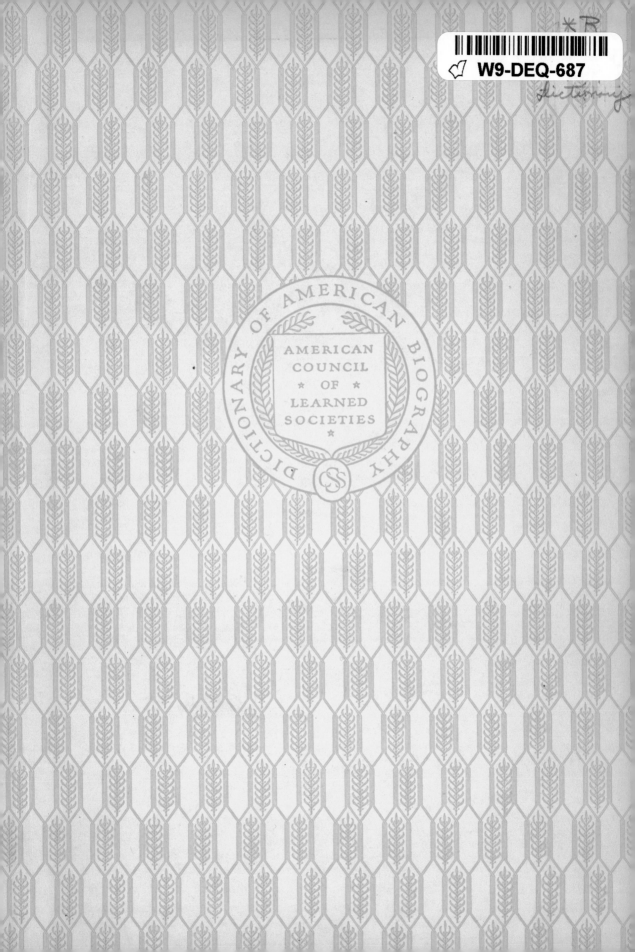

DICTIONARY OF AMERICAN BIOGRAPHY

AMERICAN
COUNCIL
* OF *
LEARNED
SOCIETIES

DICTIONARY OF
AMERICAN BIOGRAPHY

DICTIONARY OF AMERICAN BIOGRAPHY

UNDER THE AUSPICES OF THE
AMERICAN COUNCIL OF LEARNED SOCIETIES

EDITED BY
DUMAS MALONE

Troye—Wentworth

VOLUME XIX

CHARLES SCRIBNER'S SONS

NEW YORK

1936

Prompted solely by a desire for public service the New York Times Company and its President, Mr. Adolph S. Ochs, made possible the preparation of the manuscript of the Dictionary of American Biography through a subvention of more than $500,000 and with the understanding that the entire responsibility for the contents of the volumes rests with the American Council of Learned Societies.

CONTRIBUTORS TO VOLUME XIX

THOMAS P. ABERNETHY . . . . T. P. A.
ADELINE ADAMS . . . . A. A.
JAMES TRUSLOW ADAMS . . . . J. T. A.
NELSON F. ADKINS . . . . . . N. F. A.
ROBERT GREENHALGH ALBION . R. G. A.
HORACE NEWTON ALLEN . . . . H. N. A.
GEORGE M. ANDERSON . . . . . G. M. A.
RUSSELL H. ANDERSON . . . . . R. H. A.
GERTRUDE L. ANNAN . . . . . G. L. A.
MARGUERITE APPLETON . . . . M. A.
JOHN CLARK ARCHER . . . . . J. C. A.
RAYMOND CLARE ARCHIBALD . R. C. A.
FREDERICK W. ASHLEY . . . . . F. W. A.
ROLAND H. BAINTON . . . . . . R. H. B.
CARLOS H. BAKER . . . . C. H. B.
FRANK COLLINS BAKER . . . . F. C. B.
HENRY G. BARBOUR . . . . . . H. G. B.
GILBERT H. BARNES . . . . . . G. H. B.
CLARIBEL R. BARNETT . . . . . C. R. B.
HAROLD K. BARROWS . . . . . H. K. B—s.
CLARENCE BARTLETT . . . . . . C. B—t.
GEORGE A. BARTON . . . . . . G. A. B.
ERNEST SUTHERLAND BATES . . E. S. B—s.
G. PHILIP BAUER . . . . G. P. B.
HOWARD K. BEALE . . . . . . H. K. B—e.
WILLIAM G. BEAN . . . . W. G. B.
ELBERT J. BENTON . . . . E. J. B.
WILLIAM C. BINKLEY . . . . . W. C. B.
EDITH R. BLANCHARD . . . . . E. R. B.
LOUISE PEARSON BLODGET . . . L. P. B.
HELEN C. BOATFIELD . . . . . H. C. B.
LOUIS H. BOLANDER . . . . . . L. H. B.
CHARLES K. BOLTON . . . . . . C. K. B.
ETHEL STANWOOD BOLTON . . . E. S. B—n.
HENRY E. BOURNE . . . . . . H. E. B.
WITT BOWDEN . . . . W. B.
J. BARTLET BREBNER . . . . . J. B. B.
CARL BRIDENBAUGH . . . . . . C. B—h.
JOHN E. BRIGGS . . . . J. E. B.
ROBERT C. BROOKS . . . . . . R. C. B.
LAWRASON BROWN . . . . . . L. B.
C. A. BROWNE . . . . C. A. B.
WALDO R. BROWNE . . . . . . W. R. B.
ROBERT BRUCE . . . . R. B.
ISABEL M. CALDER . . . . . . I. M. C.
LESTER J. CAPPON . . . . L. J. C.
ZECHARIAH CHAFEE, JR. . . . . Z. C., JR.
O. P. CHITWOOD . . . . O. P. C.
E. CLOWES CHORLEY . . . . . E. C. C.

CHARLES E. CLARK . . . . . . C. E. C.
ELIOT CLARK . . . . E. C.
WALTER E. CLARK . . . . . . W. E. C.
RUFUS E. CLEMENT . . . . . . R. E. C.
FREDERICK W. COBURN . . . . F. W. C.
WESLEY R. COE . . . . W. R. C.
ARTHUR C. COLE . . . . A. C. C.
ROSSETTER G. COLE . . . . . . R. G. C.
THEODORE COLLIER . . . . . . T. C.
R. D. W. CONNOR . . . . . . R. D. W. C.
MARY ROBERTS COOLIDGE . . . M. R. C.
GRETA A. CORNELL . . . . . . G. A. C.
ROBERT SPENCER COTTERILL . . R. S. C.
E. MERTON COULTER . . . . . E. M. C.
ALEXANDER COWIE . . . . . . A. C.
KATHARINE ELIZABETH CRANE . K. E. C.
ARTHUR LYON CROSS . . . . . A. L. C.
WHITMAN CROSS . . . . W. C.
WILLIAM J. CUNNINGHAM . . . W. J. C.
MERLE E. CURTI . . . . M. E. C.
EDWARD E. CURTIS . . . . . . E. E. C.
CARL C. CUTLER . . . . C. C. C.
CHARLES WILLIAM DABNEY . . . C. W. D.
VIRGINIUS DABNEY . . . . . . V. D.
EDWARD E. DALE . . . . E. E. D.
TENNEY L. DAVIS . . . . T. L. D.
RICHARD E. DAY . . . . R. E. D.
JAMES QUAYLE DEALEY . . . . J. Q. D.
D. BRYSON DELAVAN . . . . . D. B. D.
WILLIAM H. S. DEMAREST . . . W. H. S. D.
EDWARD H. DEWEY . . . . . . E. H. D.
EVERETT N. DICK . . . . E. N. D.
HOBERT CUTLER DICKINSON . . H. C. D.
THEODORE DILLER . . . . . . T. D.
IRVING DILLIARD . . . . I. D.
CHARLES A. DINSMORE . . . . . C. A. D.
ARMISTEAD M. DOBIE . . . . . A. M. D.
JOHN J. DOLAN . . . . J. J. D.
ELIZABETH DONNAN . . . . . . E. D.
RANDOLPH C. DOWNES . . . . . R. C. D.
WILLIAM HOWE DOWNES . . . . W. H. D.
STELLA M. DRUMM . . . . . . S. M. D.
EDWARD A. DUDDY . . . . . . E. A. D.
ANDREW G. DU MEZ . . . . . A. G. D-M.
EDWARD DWIGHT EATON . . . . E. D. E.
WALTER PRICHARD EATON . . . W. P. E.
EDWIN FRANCIS EDGETT . . . . E. F. E.
EVERETT E. EDWARDS . . . . . E. E. E.
L. ETHAN ELLIS . . . . L. E. E.

Contributors to Volume XIX

Contributors to Volume XIX

Lester B. Mason	L. B. M
Frank Jewett Mather, Jr.	F. J. M., Jr.
William R. Maxon	W. R. M.
Robert Douthat Meade	R. D. M.
John C. Mendenhall	J. C. M.
A. Howard Meneely	A. H. M.
Newton D. Mereness	N. D. M.
George P. Merrill	G. P. M.
Perry Miller	P. M.
C. Bowie Millican	C. B. M.
Broadus Mitchell	B. M.
Carl W. Mitman	C. W. M.
Frank Monaghan	F. M.
Robert E. Moody	R. E. M.
Richard B. Morris	R. B. M.
Jarvis M. Morse	J. M. M.
Frank Luther Mott	F. L. M.
H. Edward Nettles	H. E. N.
A. R. Newsome	A. R. N.
Jeannette P. Nichols	J. P. N.
Robert Hastings Nichols	R. H. N.
Roy F. Nichols	R. F. N.
Herman C. Nixon	H. C. N.
A. B. Noble	A. B. N.
Alexander D. Noyes	A. D. N.
Francis R. Packard	F. R. P.
Stanley M. Pargellis	S. M. P.
Edd Winfield Parks	E. W. P.
William Patten	W. P.
Charles O. Paullin	C. O. P.
Frederic Logan Paxson	F. L. P.
C. C. Pearson	C. C. P.
Edmund L. Pearson	E. L. P.
Henry G. Pearson	H. G. P.
James H. Peeling	J. H. P.
Hobart S. Perry	H. S. P.
Henry J. Peterson	H. J. P.
James M. Phalen	J. M. P—n.
Francis S. Philbrick	F. S. P.
Paul Chrisler Phillips	P. C. P.
John A. Pollard	J. A. P.
David deSola Pool	D. deS. P.
John M. Poor	J. M. P—r.
Jennie Barnes Pope	J. B. P.
Dorothy B. Porter	D. B. P.
Louise Pound	L. P.
Julius W. Pratt	J. W. P.
Richard J. Purcell	R. J. P.
Arthur Hobson Quinn	A. H. Q.
Lowell Joseph Ragatz	L. J. R.
P. L. Rainwater	P. L. R.
P. O. Ray	P. O. R.
Thomas T. Read	T. T. R.
Herbert S. Reichle	H. S. R—e.
Elizabeth M. Richards	E. M. R.
Leon B. Richardson	L. B. R.
Robert E. Riegel	R. E. R.
Donald A. Roberts	D. A. R.
Benjamin L. Robinson	B. L. R.
Herbert Spencer Robinson	H. S. R—n.
William A. Robinson	W. A. R.
William M. Robinson, Jr.	W. M. R., Jr.
L. Harding Rogers, Jr.	L. H. R., Jr.
Flora Rose	F. R.
Harold E. Ross	H. E. R.
Frederick D. Rossini	F. D. R.
Peyton Rous	P. R.
W. Carl Rufus	W. C. R.
William Sener Rusk	W. S. R.
Verne Lockwood Samson	V. L. S.
Carl Sandburg	C. S.
Louis Bernard Schmidt	L. B. S—t.
William O. Scroggs	W. O. S.
Elias Howard Sellards	E. H. S.
James Lee Sellers	J. L. S.
Thorsten Sellin	T. S—n.
Joseph J. Senturia	J. J. S.
Henry Sewall	H. S—l.
Robert Francis Seybolt	R. F. S.
William E. Shea	W. E. S—a.
Augustus H. Shearer	A. H. S.
Lester B. Shippee	L. B. S—e.
Richard H. Shryock	R. H. S.
George N. Shuster	G. N. S.
Eleanor M. Sickels	E. M. S.
Wilbur H. Siebert	W. H. S.
Kenneth C. M. Sills	K. C. M. S.
Marian Silveus	M. S.
Lesley Byrd Simpson	L. B. S—n.
Theodore Sizer	T. S—r.
Emily E. F. Skeel	E. E. F. S.
David Eugene Smith	D. E. S.
Harry Worcester Smith	H. W. S.
William E. Smith	W. E. S—h.
Herbert Solow	H. S—w.
Raymond J. Sontag	R. J. S—g.
George A. Soper	G. A. S.
J. Duncan Spaeth	J. D. S.
E. Wilder Spaulding	E. W. S.
Oliver L. Spaulding, Jr.	O. L. S., Jr.
Thomas M. Spaulding	T. M. S.
Robert Elliott Speer	R. El. S.
Robert Ernest Spiller	R. Er. S.
Richard J. Stanley	R. J. S—y.
Harris Elwood Starr	H. E. S.
Bertha Monica Stearns	B. M. S.
Raymond P. Stearns	R. P. S.
Wayne E. Stevens	W. E. S—s
De Lisle Stewart	D-L. S.
Edgar I. Stewart	E. I. S.
George R. Stewart, Jr.	G. R. S., Jr.
Randall Stewart	R. S.
Anson Phelps Stokes	A. P. S.
Richard G. Stone	R. G. S.

Contributors to Volume XIX

Lionel M. Summers	L. M. S.	Luther Allan Weigle	L. A. W.
Charles S. Sydnor	C. S. S.	Elizabeth Howard West	E. H. W.
Thomas E. Tallmadge	T. E. T.	Allan Westcott	A. W—t.
William A. Taylor	W. A. T.	Alexander Wetmore	A. W—e.
David Y. Thomas	D. Y. T.	George F. Whicher	G. F. W.
Milton Halsey Thomas	M. H. T.	Arthur P. Whitaker	A. P. W—r.
Herbert Thoms	H. T.	Isabel M. S. Whittier	I. M. S. W.
Irving L. Thomson	I. L. T.	Robert H. Wienefeld	R. H. W.
Edward Larocque Tinker	E. L. T.	Jerome K. Wilcox	J. K. W.
Bruce R. Trimble	B. R. T.	Vernon L. Wilkinson	V. L. W.
Alonzo H. Tuttle	A. H. T.	Mary Wilhelmine Williams	M. W. W.
Edward M. Van Cleve	E. M. V-C.	Samuel C. Williams	S. C. W.
Lewis G. Vander Velde	L. G. V-V.	Tyrrell Williams	T. W.
Arnold J. F. van Laer	A. J. F. v-L.	Albert Potter Wills	A. P. W—s.
George Van Santvoord	G. V-S.	Maude H. Woodfin	M. H. W.
Henry R. Viets	H. R. V.	Vann Woodward	V. W.
Harold G. Villard	H. G. V.	Walter L. Wright, Jr.	W. L. W., Jr.
Edna Vosper	E. V.	James Ingersoll Wyer	J. I. W.
Rufus W. Weaver	R. W. W.		

DICTIONARY OF

AMERICAN BIOGRAPHY

——

Troye—Wentworth

TROYE, EDWARD (1808–July 25, 1874), painter of American blood horses, was born near Geneva, Switzerland, and died in Georgetown, Ky. He was of French descent, his grandfather, a nobleman, having been exiled from France for political reasons. Jean Baptiste de Troy, Edward's father, was an artist of note, and one of his paintings, "The Plague of Marseilles," now hangs in the Louvre. All his children were educated in the arts, and several of them gained distinction in their several fields. For some years Edward lived with his father in England, but at the age of twenty emigrated to the New World, changing his name to Troye.

In the West Indies, where he first resided, he was connected with a sugar plantation and employed his leisure time in sketching and painting. Ill health compelling him to seek a different climate, he went to Philadelphia, Pa., and soon found employment with the art department of *Sartain's Magazine*. In July 1839 he was married, in Kentucky, to Cornelia Ann Van der Graff, a grand-daughter of one of the Dutch governors of Ceylon.

Troye's best work, which was done between 1835 and 1874, is to be seen in his paintings of blood horses. Since photography did not become commercial until after the seventies, Troye's portraits are the truest delineations of the forebears of the great racers of the American turf, and so have much historical as well as artistic value. Before the Civil War he painted for the plantation owners of the South, where the leading thoroughbred studs of the United States were to be found. His chief patrons were A. Keene Richards of Georgetown, Ky., and the Alexander family of Lexington, and with them he spent the middle and latter part of his life. With Richards

he made a trip in the fifties to Arabia and the Holy Land, where Richards selected and purchased a number of Arab horses, while Troye painted horses, Damascus cattle, the Dead Sea, the bazaar of Damascus, and other scenes and objects. Copies of some of these paintings are preserved at Bethany College, Bethany, W. Va.

Troye's most notable paintings are those of American Eclipse and Sir Henry, heroes of the memorable North-South match in 1823; the mighty Boston and his son Lexington, the leading sire in America for sixteen years; Lecomte, Lexington's valiant foe in the four-mile heat match at the Metairie course in New Orleans; Reel, a great brood mare, dam of Lecomte; Glencoe, sire of Reel; Revenue, Bertrand, Richard Singleton, Reality, Black Maria, Leviathan, Wagner, Ophelia—dam of Gray Eagle, and numerous others. Hanging in the Capitol at Washington is Troye's great painting of Gen. Winfield Scott, mounted on a son of Glencoe, a charger given by A. Keene Richards to John Hunt Morgan [*q.v.*], the daring leader of Morgan's cavalry, and painted from life.

Up to 1912 not more than twenty of Troye's paintings were known in the East, but since that time over three hundred of them have been located and three-quarters of them photographed. The chief collections in America are in the hands of the Jockey Club, New York; the Alexander family in Kentucky; Walter Jeffords, Pennsylvania; Harry Worcester Smith, Massachusetts; A. Kenneth Alexander, New York; Louis Lee Haggin, Kentucky; David Wagstaff, and Harry T. Peters of New York; Robert Gilmor, Long Island; and the Francis P. Garvan collection given to Yale University in memory of Harry Payne and Payne Whitney. Troye was the au-

I

thor of *The Race Horses of America* (1867), of which only the first number was published. At his death he was survived by a daughter.

[Information from Troye's daughter, the late Anna V. T. Christian; Mrs. John C. Pack, of Singleton, Ky., and Mrs. E. K. Schwartz, of New Orleans, daughters of A. Keene Richards; W. S. Vosburgh, "Horse Portraiture in America," in *Daily Racing Form* (Chicago), Mar. 18, 1919; C. E. Fairman, *Art and Artists of the Capitol of the U. S. A.* (1927); Harry Worcester Smith, "Edward Troye (1808–1874), The Painter of American Blood Horses," *The Field* (London), Jan. 21, 1926.]

H. W. S.

TRUDE, ALFRED SAMUEL (Apr. 21, 1847–Dec. 12, 1933), lawyer, was born on shipboard in New York harbor. His parents, Samuel and Sallie (Downs) Trude, were immigrants from England, who shortly settled at Lockport, N. Y. Here Alfred spent his boyhood, attending the public schools. At seventeen he set out to seek his fortune in Chicago, which was his home thereafter. On Apr. 7, 1868, he married Algenia Pearson of Lockport, by whom he had three sons and two daughters.

Shortly after his marriage, he enrolled in the Union College of Law (now the Northwestern University Law School) at Chicago, at the same time pursuing office study under A. B. Jenks. Admitted to the bar in 1871, he soon attracted the attention of Joseph Medill [*q.v.*], editor and proprietor of the *Chicago Tribune* and mayor of the city, who in 1872 appointed the young man city prosecutor. After their official relation had ceased, Trude long remained the *Tribune's* attorney. His success in that connection brought him another valuable client in Wilbur F. Storey [*q.v.*] of the *Chicago Times,* whose attorney he became in 1876, when he prevented, on the ground that Storey was not a fugitive from justice, the latter's extradition to Wisconsin on the charge of libeling Milwaukee's chief of police. In one decade, it is said, Trude appeared for Storey and the *Times* in about five hundred cases, and the wide publicity given to the first of these led to retainers in many other extradition cases, notably the "Newburg Poker Case," in which he prevented the discharge on *habeas corpus* of two gamblers who had taken $150,000 from a client. Another early case which enhanced his reputation was the divorce suit of *Linden* vs. *Linden,* in which the plaintiff, the daughter of a wealthy packer, had married a coachman in the belief that he was a British peer. Trude appeared for the defendant, and a decree was denied. After successfully prosecuting actions against various railway companies, Trude was retained by such important corporations as the Chicago & Alton Railroad and the Chicago City Railway Company. He also appeared in famous testamentary

litigation, such as contests of the wills of Wilbur F. Storey and Henrietta Snell.

Although his success in civil practice was phenomenal, it was his frequent appearance in criminal causes which brought his name into the headlines of the daily newspapers. Almost a half century before his death, he had already appeared in thirty-four murder cases and had been successful in all but three. Among his successful defenses was that of the Reno brothers who, however, were lynched after his acquittal. In some famous cases he was the prosecutor—notably in *State* vs. *Prendergast,* in which the defendant was convicted and hanged for murdering Mayor Carter Henry Harrison [*q.v.*] on the last night of the World's Columbian Exposition (1893). One of the most successful trial lawyers of his time—before the age of excessive specialism—Trude was a product of the jury system and his forte lay in resourcefulness, adroitness, and persuasive address rather than in profound legal learning. In the latter, nevertheless, he was by no means deficient and his wide range of practice gave him a technical knowledge of many diverse branches of the law.

In the midst of his professional activities, he found time for public and party service. During the last eight years of the century, he was a member of the Chicago School Board. For a long period he was active in local politics, and in 1896 and again in 1900 he was a delegate to the National Democratic Convention. His last years were spent in retirement.

[*The Bench and Bar of Chicago* (n.d.), published before 1886; John Moses and Joseph Kirkland, *Hist. of Chicago* (1895), vol. II; J. W. Leonard, *The Book of Chicagoans,* 1905 and 1926; *Who's Who in America,* 1918–19; *Chicago Daily Tribune,* Dec. 14, 1933; *N. Y. Times,* Dec. 13, 1933.]

C. S. L.

TRUDEAU, EDWARD LIVINGSTON (Oct. 5, 1848–Nov. 15, 1915), physician, pioneer scientific student of tuberculosis in America, was born in New York City, the third child of James and Céphise (Berger) Trudeau. His father, the grandson of Zenon Trudeau, lieutenant governor of upper Louisiana from 1792 to 1799, was a Confederate officer, a friend and companion of John J. Audubon [*q.v.*], a sculptor of some ability, and a physician. Soon after the boy's birth his parents separated. His mother returned to Paris, with her father, François Eloi Berger, the son of a long line of physicians and a successful practising physician of New York. There young Trudeau lived until his eighteenth year, studying at the Lycée Bonaparte. Returning to New York, he prepared to enter the United States Naval Academy, but, when his brother developed tuberculosis, he resigned in order to nurse him until he died. Tiring of the work in the School of Mines of Columbia College, now part of the School of Engineering of Columbia University, and caring little for the life of a stock broker, he began in 1868 the study of medicine and was graduated from the College of Physicians and Surgeons, now a part of Columbia University. He was steadied in his determination for a career by his desire to win the confidence, approbation, and love of Charlotte G. Beare of Douglaston, Long Island. He was married to her on June 29, 1871, and in his autobiography he repeatedly acknowledged her influence throughout his life. After a short hospital experience he began practice on Long Island but soon, in 1872, removed to New York, associated himself with Fessenden Nott Otis [q.v.], and engaged in teaching and dispensary work. Infected no doubt by his brother, he developed in 1873 rather extensive pulmonary tuberculosis, which led him to the Adirondacks, where he continued to live, considering himself always an exile from New York. Having inherited a modest income, he fished and hunted until 1880, when he began to devote more time to medical practice, at Paul Smiths in the summer and in Saranac Lake during the winter.

He was interested chiefly in two phases of tuberculosis, early diagnosis and the discovery of a cure, both closely related to his consuming passion, aiding in recovery from tuberculosis. The cure he sought in the laboratory; early diagnosis and treatment he pursued in the sanatorium. He was a keen diagnostician, his grasp of prognosis was as excellent as it was cautious. He published little upon clinical tuberculosis, much from the laboratory. He spoke optimistically, he wrote guardedly, with the result he had little to retract. Impressed with the need of caring for patients with pulmonary tuberculosis and small means, stimulated by an article by Herman Brehmer, in 1884 he established on sixteen acres, bought and presented to him by Adirondack guides, lifelong friends, the Adirondack Cottage Sanitarium, now the Trudeau Sanatorium, the first in America. For thirty years, practically unaided, he met the yearly deficit, ultimately $30,-000, by soliciting contributions and by donations from his own modest income, and he left an endowment fund of $600,000. At his death the sanatorium accommodated 150 patients and consisted of 36 buildings on 60 acres. He was already familiar with the work of Pasteur and Tyndall, when a translation of Robert Koch's paper on the etiology of tuberculosis came into his hands. This led to the establishment of a small, very primitive laboratory in his home, eventually causing a fire that destroyed his house in 1893 and prompted George C. Cooper to build the present Saranac Laboratory in 1894. There the first immunity experiments in tuberculosis in America were performed, various substances tested on animals, and in a hole nearby the beneficial influence of fresh air on tuberculous rabbits was controlled. Among his earlier publications were "An Experimental Study of Preventive Inoculation in Tuberculosis" (Medical Record, Nov. 22, 1890) and "The Treatment of Experimental Tuberculosis by Koch's Tuberculin, Hunter's Modification and Other Products of the Tubercle-Bacillus" (Medical News, Sept. 3, 1892, and also in Transactions of the Association of American Physicians, vol. VII, 1892, pp. 99–101). Two of his later studies were reported as "Artificial Immunity in Experimental Tuberculosis" (Ibid., vol. XVIII, 1903, p. 97 and in New York Medical Journal, July 18, 1903) and "Two Experiments in Artificial Immunity against Tuberculosis" (Medical News, Sept. 30, 1905, and Transactions of the National Association for Study and Prevention of Tuberculosis ...1905, 1906). In 1915 An Autobiography was published posthumously (title page 1916). He became in 1904 the president of the National Association for the Study and Prevention of Tuberculosis, later the National Tuberculosis Association; in 1905 president of the Association of American Physicians; in 1910 president of the Congress of American Physicians and Surgeons, where, too weak to be heard, he spoke on "Optimism in Medicine" (for extensive quotation see Chalmers, post, introduction).

His most striking characteristics were his personal charm, his optimism, his wonderful never flagging enthusiasm, his wide sympathies, his choice of forceful picturesque diction in speech and writing, his ability to interest others, to make and keep friends, his love of people. Such characteristics made him a keen scientist and a great physician. Strongly influenced after the death of his brother by broad and tolerant religious views, he led in the organizations of the churches at Paul Smiths and in Saranac Lake, in the affairs of which he took deep interest until his death. Of his four children, one, a physician, survived him, another boy died in infancy, a daughter was claimed by the disease he was struggling to control, and in 1906 his eldest son died suddenly while convalescing from pneumonia. Trudeau never recovered from this blow, and gradually his disease, long quiescent, becoming more active, required collapse therapy that for a time relieved him. He died in Saranac

Lake and was buried at St. Johns-in-the-Wilderness, at Paul Smiths.

[*Autobiog., ante*; Stephen Chalmers, *The Beloved Physician* (1916), and in *Atlantic Monthly*, Jan. 1916; *Jour. of Outdoor Life*, Jan. 1925; *N. Y. Times*, Nov. 16–18, 21, 23, 1915; personal association.]   L. B.

TRUDEAU, JEAN BAPTISTE [See TRU-TEAU, JEAN BAPTISTE, 1748–1827].

TRUE, ALFRED CHARLES (June 5, 1853–Apr. 23, 1929), leader in agricultural education, was born at Middletown, Conn., the son of Charles Kittredge and Elizabeth Bassett (Hyde) True. Frederick William True [*q.v.*] was his younger brother. Their father, a Methodist minister, was then a professor at Wesleyan University. Following a boyhood spent in rural communities of Connecticut, Massachusetts, and New York, True prepared for college at the Boston Latin School and graduated from Wesleyan University in 1873. After two years as principal of the high school at Essex, N. Y., he taught in the state normal school at Westfield, Mass., for seven years. On Nov. 23, 1875, he married Emma Fortune of Essex, N. Y., by whom he had a daughter and a son. Following graduate work at Harvard from 1882 to 1884 he returned to Wesleyan University, where during the next four years he gave instruction in Latin and Greek.

At Wesleyan he formed an acquaintance with Wilbur O. Atwater [*q.v.*], who in 1888 founded the office of experiment stations in the United States Department of Agriculture. The following year True was induced to join the staff of the department and remained connected with it until his death. As editor in the office of experiment stations, one of his first duties was the preparation of an article on the experiment-station movement and the history of agricultural education and research in the United States for use in connection with the Paris Exposition of 1889. This task enabled him to approach the problems of agricultural education and research from a national point of view and to visualize agricultural colleges and stations as permanent agencies for the general welfare. During the early nineties when the office functioned largely as a clearing house of information, True prepared publications and encouraged the dissemination of accurate information on agricultural matters. After his appointment to the directorship (1893) the functions of the office expanded greatly. Investigations in human nutrition resulted in his assuming leadership in research and education in the field of home economics. He also aided in making farmers' institutes a vital means of popular education. The irrigation and drainage inves-tigations of the department and the agricultural experiment stations in the territories likewise came under his supervision. Owing largely to confidence in True's breadth of view and liberality and his sound and unbiased judgment, the office of experiment stations became "an unique example of national administration" in which "influence rather than coercion is the policy" (Conover, *post*, p. 104). In 1915 the office became part of the states relations service, of which True was director until 1923; in this capacity he was spokesman for the department in programs of cooperation in the research and education carried on pursuant to the Smith-Lever Act of 1914.

True's influence as an official was supplemented by his leadership in the Association of American Colleges and Experiment Stations, finally known as the Association of Land Grant Colleges and Universities. He contributed frequently to its programs; served on its committees, notably that on agricultural instruction, was its editor and bibliographer for many years, its president in 1913, and dean of the seven successive graduate schools of agriculture which it sponsored between 1902 and 1916. In 1913 he was chairman of the official delegation of the United States at the General Assembly of the International Institute of Agriculture at Rome. During the World War he was a leader in the efforts to increase food production and conservation. After 1923 he was engaged mainly in the preparation of three monographs, *A History of Agricultural Extension Work in the United States, 1785–1923* (1928), *A History of Agricultural Education in the United States, 1785–1925* (1929), and "A History of Agricultural Experimentation and Research in the United States" (unpublished)—a trilogy such as no other person could have produced, for no one else was privileged to study more intensively from a national point of view the growth of the entire movement for agricultural education over a period of forty years.

[*Am. Men of Sci.* (4th ed., 1927); H. P. Sheldon, "Uncle Sam's Hired Men Who Serve You," *Hoard's Dairyman*, Aug. 27, 1920; *Wis. Country Mag.*, Nov. 1929; *Proceedings* of the Asso. of Am. Agric. Colls. and Experiment Stations and its successors, especially vols. XXVII (1914), XXXVII (1924), XLIII (1930); *Experiment Station Record*, Mar., July 1923, Apr., July, Oct. 1929; *Jour. of Home Economics*, July 1929; *U. S. Dept. Agric. Official Record*, May 2, 1929; U. S. Dept. of Agric., press release, Apr. 24, 1929; L. S. Ivins and A. E. Winship, *Fifty Famous Farmers* (1924); *Rus*, 1925; *Who's Who in America*, 1928–29; Milton Conover, *The Office of Experiment Stations* (1924); *Evening Star* (Washington, D. C.), Apr. 24, 25, 1929; *Washington Post*, Apr. 25, 1929; manuscript letters in U. S. Dept. of Agric. Lib.; manuscript bibliog. of True's writings in Office of Experiment Stations Lib., U. S. Dept. of Agric.]   E. E. E.

TRUE, FREDERICK WILLIAM (July 8, 1858–June 25, 1914), zoölogist, born in Middletown, Conn., brother of Alfred Charles True [*q.v.*], was a son of the Rev. Charles Kittredge and Elizabeth Bassett (Hyde) True, and a descendant of Henry Trew of England who settled at Salem, Mass., about 1636. He received his collegiate education at the University of the City of New York, where he was graduated with the degree of bachelor of science in 1878. In November of that year he entered the service of the federal government as a clerk with the fish commission and in 1879 was expert special agent in the fisheries branch of the Tenth Census. In 1880 he was custodian of the exhibits of the United States fish commission at the Berlin Fisheries Exhibition.

In July of the following year he went to the Smithsonian Institution as a clerk in the National Museum. His service under the Smithsonian continued with steady advancement until his death and covered difficult scientific and administrative labors. From 1881 to 1883 he was librarian for the National Museum, serving also for the first two years as acting curator of the division of mammals. In 1883 he became curator and retained direct supervision of the division until 1909. In the early eighties he was designated curator-in-charge and had administrative supervision of the entire museum at such times as the assistant secretary was absent; this designation was changed in 1894 to executive curator, which title carried with it additional duties.

When the National Museum was reorganized in 1897 True was made head curator of the department of biology, with direction of all of the biological work of the organization, a position in which his duties were largely administrative. During the absence of Samuel P. Langley [*q.v.*] that year, True served for a period as acting secretary of the Smithsonian Institution, and until 1901 he bore the major burden of administration in the National Museum. On June 1, 1911, he became assistant secretary of the Smithsonian in charge of the library and of the international exchange service, a position that he occupied until his death. In the exposition work that was an important feature of the activities of the Institution during this period True had a prominent part. He directed the preparation of exhibitions shown at Nashville, Tenn., in 1897; at Omaha, Nebr., in 1898; at Buffalo, N. Y., in 1901; at Charleston, S. C., in 1902; at St. Louis, Mo., in 1904; and at Portland, Ore., in 1905. He was, also, an official representative of the United States government at the Seventh International Zoölogical Congress in 1907.

True was profound as a student, and exact and punctilious as an administrative officer. He cared little for sports or pastimes, finding his recreation in music, literature, and art. Of a retiring disposition, he was not interested in social activities beyond association with friends and colleagues and when not at the museum was usually engaged in studies at home. His early scientific interests were directed toward the lower groups of animals, but, finding that his eyesight would not permit continued use of the microscope, he turned to the mammals and in research on this group made his outstanding scientific contributions. He published many papers, and was known especially for his studies of the whales and their allies. A collection of these which he began for the National Museum is one of the most extensive in the world. His memoirs on the family *Delphinidae,* on the whalebone whales, and on the beaked whales were of much significance, and in later years he was occupied with studies of fossil cetaceans, a subject to which he made noteworthy contributions. In his investigations he went to many other museums and visited whaling stations in Newfoundland. At the time of his death he was recognized as the foremost living authority on the *Cetacea.* On Feb. 16, 1887, he married Louise Elvina Prentiss of Washington, D. C.; two of their children survived him.

[*Ann. Report of the Board of Regents of the Smithsonian Institution, 1914* (1915); J. M. Cattell, *Am. Men of Sci.* (2nd ed., 1910); *Who's Who in America, 1914–15*; *Evening Star* (Washington), June 25, 1914; records in the Smithsonian Institution; family sources.]

A. W—e.

TRUEBLOOD, BENJAMIN FRANKLIN (Nov. 25, 1847–Oct. 26, 1916), educator, publicist, and professional worker for international peace, was born in Salem, Ind., and adhered throughout his life to the Quaker principles of his parents, Joshua and Esther (Parker) Trueblood. After graduating from Earlham College in 1869, he began his educational work as professor of classics at Penn College, Iowa. From 1874 to 1890 he served as president of Wilmington College, Ohio, and of Penn College. His thorough scholarship, his virility, and his high moral principles won the respect of his colleagues and students; his faculty for using homely and terse words, his humane and charming strain of humor, and his rare combination of modesty and heartiness won their love and devotion. On July 17, 1872, he married Sarah H. Terrell of New Vienna, Ohio. In 1890 he broadened his educational activity by becoming a professional worker for international peace. A year abroad as agent for the Christian Arbitration and Peace

Society provided an opportunity for studying European conditions and for becoming acquainted with leaders in the peace movement. From that time until his death he was important in its councils, both in England and on the Continent, and the more influential because of his mastery of several modern languages. From 1892 until 1915 he served as secretary of the American Peace Society and as editor of its periodical, the *Advocate of Peace*. The fortunes of the peace movement in the United States were at a low ebb, and much of the organizing work of his predecessors, William Ladd and Elihu Burritt [*qq.v.*], had to be done over again. The first western man to assume the leadership of organized pacifism in the United States, he made the movement a truly national one. As a result of his tireless activity in organizing branch peace societies, of writing not only for peace periodicals but for other magazines, and of lecturing on innumerable occasions, he played a responsible part in the rapid expansion of the peace movement. A repeated visitor at the state department and at the White House, he was treated at the national capital with greater respect than most pacifists. His influence was extended by his active participation in the Lake Mohonk arbitration conferences, the International Law Association, and the American Society of International Law.

As editor of the *Advocate of Peace* he set a new standard for pacifist journalism. Without sacrificing the moral, ethical, and religious elements that had given so much impetus to pacifism, he interpreted the peace movement and the forces promoting war with realism as well as vision. His analyses of contemporary events were characterized by shrewdness, insight, and literary merit. Himself an uncompromising foe of all wars, militarism, and violence, he believed it was necessary to enlist the support of every shade of opinion if pacifism and internationalism were to be translated into actualities. An intelligent advocate of arbitration and the limitation of armaments, he believed that, as a result of the solidarity of humanity and the principle of progress that governed history, the groping steps and strivings toward world organization must inevitably, and in the relatively immediate future, lead to a true world federation. He gave to the peace movement an historical sense, a more substantial ground for its optimism, and a sense of realism that did much to mitigate the sentimentalism of many of its friends. In spite of the catholic character of his philosophy and program of peace, he only partly understood the relationships between industrial and financial capitalism and

war; and his appreciation of the importance of socialism and the labor movement for eliminating war did not lead him to make an effective alliance with those forces. Among his numerous publications perhaps the most important were *The Federation of the World* (1899) and *The Development of the Peace Idea and Other Essays* (1932), with an introduction by Edwin D. Mead.

[Letters of Trueblood in the Roosevelt Papers in the Lib. of Cong., in the Frederick Bayer Papers in the Kongelig Bibliothek in Copenhagen, and in the files of the International Peace Bureau in Geneva; C. E. Beals, *Benj. Franklin Trueblood* (1916); E. L. Whitney, *The Amer. Peace Soc.* (1928); *Who's Who in America*, 1916–17; *N. Y. Times*, Oct. 27, 1916.]

M. E. C.

TRUMAN, BENJAMIN CUMMINGS (Oct. 25, 1835–July 18, 1916), journalist, author, eldest son of Henry Hammond Truman and his first wife, Susan (Cummings), and a descendant of Joseph Truman who settled in New London (Conn.) about 1666, was born in Providence, R. I. He attended public school there and a Shaker school in Canterbury, N. H., and at seventeen took charge for a year of a district school in Merrimack County, N. H. Returning to Providence, he learned typesetting, and from 1855 until late in 1859 was a compositor and proofreader on the *New York Times*. In the latter year he entered the employ of John W. Forney [*q.v.*] of Philadelphia, publisher of the *Press,* and in 1861 went to Washington to work on Forney's *Sunday Morning Chronicle.* Upon the outbreak of the Civil War he was sent to the front as a correspondent and in March 1862, declining a commission in a regiment of volunteers, became an aide on the staff of Andrew Johnson, military governor of Tennessee. Nominally he so remained until near the end of the war, though his talent for doing many things at the same time enabled him to render distinguished service as a correspondent and to serve from time to time on the staffs of Generals J. S. Negley, John H. King, and Kenner Garrard.

In the late summer of 1865 Truman was sent by President Johnson as a confidential agent to investigate opinion and conditions in the far South, and from the first of September 1865 to the middle of March 1866 he traveled in Alabama, Georgia, Florida, Tennessee, Arkansas, Mississippi, Louisiana, and Texas, sending frequent illuminating letters to the *New York Times* and making observations which he submitted to the President in the form of a report, dated Apr. 9, 1866 (*Senate Executive Document No. 43, 39 Cong., 1 Sess.*). He testified before the congressional Committee on Reconstruction on Apr. 5 (*House Report No. 30,* pt. IV, pp. 136–40, 39

Cong., 1 Sess.) and shortly thereafter was sent as a special treasury agent to South Carolina and Florida. Declining appointment as paymaster with the rank of major in the Regular Army, he served from December 1866 until late in 1869 as special agent of the Post Office Department on the Pacific Coast, in this capacity visiting China, Japan, and Hawaii. On Dec. 8, 1869, at Los Angeles, he married Augusta Mallard and soon afterward went to Washington as a correspondent of the *New York Times* and the San Francisco *Bulletin*. He was again in California in 1870, became interested in the *San Diego Bulletin,* and in February 1872 assumed the editorship of the *Evening Express* of Los Angeles. In the following year he bought the *Los Angeles Star,* but four years later sold it and again became a special agent of the Post Office Department. For eleven years (1879–90) he was chief of the literary bureau of the Southern Pacific Railway; for the next two years the manager of a Southern California exhibit in Chicago; and subsequently for a time assistant chief of floriculture at the World's Columbian Exposition there. Returning to Los Angeles, he edited for some years the weekly *Western Graphic.* In 1900 he was one of the California commissioners to the Paris exposition and toured the Near East as a correspondent.

Besides his newspaper articles and sketches, Truman produced a number of books and pamphlets, including: *Life, Adventures, and Capture of Tiburcio Vasquez, the Great California Bandit and Murderer* (1874); *Semi-Tropical California* (1874); *Occidental Sketches* (1881); *The Field of Honor* (London, 1883; New York, 1884), a history of dueling; and a *History of the World's Fair* (copr. 1893). He also produced two plays, one of them a dramatization of Tennyson's *Enoch Arden.* He died in Los Angeles, survived by his wife and one of their two children.

Truman was jovial and expansive in manner, had amazing energy, and wrote voluminously. He has been called one of the most brilliant and successful of the Civil War correspondents, since by ingenuity or luck he was often enabled to get important news to the press ahead of his rivals, and in at least one notable instance ahead of the War Department (Elmer Davis, *History of the New York Times,* 1921, p. 57). His letters to the *Times* and his report and testimony on conditions in the South during the early period of Reconstruction are among the valuable sources of information covering that field.

[Autobiog. letter and other data in E. M. Treman and M. E. Poole, *The Hist. of the Treman, Tremaine, Truman Family in America* (1901), I, 193–98; *Who's Who in America,* 1916–17; *Printers and Printing in* *Providence, 1762–1907* (n.d.), p. lxxxv; *The New Internat. Year Book, 1916* (1917); *Mil. Order of the Loyal Legion . . . Commandery of Cal., Circular No. 24, Ser. of 1916* (1916); *Sixty Years in Southern Cal. . . . Reminiscences of Harris Newmark* (3rd ed., 1930), ed. by M. H. and M. R. Newmark; *N. Y. Times,* July 30, 1916, pt. III, p. 4; *Los Angeles Times,* July 19, 1916.]
W. J. G.

TRUMBULL, BENJAMIN (Dec. 19, 1735–Feb. 2, 1820), Congregational clergyman, historian, was born in Hebron, Conn., the eldest child of Benjamin and Mary (Brown) Trumble and a descendant of John Trumble who came to Roxbury, Mass., in 1639 and was made a freeman of Rowley in 1640. The spelling of the family name was changed to Trumbull about 1768. After preliminary study with the Rev. Elijah Lathrop, Benjamin entered Yale College and was graduated in 1759. Having completed his theological studies with the Rev. Eleazar Wheelock, he was licensed to preach on May 21, 1760, by the Windham Association of Ministers, and in August of the same year was called to the Congregational Church in North Haven, Conn. There on Dec. 24, 1760, he began services as pastor which were to continue until his death sixty years later, interrupted only by a period of six months during the Revolution when he served as chaplain of General Wadsworth's brigade (June 24 to Dec. 25, 1776). Upon his return to North Haven, he was chosen captain of a company of sixty volunteers.

Trumbull was a man of great energy and character. Though he never neglected his duty to his parish, he felt obligated to serve the state. This sentiment, combined with the repeated pleas of his friends, among whom were his father's first cousin, Gov. Jonathan Trumbull [*q.v.*], and Secretary of State George Wyllys, induced him to undertake the writings of a history of Connecticut. He worked under great difficulties, his pastoral activities often necessitating the suspension of his writing for months at a time. In 1797, more than twenty years after he had undertaken the task, he published the first volume—*A Complete History of Connecticut, Civil and Ecclesiastical from the Emigration of Its First Planters, from England, in MDCXXX, to MDCCXIII.* This was followed by a two-volume edition in 1818—*A Complete History of Connecticut . . . to the Year 1764.* A reprint of the 1818 edition, limited to one thousand copies, was published in 1898 by H. D. Utley of New London. From the date of its appearance until the present time, Trumbull's work has proved invaluable to the student of Connecticut history. Though more a chronicle than a history, it faithfully records the events which took place during the period covered. In recent years, a certain amount of new material has been discovered which makes necessary some corrections and modification in Trumbull's statements; but the book yet remains one of the most important single pieces of writing devoted to the history of Connecticut. After its completion he set to work on his *A General History of the United States of America . . . 1492–1792.* It was to have been a three-volume work, but he lived to complete only the first volume, covering the period to 1765, which appeared in 1810. Although Trumbull's lasting fame rests on his historical writing, he published sixteen other books and pamphlets, thirteen of which were either sermons or theological treatises, and the remaining three discussions of current political problems. Worthy of special mention perhaps are *A Plea, in Vindication of the Connecticut Title to the Contested Lands, Lying West of New York* (1774) and *An Appeal to the Public . . . with Respect to the Unlawfulness of Divorces* (1788). From material he had collected was published in 1924 *A Compendium of the Indian Wars in New England,* edited by F. B. Hartranft.

A portrait of Trumbull, painted by George Munger in 1818, was reproduced as the frontispiece to the 1818 edition of the history of Connecticut. From this portrait one gathers the impression that Trumbull was a man of great melancholy. The statement of his contemporaries is to the effect that such he was. So keenly did he feel the weight of the sins of the world upon his shoulders that the fact was manifest not only in his sermons but also in his general demeanor. Those who listened to his preaching felt that he was about to weep at any moment. This lugubriousness was not conducive to inspiring sermons, and the large attendance at his church services was due rather to his reputation as a patriot and historian than to any personal magnetism.

He was married on Dec. 4, 1760, to Martha, daughter of Ichabod and Martha Tillotson Phelps of Hebron, Conn., by whom he had seven children, two of whom were sons; Lyman Trumbull [*q.v.*] was his grandson.

[Introduction to Trumbull's *Complete Hist. of Conn.* (edition of 1898); F. B. Dexter, *Biog. Sketches Grads. Yale Coll.,* vol. II (1896); *Christian Spectator,* Mar. 1820; H. P. Johnston, *Yale and Her Honor-Roll in the Am. Revolution* (1888); *Proc. Mass. Hist. Soc.,* vol. XVII (1880); W. B. Sprague, *Annals of the Am. Pulpit,* vol. I (1857); S. B. Thorpe, *North Haven Annals* (1892); J. H. Lea, *Contributions to a Trumbull Geneal.* (1895); *A Geneal. Chart of Some of the Descendants of John Trumbull* (n.d.); *Columbian Reg.* (New Haven, Conn.), Feb. 12, 19, 1820.]   R. M. H.

TRUMBULL, HENRY CLAY (June 8, 1830–Dec. 8, 1903), Sunday-school missionary, editor, and author, was born in Stonington, Conn., the sixth child of Gurdon and Sarah Ann (Swan) Trumbull, and a younger brother of James Hammond Trumbull [*q.v.*]. He was of Puritan stock, a descendant of John Trumbull, mariner, who settled in Charlestown, Mass., about 1636, and of William Cheseborough and Walter Palmer, earliest settlers of Stonington. The boy's father was a man of varied business interests—whaling and sealing, the New York and Stonington Railroad, and the local banks—who served at different times as postmaster, representative and senator in the General Assembly of Connecticut, and commissioner of the state school fund. Henry attended Stonington Academy and Williston Seminary, but because of ill health had little formal education after the age of fourteen, being employed in later youth as a clerk in the Stonington bank. Beset by lung trouble, he gave up thought of a college education and at twenty-one removed to Hartford, where he became a clerk in the offices of the Hartford, Providence & Fishkill Railroad.

Under the influence of revival meetings conducted by Charles G. Finney [*q.v.*], he became superintendent of a mission Sunday-school in April 1852, and on June 1 united with the historic First (Center) Church in Hartford. Common interest in the revival and the Sunday-school brought him into intimacy with the family of Dr. Thomas Hopkins Gallaudet [*q.v.*], whose daughter Alice Cogswell he married on May 23, 1854. From 1856 to 1858 he was an apothecary, an editor, and a cotton and wool broker successively; he was also prominent in the state campaigns of the newly organized Republican party. As secretary of the first Connecticut Sunday-school Convention, 1857, he prepared so thorough and pointed a report that plans were made, with the cooperation of the American Sunday School Union, to employ a state Sunday-school missionary, and he was offered and accepted the post, giving full time to its duties after Sept. 1, 1858. On Sept. 10, 1862, he was ordained in order that he might qualify for the chaplaincy of the 10th Connecticut Regiment, then stationed at New Bern, N. C., where he joined it. He was captured by Confederates while ministering to the wounded after the assault on Fort Wagner in July 1863, and was held prisoner, suspected as a spy, for four months. After exchange, he was in active service on the Virginia front until the end of the war, being mustered out with his regiment, Aug. 25, 1865.

Refusing attractive offers in various editorial, educational, and business relationships, he resumed his work for the Sunday-schools, becoming secretary for New England of the American Sunday School Union. As chairman of the executive committee of the National Sunday School Convention, he issued the call for the meeting of 1872 which initiated the International Uniform Sunday School Lessons. In 1875 he became editor and part owner of the *Sunday School Times,* and removed with his family to Philadelphia, which was henceforth his home. Through this periodical, he contributed powerfully to the development of the Sunday-school movement in the United States and throughout the world, and gave stimulus and guidance to the spread of Bible study under the regimentation of the uniform lesson system. In 1888 he delivered the Lyman Beecher Lectures at Yale, which were published under the title *The Sunday School, Its Origin, Mission, Methods and Auxiliaries* (1888). Visiting Palestine in 1881, he succeeded in identifying the site of Kadesh-Barnea, and his book entitled *Kadesh-Barnea,* published in 1884 after two years of further study and research, remains the most important work on this subject. From 1886 to 1897, he served as chaplain-in-chief of the Loyal Legion.

Trumbull was an effective speaker and a stimulating and resourceful writer. He was, in the best sense of the term, a nineteenth-century Puritan. He wrote thirty-three books, notable among which, besides the two already mentioned, are: *Teaching and Teachers* (1884), *The Blood Covenant* (1885), *Hints on Child-Training* (1891), *Friendship the Master-Passion* (1892), *A Lie Never Justifiable* (1893), *War Memories of an Army Chaplain* (1898), *Border Lines in the Field of Doubtful Practices* (1899), *Illustrative Answers to Prayer* (1900), *Individual Work for Individuals* (1901), *How to Deal with Doubts and Doubters* (1903). At his death he was survived by six of his eight children.

[J. H. Lea, *Contributions to a Trumbull Geneal.* (1895); P. E. Howard, *The Life Story of Henry Clay Trumbull* (1905); *Congregationalist,* Nov. 7, Dec. 19, 1903; *Sunday School Times,* Dec. 12, 19, 1903; *The Congregational Year-Book, 1904* (1904); *Pub. Ledger* (Phila.) and *Phila. Inquirer,* Dec. 9, 1903.]

L. A. W.

TRUMBULL, JAMES HAMMOND (Dec. 20, 1821–Aug. 5, 1897), historian, philologist, and bibliographer, was the son of Gurdon and Sarah Ann (Swan) Trumbull of Stonington, Conn., and a brother of Henry Clay Trumbull [*q.v.*]. Prepared at Tracy's Academy, Norwich, he entered Yale College in 1838 but withdrew two years later because of poor health. After assisting James Harvey Linsley in cataloging the mammalia, birds, reptiles, fish, and shells of Connecticut, he was appointed assistant secretary of state in Connecticut in 1847. He received the nomination of the Whig party for the office of

secretary of state in 1852, but failed to win the election and declined similar nominations in 1853 and 1854. Following service as state librarian and registrar, he was again appointed assistant secretary of state in 1858. Three years later he was elected secretary of state on the Republican ticket and held the office until 1866. Upon the establishment of the Watkinson Library of Reference at Hartford, he was appointed trustee and librarian, and after 1866 devoted his full time to the duties of librarian. In 1890 he was appointed librarian emeritus.

While serving as assistant secretary of state Trumbull transcribed, edited, and published *The Public Records of the Colony of Connecticut, Prior to the Union with New Haven Colony, May, 1665* (1850). This was followed in 1852 by a second volume, covering the period from 1665 to 1677; and in 1859 by a third, covering the period from 1678 to 1689. In the appendix of the third volume was printed "Extracts from the Records of the United Colonies of New England," comprising such portions of the records as were not published in the second volume (1794) of Ebenezer Hazard's *Historical Collections*; these "Extracts" appeared as a separate publication in 1859. He contributed "A Sketch of the Life of Thomas Lechford" to Lechford's *Plain Dealing* (1867), and to the *Note-Book Kept by Thomas Lechford* (1885). The caustic criticism of Connecticut by Samuel Andrew Peters [*q.v.*] evoked from Trumbull's pen *The True-Blue Laws of Connecticut and New Haven and the False-Blue Laws Invented by the Rev. Samuel Peters* (1876), and *The Rev. Samuel Peters, His Defenders and Apologists* (1877), reprinted from the *Hartford Courant.* He also edited *The Memorial History of Hartford County, Connecticut, 1633–1884* (2 vols., 1886).

Trumbull made his most noteworthy contributions as the historian and philologist of the Indians. He published in 1865 a translation of John Eliot's Catechism for the Indians, and edited Roger Williams' "A Key into the Language of America" (*Publications of the Narragansett Club,* vol. I, 1866). Between 1869 and 1876 he contributed seven papers on the language of the Indians to the *Transactions* of the American Philological Association. He prepared "The Composition of Indian Geographical Names, Illustrated from the Algonkin Languages," for the *Collections of the Connecticut Historical Society* (vol. II, 1870); "On Some Alleged Specimens of Indian Onomatopoeia," for the *Transactions of the Connecticut Academy of the Arts and Sciences* (vol. II, 1871–73); and an introduction for Abraham Pierson, *Some Helps for the Indians,* published at Hartford in 1873 and included in *Collections of the Connecticut Historical Society* (vol. III, 1895). His "Origin and Early Progress of Indian Missions in New England, with a List of Books in the Indian Language" appears in the *Proceedings of the American Antiquarian Society* (1874), and his *Indian Names of Places, Etc., in and on the Borders of Connecticut: with Interpretations of Some of Them* was published at Hartford in 1881. To *The Memorial History of Hartford County* he contributed "Indians of the Connecticut Valley." Upon Trumbull's death, a "Natick Dictionary" in manuscript was deposited in the library of the American Antiquarian Society; it was published by the Smithsonian Institution in 1903 (*Bureau of American Ethnology, Bulletin 25,* 1903). Trumbull was also a bibliographer of note. His *Catalogue of the American Library of the Late Mr. George Brinley of Hartford, Conn.* (5 vols., 1878–97) still serves as a guide to Americana. At the time of his death a "List of Books Printed in Connecticut, 1709–1800," existed in manuscript and it was subsequently edited by his daughter and published in 1904 by the Acorn Club.

Trumbull's work brought him several honorary degrees, the complimentary appointment as lecturer on Indian languages at Yale, and membership in many historical, philological, and scientific societies. After a brief illness he died at Hartford. He was survived by his widow, Sarah A. (Robinson) Trumbull, whom he had married in 1855, and a daughter, Annie Eliot Trumbull.

[A. W. Wright, "Biog. Memoir of James Hammond Trumbull, 1821–1897," *Nat. Acad. of Sciences, Biog. Memoirs,* vol. VII (1913), separately printed in 1911; *Proc. Am. Antiquarian Soc.,* n.s., vol. XII (1899); *Cat. of the Officers and Grads. of Yale Univ. in New Haven, Conn., 1701–1924* (1924); *Hartford Courant,* Aug. 6, 1897.]   I. M. C.

TRUMBULL, JOHN (Apr. 13, 1750 o.s.–May 11, 1831), poet and jurist, was a member of an illustrious Connecticut family whose first American representative, John Trumble, was in Roxbury, Mass., in 1639, and the following year was made a freeman of Rowley. John Trumbull the poet was born at Westbury (now a part of Watertown), Conn. His father, John, a Congregational minister and a fellow of Yale College, was known as a man of sound judgment in practical affairs; he was a first cousin of Jonathan Trumbull, 1710–1785 [*q.v.*], Revolutionary governor of Connecticut. The poet's mother, Sarah (Whitman), a grand-daughter of Solomon Stoddard [*q.v.*], instructed and encouraged the boy while he made an almost incredible but well authenticated record of precocity, which culminated in a successful examination for entrance into Yale College at the age of seven. Being over-young for college life, Trumbull was honorably rusticated to Westbury until he was thirteen. He matriculated at Yale in 1763.

Although a faithful student, he disapproved of the Yale curriculum because of its concentration on "solid learning," *i.e.,* theology, mathematics, and linguistics, to the neglect of English composition and the interpretation of literature. Accordingly, with the cooperation of friends, including Timothy Dwight and David Humphreys [*qq.v.*], he satirized the course of study and attempted by example to create among the students a love of belles-lettres. The poetry which he wrote as a student was chiefly of two kinds: "correct" but undistinguished elegies written under the aegis of the neo-classical school, and brilliant, if fragmentary, comic verses with an occasional admixture of mild bawdry. From the former type he hoped ultimately for fame; the latter, which exhibited his true talents, he circulated privately among friends. His burlesque "Epithalamium," written in 1769, artfully combined wit and scholarship. In prose he produced a series of polished Addisonian essays, which were published in *The Boston Chronicle* (Sept. 4–7, 1769–Jan. 18–22, 1770). His valedictory oration, *An Essay on the Uses and Advantages of the Fine Arts,* which was promptly printed in 1770, was distinguished by its early plea for the abandonment of neo-classical rules in poetry; but the verses which concluded the oration were an egregious example of the very practices its thesis had condemned. Graduated and awarded a Berkeley fellowship in 1767, he continued his studies at Yale for three years more.

After receiving his master's degree in 1770, he spent a year in Wethersfield, Conn., studying law, writing verse, and (probably) teaching school. Upon returning to Yale in 1772 as a tutor, he soon commenced the composition of his comic satire on the abuses of collegiate instruction, *The Progress of Dulness,* a poem of seventeen hundred lines in octosyllabic couplets. Published in three parts during 1772 and 1773, it provoked local storms of criticism; but it pleased impartial judges and was reprinted in 1794, 1797, and 1801. During the second year of his tutorship Trumbull also brought to completion a series of thirty-eight essays, begun in 1770 under the pen-name, "The Correspondent," which he published in *The Connecticut Journal* (Feb. 23–July 6, 1770; Feb. 12–Sept. 3, 1773).

Having passed his bar examination in 1773, Trumbull moved to Boston, there to continue his legal studies under John Adams, whose confidential friend he remained for many years. In

Boston, Trumbull gained some of the political background for his comic epic, *M'Fingal*; but the poems that he wrote at the time showed him to be still dominated by the duller vices of the age of Pope. His first poem reflecting national affairs, *An Elegy on the Times* (1774), a glittering, bombastic piece, bore a patriotic message that was vitiated by the poet's untimely note of caution against violence. When Adams left Boston in August 1774, Trumbull retired to the relative security of New Haven, where he commenced the practice of law. He remained at New Haven until the menace of a British invasion in 1777 influenced him to withdraw to his native hamlet, Westbury. In 1781 he established himself at Hartford.

In the fall of 1775, at the suggestion of "some leading members of the first Congress," Trumbull wrote the initial canto of *M'Fingal*. This was published early in 1776 with a 1775 imprint. After the war, he divided this part into two cantos and wrote two additional ones. The whole work, containing approximately three thousand lines, was first published at Hartford in 1782. The framework of the poem is a loosely unified narrative of the misfortunes of the Tory squire, M'Fingal; but the poem virtually constitutes a comprehensive review of the blunders and cowardice of the British leaders throughout the Revolution. Despite its pro-Whig bias, the efficacy of *M'Fingal* as an agent of anti-Tory propaganda has been exaggerated. It had but three editions during the war, whereas Paine's *Common Sense,* published at the same time, had a sale of more than one hundred thousand copies within a few months. Though a patriot, Trumbull was not a fiery revolutionist of the stripe of Paine or Freneau. His principal powers were intellectual and critical rather than emotional. Consequently he invested his poem with literary qualities which received their fullest recognition after the war, when, despite Puritan prejudice against satirical poetry, *M'Fingal* was accepted as an important contribution to belles-lettres. Its inexhaustible wit, its air of learning without pedantry, and its buoyant Hudibrastic couplets that fitted snugly in the memory made it a cherished possession of the American people in an era when good native poets were not plentiful. Reprinted more than thirty times between 1782 and 1840, it was the most popular American poem of its length before Longfellow's *Evangeline.*

The merits of *M'Fingal* gave Trumbull the position of literary leader of the "Hartford Wits" during the eighties and nineties. Notwithstanding the grave competition of Dwight and Barlow, however, he did little to sustain his reputation. After 1782 he commenced no poetry of major importance; his small part in "The Anarchiad," which appeared in *The New Haven Gazette and the Connecticut Magazine* (1786–87), and in *The Echo* (1807), first published in the *American Mercury,* his miscellaneous newspaper verses and critical essays, and his lexicographical assistance to Noah Webster merely called attention to his declining creative powers. His literary defection, however, was balanced by his increasing interest in law and politics. After the Revolution, like most of the "Hartford Wits," he became a strong Federalist. He first held office in 1789, when he became state's attorney for the county of Hartford. In 1792 and 1800 he was elected to the state legislature. He was appointed judge of the superior court of Connecticut in 1801 and judge of the supreme court of errors in 1808. Both of these positions he held until he was removed from office by politics in 1819. Although the jurist thus survived the poet, the latter was not forgotten. In 1820 *The Poetical Works of John Trumbull* was issued in two volumes. The last six years of his life Trumbull spent at Detroit, Mich., where he died at two in the morning on May 11, 1831. On Nov. 21, 1776, he married Sarah Hubbard, by whom he had two sons and two daughters.

[The two principal collections of Trumbull MSS. are in the possession of Cornell Univ. Lib. and the Burton Hist. Coll. (Detroit). Yale Univ. possesses indispensable biog. material; the best collection of editions of *M'Fingal* is in the Watkinson Library (Hartford); the "Memoir of the Author" prefixed to Trumbull's *Poetical Works* is autobiographical but not infallible as to fact; the only full-length work on Trumbull is Alexander Cowie, *John Trumbull: Connecticut Wit* (1936); useful articles and books include Henry Bronson, *The Hist. of Waterbury, Conn.* (1858); Alexander Cowie, "John Trumbull as Revolutionist," in *Am. Lit.,* Nov. 1931; F. B. Dexter, *Biog. Sketches of the Grads. of Yale Coll.,* vol. III (1903); S. G. Goodrich, *Recollections of a Lifetime* (1857); Annie Marble, *Heralds of Am. Literature* (1907); V. L. Parrington, *The Connecticut Wits* (1926), and *The Colonial Mind* (1927); A. P. Stokes, *Memorials of Eminent Yale Men* (1914); J. H. Trumbull, *The Origin of M'Fingal* (1868); M. C. Tyler, *The Lit. Hist. of the Am. Revolution* (1897); R. J. Purcell, *Conn. in Transition* (1918); *A Geneal. Chart of Some of the Descendants of John Trumbull* (n.d.); J. H. Lea, *Contributions to a Trumbull Geneal.* (1895); *Detroit Courier,* May 12, 1831; *Proc. Am. Antiquarian Soc.,* Oct. 17, 1934.]　　A. C.

TRUMBULL, JOHN (June 6, 1756–Nov. 10, 1843), the painter of the Revolution, was born in Lebanon, New London County, Conn. The youngest of six children of Gov. Jonathan Trumbull [*q.v.*] and Faith (Robinson) Trumbull, he was "emphatically well born." Soon after his birth he was subject to convulsions caused by the overlapping of the bones of the cranium, but the natural form of his head was restored at the age of three. A year or so later he severely injured his left eye. Gilbert Stuart, once puzzling over one of Trumbull's drawings, remarked, "This looks as if it was drawn by a man with but one eye" (Dunlap, *post,* I, 217). The sickly child attended the local school, learning to read Greek at the age of six, and was ready for college at twelve. His predilection for drawing began at an early age. He begged his father to allow him to study under John Singleton Copley [*q.v.*], but the governor packed him off to Harvard at the age of fifteen in the middle of his junior year. He graduated in 1773, the youngest boy in his class. On the side he learned French and copied engravings. Returning to Lebanon, he taught school temporarily, copied more engravings, and made his first essays at historical composition.

Shortly after the outbreak of the Revolution the governor secured his son's appointment as adjutant, and a "sort of aid-du-camp" to Gen. Joseph Spencer of the 1st Connecticut Regiment. Brought to Washington's attention by the accurate drawings he had made of the British gun emplacements, Trumbull was appointed second aide-de-camp to the new commanding general (General Order, July 27, 1775, *Proceedings of the Massachusetts Historical Society,* vol. XV, 1878, p. 132), but he felt himself unequal to the "elegant duties" of this post and was thankful when commissioned major of brigade (August 1775). He participated in the action at Dorchester Heights the following March and witnessed the British evacuation of Boston, proceeding afterwards to New York. On June 28, 1776, he became deputy adjutant-general with the rank of colonel under Gen. Horatio Gates, going with him to Crown Point and Ticonderoga, and later into Pennsylvania; he afterwards accompanied Gen. Benedict Arnold to Rhode Island, wintering in Providence. When in February he finally received his signed commission from Congress, he returned it "within an hour" because it was dated three months late.

His military career suddenly terminating, Trumbull, now twenty-one, went to Boston to take up art. For a time he rented the famous painting rooms occupied by John Smibert [*q.v.*], but in the summer of 1778 he offered his services to Gen. John Sullivan as a volunteer aide-de-camp in the Rhode Island campaign, during which he conducted himself gallantly. The following year Trumbull was in Boston once more, pursuing his study of painting. In the fall of 1779, however, he undertook a speculation for the supply of military stores to the American army. Foreseeing the possible failure of the project, the rebel officer secured through his father's friend John Temple, afterwards British consul-general,

permission to study painting in London and in May 1780 sailed for France. He obtained a letter to Benjamin West [*q.v.*] from Franklin in Paris, proceeded to London, and was received with the usual kindness by West, who accepted him as a pupil. The pleasant life of making twice-removed copies after the old masters at West's studio on Newman Street was rudely interrupted by Trumbull's arrest on Nov. 19, 1780, on "suspicion of treason" under suspension of the *habeas corpus* act. His imprisonment in Tothill Fields Bridewell was said to have been a reprisal for the tragic hanging of Major André. Both Charles James Fox and Edmund Burke interested themselves in the case and ultimately secured his release (see Lewis Einstein, *Divided Loyalties,* 1933, p. 374). Trumbull immediately crossed to the Continent, where he attempted to negotiate a loan for Connecticut through his father's Amsterdam bankers, M. de Neufville & Son, for whom he painted a full-length portrait of Washington (1780). This was engraved by Valentine Green and published the following year, the first authentic portrait of Washington issued in Europe. After a vexatious delay in Spain he returned to Boston. During the winter of 1782 and the fall of 1783 he acted as confidential agent for his brother Joseph [*q.v.*], then engaged in a contract for army supplies, at New Windsor, N. Y. At the end of the war he again considered entering "regular commerce." His practical father urged law. When the painter "dwelt upon the honors paid to artists" in antiquity, his father rejoined in the oft-quoted phrase, "You appear to forget, sir, that Connecticut is not Athens" (*Autobiography,* p. 89).

In December 1783 Trumbull embarked for London. When hoped-for commercial connections did not develop he went to the benevolent Mr. West and was again accepted as a pupil, working in the studio by day and attending the Royal Academy school evenings. In 1785, after copying West's celebrated "Battle of La Hogue" for his master, and composing his "Priam and the Dead Body of Hector," he fortunately abandoned the Greeks and the Romans for contemporary history. His first subjects, the "Battle of Bunker's Hill" and the "Death of General Montgomery in the Attack of Quebec," were painted in West's studio and under his direction, and were completed in the spring of 1786. Inspired by Boydell's publications and encouraged by his master, he embarked on a plan of publishing engravings after the paintings and associated himself in this undertaking with Antonio C. de Poggi, an Italian artist and publisher of Bond Street, London, by whom six plates were issued.

Armed with letters from John Adams, the minister to Great Britain, Trumbull proceeded to Paris in the summer of 1785 in search of suitable engravers, and there was encouraged by Thomas Jefferson to continue the scheme. After traveling in France and in Germany, where he left his paintings with his agent Poggi, he returned to London in November 1786. "Bunker's Hill" was ultimately engraved by John G. von Müller of Stuttgart, and "Quebec" by J. F. Clemens of Denmark, both dated 1798, twelve years after the completion of the paintings.

The next three years in London, stimulated by travel, broadened by study, and encouraged by praise, were the most creative in the artist's life. The small painting of the "Declaration of Independence," which occupied eight years, was begun. This brilliant and dignified achievement remains the most important visual record of the heroic period of American history, although not historically accurate in every detail. Thirty-six of the forty-eight portraits were from life, the rest from portraits by others and from memory; thirteen signers were not represented; and four non-signers were included. The "Surrender of Lord Cornwallis at Yorktown," the "Death of General Mercer at the Battle of Princeton," and the "Capture of the Hessians at Trenton" followed, all painted in West's studio. Finding his American Revolutionary subjects none too popular in England, Trumbull expediently undertook to celebrate a feat of British arms, selecting the "Sortie Made by the Garrison of Gibraltar" and producing a little masterpiece (Jean L. Brockway, "Trumbull's Sortie," *Art Bulletin,* March 1934, with checklist of replicas. In 1787 and again in 1789 Trumbull was in Paris, painting French and British officers, staying with Jefferson, who tentatively offered him a post of private secretary in the American legation in Paris at £300 a year (letter, May 21, 1789, *Autobiography,* p. 155). Trumbull declined this offer, however, and returned to America to further his "national work."

Congress was then meeting in New York, whither Trumbull repaired in December 1789 to obtain portraits for the four historical compositions already undertaken and to secure subscriptions for the engravings of the first two. Washington headed the list with four sets and, as his *Diary* records, obligingly sat a number of times for his former aide. Later in the same city Trumbull solicited commissions from the city council and painted twelve portraits in all. "Heads" and subscribers were collected in New England, Pennsylvania, Virginia, and South Carolina. Yorktown was visited and the terrain for the "Surrender of Cornwallis" studied. In 1792 Trumbull was again in Philadelphia, where he painted the large portrait of "Washington before the Battle of Princeton" (engraved in stipple by Thomas Cheesman) for Charleston, S. C. The picture was rejected, and another had to be painted. Subscriptions languished, and Trumbull, the best portrait-painter in America, Stuart excepted, again abandoned painting, never to resume it on the same plane or with so little competition.

In 1793 at the particular request of John Jay, envoy extraordinary to Great Britain, Trumbull became his private secretary, prompted perhaps by the realization of an earlier ambition (he had solicited a foreign secretaryship from Congress after his resignation from the army) or by the opportunity to supervise the engraving of his paintings. The mission set out from New York in May 1794, and the complicated negotiations were concluded in November. After committing Jay's Treaty to memory, Trumbull proceeded to Paris to repeat it to Monroe, visited Stuttgart to ascertain what progress had been made with his "Bunker's Hill," and then returned to Paris, where he undertook a series of unsuccessful commercial ventures. Paintings from broken-up noble collections were purchased with funds supplied by West and auctioned at Christie's in London in 1797 (W. Buchanan, *Memoirs of Painting,* 1824, I, 257). The second speculation, the purchase of brandy in France, a business involving eight months' time, ended disastrously. In August 1796 Trumbull was appointed the fifth member of the commission to oversee the execution of the seventh article of the Jay Treaty, a post which he accepted with some hesitancy, but in which he acquitted himself with distinction. In the summer of 1797 he revisited Stuttgart to get his picture and the engraved plate. Returning via Paris, he found himself listed among the suspect and was denied permission to proceed to Calais, but his friend, the painter David, got him out of his uncomfortable predicament (see C. L. Lokke, in *New England Quarterly,* March 1934). In London once more (November 1797) the work of the commission was resumed, terminating in May 1804.

The years between 1799 and 1804 are passed over without comment in Trumbull's *Autobiography.* He resided in Bath in 1801 and 1802. He married, without consulting or advising his family, a pretty Englishwoman, Sarah (Hope) Harvey, Oct. 1, 1800, about whom there has been much mystery (see *Diary of William Dunlap,* 1930, III, 738–39, 800–01, for gossip). Whoever she was, her social position was inferior to that of her husband, who devoted only six lines to her in the *Autobiography,* on the occasion of her death in 1824. Two pleasing portraits exist of her at Yale, one by Samuel L. Waldo and the other by her husband (1800), who also painted her on her death bed. There were no children. As a young man in Connecticut, Trumbull, with a number of others, was involved with a country girl. A child was born, and Trumbull, the most affluent of the group, was claimed as father. He contributed towards the support of the child, John Trumbull Ray, as he was later named, apprenticing him to a gentleman farmer in England and finally purchasing him a lieutenant's commission in the British army. (A miniature portrait of Ray in a scarlet uniform is in the possession of Maria Trumbull Dana of New Haven.)

Wearying of Europe, Trumbull decided to settle in Boston, sailing with his wife in April 1804, but he found Gilbert Stuart [*q.v.*] so well established there that he wisely decided to go to New York. Trumbull was a rapid painter, averaging five sittings to a head, for which he charged one hundred dollars, and correspondingly more for half and full lengths. The Timothy Dwight and the Stephen van Rensselaer at Yale are in the new and less fortunate style of the erstwhile diplomat and merchant, to whose art the constant interruptions in his work proved fatal. A large collection of pictures purchased in Paris was hung in the Park Theatre, the "first public exhibition of original pictures by the old masters of Europe . . . in America" (Dunlap, *post,* II, 49), did not pay the costs, and was returned to London. In December 1808, thoroughly soured by lack of patronage, Trumbull sailed for London for the fourth and last time, but neither portrait painting, a projected panorama of Niagara Falls, nor his "large pictures" proved successful. Hope of a speedy return to America was destroyed by the declaration of war in 1812.

As soon as hostilities ceased, Trumbull embarked for New York, arriving in September 1815. There, because of his own waning talents and competition from such men as S. F. B. Morse, Thomas Sully, John Wesley Jarvis, John Vanderlyn [*qq.v.*], and others, he met with little success. In Washington, however, where Congress was in session, Timothy Pitkin championed the aging painter's "long suspended" plan for the painting of his Revolutionary subjects in the Capitol. The subjects already executed (in miniature for the engraver) were exhibited in the House in 1816; and at length Trumbull was commissioned by Congress (Feb. 6, 1817) to paint four pictures in the Rotunda. A contract was eventually drawn up (March 1817) for the execution of the "Surrender of General Burgoyne at Saratoga," the "Surrender of Lord Cornwallis at Yorktown," the "Declaration of Independence," and the "Resignation of Washington," the price being settled at $8,000 each.

President Madison unhappily insisted that the figures be "as large as life," which the monocular Trumbull rarely painted well even in his best period. Other painters, especially Vanderlyn, resented the award to the combative and overbearing ex-Revolutionary soldier. The last of the four twelve-by-eighteen-foot canvases—all painted in New York—, replicas of the miniature paintings now at Yale, was finished in April 1824 after seven years of effort, twenty-five years or more after their conception. The heavy-handed, chalky-colored replicas (see Trumbull's *Description of the Four Pictures . . . in the Rotunda of the Capitol,* 1827) were not successful. John Quincy Adams records his disappointment in seeing the enlarged "Declaration" (*Diary,* Sept. 1, 1818), which Trumbull exhibited commercially before its installation, in New York, Philadelphia, and Baltimore. The other enlargements were exhibited in like manner and with considerable profit. The pictures were installed under the supervision of the artist in 1824. Four years later it was found necessary to remove and repair them on account of dampness and wanton injury (*Autobiography,* p. 281).

In the meantime other troubles beset the aging painter. His wife died in 1824, and the apartments at Park Place and Church Street were given up. Negotiations were undertaken for the engraving of the "Declaration," subscriptions for which were solicited in advance, the work finally being entrusted (contract December 1820) to the young Asher Brown Durand [*q.v.*]. Although the print established the reputation of the engraver it was another financial disappointment to Trumbull. In 1817 Trumbull had become president of the American Academy of Fine Arts; but lack of public interest, the opposition of cliques, and finally the secession of most of the artists resulted in the founding of the National Academy of Design (1826) under the presidency of Morse, leaving the dictatorial and cantankerous Trumbull the captain of a sinking ship. For years he had been in debt to his bankers, and at length, pressed for settlement, he liquidated his New York State land holdings. In 1832 a military pension was secured. Replicas of earlier work and large religious paintings, "nearly all of which should have been destroyed" (Weir, *post,* p. 42), were unhappily completed by the artist.

At this juncture Prof. Benjamin Silliman of Yale, Trumbull's nephew by marriage, suggested the establishing of a gallery at New Haven to contain Trumbull's unsalable pictures. He induced friends to finance an annuity of one thousand dollars on condition that Trumbull's collection be turned over to Yale College, which agreed to erect a gallery after the artist's design for the reception of the pictures. The Trumbull Gallery, the earliest art museum connected with an educational institution in America, was opened to the public in October 1832. The artist wrote a carefully prepared catalogue (1832), and Silliman became curator. Silliman was also somewhat responsible for the publication of Trumbull's *Autobiography*. When William Dunlap [*q.v.*] wrote his history of American painting in 1834 he used the manuscript biography that Trumbull had dictated to James Herring [*q.v.*], adding his own emotional observations and gossip. Trumbull justly attacked the *Arts of Design* (*New York American*, Dec. 13, 1834), Dunlap replying. Silliman urged the aged artist to elaborate and publish his early notes, and in 1841 the defensive *Autobiography, Letters, and Reminiscences of John Trumbull, from 1756 to 1841* appeared. It has remained the chief source for all later writers. In 1841 the old man returned from New Haven to New York, where he died two years later at the age of eighty-seven. According to his instructions he was buried beside his wife beneath the Trumbull Gallery. The bodies were removed, along with the pictures, in 1866 to a new and larger building, and again, April 1928, to the new Yale Gallery of Fine Arts.

Trumbull was a handsome man, as can be seen from Stuart's early portrait, his two self-portraits, the small full-length by George W. Twibill, and especially the Waldo and Jewett at Yale. Ball Hughes's marble bust of Trumbull is at Yale. In 1849 the American Art-Union issued a portrait medal. Trumbull was dignified and courtly in bearing, punctilious, frank and abstemious, high-strung, excitable, impetuous, exceedingly sensitive and ready to take offense. As an old and disappointed man he was irritable, uncompromising, and haughty. He was, however, a gentleman by birth, education, and instinct.

Some notice should be paid to Trumbull, the amateur architect. He drew up plans for a series of dormitory buildings for Yale in 1792 and designed the Barclay Street quarters of the American Academy (1831), the Trumbull Gallery, and the Congregational church in Lebanon (1804). He might have become a better architect than he was painter; the opportunity, as Edmund Burke had once told him, was far greater. Yet it is impossible not to be grateful for Trumbull's determined devotion to historical painting. Far

as he is from being America's greatest painter, he is nevertheless inextricably a part of America's past; no schoolboy but sees the Revolution through his eyes. His 250 to 300 faithful representations, drawn from life, of the principal actors and actions of the Revolution make him at once the chief, the most prolific, and the most competent visual recorder of that heroic period.

[For biog. materials, in addition to the incomplete and stuffy *Autobiog., Reminiscences, and Letters of John Trumbull* (1841), and William Dunlap, *The Hist. of the Rise and Progress of the Arts of Design in the U. S.* (3 vols., 1918), ed. by F. W. Bayley and C. E. Goodspeed, see *A Geneal. Chart of Some of the Descendants of John Trumbull of Newcastle-on-Tyne* (n.d.); J. H. Lea, *A Geneal. of the Ancestors . . . of George Augustus and Louisa (Clap) Trumbull* (1886); Trumbull's *Letters Proposing a Plan for the Permanent Encouragement of the Fine Arts by the Nat. Government* (1827), *Address Read before the Am. Acad. of Fine Arts* (1833), and a series of cats. and explanations of his pictures prepared by Trumbull; *Cat. of Paintings by Col. Trumbull . . . Am. Acad. of the Fine Arts* (1831); S. F. B. Morse, *Examination of Col. Trumbull's Address* (1833); Benjamin Silliman, in *Am. Jour. of Science and Arts*, vol. I, no. 2 (1819), vol. VIII, no. 1 (1824), July–Sept. 1840, and Oct.–Dec. 1843; *Am. Acad. of Fine Arts, Charter and By-Laws* (1817); T. S. Cummings, *Hist. Annals of the Nat. Acad. of Design* (1865); and obituaries in *N. Y. American*, Nov. 10, *N. Y. Spectator, Columbian Reg.* (New Haven), Nov. 11, and *Daily Morning Courier* (New Haven), Nov. 11, 13, 1843. See also John Durand, *John Trumbull* (1881); J. F. Weir, *John Trumbull* (1901), with an excellent appraisal of the paintings; Theodore Bolton, *Early Am. Portrait Painters in Miniature* (1921), with a checklist; J. H. Morgan, *Paintings by John Trumbull at Yale Univ.* (1926); with good illustrations and keys to the eight hist. pictures; B. L. Belden, *Indian Peace Medals Issued in the U. S.* (1927), pp. 23–24; Theodore Sizer, "The Trumbull Gallery, 1832–1932," *Yale Alumni Weekly*, Oct. 28, Nov. 4, 1932; *Conn. Tercentenary . . . John Trumbull and Trumbull Memorabilia . . . Yale Univ.* (1935), a convenient checklist; Theodore Bolton and H. L. Binsse, in *Antiquarian*, July 1931. The Trumbull and Silliman papers at Yale, which include Trumbull's marriage certificate, are the largest manuscript source. Important material is in the possession of the Robert Fridenberg Gallery, New York; the N. Y. Pub. Lib.; the N. Y. Hist. Soc.; the Conn. Hist. Soc.; the Mass. Hist. Soc.; the Boston Athenaeum; M. B. Brainard of Hartford, Conn.; and in the records of the First Ecclesiastical Soc., Lebanon, Aug. 13, 1804. Many references to Trumbull occur in the writings of Jefferson, Rufus King, J. Q. Adams, and others. Trumbull's paintings and drawings, and engravings after his designs are scattered in pub. and private colls., among them those at Yale; the Wadsworth Athenaeum, Hartford; the City Hall and Chamber of Commerce, New York, and the coll. of Mrs. I. Sheldon Tilney, N. Y. City. His painting cabinet, etc., is at Yale. Forgeries abound, particularly of his pencil and sepia portrait studies; the largest group appears in the Ed. Frossard sale of 1894. The most important of many auction sales were those of Dec. 1896 and Feb. 1897 (the "Silliman Sale"), Jan. 1926, and Mar. 1931 (Trumbull-Silliman correspondence), Am. Art Asso., N. Y.]   T. S—r.

TRUMBULL, JONATHAN (Oct. 12, 1710–Aug. 17, 1785), governor of Connecticut, was born at Lebanon, Conn., the second son of Joseph and Hannah (Higley) Trumble. He did not adopt the present spelling of the name until 1766. His great-grandfather, John Trumble, had emigrated from England to Roxbury, Mass., in 1639 and the following year was made a freeman of Rowley; his father was an early settler in Lebanon, where he developed a considerable mercantile business. In 1727 Jonathan graduated from Harvard and returned to Lebanon to prepare for the ministry. He was licensed to preach by the Windham Association and in 1731 was considering a call to the church of nearby Colchester when his elder brother Joseph, their father's business associate, died. Recognizing a call to duty, Jonathan abandoned his own plans and took his brother's place. On Dec. 9, 1735, he married Faith Robinson, daughter of Rev. John Robinson of Duxbury, Mass., a union which raised his social standing considerably. To them were born four sons and two daughters. Joseph [q.v.], the eldest son, was the first commissary-general of the Continental Army; Jonathan [q.v.], after a military and political career, also became governor of Connecticut; and John, 1756–1843 [q.v.], acquired fame as a painter. John Trumbull, 1750–1831 [q.v.], the poet and wit, was a second cousin of these three.

Trumbull soon disclosed an exceptional aptitude for commerce. With various partners he developed an extensive trade, establishing direct commercial connections with Great Britain instead of dealing only indirectly through Boston and New York as did most Connecticut merchants. By the 1760's Trumbull was one of the outstanding figures of Connecticut commerce; but in 1766 came a change. For reasons not entirely clear, his business suffered a reversal from which it never recovered. He was forced into virtual—though not legal—bankruptcy, and at the outbreak of the Revolution still owed large sums to his British creditors.

While Trumbull was still in his early twenties he entered politics. First sent to the General Assembly in 1733, he was returned frequently and in 1739 served as speaker. His abilities soon attracted attention and he was chosen assistant in 1740, the first time his name appeared in nomination—an unusual achievement for a man of thirty. For the next ten years he was regularly reëlected until a political reversal in 1750–51 led to his loss of the assistantship. Elected again to the Assembly, he served twice more as speaker. He was restored to the Council in 1754 in his previous order of seniority. In 1766 Gov. Thomas Fitch [q.v.], who had taken the oath required of all governors by the Stamp Act, was defeated for reëlection. Trumbull, now second councilor, had sided with the majority in this dispute and was in consequence advanced to the deputy governorship. In this capacity he served for three and a half years. As deputy governor he was also regularly named chief justice of the superior court. Though not trained in the law, he had judicial experience. In 1744 he had become a justice of the quorum and two years later was named judge of the Windham county court, a position which he had held, with one three-year interruption, ever since. He had also served continuously as judge of the Windham probate court since 1747. His most conspicuous action as chief justice was in successfully turning aside the application of the royal customs officers for writs of assistance (1768–69).

Upon the death of Gov. William Pitkin, 1694–1769 [q.v.] in October 1769, the Assembly named Trumbull to the governorship, a position which he continued to fill until his voluntary retirement in 1784. In the period of increasing tension between the colonies and the mother country Trumbull stood as a stanch supporter of colonial rights. As early as 1770 he foresaw the possibility of independence, distressing as the thought still seemed to him ("The Trumbull Papers," post, I, 403). When hostilities actually began he was the only colonial governor to take the radical side. He threw himself at once into active support of the Continental Army, and when independence was proclaimed, welcomed its declaration. The scene of little actual fighting, but close to several major fields of operation, Connecticut became a principal source of supply for the American troops. In supervising this work, for which his previous business experience well fitted him, Trumbull made his chief contribution to the cause. His relations with Washington became close, the commander writing him on an average of every ten days until 1778, letters appearing less frequently thereafter except in times of emergency. The General counted heavily upon the Governor's supplying him with food, clothing, and munitions. To a large extent Trumbull was able to meet Washington's expectations —if not his hopes—but at times the General expressed bitter disappointment at what seemed indifference to his most pressing needs. Neither man could always comprehend the other's situation. Trumbull sometimes failed to appreciate the inevitable waste of *matériel* incident to military operations and felt that Washington's demands exceeded what Connecticut could reasonably be expected to provide. The General similarly failed to understand the difficulty of Trumbull's position as head of a community that had always been freer from outside control than any other colony and was now living in terror of occasional British raids. At one time Trumbull seemed to show a greater admiration for Gates than for Washington, but there is at present no available evidence that he was involved in the "Conway cabal." In spite of difficulties, Trumbull and Washington cooperated loyally. Without the former's help as a civilian leader the army's sufferings would have been immeasurably increased, and on his death Washington acknowledged that his services "justly entitled him to the first place among patriots" (*Colonial Society of Massachusetts Publications*, vol. VII, 1905, p. 183). In 1846 a newspaper story appeared telling how Washington's reliance upon Trumbull's advice and help had led the General to remark at a moment of perplexity, "We must consult Brother Jonathan." The expression is said to have spread throughout the army and the people until "Brother Jonathan" became a generic term to describe America and Americans. The historical accuracy of the legend must be doubted, however. The British, indeed, used the term "Brother Jonathan" to designate the Americans as early as March 1776, but there is no contemporary evidence to connect Jonathan Trumbull with the origin of the phrase (Albert Matthews, "Brother Jonathan," *Ibid.*, pp. 95–125).

While Trumbull was devoting his energies to the prosecution of the war, he was also facing political difficulties at home. He became the victim of a whispering campaign to the effect that he was secretly trading with the enemy. The rumor helped reduce his popular majority to a mere plurality in the elections of 1780 and 1781, although in both years the Assembly returned him to office over his rivals. In January 1782 he demanded a legislative investigation, which led to his complete vindication, the committee expressing the belief that the rumors were circulated by the British in an effort to discredit a leading patriot. The committee's report quieted the opposition but a year later political storms broke once more. Trumbull's firm belief in the necessity of a stronger central government and his support of the unpopular plan for half pay for disbanded officers brought renewed opposition in May 1783. Again he was chosen only by the Assembly. Wearied by his years of strenuous service and disliking the prospect of further opposition, the old man, just passing his seventy-third birthday, informed the October Assembly that he would not again be a candidate. His *Address . . . Declining Any Further Election to Public Office* (1783), which pled for a federal union stronger politically and financially than the existing government, marks him as a John the Baptist of Federalism. In May 1784 he retired from office and devoted the remaining fifteen months of his life to his long-neglected personal affairs and to the subject of his youthful interest, the study of theology.

Trumbull, as described by a contemporary, was "about five feet, seven inches high, has dark eyes, a Roman nose, sallow countenance, long chin, prominent forehead, high and broad cheek bones, hollow cheeks and short neck. In person of a handsome figure and very active" (Peters, *post*, p. 10). He had little interest in what seemed the lighter things of life. His son John's artistic ambitions gained no sympathy from him and his own election to the American Academy of Arts and Sciences in 1782 would have remained unacknowledged but for the prompting of Ezra Stiles ("Trumbull Papers," IV, 404, 412). For Hebrew, Greek, and Latin, however, he retained a lasting affection. Yale and the University of Edinburgh conferred the degree of LL.D. upon him. A strong sense of duty and of divine leadership was part of his Puritan heritage. Throughout the war, in times of deepest gloom as well as in the hour of final triumph, his letters repeat the thought "the Lord reigneth," which conviction was the unshakable foundation of his faith.

[Sources include Trumbull MSS., Conn. State Lib. and Conn. Hist. Soc., Hartford; "The Trumbull Papers," 4 vols., in *Colls. Mass. Hist. Soc.*, 5 ser. IX and X (1885), 7 ser. II and III (1902); Peter Force, *Am. Archives* (9 vols., 1837–53); Jared Sparks, *The Writings of George Washington* (12 vols., 1834–37); W. C. Ford, *The Writings of George Washington* (14 vols., 1889–93), J. C. Fitzpatrick, *The Writings of George Washington*, vols. I–XI (1931–34); C. J. Hoadly, *The Public Records of the Colony of Conn.*, vols. VII–XV (1873–90), and *The Public Records of the State of Conn., 1776–81* (3 vols., 1894–1922); Zebulon Ely, *The Death of Moses the Servant of the Lord; a Sermon Preached at the Funeral Solemnity of His Excellency Jonathan Trumbull* (1786). I. W. Stuart, *Life of Jonathan Trumbull, Sen., Gov. of Conn.* (1849); Jonathan Trumbull, *Jonathan Trumbull Gov. of Conn., 1769–1784* (1919); Samuel Peters, "Hist. of Jonathan Trumbull, the Present Rebel Governor of Conn.," *Political Mag.*, Jan. 1781. For family connections see J. H. Lea, *Contributions to a Trumbull Geneal.* (1895); *A Geneal. Chart of Some of the Descendants of John Trumbull* (n.d.). Portraits of Trumbull by his son John are in the Gallery of Fine Arts and Trumbull College, Yale University, and in the Wadsworth Athenaeum, Hartford, Conn.] L. W. L.

TRUMBULL, JONATHAN (Mar. 26, 1740–Aug. 7, 1809), Revolutionary soldier, governor of Connecticut, congressman, and senator, was born in Lebanon, Conn., the son of Jonathan Trumbull [*q.v.*] and his wife Faith (Robinson) Trumbull. At the age of fifteen he entered Harvard College and was graduated in 1759 as salutatorian of his class. Three years later he was awarded the degree of M.A. and delivered the valedictory oration at the commencement exercises. In March 1767 he married Eunice Backus of Norwich, Conn., by whom he had a son and four daughters.

His political career began with his election in 1770 as selectman of Lebanon, an office which he held during the succeeding five years. He also represented Lebanon in the state legislature at various times—in 1774, 1775, 1779, 1780, 1788. In May of the last-mentioned year he was elected speaker of the House. On July 28, 1775, the Continental Congress unanimously chose him "Pay master of the forces for the New York department," an office which he occupied, in the face of grave difficulties arising from an impoverished treasury, until July 29, 1778, when he retired in order to undertake the task of settling the accounts of his brother Joseph [q.v.], commissary-general of the army, who had recently died. He was the first person to serve as comptroller of the treasury, a position to which he was unanimously elected by Congress on Nov. 3, 1778. He resigned in April 1779, and on Nov. 9 was chosen commissioner of the board of treasury but declined the office. On June 8, 1781, he was appointed secretary to Washington and remained a member of the latter's military family until the close of the war, when he retired for a period from public life in order to look after his private affairs.

Upon the erection of the new government under the Constitution, he was elected to the First, Second, and Third congresses. The esteem in which he was held by his fellow legislators is attested by the fact that in October 1791 he was chosen speaker of the House. In October 1794 he was elected to succeed Stephen Mix Mitchell [q.v.] in the Senate of the United States. After serving from Mar. 4, 1795, to June 10, 1796, he resigned in order to become deputy governor of Connecticut. Upon the death of Oliver Wolcott [q.v.] in December 1797, he succeeded to the governorship, an office which he held by annual election during the remainder of his life. Ever a stanch Federalist, he viewed the policies of Jefferson and his followers with repugnance. When Henry Dearborn [q.v.], the secretary of war, requested the use of the militia in conformity with the act passed by Congress on Jan. 9, 1809, for the enforcement of the Embargo, Trumbull refused on the ground that the measure in question was an unconstitutional invasion of the rights of the states. On Feb. 23, in an address (published in the *Connecticut Courant*, Mar. 1, 1809) to the legislature which had been called into special session to consider the situation, he justified the opposition of Connecticut to the Embargo by ironically employing the language of the Virginia Resolves of 1798, of which James Madison, president-elect and heir to Jefferson's

policies, was the author (Henry Adams, *History of the United States*, vol. IV, 1890).

Trumbull died of dropsy of the heart and was buried at Lebanon. While his successes in public life may be ascribed in part to family influence, they were mainly due to his natural capacity for the management of large affairs. In the transaction of business he was orderly and unhurried. A man of cheerful spirit and affable manners, he possessed the gift of easy intercourse with all ranks of society.

[Manuscript correspondence of Trumbull in the Conn. Hist. Soc.; Zebulon Ely, *The Peaceful End of the Perfect Man* . . . (1809); Timothy Dwight, *A Discourse Occasioned by the Death of His Excellency Jonathan Trumbull* (1809); O. D. Hine, *Early Lebanon* (1880); W. C. Ford, *The Writings of George Washington* (14 vols., 1889–93); J. C. Fitzpatrick, *The Writings of George Washington*, vols. I–XI (1931–34); "The Trumbull Papers," *Mass. Hist. Soc. Colls.*, 7 ser. II, III (1902); W. C. Ford and J. C. Fitzpatrick, *Jours. of the Continental Congress*, vols. I–XXXI (1904–34); Jonathan Trumbull, *Jonathan Trumbull, Gov. of Conn., 1764–1784* (1919); E. C. Burnett, *Letters of Members of the Continental Congress*, vols. I–VI (1921–33); R. J. Purcell, *Conn. in Transition* (1918); *Conn. Courant* (Hartford), Aug. 16, 1809.] E. E. C.

TRUMBULL, JOSEPH (Mar. 11, 1737–July 23, 1778), commissary-general of the Continental Army, was born at Lebanon, Conn., the eldest son of Jonathan Trumbull [q.v.] and his wife, Faith Robinson; the younger Jonathan and the painter John Trumbull [qq.v.] were his brothers. After graduating from Harvard in 1756, he was engaged for eleven years in his father's firm, making two trips to England in behalf of its interests. In 1767 he was elected to the General Assembly of Connecticut and served therein almost continuously for six years. In May 1773 he was chosen a member of the state committee of correspondence, and in August 1774 was selected to represent Connecticut in the Continental Congress as alternate to Roger Sherman [q.v.]. He had in the meantime joined to his knowledge of business affairs some acquaintance with military matters by serving as captain of a trainband. Hence in April 1775 he was appointed by the Assembly commissary-general of the Connecticut troops, concentrated near Boston. His efficiency in provisioning them so favorably impressed Washington that on July 10, 1775, he urged Congress to entrust Trumbull with the task of victualing all the patriot forces, and on July 19 Congress appointed him commissary-general of the army with the rank and pay of colonel.

His problem was to produce order out of the chaos which characterized the business of feeding the army. It was a task fraught with numerous difficulties. Transportation was slow and laborious. Purchasing was hampered by currency depreciation, lack of funds, and state embargoes. Both Congress and the states appointed numerous commissaries who disputed his authority. Such disputes were often intensified by personal and sectional animosities. A court of inquiry appointed by Washington in December 1775 to examine complaints against him found fault with the prices fixed by him for provisions but acquitted him of any fraudulent intent. In 1776 he was drawn into controversy with General Schuyler regarding the right of the commissary-general to exercise plenary control over the provisioning of the northern army. While Trumbull's conduct in the matter was not without blemish, his claim of authority was sustained by both Washington and Congress (J. C. Fitzpatrick, *The Writings of George Washington*, vol. V, 1932, pp. 257, 357–58).

In the spring of 1777 Congress voted to reorganize the commissary department by creating two commissary-generals, one of purchases and the other of issues. Trumbull was offered the former post, but declined it on the ground that the new scheme was unworkable since the deputy commissaries were to be appointed by and made responsible to Congress. Subsequent events seemed to justify his contention, for in the following year Congress reëstablished the previous system. In the meantime Trumbull had been elected to membership on the board of war, but after brief service (November 1777–April 1778) was compelled to resign by reason of poor health. Retiring to Lebanon, he succumbed to illness induced by his exhausting labors as commissary-general. While his services to the Continental Army were undramatic, they were indispensable. "Few armies, if any," wrote Washington, "have been better and more plentifully supplied than the troops under Mr. Trumbull's care" (*Ibid.*, V, 192). In March 1777 Trumbull was married to Amelia Dyer.

[Papers of Joseph Trumbull in possession of the Conn. Hist. Soc.; Jonathan Trumbull, "Joseph Trumbull," in *Records and Papers of the New London County Hist. Soc.*, Pt. III, vol. II (1897); C. J. Hoadly, *The Pub. Records of the Colony of Conn.*, vols. XII–XIV (1881–87), and *The Pub. Records of the State of Conn.* (3 vols., 1894–1922); "The Trumbull Papers," in *Mass. Hist. Soc. Colls.*, 7 ser. II (1902); Jonathan Trumbull, *Life of Jonathan Trumbull, Gov. of Conn.* (1919); E. C. Burnett, *Letters of Members of the Continental Cong.*, vols. I–IV (1921–28), and "The Continental Cong. and Agric. Supplies," in *Agric. Hist.*, July 1928.]   E. E. C.

TRUMBULL, LYMAN (Oct. 12, 1813–June 25, 1896), jurist, United States senator, was born in Colchester, Conn., the son of Benjamin and Elizabeth (Mather) Trumbull, and a grandson of Benjamin Trumbull [*q.v.*]. He attended Bacon Academy in his native town, and when twenty years old went to Greenville, Ga., where he taught school for three years. In the meantime he read law and in 1836 was admitted to the bar. The following year he began practice in Belleville, Ill., and soon entered politics. He was elected to the state legislature as a Democrat in 1840, but resigned in 1841 to accept appointment as secretary of state, in which capacity he served until removed by the governor in 1843. He then practised law and was a candidate for various offices until 1848, when he was elected justice of the state supreme court; in 1852 he was reëlected for a term of nine years.

He had served but two years of this term, however, when he was elected to the United States House of Representatives as an anti-Nebraska Democrat, but before taking his seat a three-cornered legislative contest, in which Lincoln, in order to elect a free-soiler, threw his Whig support to Trumbull, resulted in his being sent to the Senate. The three terms that he served (1855–73) were marked by the bitter struggle over slavery and reconstruction, during which he was first a Democrat, next a leading Republican, and ultimately a supporter of the ill-starred Liberal Republican movement. The failure of this movement left him no haven but the long-deserted Democratic fold. This pilgrimage appears opportunistic, but it was fundamentally dictated by convictions determined by considerations of law as well as of politics.

In the Kansas controversy Trumbull and his colleague, Stephen A. Douglas [*q.v.*], were diametrically opposed in matters of principle. Countering Douglas' proposal to admit Kansas (1856), Trumbull presented a bill uniting Kansas and Nebraska (*Congressional Globe*, 34 Cong., 1 Sess., p. 1369). Both senators opposed the Lecompton constitution, but on differing grounds. Douglas would have the people settle the question of slavery by vote; Trumbull, now a full-fledged Republican, asserted plenary congressional jurisdiction. When secession became an issue, he opposed the Crittenden compromise and supported a resolution declaring that the Constitution was ample in its scope and needed to be obeyed rather than amended—an earnest of his later war-time defense of that much transgressed document.

During the war he was at once Lincoln's able helper and stanch opponent, his attitude being determined by that of the executive toward the Constitution. An authoritative spokesman of the administration, he often tried to school his master in matters of executive propriety. He opposed legalizing Lincoln's extraordinary acts performed while Congress was in recess, saying: "I am disposed to give the necessary power to the

Administration to suppress this rebellion; but I am not disposed to say that the Administration has unlimited power and can do what it pleases, after Congress meets" (*Congressional Globe*, 37 Cong., 1 Sess., p. 392). In introducing his radical confiscation bill (December 1861) he declared that he wanted "no other authority for putting down even this gigantic rebellion than such as may be derived from the Constitution properly interpreted." He would suppress the "monstrous rebellion according to law, and in no other way" (*Ibid.*, 2 Sess., p. 18). He censured the method, but not the motive, of Lincoln's arbitrary arrests and led the movement which, while indemnifying the President for previous suspensions of the writ of *habeas corpus,* regulated further suspensions. In 1864, as chairman of the judiciary committee, he introduced the resolution which became the basis of the thirteenth amendment to the Constitution. When the first state sought admission under Lincolnian reconstruction he was the President's agent, but was foiled by Sumner and the Democrats.

Trumbull's powerful personal and committee influence aided the Radicals in the early stages of the fight with Johnson. His bill to enlarge the powers of the Freedmen's Bureau failed to pass over the veto. The veto of his civil rights bill, designed to give effect to the thirteenth amendment, alienated him from the Administration after a period of patient tolerance and dignified expostulation. He urged its repassage to offset the actions of the executive, and spoke of "the spirit of this message, of the dangerous doctrines it promulgates, of the inconsistencies and contradictions of its author, of his encroachments upon the constitutional rights of Congress, of his assumption of unwarranted powers, which, if persevered in and not checked by the people, must eventually lead to a subversion of the Government and the destruction of liberty" (*Ibid.,* 39 Cong., 1 Sess., p. 1760). These episodes mark an opposition which lasted until the impeachment furor. They also presage his departure from the leadership of radicalism. His decreasing activity in the Stevens-Sumner program was followed, as this group insisted on more and more humble submission of the rebel states, by participation with the moderates who attempted rather ineffectually to check the Radicals. Again, his was a legal criterion; he was one who was "willing to be radical lawfully" rather than one "who would rather be radical than right" (*Chicago Tribune,* May 26, 1870). This viewpoint drove him to oppose the impeachment proceedings and he was one of the famous seven who saved Johnson from conviction. This heresy,

together with his reconstruction attitude, lost him Republican leadership. The excesses of the Grant administration drove him into the Liberal Republican movement. He was among those suggested for the presidential nomination, but loyally stumped several states for Greeley. After the movement collapsed he finished his senatorial term and then retired to Chicago, where he practised law.

His appearance as counsel for the Tilden side in the disputed election of 1876 marked his return to the Democratic fold and he was that party's unsuccessful candidate for the governorship of Illinois in 1880. His last political excursion found him skirting the edges of Populism; in 1894 he drafted a platform which Chicago Populists took to a national conference in St. Louis. His death removed one of the ablest statesmen of his generation, an unpretentious, scholarly constitutionalist, who failed to scale political heights because of a conscience and a lack of popular appeal. The conscience drove him from party to party seeking a place where he could abide, and his colorless public personality denied him the kind of support on which spectacular careers are built. He was twice married: first, June 21, 1843, to Julia Maria Jayne, who died in August 1868; and second, Nov. 3, 1877, to Mary Ingraham; three sons by his first wife survived him.

[Trumbull Papers, Lib. of Cong.; Horace White, *The Life of Lyman Trumbull* (1913); A. H. Robertson, "The Political Career of Lyman Trumbull" (1910), M. A. thesis, Univ. of Chicago; L. E. Ellis, "A Hist. of the Chicago Delegation in Cong., 1843–1925," *Trans. Ill. State Hist. Soc.*, 1930; E. D. Ross, *The Liberal Republican Movement* (1919); *Chicago Tribune*, June 26, 1896.]
L. E. E.

TRUTEAU, JEAN BAPTISTE (Dec. 11, 1748–Jan. 30?, 1827), Indian trader, explorer, school-master, was born in Montreal, Canada, the son of Joseph and Catherine (Menard) Truteau. He always spelled the name Truteau but was generally referred to as Trudeau. His own children adopted this corrupt spelling. He established himself as school-master of the village of St. Louis in 1774 and continued to teach for more than forty years. In June 1794 he was engaged by the Missouri Trading Company for a term of three years to take charge of an exploring expedition under the direction of Jacques Clamorgan and Antoine Reihle. This company was organized in that year by some St. Louis merchants under the advice of Zenon Trudeau, the Spanish lieutenant-governor, who took a great interest in the exploration of the Upper Missouri country and the expansion of the fur trade. The avowed object was to exploit the fur trade of the Upper Missouri and to penetrate the sources of the Missouri River, and "beyond to the Southern Ocean," a term applied in that day to the Pacific Ocean. The instructions given to Truteau, approved by the governor, directed him to keep a record of all that should come under his observation. Accordingly, Truteau began his journal June 7, 1794, the day of his departure. It was in two parts, the first to Mar. 26, 1795 (in *American Historical Review,* Jan. 1914), and the second from May 24, 1795, to July 20, 1795 (in *Missouri Historical Society Collections,* vol. IV, 1912, with biographical sketch). This journal came to the attention of Thomas Jefferson, who sent extracts from it to Capt. Meriwether Lewis on Nov. 16, 1803, and on Jan. 22, 1804, a translation of the whole journal. Truteau's journal proved a valuable contribution to the knowledge of the Upper Missouri and its tribes of Indians, especially applicable to the years 1794 and 1795. The expedition, however, was not a profitable venture on account of desertions, jealousies, and lack of confidence in Jacques Clamorgan, who was one of the most active among the organizers.

He was at home in 1798, and the following year Governor Trudeau made a gift of a mortgage debt on Truteau's dwelling, amounting to four hundred dollars, to the school-master's two sons, "under grateful acknowledgments . . . for having educated my numerous family and for many favors." This dwelling was a stone house known as 18 and 20 North Main Street in St. Louis. Governor Trudeau described the school-master as his kinsman. Jean Baptiste Truteau was a man of importance in the village of St. Louis, and his name appeared in public documents of the time with many of the principal citizens. A subscription list of "well-to-do people," making patriotic gifts to aid Spain in war, mentions his name. He was married on May 1, 1781, to Madeleine Le Roy, the widow of François Herbert dit Bellhomme and the daughter of Julien and Marie (Saucier) Le Roy. They had five children. He died in the neighboring village of St. Louis and was buried in Carondelet.

[Cyprien Tanguay, *Dictionnaire Généalogique des Familles Canadiennes,* vol. VII (1890), p. 377; St. Louis Cathedral marriage and burial registers; Trudeau letters in possession of Mo. Hist. Soc.; journals, *ante*; Louis Houck, *A Hist. of Mo.* (1908), vol. II and *Spanish Regime in Mo.* (1909), vols. I–II; "Trudeau's Journ.," in *S. D. Hist. Colls.,* vol. VII (1914); "Trudeau's Description of the Upper Missouri," in *Miss. Valley Hist. Rev.,* July, Sept. 1921; *Original Journals of the Lewis and Clark Expedition,* vol. VII (1905), ed. by R. G. Thwaites.]   S. M. D.

TRUXTUN, THOMAS (Feb. 17, 1755–May 5, 1822), naval officer, was born near Hemp-stead, Long Island, the son of Thomas and Sarah (Axtell or Axtill) Truxtun. His father was an English barrister practising in New York, and an incorporator of Grace Church, Jamaica, L. I. The son in 1761 attended the Rev. Samuel Seabury's school at Hempstead. After his father's death about 1765, he came under the guardianship of his father's executor, John Troup of Jamaica, and at twelve went to sea, sailing under Capt. Joseph Holmes and later Capt. James Chambers in the London trade. At fifteen he was impressed and served briefly in H.M.S. *Prudent,* attracting the attention of the commander, who noted his abilities and offered him aid in advancement. He obtained his release, however, and, reëntering the merchant service, was at twenty a ship commander. In 1775 he brought a powder shipment to the colonies, and later that year he was captured with his vessel and cargo in the West Indies.

Subsequently, in the Revolution, he became an ardent privateersman, serving as lieutenant in the *Congress,* and then in command successively of the *Independence,* 10, which in 1777 captured a sugar ship of sixteen guns and other prizes; of the *Mars,* 24, which aroused British protests by sending into French ports prizes taken in the Channel; of the *Independence* again in 1780, in which at L'Orient he was reprimanded by John Paul Jones for flying "a kind of broad pennant"; and of the *St. James,* 20, which in 1781–82 sailed for France after beating off a 32-gun British blockader. The *St. James* brought back the most valuable cargo entered at Philadelphia during the Revolution, and Washington, at a dinner in Truxtun's honor, declared his services worth a regiment. He was master or part owner of other privateers (Naval Records of the American Revolution, MSS., Library of Congress), and in 1780 paid taxes in Philadelphia on $15,200 (*Pennsylvania Archives,* 3 ser. XV, 1897, p. 210).

After the war he returned to commerce, making many voyages and taking out the first Philadelphia ship to China, the *Canton,* in 1786. In June 1794 he was made a captain in the new American navy, ranking fifth among the six captains then appointed. In this year he published *Remarks, Instructions, and Examples Relating to Latitude and Longitude,* together with a chart of his voyages showing favorable routes, a treatise on winds and currents, and appendices on the masting of warships and the duties of naval officers. Three years later he published *Instructions, Signals, and Explanations Offered for the U. S. Fleet* (1797), and in 1806, *A Few Extracts from the Best Authors on Naval Tac-*

tics; all of these evidence a keen mind and high professional attainments. In June 1798 at the outbreak of naval warfare with France, he sailed in the frigate *Constellation,* whose construction he had supervised in Baltimore, and after two short cruises commanded a squadron consisting of the *Constellation* and four smaller vessels stationed between St. Christopher and Puerto Rico. In these waters, Feb. 9, 1799, he won the first of his two celebrated victories, capturing after an hour's fighting the French frigate *Insurgente.* His return home in May was greeted with general acclamation. "I wish," wrote President Adams (*Works,* VIII, 636), "all the other officers had as much zeal." Though in August the restoration of two former captains, Silas Talbot and Richard Dale [*qq.v.*], with senior rank, angered Truxtun to the point of resignation, he was persuaded to continue in the service, and in December sailed in the *Constellation* for his former station, with his command increased to ten vessels. On the night of Feb. 1–2, 1800, after an all-day chase, occurred his battle with *La Vengeance,* lasting from 8 P.M. to 1 A.M. Reversing the odds of the *Insurgente* action, the *Vengeance* had a broadside of 555 pounds to the *Constellation's* 372. After "one of the warmest combats between frigates that is on record" (Cooper, *post,* I, 354), the guns of the *Vengeance* were completely silenced, but as Truxtun was about to board his mainmast was carried away and the enemy escaped in the darkness. The *Constellation,* after repairs at Jamaica, returned late in March to Norfolk. For his hard-fought action Truxtun received the thanks of Congress and a gold medal, and in popular regard he became unquestionably the hero of the war.

After commanding the *President* during the last months of hostilities, he retired to his home at Perth Amboy, N. J., opposite the governor's mansion. A visitor at this time described him as suffering from gout: "Hercules at his distaff and Achilles in female attire were not stranger figures, than the brave commodore, sitting at his desk, penning his instructions for the American Navy, arrayed in his uniform coat, cocked hat and cockade, a flannel petticoat in place of breeches, and his feet rolled up in pieces of the same texture." The visitor added: "But he is now about to leave us, perhaps forever, and as he rises in his wrath, let the Bey [*sic*] of Algiers and all perfidious pirates tremble" ("A Colonial Capital," *Proceedings of the New Jersey Historical Society,* 4 ser. III, 1918, p. 15). The new assignment to which the visitor referred, in the spring of 1801, was to the *Chesapeake* at Norfolk, to command the second squadron

against Tripoli. But the new Jefferson administration, hostile politically, refused Truxtun a captain for his flagship, and construed his consequent withdrawal from the command as resignation from the navy. The loss to the country was serious, for Truxtun was only forty-seven, and his positive, energetic character would have animated the Tripolitan campaign. His fighting spirit and rigid discipline, however, had already set excellent standards for the young navy. He lived for four or five years after his retirement at Perth Amboy, and later in Philadelphia. In 1806 he was approached by Aaron Burr [*q.v.*] with offers of a naval command in connection with Burr's projected western state, but he declined on discovering Burr's schemes to be unsanctioned by the President. He was prominent in Philadelphia politics, a leader in the agitation of 1809 against the Embargo, unsuccessful Federalist candidate for Congress in 1810, and sheriff of Philadelphia, 1816–19. He was married, May 27, 1775, to Mary Fundran (probably anglicized from Vaudreuil or Von Drieull) of Perth Amboy, and had two sons and eleven daughters. He was buried in Christ Church yard, Philadelphia. William Talbot Truxtun [*q.v.*] was his grandson.

[For parentage, etc., see "Records of St. George's Church, Hempstead, L. I.," *N. Y. Geneal. and Biog. Record,* July 1881, p. 145; Henry Onderdonk, *Antiquities of the Parish Church, Jamaica, L. I.* (1880); "Abstract of Wills, N. Y., 1760–66," *N. Y. Hist. Soc. Colls., 1897* (1898), p. 421. Truxtun's biography appeared first in Isaac Bailey, *Am. Naval Biog.* (1815), and was included with slight additions in the later compilations of Frost and Peterson; see also J. F. Cooper, *Hist. of the Navy of the U. S.* (1839), esp. I, 354; G. W. Allen, *Our Naval War with France* (1909), containing references to manuscript sources; S. S. Robison, "Commodore Thomas Truxtun, U. S. Navy," *Proc. U. S. Naval Inst.,* Apr. 1932; Truxtun Papers (1798–1800) in Hist. Soc. of Pa., Phila.; Letters to Officers, vols. I–V (1794–98) and other papers in Navy Dept. Lib.; *The Works of John Adams,* vols. VIII (1853), IX (1854); *The Works of Alexander Hamilton* (1851), vols. V, VI; S. H. Wandell and Meade Minnigerode, *Aaron Burr* (2 vols., 1925); James Parton, *The Life and Times of Aaron Burr* (1886), II, 141; J. T. Scharf and Thompson Westcott, *Hist. of Phila.* (1884), vol. I; *Poulson's Am. Daily Advertiser* (Phila.), May 7, 1822.]   A.W—t.

TRUXTUN, WILLIAM TALBOT (Mar. 11, 1824–Feb. 25, 1887), naval officer, was born in Philadelphia, Pa., grandson of Commodore Thomas Truxtun [*q.v.*], and only son of William Truxtun by his marriage to Isabelle Shute Martin of South Carolina. His father was a naval lieutenant who died at Key West in 1830. The son became a midshipman on Feb. 9, 1841, and his early service at sea was in the *Dolphin* and *Falmouth* of the Home Squadron. He next cruised in the brig *Truxtun* on the African coast, in the suppression of the slave trade, and after six months at the newly established Naval Academy was made passed midshipman, Aug. 10, 1847. In 1847–48 he was on the Brazil station, and came home as prize-master of the former slaveship *Independence,* captured off Rio. After three years in the Pacific, he served on board the *Dolphin* in 1853 in soundings for the first Atlantic cable, and in 1854 in the Strain expedition, surveying the Isthmus of Darien for a canal route. Only his iron constitution carried him through the hardships of this latter duty in the tropics, which is believed to have caused some permanent injury to his health.

After the outbreak of the Civil War, he was assigned in June 1861 as executive of the sailing sloop-of-war *Dale* in the North Atlantic Blockading Squadron, and subsequently commanded her on the southeast coast blockade, being senior officer during the summer of 1862 in St. Helena Sound, S. C. Made lieutenant commander July 16, 1862, he commanded the *Chocura* from October 1862 to November 1863, chiefly on the Wilmington blockade, and thereafter the gunboat *Tacony* until the close of the war. The *Tacony* operated in the North Carolina sounds during the summer of 1864, took part in an hour's sharp action with batteries at Plymouth, N. C., Oct. 31, 1864, before its occupation, and was engaged in Admiral Porter's squadron in both attacks on Fort Fisher, December 1864 and January 1865. Porter in a letter to Truxtun (Feb. 18, 1865) remarked: "There has been no other officer in this squadron in whom I have more confidence or for whom I have a higher respect" (*Official Records, post,* XI, 473).

His post-bellum service included duty as superintendent of naval coal shipments, 1866–67; in command of the *Jamestown,* North Pacific Squadron, 1868–70; in command of the *Brooklyn* in the North and South Atlantic, 1873–75; and at the Boston and Norfolk navy yards, 1876–80. Thereafter he had special duty on the Norfolk harbor commission, and from 1885 until his retirement he commanded the Norfolk yard. He was commissioned commodore May 1, 1882, and was nominated for rear admiral in February 1886, but he had aroused some political opposition during his navy-yard administration, and his promotion was delayed until prevented by his retirement for age Mar. 11, 1886. Truxtun was popular at Norfolk, where he had made his home for a considerable period and identified himself with commercial and social interests, and his funeral in Christ Church was described as the most imposing and largely attended in that city since the war. He was twice married: first, Oct. 15, 1856, to Annie Elizabeth, daughter

of John E. Scott of Philadelphia, who died in 1873; and second, Sept. 2, 1875, to Mary Calvert Walke of Norfolk. There were three children of the first marriage, and five of the second; one of the sons, William, became a lieutenant commander in the navy and died in 1905.

[L. R. Hamersly, *The Records of Living Officers of the U. S. Navy and Marine Corps* (4th ed., 1890); *War of the Rebellion: Official Records* (*Navy*), see Index; W. H. Powell and Edward Shippen, *Officers of the Army and Navy Who Served in the Civil War* (1892); *The Virginian* (Norfolk), and the *Norfolk Landmark,* Feb. 26, 1887; *Army and Navy Journal,* Mar. 12, 1887; other material from family sources.]   A. W—t.

TRYON, DWIGHT WILLIAM (Aug. 13, 1849–July 1, 1925), landscape painter, was born at Hartford, Conn. His mother was Delia O. (Roberts) Tryon. His father, Anson Tryon, the descendant of New England artisan stock, died in Dwight's infancy, and the boy came up in narrow circumstances with only a common-school education. From early childhood he drew and drew well. At fifteen he became clerk and bookkeeper for Brown & Gross, booksellers, at Hartford. The work brought before him handsomely illustrated books, among them some with illustrations after Turner, for whom he conceived an admiration that was to be life long. To the shop came such notables as Horace Bushnell, Samuel L. Clemens (Mark Twain), Harriet Beecher Stowe [*qq.v.*], all of whom Tryon came to know. Meanwhile he began to paint in such spare moments as his work in the book store permitted. Thus he had to cultivate the useful habit of working much from memory. His mother was custodian of the Wadsworth Athenaeum, where hung impressive landscapes by Thomas Cole and Frederick Edwin Church [*qq.v.*]. At twenty-one Tryon sold his first picture. About this time he considered studying medicine, and his reading to this end grounded him in anatomy. In 1872 he exhibited, at the National Academy of Design in New York, a picture that was bought by the dealer Samuel Putnam Avery [*q.v.*]. In 1873 he married Alice H. Belden and, against the advice of "Mark Twain" and others of his notable acquaintances, set up a studio at Hartford. His support was giving lessons—as was to be the case all his life—but he soon began to sell his pictures. His first really notable picture, "Clay Cliffs, Block Island," painted for the Centennial Exhibition of 1876 in Philadelphia, is a stately affair executed rather tightly in the manner of such older contemporaries as John Frederick Kensett or William Trost Richards [*qq.v.*], but in every way a remarkable performance for a self-trained artist of twenty-seven.

Feeling the defects of such training, at the

end of 1876, having auctioned off his pictures and effects for $2,000, he sailed for Paris. Living with his young wife, he escaped the usual Bohemian contacts. Nothing better showed his ever stoical perception of what concerned himself than his disregard of the new Impressionism and his avoidance of the big popular ateliers in favor of the small private class of that austere disciple of Ingres, Jacquesson de la Chevreuse. From him Tryon learned a sound but unassertive construction, methods always thoughtful, restrained and highly selective, much dependence on delicately modulated edges—precision and refinement in all things. Among French landscapists he knew Daubigny well, and Harpignies slightly, while he deeply valued the advice of J. B. A. Guillemet. There were summers in Brittany and Normandy, excursions to Holland and Venice, all productive of pictures in his new mature manner—notable among these "The River Maas," at Smith College and three pictures he showed at the Salon of 1881. The $2,000 ran out in five years; so at thirty-two, in 1881, he returned to America, took a studio in New York, and after a couple of years settled for good on the harbor of South Dartmouth, often called Padanaram, near New Bedford. He was soon successful as a teacher in New York, and in 1885 he was appointed visiting professor of art at Smith College. This position he held for thirty-eight years. Honors followed him. In 1882 he was elected to the Society of American Artists; in 1890 made an associate of the National Academy and next year a member. In America and Europe he received no less than eighteen medals or awards.

Secure financially through his teaching, he painted rather few pictures, took infinite pains with them, always sold them well, and through saving and prudent investment gradually built up a handsome fortune. In 1889 Charles Lang Freer [q.v.], the collector, bought from Tryon that exquisite and eventually much medaled picture, "The Rising Moon." It was the harbinger of some forty Tryons that are preserved in the Freer Gallery at Washington. The relation between artist and patron soon ripened into friendship. Tryon did four big landscape decorations, "The Seasons," for Freer's house at Detroit, and in a modest way he followed Freer's example as a fastidious and enthusiastic collector. The preciousness that characterized Tryon's taste and art was reflected neither in his manner of life nor yet in his personal appearance. The months from April to November he spent at Padanaram, fishing and sailing on the lumpy waters of Buzzards Bay, in admirable little boats of his own

design. The remaining six months, at New York, were passed in teaching and a carefully restricted output of painting. Never quite a recluse, he was always most at ease in rustic company, avoiding general social relations, and disregarding freely the conventions of speech and dress. His aspect was that of a Yankee sailor—bronzed and wrinkled by the sun and wind, with steady blue eyes shading to brown, and an undersized but stocky and powerful frame that tipped the scales at 140 pounds.

His art is on the whole crepuscular. He loved the moments at dusk when infinitesimal differences of tone retain and assert pensively the almost lost definition of objects about to disappear. The foreground is generally deep, the interest lies in a few well chosen and placed forms—trees or farm houses in far middle distance—with skies thinly veiled and saturated with faint light. His exquisiteness carries with it a certain thinness and monotony, yet one cannot comprise with such words a performance that won the admiration of Homer D. Martin and Whistler. In technique Tryon was highly experimental and ingenious. For greater durability he preferred to canvas a carefully made ply board; in his latter years he painted on a white ground; his underpainting was generally bold and highly colorful. After scraping down and over-painting, something of the underlying richness qualified the apparent monochrome. He made curious and successful ventures in heavily loaded and permanently fixed pastels. Practising an art rather of taste and reflection than of vigorous imagination, his place is not with our greater landscapists. Among those of second order he is surely one of the most accomplished.

His powerful frame broke rather suddenly. He had tramped the woods, sailed a canoe from New York to New Bedford, shipped on fishing smacks. In his early seventies he still took the *Skat*, the little catboat that he had designed himself, single-handed about Buzzards Bay. At seventy-five cancer of the stomach developed, and the next year he died. Two years earlier he had provided for the art museum at Smith College. It was completed only after his death, and after that of his wife, four years later, it received a handsome endowment.

[C. H. Caffin, *The Art of Dwight W. Tryon. An Appreciation*, privately printed (1909), with excellent illustrations; H. C. White, *The Life and Art of Dwight William Tryon* (1930); F. F. Sherman, *Am. Painters of Yesterday and Today* (1919); *Smith Alumnae Quart.*, Nov. 1925; *Who's Who in America*, 1924–25; *N. Y. Times*, July 2, 12, 19, 22, 1925.]   F. J. M., Jr.

TRYON, GEORGE WASHINGTON (May 20, 1838–Feb. 5, 1888), conchologist, was born in Philadelphia, the eldest son of Edward K. and Adeline (Savidt) Tryon. He was named for his grandfather, a gunsmith. After passing through several private schools, he entered the Friends' Central School in 1850, completing a three years' course in June 1853. Soon afterward he studied French, German, and music with private tutors, thus completing his formal education. Edward K. Tryon had carried on successfully the well-established business of manufacturing and selling firearms and sportsman's accoutrements which he had inherited from his father, and in due course his son succeeded him. The younger George Washington Tryon, however, retired from business about 1868 with a modest sum, sufficient in his estimation to justify unrestrained pursuit of science and letters.

Tryon began when he was seven years old to collect natural history specimens, especially shells of mollusks, which were favorites from the start. Orderliness was one of the child's notable mental qualities and even before his undeveloped mind could grasp the meaning of taxonomy he arranged his specimens according to an original system. In 1859, at the age of twenty-one, he was elected a member of the Academy of Natural Sciences of Philadelphia, and from that time until his death in 1888 he was active in promoting its welfare. Largely through his efforts a new building was erected. In 1866 the conchological section of the Academy was formed and under its auspices large collections were gathered, including Tryon's own private collection which numbered more than 10,000 species. At the time of his death, the section had one of the largest and most complete collections of Mollusca in the world. Tryon was a curator of the Academy from 1869 to 1876 and conservator of the conchological section from 1875 until his death.

His first paper on conchology, "On the Mollusca of Harper's Ferry, Virginia," was presented in 1861 (*Proceedings of the Academy of Natural Sciences of Philadelphia*, 2 ser. V, 1862), and subsequently more than seventy papers on land, freshwater, and marine mollusks came from his pen. Among his contributions were *A Monograph of the Terrestrial Mollusca Inhabiting the United States* (1866); *A Monograph of the Freshwater Univalve Mollusca of the United States (In Continuation of Prof. S. S. Haldeman's Work . . .)*, with a preface dated 1870; Part IV, "Strepomatidae" (1873), of W. G. Binney's *Land and Fresh Water Shells of North America* (4 vols., 1865–73); and *Structural and Systematic Conchology* (3 vols., 1882–84). He also edited and published the *American Journal of Conchology* from 1865 to 1872. His

chief work, however, was his *Manual of Conchology, Structural and Systematic, with Illustrations of the Species,* in which it was designed to describe and figure all of the living species of the Mollusca known to science. The first volume appeared in 1879. Of the first series on the marine shells, nine volumes had been completed and of the second series, the land shells, three volumes had been issued at the time of his death. Fortunately for the science of malacology, the work was continued under Dr. Henry A. Pilsbry.

Tryon was very fond of music and made an effort to spread a love of music among the people and to elevate popular taste. To this end he arranged a series of songs for amateur singers. He also edited and published librettos of more than fifty standard operas and himself wrote an unsuccessful comic opera, *Amy Cassonet or the Elopement,* published in 1875. Interested likewise in art, he occasionally painted for his own pleasure. He twice visited Europe, in 1874 and 1877, publishing an account of the earlier trip in *The Amateur Abroad* (1875). Tryon was a bachelor, of a quiet, frank, and unpretentious disposition. He was a member of the Society of Friends for a number of years and later attended the services of the Unitarian Church of Philadelphia.

[*Conchologists' Exchange,* Mar.–Apr. 1888, reprinting article from *Public Ledger* (Phila.), Feb. 7, 1888; *Am. Naturalist,* Mar. 1888; W. S. W. Ruschenberger, "A Biog. Notice of George W. Tryon, Jr.," in *Proc. Acad. Nat. Sci. of Phila.,* 3 ser. XVIII (1889), and separately reprinted.] F. C. B.

TRYON, WILLIAM (1729–Jan. 27, 1788), colonial governor, was born at "Norbury Park," Surrey, England, the son of Charles Tryon of "Bulwick," Northamptonshire, and Lady Mary Tryon, the daughter of Robert Shirley, the first Earl Ferrers. He was commissioned lieutenant in the 1st Regiment of Foot Guards in 1751 and promoted to be captain with army rank of lieutenant-colonel seven years later. Marriage with Margaret Wake of London in 1757 brought him control of an estate of £30,000 and, in 1764, probably through her connection with Lord Hillsborough, appointment as lieutenant-governor of North Carolina. Upon the death of the governor, Arthur Dobbs, in March 1765, Tryon took command of the province and a few months later was commissioned governor. In his long service in America he was faced with one difficulty after another which his military background hardly prepared him to handle in a pacific spirit. During the Stamp Act controversy he actively supported the customs and naval officers in their refusal to permit the entrance and clearance of vessels whose papers lacked the required stamps. Commerce in the Cape Fear region came to a standstill. When the inhabitants intimidated the officers into abandoning their policy, he was helpless and hinted at the need of British troops.

Disturbances of a different origin soon gave him an opportunity for more forceful action. The movement known as the Regulation developed in the frontier counties largely because of inadequate currency, inequitable taxation, and the greed of officials. The governor was not altogether deaf to the grievances of the Regulators and urged a few reforms. But some of the accused officials, especially Edmund Fanning [q.v.], the register of Orange County, were his personal friends, and he answered the riotous demonstrations of the Hillsboro mob in 1768 by leading a force of militia into the disaffected region to restore order. Conditions grew no better, and in September 1770 the Regulators broke up the superior court at Hillsboro and severely mishandled several officials and lawyers. Under a drastic riot act the ringleaders were indicted and outlawed, and in the following March the governor again organized an armed force. His column, consisting of about 1,100 militia, met some 2,000 Regulators at the Alamance on May 16, 1771, and inflicted a crushing defeat upon them. While still on this campaign, he received word of his transfer to New York to replace Lord Dunmore, who was going to Virginia. Tryon, who had long sought the change, left his troops still engaged in the work of pacification and sailed to New York in July. Although marred by the violence of its close, his administration had been on the whole successful. He was responsible for establishing the provincial capital at New Bern and the erection there of an executive residence, "Tryon's Palace," one of the finest buildings in colonial America. His negotiations with the Cherokee had led to the establishment of a satisfactory boundary. Personally he was popular in the eastern counties, and his departure was witnessed with regret.

In New York he was again beset with frontier disturbances, the result of conflicting grants by New York and New Hampshire, within the present state of Vermont. The violent actions of Ethan Allen and his followers led the governor to seek the use of British regulars, but his request was denied by General Haldimand. Difficulties also arose over the purchase of large tracts of lands from the Indians in the Mohawk Valley, an operation in which the governor was personally interested to the extent of 40,000 acres. To consult on these problems, he was finally summoned to England. Leaving New York in April 1774 he did not return until fourteen months later, after the commencement of the Revolution. In October 1775, fearing for his personal safety, he took refuge on board ship in New York harbor, where he remained until the landing of Lord Howe's troops in August 1776. Wartime conditions prevented the restoration of his civil functions, although he busied himself in administering the oath of allegiance to all available Loyalists. Yet he was essentially a military man and longed for a more active part in the war. He had been advanced to the rank of colonel in 1772 and in 1777 obtained permission to command a force of Loyalists. He was promoted to the rank of major-general in America in 1778 and made colonel of the 70th Foot. His chief military activities consisted in a series of raids upon Connecticut, which succeeded well in their purpose of destroying supplies and diverting some of Connecticut's energies from support of Washington's army to home defense. As the war continued, Tryon's vindictive spirit mounted. He frankly expressed a wish to "burn every Committee Man's house within my reach" (O'Callaghan, post, VIII, 736), and Sir Henry Clinton was said to have privately disapproved the extremes to which he carried his acts of retaliation (Dartmouth MSS., post, Eleventh Report, p. 423). In 1780 illness, which had frequently incapacitated him throughout his American career, compelled his return to England. Although promoted lieutenant-general in 1782 and made colonel of the 29th Foot the next year, his active career was over. He died at his London home and was buried in the family tomb at Twickenham.

Against Tryon's proneness to settle disputes with force must be set the fact that he achieved a very real popularity with most of those with whom he came in personal contact. He was a stanch supporter of the established church and gave active encouragement to education. His inquiring mind led him to make extensive tours through both his provinces. He was intensely loyal to the crown but always expected rewards for his faithful services—the suppression of the Regulators was, he thought, worth at least a baronetcy. The conflicting qualities of his nature were well summed up by an unfriendly Loyalist in New York who wrote of him as "the pink of politeness, and the quintessence of vanity. . . . The man is generous, perfectly good-natured, and no doubt brave, but weak and vain to an extreme degree. You should keep such people at home; they are excellent for a Court parade" (Colonial Records of North Carolina, post, vol. VIII, p. xxxix).

[*The Colonial Records of N. C.*, vols. VII, VIII (1890); *Documents Relative to the Colonial Hist. of the State of New-York*, VIII (1857), ed. by E. B. O'Callaghan; "The MSS. of the Earl of Dartmouth," *Great Britain. Hist. MSS. Commission Eleventh Report*, app. pt. 5 (1887), *Fourteenth Report*, app. pt. 10 (1895); *Gentleman's Mag.*, Dec. 1757, p. 577, Feb. 1788, p. 179; *Army Lists*, 1755–1783; R. D. W. Connor, *Hist. of N. C.*, vol. I (1919); J. S. Bassett, "The Regulators of North Carolina," *Amer. Hist. Assn. Report . . . 1894* (1895); M. D. Haywood, *Gov. William Tryon and his Administration of the Province of N. C.* (1903); Lorenzo Sabine, *Biog. Sketches of Loyalists of the Amer. Rev.*, new ed. (1864), vol. II. The date for birth given in this sketch is taken from copy of epitaph in Haywood, *ante*, and for death *Ibid.*, and from *Gentleman's Mag.*, *ante*, although the *D. N. B.* gives birth-date as 1725 and death-date as Dec. 27, 1788.]
L. W. L.

TSCHERINOFF, MARIE VAN ZANDT
[See VAN ZANDT, MARIE, 1858–1919].

TUBMAN, HARRIET (*c.* 1821–Mar. 10, 1913), fugitive slave, abolitionist, was born in Dorchester County on the Eastern Shore of Maryland, the daughter of Benjamin Ross and Harriet Greene, both slaves. She was first named Araminta, but early assumed the name Harriet. In childhood she received a head injury to which have been attributed spells of somnolence which overtook her without warning at intervals during the rest of her life. From her early teens she worked as a field hand—plowing, loading and unloading wood—an activity which developed in her great strength and remarkable powers of endurance. In 1844, her master forced her to marry a man named John Tubman who was unfaithful to her. Much later she married a man named Nelson Davis. About 1849 she made her escape from slavery, guided in her flight only by the north star. It was not long afterwards that she became one of the most conspicuous figures in the work of the "Underground Railroad," winning the appellation "Moses" by leading, in all, more than three hundred slaves from bondage to freedom in the North and Canada.

From the time of her escape until the beginning of the Civil War she was busy making journeys into the South to lead out slaves. An important "station" on one of her routes was the home of the Quaker Thomas Garrett [*q.v.*] of Wilmington, Del., who gave her all the help within his power. Between her journeys she worked as a cook in order to raise the money she needed to aid the fugitives. In 1857 she rescued her own parents, who were very old, and settled them in Auburn, N. Y., on a little tract of land purchased from William H. Seward. Although she could neither read nor write, her shrewdness in planning hazardous enterprises and skill in avoiding arrest were phenomenal. When rescu-

ing a group of slaves, she enforced a rule which she herself had laid down, threatening with death any passenger who thought of surrender or attempted to return. She seemed absolutely fearless and was willing to endure any hardship. To a remarkable degree she was guided in her work by visions and sustained by her faith in God. John Brown, who met her in Canada and subsequently referred to her as "General" Tubman, confided in her and relied on her for assistance in his campaign against slavery in Virginia. She was well known in the office of the *National Anti-Slavery Standard* in New York and in abolition circles in Boston and from time to time was presented as a speaker at anti-slavery meetings. After the outbreak of the Civil War she was sent to Gen. David Hunter in South Carolina with a letter from Governor Andrew of Massachusetts and attached herself to the Union army, working as cook, laundress, and nurse; frequently acting as guide in scouting parties and raids; and rendering noteworthy service as a spy within the Confederate lines.

After the war Harriet continued to labor for her people. For a time she was concerned with an attempt to establish schools for freedmen in North Carolina. She was able to finish paying for her home in Auburn with the proceeds of a little book, *Scenes in the Life of Harriet Tubman* (1869), written for her benefit by Mrs. Sarah Hopkins Bradford and published through the generosity of Gerrit Smith, Wendell Phillips [*qq.v.*], and certain Auburn neighbors. Here in her own home she supported several children and penniless old people, being further aided by the proceeds of a revised edition of Mrs. Bradford's book, *Harriet the Moses of Her People* (1886). The Harriet Tubman Home for indigent aged negroes continued to exist for a number of years after her death, and the citizens of Auburn erected a shaft in her memory.

[S. H. Bradford, *Harriet the Moses of Her People*, which was reprinted in 1901, contains reminiscences and testimonials from all the prominent Abolitionists mentioned above, a number of the Union officers under whom Harriet served, and others. See also P. E. Hopkins, "Harriet Tubman (Moses)," *Colored American Mag.*, Jan.–Feb. 1902; *Freedmen's Record*, Mar. 1865; Lillie B. C. Wyman, "Harriet Tubman," *New England Mag.*, Mar. 1896; *American Mag.*, Aug. 1912; W. H. Siebert, *The Underground Railroad* (1898); H. H. Swift, *The Railroad to Freedom* (1932); *Albany Evening Jour.*, Mar. 11, 1913; *N. Y. Times*, Mar. 14, 1913.]
D. B. P.

TUCK, AMOS (Aug. 2, 1810–Dec. 11, 1879), congressman, was born at Parsonsfield, Me., fourth of six children of John and Betsey (Towle) Tuck, and a descendant of Robert Tuck who settled on the New Hampshire coast in 1638. His parents were people of strong character, intelligent, industrious, ambitious for their children, but handicapped by the grinding struggle for a livelihood on a New England farm. The boy farmed at home until he was seventeen, then, with intermittent attendance at various schools, worked as a common laborer, taught district school, and in time accumulated resources financial and scholastic for admission to Dartmouth College.

After his graduation in 1835 he taught school, studying law in the meantime, and upon his admission to the bar in 1838 began practice in Exeter where within a few months he was admitted to partnership with James Bell, his former preceptor. In 1842, as a Democrat, he served a term in the New Hampshire legislature, but in 1844 definitely broke with the Democratic party on the Texas question and three years later, after an exciting and embittered contest, was elected to the Thirtieth Congress by a fusion of independent Democrats and Whigs. The contest conducted in New Hampshire by Amos Tuck and John P. Hale [q.v.], who was elected to the Senate as a result of the same campaign, was in many respects a forerunner of the great party upheavals of the next decade and attracted national attention. Tuck served three terms in Congress (1847-53). His independent position in the House, where with Joshua R. Giddings [q.v.] of Ohio and John G. Palfrey [q.v.] of Massachusetts he constituted a nucleus of anti-slavery sentiment, was prominent rather than influential. His views, however, well expressed in his speech of Jan. 19, 1848, against the Mexican War and extension of slavery, were eventually to become predominant in the Northern states.

Defeated for a fourth term because of a temporary waning of anti-slavery fervor in his state together with an effective gerrymander by the legislature, he continued active in the movement against slavery, but his essential sanity and political acumen kept him out of its more extravagant manifestations and his activity was therefore vastly more effective—so effective, indeed, that his admirers have often claimed that the Republican party was really a New Hampshire creation. At all events, he was instrumental in 1853 and 1854 in bringing about a merger of the dissatisfied into a new party alignment. At the Republican convention of 1856 he was a vice-president and in 1860 he was a member of the platform committee; in 1861 he attended the unsuccessful conference at Washington which endeavored to avert the final break between North and South. He was a loyal adherent of President Lincoln, with whom he had formed a personal friendship in Congress and from whom in 1861 he accepted the post of naval officer for the district of Boston and Charlestown. He served in this capacity until removed by President Johnson in 1865.

From the professional standpoint the most successful period of Tuck's career followed the Civil War. Although he retained his residence at Exeter, his clients were now of national importance and their affairs took him into courtrooms and business offices in the financial centers of the country. He was interested in the Western railroad development and his shrewd sense of investment values enabled him to accumulate a large estate. He was a trustee of Phillips Exeter Academy from 1853 to 1879, and from 1857 to 1866 of Dartmouth College, where in 1900 his son Edward Tuck established the Amos Tuck School of Administration and Finance. Tuck's fine appearance, personal charm, and public spirit gave him a prominent place in that group of lawyers and party leaders which made Exeter one of the influential centers of New England life of the nineteenth century. He was twice married, first to Sarah Ann Nudd, who bore him eight children, and after her death early in 1847, on Oct. 10 of the same year to Mrs. Catharine (Townsend) Shepard, daughter of John Townsend of Salisbury. Three of his children survived him.

[*Autobiog. Memoir of A. Tuck* (privately printed, 1902); C. R. Corning, *Amos Tuck* (1902); J. W. Dearborn, *Sketch of the Life and Character of Hon. Amos Tuck* (n.d., 1889); Joseph Dow, *Tuck Geneal.: Robert Tuck of Hampton, N. H. and His Descendants* (1877); C. H. Bell, *The Bench and Bar of N. H.* (1894) and *Hist. of the Town of Exeter, N. H.* (1888); L. M. Crosbie, *The Phillips Exeter Acad.* (1923); J. K. Lord, *A Hist. of Dartmouth Coll.* (1913); *Biog. Dir. Am. Cong.* (1928); J. O. Lyford, *Life of Edward H. Rollins* (copr. 1906); *Concord Daily Monitor*, Dec. 12, 1879; MSS. in Dartmouth Coll. archives.]   W. A. R.

TUCKER, GEORGE (Aug. 20, 1775–Apr. 10, 1861), political economist, author, was born in Bermuda, the son of Daniel Tucker, mayor of Hamilton, and his first wife, Elizabeth (Tucker) Tucker, a distant relative. George was sent to Virginia at the age of twelve, and placed in the charge of his distant kinsman, St. George Tucker [q.v.], also a native of Bermuda, who had succeeded George Wythe as professor of law in the College of William and Mary. Here George graduated in 1797; he afterwards practised law in Richmond, then in Pittsylvania Court House (now Chatham), and Lynchburg. After serving in the Virginia legislature he was elected to Congress for three successive terms, obtaining there (1819-25) a reputation as debater and constitutional lawyer. Having attracted the attention of James Madison, whom he came to know intimately—as he also knew Jefferson, he was appointed professor of moral philosophy in the University of Virginia when it opened in 1825, and as the oldest member of the staff was elected the first chairman of the faculty. He had already published *Essays on Subjects of Taste, Morals, and National Policy, by a Citizen of Virginia* (1822), *The Valley of Shenandoah* (2 vols., 1824), and other works. He now issued, under the name "Joseph Atterley," *A Voyage to the Moon* (1827), a satirical romance, not very diverting or pointed, with occasional unimportant references to political economy and a good deal of bastard astronomy and botany. He worked hard for six months in 1829 as contributing editor of an ill-starred weekly inaugurated at the University, *The Virginia Literary Museum*. His humor was not appreciated in the academically self-conscious atmosphere of the new institution.

He must have labored for a long period on *The Life of Thomas Jefferson* (2 vols., 1837), in which he supplemented extensive research, often in out-of-the-way journals, by many conferences with Madison. He tried honestly to hold even justice between Republicans and Federalists, and on the whole succeeded. The advantages which he enjoyed of personal association with the chief Republican actors had, of course, their corresponding embarrassments. Tucker's sins are sometimes of commission, but oftener of omission. It must be remembered, however, that his own sympathies were on the side of Jefferson's opinions. He frequently does not understand, or does not admit, the degree to which Jefferson controlled the actions of such men as Madison and Giles. However, Tucker's exposition of the national problems that arose, and of the conflict over them, is a genuine contribution to history, for he often was able to see what was involved better than did many of the actors themselves. This same year he published *The Laws of Wages, Profits, and Rent Investigated* (1837), and in 1839 *The Theory of Money and Banks Investigated*. Apart from his own wisdom, Tucker had sufficient reason, in the recent panic and current depression, for upholding the policy of a national bank, or rather of several national banks, in order to prevent the excesses of local banks of issue. His *Progress of the United States in Population and Wealth in Fifty Years* (1843, appendix 1855), while noticing the tendency of the rate of population growth to decrease, calculated that the population three generations from the time he wrote would be just twice what it actually turned out to be.

In 1845, at the age of seventy, he retired from the University of Virginia, and thereafter lived in Philadelphia. When seventy-five, he commenced *The History of the United States* (4 vols., 1856–57), much of which embraced an account of his own times. When eighty-four he was his own publisher of *Political Economy for the People* (1859), and the next year issued *Essays, Moral and Metaphysical*. His mental activity was matched by surprising bodily stamina; in 1860 he traveled throughout Virginia and to Chicago, and the next year visited Southern cities as far down as Mobile. At the last place, in disembarking from a steamboat, he was struck by a bale of cotton and rendered unconscious for days. He survived long enough to be brought back to the home of his son-in-law, "Sherwood," in Albemarle County, Va. Tucker married, in 1801, Maria Ball Carter, grand-daughter of Elizabeth Lewis, Washington's sister; before her death in 1823, she bore him four daughters and a son, of whom two daughters and possibly the son survived him. His second marriage to Mary (Byrd) Farley, daughter of Mary Byrd of "Westover," was childless. His third wife, Louisa (Bowdoin) Thompson of the Eastern Shore of Virginia, died in 1859 without issue.

Tucker's principal formal works on economic theory belong to periods separated by twenty years. The two first, *The Laws of Wages, Profits, and Rent Investigated* (1837) and *The Theory of Money and Banks Investigated* (1839), published while he was teaching these subjects in the University of Virginia, are detailed and vivid, with frequent spirited criticism of other writers. The last, *Political Economy for the People* (1859), was prepared a decade and a half after his retirement; much detail has dropped out, there is little or no controversial matter, and the whole subject is treated as a summary of his wisdom and experience. His essential views, however, did not change. Tucker was always the political economist in the proper meaning of that term, that is, he cultivated the science because it could "exert a great influence on the public prosperity, in teaching governments how best they may improve the sources of national wealth, whether by regulation or forbearance, may least injuriously raise the public revenue, and most beneficially expend it" (*Wages, Profits, and Rent*, p. v). He followed his investigations of theory, therefore, with positive recommendations as to public policy. In general he was an adherent of the English and French classical school; his American environment, exhibiting in his lifetime prodigious economic progress, never dissuaded him, as it did Henry Charles Carey and Mathew Carey, Daniel Raymond, John Rae, and Georg Friedrich List [*qq.v.*], from the apprehensions and pessimism born of older civilizations. He sometimes approached the more optimistic position, but these inklings never formed themselves into anything like a system which should overset the old preoccupation with diminishing returns. This was in spite of the fact that he knew H. C. Carey's work from an early period, and certainly must have been thrown with him in Philadelphia, especially as they were both members of the American Philosophical Society. Tucker's mentor was Adam Smith, and his chief theoretical differences were with David Ricardo. This in itself indicates the narrow dimension of his contribution. He declared that Ricardo, though "entitled to all his reputation for a thorough knowledge of the subjects of money and finance, is mistaken in his elementary principles of the science; that the origin and progress of rents admits of a more simple and natural explanation than he has given; that his theory of wages is inconsistent with itself, and that of profits [is] contradicted by the whole history of capital in the civilized world" (*Wages, Profits, and Rent*, p. iv). Yet his criticism of Ricardo is mainly textual; it is in part based upon misapprehension, due perhaps to Ricardo's elliptical style; in fact, he virtually argues himself around to Ricardo's position of ascribing prime importance in the origin of rent to the differences in qualities of soils (*Ibid.*, p. 113). Tucker, while introducing judicious refinements of the doctrine, was permanently impressed with Malthus' principle of population, and applied it consistently throughout his thinking; it had much to do, doubtless, with leading him to his elaborate studies of the census, and bore immediately upon his insistence that American negro slavery would extinguish itself (about the year 1925 he thought) by becoming unprofitable to the masters. This would be in consequence of the progressive lessening of the value of labor, to the point where the earnings of a slave would not repay the cost of rearing him. "This," he said, "may be called the euthanasia of the institution, as it will be abolished with the consent of the master no less than the wishes of the slave" (*Progress of the United States*, p. 110). Tucker gave an early indication of the propriety of separating, in economic analysis, the functions of capitalist and enterpriser (*Wages, Profits, and Rent*, p. 91 and note). He condemned usury laws in unmeasured terms, not only as violating his general principle of governmental non-interference in commercial transactions, but as positively injurious to debtors by circumventions of the laws.

Of all the great economic and social questions of Tucker's time—tariff protection, internal improvements, banking regulation, and slavery—the last was the most portentous for the welfare of the country and especially of the South. As a resident on Virginia plantations, as a member of Congress at the time of the Missouri Compromise, as a teacher of the social sciences within the South, and as a witness of the preliminaries of the Civil War, he saw the political and economic situation of his section become increasingly critical. Though his opposition to slavery was unmistakable, and he steadily looked forward to the attenuation of the institution—earlier through deportation and manumission, and later as a consequence of the increase of population—his utterances were discreetly academic. Though, except upon specific minor points, he was never seduced into becoming its advocate, refusing to indulge in the imbecilities of his colleague Albert Taylor Bledsoe [*q.v.*], he was far removed from the fiery and effective opposition of such a man as Hinton Rowan Helper [*q.v.*]. The *Letters from Virginia* (1816), giving every appearance of Tucker's authorship, though also attributed to William Maxwell and James Kirke Paulding [*qq.v.*], condemned slavery in unmeasured terms, and ridiculed the planters, all under the cover of anonymity; the *Speech of Mr. Tucker, of Virginia, on the Restriction of Slavery in Missouri . . . February 25, 1820* (1820) discovered insuperable constitutional objections to preventing the extension of slavery; and the criticism of slavery, sufficiently explicit in his books of the 'thirties and 'forties, was reduced to a pallid mention in his *Political Economy for the People* published almost on the eve of the Civil War.

[Robley Dunglison, "Obituary Notice of Professor George Tucker," in *Proc. Am. Philosophical Soc.*, IX (1865), 64–70; T. A. Emmet, *An Account of the Tucker Family of Bermuda* (1898); Albert Welles, *The Pedigree and Hist. of the Washington Family* (1879); P. A. Bruce, *Hist. of the Univ. of Va., 1819–1919*, II (1920), III (1921); J. S. Patton, *Jefferson, Cabell and the Univ. of Va.* (1906), pp. 101–02; *Daily Richmond Enquirer*, Apr. 13, 1861.]
B. M.

TUCKER, GILBERT MILLIGAN (Aug. 26, 1847–Jan. 13, 1932), editor, author, publicist, was the son of Luther Tucker [*q.v.*] and his third wife, Margaret Lucinda (Smith) Burr Tucker. He was born at Albany, N. Y., where his father was conspicuous in the field of agricultural journalism. After preparation at the Albany Academy, he entered Williams College in 1864 and completed the four-year course in three years, earning the degree of A.B. with honors in 1867. He at once became associated with his father and elder brother in the publication of the *Cultivator and Country Gentleman*. In 1897, when the first part of the title was dropped, he became editor-in-chief, so continuing until the *Country Gentleman* was sold to the Curtis Publishing Company in 1911, when he retired from active business.

Tucker's editorial policy was vigorous and forthright. He had strong opinions and limitless courage in their support, yet was open-minded and tolerant withal. He opposed strongly, and believed detrimental to agricultural interests, such policies as the expansion of the state canal system and the development of western farm lands—particularly by irrigation—at public expense, foreseeing the danger of over-production and consequently injury to agriculture. He also disapproved of the Eighteenth Amendment to the Constitution, calling it "an absurd and dangerous anomaly." He spoke and wrote frequently on these and kindred subjects. During his connection with the *Country Gentleman,* he served on various federal and state commissions dealing with agricultural affairs. He was deeply interested in, and at one time president of, the old New York State Agricultural Society. He was a trustee of Cornell University, 1905–06; a member, elder, and trustee of the Reformed Church; a Mason; a member of the Order of Founders and Patriots; and in politics a Republican, although in later life he came to disbelieve in the policy of tariff protection.

Deeply interested in philological subjects, he was a student of New Testament Greek and a frequent writer on the English language, with special reference to the differences in its usage in England and America. He maintained that the purity of English has been better preserved on the West side of the Atlantic, and held that most of the so-called "Americanisms" originated many years ago in the mother country. He was the author of *Our Common Speech* (1895); *American English* (1921); *A Layman's Apology* (1913), a volume of essays on religious subjects; *American Agricultural Periodicals* (an historical sketch, privately printed, 1909); and contributions to the daily press, *North American Review, New Englander, Presbyterian Review,* and other journals.

On June 7, 1877, Tucker married Sara Edwards Miller, daughter of the Rev. William Augustus Miller of Albany. She died in 1930. They had one son, who survived his father, and one daughter who died unmarried in 1926. Tucker died at Albany in his eighty-fifth year.

[Ephraim Tucker, *Geneal. of the Tucker Family* (1895); *Who's Who in America,* 1930–31; *N. Y. Times,* Jan. 14, 1932; *Knickerbocker Press* (Albany), Jan. 14, 1932; family material; personal acquaintance.]

J. I. W.

TUCKER, HENRY HOLCOMBE (May 10, 1819–Sept. 9, 1889), Baptist clergyman, was born near Camak, Warren County, Ga., the son of Germain Tucker and Frances Henrietta, daughter of Henry Holcombe [*q.v.*]. Both his parents were of Virginia ancestry; his paternal grandfather, Isaiah Tucker, was a wealthy planter. After the death of his father at the age of twenty-seven, Henry's mother married again and the family removed to Philadelphia. The boy was prepared for college in the academic department of the University of Pennsylvania, and in 1834 he entered the freshman class of the University. In his senior year he transferred to Columbian College (now George Washington University), Washington, D. C., where he was graduated with the degree of A.B. in 1838.

Returning to the South, he entered business in Charleston, S. C. In 1842 he decided to study law and repaired to Forsyth, Ga., where he was admitted to the bar in 1846. Two years later he married Mary Catherine West, who lived but a few months after their marriage. Her death seems to have turned his mind toward the ministry, for he soon gave up the practice of law, sold his library, was licensed to preach, and removed to Penfield in order to take private instruction in theology under John L. Dagg [*q.v.*], then president of Mercer University. Although he preferred to enter the pastorate, he was persuaded to undertake educational work and accepted a position with the Southern Female College at Lagrange, Ga., where he was ordained to the Baptist ministry in 1851. For a short time subsequently he was professor in the Richmond Female Institute, Richmond, Va. In 1853 he was offered the presidency of Wake Forest College, Wake Forest, N. C., but since he had just accepted the pastorate of a church at Alexandria, Va., he declined. While in Alexandria, he married Sarah O. Stevens. In 1856 he became professor of belles-lettres and metaphysics in Mercer University, a position which he held until the institution was closed by the Civil War in 1862.

He was opposed to secession and used his utmost influence against it, but when Georgia seceded he remained loyal to the South. Foreseeing a salt famine, he organized a company for the manufacture of salt, which was extremely helpful in the dark days of the war. He also organized the Georgia Relief and Hospital Association, a voluntary organization for the care of sick and wounded soldiers. After the war he was elected editor of the *Christian Index,* Jan. 1, 1866, but resigned in July to accept the presidency of Mercer University, in which office he served until 1871. The period was one of extreme difficulty for all educational institutions of the South, but Mercer made progress. In 1870 the institution was moved from Penfield to Macon. This removal, which was favored by Tucker, caused much resentment and friction, which probably was in part the cause of his resignation in 1871. The following fourteen months he spent in Europe, chiefly at Rome and Paris. In Rome he assisted in establishing a Baptist Church and himself baptized in the Tiber the first candidate for membership. In Paris he preached for the American Church most of the winter. On returning to America he became chancellor of the University of Georgia, at Athens, and served as such from 1874 to 1878. In the latter year he became proprietor and editor of the *Christian Index,* which he conducted until his death in 1889. Under his control the paper attained a position of wide and commanding influence not only in Georgia but far beyond its borders.

Tucker was not a great scholar, but he was a logical and consistent thinker and an excellent teacher. As a speaker and writer he was master of a clear style characterized by conciseness and finish. In his preaching he was ardent and earnest, and his discourses were enlivened by flashes of wit and humor. Though he held but one pastorate, he did much preaching throughout his life. He published a volume of sermons in 1884 under the title *The Old Theology Re-stated in Sermons,* and in 1869, a small volume entitled *The Gospel in Enoch,* which occasioned much favorable comment. After his death, *Select Writings by the Late Henry Holcombe Tucker* (copr. 1902), edited by B. J. W. Graham, was issued. He died at Atlanta, Ga., survived by his wife and two children.

[William Cathcart, *The Baptist Encyc.* (1881); *Hist. of the Baptist Denomination in Ga.* (1881); R. L. Robinson, *Hist. of the Ga. Baptist Asso.* (1928); B. D. Ragsdale, *Story of Ga. Baptists* (copr. 1932); T. H. Martin, *Atlanta and Its Builders* (1902), vol. II; W. J. Northen, *Men of Mark in Ga.,* vol. III (1911); *Atlanta Constitution,* Sept. 10, 1889.]   W. J. M.

TUCKER, HENRY ST. GEORGE (Dec. 29, 1780–Aug. 28, 1848), jurist, was born at "Matoax," in Chesterfield County, Va., the son of St. George Tucker [q.v.] and Frances (Bland) Randolph Tucker. John Randolph of Roanoke, 1773–1833 [q.v.] was his half-brother and Nathaniel Beverley Tucker, 1784–1851 [q.v.] was his brother. In 1799 he graduated from the College of William and Mary, where he studied law under his father. Shortly after he attained his majority he went to Winchester, Va., where he began the general practice of law. In spite of his youth, his outstanding talents were swiftly recognized, and his practice grew rapidly in volume and in importance. He appears to have gained no little reputation by his handling of litigation involving the estates of Lord Fairfax. On Sept. 23, 1806, he married Anne Evelina Hunter. John Randolph Tucker, 1823–1897 and Nathaniel Beverley Tucker, 1820–1890, were their sons and Henry St. George Tucker, 1853–1932 [qq.v.] their grandson. He served for the session of 1807–08 in the Virginia House of Delegates. Upon the outbreak of the War of 1812 he enlisted as a volunteer. From 1815 to 1819 he sat in the federal House of Representatives. Though the House then included among its members such men as Clay, Calhoun, and Webster, he took a prominent part in its activities. In 1816 he opposed the act to increase the salaries of members of Congress and refused to accept the increase in his own salary. From 1819 to 1823 he served in the state Senate.

His judicial career, which absorbed seventeen years of his life and in which he added no little to his renown, began in 1824, when he was elected judge of the superior courts of chancery for the Winchester and Clarksburg districts. An indefatigable worker, he gave unstintedly of his time and labor to his judicial duties. Yet he organized and taught with signal success during the seven years of his chancellorship a private law school at Winchester. In this period he wrote his *Commentaries on the Laws of Virginia* (2 vols., 1836–37). This work, with such other publications as *A Few Lectures on Natural Law* (1844) and *Lectures on Constitutional Law* (1843) firmly established his reputation in the field of legal authorship. In 1831 he was elected president of the supreme court of appeals of Virginia. For a decade he presided with dignity and distinction over that high court, winning the acclaim of his colleagues on the bench, the members of the Virginia bar, and the people of the State. So highly did he consider his office that he declined an appointment as federal attorney-general at the hands of President Jackson. In 1841 he resigned from the court to accept the professorship of law in the University of Virginia. Though handicapped by lack of health, he yet taught with such vigor and enthusiasm as to win the warm plaudits of his students. In 1842, when he was chairman of the faculty, upon his motion, the "Honor System" was adopted at the University of Virginia, which has operated there for more than ninety years as a spiritual asset of the institution. His failing health compelled him, in 1845, to retire, and he returned to Winchester, where he died.

Glowing tributes were paid to him after his

death. His varied activities had brought him into contact with most of the distinguished Virginians of his day. Though his restless energy had been scattered over many fields, he literally touched nothing that he did not adorn. It is quite remarkable how closely his career paralleled that of his father. Each was a lawyer, a legislator, a judge, a teacher of law, and a judicial writer. Each was a soldier in his country's service, and each ventured into the field of light poetry. Yet Henry St. George Tucker need shine in no reflected glory.

[S. N. Hurst and R. M. Brown, *A Complete Alphabetical, Chronological Annotated Digest of All the Reported Decisions of . . . Va.*, vol. I (1897), p. 35; J. R. Tucker, "The Judges Tucker of the Court of Appeals of Va.," *Va. Law Register*, Mar. 1896; S. S. P. Patteson, "The Supreme Court of Appeals of Va.," *Green Bag*, July 1893; S. E. M. Hardy, "Some Va. Lawyers," *Ibid.*, Jan. 1898; P. A. Bruce, *Hist. of the Univ. of Va.*, vols. I–IV (1920–21); faculty minutes of the Univ. of Va.]　　　　　　　　　　　　　A. M. D.

TUCKER, HENRY ST. GEORGE (Apr. 5, 1853–July 23, 1932), congressman from Virginia and lawyer, was born at Winchester, Va., the great-grandson of the emigrant, St. George Tucker, the grandson of Henry St. George Tucker, 1780–1848, and the son of John Randolph Tucker, 1823–1897 [*qq.v.*]. His mother was Laura (Powell) Tucker. After attending private schools in Loudoun County and at Richmond, he entered Washington and Lee University, where he received the degrees of master of arts in 1875 and bachelor of laws in 1876. On Oct. 25, 1877, he was married to Henrietta Preston Johnston, the daughter of William Preston Johnston [*q.v.*]. She died in 1900 leaving six children. He practised law at Staunton, Va., from 1876 to 1889, when he succeeded his father as Democratic representative in Congress. He served there until 1897. His advocacy of the popular election of federal senators and his attitude toward silver stand out in his congressional career of this period. Denouncing the control of legislative bodies by corporate wealth, he declared that "an aptness for percentages and the successful manipulation of railroads and stock boards are often regarded as the most essential of Senatorial equipments" (*Cong. Record,* 52 Cong., 1 Sess., p. 6063). A bi-metallist, he voted for the repeal of the Sherman Silver Act and, thereafter, consistently opposed the remonetization of silver except at the ratio of 20 to 1. At the Democratic State convention at Staunton, Va., in June 1896 he alone defended Cleveland. "I am not going," he said, "to stand before a crowd of Virginia Democrats and blackguard a man that you elected" (*Rockbridge County News,* June 11, 1896). His refusal to indorse the plat-

form of 16 to 1 in that campaign, although he supported Bryan, cost him the political support of his district.

From 1897 to 1902 he was associated with Washington and Lee University as professor of law, as dean of the law school, and, after the death of William L. Wilson [*q.v.*], as acting president, 1900–01. On Jan. 13, 1903, he was married to Martha Sharpe of Wilkes Barre, Pa., who died in 1928. He was dean of the department of law and jurisprudence at Columbian University (George Washington University) from 1903 to 1905, president of the American Bar Association, 1904-05, and president of the Jamestown Tercentennial Exposition, 1905-07. An anti-machine Democrat, he was an unsuccessful candidate for the governorship of Virginia in 1909 and in 1921. He was the author of *Limitations on the Treaty-Making Power Under the Constitution of the United States* (1915) and *Woman's Suffrage by Constitutional Amendment* (1916), and he edited *The Constitution of the United States* by John Randolph Tucker, 1823–1897 [*q.v.*], in two volumes (1899).

Reëlected to Congress in March 1922, he served continuously until his death. In that postwar era he was regarded as one of the most ardent exponents of state rights and as one of the zealous defenders of the *laissez-faire* interpretation of the Constitution in Congress; and he was opposed generally to the social and economic legislation of that period, the proposed child labor amendment, woman's suffrage, the Eighteenth Amendment, and similar legislative proposals. "When the powers of the Government can be used to settle the question of competition in commercial life, the act becomes tryanny," is an apposite expression of his political philosophy (*Cong. Record,* 67 Cong., 2 Sess., p. 7596). He attracted nation-wide attention in 1925 by refusing to accept an increase in salary for that session, citing as a precedent for his action his grandfather's refusal in Congress in 1816 in similar circumstances. He died in Lexington, survived by his third wife, Mary Jane (Williams) Tucker, to whom he had been married on June 26, 1929.

[Letters in possession of the family; L. G. Tyler, *Men of Mark in Va.*, V (1909); *Memorial Services Held in the House of Representatives* (1933); Allan Nevins, *Grover Cleveland* (1932); *Who's Who in America*, 1930–31; *Colonial Families of the U. S.*, V (1915), ed. by G. N. Mackenzie; *Rockbridge County News* (Lexington), July 28, 1932; *N. Y. Times*, July 24, 1932; dates for degrees from contemporary catalogs of the university and *Lexington Gazette and Citizen* (Lexington), June 25, 1875, and June 23, 1876.] W. G. B.

TUCKER, JOHN RANDOLPH (Jan. 31, 1812–June 12, 1883), naval officer, the son of

Susan (Douglas) and John Tucker, lately of Bermuda, was born at Alexandria, Va., then within the limits of the District of Columbia. He received his early education in local schools, and on June 1, 1826, he was appointed to the United States Navy as a midshipman. He became passed midshipman on June 10, 1833. He was commissioned lieutenant from Dec. 20, 1837. On June 7, 1838, he was married at Norfolk, to Virginia Webb. They had three children. Tall, with imposing presence, he was known to the sailors as "Handsome Jack." He had the reputation of being a resolute fighter, a strict disciplinarian, and a splendid seaman. Alternating with duty at the Norfolk yard, he served in the Home Squadron, in the East Indies, during the Mexican War on the *Stromboli,* first as executive officer, then as commander, in the Home Squadron, and in the Mediterranean Squadron. He was promoted to be commander from Sept. 14, 1855. He commanded the receiving ship at Norfolk for three years, was on "waiting orders" for nearly two years, broken by a short tour on a board of inspection, and was rounding out a year as ordnance officer at the Norfolk yard when Virginia seceded. He resigned on Apr. 18, 1861, but under the policy of the Lincoln administration his separation from the service was recorded as a dismissal.

He was immediately appointed in the short-lived Virginia state navy and in the Confederate States Navy on June 8, 1861, to rank as commander from Mar. 26, 1861. He was placed in charge of the naval defenses of the James River and was ordered to command the steamer *Yorktown,* which under his superintendency was converted into the protected cruiser *Patrick Henry.* His vessel was stationed at Mulberry Island to protect the right flank of the Confederate Army of the Peninsula. He participated in the battle of Hampton Roads on Mar. 8–9, 1862, in the demonstration against the enemy's fleet below Fort Monroe in April 1862, and after the evacuation of Norfolk commanded the fleet in its retirement up the James River to Drewry's Bluff, where the pursuing ships were severely repulsed on May 15, 1862. He left the *Patrick Henry* in August 1862 for Charleston, S. C., where he assumed command of the ironclad ram *Chicora.* He took part in the night attack upon the blockading squadron off Charleston on Jan. 31, 1863, and was shortly afterward given command of the Charleston Squadron. He was promoted to captain of the Provisional Navy of the Confederate States from May 13, 1863. When Charleston was evacuated in February 1865, he destroyed his vessels and formed his crews into a naval brigade,

which was assigned to duty at Drewry's Bluff, where he commanded ashore and Rear Admiral Raphael Semmes afloat. Upon the evacuation of Richmond, his command was assigned to the rear guard of Lee's army and distinguished itself at the battle of Sailor's Creek on Apr. 6, only to be surrendered by the corps commander in consequence of losses elsewhere on the field. He was imprisoned at Fort Warren, from where he was released on July 24, 1865, upon taking the oath of allegiance to the United States.

After much difficulty he obtained employment as agent of the Southern Express Company at Raleigh, N. C., where he remained until he received a commission as rear admiral in the Peruvian navy. He commanded the combined fleets of Peru and Chile in the war with Spain, but the war was concluded in 1869 without an opportunity to engage the Spanish fleet. He was then appointed president of an hydrographical commission to survey the upper waters of the Amazon, which he accomplished in the face of hostile Indians. He was sent to New York to prepare the charts for publication but the financial difficulties of Peru caused the termination of the commission in 1877. He retired to Petersburg, Va., where he died from heart failure.

[*War of the Rebellion: Official Records (Navy)* and *(Army)* indexed as John R. Tucker and not to be confused with John Randolph Tucker, the attorney-general of Va.; records of the Naval Lib. and of the Navy Dept.; J. H. Rochelle, *Life of Rear Admiral John Randolph Tucker* (1903); L. G. Tyler, *Encyc. of Va. Biog.* (1915), vol. III; W. H. Parker, *Recollections of a Naval Officer* (1883), pp. 253–322; J. T. Scharf, *Hist. of the Confederate States Navy* (1887); *Richmond Dispatch,* June 14, 1883.]   W. M. R., Jr.

TUCKER, JOHN RANDOLPH (Dec. 24, 1823–Feb. 13, 1897), lawyer, teacher, and congressman from Virginia, was born at Winchester, Va., the son of Anne Evelina (Hunter) and Henry St. George Tucker, 1780–1848 [*q.v.*], the nephew of Nathaniel Beverley Tucker, 1784–1851, and the grandson of St. George Tucker [*qq.v.*]. His brother was Nathaniel Beverley Tucker, 1820–1890 [*q.v.*]. He attended private schools at Winchester and Richmond, and in 1839 he entered the University of Virginia, where he studied moral and political philosophy under his kinsman, George Tucker [*q.v.*], and also mathematics and physical science, the teaching of which he was urged by his preceptors to follow. However, he studied law under his father at the university and received the law degree there in 1843. On Oct. 5, 1848, he married Laura Holmes Powell of Loudoun County, Va. Henry St. George Tucker, 1853–1932 [*q.v.*], was their son. From 1845 until 1857 he practised law at Winchester. An ardent believer in state-rights principles he took an active part in politics, serving as Democratic elector in 1852 and 1856, participating in the gubernatorial campaign in 1855 against the Know-Nothing party, and supporting Breckinridge in 1860. As attorney-general of Virginia from 1857 to 1865, he represented the state in important civil and criminal cases before the state courts. From 1865 to his death, though he was during most of this time either teaching law at Washington and Lee University (1870–74; 1889–97) or serving in Congress (1875–87), he still engaged in the practice of law. It is said he appeared before the federal Supreme Court oftener, with one exception, than any other Virginian during this period. He represented the Chicago anarchists before this body, and, when surprise was expressed by some friends, he replied, "I do not defend anarchy; I defend the Constitution" (Hamilton, *post*, pp. 152, 153). Other notable cases with which he was associated were the trial of Jefferson Davis and the Florida case before the electoral commission.

Upon entering Congress in 1875, he immediately became a leader on the Democratic side of the House and showed himself to be "an old-fashioned, strict-constructionist, state-rights logician" (Smith, *post*, I, 589), resisting every tendency toward centralization and applying the yard stick of constitutionality to every measure before Congress. "It is unfashionable, I know," he once remarked, "to stickle for the Constitution" (*Cong. Record*, 49 Cong., 1 Sess., App. p. 59). He championed tariff reform, characterizing the perversion of the taxing power "from the purpose of revenue to the grant of a bounty or special privilege . . . if . . . directly . . . a robbery; if indirectly . . . a fraud" (*Cong. Record*, 47 Cong., 1 Sess., App. p. 275). He advocated the repeal of the internal revenue system—"nests of Federal patronage which have infested the States for twenty years, and have been the source of more petty tyranny and of more interference with the freedom of elections . . . than has ever been known before in the history of the country" (*Ibid.*, p. 475); favored the Chinese exclusion bill in order to protect "the young Hercules of the Pacific" (*Ibid.*, App. p. 56); aided in the defeat of the Blair education bill; supported a sound money policy; and in 1880 introduced a quorum-counting rule that was subsequently adopted by the House under the speakership of Thomas B. Reed.

After his retirement from Congress, he returned to Washington and Lee University as professor of constitutional and international law and in 1893 was made dean of the law school.

In 1892–93 he was president of the American Bar Association. He was the author of *The Constitution of the United States* (2 vols., 1899, published posthumously). Among his published public addresses were *The Southern Church Justified in its Support of the South* (1863), *Paper Read Before Social Science Association . . . at Saratoga Springs, N. Y., on the Relations of the United States to Each Other as Modified by the War and the Constitutional Amendments* (1877), and *The History of the Federal Convention of 1787* (1887) read before the graduating class of the Yale Law School. His speeches were polished, and he was known for his witticism, oratory, and ability as a story teller.

[Alexander Hamilton, *Memorial of John Randolph Tucker* (1897) and in *Report of . . . Va. State Bar Asso. . . . 1897* (1897); *Report of . . . the Am. Bar Asso. 1897* (1897); R. T. Barton, "John Randolph Tucker," *Va. Law Register*, May 1897; T. C. Smith, *The Life and Letters of James Abram Garfield* (2 vols., 1925); O. F. Morton, *A Hist. of Rockbridge County, Va.* (1920); Philip Slaughter, *A Hist. of Bristol Parish, Va.* (2nd ed., 1897); *Rockbridge County News* (Lexington), Feb. 18, 1897.]   W. G. B.

TUCKER, LUTHER (May 7, 1802–Jan. 26, 1873), agricultural journalist, was born in Brandon, Vt., the youngest of six children of Stephen and Olive (Green) Tucker and a descendant of Robert Tucker who settled in Weymouth, Mass., about 1635. His mother died soon after his birth, and the family scattered, leaving Luther in the care of a neighbor. His formal schooling was meager, but through his own efforts he acquired a good education and became adept as a writer. At the age of fourteen he was apprenticed to a printer of Middlebury, Vt., and in 1817 moved with his master to Palmyra, N. Y. During his journeyman years he worked in New York, Philadelphia, Baltimore, and Washington. In the spring of 1825 he entered into a partnership with Henry C. Sleight of Jamaica, Long Island, printer of standard works for New York houses; some of these bear the imprint of Sleight & Tucker.

A little more than a year later, under the firm name of Luther Tucker & Company, Sleight and Tucker established the *Rochester Daily Advertiser* in Rochester, N. Y., where Tucker took up his residence. With Henry O'Reilly [*q.v.*] as its editor, the *Advertiser* began publication in October 1826; two years later Tucker bought his partner's interest. The success of the *Advertiser*, together with his interest in agriculture, led him to establish the *Genesee Farmer*, Jan. 1, 1831, which despite strong prejudice against "newspaper farming," soon gained a large following. The *Genesee Farmer* was published weekly, but from January 1836 to December 1839

Tucker published also the *Monthly Genesee Farmer and Horticulturist,* made up of selections from the weekly.

In 1839 he sold the *Advertiser* to devote his full time to farming and his agricultural journal. In October of that year, however, the death of Jesse Buel [*q.v.*] left the Albany *Cultivator* without a head, and at the solicitation of his friends and Buel's family Tucker purchased it, merging with it his *Genesee Farmer,* and early in 1840 moved to Albany to carry on the *Cultivator* at that place. Here he became an outstanding member of the New York State Agricultural Society and held various offices. At the annual meeting in 1841 a new constitution which he had prepared was adopted by the Society. This document provided for the holding of state fairs, and thus to Tucker much credit is due for the long series of New York fairs, held annually without a break since 1841, which have contributed largely to the progress of New York agriculture.

In July 1846 Tucker established the *Horticulturist,* under the editorship of his friend Andrew J. Downing [*q.v.*]. It at once assumed a position of influence and is still considered America's most notable contribution to the periodical literature of horticulture. Tucker sold it in 1852, however, the year of Downing's death, and in 1853 began to issue a weekly edition of the *Cultivator* which he called the *Country Gentleman.* Since this gradually took the place of the monthly in the interest and preference of the public, he consolidated the two papers in January 1866 under the title of *Cultivator and Country Gentleman.* At the time Tucker established the *Country Gentleman* his eldest son, Luther H. Tucker, became associated with him as business manager, the firm name being changed to Luther Tucker & Son. Another son, Gilbert Milligan Tucker [*q.v.*], entered the firm in 1867. The senior Tucker continued as editor until his death, when his sons took over the conduct of the paper.

In disposition Tucker was unassuming, kindly, and generous. He exerted for many years an important influence on agricultural matters, and did perhaps more than any other American of his time to promote the literature of agriculture. He was regarded by his contemporaries as the leader and model of agricultural journalists of the country and no fewer than ten other agricultural editors received their training under him. He was remarkably successful in enlisting large numbers of the best farmers of the country as contributors to his publications. With Willis Gaylord [*q.v.*] he compiled in 1840 a work in two volumes entitled *American Husbandry,* being a series of essays on agriculture first published principally in the *Cultivator* or the *Genesee Farmer.*

Tucker was married three times: first, Nov. 19, 1827, to Naomi Sparhawk, who died Aug. 4, 1832, at Rochester, a victim of the cholera; second, Oct. 4, 1833, to her sister, Mary Sparhawk, who died Mar. 8, 1844, of consumption; and third, June 1, 1846, to Mrs. Margaret Lucinda (Smith) Burr, who survived him. A son and a daughter were born of the first marriage, a son and three daughters of the second, and two sons of the third. Tucker died in Albany after a few weeks' illness and was buried in the Albany Rural Cemetery.

[*Cultivator and Country Gentleman,* Jan. 30, Feb. 6, 13, 20, Mar. 6, 13, Apr. 10, 1873; *Country Gentleman,* Jan. 4, 1906; Ephraim Tucker, *Geneal. of the Tucker Family* (1895); W. E. Ogilvie, *Pioneer Agricultural Journalists* (1927); *N. Y. Tribune,* Jan. 28, 1873; *Horticulturist,* Mar. 1873; *Moore's Rural New Yorker,* Feb. 8, 1873; *Gardener's Monthly,* Mar. 1873; *Rochester Hist. Soc. Pub. Fund Ser.,* VI (1927), 263–64, 270–71, 279–90.]

C. R. B.

TUCKER, NATHANIEL BEVERLEY (Sept. 6, 1784–Aug. 26, 1851), author, professor of law, was born at "Matoax," Chesterfield County, Va. He was usually referred to as Beverley Tucker. He was the son of St. George Tucker [*q.v.*] and Frances (Bland) Randolph Tucker. Along with his brother, Henry St. George Tucker, 1780–1848, and his half-brother, John Randolph, 1773–1833 [*qq.v.*], he was privately tutored, and he graduated from the College of William and Mary in 1801. He began the practice of law in Charlotte County, Va., but with little success. There he married Mary Coalter and devoted his ample leisure to the study of history and politics. In 1809 he removed to "Roanoke," where he struggled with the law and lived largely on the bounty of John Randolph, who exercised an important influence over his political views. In the War of 1812 he served as a lieutenant and later was promoted to a staff appointment. In 1815, although his practice was improving, he removed with his family to Missouri. There his wife died, and he married Eliza Taylor. After her death he was married a third time, on Apr. 13, 1830, to Lucy Anne Smith. He was instrumental in the organization of Jefferson County and served as a judge in the circuit courts of the territory and later of the state. He resisted unsuccessfully the admission of "Yankeys" to the new state and was a violent opponent of the Missouri Compromise.

In the winter of 1833–34 he returned to Virginia and shortly afterward was appointed professor of law at William and Mary, a post he held until his death. From his academic retreat he poured forth letters, books, and speeches in defense of the rights of the South. As a lecturer and letter writer he had his greatest influence. During his fifteen years as professor he gave his political views wide currency among his students. He published books on political economy that are permeated with his doctrine of state sovereignty and reflect the theories of his colleague, Thomas R. Dew. Probably his greatest political influence was effected by his extensive letter writing. Among his correspondents were Calhoun, Tyler, Jefferson Davis, Hammond, Wise, and William G. Simms. His ideas were important in the development of President Tyler's "exchequer plan" (Tyler, *post,* II, 29–30). His last public appearance was as a delegate from Virginia to the Nashville Convention of 1850, and he died in the following year at Winchester, Va.

His principal works include three novels: *George Balcombe* (1836), published anonymously; *The Partisan Leader* (2 vols., 1836); and *Gertrude,* published as a serial in the *Southern Literary Messenger,* September 1844 to December 1845 as well as numerous writings on political economy and law, of which *A Discourse on the Importance of the Study of Political Science as a Branch of Academic Education in the United States* (1840) and *The Principles of Pleading* (1846) are the most significant. *George Balcombe,* the most thoroughly literary in purpose, received high praise at the time. Edgar Allan Poe wrote, "George Balcombe, we are induced to regard, upon the whole, as *the best* American novel . . . its interest is intense from beginning to end . . . its most distinguishing features are invention, vigor, almost audacity, of thought" ("Marginalia," ccxxv). Tucker's books were nearly all devoted to an exposition of extreme state rights. As early as 1820 he expressed himself boldly in favor of secession and for thirty years maintained this view with inflexible consistency. His philosophy was firmly rooted in eighteenth-century agrarianism; he believed in aristocratic government and had no patience with Jacksonian Democracy—especially as it began to invade his own beloved state. The Nullification Proclamation and the Force Bill outraged his doctrine of state sovereignty and led to the writing of his best known novel, *The Partisan Leader*. At the request of friends in South Carolina, the book was secretly printed before its completion in the hope of swaying the election of 1836—though Tucker believed Van Buren's triumph assured. The title page bore the fictitious date of 1856, and the situation described is almost prophetic in its exactness. The modern reader marvels at the clearness with which he

foresaw the approach of civil war, and that as early as 1835 some in the South felt that secession was inevitable. The novel was suppressed but was reprinted as propaganda by both sides in the later struggle. Today it cannot claim a high place in literature; the language seems stilted, the seriousness unrelieved by humor, and the outlook limited. His position in literary history rests on the fact that he was one of the earliest American disciples of Scott, though his execution, praised in 1836, is now (1936) outmoded and unnatural. Tucker represented the survival of eighteenth century thought in pre-war Virginia. Hatred of centralization in government, "shirt-sleeve democracy," and "Yankee industrialism," along with his intense love for Virginia, agrarianism, and the idealized slave characterize his thought. He was among the last of Virginia's political thinkers and is perhaps excluded from the fame of his predecessors because his philosophy belonged to a time that was past and was based upon a dying economy.

[Letters in possession of his grandson, George P. Coleman, Williamsburg, Va.; M. H. Woodfin, "Nathaniel Beverley Tucker," *Richmond College Hist. Papers,* vol. II, no. 1 (1917); W. C. Bruce, *John Randolph of Roanoke* (2 vols., 1922); *Hist. Mag.,* June 1859; L. G. Tyler, *Letters and Times of the Tylers* (2 vols., 1884–85); Carl Bridenbaugh, "Introduction," *Partisan Leader* (1933); V. L. Parrington, *The Romantic Rev. in America* (1927); a more favorable view by Poe, *ante,* and lxv as well as Carl Van Doren in *Cambridge Hist. Am. Lit.* (1917), vol. I, and H. Findlay in *Lib. of Southern Literature,* vol. XII (1907); a biog. with letters in preparation by P. W. Torrentine, Cambridge, Mass.; *International Mag.,* Oct. 1851.]   C. B—h.

TUCKER, NATHANIEL BEVERLEY (June 8, 1820–July 4, 1890), Confederate agent, was born in Winchester, Va., the grandson of St. George Tucker [*q.v.*], an emigrant from Bermuda, the nephew of Nathaniel Beverley Tucker, 1784–1851, and the son of Henry St. George Tucker, 1780–1848 [*qq.v.*]. His mother was Anne Evelina (Hunter) Tucker, and John Randolph Tucker, 1823–1897 [*q.v.*], was his brother. In 1831 the family removed to Richmond. The boy was prepared for college at the Richmond Academy and in 1837 went to the University of Virginia. For a year he worked under Charles Ellet [*q.v.*] on the building of the James River & Kanawha Canal and then undertook the management of one of the family plantations. On Jan. 21, 1841, he was married to Jane Shelton Ellis and shortly afterward established himself at "Hazelfield" in Jefferson County. They had eight children. Leaving "Hazelfield" after a few years, he occupied himself with various undertakings, lost his capital and acquired debts in a business in Richmond, manufactured munitions for a time during the Mexican War, built up a practice in representing claims before Congress and before the federal departments, and was active in politics. From 1853 to 1856 he edited the *Washington Sentinel*. In 1857 he succeeded Nathaniel Hawthorne as consul at Liverpool. He enjoyed his personal and family connections in Europe, the friends and family of his late cousin, Henry St. George Tucker, who had been director and treasurer of the East India Company, as well as such Americans as George M. Dallas and John Y. Mason [*qq.v.*], the ministers to Great Britain and France and both friends and relatives by marriage. More than six feet tall and fine-featured, he possessed a manner and personality that made him many friends. In 1861 in a notice seeking his recognition and arrest, Seward described him as "a large man, upwards of fifty, florid complexion" with "plausible and boisterous manners" (*Official Records, post, 2* ser., vol. II, p. 176).

Upon the secession of Virginia he returned home and joined the Confederate army. Soon he entered into a contract to provide supplies for the army, and in 1862 he was in New Orleans seeking passage abroad. He reached Paris and for a time entertained high hopes, but, thwarted on every hand, he returned home unsuccessful. In 1864 he was sent to Canada on a delicate mission to arrange for an exchange of cotton for bacon and, apparently, to make some kind of secret diplomatic representations to Northern men of influence. He was successful in making a contract for the exchange of the two commodities, pound for pound, but in the confusion at the end of the war the terms were never carried out.

After the war he was harassed by the unfounded suspicions and animosities of the period. Accused of complicity in the plot to murder Lincoln, a reward of $25,000 was offered for him until November 1865, when the offer was revoked. In spite of the entire lack of evidence against him and in spite of his own knowledge of the partisan reasons for such persecution, this charge continued to be a source of distress to him (see his *Address . . . to the People of the United States*, 1865, and Rowland, *post*). He spent a series of unprofitable years in England, Mexico, and Canada and in 1872 returned to the United States. He lived the remaining years of his life at Washington and, in the summer, at Berkeley Springs, W. Va., advocating the claims of various interests to Congress, to the federal departments, and to the public, writing for newspapers, and valiantly struggling with the difficulties of poverty and illness. Such stanch Republicans as James G. Blaine and Hamilton Fish professed to be his friends, and at his death the

Washington Post (*post*) said of him that "he was perhaps as well known personally to leading politicians throughout the country as any man of his time."

[J. E. Tucker, *Beverley Tucker. A Memoir by his Wife* (n.d.), in possession of Beverley Tucker of Richmond, Va.; *War of the Rebellion: Official Records (Army)*, 1 ser., XLVI, pt. 3, XLIX, pt. 2, LII, pt. 2, LIII, 2 ser., II, VIII, 4 ser., II, III; J. B. Jones, *A Rebel War Clerk's Diary* (1935), ed. by Howard Swiggett, vol. II, p. 319; *Jefferson Davis* (1923), ed. by Dunbar Rowland, vols. II, VII; *Richmond Dispatch* and *Washington Post*, July 5, 1890.]   K. E. C.

TUCKER, ST. GEORGE (June 29, 1752 o.s.–Nov. 10, 1827), jurist, was born at Port Royal, Bermuda, the son of Henry and Anne (Butterfield) Tucker. He was distantly related to George Tucker [*q.v.*]. In his late teens he emigrated to Virginia. He enrolled as a student in the College of William and Mary and graduated in 1772. He was admitted to the bar and began the practice of his chosen profession in Williamsburg. His career as a lawyer was interrupted by the outbreak of the Revolutionary War, into which he threw himself on behalf of the struggling colonies. At the battle of Guilford Court House he distinguished himself by his bravery and military skill as a colonel of the Chesterfield County militia. Later he became lieutenant-colonel of a troop of horse and took part in the siege of Yorktown, where he was wounded. On Sept. 23, 1778, he married Frances (Bland) Randolph, the widow of John Randolph of "Matoax," Chesterfield County, and mother of John Randolph of Roanoke, 1773–1833 [*q.v.*]. Nathaniel Beverley Tucker, 1784–1851, and Henry St. George Tucker, 1780–1848, were their sons, John Randolph Tucker, 1823–1897 and Nathaniel Beverley Tucker, 1820–1890, grandsons, and Henry St. George Tucker, 1853–1932 [*qq.v.*], a great-grandson. She died in 1788. His letters to her while he was in the Revolutionary Army bear testimony of his devotion as a husband. They are, at the same time, historical documents of no mean importance ("Southern Campaign, 1781," in *Magazine of American History*, July, Sept. 1881). On Oct. 8, 1791, he married Lelia (Skipwith) Carter, the daughter of Sir Peyton Skipwith.

In public office he spent virtually the whole remainder of his life. In 1786 he became one of the commissioners at the Annapolis convention. His judicial career, in which he was to attain distinguished eminence, began when he became judge of the general court of Virginia in 1788. In 1800 he became professor of law in the College of William and Mary. In 1803 he was elected to the supreme court of appeals of Virginia as the successor of Edmund Pendleton [*q.v.*].

He sat for eight years, adding no little to his own growing fame and enhancing the reputation of the court. He resigned from this court in 1811, but in 1813 he was appointed by President Madison judge of the district court for the district of Virginia. For nearly fifteen years he continued as a federal judge before failure in health prompted his resignation. He then retired to the home of Joseph C. Cabell [*q.v.*] in Nelson County, Va., where he died. His grandson, John Randolph Tucker, 1823–1897 [*q.v.*], many years later cited his opinion in *Kamper* vs. *Hawkins* (1 *Va. Reports,* 20), in the general court, that the state constitution of 1776 was a sovereign act of the people of Virginia and therefore the supreme law, and that any act of the legislature or the government in conflict with it was null and void. Among his other important opinions are his dissenting opinion in *Woodson* vs. *Randolph,* also in the general court, holding that it was a violation of the federal Constitution for Congress to undertake to change the rules of evidence with reference to a state contract sued upon in a state court (1 *Brockenbrough and Holmes Reports,* 128) and his opinion, in the supreme court of appeals of Virginia, in *Turpin* vs. *Locket* (6 *Call Reports,* 113) sustaining the constitutionality of the act of 1802 by which the glebes of the Episcopal Church were to be applied to the relief of poor of each parish (for discussion see Call, *post,* and Hardy, *post,* p. 58).

His reputation rests in no small part on his juridical writings. His pamphlet *Dissertation on Slavery: with a Proposal for its Gradual Abolition in Virginia* (1796 and reprinted in Philadelphia 1861), advocating the emancipation of children born to slave mothers, was widely read and acclaimed. His annotated edition of *Blackstone's Commentaries* (5 vols., 1803) was one of the most important law books of its day. In an appendix he discussed the principles of government as related to the nature and interpretation of the federal Constitution. He also wrote minor poetry of some charm, as *Liberty, a Poem on the Independence of America* (1788) and *The Probationary Odes of Jonathan Pindar* (2 pts. 1796), originally published in the *National Gazette* and often erroneously attributed to Philip M. Freneau.

[Daniel Call, "Memoir," 4 *Call Report* (Va.), p. xxvi; J. R. Tucker, "The Judges Tucker of the Court of Appeals of Va.," *Va. Law Register,* Mar. 1896; S. S. P. Patteson, "The Supreme Court of Appeals of Va.," *Green Bag,* July 1893; S. E. M. Hardy, "Some Va. Lawyers," *Ibid.,* Jan. 1898; H. St. George Tucker, "Patrick Henry and St. George Tucker," *Univ. of Pa. Law Rev.,* Jan. 1919; W. C. Bruce, *Life of John Randolph of Roanoke* (2 vols., 1922); S. N. Hurst and R. M. Brown, *A Complete Alphabetical, Chronological Annotated Digest of All the Reported Decisions of ... Va.,* vol. I (1897); *Colonial Families of the U. S.,* vol. V (1915), ed. by G. N. Mackenzie; T. A. Emmett, *An Account of the Tucker Family of Bermuda* (1898); *Gentleman's Mag.,* Nov. 1828.]   A. M. D.

TUCKER, SAMUEL (Nov. 1, 1747–Mar. 10, 1833), naval officer, was born in Marblehead, Mass., third of the eight children of Andrew and Mary (Belcher) Tucker. His father was a prosperous ship captain, said to have come from Dundee, Scotland, and his mother was of English extraction. At the age of eleven the boy ran away from home and went to sea, enlisting on board the *Royal George* bound for Louisbourg. At seventeen he was a second mate. Rising to first mate, he later became a master and on the eve of the Revolution was in command of the *Young Phoenix,* trading with Spain and England and importing salt. In the meantime, on Dec. 21, 1768, he had married Mary Gatchell of Marblehead, who bore him several children.

It is said that Tucker saw his first Revolutionary service in 1775 as lieutenant of a company of soldiers. On Jan. 20, 1776, Washington commissioned him captain of the *Franklin,* an army warship, and directed him to cruise against British vessels. A few months later he was transferred to the *Hancock,* a superior command. During 1776, alone or in company with another ship of the army, he captured several valuable prizes, including two transports carrying Scottish troops and two ships laden with beef, pork, and other supplies. Congress on Mar. 15, 1777, recognized his services by appointing him a captain in the navy, but several months elapsed before he received a command, the frigate *Boston.* On Feb. 17, 1778, he weighed anchor at Marblehead and sailed for France, carrying as passengers John Adams, recently appointed commissioner to France, and his son John Quincy Adams. The elder Adams, who characterized Tucker as an able seaman, and a brave, vigilant officer, though of no great erudition, has left a description of this eventful voyage (*The Works of John Adams,* vol. III, 1851, esp. p. 97). Noteworthy were the rough weather that shattered the mainmast, the escape of the *Boston* from the watchful enemy, the chasing of prospective prizes, the capture of the valuable privateer *Martha,* whose captain had served twenty years in the Royal Navy, and the anxieties of all as the ship neared her destination. On Aug. 22, after a successful cruise in French waters in which he captured four small prizes, Tucker sailed for America, accompanied by the *Providence,* Commodore Abraham Whipple [*q.v.*], and the *Ranger,* Capt. John Paul Jones [*q.v.*]. The little fleet captured three prizes before arriving at its destination, Portsmouth, N. H.

In the spring of 1779 Tucker sailed southward

to Chesapeake Bay and on July 29, accompanied by the *Deane,* Commodore Samuel Nicholson [*q.v.*], two ships of the Virginia navy, and a convoy of merchantmen, sailed out of the bay. The two frigates made a successful cruise of about five weeks, capturing eight prizes, including four New York privateers, and the packet *Sandwich* and the sloop of war *Thorn,* each of sixteen guns. On Sept. 6 they arrived at Boston, with 250 prisoners, among whom were several officers. In November the *Boston* with several other naval ships sailed on important service. After a brief cruise, during which a privateer of twelve guns was captured, the fleet arrived at Charleston, S. C., where Tucker participated in the siege of Charleston, with the *Boston* anchored in the Cooper River. On the surrender of the city he and his vessel fell into the hands of the enemy. He was almost immediately paroled and his vessel was taken into the Royal Navy and renamed the *Charleston.* Exchanged for the captain of the *Thorn,* Tucker obtained leave of absence from the navy and in 1781 made several cruises in that vessel, now a privateer, and captured among other ships the packet *Lord Hyde.* About Aug. 1 near the mouth of the St. Lawrence the *Thorn* was captured by the frigate *Hind* and Tucker and his officers were landed on the island of St. John's (now Prince Edward Island). Furnished with an open boat to carry them to Halifax, they laid a course for Boston, where in due time they arrived. This ended Tucker's active service in the navy.

In comfortable circumstances by reason of prize money, Tucker lived for several years in a house on Fleet Street, Boston. Returning to the merchant service, in 1783–85 he commanded several vessels trading with West India and European ports. In 1786 the *Cato,* a ship in which he had a large pecuniary interest, sank in the harbor of Lisbon. Giving up the sea, he moved to Marblehead and purchased there an interest in two grist mills and a granary. Failing in this enterprise, in 1792 he purchased a farm in Bristol, Me., on which he spent the rest of his life. From 1814 to 1818 he was a member of the Massachusetts house and later he was twice elected to the Maine house. In 1820 he carried to Washington the electoral vote of Maine, making the journey of 600 miles in less than five days. A statement made at this time (*Daily National Intelligencer,* Washington, Dec. 16, 1820) that he had taken sixty-two prizes, more than 600 cannon, and 3,000 prisoners probably exaggerated his Revolutionary services. In 1821 a private act of Congress pensioned him at the rate of twenty dollars a month and ten years later a general act

increased his pension to $600 a year. His wife died Dec. 30, 1831, and Tucker some fifteen months later, at Bremen, Me.

[J. H. Sheppard, *The Life of Samuel Tucker* (1868), is not free from legendary materials. See also Sheppard's briefer sketch in *New-Eng. Hist. and Geneal. Reg.,* Apr. 1872; G. W. Allen, *A Naval Hist. of the Am. Rev.* (2 vols., 1913); C. O. Paullin, *Out-Letters of Continental Marine Committee and Board of Admiralty* (1914); Ephraim Tucker, *Geneal. of the Tucker Family* (1895); Samuel Roads, *Hist. and Traditions of Marblehead* (1880); *Niles' Weekly Register,* Apr. 6, 27, 1833. W. P. Chipman, *In Ship and Prison* (copr. 1908) is a fictional account of Tucker.] C. O. P.

TUCKER, STEPHEN DAVIS (Jan. 28, 1818–Oct. 9, 1902), inventor and manufacturer, was born at Bloomfield, N. J. His parents were Benjamin and Jane (Davis) Tucker; his first American ancestor, grandfather of Benjamin, was Timothy Tucker, who came to America prior to 1732. On June 3, 1834, young Tucker was apprenticed to a member of the firm of R. Hoe & Company of New York, manufacturers of printing presses, to learn "the art, trade and mystery of finisher or whitesmith," and with the same firm he remained for fifty-nine years, until his retirement as senior partner. In 1842 he was set to work in the experiment room which had just been established. At first his work there consisted merely in the fabrication and testing of models, but his inventive genius soon manifested itself. He proved to be "one of the most brilliant mechanics that this country ever produced" (*Scientific American,* June 5, 1915), and in the course of his long service with the company took out nearly one hundred patents for improvements in printing, some in his own name alone and some in conjunction with Richard M. Hoe [*q.v.*]. Among his most important inventions were those which made (or helped to make) practicable the printing of both sides of a paper at once, the printing of a continuous web of paper instead of individual sheets, and the folding of newspapers by machinery as they come off the press. In 1846 he became foreman of his department, and in 1848 was sent to Paris to set up new Hoe presses for *La Patrie* and start their operation. Further business of the firm kept him in France for two years. He was admitted as a partner May 28, 1860, and finally retired on Aug. 31, 1893, transferring his share to Robert Hoe, 1839–1909 [*q.v.*].

Tucker continued to live in New York, but traveled abroad extensively. He devoted much of his leisure to the study of sundials and assembled a collection of more than sixty specimens in ivory, bone, silver, and wood, illustrating both artistic and scientific aspects; this he left to the Metropolitan Museum of Art in New York.

He also wrote a "History of R. Hoe & Company," which is of great value for the study of the printing art in the nineteenth century. It was not intended for publication and was never printed, but there are copies in the Library of Congress, the Newberry Library (Chicago), and the Stephen Spaulding Collection at the University of Michigan, besides three or four in private possession. He died in London. He was twice married: first, about 1852, to Aimée Désirée, daughter of Jean Cherouvrier of Le Mans, who died Sept. 12, 1860; and second, Nov. 4, 1862, to Sarah Ann, daughter of William Conquest of London, who survived him.

[This account is based mainly on information supplied by Tucker's daughters; only scattered references to him or to his work are to be found in print. Something can be gleaned from his own "History of R. Hoe & Company," but it is quite impersonal and deals mostly in "we," not in "I."]   T. M. S.

TUCKER, WILLIAM JEWETT (July 13, 1839–Sept. 29, 1926), clergyman, educator, was born at Griswold, Conn., the son of Henry and Sarah White (Lester) Tucker, and a descendant of Robert Tucker, who settled in Weymouth, Mass., in 1635. His mother died when he was a child and he spent the greater part of his youth in the home of his maternal uncle, the Rev. William R. Jewett, at Plymouth, N. H. He was educated at Plymouth, at Kimball Union Academy, and at Dartmouth College, where he graduated in 1861. After teaching for a period at Columbus, Ohio, he entered the Andover Theological Seminary and was graduated from that institution in 1866. During his course in the Seminary he served for a time as agent of the United States Christian Commission with the Army of the Cumberland in the campaign before Atlanta. After a period spent as representative of the American Home Missionary Society in Kansas and Missouri, he was ordained, Jan. 24, 1867, and assumed the pastorate of the Franklin Street (Congregational) Church in Manchester, N. H., transferring his activities to the Madison Square (Presbyterian) Church in New York in 1875. In 1880 he became professor of sacred rhetoric in the Andover Theological Seminary.

At Andover, in addition to the usual duties of his professorship, Tucker was specially concerned with the social responsibilities of the church. In connection with his lectureship in pastoral theology he developed courses in sociology, then a novelty in divinity schools. In 1891 he founded a social settlement in Boston called Andover House (afterwards South End House) modeled after Toynbee Hall in London, which, under the immediate supervision of Robert A. Woods, soon achieved a distinguished success. His Andover period was far from peaceful, however. In 1884 five professors in the Seminary, including Tucker, founded a periodical called the *Andover Review*. The articles in this journal, some of them republished in book form under the title *Progressive Orthodoxy* (1886), soon attracted the unfavorable attention of the conservative wing of Congregationalism. While numerous utterances of the editors were considered to be heterodox, particular objection was raised to their refusal to admit that infants and members of races which had never enjoyed the advantage of Christian teaching are necessarily doomed to eternal perdition. This doctrine of a "second probation" was especially objectionable to the missionary organizations of the church. Charges were filed against the five professors in 1886, at the end of that year they were tried before the board of visitors of the seminary, and Prof. Egbert C. Smyth [*q.v.*] was found guilty, while the other four (against whom the evidence was practically the same as against Professor Smyth) were acquitted by a tie vote. Upon appeal, the supreme court of Massachusetts in 1890 pronounced the proceedings faulty, and in 1892, at a second trial, Smyth was acquitted. The "Andover controversy" thus ended in a complete victory for the faculty.

In 1893 Tucker became president of Dartmouth College. Serious problems confronted him upon his accession. The institution had long been a stronghold of conservatism—dominated by a reactionary theology, averse to educational experimentation, and working in large part with the material facilities of the eighteenth century. To the solution of these problems Tucker brought educational vision and insight of a rare order, acumen and resource in business management, adroitness in matters of finance, and powers of leadership which ensured harmonious cooperation of all the branches of the college. As a result of his efforts student attendance rose from three hundred to eleven hundred, the teaching body was increased in like proportion, material facilities were modernized, finance reorganized and placed upon a sounder basis. The spirit of contention which had marked much of the previous history of the institution disappeared, theological dictation vanished, and, most of all, the spirit of the college became such as to enable it more intelligently to meet the educational demands of the age.

Tucker's moral leadership was also impressive. Exerted under the advantage of direct personal contact at Andover, it was no less effective at Dartmouth where his opportunities, for the most part, were limited to chapel services and other public exercises. His personality awakened veneration, respect, and sincere affection, and through the strength of his appeal he became an influence for good in generations of college graduates. He retired from the presidency of Dartmouth in 1909. The remainder of his life, so far as his health permitted, was devoted to literary activity. In addition to numerous articles in the magazines and to his contributions to books issued by the Andover faculty, he had already published *The Making and the Unmaking of the Preacher* (1898). In 1910 appeared two volumes, *Personal Power* and *Public Mindedness*; in 1911, *The Function of the Church in Modern Society*; in 1916, *The New Reservation of Time,* and in 1919 an autobiography, *My Generation.*

Tucker was twice married: on June 22, 1870, to Charlotte Henry Rogers of Plymouth, N. H., who died in 1882, and in June 1887 to Charlotte Barrell Cheever of Worcester, Mass. Two daughters were born of the first marriage and one of the second; all three survived their father.

[In addition to Tucker's autobiography, see J. K. Lord, *A Hist. of Dartmouth Coll.* (1913); L. B. Richardson, *Hist. of Dartmouth Coll.,* vol. II (1932); J. W. Buckham, *Progressive Religious Thought in America* (1919); *Granite Monthly,* June 1903; E. M. Hopkins, *William Jewett Tucker, a Tribute* (1926); *Who's Who in America,* 1926–27; Ephraim Tucker, *Geneal. of the Tucker Family* (1895); *Manchester Union* (Manchester, N. H.), Sept. 30, 1926.]   L. B. R.

TUCKERMAN, BAYARD (July 2, 1855–Oct. 20, 1923), author, the son of Lucius and Elizabeth Wolcott (Gibbs) Tuckerman, was born in New York City. Through his father, an iron manufacturer, son of the Rev. Joseph Tuckerman [q.v.], he was descended from John Tuckerman who came to Massachusetts Bay about 1649; his mother, daughter of the elder George Gibbs [q.v.] and sister of the younger George and of Oliver Wolcott Gibbs [qq.v.], was a granddaughter of Oliver Wolcott [q.v.], signer of the Declaration of Independence. Having studied with private tutors, Bayard Tuckerman spent two years at the Pension Roulet at Neuchâtel, Switzerland, before entering Harvard College, where he graduated with the class of 1878. Returning to Paris the year of his graduation, he soon undertook a serious study of English literature, producing after four years *A History of English Prose Fiction from Sir Thomas Malory to George Eliot,* published in New York in 1882. While this volume has long since been superseded, it was much esteemed by the author's contemporaries. In September 1882, at Ipswich, Mass., Tuckerman married Annie Osgood Smith, daughter of the Rev. John Cotton Smith [q.v.], and settled down to a life of domestic felicity and

the joys of authorship; a son and three daughters were born to them.

His *Life of General Lafayette* (2 vols., 1889), a thorough, careful, and interesting biography, written in a clear and unpretentious style, was the first account of Lafayette based upon an adequate, modern critical apparatus. The same year was marked by his publication of *The Diary of Philip Hone, 1828–1851* in two volumes; this was a satisfactory collection of excerpts from Hone's voluminous diary, but otherwise the editing was slight, for Tuckerman's edition contains almost no notes. In 1893 he published, in the Makers of America Series, a biography, *Peter Stuyvesant,* which was useful and well-written, but hardly an important contribution to American historiography. His *William Jay and the Constitutional Movement for the Abolition of Slavery* (1894) was a significant addition to the literature of the anti-slavery movement, for it was based upon voluminous manuscript materials that have never been utilized by any other historian. His *Life of General Philip Schuyler, 1733–1804* (1903), although still standard in its field, is not marked by any great biographical skill, but it was based upon valuable manuscript materials which have since been scattered and probably lost. Although Tuckerman later compiled two small genealogies —*Notes on the Tuckerman Family of Massachusetts* (privately printed, 1914) and *A Sketch of the Cotton Smith Family of Sharon, Connecticut* (privately printed, 1915)—his book on Schuyler was his last important literary production. Increasing ill health prevented the completion of a history of chivalry, upon which he had spent several years of research.

From 1898 to 1907 Tuckerman lectured on English literature at Princeton University, but while he enjoyed academic life his first choice was for the quiet and severe life of the country, and a private income made him independent and permitted him to indulge his inclinations. He never became a great scholar, but he fully deserved the old-fashioned title of "scholar and gentleman" which his intimate friends bestowed upon him.

[Sources include *Harvard College, Class of 1878, Fiftieth Anniversary Report, 1878–1928* (n.d.); *Harvard Graduates' Magazine,* Dec. 1923; *Who's Who in America,* 1922–23; Tuckerman's genealogical books, mentioned above; George Gibbs, *The Gibbs Family of Rhode Island and Some Related Families* (1933); death notice in *Boston Transcript,* Oct. 22, 1923; information from a daughter, Mrs. Wm. M. Elkins. Tuckerman's MSS. are in the possession of Mrs. Bayard Tuckerman, Ipswich, Mass., and Bayard Tuckerman, Jr., Hamilton, Mass.]   F. M.

TUCKERMAN, EDWARD (Dec. 7, 1817–Mar. 15, 1886), botanist, distinguished authority upon lichens, was born in Boston, Mass., the eldest son of a merchant of the same name and Sophia (May) Tuckerman. He was a brother of Frederick Goddard Tuckerman and a nephew of the Rev. Joseph Tuckerman [qq.v.]. Prepared for college at Boston Latin School, he graduated (B.A.) from Union College in 1837 and from Harvard Law School in 1839. Two years later he visited Europe, to pursue special studies in philosophy, history, and botany, an important influence in his later work being his studies at Upsala, Sweden, under the famous lichenologist Elias Fries. Returning in 1842, he reëntered Union College and received the degree of M.A. the next year. Desiring then to obtain an academic degree from Harvard, he matriculated as a senior in 1846, graduating (B.A.) in 1847. Subsequently he entered Harvard Divinity School, and completed the courses of study in 1852. He married Sarah Eliza Sigourney Cushing, in Boston, May 17, 1854, and shortly thereafter removed to Amherst, Mass., to lecture in history at Amherst College. He was appointed professor of botany in 1858, and held this position the rest of his life, which was passed at Amherst. During his later years he became almost totally deaf; he died from complications of Bright's disease, without issue.

Tuckerman was a man of uncommonly broad scholarly culture, whose life was devoted unreservedly to study. He was early attracted to lichens, and his botanical publications up to 1841 dealt with New England plants of this group, largely of his own collecting in the White Mountains. By that time, however, he had also contributed to the New York *Churchman* no less than fifty-four articles upon biographical, historical, and theological topics. In 1842 he described *Oakesia*, a new genus of flowering plants from New England. While a student at Union he was appointed curator of the college museum, and here also he issued privately, *Enumeratio Methodica Caricum Quarundam* (1843), an erudite revision of the sedges (*Carex*), which Asa Gray (*post*, p. 541) mentions as early displaying Tuckerman's genius as a systematizer. This was followed by three other papers on New England flowering plants, including (1849) an elaboration of the American pondweeds (*Potamogeton*). But otherwise, aside from his *Catalogue of Plants Growing without Cultivation within Thirty Miles of Amherst College* (1875), summarizing twenty years' study, his published botanical work is chiefly upon lichens.

In the field of American lichenology Tuckerman is outstanding. Lichens had been studied scarcely at all by American students, and he himself was the first to explore for them in the mountains of New England. This he did with notable success and thoroughness, in the most difficult regions. In 1845 there appeared his *Enumeration of North American Lichenes*; then his "Synopsis of the Lichenes of New England, the other Northern States, and British America" (*Proceedings of the American Academy of Arts and Sciences*, vol. I, 1848, pp. 195–285). The latter was the first attempt to describe and classify all the lichens known from temperate North America, and it proved a great stimulus to the study of this group. From 1848 to 1872 Tuckerman published numerous other papers, of which the more important are a supplement to his *Enumeration* describing many new species from California and the southern United States (*American Journal of Science*, 1858, 1859); four parts of a continued series of critical notes in *Proceedings of the American Academy* (vols. IV–VII, 1860–68, vol. XII, 1877), relating largely to the Cuban lichens collected by Charles Wright; an illustrated brochure (1862) upon the lichens of the United States Exploring Expedition under Wilkes; *Lichens of California, Oregon, and the Rocky Mountains* (1866); besides accounts of species from many foreign regions, as well as of material collected on several governmental surveys. These studies were definitely contributory to *Genera Lichenum: An Arrangement of North American Lichens* (1872), regarded as Tuckerman's greatest work. He planned also a comprehensive treatise containing descriptions of all the lichens known from the United States, and the first volume appeared in 1882 as *A Synopsis of the North American Lichens: Part I*; the second, completed by Henry Willey, was published two years after Tuckerman's death.

Though never robust, Tuckerman was in early life an intrepid explorer; Tuckerman Ravine on Mount Washington was named in his honor. He is commemorated also by a genus of Compositæ, *Tuckermania*. He was elected a member of the National Academy of Sciences in 1868. Of gentle, sensitive disposition and retiring temperament, he was noted for his amiability, helpfulness, and exquisite taste, and equally for his keen independent criticism, his fondness for antiquarian and genealogical research, and his studious attention to philosophy, divinity, and law. In the words of his friend Asa Gray (*post*, p. 544), he was "much more than an excellent specialist."

[Asa Gray, "Edward Tuckerman," *Proc. Am. Acad. Arts and Sci.*, XXI (1886), 539–47, with bibliog., repr. in *Am. Jour. Sci.*, July 1886 (3 ser., XXXII, 1–7); H. H. Goodell, "Edward Tuckerman: Biog. Sketch," and Henry Willey, "Bibliog. Sketch," *Bot. Gaz.*, Apr. 1886

(XI, 73–74 and 74–78); W. G. Farlow, "Memoir of Edward Tuckerman," with bibliog., *Nat. Acad. Sci. Biog. Memoirs,* vol. III (1895), preprint, 1887; Bruce Fink, in *Proc. Iowa Acad. Sci.,* XI (1904), 25–29, portr.; *Am. Naturalist,* June 1886 (XX, 578–79); Bayard Tuckerman, *Notes on the Tuckerman Family* (priv. printed, 1914).]

W. R. M.

TUCKERMAN, FREDERICK (May 7, 1857–Nov. 8, 1929), comparative anatomist and naturalist, was born in Greenfield, Mass., the son of Frederick Goddard Tuckerman [*q.v.*] and Hannah Lucinda (Jones), and a nephew of the botanist Edward Tuckerman [*q.v.*]. He received the degree of B.S. from both the Massachusetts Agricultural College and Boston University in 1878 and that of M.D. from the Harvard Medical School in 1882. After a period of study in London and Berlin, 1882–83, he lectured on anatomy and physiology at the Massachusetts Agricultural College until 1886. Subsequently he was a fellow of Clark University, 1889–90, and again went abroad to study in London, Berlin, and Heidelberg; from the University of Heidelberg he received the degrees of A.M. and Ph.D. in 1894. After his return to America, he made his home at Amherst, Mass. Having adequate means, he sought no university position, but gave his time to independent research in comparative anatomy and natural history and to genealogical studies. He also took an active interest in local church and town affairs.

Tuckerman's best genealogical work concerned his wife's family, the Coopers of Boston. He published "Thomas Cooper of Boston and His Descendants" and "Notes from the Rev. Samuel Cooper's Interleaved Almanacs of 1764 and 1769" in the *New-England Historical and Genealogical Register* (January 1890, April 1901) and "Diary of Samuel Cooper, 1775–1776" and "Letters of Samuel Cooper to Thomas Pownall, 1769–77," in the *American Historical Review* (January 1901, January 1903). An excellent biography of Charles Anthony Goessmann [*q.v.*], professor of chemistry in the Massachusetts Agricultural College, was written by him in 1911 (*United States Catholic Historical Society, Historical Records and Studies,* vol. VI, pt. 1, 1911) and, in 1929, his *Amherst Academy: A New England School of the Past* was published posthumously. He was also a contributor to the *Dictionary of American Biography*. He supported the Appalachian Mountain Club, contributing to their publication *Appalachia* in 1918, 1921, and 1926, and was considered an authority on the history of the White Mountains. His researches in comparative anatomy, especially on the gustatory and taste organs, were sound (*Journal of Anatomy and Physiology,* vols. XXIII, XXIV, XXV, 1889–91, and *Journal of Morphology,* vols. II,

IV, VII, 1889–92). He held membership in the American Society of Naturalists, the Boston Society of Natural History, Anatomische Gesellschaft (Jena), and the American Association of Anatomists. On Sept. 6, 1881, he married Alice Girdler Cooper, daughter of James Sullivan Cooper; she and two daughters survived him.

[Bayard Tuckerman, *Notes on the Tuckerman Family* (privately printed, 1914); *Who's Who in America,* 1928–29; *Boston Transcript,* Nov. 8, 1929; *Amherst Record,* Nov. 13, 1929; reports from Tuckerman's family.]

H. R. V.

TUCKERMAN, FREDERICK GODDARD (Feb. 4, 1821–May 9, 1873), poet, son of Edward and Sophia (May) Tuckerman, was born in Boston, Mass. He came from a distinguished family; his elder brother, Edward Tuckerman [*q.v.*], became professor of botany at Amherst College; his cousin, Henry Theodore Tuckerman [*q.v.*], was a critic and essayist of some repute; his uncle, Joseph Tuckerman [*q.v.*], was a noted philanthropist and Unitarian clergyman. Tuckerman entered Harvard College with the class of 1841, but left at the end of his first year on account of serious eye trouble. After a year of rest, however, he persisted in his education and was graduated from the Harvard Law School in 1842. He was admitted to the bar in 1844, but practised only a few years, since private means enabled him to devote himself to his chief interests—literature, botany, and astronomy. Retiring to Greenfield, Mass., in 1847, he lived there, except for two holidays in Europe, until his death in 1873. He published some of his observations on eclipses and won a reputation as an authority on the local flora, but for the most part his life was passed in seclusion from the world. He married Hannah Lucinda Jones, June 17, 1847; she died at the birth of her third child, Frederick [*q.v.*], in 1857.

A number of Tuckerman's poems—several of which had first appeared in the *Living Age, Putnam's,* or the *Atlantic Monthly*—were collected and privately printed at Boston under the title *Poems* in 1860, and published in England in 1863 and in Boston in 1864 and 1869. Some of them won favorable comment from Emerson and Longfellow, but Tuckerman was overlooked by Stedman in compiling his *American Anthology* and as a poet had virtually slipped from memory when he was rediscovered by Walter Prichard Eaton in 1909 ("A Forgotten American Poet," *Forum,* January 1909). In 1931, Witter Bynner edited and published, with a critical introduction, *The Sonnets of Frederick Goddard Tuckerman,* containing in addition to some which had appeared in the *Poems,* three previously unpublished sequences. Although Tuckerman's sonnets were unnoticed by his contemporaries—even by Emerson and Longfellow—Bynner ranks them "with the noblest in the language" (Introduction, *post,* p. 36), finding in them "not only . . . the fine thoughts of a devout stoic," but "the subtly fine craft of a devout poet." Not bound by conventional sonnet forms, Tuckerman "shuffled the rhyme-scheme to suit the rise and fall of his meaning" and revealed "an anachronistic fondness for the juxtaposition of fine and homely phrases and images," together with "an . . . emotional use of words that Edgar Allan Poe might have envied" (*Ibid.,* pp. 18–19). He died at Greenfield, in his fifty-third year.

[Bayard Tuckerman, *Notes on the Tuckerman Family* (privately printed, 1914) ; Witter Bynner, Introduction, in *Sonnets of Frederick Goddard Tuckerman* (1931), portr.; *Bookman,* Apr. 1931 ; death notice in *Boston Daily Globe,* May 12, 1873.]   H. R. V.

TUCKERMAN, HENRY THEODORE (Apr. 20, 1813–Dec. 17, 1871), critic, essayist, and poet, was born in Boston, Mass., a nephew of Joseph Tuckerman [*q.v.*] and the son of Henry Harris and Ruth (Keating) Tuckerman. His sister Ruth became the mother of Henry Cuyler Bunner [*q.v.*]. The elder Tuckerman, a prosperous merchant, sent his son to the Latin School and thence to Harvard, where, however, the young man remained for only two years. Ill health caused him to seek relaxation in foreign travel, and he spent the years 1833–34 mostly in Italy, where he began his lifelong, romantic devotion to literature and art. Upon his return he published *The Italian Sketch Book* (1835). The years 1836–38, passed again in Italy and Sicily, resulted in a travel romance, *Isabel, or Sicily, a Pilgrimage* (1839). Tuckerman now determined upon a literary career, and with his return to Boston started contributing poems and essays to periodicals. For a time in 1843 he edited the *Boston Miscellany of Literature and Fashion,* but in 1845 he removed to New York City, where he settled down to a quiet literary and social life. A brief visit to England in 1852–53 was the basis of a small volume, *A Month in England* (1853), which embodied reflections on English life and art.

A man of independent financial means, Tuckerman had ample opportunity to indulge his love of meditation and study. In his essay "New England Philosophy" (*The Optimist*), he decries the national spirit of commercialism, which carries with it "want of serenity" and of poetic feeling. His works of travel, in their emphasis on the picturesque and on the historic and literary associations of European life, as well as in their quiet, leisurely style, show the influence of Irving and sometimes of Sterne. As a literary critic, Tuckerman is best understood in the light of his essay on Hazlitt (*Characteristics of Literature,* second series), where he finds the function of the critic that of feeler and sympathizer, as well as that of analyst. Following more or less Hazlitt's critical manner are his *Thoughts on the Poets* (1846) and the two series of *Characteristics of Literature* (1849, 1851). Always fascinated by pictorial art and sculpture, Tuckerman produced in 1847 *Artist-Life, or Sketches of American Painters,* which twenty years later he expanded into a significant volume, *Book of the Artists: American Artist Life* (1867). His interest in biography found expression in *The Life of Silas Talbot* (1850), *Mental Portraits* (1853), *Essays, Biographical and Critical* (1857), and *The Life of John Pendleton Kennedy* (1871). Characteristic familiar essays are collected in *The Optimist* (1850) and *The Criterion* (1866), and a series of Irvingesque sketches in *Leaves from the Diary of a Dreamer* (1853). A volume of *Poems* (1851) shows many of the traits discernible in his prose—love of retirement, interest in art, fascination with the historic and literary associations of Italy, and indulgence in sentiment that sometimes passed into sentimentality. Perhaps his work of greatest lasting importance is *America and Her Commentators: with a Critical Sketch of Travel in the United States* (1864).

Although of a quiet, retiring nature, Tuckerman entered freely into the social life of New York, having as friends such men as Washington Irving, Dr. John W. Francis, and Fitz-Greene Halleck [*qq.v.*]. His love of the city of his adoption is evinced in his edition (1865) of Dr. Francis' *Old New York.* Representing with Rufus W. Griswold and Evert A. Duyckinck [*qq.v.*] the easy, romantic scholarship of the forties and fifties in America, he readily passed in his day for a man of genius, having even a small English audience. Harvard in 1850 gave him the honorary degree of M.A.; and the king of Italy conferred upon him an order "in recognition of his labors on behalf of Italian exiles in the United States." Tuckerman never married. He died in New York City and was buried in Mount Auburn Cemetery, Cambridge, Mass.

[See Bayard Tuckerman, *Notes on the Tuckerman Family of Mass.* (priv. printed, 1914) ; *N. Y. Tribune,* Dec. 18, 1871 ; *Evening Post* (N. Y.), Dec. 18, 20, 1871 ; R. W. Griswold, *Poets and Poetry of America* (1842), and *The Prose Writers of America* (1847) ; E. A. and G. L. Duyckinck, *Cyc. of Am. Lit.* (1875), vol. II ; E. A. Duyckinck, *A Memorial of Henry T. Tuckerman* (1872) ; N. F. Adkins, *Fitz-Greene Halleck* (1930), *passim* ; F. L. Mott, *A Hist. of Am. Mags.* (1930). For a full list of Tuckerman's works, as well as for many critical articles, see S. A. Allibone, *A Critical Dict. of Eng. Lit.,* vol. III (1871). Some information has been furnished by Miss Sydney R. McLean, who is preparing a biography of Tuckerman.]   N. F. A.

TUCKERMAN, JOSEPH (Jan. 18, 1778–Apr. 20, 1840), Unitarian clergyman, the son of Edward and Elizabeth (Harris) Tuckerman and a descendant of John Tuckerman who came from England to Massachusetts Bay about 1649, was born in Boston, Mass. He was educated at the Boston Latin School and Harvard College, graduating in 1798. William Ellery Channing and Joseph Story were his classmates, the latter his roommate. Tuckerman studied for the Unitarian ministry with Rev. Thomas Thacher and must have been an outstanding pupil, for he was invited by the Boston Mechanic Association to preach for them on Feb. 22, 1800, and was generously thanked for his "pathetic Elegant and Judicious Oration, commemorative of the Sublime virtues and preëminent services of the late General Washington," which was then printed, under the title, *A Funeral Oration: Occasioned by the Death of General George Washington.* In 1801, on Nov. 4, he was ordained to his first and only pastorate, in Chelsea, to receive the munificent sum of five hundred dollars a year. He was now settled, with a salary, and on July 5, 1803, he married Abigail Parkman of Boston. She died July 28, 1807, leaving him with three young children, and on Nov. 3, 1808, he married Sarah Cary, of a family prominent socially in Chelsea, who bore him seven children. Bayard Tuckerman [*q.v.*] was his grandson.

In 1805, Tuckerman became one of the original members of the Anthology Society, publishers of the *Monthly Anthology and Boston Review.*

During his ministry in Chelsea, he started (1812) the Boston Society for the Religious and Moral Improvement of Seamen ("Report," *Christian Disciple,* July 1813), said to have been the first of its kind in the United States. He wrote a number of tracts for the benefit of this movement. His interest in seamen was duplicated by his interest in those he called "the neglected poor in our cities," and when he removed from Chelsea to Boston in 1826, on account of ill health, he began a "ministry-at-large," which was in effect a city mission for the poor. His work in this field was described in his book, *The Principles and Results of the Ministry at Large, in Boston* (1838). Many of his sermons and tracts dealing with charitable subjects were also printed. The idea of the ministry-at-large took him to England in 1833–34; he established missions in London and Liverpool and stimulated those already established in other places, and his influence extended into France. He continued his work in Boston on his return, but his health broke down in 1836. Seeking its restoration, he went to Santa Cruz and in 1838 to Cuba; he died in Havana.

Tuckerman had "a thin, aquiline face, and hair combed back from the brow" (Sprague, *post,* p. 350), and both dress and manner proclaimed his profession. He cared little for doctrines, and criticized Channing as well as those not of his communion. Devoted to his calling, he labored throughout his life for the good of others. The power of his personality is indicated by the fact that a society of ladies calling themselves the "Tuckerman Sewing Circle" were still sewing and selling what they made for the "Poor's Purse" as late as 1888; while in *A Memorial of Joseph Tuckerman* printed that year the statement is made that "the impetus which he gave to intelligent philanthropy has not yet passed away either in this country or in England."

[W. B. Sprague, *Annals Am. Pulpit,* vol. VIII (1865); *A Memorial of Joseph Tuckerman* (Worcester, 1888); *Proc. Mass. Hist. Soc.,* 1 ser. II (1880); Mellen Chamberlain, *A Doc. Hist. of Chelsea, Mass.* (1908), vol. II; *Vital Records of Chelsea, Mass.* (1916); *Seventy-fifth Anniv. of the Founding of the Ministry-at-Large in Boston, 1826–1901* (1901); W. E. Channing, *A Discourse on the Life and Character of the Rev. Joseph Tuckerman* (1841); Bayard Tuckerman, *Notes on the Tuckerman Family* (privately printed, 1914); *Boston Transcript,* May 8, 1840.]
E. S. B—n.

TUCKEY, WILLIAM (c. 1708–Sept. 14, 1781), organist, choirmaster, composer, was born in Somersetshire, England. The date of his birth is established only through the statement on his tombstone that he died in his seventy-third year. From an advertisement in the *New-York Mercury* (Mar. 11, 1754) it is known that he was for a time vicar choral and parish clerk of the Bristol Cathedral.

On Jan. 31, 1753, he was appointed parish clerk of Trinity Church, New York, at a salary of twenty-five pounds per annum (Dix, *post,* p. 262). That he had a wife and several children is disclosed by the fact that the vestry made provision for their transportation to America (*Ibid.*). He was also given charge of the music at the church, and he soon convinced the vestry of the necessity of teaching vocal music to the pupils of the Charity School. Through such teaching he developed the Trinity Church choir, which became noted both in and outside the city. In 1756 he was summarily dismissed from the office of parish clerk because of his "refusal to officiate in time of Divine Service" (*Ibid.,* p. 300), but he evidently continued to act as musical director of the church. It is certain that he continued his career as chorus master, for in 1762 he advertised for volunteers for a chorus to sing the *Te Deum* (*New York Weekly Post Boy*, Sept. 4), and four years later he announced a "Rehearsal of Church-Musick," and a forthcoming concert (*New-York Mercury*, Oct. 6, 1766). On Oct. 30, 1766, he was paid fifteen pounds for playing the organ at the dedication of the "new Episcopal chapel . . . called St. Paul's," assisted by a "suitable Band of Music, vocal and instrumental" (*Ibid.*, Nov. 3, 1766). On Jan. 16, 1770, he conducted a performance of the overture and sixteen numbers from Handel's *Messiah*, the first American rendering from this oratorio. The performance was held in "Mr. Burns's Room," New York.

During these years Tuckey had also been offering concerts of secular music. The earliest of these was announced in the *Post Boy* (Dec. 15, 1755) as a "Concert of Vocal and Instrumental musick," "for the benefit of Messrs. Cobham and Tuckey." At a benefit concert, "followed by a ball" (Apr. 21, 1769), Tuckey announced that "by particular desire" the concert would end with "God Save the King." It is possible that this was the first appearance of the British national hymn on an American concert program (Sonneck, *post*, p. 179).

After the *Messiah* performance in 1770 Tuckey's name does not appear in connection with concerts in New York. In 1771 he advertised for subscriptions to the publication of a number of his compositions—"an Hymn . . . together with a Psalm Tune; . . . a performance adapted for a FUNERAL, consisting of three Dirges . . . together with an anthem . . ." (*New-York Mercury*, Mar. 11), and he was probably the anonymous author of a collection of church music proposed in an advertisement in the *New-York Journal*, July 1, 1773. He died in Philadelphia, and was buried in the burial grounds of Christ Church. As a choir master, Tuckey takes rank with William Selby of Boston and Andrew Adgate [*qq.v.*] of Philadelphia. He labored hard to establish regular choral singing, but the time was not ripe for his efforts, though he achieved some remarkable results. As a composer he contributed to the literature of early American choral music, even though solicitations for subscriptions to his works were apparently not successful enough to warrant their publication. There is record of a "Thanksgiving Anthem," performed in Trinity Church, Boston, "before his excellency, General Amherst" (*Boston Evening Post*, Dec. 15, 1760); and an "Ode on Masonry," performed at the Cobham-Tuckey concert, was no doubt of Tuckey's composition. The only work by him now extant is an "Anthem Taken Out of the 97th Psalm," subsequently called "Liverpool," and as

such included in James Lyon's collection, *Urania* (c. 1761).

[O. G. Sonneck, *Early Concert-Life in America* (1907); H. E. Krehbiel, "Music in Trinity Church," *N. Y. Tribune*, July 26, 1903; Morgan Dix, *A Hist. of the Parish of Trinity Church in the City of N. Y.*, vol. I (1898); A. H. Messiter, *A Hist. of the Choir and Music of Trinity Church, N. Y.* (1906); *Grove's Dict. of Music and Musicians, Am. Supplement* (1931); J. T. Howard, *Our Am. Music* (1931); E. L. Clark, *A Record of the Inscriptions on the Tablets and Grave-Stones in the Burial-Grounds of Christ Church, Phila.* (1864).] J.T.H.

TUDOR, FREDERIC (Sept. 4, 1783–Feb. 6, 1864), known as the "Ice King" from his success in building up the business of shipping ice from Boston to cities in tropical latitudes, was born in Boston, Mass. Son of a family that was prominent in Boston in the years following the Revolution (his father was William Tudor, who married Delia Jarvis), he did not, like his brothers, attend Harvard College, but went into business at the age of thirteen. When he was twenty-one he and his brother William [*q.v.*] conceived the idea of sending a cargo of ice to Martinique, and, in spite of the ridicule of their friends, with the aid of their cousin, James Savage [*q.v.*], they put their plan into effect, the vessel arriving at Saint-Pierre in March 1806. For the next fifteen years, alone, in debt and sometimes in jail for it, Tudor persisted in his scheme. By 1821 he had established himself in Havana and Charleston, and had undertaken a venture in New Orleans. His assistant, Nathaniel J. Wyeth [*q.v.*], had mastered the technique of ice-cutting on the ponds around Boston; Tudor himself, through much experiment, had learned how to ship his ice with the least possible loss, had devised a structure that would keep his commodity in warm climates, and had succeeded in making the use of ice an accepted thing in cities there. In the next ten or a dozen years he had to meet a good deal of competition; but his vigorous, not to say ruthless methods, his fanatical belief in his business, and his determination to become rich and enjoy the "delicious essence" of flattery overcame all obstacles. In May 1833 he sent his first cargo to Calcutta, and the success of this long-dreamed-of project made possible a worldwide expansion of his business. The number of tons of ice shipped from Boston, beginning with 130 in 1806, rose to 1,200 in 1816; to 4,000 in 1826; to 12,000 in 1836; to 65,000 in 1846; to 146,000 in 1856 (*Boston Board of Trade, Third Annual Report*, 1857, p. 80). In this last year 363 cargoes were sent to fifty-three different places in the United States, the West Indies, the East Indies, China, the Philippines, and Australia (*Ibid.*, pp. 79–82, and Justin Winsor, *The*

Memorial History of Boston, vol. IV, 1883, p. 221). To Boston the trade was invaluable. "Mr. Tudor and his ice came just in time to preserve Boston's East-India commerce from ruin. Our carrying trade between Calcutta and Europe had declined almost to extinction. . . . For a generation after the Civil War, until cheap artificial ice was invented, this export trade increased and prospered. Not Boston alone, but every New England village with a pond near tidewater was able to turn this Yankee liability into an asset, through the genius of Frederic Tudor" (S. E. Morison, *The Maritime History of Massachusetts,* 1921, pp. 282–83). Notwithstanding the growth of his enterprise, Tudor's embarrassments continued: the loss of over $200,000 in an unlucky coffee speculation kept him dependent on his creditors; for years he carried on a fierce fight with his agent in Havana for the control of the business there. It was not until he had reached the age of sixty-five that, with his debts extinguished and his lawsuit won, he was a free man. Characteristic of him was the sentence he printed on the cover of his "Ice House Diary"—"He who gives back at the first repulse and without striking the second blow despairs of success, has never been, is not, and never will be a hero in war, love, or business . . ."

Masterful in all his dealings and not without a power of fascination which compelled men to obey him ("I have so willed it"), Frederic Tudor was an extreme example of militant, despotic, and punitive individualism. With his quick and originating mind, he initiated many undertakings: he brought to Boston the first steam locomotive, a toy affair of one horse-power, which ran on the sidewalk; he designed a new type of hull for sailing vessels; he developed a graphite mine in Sturbridge, Mass.; he created the Maolis Gardens at Nahant, probably the first amusement park in the United States. Living at the age of eighty, he was in his last years a marked man in the life of Boston, already, as "Ice King," the hero of a legend in the "romance" of American business—a legend that only grows with the passage of time. On Jan. 2, 1834, at the age of fifty, he married Euphemia Fenno, aged nineteen, of Mount Upton, N. Y.; by her he had six children. He died in Boston.

[See *Deacon Tudor's Diary* (1896), ed. by William Tudor; memoir to be published in *Proc. Mass. Hist. Soc.,* vol. LXV (in preparation); Tudor's letter on the ice trade, *Proc. Mass. Hist. Soc., 1855–58,* vol. III (1859); *Bull. of the Business Hist. Soc.,* Sept. 1932, which contains three of Tudor's business letters taken from the Tudor papers in the lib. of the Grad. School of Business Administration, Harvard Univ.; F. A. Wilson, *Some Annals of Nahant, Mass.* (1928); and obituary in *Boston Transcript,* Feb. 8, 1864. The bulk of his papers, including the "Ice House Diary," is in the possession of Frederic Tudor of Sandwich, Mass.]

H. G. P.

TUDOR, WILLIAM (Jan. 28, 1779–Mar. 9, 1830), author, the son of Col. William and Delia (Jarvis) Tudor, was born in Boston, Mass. His father was a prominent merchant and scholar, the son of Deacon John Tudor who was taken from England to Boston about 1714 at the age of six. After graduation from Harvard in 1796, young Tudor entered John Codman's counting-room and was sent to Paris on business. A year later he sailed for Leghorn on another mission. Both ventures were disappointing, but Tudor made many friendships and strengthened his love of letters. He next went to the West Indies at the request of his brother Frederic [*q.v.*] to develop a trade in ice. On his return he was elected to the Massachusetts legislature, where he served a number of times, and in 1809 he delivered the annual Fourth of July oration in Boston, which went through two editions. At this period he was employed by Stephen Higginson [*q.v.*] in a none-too-successful attempt to force quantities of English manufactures into Europe against the hostile decrees of Bonaparte. He also aided a group of Americans in a futile attempt to establish at Birmingham the manufacture of cut nails.

Turning at last to other activities, he became the founder and first editor (1815–17) of the *North American Review,* and was the largest contributor to the first four volumes. An original member of the Anthology Society (1805), he frequently contributed to the pages of its magazine, the *Monthly Anthology and Boston Review.* He helped to found the Boston Athenaeum, a library and art museum; suggested a plan for the purchase of land on Bunker Hill in Charlestown on which the American redoubt had been raised and where Warren fell; and was active in the affairs of the Massachusetts Historical Society, to which he had been elected in 1816. Tudor was a keen critic of contemporary manners, and his *Letters on the Eastern States* (1820), now forgotten, contains much that is of permanent value. In this book he fell foul of Mathew Carey [*q.v.*], an excitable Irishman then living in Philadelphia, whose *The Olive Branch* (1814) had been intended to soften political asperities caused by the war with England. He received little epistolary comfort from Tudor, and his pamphlet on the encounter (1821) ran to almost seventy pages. In 1821 Tudor gathered into a small book under the title *Miscellanies* various essays, some from the *Anthology,* others from the *North American Review.* They have a human touch and interest that make them readable today. They range from "Secret Causes of the American and French Revolutions" to essays on cranberry sauce, purring cats, and the miseries of human life. Two years later Tudor published *The Life of James Otis, of Massachusetts,* which is said to be his best effort. The same year he was appointed United States consul at Lima and for the ports of Peru (appointment confirmed, Dec. 9, 1823), and was of service during the feud between Peru and Colombia. In 1827 he was advanced to be chargé d'affaires at Rio de Janeiro (appointment confirmed, Dec. 27). While in Brazil he wrote an allegory on current international politics which was published anonymously under the title *Gebel Teir* (1829). His health was affected by the climate at Rio de Janeiro, and he died there of fever. He was buried at Rio. He never married.

[See *Deacon Tudor's Diary* (1896), ed. by William Tudor; C. C. Smith, in *Proc. Mass. Hist. Soc.,* vol. I (1879), p. 429; Josiah Quincy, *The Hist. of the Boston Athenaeum* (1851); J. S. Loring, *The Hundred Boston Orators* (1853); *Jour. of the Proc. of the Soc. Which Conducts the Monthly Anthology* (1910), with intro. by M. A. De Wolfe Howe; death notice in *Boston Daily Advertiser,* May 3, and letter, May 8, 1830. Stuart's portrait of Tudor is reproduced in Lawrence Park, *Gilbert Stuart, an Illustrated Descriptive List of His Works* (4 vols., 1926).]　　　　　　　C.K.B.

TUFTS, CHARLES (July 17, 1781–Dec. 24, 1876), a founder of Tufts College, son of Daniel and Abigail (Tufts) Tufts, was born in a part of Medford later incorporated in Somerville, Mass. He was a lineal descendant of an early English colonist, Peter Tufts, who settled in Charlestown, Mass., about 1638. It is believed that he was long associated with his father in farming and brickmaking, pursuits which he followed in later years. On Apr. 8, 1821, he married Hannah, daughter of Jacob and Hannah Robinson, of Lexington, Mass., an earnest and liberal-minded young woman fourteen years his junior, who exerted a strong guiding influence upon her husband.

Tufts received very little formal education but contrived, nevertheless, to acquire a considerable fund of knowledge. A strongly religious man in adult life, he became deeply interested in the work of the Universalist Church, first in Charlestown and later in Somerville, and it was to a considerable extent his proselyting interest in Universalist doctrines that impelled him to set aside a portion of his extensive farm properties for educational purposes. When in 1840 the Massachusetts Convention of Universalists proposed the establishment of a theological seminary, Tufts offered a building site. Before the plan could materialize, however, it became identified with attempts to bolster up the Clinton Liberal

Institute (1845) and resulted finally in a project for a Universalist college (May 1847). As the movement progressed, Tufts offered approximately twenty acres of land on the Medford-Somerville line. Although some of the conditions attached to the grant caused hesitation, the site, known as Walnut Tree Hill, was formally approved by the trustees of the nascent institution on Jan. 8, 1852, and a charter of incorporation was presently obtained for Tufts College. In 1856 and 1864 Tufts deeded other properties to the college under various conditions, one of which was that its name should never be changed. He also served as a trustee of the college from 1856 until his death. His gifts, amounting altogether to more than one hundred acres of land, together with lesser adjacent tracts from other sources, established the college in a physical sense and placed it in a unique position within the Boston metropolitan area.

Tufts was a man of medium stature, with small, mild features and a gentle manner which gave little hint of his decided opinions and inflexible will. He was shrewd in his calculations, but "without a particle of deceit." Both natural inclination and extreme deafness caused him to live somewhat as a recluse, and it was only through his benefactions that he came into public notice.

[Records of the Trustees of Tufts Coll., 1852–78, vol. I; Trustees of Tufts Coll., Fund File: original Tufts papers; C. D. Elliot, in *Tufts Coll. Grad.,* Jan. 1910; H. S. Ballou, *Hosea Ballou, 2d, D.D., First President of Tufts Coll.* (1896); Charles Brooks, *Hist. of the Town of Medford, 1630–1855* (1886), revised by J. M. Usher; L. T. Tufts and E. C. Booth, "Tufts Geneal.: Descendants of Peter" (1925) New-Eng. Hist. Geneal. Soc.; *Universalist Reg.,* 1842, 1844; *Hist. of Tufts Coll., 1854–1896* (1896), ed. by A. B. Start; *Universalist,* Jan. 6, 1877; *Christian Leader,* Apr. 28, 1928; obituary in *Boston Transcript,* Dec. 27, 1876.]

　　　　　　　　　　　　　　　　　H.L.H.

TUFTS, COTTON (May 30, 1732–Dec. 8, 1815), physician, was born in Medford, Mass., the fourth child of Simon and Abigail (Smith) Tufts, and a nephew of John Tufts [*q.v.*]. His great-grandfather, Peter Tufts, emigrated from England to Charlestown about 1638. His father, who was a graduate of Harvard College, was the first physician to practise in Medford. Young Cotton, a serious student, entered Harvard at fourteen and, having received three scholarships, the last one of fifteen pounds, was graduated with the degree of A.M. in 1749. After a short period of teaching school, he studied medicine with his elder brother Simon, a graduate of Harvard College, who had followed in his father's footsteps in Medford, and began practice in Weymouth, April 1752. It appears, however, that he spent part of the preceding year in Weymouth, for during an epidemic of diphtheria he took an active part in assisting the older physicians; as a result he settled there and spent the rest of his life in that community.

Tufts not only became the leading practitioner of Weymouth but was also an important figure in medical, scientific, and political affairs of Massachusetts. In 1765 he planned a state medical society, a project which fell through for lack of adequate support, and in 1781 it was he who was most forceful in organizing the Massachusetts Medical Society. He was elected president in 1787. It is said that he missed attending only two out of forty meetings in Boston during a period of thirteen years, although he lived twelve miles away and travel was often difficult in winter. In 1780 he became one of the charter members of the American Academy of Arts and Sciences. He represented the town of Weymouth in the meetings against the Stamp Act, and after the Revolution, although he had not entered the army, he voted affirmatively in the Massachusetts convention to ratify the new United States Constitution in 1788. Locally, he was a deacon of his church, a trustee of Derby Academy in Hingham, and president of the society for the Reformation of Morals. Harvard College granted him an honorary degree of M.D. in 1785. He was a friend of John Adams [*q.v.*], whose private affairs he administered while Adams was at his London post (*The Works of John Adams,* vol. IX, 1854, pp. 548–49). He was twice married, first (Dec. 2, 1755) to Lucy Quincy, daughter of John Quincy of Braintree, by whom he had one son, Cotton, graduate of Harvard College in 1777; second (Oct. 22, 1789) to Mrs. Susanna Warner of Gloucester, who survived him.

[The date of birth is from *Vital Records of Medford, Mass.* (1907); the marriage dates from *Vital Records of Weymouth* (1910), vol. II. The principal biog. source is Jacob Norton, *Sermon Delivered . . . at the Interment of the Hon. Cotton Tufts* (1816), a somewhat rare pamphlet. See also *New-Eng. Hist. and Geneal. Reg.,* Apr. 1847, Apr. 1855, Jan. 1857; *Proc. Mass. Hist. Soc.,* 3 ser., vol. II (1909), which contains Tuft's diaries for 1772 and 1784; W. L. Burrage, *A Hist. of the Mass. Medic. Soc.* (1923); *Pubs. Colonial Soc. of Mass.,* vol. XVI (1925); James Thacher, *Am. Medic. Biog.* (1828); obituary in *New-England Palladium and Commercial Advertiser,* Dec. 15, 1815; letters and memorabilia in the Boston Medic. Lib.]
H. R. V.

TUFTS, JOHN (May 5, 1689–Aug. 17, 1752), pioneer compiler of church music, Congregational minister, was born in Medford, Mass., the third of twelve children of Capt. Peter Tufts and his second wife, Mercy (Cotton) Tufts. His father was a son of Peter Tufts who emigrated from England to America about 1638; his mother was a daughter of the Rev. Seaborn Cotton

and Dorothy, daughter of Gov. Simon Bradstreet [*q.v.*]. He was graduated from Harvard College in 1708 and was ordained as minister of the Second Church of Christ in West Newbury, June 30, 1714. A few references to Tuft's ministerial activities may be noted in town histories of Essex County, but his career as a country minister was notable mainly by reason of the influence exerted upon American music by the publication, probably in 1714 or 1715, of his *A Very Plain and Easy Introduction to the Art of Singing Psalm Tunes: with the Cantus or Trebles of Twenty-eight Psalm Tunes, Contrived in Such a Manner, As That the Learner May Attain the Skill of Singing Them, with the Greatest Ease and Speed Imaginable* (Hood, *post,* p. 65). No copy of the first edition is known. This book, in which letters were used on the staff instead of notes, was considered "a daring and unjustifiable innovation," and Tufts's carefully chosen selection of tunes met with caustic criticism. One writer said: "Truly, I have a great jealousy that if we once begin to sing by rule the next thing will be to pray by rule and preach by rule, and then comes popery" (quoted in Coffin, *post,* p. 186). Another critic objected to the book as "Quakerish and Popish, and introductive of instrumental musick; the names given to the notes are blasphemous; it is a needless way since the good Fathers are gone to heaven without it; its admirers are a company of young upstarts; they spend too much time about learning, and tarry out a-nights disorderly" (quoted in Fisher, *post,* pp. 6–7). Despite such objections Tufts's book achieved wide popularity. The music was simple, but for its purpose very effective. Under varying titles the book went through at least eleven editions, some of them prepared to be bound up in the Bay Psalm Book, the last one printed in 1774. In its defense the Rev. Thomas Symmes wrote his tract on the *Reasonableness of Regular Singing* (1720), Tufts's name appearing in it as one of "the subscribers willing to countenance and promote *Regular Singing,* or Singing by Note." Other publications of Tufts's were *Anti-Ministerial Objections Considered* (1725) and *A Humble Call to Archippus, Or the Pastor Exhorted, To Take Heed That He Fulfill His Ministry* (1729).

Apart from his activity as an innovator in the field of church music Tufts appears to have led for many years the uneventful life of a rural minister. He married, Nov. 9, 1714, Sarah Bradstreet, daughter of Dr. Humphrey Bradstreet, by whom he had four children. On Feb. 26, 1738, a council of ten ministers and twenty delegates was called to consider " 'the distressed state and condition of ye second church of Christ in Newbury by reason of their reverend pastor Mr. John Tufts being charged by a woman or women of his indecent carriage and also of his abusive and unchristian behavior towards them'" (Coffin, *post*, p. 207–08). Tufts vehemently opposed the investigation and demanded his dismission, which was granted Mar. 2, his church refusing to recommend him for employment as a Christian minister. He thereupon retired to the adjoining town of Amesbury, where he died (*Vital Records of Amesbury, Mass.,* 1913).

[For a discussion of the bibliog. problems, see Joseph Sabin, *A Dict. of Books Relating to America,* pt. CLI (1935), continued by R. W. G. Vail. In addition to Charles Brooks, *Hist. of the Town of Medford* (1886), and T. B. Wyman, *The Geneals. and Estates of Charlestown* (1879), vol. II, see F. J. Metcalf, *Am. Writers and Compilers of Sacred Music* (copr. 1925); George Hood, *A Hist. of Music in New England* (1846); N. D. Gould, *Church Music in America* (1853); W. A. Fisher, *Notes on Music in Old Boston* (1918); *New-Eng. Hist. and Geneal. Reg.,* Apr. 1847, Apr. 1855, Jan. 1856, July 1875; E. H. Pierce, in *Musical Quart.,* Apr. 1930; J. J. Currier, *Hist. of Newbury, Mass.* (1902); and Joshua Coffin, *A Sketch of the Hist. of Newbury* (1845).]

F. W. C.

TULANE, PAUL (May 10, 1801–Mar. 27, 1887), merchant and philanthropist, was the son of French parents. His father, Louis Tulane, born in 1767 at Rillé, near Tours, France, of a line of local judges, removed to Santo Domingo in young manhood, with his wife and a brother-in-law, to engage in commercial pursuits. In a slave insurrection the brother-in-law's family perished, but Louis and his wife escaped to the United States and settled in 1792 near Princeton, N. J., and here Paul was born. He attended a private school and Somerville Academy and at fifteen, after the death of his mother, became a clerk for about a year in the store of Thomas White at Princeton. This experience was followed by a tour of the South and West with a cousin of means visiting from France.

In 1822 Paul Tulane established himself in business in New Orleans with a strong faith in the future of the region. As head of the house of Paul Tulane & Company of New Orleans, and of Tulane, Baldwin & Company of New York, he built up a retail and wholesale trade in dry goods and clothing, with a large clientele in the Mississippi Valley, and by 1840 had acquired a fortune estimated at a quarter of a million dollars. About 1858 he busied himself chiefly with real-estate transactions and acquisitions, dividing his time and his investments between New Orleans and New Jersey in anticipation of a Southern backset from the slavery controversy. After a residence of fifty-one years in New Orleans, he removed permanently to an elegant stone mansion in Princeton, where he died. A bachelor, of reserved disposition, he survived all members of his immediate family.

Tulane's was a rugged personality. Physically, he was short and heavily built; as a business man he was frugal, industrious, and tenacious, exacting to the last penny. He was liberal in his philanthropy, however, spending thousands of dollars on individuals and local organizations in the interest of religion, charity, and education. The First Presbyterian Church of Princeton was a special recipient of his donations, but his most significant gifts were those by which the University of Louisiana, a state institution founded in 1834 at New Orleans, was converted in 1884 into the independent Tulane University of Louisiana in the same city. Tulane's first donation was made in 1882, through his own initiative and without solicitation. It consisted of all his New Orleans real estate and was valued at $363,000. Other gifts from him followed making a total estimated at more than a million dollars. He expressed the intention to make still further contributions, but his death without a will intervened and his property was divided among his nieces and nephews. At the time of his first donation he chose with care the first members of a board of administrators for his fund, headed by Randall L. Gibson [q.v.], and gave them general instructions to provide for the higher education of the white youth of New Orleans. This group arranged with the state to absorb the existing University of Louisiana, with "Tulane" prefixed to the name, instead of starting a rival university in the city.

[W. P. Johnston, "Tulane University of Louisiana," in E. W. Fay, *The Hist. of Educ. in La.* (Bur. of Educ., Circular of Information No. 1, 1898, ch. viii); Alcée Fortier, *Louisiana* (1909), vol. II; *Princeton Press,* Apr. 2, 1887; *Times-Democrat* (New Orleans), Mar. 29, Apr. 2, 1887.]

H. C. N.

TULLY, WILLIAM (Nov. 18, 1785–Feb. 28, 1859), physician, was born at Saybrook Point, Conn., the only child of Col. William Tully, an officer of the Revolution, who married Eunice (Tully), his cousin. He was a descendant of John Tully of Horley, Surrey County, England, whose widow came with her son and daughter to Saybrook about 1647. As a boy Tully attended the district school and was later prepared for college by the Rev. Frederick W. Hotchkiss, of Saybrook. Entering Yale in 1802, he graduated in 1806, and then taught school for a short time in his native town. In the spring of 1807 he began the study of medicine with Dr. Mason F. Cogswell of Hartford and in the fall of the following year attended the medical school of Dartmouth under Dr. Nathan Smith, 1762–1829

51

[*q.v.*]. Returning to Saybrook in 1810, he studied for a time with Dr. Samuel Carter. In March of this year he entered the office of Dr. Eli Ives [*q.v.*] of New Haven, professor of materia medica at Yale. In October 1810 Tully was licensed by the Connecticut Medical Society, and in May 1811 he began to practise in Enfield, Conn.

For the next few years he changed his location so rapidly that a biographer refers to him as "The Peregrinating Dr. William Tully" (Ferris, *post*). On Jan. 5, 1813, he married Mary, daughter of the Rev. Elam Potter, and in March of that year removed to Milford, Conn. Two years later he went to Cromwell, Conn., and in September 1818, to Middletown. In the latter place he became an intimate friend of Dr. Thomas Miner, a physician and scholar of considerable repute, who is said to have had a noteworthy influence on Tully's subsequent literary career. In 1807 Yale conferred the degree of A.M. on him and in 1819 the honorary degree of M.D. The following year he published an article, "On the Ergot of Rye," in the *American Journal of Science* (April 1820) and another, "Scutellaria Laterifolia," in the *Middlesex Gazette* (Nov. 30, 1820). An article by him entitled "Diversity of the Two Sorts of Datura Found in the United States" appeared in the former journal in 1823, and in this same year, with Dr. Thomas Miner, he published *Essays on Fevers*. In June 1822 Tully removed to East Hartford and in July 1824 was appointed president and professor of theory and practice and medical jurisprudence in the Vermont Academy of Medicine, at Castleton. When this school was reorganized in 1830 he retired as president but continued for eight years as professor of materia medica and therapeutics.

In January 1826 he removed to Albany, N. Y., where he practised as a colleague of Dr. Alden March [*q.v.*], but continued his lectures at Castleton. In 1828 he wrote "An Essay, Pharmacological and Therapeutical, on Sanguinaria-Canadensis," which appeared in the *American Medical Recorder* (January, April 1828), and won him a prize. Appointed professor of materia medica and therapeutics at Yale in 1829, he removed to New Haven and taught there as well as at Castleton. In collaboration with Ives and M. C. Leavenworth, he published *Catalogue of the Phenogamous Plants and the Ferns Growing without Cultivation, within Five Miles of Yale College* (1831). Other papers, on sanguinaria, chlorite of potassa, congestion, narcotine and sulphate of morphine, were prepared by him during this period. He is said to have made the first

half ounce of quinine sulphate from cinchona bark produced in the United States (Ferris, p. 24). In August 1842, as a result of strained relations with his colleagues, he resigned his chair at Yale and in 1851 removed to Springfield, Mass. Here was published his compendious work of more than 1,500 pages, *Materia Medica, or, Pharmacology and Therapeutics* (2 vols., 1857–58). In this work appears his modification of the well-known Dover's powder which later became known as Tully's powder.

Tully died in Springfield and was buried in the Grove Street Cemetery, New Haven. He had eleven children, but of these only a son and two daughters survived him. According to his successor at Yale, he was "doubtless the most learned and thoroughly scientific physician of New England" (Bronson, *post*, p. 5). "As a teacher he stimulated scientific zeal in his students, as a physician he studied his patients carefully and was a good diagnostician" (Ferris, p. 35). In appearance he was tall and square-shouldered, with large head and prominent eyes. As a lecturer "he spoke distinctly and without gesticulation, reading from his manuscript in a loud, almost stentorian voice, with an uniform and slightly nasal tone, and assured air" (Bronson, p. 5). His eminence in his day is attested by the large number of medical and scientific societies to which he belonged.

[H. B. Ferris, in *Yale Jour. of Biology and Medicine*, Oct. 1932; Henry Bronson, in *Proc. and Medic. Communications of the Conn. State Medic. Soc.*, 2 ser. vol. I (1863); Kate C. Mead, in *Bull. of the Johns Hopkins Hospital*, Mar. 1916, and in H. L. Kelly and W. L. Burrage, *Am. Medic. Biogs.* (1920); S. H. Parsons, "The Tully Family of Saybrook, Conn.," *New-England Hist. and Geneal. Reg.*, Apr. 1849; F. B. Dexter, *Biog. Sketches, Grads. Yale Coll.*, vol. VI (1912); G. C. Gates, *Saybrook at the Mouth of the Conn.* (1935); *Springfield Republican*, Mar. 1, 1859; diary and letters in Yale Univ. Lib.]   H. T.

TUPPER, BENJAMIN (Mar. 11, 1738–June 7, 1792), Revolutionary soldier, pioneer, was born in Stoughton, Mass., the son of Thomas and Remember (Perry) Tupper. Since his father died early, Benjamin had but a common-school education, and was apprenticed to a tanner in Dorchester until he was sixteen. Subsequently he worked as a farm hand until the outbreak of the French and Indian War, when he enlisted in the company of his uncle, Capt. Nathaniel Perry. At the close of the war he left the army with the rank of sergeant. After teaching school for a few years in Easton, he married, Nov. 18, 1762, Huldah White of Bridgewater, and migrated to Chesterfield, Hampshire County, in western Massachusetts.

In 1774, Tupper joined the Revolutionary

cause, serving as militia lieutenant in purging western Massachusetts of Loyalist sentiment. In 1775 he took a heroic part in the siege of Boston and in the destruction of the British lighthouse on Castle Island. From 1776 to the end of the war he served as lieutenant-colonel and then colonel of Massachusetts troops, participating in the battle of Long Island, the Saratoga campaign, and the battle of Monmouth, and constructing defenses at West Point and on the Mohawk–Lake George Indian frontier. He retired from the army in 1783 with the brevet rank of brigadier-general and on his return to Chesterfield was elected representative in the state legislature. In 1786 he returned to the field and took an active part in defending Springfield against the insurgent, Daniel Shays [q.v.].

The last ten years of Tupper's life were identified with the westward movement. He was one of the 288 Continental officers to sign the Newburgh Petition in 1783, seeking the creation of a new territory in the Northwest for occupation by soldiers. With the settlement of the Indian and land problems by ordinances and treaties between 1783 and 1785, Tupper represented Massachusetts on the corps of state surveyors sent west by Congress under Thomas Hutchins. He personally conducted in 1785 preliminary surveying in numbers three and four of the Seven Ranges. On his return to the East, he joined with Gen. Rufus Putnam [q.v.] in inaugurating the movement that led to the formation of the Ohio Company. In an "Information" that appeared in Boston and Worcester papers early in 1786, the Ohio country was described and Revolutionary officers and soldiers were invited to form a settlement association. Tupper was elected delegate to represent Hampshire County at the appointed organization meeting in March in Boston. By this body the Ohio Company was formed and a petition was sent to Congress for a purchase which resulted in the grant and settlement of Marietta at the mouth of the Muskingum and in the creation of the Northwest Territory.

Tupper took an active part in the affairs of the Company and of his adopted home. He accompanied the original settlers to Marietta in 1788, and served on committees for determining the place and value of sites for settlement, for receiving applications for mills, for devising donation methods to attract settlers, for the location of roads and the leasing of city lots. With Putnam he was made judge of common pleas and quarter sessions and held the first civil court in the Territory on Sept. 9, 1788. Subsequently, as Putnam was occupied with other duties, Tupper was practically sole administrator of local justice on the Muskingum until his death.

Tupper had seven children. His daughter Rowena was the first wife of Winthrop Sargent, 1753–1820 [q.v.], secretary of the Northwest Territory.

[A. B. Hulbert, *The Records of the Original Proceedings of the Ohio Company* (2 vols., 1917) and *Ohio in the Time of the Confederation* (1918); *Life, Journals and Correspondence of Rev. Manasseh Cutler* (1888), vol. I; A. T. Nye, "Gen. Benjamin Tupper," in S. P. Hildreth, *Biog. and Hist. Memoirs of the Early Pioneer Settlers of Ohio* (1852); W. L. Chaffin, *Hist. of the Town of Easton, Mass.* (1886), F. B. Heitman, *Hist. Reg. of Officers of the Continental Army* (1914).]

R. C. D.

TUPPER, HENRY ALLEN (Feb. 29, 1828–Mar. 27, 1902), Baptist clergyman, denominational leader in foreign missionary enterprises, was born in Charleston, S. C., the son of Tristram—a native of Dresden, Me.—and Eliza (Yoer) Tupper. His first American ancestor was Thomas Tupper, a descendant of exiles from Hesse Cassel to England, who emigrated to New England in 1635, and in 1637 was one of the founders of Sandwich, Mass. Tristram settled in Charleston in 1810 and thereafter conducted a commission house. For more than fifty years the Tupper family was prominent in the business, social, and religious affairs of the city. Henry attended local schools and from 1844 to 1846 was a student in the College of Charleston. He then enrolled at Madison University (now Colgate University), Hamilton, N. Y., where he was graduated with the degree of A.B. in 1849. The following year he spent at the theological seminary connected with the University, and was much influenced by the prevailing missionary zeal. On Nov. 1, 1849, he married Nancy Johnstone Boyce, by whom he had twelve children, six of whom survived him.

In 1850 he was ordained to the Baptist ministry and became pastor of the church in Graniteville, S. C. Three years later he accepted a call to the church at Washington, Ga., where he served until 1872. He was active in local temperance work, preached to the colored people twice a week, and gave the community a varied leadership. He traveled abroad and dreamed of active mission work in foreign fields, even going so far as to plan a self-sustaining colony in Japan. With the advent of the Civil War, however, he took part in that struggle as chaplain of a Georgia regiment in the Confederate army.

His real life work began when he accepted, in 1872, the office of corresponding secretary of the Board of Foreign Missions of the Southern Baptist Convenion, with headquarters in Richmond. To the missionary enterprises of his denomination he now gave tirelessly of his strength, thought, and means. In 1883–84 he went to Mexico and consummated plans for establishing mission schools for girls in Coahuila. His liberality was proverbial. In 1883 he recorded that he had received "from the Lord" since 1854 in income $279,500.98, and of that sum had donated $124,541.39 for religious work. In his vacations he wrote several books for young people of a type considered suitable for Sunday school libraries. They included *The Truth in Romance* (1887), published under the pseudonym Tföffer, the old German spelling of his family name; and *The Carpenter's Son* (1889), an interpretation of the life of Christ. His major works, however, were a lengthy history and survey of the mission enterprise, under the title *The Foreign Missions of the Southern Baptist Convention* (1880) and *A Decade of Foreign Missions, 1880–90* (1891). He retired from the secretaryship of the mission board in 1893. For a time he was president of the board of trustees of the Woman's College of Richmond, and he served, also, as a trustee of Hollins College and of Richmond College. In his closing years, 1896–1902, he was instructor in Bible in Richmond College.

[Tupper's surviving children have many of his letters and other papers, including a manuscript diary kept over a long period of years; the files of the Foreign Mission Board of the Southern Baptist Convention, in Richmond, Va., contain much of his correspondence; for printed sources, see *Am. Ancestry,* vol. V (1890); G. B. Taylor, *Va. Baptist Ministers, Fifth Series, 1902–14* (1915); H. A. Tupper, *The First Century of the First Baptist Church of Richmond* (1880); *The Religious Herald,* Apr. 3, 1902; *Foreign Mission Jour.,* May 1902; *Who's Who in America,* 1901–02; *Times* (Richmond), Mar. 28, 1902.]   M. H. W.

TURELL, JANE (Feb. 25, 1708–Mar. 26, 1735), poet, daughter of the Rev. Benjamin Colman [*q.v.*] and his first wife, Jane Clark, was born in Boston, Mass., where her father was pastor of the Brattle Street Church. As the only girl in the family until her seventh year and as a child afflicted with a constitution "wonderful weak and tender," she received an uncommon share of attention from her father and responded by developing a precocious memory for Scripture texts, Biblical stories, and passages from the catechism. Gov. Joseph Dudley and other gentlemen who frequented Mr. Colman's house used to place little Jane on the table to hear her talk and "owned themselves diverted" by her recitations. At a very early age she learned to read and rapidly went through her father's library. A hymn written in her eleventh year was followed a few years later by verse-paraphrases of the Psalms, which Mr. Colman criticized and returned to her with edifying poems of his own. He made it clear to her, however, that "a Poeti-

cal Flight now and then" was not to be allowed to interrupt her daily hours of reading and devotion. Jane Colman's marriage to the Rev. Ebenezer Turell, graduate of Harvard College in the class of 1721 and minister at Medford, took place on Aug. 11, 1726. Her husband cultivated her literary gifts by reading aloud to her books of "Divinity, History, Physick, Controversy, as well as Poetry," as they sat together during the long winter evenings. Mrs. Turell continued her writing, both in verse and in prose. Besides keeping a religious diary, she composed a poetic eulogy on Sir Richard Blackmore, whom she admired "not as the first of Poets, but as one of the best; consecrating his Muse to the cause of Virtue and Religion"; an appreciative tribute to Edmund Waller "for the Purity of his Style and delicacy of Language"; and "An Invitation into the Country, in Imitation of Horace." She died, with all the pious expressions that the occasion demanded, at Medford, aged twenty-seven. The only one of her four children who survived her died a year later.

Immediately after her death Mrs. Turell was immortalized in a volume entitled *Reliquiae Turellae, et Lachrymae Paternae* (Boston, 1735), published in London under the title of *Memoirs of the Life and Death of the Pious and Ingenious Mrs. Jane Turell . . . Collected Chiefly from Her Own Manuscripts* (1741). This contains a poetic epistle by the Rev. John Adams, two funeral sermons preached in her honor by her father, and a memoir by her husband. It is the only source of first-hand information about Mrs. Turell's life and character, and the only form in which her poems were published. It also contains selections from her religious meditations and specimens of her letters to her father and his replies. The image presented to the world by the joint efforts of husband and father was that of a devout woman according to the strict Puritan pattern. Piety was her grace, poetry merely a grace note. Her verse has no importance except as an indication of the literary taste of Boston during the first quarter of the eighteenth century.

[The date of birth is given in *A Report of the Record Commissioners of the City of Boston . . . Births* (1894) as Feb. 25, 1707; in *Records of the Church in Brattle Square, Boston* (1902), however, the date of baptism is given as Feb. 29, 1708. In addition to *Reliquiae Turellae* (1735), see Ebenezer Turell, *The Life and Character of the Rev. Benjamin Colman, D.D.* (1849); E. A. and G. L. Duyckinck, *Cyc. of Am. Lit.,* vol. I (1855), for specimens of Mrs. Turell's verse; and *Vital Records of Medford, Mass.* (1907) for the date of her death.]   G. F. W.

TURNBULL, ANDREW (*c.* 1718–Mar. 13, 1792), was a Scotch physician and colonizer, who, after visting Mediterranean lands and marrying Maria Gracia Dura Bin, a Grecian lady of Smyrna, undertook to cultivate sub-tropical products in the new British province of East Florida. In June 1766 he was granted by *mandamus* 20,000 acres of land therein, and five months later, with his wife and four children, he landed at St. Augustine. He located his land at Mosquito (now Ponce de Leon) Inlet, hired a manager, and ordered cattle. Returning alone to England in the spring of 1767, he allied himself with Sir William Duncan and Lord George Grenville—the latter represented by Sir Richard Temple—in a project for colonizing 500 indentured Greeks, who, after seven or eight years of service, were to receive fifty acres each and five for each child. His partners added 81,400 acres and promised £6,000 for expenses. The government provided a vessel and a bounty of forty shillings a head for the adult Greeks.

In the summer of 1768 Turnbull brought back in eight vessels 200 Peloponnesian Greeks, 110 south Italians, and nearly 1,100 Minorcans, who found buildings and provisions awaiting them. In August, during his temporary absence, a sizable band of Italians and Greeks mortally wounded his manager and carried stores on board the schooner *Balmar* for flight to Havana. Gov. James Grant dispatched two vessels with troops in time to halt the *Balmar,* although some thirty insurgents escaped in her boat. These were subsequently taken at the Florida Keys and two were hanged for piracy. During these first months about 300 colonists died of scurvy and gangrene. Malaria carried off hundreds more while they were clearing seven miles of low land along the Halifax and Hillsboro rivers, constructing walled canals, planting maize, making gardens, and producing indigo for export. The cost of the enterprise for the first year had been about £28,000 and provisions were nearly exhausted when the Lords of the Treasury granted £2,000 for relief.

Early appointed to the Provincial Council and secretaryship by Grant, Turnbull resigned the former office under Lieut.-Gov. John Moultrie [*q.v.*] on account of differences of opinion. He also quickly antagonized Gov. Patrick Tonyn by participating in a scheme to lease lands from the Indians and by opposing, with Chief Justice William Drayton [*q.v.*] and others, Tonyn's measures as the Revolution approached. When the governor denounced them as disloyal, they adopted a loyal address, which Drayton and Turnbull carried to England early in 1776. Tonyn then broke up the latter's colony of New Smyrna by drafting many recruits therefrom for his

militia and galleys and by welcoming the other colonists to St. Augustine.

In August 1778 Turnbull removed thither with his family, and was soon sued for debt by his partners' heirs. Tonyn heard the case and had the debtor detained two years for want of the bond he imposed. Released in May 1781 by surrendering all but a fraction of New Smyrna, Turnbull and his family sailed for Charleston. There he practised medicine until his death. On his and his children's joint claims of over £15,-000 for their losses in Florida, they received £916 13s d4; on his individual claim of over £6,400 he got nothing. He had three daughters and four sons; one of the sons being Robert J. Turnbull [*q.v.*].

[Carita Doggett, *Dr. Andrew Turnbull and the New Smyrna Colony of Florida* (1919); W. H. Siebert, *Loyalists in East Florida, 1774 to 1785* (2 vols., 1929); *Acts of the Privy Council of England, Colonial Series,* IV (1911), 815, V (1912), 564–65, 591; A. J. Morrison, *Travels in the Confederation* (1911), translated from the German of J. D. Schöpf; *S. C. and Am. Gen. Gazette,* Oct. 31–Nov. 7, 1766, Jan. 30–Feb. 6, 1767; *S. C. Gazette,* Aug. 3–10, 1767, July 4, 11, 1768, Feb. 28, Dec. 19, 1771, Oct. 11, 1773; *Ga. Gazette,* June 29, July 6, Oct. 19, 1768.]   W. H. S.

TURNBULL, ROBERT JAMES (Jan. 1775– June 15, 1833), publicist, was born in New Smyrna, Fla., the third son of Andrew [*q.v.*] and Maria Gracia (Dura Bin) Turnbull, the latter a native of Smyrna. His father was an English physician who had obtained a British grant in 1766 and soon thereafter had led to Florida several thousand colonists from the region of the Mediterranean. The project failed, Dr. Turnbull embraced the colonial cause in the Revolution, thereby forfeiting his grant, and he moved to South Carolina in 1782. The son was educated at an academy at Kensington (London), and studied law in Philadelphia, and under John Julius Pringle [*q.v.*] in Charleston. Admitted to the bar in 1794, Turnbull began practice in Charleston, but in 1810 he gave up his profession and retired to a large plantation, maintaining, however, a residence in Charleston. Though widely popular and distinctly politically-minded, he took no part in public affairs, except to serve on the special court in 1822 for the trial of the Denmark Vesey conspirators. His influence was largely developed during the last decade of his life, and by his writings rather than by the speaker.

spoken word, though he was no mean public

He wrote *A Visit to the Philadelphia Prison* (1796), which was published in French in 1800 and attracted considerable attention. He contributed a communication on plantation management and the treatment of slaves in South Carolina to the anonymous work of Edwin Clifford Holland [*q.v.*], entitled *Refutation of the Calumnies Circulated Against the Southern and Western States, Respecting the Institution and Existence of Slavery among Them* (1822). There is no record of any other product of his pen for several years, but his later writings indicate that he was an interested observer of prevailing tendencies in American life and government. An ardent Jeffersonian, he became haunted by the spectre of national consolidation under the doctrine of implied power, angered by the sectional aspects of the protective tariff—a scheme "for rendering the South *tributary* to the North," and convinced that the growth of anti-slavery agitation imperiled the South. The South, he felt, must resist. "Let us say *distinctly to Congress, 'Hands off*—mind your *own* business.' . . . If this fails, let us separate. It is not a case for reasoning or for negotiation" (*The Crisis*, no. 27, p. 137).

In 1827 he published his most important work, *The Crisis: or, Essays on the Usurpations of the Federal Government*, which appeared after two-thirds of the essays had been published in the *Charleston Mercury* over the pen name, "Brutus." It is doubtful if the thinking of the people of any other state has ever been so impressed and influenced by a single publication as was that of South Carolina by this work. It is often said incorrectly that in it Turnbull originated the doctrine of nullification in its South Carolina form, but it cannot be denied that it was "the first bugle-call to the South to rally" (Hamilton, *post*, p. 15), and it prepared the ground admirably for the seed others were soon to sow. Frankly confessing his feelings to be more sectional than national, he "struck at every evil in sight in such a bold, fearless, direct manner as to win the unbounded admiration of the masses" (Houston, *post*, p. 50). Seeking to show that Congress and the Supreme Court had transformed the Constitution into a "dead letter" which might mean anything or nothing, he attacked the nationalism of Monroe and Calhoun. He declared that since the chief interest of the North and West was in usurpation, while that of the South lay in the preservation of the compact, the interest of the former demanded that the government become more national, and that of the latter that it become more federal. The remedy lay in resistance to implied power, to the tariff, and to the anti-slavery movement, in insistence upon the compact theory, and in reliance upon the sovereignty of the states, even to the point of separation. The essays are effectively written,

well-reasoned, and, admitting their premises, unanswerable.

Having tasted blood, Turnbull was in the thick of the fight for the rest of his life. The legislature in 1828 passed a series of resolutions written by him affirming the compact theory with each state as judge. In 1828 Hamilton and Calhoun proclaimed the nullification doctrine. Turnbull had supported Jackson in 1824 and 1828, but in 1830 he became his caustic critic. In that year he wrote *The Tribunal of Dernier Ressort*, and in a notable public address, declaring that he had "trodden no path which has not been hallowed by the footsteps of Jefferson" (*Proceedings of the State Rights Celebration at Charleston, S. C., July 1, 1830*, p. 38), he again passionately proclaimed his principles and his adherence to the "Carolina doctrine." Just a year later, he addressed the State Rights and Free Trade party, defending nullification as the "Rock of Safety for the Union," and declaring his readiness to oppose secession with his last breath, except as a last resort from tyranny (*Proceedings of the Celebration of the 4th of July, 1831, . . . by the State Rights and Free Trade Party*, p. 55). He was in the same year a member of the Free Trade convention at Columbia and wrote its report. In February 1832 he attended and addressed a similar convention in Charleston, and on July 4 he delivered an oration in which he characterized nullification as the "inherent, unmodified, all preserving principle of American liberty," as "the ground-work of Mr. Jefferson's faith," and, as "a medium course between those unspeakably dreadful evils *Submission* and *Secession*," the rightful remedy for usurpation. He pleaded for the preservation of a federal Union of sovereign states, arguing that the state governments could not enslave the people because they could impose none but direct taxes. "As long as these republics remain free, sovereign, and independent, it is impossible that tyranny can ever advance a single step in our country." (*An Oration . . . Before the State Rights & Free Trade Party, . . . on the 4th of July, 1832*, 1832, pp. 7, 8, 17, 20.)

In the nullification convention he took a leading part, writing its *Address*. Upon Jackson's proclamation, he volunteered for military service. He refused to believe the experiment a failure. "Is it little to have put a bit in the teeth of the Tariff-Mongers?" He thought it no little victory to have "foiled the barbarian fury" of Jackson. "With but our one-gun battery of Nullification, we have driven the enemy from his moorings, compelled him to slip his cable, and put to sea." But, he added, the contest was only well begun, and at the second session of the convention he made an elaborate speech in advocacy of the ordinance which he wrote and proposed requiring a test oath and nullifying the "Bloody Bill" of Congress. (*Speeches Delivered in the Convention, of the State of South-Carolina . . . March, 1833,* 1833, pp. 35, 52–62.)

He died suddenly in the summer and his funeral was the occasion of a tremendous demonstration by the State Rights party. Great as was his influence in life, it was perhaps greater afterwards, since with James Hamilton he largely determined the pattern of the thinking of Robert Barnwell Rhett [*q.v.*]. Turnbull was three times married: first, on Jan. 10, 1797, to Claudia Butler Gervais of Charleston; second, to Valeria, the daughter of John Lightwood of Charleston; and, third, to Anna Beresford McCall of Charleston.

[C. S. Boucher, *The Nullification Controversy in South Carolina* (1916); D. F. Houston, *A Critical Study of Nullification in South Carolina* (1896); *Proc. of the Convention of the State of S. C. upon the Subject of Nullification* (1832); *Speeches Delivered in the Convention of the State of S. C. in March, 1833* (1833); Dumas Malone, *The Public Life of Thomas Cooper* (1926); James Hamilton, *An Eulogium on the Public Services and Character of Robert J. Turnbull, Esq.* (1834); Gaillard Hunt, *John C. Calhoun* (1907); Laura A. White, *Robert Barnwell Rhett: Father of Secession* (1931); *Charleston Mercury,* June 17, 18, 19, 1833; *Southern Patriot* (Charleston), June 15, 1833; *Charleston Courier,* June 17, 1833; Carita Doggett, *Dr. Andrew Turnbull and the New Smyrna Colony of Florida* (1919).]   J. G. deR. H.

TURNBULL, WILLIAM (1800–Dec. 9, 1857), soldier, engineer, was born in Philadelphia, Pa., the son of William Turnbull by his second wife, Mary, daughter of Charles Nisbet [*q.v.*]. The elder Turnbull emigrated to Philadelphia from Scotland about 1770. He was a shipping merchant and later an ironmaster with a blast furnace near Pittsburgh. In 1798 he returned to Philadelphia. Young William entered the United States Military Academy Sept. 30, 1814, and graduated July 1, 1819. He was assigned as second lieutenant in the Corps of Artillery and served in this arm, principally engaged on topographic duty, until Aug. 20, 1831, being promoted to first lieutenant Jan. 15, 1823. Transferred with the rank of captain to the topographical engineers, he was engaged in 1831–32 on the survey of a railroad route in the state of Mississippi and then assigned to the construction of the Potomac Aqueduct across the Potomac River at Georgetown. This was his most important work and engaged his time for eleven years, during which he was promoted to the grade of major. The masonry piers of this aqueduct were founded on bed rock which lay thirty to forty feet below the water surface and was covered with

about twenty feet of mud. The river itself was subject to floods and, in winter, to floating ice. The method of construction was by coffer dams, which Turnbull designed. This aqueduct was one of the first important works of American engineering and gave Turnbull a wide reputation. Two reports by him were published (*House Document 261,* 24 Cong., 1 Sess., 1836, and *House Document 459,* 25 Cong., 2 Sess., 1838). After his death, both of these being out of print, the demand for them by engineers called forth the publication of *Reports on the Construction of the Piers of the Aqueduct of the Alexandria Canal across the Potomac River at Georgetown, District of Columbia* (1873). After the aqueduct was completed Turnbull was engaged in the improvement of harbors on some of the Great Lakes and on Lake Champlain until the Mexican War.

In this conflict he served as chief topographical engineer on the staff of Gen. Winfield Scott and took an active part in all operations from the siege of Vera Cruz to the capture of the city of Mexico. For his services he was awarded the brevet of lieutenant-colonel for gallant and meritorious services in the battles of Contreras and Churubusco, and that of colonel for similar services in the battle of Chapultepec. After the war, he was superintending engineer of the construction of the custom house at New Orleans (1848–49); he surveyed Whale's Back Rock, Portsmouth, N. H., for a lighthouse site and examined into the practicability of bridging the Susquehanna River at Havre de Grace (1850–52); he served on a board to examine into the feasibility of an additional canal around the Falls of the Ohio (1852–53); and as engineer in charge of harbor improvements on Lake Erie and Lake Ontario (1853–56) and of lighthouse construction at Oswego, N. Y. (1853–55).

Early in 1826 he married Jane Graham Ramsay, sister of George Douglas Ramsay [*q.v.*], and established a home in Washington. Of six sons and four daughters, five sons and three daughters survived him. One son, Charles N. Turnbull (1832–1874), was also a graduate of the Military Academy and an officer of the topographical engineers, serving with distinction in the Civil War.

[A. D. Turnbull, *William Turnbull 1751–1822, with Some Account of Those Coming After* (privately printed, 1933); G. W. Cullum, *Biog. Reg. Officers and Grads. U. S. Mil. Acad.* (1st ed., 1879), vol. I; *Daily Jour.* (Wilmington, N. C.), Dec. 11, 1857; *Daily Nat. Intelligencer* (Washington), Dec. 11, 12, 1857.]   G. J. F.

TURNER, ASA (June 11, 1799–Dec. 13, 1885), Congregational clergyman, educator, brother of Jonathan Baldwin Turner [*q.v.*], was born in Templeton, Mass., the son of Asa and Abigail

(Baldwin) Turner, and a descendant of John Turner who emigrated from England in 1635 and settled in Roxbury, Mass., through his son John who was admitted freeman of Medfield, Mass., in 1649. Asa attended a district school and later worked on his father's farm, teaching during the winter months. In the fall of 1821, having decided to become a minister, he entered Amherst Academy in order to prepare for college, and within two years was able to meet the requirements for admission to Yale. Graduating in 1827, he enrolled at the Yale Divinity School, where he was soon recognized as a student of unusual ability. On Sept. 6, 1830, he was ordained at New Haven by the New Haven West Association.

That same year he became one of a group of seven theological students, known as the "Yale Band." Formally organized as the "Illinois Association," these students signed a pledge, Feb. 21, 1829, indorsed by the president of Yale College, expressing their willingness to go to Illinois for the purpose of establishing a seminary of learning, where some of them would teach, while the others occupied preaching stations in the surrounding country. Elected a trustee of the proposed educational institution Dec. 18, 1829, a position in which he served until 1844, Turner took an active part in the campaign for endowment, soliciting funds in Andover, Boston, Troy, Albany, and New York City. The money was secured within a few months, and on Jan. 4, 1830, Illinois College, at Jacksonville, was opened for instruction. On Aug. 31, 1830, Turner married Martha Bull, daughter of Dr. Isaac Dickerman and Mary (Watson) Bull, of Hartford, Conn.

Having decided to establish himself in Quincy, Ill., he set out on the westward journey, Sept. 14, 1830. The spot which he had chosen for his labors was sadly in need of spiritual and intellectual cultivation; there were no schools or churches. Working against indifference and actual opposition, he established a Presbyterian Church in December 1830. Early in the following year he persuaded a schoolmaster to settle in the town and open a school. Turner soon became the leading spirit in the development of the civic and intellectual life of Quincy. In the summer of 1832, at the request of Illinois College, he went East to solicit additional funds and to assist in securing instructors. His mission for the college successfully fulfilled, he returned late in the spring of 1833 accompanied by twenty people pledged to help in the work of "colonizing and civilizing." Many others had been persuaded to follow as settlers. Once more he entered vigorously into his work as missionary and preacher.

A Presbyterian when he first arrived in Quincy, he decided to become a Congregationalist, and on Oct. 10, 1833, by unanimous vote, his church adopted the Congregational form of government, becoming the first of this order in Illinois. Turner traveled throughout the northern part of the state—visiting Iowa, also, in 1834 and 1836—promoting camp meetings and urging the erection of churches. Late in 1837, after having organized thirteen churches, he went again to New England.

After his return the following spring, he and the Rev. J. A. Reed, of Warsaw, Ill., established at Denmark, Iowa, May 5, 1838, the first Congregationalist Church west of the Mississippi, and three months later Turner became its pastor. His ministry in Denmark, which began Aug. 3, 1838, continued for thirty years. In July 1839 the American Home Missionary Society appointed him first missionary agent for Iowa. Within a few months he was exploring northern Iowa, which was then uninhabited. His letters to Eastern friends and societies induced many families to move thither. He pleaded with Eastern churches for missionaries, and by 1842 had persuaded twelve young ministers to join him in developing the frontier country. Before his active missionary work ceased, he had inspired more than one hundred others to follow their example. He was also responsible for the organization of the "Iowa Association," formed by seven Yale theological students in 1837, for the purpose of establishing an educational institution in Iowa. After much effort, he obtained from the territorial Assembly, Feb. 3, 1843, a charter for Denmark Academy, and later in the year he went East to raise money for its support. Instruction at the academy was begun in September 1845, and three years later, Nov. 1, 1848, Iowa College was opened at Davenport. For the establishment of these pioneer institutions, Turner's labors were chiefly responsible, and he served as trustee of both until his death. He was also an active participant in the movement for the organization of a system of public schools. In the anti-slavery campaign in Iowa he took a vigorous part, expressing his views courageously at various political conventions. During the Civil War he supported the cause of abolition in his sermons and in articles published in Eastern religious journals. Failing in health in 1868, he withdrew from his pastorate and retired to Oskaloosa, where he died.

[Obit. Record Grads. Yale Coll. (1886); T. O. Douglass, The Pilgrims of Iowa (1911); C. F. Magoun, Asa Turner, a Home Missionary Patriarch, and His Times (1889); Manual of the First Congregational Church of Quincy, Ill. (1865); C. H. Rammelkamp, Ill. Coll.: A

Centennial Hist., 1829–1928 (1928); Iowa State Reg. (Des Moines), Dec. 16, 1885.]   R. F. S.

TURNER, CHARLES YARDLEY (Nov. 25, 1850–Dec. 31, 1918), mural painter, was born in Baltimore, Md., the son of John C. and Hannah (Bartlett) Turner. The Turners were Friends, and years later the quiet interior of the meeting-house often inspired the painter. The boy's home was one of culture, but his father's three marriages left little for his maintenance after preparatory schooling at the public and Friends' schools. He soon began to support himself as photographic finisher, attending at night the art classes of the Maryland Institute for the Promotion of the Mechanic Arts. After his graduation from the Maryland Institute in 1870, he spent several days as apprentice in the architectural office of Frank E. Davis and then set out for New York (1872). He studied for the next six years at the National Academy and at the Art Students' League, which he helped to organize, and continued to earn his living by photographic work. In 1878 he began study in Paris under Jean Paul Laurens, the mural decorator, Munkácsy, the Hungarian colorist, and Léon Bonnat, the figure painter. On his return to America he became an instructor in drawing and painting at the Art Students' League (1881–84) and a director of the Maryland Institute.

His earliest popular success was his "Grand Canal at Dordrecht" (1882), but he struck his stride as figure painter in the literary and historical field, a Miles Standish series being much in demand. The "Bridal Procession" (1886), now in the Metropolitan Museum of Art, "Days That Are No More," suggested by Tennyson's lines, and the etching of Hannah Thurston, Bayard Taylor's heroine, are further examples. His water colors were also frequently successful, especially his "Dordrecht Milkmaid" (1882), while "Chrysanthemums," a decorative oil in the Brooklyn Institute of Arts and Sciences, illustrates his versatility in color. In 1886 he became an Academician. He was assistant director of decoration at the Chicago World's Fair (1893) and director of color at the Pan-American Exposition (1901) at Buffalo. Increasingly, however, his interests turned to mural painting, reaching their fullest development in the Baltimore Court House panels, "The Burning of the Peggy Stewart" (1905). The fact that the decorations by John La Farge, E. H. Blashfield, and J. P. Laurens in the same building do not subordinate the Turners indicates at least their admirable adaptation to their position. Other Turner murals are to be seen in the DeWitt Clinton High School, the Appellate Courts Building, the National Bank of Commerce, the Manhattan, Martinique, and Waldorf-Astoria hotels, all in New York; the Hotel Raleigh in Washington, court houses in Jersey City, Newark, Baltimore, Youngstown, and Cleveland, and the state Capitol, Madison, Wis.

In 1912 Turner became the director of the Maryland Institute School of Art and Design, and in the same year received the medal of honor for painting given by the Architectural League of New York. He was engaged in painting a poster-picture, "The Madonna of the War," in the plaza outside the Baltimore Court House in connection with the United War Work drive when he contracted the influenza which resulted in his death. He died in New York and was buried in the Friends Burial Grounds, Baltimore. He never married. In his later years he was affiliated with a firm of interior decorators. Turner is recalled as a man of unusual kindliness, charm, and simplicity. His later pictures show well-formed features, a Vandyke beard, and brilliant eyes.

[Who's Who in America, 1918–19; Addresses Delivered on the Occasion of the Unveiling of . . . "The Burning of the Peggy Stewart" (copr. 1905), Municipal Art Soc. of Baltimore; Pauline King, Am. Mural Painting (1902), ch. xiii; The Brochure of the Mural Painters (copr. 1916); Am. Art Ann., 1919, Am. Art News, Jan. 4, 1919; obituaries in Sun (Baltimore) and N. Y. Times, which also contains a death notice, Jan. 2, 1919.]
W. S. R.

TURNER, DANIEL (1794–Feb. 4, 1850), naval officer, was born probably at Richmond, Staten Island, N. Y., although there is a possibility that he was born in Rhode Island, where at Newport he made his home for many years, and one obituary notice gives New Jersey as his birthplace. On Jan. 1, 1808, he was appointed to the navy as a midshipman. After a period of service at the New York naval station he cruised on board the Constitution, 1809–11. On June 8, 1812, he was ordered to take command of the gunboats at Norwich, Conn. He was commissioned lieutenant on Mar. 12, 1813, and two days thereafter received orders to proceed to Sacketts Harbor, N. Y. For a time he commanded the Niagara, the second vessel in the squadron of Commodore O. H. Perry [q.v.], but previous to the battle of Lake Erie he was succeeded by Capt. J. D. Elliott [q.v.] and was given the command of the Caledonia, thus being the third officer in rank during the battle. His conduct on that occasion was highly commended by Perry, who described him as "an officer that in all situations may be relied on" (American State Papers, Naval Affairs, vol. I, 1834, p. 295). He was one of those who received the thanks of Congress and was awarded a silver medal. In the summer of 1814 he commanded the *Scorpion* of the fleet of Commodore Arthur Sinclair and participated in the capture of several British vessels on Lake Huron, the burning of the fort and barracks at St. Joseph, and the attack on Mackinac. On Sept. 5 the *Scorpion* was surprised and captured by the enemy under circumstances that were regarded as not discreditable to Turner. A court of inquiry decided that his conduct on this occasion was that of a discreet and vigilant officer. After a period of imprisonment he was exchanged.

In 1815–17 he was with the frigate *Java* and in 1819–24 with the cruiser *Nonsuch,* cruising part of the time in the Mediterranean. On Mar. 3, 1825, he was promoted master commandant. After a tour of duty at the naval rendezvous at Boston he cruised in the West Indies, 1827–30, as commander of the *Erie.* For three years he was stationed at the Portsmouth (N. H.) navy yard. On Mar. 3, 1835, he was promoted captain. After a long period on waiting orders he commanded the *Constitution* of the Pacific Squadron, 1839–41. From 1843 to 1846 he was in command of the Brazil Squadron. His last duty was performed at the Portsmouth navy yard as its commandant. He died suddenly at Philadelphia of a heart affection, leaving a wife and daughter. On May 23, 1837, he had married in that city Catharine M. Bryan.

[Bureau of Navigation, Records of Officers, 1804–58; Navy Register, 1815–50; Usher Parsons, *Brief Sketches of the Officers Who Were in the Battle of Lake Erie* (1862); *Daily National Intelligencer* (Washington, D. C.), Feb. 7, 1850; *Newport Mercury,* Feb. 9, 1850; *Public Ledger* (Phila.), Feb. 6, 7, 1850; Veterans Administration, Pension Files, War of 1812; Theodore Roosevelt, *The Naval War of 1812* (1889).]

C. O. P.

TURNER, EDWARD (Nov. 25, 1778–May 23, 1860), jurist, was born in Fairfax County, Va., the son of Lewis Ellzey and Theodosia (Payne) Turner, and a grandson of William Payne who, according to "Parson" Weems, once knocked George Washington down (M. L. Weems, *A History of the Life . . . of . . . George Washington,* 2nd ed., 1800, p. 49). In 1786 the Turners moved to Kentucky. Becoming a student in Transylvania University, Edward attended at intervals, as time and means permitted, and studied law while serving as clerk in the office of George Nicholas [*q.v.*]. About this time Nicholas was championing Jefferson's Kentucky resolutions (1798). With a Democratic background, therefore, and with letters of introduction from Gen. Green Clay [*q.v.*] of Kentucky, late in 1801 Turner went to Natchez, Miss., where the Democrats were just coming into power.

The young lawyer was well received, for within a few months he was made aide-de-camp and private secretary to the governor and clerk of the lower house of the territorial legislature. On Sept. 5, 1802, he was married to Mary, daughter of Cato West, a prominent Democrat of Jefferson County, and about the same time became clerk of the court of that county. In the summer of 1803 he was appointed by the federal government register of the newly established land office at Washington, Miss. Losing this place in December 1804, he returned to Jefferson County, where he practised law until 1810 and then moved to a plantation he had acquired in Warren County. He was elected to the legislature in 1811. In February of that year his wife died, and on Dec. 27, 1812, he married Eliza Baker, daughter of a wealthy planter from New Jersey. Returning to Natchez in 1813, he became city magistrate and president of the board of selectmen. Two years later, he was again elected to the legislature and was chosen to prepare a digest of the laws of the territory. This was published in 1816—*Statutes of the Mississippi Territory . . . Digested by Authority of the General Assembly.* As a representative of Adams County in the convention of 1817 he was a member of the committee that drafted the first constitution of Mississippi, and he continued to shape the affairs of the new state as chairman of the judiciary committee in the first state legislature (1817–18), and as speaker of the house in 1819 and 1820. For a short time in 1820–21 he was attorney-general.

In 1822 he was appointed judge of the criminal court of Adams County and in 1824 was advanced to the supreme court of Mississippi. Five years later he became chief justice and remained in this office until the adoption of the constitution of 1832, which provided for the popular election of judges. In 1834 he was elected chancellor, serving until 1839, in which year he was an unsuccessful candidate for governor on the Whig ticket. In 1840 he was again elected to the supreme court to fill a term which expired in 1843. He was not a candidate for reëlection, but in 1844 he was sent to the state Senate and served one term.

The last twelve years of his life he held no political office, but continued for several years to serve as president of the trustees of Jefferson College at Washington, Miss. By his marriages and by the practice of law he had become comparatively wealthy and he lived in comfort in his home near Natchez. He was survived by his wife and two daughters. Although Turner is remembered chiefly as a jurist, "his warmest friends," according to Henry S. Foote (*post*, p. 19), "did not claim for him any very extraordinary knowledge of law as a science." His success in public and private life was due to the fact that his "intellect was of a sound and practical cast, and his industry most remarkable." He was also "of unsurpassed integrity" and he had "exceedingly kind and conciliatory manners."

[9 *Miss. Reports*, 10–12; H. S. Foote, *The Bench and Bar of the South and Southwest* (1876); J. D. Lynch, *The Bench and Bar of Miss.* (1881); Dunbar Rowland, *Official Letter Books of W. C. C. Claiborne, 1801–1816* (1917), vols. I, II, and *Mississippi* (1907), vol. II; *Biog. and Hist. Memoirs of Miss.* (1891), vol. II; *Frank Leslie's Illustrated Newspaper*, Nov. 6, 1858; J. F. Claiborne, *Miss., as a Province, Territory and State* (1880); manuscript diary of B. L. C. Wailes [*q.v.*]; information supplied by L. P. Conner of Natchez, from family records.]   C. S. S.

TURNER, EDWARD RAYMOND (May 28, 1881–Dec. 31, 1929), historian, was born in Baltimore, Md., the son of Charles and Rosalind (Flynn) Turner. After attending the public schools of Baltimore he matriculated at St. John's College, Annapolis, receiving the degree of B.A. in 1904. Shortly thereafter he entered the graduate school of the Johns Hopkins University, where he devoted himself to the study of history. The American Historical Association awarded him the Justin Winsor Prize in 1910 for his dissertation, published the following year with the title *The Negro in Pennsylvania*. In the same year that he received the degree of Ph.D. (1910), he was called to Bryn Mawr College as associate in history; and, after remaining there one year, he accepted a professorship of European history at the University of Michigan. While occupying that chair, from 1911 to 1924, Turner established himself as an able and attractive lecturer.

In the field of historical research he devoted himself to English constitutional history. At first he planned to study the development of the cabinet during the reign of the early Hanoverians, but he eventually extended his research through the seventeenth and eighteenth centuries. His early contributions to the *English Historical Review* (such as the one published in April 1915) and the *American Historical Review* brought him into prominence both in England and the United States, and during the remainder of his life he continued his study of conciliar development. By reason of his abundant learning and energy Turner was also able, during the same time, to produce numerous manuals that enjoyed wide popularity. Thus there appeared: *Ireland and England* (1919); *Europe, 1789–1920* (1920); *Europe since 1870* (1921); *Europe,*

1450–1789 (1923); and *Europe since 1789* (1924).

In 1924 Turner accepted the professorship of English history at Yale University. The following year he was selected to succeed his former teacher, John Martin Vincent, as professor of European history at the Johns Hopkins University, and he returned to his native city. On Sept. 1, 1917, he had married Eleanor Howard Bowie of Baltimore. There were three children, of whom two survived him. At the Johns Hopkins he entered upon his new duties with great enthusiasm, invigorating the department of history and injecting new interest in the study of recent European diplomatic history. Strenuous academic duties, however, did not prevent him from progressing toward the completion of his *magnum opus*, for in 1927–28 appeared two volumes on *The Privy Council of England in the Seventeenth and Eighteenth Centuries*. Unfortunately, the premature death of Turner prevented him from completing his work, but two more volumes, left by him in type, were published in 1930–32 under the title, *The Cabinet Council of England in the Seventeenth and Eighteenth Centuries*, while materials for another were left with his widow. It was his desire "to make these four volumes a repository of all the available information on his subject" (Adair, *post*, p. xvi). Final conclusions, "flowing from the evidence," were to follow.

During almost his entire professional life, Turner spent his summers and sabbatical years in England, carrying on his research. During his last years he devoted much attention to the origins of the World War, being a frequent contributor to the *American Historical Review, Current History*, and other journals. Occasionally he became involved in controveries with certain "revisionists," but he defended his position with learning and conviction. His wide research, his mastery of numerous languages, and his love of literature are constantly reflected in his works.

[Information from Mrs. Eleanor Bowie Turner; personal recollection of the author; E. R. Adair, sketch of Turner and discussion of his work in introduction of *The Cabinet Council*, vol. II (1932); *The Johns Hopkins Alumni Mag.*, Mar. 1930, in "Necrology"; "Edward Raymond Turner, 1881–1929," in *Jour. of Modern Hist.*, Mar. 1930; editorial note in *Current Hist.*, Feb. 1930; *Am. Hist. Rev.*, Apr. 1930, p. 689, and reviews, *Ibid.*, Jan., Oct. 1928; *Sun* (Baltimore), Jan. 1, 1930; *Times* (London), Jan. 2, 1930.]   R. H. W.

TURNER, FENNELL PARRISH (Feb. 25, 1867–Feb. 10, 1932), missionary executive, was born in Danielsville, Dickson County, Tenn., the son of William Allen and Mary Jane (Pickett) Turner. Reared in the family of a Methodist minister and descended from a long line of ministers, he was naturally predisposed to the profession of his father and began preaching when in his teens. The oldest of the family, he shared the responsibility of helping to educate the younger children. He himself attended the common schools, then the Wall School at Chapel Hill, Tenn., and in 1891 graduated from Vanderbilt University. He interrupted his college course for two years, 1888–1890, to be principal of Dixon Academy, at Shelbyville, Tenn. For a year, 1891–92, he was a student in the Biblical department of Vanderbilt University but left to give full time to the *Tennessee Methodist,* of which he became assistant editor and business manager in 1891.

In 1895 he became state secretary of the Young Men's Christian Association for North Carolina. From this position he passed in 1897 to that of general secretary of the Student Volunteer Movement for Foreign Missions, then closely associated with the student department of the international committee of the Young Men's Christian Association; that same year, Nov. 3, he was married to Rose Vaughan of Nashville, Tenn. The Student Volunteer Movement, at the time Turner took charge of it, was scarcely ten years old. As a recruiting and educating agency for Protestant foreign missions, it had a large part in the religious life of the colleges and universities of the United States and Canada and in the growth of American foreign missions. The quadrennial conventions held by the Movement drew more students from more of the colleges and universities of North America than any other gatherings, secular or religious. Turner's twenty-two years (1897–1919) as its secretary spanned the Movement's most prosperous years, and for its development he was to no small degree responsible. In 1911 he brought about the organization of the Board of Missionary Preparation and was chiefly responsible for it until 1916. In 1918 he became the secretary of the Committee of Reference and Counsel of the Foreign Missions Conference of North America—the body coördinating the Protestant foreign mission boards of the Continent—and the following year he resigned from the secretaryship of the Student Volunteer Movement to give his entire time to the new post. From 1919 to 1928 he was also recording secretary of the Foreign Missions Conference. During these years in New York, he found time to serve with several other organizations whose work was closely related to that in which he was chiefly engaged: from 1912 to 1919 he was a member of the general committee of the World's Student Christian Federation; in 1910 he attended the World Missionary Conference at Edinburgh; from 1920 to 1928 he was a member of the committee of the newly formed International Missionary Council, and was present at four of the meetings of that body, including the memorable one at Jerusalem in 1928; he was a member of the executive committee of the World Alliance for Promoting International Friendship through the Churches, and of the administrative committee of the Federal Council of the Churches of Christ in America; and he was a delegate to international gatherings which planned for Protestant activities in Latin America—at Panama in 1916, at Montevideo in 1925, and in Havana in 1929. In these and many other connections he had a share in the formulation of the policies for the international outreach of Protestant Christianity.

In 1928, when the strain of the years of heavy administrative duties had at last become insupportable, he severed most of his major New York connections and became secretary for missionary education and foreign extension of the General Sunday-school Board of the denomination of his youth, the Methodist Episcopal Church, South, and served until 1930. In 1930–31 he traveled in Asia as a member of the research staff of the Laymen's Foreign Missions Inquiry. His report, "Missionary Personnel in India, Burma, China, and Japan," was published in *Laymen's Foreign Missions Inquiry: Fact-Finders' Reports,* vol. VII (1933). Shortly after his return from the East, increasing ill health forced him to retire to Southern California and a few months later he died at Santa Cruz. Not especially gifted in public address, and never writing much under his own name, Turner gave most of his energy to administration, to personal counsel, to service on boards and committees, and to editing papers and reports. A prodigious and not a quick worker, he willingly and patiently bore burdens which, as the years passed, broke his health. Kindly, companionable, unassuming, and unselfish, he won and held a wide circle of friends.

[*Who's Who in America,* 1932–33; *Missionary Rev. of the World,* May 1932, and *Christian Advocate* (Nashville), Feb. 19, 1932, both giving Feb. 9 as day of death; *N. Y. Times,* Feb. 11, 1932, which gives day of death as Feb. 10; material furnished by family and friends.]   K. S. L.

TURNER, FREDERICK JACKSON (Nov. 14, 1861–Mar. 14, 1932), historian, was born at Portage, on the northern fringe of agricultural Wisconsin, and passed his boyhood near the route over which explorers and missionaries had made their way from the St. Lawrence Valley to that of the Mississippi. He had local schooling, reënforced from a background of New England culture by his parents Andrew Jackson and Mary (Hanford) Turner, who were able to give him the best in education that the state afforded. His father, from Plattsburg, N. Y., a journalist and a politician, was a local historian as well. While Turner was at the University of Wisconsin, Prof. William Francis Allen [q.v.] taught him to examine sources and to weigh the inferences they suggested. Between 1884, when he was graduated, and 1888, when he took the degree of M.A., Turner gave up youthful ideas of journalism and elocution and determined to venture upon the new career of professor of history. Allen had already set him to work on the manuscripts of Lyman C. Draper [q.v.] in the State Historical Society, where his young friend Reuben Gold Thwaites [q.v.] had now been installed as Draper's successor. Out of these initial studies came material for "The Character and Influence of the Indian Trade in Wisconsin," which Turner offered as his dissertation for the doctorate at the Johns Hopkins in 1890 (*Johns Hopkins University Studies in Historical and Political Science*, 9 ser., 1891). At the University of Wisconsin, where he was assistant professor of history, 1889–91, professor of history, 1891–92, and professor of American history, 1892–1910, he took part in a deliberate attempt to erect a distinguished school of social studies.

Turner was a teacher with unusual power to inspire devotion, and an appearance of youth and simplicity that never quite deserted him. He became a useful professor, with a practical political instinct that made him a central figure in his university and threatened to divert him from paths of quiet scholarship. But he was aware of the nearness of unique archives in which American life could be investigated at its beginnings, and he never strayed far from the themes of his early studies. Invited to present a brief paper at the special meeting of the American Historical Association to be held at the World's Fair in Chicago, he assembled data for an essay on "The Significance of the Frontier in American History," which he read July 12, 1893 (first printed in 1894 in *Proceedings of the State Historical Society of Wisconsin . . . 1893,* and reprinted that year in *Annual Report of the American Historical Association . . . 1893*). Without warning he set forth a new hypothesis, and then and there opened a new period in the interpretation of the history of the United States. At the age of thirty-two he found himself treated as one of the significant figures in historical writing. Returning to his teaching work, where his distinctive course soon became the "History of the West," he adjusted himself slowly to the idea of his own importance.

He wrote little. His relatively small output may be attributed in part to a caution inspired by early success, in part to his endless patience with his students, and largely to the painstaking procedure by which he assembled and verified his facts. He was not working in a field already standardized, or yielding to easy narration, but in one in which small fragments, each of slight importance, needed to be brought together for impressive aggregates. Brief essays came from his study; but there were only a dozen which he cared to reprint, along with "The Significance of the Frontier," in *The Frontier in American History* (1920) ; and only a dozen more for *The Significance of Sections in American History* (1932), a posthumous recipient of the Pulitzer Prize. He edited "Correspondence of the French Ministers to the United States, 1791–1797" (*Annual Report of the American Historical Association . . . 1903*, vol. II, 1904). He was persuaded by A. B. Hart to prepare the *Rise of the New West* (1906), as a volume in the cooperative work, *The American Nation*. In this he disclosed the various sectional unities in the period 1819–29. He left incomplete at death a continuation of this; it was later published as *The United States, 1830–1850: The Nation and Its Sections* (1935), with an introduction by Avery Craven.

It was neither the bulk of his writing that brought Turner international recognition, nor the number of advanced students whom he trained at Wisconsin, for these were relatively few. It was rather the penetrating influence of his hypothesis, which incited investigation by his co-workers and led to a change in the trend of historical writing upon the United States. Trained historical craftsmen came into American historiography only in the decade at the close of which Turner took his doctorate; they told the American story with increasing accuracy, but without developing any convincing formula to account for the obvious fact that emigrants from western Europe and their descendants had brought into being a nation as variant from any of those from which they came as though it were of a different breed. Earlier historians had written in terms of religious liberty and revolt against the tyranny of England, or in admiration of the triumph of the principle of democracy. Where their writings were not antiquarian in character they were often nationalist or party tracts. Turner made necessary a new synthesis.

Seeking an explanation for that quality that appeared not to derive from the European sources of American culture, Turner looked for elements in the American environment that were novel in it. He observed that for three centuries the immigrants had found lodgment in an open continent where there was little to impede their free access to good land. He observed as well that for many centuries the peoples of Europe had lived in an environment of owned land, where the individual not born to estate had little chance to acquire it. The "hither edge of free land" became the magic element in the Turner hypothesis. Once recognized, it led him to see in the American frontier an influence unusual in history and perhaps formative in shaping American culture. He stated the formula with modesty, often asking his students whether they could "prove an inference." Some of his followers were prompted to state it dogmatically, and to go far beyond the master in applying it; but Turner was content to point out the possibility that human nature in a free environment might behave differently from the same nature under social and economic pressure, that equality of opportunity might have something to do with democracy in politics, that isolation on a new frontier might encourage the survival of the robust and the opinionated, that the necessity of repeatedly setting up social and governmental institutions brought about a laboratory process in which nonessentials dropped out while tested principles survived, that the relationship between frontiersmen and government led naturally to a nationalism more intense than that of the older communities. He traced in his famous essay the spread over the continent of a series of frontiers: of the discoverer and explorer, the missionary, the soldier, the trapper, and the farmer. But his hypothesis was derived largely from the experiences of the frontier farmers who first changed the face of nature, and who added new units of social and economic life to the United States. He pointed out, as well, that whatever the influence of the frontier had been, it was now in 1893 about to terminate. Free land had gone, after three centuries of access to its "hither edge"; and he foretold a future different from the past in so far at least as the open frontier had been a positive force.

For the rest of his creative life Turner tested his hypothesis, applying it at times to microscopic examination of limited regions and periods, and trying at other moments to reconcile it with larger views of American development. He regarded the frontier less as a place than as a continuous process sweeping the continent, and regarded the region where it was temporarily operating as a section with aspects and interests

deriving from its cultural state. This led him easily to a consideration of other varieties of sections, owing their identity to topography, natural resources, or the racial components of their people. He observed in these the American equivalents of the distracted nationalities of Europe. On this note he ended.

From the day that he read his essay Turner was a marked man, but, declining all calls to other institutions, he continued until 1910 to serve his university. Soon welcomed to the inner councils of the American Historical Association, he served as its president in 1909–10. During the period 1910–15, he was a member of the board of editors of the *American Historical Review*. In 1910 he accepted a professorship at Harvard. Here, in an atmosphere less hospitable to his trend of thought than that of Wisconsin, he continued until retirement in 1924. He planned thereafter to reside in Madison, but poor health intervened and winters in California gave way to residence in Pasadena, where the Huntington Library welcomed him as research associate. He died at the age of seventy-one. He was married on Nov. 25, 1889, to Carolina Mae Sherwood of Chicago, who, with one of their children, survived him.

[Turner's reference books and notes were presented by him to the Huntington Lib., and the bulk of his correspondence is deposited there. See Max Farrand, in the *Huntington Lib. Bulletin*, no. 3, Feb. 1933, pp. 157–64. Carl Becker, in H. W. Odum, ed., *American Masters of Social Science* (1927), gives an appraisal of Turner's work and a careful bibliography of his writings. Other friendly appreciations are: E. E. Robinson, in *N. D. Hist. Quart.*, July 1932; Joseph Schafer, in *Wis. Mag. of Hist.*, Sept. 1931, June 1932, June 1933, June 1934; Constance L. Skinner, *Ibid.*, Sept. 1935; M. E. Curti, "The Section and the Frontier in American History: The Methodological Concepts of Frederick Jackson Turner," in S. A. Rice, ed., *Methods in Social Science* (1931); F. L. Paxson, "A Generation of the Frontier Hypothesis," in *Pacific Hist. Rev.*, Mar. 1933. Destructive criticism is offered in J. C. Almack, "The Shibboleth of the Frontier," in *Historical Outlook*, May 1925; B. F. Wright, Jr., "American Democracy and the Frontier," in *Yale Rev.*, Winter, 1931; L. M. Hacker, "Sections—or Classes," in *The Nation*, July 26, 1933, with reply by Benjamin Stolberg, *Ibid.*, Sept. 13, 1933. A valuable aid is E. E. Edwards, "References on the Significance of the Frontier in American History," *Bibliographical Contributions*, No. 25, Oct. 1935, U. S. Dept. of Agriculture Lib. See also R. G. Thwaites, *The Univ. of Wisconsin* (1900); *Am. Hist. Rev.*, July 1932, pp. 823–24; review of Turner's last book by J. D. Hicks, in *Am. Hist. Rev.*, Jan. 1936; obituary and editorial, *N. Y. Times*, Mar. 16, 17, 1932.] F. L. P.

TURNER, GEORGE (Feb. 25, 1850–Jan. 26, 1932), lawyer, United States senator, was born in Edina, Mo., the son of Granville Davenport and Maria (Taylor) Turner. His father, a cabinet maker, was of English and Dutch ancestry; his mother, of Scotch-Irish. They had moved from Kentucky to Missouri in 1825. The boy's schooling was meager, and at the age of thirteen, the Civil War then being in progress, he became a military telegrapher in the Union service. After the war, he studied law in the office of a brother in Mobile, where he was admitted to the bar in 1870. President Grant in 1876 appointed him United States marshal for the middle and southern districts of Alabama, and he served until 1880. During this period he was the acknowledged Republican leader of the state. He was chairman of the Alabama delegation at the Republican National Convention of 1880, and held his negroes in line for Grant through the six days' battle between the Grant and Blaine forces.

In 1885 President Arthur appointed him associate justice of the supreme court of Washington Territory. Resigning in 1888, he entered upon the practice of law in Spokane. He was a member of the state constitutional convention of 1889 and chairman of its judiciary committee. He is credited with the authorship of the bill of rights, regarded by jurists as exceedingly comprehensive. The Puget Sound tidelands were coveted by railway interests, and his successful campaign in the convention to save them for the state created an opposition to him which repeatedly prevented his election to public office later. Working with scanty capital in the panic years of the nineties, Turner and some Spokane friends developed the Le Roi mine, at Rossland, B. C. It became a rich producer and was sold to a British syndicate for $4,000,000. Turner's sagacity and his skill in bending insurgent stockholders to his purpose were largely responsible for this success. He was president of the Le Roi and, later, of the Constitution mine and the Sullivan group, near Cranbrook, B. C. With profits from the Le Roi, he joined Frank Graves of Spokane in the purchase of the *Seattle Post-Intelligencer*. They paid $50,000 for the paper in September 1897 and some two years later sold it for $350,000 to Senator John L. Wilson backed by James J. Hill [*qq.v.*]. This paper was the principal Republican organ of the state; Turner made no effort to change its policy while he was an owner, and it continued to attack his acts as United States senator.

Turner was elected to the Senate on a fusion ticket of Silver Republicans, Democrats, and Populists, and served from Mar. 4, 1897, to Mar. 3, 1903. At the expiration of his term, the legislature was under Republican control, and there was no possibility of his reëlection. He had won high regard as a constitutional lawyer, and on the day following his retirement President Theodore Roosevelt notified him of his appointment, with Secretary of War Elihu Root and Senator Henry Cabot Lodge [*q.v.*], as a member of the Alaska Boundary Tribunal. In 1910 President Taft appointed him as counsel for the United States in the Northeastern fisheries dispute with Great Britain, which was arbitrated at The Hague. President Taft also appointed Turner to the International Joint Boundary Commission, on which he served in 1913 and 1914, resigning because of the demand for his legal services in Spokane. From 1918 to 1924, however, by President Wilson's appointment, he acted as counsel for the United States before this commission.

Turner was always a dramatic figure. He belonged to the pioneer tradition, with its vision, independence, and fighting spirit. He was most happy in the stress of the old party conventions, which released his vivid eloquence. His rise to eminence in the face of educational disadvantages was due to an orderly mind, phenomenal memory, and untiring will. On June 4, 1878, he married Bertha C. Dreher, daughter of George and Catherine Dreher of Montgomery, Ala. He died at his home in Spokane, survived by his widow.

[N. W. Durham, *Hist. of the City of Spokane* (1912), I, 421, 481, 488, II, 116; *Who's Who in America*, 1930–31; *Biog. Dir. Am. Cong.* (1928); Jonathan Edwards, *An Illustrated Hist. of Spokane County* (1900); *Spokesman-Review* (Spokane), Jan. 27, 1932; information as to certain facts from relatives and associates.]   G. W. F.

TURNER, HENRY McNEAL (Feb. 1, 1834– May 8, 1915), bishop of the African Methodist Episcopal Church, editor, author, was born near Abbeville, S. C. He was the son of Hardy Turner and Sarah (Greer) and came of mixed blood. Losing his father when still young, Turner worked for a time in the cotton fields and was then apprenticed to a blacksmith. He was fifteen before he was taught to read. He was next employed by a law firm, learned to write, and mastered arithmetic. He joined the Methodist Episcopal Church, South, and in 1853 was licensed to preach. He became a successful revivalist among the negroes and held meetings in most of the Southern states until 1857, when he settled in St. Louis. In the following year he was admitted to the Missouri Conference of the African Methodist Episcopal Church, to which he thereafter adhered.

Placed in charge of a mission in Baltimore and criticized locally for his imperfect command of English, he studied grammar, Latin, Greek, and Hebrew. He was ordained deacon in 1860 and elder in 1862. In the latter year he was installed as pastor of Israel Church, Washington, where he came into contact with many prominent men. In 1863 he was made an army chaplain by President Lincoln—the first colored man to be appointed to such a position—and was attached to the 1st Regiment, United States Colored Troops. Mustered out in 1865, he was appointed chaplain in the regular army by President Johnson and assigned to the Georgia office of the Freedmen's Bureau. He soon resigned in order to build up the African Methodist Episcopal Church in Georgia. Under his vigorous proselyting a large number of churches were established, which became rallying points for the freed negroes. One of the founders of the Republican party in Georgia, Turner was elected a delegate to the Georgia Constitutional convention in 1867, and a member of the state legislature for Bibb County in 1868. Here he aroused the jealousy of the white Republicans, while his outspoken and provocative language made him bitterly hated by the Democrats. In 1869 he was appointed postmaster at Macon by President Grant at the request of Senator Charles Sumner, which office he relinquished because of the opposition of the white patrons. He subsequently served as a United States customs inspector and as a government detective.

In 1876 he was made manager of the African Methodist Episcopal Book Concern in Philadelphia, and from 1880 until 1892 he was bishop of his Church for Georgia. For twelve years he was chancellor of Morris Brown College (now Morris Brown University) in Atlanta. He visited South and West Africa, introduced African Methodism there, and advocated the return of the negroes to Africa. He founded several periodicals, including the *Southern Christian Recorder* (1889) and the *Voice of Missions* (1892) and was the author of *The Genius and Theory of Methodist Polity* (copr. 1885) and the compiler of a catechism and a hymn book.

Turner was very tall, with an elephantine frame and massive head. He possessed a coarse nature, his manners and movements were crude, and he cared nothing about his dress or personal appearance. He was an eloquent speaker, had a guttural voice, and was given to angry tirades and bitter sarcasm against both negroes and whites. He was married four times and had numerous children, of whom only two survived him. His first marriage, to Eliza Ann Peacher, occurred on Aug. 31, 1856, in Columbia, S. C.; his second, to Mrs. Martha De Witt of Bristol, Pa., in August 1893; his third, to Harriet A. Wayman of Baltimore, Md., widow of Bishop Alexander Wayman [q.v.], on Aug. 16, 1900; and his last to Laura Pearl Lemon of Atlanta, Ga., divorced wife of a minister named Powell. Turner died in Windsor, Ontario, and was buried in Atlanta.

[M. M. Ponton, *Life and Times of Henry M. Turner* (1917); R. R. Wright, *Centennial Encyc. of the Afri-* *can Methodist Episcopal Church* (1916); *Who's Who in America*, 1914–15; *Atlanta Constitution*, Aug. 17, 1900, Dec. 4, 1907, May 9, 1915; *Atlanta Jour.*, May 9, 1915.]

H. G. V.

TURNER, JAMES MILTON (May 16, 1840– Nov. 1, 1915), negro leader, minister to Liberia, was born a slave in St. Louis County, Mo., on the St. Charles Road plantation of Charles A. Loring. His father, John Turner, also known as John Colburn after a master, had been removed from Virginia by one Benjamin Tillman, following the 1831 slave insurrection led by Nat Turner [q.v.]. Taught veterinary medicine by Tillman, Turner subsequently bought his freedom and in 1843 purchased his wife Hannah and their son, then in his fourth year. The boy's aptitude displayed at a clandestine school so pleased his parents that they sent him to Oberlin College, where he spent his fourteenth year in the preparatory department under the tutelage of James Harris Fairchild [q.v.].

In the Civil War he served as a Northern officer's servant, and is said to have received at Shiloh an injury that caused a lifelong limp. After the war he directed his attention to negro public education as required by the Missouri constitution of 1865. In April 1866 he was appointed by the Kansas City school board to conduct a school for negroes during the winter; no earlier negro public school in Missouri is recorded. In June 1868 he was reappointed. Meanwhile, he had become interested in plans for a negro institute in Jefferson City, Mo. For this undertaking, now Lincoln University, he gave and collected money and served as trustee. Oratorical ability soon made him the acknowledged leader of Missouri negroes and as such a figure in Republican politics. The Columbia (Mo.) *Statesman* in 1870 pictured him as "possessed of a fine flow of language and never wanting an idea" (quoted in Dilliard, *post*, p. 379).

On nomination of President Grant, confirmed by the Senate, Mar. 1, 1871, Turner became minister resident and consul general to Liberia, the first negro, it is said, to serve in the diplomatic corps. He presented his credentials at Monrovia on July 25 of that year and served until May 20, 1878. Liberia's frequent governmental changes and native uprisings kept him busy writing long, apologetic dispatches to the Department of State. Thorough observation of conditions led him to oppose settlement by American negroes on the ground that they were unfitted for equatorial life. Colonization activities of philanthropists he described as "well-meaning" but "absolutely injurious in results" (see *Papers Relating to the Foreign Relations of the United States*, 1877, pp. 370–75); he urged instead help for native tribes. After European receptions, Turner returned to the United States to be fêted widely; admiring negroes hauled his carriage through the streets of St. Louis. Later he married Ella De Burton of St. Joseph's Parish, La., who died Mar. 2, 1908; they had no children. On Apr. 18, 1882, he appeared before the Missouri Historical Society, St. Louis, to eulogize Dred Scott [q.v.] and to present an oil painting of him to the society in behalf of the widow of Theron Barnum, to whose family Scott had been attached. In 1886 he presented to President Cleveland the claim that negro members of the Cherokee nation were entitled to a proportionate share of $300,-000 allotted that nation by Congress, and as their attorney was instrumental in securing an appropriation of $75,000 for them in 1889. He also interested himself in claims for Choctaw and Chickasaw freedmen.

Caught in the débris of an explosion in Ardmore, Okla., Turner died there. His funeral, conducted by Missouri negro Masons, was the largest ever held in St. Louis for a member of his race. Crowds thronged to the service, where tribute was paid to his leadership and generosity. He was buried in Father Dickson Cemetery, near his birthplace. A "citizen's memorial service" was held two weeks later.

[The fullest source of information is Irving Dilliard, "James Milton Turner, a Little Known Benefactor of His People," *The Jour. of Negro Hist.*, Oct. 1934; it cites newspaper articles, letters, memoranda, and quotes at length from Turner's dispatches to the Department of State.]   I. D.

TURNER, JOHN WESLEY (July 19, 1833–Apr. 8, 1899), soldier, son of John Bice and Martha (Voluntine) Turner, was born near Saratoga, N. Y. His father was a prominent railroad and canal constructor, and in 1843 the family removed to Chicago, where the elder Turner helped build the Galena & Chicago Union Railroad. John Wesley was appointed to the United States Military Academy from Illinois, graduated in 1855, and was commissioned lieutenant of artillery. As a subaltern he served in Oregon and in hostilities against the Seminoles in Florida.

In August 1861 he was commissioned captain in the commissary department and served as chief commissary under Gen. David Hunter [q.v.] in Kansas from December 1861 to March 1862, and in the same capacity under General Hunter when the latter was in command of the Department of the South in April 1862. During this tour of duty he was employed as an artillery officer in the attack on Fort Pulaski, Apr. 10–11, 1862. In May of the same year he was assigned as chief commissary on the staff of Gen. Benjamin F. Butler [q.v.] at New Orleans and remained with him to the end of the year. In the spring of 1863 he returned to General Hunter in the Department of the South, and when Hunter was relieved by Gen. Quincy A. Gillmore [q.v.], Turner was made chief of staff and chief of artillery, June 13, 1863, and as such took part in the siege of Fort Wagner and the attack on Fort Sumter. For his services he received the brevet of major, United States Army, and was commissioned brigadier-general of volunteers. In the operations of 1864 Turner commanded a division in the Army of the James under General Butler on Bermuda Hundred and in front of Petersburg, and received the brevet of lieutenant-colonel, United States Army, for gallant services in action at the Petersburg mine, and the brevet of major-general of volunteers for gallant services in the campaign of 1864. From Nov. 20, 1864, to Jan. 12, 1865, he was chief of staff of the Army of the James. In the campaign of 1865 he commanded a division of the XXIV Army Corps and took an active part in the operations leading to the surrender of Lee at Appomattox. For his services at the capture of Fort Gregg he received the brevet of colonel, United States Army, and later those of brigadier and major-general. At the end of active operations he was appointed to the command of the District of Henrico, which included the city of Richmond; this position he held from June 1865 to April 1866. His administration was both efficient and tactful. On being mustered out of the volunteer service in 1866 he became purchasing and depot commissary at St. Louis. In September 1871 he resigned from the army.

Being accustomed to command and to assume great responsibilities, and having a pleasing personality and great tact, he was as successful in civil life as he had been in his military career. From 1872 to 1877 he was president of the Bogy Lead Mining Company, and for eleven years (1877–88), street commissioner of St. Louis. He served, also, as president of the St. Joseph Gas and Manufacturing Company (1888–97), and as a director of the American Exchange Bank and of the St. Louis Savings and Safe Deposit Company (1893–99). On Sept. 18, 1869, he married Blanche Soulard of St. Louis, by whom he had seven children. His death occurred in St. Louis and his wife and children survived him.

[G. W. Cullum, *Biog. Reg. . . . Grads. U. S. Mil. Acad.* (3rd ed., 1891); *Thirteenth Ann. Reunion, Asso. Grads. U. S. Mil. Acad.* (1899); *War of the Rebellion: Official Records* (Army); William Hyde and H. L. Conard, *Encyc. of the Hist. of St. Louis* (1899, vol. IV); *St. Louis Globe-Democrat*, Apr. 8, 9, 1899.]
G. J. F.

TURNER, JONATHAN BALDWIN (Dec. 7, 1805–Jan. 10, 1899), educator, agriculturist, was born in Templeton, Mass., the son of Asa and Abigail (Baldwin) Turner, and a brother of Asa Turner [*q.v.*]. He obtained his early education in local district schools, in which he later became a teacher. When his brother Asa graduated from college in 1827, he persuaded his father to let Jonathan go to New Haven to prepare for Yale, and at the end of two years he was admitted to the college. Early in the spring of his senior year a call came to Yale from Illinois College, at Jacksonville, for an instructor in Latin and Greek. The president of Yale recommended Turner and offered to excuse him from final examinations and to forward his diploma if he would accept. As a result, in May 1833 he became a member of the Illinois faculty. The following year he was appointed professor of rhetoric and belles-lettres. He returned to the East in 1835 to marry, on Oct. 22, Rhodolphia S. Kibbe of Somers, Conn. He early became a leader in the movement for public schools in Illinois, lecturing in its behalf throughout the central part of the state. One of the organizers of the Illinois State Teachers' Association in 1836, he enlisted the aid of teachers and parents in his campaign. He was successful as an instructor, but in 1843–44 he edited the *Statesman,* a local paper, and by his vigorous condemnation of slavery alienated the Southern students in the college and the slavery advocates in Jacksonville. In 1847 he resigned his professorship because of ill health and disagreement with the college officials over slavery and denominational questions.

He now devoted himself primarily to his gardens and orchards, which he had been developing since 1834, and to agricultural experiments. He made the Osage orange popular for farm hedges, and invented various implements for planting and cultivating crops. The preservation of game life and of national resources also engaged his attention. When the Illinois State Natural History Society was organized, June 30, 1858, he was elected president. In spite of these activities he found time to further various educational projects. The free school law of 1855 was largely the result of his untiring efforts, and his influence had much to do with the establishment of the first normal school in Illinois in 1857. His most notable contribution to education, however, was in connection with the campaign for land grant colleges. At a county institute of teachers held at Griggsville, May 13, 1850, he presented a plan for a state university for the industrial classes in each of the states of the

Union. This he presented, also, to a convention of farmers which convened in Granville on Nov. 18, 1851. The plan was approved by this convention, which also adopted certain resolutions including one which pledged the members to "take immediate steps for the establishment of a university in the State of Illinois." These resolutions and Turner's plan were printed and widely circulated. Other conventions were held later, and at one which met at Springfield, Jan. 4, 1853, a petition was drawn up requesting the legislature to ask Congress to appropriate lands to each state for the establishment of industrial universities. Such a request, the first probably from any state, was made by the Illinois legislature in 1853 (*Journal of the House of Representatives of ... Illinois,* 1853). Through the Industrial League, organized to carry on propaganda in behalf of industrial education, of which he became principal director, Turner gave time and strength to the movement for years. Meanwhile, it was gathering strength in other parts of the country, and in 1857 Justin Morrill [*q.v.*], then a representative from Vermont, introduced a bill in Congress providing that public lands be donated to the states and territories to provide colleges of agriculture and the mechanic arts. This failed to pass over a presidential veto, but a similar bill became a law in 1862. Shortly after its passage, the small colleges of Illinois united to secure the advantages of the land grant, but chiefly through Turner's activities the legislature of 1867 decided to establish "a single new industrial university" (now the University of Illinois), which was located at Urbana, Champaign County. After the university was incorporated, Feb. 28, 1867, he devoted the remainder of his life to a study of the Bible and its teachings. His published works included *Mormonism in All Ages* (1842); *The Three Great Races of Men* (1861); *Universal Law and Its Opposites* (1892); and *The Christ Word Versus the Church Word* (1895). He died in Jacksonville, Ill., survived by four of his seven children.

[*Obit. Record Grads. Yale Univ. . . . 1890–1900* (1900); M. T. Carriel, *The Life of Jonathan Baldwin Turner* (1911); J. W. Cook, *Educational Hist. of Ill.* (1912); E. J. James, *The Origin of the Land Grant Act of 1862* (1910); I. L. Kandel, *Federal Aid for Vocational Education* (1917); C. H. Rammelkamp, *Ill. Coll., A Centennial Hist., 1829–1929* (1928); *Chicago Tribune,* Jan. 12, 1899.]　　　　　R. F. S.

TURNER, JOSIAH (Dec. 27, 1821–Oct. 26, 1901), editor, the eldest son of Josiah and Eliza (Evans) Turner, was born in Hillsboro, N. C. He was educated at Caldwell Institute and at the University of North Carolina. Admitted to the bar about 1845, he built up a considerable practice, more by native cleverness than by legal learning and ability. In 1856 he married Sophia Devereux of Raleigh, by whom he had four sons and a daughter. His public life began with his election to the House of Commons in 1852 as a Whig. Reëlected for the succeeding term, he was defeated for the state Senate in 1856, but was elected in 1858 and again in 1860. At the session of 1861 he contested every move of the secessionists and voted against calling the secession convention, but upon the passage of the ordinance, he enlisted immediately in the state forces and became a captain of cavalry. He participated in the battle of New Bern and was soon afterwards wounded and disabled. In November 1862 he resigned his commission and in 1863 was elected as a peace candidate to the Confederate Congress, where he was actively hostile to the administration and frankly urgent for making terms with the United States.

When the war ended he was no less eager for the restoration of the state but, distrusting William W. Holden [q.v.], the provisional governor, as a former Democrat and a secession leader, he was active in the movement which led in November 1865 to Holden's defeat. In the same campaign Turner won election to Congress, but he was denied his seat. He was subsequently for two years president of the North Carolina Railroad. In 1868, when Holden was elected governor, Turner was elected to the state Senate, but was denied his seat because of disabilities. In this same year he purchased the Raleigh *Sentinel,* in the editorial conduct of which he made his chief reputation. Bitterly hostile to congressional reconstruction, he threw himself into the task of discrediting and defeating the "Carpet-bag" government. With a positive genius for political polemics, sparing little nor caring where he struck, quick-witted, ingenious in keeping political opponents on the defensive, he now, by ridicule and telling nicknames, brought the Republican leaders into contempt, and again, with a lash of scorpions held them up to public condemnation. No man was so bitterly hated and feared by them. He never overlooked a vital point, never lost his temper, and never forgot or forgave. To him more than to any one man belongs the credit for the overthrow of reconstruction in North Carolina. When in 1870 Governor Holden sought to sustain his administration and carry the election by armed force, Turner roused the state to effective opposition. His own illegal arrest and imprisonment under the Governor's orders was the great event in his life and furnished one of the charges upon which Holden was later impeached.

Turner's later career was pathetic. Essentially destructive, when the crisis was past he could not find peace but continued to fight. He expected high office, but his party regarded him as too erratic and too violent, and he soon turned on his late associates. He declined a nomination to Congress in 1872 and was denied one in 1874. He was a delegate to the convention of 1875, where he loudly clamored for the repudiation of the "Carpet-bag" bonds before his party was ready for such drastic action. He lost his newspaper, which was sold in 1876 under mortgage. Defeated for the state Senate in that year, he ran for Congress as an independent in 1878 and was defeated. He had already been elected to the lower house of the legislature for the term of 1879, but was so persistently disorderly that he was finally expelled. After another defeat for Congress in 1884, he retired and ended his life a partisan Republican. He died at his home near Hillsboro.

[S. A. Ashe, *Biog. Hist. of N. C.,* vol. III (1905); J. G. deR. Hamilton, *Reconstruction in N. C.* (1914); *Alumni Hist. of the Univ. of N. C.* (1924); R. D. W. Connor, *North Carolina,* vol. II (1929); *News and Observer* (Raleigh, N. C.), Oct. 27, 1901; files of the *Sentinel.*]   J. G. deR. H.

TURNER, NAT (Oct. 2, 1800–Nov. 11, 1831), leader of slave insurrection, the son of Nancy, a slave woman and native of Africa, was born on the plantation of her owner, Benjamin Turner, in Southampton County, Va. He successively became the property of Samuel Turner, Thomas Moore, and Putnam Moore, and in 1830 he was hired to Joseph Travis, whom Mrs. Thomas Moore had married. His mother was little removed from savagery at the time of his birth, and his father, whose name has not survived, ran away while Nat was a child. Nat, who was precocious, was given the rudiments of an education by one of his master's sons, and, early developing a religious fanaticism, under his mother's encouragement came to believe himself inspired. A fiery preacher, he soon acquired leadership among the negroes on the plantation and in the neighborhood. According to his sworn confession, he deliberately set about convincing them of his divine inspiration, and presently believed himself chosen to lead them from bondage. He began to see signs in the heavens and on the leaves, and to hear voices directing him. An eclipse of the sun in 1831 convinced him that the time was near and caused him to enlist four other slaves, to whom he communicated his plans. They plotted an uprising for July 4, but abandoned it. After a new sign was seen in a peculiar solar phenomenon on Aug. 13, they settled upon Aug. 21 as the day of deliverance.

With seven others Nat attacked the Travis family and murdered them all. Securing arms and horses, and enlisting other slaves, they ravaged the neighborhood. In one day and one night they butchered horribly and mangled the bodies of fifty-one white persons—thirteen men, eighteen women, and twenty-four children. With the blood of the victims Nat sprinkled his followers. At the first armed resistance the revolt collapsed and on Aug. 25 Nat went into hiding in a dugout, less than two miles from the Travis farm, where he remained, successfully concealed in the daytime, for six weeks. Discovered by accident, he was at once tried, and after conviction was hanged at Jerusalem, the county seat. He faced his fate with calmness. Thomas R. Gray, who was assigned to defend him, said: "He is a complete fanatic, or plays his part most admirably" (Gray, *post*, p. 19). Of his sixty or seventy followers, twenty-eight were convicted and condemned; sixteen, including the one woman involved, were executed, and twelve were transported. The number that were killed in the suppression of the uprising has never been ascertained.

The revolt, following closely upon slave insurrections in Martinique, Antigua, Santiago, Carácas, and the Tortugas, caused a profound shock in the slaveholding states. Exaggeration magnified both the real and the false, and for weeks there was widespread terror. As a result almost every Southern state enacted new laws which greatly increased the severity of the slave codes, though, after a brief time, most of them were more honored in the breach than in the observance. The insurrection dealt a death blow to the manumission societies which had flourished in the South, and put an end there to the organized emancipation movement. Further, the blame for the uprising was placed upon the Garrisonian abolitionists, though not a scintilla of evidence ever connected them with it, and intensified the detestation and dread with which the South regarded them. Perhaps the most important result of all was that never again was the slaveholding South free from the fear, lurking most of the time, of a wholesale and successful slave uprising, a fact potent in the history of the republic during the next thirty years.

[W. S. Drewry, *The Southampton Insurrection* (1900), S. B. Weeks, "The Slave Insurrection in Virginia, 1831," in *Mag. of Am. Hist.*, June 1891; R. R. Howison, *A Hist. of Virginia*, vol. II (1848), pp. 439–41; W. S. Forrest, *Hist. and Descriptive Sketches of Norfolk and Vicinity* (1853); T. R. Gray, *The Confession, Trial, and Execution of Nat. Turner* (1881), published earlier as *The Confessions of Nat Turner . . . to Thomas R. Gray* (1832); *Richmond Enquirer*, Aug. 26, 30; Sept. 2, 6; Nov. 15, 18, 1831.] J. G. deR. H.

TURNER, ROSS STERLING (June 29, 1847–Feb. 12, 1915), painter, teacher of art, was born at Westport, N. Y. His parents, David and Eliza Jane (Cameron) Turner, moved in his boyhood to Williamsport, Pa., where Ross attended the local academy, showing special aptitude for freehand and mechanical drawing. He was for several years a draftsman at the Patent Office, Washington, doing work which has been deplored as too mechanical and irksome for a man with Turner's "delicate touch and freedom of brush stroke" (Walker, *post*), but which in reality may have been good training toward his spontaneous water colors and exquisite illuminations, his chief contributions to the art of his period. In 1876 Turner went to Munich, where as an art student he was associated with Frank Duveneck, Joseph Rodefer DeCamp, Julius Rolshoven [*qq.v.*], and other young Americans. He was at Venice when Whistler was there, and he gave, shortly before his death, a talk at the Whistler House, Lowell, Mass., on his recollections of Whistler. Turner settled in 1882 in Boston where, two years later, he married Louise Blaney, sister of Dwight Blaney, a fellow artist. They made their home at Salem. Turner soon became one of the most popular teachers of water color in New England, instructing literally thousands of young people at his Boston studio, at the Massachusetts Institute of Technology (1884–1914), and for a time at the Massachusetts Normal Art School. Among his publications the most important is a manual, *On the Use of Water Colors for Beginners* (1886). He made many illustrations, and he exhibited frequently at the American Water Color Society, New York. He was a pioneer in the movement for decoration of school rooms.

Commuting for many years between Salem and Boston, with a summer studio at Wilton, N. H., Turner had an uneventful though busy and useful career. He was modest, friendly, and possessed of a wide range of interests. His chief recreation was outdoor painting in water color, in which he was facile and proficient. In his later life he discovered the charm of the Bahamas as a sketching ground, and there, at Nassau, he died. He was survived by his wife and two sons. He had previously developed a form of art of which he was one of the few modern exponents, that of the illuminated manuscript, where he used the materials and followed the manner of the medieval craftsmen. His illuminations were exhibited from time to time at the Society of Arts and Crafts, Boston. He was a charter member of the Guild of Boston Artists (formed in 1913), which in March 1915 held a memorial exhibition of his works. According to a friend, he was a "charming companion, simple as a child with the broader wisdom that declines to see evil" (Walker, *post*, p. 299).

[*Who's Who in America*, 1914–15; C. H. Walker, in *Technology Rev.*, Apr. 1915; F. T. Robinson, *Living New England Artists* (1888), with reproductions of several early water colors; cat. of the memorial exhibition, Guild of Boston Artists, Mar. 22, 1915; *Artists Year Book*, 1905; *Am. Art Ann.*, 1915; *Am. Art News*, Feb. 20, 1915; obituary in *Boston Globe*, Feb. 13, 1915.]   F. W. C.

TURNER, SAMUEL HULBEART (Jan. 23, 1790–Dec. 21, 1861), Protestant Episcopal clergyman, educator, was born in Philadelphia, Pa., the son of the Rev. Joseph Turner, a native of England, and Elizabeth (Mason), the daughter of a physician of Devonshire, England. He received his early education under private tutors and at the Quaker Academy on Fourth Street, near Chestnut, and in January 1806 entered the University of Pennsylvania. Graduating in 1807, he prepared for the ministry under the personal direction of Bishop William White [*q.v.*]. Looking back on this course of study in later years, he acknowledged his great indebtedness to the learned bishop, but confessed that "a good deal of reading without much thought . . . left my mind poorly disciplined" (*Autobiography, post*, p. 33). His awareness of this defect led him to seek the remedy, and he early developed habits of exact scholarship and sustained thinking. He was ordained deacon Jan. 27, 1811, and priest in 1814. His first charge was that of the church at Chestertown, Md. The parish was a small one and the young minister was free to devote much of his time to the further pursuit of his studies without neglecting his pastoral duties. His reputation for scholarship grew and he was offered a Latin professorship in St. John's College at Annapolis, which he declined. Removing to Philadelphia in 1817, he was appointed, early the following year, superintendent of theological students in the diocese of Pennsylvania. The duties were not onerous, for only two young men were in his care; but one of these was Alonzo Potter [*q.v.*], who was later to attain eminence as bishop of Pennsylvania.

At this time the Protestant Episcopal Church was formulating plans for a theological school, and on the establishment of the General Theological Seminary in New York, Turner was made professor in historic theology, his appointment dating from Oct. 8, 1818. When the institution was moved to New Haven in 1820, Turner went with it. On its reorganization in New York in 1822 he became professor of Biblical learning and interpretation, a position which he held for forty years. He had, therefore, a large part in shaping the traditions of the seminary, and since theological education in the United States was then in its formative stage, his influence was not inconsiderable in wider circles.

Along with his chair at the seminary he held for some years, beginning in 1830, the professorship of the Hebrew language and literature in Columbia College. His earlier writings, all of them on Biblical subjects, were for the most part translations of the more conservative German books of the day; but in 1841 he published an original work entitled *A Companion to the Book of Genesis,* and this was followed by a series of commentaries dealing with other parts of the Bible. They were all characterized by solid learning and sober judgment. A reviewer remarked that his books showed an "intimate acquaintance with German theology" but were "in no respects tainted by its neology" (Johnson, *post*, p. 29). At the same time, his sturdy, matter-of-fact exegesis with its resolute rejection of forced and fantastic interpretation of Holy Scripture played its part in paving the way for a just appreciation of that Biblical criticism which was later to revolutionize the study of the Bible, and would have sadly disturbed him.

During the latter half of his ministry the effects of the Oxford Movement were making themselves felt in the Episcopal Church in the United States, and the seminary was necessarily involved in the long controversy which followed. Turner, who opposed the movement but would have classed himself among the "moderates," defended his position throughout with a becoming sobriety of argument. His appeal was always to learning, "without which," in his own words, "piety is the more likely to degenerate into fanaticism and the suggestions of fancy to be taken for illapses of inspiration." He was married on May 23, 1826, to Mary Esther Beach of Cheshire, Conn., who died Sept. 2, 1839. At his death in New York City, he was survived by two sons and a daughter. His own account of his life, *Autobiography of the Rev. Samuel H. Turner, D.D.,* appeared in 1863.

[In addition to the *Autobiog.*, see S. R. Johnson, *Sermon Commemorative of the Life and Services of Rev. Samuel H. Turner* (1863); *N. Y. Times* and *N. Y. Tribune*, Dec. 23, 1861.]   H. E. W. F.

TURNER, WALTER VICTOR (Apr. 3, 1866–Jan. 9, 1919), engineer, inventor, son of George and Beatrice (Brandon) Turner, was born in Epping Forest, Essex, England. After completing his education in the Textile Technical School at Wakefield, Yorkshire, he engaged in the woolen textile business in that country. In 1888 he was sent by his employer to the United

Turner

States to investigate wool growing. In 1893 he became secretary and manager of the Lake Ranch Cattle Company, Raton, N. Mex., and a year or two later, with a partner, started a similar business of his own, which, however, was not successful.

One day he happened to pick up parts of an airbrake triple valve from a wrecked freight train, which so fascinated him that he spent days studying it until he had mastered its intricacies. Ideas for improvements came to him and in 1897, to gain mechanical experience, he obtained a job as a car repairer for the Atchison, Topeka & Santa Fé Railway. During the succeeding six years he rose to be mechanical instructor for the entire system and gained a wide reputation as a mechanical genius, particularly in the airbrake field. Meanwhile, he devised and patented several airbrake improvements. In 1903 he entered the employ of the Westinghouse Air Brake Company at Wilmerding, Pa., as mechanical expert and applied himself to the betterment of the existing braking equipment. His advancement was rapid; in 1910 he was made chief engineer and in 1916, manager of engineering, which position he held at the time of his death. During his career Turner acquired over 400 patents and gained the reputation of being the foremost pneumatic engineer in the world. One of his greatest inventions was the "K" triple valve, first patented Oct. 25, 1904, of which at the time of his death there were more than 2,000,000 in use. This valve solved many difficulties connected with the operation of long freight trains, making it possible to handle a train of 100 or more cars, whereas previously the maximum had been fifty; this gain led in its turn to the building of heavier locomotives and larger capacity cars. By the use of this valve, also, passenger trains could be brought to a stop in half the distance formerly required. Another invention, the electro-pneumatic brake, permitted a vast increase in traffic in subways and elevated railways without any increase in rolling stock. One of his last achievements was the system for automatically increasing or decreasing the braking power of a car as the number of passengers increased or decreased.

Turner was a frequent contributor to technical publications and often lectured before engineering societies of which he was a member. He was also the author of books regarded as classics in their field. Among these are *Development in Air Brakes for Railroads* (1909), and *Collection of Air Brake Papers* (n.d.). In 1911, for his paper "The Air Brake as Related to Progress in Locomotion" (*Journal of the Franklin Institute*, December 1910, January 1911), he was awarded

Turney

the Edward Longstreth medal of merit by the Franklin Institute, Philadelphia, which organization likewise awarded him the Elliott Cresson gold medal in 1912 for his airbrake inventions and developments. On Dec. 9, 1887, he married Beatrice Woolford at Wakefield, England, and at the time of his death at Wilkinsburg, Pa., he was survived by his widow and three children.

[*Jour. of the Franklin Institute*, Mar. 1919; *Mechanical Engineering*, Apr. 1919; *Railway Rev.*, Jan. 11, 1919; *Railway Age*, Jan. 10, 1919; *Railway and Engineering Rev.*, Mar. 24, 1906; *Pittsburgh Post* and *Pittsburg Dispatch*, Jan. 10, 1919; *Who's Who in America*, 1918–19; Patent Office records.] C. W. M.

TURNEY, PETER (Sept. 22, 1827–Oct. 19, 1903), jurist, governor of Tennessee, Confederate soldier, the son of Hopkins Lacy and Teresa (Francis) Turney, was born at Jasper, Marion County, Tenn. His father, the son of a German immigrant, was a prominent figure in Tennessee politics, serving as a member of the state legislature (1828–37), representative in Congress (1837–43), and United States senator (1845–51). His mother's family was of prominent Virginia stock which emigrated to Tennessee late in the eighteenth century. Peter was educated in the public schools at Winchester, Franklin County, and at a private school in Nashville. At the age of seventeen he became surveyor but soon abandoned this work to read law in his father's office. Following his admission to the bar in 1848, he practised in partnership with his father until the latter's death in 1857. He was twice married: first, in 1851, to Cassandra Garner of Winchester, who died in 1857; and second, in 1858, to Hannah F. Graham of Marion County; by his first wife he had three children, and by his second, nine.

Following the election of Lincoln in 1860, Turney became an active advocate of secession, and was one of the leaders in the attempt to secure a convention to take Tennessee out of the Union. When this proposal was rejected by popular vote in February 1861, he led the citizens of Franklin County in the adoption of an ordinance withdrawing their county from Tennessee and attaching it to Alabama. He at once raised a volunteer regiment and marched it to Virginia, where it was mustered into the Confederate service as the 1st Tennessee, with himself as colonel. He was attached to the Army of Northern Virginia, and served under "Stonewall" Jackson until the battle of Fredericksburg, Dec. 13, 1862, when Turney was wounded. On his recovery he was transferred to Florida, where he surrendered in May 1865.

At the close of the war he resumed his law practice at Winchester, and soon gained political

72

prominence through his opposition to the reconstruction program of Gov. William G. Brownlow [*q.v.*]. When the Democrats gained control of the state in 1870, he was elected a member of the supreme court and was reëlected in 1878 and 1886, serving as chief justice from 1886 to 1893. In his work as a judge he was described by a contemporary as "one who refuses to conform to custom and defies classification" (Pitts, *post*, p. 72). He impressed his associates as a man of strong common sense with a clear perception of practical justice, who framed his opinions by going at once to the heart of a case and deciding it and then giving briefly his reasons with little citation of authorities.

Although he had taken little active part in politics, he was known to be a Democrat of the conservative school, and therefore was selected by that element of his party to become its candidate for governor in 1892, with the hope that the party might be saved from the threatened domination of the agrarian movement. He won the election and during his first term was able to preserve nominal harmony in the party, although he failed to appeal to the younger and rural element. As a result his candidacy for reëlection in 1894 was a close contest in which H. Clay Evans [*q.v.*], his Republican opponent, received a bare majority of the votes on the face of election returns. The Democratic leaders at once raised a charge of fraud and demanded a recount by the legislature. A legislative investigating committee finally reported that an "honest count" gave the victory to Turney by a majority of over 2,000 votes. As a result of the antipathy thus aroused, he was not considered again for public office and at the close of his term, in 1897, he returned to his home at Winchester, where he died.

[Sources include John Allison, *Notable Men of Tenn.* (1905) ; J. T. Moore and A. P. Foster, *Tenn. the Volunteer State* (4 vols., 1923) ; D. M. Robison, *Bob Taylor and the Agrarian Revolt in Tenn.* (1935) ; J. A. Pitts, *Personal and Professional Reminiscences of an Old Lawyer* (1930) ; O. R. Temple, *East. Tenn. and the Civil War* (1899) ; *Biog. Dir. Am. Cong.* (1928) ; *Who's Who in America*, 1903–05 ; *Nashville Banner*, Oct. 19, 1903. Turney's supreme court opinions are in 47–92 *Tenn. Reports* ; official records of his terms as governor are in House and Senate Jours. of the 48th and 49th Tenn. Gen. Assemblies ; the legislative report on the election of 1894 was published with the title, *Contest for Gov. of Tenn., Complete Proceedings of the Joint Convention and the Investigating Committee* (2 vols., 1895).]   W. C. B.

TUTHILL, WILLIAM BURNET (Feb. 11, 1855–Aug. 25, 1929), architect, was born in New York City, the son of George F. and Jane (Price) Tuthill. On his father's side he was descended from Henry Tuthill who came to America about 1637 and about 1644 settled in Southold, L. I. After graduating from the College of the City of New York in 1875, Tuthill entered the office of Richard Morris Hunt [*q.v.*], where he carried on his architectural studies for two years. In 1877 he opened his own office. He had an extensive practice for over fifty years. His most important work was Carnegie Hall in New York City (1891), with Dankmar Adler and Louis H. Sullivan of Chicago as associate architects. Adler and Sullivan were engaged because of the Auditorium in Chicago, which they had just completed, but there is little evidence that they exercised more than a general supervision of practical matters. Carnegie Hall was acoustically a tremendous success. In its design Tuthill studied the acoustics of all the more important European concert halls, and as a result developed an unusual empirical command of the subject that led him to be called in as consultant for many churches and concert halls. A valuable manuscript monograph on the subject still exists (1936) in the possession of his son. Among Tuthill's other buildings were the Harlem Young Women's Christian Association (1888), the Jekyl Island Club, Jekyl Island, Ga. (1888), the Princeton Inn, Princeton, N. J. (1893), a Carnegie library, Pittsburgh (1894) ; and the Post Graduate Medical School and Hospital (1892), the Women's Medical College of the New York Infirmary (1900), the Columbia Yacht Club (1900), the Home for the Friendless (1902), and the white marble Schinasi residence (1909), all in New York City. He also had charge of the alteration of the Church of the Messiah, New York City (1918). Tuthill's architecture is on a broadly eclectic basis ; often, as the taste of the time decreed, over-lavish in surface decoration. But beneath its peculiarities of detail the basic creative planning is sound and practical ; after over forty years Carnegie Hall is still the musical center of New York, and the wide-spreading, low-pitched roofs of the Columbia Yacht Club are inviting and excellent in mass.

In addition to being an able architect, Tuthill was one of those born musicians who seem to develop naturally into the art, without much training. Possessed of an excellent tenor voice, he joined the Oratorio Society of New York in 1878 and for many years served as its secretary (1881–1917). He was also an accomplished 'cellist and was a member of an amateur quartet, which, with changing membership, played weekly for over thirty-six years. He was an intimate friend of most of the musical world of New York of his time. In 1891 he was a member of the board of directors of the concerts given in Carnegie Hall under Walter Damrosch. In 1919 he and his son were the founders of the Society for the Publication of American Music, and served as executive officers. His exuberant vitality can be seen in the fact that in addition to his architecture and his music, he found time to write several once-popular architectural books: *Practical Lessons in Architectural Drawing* (copyright 1881), which passed through many editions; *Interiors and Interior Details* (1882); *The City Residence, Its Design and Construction* (1890); *The Suburban Cottage, Its Design and Construction* (2nd ed., 1891); and *The Cathedral Church of England* (1923). In 1881 he married Henrietta Elizabeth Corwin of Newburgh, N. Y., who died Mar. 11, 1917. She was an organist and pianist. They had two children, a daughter who died as an infant, and a son who became a musician.

[For information on Henry Tuthill, see G. F. Tuttle, *The Descendants of William and Elizabeth Tuttle* (1883). See *Music Festival . . . for the Inauguration of the Music Hall Founded by Andrew Carnegie* (1891) and *Festival of Music: the Oratorio Soc. of N. Y., 1920* for Tuthill's musical activities, and obituary in *N. Y. Times,* Aug. 27, 1929. Family information has been supplied by Burnet C. Tuthill, Tuthill's son.]

T. F. H.

TUTTLE, CHARLES WESLEY (Nov. 1, 1829–July 17, 1881), astronomer, writer on historical and antiquarian subjects, lawyer, was born at Newfield, Me., the eldest of the seven children of Moses and Mary (Merrow) Tuttle. His father was descended from John Tuttle (or Tuthill) who by 1640 had settled at Dover, N. H., and his mother from Dr. Samuel Merrow (or Merry) who as early as 1720 was living at Dover. At Newfield he became especially interested in natural history and astronomy, and in his teens he constructed a small telescope. Following his mother's death in 1845, he lived with relatives at Dover. Under the influence of an uncle, he became a carpenter's apprentice, devoting his spare time to astronomy, mathematics, and history. In 1849 he went to Cambridge, Mass., and began work as a carpenter. With the aid of Truman Henry Safford [q.v.], whom he met there, he gained admission to the Harvard Observatory, where he so impressed the director, William Cranch Bond [q.v.], by his knowledge of astronomy that in October 1850 he was appointed an assistant. He immediately began taking part in the program set for the great equatorial. On Nov. 15, 1850, he made his most important contribution to astronomy by explaining Saturn's "dusky" ring (see W. C. Bond, "Observations on the Planet Saturn," *Annals of the Astronomical Observatory of Harvard College,* vol. II, 1857). Outside the routine of the Observatory he compared "the lustre of the stars" at sea level (the Isles of Shoals) and on

the summit of Mount Washington (1852), independently discovered Comet 1853 I (*Astronomical Journal,* Mar. 15, p. 47, Apr. 25, 1853, p. 72), computed cometary orbits and ephemerides, and took part in the eclipse expedition to the summit of Mount Washington in May 1854. By this time the effects of observation on his eyes made it clear that he must give over his ambitions in practical astronomy, and he resigned as observer to begin the study of law at the Harvard Law School in September 1854. In August 1855 he visited England on an expedition for the United States Coast Survey. He was admitted to the bar in March 1856 at Boston, where he began practice. In 1857 he opened an office in Newburyport, Mass., but returned to Boston about 1858. He was admitted to practice in the United States circuit courts (1858) and before the United States Supreme Court (1861). In 1860 he was appointed a United States commissioner and in 1874 took testimony for use before the Court of Alabama Claims.

As a result of historical and antiquarian studies connected with Maine and New Hampshire, he contributed many articles, often brief but of rich content, to such publications as the *New-England Historical and Genealogical Register,* the *Proceedings of the Massachusetts Historical Society, Notes and Queries,* and to newspapers of Dover and Boston. After his death appeared his *Capt. John Mason* (1887), edited by J. W. Dean, and *Capt. Francis Champernowne . . . and Other Historical Papers* (1889), edited by A. H. Hoyt. He was always the discriminating, accurate scholar, the master of clear, concise expression, interested only in bringing the facts to light. From time to time he addressed historical societies, and showed his continued interest in astronomy by occasional lectures as well as by observations and computations. He was a member of many historical and antiquarian societies. He received the honorary degree of A.M. from Harvard in 1854 and of Ph.D. from Dartmouth in 1880. He married, Jan. 31, 1872, Mary Louisa Park, daughter of John C. Park of Boston, who survived him.

[See C. W. Tuttle, "The Tuttle Family of New Hampshire," *New-Eng. Hist. and Geneal. Reg.,* Apr. 1867; John Wentworth, *The Wentworth Geneal.* (2nd ed., 1878), vol. I, p. 260, vol. II, p. 284; J. W. Dean, in C. W. Tuttle, *Capt. Francis Champernowne* (1889), the most complete account, and in *New-Eng. Hist. and Geneal. Reg.,* Jan. 1888; E. F. Slafter, in *Proc. Mass. Hist. Soc.,* 2 ser., vol. I (1885); *Annals of the Astronomical Observatory of Harvard Coll.,* vol. I (1856), p. clxxix; S. I. Bailey, *The Hist. and Work of Harvard Observatory* (1931); obituary in *Boston Daily Advertiser,* July 18, 1881. In the lib. of the New-Eng. Hist.-Geneal. Soc., Boston, is galley proof of an article on Tuttle written during his lifetime.] J. M. P—r.

TUTTLE, DANIEL SYLVESTER (Jan. 26, 1837–Apr. 17, 1923), bishop of the Protestant Episcopal Church, was a descendant of William Tuttle, or Tothill as the name was spelled in Devonshire, who settled in New Haven (Conn.) in 1639. His great-grandfather, Jehiel Tuttle, was an officer in the French and Indian War, his grandfather, Charles, a soldier of the Revolution. Second son among four children of Daniel Bliss Tuttle and Abigail Clark (Stimson), Daniel Sylvester was born in Windham, N. Y., where his father was the village blacksmith. Family devotions were regularly held in his parents' Methodist home, but it was Thomas S. Judd, Windham's Episcopal rector, whose kindly interest in the boy inclined him toward the ministry. Following such education as the district school afforded and three years under Judd's tutelage, he entered the academy in Delhi, N. Y., in 1850, paying part of his way by milking cows and by assistant teaching. In 1853 he was baptized in the Episcopal Church and confirmed by Bishop Wainwright. Using money he earned by teaching for a year in Scarsdale, N. Y., he enrolled in Columbia College as a sophomore in 1854 and graduated in 1857, second in his class. After two years as a tutor in New York, he entered the General Theological Seminary, from which he was graduated in 1862. On June 29 of that year he was ordered deacon and on July 19, 1863, he was elevated to the priesthood having gone meanwhile to Morris, N. Y., to assist Rev. George L. Foote, whom he succeeded, and whose daughter, Harriet Minerva, he married on Sept. 12, 1865.

While ministering diligently among his rural parishioners, he was surprised, Oct. 5, 1866, by election as missionary bishop of Montana with jurisdiction in Utah and Idaho. Not yet thirty, he remained in Morris till he reached the required age and then after consecration in Trinity Chapel, New York, May 1, 1867, left his wife and infant son behind and went to his new field. For the next nineteen years he labored in the rocky vineyard of the Northwest. Of powerful frame and democratic, "Bishop Dan" was well fitted for frontier life. His letters to his wife (*Reminiscences, post*) present a vivid picture of the region and its hindrances to the advancement of the gospel. In 1868 he was elected bishop of Missouri, but because he felt that his part in the winning of the West had just begun, did not accept. The following year he established his family in Salt Lake City, where he and the Mormons grew to respect each other, despite their religious differences (*Ibid.*, ch. xii). A second call to Missouri he accepted in 1886, and thereafter St. Louis was his home.

On Sept. 7, 1903, through seniority, he became presiding bishop of his church. A harmonizer whose utterances were marked by liberality and courtesy, he took virtually no part in church controversy, although he vigorously opposed the movement toward the election of presiding bishops, on the ground that God should designate the church's head (*Churchman*, Aug. 23, 1913). His humility, kindly wit, sagacity, and long years of service endeared him to all groups. A deep, resonant voice made the more impressive his carefully prepared sermons, while his long snow-white beard, high bald head, and dignified bearing gave him a striking presence. From middle life he was quite deaf and presided over meetings only with the aid of an informer. He was physically strong, however, made a practice of walking the two miles from his St. Louis home to the downtown cathedral, and at his summer place at Wequetonsing, Mich., he was swimming and cutting wood after he was eighty. From its founding he was a trustee of the Missouri Botanical Garden.

He died at the age of eighty-six, of grippe contracted while conducting a funeral. He had been a bishop for fifty-six years, and had helped consecrate eighty-nine bishops. Predeceased by his wife (1899) and four children, he was survived by two sons. St. Louis mourned him as its most distinguished citizen, and a $500,000 building was reared in his memory, adjoining his beloved Christ Church cathedral. Wholly expressive of the man was the inscription placed by his desire on his gravestone in Bellefontaine Cemetery: "God be merciful to me a sinner."

[Tuttle's own *Reminiscences of a Missionary Bishop* (1906) chronicle his life until his removal to the Missouri diocese. See also: G. F. Tuttle, *The Descendants of William and Elizabeth Tuttle* (1883); *Who's Who in America*, 1922–23; Wm. Hyde and H. L. Conard, *Encyc. of the Hist. of St. Louis* (1899), vol. IV; *Church News* (St. Louis), May 1923, and Sept.-Oct. 1924; *The Living Church Annual, 1924* (1923); *St. Louis Post-Dispatch*, Oct. 23, 1921, Apr. 17, 18, 20, 1923; *Living Church*, Oct. 11, Dec. 6, 1924; *Churchman*, Apr. 28, 1923; information from Mrs. George M. Tuttle of St. Louis. A life-size portrait by Charles F. Galt hangs in the Tuttle Memorial.]   I. D.

TUTTLE, HERBERT (Nov. 29, 1846–June 21, 1894), historian, college professor, was born in Bennington, Vt., the son of Charles J. Tuttle and Evaline (Boynton) Tuttle. In 1853 the family moved to Hoosick Falls, N. Y. As a student in the University of Vermont, from which he was graduated in 1869, Tuttle attracted the attention of President James B. Angell [*q.v.*], his first teacher of history, who noted the orderliness of his mind and his keen interest in the growth of political institutions. Tuttle desired to make journalism his profession, and President Angell aided him in securing a position on the *Boston Daily Advertiser,* which he held nearly two years, for a time acting as Washington correspondent. Still richer opportunities for observation came in October 1871, when he began a long residence in Europe, at first as special correspondent of the *Advertiser* in Paris, and from 1873 to 1879 as Berlin correspondent of the London *Daily News.* In 1872 he reported the proceedings of the Court of Alabama Claims at Geneva for the *New York Tribune,* and it was probably upon the recommendation of George W. Smalley [*q.v.*], London correspondent of the *Tribune,* that the great London daily offered this young American of twenty-six so important a post as Berlin.

Tuttle had not been in Berlin long before he conceived the idea of writing a history which should show the relation of the earlier Prussia, and especially the work of Frederick the Great, to the triumphant Prussia and Germany of the seventies. He had discovered "how inadequate was Carlyle's account . . . of the working system of the Prussian government" (*History of Prussia,* 1888, vol. II, p. vi). When Andrew D. White [*q.v.*] went to Berlin in 1879 as American minister, he encouraged Tuttle's project and suggested an academic career. President Angell, now at the University of Michigan, gave him his first appointment, inviting him to lecture on international law (1880–81) during his own absence in China. In the fall of 1881 White, as president of Cornell University, gave him a similar appointment, and until 1883 he divided his time between Michigan and Cornell. In 1883 he was made associate professor at Cornell. In 1887 he was promoted to a full professorship, with the history of political institutions added to his title. In 1890 he was made professor in his chosen field, Modern European history. While he was still in Berlin he had published a volume of essays on *German Political Leaders* (New York, 1876). The first volume of his *History of Prussia* (dated 1884) appeared late in 1883, an introduction covering the period from 1134 to 1740. Of the five planned (an introduction and four volumes on Frederick the Great), Tuttle lived to complete only the introduction, two volumes on Frederick (1888), and part of a third (1896). His health broke down in 1893, and he died in Ithaca on June 21, 1894. His *History of Prussia* is based upon documentary collections, edited mainly by German scholars, and upon monographs published since Carlyle wrote. His career as a teacher was equally significant. His

students remembered him as incisive and judicial, with a horror of exaggeration or inaccuracy. His comments were occasionally touched by a sub-acid wit. He had little sympathy with the more radical plans of departmental organization, and when, upon the recommendation of President Charles Kendall Adams [*q.v.*], the trustees of the university created "The President White School of History and Political Science," in recognition of White's gift of his noble library, Tuttle so vigorously opposed the appointment of a dean of the School that the plan was not fully carried through. Tuttle was one of the original members of the American Historical Association, and was a frequent contributor to learned and critical journals. On July 6, 1875, he married Mary McArthur Thompson of Hillsboro, Ohio, who survived him.

[Tuttle's full name was Charles Herbert Tuttle, but he dropped the first name before 1876. Sources include J. F. and C. H. Boynton, *The Boynton Family* (1897); H. B. Adams, in Tuttle's *Hist. of Prussia,* vol. IV (1896), pp. xi–xlvi, an amplification of an article in *Ann. Report Am. Hist. Asso. . . . 1894* (1895); W. T. Hewett, *Cornell Univ.: A Hist.* (1905), vol. II; H. M. Jones, *The Life of Moses Coit Tyler* (1933), based on an unpublished dissertation by T. E. Casady; Mary M. T. Tuttle, *Memorial to Herbert Tuttle* (priv. printed, 1910); obituaries in *Evening Post* (N. Y.) and *N. Y. Tribune,* June 22, 1894; recollections of Tuttle's colleagues. A bibliog. of Tuttle's writings appears in his *Hist. of Prussia,* vol. IV (1896).] H. E. B.

TUTWILER, HENRY (Nov. 16, 1807–Sept. 22, 1884), Alabama educator, was born in Harrisonburg, Va., the son of Henry and Margaret (Lorchbaugh) Tutwiler. He was of German descent, and there was a family tradition that his ancestors came from the German section of Switzerland, settling first in Pennsylvania and moving later into the Valley of Virginia. The boy was for the most part self-taught, although for a short time he attended a school kept by a Presbyterian minister, the Rev. Daniel Baker [*q.v.*]. When the University of Virginia opened its doors in 1825, Tutwiler was one of the first students to enroll. He devoted himself to mathematics and the classics and completed his course in 1829, but spent another year in the University studying law. More than fifty years later he delivered an address before the alumni of the University published under the title *Early Years of the University of Virginia* (1882). In 1831, when the newly established University of Alabama was seeking a faculty, the trustees turned to the University of Virginia to find professors, and Henry Tutwiler was highly recommended for the chair of ancient languages. He moved to Alabama in that same year and made his home there for the remainder of his life.

It was said of Tutwiler that although he held

the professorship of ancient languages he was really a whole faculty, for he had a knowledge of law and was a student of science as well, showing special interest in chemistry and astronomy. The early years of the University of Alabama were not happy, and in 1837 the entire faculty resigned. For the next ten years Tutwiler held professorships in various small colleges in Alabama and at the end of that time turned to the fulfilment of a life-long ambition, the education of boys. Near the village of Havana, in the present Hale (then part of Greene) County, he opened in 1847 Greene Springs School for Boys, which soon attained wide recognition for the advanced ideas of education it embodied. Called the "Rugby of the South," it gave training primarily in the classics and mathematics, but laid an emphasis on the sciences which was unusual. Even more unusual in the equipment of a preparatory school of that time were its chemical laboratory, telescope, and library of 1,500 volumes.

Tutwiler insisted that trained teachers were as important for his boys as for college students, and the faculty of the Greene Springs School compared very favorably with those of the colleges of the day. Respect for the individual student was an important tenet of his educational creed: corporal punishment was forbidden, and students were not divided into classes, but in each study the student was placed in the class which he was prepared to enter. Tutwiler remained at the head of the Greene Springs School until his death in 1884, twice declining the presidency of the University of Alabama with the statement that he was determined never again to put himself in any position where he could not be his own master. His scholarly interests filled his life and left small place for other things. He was a Whig and opposed secession, but he took no active part in the political events of his day. Nevertheless, though indirect, his influence in the life of the South through the students who went out from the Greene Springs School was very great. Tutwiler was married in Tuscaloosa, Dec. 24, 1835, to Julia Ashe, of a distinguished North Carolina family. He died at Greene Springs, survived by eleven children, one of whom, Julia Strudwick Tutwiler [q.v.], was also a noted educator.

[T. M. Owen, *Hist. of Ala. and Dict. of Ala. Biog.* (1921), vol. IV; Willis Brewer, *Alabama* (1872); W. G. Clark, *Hist. of Educ. in Ala.* (1889); A. B. Moore, *Hist. of Ala.* (1927), vol. I; T. C. McCorvey, "Henry Tutwiler and the Influence of the University of Virginia on Education in Alabama," *Trans. Ala. Hist. Soc.* (1904), vol. V; P. A. Bruce, *Hist. of the Univ. of Va.*, vols. II, III (1920–21); *Montgomery Advertiser*, Sept. 26, 1884; *Daily Register* (Mobile), Sept. 27, 1884.]

H. F.

TUTWILER, JULIA STRUDWICK (Aug. 15, 1841–Mar. 24, 1916), educator, social reformer, was born in Greene Springs, Ala., the daughter of Henry Tutwiler [q.v.] and Julia (Ashe). Her father had views of education far in advance of the practices of his day and in 1847 established at Greene Springs a boys' school in which to carry out his ideas. One of his convictions was that his daughters should be as well educated as his sons. Julia, who was the third girl in the family, responded eagerly to the teaching offered her and after receiving her early training from her father, was sent for two years of study in Philadelphia. In January 1866 she enrolled in Vassar College, where she remained for half a school year. She showed unusual ability in languages, and was subsequently permitted to spend a year in Lexington, Va., studying Greek and Latin under the tuition of professors in Washington and Lee University. Still later, after teaching for a time in the Tuscaloosa Female Seminary, she spent three years in advanced study in Germany and France at a time when such study was most unusual for a woman. At the end of this period she passed the government examinations required of teachers in the Prussian schools and received a teacher's certificate.

She returned to Alabama in 1876 and devoted the rest of her life to education and social service there. She introduced kindergarten methods which she had learned in Germany and taught for a time in her father's school at Greene Springs, but her primary interest was in the education of women. In 1882, while she was co-principal of the Livingston Female Academy at Livingston, Ala., she persuaded the state legislature to appropriate $2,500 to establish a normal department in the school—the first gift, according to her own statement (Bennett, *post*, p. 13), which the women of Alabama had ever received from the state. As a result, the Alabama Normal College was incorporated Feb. 22, 1883, with Julia Tutwiler as co-principal. In 1888 she became sole principal, and later her title was changed to president.

The creation of a normal school was only the first step in her long struggle to secure vocational training for women in Alabama. Her paper, "The Technical Education of Women" (*Education*, Boston, November 1882), attracted wide attention and had considerable influence. In 1893 with the support of the women of the state and the agricultural interests, she secured a grant from the legislature for the Alabama Girls Industrial School, which was opened in October 1896 at Montevallo, Shelby County. She was offered the presidency of this school but declined. In 1896 she persuaded officials of the University of Alabama to permit several young women prepared at the Alabama Normal College to enter the junior year in the University and to reside in a cottage on the campus. In this first year these women captured sixty per cent. of the honors awarded to the junior class, and in 1900, when the first women received degrees from the University, four of the six honors awarded to graduates went to "Miss Julia's" students. After that experiment the doors of the University were thrown open to women on equal terms with men.

Active also in prison reform in Alabama, she was for many years the superintendent of prison and jail work for the Woman's Christian Temperance Union. Her efforts were instrumental in securing the classification of prisoners and the separation of the sexes, the first juvenile reform school, and the first law providing for the inspection of jails and prisons. She labored to secure the establishment of night schools and vocational education in prisons, and fought the convict leasing system, although she never succeeded in driving it from the state. She wrote many magazine articles on subjects relating to prison reform and the education of women, and composed poems for her own pleasure. One of these, "Alabama," has become the state song. In 1910 she became president emeritus of the Alabama Normal College, and six years later died in Birmingham.

[T. M. Owen, *Hist. of Ala. and Dict. of Ala. Biog.* vol. IV (1921); *A Woman of the Century* (1893), ed. by F. E. Willard and M. A. Livermore; *Who's Who in America*, 1916–17; I. H. Weed, in *Am. Mag.*, Sept. 1911; Helen C. Bennett, "Julia Tutwiler, First Citizen of Alabama," *Pictorial Rev.*, Apr. 1913; Edna Kroman, "Julia S. Tutwiler, Pioneer in Education of Women in Alabama," *Birmingham News*, July 22, 1923; H. L. Hargrove, *Julia S. Tutwiler of Alabama* (n.d.); *Montgomery Advertiser* (Montgomery, Ala.), Mar. 25, 1916.]
H. F.

TWACHTMAN, JOHN HENRY (Aug. 4, 1853–Aug. 8, 1902), painter, was born in Cincinnati, Ohio, the son of Frederick Christian and Sophia (Droege) Twachtman. Both his parents came from the province of Hanover, Germany. His father, born in Erichshagen, where his forebears had been for several generations prosperous farmers, came to America at an early age and settled in Cincinnati. As a boy John helped his father in making decorated window shades. Later he studied drawing at the night school of the Ohio Mechanics' Institute, and at the University of Cincinnati School of Design. In 1875, with Frank Duveneck [q.v.], the son of family friends, Twachtman went to Munich. After working there two years under Ludwig Löfftz, he joined Duveneck and William Merritt Chase [q.v.] at Venice for a year. Returning to America in 1878, he painted in New York (1879) and at Avondale, near Cincinnati. He spent the winter of 1880 in Florence, where Duveneck had settled the year before. After his marriage in the spring of 1881 to Marthe Scudder, daughter of Jane (Hannah) and John Milton Scudder [q.v.], he traveled abroad, visiting London and spending a short time in Holland. At Schleissheim, near Munich, he painted a number of large canvases directly from nature and, after a short stay in Venice, returned to New York. In 1883 he was again in Europe, this time studying in Paris at the Julian Atelier under Jules Joseph Lefebvre and Gustave Boulanger. In the summer he painted at Honfleur and at Arques-la-Bataille, near Dieppe, where he produced many of the most characteristic examples of this period. After wintering in Venice (1884), he returned to the United States. He had sent many of his pictures in advance, but unhappily the ship was lost at sea and with it much of the best work of Twachtman's continental experience.

After unsuccessfully endeavoring to combine farming and painting, Twachtman worked in Chicago on one of the great war cycloramas, then popular, picturing the battle of Gettysburg. In 1888 he joined his friend, Julian Alden Weir [q.v.], at Branchville, Conn. In the fall of 1889 he acquired a place near Greenwich, Conn., and there during the following ten years many of his finest pictures were painted. At this time he became an instructor of the antique class at the Art Students' League, a position he held until his death. From his anchorage at Round Hill he made several more distant excursions in order to paint Niagara Falls and Yellowstone Park. Later he spent the summers at Gloucester, Mass., in company with Duveneck, J. R. De Camp, C. A. Corwin, and E. H. Potthast, whom he had known in Florence. Separated from his family, he lived much alone. Never robust in physique, he was somewhat indifferent and careless about his health. He died at Gloucester, still comparatively young, survived by his wife and five children. Prizes awarded him included a medal at the World's Columbian Exposition, Chicago (1893); the Webb Prize, Society of American Artists (1888); the Temple gold medal, Pennsylvania Academy of the Fine Arts (1895); and a silver medal, Pan-American Exposition, Buffalo (1901). He was a member of the Society of American Artists, from which he later resigned, the Ten American Painters, the New York Etching Club, and the Pastel Club, New York.

The art of John Twachtman falls into three distinct periods. The work of the first period (1875–81) is characterized by strong contrast of values, in subdued variations of brown and black; vigorous brushwork, the pigment heavily applied; and direct rendering from nature. The small decorative panels of buildings, shipping, and waterways painted at Venice are more spirited and personal than the larger and more ambitious landscapes of the same time. Among the pictures of the early period are the highly original "Brooklyn Bridge"; the "Italian Landscape," dated 1878, in the Museum of Fine Arts, Boston; the graphic and powerfully realistic "Oyster Boats," dated New York, 1879, and the "Venice" with the dogana in the background.

The second period is marked by a reaction against the heavy impasto and dark tones of the Munich tradition. The color is in variations of silvery greys and greens, showing a close study of relative values and atmospheric perspective; the pigment is applied thinly with a delicate but precise technique over a fine French linen; the composition is restricted to very simple themes. There is seldom an attempt at sunlight or full color. Most characteristic of Twachtman's style at this time are the pictures painted in France and Holland, notably the "Arques-la-Bataille" dated 1885; "Windmills," with striking silhouette and effective spatial arrangements; "Canal Boats"; "Winding Path"; the "Sketch" in the Museum of Fine Arts, Boston; and "L'Étang."

The final period belongs to America. It was not until Twachtman settled at Greenwich in 1889 that he seems definitely to have found himself. Impressionism had in the meantime an obvious influence on his development. From subdued hues of neutral greys the color changes to the higher key of sunlight, the delicately attuned relations of gold, blue, and violet, or the ethereal and pallid harmony of winter landscape. The painter's artistic nature is revealed in delicacy rather than strength, in the sensitive rather than the striking, in the subtle rather than the obvious. He was a master of nuance; his mood is one of intimacy and charm. He was not a realist in the literal sense of the term and openly declared the decorative intention of his work. Particularly worthy of note in the final period are the series of waterfalls painted on Twachtman's own place at Greenwich and the pictures of winter—"Falls in January," the ice and snow patterned against the turbulent brook; "The Cascade"; and similar motives in the Metropolitan Museum and the Worcester Art Museum, Worcester, Mass.; "Snow," in the Worcester Art Museum; "Old Mill in Winter"; "Round Hill Road," in the National Gallery of Art, Washington; "February," in the Museum of Fine Arts, Boston; "Snowbound" and "Hemlock Pool," which Twachtman himself considered one of the best of his pictures. The figure subjects are less widely known, but they remain among the most personal and distinguished examples of Twachtman's brush. Most of the subjects are his own family, painted in the intimate environment of his home.

Twachtman occupies a unique position in American painting. Not following the earlier tradition, which portrayed the scenic aspects of nature or its romantic associations, he found his interest in the expressive organization of form, and the harmonic relation of line and color. His intention was more truly esthetic than pictorial. His art is therefore related to the doctrine of Whistler and the cult of "art for art's sake" so prevalent in the nineties. He had a militant dislike of conventional composition, banalities, and sentimentality. He took a purely sensuous delight in the beauty of the visible world, and a keen enjoyment in esthetic adventure. But if Whistler quickened Twachtman's artistic sensibility and stimulated the search for new discoveries in line and form, Monet awakened his appreciation of light and color. He thus responds to the two dominant influences of his generation. Dependent upon optical stimulation and the exhilaration of the moment, Twachtman's art lacks something of the intellectual and universal; finely attuned to the fleeting, it misses the eternal. Both his expression and presentation were nevertheless very personal and original. The distinction of his art rests upon beauty of design, harmonic tonal relations, and the sensitive interpretation of evanescent effect.

[Who's Who in America, 1901–02; Samuel Isham, The Hist. of Am. Painting (1927 ed.); Eliot Clark, in Art in America, Apr. 1919, Internat. Studio, Jan. 1921, Scribner's Mag., Dec. 1922, and John Twachtman (1924); Allen Tucker, John Twachtman (copr. 1931); R. J. Wickeden, "The Art and Etchings of John Henry Twachtman," booklet published by Frederick Keppel & Co., New York; Carolyn C. Mase, in Internat. Studio, Jan. 1921; Margery A. Ryerson, in Art in America, Feb. 1920; Royal Cortissoz, in N. Y. Tribune, Jan. 12, 1919, reprinted in American Artists (1923); Charles De Kay, in Arts and Decoration, June 1918; C. C. Curran, in Lit. Miscellany, Winter 1910; J. Alden Weir and others, in North Am. Rev., Apr. 1903; obituary in N. Y. Times and editorial in N. Y. Daily Tribune, Aug. 9, 1902; information from Mrs. Twachtman.] E. C.

TWAIN, MARK [See CLEMENS, SAMUEL LANGHORNE, 1835–1910].

TWEED, WILLIAM MARCY (Apr. 3, 1823– Apr. 12, 1878), political boss, was born in New York City, the son of Richard and Eliza Tweed. His great-grandfather, a blacksmith, emigrated from Kelso, Scotland, in the middle of the eighteenth century. His father was a chairmaker, and young William was taken from the public school to begin learning the same trade at the age of eleven. At thirteen, however, he was apprenticed to a saddler and worked with him nearly two years. He then attended a private school at Elizabeth, N. J., for one winter, learned bookkeeping, and became a junior clerk in a mercantile office in New York. Meanwhile, his father had bought an interest in a small brush factory, and William at seventeen became its bookkeeper. He was made a member of the firm at nineteen. At twenty-one he married the daughter of the principal owner of the factory, Mary Jane Skaden. She bore him eight children and died in 1880. Tweed was a sober, steady young man, but big-bodied and powerful, and on occasion he could use his fists effectively. He became a volunteer fireman, and in 1848 helped to organize a new engine company, Americus No. 6. At the age of twenty-seven he was elected its foreman. The head of a tiger which was painted on the engine became in time the symbol of Tweed's political organization, Tammany Hall.

Volunteer fire companies were often stepping stones to political power, and Tweed's capacity for leadership, which began to display itself at an early age, inevitably led him into politics and alliance with Tammany. In 1850, the year he became foreman of "Big 6," he ran for assistant alderman in his home ward, but was defeated by a small margin. In 1851 he was nominated by the Democrats for alderman. There seemed small chance for him to win, but he persuaded a friend, a prominent educator, to run as an independent Whig, which split the Whig vote sufficiently to insure Tweed's election—his first venture in political strategy. The common council to which he was elected came to be known in New York as "The Forty Thieves." Tweed's capacity as an aldermanic grafter soon rendered further honest toil unnecessary. In 1852 he was elected to Congress, but served only two years (1853–55), continuing to sit as alderman. He preferred municipal politics. A wave of Know-Nothingism, however, caused his defeat for alderman in 1855. He and two other men, Peter B. Sweeny [q.v.] and Richard B. Connolly, later his chief partners in the "Tweed ring," had now begun to be drawn together in the faction of Tammany Hall opposing Mayor Fernando Wood [q.v.], who was finally forced out of the Hall. In 1856 Tweed was chosen as a member of the newly created, bi-partisan, popularly elected board of supervisors, intended to check corruption at elections, but which itself became an agency for graft.

Tweed was also appointed school commissioner. In 1857 he succeeded in having his friend Sweeny nominated for district attorney, and another ally, George G. Barnard, for recorder, and both were elected. Connolly was elected county clerk. Thus was the foundation laid for the Tweed machine.

He was now a sachem of Tammany, and by 1859 was considered one of the most powerful men in the organization. He well-nigh dominated the state Democratic convention of 1860 and sent his friend Barnard to the state supreme court bench. In 1861 he ran for sheriff, but lost. Nevertheless, he succeeded in bringing about the defeat of Wood for mayor, and one of his dearest aims was accomplished. But the campaign had cost him his entire fortune of about $100,000. He made the office of supervisor pay, however, and within two years, it is said, he had recovered practically half his loss. He was made chairman of the Democratic central committee of New York County in 1860. Another cog in his machine, A. Oakey Hall [q.v.], was now district attorney. Tweed had become chairman of Tammany's general committee, and thereafter was supreme dictator of nominations for mayor and other positions. He opened a law office in the autumn of 1860. His knowledge of law was small, but he collected some huge fees for "legal services," the Erie Railroad alone paying him more than $100,000. In 1864 he bought a controlling interest in a printing concern, which thereafter did all the city's printing and which all railroads, ferries, and insurance companies must patronize if they wished to stay in business. He also organized a marble company and bought a quarry in Massachusetts from which the stone for the new county court house—for that gigantic swindle was now under way—was bought at extortionate prices. By 1867 Tweed was doubtless a millionaire, and had moved his family from the lower East Side up to a Murray Hill residence just off Fifth Avenue. He assisted in launching the Brooklyn Bridge project in 1866, and received a $40,000 block of stock as his perquisite.

He practically secured control of the State in 1868, when he placed in the governor's chair John T. Hoffman [q.v.], who had been Tammany mayor of the city for two years. In Hoffman's stead as mayor the Tweed henchman, A. Oakey Hall, was elected. Another puppet was made speaker of the Assembly. Tweed had been elected state senator in 1867, and his luxurious, seven-room hotel suite in Albany was virtually state Democratic headquarters. He was still New York County Democratic chairman, and for New York City was school commissioner, assistant street commissioner, and president of the Board of Supervisors. In 1868 he realized a life-long ambition when he was made grand sachem of Tammany. In 1869 the "ring," convened in Albany, decided that all bills thereafter rendered against the city and county must be one-half fraudulent. Later the proportion was raised to 85 per cent. ("Report of the Special Committee of the Board of Aldermen," pp. 74-76, 397, 403). The money thus gained was to be divided into five parts, of which Tweed, City Chamberlain Sweeny, Comptroller Connolly, and Mayor Hall received one share each, while the fifth was used to bribe smaller politicians. Bogus naturalization of immigrants and repeating at elections were now carried to hitherto unknown lengths. Tweed was a partner with Jay Gould and James Fisk [qq.v.] in the plundering of the Erie Railroad, and was a director (often without investment) in banks, gas, and street railroad companies.

By this time Harper's Weekly, with Thomas Nast [q.v.] as its cartoonist, was beginning its long campaign against Tweed and his group (especially Jan. 22, 1870, and thereafter). But many leading citizens, Peter Cooper and Horace Greeley among the rest, were so deceived that they gave approval to the new city charter in 1870, which riveted the rule of the "ring" more firmly on the city. Samuel J. Tilden [q.v.] asserted that it cost Tweed more than a million dollars to put the charter through the legislature, and Tweed himself testified that he paid about $600,000 ("Report . . . of the Board of Aldermen," p. 73). The New York Times, under the ownership of George Jones [q.v.], began its attacks on Tweed late in 1870 (editorial, Sept. 20, 1870). The uncompleted county courthouse (its final cost was $12,000,000, of which two-thirds was fraudulent) had begun to arouse suspicion, but most of the newspapers and leading citizens were still servile in loyalty to the "ring" (see report of a committee of business men, Nov. 1, 1870, in N. Y. World, Nov. 6, N. Y. Times, Nov. 7). When Tweed's daughter was married in May 1871, gifts to her from prominent citizens were valued at $700,000. That spring Sheriff O'Brien and another discontented official turned over to the Times proofs of enormous swindling by the "ring." Learning that the Times had these figures, the boodlers offered Jones $5,000,000 not to publish them. Nast was offered $500,000 to cease his attacks. Both offers were rejected, and the Times published the evidence (especially July 8, July 20-29, 1871). On Sept. 4, 1871, at a mass meeting in Cooper Union, a committee of seventy was formed to

take action. An injunction was obtained against further taxation or payment of money. On Oct. 26, on Tilden's affidavit, a civil suit was brought to recover stolen money (N. Y. Times, Oct. 26, 27, 1871). Tweed's $2,000,000 bail was quickly raised, Jay Gould supplying $1,000,000. By fraud at the polls he was reëlected to the state Senate that autumn. On Dec. 16 he was arrested in a criminal action. Connolly, Sweeny, and others implicated had fled to Canada and Europe.

At Tweed's first criminal trial, the jury disagreed; but at the second, in November 1873, he was convicted and sentenced to twelve years in prison and a fine of $12,750. The court of appeals reduced the sentence to a year and a $250 fine, and in January 1875 Tweed left the prison on Blackwell's Island. He was at once rearrested on a civil action brought by the state to recover $6,000,000 of the "ring's" stealings. Failing to procure $3,000,000 bail, he was sent to prison. Here he was treated leniently, taking a carriage ride almost every afternoon, and frequently visiting his home, accompanied by two turnkeys. On Dec. 4, while visiting his home, he escaped by the back door while the turnkeys sat in the parlor. Aided by friends, he lay in hiding near New York for several weeks, then got away to Cuba, and from there went to Spain disguised as a common seaman. Identified by Spanish officials through a Nast cartoon (in Harper's Weekly, July 1, 1876), he was arrested and returned to America in November 1876. Judgment in the civil suit had been obtained against him in his absence, and in default of payment he was again committed to Ludlow Street Jail, this time in strict confinement. He was now failing steadily in health. Hoping that he might secure release from jail in return for his testimony, he supplied considerable information to the state, and before an aldermanic investigating committee in the winter of 1877-78 he testified frankly about many of his crooked transactions. He died in his room at the jail at the age of fifty-five. At his request, his wife and a married daughter had gone abroad to escape humiliation, and they were in Paris at the time of his death.

Tweed was genial and generous in disposition, and not vindictive toward his enemies. Nast's cartoons were not bad portraits of him, though his facial expression was milder and his photographs show that he might easily have been mistaken for a thoroughly respectable man. He was crafty, but even more remarkable for boldness and plausibility. The amount which his "ring" filched from the city has been variously estimated at from $30,000,000 to $200,000,000.

[D. T. Lynch, *"Boss" Tweed* (1927); M. R. Werner, *Tammany Hall* (1928); R. H. Fuller, *Jubilee Jim: The Life of Colonel James Fisk, Jr.* (1928); obituaries and articles in *Evening Post* (N. Y.), *N. Y. Times, Sun* (N. Y.), *N. Y. Herald, N. Y. Tribune, World* (N. Y.), Apr. 12–14, 1878; "Report of the Special Committee of the Board of Aldermen Appointed to Investigate the 'Ring' Frauds," *Documents of the Board of Aldermen of the City of N. Y.... Part II—1877,* Doc. No. 8 (1878); C. F. Wingate, "An Episode in Municipal Government," *North American Review,* Oct. 1874, Jan., July 1875, Oct. 1876; W. C. Gover, *The Tammany Hall Democracy of the City of New York and the General Committee for 1875* (1875); A. P. Genung, *The Frauds of the New York City Government Exposed* (1871); S. J. Tilden, *The New York City "Ring"* (1873); Charles O'Conor, comp., *Peculation Triumphant* (1875), a collection of documents on the trials; J. D. Townsend, *New York in Bondage* (1895), by Tweed's counsel, 1876–78; H. L. Clinton, *Celebrated Trials* (1897); Harold Zink, *City Bosses in the United States* (1930), with good chapter on Tweed and definite references; scrapbooks of newspaper clippings relating to N. Y. City politics, N. Y. Pub. Lib.]
A. F. H.

TWICHELL, JOSEPH HOPKINS (May 27, 1838–Dec. 20, 1918), Congregational clergyman, was a native of Connecticut and spent practically his entire life there, becoming one of its best known and most beloved citizens. Born in the nearby town of Southington, he was called to Hartford in 1865 to take charge of the newly organized Asylum Hill Congregational Church and remained as pastor and pastor emeritus until his death more than fifty years later. He was the son of Edward Twichell, a tanner and manufacturer, by his first wife, Selina Delight Carter, his ancestry running back to Benjamin Twichell, born in Chesham Parish, Buckinghamshire, England, who emigrated to Massachusetts about 1630. Prepared for college in the schools of Southington, Joseph graduated from Yale with the class of 1859. He began his theological studies at Union Seminary, New York, but they were interrupted by the outbreak of the Civil War. From 1861 to 1864 he saw active service as chaplain of the 71st New York Volunteers, in the meantime, Jan. 30, 1863, being ordained in his native town. When mustered out, he entered Andover Theological Seminary, from which he graduated in 1865. That same year, recommended to the Asylum Hill Church by Horace Bushnell [q.v.], he began his Hartford pastorate, and on Nov. 1, married Julia Harmony Cushman of Orange, N. J., by whom he had nine children. For thirty-nine years (1874–1913) he was an active member of the Board of Fellows of Yale University.

During his half century in Hartford he exerted much influence in the religious and civic affairs of his city and state. He was handsome, athletic, abounding in good humor, and had a sympathetic understanding of all sorts and conditions of men, derived in part from his army experiences. His humanness is indicated by the fact that he was invariably alluded to as "Joe" Twichell. Although not a scholar in the academic use of the term, he had a well stocked and well disciplined mind, keen discernment, sound judgment, and a fine literary taste. His influence was exerted not only directly, but indirectly through his close association with newspaper editors, writers, and public officials, who held him in high esteem. He was so often introduced into Charles Dudley Warner's conversation "that many persons felt they had a certain acquaintance and wished they knew him better" (Mrs. J. T. Fields, *Charles Dudley Warner,* 1904, p. 41). Upon taking up his residence in Hartford, he at once became a member of the circle that included Warner, Calvin and Harriet Beecher Stowe [qq.v.], and other notable people. When Samuel L. Clemens [q.v.] came to the city in 1868 to supervise the publication of a book, he met Twichell and a most intimate friendship began. Twichell was one of the officiating clergymen at Clemens' wedding in Elmira; later the two were neighbors in Hartford; they tramped together, and traveled together. They were companions on the trip described in *A Tramp Abroad,* in which Twichell figures as "Harris" (Paine, *post,* II, 629, 666), and it was Twichell who made the suggestion that prompted the writing of the sketches which formed the basis of *Life on the Mississippi (Ibid.,* I, p. 531). In his description of the pastor's appearance in the pulpit with "green hair," the humorist affectionately immortalized his friend in a most amusing skit (*Mark Twain's Autobiography, post,* I, 342–43). They stood together, in a Republican stronghold, in support of Cleveland rather than Blaine for the presidency, a stand which almost cost Twichell his pastorate (*Ibid.,* II, 20–26). When apart, the two corresponded at length, their letters disclosing that there was no one to whom Clemens revealed his soul more fully than to Twichell. The latter's own literary output was not great. He made contributions to periodicals, among them "Mark Twain" (*Harper's Monthly,* May 1896), and "Qualities of Warner's Humor" (*The Century,* January 1903); and he published two more substantial works, *John Winthrop* (copr. 1891), in the Makers of America Series, and *Some Old Puritan Love-Letters* (1893), being the correspondence of John and Margaret Winthrop.

[R. E. Twichell, *Geneal. of the Twichell Family* (1929); *Yale Univ. Obit. Record ... 1919* (1920); A. B. Paine, *Mark Twain* (3 vols., 1912); *Mark Twain's Autobiog.* (2 vols., 1924); and *Mark Twain's Letters* (2 vols., 1917); *Who's Who in America,* 1918–19; *Congregationalist,* Jan. 2, 1919; *Hartford Daily*

Times, Dec. 20, 1918; *Hartford Daily Courant*, Dec. 21, 1918.]
H. E. S.

TWIGGS, DAVID EMANUEL (1790–July 15, 1862), soldier, the son of Brigadier- General John Twiggs, who was called the "Savior of Georgia" in the Revolution, and his wife, Ruth Emanuel, was born in Richmond County, Ga. He was appointed a captain in the 8th United States Infantry in March 1812, and served in minor capacities during the war with Great Britain. He became a major of the 28th Infantry in September 1814, but his regiment was disbanded the following June, and he was without a commission. When interest in military affairs revived, he was commissioned a major of the 1st Infantry on May 14, 1825, lieutenant-colonel of the 4th Infantry, July 15, 1831, and colonel of the 2nd Dragoons, June 8, 1836. It was in the last capacity that he joined Zachary Taylor's forces at the beginning of the War with Mexico. Shortly thereafter arose the unfortunate dispute between himself and Brevet Brigadier-General William J. Worth [*q.v.*], whose regular rank was that of colonel, junior to Twiggs. Through the awkward handling of this controversy over prestige and rank by Taylor, the troops lost confidence in all three of their superiors. Twiggs, however, gave a good account of himself at Palo Alto and Resaca de la Palma, so that, on June 30, 1846, he was promoted to the grade of regular brigadier-general. After the capture of Monterey, Taylor asked for another promotion for him, although Twiggs had ostensibly been ill and had taken no part in the fight. Singularly enough, he was brevetted a major-general for gallantry at Monterey.

Throughout the northern campaign he had commanded the 1st Division, but when Scott's southern campaign began he was withdrawn to the south. He served at Vera Cruz and commanded the vanguard of that army in its progress toward Mexico city. Although his leadership at Cerro Gordo was more intrepid than intelligent and his feint before Mexico city lacked vigor, his work mainly showed dogged perseverance and bravery. He was a stanch and loyal supporter of his commander when too many of the other commanders about him were insubordinate and conniving. On Mar. 2, 1847, Congress voted him a sword, with a jeweled hilt and a gold scabbard, in testimony of his gallantry at Monterey, and he was subsequently presented two others by the legislature of Georgia and by the city of Augusta. He was a member of the court of inquiry on Worth's defiant conduct, and was military governor of Vera Cruz from December 1847 to March 1848. Twiggs was a robust, powerfully built man, nearly six feet tall, with thick red face, heavy white hair, and an abundant beard. To his soldiers he was the embodiment of dynamic physical energy. They called him variously "Old Davy," "The Horse," and "Bengal Tiger."

After the war his peace-time duties of departmental commander, mostly in the South, simmered into the routine of the decade preceding the Civil War. In February 1861, he was in command of the Department of Texas. It was then, because of his Southern affiliations, that he surrendered all of the Union forces and stores under his control to the Confederate general, Ben McCulloch [*q.v.*]. He was, accordingly, promptly dismissed from the United States Army. On May 22, 1861, he was made a major-general of the Confederate army and assigned to the command of the district of Louisiana. At this time he was the ranking general of the Confederate forces, but he was too old to take the field. He died and was buried near his birthplace in the old Twiggs Cemetery, about ten miles from Augusta. He was survived by his second wife and two children. His first wife was Elizabeth Hunter, of Virginia; and his second was a Mrs. Hunt, of New Orleans, La. His daughter became the wife of Abraham C. Myers [*q.v.*], of the Confederate army.

[*Georgia's Roster of the Revolution* (1920); F. B. Heitman, *Hist. Reg. and Dict. of the U. S. Army* (1903); W. A. Ganoe, *The Hist. of the U. S. Army* (1924); *Men of Mark in Ga.*, vol. II (1910); J. H. Smith, *The War with Mexico* (2 vols., 1919); *Battles and Leaders of the Civil War* (1887–88), vol. I; *Confed. Mil. Hist.* (1899), vol. VI; records in the Old Files Section, Adjutant-General's Office, Washington, D. C.; information from the family.]
W. A. G.

TWINING, ALEXANDER CATLIN (July 5, 1801–Nov. 22, 1884), inventor, engineer, astronomer, was the son of Stephen and Almira (Catlin) Twining, and was born in New Haven, Conn., where his father for many years was steward and treasurer of Yale College. He was a descendant of William Twining who was in Yarmouth in 1643. Upon completing his preparatory school work at Hopkins, N. H., Twining entered Yale and graduated in 1820 with the degree of A.B. He then took two years of post-graduate work for his master's degree and entered Andover Theological Seminary to study for the ministry. He did not complete the course, however, for the reason that he had meanwhile become intensely interested in mathematics and engineering. Subsequently he returned to Yale, where for two years he served as a tutor (1823–24), and engaged in further study in natural philosophy and mathematics. Later he entered the United States Military Academy at West Point, and took a course in civil engineering, specializing at the same time in mathematics and astronomy. While there Twining observed the remarkable star shower of November 1833. As a result he formulated independently a theory of the cosmic origin of meteors, which was also propounded at the time by Denison Olmsted [*q.v.*]; that is, that shooting stars are bodies coming into the air from external space, and that their discussion belongs to astronomy and not to terrestrial physics (*American Journal of Science and Arts,* vol. XXVI, no. 2, 1834). Between 1834 and 1839 Twining engaged in railroad engineering, chiefly for the Hartford & New Haven Railroad Company, locating most of its northern routes out of New Haven. He later served for many years as a railroad consultant not only in New England but in the Middle West. In 1839 he accepted the chair of mathematics and natural philosophy at Middlebury College, Middlebury, Vt. Ten years later he resigned, and returned to New Haven in order to resume his engineering practice and the inventive work which he had undertaken in the meantime.

His most important invention was a method of manufacturing ice, the initial patent for which was granted on Nov. 8, 1853 (patent no. 10,221), although he filed a caveat of the invention in 1849. Because this was one of the earliest applications of the absorption process for the manufacture of ice on a commercial scale, Twining was granted extensions of his patent in 1864 and 1871. Although he devoted all his time to it after 1849, he never succeeded in having his process introduced commercially. He wrote a number of papers on mathematical problems. He married Harriet Amelia Kinsley of West Point on Mar. 2, 1829, and at the time of his death in New Haven was survived by six children.

[T. J. Twining, *Geneal. of the Twining Family* (1890); *Obit. Record Grads. Yale Coll.* (1885); *Cat. of the Officers and Grads. of Yale Univ.* (1895); E. H. Knight, *Knight's Am. Mechanical Dict.,* vol. II (1875); A. C. Twining, *The Rights of Am. Inventors: A Petition in the 45th Cong., Jan. 28, 1879* (1879); obituaries in *New Haven Evening Reg.,* Nov. 22, and *New Haven Morning Courier,* Nov. 24, 1884.]   C. W. M.

TWITCHELL, AMOS (Apr. 11, 1781–May 26, 1850), pioneer New Hampshire surgeon, was born in Dublin, N. H., the son of Samuel and Alice (Willson) Twitchell, and a descendant of Benjamin Twitchell who emigrated from England to Dorchester about 1630. He was the seventh of nine children. His father, a patriot-farmer of 1775, served in the state legislature and established a library in Dublin as early as 1793.

Following a preliminary education in the New Ipswich Academy, Twitchell entered Dartmouth College and, after a struggle against poverty and poor health, was graduated with the degree of A.B. in 1802. While in college he formed warm friendships with Daniel Webster and the elder George Cheyne Shattuck [*qq.v.*]. Stimulated to study medicine by the energetic Nathan Smith, 1762–1829 [*q.v.*], then forming the medical school at Dartmouth, he became one of Smith's most ardent pupils, and later his life-long admirer and friend. Receiving the degrees of A.M. and B.M. in 1805, Twitchell first practised medicine in Norwich, Vt., then in Marlborough, N. H., and finally in Keene, N. H., where he settled in 1810 and remained until his death. He married Elizabeth, daughter of Dr. Josiah Goodhue, one of his teachers, in 1815; there were no children. Honors came to him, and he was offered many teaching positions in medicine, all of which he refused in order to continue his arduous practice. He became an overseer of Dartmouth College in 1816, having received the degree of M.D. there in 1811, served as president of the New Hampshire Medical Society (1829–30), and held membership in the American Medical Association, the College of Physicians of Philadelphia, and the National Institution for the Promotion of Science (1841). He died in Keene, May 26, 1850, after a period of over forty years as the leading surgeon of northern New England.

Twitchell became an outstanding figure in his time at an early age, owing to a bold and dramatic operation. At the age of twenty-six, on Oct. 18, 1807, while in practice at Marlborough, he saved the life of a man severely injured by a gun-shot wound in the neck, by tying the carotid artery, an operation not previously thought possible without fatal results. The scene in the farmhouse, with the mother holding open the wound and the young surgeon acting under great pressure in the dire emergency, was modestly but effectively described by Twitchell many years later (*New England Quarterly Journal of Medicine and Surgery,* October 1842). Only once had this operation been performed before, by a surgeon in the British navy, unknown to Twitchell.

In Keene, Twitchell led the life of a country practitioner, performing many operations with exceptional skill. He was one of the first in the United States to perform extensive amputations for malignant disease, operations for stone in the bladder and ovarian tumors, tracheotomy, and trephining of the long bones for suppuration. He traveled by chaise, with frequent changes of horses; known throughout the countryside, "the doctor" got the best and fastest horse, and he often covered a hundred miles or more a day. His health, never very good, was carefully guarded by a rigorous diet, total abstinence from tobacco and alcohol, and frequent short rest periods. He was a stanch upholder of the best of American medical traditions, although a frequent advocate of conservative reforms in the American Medical Association during its period of formation. Honest, intellectual, with both surgical acumen and originality, Twitchell should be regarded as one of the outstanding early American physicians.

[The date of Twitchell's birth, given by Bowditch as Apr. 14, is from Dartmouth Coll. records. The chief source is H. I. Bowditch, *Memoir of Amos Twitchell* (1851), with portrait. See also R. E. Twitchell, *Geneal. of the Twitchell Family* (1929); Albert Smith, in *N. H. Jour. of Medicine*, June 1851; *Am. Jour. of the Medic. Sciences*, July 1850; H. J. Bowditch, in *Charleston Medic. Jour.*, Nov. 1849; *Medic. Communications, Mass. Medic. Soc.* (1854); L. W. Leonard and J. L. Seward, *The Hist. of Dublin, N. H.* (1920); obituary in *N. H. Statesman* (Concord), June 7, 1850; Twitchell MSS. in the Boston Medic. Lib.]　　　H. R. V.

TYLER, BENNET (July 10, 1783–May 14, 1858), theologian and educator, was born in Middlebury, Conn., the son of James and Anne (Hungerford) Tyler. An accident when he was fifteen years of age incapacitated him for a life of manual labor and his family determined out of their meager resources to send him to college. He prepared under his pastor, the Rev. Ira Hart, and entered Yale in 1800, graduating four years later. After teaching a year in the academy at Weston, Conn., he studied theology with the Rev. Asahel Hooker of Goshen. In 1807 he was invited to the church in South Britain, Conn., and on Nov. 12 of that year was married to Esther Stone of Middlebury. Ordained and installed over the church June 1, 1808, he continued a highly successful ministry for fourteen years, then to his surprise, Mar. 6, 1822, he was called to the presidency of Dartmouth College. This institution he served acceptably for six years, his most outstanding service being the raising of a fund of ten thousand dollars to aid students fitting for the ministry. His inclinations, however, turned strongly towards the pastorate and he accepted an urgent call to the Second Church of Portland, Me., being installed in September 1828.

In this same year a sermon preached by Dr. Nathaniel W. Taylor [*q.v.*] at the Yale Commencement let loose a flood of theological controversy among the New England churches, especially in Connecticut, between the "Old School" Calvinists and the "New Divinity" as promulgated from New Haven. Being an ardent conservative and one of the ablest interpreters of the old theology, Tyler was drawn into the debate and became a recognized leader of the

conservatively orthodox. On Sept. 10, 1833, forty ministers met in East Windsor, Conn., and resolved to establish a theological seminary—if twenty thousand dollars could be raised—to counteract, as far as possible, the harmful effects of the "New Divinity" as taught in New Haven. The money was raised in a few weeks, the corner-stone of the Theological Institute of Connecticut, now the Hartford Theological Seminary, was laid May 13, 1834, and Tyler was inducted into office as president and professor of Christian theology on the same day. This position he held for twenty-three years, resigning on account of the infirmities of age July 16, 1857.

In closing his services with the Theological Institute he delivered an address in which he set forth with great clarity and force the convictions that had governed his thinking and actions—the absolute sovereignty of a perfect God, the total depravity of human nature, the federal headship of Adam, the substitutionary death of Christ, man's natural ability but moral inability to repent, the elective grace of the Almighty, regeneration effected by the direct agency of the Holy Spirit, the endless punishment of the wicked. These doctrines he had held consistently and unchanged during all his years of public service. After his retirement he lived less than a year, dying some two months after Nathaniel W. Taylor, his chief opponent. Not an original or speculative thinker, Tyler dwelt contentedly in the Calvinistic system as modified by Jonathan Edwards and tempered by Timothy Dwight [*qq.v.*]. To him it was real Christianity, the complete and final revelation of the divine plan; whosoever sought to mitigate its severities or deny its logical implications, him he conscientiously opposed. Although a fearless controversialist, he was a man of amiable disposition, genial temper, and genuine humility. He had six sons and six daughters; one of the daughters became the first wife of Calvin E. Stowe [*q.v.*]. In addition to numerous sermons and tracts he published *Letters on the Origin and Progress of the New Haven Theology* (1837), *A Review of President Day's Treatise on the Will* (1838), *A Treatise on the Sufferings of Christ* (1845), *New England Revivals* (1846), *Letters to the Rev. Horace Bushnell Containing Strictures on His Book Entitled "Views of Christian Nurture"* (two series, 1847, 1848). After his death, *Lectures on Theology with a Memoir by Rev. Nahum Gale* (1859) was issued.

[In addition to the memoir by Gale, his son-in-law, see F. B. Dexter, *Biog. Sketches Grads. Yale Coll.*, vol. V (1911); C. M. Geer, *The Hartford Theological Sem.* (1934); J. K. Lord, *A Hist. of Dartmouth Coll.*, vol. II (1913); William Cothren, *Hist. of Ancient Wood-*

bury (2 vols., 1854-72); *Am. Congregational Year Book* (1859).]   C. A. D.

TYLER, CHARLES MELLEN (Jan. 8, 1832–May 15, 1918), Congregational clergyman, college professor, was born in Limington, Me., the son of Daniel and Lavinia (Small) Tyler. He was a descendant of Job Tyler who emigrated from England to Newport, R. I., as early as 1638, and later settled in Andover, Mass. He received his early education from his father, a lawyer by profession, in the common schools, and at Lewiston Academy. Financial reverses interrupted his schooling, and for a time he worked in a ship-chandler's shop at Belfast and later for the wholesale grocery house of D. L. Gibbons, Boston. Subsequently, after taking the senior year at Phillips Academy, Andover, he entered Yale and graduated with the class of 1855. He distinguished himself as a scholar and won prizes in Latin, English composition, and oratory. Having spent a year in Union Theological Seminary, New York, he accepted a call to the First Congregational Church, Galesburg, Ill., and was ordained and installed in June 1857. A year later he became pastor of the Congregational Church in Natick, Mass., which position he held until 1867. During this period he took an active interest in civic affairs and in 1861–62 was a member of the Massachusetts legislature. He came of fighting stock, both his grandfather and his great-grandfather having been soldiers in the Revolution, and he and his father served in the Civil War, the latter as a paymaster under General McClellan, and Charles as chaplain of the 22nd Massachusetts Volunteers, with rank of captain. He was with the army in the Wilderness Campaign and about Petersburg. An outcome of his war experiences was the publication of a little book, *Memorials of Lieut. George H. Walcott, Late of the 30th U. S. Colored Troops* (1865). From 1867 to 1872 he was pastor of the South Church, Chicago.

In the latter year he took charge of the Reformed Dutch Church, Ithaca, N. Y., which later became the First Congregational Church. Thereafter until his death he was intimately connected with the affairs of Ithaca and Cornell University. He became a trustee of the University in 1886 and was active in this position until 1892, at which time he had assumed a professorship there. Two years before, Henry W. Sage [q.v.], a friend of Tyler, had endowed the Susan Linn Sage School of Philosophy, the organization of which included a chair of history and philosophy of religion and Christian ethics. Tyler was chosen in 1891 to be its first occupant and served in this capacity for twelve years, becoming professor

emeritus in 1903. In addition to contributions to periodicals, he published a substantial work, entitled *Bases of Religious Belief, Historic and Ideal* (1897). A résumé of modern thought on the subject with some critical comment, rather than an original treatise, it was valuable in its day to students as an introduction and guide. In 1907 he was again elected a trustee of the University, and served until his death. He was twice married: first, in New Haven, Conn., Dec. 10, 1856, to Ellen A., daughter of Thomas and Harriet N. (Rich) Davis, who died Jan. 14, 1891; second, June 1892, to Kate E. Stark, professor of music at Syracuse University. By his first wife he had two daughters; he died at the home of one of them, in Scranton, Pa.

[W. I. T. Brigham, *The Tyler Geneal.* (1912); *Obit. Record Grads. Yale Univ. . . . 1918* (1919); W. T. Hewett, *Cornell Univ., A Hist.* (1905); *Who's Who in America*, 1918–19; *Cornell Alumni News*, May 23, 1918.]   H. E. S.

TYLER, DANIEL (Jan. 7, 1799–Nov. 30, 1882), soldier, industrialist, was born in Brooklyn, Windham County, Conn. His parents were Daniel Tyler, III, a Revolutionary officer, descended from Job Tyler, one of the early settlers of Andover, Mass., and Sarah (Edwards) Chaplin Tyler, a grand-daughter of Jonathan Edwards [q.v.]. After attending the public schools, the boy was sent in 1812 to Plainfield Academy to prepare for Yale, but secured instead an appointment to the United States Military Academy in 1816. Three years later, as a lieutenant of light artillery, he began service in New England, and in 1824 he was ordered to the Artillery School of Practice at Fortress Monroe, Va. His own need for professional knowledge led him to import the best books on the subject and then to translate from the French a work on drill and maneuvers originally published in Paris in 1824. This translation was used by a commission appointed in 1826 to prepare a light artillery system for the American army, and in 1828 Tyler was sent to France to make further study of the French system. Admitted to the artillery school at Metz, he found it so far superior to that at Fortress Monroe that he proceeded at great expense to obtain copies of every drawing and treatise on the French system and to translate their latest manual of exercise and instruction for field artillery (1829). His detailed inspection of French armories and construction of small arms he turned to good advantage in 1830 when he investigated the armory at Springfield, Mass., exposing the inferior quality of the arms produced there and pointing to political influence as the cause. Likewise, as superintendent of inspectors of contract arms in 1832, he rejected as defective most of the muskets delivered by manufacturers. When the Ordnance Corps was reorganized, he was recommended for the commission of captain, but President Jackson, doubtless owing to political pressure, refused to appoint him. Tyler then resigned from the army, May 31, 1834. On May 28, 1832, in Norwich, Conn., he married Emily Lee.

After an unsuccessful venture in iron-making in Lycoming County, Pa., he turned to the financing and engineering of a series of transportation projects. In the early 1840's, as president of the Norwich & Worcester Railroad and the Morris Canal & Banking Company, he rescued both from bankruptcy. During 1844–45 he was asked to complete the construction of a railroad from Macon, Ga., to Atlanta, then for sale at $150,000, scarcely one-tenth of the capital already expended. Through Tyler's financial aid and the backing of a group of Macon men, the rechartered Macon & Western Railroad was opened for traffic in ten months and was soon paying a dividend of eight per cent. Anticipating disunion, Tyler resigned in 1849 from the presidency of the road and returned to Connecticut. During the 1850's he reorganized and improved a number of railroads in Pennsylvania, New Jersey, and Kentucky.

With the outbreak of the Civil War, in April 1861 Tyler was chosen to command the 1st Connecticut Regiment; in May he was commissioned brigadier-general, and shortly before the Bull Run campaign he was given a division command. Whether or not this campaign "was gotten up," as Tyler said, "by Gen. McDowell . . . to make him the hero of a short war" ("Autobiography," Mitchell, *post*, p. 49), Tyler disobeyed orders by failing to go to Centreville to intercept the Confederates' communication with Fairfax Court House and by bringing on a premature engagement, July 18, at Blackburn's Ford, where he was repulsed by Beauregard (*War of the Rebellion: Official Records, Army,* 1 ser., II, 311–12; Fry, *post,* pp. 17–25). His opponent failed to follow up the advantage, but during the main battle of Bull Run, July 21, Tyler did not press the attack when he could have, and he must bear some of the blame for the disastrous outcome of that battle. He was in action at Corinth in 1862 and in command of Maryland Heights and Harpers Ferry during the summer of 1863, and he also aided in recruiting, prison-camp administration, and army investigations.

After the death of his wife in 1864 he moved to New Jersey and traveled extensively year after year in Europe and in the South. In Charleston, S. C., in 1872, he met Samuel Noble [*q.v.*],

who induced him to examine the iron deposits of Eastern Alabama. They explored the country on horseback, and the upshot of the visit was the organization of the Woodstock Iron Company by Tyler, his son Alfred, and Noble in 1872. Furnace No. 1 was erected immediately at a cash investment of $200,000, and gave rise to the town of Anniston, named for Tyler's daughter-in-law. The company and the town enjoyed a steady growth despite the depression years immediately following: a second furnace was added in 1879; a cotton mill with 10,000 spindles, a water works, and a car factory were built; improvements in agriculture were introduced. During his last years he served as president of the Mobile & Montgomery Railroad with his residence in Montgomery and spent his winters in Guadalupe County, Tex., where he had invested in railroad lands, but he visited Anniston frequently. He died in New York City, but was buried in Anniston. Three sons and two daughters survived him.

[W. I. T. Brigham, *The Tyler Geneal.* (1912), vol. I; D. G. Mitchell, *Daniel Tyler: A Memorial Vol. Containing His Autobiog. and War Record* (1883); J. B. Fry, *McDowell and Tyler in the Campaign of Bull Run, 1861* (1884); T. M. Vincent, "The Battle of Bull Run," *Military Order of the Loyal Legion of the U. S., Commandery of D. C., War Papers,* no. 58 (1905); G. W. Cullum, *Biog. Reg. . . . U. S. Mil. Acad.* (3rd ed., 1891), vol. I; *Fourteenth Ann. Reunion, Asso. Grads. U. S. Mil. Acad.* (1883); Ethel Armes, *The Story of Coal and Iron in Ala.* (1910); U. B. Phillips, *A Hist. of Transportation in the Eastern Cotton Belt* (1908); *N. Y. Times,* Dec. 1, 1882; *Army and Navy Journal,* Dec. 2, 1882.]   L. J. C.

TYLER, JOHN (Feb. 28, 1747–Jan. 6, 1813), Revolutionary patriot, judge, governor of Virginia, and father of President John Tyler [*q.v.*], was the son of John Tyler, marshal of the colonial vice-admiralty court of Virginia, and his wife Anne Contesse. He was descended from Henry Tyler who had emigrated from England before the middle of the seventeenth century and settled in York County. Here at the ancestral home the fourth John Tyler was born, and hence he went at an early age to the College of William and Mary. Versifying and fiddling broke the monotony of his student days, and upon completion of his collegiate course he devoted five years to the reading of law under direction of Robert Carter Nicholas [*q.v.*]. During this impressionable period he became a friend of Thomas Jefferson and an admirer of Patrick Henry, whose speech against the Stamp Act he heard in 1765; the famous comparison with which it closed was repeated by him to William Wirt for the benefit of future generations (Wirt, *Sketches of the Life and Character of Patrick Henry,* 1817, p. 65). Having completed his legal training, he removed to Charles City County and took up the practice of his profession.

As the Revolutionary movement was already under way, a young man of ability had many opportunities to distinguish himself. The first of these came in the form of an appointment to the committee of safety of Charles City County in 1774. The following year Tyler raised a company of volunteers and accompanied Patrick Henry on his march against Lord Dunmore to recapture the powder which His Lordship had removed from Williamsburg. In 1776 the young lawyer married Mary Marot Armistead, daughter of Robert Armistead of York County, and established his home at "Greenway," near the court house of Charles City County. During the same year Tyler was appointed one of the judges of the newly organized high court of admiralty for Virginia. In 1777 he, along with Benjamin Harrison "the Signer" [q.v.], was elected to represent Charles City County in the House of Delegates. During 1780 he was appointed a member of the Council of State, but finding it impossible to execute the functions of this office in addition to other duties, he resigned it in 1781. This year Benjamin Harrison was elected governor of Virginia, and Tyler succeeded him as speaker of the House of Delegates. After Harrison retired from the governorship in 1784, he again sought a seat in the House, but was defeated by Tyler (W. C. Ford, ed., *Letters of Joseph Jones of Virginia*, 1889, p. 145). Harrison, however, secured an election from another county and then defeated Tyler for the speakership by a narrow margin (Breckinridge papers, Library of Congress, Archibald Stuart to John Breckinridge, Oct. 24, 1785). During all these years in the Assembly, Tyler maintained his friendship for Patrick Henry. They worked together in their support of congressional authority and strenuous opposition to Great Britain. Tyler favored a congressional impost on imports, and opposed the negotiation of a separate peace with Great Britain. At the end of the war he refused to support Henry in his lenient policy toward the Loyalists, but worked with him to defeat Madison's attempt to provide for the payment of British debts until Great Britain should comply with the terms of the treaty of peace (I. S. Harrell, *Loyalism in Virginia*, 1926, pp. 128, 132, 193; L. G. Tyler, *Judge John Tyler, Sr., and His Times*, pp. 14–16). His most important act as a member of the House was to present in 1785 a resolution calling a federal convention to meet at Annapolis in 1786 (J. B. McMaster, *A History of the People of the United States*, I, 1883, p. 279).

In the Virginia convention of 1788, Tyler was elected vice-president, and stood with Henry against the adoption of the federal Constitution. When the point was carried against them, the public life of the Admiralty Judge was seriously affected. The new government now took over the duties of his court, and he was transferred to the general court of Virginia. In this position he was one of the first judges to assert the overruling power of the judiciary. The relative aloofness of this position was not disturbed for some years, but Tyler retained his interest in politics. When national parties began to develop, he became an ardent Republican and kept in touch with his old friend Thomas Jefferson (Lipscomb and Bergh, *The Writings of Thomas Jefferson*, XI, 1904, pp. 32–35, 69–70; XIII, 1904, pp. 165–68). In 1808 he was elected governor of Virginia and held that post until 1811, when he accepted an appointment as judge of the federal court for the district of Virginia. As governor he opposed submission to the maritime policy of Great Britain and advocated a progressive policy in regard to public education and improved communications. The state Literary Fund sprang from one of his urgent messages.

His life was lived in troubled times, but despite his vehemence there was an air of benevolence in his manner and a touch of humor in his blue eyes. His facial features were much like those of his distinguished son, with a large Roman nose. He was an aristocrat by nature, but a democrat by choice. In politics he was a liberal, but an unruffled conservative in his private life. While war was still raging in the country, he died and was buried beneath the quiet shades of "Greenway."

[The most extensive account of the life of Judge Tyler is given by his grandson Lyon G. Tyler, in *The Letters and Times of the Tylers*, vols. I, II (1884–85). Another account by the same author is *Judge John Tyler, Sr., and His Times* (1927). Briefer sketches appear in Margaret V. Smith, *Virginia, 1492–1892 . . . A Hist. of the Executives* (1893), pp. 313–14; H. B. Grigsby, *The Hist. of the Va. Federal Convention of 1788*, vol. I (1890), 247–54; and Charles Campbell, *Hist. of the Colony and Ancient Dominion of Va.* (1860), pp. 723–24. For an obituary, see *Enquirer* (Richmond), Jan. 12, 1813.]   T. P. A.

TYLER, JOHN (Mar. 29, 1790–Jan. 18, 1862), tenth president of the United States, was the second son of Judge John Tyler [q.v.] and Mary (Armistead) Tyler. There was something classical in the simple dignity of Virginia's aristocratic republicans of that day, and the life of the Tyler homestead, "Greenway," in Charles City County, where young John was born, represented these qualities in full measure. There was a certain delicacy in the boy's manner, but he had his share of sterner stuff and was, on one occasion at least, a ringleader in a rebellion against his schoolmaster. *"Sic Semper Tyrannis"* was his father's only comment upon the incident. Completing his career at the local school, at the age of twelve he was bundled off to the College of William and Mary. Here he followed in the footsteps of his father, finding relaxation from studies in fiddling and poetry. He was also deeply interested in political subjects, and often sought his father's advice concerning them. Finishing his collegiate course at the age of seventeen, he read law under the direction of his father for two years and then entered upon the practice of his profession in his native county. It was only two more years before he was elected to the House of Delegates, and on Mar. 29, 1813, he married Letitia Christian, daughter of Robert Christian of New Kent County.

The War of 1812 was in progress. Tyler served for a month around Richmond as captain of a company of volunteers, but the enemy did not appear and he returned to civil life. In the Assembly he supported President Madison and the war and gave early notice that he was a strict constructionist of the school to which his father belonged. The Assembly had passed resolutions instructing Virginia's senators to vote against a bill proposing to recharter the Bank of the United States. One senator refused to comply, and the other complied under protest. Tyler introduced resolutions to censure them for their conduct. With a gracious manner and a definite gift for public speaking, the young member from Charles City became increasingly popular with his constituents and in the House of Delegates. He was elected to that body for five successive years, and finally, during the session of 1815–16, was chosen to sit on the executive council of the state. This service, however, was cut short by his election in 1816 to the federal House of Representatives. His membership in this body continued until 1821, when ill health forced him to resign. During these five years he put himself still further on record as a strict constructionist. As a member of a committee to report on the operation of the Bank of the United States, he favored the revocation of its charter (*House Document No. 92*, 15 Cong., 2 Sess., 1816). He voted against Calhoun's "bonus" bill for the aid of internal improvements, against a protective tariff, for the censure of Andrew Jackson's conduct in the Florida campaign, and against the adoption of the Missouri Compromise measure of 1820. His Virginia colleagues in Congress, with few exceptions, and the powerful *Richmond Enquirer,* supported him in his denial that the federal government had the right to control the question of slavery in the territories. The Tylers, both fa-

ther and son, were consistent in their opposition to the slave trade, and wished to see slavery pass away, but they trusted to time and climate for its ultimate abolition. They held that good faith to the Southern states required that while slavery existed, it should have all the protection of any other property (Tyler, *post,* I, 313).

On his retirement from Congress, Tyler bought "Greenway," which on the death of his father in 1813 had descended to an older brother, Dr. Wat Henry Tyler; and there for two years he lived the life of a private citizen. In 1823 he was again elected to the House of Delegates and from this post took a leading part in the exciting events connected with the presidential campaign of 1824. Along with the majority of the Jeffersonian Republicans of Virginia, he supported William H. Crawford in that contest. Andrew Jackson he considered a mere military hero, and of little value as a civilian. After the election of Adams and the appointment of Clay as secretary of state, Tyler refused to believe the "bargain and corruption" story, and wrote to Clay stating his opinion (Calvin Colton, ed., *The Private Correspondence of Henry Clay,* 1856, pp. 119–20). In 1825 and again in 1826 Tyler was elected governor of Virginia, and in this capacity worked for the development of roads and schools, as his father had done before him. While not a supporter of the Adams administration, Tyler did not at once follow John Randolph and the *Enquirer* into the Jackson camp (C. H. Ambler, *Thomas Ritchie,* 1913, p. 111; Tyler, *post,* I, 375–76). In 1827 he was elected to the United States Senate by the anti-Jackson element in the Assembly. In 1828 he voted against the "tariff of abominations" and supported Jackson for the presidency as a "choice of evils." However, Tyler soon flew in the face of the President by opposing his appointment of several newspaper editors to high federal posts (C. G. Bowers, *The Party Battles of the Jackson Period,* 1922, p. 82). There were apparently some phases of Jackson's democracy with which he did not sympathize. This fact is further illustrated by his stand, as a member of the Virginia constitutional convention of 1829–30, in favor of the "federal ratio" of apportionment for the upper house of the Assembly (Tyler, I, 397–404). Jackson's veto of the Maysville road bill was an action after Tyler's own heart, and so was the President's opposition to the rechartering of the Bank of the United States, but the removal of the deposits was another matter. In the Senate he supported the resolutions which condemned the President for this act. While not a believer in nullification, Tyler considered Jackson's nullification proclamation as subversive of the Constitution and he cast the only vote recorded in the Senate against the Force Bill. But his state-rights views did not lead him into merely obstructionist tactics. It was he who first formulated a plan of conciliation and brought Calhoun and Clay together to agree upon the compromise tariff of 1833 (Tyler, I, 455–60; A. C. Cole, *The Whig Party in the South*, 1913, pp. 24–25).

It cannot be said that Tyler was ever a Jackson man in the strict sense of the term. He supported him in 1828 and again in 1832, but not without reservations, and considered him distinctly unsound on constitutional principles. Coming finally to a definite break with the administration, he became a member of the Southern state-rights group in Congress which cooperated and acted with the National Republicans within the newly forming Whig party. Neither Tyler nor any of his group pretended to accept the nationalistic doctrines of Clay and his following.

In 1833 Tyler was reëlected to the Senate. Virginia supported him without reservation in his stand on the Force Bill (C. H. Ambler, *Thomas Ritchie*, p. 152). But times were changing. The Jacksonians, under the lead of John Randolph and Thomas Ritchie of the *Enquirer*, got control of the state, and Tyler became a member of the opposition. In 1836 the legislature instructed him to vote for the expunging of resolutions censuring Jackson for removal of the deposits, and he resigned his senatorship rather than comply (*Letter of John Tyler ... to the ... General Assembly of Virginia*, 1836). In this year the Virginia Whigs supported him as their vice-presidential candidate on a ticket which was split between Harrison and White as to the first place. William C. Rives [*q.v.*] was elected to the seat in the Senate vacated by Tyler, but by 1839 the Whigs had ousted the Democrats from the control of the Assembly and Tyler was again a member of that body. In this year Rives came up for reëlection. Meanwhile, he had broken with the Democrats on the sub-treasury issue, and the Whigs were anxious to win him over. In the election, John Y. Mason was the regular Democratic candidate and Tyler the regular Whig. A number of Whigs, however, deserted Tyler and voted for Rives with the result that none of the candidates was able to secure a majority. It appears that Henry Clay was cognizant of this scheme to desert Tyler in order to win Rives, and that he had held out hopes of the vice-presidential nomination for Tyler in case his friends would cooperate. But Tyler had no part in any of these schemes (Henry A. Wise, *Seven Decades of the Union*, p. 158; Tyler, I, 588–93).

It did, nevertheless, come about that Tyler was nominated for the second place on the Harrison ticket of 1840; that he was elected in the boisterous campaign of that year; and that, Harrison dying within a month of his inauguration, he became president of the United States by right of succession. No vice-president had ever thus become president, and there were those who would have withheld from him the full title, but Tyler maintained his claim. Henry Clay certainly intended to withhold from him the leadership of the Whig party, and in this he was successful. Tyler's constitutional views were well known when he was nominated and elected, but the majority of the Whigs were nationalists, with Clay as their leader, and they could not refrain from bringing forward the old measures of the National Republican party, which they had minimized in the recent canvass. Tyler regarded this as an act of bad faith, but, hoping to avoid a break, he held a conference with Clay and tried to reach an agreement with him on the bank question (Tyler, II, 127–28; *Speech of Mr. Cushing ... on the Post Office Bill*, 1841). Clay, however, wished no agreement. This was the last meeting between the two men. Clay said, "I'll drive him before me," but Tyler still hoped for conciliation. His retention of Harrison's cabinet could have had no other meaning, but he found that Harrison's plans as to the use of the patronage were a bit too strong for him (Tyler, II, 310). He signed an act abolishing the sub-treasury system, but insisted that the "distribution" measure be dropped from the tariff bill of 1842 before he would sign it (Thomas H. Benton, *Thirty Years' View*, 1856, II, 413–17). Furthermore, his policy on the question of internal improvements was far more conservative than had been that of Jackson or Adams.

It was the bank question that brought on the crisis between the President and the party. Tyler had made it clear from the beginning that he would not sanction a measure which permitted a National Bank to establish branches in the states without their previous consent. He devised a plan, known as the "exchequer system," which would have avoided this difficulty, and recommended it to Congress, but Clay did not wish to satisfy Tyler on that point (Wise, *Seven Decades*, pp. 204–05; Tyler, II, 15–16, 131, 134). A bill was passed chartering a bank along the lines desired by Clay, and Tyler promptly vetoed it. Conferences were thereupon held. Three members of the cabinet, followers of Clay, later averred that the President had agreed to a revised plan for a bank, and a second bill was presented to Congress, but Tyler had never seen it

(A. C. Gordon, *John Tyler*, pp. 30–31; Wise, pp. 185–90). Feeling that it did not properly safeguard the rights of the states, he vetoed it when it was passed (J. F. Jameson, ed., "Correspondence of John C. Calhoun," *Annual Report of the American Historical Association for the Year 1899*, vol. II, 1900, pp. 487–89). At the behest of Clay, the cabinet members then resigned, with the exception of Webster who saw no reason for such action. Thus Tyler became a president without a party.

It was not believed that his administration would result in much constructive work, but this did not prove to be the case even on the legislative side, while as an administrator and negotiator Tyler made a remarkable record. His hand was seen in many constructive acts of Congress, prominent among which was the entire reorganization of the Navy, the establishment of a depot for nautical charts and instruments, which developed into the National Observatory; and the act to test the practicability of establishing a system of magnetic telegraphs for the use of the United States, which has had a many-sided development, especially in the Weather Bureau. The government was conducted with a minimum of waste and extravagance despite the fact that Congress had provided no system for the keeping of public funds. The Seminole War was brought to an end. Dorr's Rebellion was quieted without Federal interference (Edward Everett, ed., *The Works of Daniel Webster*, 1851, vol. VI, 237–38), a treaty was negotiated with China opening the doors of the Orient for the first time, and the Monroe Doctrine was enforced in the case of Texas and the Hawaiian Islands.

The greatest achievements were the negotiation of the Webster-Ashburton treaty and the annexation of Texas. Webster has usually been given all the credit for the settlement of the northeastern boundary dispute with Great Britain, but many of the provisions were Tyler's own, and it was Tyler who oiled the wheels of the negotiation which not only settled the question of the boundary, but dealt with several other difficult though lesser causes of friction between the two countries (J. H. Latané, *A History of American Foreign Policy*, 1927, pp. 210–22; *William and Mary College Quarterly Historical Magazine*, July 1916, pp. 1–8; *Tyler's Quarterly Historical and Genealogical Magazine*, III, 255–57; Tyler, II, 216–18). Early in his administration Tyler broached the Texas question to Webster, but he hesitated to press it on account of the slavery issue (Tyler, II, 126–27). After Webster's resignation, Upshur negotiated the treaty of annexation, but the latter's untimely death left the mat-

ter still unsettled. The appointment of a new secretary of state to finish the work was a delicate matter. In this crisis, Henry A. Wise [*q.v.*] committed the President to the appointment of Calhoun (Wise, *Seven Decades*, pp. 221–25). On the score of friendship and policy, the President accepted the situation and Calhoun took over the Texas negotiation. His partisans hoped to capitalize the appointment and make the South Carolinian the Texas candidate for the succession (C. H. Ambler, ed., "Correspondence of R. M. T. Hunter," *Annual Report of the American Historical Association for the Year 1916*, vol. II, 1918, pp. 51–55; Ambler, *Thomas Ritchie*, pp. 227, 232). But Tyler's reluctance to appoint Calhoun received ample justification when Clay and Van Buren came out against immediate annexation and the Senate rejected the treaty. Tyler was then supported for the presidency by a strong element in many states, but when the Democrats selected Polk as their candidate on an annexationist platform Tyler withdrew in his favor (U. B. Phillips, ed., "The Correspondence of Robert Toombs, Alexander H. Stephens, and Howell Cobb," *Annual Report of the American Historical Association for the Year 1911*, vol. II, 1913, p. 59; *The Madisonian Pamphlet*, Letter of John Tyler "To my Friends throughout the Union," 1844; Tyler, II, 341, III, 139–43, 147, 153, 169; *Tyler's Quarterly Historical and Genealogical Magazine*, Oct. 1924, pp. 81–97). Polk was elected, but Texas was annexed by joint resolution while Tyler was still president. He could retire with the satisfaction of knowing that he had accomplished much for his country.

One who saw him at the time he occupied the White House said: "In his official intercourse with all men, high or low, he was all that could be asked: approachable, courteous, always willing to do a kindly action, or to speak a kindly word.... He was above the middle height, somewhat slender, clean-shaven, with light hair. His light blue eyes were penetrating, and had a humorous twinkle which aided the notable faculty he possessed for telling a good story, and for making keen conversational hits" (W. O. Stoddard, *William Henry Harrison, John Tyler, and James Knox Polk*, 1888, p. 55). It was this amiability and efficiency which enabled him to accomplish so much as an administrator.

The ex-President retired to "Sherwood Forest." His first wife, who bore him seven children, died in 1842. Two years later he himself had narrowly escaped death when a large gun exploded during trials on board the warship *Princeton*. One of the victims of that accident was David Gardiner of New York; and his daughter, Julia, being thrown with Tyler under these tragic circumstances, became his bride within a few months (June 26, 1844). She presided as mistress of the White House during the closing scenes of the administration, and now became mistress of "Sherwood Forest." She had seven children. The family lived the quiet life of rural Virginia until the outbreak of the Civil War called Tyler again into public activity. Believing in the desirability of conciliation, he proposed a convention of the border states to meet and consider compromises which might save the Union. The Virginia Assembly proposed a convention of all the states for this purpose, and when it met in Washington in February 1861 Tyler acted as its chairman. These efforts failing, Tyler in March was a member of the Virginia convention which met to consider the question of secession. As soon as all compromise measures had failed, he declared for separation. When Virginia seceded he urged that Southern troops occupy Washington and that the South appropriate the name and the flag of the old Union. He believed an offensive to be better than a defensive policy (Tyler, II, 658–62). These proposals were rejected, but Tyler served in the provisional Congress of the Confederacy and was elected to a seat in the Confederate House of Representatives. He died before he was able to take his place, and lies buried in Hollywood Cemetery, Richmond. His memory has been dimmed by the writings of historians who find a record of courageous consistency bewildering.

[The most complete account of the life of President Tyler is in *The Letters and Times of the Tylers* (3 vols., 1884, 1885, 1896), by his son Lyon G. Tyler. Other accounts are in H. A. Wise, *Seven Decades of the Union* (1872); *Observations on the Political Character and Services of President Tyler and His Cabinet* (1841), by "A Native of Maryland" (John L. Dorsey); anonymous, *Life of John Tyler* (1843); J. R. Irelan, "History of the Life, Administration and Times of John Tyler," *The Republic*, vol. X (1888); *John Tyler* (1932), address of C. G. Bowers; A. C. Gordon, *John Tyler* (1915), an address, reprinted in substance in *Virginian Portraits* (1924). Special phases of his administration are discussed by J. H. Smith, *The Annexation of Texas* (1911); J. S. Reeves, *American Diplomacy under Tyler and Polk* (1907); and C. M. Fuess, *The Life of Caleb Cushing* (1923). Some of Tyler's later papers are published in "An Echo from the Civil War," by Stephen F. Peckham, in *Journal of Am. History*, Oct. 1911, pp. 611–63, and Mar. 1912, pp. 73–86. There is a collection of Tyler papers (8 vols.) in the Lib. of Cong. and another in the library of Duke Univ. *The William and Mary College Quart. Hist. Mag.* and *Tyler's Quart. Hist. and Geneal. Mag.* contain many letters and other articles bearing on his administration. For an obituary see *Daily Richmond Enquirer*, Jan. 20, 1862.]

T. P. A.

TYLER, MOSES COIT (Aug. 2, 1835–Dec. 28, 1900), historian and educator, son of Elisha and Mary (Greene) Tyler and a descendant of Job Tyler, an early settler of Andover, Mass.,

was born in Griswold, Conn. After various wanderings the family settled in Detroit, where Moses attended the public schools, and whence he entered the University of Michigan. In Detroit he came strongly under the influence of the Rev. Harvey D. Kitchel, who strengthened his lifelong tendency to religious preoccupation. In 1853 Tyler withdrew from the institution at Ann Arbor to enter Yale, where he was graduated in 1857. After attending the theological seminaries at New Haven and Andover, but without a degree from either, he was ordained to the Congregationalist ministry at Owego, N. Y., in August 1859, and after a year there became pastor of a Congregational Church in Poughkeepsie, where he was formally installed in February 1861. During this period he was an ardent disciple of Henry Ward Beecher [*q.v.*]. On Oct. 26, 1859, he had married Jeannette Hull Gilbert, by whom he had a daughter and a son. Failing health and dissatisfaction with orthodox theology led him to resign his pulpit in October 1862.

At one time or another Tyler took up various reforms, including the temperance movement, abolition, and the cause of women's rights, but the one to which he gave most time was the advocacy of "musical gymnastics," a system of calisthenics invented by Dio Lewis [*q.v.*], under whose influence the future historian fell after leaving Poughkeepsie for Boston. At Lewis' suggestion, Tyler went to England in April 1863 to crusade for physical education. He was extraordinarily successful as a lecturer on calisthenics, and gradually extended the range of his topics to include literary addresses and a defense of the Union cause. He was gradually drawn into journalism, and thought for a time of making it his career. The best of Tyler's essays from this period, reprinted in *Glimpses of England* (1898), reveal him as an ardent liberal.

After returning to the United States, in December 1866, Tyler was for a time at a loss, but in 1867 received appointment as professor of rhetoric and English literature at the University of Michigan. He did much to modernize instruction in literature at Ann Arbor, for he was an extraordinarily effective teacher. In the meantime his own interests were increasingly directed to the interpretation of American colonial history, the reading of H. T. Buckle's *History of Civilization* helping to arouse his enthusiasm and his curiosity. Finding no way to carry forward effective investigation at Michigan, Tyler resigned his professorship in 1873 and secured an appointment to the staff of the *Christian Union,* then under Beecher's control, believing that it would give him leisure and access to

Eastern libraries. The association proved unhappy, however, owing to the Tilton-Beecher scandal and to Tyler's moral disgust with "the gilded age," and he returned thankfully to Michigan in 1874. Here he remained as professor of English literature until 1881, when Andrew D. White [*q.v.*], a lifelong friend, called him to Cornell as the first professor of American history in the country. In both institutions Tyler helped to introduce German methodology into graduate instruction. Except for a personal controversy with President Charles Kendall Adams over the organization and control of the Cornell department of history, Tyler's years in Ithaca were uneventful, though he was occasionally troubled by a mild religious melancholia. In 1881 he was ordered deacon and in 1883 ordained priest in the Protestant Episcopal Church. The last fifteen years of his life were in many ways the most effective, for he labored happily at American history, helped to found the American Historical Association (1884), gained wide recognition as an authority on the colonial literature of the country, and was generally recognized as a leader in the cause of "critical" as opposed to "patriotic" history. He died at Ithaca, survived by his wife and both children. Personally, he was a genial, humorous, quick-tempered, ever-active man.

Tyler produced a mass of more or less ephemeral essays and reviews, a group of scholarly articles, one or two minor volumes, and a few textbooks, but his permanent reputation is due to his historical and biographical researches. During his second period at Michigan he wrote *A History of American Literature during the Colonial Time, 1607–1765* (2 vols., 1878). This he followed by *Patrick Henry* (1887), the first modern biography of the Virginia leader, and by *The Literary History of the American Revolution 1763–1783* (2 vols., 1897), written at Cornell. With the last-named work should be associated his *Three Men of Letters* (1895), critical biographies of George Berkeley, Timothy Dwight, and Joel Barlow, characterized by great charm and insight; these he planned to follow by a book to be called *"Vivi Memorabiles,"* which was not completed. Because of Tyler's thorough preparation, clearness of style, and sanity of judgment, his four volumes of literary history have become by common consent the standard account of the first two centuries of American literary development.

[The Tyler papers in the library of Cornell Univ. were used in H. M. Jones, *The Life of Moses Coit Tyler* (1933), based on an unpublished dissertation from original sources by T. E. Casady. Tyler's daughter, Jessica Tyler Austen, published *Moses Coit Tyler:*

Selections from His Letters and Diaries (1911). See also W. I. T. Brigham, *The Tyler Geneal.* (2 vols., 1912); W. P. Trent, in *Forum*, Aug. 1901; G. L. Burr, in *New Eng. Hist. and Geneal. Reg.*, Apr. 1901, supp.; *Who's Who in America*, 1899–1900; *Yale Univ. Obit. Record*, 5 ser. (1910); *N. Y. Times*, Dec. 29, 1900.]
H. M. J.

TYLER, RANSOM HUBERT (Nov. 18, 1815–Nov. 21, 1881), legal writer, son of Peter and Eunice Tyler, was born in Franklin County, Mass., whence, when he was three, his family moved to Oswego County, N. Y. During his boyhood he worked on his father's farm and in the winter attended public school. Having shown an eagerness for an education, he was sent to Mexico Academy, where he acquired a good classical schooling. In 1836 he began the study of law, at the same time taking charge of the principal school of Fulton village, and in 1840 he was admitted to practice. Four years later he was appointed master in chancery, keeping this office until its termination, as the result of constitutional changes, in 1846. After serving as district attorney for three years, he was elected county judge for a term running from Jan. 1, 1852, to Dec. 31, 1855, and again for a similar term beginning Jan. 1, 1864.

Between his judgeships Tyler edited gratuitously for one year the *Oswego County Gazette* and in 1858 ran unsuccessfully for Congress on the Democratic ticket. In 1861, however, he changed his political allegiance to support Lincoln. During this same period his strong religious tendencies led him to publish a book entitled *The Bible and Social Reform or, the Scriptures as a Means of Civilization* (1860). The hold that theology had on him was further demonstrated by his first legal textbook, *American Ecclesiastical Law* (1866), in which he not only discussed the laws of the several states bearing on ecclesiastical organizations, but also dissected the dogmas of the various creeds with a skill that won contemporary praise.

Closely following this publication came texts and treatises on various aspects of civil law, namely *Commentaries on the Law of Infancy, including Guardianship and Custody of Infants, and the Law of Coverture, embracing Dower, Marriage and Divorce, and the Statutory Policy of the Several States in Respect to Husband and Wife* (1868, 2nd ed., 1882); *A Treatise on the Law of Boundaries and Fences* (1874); *A Treatise on the Remedy by Ejectment and the Law of Adverse Enjoyment in the United States* (1870, 1874, 1876); *A Treatise on the Law of Usury, Pawns or Pledges, and Maritime Loans* (1873); and *A Treatise on the Law of Fixtures* (1877). In addition, he contributed to periodical literature. All his books were the products of considerable research and valuable for their wealth of material, but they were subject, as a whole, to the criticism of prolixity, poor arrangement, and, ofttimes, lack of clarity.

Apart from his legal interests, Tyler was at one time a bank president and for a period was an officer in the New York militia, attaining the rank of brigadier-general before resigning. He took an abiding interest in religious and social activities and traveled extensively, through Europe, Asia, and Africa. Friendly and generous by nature, he was liked and respected by his community. He was married twice, first to Nancy D. Cadwell, and after her death, to Mary E. Douglas. He died at his home in Fulton, N. Y., survived by his second wife and one child.

[Sources include *Landmarks of Oswego County, N. Y.* (1895), ed. by J. C. Churchill; Crisfield Johnson, *Hist. of Oswego County, N. Y.* (1877); clippings from an unidentified newspaper preserved by the Am. Antiquarian Soc. in "Roe Contemporary Biography," vol. II, p. 42. Tyler's middle name is given as Hebbard in some accounts, but appears as Hubert in the Alumni Register of Hamilton College, which in 1853 awarded him the honorary degree of A.M. (*The Hamilton Coll. Bull.*, Nov. 1922).]　　　L. M. S.

TYLER, ROBERT (Sept. 9, 1816–Dec. 3, 1877), lawyer, politician, and editor, son of President John Tyler [*q.v.*] and Letitia (Christian), was born in Charles City County, Va. Like his father and grandfather, he was educated at the College of William and Mary, graduating in 1835. He then studied law under Prof. Beverley Tucker and began practice in Williamsburg. On Sept. 12, 1839, he married Elizabeth Priscilla, daughter of Thomas Abthorpe Cooper, the famous Irish tragedian and protégé of William Godwin (John Bernard, *Retrospections of America*, 1887, p. 164). When John Tyler became president in 1841, Robert took up his residence in Washington, acting as private secretary to his father, while his wife presided as mistress of the White House during the first year of the administration. The young man found time while thus engaged to write two serious poems of a religious nature; *Ahasuerus,* and *Death: or Medorus' Dream,* published in 1842 and 1843 respectively.

Toward the close of President Tyler's term of office, Robert moved to Philadelphia and at once began to take a leading part in the politics of that city. In 1844 he was elected president of the Irish Repeal Association. In 1847 he became solicitor to the sheriff of Philadelphia, and a little later was made prothonotary to the supreme court of Pennsylvania. During the Mexican War he recruited a regiment in Philadelphia, but its services were declined (L. G.

Tyler, *post,* II, 456). Meanwhile, he had become a political friend of James Buchanan, secretary of state under President Polk. Buchanan had not been friendly to the Tyler administration, and the ex-president seems to have had no part in making this alliance nor in shaping the career of his son at this time (*Ibid.,* II, 494). In 1852 Robert Tyler supported Buchanan for the Democratic nomination for the presidency. In 1854 he became one of the earliest advocates of a Pacific railway. In 1856 Henry A. Wise, a close friend of the Tylers, was elected governor of Virginia, and he and Robert Tyler were able to bring Virginia to the support of the Pennsylvanian in the Cincinnati convention of 1856. This service was followed by Tyler's appointment in 1858 to the chairmanship of the Democratic executive committee of Pennsylvania (C. H. Ambler, "Correspondence of Robert M. T. Hunter," *Annual Report of the American Historical Asso. . . . 1916,* 1918, II, 299–300).

When the Civil War broke out, a Philadelphia mob attacked the home of the Virginian because of his well-known Southern sympathies, and he was forced to flee to Richmond. It was not long before President Davis appointed him to be register of the Confederate Treasury. In this capacity he published valuable reports on Confederate shipping and finance. At the end of the war, he removed his family to Montgomery, Ala., and in 1867 became editor of the Montgomery *Mail and Advertiser.* This position enabled him to take a leading part in the expulsion of Carpet-bag rule from Alabama, and his work was recognized by his appointment as chairman of the Democratic state central committee, in which capacity he served for several years. Thus, in very different scenes and circumstances, he twice became the leader of his party in the state of his residence. Strong convictions, fervor of temperament, and ability as a political speaker and writer enabled him to attain his position quite independently of any aid from his more famous father. When he died, at the age of sixty-one, his remains were interred in Montgomery.

[The most complete sketch of Tyler's career is in T. M. Owen, *Hist. of Ala. and Dict. of Ala. Biog.* (1921), vol. IV; see also L. G. Tyler, *The Letters and Times of the Tylers,* vol. II (1885); William Brewer, *Ala., Her Hist., Resources, War Record, and Public Men* (1872); P. G. Auchampaugh, *Robert Tyler, Southern Rights Champion* (1934) and "John W. Forney, Robert Tyler, and James Buchanan," in *Tyler's Quart. Hist. and Geneal. Mag.,* Oct. 1933; *Mobile Daily Reg.,* Dec. 5, 6, 1877. The Confederate treasury reports are in the Lib. of Cong., in pamphlet form.]　　T. P. A.

TYLER, ROBERT OGDEN (Dec. 22, 1831–Dec. 1, 1874), soldier, was born at Hunter,

Greene County, N. Y., the son of Frederick and Sophia (Sharp) Tyler and a nephew of Daniel Tyler [*q.v.*]. He was descended from Job Tyler who was in Newport, R. I., in 1638 and later went to Massachusetts. Robert's grandfather, Daniel Tyler, was adjutant to Gen. Israel Putnam during the Revolution, and three uncles were army officers. Given an excellent preparatory education, he entered the United States Military Academy in 1849, graduated in 1853, and became a second lieutenant of the 3rd Artillery. He soon participated in a movement of troops from the Missouri River to Salt Lake and San Francisco (1854–55). In 1856—he was promoted first lieutenant on Sept. 1 of that year—he was engaged in Indian wars in what is now the state of Washington. In 1859, he went to the Sioux country in Minnesota.

At the opening of the Civil War he was in garrison at the Fort Columbus Recruiting Station, N. Y. He accompanied the relief expedition to Fort Sumter, S. C., in April 1861, and then went to Baltimore to assist in the opening of that city to Federal forces. In May 1861 he transferred as a captain to the quartermaster's department and opened a supply depot at Alexandria, Va. In September he became colonel of the 1st Connecticut Heavy Artillery. He found this regiment, considerably demoralized, within the defenses of Washington, but soon brought it to a state of high efficiency. The following spring he participated in the Peninsular campaign. He prepared his batteries to bombard Yorktown, but owing to the fact that the Confederates withdrew just before the batteries were ready to fire, there was no engagement. With great effort the batteries were moved up for an attack on Richmond, which also never occurred. At Gaines's Mill, June 27, 1862, the batteries did good work in assisting the Federals north of the Chickahominy. In the retreat to Malvern Hill, Tyler brought off all his guns but one and used them in repulsing the Confederate attack on July 1. For these services he was appointed a brigadier-general of volunteers on Nov. 29, 1862. The following month he had charge of the Federal batteries which fired upon Fredericksburg. In the Gettysburg campaign he commanded the artillery reserve of 130 guns and, under direction of Gen. Henry J. Hunt [*q.v.*], chief of artillery, disposed these guns to maximum advantage, especially in stopping Pickett's charging infantry. In 1864 Tyler's artillery served as infantry throughout the Wilderness campaign. It distinguished itself at Spotsylvania, May 17–24, driving back the Confederate forces under Gen. Richard Ewell

[*q.v.*]. At Cold Harbor, on June 1, it was one of the brigades selected for the famous bloody assault. Early in this action Tyler was shot through the ankle, a wound from the effects of which he never recovered.

Returning to duty in December, he was assigned to board duties, and to the command of districts outside of the theatre of active operations. On Mar. 13, 1865, he was brevetted major-general for gallant conduct and meritorious services. He was mustered out of the volunteer service Jan. 15, 1866, and on July 29 was appointed to the Regular Army as a lieutenant-colonel in the quartermaster's department. In this capacity he served at many important military headquarters, with constantly declining health. In an effort to recuperate he took a year's leave in 1872, visiting the Far East. A diary relating to part of this trip was published in *Memoir of Brevet Major-General Robert Ogden Tyler* (1878). Failing to find the relief he had sought, Tyler died at Boston in the year after his return from the East, and was buried in Hartford, Conn. He never married. He was noted for strictness and justice, but was of kindly disposition.

[W. I. T. Brigham, *The Tyler Geneal.* (1912, vol. I); G. W. Cullum, *Biog. Reg. Officers and Grads. U. S. Mil. Acad.* (3rd ed., 1891), vol. II; *War of the Rebellion: Official Records (Army)*; F. B. Heitman, *Hist. Reg. and Dict. U. S. Army* (1903), *Sixth Ann. Reunion Asso. Grads. U. S. Mil. Acad.* (1875); *N. Y. Tribune*, Dec. 2, 1874.]   C. H. L—a.

TYLER, ROYALL (July 18, 1757–Aug. 26, 1826), playwright, novelist, jurist, was born in Boston, Mass., the son of Royall and Mary (Steele) Tyler. His father, grandson of Thomas Tyler who settled in Boston about 1680, was a graduate of Harvard, a merchant, and a member of the King's Council from 1765 to 1771. Royall, junior, was christened William Clark, but his name was afterwards changed to Royall by action of the General Court. Entering Harvard College July 15, 1772, he attracted attention by his ability, his wit, and his lively nature. Upon his graduation in 1776, Yale College bestowed the degree of B.A. upon him, in early recognition of those intellectual qualities of which he had already given evidence. While engaged in the study of law with Francis Dana [*q.v.*] in Cambridge, he was one of the leaders of a group of young men who were interested in writing, painting, and politics.

He joined the Independent Company of Boston and in 1778 served as aide to General Sullivan, with the rank of major, in the attack on Newport, but owing to his mother's widowhood, his military service was not continuous. On

Aug. 19, 1780, he was admitted to the bar, practising first in Falmouth, now Portland, Me., then in Braintree, Mass., where he became engaged to be married to Abigail Adams, daughter of John Adams [*q.v.*], then in France. Adams, however, insisted that his wife and daughter join him at Auteuil in the summer of 1784, and in 1785 Tyler received word that the engagement was cancelled. No reason was given, but the subsequent marriage of Abigail Adams to her father's secretary of legation, Col. William Stephens Smith [*q.v.*], makes it unnecessary to lay too much stress on the persistent tradition that John Adams distrusted the stability of Tyler. The latter was of an extremely sensitive nature, however, and retired for some months to his mother's home at Jamaica Plain; but before the close of the year he resumed active practice, this time in Boston, where he resided with Joseph Pearce Palmer and renewed his friendship with little Mary Palmer, who was afterward to be his wife.

Early in 1787 he joined the staff of Gen. Benjamin Lincoln [*q.v.*], again with the rank of major, and assisted in the suppression of Shays's Rebellion, partly by his eloquence in addressing the rioters. He was less successful in his diplomatic journey into Vermont to secure Shays, but it was on a mission connected with the fugitives that he was sent by Governor Bowdoin to New York City. He arrived on Mar. 12, 1787.

In New York, inspired by the production of *The School for Scandal* and other plays he undoubtedly saw at the old John Street Theatre, and by his acquaintance with the well-known low comedian, Thomas Wignell [*q.v.*], he wrote *The Contrast,* produced Apr. 16, 1787, by the American Company, the second play and the first comedy written by a native American and produced by a professional company. It was instantly successful, being repeated five times in New York and soon played in Baltimore, Philadelphia, Boston, and Charleston. Tyler gave the copyright to Wignell, who published it in Philadelphia in 1790 as by "a citizen of the United States," with a list of subscribers headed by Washington. The play is a sterling social comedy, comparing the American officer and gentleman, in Colonel Manly, with Dimple, the imitator of British affectations. Charlotte, the flirt of that day, is as real today as she was then, and Jonathan was the prototype of a long succession of stage Yankees. The scene in which Jonathan goes to the play without knowing it has become a classic. During recent years *The Contrast* has been produced at many of the leading American universities and little theatres, and always with

effect; and its influence upon playwrights like William Dunlap [*q.v.*], who were inspired by its success in its own day, can hardly be estimated.

Tyler followed *The Contrast* with a comic opera in two acts, *May Day in Town; or, New York in an Uproar,* performed at the John Street Theatre, May 19, 1787. It probably reflected the confusion occasioned by the custom of moving households on May 1 in New York, but it has not survived, even in manuscript. Neither has *The Georgia Spec; or, Land in the Moon,* a comedy in three acts which ridiculed the land speculations in the Yazoo country in Georgia. It was first played in Boston, at the Haymarket Theatre, Oct. 30, 1797, and in New York, Dec. 20 and later. According to the memoir of Tyler, prefaced by his son, he also wrote a farce, *The Farm House; or, The Female Duellists,* which, according to the son (T. P. Tyler, *post*), "was performed and was especially popular." It has not survived, and the cast as given at the Boston Theatre is identical with that of Kemble's farce of the same name. Tyler may have adapted the English play. The same authority attributes to Tyler *The Doctor in Spite of Himself,* evidently an adaptation of Molière.

Tyler's ability as a playwright must be judged by *The Contrast* and by four unpublished manuscripts. The first, bearing two titles, *The Island of Barrataria* [*sic*] and *Tantalization or The Governor of a Day,* is an amusing farce in three acts based upon the second part of *Don Quixote.* Through Sancho Panza, who is made governor of the island for one day and decides the cases brought before him with a shrewd common sense which contrasts sharply with the verbiage of the lawyers, Tyler satirizes cleverly the methods of his own profession. It would act well, though no sure record exists of its production. Three sacred dramas, *The Origin of the Feast of Purim, or The Destinies of Haman and M∟rdecai; Joseph and His Brethren;* and *The Judgment of Solomon,* are written in blank verse of a flexible and even distinguished character, but could hardly have been placed upon the stage. They represent Tyler as a writer of verse, in which he had a facility that resulted in a large quantity of satiric and occasional poems contributed to periodicals. Practically all of these were printed anonymously and it is not now possible to identify them with surety.

In 1794, Tyler entered into a literary partnership with his friend Joseph Dennie [*q.v.*] under the name of "Colon and Spondee," which proposed to furnish verse and prose of a familiar and satiric nature. Tyler was "Spondee," and the pieces so signed in the *Eagle; or Dartmouth Centinel,* and later in *The New Hampshire Journal; or The Farmers' Weekly Museum,* and probably in the *Portfolio,* are Tyler's. They are clever and to the historian are of value in their description of customs and in their representation of Federalist opinion. The best are probably contained in a collection, *The Spirit of the Farmers' Museum* (1801). In more serious vein his long reflective poem, *The Chestnut Tree,* written in 1824 but not published until 1931, is of importance not only for its picture of the village life of his time, but also for its prophecies of the results of the machine age.

More important than Tyler's fugitive verse was his novel *The Algerine Captive,* published in 1797 and republished in London in 1802. Through the career of the hero of this picaresque story, Dr. Updike Underhill, Tyler satirizes college education and medical quackery in the North, and slavery in the South; then, through the capture of Underhill by the Algerines, he paints the miseries of prisoners in that country. One of his uncles had indeed been lost in that manner, and, though Tyler's picture is imaginary, it is vivid. In fact, his fancy was so fertile that his *Yankey in London* (1809), a series of letters supposed to be written by an American living there, deceived some of the English critics.

Tyler's literary work did not interrupt his professional career. It was disturbed, however, by that curious melancholy which had visited him earlier and which apparently caused him to retire from Boston in 1791 and begin his career again in Guildford, Vt. Perhaps some explanation may be found in the charming diary of Mary Palmer, who, against his mother's opposition, became his wife in 1794. He held many professional positions of distinction, being state's attorney for Windham County, 1794–1801; side or assistant judge, 1801–07; and chief justice of the supreme court of Vermont, 1807–13. He was also professor of jurisprudence at the University of Vermont from 1811 to 1814, and trustee from 1802 to 1813. Indeed the only publication in book form in which his name is printed is his two-volume *Reports of Cases Argued and Determined in the Supreme Court of Judicature of Vermont 1800 to 1803* (1809–10). In his most important decision, rendered in 1802, he stated that since according to the constitution of Vermont no inhabitant could own a slave, the bill of sale could not operate in favor of any master who brought a slave within Vermont territory, and that the question was not affected by the laws of the United States.

Undaunted by suffering during his last few years through cancer of the face, which caused blindness and finally ended fatally, Royall Tyler died in Brattleboro, Vt., where he had been living since 1801. He left a tradition there of charm and high spirit, of energy and versatility. Up to two weeks before his death he had been writing a semi-autobiographical story, "The Bay Boy." His ultimate fame will rest upon *The Contrast* and *The Algerine Captive,* pioneer achievements in drama and fiction, to neither of which did he permit his name to be attached.

[Biographical details are based on an unpublished manuscript memoir by Rev. Thomas P. Tyler, son of Royall Tyler, in the Vt. Hist. Soc.; and on *Grandmother Tyler's Book* (1925), the autobiography of Mary Palmer Tyler, ed. by Frederick Tupper and Helen Tyler Brown. The Tyler papers have been deposited in the Vt. Hist. Soc. by Miss Brown, great-granddaughter of Tyler, who has in preparation a biography with A. W. Peach and H. S. Wardner, to all of whom the present writer is indebted. A brief account by Miss Brown is given as an introduction to the limited edition of *The Contrast* (1920). See also B. H. Hall, *Hist. of Eastern Vt.* (1858); M. R. Cabot, *Annals of Brattleboro* (2 vols., 1921); Henry Burnham, *Brattleboro, Vt.* (1880); Frederick Tupper, "Royall Tyler, Man of Law and Man of Letters," *Proc. Vt. Hist. Soc.* (1928); H. M. Ellis, *Joseph Dennie and His Circle* (1915); A. H. Quinn, *A Hist. of the Am. Drama from the Beginning to the Civil War* (1923).]
A. H. Q.

TYLER, SAMUEL (Oct. 22, 1809–Dec. 15, 1877), lawyer, writer, the elder son of Grafton and Anne (Plummer) Tyler, was born in the Forest of Prince George's County, Md., on the Patuxent River tobacco plantation which had been owned by his paternal ancestors since 1660. After a classical education in the academy of Dr. James Carnahan [*q.v.*] at Georgetown, D. C., he attended Middlebury College, Vt. (1826–28) and studied law in the office of John Nelson in Frederick, Md., where he was admitted to the bar in 1831 and practised for thirty-five years. Though often in court in this period, he was more an office lawyer than an advocate. To the quiet of the office and the seclusion of the library his scholarly temperament inclined him, and from the boundless book-learning he acquired therein his principal achievements in the legal field resulted. On the ancient refinements of the adjective law he became an especial authority, and in 1852 the Maryland legislature appointed him one of three commissioners to simplify the practice and pleading in the various courts of the state. In the allotment of work among the commissioners his particular task was the reform of preliminary procedure; when his recommendations therefor were accepted he drew up a statute incorporating them (*Laws Made and Passed by the General Assembly of . . . Maryland,* 1856, ch. 112) and subsequently published *A Treatise on the Maryland Simplified Preliminary Procedure and Pleading* (1857), thus rendering invaluable service to the administration of justice and to the legal profession in the state.

Meanwhile, through articles on logic and metaphysics which he contributed to the *Princeton Review* he gained the approval of Europe and the esteem and correspondence of Sir William Hamilton, celebrated philosopher of the Scottish school of Realism. Several of these papers were collected under the titles *A Discourse of the Baconian Philosophy* (1844) and *The Progress of Philosophy in the Past and in the Future* (1858), and brought him certain academic honors, yet he contributed nothing original to the history of thought and his works on the subject have been long since consigned to the philosophic potter's field.

Abandoning active practice, he lectured from 1867 until his death as professor of law in Columbian (now George Washington) University in Washington, D. C., and during these years published the works that more than any others have caused the survival of his name. His American edition (1871) of H. J. Stephen's *Treatise on the Principles of Pleading* and his *Commentary on the Law of Partnership* (1877), both elementary works for students, are still in frequent use. His authorized *Memoir of Roger Brooke Taney, LL.D.* (1872), notwithstanding the fact that it is an undiluted panegyric of his most intimate friend and a partisan defense of the cause of the Confederacy, long remained the standard biography of the Chief Justice. Indeed, the fragment of Taney autobiography and the anecdotes contained therein would seem to assure its permanence as a source book. Other minor works from his pen were *Robert Burns as a Poet and as a Man* (1848) and *The Theory of the Beautiful* (1873). Tyler was tall, lean, dark, bookish, something of a recluse, but jovial. He died at Georgetown, D. C., and was buried there in Oak Hill Cemetery. His wife, Catherine M. Bayly, whom he married at Frederick, Apr. 16, 1833, and two of their four children survived him.

[Sources include records in the possession of a descendant, Miss Dorothy F. Williams, Chicago, Ill.; Frederick County Marriage Record, 1778–1865, Clerk's office, Frederick, Md.; *Washington Post*, Dec. 17, 18, 19, 1877; *The Sun* (Baltimore), Dec. 17, 19, 1877; E. A. and G. L. Duyckinck, *Cyc. of Am. Lit.* (1875), II, 382; *The Biblical Repertory and Princeton Rev. Index Vol.* (1871); list of other periodical contributions in S. A. Allibone, *A Critical Dict. of Eng. Lit. and British and Am. Authors* (1871); review by Moorfield Storey of *Memoir of Roger Brooke Taney* in *North Am. Rev.*, Jan. 1873. The date of Tyler's death is often given erroneously as Dec. 15, 1878.]

J. J. D.

TYLER, WILLIAM (June 5, 1806–June 18, 1849), Roman Catholic prelate, son of Noah and Abigail (Barber) Tyler, was born at Derby, Vt., from which his parents soon removed to a small farm near Claremont, N. H. The family of the Rev. Daniel Barber (brother of Abigail Tyler) became famous in Catholic circles as the first family of Puritan stock to be converted to Catholicism, the Rev. Daniel and his wife entering the church, their two sons becoming Jesuits, their four daughters Ursuline nuns, and their daughter-in-law a Visitation nun. About 1821 the Tylers were also converted. William was educated in the classical school at Claremont conducted by his cousin, the Rev. Virgil H. Barber. As a convert, and a promising youth of sound training and musical ability, Tyler challenged the attention of Bishop Benedict J. Fenwick [*q.v.*], who took him into his household and instructed him in theology (1826), and apparently sent him to a seminary in Montreal for a brief sojourn. Ordained a priest by Fenwick (June 3, 1829), Father Tyler rejoiced in seeing four sisters join the Sisters of Charity, though his three brothers continued in the world. As perverts, the Tylers aroused some Protestant hostility, but, on the whole, Tyler found no unusual difficulties as a curate at the cathedral in Boston or as a missionary at Canton and Sandwich, Mass., and at Aroostook and Benedicta, Fenwick's Catholic colony, in Maine. A tall, slender, delicate man, his quiet meekness, saintly zeal, methodical life, and humility disarmed criticism, and won the affection of Irish immigrants who were ordinarily suspicious of Yankee priests. As a priest at the cathedral, he made missionary tours of the countryside and visits to the shanty-chapels on public works, and served as vicar-general of the diocese.

At the Fifth Provincial Council of Baltimore, the bishops petitioned Rome to erect a new see at Hartford, Conn., with Tyler as bishop. Consecrated by Fenwick (Mar. 17, 1844), Tyler found that southern New England was even less fertile soil for Catholicism than Massachusetts. As Hartford was a small town with only a wooden church, he moved his headquarters to Providence, with a Catholic population of 2,000. There he lived in a wretched cottage, but, aided by gifts from the Leopoldine Society of Vienna and the Society for the Propagation of the Faith of Lyons, he managed to enlarge his Cathedral of SS. Peter and Paul into one of the best churches in New England (1847). With assistance from All Hallows Seminary, Dublin, and with the beginning of Irish immigration on a large scale, the little diocese of 10,000 doubled its population and increased the number of its priests from six to fourteen. Constant crusading against liquor sellers and intemperance resulted in a reformation of conduct, but made Tyler rather unpopular among wealthy Catholics of Providence (*American Catholic Historical Researches,* Jan. 1895). While he built only four primitive churches and made a contribution that seems intangible and undramatic, he quietly laid the foundations of the church in an unfriendly region with a minimum of nativist friction. In summary of his character, Bishop John Bernard Fitzpatrick [*q.v.*] of Boston confided to his diary that though Tyler was neither learned nor brilliant, he was a model for young priests because he was a firm, diligent man of sound prudence, who squandered no time from his duty.

[L. M. Wilson, *Barber Geneal.* (1909); R. H. Clarke, *Lives of the Deceased Bishops of the Cath. Church in the U. S.,* vol. II (1888); William Byrne, *The Hist. of the Cath. Church in the New Eng. States* (1899), vol. II, p. 122; *Cath. Encyc.,* vol. VII (1910), p. 144; Louis de Goesbriand, *Cath. Memoirs of Vt. and N. H.* (1891); T. S. Duggan, *The Cath. Church in Conn.* (1930); *Metropolitan Cath. Directory* (1850), p. 216; *Cath. Observer* (Boston) and *Pilot* (Boston), June 1849; obituary in *Republican Herald* (Providence, R. I.), June 20, 1849.]
R. J. P.

TYLER, WILLIAM SEYMOUR (Sept. 2, 1810–Nov. 19, 1897), college professor, was the eldest of three sons of Joab and Nabby (Seymour) Tyler, and a descendant of Job Tyler, an early settler of Andover, Mass. He was born in Harford, Pa., a pioneer village in the beechwood forests along the Susquehanna, where his father and grandfather, natives of Attleboro, Mass., had been among the earliest settlers. As a boy he learned the frugal, industrious habits, the sturdy self-reliance, and the intense aspirations of a New England community transplanted into the wilderness. His education, begun in the schoolroom under his father's roof, was intermittently continued at various local academies and under the tutelage of neighboring ministers. He entered the junior class at Hamilton College in September 1827, but left to teach school after completing one term. In February 1829 he joined the junior class at Amherst College, where he graduated as valedictorian in 1830. There followed one year of teaching at Amherst Academy, two years of theological study at Andover interrupted by two years as a tutor in Amherst College, and a final year of divinity under the Rev. Thomas H. Skinner of New York. Tyler was then ready to become a home missionary in the West, but was recalled to Amherst unexpectedly to fill a tutorship vacated by his brother. At the end of his term (August 1836) he was appointed professor of Latin and Greek, and remained in the active service of the college—as Williston Professor of

Greek from 1847—for fifty-six years. In 1893 he became professor emeritus.

Within this exceptionally long term of active service, which was only twice interrupted by periods of travel in Europe and the Holy Land, Tyler taught every member of fifty-one successive classes, until in 1888 Greek was made an optional study. His conception of Greek civilization as a dramatic moment in the unfolding of human nature's highest possibilities so vitalized his treatment of ancient literature that his students often felt that they were hearing the authentic voice of Demosthenes or Plato. Besides performing countless services for the college outside the range of his classroom duties, Tyler was ceaselessly interested in the religious and educational affairs of western Massachusetts. He was ordained to the Congregational ministry at North Amherst on Oct. 16, 1859, and frequently supplied pulpits in nearby towns. His activity at convocations was so great that he was playfully called the bishop of Hampshire County. His sermons from the college pulpit were remembered by generations of undergraduates because of their pointed applications and robust fervor. Tyler was chiefly responsible for framing the constitution and policy of Williston Seminary, and was president of its board of trustees from its foundation. He was also a trustee of Mount Holyoke Seminary (later College) from 1862, and of Smith College from 1871, and president of the board of trustees of both institutions. He was a founder of the Amherst chapter of Phi Beta Kappa and its first president, and a member of many national societies concerned with the study of classical philology and archeology.

Tyler was married on Sept. 4, 1839, to Amelia O. Whiting of Binghamton, N. Y. They had four sons, all graduates of Amherst; one became a professor of Greek in Smith College and one returned to Amherst as professor of biology. The Tyler home inevitably became a center of pilgrimage for visiting dignitaries and alumni. In spite of the many calls upon his time, however, Tyler worked untiringly as a scholar, editing numerous Latin and Greek authors for classroom use, writing popular or learned articles for magazines and encyclopedias, and composing the sermons, occasional discourses, and memorial addresses that were constantly demanded of him. His finest book was a labor of love, the *History of Amherst College during its First Half Century* (1873), later abridged and continued as *A History of Amherst College during the Administrations of its First Five Presidents* (1895), to the writing of which the author brought both an intimate knowledge of personalities and events and the deep feeling of consecration characteristic of the founders of the college. More than any other one man Tyler had given himself to the making of Amherst College, and his history of its achievement is his best monument.

[*Autobiog. of William Seymour Tyler* (1912), ed. by C. B. Tyler; W. I. T. Brigham, *The Tyler Geneal.* (2 vols., 1912); *Obit. Record Grads. Amherst Coll.*, vol. IV (1898); *Amherst Coll. Biog. Record* (1927); *Springfield Republican*, Nov. 20, 1897.]   G. F. W.

TYNDALE, HECTOR (Mar. 24, 1821–Mar. 19, 1880), merchant, Union soldier, was the son of Robinson and Sarah (Thorn) Tyndale. His father, who was reputed to be a lineal descendant of William Tyndale the Bible translator and martyr, had emigrated from Ireland to Philadelphia early in the nineteenth century and become a dealer in china and glass; his mother was a Philadelphian by birth and a member of the Society of Friends. Young Tyndale was educated at a Philadelphia school, upon leaving which he was offered an appointment to the United States Military Academy. Yielding to the wishes of his mother he declined the appointment, and went into business with his father. In August 1842 he married Julia Nowlen, and, at the death of his father in 1845, he and his brother-in-law, Edward P. Mitchell, formed a partnership in the business of importing glass. He subsequently made numerous trips to Europe, visiting the leading factories there, collecting many specimens of pottery, and becoming an authority in the field of ceramics.

A Free-soiler in politics, he affiliated himself with the rising Republican party, and served as a member of the first Republican committee in Philadelphia. In 1859 the wife of John Brown stopped at Philadelphia on her way to Charles Town, Va. (now W. Va.), to visit her imprisoned husband, and, after his execution, to bring his body North for burial. Tyndale believed her to be in such personal danger at that time that he voluntarily served as her escort. He was never an abolitionist, but years after this incident occurred his political enemies accused him of disloyalty to the Union because of his gallant gesture in behalf of a defenseless woman.

Tyndale was in Paris at the outbreak of the Civil War. He immediately hastened home, and in June 1861 was commissioned major of the 28th Regiment, Pennsylvania Volunteers. This regiment participated in a total of forty-three engagements during the war, Tyndale taking part in practically all of them. He commanded the forces near Harpers Ferry in August 1861, and at that time received several wounds. In April 1862 he was promoted lieutenant-colonel. He

next served in Banks's Corps in the Shenandoah Valley campaign, and under Pope in the battles of Chantilly and second Bull Run. At Antietam, where three horses were shot from under him, he was twice wounded and left on the field for dead. Because of his conspicuous bravery at that battle he was promoted brigadier-general, Nov. 29, 1862. He subsequently went to the support of Thomas at Chattanooga; led a bayonet charge to relieve Geary at Wauhatchie, Tenn.; distinguished himself at Missionary Ridge; and, with Sherman, participated in the campaign to relieve Knoxville. With health seriously impaired by disease and strenuous campaigning, he resigned from the service in August 1864. He was brevetted major-general the following March for gallant and meritorious service during the war.

As a civilian, Tyndale was highly esteemed. He was a successful merchant; a member of many patriotic and scientific societies; and, as the Republican candidate for mayor of Philadelphia in 1868, was defeated by a narrow margin. He was trustee of a fund which provided a number of university scholarships in physics, and one of these, at the University of Pennsylvania, bears his name. He died in Philadelphia; his wife, but no children, survived him.

[John McLaughlin, *A Memoir of Hector Tyndale* (1882); *Re-union of the 28th and 147th Regiments, Pa. Volunteers* (1872); F. B. Heitman, *Hist. Reg. and Dict. U. S. Army* (1903); *Public Ledger* (Phila.) and *Phila. Press*, Mar. 20, 1880; *Phila. Record*, Mar. 22, 1880; *N. Y. Tribune*, Mar. 21, 1880; *Pa. Mag. of Hist. and Biog.*, Jan. 1916, pp. 1–3; *Univ. of Pa. Cat., 1931–32* (1931), p. 163.]   R. W. I.

TYNG, EDWARD (1683–Sept. 8, 1755), naval officer, was born in Boston, Mass., the grandson of Edward Tyng who came to Massachusetts from England about 1630 and died in Dunstable in 1681, and the son of Col. Edward Tyng, whose wife was a daughter of Ensign Thaddeus Clarke of Portland, Me. The father was appointed governor of Annapolis Royal, Nova Scotia, and on his way to the colony was captured by the French and taken to France, where he died in prison. In 1736 in consideration of the sufferings and great expense of the father the Massachusetts General Court granted the son a tract of land (*The Acts and Resolves of the Province of the Massachusetts Bay*, vol. XII, 1904, pp. 325, 462). As a youth Edward followed the sea and later was a merchant in Boston. His first wife, whom he married Jan. 8, 1725, was Elizabeth, daughter of Capt. Cyprian Southack [*q.v.*] and widow of Francis Parnel; his second, a sister of Gen. Samuel Waldo [*q.v.*], Ann Waldo, to whom he was married Jan. 27, 1731, and by whom he had seven children.

On Apr. 16, 1740, Governor Belcher appointed Tyng captain of the batteries and fortifications in Boston and a few months later made him commander of the province snow *Prince of Orange,* recently built for the protection of the navigation and trade of the colony. During 1741–43 Tyng cruised after Spanish privateers chiefly off the New England coast, but on one cruise he went as far southward as St. Augustine, Fla. On the outbreak of King George's War in 1744, after a chase off Cape Cod of some twelve hours, he overtook a French privateer commanded by Captain Delabroitz and forced her to strike her colors. Out of gratitude Boston voted him its thanks and the merchants of the town presented him with a silver cup. In July he was sent to Annapolis Royal with reinforcements. His arrival there proved most opportune, for the place was besieged by the Indians and French, who fled on his approach, to the great relief of the besieged. For the rest of the year he was employed in convoy duty off the New England coast and to the eastward as far as the Grand Banks. Early in 1745 he was promoted to the command of the frigate *Massachusetts,* in which vessel, alone or in company with provincial or Royal vessels, he cruised after French ships. He was also employed in blockade and transport duties. As senior officer of the Massachusetts navy, he participated in the taking of the *Vigilante,* of 64 guns, the capture of Louisbourg, and the destruction of St. Ann. He was one of the leading American naval officers of the colonial period. His death occurred at Boston, after a stroke of paralysis. His residence was on Milk Street and he also owned property on Fleet Street and near Windmill Point.

[*Mass. Hist. Soc. Colls.,* 1 ser. X (1809), 180–83; Timothy Alden, *A Coll. of Am. Epitaphs* (1814), II, 97–101; Elias Nason, *A Hist. of the Town of Dunstable* (1877); Waldo Lincoln, *The Province Snow "Prince of Orange"* (1901); S. G. Drake, *A Particular Hist. of the Five Years' French and Indian War* (1870); L. E. de Forest, *Louisbourg Journals, 1745* (1932); H. M. Chapin, *Privateering in King George's War* (1928); *A Report of the Record Commissioners of the City of Boston* (1898), containing Boston marriages, 1700–1751; Justin Winsor, *The Memorial Hist. of Boston,* vol. II (1882).]　　　　　　　　　　　　　　C. O. P.

TYNG, STEPHEN HIGGINSON (Mar. 1, 1800–Sept. 3, 1885), Episcopal clergyman, born at Newburyport, Mass., was the fourth child of Dudley Atkins, who adopted the name of Tyng on inheriting the estate of his kinswoman, Sarah (Tyng) Winslow. He was a descendant of Joseph Atkins, who came to Newbury, Mass., in 1728, and also of Edward Tyng, who died in Dunstable, Mass., in 1681. Stephen's mother, Sarah, was the eldest daughter of the Hon. Stephen Higginson of Salem, Mass., a descendant of Francis Higginson [*q.v.*], one of the founders of Salem in 1629. After attending private schools young Tyng entered Harvard College, where he was graduated at the age of seventeen. Two years later he abandoned an unusually promising business career to prepare for the ministry of the Episcopal Church and studied theology under the direction of the Rt. Rev. Alexander V. Griswold [*q.v.*]. He was ordered deacon on Mar. 4, 1821, by Bishop Griswold, whose daughter, Anne, he married on Aug. 5 of that year; he was ordained priest in 1824 by Bishop Kemp of Maryland. His fifty-seven years of active ministry were spent at St. John's Church, Georgetown, D. C. (1821–23); Queen Anne's Parish, Prince Georges County, Md. (1823–29); St. Paul's Church, Philadelphia (1829–34); Church of the Epiphany, Philadelphia (1834–45) and St. George's Church, New York (1845–78).

Tyng was one of the outstanding figures in religious circles. He was a man of imperious temper—which he did not always control—and of commanding personality; he did not take kindly to opposition and was at times autocratic. He was described as "the prince of platform orators" and Henry Ward Beecher said of him, "He is the one man that I am afraid of. When he speaks first I do not care to follow him" (T. L. Cuyler, *Recollections of a Long Life,* 1902, p. 200). He shared with the Rev. Dr. Francis Lister Hawks [*q.v.*] the distinction of being the greatest preacher in the Episcopal Church. Noted for his fearlessness in the pulpit, at times he rose to great heights of eloquence and moved his hearers like a wind-swept sea. Vast congregations flocked to hear him; St. Paul's Church in Philadelphia, when he was rector, was popularly known as "Tyng's Theatre." He was one of the first to recognize the importance of Sunday schools and his own school in Philadelphia had more than two thousand children. This work in religious education he continued in New York, and under his direction St. George's parish was the first to establish mission chapels for the poor on the East Side of the city.

Tyng's ministry covered a period of great importance in the development of the Episcopal Church in the United States. At the outset the Evangelicals were dominant. That dominance was challenged by the high churchmen who were profoundly influenced by the Tractarian movement. The development of ritual in the services of the church followed. A few years after he went to St. George's, broad churchmanship became dominant under the leadership of men like Phillips Brooks and David H. Greer [*qq.v.*]. Against all these developments Tyng set his face like steel; he was a typical low churchman. Trained in the straitest school of the Evangelicals, he never faltered in his allegiance; broad churchman was just as obnoxious to him as high churchman, and both he fought tooth and nail. He was content to walk in the old paths. In his early ministry in Maryland he crossed swords with Bishop James Kemp and in his later years in New York he entered the lists against Bishop Horatio Potter. Like Bishop Manton Eastburn of Massachusetts, Tyng never changed a theological opinion, with the unhappy result that he never rose above the position of being the leader of a party in the church.

Among his publications were *Lectures on the Law and the Gospel* (3rd ed., 1844), *Recollections of England* (1847), *The Israel of God* (1849), *Christ Is All* (1849), *Christian Titles* (1853), *Fellowship with Christ* (1854), *The Rich Kinsman; the History of Ruth the Moabitess* (1855), *The Captive Orphan; Esther, Queen of Persia* (1860); *Forty Years Experience in Sunday Schools* (1860); *The Spencers, a Story of Home Influence* (1869). He also served as an editor of the *Episcopal Recorder* (Philadelphia), and of the *Protestant Churchman* (New York). He resigned the rectorship of St. George's, New York, in 1878 and was made rector emeritus. The closing years of his life were marked by mental decline, and he died at Irvington-on-Hudson, N. Y. His first wife died in 1832, and in July 1833 he married Susan Mitchell. He had four children by his first wife, and five by his second.

[F. H. Atkins, *Joseph Atkins, the Story of a Family* (1891); C. R. Tyng, *Record of the Life and Work of the Rev. Stephen Higginson Tyng, D.D., and Hist. of St. George's Church, N. Y., to the Close of His Rectorship* (1890); Henry Anstice, *Hist. of St. George's Church in the City of N. Y.* (1911); *Churchman*, Sept. 12, 1885; *N. Y. Tribune*, Sept. 5, 1885.]   E. C. C.

TYSON, GEORGE EMORY (Dec. 15, 1829–Oct. 18, 1906), whaler, Arctic explorer, was born at Red Bank, N. J., son of Peter and Clarica Tyson. In his infancy his parents moved to New York City, where he attended the public schools and afterwards worked in an iron foundry. An early interest in Arctic adventure led him in February 1850 to ship from New London in the whaler *M'Clellan,* and he was one of twelve volunteers from the ship who wintered in 1851–52 in Cumberland Sound. He rose to mate and master, and in 1860–70 was steadily engaged in command of Arctic whalers, taking the *Antelope* in 1864 to Repulse Bay, furthest north for whaleships of the time. He had frequently met the explorer Charles Francis Hall [*q.v.*], and in 1870 was invited by Hall to be sailing-master and ice-

pilot in his projected Arctic expedition in the *Polaris.* Though at first prevented by other engagements, he finally joined in a specially created post as assistant navigator. With seven officers, three scientists, and fifteen seamen, the *Polaris* left Brooklyn, June 29, 1871, and after making a furthest north record (82° 11′) wintered in Hall Basin, North Greenland. Hall died in November. In the ensuing period, marked by much friction and indiscipline, Tyson, now second in command, was apparently a neutral and stabilizing influence. In subsequent investigations his honesty and modesty were recognized, as well as his stamina and temperamental fitness for Arctic hardships. Capt. Edwin White, a fellow whaler, described him as "the best man to consult with that I have ever met . . . his power of endurance ahead of anyone I ever traveled with" (*Arctic Experiences, post,* p. 423). In the autumn of 1872, on Oct. 15, the *Polaris,* endeavoring to work southward and leaking badly, was nearly crushed by ice. Having built a storehouse on the ice, Tyson and others were shifting supplies to it when the ship broke loose in the darkness, leaving nineteen of them—Tyson, the meteorologist Meyers, eight seamen, and two Eskimos with their wives and five children—adrift on the floe. Their ensuing experience is among the most extraordinary in Arctic annals. For six and a half months they drifted southward through winter darkness, dependent for food chiefly on the desperate efforts of the Eskimo hunters, and forced toward the last to shift from floe to floe and cling to their boat to prevent its being washed away by stormy seas. Without a life lost, they were picked up, Apr. 30, 1873, by the sealer *Tigress* off Labrador.

Later that year Tyson was made temporary lieutenant and ice-master in the *Tigress,* purchased by the United States Navy, and sent north to seek the remaining *Polaris* party, who, it was learned later, had left her and been rescued by a whaler. In 1877–78 he also commanded the *Florence,* sent to the Arctic to establish a preliminary base for the Howgate expedition, subsequently abandoned. During his later years he lived in Washington, D. C., where he had a position as captain of the guard in the Navy Department. He was married, probably about 1870, to Helen (McElroy) Myers, a widow with three sons.

[*Arctic Experiences: Containing Capt. George E. Tyson's Wonderful Drift on the Ice-Floe, A History of the Polaris Expedition* (1874), ed. by E. V. Blake; C. H. Davis, *Narrative of the North Polar Expedition: U. S. Ship Polaris* (1876); J. E. Nourse, *Narrative of the Second Polar Expedition Made by Charles F. Hall* (1879), being *Sen. Exec. Doc. 27,* 45 Cong., 3 Sess.; *The Cruise of the Florence* (1879), ed. by H. W. Howgate; *Who's Who in America*, 1903–05; obituary articles in *Washington Post*, Oct. 20, 21, 1906.]

A. W—t.

TYSON, JAMES (Oct. 26, 1841–Feb. 21, 1919), physician and teacher, was born in Philadelphia, Pa., the son of Dr. Henry Tyson and Gertrude (Haviland) Caswell Tyson. His father, who practised medicine in Reading, Pa., was a direct descendant of Cornelius Teisen of Germantown (born in Crefeld), one of the many Germans who emigrated to America from the Palatinate about the beginning of the eighteenth century. After getting his schooling at the Friends' Central School in Philadelphia, Tyson entered Haverford College, from which he received the degrees of A.B. (1861) and A.M. (1864). He studied medicine in the medical department of the University of Pennsylvania and was graduated in 1863. During his last year in the medical school he was a medical cadet in the United States army hospital at Broad and Cherry Streets, Philadelphia. After his graduation he served as an acting assistant surgeon in the United States Army until July 1863, when he resigned to become resident physician in the Pennsylvania Hospital. Later he again became an acting assistant surgeon in the army, serving in that capacity until the close of the Civil War. He then entered into private practice in Philadelphia. In 1868 began his long association with the University of Pennsylvania. He was lecturer on microscopy (1868), on urinary chemistry (1870), and on pathological anatomy and histology (1874), professor of general pathology and morbid anatomy (1876), and professor of clinical medicine (1889). In 1899 he succeeded the younger William Pepper [*q.v.*] in the chair of medicine, which he held until 1910, when he was retired as emeritus professor of medicine. From 1888 to 1892 he was dean of the medical faculty. He was on the staffs of many hospitals, including the Pennsylvania and the Philadelphia, and was one of the incorporators and very active in the affairs of the Rush Hospital for Consumptives. He was consulting physician to St. Mary's Hospital, the Kensington Hospital for Women, and the Jewish Hospital.

He was a frequent contributor to periodical medical literature and the author of a number of successful books: *The Cell Doctrine, Its History and Present State* (1870), *A Guide to the Practical Examination of Urine* (1875), *A Treatise on Bright's Disease and Diabetes* (1881), *Manual of Physical Diagnosis* (1891), and *The Practice of Medicine* (1896), all of which went through several editions. For some years he was an assistant editor of the *Philadelphia Medical Times* and a member of the editorial board of the *Philadelphia Medical News*; from 1871 to 1877 he edited the *Transactions* of the Pathological Society of Philadelphia. Tyson served as president of the Philadelphia County Medical Society (1897), the Pathological Society of Philadelphia (1882–84), the College of Physicians of Philadelphia (1907–10), and the Pennsylvania State Medical Society (1911). He was one of the founders of the Association of American Physicians (1886), its first secretary, and in 1907 its president. In 1887 he was elected a member of the American Philosophical Society. For some years he was recorder of the biological and microscopical section of the Academy of Natural Sciences of Philadelphia. In 1894 an undergraduate society, named in his honor the James Tyson Medical Society, was founded among the medical classes at the University of Pennsylvania. On Dec. 5, 1865, Tyson married Frances Bosdevex, of Belgian descent. They had a son, who became a physician, and a daughter. There are excellent oil paintings of Tyson at the University of Pennsylvania and in the College of Physicians of Philadelphia.

[J. W. Jordan, *Colonial and Revolutionary Families of Pa.* (1911), vol. I; *Who's Who in America*, 1918–19; M. H. Fussell, in *Trans. Coll. of Physicians of Phila.*, 3 ser., vol. XLIII (1921); *Jour. Am. Medic. Asso.*, Mar. 3, 1919; *Medic. Record* (N. Y.), and *N. Y. Medic. Jour.*, Mar. 1, 1919; obituary in *Pub. Ledger* (Phila.), Feb. 22, 1919; personal acquaintance; autobiog. notes in MS. in the possession of Mrs. H. W. Stokes of Phila., Tyson's daughter; information from Mrs. Stokes.]

F. R. P.

TYSON, JOB ROBERTS (Feb. 8, 1803–June 27, 1858), lawyer, congressman, historical writer, was born in or near Philadelphia, the son of Joseph and Ann (Trump) Tyson and a descendant of Reynier Tyson who settled in what is now Germantown, Pa., in 1683. Joseph Tyson, a Philadelphia merchant, started his son on a business career, but the youth turned to school teaching and the study of law, and in 1827 was admitted to the bar. On Oct. 4, 1832, he married Eleanor, daughter of Thomas P. Cope [*q.v.*], a prominent Philadelphia merchant and philanthropist. He was vice-provost of the Philadelphia Law Academy, 1833–58; a solicitor of the Pennsylvania Railroad, 1847–55; an early director of the Philadelphia public schools; a member of the Select Council of Philadelphia, 1846–49; and a Whig congressman for one inconspicuous term, 1855–57. He was an effective writer and an excellent speaker; a score or more of his speeches were printed. Participating actively in the reforms of the thirties, he was a friend of temperance and a foe of lotteries. He hoped to solve the slavery problem by colonization, served in the ranks of the Society for Alleviating the Miseries of Public Prisons, and drafted a report on the impropriety of capital punishment. He was a manager of the Apprentices' Library in Philadelphia, and a trustee of Girard College and of the Pennsylvania Female College. On Jan. 15, 1836, he was elected a member of the American Philosophical Society.

His greatest interest was history. One of the early members of the Historical Society of Pennsylvania and an officer from 1829 to 1848, he was among the first to grasp the importance of intensive study of Pennsylvania history. The Indians, the Revolution, the social and intellectual state of Penn's colony, the life of William Penn, the history of art in America, were objects of his study. In his *Discourse . . . on the Colonial History of the Eastern and Some of the Southern States* (1842), also published in *Memoirs of the Historical Society of Pennsylvania* (vol. IV, pt. 2, 1850), he attacked New England historians for their claims, denying that enlarged social freedom owed its existence to the Puritans and maintaining rather that it triumphed in spite of their hostility, and that Penn's contribution to liberty was more significant. This paper marks him as a pioneer in readjusting the balance of historical interpretation. The most tangible results of his historical interest are the first volumes of the printed archives of Pennsylvania. As a member of a joint committee of the Philosophical and Historical societies he was instrumental in petitioning the legislature (1836) to provide for the printing of the archives, and his brother, J. Washington Tyson, as chairman of a committee of the legislature, reported favorably upon the project. Thus a beginning was made with three volumes (1838–40) containing the minutes of the Provincial Council, and the series has been continued intermittently ever since. Tyson planned to write a history of the state, but died before he could make systematic use of his collected material.

[F. W. Leach, "Old Philadelphia Families—The Tyson Family," *North American* (Phila.), July 21, 1912; H. L. Carson, "A History of the Historical Society of Pennsylvania" (MSS. in Hist. Soc. of Pa. and Free Library of Phila.); *Biog. Dir. Am. Cong.* (1928); *Dollar Newspaper* (Phila.), June 30, 1858; *North American and United States Gazette* (Phila.), June 28, 1858.]
R. F. N.

TYSON, LAWRENCE DAVIS (July 4, 1861–Aug. 24, 1929), soldier, newspaper publisher, and senator from Tennessee, was born near Greenville, N. C., the son of Richard Lawrence and Margaret Louise (Turnage) Tyson. His ancestors had settled in Pitt County, N. C., about 1720; his father served with the Confederate forces throughout the Civil War. Tyson graduated from the United States Military Academy in 1883, was commissioned lieutenant of the 9th Infantry, and took part in the campaign against the Apache Indians. On Feb. 10, 1886, he married Bettie Humes McGhee, daughter of Charles M. McGhee [*q.v.*], a leading railroad financier of the South. From 1891 to 1895, by appointment of the War Department, he was professor of military science in the University of Tennessee at Knoxville. While here he studied law, receiving the degree of LL.B. in 1894; in April 1896 he resigned his commission in the army and entered on the practice of law in Knoxville. Two years later, during the war with Spain, he was appointed colonel of the 6th United States Volunteer Infantry and served in Puerto Rico; in 1899, after peace was declared, he was for some months military governor of the north-central portion of that island. He was mustered out of the service, May 15, 1899.

Resuming practice in Knoxville, he was elected to the House of Representatives of the Tennessee General Assembly of 1903, and was chosen speaker; he was delegate-at-large to the Democratic National Convention of 1908; and in 1913 was an unsuccessful candidate for the United States senatorship. He served for a number of years as brigadier-general and inspector-general of the Tennessee National Guard. When the United States entered the World War, he was placed by the governor in command of the Tennessee National Guard but in August 1917 was appointed by President Wilson brigadier-general, National Army, and assigned to the 59th Brigade of the 30th Division, at Camp Sevier, S. C. His brigade of 8,000 men, made up in large part of soldiers from Tennessee, embarked for France on May 10, 1918, and in July was sent to join the British forces in Belgium. It was in almost continuous action from July 5 to Oct. 20, 1918, suffering losses of some 3,000 in killed and wounded. Its signal achievement was its participation in the breaking of the Hindenburg line: "The 59th brigade went through the line at St. Quentin tunnel, advancing further to Bellicourt and neighboring towns. This was accomplished in three days of terrific fighting" (Official Records, quoted by Hamer, *post,* p. 23). Tyson subsequently received the Distinguished Service Medal.

Returning to his home in Knoxville, he purchased and became publisher of the Knoxville *Sentinel*. In 1920 he was indorsed by the state Democratic convention for the vice-presidential nomination, but in the Democratic National Convention he withdrew his name and seconded the nomination of Franklin D. Roosevelt. Nominated by a primary election in 1924, he won election as United States senator for the term beginning in 1925. In the Senate he advocated adherence to the World Court and was joint author of the Tyson-Fitzgerald bill which gave full retirement compensation to disabled emergency officers of the United States in the World War. In 1927 he was a delegate to the conference of the Interparliamentary Union held in Paris. He was interested in the larger industrial concerns of his city and region, was president of coal companies and textile mills, and in 1923 was president of the American Cotton Manufacturers' Association. With his wife he gave Tyson Park to the city of Knoxville. He died in Philadelphia, survived by his wife and a daughter; his only son died in the World War.

[P. M. Hamer, *Tenn., A Hist.* (1933), vol. III; W. T. Hale and D. L. Merritt, *A Hist. of Tenn.* (1913), vol. VII; G. W. Cullum, *Biog. Reg. Officers and Grads. U. S. Mil. Acad.*, vols. III (1891), VI (1920), VII (1930); *Who's Who in America*, 1928–29; *Biog. Dir. Am. Cong.* (1928); *Lawrence D. Tyson: Memorial Addresses in the Senate and House of Representatives* (1930); *News-Sentinel* (Knoxville), Aug. 25, 1929; *Knoxville Jour.*, Aug. 24, 25, 1929.]   S. C. W.

TYSON, STUART LAWRENCE (Nov. 12, 1873–Sept. 16, 1932), Protestant Episcopal clergyman, was born in Pennllyn, Pa., the son of Herbert Benezet and Mary (Stuart) Tyson. His father was a nephew of Job Roberts Tyson [*q.v.*] and a descendant of Reynier Tyson who emigrated to Pennsylvania from Crefeld, Prussia, in 1683. Reynier was probably a brother of Cornelius, ancestor of James Tyson [*q.v.*]. After routine schooling, Stuart went to Nashota House, Wisconsin, the Anglo-Catholic seminary of the Episcopal Church, to prepare for the ministry. He was graduated in 1895, and in this same year, Apr. 25, he married Katharine Emily Rosengarten of Philadelphia, who was killed in an accident in 1915. In 1895, also, he was ordained deacon, and two years later, priest. After a brief pastorate in Milwaukee, Wis., he went to Oxford, England, in 1899, where he remained eight years as student at St. John's College, special preacher at the University (1899–1903), assistant at St. Paul's Church (1904–07), and tutor (1903–05). He received three degrees from Oxford—M.A., B.D., and D.D., the last awarded in 1923 "in course."

Tyson returned to America in 1907 to become professor of New Testament at the Western Theological Seminary, Chicago. From here he went in 1908 to the University of the South, where he served five years as professor of New Testament and liturgics. He resigned in 1913 to give his chief time and labor to lecturing under the auspices of the Tyson Lectureship Foundation for the Promotion of Christian Knowledge, an organization of Episcopalian clergymen, laymen, and laywomen which he was instrumental in establishing for the popular interpretation of the Scriptures in the light of scientific truth. In 1919 he accepted appointment as lecturer, special preacher, and honorary vicar at the Cathedral of St. John the Divine, New York. In 1924 he was transferred to the staff of St. George's Church.

This last appointment may be said to mark the climax in the long process of his theological development. Educated in a conservative school, Tyson was led by his Biblical studies, continued through many years, into the liberal wing of contemporary religious thought. His preaching became a vigorous advocacy of liberalism. His lecturing, which long absorbed his best attention, was devoted to expounding the modern significance of the Bible. In the controversies which broke out in the Episcopal Church in the decades before and after the World War, he was a consistent modernist. He sprang quickly to the defense of priests who fell under attack of their bishops for heresy. Thus, in 1914, he was chairman of the Heaton Defense Committee, when the Rev. Lee W. Heaton, a Texas rector, was cited by Bishop Harry T. Moore for trial on charges that he "had denied the supernatural and the divinity of Jesus." Tyson also figured prominently in the cases of Bishop-elect Herbert Shipman and of the Rev. Percy Stickney Grant [*q.v.*]. It was his steadfast contention that clergymen should have full right to "think freely, and to use present-day knowledge in religion as well as in all other relations of life." As the New York diocese fell more and more into the hands of conservatives, it was natural that he should move from the Cathedral to St. George's. A year later (1925) his divorce of his second wife, Anna Gertrude W. Mullins—whom he married Mar. 17, 1917—on grounds of cruelty, created a situation which led to his retirement from the Episcopal ministry. Tyson declared that the resignation, thus precipitated by unhappy outward events, was in reality "the final result of a process" within himself which had begun long before. In 1925 he entered the Congregational ministry, and in his last years was pastor of the Community Church, Summit, N. J., a society composed predominantly of Unitarians and Universalists.

Tyson died in New York after a week's illness from pneumonia. He was survived by his third wife, Margaretta Wentz, whom he married Apr. 18, 1927, and by twelve of thirteen children by his first wife. He was the author of *The Eucharist in St. Paul* (1923), and numerous lectures, sermons, and articles.

[*Who's Who in America*, 1918–19, 1932–33; *N. Y. Times*, Sept. 17, 1932; *N. Y. Herald Tribune*, Sept. 17, 1932; *Churchman*, Sept. 24, 1932; F. W. Leach, "Old Philadelphia Families—The Tyson Family," *North American* (Phila.), July 21, 1912.]   J. H. H.

UDDEN, JOHAN AUGUST (Mar. 19, 1859–Jan. 5, 1932), geologist, was born in Uddabo, Lekasa parish, Vestergötland, Sweden, the son of Andrew Larsen and Inga Lena (Andersdotter) Udden. Two years after his birth his parents emigrated to America, and settled in Minnesota, where Udden spent his early youth. He was graduated with the B.A. degree from Augustana College, Rock Island, Ill., in 1881, studied at the University of Minnesota in 1886, and received the M.A. degree from Augustana in 1889. From 1881 to 1888 he taught natural science, German, and civics at Bethany College, Lindsborg, Kan., and from 1888 to 1911 was professor of geology and natural history at Augustana College. He held membership in several scientific societies, and was a fellow of the American Association for the Advancement of Science. His fields of investigation included stratigraphic and areal geology, work of the atmosphere, till in the upper Mississippi Valley, clastic sediments, and related subjects. His published papers on these subjects number about one hundred titles.

The geologic activities of Udden had far-reaching effects upon the development of both theoretical and economic geology. The qualities of his mind and the circumstances of his early scientific training combined to give him preeminent characteristics as a research geologist. Because of the slight development of specialized geological training in his early school days, he received relatively little professional guidance in the subject. He early determined to rely upon his own powers of observation and reasoning. The richness and originality of his work and the independence of his geological thought are attested by all his principal papers. His study on the "Mechanical Composition of Clastic Sediments," published in the *Bulletin of the Geological Society of America*, Dec. 14, 1914, established an adequate quantitative method of treating the material, and outlined the major features of this early branch of sedimentology.

His active mind was ever alert for the development of new geological methods. He was one of the first in America to point out and stress the value of seismograph observations for locating geologic structure. His work on the technique of examining subsurface material, now universal-

ly followed, was purely pioneer research. In Texas he worked on a virgin field with an observant, open, and critical mind, and his labors found their rich reward in the contributions made to the science of geology and to the economic development of the state. In grateful recognition of services that he gave, his many friends joined in establishing in his honor the Johan August Udden Publication and Research Fund of The University of Texas.

Udden was geologist of the Bureau of Economic Geology and Technology of The University of Texas from 1911 to 1915, and director of the Bureau from that time until his death. He was a special assistant with the Iowa Geological Survey, 1897–1903, geologist for the University of Texas Mineral Survey, 1903–04, geologist for the Illinois Geological Survey, 1906–11, and special agent of the United States Geological Survey, 1908–14. His distinguished services were recognized by his native country in 1911, when he was decorated with the Order of the North Star by the king of Sweden. At his death he was survived by his widow, Johanna Kristina Davis, to whom he had been married in 1882, and one of their four children.

[*Who's Who in America*, 1930–31; C. L. Baker, "Memorial of Johan August Udden," *Bull. Geological Soc. of America*, Apr. 30, 1933 (includes a bibliography of Udden's publications); E. H. Sellards, *Bull. Am. Asso. Petroleum Geologists*, Mar. 1932; *Memorial to Dr. Johan August Udden: The Univ. of Tex. Bull.*, No. 3201, Nov. 1932; *Alcalde* (Univ. of Tex.), Mar. 1932; *Dallas Morning News*, Jan. 6, 1932.]

E. H. S.

UHLER, PHILIP REESE (June 3, 1835–Oct. 21, 1913), entomologist, librarian, was born in Baltimore, Md., the son of George Washington Uhler, a merchant of that city, and Anna Maria (Reese) Uhler. His great-grandfather, Erasmus Uhler, emigrated to America from England and served as a private in the Revolutionary War. Uhler was educated at the Latin School conducted by Daniel Jones and at Baltimore College. He began to collect insects after his father had bought a farm near Baltimore, and in this he was encouraged by the Rev. John Gottlieb Morris [q.v.], a well-known entomologist. One of Uhler's earliest published papers was his "Descriptions of a Few Species of *Coleoptera* Supposed to be New" (*Proceedings of the Academy of Natural Sciences of Philadelphia*, vol. VII, 1856). In 1860 he wrote his first paper on *Hemiptera* (*Ibid.*, vol. XII, 1861), and from that time on for the rest of his life his entomological papers related almost entirely to this group. He described many new forms and had a broad, comprehensive view of the whole complex. In 1861 his *Synopsis of the Neuroptera of North Amer-*

ica, translated from the Latin of Hermann August Hagen, was published by the Smithsonian Institution. In 1863 he was appointed librarian of the Peabody Institute in Baltimore, and early in 1864 was called to Cambridge by J. L. R. Agassiz [*q.v.*], for whom he worked as an assistant and as librarian in the Museum of Comparative Zoology. He taught entomology to some of the Harvard undergraduates and gave a series of lectures in the museum. At the same time he attended lectures at Harvard by Asa Gray, Jeffries Wyman, Agassiz and his son, and Nathaniel Southgate Shaler. He returned to Baltimore in 1867 to become assistant librarian of the Peabody Institute, and in 1870 was made librarian, a position he held for the rest of his life. In addition to his entomological work he wrote several geological papers, and with N. H. Morison he prepared an elaborate catalogue of the Peabody library (5 vols., 1883–92), which was a model of its kind. He was of much assistance in the early days of the Johns Hopkins University and was associate in natural history from 1876 until the last year of his life. He was married in 1869 to Sophia Werdebaugh, who died in 1883; on Apr. 29, 1886, he married Pearl Daniels of Baltimore. He had a son by his first wife and a daughter by his second.

His last entomological paper, "Recognition of Two North American Species of Cicada," published in *Entomological News* in March 1905, completed practically fifty years of active publishing life. He built up a very large collection, which he presented before his death to the United States National Museum. He was a modest man but an excellent speaker, and, like nearly all great naturalists, he was always ready to help younger workers. Probably his last work was done on a monograph of the *Capsidae,* which, although an enormous manuscript accumulated, was never published as a whole. His eyesight failed him almost completely in 1907, and at that time he virtually stopped work. His entomological writings in 1903 covered fifty-two titles. This is not a large number; but his work was careful and sound and broad. For many years he was the leading American worker in a very important group and a world authority on entomology.

[Uhler's middle name appears in the Johns Hopkins official publications as Rhees. For biog. materials, see *Who's Who in America,* 1912–13; L. O. Howard, in *Entomological News,* Dec. 1913; *Proc. Entomological Soc. of Washington,* vol. XVI (1914); obituary in *Sun* (Baltimore), Oct. 22, 1913. A list of his writings appeared in *Psyche,* Feb., Apr. 1903.]   L. O. H.

ULLOA, ANTONIO DE (Jan. 12, 1716–July 5, 1795), first Spanish governor of Louisiana, was born in Seville, Spain, the second son of

Bernardo de Ulloa y Sousa, the economist, and his wife, Josefa de la Torre Guiral. He had a long and varied career in the service of the crown —in the navy, in the colonial administration, and on special missions. Several conspicuous failures marred his record, but later investigations always showed that he was the victim either of circumstances beyond his control or of influential officials whose misconduct he tried to correct. Moreover, his failures as an administrator were outweighed by the success of his writings. His two most important works were the result of an expedition to South America (1735–44) which he and Jorge Juan y Santacilia made in company with La Condamine and other French scientists. One of these works, *Relación histórica del viage a la América meridional* (Madrid, 1748), published in English as *A Voyage to South America* (1758), was translated into several other languages and won him an enviable reputation both at home and abroad. The other, a confidential report on conditions in the viceroyalty of Peru written about 1749 in collaboration with Jorge Juan, revealed grave abuses in the Spanish régime and probably stimulated the reform movement already in progress at court. Published with some alterations at London under the title *Noticias Secretas de America* (1826), it is one of the best-known accounts of Spanish America.

At the close of a disastrous administration as governor of Huancavélica (Peru) and superintendent of its important quicksilver mine (1758–64), Ulloa was appointed governor of Louisiana, which had just been ceded to Spain by France. Arriving at New Orleans in March 1766, he found that the resources at his command were utterly inadequate to his needs and throughout the period of his residence there he had to let the last French governor, Aubry, continue to govern the province in the name of the king of Spain. The situation was not only anomalous: it was impossible. In October 1768, the publication of a Spanish order altering the commercial regulations provoked a Creole uprising, and Ulloa was expelled from the province. Though again he appears to have been not wholly responsible for his failure—his government had not supported him properly, and Aubry wrote that the trouble had been brewing for a decade and that a storm was necessary to clear the air—the task of pacifying Louisiana was entrusted to another man, Alejandro O'Reilly [*q.v.*], and Ulloa returned to Spain. His conduct as commander of a squadron in the war with Great Britain (1779) resulted in his being court-martialed (1779–81), but he was vindicated, and during the last years of his life he held high office in the Spanish navy. By his wife, Francisca Ramírez de Laredo, daughter of the Conde de San Javier, he had nine children, one of whom—Francisco Javier de Ulloa—rose to the rank of admiral and secretary of the navy.

[A. P. Whitaker, "Antonio de Ulloa," *Hispanic American Hist. Rev.*, May 1935, with bibliographical references, particularly to Spanish sources; J. W. Caughey, *Bernardo de Gálvez in La.* (1934); J. E. Winston, "The Cause and Results of the Revolution of 1768 in Louisiana," *La. Hist. Quart.*, Apr. 1932; E. W. Lyon, *Louisiana in French Diplomacy* (1934).]

A. P. W—r.

UNANGST, ERIAS (Aug. 8, 1824–Oct. 12, 1903), Lutheran missionary, was born in Easton, Pa., the son of Jacob and Eleanora Unangst. He attended the local schools for several years and in 1847 registered in the academy of Pennsylvania (now Gettysburg) College. In 1854 he received the B.A. degree from the college. He studied at the Lutheran Theological Seminary at Gettysburg thereafter and was ordained to the ministry by the Allegheny Synod in 1857. He then read medicine for several months in preparation for his work as a foreign missionary. On Sept. 24, 1857, he was married to Phebe Ann Miliken, of Lewistown, Pa., and a month later they sailed from Boston for India, where they arrived in April 1858, during the Sepoy rebellion. After thirteen years in India he returned to America on a furlough in 1871, but was called back to the Guntur mission in less than a year. In 1882 he was again in America on a furlough, and again returned to India earlier than he had planned because of the death of a fellow missionary. In 1895, at the age of seventy-one, Unangst returned to America, after having labored in India as a missionary more than thirty-five years. He spent the remainder of his life in Hollidaysburg, Pa., at the home of one of his eight children. His wife had died while engaged in active service in India in 1888.

When Unangst arrived in the Guntur mission field of the General Synod of the Lutheran Church, it had scarcely emerged from the period of its beginnings. He was the connecting link between its founder, John C. F. Heyer [*q.v.*], and a later generation of missionaries. Accordingly, he had many of the hardships and perplexing responsibilities of the pioneer. At times he worked under great difficulties; once for a period of four years, 1866–70, he was the only missionary in the field. But his patience and zeal, his tact and devotion triumphed, and under his leadership the Guntur mission prospered in spite of obstacles. He had the restless spirit of a creator of new enterprises. He planned and urged

the development of special work among the women of the middle and upper classes, and a similar program for work among the men of these classes. He saw the need of a trained native ministry, and assisted in establishing an institution for that purpose. He excelled as a linguist, both in the original languages of the Bible and in Telugu. For a quarter of a century he was associated with other missionaries of the Telugu country in preparing for the revision of the Telugu translation of the Bible, and in completing the revision. This was done under the Madras Auxiliary Bible Society and the British and Foreign Bible Society. He made several trips to London to meet with the group who were engaged in this enterprise. He published *Historical Sketch of India Missions* in 1879. He also translated hymns into Telugu and wrote several original hymns.

[L. B. Wolf, *After Fifty Years; or, an Hist. Sketch of the Guntur Mission* (1896); A. R. Wentz, *Hist. of the Gettysburg Theological Seminary* (1927); *The Alumni Record of Gettysburg Coll.* (1932); *Luth. Missionary Jour.*, Dec. 1903; *Pittsburg Dispatch*, Oct. 13, 1903.]

S. G. H.

UNCAS (*c.* 1588–*c.* 1683), sachem of the Mohegan Indians, was the son of Oweneco, a Pequot sachem, and of Meekunump, daughter of another Pequot sachem. In 1626 he married a daughter of Sassacus [*q.v.*], chief sachem of the Pequots, and later a daughter of Sebequanash, a Hammonassett sachem. Rebelling against Sassacus, Uncas was defeated and banished. He fled to the Narragansetts, but later made his peace with his kinsmen and returned to the Pequots. It is said that he rebelled thus more than once. On his final revolt the Pequot territory was divided, and Uncas became ruler of the western part, called Moheag, his tribe becoming known as the Mohegans. He courted the favor of the English and in May 1637, with Miantonomo [*q.v.*], chief sachem of the Narragansetts, joined them in war on the Pequots. He was not wholly trusted, however, and was accused of harboring the enemy. In June 1638 he went to Boston with an escort of thirty-seven men and offered the Governor a present of wampum, which was refused until he had satisfied the government of his loyalty; he was then given "a fair, red coat" and food for his homeward journey, and "departed very joyful" (*Winthrop's Journal, post*, I, 271). Later that year he signed a treaty of peace with Miantonomo and with the English at Hartford.

In 1643 he complained to the Commissioners of the United Colonies that Miantonomo had hired a Pequot to kill him, and that some of the followers of Sequasson, an undersachem of the Narragansetts, had shot at him as he was going down the Connecticut. An attempt by John

Haynes [*q.v.*], governor at Hartford, to make peace between Uncas and Sequasson failed, and in the war which followed, through treachery, Uncas captured Miantonomo and delivered him to the English at Hartford. The Commissioners of the United Colonies at Boston now gave Uncas permission to kill the Narragansett chief, and agreed to assist him should the Narragansetts make war on him. Accordingly, Miantonomo was killed by a brother of Uncas, and when the Narragansetts demanded satisfaction the English intervened. The peace agreement made in September 1644 was of short duration, however, and in the spring of 1645 Uncas was besieged in his stronghold on the Connecticut by the Narragansett sachem Pessacus and almost forced to surrender, but was saved by the English under Thomas Leffingwell, to whom he gave a grant of the lands forming the site of the present Norwich. Another agreement between the hostile tribes was reached but soon Uncas undertook to chastise a Narragansett sachem for an alleged offense, and thus created further trouble. Ordered to appear before the English at New Haven to answer for his conduct, he acknowledged himself guilty on some points and was released. In July 1647 many Indians brought complaints against him to the United Colonies; one complained that Uncas had captured his wife, and the Commissioners made him give her up; but in answer to the Pequot complaint that he was unjust and had many times over collected the fines due the English, they merely reproved Uncas. In 1661, however, when he made war without cause on Ousamequin or Massasoit [*q.v.*], the good friend of the Massachusetts colony, the English forced him to give up his captives and stolen goods, and in 1675 he was ordered to appear in Boston to surrender his arms and to leave two of his younger sons as hostages to secure his neutrality or cooperation in King Philip's War.

Uncas was tricky, untrustworthy, and dissolute. Daniel Gookin [*q.v.*], governor of the "praying Indians," described him in his late years as "an old and wicked, wilful man, a drunkard, and otherwise very vicious; who has always been an opposer and underminer of praying to God" (*Collections of the Massachusetts Historical Society*, I ser. I, 1792, p. 208). The apparent forbearance toward him displayed by the English of Connecticut and Massachusetts was probably owing to the fact that Uncas was neighbor to Connecticut whereas his enemies, the Narragansetts, lived in the much detested colony of Roger Williams.

[*Winthrop's Journal* (2 vols., 1908), ed. by J. K. Hosmer; "Acts of the Commissioners of the United Colonies of New England," *Records of the Colony of New Plymouth*, vols. IX–X (1859), ed. by David Pulsifer; F. M. Caulkins, *Hist. of Norwich, Conn.* (1866); S. G. Drake, *The Book of the Indians* (8th ed., 1841); F. W. Hodge, *Handbook of Am. Indians* (1910).]

J. T. A.

UNDERHILL, FRANK PELL (Dec. 21, 1877–June 28, 1932), pharmacologist, toxicologist, was born in Brooklyn, N. Y., the son of David Bonnett and Emma (Housie) Underhill, and a descendant of the ninth generation from John Underhill [*q.v.*]. After attending the public high school of Norwalk, Conn., his entire academic career was devoted to Yale University, where he received the degrees of Ph.B. in 1900, and Ph.D. in 1903. Until 1918 he was on the staff of the Sheffield Scientific School, where he was associated with Russell H. Chittenden and Lafayette B. Mendel. He was professor of pathological chemistry from 1912 to 1918, held the chair of experimental medicine from 1918 to 1921, and that of pharmacology and toxicology from 1921 until his death. The most significant of his earlier researches pertained to the physiologic action of proteins and tartrates, and to the effects of chemical substances upon the behavior of sugars, salts, and water within the body. With H. Gideon Wells, he was the co-discoverer of tartrate nephritis.

Closely identified with the beginnings of the Chemical Warfare Service, Underhill attained therein the rank of lieutenant-colonel. He was appointed the United States representative to the Interallied Gas Warfare Conference at Paris, in October 1918, and became vice-president of the conference. With a staff of experts he investigated chlorine, phosgene, and chlorpicrin, and detailed their effects upon the animal body in his book, *The Lethal War Gases: Physiology and Experimental Treatment* (1920). These investigations laid bare in striking fashion the significance of bodily water exchange in lethal gas poisoning. A method of treatment for war-gas victims was evolved, based upon blood-letting in the period of blood dilution, and the introduction of fluid during the period of blood concentration. The value of such treatment was fully demonstrated in animals, and Underhill arranged for extensive application on the western front just as the World War closed.

Returning to the Yale University School of Medicine after the war, he next traced a close relationship between war-gas poisoning and the acute devastating form of influenza. In both he regarded water as of prime significance. Still another condition, that of extensive superficial burns, he attacked intensively from a like viewpoint, and discovered the effects of fluid administration to be very beneficial. He described the successful treatment of twenty-one patients seriously burned in a New Haven theatre fire. During his last years, he was deeply interested in pellagra. He investigated this disease in its possible relationships to vitamin deficiencies as well as to a canine condition known as "black tongue."

In person, Underhill was of the scholarly type, reserved and quiet; in action and speech, he was unhurried and certain. He was single in purpose; no compelling hobby distracted him. Throughout his career, he exhibited remarkable and careful industry, a discriminating intellect, and unquestionable scientific honesty. Many research associates and a still greater number of medical and chemical pupils profited by his guidance. The influence of his research contributions, numbering nearly two hundred, has extended throughout the world to benefit workers in widely varying fields, both theoretical and clinical. Among his major works are: *The Physiology of Amino Acids* (1915), *A Manual of Selected Biochemical Methods* (1921), and *Toxicology; Or the Effects of Poisons* (1924, second edition, 1928). He was frequently consulted on commercial questions, and was likewise a very effective medico-legal expert. He was chairman of the committee on biological chemistry of the National Research Council, and an associate editor of *Chemical Abstracts*. His many memberships in medical and other scientific societies included Die Kaiserlich Leopoldinisch-Carolinisch Deutsche Akademie der Naturforscher zu Halle. At his death in New Haven, he was survived by his widow, Lavina Reed Chasmar, of Norwalk, Conn., to whom he had been married on Sept. 2, 1903. Their two children died in infancy.

[*Who's Who in America*, 1932–33; J. C. Frost, *Underhill Genealogy* (1932), vol. III; H. G. Barbour, "The Scientific Activities of Frank Pell Underhill," *Yale Jour. of Biology and Med.*, Mar. 1933 (contains complete bibliography); *Bull. of Yale Univ.*, Oct. 15, 1933; *New Haven Jour.-Courier*, June 29, 1932.] H. G. B.

UNDERHILL, JOHN (c. 1597–Sept. 21, 1672), colonial military leader and magistrate, was a son of John and Honor (Pawley) Underhill originally of Kenilworth, Warwickshire. His father was a military adventurer in the Dutch service, and John, "bred to arms" in the Netherlands, evidently received little education. Influenced by English refugees, he adopted the outward forms of Puritanism, but he displayed little of the moral stamina which characterized the Puritan fathers. When, on Dec. 12, 1628, he married Helena de Hooch he was "a Cadet in the guard" of the Prince of Orange. He was an apt pupil in a great military school.

In 1630 he moved to Boston to help organize the militia of the Massachusetts Bay. The Boston church accepted him (Aug. 27, 1630); the colony appointed him, with Daniel Patrick, captain of the militia, voted him supplies and money, and allotted him land; and, in 1634, the town chose him one of its first selectmen. In colonial military affairs he encountered popular apathy and insufficient supplies, and in an effort to enlarge the military stores he went to England in the winter of 1634–35.

When Indian troubles arose, Underhill helped in avenging Oldham's death at Block Island (August 1636). Lent to Saybrook Plantation in April 1637, he cooperated with Mason's Connecticut forces in destroying Mystic Fort and scattering the Pequots. He might have returned to Massachusetts a hero, had it not been for the bitter theological controversy going on there. Underhill had allied himself with the Antinomians and signed the petition in behalf of the Rev. John Wheelwright [*q.v.*]; the orthodox party was now in control, and Underhill was received as a seditious person. He made the situation worse for himself by imprudent words (*Massachusetts Historical Society Collections*, 4 ser., vol. VII, 1865, pp. 170–74), and was disfranchised, discharged from military service (Nov. 15, 1637), and disarmed (Nov. 20, 1637). Humiliated, he spent the winter of 1637–38 in England and published in 1638 *Nevves from America* (reprinted *Ibid.*, 3 ser., vol. VI, 1837), now a classical account of the Pequot troubles. Returning to Boston, he was accused of making contemptuous speeches and was brought before the General Court which, for "his gross & palpable dissimulation & equivocation," banished him (Sept. 6, 1638). He fled to Dover (N. H.) just in time to escape a church trial for adultery.

At Dover, he organized a church of which Hanserd Knollys became pastor, secured the governorship, and scorned Massachusetts' claims upon the region and Boston's summons for a church trial. By publishing their accusations, however, Massachusetts officials so reduced Underhill's Dover adherents that, by October 1639, he begged forgiveness and thereafter, in expiation, supported Massachusetts claims to New Hampshire (*Ibid.*, 4 ser., VII, 178–79). Before the Boston church (Mar. 5, 1640), he confessed to adultery (Records of the First Church of Boston, *post*, p. 13); but his repentance was judged insincere, and he was excommunicated. Subsequently, however, he satisfied the church and on Sept. 3, 1640, he was reinstated (*Ibid.*, p. 15); shortly afterwards (Oct. 7, 1640) the General

Court suspended his sentence of banishment and on June 2, 1641, repealed it.

Offers from New Amsterdam tempted him, but he yielded temporarily to pleas to move to Stamford, Conn., which in 1643 he represented in the New Haven Court. Soon afterwards, being employed by the Dutch to fight Indians, he acquitted himself well, moved to Long Island, and later became member of the Council for New Amsterdam and schout of Flushing. After the Anglo-Dutch war began, he narrowly escaped imprisonment for sedition, because in May 1653 he denounced Stuyvesant's "iniquitous government" for its dealings with the Indians, unjust taxation, and other oppressive measures toward the English. He offered his services to the United Colonies, was refused, secured commission as a privateer at Providence (May 19, 1653), and endangered the United Colonies' unpatriotic neutrality by seizing the Dutch West Indies Company's property at Hartford (June 27, 1653), precipitating a ten-year dispute with the Hartford government. After his wife's death in 1658, he married Elizabeth Feake, probably became a Quaker, and moved to Oyster Bay, establishing an estate (Killingworth) on land given by the Indians. He helped reduce the New Amsterdam Dutch to English control (1664–65), was a member of the Hempstead Convention (Mar. 1, 1664/5), surveyor of customs for Long Island (Apr. 22, 1665), and, later, high constable and under sheriff of North Riding, Yorkshire, Long Island. Retiring from public life, Mar. 14, 1666/7, he died at Killingworth, survived by at least two daughters and one son by his first wife and three daughters and two sons by the second.

[The Underhill Soc. of America, sponsored by M. C. Taylor, has pub. valuable material concerning Underhill in J. C. Frost, *Underhill Geneal.* (4 vols., 1932) and H. C. Shelley, *John Underhill* (1932); these are decidedly favorable to Underhill and should be read in connection with J. K. Hosmer, *Winthrop's Jour.* (2 vols., 1908), "Records of the First Church of Boston" (manuscript in Mass. Hist. Soc. Lib.), Nathaniel Shurtleff, *Records of the Gov. and Company of the Mass. Bay,* vol. I (1853), and L. E. and A. L. de Forest, *Capt. John Underhill* (1934). See also *Docs. Rel. to the Colonial Hist. of . . . N. Y.,* vols. II (1858), XIV (1883).]   R. P. S.

UNDERWOOD, BENJAMIN FRANKLIN (July 6, 1839–Nov. 10, 1914), freethinker, lecturer, editor, the son of Raymond C. and Harriet (Booth) Underwood, was born in the city of New York. He received a slender education in the common schools and at Westerly Academy in Westerly, R. I., which he supplemented by wide reading in philosophy, science, and literature. Having enlisted at the outbreak of the Civil War in the 15th Massachusetts Volunteer Infantry, he was wounded and captured at the battle of Ball's Bluff, Oct. 21, 1861, and was confined for some months in Libby Prison. Released through an exchange of prisoners, he returned to Massachusetts, where he married Sara A. Francis, a young suffragist leader, on Sept. 6, 1862. Reënlisting, in the 5th Rhode Island Heavy Artillery, he served with it for the duration of the war, being promoted to first lieutenant and commended for bravery in action.

After the war he took up platform work as a freethinker. Unlike Robert Green Ingersoll [q.v.], he possessed a logical rather than rhetorical type of mind and had considerable philosophic acumen. During the seventies and eighties he terrorized the churches of the East by his custom of issuing a public challenge to the clergy of the large cities to meet him in a series of debates, these series running from three to as many as thirty meetings. It was an unusual clergyman who was able to rival him in forensic ability, and gradually ministers became so wary of accepting his challenges that only the boldest ventured to enter the lists against him. The issue usually turned upon the acceptance or interpretation of the theory of evolution, of which he was one of the earliest and most zealous American supporters. The most notable of these intellectual combats was one in which Prof. Asa Gray [q.v.] of Harvard participated, in a symposium organized by Underwood in Boston (1873). Although influenced by the deism of Thomas Paine as well as by the agnosticism of Herbert Spencer, Underwood's own position approached that of orthodox materialism. During his earlier, more aggressive years he published a number of lectures and pamphlets on such topics as *Darwinism* (1875), *The Crimes and Cruelties of Christianity* (1877), *Christianity and Materialism, Will the Coming Man Worship God?, Modern Scientific Materialism, Naturalism vs: Supernaturalism, Spiritualism from a Materialistic Standpoint, Paine, the Religious and Political Reformer, Woman: Her Past and Present, Her Rights and Wrongs*—little materialistic tracts containing much trenchant argument. From 1880 to 1886 he edited the Boston *Index*; then, moving to Chicago, he edited the *Open Court* in 1887 and the *Illustrated Graphic News* in 1888; from 1893 to 1895 he was editorial writer for the *Philosophical Journal*; in 1893 he acted as chairman of the Congress of Evolution held in connection with the World's Columbian Exposition. He moved to Quincy, Ill., in 1897 to assume the editorship of the *Quincy Journal,* a position which he held until within a year of his death. In spite of his penchant for debate, he was of a genial, kindly disposition, and during his later life he became much more reserved in the expression of his anti-religious views and seems to have modified them to a considerable extent. In 1913 he retired from active work and returned to his boyhood's home in Westerly, R. I., where he died.

[L. M. Underwood, *The Underwood Families of America* (2 vols., 1913); *Who's Who in America,* 1914–15; editorial by H. N. Wheeler and obituary in *Quincy Jour.,* Nov. 12, 1914; manuscript copy of debate with the Rev. C. S. Bates of Cleveland, Mar. 21, 22, 23, 1889.]   E. S. B—s.

UNDERWOOD, FRANCIS HENRY (Jan. 12, 1825–Aug. 7, 1894), author, lawyer, and United States consul, was the son of Roswell Underwood, a farmer of Enfield, Mass., and Phoebe (Hall) Underwood. He was probably a descendant of Joseph Underwood who emigrated from England to Massachusetts in 1637. In spite of extreme poverty he managed to prepare himself for college and entered Amherst with the class of 1847. After one year, however, he left college to teach school in Kentucky, declining the offer of an uncle to pay the expenses of his education on condition that he become a minister. In the South he studied law, was admitted to the bar (1847), and married, in Taylorsville, Ky., May 18, 1848, Louisa Maria Wood. His original antipathy to slavery was increased by what he saw of the institution, and he returned to Massachusetts in 1850 an ardent advocate of Free Soil principles. After twelve months of private law practice in Webster, Mass., he was appointed clerk of the state Senate for the session of 1852. Political feeling in the North had been roused by the passage of the Fugitive Slave Law, but had not yet taken form. Underwood succeeded in interesting John Punchard Jewett [q.v.], the publisher of *Uncle Tom's Cabin,* in a scheme for establishing a magazine which should enlist the literary forces of New England in a crusade against slavery. He secured the cooperation of a distinguished list of contributors and was ready to launch the new venture in December 1853. But at the last moment the publishers declined to proceed and the whole scheme had to be temporarily abandoned.

Underwood next entered the publishing house of Phillips, Sampson & Company, Boston, as literary editor, and for some time devoted himself to extending his acquaintance among Boston and Cambridge authors. He then revived the project of a magazine. The cautious Phillips was slow to accept the proposal, but Underwood's efforts were warmly seconded by William Lee, a junior member of the firm, and by Harriet Beecher Stowe. Their united persuasions at length overcame the publisher's reluctance. On May 5, 1857, occurred the memorable dinner at the Parker House when Emerson, Lowell,

Holmes, Longfellow, John Lothrop Motley, and James E. Cabot joined Phillips and Underwood in discussing plans for the yet unnamed magazine. In consequence of this and several succeeding dinners Underwood, who naturally expected to act as editor, was sent abroad to solicit contributions from British authors. He returned in midsummer to find the success of the project imperiled by the financial panic of 1857. Realizing at once that the prestige of James Russell Lowell [q.v.] as editor would strengthen the undertaking, Underwood, "without a suggestion from any person," nominated his friend for the position, and Lowell accepted. At the same time Holmes christened the new publication the *Atlantic Monthly.* The first number appeared under the date of November 1857, and almost at once the magazine assumed the lead among American periodicals. Underwood's connection with the enterprise that he had projected and brought into being lasted only two years, during which time he loyally performed the routine work of assistant editor, sifting all contributions and making up numbers subject to Lowell's approval. In 1859 both Phillips and Sampson died, their firm was dissolved, and the *Atlantic* became the property of Ticknor & Fields. Underwood, to his deep regret, was not retained by the new proprietors.

After leaving the *Atlantic* he was elected (1859) clerk of the Superior Criminal Court of Boston. Social, literary, and civic affairs occupied much of his time. He was an original member and second president of the Papyrus Club, and for ten years served on the Boston school committee. To secure leisure for more sustained literary work he resigned his clerkship in 1866 and engaged in private business ventures, some of which proved to be unfortunate. Meanwhile he wrote manuals of English and American literature; *Cloud-Pictures* (1872), a volume of short stories; *Lord of Himself* (1874), *Man Proposes* (1885), and *Doctor Gray's Quest* (1895), novels; and biographies of Longfellow, Lowell, and Whittier. His wife, by whom he had had five children, died in 1882. By appointment of President Cleveland (confirmed, Apr. 28, 1886) Underwood succeeded Francis Brett Harte [q.v.] as United States consul at Glasgow. He was recalled when the Democrats went out of office, but returned to Scotland (appointment confirmed, Sept. 2, 1893) at the beginning of Cleveland's second term, this time to be consul at Leith. He died in Edinburgh. Underwood's life abroad brought him many friendships and new distinctions, including an honorary LL.D. from the University of Glasgow. He also found consolation in a young Scotch wife, Frances

Findlay of Callendar, near Glasgow. In the interval between his consulships he wrote his best book, *Quabbin, the Story of a Small Town* (1893), a pleasantly discursive account of Enfield as he remembered it from his boyhood. Nevertheless, his last years were not entirely happy. He was painfully conscious that he had not won the recognition that his industry, talent, and genial nature deserved. Always it had been his fate to play a secondary rôle, contributing much to the fame of others but gaining little credit for himself. As Francis Parkman lucidly pointed out to him, he was "neither a Harvard man nor a humbug" and so, being both unassuming and unsupported, a victim of his own merit.

[L. M. Underwood, *The Underwood Families of America* (2 vols., 1913); *Amherst Coll. Biog. Record* (1927); J. T. Trowbridge, "The Author of Quabbin," *Atlantic Monthly*, Jan. 1895; Bliss Perry, "The Editor Who Was Never the Editor," *Park-Street Papers* (1908); M. A. DeW. Howe, *The Atlantic Monthly and Its Makers* (1919); obituary in *Times* (London), Aug. 9, 1894; scrapbook of newspaper clippings relating to Underwood's years in Scotland in the Jones Lib., Amherst.]
G. F. W.

UNDERWOOD, HORACE GRANT (July 19, 1859–Oct. 12, 1916), missionary, was born in London, England, the fourth of six children of John and Elizabeth Grant (Maire) Underwood. His father, whose inventive work as a manufacturing chemist had won him recognition from the Royal Society of Arts, emigrated to New Durham, N. J., in 1872, and engaged in the manufacture of inks and special papers, a business which developed into the Underwood Typewriter Company. At ten Horace was sent to a Catholic school in France; he continued his studies in America at Hasbrouck Institute, Jersey City; at the University of the City of New York (later New York University), from which he graduated in 1881; and at the New Brunswick Theological Seminary, where he completed his course in 1884.

Having had a missionary career in view from childhood, he was ordained in November 1884 to the Dutch Reformed ministry and commissioned missionary to Korea by the Presbyterian Board. He arrived at Chemulpo, Apr. 5, 1885, and, though missionaries were not welcomed in that newly opened land, he was given duties at the government hospital just established. He soon acquired the language, and in 1890 published *A Concise Dictionary of the Korean Language*. He began the translation of the Scriptures into Korean, and was chairman of the board of translators until his death. In 1886 he opened an orphanage at Seoul, which became the John D. Wells Academy. In 1889 he organized the Sai Mun An Church, of which he was still the pastor when he died. At Seoul he married, Mar. 13, 1889, Dr. Lillias Stirling Horton, then serving as physician to the queen. On their wedding trip to the northern border, Underwood crossed over into Manchuria with thirty Koreans, whom he there baptized, thus conforming with the letter of his promise not to engage in such work while so traveling in Korea. This promise was exacted because of a proselyting trip he had made with the Rev. Henry Gerhard Appenzeller [*q.v.*] in 1888, which resulted in the issuance of a decree, later recalled, forbidding the teaching of Christianity in Korea. Underwood's work, with that of his associate missionaries, raised Korea to the foremost place among mission fields. From 1897 to 1901 he published at his own expense a native paper, the *Christian News*. He was instrumental in organizing the Seoul branch of the Young Men's Christian Association, and aided in establishing the Severance Hospital and the Chosen Union Christian College (Presbyterian-Methodist). After the assassination of the queen in 1895, he became the trusted intermediary of the king, even conveying his food from his own table to avoid the danger of poisoning. This activity was criticised, certain publications calling him "Underwood the schemer" (*Underwood of Korea, post*, p. 154). He died at Atlantic City and was buried at New Durham, N. J. He was the author of *An Introduction to the Korean Spoken Language* (1890), *The Call of Korea* (1908), and *The Religions of Eastern Asia* (1910). He was a member of the Royal Asiatic Society and the British Foreign Bible Society. He lectured on missions at Princeton in 1908 and at New York University in 1909. His wife died in Seoul, Oct. 20, 1921. She was the author of *Fifteen Years among the Topknots* (1904), *Tommy Tompkins in Korea* (1905), and *Underwood of Korea* (1918). Their only son became an author and a missionary in Korea.

[L. M. Underwood, *The Underwood Families of America* (1913), vol. II; *Who's Who in America*, 1916–17; *Biog. Record, Theological Seminary, New Brunswick* (1912); Lillias H. Underwood, *Underwood of Korea* (1918); W. E. Griffis, *A Modern Pioneer in Korea* (1912); H. H. Underwood, *Modern Educ. in Korea* (1926); H. N. Allen, *A Chronological Index of Korea* (1901), and *Things Korean* (1908); J. S. Gale, *The Vanguard* (1904); Lillias H. Underwood, and A. J. Brown, in *Missionary Review of the World*, Dec. 1916; obituary in *N. Y. Times*, Oct. 13, 1916; personal recollections; information from Underwood's family.]
H. N. A.

UNDERWOOD, JOHN CURTISS (Mar. 14, 1809–Dec. 7, 1873), jurist, was the son of John and Mary (Curtiss) Underwood of Litchfield, Herkimer County, N. Y. On his father's side he was a direct descendant of William Underwood, who came from England to Concord, Mass., probably prior to 1640, and in 1652 moved to Chelmsford. One of William's descendants, Parker Underwood, removed from Chelmsford to Litchfield, where his grandson, John Curtiss Underwood, was subsequently born and reared. He was graduated from Hamilton College in 1832. While there he became one of the founders of the Alpha Delta Phi fraternity. After his graduation he went to Virginia; obtained employment as a tutor; began the study of law; and later returned to Herkimer County to begin practice. On Oct. 24, 1839, he married Maria Gloria Jackson of Clarksburg, Va. (now W. Va.)—a double cousin of "Stonewall" Jackson, and a member of the family in which Underwood had formerly served as tutor. The couple soon acquired about eight hundred acres of land in Clarke County, established their home there, and sought to introduce dairying into that portion of Virginia (*Underwood Families, post,* I, 364–77). Three children were born to them.

A Free-soiler in politics, Underwood was a delegate to the Republican National Convention of 1856, and during the ensuing campaign incurred such unpopularity by his utterances on the subject of slavery that he removed from Virginia. In 1860 he was a delegate to the convention which nominated Lincoln, in behalf of whose candidacy he stumped New England and the Middle States. After the election he was nominated as United States consul to Callao, Peru, the nomination being confirmed July 26, 1861. On July 25, however, Lincoln nominated him fifth auditor of the Treasury and the appointment was confirmed on Aug. 1. On Jan. 25, 1864, he was appointed judge of the district court of Virginia, in which capacity he asserted the right of the United States to confiscate property of "persons in rebellion," and advocated extension and protection of negro civic rights. The most noteworthy case with which he was connected was that of Jefferson Davis. At the session of the grand jury held at Norfolk in May 1866, at which Davis was indicted for treason, Underwood delivered a charge of some length and severity. The session adjourned to meet in Richmond on June 5, and local feeling was running so high that there was speculation as to whether Underwood would risk assassination by appearing. He was present at the appointed time, however, and in another charge to the grand jury scathingly denounced the press and many residents of Richmond. Later, he refused to admit Davis to bail, on the ground that he was a military prisoner, and not, in consequence, within

the power of the civil authorities (*New York Herald,* May 12, June 6, 7, 12, 1866).

When the drastic Reconstruction acts of March 1867 were applied to Virginia, Underwood was chosen delegate to, and president of, the constitutional convention which assembled at Richmond, Dec. 3, 1867. This convention drew up what came to be known as the "Underwood Constitution" (*Underwood Families,* I, 376). Certain of its provisions, subsequently eliminated by popular vote on ratification in 1869, would have placed the government "based on such a constitution, in the hands of negroes, 'scalawags' and 'carpet-bag' adventurers" (Burgess, *post,* p. 227). With its proscriptive features removed, however, the constitution proved to be satisfactory, and remained the organic law of Virginia from 1869 until 1902.

Underwood eventually acquired several thousand acres of land. To a portion of this he obtained title at the close of the war by methods which evoked widespread criticism, involved him in litigation, and even caused him to be subjected to physical assault. His death from apoplexy occurred at his residence in Washington, D. C.

[L. M. Underwood, *The Underwood Families of America* (1913); *N. Y. Herald,* May 12, June 6, 7, 12, 1866, Dec. 9, 1873; *N. Y. Times,* May 12, June 6, 8, 1866, Nov. 12, Dec. 9, 1873; *The Debates and Proceedings of the Constitutional Convention of the State of Va.* (1868); J. W. Burgess, *Reconstruction and the Constitution* (1902); H. J. Eckenrode, *The Pol. Hist. of Va. During the Reconstruction* (1904); R. F. Nichols, "U. S. vs. Jefferson Davis," *Am. Hist. Rev.,* Jan. 1926.]   R. W. I.

UNDERWOOD, JOSEPH ROGERS (Oct. 24, 1791–Aug. 23, 1876), jurist, representative and senator from Kentucky, was born in Goochland County, Va., the eldest of eight children of John and Frances (Rogers) Underwood. He was a descendant of Thomas William (or William Thomas) Underwood, who was born about 1675 and came to Virginia from England as a boy. Joseph's father was a person of standing in his community and often represented the county in the legislature. His resources were so meager, however, that he found it impossible properly to educate all his children. Hence, when twelve years old, Joseph was sent to his uncle, Edmund Rogers, in Barren County, Ky., who gave him the attention of a parent. He was instructed for a year by Rev. John Howe, near Glasgow, spent a term under Samuel Findley at Danville, and later attended a school at Lancaster. He entered Transylvania University and was graduated in 1811. He immediately began the study of law in Lexington under the instruction of Robert Wickliffe, but before he had secured a license to practise he volunteered in a regiment recruited to avenge the massacre at the River Raisin. Elected lieutenant in the 13th Kentucky Regiment, he became a part of the army commanded by Gen. William Henry Harrison [q.v.]. On May 5, 1813, his company was defeated and captured at Fort Meigs, and he was imprisoned at Fort Wayne.

In July he returned to Kentucky, received his license to practise law, and before the end of the year settled at Glasgow. He was town trustee and county auditor until 1823, when he removed to Bowling Green, where he maintained a residence for the rest of his life. In 1816, when everybody in the state was a Jeffersonian Democrat, he entered politics and secured membership in the lower house of the legislature, representing Barren County. After serving four years, he decided to retire from politics; but in 1825, during the excitement of the "Old Court, New Court" parties, he returned to the legislature as a representative of the former. He was reëlected the next year, and in 1828 he ran for lieutenant-governor as an anti-Jackson man, but was defeated. The same year Gov. Thomas Metcalfe appointed him associate justice of the court of appeals, in which capacity he served until his resignation in 1835.

Immediately thereafter he was elected to the lower house of Congress as a Whig, where he served four successive terms (Mar. 4, 1835–Mar. 3, 1843). He declined another term, and in 1845 was elected to the state legislature and chosen speaker. In 1847 he was elected to the United States Senate, of which he was a member until Mar. 3, 1853. As a national legislator he favored the distribution of the surplus revenues among the states, and in 1837, even when the panic was upon the country, demanded of Congress the completion of the payments promised. He opposed the famous rule of the House excluding slavery petitions, on the ground that the abolitionists would wax strong as the result of the agitation which would be raised if it were passed. He took the Whig position of opposition to the Mexican War and the acquisition of territory. Being a strong believer in liberty for all, he applauded the revolutionary movement in Europe in 1848, though he opposed the reception of Kossuth by Congress as meddling. In the troubles of 1850 he took a calm attitude and supported the compromise measures. Though he strongly supported the South on slavery, he never mentioned secession. He thoroughly believed in the colonization movement, and sought federal aid in returning free negroes to Africa. He was a consistent advocate of national economy, opposing large armies and navies, the extension of pensions, the padding of mileage accounts, and various petty expenditures by public officials. A great admirer of Henry Clay, he served as a presidential elector on his ticket in 1824 and in 1844.

Underwood remained a Unionist throughout the Civil War, though he had a son in the Confederate army. In 1860 he again entered the Kentucky legislature and served until 1863, when he finally relinquished public office for the practice of law and agriculture. The war made him a Democrat; he attended the national convention in Chicago in 1864, and the next year he was instrumental in reorganizing the party in Kentucky. He was a large man physically, benevolent, public-spirited, and truly a man of the people. He accumulated a considerable fortune. On Mar. 26, 1817, he married Eliza M. Trotter; she died in 1835, and on Feb. 27, 1839, he married Elizabeth Cox, a daughter of the mayor of Georgetown, D. C.; by each marriage he had eight children. A son by his second wife, John C. Underwood, became lieutenant-governor of Kentucky, and a grandson, Oscar W. Underwood [q.v.], became a senator from Alabama; a brother, Warner Lewis Underwood, was a Kentucky congressman and United States consul at Glasgow, Scotland.

[For sources, see L. M. Underwood, *The Underwood Families of America* (1913) ; Lewis and R. H. Collins, *Hist. of Ky.* (1882) ; *The Biog. Encyc. of Ky.* (1878) ; *Biog. Dir. Am. Cong.* (1928) ; *Am. Rev.*, June 1848 ; *Louisville Commercial*, Aug. 25, 1876. A few letters from Underwood to J. J. Crittenden are in the Crittenden MSS. in the Lib. of Cong.] E. M. C.

UNDERWOOD, LORING (Feb. 15, 1874– Jan. 13, 1930), landscape architect, was born at Belmont, Mass., the youngest of three children of William James and Esther Crafts (Mead) Underwood. His grandfather, William Underwood, emigrated to Boston from England in 1817. Having completed his preparatory work at the Noble & Greenough School, Boston, Underwood entered Harvard College, from which he received the degree of A.B. in 1897. On Oct. 14, 1897, he married Emily Walton of Newark, N. J., who with three daughters survived him. The year 1898–99 he spent in study at the Bussey Institution at Harvard, and the following year he spent in travel and study abroad. In Paris he attended the École d'Horticulture, studying under Edouard André, the celebrated French landscape architect. Thus was laid the educational foundation which, coupled with his sensitiveness to beauty and his intense love of nature, made him one of the outstanding landscape architects of his day. On his return from abroad in 1900 he established his home in Belmont and soon afterwards began the practice of his profession in Boston, where he maintained an office until his death. During the World War he rendered notable service as landscape architect of the housing development at Bath, Me., one of the United States Housing Corporation's villages for war workers. He was also a member of the Fuel Administration. In 1919 Laurence S. Caldwell joined him as partner.

Although he was landscape architect for the Mother Church, the First Church of Christ, Scientist, Boston, and other New England institutions, designed several subdivisions, and was for many years consulting landscape architect for Vassar College, it is not so much for these as for the many smaller home gardens which he designed that he will be long remembered. His field was largely New England. He was much sought after as a lecturer upon old New England gardens, and upon village and landscape improvement. His lectures were illustrated by lantern slides made by a direct color process, in the use of which he was a pioneer. For the display of these lantern slides he invented an ingeniously devised five-sided standard with interior illumination. His book, *The Garden and Its Accessories* (1906), remains after thirty years the outstanding American work on the subject. He was also the author of *A Garden Diary and Country Home Guide* (copyright 1908). Of a generous nature and keenly interested in all that pertained to his chosen profession, he gave freely of his time and abilities in many positions of responsibility. He was at one time president of the Boston Society of Landscape Architects; at the time of his death he was a member of the visiting committee of the School of Landscape Architecture of Harvard University, a director of the Massachusetts Horticultural Society, and a trustee of the Lowthorpe School.

[See L. M. Underwood, *The Underwood Families of America* (1913), vol. II; *Who's Who in America*, 1930–31; *Harvard Coll. Class of 1897, Twenty-fifth Anniversary Report* (n.d.); *Harvard Grads.' Mag.*, Mar. 1930; obituary notice in *Landscape Architecture*, Apr. 1930; obituaries in *Boston Transcript*, Jan. 13, and *Boston Herald*, Jan. 14, 1930; unpublished data in the possession of L. S. Caldwell, Boston. A large part of Underwood's collection of lantern slides is in the lib. of the School of Landscape Architecture, Harvard Univ.]   K. McN.

UNDERWOOD, LUCIEN MARCUS (Oct. 26, 1853–Nov. 16, 1907), botanist, was born in New Woodstock, N. Y., the son of John Lincklaen and Hannah Jane (Smith) Underwood. He was descended probably from Joseph Underwood (1614–1677) of Hingham and later of Watertown, Mass. Farm duties greatly ham-

pered Underwood's early education. Having prepared for college intermittently at near-by Cazenovia Seminary, he entered Syracuse University (1873), where he became greatly interested in geology and entomology, and, self-instructed, began his lifelong study of ferns. Upon graduation (1877) he taught school for a year and obtained the degree Ph.M. from Syracuse. In July 1878 he published in *L. B. Case's Botanical Index* an enumeration of the ferns growing near Syracuse, his first paper. During the following school year he taught natural sciences at Cazenovia and completed graduate studies in geology at Syracuse, receiving the degree Ph.D. (1879). He taught in Hedding College, Abingdon, Ill., the next year, and in 1880 became professor of geology and botany at Illinois Wesleyan University, where he remained three years. Here he published his first book, *Our Native Ferns and How to Study Them* (1881), a synoptical work which (under a slightly changed title) passed through six editions in twenty years, serving more than any other agency to stimulate the study of ferns in the United States. Here began also his special interest in the *Hepaticae,* a group upon which he published subsequently more than a score of important papers, the most widely known being his *Descriptive Catalogue of the North American Hepaticae North of Mexico* (1884). His keen zoölogical interest at this time is shown by several papers, mainly bibliographical, on spiders, myriapods, and crustaceans. The organization of the Indiana Academy of Sciences (1885) resulted largely through his efforts.

In 1883 Underwood was called to Syracuse University as instructor in geology, zoölogy, and botany, and in 1886 became professor. He taught here seven years, meanwhile gradually giving up zoölogy for cryptogamic botany and contributing the text on the *Hepaticae* to the sixth edition (1890) of Asa Gray's *Manual of the Botany of the Northern United States.* There followed a year given to study as Morgan Fellow at Harvard and to botanical work in Florida. In 1891 he accepted the professorship of botany at De Pauw University, transferring after four years to the Alabama Polytechnic Institute as professor of biology. He became professor of botany at Columbia University in July 1896, and remained in this position until his death. In 1899 he published *Moulds, Mildews, and Mushrooms,* an introduction to the study of fungi. This and the two synoptical works on ferns and hepatics afford the clew to much of Underwood's effort—an impelling desire to popularize botanical knowledge. From early boyhood he exhibited genius in classifying not only objects of natural history but historical data of all sorts. He compiled an elaborate genealogy, *The Underwood Families of America* (2 vols., 1913), which appeared posthumously.

Underwood's eleven years at Columbia University, the botanical department of which is affiliated with the New York Botanical Garden, left a notable impress. They were given not only to botanical exploration in the West Indies, the examination of fern "types" in European herbaria, and the publication of numerous papers on ferns (chiefly American), but also to the trenchant advocacy of sounder methods in taxonomy and of radical reform in botanical nomenclature. From 1901 he served as chairman of the board of scientific directors of the Botanical Garden, and in this capacity took a leading part in initiating, in 1905, publication of the *North American Flora,* a project he had long cherished. Temporarily deranged by overwork and worry, he died by his own hand at his home in Redding, Conn. He was married, Aug. 10, 1881, to Marie Annette Spurr, of Oakland, Cal., descended in the seventh generation from Jan Wybesse Spoor of Albany, N. Y.

In personality Underwood was uncommonly genial and forthright, keen, sympathetic, and imbued with a spirit of unselfish helpfulness. His professional accomplishment was essentially that of an inspiring pioneer and exceptionally energetic organizer.

[Biographical and memorial sketches by C. C. Curtis, M. A. Howe, J. H. Barnhart, and N. L. Britton, in *Bull. Torrey Botanical Club*, vol. XXXV, pp. 1–40 (Jan. 1908); N. L. Britton, in *Columbia Univ. Quart.*, Dec. 1907; H. H. Rusby, in *Jour. N. Y. Botanical Garden*, vol. VIII, pp. 263–69, portr. (Dec. 1907); obituary in *Hartford Times*, Nov. 18, 1907; private information.]   W. R. M.

UNDERWOOD, OSCAR WILDER (May 6, 1862–Jan. 25, 1929), representative and senator from Alabama, was born in Louisville, Ky., the son of Eugene Underwood and the latter's second wife, Frederica Virginia (Smith) Wilder Underwood. His earliest paternal ancestor in America, Thomas William (or William Thomas) Underwood, born *c.* 1675 near Norfolk, England, came to Virginia as a boy; and his grandfather, Joseph Rogers Underwood [*q.v.*], a native of Virginia, was representative and senator from Kentucky. When Oscar was three years old, his parents took him with them to St. Paul, Minn., and he spent the next decade at that frontier outpost. In 1875 his father and mother returned to Louisville, and he attended the common schools and the Rugby School there. He was a student at the University of Virginia from 1881 to 1884, and was elected to the presidency of the Jefferson Society, one of the highest honors within the gift of the student body. In 1884 he was admitted to the bar. After a brief period of practice in Minnesota, he removed to Birmingham, Ala., then a small but growing town. In 1894 he announced his candidacy for the House of Representatives from the Birmingham district. He took his seat in March of the following year and served until June 1896, when he was succeeded by Truman H. Aldrich, who had contested his election. He was then elected to the nine succeeding Congresses, and served continuously from Mar. 4, 1897, until Mar. 3, 1915. The following day he took his seat in the Senate, where he remained for two terms (1915–27).

Early in his career as a congressman Underwood proclaimed his belief in the principle of a tariff for revenue only enunciated by President Grover Cleveland. The fact that he stood on this platform was evidence of his independence of mind, for Birmingham was already a center of the iron and steel industry, an industry which believed in protection. In no sense a spectacular figure, Underwood forged to the front by virtue of his high character, his winning personality, and his unflagging industry. Those who knew him best respected him most, and after the Democrats captured control of the House in the elections of 1910, he was chosen by his party as floor leader (1911–15). At the same time he became chairman of the powerful ways and means committee. In the years immediately preceding, the Democrats had given little evidence of a coherent policy, and there was some uneasiness in the country as to whether Underwood, who was without great experience as a party helmsman, could mold them into a compact fighting force. Not only was he able to convince his party and the public of his ability to lead, but at the same time his detailed knowledge of the tariff, gained through years of close study, was an invaluable asset. The tariff was the issue of the hour.

President Taft called Congress in special session in 1911 to act on his Canadian reciprocity program. Putting aside narrow partisanship, Underwood gave unstinted support to reciprocity, since he felt it to be to a considerable degree compatible with the principles and purposes of the Democratic party. But at the same time he took the lead in revising many of the tariff schedules downward. This tariff legislation was all vetoed by President Taft. Thus was created an outstanding issue of the presidential campaign of 1912. Underwood's leadership at the special session of 1911 met and overcame a serious challenge from the powerful William Jennings Bryan. Bryan charged him publicly with protecting certain interests in his tariff schedules. Underwood abandoned his usual suavity as he lashed back at the Commoner in denial of the accusation (*Congressional Record,* 62 Cong., 1 Sess., pp. 3510–12), and his colleagues of the ways and means committee came to the floor of the House and supported him. The episode was a boomerang for Bryan, for the applause that greeted the Underwood statement left no doubt as to the attitude of the House.

Underwood conducted himself with such conspicuous ability in Congress that by the time the Democrats convened at Baltimore in 1912 to nominate a candidate for the presidency, he was among the leading contenders. In fact William F. McCombs, manager for Woodrow Wilson, felt when the convention opened that Underwood had the greatest potential strength of any of the aspirants (McCombs, *post,* p. 138). He polled 117½ votes on the first ballot, but his candidacy was opposed bitterly by Bryan, and his potential strength was never realized. He declined to be considered for the nomination for vice-president after Wilson had been named to head the ticket. Following Wilson's election, Underwood cooperated to the fullest in carrying out the new President's legislative program. His work in framing the important tariff bill which bears his name and in holding the Democratic majority in line behind the Federal Reserve act was especially noteworthy.

Taking his seat in the Senate in 1915, he was recognized as one of its most influential members. As a member of the appropriations committee during the World War, he had charge of some highly important appropriation bills during the illness of Senator Thomas S. Martin [*q.v.*]. In the Senate fight over the League of Nations, Underwood stood with Wilson, although he personally was of the opinion that the President ought to have agreed to certain mild reservations. He was strongly dissatisfied with the Senate rules, and in 1923, after two years as floor leader, he declined to offer for that position again. His acceptance of President Harding's appointment as one of the four representatives of the United States at the conference on limitation of armament in 1921–22, and his work in securing the ratification of the treaties drafted there, was looked at askance by his more partisan colleagues. He would probably have had opposition if he had sought the post of floor leader again.

In 1923 he announced that he was going to give the South a chance to select a Southerner to carry the banner of Democracy in the presidential election of the following year. The Ku Klux Klan was sweeping the country, and was in control in many states, especially in the South, where much of Underwood's strength lay. He was strongly advised to say nothing to offend the Klan, but that organization seemed to him fundamentally un-American, and he felt in duty bound to denounce it in no uncertain terms. On the eve of the Democratic National Convention in New York City, he declared that the Klan would be the paramount issue, and when the convention met he and others failed by a margin of only one vote to have an anti-Klan plank included in the platform. After the prolonged deadlock between the forces of William G. McAdoo and Alfred E. Smith had continued for fifty ballots, it is said that Smith offered to throw all his strength to Underwood if he could get the support of two Southern states, in addition to Alabama (Kent, *post,* p. 494). However, Underwood's uncompromising hostility to the Klan and national prohibition had alienated the South, so there was slight chance of his becoming a real contender.

Before the expiration of his second senatorial term in 1927, he announced that he would not be a candidate for reëlection, and at the close of the term he retired to his handsome estate, "Woodlawn," near "Mount Vernon" in Virginia. He was nearly sixty-five years of age and anxious to spend his remaining years in literary and other congenial pursuits. During his retirement he wrote *Drifting Sands of Party Politics* (1928), in which he discussed governmental principles. In the pages of this book he revealed himself as a devout follower of Thomas Jefferson, an advocate of a minimum of government and a maximum of personal liberty. He elaborated upon his oft-expressed opposition to sumptuary legislation, particularly the Eighteenth Amendment, as well as his objections to federal regulation of child labor. His strong aversion to all extensions of the federal authority caused him to be regarded by many as an ultra-conservative. While in the Senate he had taken a leading part in the fight against government operation of a power plant at Muscle Shoals, his position being that it should be used for the manufacture of nitrates, the purpose for which it was erected. He also opposed the woman's suffrage amendment.

Underwood was offered an appointment to the United States Supreme Court by President Harding (*New York Times,* Jan. 26, 1929; information from family), but such a position was not congenial to his temperament. He accepted two appointments from President Coolidge, one in 1927 as a member of the international commission between the United States and France, under the treaty of Sept. 15, 1914, and the other in 1928 as a delegate to the sixth international conference of American states held in Havana, Cuba, in that year. He attended this conference, but his health was beginning to fail, and in December he suffered a cerebral hemorrhage. This was followed by a paralytic stroke which proved fatal. Word of his death was received with unaffected and sincere expressions of sorrow in official Washington. His body was taken to Birmingham for burial, and the demonstrations which marked the obsequies there had seldom been equaled in the history of the state. He was married on Oct. 8, 1885, to Eugenia Massie of Charlottesville, Va., who died in 1900. On Sept. 10, 1904, he married Bertha Woodward of Birmingham. She and two sons by his first marriage survived him.

[O. W. Underwood, *Drifting Sands of Party Politics* (2 ed., 1931), with sketch of Underwood by C. G. Bowers; F. R. Kent, *The Democratic Party* (1928); W. F. McCombs, *Making Woodrow Wilson President* (1921); *Biog. Directory of the Am. Congress: 1774–1927* (1928); *Who's Who in America*, 1928–29; T. M. Owen, *Hist. of Alabama and Dictionary of Alabama Biography* (1921), vol. IV; obituary compiled by the Associated Press and published in afternoon papers, such as *Evening Star* (Washington), Jan. 25, 1929; obituary and editorial, *N. Y. Times*, Jan. 26, 1929, and funeral notice, Jan. 29, 1929; L. M. Underwood, *The Underwood Families of America* (1913), vol. II; newspaper clippings in possession of his widow relative to his fight against the Ku Klux Klan; letters from his former colleagues in Congress; correspondence with his family.]   V.D.

UPCHURCH, JOHN JORDAN (Mar. 26, 1820–Jan. 18, 1887), founder of the Ancient Order of United Workmen, was born on a farm in Franklin County, N. C., one of four children of Ambrose and Elizabeth (Hill) Upchurch. After 1824, when the father was shot dead by his wife's brother-in-law, the family was extremely poor. In 1837 Upchurch left the farm to learn the trade of millwright. Four years later, June 1, 1841, he married Angelina Green, a Pennsylvanian, who became the mother of his fifteen children. Soon afterward, with his wife's uncle, John Zeigenfuss, he opened a hotel in Raleigh, said to have been the first temperance house south of the Mason and Dixon line. When this venture failed, he worked briefly for the Raleigh & Gaston Railroad, attempted horse taming for a time, and in 1846 moved to Pennsylvania, where he entered the employ of the Mine Hill & Schuylkill Haven Railroad, in 1851 becoming master mechanic.

In June 1864, train hands, seeking a raise, went on strike, and for two weeks, according to his own account, Upchurch operated the road in the interest of the government with men provided by the War Department. The strike was broken, and Upchurch determined to unite employers and employees "in one grand organization" opposed to trade unions (*Life, post,* pp. 22, 24). On Jan. 1, 1865, he resigned from the railroad to engage in oil speculation, but with its collapse at the end of the Civil War, returned, off and on, to railroading. In 1868 he settled in Meadville, Pa., where he joined the League of Friendship, Supreme Mechanical Order of the Sun, one of the many secret workers' orders then springing up. The Meadville lodge soon split, and on Upchurch's initiative a section reorganized, Oct. 27, 1868, as Jefferson Lodge No. 1 of the Ancient Order of United Workmen. One of the main objects of the new order was "To discountenance strikes" (*Ibid.*, p. 57), but since the organization had the character of a lodge rather than a trade union, it proved impotent to affect strike movements seriously one way or the other. When, a year after its inception, it levied a dollar per capita assessment to pay substantial death benefits, it began to transform itself into a fraternal benefit society, and became the model for a movement characteristic of the period in America.

The demand of a rising but propertyless working class for a bulwark against sickness, old age, and funeral expenses underlay the rapid expansion of mutual-benefit societies. Impetus was given by the policies of the oldline commercial insurance houses, whose rates were very high. Indirectly, the societies were influenced by the English friendly societies of the sixteenth century and directly, although subordinately, by the secrecy, ritualism, and sociability of Freemasonry. Dozens of them went bankrupt until, late in the eighties, actuarial calculations were adopted and reserves built up. The Ancient Order of United Workmen pioneered in this field under the direction of Upchurch, who in 1873 had been made Past Supreme Master Workman, and today he is generally regarded as the founder of the mutual-benefit system, which in 1919 numbered two hundred fraternal societies in the United States and Canada, with more than 120,000 subordinate lodges and some 9,000,000 members.

Upchurch continued to work as master mechanic for various railroads until about 1881, after which time he had no regular employment. In 1885, at the solicitation of the Order he visited California, where he was fêted by many lodges, and the next year visited Boston and Philadelphia. He wrote an autobiography, *The Life, Labors, and Travels of Father J. J. Up-*

church (1887), which was edited and published posthumously by his fraternal brother, Sam Booth. He died in Steelville, Mo., where he had settled, and was buried in Bellefontaine Cemetery, St. Louis.

[Sources include M. W. Sackett, *Early Hist. of Fraternal Beneficiary Societies in America* (1914) ; Walter Basye, *Hist. and Operation of Fraternal Insurance* (copr. 1919); F. H. Hankins, "Fraternal Orders," *Encyc. of the Social Sciences,* VI (1931), 423 ; Arthur Preuss, *A Dict. of Secret and Other Societies* (1924) ; A. C. Stevens, *The Cyc. of Fraternities* (1899) ; *St. Louis Globe-Democrat,* Jan. 19, 1887. In Upchurch's autobiog. (*Life,* p. 13), the year of his birth is given as 1822, but all other references to year of birth in the *Life,* including description of coffin plate (p. 228), give 1820.]   H. S—w.

UPDEGRAFF, DAVID BRAINARD (Aug. 23, 1830–May 23, 1894), Quaker preacher, evangelist, editor, was descended from the family of Op den Graeff, German Mennonites with Dutch names who settled in Germantown, Pa., with Pastorius in 1683. He was born in Mount Pleasant, Ohio, the youngest son of David and Rebecca (Taylor) Updegraff. His mother was a preacher, and on both sides of his line of ancestry there were prominent Quaker preachers, the most noted of whom was his maternal grandmother, Ann Taylor. He was prepared for college in the local schools of Ohio and in 1851 entered Haverford College, where he remained for only one academic year. Returning to Mount Pleasant, he entered business. He was twice married, first, on Sept. 23, 1852, to Rebecca B. Price and, second, on Sept. 4, 1866, to Eliza J. C. Mitchell. There were four children by each marriage.

Updegraff's main interest lay in religious interpretation, and he had marked gifts as an evangelist of the type which flourished in America in the seventies and eighties of the nineteenth century. His successful career in this field dates from 1869, when he began to have meetings for prayer in his own home. In the early stages of his public ministry he worked for the most part among his own Quaker fellowship in the Middle West, especially in Ohio. He soon, however, widened his range of service and became a noted leader in the popular summer gatherings at Mountain Lake Park, Garrett County, Md., at Pitman Grove, N. J., and in the great interdenominational camp-meetings then being held both in the East and the West. As his views took final shape in his preaching he became noted as the fervid exponent of a special type of religious thought, which may fitly be called "Pentecostal Christianity." He advocated two stages of religious experience, which he called justification and sanctification. Justification for him meant the divine act by which a sinner is ab-

solved from the guilt and penalty of his sin; sanctification was represented as a state of baptism by the Holy Spirit, perfect peace, joy, love, and freedom from the power of sin.

Within the Society of Friends itself to which he belonged, he was widely known as an innovator and as a leader of a transformed Quakerism. He represented an intense form of evangelical thought and a dramatic style of preaching. He advocated the introduction of singing and set pastoral leadership, believed in conversion at a definite moment, and had a critical attitude toward silence in worship and toward the Quaker doctrine of the inward light. Midway in his career he was baptized with water in the Berean Baptist Church of Philadelphia. This brought him into sharp conflict with the leaders of the Society of Friends in America, which throughout its history had been opposed to the practice of outward baptism on the part of its members. He carried many Ohio Friends with him, and many other Friends elsewhere, influenced by his powerful personality, remained loyal to him through the controversies which followed. From 1887 to 1893 he edited a periodical entitled the *Friends' Expositor,* in which he vigorously interpreted his views and defended his position. In 1892 he published a volume of sermons and addresses with the title, *Old Corn,* which contains the substance of his teaching. He defended his position on baptism in two printed booklets. The more important one was printed in Columbus, Ohio, in 1885, as *An Address to the Ohio Yearly Meeting on the Ordinances;* the other was *The Ordinances: an Interview* (Richmond, Ind., 1886). He died at his home in Mount Pleasant, May 23, 1894.

[Dougan Clark and J. H. Smith, *David B. Updegraff and His Work* (1895) ; *Biog. Cat. of the Matriculates of Haverford Coll., 1833–1922* (1922) ; files of *Friends' Expositor, Christian Worker,* and *Friends' Review;* obituary in *Wheeling Reg.* (Wheeling, W. Va.), May 25, 1894.]   R. M. J.

UPDIKE, DANIEL (*c.* 1693–May 15, 1757), attorney-general of Rhode Island, son of Ludowick and Catherine (Newton) Updike, was born in North Kingstown, R. I. His grandfather was Gilbert Updike (Gysbert Opdyck), who came to New Amsterdam from Wesel sometime before 1638. When New Amsterdam was taken over by the English, in 1664, he emigrated to Rhode Island, and there married the daughter of Richard Smith, who had purchased a very large tract of land from the Narragansett Indians. Daniel was instructed at home by a private tutor and supplemented his education by a period of travel. He then took up the study of law, and after his admission to the bar established himself at Newport. Natural ability and an attractive personality quickly brought him to the front in the affairs of the colony. In 1722 he was elected attorney-general, which office he held continuously for the next ten years. One of his most important cases was the trial in 1723 of thirty-six pirates captured by an English vessel off the coast of Long Island. In 1724 he was appointed one of the commissioners who, with representatives from Connecticut, sought to locate definitely the boundary line between that colony and Rhode Island. The settlement of this controversy was protracted until 1726 when, since no agreement could be reached, the final decision was made by the King in Council.

Updike declined election as attorney-general in 1732 to accept nomination for governor; he was defeated, however, by his opponent, William Wanton. In 1740 he again represented his colony in a boundary line debate, this time with Massachusetts. The case was discussed before commissioners appointed by the King, Updike's speeches being described by a contemporary, Judge Lightfoot, as a brilliant performance (Wilkins Updike, *Memoirs, post,* p. 49). The decision reached by the commissioners proved unsatisfactory to the Massachusetts delegation, and the location of this boundary also was eventually settled by the King in Council.

Since Updike's retirement from the attorney-generalship, a law had been passed providing that each county of Rhode Island Colony should have its own attorney-general, and in 1741 Updike was elected to the office for Kings County, and held it until 1743 when the law was repealed. He was then again elected attorney-general for the whole colony, remaining as such until his death. In 1749, when the supreme court of Rhode Island ruled that no English statutes could be considered in force unless definitely adopted by the colony, Updike was one of the group of lawyers who selected the statutes to be proposed for adoption.

Not only was he an outstanding leader in the political life of Rhode Island, he was active, also, in its literary and social interests. He was a charter member of the society for the promotion of knowledge and science which was founded in Newport in 1730, and out of which grew the Redwood Library. Dean Berkeley, during his stay in Newport, was the friendly counselor of this society, and Updike became intimately associated with him. Updike was married first, Dec. 20, 1716, to Sarah, daughter of Gov. Benedict Arnold: she died in 1718, and on Dec. 22, 1722, he married Anstis Jenkins, whose inheritance added considerably to his own ample patrimony;

his third wife was Mary (Godfrey) Wanton, whom he married Mar. 14, 1745. In appearance he was a man slightly above the average height, with a dignified bearing, and a clear, pleasing voice, which contributed to his success as a speaker.

[C. W. Opdyke, *The Op Dyck Geneal.* (1889); J. O. Austin, *The Geneal. Dict. of R. I.* (1887), p. 397; Wilkins Updike, *Memoirs of the R. I. Bar* (1842); J. R. Cole, *Hist. of Washington and Kent Counties, R. I.* (1889); *The Biog. Cyc. of Representative Men of R. I.* (1881); J. R. Bartlett, *Records of the Colony of R. I.,* vols. IV, V (1859–60); Wilkins Updike, *A Hist. of the Episcopal Church in Narragansett, R. I.* (2nd ed., 3 vols., 1907), ed. by Daniel Goodwin.]   E. R. B.

UPHAM, CHARLES WENTWORTH (May 4, 1802–June 15, 1875), Unitarian clergyman, congressman, and historian of the Salem witchcraft delusion, was born in St. John, New Brunswick, the son of Joshua and Mary (Chandler) Upham. He was a descendant of John Upham who emigrated from England to Weymouth, Mass., in 1635. Joshua Upham, a native of Brookfield, Mass., a graduate of Harvard, and a Loyalist during the American Revolution, had served in the British army during the war, and at its close had emigrated to New Brunswick, where he held the office of judge of the supreme court until his death in 1808. Charles attended school in St. John, and at the age of twelve he was apprenticed to an apothecary. In 1816 he went to Boston to work for his cousin, Phineas Upham, a merchant; but this benevolent kinsman, soon perceiving that the boy's inclination was for study rather than business, placed him under the tutelage of Deacon Samuel Greele, and in 1817 sent him to Harvard College. Upham amply justified his kinsman's aid by graduating in 1821, second in his class. He next spent three years in the Cambridge Divinity School, and on Dec. 8, 1824, was ordained as associate pastor of the First Church (Unitarian) of Salem. Here he served until 1844—twelve years as the colleague of the Rev. John Prince—when, suffering from a bronchial ailment, he resigned.

During his career as clergyman, he distinguished himself as a learned champion of Unitarianism. In his discourse *Principles of the Reformation* (1826), he urged the necessity of advancing beyond the religious beliefs of the Pilgrim fathers. In 1833–34 he engaged in an extended controversy with the Rev. George B. Cheever [q.v.] in the columns of the *Salem Gazette* on the subject of Unitarian versus Trinitarian principles. Upham's chief proposition, in the support of which he displayed a formidable knowledge of the history and literature of the Reformation, was that Ralph Cudworth, who had been quoted by Cheever in defense of the Trinitarian doctrine, was in reality a Unitarian. By 1840, in *The Scripture Doctrine of Regeneration*, he could rejoice in the "abandonment of Calvinism" and the "general diffusion of rational Christianity."

Having partially recovered his health, in 1848 Upham turned to politics, aligning himself with the Whig party. In 1849–50 he was a member of the state House of Representatives and in 1850–51, of the state Senate. He warmly supported the presidential candidacy of Zachary Taylor, and at the request of the city authorities of Salem he delivered a eulogy, July 18, 1850, on the late President's life and character. He was a delegate to the state constitutional convention of 1853, and was a member of the Thirty-third Congress (1853–55). As a congressman he opposed the Kansas-Nebraska Act, approaching the subject not as an abolitionist or moral reformer, but as a historian, insisting upon the validity of the principles involved in the ordinance of 1787 and the Missouri Compromise. An active supporter in 1856 of the newly organized Republican party, he wrote a campaign biography of John C. Frémont. He was a member of the state Senate from 1857 to 1859 and served as its presiding officer. From 1859 to 1861 he was again a member of the state House of Representatives.

Retiring from political life in 1860, Upham devoted his energies to historical research. He is remembered chiefly as the author of *Salem Witchcraft* (2 vols., 1867). To furnish a background for the events of 1692, he reconstructed in admirable detail the local family history of Salem Village. His account of the witch trials is still of use to historians. A controversy arose as to the part taken by Cotton Mather [*q.v.*] in the persecution of the witches: Upham had argued that Mather fomented the delusion to increase his power in the community; William F. Poole [*q.v.*] defended Mather in the *North American Review* (April 1869); Upham, with characteristic love of debate, replied in a spirited brochure of ninety finely printed pages (*Salem Witchcraft and Cotton Mather*, 1869). Although the question is still a disputed one, recent scholarly opinion seems inclined to exculpate Mather (K. B. Murdock, *Selections from Cotton Mather*, 1926, p. xv).

It seems likely that Upham's reputation as a man will suffer as a result of his having incurred the ill will of Nathaniel Hawthorne. Because of Upham's activity in securing the removal of Hawthorne as surveyor of customs at Salem, the novelist is believed to have drawn, in the character of Judge Pyncheon, a satirical portrait of his political opponent (see W. S. Nevins,

"Nathaniel Hawthorne's Removal from the Salem Custom House," *Historical Collections of the Essex Institute*, April 1917; Julian Hawthorne, *Nathaniel Hawthorne and His Wife*, 1885, I, 339, 438). Pyncheon, in the words of Henry James, is "a superb, full-blown hypocrite, a large-based, full-nurtured Pharisee" (*Hawthorne*, 1879, p. 124). This portrait, however, contains elements of caricature, and, like many other famous satirical sketches, it is doubtless unfair to its prototype. Upham was apparently held in high esteem by many of his contemporaries. He numbered Edward Everett among his friends, and Emerson, his classmate at Harvard, referred to his "frank and attractive" manners, and his large "repertory of men and events" (Ellis, *Memoir, post*, p. 12). He died in Salem. On Mar. 29, 1826, he married Ann Susan, daughter of the Rev. Abiel Holmes [*q.v.*] of Cambridge, and sister of Oliver Wendell Holmes; they had fourteen children, all but three of whom died either in infancy or in early life.

[F. K. Upham, *The Descendants of John Upham of Mass.* (1892); G. E. Ellis, *An Address . . . at the Funeral Services of Charles W. Upham* (1875), and *Memoir of Charles Wentworth Upham* (1877); *Biog. Dir. Am. Cong.* (1928); S. A. Eliot, *Heralds of a Liberal Faith* (1910), vols. I, II; *Salem Gazette*, June 18, 1875; *Boston Transcript*, June 15, 1875.]   R. S.

UPHAM, SAMUEL FOSTER (May 19, 1834–Oct. 5, 1904), Methodist Episcopal clergyman, for many years professor in Drew Theological Seminary, was born in Duxbury, Mass. His father, Frederick Upham, also a Methodist minister, was descended from John Upham who emigrated from England to Weymouth, Mass., in 1635; his mother, Deborah Bourne of Sandwich, Mass., was a descendant of Richard Bourne, missionary to the Indians, who died in Sandwich in 1682. Samuel prepared for college at East Greenwich (R. I.) Academy, and graduated from Wesleyan University in 1856. He was immediately admitted to the Providence Conference of the Methodist Episcopal Church on trial, was ordained deacon in 1858, and elder in 1860. From the beginning of his ministry he was a popular preacher, and his advancement was rapid. From 1856 to 1864 he served churches in Taunton, Mass., Pawtucket, R. I., New Bedford, Mass., and Bristol, R. I. In 1864 he transferred to the New England Conference, where at different times he was pastor of three Boston churches, and also of churches in Lowell, Lynn, and Springfield, Mass. In 1865 he was chaplain of the Massachusetts House of Representatives. Appointed professor of practical theology at Drew Theological Seminary, Madison, N. J., in 1880, he began his duties there on Mar. 13, 1881, and continued in the performance of them until his death some twenty-three years later.

Samuel, or "Sammy" Upham, as he was affectionately called, was one of the best known and most highly esteemed of the Methodist ministers of his day. If some excelled him in learning and scholarly productivity, not many surpassed him in personal attractiveness, shrewd wisdom and sound judgment, ability and disposition to be helpful to individuals, and power to interest and influence an audience. He was a kindly, companionable, sagacious person with whom young and old felt at home, and at Drew he was the friend, counsellor, and prophet of many. He was blessed with wit and humor, was fond of his cronies, and "loved a joke no matter what its age" (Tipple, *post*, p. 108). He was an adept in the use of ridicule and could be merciless in exposing error. His preaching was trenchant, practical, and arousing, and few were called upon more often for sermons and addresses on special occasions. In the councils of the Church and in the management of its institutions his influence was strong and lasting. From 1871 until his death he was a trustee of Wesleyan University and from 1880 till his death, of the Methodist preparatory school, Wilbraham Academy, Wilbraham, Mass. He was a member of all the General Conferences from 1880 to 1904 inclusive; one of the board of managers of the Missionary Society and for sixteen years its representative on the General Missionary Committee; member and secretary of the committee on constitutional law; and chairman of the hymnal commission, which prepared the official Methodist hymnal. As a member of the committee on itinerancy in the General Conference of 1900, he was instrumental in having the time limit to pastorates removed. On several occasions he received votes for the office of bishop. He was married, Apr. 15, 1857, to Lucy Graves Smith of Middletown, Conn.; they had five sons.

[F. K. Upham, *The Descendants of John Upham of Mass.* (1892); *Alumni Record of Wesleyan Univ.* (4th ed., 1911); *Official Minutes of the ... New Eng. Conf. of the M. E. Ch.*, 1905 (n.d.); E. S. Tipple, *Drew Theological Sem., 1867–1917* (copr. 1917); *Who's Who in America*, 1903–05; *Christian Advocate* (N. Y.), Oct. 13, 1904; *Zion's Herald* (Boston), Oct. 12, 1904.]
H. E. S.

UPHAM, THOMAS COGSWELL (Jan. 30, 1799–Apr. 2, 1872), teacher, metaphysician, and author, was born at Deerfield, N. H., a member of a distinguished family descended from John Upham who settled in Weymouth, Mass., in 1635. His father, Nathaniel Upham, served in Congress; one brother, Nathaniel, was a judge of the supreme court of New Hampshire; another,

Francis, a well-known professor of mental philosophy at Rutgers Female College, New York. His mother was Judith Cogswell, daughter of Thomas Cogswell, of Gilmanton, N. H. Upham graduated from Dartmouth College in 1818, and from Andover Theological Seminary in 1821. He made there such an outstanding record for indefatigable study and scholarship that he became tutor in Hebrew under Prof. Moses Stuart [*q.v.*]; and in 1823 he published an excellent translation, *Jahn's Biblical Archaeology*, from the Latin of Johann Jahn, with additions and corrections. From 1823 to 1824 he served as associate pastor of the Congregational Church at Rochester, N. H. In 1824 he was chosen professor of mental and moral philosophy at Bowdoin College, which chair he held until his retirement in 1867. His remaining years were spent in study and writing at Kennebunkport, Me., and later in New York City, where he died.

At Bowdoin he was one of the best known teachers in a rather distinguished faculty. Although he came to his professorship from a pastorate, he soon gave up preaching and public speaking, and made his strong religious influence felt in the classroom, in small groups of students, and with individuals. He was actively interested in the social reforms of the day, was an earnest and liberal patron of the colonization of negroes, a strong supporter of the temperance movement, and one of the earliest American advocates of international peace, collaborating with William Ladd [*q.v.*] and writing one of the essays published in *Prize Essays on a Congress of Nations* (1840). In 1852 he spent a year in European and Eastern travel, publishing in 1855 *Letters Aesthetic, Social, and Moral, Written from Europe, Egypt, and Palestine*. He also served Bowdoin well in practical affairs, at one time raising by his own efforts the then surprisingly large sum of nearly $70,000. Yet it is as an author in his chosen field of mental philosophy that Upham was best known. Brought to Bowdoin to oppose the doctrines of Kant and his school, he found himself after long effort unable to refute the teachings of the German metaphysician, and was on the point of resigning his professorship when suddenly he conceived a distinction between the intellect, the sensibilities, and the will which he embodied in his *A Philosophical and Practical Treatise on the Will* (1834), his outstanding work. This has been called "one of the first original and comprehensive contributions of American scholarship to modern psychology" (Foster, *post*, p. 249). This work and a succeeding volume, *Outlines of Imperfect and Disordered Mental Action* (1840), made him to be regarded more as a psychologist than a theologian, and did much to liberate American philosophy and theology from the thraldom of the elder Jonathan Edwards [*q.v.*]. A bibliography of Upham's works contains more than sixty items, and includes, in addition to philosophical treatises, a religious classic, *Principles of the Interior or Hidden Life* (1843), and some books of verse, notably *American Cottage Life* (1851), first published anonymously about 1828 as *Domestic and Religious Offering*.

In character and appearance, Upham was distinctly of the academic type of the early nineteenth century. Modest, retiring, very reserved, almost secretive, absent-minded, kindly, with remarkable self-control, he was "in the best sense a quietest [*sic*], and seemed . . . to have attained to a high state of repose in God" (Packard, *post*, p. 21). Having no children, he and his wife, Phebe Lord, whom he married on May 18, 1825, and whose portrait by Gilbert Stuart in the Bowdoin Art Museum reveals an unusual loveliness of person and character, adopted several children, and made their home, in the words of Harriet Beecher Stowe, who was received there on her arrival in Brunswick, "delightful . . . a beautiful pattern of a Christian family, a beautiful exemplification of religion" (Hatch, *post,* p. 60).

[F. K. Upham, *The Descendants of John Upham* (1892); A. S. Packard, *Address on the Life and Character of Thomas C. Upham, D.D.* (1873); L. C. Hatch, *The Hist. of Bowdoin Coll.* (1927); F. H. Foster, *A Genetic Hist. of New England Theology* (1907); death notice in *N. Y. Times,* Apr. 3, 1872; letters and newspaper articles in Bowdoin Coll. lib.]   K. C. M. S.

UPHAM, WARREN (Mar. 8, 1850–Jan. 29, 1934), geologist, archeologist, writer on historical subjects, was born at Amherst, N. H., the son of Jacob and Sarah (Hayward) Upham, and a descendant of John Upham who emigrated from England to Weymouth, Mass., in 1635. After his graduation from Dartmouth College in 1871, he was engaged on the geological survey of New Hampshire (1874–78), and on the geological survey of Minnesota and the United States Geological Survey (1879–95). He went to Minnesota in 1879. On Oct. 22, 1885, he married Addie M. Bixby of Aurora, Minn.; there was one child, who died at birth. From 1895 to 1914 he was secretary and librarian of the Minnesota Historical Society, and from 1914 to 1933 archeologist of the society.

Upham's life affords the unusual example of a diligent scholar at the height of his career in one science changing his major field after the age of fifty. Before 1905 most of his work was in geology; after 1905, in archeology and history. An indefatigable and patient worker, he published almost two hundred papers on geology. Of these all but about twenty are on glacial geology and nearly related subjects, which were his principal fields of work. His greatest contribution to geology probably is contained in the fine series of county reports issued by the Minnesota Geological Survey, but his best known paper is "The Glacial Lake Agassiz," *United States Geological Survey Monographs,* vol. XXV (1896), which includes many of the principal results of his studies in Minnesota, North Dakota, and Manitoba. This monograph, a classic on the subject of post-glacial physiography, describes an ancient lake vastly greater than the present Lake Superior, its beaches, deltas, and other shore features that became wonderfully well exposed when the lake shrank to become the present Lake Winnipeg. In 1896 Upham issued, jointly with G. F. Wright, a volume entitled *Greenland Ice Fields and Life in the North Atlantic.*

His most important historical publications appeared in the *Collections of the Minnesota Historical Society,* among them "Groseilliers and Radisson, the First White Men in Minnesota" (vol. X, pt. 2, 1905), "Minnesota Biographies" (vol. XIV, 1912), which he compiled with Rose B. Dunlap, and "Minnesota Geographic Names" (vol. XVII, 1920). He was one of the editors of *Minnesota in Three Centuries* (1908). He was particularly interested in the history of man before the period of the graphic arts, and published two noteworthy contributions on the subject: "Man in the Ice Age at Lansing, Kan., and Little Falls, Minn." (*American Geologist,* Sept. 1902), and "Valley Loess and the Fossil Man of Lansing, Kan." (*Ibid.,* Jan. 1903). Although the conclusions of these discourses were not generally accepted as indisputable proof of the presence of man in North America during the Ice Age, Upham died with the conviction that man inhabited the region beyond the ice edge during at least a part of that period, and recent discoveries in Minnesota lend strong support to that theory. Upham was courtly, modest, unobtrusive, almost retiring until his own field was mentioned; he then became alert, authoritative, and entertaining. He was endeared to all his associates by his modesty regarding his own attainments, his thoughtfulness for others, and his willingness to give without stint both his time and his knowledge. He died at St. Paul, Minn., where he had lived for many years.

[See F. K. Upham, *The Descendants of John Upham* (1892); Mary U. Kelly and Warren Upham, *Upham and Amherst, N. H.* (1897); *Who's Who in America,* 1932–33; *Am. Men of Sci.* (5th ed., 1933), ed. by J. M. and Jaques Cattell; "Minn. Biogs.," *Minn. Hist. Soc.*

Colls., vol. XIV (1912) ; obituary in *Minneapolis Jour.*, Jan. 30, 1934. A bibliog. of Upham's articles on geology appears in *U. S. Geological Survey Bull. 746* (1923).]   W. H. E.

UPJOHN, RICHARD (Jan. 22, 1802–Aug. 17, 1878), architect, born in Shaftesbury, Dorsetshire, England, was the son of James Upjohn, surveyor and master in the grammar school, and of Elizabeth Plantagenet Dryden Michell, daughter of the rector of Holy Trinity Church, Shaftesbury. His parents had planned that he should enter one of the learned professions, but he insisted on becoming a draftsman and was accordingly apprenticed to a cabinetmaker. A master craftsman at twenty-two, he established his own business in Shaftesbury, and on Nov. 14, 1826, he married in London Elizabeth Parry, daughter of the Rev. John Parry of Denbigh, North Wales. He prospered, but, ambitious, headstrong, and incautious, he became entangled in grandiose schemes and was soon hopelessly in debt. During his early childhood, the Upjohn family had spent some time in St. John's, Newfoundland, where James Upjohn had established a business. Now, refusing to let an uncle shoulder his debts, Richard set out for America with his wife and young son, Richard Michell [*q.v.*], and landed in New York on June 1, 1829 (diary in the possession of his grandson, Hobart Upjohn). In the fall of 1830 he finally settled in New Bedford, Mass., became a draftsman for Samuel Leonard, builder and sperm-oil merchant, and opened an evening school of drawing. Upon seeing some drawings for the Boston Custom House, he exclaimed, according to a family story, "If that is architecture, I am an architect," and forthwith opened his office and advertised for work.

In February 1834 he moved to Boston, and for four years worked spasmodically for Alexander Parris [*q.v.*]. He also did considerable work of his own, including numerous Greek villas, and a Gothic iron fence for Boston Common. In 1837 he completed St. John's Church, Bangor, Me., his first Gothic Church, and the first of much Maine work, which culminated in the large stone mansion for R. H. Gardiner at Gardiner, Me. In the spring of 1839 he was chosen draftsman for repairs and alterations in Trinity Church, New York, and when a new building was decided upon he was retained officially as architect. In August he moved to New York. The new Trinity Church, begun in 1841 and consecrated in 1846, of unprecedented richness and purity of style, won immediate fame, equalling, if not surpassing, that of Grace Church, New York, by the younger James Renwick [*q.v.*]. From that time

on, work flowed into Upjohn's office faster than he could handle it. He designed not only Gothic churches, but houses and civil buildings as well. Many of his houses were in the Italian or "bracketed" styles, and the Trinity Building (1852)—at the time New York's finest office building—was called Italian Renaissance.

The long list of Upjohn's important work includes an "Italian villa" for Edward King, Newport (see A. J. Downing, *The Architecture of Country Houses*, 1850, pp. 317–21) ; the alterations of the Van Rensselaer Manor-house, Albany, N. Y., in a kind of pseudo-Colonial ; of the Van Buren house, Kinderhook, N. Y. ; and of the Pierrepont house, Brooklyn, N. Y., all done between 1840 and 1850. Other buildings, designed between 1840 and 1855, include the city hall and Taunton Academy, Taunton, Mass., and the much praised Corn Exchange Bank Building, New York ; the Church of the Ascension, New York ; Bowdoin College Chapel ; the Church of the Pilgrims, Brooklyn, a building of marked originality ; Grace Church, Newark, N. J. ; St. James', New London, Conn. ; the Church of the Holy Communion, Twentieth Street and Sixth Avenue, New York ; St. Paul's Church, Buffalo, N. Y. ; St. Mark's, Augusta, Me. ; St. Paul's, Brookline, Mass. ; and Grace Church, Utica, N. Y. During the period of the growing influence of Richard Michell Upjohn upon the office work, the best works were the Central Congregational Church, Boston, Mass., and St. Thomas's, New York. Upjohn's favorite work, and in many ways his best, is Trinity Chapel, West Twenty-fifth Street, New York (1853), with unusual direct simplicity of design and unusual height. The delicate detail of the monument to unknown Revolutionary soldiers, Trinity Churchyard, is also an achievement rare for the time. Upjohn's careful and sensitive use of the precedent of English Gothic was widely imitated but rarely equalled ; his influence in the United States was in many ways similar to the influence in England of A. W. N. Pugin. Like most early Gothic Revival architects, Upjohn was more interested in effect than in structure and used lath-and-plaster vaults frequently, apparently without compunction. Yet in Trinity Chapel there is an honest use of materials everywhere, and in *Upjohn's Rural Architecture* (1852) the designs show a simple and functional use of wood.

Upjohn is important as the chief instrumentality in the founding of the American Institute of Architects, of which he was president from its beginning (1857) until his resignation in 1876. At the first meeting, in his office and at his invitation, the group took the name "New York Society of Architects," but soon adopted the present name, and the new society became the successor to the short-lived American Institution of Architects, founded in 1837. As president Upjohn supported the highest possible professional standards. The foundations of the present competition code and the present standards of professional ethics were laid during his administration, and largely at his instigation. The same high ethical standards controlled his personal life. He refused to design the Arlington Street Unitarian Church, Boston, since it seemed to him an anti-Christian, because Unitarian, enterprise; his attitude in this probably caused the loss to him of the Harvard College Chapel, designs for which he had prepared the same year. He made it a practice to do at least one mission church a year free. His influence was spread indirectly by many architects who were trained in his office or worked for him, among them Leopold Eidlitz [*q.v.*], Alpheus Morse, Charles Babcock (later professor of architecture at Cornell), Joseph C. Wells, and Charles Clinton, of Clinton and Russell. His great hobby was painting, and he brought back from a European trip in 1850 many landscapes of high merit. He was an honorary member of both the Royal Institute of British Architects and the Institute of Portuguese Architects. He died at Garrison, N. Y., survived by his wife and five children.

[I. N. P. Stokes, *The Iconography of Manhattan Island*, vols. III (1918), V–VI (1926–28); Glenn Brown, *The Am. Institute of Architects, 1857–1907* (n.d.); obituaries in *Am. Architect and Building News*, Aug. 24, *N. Y. Times*, Aug. 18, and *N. Y. Tribune*, Aug. 19, 1878; biog. in MS. by Upjohn's grandson, Hobart B. Upjohn; office records and drawings in the possession of H. B. Upjohn of New York.]					T. F. H.

UPJOHN, RICHARD MICHELL (Mar. 7, 1828–Mar. 3, 1903), architect, the son of Richard Upjohn [*q.v.*] and Elizabeth (Parry) Upjohn, was born in Shaftesbury, England, and was brought to America in his second year. He received a good education in private schools, and in 1846 entered his father's office, where during his father's extended European trip in 1850 he had full charge. In 1851–52 he studied in Europe. On his return he opened his own office but soon returned to his father's as a full partner (1853) and exercised a growing influence on the design. During the sixties and seventies, it is sometimes difficult to determine which was the controlling mind. St. Thomas's Church, New York, is typical of the work of this period; its towers probably indicate the son's taste.

Upjohn's work was less dominantly ecclesiastical than his father's. He was the architect of the Mechanics' Bank, New York (1858), one of the early buildings to use rolled-iron beams and brick floor arches; the building of the Newark Banking and Insurance Company, Newark, N. J.; a large school in Hartford, Conn., and the first building for Trinity School, New York. Among his noteworthy churches were the old Madison Square Presbyterian Church, New York; Park Church, Hartford, Conn.; the Presbyterian Church and manse, Rye, N. Y.; the De Lancey Memorial, Geneva, N. Y.; St. Mark's Pro-Cathedral, San Antonio, Tex.; and St. Paul's Cathedral at Fond du Lac, Wis. One of his best churches was the American church, St. John's, in Dresden, Germany. The main entrance gateway of Greenwood Cemetery, Brooklyn, is his design (1861); and it is probable that the Central Congregational Church, Boston, with its simple and exquisite 235-foot stone tower and spire is his also. His most famous work was the state capitol at Hartford, Conn. (1885), for which drawings were begun in 1872. The only such building in America to combine a dome with wings in a Gothic style, it presented problems of exceptional difficulty. Upjohn had intended to use a square tower, but the state authorities were unable to conceive of a capitol without a dome and forced him to design one; the resulting dome is, nevertheless, a brilliant adaptation. Under the influence of Ruskin, Upjohn's work is often full of such "Victorian Gothic" mannerisms as polychromy and the dominance of the horizontal line. The Trinity school building, with its erratic detail and its rich plate tracery over flat-headed windows, is typical, and the lavish color and carving of the Hartford capitol, in which the modern eye often sees only the bizarre, is an excellent example of Ruskinian principles conscientiously applied.

Upjohn was a fellow of the American Institute of Architects from its beginning, and for two years a president of its New York chapter; he was also a member of the Institute's important committee for examining unsafe buildings. He lived in Brooklyn for most of his later life. Much interested in local history, he was one of the founders of the Long Island Historical Society. In character he was reserved, in his later years almost a recluse. Strong-willed, impulsive, at times hot-tempered, he was an indomitable worker, making many of the office drawings himself. He retired gradually from the practice of architecture during the nineties, his interests becoming more and more financial; by 1895 his architectural career had ceased. On Oct. 1, 1856, he married Emma Degen Tyng, daughter of the Rev. James H. Tyng, in Morristown, N. J. There were nine children, of whom the youngest became an architect. Upjohn died in Brooklyn, survived by five sons and three daughters.

[*Who's Who in America,* 1901–02; *Proc. . . . Am. Institute of Architects . . . 1903,* vol. XXXVII (1904); *Am. Architect and Building News,* Mar. 14, 1903; *Am. Art Ann.,* 1903; R. M. Upjohn, *The State Capitol, Hartford, Conn.* (1886); obituaries in *Brooklyn Daily Eagle,* Mar. 3, and *Evening Post* (N. Y.), Mar. 4, 1903; family records, office drawings and records in the possession of Upjohn's son, Hobart B. Upjohn of New York.]   T. F. H.

UPSHUR, ABEL PARKER (June 17, 1791–Feb. 28, 1844), jurist, cabinet officer, publicist, one of twelve children of Littleton Upshur and Ann (Parker) Upshur, and a descendant of Arthur Upshur who settled on the Eastern Shore of Virginia in the seventeenth century, was born in Northampton County, Va. His father, a Federalist member of the Virginia legislature of 1809, voted against the resolutions thanking Jefferson for his services to the country and later served as a captain in the War of 1812. Abel Upshur studied at the College of New Jersey (Princeton) until his expulsion as a participant in a student rebellion in 1807 and then continued his studies at Yale, but did not graduate. After reading law in the office of William Wirt of Richmond, he began practice in that city. In 1812–13 he was a member of the House of Delegates from his native county, and served again in that capacity, 1825–27. He was also a member of the Virginia constitutional convention of 1829–30, in which he was an opponent of the proposed democratic changes in the constitution. He denied the existence of any original principles of government, insisting instead that the interests and necessities of the people determined the principles of government (*Proceedings and Debates, post,* p. 69). He rejected the theory of "natural law," maintaining that the only natural law was "the law of force . . . the only rule of right" (*Ibid.,* p. 67). From 1826 to 1841, he was a member of the supreme court of Virginia, and in politics he was associated with the extreme state-rights, proslavery group.

In September 1841, Upshur was appointed secretary of the navy by President Tyler, and in 1843 he succeeded Webster as secretary of state. An ardent advocate of the annexation of Texas as vital to the security of the South, he reopened negotiations with that republic, but they were interrupted by his death in the explosion of a gun on board the battleship *Princeton,* and were completed by his successor, Calhoun.

A particularistic jurist and planter-philosopher of Tidewater Virginia, Upshur often ex-pressed his views upon slavery, government, and banks. The South constituted, in his opinion, the only bulwark of conservatism in America against the rising tide of agrarianism, leveling democracy, and all the *isms* of the free North. "It is clear," he wrote pessimistically, "that in this country Liberty is destined to perish a suicide. . . . And perish when she may, I am much deceived if her last entrenchment, her latest abiding place, will not be found in the slave holding states" ("Domestic Slavery," *Southern Literary Messenger,* October 1839). Law, and not the principle of numerical majority, he held to be the basis of liberty—a juridical conception. In a letter to his intimate friend, Judge Beverley Tucker, commenting upon Dorr's Rebellion, Upshur wrote: "This is the very madness of democracy, and a fine illustration of the workings of the majority principle" (Tyler, *post,* II, 198). His pamphlet, *A Brief Enquiry into the True Nature and Character of our Federal Government* (1840), a review of Story's *Commentaries,* was regarded by his friends as a complete refutation of the nationalistic theory of the Constitution. It was reprinted in 1863 by Northern Democrats as a means of setting forth the political philosophy of the Confederacy (Adams, *post,* p. 77). In an address (1841) before the literary societies of the College of William and Mary upon "The True Theory of Government," Upshur rejected almost *in toto* the natural rights philosophy, characterizing it as one that "overlooks all social obligations, denies the inheritable quality of property, unfrocks the priest, and laughs at the marriage tie" (*Southern Literary Messenger,* June 1856, p. 410). A supporter of banks, he opposed the requirement of specie as the basis of credit and also opposed laws which declared banks insolvent when unable to redeem their notes in specie. "A bank," he wrote, "without a single dollar in specie, yet having good notes of others, equal to its own notes outstanding, and its other indebtedness, is perfectly solvent, and entitled to credit" (*A Brief Enquiry into the True Basis of the Credit System,* 1840, p. 11). He furthermore urged the minimum regulation of banks, believing that the "general law of the land, the common law . . . affords ample means . . . of keeping them within proper limits" (*Ibid.,* p. 20).

Upshur was married twice: first, to Elizabeth Dennis, and second, in 1826, to his cousin, Elizabeth Upshur; she, with their daughter, survived him.

[C. H. Ambler, *Thomas Ritchie, A Study in Virginia Politics* (1913); T. H. Benton, *Thirty Years' View,* vol. II (1856), J. P. Kennedy, *Memoirs of the Life of William Wirt* (1849), I, 399; *Niles' National*

Register, Sept. 18, 1841, Feb. 12, 26, 1842, Mar. 2, 1844; L. G. Tyler, *The Letters and Times of the Tylers* (2 vols., 1884–85); *Proc. and Debates of the Va. State Convention of 1829–30* (1830); *Wm. and Mary Coll. Quart.*, Apr. 1895, Oct. 1907, Jan. 1928, Jan. 1931; H. A. Wise, *Seven Decades of the Union* (1872), pp. 197–200; Mary Upshur Sturges, "Abel Parker Upshur," *Mag. of Am. Hist.*, Sept. 1877; R. G. Adams, "Abel Parker Upshur," in S. F. Bemis, *The Am. Secretaries of State*, vol. V (1928); *Daily Nat. Intelligencer* (Washington), Feb. 29, 1844.]   W.G.B.

UPSHUR, JOHN HENRY (Dec. 5, 1823–May 30, 1917), naval officer, was born at Eastville, Northampton County, Va., and had originally the surname Nottingham, being the son of Elizabeth Parker (Upshur) and John Evans Nottingham. He was a nephew of Abel Parker Upshur [*q.v.*] and of Capt. George P. Upshur, U. S. N., and perhaps because of these relationships both he and his brother, Dr. George L. Upshur, were given in childhood their mother's family name, upon authorization of the Virginia legislature. After attending the grammar school connected with the College of William and Mary (1834–41), he entered the navy, Nov. 4, 1841, as a midshipman. A Mediterranean cruise in the *Congress* (1842–43) was followed by service throughout the Mexican War in the sloop *St. Mary's,* including duty ashore, Mar. 10–25, 1847, with the naval battery at the siege of Vera Cruz. During the next year he attended the United States Naval Academy, then under the superintendency of his uncle, George P. Upshur, and graduated as passed midshipman, Aug. 10, 1848, ranking 17 in his class of 235 members. During the next decade his chief assignments were in the Mediterranean Squadron (1849–50), in the storeship *Supply* with Perry's mission to Japan (1852–55), as flag lieutenant in the *Cumberland,* African Squadron (1857–59), and as an instructor at the Naval Academy (1859–61). In the Civil War he served in the *Wabash* at the capture of Hatteras Inlet, in subsequent operations in the North Carolina sounds, and at the capture of Port Royal, Nov. 7, 1861. As senior lieutenant of the *Wabash* and one of the officers commanding gundeck divisions, he could share considerably in Commander C. R. P. Rodgers' praise of these officers for handling their divisions at Port Royal "in a manner which illustrated the highest power both of men and guns" (*War of the Rebellion: Official Records, Navy,* vol. XII, p. 267). Made lieutenant commander, July 16, 1862, he subsequently commanded the side-wheeler *Flambeau* in the Charleston blockade. In November 1863 Rear Admiral Samuel Phillips Lee selected him as chief of staff and commander of the flagship *Minnesota,* North Atlantic Blockading Squadron, a position he held

until September 1864. He was then assigned to the fast side-wheeler *A. D. Vance,* and commanded her in both attacks on Fort Fisher, Dec. 23–25, 1864, and Jan. 13–15, 1865. After the second action, in which he had charge of the reserve division, Admiral David Dixon Porter recommended his advancement, stating that he "was employed night and day in landing army stores and guns, and covering the troops" (*Ibid.,* vol. XI, p. 455). He was made commander, July 25, 1866; captain, Jan. 31, 1872; commodore, July 11, 1880; and rear admiral, Oct. 1, 1884. In 1870 he incurred a court martial and reprimand for having paid money to an appointee to the Naval Academy to induce the latter's withdrawal in favor of his son. There were, however, many extenuating circumstances, and it was testified at his trial that he was "in all matters of duty even fastidiously particular" (*House Executive Document, post,* p. 15). His later sea commands included the *Frolic* in the Mediterranean (1865–67), the *Pensacola* and afterwards the *Brooklyn* in South American waters (1873–76), and the Pacific Squadron (1884–85). He was a member of the Board of Inspectors (1877–80) and, after a year's leave in Europe, commandant of the Brooklyn navy yard (1882–84).

On June 1, 1885, he retired, and made his subsequent home in Washington, D. C. Here he lived until his ninety-fourth year, a well-known figure at the Metropolitan Club, in full possession of his faculties to the last, and highly respected not only for his long and notable service but for his southern charm of manner (he was called "the Chesterfield of the Navy"), his keen mind, and his strict standards of conduct. His burial was in Arlington. By his first marriage in 1851 to Kate, daughter of Capt. William G. and America (Peter) Williams, and great-grand-daughter of Martha Washington, he had two sons and two daughters. He was married, second, to Agnes, daughter of Hugh Maxwell of New York, who died July 2, 1917.

[L. G. Tyler, in *William and Mary Coll. Quart.*; Apr. 1895; *Who's Who in America*, 1916–17; L. R. Hamersly, *The Records of Living Officers of the U. S. Navy and Marine Corps* (1902 ed.); *Memoir and Correspondence of Charles Steedman* (1912), ed. by A. L. Mason; *War of the Rebellion: Official Records (Navy)*; *House Exec. Doc.* 308, 41 Cong., 2 Sess., which contains the proceedings at Upshur's court martial; Personnel Files, Navy Dept. Lib.; *Sea Power*, July 1917; *Army and Navy Jour.*, June 2, 1917; obituary in *Evening Star* (Washington, D. C.), May 31, 1917.]   A. W—t.

UPTON, EMORY (Aug. 27, 1839–Mar. 15, 1881), soldier, tactician, author, was born on a farm west of Batavia, N. Y., the tenth child and sixth son of Daniel and Electra (Randall) Upton. He was a descendant of John Upton, who seems to have been in Massachusetts as early as 1639, bought land in Salem in 1658, and later moved to North Reading. During the winter of 1855–56, Emory Upton was a student at Oberlin College. Interested from early youth in military history, he secured appointment to the United States Military Academy, which he entered on July 1, 1856. He was an excellent student, and was notably outspoken on controversial subjects. As personal feelings grew tense over the issues that provoked the Civil War, he had the most celebrated physical encounter—with Wade Hampton Gibbes of South Carolina—in the history of West Point (Schaff, *post*, pp. 143–48). Graduating number eight on the list of forty-five with the first (May 6) class of 1861, he was at once appointed second lieutenant, 4th Artillery, and sent to help drill Federal volunteers then assembling about Washington. On May 14 he was advanced to first lieutenant in the newly organized 5th Artillery (field batteries), and continued to drill volunteers until assigned to active field service under Gen. Daniel Tyler [*q.v.*] in the 1st Division of McDowell's army in northern Virginia. From that time to the close of the Civil War, Upton's career was one of the most notable in the annals of the army, comprising as it did varied service (artillery, infantry, and cavalry) and participation in a large number of engagements; it also brought him by successive promotions to the rank of brevet major-general, United States Army.

Four of the many actions in which he commanded troops brought advanced rank "for gallant and meritorious services": at Rappahannock Station, Va., Nov. 7, 1863; at Spotsylvania, Va., May 10, 1864, where Upton, wounded in the charge, was promoted to brigadier-general on the spot by Grant; at the Opequon (or Winchester, Va.), Sept. 19, 1864, where after the death of Gen. D. A. Russell, Upton succeeded to command of the 1st Division, VI Army Corps, and though soon dangerously wounded, continued in active command while being carried about the field on a stretcher until the battle had been won (Wilson, *post*, I, 554); and at Selma, Ala., Apr. 2, 1865, where dismounted Federal cavalry, of which he led a detachment, broke through and surmounted stockaded fortifications defended by sheltered infantry and superior artillery, capturing the city and arsenal. For nearly three months after the Opequon engagement, Upton was disabled and on sick leave; meanwhile, J. H. Wilson [*q.v.*], assigned to command the cavalry in the farther South, requested and

secured his services for the latter part of the Tennessee-Alabama-Georgia campaign. Upton also participated in the Antietam and Fredericksburg campaigns, the thirty-five-mile march by the VI Corps from Manchester, Md., to Gettysburg, Pa., mostly through the night of July 1–2, 1863, and in the battles of the Wilderness and Cold Harbor, and about Petersburg. The timeliness, good judgment, and precision with which he executed orders were frequently commended in the reports of his superiors.

After the Civil War, Upton continued in the Regular Army, with much lower rank because of the reduction of the military establishment. For short periods he was stationed in Tennessee and Colorado; then transferred to West Point as a member of the board of officers appointed to consider the system of infantry tactics which he had prepared. That system, with which his name has since been associated, was adopted in 1867. After a short station in Kentucky, he secured leave of absence and with his wife spent several months in Europe. Returning in the late summer of 1868, he was again assigned to regular duties for short periods. From July 1, 1870, to June 30, 1875, he was commandant of cadets and instructor in artillery, infantry, and cavalry tactics at West Point. Those five years were the height of Upton's career in time of peace, and his influence upon the corps of cadets was particularly marked; meanwhile, he served on the board appointed to assimilate the tactics adopted in 1873. In the summer of 1875 he was relieved at the Military Academy and assigned to professional duty on a trip around the world via San Francisco and the Orient, and for the greater part of two years studied the army organizations of Asia and Europe. At Shanghai, October 1876, he wrote out an elaborate plan for a military academy in China on the model of West Point. Returning, he was appointed superintendent of theoretical instruction in the Artillery School, Fort Monroe, Va., where he was stationed nearly three years and during two periods commanded the post. After service as member of the board to codify army regulations, he was assigned to command the 4th Artillery and the Presidio of San Francisco.

There, before reaching the age of forty-two, he died by a shot from his own hand, an act explained in brief by "an incurable malady of the head and its passages that ultimately became unbearable" (Wilson, II, 368; Michie, *post*, pp. 474–97). His resignation as colonel of the 4th Artillery was written out and signed on the day before. Upton's tragic death was a shock to the nation, and particularly to the army, which had looked to him as a model of life and conduct as well as its leading tactician. Known always as a strict disciplinarian who drilled his men in all weathers and occasionally put them through new evolutions, he won and held their confidence and loyalty to a remarkable degree. His face, somewhat "pointed," was habitually in an attitude of concentration, "with force and determination in every line." In the field he took nothing for granted; was enterprising, resourceful, and energetic; acted upon personally ascertained or well-assimilated facts; and carried military books on campaigns which he studied in connection with situations developing from day to day. He was of strong religious nature and was in the habit of saying his prayers every night. On occasions he was excitable and angry, and after the great sacrifices at Cold Harbor, Va., in June 1864, he severely criticized the chief command (Michie, pp. 108–09). He rose to his greatest heights in the excitement and turmoil of battle. On Feb. 19, 1868, he married Emily Norwood Martin, who died Mar. 30, 1870, after much illness. His funeral was at Auburn, N. Y., Mar. 29, 1881, and he was buried in Fort Hill Cemetery there.

Upton wrote more on tactics and critical military history than any other officer of his day. Two books were published in his lifetime—*A New System of Infantry Tactics, Double and Single Rank, Adapted to American Topography and Improved Firearms* (1867, rev. ed., 1874); and *The Armies of Asia and Europe* (1878). A monumental work, "The Military Policy of the United States from 1775," upon which he had been engaged for several years, he was able to complete only down to the second year of the Civil War. In 1903–04 the manuscript was re-examined by Elihu Root, who was then secretary of war, and in 1904 *The Military Policy of the United States* was published, under the editorship of J. P. Sanger; in 1914 a separate reprint of the Mexican War section was made. Some of the recommendations contained in Upton's treatise have been adopted; others no longer apply to changed conditions of warfare; yet it remains the most important work on a subject nowhere else treated on the same scale and in equal detail. Its outstanding features are searching analyses of the American national military policy and fearless comments upon its results. Intense application to those engrossing subjects, usually in connection with the full discharge of routine military duties, may have been a contributing factor to Upton's breakdown in the prime of life.

[G. W. Cullum, *Biog. Reg. Officers and Grads., U. S. Mil. Acad.* (1891), vol. II; *Twelfth Ann. Reunion, Asso. Grads., U. S. Mil. Acad.* (1881); Morris Schaff, *The Spirit of Old West Point, 1858–1862* (1907); *War of the Rebellion: Official Records (Army)*; U. S. Grant, *Personal Memoirs*, II (1886), 223–25, 234–36; J. H. Wilson, *Under the Old Flag* (1912); W. F. Scott, *The Story of a Cavalry Regiment* (1893); I. O. Best, *Hist. of the 121st N. Y. State Infantry* (1921); E. N. Gilpin, "The Last Campaign," *Jour. U. S. Cavalry Asso.*, Apr. 1908; *Army and Navy Jour.*, Mar. 19 and 26, 1881; *Harper's Weekly*, Apr. 9, 1881; *Morning Call* (San Francisco), Mar. 16, 1881; P. S. Michie, *The Life and Letters of Emory Upton* (1885); W. H. Upton, *Geneal. Colls. for an Upton Family Hist.* (1893); J. A. Vinton, *The Upton Memorial* (1874); information from various army officers, from E. S. Martin, New York, and from the Seymour Library, Auburn, N. Y.]   R. B.

UPTON, GEORGE BRUCE (Oct. 11, 1804– July 1, 1874), merchant, capitalist, was born in Eastport, in the District of Maine, the second of the two sons of Daniel Putnam and Hannah (Bruce) Upton. He was descended from John Upton who seems to have been in Salisbury, Mass., as early as 1639, and later owned land in Salem. George's father died in 1805, and his mother moved to Billerica, Mass., where she lived with her brother. Her sons were prepared for college in the local school, but the elder elected to go to sea, and the younger to enter business. After an apprenticeship of about three years with several retail merchants in Boston, George, in 1821, became confidential clerk in the dry goods firm of Baker & Barrett on Nantucket Island. When the senior member retired in 1825, Upton formed a partnership with Barrett. In addition to retail business, the firm engaged in sperm whaling, shipbuilding, and the manufacture of candles on a large scale. Upton became active, also, in public affairs, serving as representative in the Massachusetts legislature in 1837 and 1841, and as senator from Nantucket and Dukes County in the state Senate in 1839, 1840, and 1843. In 1844 he was a delegate to the Whig convention that nominated Henry Clay for the presidency.

Foreseeing the decline of business in Nantucket, in 1845 Upton moved to Manchester, N. H., where he acted as agent for a print works then being established. In 1846, however, he went to Boston, where he became a merchant and capitalist. From 1846 to 1854 he was treasurer of the Michigan Central Railroad, and was associated with other important business and financial organizations. On his own account, he engaged in shipping, and managed some famous clippers. Again he became active in public affairs, serving as a member of the executive council in 1853 and in the state constitutional convention of the same year. He was best known for the position he took on the question of commerce in time of war, and for his interest in the welfare of seamen. In protest against the ratification of the Clarendon-Johnson treaty in connection with the *Alabama* claims, he made representations to the United States government relative to the capture of his vessel *Nora*. Regarding these Lord John Russell made disparaging remarks (see *Selections from Speeches of Earl Russell*, 1870, II, 244–45). Whereupon Upton in a public letter, dated Mar. 23, 1870, charged the British people with being responsible for Confederate commerce raiders, and with having operated them. Through these charges, he attracted international attention. In the interest of seamen he promoted the Sailors' Snug Harbor, at Quincy, Mass., and in an article, "Shipwreck and Life-Saving," published in *Old and New,* a Boston periodical, in May 1874, he made some radical suggestions about life-saving equipment on ships. On May 2, 1826, he married Ann Coffin Hussey in Nantucket, by whom he had eight children; his widow, one son, and three daughters survived him. He died in Boston.

[*Vital Records of Nantucket, Mass., to the Year 1850,* vol. IV (1927); W. H. Upton, *Upton Family Records* (1893); J. A. Vinton, *The Upton Memorial* (1874); *New England Hist. and Geneal. Reg.,* Jan. 1875; *Boston Past and Present* (1874); *Boston Transcript* and *Boston Post,* July 2, 1874.]   S. G.

UPTON, GEORGE PUTNAM (Oct. 25, 1834–May 19, 1919), journalist, music critic, and author, was born at Roxbury, Mass., the eldest of three children of Daniel Putnam and Lydia (Noyes) Upton. His father, a first cousin of George Bruce Upton [*q.v.*], was a descendant of John Upton who purchased land in Salem in 1658. George Putnam Upton was educated at the Roxbury Latin School and at Brown University, from which he was graduated in 1854 with the A.M. degree. During the following winter he taught school at Plymouth, Mass. In October 1855, he went to Chicago where he immediately secured a position on the staff of the *Native Citizen*. Six months later he became city editor of the *Chicago Evening Journal*. The meager musical life of the young growing city soon drew his attention, and he started the first musical column to appear in a Chicago newspaper, reviewing all the earliest important musical events in the history of the city. In 1862 he joined the staff of the *Chicago Daily Tribune* and continued to serve this paper for fifty-seven years in various capacities—first as city editor and war-correspondent at the front (1862–63), then as music critic (1863–81), associate editor (1872–1905), and editorial writer from 1870 until his death. After 1909 he compiled the *Tribune's* annual review. He was one of the

founders of the Chicago Apollo Musical Club in September 1872 and served as its first president. The first concert of the Club, on Jan. 21, 1873, aroused much enthusiasm and lent new impetus to the musical life of Chicago after the great fire. Starting as a male chorus, it expanded into a mixed chorus, and later developed into one of the leading choral organizations in the West.

Upton's local reputation was established by his writings as a music critic, usually under the *nom de plume* "Peregrine Pickle." In the earlier years of his journalistic experience he was frequently called upon to combine the duties of literary, art, dramatic, and music critic. His work as such coincided with the formative period of Chicago's civic and art life. As he was for some time the only local critic able to speak with authority, his influence was very great. His position as a music critic was unusual. He had no real background of musical education, played no instrument well, and did not sing, but his natural fondness for music, his literary training, his clear judgment and keen analytical and critical abilities well fitted him for his task. His attitude towards performing artists was a singularly kindly one; he took pains to understand what he was called upon to write about and was unusually free from harshness when he could not praise. His autobiographic *Musical Memories* (1908) is a valuable and entertaining record of musical events and personalities, principally in Chicago, extending over a period of a half-century. From the beginning he was a warm friend and enthusiastic supporter of Theodore Thomas [*q.v.*], and after the great conductor's death he edited *Theodore Thomas. A Musical Autobiography* (2 volumes, 1905).

Upton's first published work as an author was *Letters of Peregrine Pickle* (1869). Soon thereafter he began a notable series of works in the field of musicology, all marked by accuracy of statement and a genial style of expression. It includes *Woman in Music* (1880, revised editions, 1886, 1909), *Standard Operas* (1886, and five later revised editions), *Standard Oratorios* (1887), *Standard Cantatas* (1888), *Standard Symphonies* (1889), *Standard Light Operas* (1902), *Musical Pastels* (1902), *Standard Concert Guide* (1908, three later revisions), *Standard Concert Repertory* (1909), *Standard Musical Biographies* (1910), *In Music Land* (1913), and *The Song, Its Birth, Evolution, and Functions* (1915). In collaboration with Mrs. G. K. Hack, he published *Edouard Remenyi* (1906). He also found time to translate for American music-lovers Max Muller's *Deutsche Liebe* with the English title *Memories,* Theodor Storm's

Immensee, and Ludwig Nohl's biographies of Haydn, Liszt, and Wagner. In *Life Stories for Young People* (1904–12), a series of thirty-six small volumes, he published translations of German studies of great historical characters. He was twice married. His first wife, Sarah E. Bliss, of Worcester, Mass., to whom he was married on Nov. 15, 1862, died on May 2, 1876. Of their two children one died at birth, the other in 1917. His second wife, Georgiana S. Wood, of Adrian, Mich., to whom he was married on Sept. 22, 1880, died on Oct. 1, 1927. In his personal contacts he was affable, modest, and possessed of a quiet humor. He died in Chicago. His remains were cremated and his ashes buried at Danvers, Mass.

[Information from Upton's personal friends and from the family records; *Who's Who in America,* 1918–19; J. A. Vinton, *The Upton Memorial* (1874); *Grove's Dict. of Music and Musicians, Am. Supp.* (1930); *A Hundred Years of Music in America* (1889), G. L. Howe, publisher, W. S. B. Mathews, associate ed.; Florence French, *Music and Musicians in Chicago* (copr. 1899); L. C. Elson, *The Hist. of Am. Music* (rev. edition, 1925); *Chicago Daily Tribune,* May 20, 1919.]   R. G. C.

UPTON, WINSLOW (Oct. 12, 1853–Jan. 8, 1914), astronomer and meteorologist, was born at Salem, Mass., and was the third son and fifth child of James Upton and his second wife, Sarah Sophia (Ropes) Upton. His father was a business man with musical talent, whose *Musical Miscellanea,* a collection of original musical compositions, was printed for private circulation in 1872. He was descended from John Upton who purchased land in Salem in 1658 and later moved to North Reading. Winslow Upton entered Brown University and graduated as valedictorian of his class in 1875. While he attained to equal excellence in his studies of ancient classics and of science, he felt that his forte lay rather in scientific investigation. He went to the University of Cincinnati for graduate work in astronomy, and was there awarded the degree of A.M. in 1877. After two years as assistant at the Harvard Observatory, a year as assistant in the United States Lake Survey at Detroit, a year as computer in the United States Naval Observatory at Washington, and two years as computer and assistant in the United States Signal Office, he was appointed professor of astronomy at Brown University in 1883, and he held this position until his death. He was secretary of the faculty (1884–91), director of the Ladd Observatory (1890–1914), and dean of the university (1900–01). He was a member of the American Philosophical Society, of the Deutsche Meteorologische Gesellschaft, and of the United States astronomical expeditions to

observe the total eclipses at Denver, Colo., in 1878 and at the Caroline Islands in 1883. He also observed solar eclipses in Russia (1887), in California (1889), in Virginia (1900), and in Manitoba, Canada (1905). During a sabbatical year (1896–97) he was a research assistant at the observatory of Harvard University in Arequipa, Peru; and during part of a later sabbatical leave (1904–05) he was connected with the observatory on Mount Wilson.

Shortly after his advent at Brown University Upton taught classes in mathematics, meteorology, and logic, as well as astronomy. At the Ladd Observatory for many years he conducted meteorological and other observations, in part for the federal government. His published papers included a number on meteorological topics in the *Annals of the Astronomical Observatory of Harvard College, Zeitschrift für Meteorologie,* and the *American Meteorological Journal.* Other notes and articles were published in the *Bulletin of the Essex Institute,* the *Memoirs of the National Academy of Science, Astronomische Nachrichten,* the *Sidereal Messenger,* and the *Astronomical Journal.* His small *Star Atlas* was published at Boston in 1896. For over twenty years (1893–1914) he wrote monthly letters on astronomical topics for the *Providence Journal,* and he was editor of the astronomical parts of the *Providence Journal Almanac* (1894–1910). He had unusual scientific ability coupled with rare clarity of thought and power of lucid exposition. In the class room he aroused enthusiasm, and he was in constant demand as a lecturer. He was an active church worker, and endowed with great kindliness of spirit and charm of personality. At different times he was glee-club and choir leader, and church organist. On Feb. 8, 1882, he married Cornelia Augusta, daughter of William H. Babcock of Lebanon Springs, N. Y., who with two daughters survived him.

[Sources include J. A. Vinton, *The Upton Memorial* (1874); W. H. Upton, *Upton Family Records* (1893); *Who's Who in America,* 1912–13; *Hist. Cat. of Brown Univ., 1764–1914* (1914); R. C. Archibald, in *Sci.,* Feb. 1914, with bibliog.; *Brown Alumni Monthly,* June 1900, p. 2, July 1901, p. 22, Feb. 1914, pp. 169–71, with portraits; resolutions adopted by faculty and Sigma Xi, Brown Univ., in *Popular Astronomy,* Apr. 1914, with portrait; obituary in *Providence Jour.,* Jan. 9, 1914; personal reminiscences. A poem on Upton's death by H. L. Koopman appeared in *Brown Alumni Monthly,* Feb. 1914; another, by V. E. Atwell, in *Popular Astronomy,* May 1915.]   R. C. A.

URBAN, JOSEPH (May 26, 1872–July 10, 1933), architect and stage designer, was born in Vienna, Austria, son of Joseph and Helen (Weber) Urban. His father, a supervising official in the Viennese school system, intended him for the law, but his artistic bent was too strong. He studied at the Staatsgewerbeschule and the art academy in Vienna, became a pupil of Baron Karl von Hasenauer, and was well grounded in architecture, at the same time practising illustration and studying interior decoration. One of his earliest commissions was to decorate the Abdin palace in Cairo. He also did the interior of the new town hall in Vienna and designed the "Tzar's Bridge" in St. Petersburg. He was prominent in the Secessionist movement and arranged its exhibition in Vienna. In 1900 he won the grand prize for decoration at the Paris exposition, and in 1901 came to America to decorate the Austrian building at the Louisiana Purchase Exposition (St. Louis), for which he won the grand prize in 1904. Returning to Vienna, he became interested in stage sets for the Hofburg Theatre, and in 1911–12, when the Boston Opera Company was started, he was invited to that city as art director. For the Boston company he made several sets, notably one for *Pelleas and Melisande,* which were revelations in America of the new stage art. He was introduced to New York by his set for *The Garden of Paradise* (1914), and in that year he left Boston for New York to design first the Ziegfeld *Follies* of 1915 (which owed much of their fame to him), and then sets for the Metropolitan Opera and for James K. Hackett's productions of *Macbeth* and *The Merry Wives of Windsor*. By this time "Urban blue" had become famous, and he was in great demand for all sorts of decorative projects. In addition to his office in New York he established a large studio and shop near his residence in Yonkers, and worked day and night on his various projects, even returning to architecture in the 1920's. He designed furniture, motor cars, modernistic interiors, stage sets, theatres, clubs, houses, and public buildings. Among his buildings and interiors are the Ziegfeld Theatre on Sixth Avenue, New York, with an interior shaped like an egg; the New School for Social Research, New York; the Tennis and Oasis clubs at Palm Beach, and certain residences there; the interior of the Central Park Casino; the St. Regis roof garden (gilt flowers on sapphire walls); and a vast design, never carried out, for a new opera house in New York. Urban had always advocated the use of clear colors in exterior as well as interior architecture, and had popularized tints of his own. He was, accordingly, chosen to devise the color chart for the Century of Progress exposition at Chicago in 1933.

A man so prodigiously fecund and versatile as Urban is often looked upon with some suspicion by his fellow craftsmen. It is perhaps true that Urban was not, as artist, an originator. His decorative style owed much to the Secessionists and *l'art nouveau* of the late nineties. In stage design he was not a great pioneer like Adolphe Appia or Gordon Craig. In architecture his name cannot be written large. But all modern decorators, scene designers, and architects in America none the less owe him a debt of gratitude, because by popularizing the new styles he made their task so much the easier. Urban's sets for the Boston Opera House, for example, were the first large-scale examples of the new stagecraft in America, and their popularity was important. Subsequently, his use of broad masses of color, his employment of broken pigmentation in scene painting to take various light effects, his pervasive beauty of costume under the play of light, in the Ziegfeld *Follies,* spread the gospel to thousands of people ordinarily little affected by new art movements. It is perhaps not far-fetched to say that Urban's sets for the *Follies* made possible the public acceptance of the architectural scheme of the Century of Progress. In architecture, the egg-shaped interior of the Ziegfeld Theatre, purely functional, may be destined to influence American theatre building in the future. In the decorative arts, his frequent use of metal had an almost immediate influence, as did his use of large spaces of clear color. How far that influence will extend to exterior architecture remains to be seen. But, at any rate, as a popularizer of artistic innovations Urban was an important figure.

He was a large, florid, genial, witty man, with a cascade of chins and an enormous capacity for work. He often worked from 9 a.m. till 2 the next morning, designing sets (built in his studios) for five operas and ten or twelve plays and musical comedies a year, in addition to his decorative jobs and architectural projects. This work entailed reading scripts, attendance at rehearsals, the supervision of lighting and of practical construction. He smoked a hundred Turkish cigarettes a day, and had a pot of coffee always on his desk. His one recreation was attending prize fights. He died in New York, from a not surprising heart ailment, July 10, 1933, after an illness which had to his bitter disappointment prevented him from going to Chicago to see his colors applied on the exposition buildings. He was admitted to American citizenship in 1917. In 1918 he divorced his first wife, Mizzi Lefler, and on Jan. 23, 1919, married Mary Porter Beegle of New York. He was survived by his wife and a daughter of his first marriage, an artist.

[*Who's Who in America*, 1932–33; "Urban, the Ambidextrous," in *N. Y. Times*, June 17, 1917; F. E. W. Freund, in *Internat. Studio*, Jan. 1923; Shepard Vogelgesang, in *Arch. Record*, Feb. 1931; *Theatre Arts Mag.*, Dec. 1932, p. 950, picture of an Urban stage set; *Outlook*, June 18, 1930; obituaries in *N. Y. Times* and *N. Y. Herald Tribune*, July 11, 1933; information from Gretl Urban, Urban's daughter.]   W. P. E.

URSO, CAMILLA (June 13, 1842–Jan. 20, 1902), violinist, was born in Nantes, France, the daughter of Salvator Urso, an organ and flute player born in Sicily, and his wife, Emilie (Girouard) Urso, a native of Portugal. Camilla began to play the violin at the time she was six years of age; at the age of seven she gave her first recital in the town of her birth. Her father took her to Paris, where, after many difficulties, she was admitted to the Paris Conservatory of Music and became a pupil of Lambert-Joseph Massart. She studied and practised for eight, and sometimes ten, hours a day. In 1852 she came to America as a child prodigy, and played in concerts with such famous stars as Henriette Sontag and Marietta Alboni. She had been engaged under a very favorable contract to make a tour of the South, but the agent proved unreliable and the child violinist was stranded for a time until the Germania Society asked her to appear as soloist at several of its concerts. She later made tours with Sontag. About 1855 Urso's parents settled in Nashville, Tenn., and for seven years she made no more public appearances, but devoted all her time to practising. In 1862 she again resumed her concert work, playing first in New York as soloist with the New York Philharmonic Society. For the next thirty years she played continually both in America and in Europe. She made two trips to Australia, in 1879 and 1894, and one to South Africa, in 1895. After this she settled permanently in New York City, where she devoted her later years to teaching. Except for a tour in vaudeville houses, she thereafter seldom appeared in concert.

According to those who knew her, and heard her play, Urso was a true artist, without affectation or conscious showmanship. George P. Upton [*q.v.*] described her in the early days as "a most serious child, with large dark eyes and with a manner and dignity that seemed strange in one so young. . . . Her face was so solemn and unchanging in its expression that it seemed as if a smile had never visited it" (Upton, *post*, p. 70). When she was about twenty-four years of age the same author said that she "still had that same pale, serious, inscrutable face, the same dark, lustrous melancholy eyes, and the same calm but gracious dignity of manner; but with the advancing years she had gained a more finished style, great individuality, and exquisitely graceful motions of the arm in bowing" (*Ibid.*, p. 71). In 1862 she was married in Paris to Frédéric Luères. She died in New York City almost in obscurity.

[*Grove's Dict. of Music and Musicians, Am. Supp.* (1930); Charles Barnard, *Camilla Urso, A Tribute* (1885); G. P. Upton, *Musical Memories* (1908); *Musical Courier*, Jan. 22, 29, 1902; *N. Y. Times*, Jan. 22, 1902.]   J. T. H.

USHER, JOHN PALMER (Jan. 9, 1816–Apr. 13, 1889), lawyer, secretary of the interior in Lincoln's cabinet, was descended from a young English Puritan, Hezekiah Usher, who settled in Boston, Mass., about the middle of the seventeenth century, becoming a bookseller and later a selectman. Among his descendants were John Usher who became lieutenant-governor of New Hampshire in 1692 and Dr. Nathaniel Usher, who with his wife, Lucy (Palmer), lived in Brookfield, Madison County, N. Y., when their son, John Palmer, was born. After receiving a common-school education Usher studied law in the office of Henry Bennett of New Berlin, N. Y., and was admitted to the bar in 1839. A year later he moved to Terre Haute, Ind., and began the practice of his profession. He rode the circuit, and was sometimes engaged with Abraham Lincoln in the argument of cases. In 1850–51 he served in the Indiana legislature.

When the Republican party was organized in 1854, Usher became an active supporter of its principles and in 1856 was an unsuccessful candidate for Congress. He was appointed attorney-general of Indiana in November 1861, but four months later resigned to accept the position of assistant secretary of the interior at Washington. In January 1863 he was appointed head of that department, following the resignation of Caleb B. Smith [*q.v.*]. In his first report he called special attention to the benefits of the new homestead law, remarking that in less than a year after it went into operation almost a million and a half acres had been taken up. He recommended a small tax on the net profits of gold and silver mines, larger Indian reservations, also larger appropriations—with a policy guided by justice and humanity—for these wards of the nation. His last report contained a comprehensive statement concerning public lands, which, he said, had included about one fifth of the entire country and had been the cause of about one fourth of all the laws passed by Congress to that date.

When the Civil War closed Usher decided to retire from political life and resume the practice of law in one of the growing Western states. He accordingly resigned as secretary of the interior on May 15, 1865, and removed with his family to Lawrence, Kan., where he accepted appointment as chief counsel for the Union Pacific Railroad—a position which he held to the end of his life. He represented the company in much important litigation in both state and federal courts. Usher's only writings were his two reports (1863, 1864) as secretary of the interior (*Executive Document No. 1,* vol. III, 38 Cong., 1 Sess.; and *House Executive Document No. 1,* pt. 5, 38 Cong., 2 Sess.) and a chapter in *Reminiscences of Abraham Lincoln* (1886), edited by A. T. Rice; but in 1925 Nelson H. Loomis published *President Lincoln's Cabinet, by Honorable John P. Usher,* a pamphlet containing the substance of an after-dinner speech delivered in 1887 together with a newspaper interview. On Jan. 26, 1844, Usher married Margaret Patterson; they had four sons. He died in a hospital in Philadelphia.

[Usher kept no diary and preserved no papers. *President Lincoln's Cabinet* (1925) contains an authoritative biog. by N. H. Loomis. See also *Kan. State Hist. Soc. Colls.,* vol. XII (1912); C. W. Taylor, *The Bench and Bar of Ind.* (1895); E. P. Usher, *A Memorial Sketch of Roland Greene Usher* (1895), containing a genealogy; *Lawrence Daily Jour.,* Apr. 14, 1889; *Lawrence Evening Tribune,* Apr. 15, 1889; *Topeka Capital-Commonwealth,* Apr. 16, 1889. Important facts have also been obtained from a son, the late Samuel C. Usher.]   T.L.H.

USHER, NATHANIEL REILLY (Apr. 7, 1855–Jan. 9, 1931), naval officer, son of Nathaniel and Pamela (Woolverton) Usher and nephew of John Palmer Usher [*q.v.*], was born in Vincennes, Ind. He entered the Naval Academy in 1871 and was graduated in 1875. After two years duty on the Asiatic Station, he was sent to the Paris Exposition of 1878 as a member of the American naval delegation. During the early gold rush days in Alaska, as an officer of the *Jamestown,* he assisted in maintaining law and order in the Territory. In 1884 he was sent with Winfield Scott Schley [*q.v.*] to the Arctic on the Greely Relief Expedition, sailing as watch officer of the *Bear* but being transferred to the *Alert,* a ship donated by the British government. In the years 1886–89 he made a cruise around the world in the *Juniata.*

During the Spanish-American War Usher commanded the torpedo boat *Ericsson* and was at Key West with her when the *Maine* was blown up in Havana Harbor. He is credited with capturing the first Spanish prize taken in the war. While Cervera's fleet lay in Santiago Harbor, Usher volunteered to run in with the *Ericsson* and torpedo the hostile vessels, but his offer was not accepted. In the battle of Santiago his vessel took a prominent part and his report of the engagement is a model of concise, vivid narrative ("Naval Operations of the War with Spain," *House Document No. 3,* 55 Cong., 3 Sess., pp. 547–48). After the war he held a succession of important posts, including service on the General Board and in the Bureau of Navigation, and the commands of the cruiser *St. Louis* and the battleship *Michigan.* He rose rapidly in the service, attaining the rank of rear admiral in 1911.

Usher commanded successively three different divisions of the Atlantic Fleet, and soon after the outbreak of the World War was made commandant of the Brooklyn Navy Yard. Recognizing the fact that the United States would very likely be drawn into the war, he did his utmost to build up and modernize the ships under his command. When war was finally declared he was obliged to commandeer docks, outfit ships, and prepare convoys for the men, munitions, and food that must be rushed to France. Under his direction a secret service was organized known as the Commandant's Aide for Information, a mine-sweeping force was developed, and the scout-patrol system was instituted. It was chiefly because of his monumental energy and organizing ability that the Port of New York was able to ship the major part of all the supplies and eighty per cent. of all the men that America sent to the aid of her Allies. In 1918 Usher was given command of the Third Naval District.

When he retired on Apr. 7, 1919, he was the guest of honor at a dinner at the Waldorf in New York, which was attended by 1,500 persons. Franklin D. Roosevelt, then assistant secretary of the navy, said of him: "No officer stands higher in his appreciation of the broad needs of this great democratic country in the matter of defence, and no one more tactfully, more forcefully, and more skillfully welded the naval reserve, the civilian, into the trained machine of the regular Navy" (*Sun,* New York, Apr. 8, 1919). France, in recognition of his services to the cause of the Allies, bestowed upon him the ribbon of the French Legion of Honor, and he was awarded the Navy Cross by his own government. He was a man of commanding presence, the idol of his men, and held in high esteem in the service. After his retirement he lived on his farm at Potsdam, N. Y. He married Anne Usher of Potsdam in 1891; he left no children.

[*Army and Navy Journal,* Jan. 17, 1931; *N. Y. Times,* Jan. 10, 1931; U. S. Navy Dept. Registers and Annual Reports; *Who's Who in America,* 1928–29; Service Record in Bureau of Navigation, Navy Dept.; L. R. Hamersly, *The Records of Living Officers of the U. S. Navy* (7th ed., 1902); E. P. Usher, *A Memorial Sketch of Roland Greene Usher, to Which is Added a Geneal. of the Usher Family in New England* (1895).]

          L.H.B.

VACA, ALVAR NÚÑEZ CABEZA de [See Núñez Cabeza de Vaca, Alvar *c.* 1490–*c.* 1557].

VAIL, AARON (Oct. 24, 1796–Nov. 4, 1878), diplomat, was born in Lorient (Morbihan), France, the son of a New York merchant, Aaron Vail, and his wife, Elizabeth Dubois, who was born in Saint Servan (Ille et Vilaine), France. The father, who seems to have come of a Quaker family of Dutchess County, N. Y., was appointed American commercial agent at Lorient in 1803 and served there usefully during the Napoleonic era, rearing a large family on a meager income. After his death in 1815 his family came to the United States. Aaron obtained a clerkship in the American legation at Paris, traveled considerably in Europe, and served as clerk in the Department of State. On Aug. 1, 1831, he was appointed secretary of legation at London. After the refusal of the Senate to confirm Van Buren's appointment as minister to Great Britain, Vail was appointed chargé d'affaires at London and filled this important position from July 13, 1832, until April 1836; he then became secretary of legation once more, and remained in London until December 1836 in that capacity. Completely at home in London society and on excellent terms with such British statesmen as Palmerston and Wellington, the bachelor chargé received the approval of President Jackson, with whom he corresponded directly, as well as that of the Department of State, for his conduct of the business of the legation. Perhaps his most difficult task was handling the American protest and claims for compensation arising out of the release of slaves from American ships forced by circumstances to put in at British West Indian ports. Vail finally persuaded the British government to refer the cases to the judicial committee of the Privy Council, but no further satisfaction was obtained during his term as chargé.

After the Canadian rebellion of 1837 it was believed that many Americans imprisoned in Canada on suspicion of having been involved were being held arbitrarily and without the prospect of a trial. On Apr. 3, 1838, Vail was appointed special agent to go to Canada to investigate. In his reports to the secretary of state, Apr. 21 and May 5, he stated his belief that Americans implicated in the revolt were being treated "in the mildest manner consistent with the demands of justice" (*House Executive Document No. 39*, 27 Cong., 1 Sess., p. 5). Appointed chief clerk of the Department of State June 26, 1838, he served until July 15, 1840. During this period he acted on numerous occasions as secretary of state. In the latter capacity he received notice from the Republic of Texas of the withdrawal of its offer of annexation to the United States; he protested vigorously the seizure by

British authorities of American fishing craft on the coast of Nova Scotia, and he attempted to prevent the outbreak of the "Aroostook war" on the border between Maine and Canada. From May 20, 1840, to Aug. 1, 1842, when Washington Irving assumed the duties of minister, Vail served as chargé d'affaires at Madrid. During the periods of his life when he was not in public service he seems to have lived in New York or in Europe. He died at Pau (Basses-Pyrénées), France.

[*Reg. of the Dept. of State*, July 1, 1933; *The Works of James Buchanan* (12 vols., 1908–11), ed. by J. B. Moore; H. M. Wriston, *Exec. Agents in Am. Foreign Relations* (1929); *Sen. Doc. 174*, 24 Cong., 2 Sess.; *Sen. Doc. 1*, 25 Cong., 3 Sess.; *Sen. Doc. 107, House Ex. Doc. 186*, 26 Cong., 1 Sess.; *House Ex. Doc. 39*, 27 Cong., 1 Sess.; MSS. in Dept. of State; birth register of Lorient, France; municipal records of Pau; Beckles Willson, *America's Ambassadors to England* (1929), extensive but in part unreliable.] E. W. S.

VAIL, ALFRED (Sept. 25, 1807–Jan. 18, 1859), telegraph pioneer, the son of Stephen and Bethiah (Young) Vail, was born at Morristown, N. J., where his father was the owner and operator of the Speedwell Iron Works. The records of the Presbyterian Church in Morristown show that he was given a middle name, Lewis, which he apparently never used. Upon completing a common-school education in his native town he entered his father's establishment. Possessed of a considerable amount of native mechanical skill, he soon became an expert mechanician and by the time he was twenty he had complete charge of the machine shop, where he continued for a number of years. About 1830 he decided to become a Presbyterian minister, and after taking some college preparatory work entered the University of the City of New York in 1832, graduating in 1836. Although his health was poor, he immediately began his theological studies.

On Sept. 2, 1837, however, at the University, he saw Prof. Samuel F. B. Morse [*q.v.*] give one of his first exhibitions of the telegraph. Vail at once perceived the significance of Morse's invention and expressed a desire to become associated with him in perfecting and exploiting it. Morse, being greatly in need of mechanical as well as financial assistance, grasped this unexpected opportunity, and on Sept. 23, 1837, a contract was drawn up between Vail and Morse, Vail binding himself to construct a complete set of instruments and to secure both United States and foreign patents at his own expense, while in return he received a fourth interest in the American rights and a half interest in patents which might be secured abroad. He had no money of his own but quickly induced his father to finance the undertaking, and thereupon Vail, Morse, and a third associate, Leonard D. Gale, went to work on the telegraph in the shops of the Speedwell Iron Works. On Jan. 6, 1838, a successful demonstration was made of the improved electric telegraph through three miles of wire stretched around one of the shops. Vail's father furnished the message for this occasion: "A patient waiter is no loser." Within the month Vail and Morse held their first public exhibition of the telegraph in New York City, when "Attention, the Universe, by kingdoms right wheel," was the terse message successfully transmitted. The mechanical perfection of practically all the instruments used was the result of Vail's skill, and he worked enthusiastically with Morse in demonstrating the telegraph before the Franklin Institute, Philadelphia, on Feb. 8, 1838, and before members of Congress on Feb. 21 of that year. The partners felt that the telegraph ought to be owned by the government and hoped that as a result of this latter demonstration Congress would purchase the invention. This hope was disappointed, but the demonstration in Washington aroused the interest of one congressman, Francis O. J. Smith, who within a month became a financial partner and received a four-sixteenths interest in the invention, brought about by the reduction of Vail's interest from four to two sixteenths.

The new capital thus acquired enabled Morse to proceed to Europe to secure his foreign patents, and with his departure Vail's interest in the telegraph waned. He did very little work on it in 1838, and in 1839 he went to Philadelphia to represent his father's interests. Here he remained until 1843; but when in March of that year Congress passed the act providing for an experimental telegraph line between Washington and Baltimore, Vail became Morse's chief assistant and received the test message "What hath God wrought!" at Baltimore on May 24, 1844. He remained with Morse for the next four years, publishing in 1845 *The American Electro Magnetic Telegraph,* but again lost interest in the work, and in 1848 resigned his position as superintendent at Philadelphia. Returning to Morristown, he lived there in retirement until his death, giving much of his time in later years to compiling material for a genealogy of the Vail family. Vail profited little from the telegraph, for he did not improve the opportunities it afforded, failing to take up the manufacture of telegraph instruments, and he died poor and unhappy. He was twice married: first, July 23, 1839, to Jane Elizabeth Cummings, who died in 1852; and second, Dec. 17, 1855, to Amanda O.

Eno, who with three sons by his first marriage survived him. He died in Morristown, in his fifty-second year.

[H. H. Vail, *Geneal. of Some of the Vail Family* (1902); F. B. Read, *Up the Heights of Fame and Fortune* (1873); *Gen. Alumni Cat., N. Y. Univ.,* vol. I (1906); *Hist. of the First Presbyt. Ch., Morristown, N. J.,* pt. II (n.d.), containing "The Combined Registers, from 1742 to 1885"; death notice in *N. Y. Times,* Jan. 20, 1859; E. L. Morse, *Samuel F. B. Morse: His Letters and Journals* (1914, vol. II); J. D. Reid, *The Telegraph in America* (1879); "The Invention of the Electro-Telegraph," *Electrical World,* July 20–Dec. 21, 1895; U. S. National Museum records.]   C.W.M.

VAIL, STEPHEN MONTFORT (Jan. 15, 1816–Nov. 26, 1880), Methodist Episcopal clergyman, educator, was born in Union Vale, Dutchess County, N. Y., the son of James Vail, a farmer, and Anna (Montfort) Vail. When he was fourteen years old he entered Cazenovia Seminary, Cazenovia, N. Y., and in 1834, Bowdoin College, from which he was graduated with honors in 1838. For his professional education he went to Union Theological Seminary, New York City, completing the course there in 1842. That same year he was admitted on trial to the New York Conference of the Methodist Episcopal Church, and in September was married to Louisa R. Cushman. He was ordained deacon in 1844, and elder in 1846. His pastoral appointments were to Fishkill, N. Y. (1842–44), Sharon, Conn. (1844–46), and Pine Plains, N. Y. (1846–47). In 1847 he became principal of Pennington Seminary, Pennington, N. J., leaving there two years later to accept the chair of Hebrew in the Methodist General Biblical Institute, Concord, N. H., which, opened in 1847, was the first distinctively theological institution established by American Methodists. In this position he served until 1869.

Two interests which Vail furthered brought him prominence. At a time when Methodists in general opposed education as a requirement for the ministerial office on the ground that the call of God and a vital personal experience were the essential requisites, Vail was a vigorous advocate of theological training. Because of articles in support of his views on this subject, published while he was at Pennington, which were deemed by some contrary to Methodist principles, he was placed on trial before the New Jersey Conference. The charges were so trivial, however, that he was speedily acquitted. During the many years he was connected with the General Biblical Institute he was indefatigable in his efforts to build up the school and also to raise the educational standards of his denomination. In 1853 he published *Ministerial Education in the Methodist Episcopal Church.* A second interest, and one that made him more widely known, was in the abolition of slavery. It led him to cross swords with prominent men of his own calling who defended the institution on Biblical grounds. In 1860 he published a sermon entitled *The Church and the Slave Power,* and in 1864, *The Bible Against Slavery.* The latter was a reply to Bishop John Henry Hopkins [*q.v.*] of the Protestant Episcopal Church who had advanced arguments to the effect that slavery is not a sin because it is not forbidden in the Scripture, and to Nathan Lord [*q.v.*], president of Dartmouth College, who contended that slavery was divinely ordained, and therefore not to be questioned.

A Methodist and a stanch Republican and supporter of the Union, he was regarded as worthy of recognition by President Grant, who in 1869 appointed him consul at Ludwigshafen, Bavaria, in which position he served until 1874. Returning to the United States, he retired to his farm at Pleasant Plains, Staten Island. He died at the home of a son-in-law in Jersey City, survived by his wife and six children. In addition to the writings already mentioned he published *Life in Earnest; or Memoirs and Remains of the Rev. Zenas Caldwell,* which appeared in 1855.

[*Commemorative Biog. Record of Dutchess County, N. Y.* (1897); H. W. Cushman, *A Hist. and Biog. Geneal. of the Cushmans: The Descendants of Robert Cushman* (1855); *Gen. Biog. Cat. of Bowdoin Coll.* (1912); sketch in *Minutes of the Ann. Conferences of the M. E. Church, Spring Conferences of 1881* (1881), reprinted in Stephen Allen and W. H. Pilsbury, *Hist. of Methodism in Me.* (1887); *Christian Advocate* (N. Y.), Dec. 2, 1880; *Zion's Herald,* Jan. 6, 1881; death notice in *N. Y. Times,* Nov. 27, 1880.] H. E. S.

VAIL, THEODORE NEWTON (July 16, 1845–Apr. 16, 1920), telephone and utilities executive, was born near Minerva, Carroll County, Ohio, the son of Davis Vail, a Quaker farmer and iron worker, and Phebe (Quinby) his wife. There were ten children, of whom seven survived childhood, and of these Theodore was the third. In 1847 Davis Vail took his family back to his former home in New Jersey, and went to work again in the Speedwell Iron Works near Morristown, well known through its association with his cousin, Alfred Vail [*q.v.*], and the electric telegraph.

Theodore went to the public schools and to the Morristown Academy until he had finished the high school grade. By this time he had become interested in reading, especially along the lines of geography and human achievement; but his real education was mainly a casual one in the school of versatile experience. At seventeen he went to work in a drugstore where there was a telegraph office; he learned to use the instrument, and by the time he was nineteen he was at

work in New York as an operator for the Western Union Telegraph Company. This career was interrupted by the decision of his father to go West. The family moved in 1866 to Waterloo, Iowa, and Theodore went with them. Here he learned what it was to be a pioneer, breaking the loam and harvesting rich crops. Baseball was the recreation of the region, and in Iowa Vail conceived his lifelong enthusiasm for the game.

In 1868 he went back into the telegraph service and was soon night operator at Pine Bluffs, in the Indian country among the Black Hills on the Union Pacific Railway. From this telegraph service he went into the mail service, and on Aug. 3, 1869, at Newark, N. J., he married Emma Louise Righter, a cousin on his mother's side. They settled in Omaha, whence he went on his mail trips across the continent. On July 18, 1870, a son was born to them. Vail was soon devising improvements in the operation and routings of the railway mail service. This initiative brought him advancement and in 1873 transfer to the office of the railway mail service at Washington; in 1874 he became assistant general superintendent. Under Postmaster-General Marshall Jewell [*q.v.*], on Sept. 16, 1875, he inaugurated the Fast Mail between New York and Chicago, over the New York Central and Hudson River Railroad; the first train, carrying only mail, started from New York at a speed of more than forty-one miles an hour, faster than any passenger train had ever traveled (Paine, *post,* p. 77). With the beginning of 1876 Theodore Vail became general superintendent of the railway mail service.

Meantime Alexander Graham Bell [*q.v.*] had invented the telephone and Gardiner Greene Hubbard [*q.v.*] had begun to organize the business. Hubbard recognized the need for a young man of vision, ability, and force to carry on the development of the telephone industry. Knowing Vail through his active interest in the postal service, Hubbard singled him out and persuaded him to undertake the work under the title of general manager of the Bell Telephone Company. Between May 1878 and September 1887, Vail organized the expanding telephone system; he merged the rapidly multiplying local exchanges into more efficient companies; he put into effect a practical system of financing the telephone industry; he provided for anticipatory technical development and for improved and more economical manufacture of telephone apparatus, with the Western Electric Company as the manufacturing unit, so as to improve the quality and extend the distance of telephone transmission. His culminating contribution in this period was to unify the industry by connecting all the operating companies and exchanges by a long-distance telephone system. For this purpose, with Edward J. Hall, Jr., as the active man, he incorporated in 1885 a special subsidiary company, the American Telephone & Telegraph Company, of which he was the first president.

By 1887 his vitality was depleted, for no plan had been too great for his quick mind to undertake, and no detail too small to receive his personal attention. He resigned from the telephone company and from all other responsibilities, and retired in 1889 to a farm he had bought at Lyndonville, Vt. There, some years before, his interest in scientific agriculture and in practical education had led him to give the funds necessary to rehabilitate and reopen (in 1884) an industrial school, Lyndon Institute.

Soon, however, a visitor from South America interested him in the industrial development of the Argentine Republic; and after several years, during which he spent much time in Europe without losing touch with the telephone company, he turned his interest and energy into utility projects in Argentina. This was his chief occupation from 1894 to 1907. He financed and developed a great water-power plant at Córdoba and electrified and made profitable a street railway system in Buenos Aires. After the death of his wife in February 1905, and of his only child, Davis, in December 1906, he sold out his South American interests and returned to Vermont. Marrying on July 27, 1907, Mabel R. Sanderson of Boston, and making his niece, Katherine Vail, his adopted daughter, he again turned his attention to agriculture and education for country life. In 1910, at Lyndonville, he was instrumental in establishing the Lyndon School of Agriculture.

Meantime the telephone had been spreading throughout the United States. The Bell Companies had grown from 180,680 telephones (Dec. 31, 1887) to 2,773,547 telephones (Dec. 31, 1906). In 1900 the American Telephone & Telegraph Company had taken over from the American Bell Telephone Company its function as the chief corporation of the telephone system, retaining its former long-distance functions in a special long-line department. With the expiration of the Bell telephone patents in 1893 and 1894, hundreds of independent telephone companies sprang up and entered into local competition with the Bell organizations. It was not yet generally realized that the telephone was a natural monopoly and that the existence of a multiplicity of telephone companies would prevent nation-wide telephone efficiency. The directors of the Bell company now urged Vail to take hold of the industry again, and on May 1, 1907, his election as president of the American Telephone & Telegraph Company was announced.

His first step was to move the headquarters of the company from Boston to New York. With the purpose of fostering and increasing public understanding and confidence he made the annual reports a medium for the frank discussion of telephone problems. He hastened the unification of the telephone industry by personally making the acquaintance of all the chief officers of the Bell companies throughout the country and by a policy of cooperation with the independent telephone companies. Under this policy, companies that preferred to remain independent could secure long distance service by contract from the adjacent Bell company; these were called Bell-connected. By such steps the Bell System came more and more to realize its natural ideal—"One Policy, One System, Universal Service." Vail went further, toward a unification of all electric communications, affiliating the Western Union Telegraph Company with the American Telephone & Telegraph Company in 1909, with himself as president of both companies, and inaugurating improvements of service such as the night letter and telephone reception of telegrams. The federal government claimed, however, that this association was in violation of the anti-trust laws, and in 1913, the two companies were separated without formal legal action in court (*Annual Report of the American Telephone & Telegraph Company,* 1913).

Meanwhile, by selecting the right men and properly supporting them in their work, Vail pushed forward the progress of telephony: scientific research resulted in new inventions and technical improvement, as well as in efficient construction; popular education increased the field of the telephone; able commercial management brought profits; and world telephony was rendered certain. The first long stride in this direction was the telephone conquest of the desert and the mountains. On Jan. 25, 1915, during the Panama-Pacific Exposition at San Francisco, the first transcontinental telephone line was opened with conversations between President Woodrow Wilson at Washington, Alexander Graham Bell at New York, Thomas A. Watson at San Francisco, and Theodore N. Vail at Jekyl Island, off the coast of Georgia. The same year telephone engineers under John J. Carty developed radio telephony so that on Oct. 21, communications sent out from Arlington, Va., were simultaneously received in Paris and at Honolulu. In 1917 a collection of Vail's papers and addresses was privately printed under the title, *Views on Public Questions*.

After the United States went into the World War, telephone battalions were organized, in accordance with plans suggested by Carty and approved by Vail, and they built an American telephone system in France. On July 31, 1918, the government took over control of all the wire communication systems, and Vail was requested to continue with his own organization the conduct of the telephone business for the government, reporting to the Postmaster General. The wires were returned to the owning companies on July 31, 1919. Just previously, June 18, Vail had resigned the presidency of the American Telephone & Telegraph Company, and become chairman of the Board of Directors. He had always lived unsparingly; in April 1920 he went to the Johns Hopkins Hospital, Baltimore, where he died on Apr. 16. He was buried in the old cemetery at Parsippany, N. J. The chief organizer of the telephone business, in little more than forty years he had "made neighbors of a hundred million people."

[A. B. Paine, *In One Man's Life* (1921), repr. as *Theodore N. Vail: A Biog.* (1929); J. W. Stehman, *The Financial Hist. of the Am. Telephone and Telegraph Company* (1925); *Ann. Reports of the Directors of the Am. Telephone and Telegraph Company*, 1907–19; *Boston Transcript*, Apr. 16, 1920; *Evening Post* (N. Y.), Apr. 17, 1920; *Evening Caledonian* (St. Johnsbury, Vt.), Apr. 16, 1920; *Wall Street Journal*, Apr. 17, 23, 1920; *Western Electric News*, May, Aug. 1920; papers in the Theodore N. Vail Collection of the Am. Telephone Hist. Lib., New York City.]
W.C.L.

VALENTINE, DAVID THOMAS (Sept. 15, 1801–Feb. 25, 1869), compiler of historical materials, was born in East Chester, Westchester County, N. Y., the second son of Daniel and Miriam (Fisher) Valentine, and a descendant of Benjamin Valentine of Holland, who settled near the town of Yonkers in 1679. On his mother's side he was descended from English stock which became established in America as early as 1611. He received his principal schooling in the Westchester Academy at White Plains, and in 1815 removed to New York City, where he found employment as a grocer's clerk. A few years later he became a member of the national guard, and after passing through the lower ranks he declined to become major of the regiment in 1826, and definitely retired from military life. Meanwhile he had acquired the friendship of persons prominent in municipal political affairs, and through their influence he became clerk of the marine court. He held his position from 1826 until 1830, when he was appointed deputy-clerk of the common council. In 1842 he became

clerk of the council and chief of the legislative department and held the position without interruption until 1868, despite numerous political changes. In January 1868, however, he was superseded in office—a circumstance which probably hastened his death.

Pursuant to a legislative resolution, Valentine published in 1841 his first *Manual of the Corporation of the City of New York,* and thereafter he added a volume annually until 1867. These volumes, copiously illustrated, and containing a jumbled mass of historical and miscellaneous matter, became so popular that they were said to have become by 1869 "almost a necessity among New-Yorkers" (*New York Times, post*). Now adequately indexed, these manuals constitute an extremely useful, if uneven, source of information relative to New York life. Other literary activities of Valentine include a *History of the City of New-York* (1853), chiefly the work of W. I. Paulding, a member of Valentine's corps of scholarly assistants, informative but badly organized, and extending only to the year 1756; *A Compilation of the Laws of the State of New York, Relating Particularly to the City of New York* (1862); *Compilation of Existing Ferry Leases and Railroad Grants Made by the Corporation of the City of New York* (1866); and *Ordinances of the Mayor, Aldermen, and Commonalty* (1859).

Popularly and affectionately referred to as "Old Uncle David" during his declining years, Valentine was one of the most respected and beloved residents of New York City. Had he not remained so absorbed in uncovering, compiling, and preserving local historical and antiquarian materials, he could probably have risen with ease to high official position. He became a member of the New-England Historic and Genealogical Society in 1855. He was twice married, first to Martha Carnell, on June 24, 1821. They had three sons and two daughters. After her death, he was married to Caroline M. Spicer, who, with the children of his first wife, survived him.

[T. W. Valentine, *The Valentines in America, 1644–1874* (1874); *New-Eng. Hist. and Geneal. Register*, Oct. 1869; Otto Hufeland, compiler, *Hist. Index to the Manuals of the Corp. of the City of N. Y.* (1900); *An Index to the Illustrations in the Manuals of the Corp. of the City of N. Y.* (1906); William Cushing, *Initials and Pseudonyms* (1885); *N. Y. Times, N. Y. Herald*, Feb. 26, 1869.]
R.W.I.

VALENTINE, EDWARD VIRGINIUS (Nov. 12, 1838–Oct. 19, 1930), sculptor, the youngest of nine children of Mann Satterwhite and Elizabeth (Mosby) Valentine, was born at Richmond, Va., where his father was a prosperous merchant, a member of a family that had been in Virginia since the middle of the seventeenth century. He received his early education from tutors and in private schools. His wish to become a sculptor led him to the study of anatomy, and in 1856 he began to attend lectures at the Medical College of Virginia, Richmond. By 1857 he had made several portrait busts, and in the fall of 1859 he went to Paris, where he studied drawing from the nude under Thomas Couture, and modeling under François Jouffroy. He then traveled to Italy, visited numerous galleries, and studied in Florence. In 1861 he was accepted as a pupil in the Berlin studio of August Kiss, where his charm and goodness completely won the old sculptor's heart. While he was in Berlin he received from the South photographs of Gen. Robert E. Lee, and made from them a portrait statuette, which he sold for the benefit of the Southern cause. In the fall of 1865 he studied for a time at the Royal Academy, Berlin.

Toward the end of 1865 he returned to Richmond, where he opened a studio. He had won praise in Berlin for a bust from life of Dr. Franz von Holtzendorff, and in London for the Lee statuette. But in Richmond, in the tragic circumstances of the Reconstruction, he at first received no orders. Undaunted, he continued to work diligently, producing the heads entitled "The Penitent Thief" and "The Woman of Samaria," and a number of portrait and genre studies of the American negro. Among the latter are "Uncle Henry," a character study of the old-time plantation negro; "The Nation's Ward," a happy-go-lucky African; and a mildly satirical statuette, "Knowledge Is Power," which suggests the "Rogers groups" and shows a darky boy sound asleep over his tattered book. A much-admired bust of General Lee, done from life, was followed by portraits of J. E. B. Stuart, Albert Sidney Johnston, Joseph E. Johnston, Col. John S. Mosby, Commodore Matthew F. Maury, and other Southern leaders, most of them done from life. At last, in 1870, came a really inspiring commission, resulting in Valentine's finest work, the marble recumbent figure of Lee for the Lee Mausoleum at Washington and Lee University, Lexington, Va. In 1908 Valentine's bronze standing figure of Lee was unveiled in Statuary Hall, Washington, D. C., as the gift of the State of Virginia. Many examples of Valentine's work are to be seen in Richmond—at the Jefferson Hotel, which has his marble statue of Thomas Jefferson, in Monroe Park, where his bronze figure of Gen. W. T. Wickham stands, and in the Valentine Museum, former home of his brother Mann. His other works include the stat-

ues of Jefferson Davis in Richmond, of which there is a replica in New Orleans, John C. Breckinridge in Lexington, Ky., Gen. "Stonewall" Jackson in Lexington, Va., and John J. Audubon in New Orleans. His classical group representing Andromache and Astyanax after their farewell to Hector was shown at the World's Columbian Exposition, Chicago, in 1893. It is said that he refused to commemorate by his work any Northern hero. Though many of his statues are historically interesting as likenesses, artistically they leave something to be desired; they are on the whole rather wooden and lifeless. Valentine served as president of the Valentine Museum, the Richmond Art Club, and the Virginia Historical Society. He was married on Nov. 12, 1872, in Baltimore to Alice Churchill Robinson (d. Aug. 23, 1883), and on Jan. 5, 1892, to Katherine Cole (Friend) Mayo (d. Feb. 5, 1927). There were no children. He died in Richmond.

[*Who's Who in America,* 1930–31; Elizabeth G. Valentine, *Dawn to Twilight; Work of Edward V. Valentine* (1929); Lorado Taft, *The Hist. of Am. Sculpture* (1924 ed.); C. E. Fairman, *Art and Artists of the Capitol of the U. S.* (1927); Margaret J. Preston, in *Am. Art Review,* May 1880, an uncritical article; obituary in *Richmond Times-Dispatch,* Oct. 20, 1930.]   A. A.

VALENTINE, MILTON (Jan. 1, 1825–Feb. 7, 1906), Lutheran theologian, educator, was born near Uniontown, Carroll County, Md., the son of Jacob and Rebecca (Picking) Valentine, and a descendant of George Valentine who emigrated from Germany in the early part of the eighteenth century and settled in Frederick County, Md., in 1740. Milton worked on the farm until he was twenty-one, meanwhile preparing for college at the Taneytown Academy. In 1846 he enrolled at Pennsylvania College, Gettysburg, and was graduated in 1850; he then entered the Lutheran Theological Seminary in the same town, where he was graduated in 1852, and was licensed as a minister. He served for a year as supply pastor at Winchester, Va., a year as missionary in Pittsburgh, a year as regular pastor at Greensburg, Pa., and four years as principal of Emmaus Institute at Middletown, Pa. In 1859 he became pastor of St. Matthew's Lutheran Church at Reading, where he ministered with conspicuous success for seven years. In 1866 he accepted the professorship of Biblical and ecclesiastical history in the Lutheran Theological Seminary at Gettysburg.

The seminary was passing through a crisis. It had been founded in 1826, and Pennsylvania College in 1832, by Samuel S. Schmucker [*q.v.*], moving spirit in the early history of the General Synod of the Lutheran Church in the United

States. Schmucker's position was that of a liberally conservative Lutheranism, based upon the Scriptures as "the inspired Word of God and the only perfect rule of faith and practice" and upon the Augsburg Confession as "a summary and just exhibition of the fundamental doctrines of the Word of God." Diverging from this central position, there began in the 1850's a movement towards the left on the part of certain zealous advocates of "American Lutheranism," impatient of liturgies and interested in revivals and other "new measures"; and toward the right, partly owing to immigration, a strong swing toward "Old Lutheranism" or "Symbolism," the supporters of which proposed as a confessional basis not only the Augsburg Confession but the whole body of Lutheran symbolical books as contained in the Book of Concord. The growing strength of the second of these movements seriously threatened the seminary at Gettysburg. Though Schmucker resigned in 1864, the Pennsylvania Ministerium withdrew to found its own seminary in Philadelphia, and led in the organization of another general body of Lutherans, the General Council, in 1867. The directors of the seminary had faced this crisis with courage and vigor, securing funds for two new professorships and calling Valentine to one of them. After two years of teaching in this post he was elected president of the college, to which he gave for sixteen years a scholarly, effective administration. In 1884 he returned to the service of the seminary, becoming professor of theology and chairman of the faculty. He retired because of increasing age and impaired hearing in 1903, with the title of professor emeritus.

Valentine was an accurate scholar, a penetrating thinker, and a stimulating teacher. He was a vigorous defender of the position of General Synod Lutheranism, which he described as "standing for the principle of union in generic and Catholic Lutheranism on the great historic Confession of Augsburg, which has always been recognized as the one decisive determining standard of our Church, apart from any of the developed specialties of explanation which have been asserted by some, and into which they have been pleased to restrict themselves" (*Lutheran Observer,* March 6, 1891). From 1871 to 1906 he was an editor of the *Quarterly Review of the Evangelical Lutheran Church* (later the *Lutheran Quarterly*). He was a member of the joint committee which, laboring from 1885 to 1888, prepared the Common Service which is now used in public worship by most English-speaking Lutheran churches. His textbooks, *Natural Theology* (1885) and *Theoretical Ethics* (1897),

were widely used. In 1898 he published *Christian Truth and Life,* a volume of sermons. His greatest work, *Christian Theology,* in two volumes, edited by his son, M. H. Valentine, appeared in 1907. On Dec. 18, 1855, he married Margaret G. Galt of Taneytown, Md., by whom he had four children.

[T. W. Valentine, *The Valentines in America* (1874); A. R. Wentz, *Hist. of the Gettysburg Theological Seminary* (1926); S. G. Hefelbower, *The Hist. of Gettysburg Coll.* (1932); *Lutheran Quart.,* Jan. 1907; *Pub. Ledger* (Phila.), Feb. 9, 1906.]   L. A. W.

VALENTINE, ROBERT GROSVENOR (Nov. 29, 1872–Nov. 14, 1916), administrator and industrial counselor, was born at West Newton, Mass., the only child of Charles Theodore and Charlotte Grosvenor (Light) Valentine. He was a descendant of John Valentine who was made a freeman of Boston, Mass., in 1675. Robert prepared for college at Hopkinson's School, Boston, and was graduated at Harvard in 1896. From 1896 to 1899 and from 1901 to 1903 he taught English at the Massachusetts Institute of Technology, the intervening period being spent in the National City Bank, New York. Beginning in 1903, through the interest of James Stillman [*q.v.*], he had a miscellaneous business experience with railroads and financial institutions in New York and Omaha until ill health from overwork forced him to retire from business in 1904. That same year, Dec. 31, he married Sophia French of South Braintree, Mass. During the administration of Theodore Roosevelt he became private secretary to Francis E. Leupp [*q.v.*], commissioner of Indian affairs, whose assistant he became in 1908. Upon Leupp's retirement in 1909, President Taft appointed Valentine to the head of the Indian Office.

His administration of that office was a notable one. He was resourceful in the protection of the enormous Indian properties against the many attempts at encroachments upon them, and was eager for the development of the best of the Indian cultures. One of his acts as commissioner created considerable political difficulties because of the religious susceptibilities that it awakened. By an Indian Office circular (Number 601), he prohibited the wearing of religious garb and the display of religious insignia in what had formerly been religious schools for Indians but had been taken over as government institutions. In the spring of 1912 the Indian Office under his administration was under political fire and a Congressional investigation followed. The committee in its report divided on political lines, the four Democratic members finding against him, and the three Republican members supporting him (*House Report No. 1279,* 62 Cong., 3

Sess.). That same year he threw in his lot with Theodore Roosevelt in the Bull Moose campaign, and resigned from the Taft administration.

The range of Valentine's experience thus far —educational, financial, administrative, sociological—was all useful though unconscious preparation for his real life work, short as that was; for his significance, apart from his enduring work at the Indian Office, is that of founder of the new profession of industrial counselor. For four years he specialized as adviser on industrial relations, and the impact of his example and achievements led to the recognition of the need of a body of specialists like himself. Others before him had diagnosed the so-called labor problem as essentially a human problem—the problem of men and women, with their impulses and desires, behind the mechanism of industry. Valentine was the first, however, to draw profound conclusions from this discernment. Just because the terms of this human equation, he argued, were subtle and excessively complicated, there was the greater necessity for making these elusive aspects of the relation of capital and labor the subject of organized study. Instead of ignoring the human problem, or leaving it to caprice, Valentine maintained that personal relations must be studied with the same scientific spirit as are the processes of production and the fiscal side of business. Such knowledge, he was convinced, could be achieved only by professionals, that is, by men who devoted their entire time to it, with a function as well-defined as that of the lawyer or the financial expert. With this insight and with astonishing courage—for he had neither funds nor backers—in the winter of 1912, Valentine advertised himself in Boston as an industrial counselor, thus inaugurating, so far as history records, the beginning of this profession.

Basic to this profession was the need of what Valentine called "an industrial audit" which would bear the same relation to the social health of an industry that a periodic financial audit bears to the solvency of a business. Such an industrial audit called for the invention of a technique adapted, by appropriate adjustments, to every variety of business. Valentine helped to install such an audit in diverse types of industrial organizations, just as he served as adviser on labor problems for diverse clients. Like an old-fashioned lawyer, he served labor unions, employees, and public officials. Notable among the services rendered the last-named was his work for Mayor John Purroy Mitchel [q.v.] in the very difficult transit strike in New York City, during the summer of 1916.

Essentially Valentine was an educator. He disseminated ideas and imparted ferment—in his work for his clients, as chairman of the first wage board under the Massachusetts minimum wage law (1913), as lecturer at Wellesley College (1915–16), in formal addresses, and through the mere contagion of casual contact. He was a poet by temperament who was dominated by scientific ardor to institutionalize sound human relations. The astonishing aspect of his career is that he succeeded in establishing recognition of his idea of scientific order in the human aspects of industry although he had so brief a period for accomplishment. He died from a sudden heart attack, survived by his widow and a daughter.

[T. W. Valentine, *The Valentines in America* (1874); *Harvard Coll. Class of 1896: Twenty-fifth Anniversary Report* (1921); *Reports of the Commissioner of Indian Affairs to the Secretary of the Interior*, 1909–12; *Bull. of the Taylor Society*, Jan. 1916; *Modern Hospital*, Apr. 1916; *Survey*, Nov. 25, 1916; *Who's Who in America*, 1916–17; *Boston Herald* and *Boston Globe*, Jan. 8, 1917; *N. Y. Times*, Nov. 15, 1916.]

F. F.

VALLANDIGHAM, CLEMENT LAIRD (July 29, 1820–June 17, 1871), politician, was born in New Lisbon, Ohio, the fifth of seven children of Clement Vallandigham, a Presbyterian minister, and his wife, Rebecca Laird. On his mother's side he was of Scotch-Irish stock; on his father's, he was descended from Michael Van Landegham, a Flemish Huguenot, who was in Stafford County, Va., as early as 1690. Vallandigham attended the New Lisbon Academy founded by his father and in 1837 entered Jefferson College, Canonsburg, Pa., as a junior. The following year he left to teach at Snow Hill, Md., but returned to the college in 1840 only to leave without graduating after a heated argument with the president over a question of constitutional law. He then read law for two years and was admitted to the Ohio bar. Though case law and argument bored him, both his practice and his reputation as a political speaker grew rapidly. In 1845 he went to Columbus as the youngest member of the Ohio legislature; he was reëlected in 1846 and chosen speaker of the House by his Democratic colleagues. The following year he formed a partnership with Thomas J. S. Smith at Dayton, Ohio. Here he soon became part owner and editor of the Dayton *Empire,* but the extent of his law practice caused him to relinquish his editorship in 1849.

Handsome, high-spirited, and self-willed, Vallandigham was devoted to the South as the home of his ancestors, and idealized Southern character. He served as an officer in the Ohio militia and became a brigadier-general in 1857, although he objected to the maintenance of a strong national army and ardently opposed centralization of government. He earnestly supported the Mexican War and although he disapproved of slavery as a moral and political evil, he advocated a policy of non-interference where it existed, opposed the Wilmot Proviso and the repeal of the Ohio "Black Laws," and supported the compromise measures of 1850. Long before the Civil War he was demanding the suppression of abolitionist fanatics and a return to Jeffersonian state rights, the Constitution as the fathers wrote it, and the Union as it had been.

He was defeated for Congress in 1852 by the abolitionists and the Liberty party, and in 1854 by the Know-Nothings. Two years later, denouncing the Republicans as dangerous sectionalists headed for civil war, he ran again for Congress. Successfully contesting the official count, which gave his opponent a majority of nineteen, he was seated by the House in May 1858, and later that year was reëlected by a scant margin. On the floor of the House, Feb. 24, 1859, he vigorously attacked the tariff of 1857 as a manufacturer's tariff. In the fall of 1859, changing trains at Harpers Ferry, Va., (now W. Va.), he interrogated the wounded John Brown and subsequently stated his conviction that Brown had been the instrument of a widespread conspiracy. For this interview he was condemned by many Republican journals which charged him with "pumping" their martyr. In the excited Thirty-sixth Congress he pleaded for freedom of speech and of the press, denounced sectionalism and ultraism on either side, and declared that the West would not allow disunion. As secretary of the National Democratic Committee in 1860 and a delegate at the Charleston convention he opposed the views of Stephen A. Douglas [q.v.] on popular sovereignty, but supported Douglas as the only "Union" candidate fit for the presidency. He vehemently denounced the radical utterances of Lincoln and Seward and declared that the Southern "fire-eaters" would vanish if the Republican party were destroyed. In a speech at Cooper Union, New York City, Nov. 2, 1860, he said he would never, "as a Representative in the Congress of the United States, vote one dollar of money whereby one drop of American blood should be shed in a civil war" (J. L. Vallandigham, post, p. 141). In Congress he supported the Crittenden Resolutions and other attempts at compromise, going to the extent of proposing (Feb. 20, 1861) a division of the Senate and of the electoral college into four sections, each to have the power of veto. His able opposition to every defense measure proposed in the

House soon incurred for him the intense hatred of the Republicans.

By the time of his return to Ohio he was suspected of treasonable intent and had become one of the most unpopular and most bitterly abused men in the North. Standing for freedom of expression, for compromise, and for the restoration of peace on any terms, he called the congressmen who condemned him radicals, rebels, and liars. In May 1862, attempting to give the Democrats a policy by which to save their party, he declared their purpose: "To maintain the Constitution as it is, and to restore the Union as it was" (Speeches, post, p. 365). His eloquent and impassioned oratory in a war-weary and uncertain North gained support among thousands of people who thought him the true apostle of liberty. His party convention enthusiastically renominated him for Congress in 1862, but he was defeated. Thenceforth he was regarded as the leader of the Peace Democrats or "Copperheads" in the Northwest. Believing that the Democratic victories in 1862 vindicated his policy, he delivered a speech in the House, Jan. 14, 1863, in which he said that the time had come to negotiate a peace, and that prolonging the war would mean that the Northwest would join the South, and the Union be permanently broken. His thrusts at the Republicans encouraged the pro-Southern element and the disloyalists in the order of the Sons of Liberty, of which he was commander; they pleased President Davis, and made the Federal administration wince.

When in the spring of 1863 Gen. Ambrose E. Burnside [q.v.] issued General Order Number 38, warning the peace party that the "habit of declaring sympathies for the enemy" would not be allowed in the Military District of Ohio, and that expressed or implied treason would not be tolerated, Vallandigham, who had promoted resistance to conscription, defied the military in speeches at Columbus and Mount Vernon, calling the "wicked and cruel" war a diabolical attempt to destroy slavery and to set up a Republican despotism. On May 5, 1863, he was arrested in Dayton and the next day was tried by a military commission in Cincinnati for expressing treasonable sympathy. He was condemned to confinement in Fort Warren, but President Lincoln shrewdly banished him (May 19) to the Confederacy. Treated kindly by the Confederates, he ran the blockade to Bermuda, thence sailed to Halifax, and in August settled at Windsor, Ont., across the river from Detroit. An appeal was taken to the federal courts in an attempt to get a decision on the validity of his trial before the military body, but in February

1864 the Supreme Court decided that it had no power to issue a writ of *habeas corpus* to a military commission (*Ex parte Vallandigham,* 1 *Wallace,* 243).

Meanwhile the Peace Democrats of Ohio, choosing him as the symbol of their principles, in July 1863 made him their candidate for governor. Mobs rioted in his behalf and committees of Democrats importuned Lincoln to return him to Ohio, but were refused on grounds of military necessity. After carrying on his campaign through friends and through correspondence, he polled a large vote, but was defeated decisively by John Brough [*q.v.*], a War Democrat running on the Republican ticket. On June 15, 1864, he suddenly appeared to deliver a speech before a Democratic convention at Hamilton, Ohio, and was afterwards escorted in triumph to Dayton. Allowed to go unnoticed by the President, he denounced "King Lincoln" and spat upon General Order Number 38. He ended his extensive pre-campaign speaking tour in Chicago, where he talked to crowds in the streets and in August irreparably damaged his party's cause by forcing into the national Democratic platform a resolution (written by himself and John McElwee) declaring the war a failure and demanding an immediate cessation of hostilities.

The Vallandigham influence and Northern victories defeated the Democracy in 1864. On Jan. 23, 1865, Vallandigham begged Horace Greeley [*q.v.*] to bring about peace, but the failure of the conference at Hampton Roads in February ended his peace efforts. He regretted the assassination of Lincoln because he feared that in retaliation the radicals would bring greater evils upon the country. In 1866 he went to Philadelphia to attend the "National Union Convention" of supporters of President Johnson, but though hundreds of people called at the Girard House to see him, he was forced to withdraw from the convention to make harmony possible in the party ranks. He entered the state elections in 1867 with his accustomed vigor and invective, and was deeply grieved when the Democratic leaders refused to choose him senator. As a member of the Ohio delegation to the National Democratic Convention of the following year, though Salmon P. Chase [*q.v.*] was his personal preference for the presidential nomination, he supported George H. Pendleton [*q.v.*] until the latter withdrew from the contest; then, after the movement toward Chase had failed, he turned to Horatio Seymour [*q.v.*]; in the subsequent campaign the Republican incumbent, Gen. Robert C. Schenk [*q.v.*], defeated Vallandigham for Congress.

In succeeding months Vallandigham reached the conclusion that it was time to accept the results of the Civil War and to drop the old issues; early in 1871 he won the Ohio Democracy to this view and invited dissatisfied Republicans to join the Democrats in turning to living issues of a new day, but he died before the movement he thus helped to start took shape in the Liberal Republican party of 1872. Whatever his policy at any time, Vallandigham advocated it with the ardor and sincerity of a fanatic. In 1871 he was retained as counsel for the defendant in a murder case and while demonstrating to a friend the way in which the victim had been shot he mortally wounded himself. On Aug. 27, 1846, he had married Louisa A. McMahon by whom he had two sons, one of whom lived to maturity.

[Sources include Vallandigham letters in Western Reserve Hist. Soc.; *Speeches, Arguments, Addresses and Letters of Clement L. Vallandigham* (1864); McClellan MSS., Blair MSS., William Allen MSS. in Lib. of Cong.; *Cong. Globe,* 36 and 37 Cong.; *War of the Rebellion: Official Records* (*Army*), 2 ser. V, VII. For accounts of Vallandigham's career see J. L. Vallandigham, *A Life of Clement L. Vallandigham* (1872), by a brother; E. N. Vallandigham, in *Putnam's Mag.,* Aug. 1907; W. H. Van Fossan, in *Ohio Archæol. and Hist. Quart.,* July 1914; Henry Howe, *Hist. Colls. of Ohio* (2 vols., 1902); S. D. Cone, *Biog. and Hist. Sketches: A Narrative of Hamilton and Its Residents* (n.d.; preface dated 1896). See also J. G. Nicolay and John Hay, *Abraham Lincoln* (1890), VII, 328–60; E. J. Benton, "The Movement for Peace without a Victory during the Civil War," *Western Reserve Hist. Soc. Colls.,* pub. no. 99 (1918); J. G. Randall, *Constitutional Problems under Lincoln* (1926); E. C. Kirkland, *The Peacemakers of 1864* (1927); H. C. Hubbart, "'Pro-Southern' Influences in the Free West, 1840–1865," *Miss. Valley Hist. Rev.,* June 1933; C. H. Coleman, *The Election of 1868* (1933); *The Am. Ann. Cyc.,* 1863 (1864), 1871 (1872); *Cincinnati Daily Enquirer,* June 19, 1871.]
W. E. S—h.

VALLEJO, MARIANO GUADALUPE (July 7, 1808–Jan. 18, 1890), prominent early California citizen and military leader, was born in Monterey, Cal., son of Ignacio Vallejo and María Antonia Lugo. At fifteen he was attached as cadet to the Monterey garrison; by 1827 he was ensign in the company at the Presidio (now San Francisco). On the occasion of the formidable Estanislao Indian rebellion of 1829, when the neophytes of the San José mission rose against the missionaries, young Vallejo was sent against the Indians with a hundred men and a number of Indian auxiliaries. He defeated and scattered the rebels, but his victory was marred by his failing to prevent the murder of some of the prisoners by his Indian allies. Elected a deputy to the territorial congress in 1830 (illegally, it seems, since he was an officer in the army), he supported the rebellion of the Californians against their Mexican governor, Manuel Victoria, in 1832. That same year, on Mar. 6, he married María Francisca Felipa Benicia Carrillo of San Diego, by whom in the course of time he had between thirteen and seventeen children. The new governor, the able and humane José Figueroa, a close friend of Vallejo's, had Vallejo removed as deputy but made him commander of an expedition to reconnoitre the northern frontier, where the activities of the Russians at Fort Ross were causing uneasiness among the Californians. Vallejo found the Russians to be peacefully engaged in the fur trade and no menace to California, but his report on the danger from the warlike Indians of that region and the encroachment of American immigrants decided Governor Figueroa to establish a military post there. The commandant of the new garrison at Sonoma was Vallejo, and his organization of the frontier defenses and his control of the Indians were, perhaps, his most valuable contributions to the state. The secularization of the mission properties carried on by Figueroa led naturally to the appointment of Vallejo as administrator of the Solano mission, a duty which he performed efficiently and humanely, befriending the Indians and settling them on the mission lands, although in so doing he ran afoul of the belligerent Father Mercado of Solano.

With the death of Figueroa in 1835 Vallejo was again forced into politics, this time against the bombastic centralist governor Mariano Chico and his lieutenant Gutiérrez. He supported his nephew, Juan Bautista Alvarado [q.v.], in the rebellion that led to the proclamation of the "free state" of California in 1836, and in 1838, under Alvarado's governorship, was named commander of the state forces. A petty quarrel over military etiquette estranged the two, and Vallejo retired to his post at Sonoma, where, with an imposing force of Indian allies and his own troops, he made himself a semi-independent chieftain, a cacique on the Spanish-American pattern, and the most powerful figure in the north. Alvarado's appointment of William Hartnell as administrator of the missions widened the gap between the two. When Hartnell invaded the Sonoma country in the discharge of his duties, he was promptly arrested and deported by Vallejo, and thereafter Vallejo was left to himself until the end of the Mexican régime in 1846. Vallejo had protected and encouraged the immigration of American families into his territory, being, as he said, powerless to prevent it. The presence of the Frémont expedition of 1846 encouraged an enemy of the Vallejos, one Merritt, and a number of idle Americans at Fort Sutter to undertake their headless and planless "Bear Flag Republic." Their single exploit was the capture and imprisonment of Vallejo and his

brother Salvador, and the theft of their cattle. The two brothers were kept prisoners for two months by the unaccountable Frémont.

A powerful agent in securing the submission of California to the United States, Vallejo was elected to the constitutional convention of 1849, and to the first state Senate of California, where he staged a long fight to have the state capital fixed at Vallejo in his own territory. Thereafter he devoted his energies largely to clearing the titles of his princely holdings, some of which he retained. In his latter years he was no longer the great cacique of the Mexican days, but he kept up his magnificent hospitality at the great house at Sonoma to the end of his life. He died in Sonoma in comparative poverty, a well loved and respected country gentleman. His unpublished "Historia de California" is a somewhat colored, but charming and valuable account of early California.

[See H. H. Bancroft, *Hist. of Cal.* (7 vols., 1884–90); T. H. Hittell, *Hist. of Cal.* (4 vols., 1885–97); Zephyrin Engelhardt, *The Missions and Missionaries of Cal.* (6 vols., 1908–30); C. E. Chapman, *Hist. of Cal., the Spanish Period* (1921); Eugène Duflot de Mofras, *Exploration du Territoire de l'Orégon, des Californies* (2 vols., Paris, 1844), valuable for its description of Spanish Cal.; Alfred Robinson, *Life in Cal. before the Conquest* (1846); P. M. G. Vallejo, "Memoirs of the Vallejos," in *Bulletin* (San Francisco), Jan. 27–Feb. 16, 1914; M. L. Lothrop, "Mariano Guadalupe Vallejo, Defender of the Northern Frontier," unpublished dissertation in the Univ. of Cal. lib., 1927; M. G. Vallejo, "Historia de California," MS. in the Bancroft Lib., Berkeley, Cal.; and obituary in *Morning Call* (San Francisco), Jan. 19, 1890. There are thirty-seven vols. of manuscript material from the archives of the Vallejo family in the Bancroft Lib.]   L. B. S—n.

VALLENTINE, BENJAMIN BENNATON (Sept. 7, 1843–Mar. 30, 1926), journalist, playwright, was born in London, the son of Benjamin Vallentine, a toy merchant, and Rosa (Nathan) Vallentine. He always gave King Edward VI's School, Birmingham, as the place of his education, but the truth seems to be that most of his education was not obtained at any school. As a youth, he spent several years in Australia, where he was clerk in a shipping firm at Sydney. He studied for the English bar, and contributed to Sydney newspapers. In 1870 he returned to England, and the next year came to New York City, where he lived until his death.

In New York he became partner in a shipping house, but after the panic of 1873 turned to journalism. He was one of the founders of *Puck* in 1877, and served as managing editor from 1877 to 1884. For *Puck* he wrote the series of papers beginning in the March 1877 issue, which constitute his chief claim to remembrance. They purport to be the letters of one Lord Fitznoodle, a musical-comedy Britisher, concerning his adventures among the Americans. The satire, which frequently cuts both ways, is always good-natured and urbane. After leaving *Puck,* Vallentine served as managing editor of Irving Bacheller's newspaper syndicate (1886–88). He did much editorial writing and dramatic criticism for New York newspapers, and held other editorial positions. Always interested in the theatre, he became a familiar figure on Broadway and had a wide circle of theatrical acquaintance. He wrote, collaborated on, or adapted, a good many plays, most of them having no pretension to depth. None of the plays seems to have been published, except a one-act version of *In Paradise,* but some, including *Fadette* (a comic opera), *A Southern Romance,* and *In Paradise,* were produced in New York, the first in 1892, the second in 1897, and the third in 1899.

In his later years Vallentine fell upon hard times. He was registered at New York University Law School in 1907–08. In 1908 he took a civil service position as audit-inspector with the municipal finance department, but the salary was low and had to be pieced out by donations from his family and "loans" from his friends. He had never married, and lived in a furnished room, spending much of his time at his old haunt, the Lotos Club. About two years before the end his health failed, and he underwent several operations. Then one day in his eighty-third year he fell unconscious in a restaurant and was taken to Bellevue Hospital. Annoyed at finding himself in a public hospital ward, he tried to get up —and fell dead.

Vallentine's friends remember him as a tiny man, with great flashing black eyes and quick, nervous gestures. He never lost his British accent nor all of his British way of looking at things. He was a good conversationalist, and had an amazing memory and wide information. Every one testifies to the essential fineness of his character. He was a lively and interesting person rather than a man of genius; yet his connection with *Puck* and his creation of the comic character which gave him his nickname of "Fitznoodle" entitle him to be remembered.

[Sources include files of *Puck;* *Who's Who in America,* 1924–25; *Who's Who in New York* (1911); *Phila. Sunday Mirror,* July 30, 1880; *N. Y. Times,* Sept. 5, 1899, Mar. 31, 1926, Apr. 4, 1926; *World* (N. Y.), Mar. 31, 1926; *Dramatic Compositions Copyrighted in the United States, 1870 to 1916* (1918); records of the Gen. Reg. Office, London, of N. Y. Univ. Law School, and of Newspaper Club, N. Y.; personal recollections of Walter R. Benjamin, Stephen L. Newman, Eva Ingersoll Wakefield, and Anna Fisch, all of New York, and of members and employees of the Lotos Club, N. Y. In his latter years Vallentine seems to have used Benton instead of Bennaton for a middle name.]

E. M. S.

VALLIANT, LEROY BRANCH (June 14, 1838–Mar. 3, 1913), jurist, was born at Moulton, Ala. His father, Denton Hurlock Valliant, a native of Tennessee, was descended from John Valliant (or Vaillant), a Londoner of French parentage, who settled on the Eastern Shore of Maryland in the seventeenth century (1658, according to family tradition), and from Jonathan Hurlock who came to the same section of Maryland from England in the first half of the eighteenth century. His mother, before marriage Narcissa Kilpatrick, a native of Tennessee, was of Irish and Scottish ancestry. An orphan at six, Valliant, helped by relatives, received a good education, first at private schools, then at the University of Mississippi, where he was graduated in 1856, and later at the Cumberland University Law School in Tennessee, where he was graduated in 1858. That same year, when the fascinating William Walker [*q.v.*] was starting one of his Nicaraguan expeditions, Valliant joined a band of Walker's "emigrants" and embarked by river for New Orleans, but because of lack of funds was put off the boat with his companions at Memphis. In later years Valliant expressed religious thankfulness for the abortive outcome of this youthful adventure.

After settling at the prosperous river town of Greenville, Miss., he was admitted to the bar in 1859, and practised law until the Civil War. In 1861 he entered the Confederate military service. At the battle of Shiloh, as captain of Company I, 22nd Mississippi Regiment, he was for a while in command of that regiment because all his ranking officers had been killed or wounded. Shortly afterwards, shattered in health and with sight permanently impaired, he returned to Greenville where eventually, with restored health, he resumed his career as a lawyer, serving for a term as chancellor of his district. In 1874, partly because of dissatisfaction with the progress of reconstruction, he left Mississippi, went to St. Louis, and there in the course of twelve years acquired considerable reputation as a lawyer and as a public speaker. Appointed by the governor in 1886 to a temporary judgeship on the circuit court of St. Louis, in the fall of that year he was elected judge of the same court for a constitutional term of six years, and reëlected in 1892. In 1898, while still a circuit judge, he was elected for a four-year term to fill a vacancy in the supreme court of Missouri, and in 1902 was reëlected for another term of ten years. After twenty-six years of useful public service in Missouri, he finally retired Dec. 31, 1912, broken in health, but still alert mentally and beloved by the legal profession. He died at Greenville; his body was taken to St. Louis and buried in Bellefontaine Cemetery. In October 1862 he had married Theodosia Taylor Worthington of Leota Landing, Miss., who with their three sons survived him.

Valliant's judicial activities on the Missouri supreme court are set forth in 147–247 *Missouri Reports*. As a judge he was sound rather than brilliant. He wrote the majority opinion of the court in *Morgan* vs. *Wabash Railroad Company* (1900), 159 *Mo., 262*, which after years of controversy finally established the so-called humanitarian doctrine as a Missouri exception to the rather harsh English common-law rule of contributory negligence. Another of his important opinions was in the case of *State ex rel. Koeln* vs. *Lesser* (1911), 237 *Mo.*, 310, holding that under the taxation statutes of Missouri the stocks in non-Missouri corporations even if owned by Missouri residents are not subject to taxation as personal property in Missouri.

[James Cox, *Old and New St. Louis* (1894); A. J. D. Stewart, *The Hist. of the Bench and Bar of Mo.* (1898); William Hyde and H. L. Conard, *Encyc. of the Hist. of St. Louis* (1899), vol. IV; *Who's Who in America*, 1912–13; "In Memoriam," 248 *Mo. Reports* (1913); Henry Lamm, "Address in Memory of Judge Leroy B. Valliant," *Proc. 31st Ann. Meeting Mo. Bar Asso.* (1913); *St. Louis Globe-Democrat*, Mar. 5, 6, 1913; newspaper clippings at Mo. Hist. Soc., St. Louis.]
         T. W.

VAN ALLEN, FRANK (Jan. 10, 1860–Aug. 28, 1923), missionary physician, the son of Martin and Martha (Bowen) Van Allen, was born in Dubuque, Iowa, to which place his parents had removed from New York State. He was a descendant of Pieter van Allen who came to New Netherland in 1658. The boy's preparatory education was obtained in Lake View High School, Chicago, Ill., where he distinguished himself as a student. Entering Yale in 1881, he received from that institution the degrees of B.A. in 1885, M.D. in 1887, and B.D. in 1888. He was ordained to the Congregational ministry at West Haven, Conn., on May 21, 1888, and in September was married in Chicago to Harriet Adelia Gurnee. Sailing with his wife from New York Oct. 13, under commission of the American Board of Commissioners for Foreign Missions, he arrived in Dindigul, Madura, South India, on Nov. 28. Except for several furloughs, he spent the remainder of his life in Madura, engaged in medical missionary service.

After a brief time in Dindigul he moved to Madura City, where he took charge of a mission dispensary which had been in operation since 1834. Under his direction it rendered a continually increasing service. In 1890 he reported the treatment of 13,000 cases; six years later the

number had doubled; and in 1897 it reached 47,-200. The following year a new men's hospital, the Albert Victoria Memorial, was completed, and on Oct. 29 it was opened by the governor of Madras. On this occasion an address was delivered by the Raja of Ramnad, one of the chief donors. The cost was $14,000, provided almost entirely by non-Christians of India, and the expense of maintenance was borne largely by "native" subscriptions. Van Allen never charged specific fees for any service, but received "thank-offerings," which, even before 1896, approximated $7,000. In 1902 the gifts amounted to 6,-300 rupees, including a donation of 1,800 from a *Zamindar* (land-owner) for the cure of his wife, who had not walked for four years previously. In 1905, another *Zamindar* gave 5,000 rupees. That year, the in-patients of the hospital numbered 346, the out-patients, 20,800, and 1,100 operations were performed, including many leg amputations. These figures indicate the extent of service rendered, and its generous support by Indians. The doctor came to hold a place of highest esteem throughout the district. Branches of the hospital were opened at Aruppukottai and Manamadura, in the latter place in connection with a leper colony. On the death of his wife in 1911 Van Allen founded for the needy the Harriet Gurnee Fund. They had four children.

His work was recognized by the government of India, which bestowed on him in 1914 the *Kaiser-i-Hind* medal. He had rendered especially conspicuous service during times of plague and cholera. Ultimately, he fell victim to the risks of his own service. Unknown to others until the last year of his affliction, he suffered for a decade from an incurable disease, contracted while he operated on a patient. Shortly before his death he resigned the headship of the hospital and retired to the nearby village of Melur to live his remaining days among the Christians there.

[*Quarter-Centenary Record of the Class of 1885, Yale Univ.* (1913); *Yale '85 Forty-five Years After* (1932); *Yale Univ. Obit. Record*, 1925; *The Congregational Year-Book*, 1923; *Missionary Herald*, 1888–1923, especially Oct. 1923; *Harvest Field*, vol. XLIII (1923); *Yale Divinity News*, Mar. 1924.]   J. C. A.

VAN ALSTYNE, FANNY CROSBY [See CROSBY, FANNY, 1820–1915].

VAN AMRINGE, JOHN HOWARD (Apr. 3, 1835–Sept. 10, 1915), professor of mathematics and dean of Columbia College, was born in Philadelphia, Pa., the son of William Frederick Van Amringe (1791–1873), the author of two scientific works, and Susan Budd Sterling, daughter of James Sterling of Burlington, N. J.

His grandfather, Leon Van Amringe, was born in Rotterdam, South Holland; married Elizabeth Oborne, a Hampshire woman, in London; and emigrated to America in 1791 (M. H. Thomas, "Van Amringe ... Family Records," *New-England Historical and Genealogical Register*, Oct. 1935, pp. 392–95). The family moved to New York City about 1840. Van Amringe was educated by his father and at the Montgomery Academy in Orange County, N. Y., whence he entered Yale in 1854. He remained there two years, and after a two-year interlude of teaching entered Columbia College, graduating in 1860 with second honors. The same year he was appointed tutor in mathematics; in 1863 he became adjunct professor. On June 20, 1865, he married Cornelia, daughter of William Goelet Bucknor of New York City; they had three sons and one daughter. Van Amringe became professor of mathematics in the School of Mines, Columbia University, in 1865 and in the School of Arts in 1873. In 1894 he succeeded Henry Drisler [*q.v.*] as dean of the School of Arts (renamed Columbia College in 1896). For a short time in 1899 he was acting president of Columbia University. He resigned his offices, June 30, 1910, and was made emeritus professor of mathematics. After the death of his former teacher and colleague, Prof. Charles Davies, he became editor of the Davies Series of mathematical textbooks. He wrote various professional papers, two pamphlets on life insurance (1872 and 1874), and many articles on Columbia and its alumni. He was one of the founders of the New York Mathematical Society (later the American Mathematical Society), and its first president (1888–90). He was one of the most popular members of the Century Association, and was vice-president at the time of his death. Long active in Episcopal organizations in New York, he served as vestryman of Trinity Church and trustee of the General Theological Seminary. He was a tall man, with a military bearing, and wore a great drooping mustache. His death occurred in Morristown, N. J.

"Van Am," as he was universally called, is a unique figure in the history of Columbia. "As a teacher he was clear, quick and incisive; having a perfect mastery of his subject, he expected and demanded hard work of his students, and was intolerant of inattention or neglect. Keen to detect a fault and sharp to reprimand, he was equally ready to recognize good work and anxious to do strict justice" (Pine, *post*, p. 192). Probably no other teacher in Columbia's history influenced the lives and ideals of his students as did Van Amringe. Probably no other teacher of

his day was so loved and revered, and "his boys" have delighted to perpetuate his memory at Columbia in song and stone and bronze and oils. Scarcely had he become an alumnus when he began to arouse an interest in the college among the alumni, and to restore the semi-moribund alumni association; imbuing others slowly with his own enthusiasm, he made the association a vital and vivifying influence in the whole university. He was at first secretary, then president of the association, and later president of the alumni of the federated schools of the university. He was unanimously elected president of the Columbia University Club in New York City on its foundation in 1901 and held office until his death. For decades no alumni gathering was complete without him. He was a fluent orator, speaking in "exquisitely phrased sentences, rich in thought and suggestion, often imbued with deep feeling and genial humor" (*Ibid.*, p. 194). He prepared the alumni necrology for many years, and used this material as a basis for nine new editions of the *General Catalogue*, which he edited from 1865 to 1906. His interest in history, originally stimulated by his courses with Francis Lieber [*q.v.*], was life-long. He compiled *An Historical Sketch of Columbia College* (1876), and wrote the section on Columbia for *Universities and Their Sons* (5 vols., 1898–1900), revising this for *A History of Columbia University, 1754–1904* (1904).

[The *Columbia Alumni News*, Nov. 5, 1915, sec. 2, is devoted to Van Amringe; it contains a biog. by J. B. Pine and memorial addresses by N. M. Butler and Seth Low; a somewhat cynical estimate by a colleague appears in J. W. Burgess, *Reminiscences of an Am. Scholar* (1934). See also *Who's Who in America*, 1914–15; *N. Y. Times* and *N. Y. Herald*, Sept. 11, 1915; J. J. Chapman, in *Evening Post* (N. Y.), Sept. 24, 1915; *Outlook*, Sept. 22, 1915; N. M. Butler, in *Columbia Spectator*, Apr. 20, 1931. The date of Van Amringe's birth, sometimes given as 1836, is from the family Bible.]   M. H. T.

VAN BEUREN, JOHANNES (*c.* 1680–July 27, 1755), physician, founder of a family of well-known physicians of New York City and vicinity, was born in Amsterdam and came to New York at the age of twenty-two. He had been a student of the renowned Dutch physician Hermannus Boerhaave, who had made the medical department of the University of Leyden famous throughout Europe. With this training he soon established a large practice in New York, where few of the so-called physicians had ever seen the inside of a medical school. In the words of a local historian, "few physicians amongst us are eminent for their skill. Quacks abound like locusts in Egypt, and too many have recommended themselves to a full practice and profitable subsistence" (William Smith, *History of New-York,* 1814, p. 325).

After practising in New York for more than twenty years, he removed about 1724 to Flatbush, Long Island, and lived there until 1728, when he returned to New York. In 1736, an almshouse, known as the "Publick Workhouse and House of Correction," was built on the site of the present City Hall. The hospital department was a room about twenty-five feet square on the second floor, containing six beds, and Van Beuren, through the influence of the governor of the colony it is said, was appointed its first medical director. He held the position until his death. His salary was £100 a year, out of which he was expected to provide his own medicines. This was the beginning of Bellevue Hospital, which may lay claim to being the oldest hospital in the United States. As Boerhaave in Holland was among the first to teach that pure air, cleanliness, and simple buildings are the first requirements for a hospital, it may be presumed that these principles were established by his former pupil in the new hospital in New York.

Van Beuren was married at New York, on June 15, 1707, to Maria Meyer, the daughter of Pieter Meyer and his wife, Batje Jans, of New York. They had fifteen children. His marriage and the baptisms of all but two of the children are recorded in the register of the Dutch Church. Five of his sons were physicians, and one of them, Beekman Van Beuren, who was the physician at the almshouse from 1765 to 1776, is credited with the introduction of inoculation for smallpox in the public institutions of the city. William Holme Van Buren [*q.v.*] was a descendant.

[*An Account of Bellevue Hospital* (1893), R. J. Carlisle, ed. ; William Jones, "The Van Beuren Family of New York and New Jersey," *N. Y. Geneal. and Biog. Record,* Jan. 1932.]   W. J.

VAN BRUNT, HENRY (Sept. 5, 1832–Apr. 8, 1903), architect and writer, was born in Boston, Mass., the son of Commodore Gershom Jaques Van Brunt, of the United States Navy, and Elizabeth Price (Bradlee) Van Brunt. On his father's side he was descended from Rutger Joesten van Brunt, who emigrated from the Netherlands in 1653 and in 1657 settled in New Utrecht, Long Island (now part of Brooklyn). One of his mother's ancestors is said to have been Nathaniel Bradlee, a participant in the Boston Tea Party. Van Brunt was educated at the Boston Latin School and at Harvard University. During his freshman year, he had a serious accident to his hip, which left him at least a partial invalid for the rest of his life. He graduated in 1854. He

then entered the Boston office of George Snell, architect, as a student; in 1856 he went to New York and became a student in the famous office-atelier of Richard Morris Hunt [*q.v.*], where he remained for several years. During the Civil War he was for two years clerk to Commodore L. M. Goldsborough of the North Atlantic Squadron and saw service in Virginia and North Carolina. In 1863 he formed a partnership, Ware and Van Brunt, with William Robert Ware [*q.v.*], whom he had met in Hunt's office. The work done with Ware included the First Church, Boston, Memorial Hall, Weld Hall, and the east wing of the college library at Harvard, and the library of the University of Michigan. Ware retired completely from the partnership in 1881; it was not formally dissolved, however, till 1883. Van Brunt thereupon took into partnership Frank M. Howe, who had been an employee of the firm since 1868, and the remainder of his architectural work was done under the firm name of Van Brunt and Howe. Commissioned by his friend Charles Francis Adams [*q.v.*], president of the Union Pacific Railway (1884–90), to design a large number of railroad stations in the West, Van Brunt sent Howe to Kansas City to open an office in 1885 and followed him soon after. Few architects of their training were then settled in the Middle West, and a large amount of work came to them. It included the railroad stations at Ogden, Utah; Sioux City, Iowa; Portland, Ore.; and Omaha, Nebr.; the store of the Emery, Bird, Thayer Dry Goods Company at Kansas City, large houses for the Armour and Griffiths families and for August R. Meyer, and other work largely residential and commercial. They were associated with McKim, Mead and White in the New York Life Insurance Building at Kansas City and, as the most important architectural firm west of Chicago, were commissioned to design the Electricity Building at the World's Columbian Exposition of 1893 at Chicago. Van Brunt had been one of the earliest members of the American Institute of Architects, and a fellow since 1864; he was secretary in 1861 and president in 1899. He declined to run for the office a second time because he was planning a long tour in Europe for study and rest, his first trip out of the United States. It signalled his practical retirement from active practice.

Van Brunt's architectural work is characteristic of the eclecticism of his time. He started with a strong bias towards Ruskin-inspired Gothic, but later worked in the popular Romanesque and in various types of classic as well; the work which seems best today, however, is characterized by a strong personal search for original and honest expression. His most important contribution was in his writings; many magazine articles on architectural subjects are distinguished for their keen analysis, and their graceful and persuasive style. Some of these were republished (with other material) in *Greek Lines and Other Architectural Essays* (1893). Van Brunt was also the translator of Viollet-le-Duc's *Entretiens sur l'Architecture* (2 vols., 1863–72) as *Discourses on Architecture* (1875). The courtliness, dignity, and gentleness which so characterized his manner are well expressed in his writing. His accomplishments are all the more remarkable in view of the physical disability against which he labored. He married Alice Sterritt Osborn at Salem, Mass., Oct. 6, 1869. He died in Milton, Mass., survived by his wife and their seven children.

[T. G. Bergen, *Geneal. of the Van Brunt Family* (1867); *Who's Who in America*, 1901–02, with an error in the mother's name; *Harvard Coll. . . . Class of 1854* (1894); Élie Brault, *Les Architectes par Leurs Oeuvres* (3 vols., 1892–93); *Proc. Thirty-seventh Ann. Convention Am. Inst. of Architects* (1904); G. C. Mitchell, *There Is No Limit: Architecture and Sculpture in Kansas City* (1934); *Am. Architect and Building News*, Apr. 11, 1903; obituaries in *N. Y. Tribune* and *Kansas City Jour.*, Apr. 9, 1903; information from Van Brunt's son, Courtlandt Van Brunt.]   T. F. H.

VAN BUREN, JOHN (Feb. 10, 1810–Oct. 13, 1866), lawyer, politician, was born in Kinderhook, N. Y., the son of Martin Van Buren [*q.v.*] and Hannah (Hoes) Van Buren. He was sent first to the Albany public schools, then to Albany Academy whence he went to Yale. In college he drank and gambled freely, studied little, worried the faculty and president of Yale, and cost his father unnecessary expense and sleepless nights. Upon graduation he read law with Benjamin F. Butler and later with Aaron Vanderpoel, whose niece Elizabeth he afterward married (June 22, 1841). In July 1831 he was admitted to the Albany bar, and one month later he sailed with his father to London to become an attaché of the American legation. His fine physique, ready wit and good humor, and aristocratic and gracious bearing made him a favorite at the English court. The Whig press of America dubbed him "Prince John." Before returning home he traveled on the Continent, and in 1838 he again visited England and Ireland.

His activities in politics were so like his father's that he soon won another title, "Young Fox." By 1834 he was a member of the "Albany regency." For a time he was a law examiner in Albany and a law partner of James McKnown (1837–45), later taking as a partner Hamilton W. Robinson. In 1845 he joined the radical wing of the New York Democracy and won the office of attorney general (1845). He prosecuted the anti-rent cases and after his resumption of private practice took part in the notorious Forrest divorce suit, in which he lost prestige. Although he was popular with the New York bar and powerful with juries, his political activities during the forties rather obscured his legal career (McAdam, *post,* I, 505).

Much of his time was consumed in lobbying in the state legislature. His power was felt in nearly every Democratic state convention from 1836 to 1848, and especially in campaigns for his father. He published a pamphlet, *The Syracuse Convention,* in 1847. He was influential in organizing the "Barnburners," and in behalf of them and the Free-soil groups he persuaded his father to accept the nomination for president at Buffalo in 1848. His zeal and oratory stirred the Free-soilers deeply. Some of their leaders wanted him for their standard bearer, but he chose to fight for his father, who had lost the Democratic presidential nomination to Polk at Baltimore (1844). John as a delegate to the convention led the enraged "Barnburners" in their withdrawal. He stumped the state, denouncing the Fugitive-slave Law and everywhere electrifying his audiences with his Free-soil evangelism. Had he grasped the full significance of the Free-soil movement he could have been one of the chief leaders of the forthcoming Republican party, but he was unhappy outside the Democracy and returned to it in 1849. He supported the compromise measures of 1850. In 1853 he threatened to denounce Pierce (R. F. Nichols, *The Democratic Machine, 1850–1854,* 1923, p. 212), but was kept quiet by Marcy and Tilden, and finally came out strongly for popular sovereignty in Kansas. He wanted a convention of states (1860) to arrange for guarantees to the slavery interests and to prevent war. He denounced Lincoln for calling for troops so soon after the firing on Fort Sumter. In many speeches he defended General McClellan, bitterly assailed the draft, the suspension of the writ of *habeas corpus,* and the use of colored troops. He supported Seymour for governor in 1862 and McClellan for president in 1864, and was himself defeated in his candidacy for the attorney generalship of the state in 1865. He threw his waning influence to Andrew Johnson (1866), but his failing health caused him to seek its improvement in England. He died of a kidney disease while on the *Scotia* en route to New York, leaving his only child, Anna, and was buried in Albany beside his wife, who had died in 1844.

[Van Buren MSS. and Marcy MSS. in Lib. of Cong.; the private collection of Blair MSS.; Van Buren letters in N. Y. State Lib., Albany; D. S. Alexander, *A Political History of the State of N. Y.,* vol. II (1906); D. T. Lynch, *An Epoch and a Man: Martin Van Buren and His Times* (1929); W. L. Mackenzie, *The Life and Times of Martin Van Buren* (1846); E. M. Shepard, *Martin Van Buren* (1888); H. D. A. Donovan, *The Barnburners* (1925); John Bigelow, *Retrospections of an Active Life,* vol. I (1909), pp. 86–90; David McAdam and others, *Hist. of the Bench and Bar of New York,* vol. I (1897); Harriet C. W. Van Buren Peckham, *Hist. of Cornelius Maessen Van Buren . . . and His Descendants* (1913); G. B. Vanderpoel, *Genealogy of the Vanderpoel Family* (1912); obituaries in *Evening Post* (N. Y.), Oct. 16, 19, 1866; *N. Y. Tribune,* Oct. 17, 20, 1866.]   W. E. S–h.

VAN BUREN, MARTIN (Dec. 5, 1782–July 24, 1862), eighth president of the United States, was born in Kinderhook, near Albany, N. Y., the third of five children of Abraham and Maria (Hoes) Van Buren, both of whom were of Dutch descent. Abraham was descended from Cornelis, who was the son of Maes of Buurmalsen and came to New Netherland in 1631 as a leaseholder of Van Rensselaer. Maria Hoes was the widow Van Alen and mother of two children when she married the bachelor Abraham. Martin's parents were frugal truck farmers and keepers of an inherited tavern who became respectable slave-owning citizens in the village. In the inadequate village schools the boy gained a fair knowledge of English and a smattering of Latin. After graduation at the age of fourteen, he became a clerk in the law office of Francis Silvester, a Federalist. He read little from law books, but devoured every Republican pamphlet, journal, or periodical that he could find. Obstinately, but good-naturedly, he refused from the beginning to adopt Silvester's Federalism. By 1800 the yellow-haired law clerk had won a local reputation for his clear thinking, clever presentation and summaries of his petty cases, extemporaneous debating, and stanch Republicanism. As a reward for his campaign for Jefferson (1800) he was sent as a delegate to the congressional caucus in Troy. In 1801 he entered as a clerk the almost clientless office in New York City of the young William Peter Van Ness [*q.v.*], a devotee of Aaron Burr.

Upon his return to Kinderhook (1803) he was licensed to practice law and became the partner of his half-brother, James I. Van Alen. He flung himself immediately into Republican politics as the champion of the Clinton-Livingston factions, in opposition to Burr, thereby annoying the Van Nesses. His income came from the pockets of Jeffersonian-Republican small landholders in whose cases in court he had often to oppose the eloquent Elisha Williams. By 1807 he was affluent enough to marry, on Feb. 21, the sweetheart

of his youth, his kinswoman Hannah Hoes. She bore him four sons: Abraham, John [*q.v.*], Martin, and Smith Thompson. Soon he moved to Hudson, where as the newly appointed surrogate (1808–13), he launched himself on an ambitious political career. Already his enemies had pronounced him a hypocrite, a heartless, selfish, intriguing politician. He was a manipulator in politics, but he was honest and generous in his private and public relations. In taverns as well as court rooms his ready wit, friendly smile, and cheerful disposition won voters and juries to his side. He was only five feet six and was slender but stood erect like a soldier. He dressed immaculately, as his preceptor Silvester had taught him. Rarely was he incensed at even his worst enemies. He could see no reason why political opponents could not be personal friends.

Until 1821 he was enmeshed in state politics. In his fight for state leadership he moved in a maze of political intrigue and bitterness, but always remained a partisan Republican. In 1807 he was admitted as counselor to practise before the state supreme court. In a race against Edward P. Livingston he was elected state senator in April 1812 on an anti-Bank platform. In August he was deeply chagrined at his failure to receive the appointment as attorney general of the state, which went to Thomas Addis Emmet, and at first blamed DeWitt Clinton. In November, in the legislative session to select presidential electors, he supported Clinton, as the nominee of the Republican caucus, though the rivalry of the two men was becoming intense. He helped to secure the election of Daniel D. Tompkins [*q.v.*] as vice-president in 1816 and annoyed Clinton that year by opposing certain details of the canal bill. The next year, however, he supported the canal project against the wishes of his group, defending his course by saying that he could not sacrifice a popular blessing to humiliate Clinton. Van Buren was soon chosen regent of the University of the State of New York (1815), a recognition of his importance. In 1816 he was re-elected senator (1816–20) and chosen attorney general of New York (1816–19). He then moved his family to Albany. His wife died in 1819. He never attempted to marry again until late in life when he was rejected by the spinster, Margaret Silvester, who was the daughter of his old preceptor. In the state Senate he was establishing himself as a leader. In 1817, however, Clinton was elected governor, and in 1819, gaining control of the Council of Appointment, he removed Van Buren from the attorney generalship. While bitterly attacking Clinton for cooperating with Federalists, Van Buren acted secretly to reëlect

Rufus King [*q.v.*] to the United States Senate (1820) and to gain Federalist aid in defeating Clinton. He asked for a state constitutional convention, which convened in 1821, largely because he opposed the arbitrary power of Chief Justice Ambrose Spencer [*q.v.*] and favored a reorganization of the judicial system. His chief work in the convention was in securing an agreement between extreme radicals and conservatives that could be accepted by all. As chairman of the committee on appointments, he advocated the decentralization of the power held by the old Council of Appointment, by the distribution of the appointing power among local authorities, the legislature, and the governor. He was unsuccessful in his opposition, probably for the sake of patronage, to the popular election of all judicial officers. (N. H. Carter and W. L. Stone, *Reports of the Proceedings and Debates of the Convention of 1821 Assembled for the Purpose of Amending the Constitution of New York*, 1821.)

Clinton had been reëlected governor in 1820, largely because of his canal policy, but the "Bucktails" won control of the legislature and in February 1821 elected Van Buren to the United States Senate. In August 1820 his brother-in-law, Moses I. Cantine, and Isaac J. Leake bought the *Albany Argus*. The paper was given the contract for the state printing. In 1823, when Edwin Croswell [*q.v.*] became editor, Van Buren wrote that without a paper edited by "a sound, practicable and above all discreet republican . . . we may hang our harps on the willows" (quoted in Mackenzie, *post*, p. 190). Croswell made the *Argus* a highly influential organ. Van Buren was chief of a group of leaders, soon nicknamed the "Albany regency," which included William L. Marcy, Azariah C. Flagg, Benjamin F. Butler (1795–1858), Edwin Croswell, Michael Hoffman, and later Silas Wright and John A. Dix [*qq.v.*]. "They were formidable in solidarity," and achieved extraordinary success (Fox, *post*, pp. 281–86). Van Buren's primacy among them was not owing merely to his amiability and caution, but to his shrewd judgment of measures and men, to his power of analysis and exposition. His political philosophy was practical and sincere. Reckless opposition to public sentiment seemed to him inconsistent with good statesmanship, and he thought that those who dispensed the public bounty would, to a greater or less degree, influence and control the public mind. However, in attacking Clinton he said that a good administration would rally around "the governmental standard the good the virtuous and the capable" (Lynch, p. 175), and he and the other members of the "regency" faithfully performed the duties of the important offices they obtained.

As United States senator he was still preoccupied with factional fights from which he hoped to emerge as the leader of a unified national party. Not until 1823 did he avow his intention openly to support William H. Crawford for president, hoping that by delay he could avoid party strife in New York and give his state a chance finally to choose between opposing candidates. In Washington he was considered the leader of the Crawford faction and he was active in the last and well-known congressional caucus, called to nominate his candidate (*Daily National Intelligencer*, Feb. 16, 1824). He considered Jackson unpromising and tried to persuade either Clay or Gallatin to run with Crawford. In New York in 1824, Clinton, who was a Jacksonian, was again elected governor, routing the "regency" (C. H. Rammelkamp, "The Campaign of 1824 in New York," *Annual Report of the American Historical Association . . . 1904*, 1905, pp. 175–201). Van Buren tried to produce a deadlock in the House of Representatives while it was voting for presidential candidates, in order that the Clay-Adams men would have to appeal to New York for a decision, but the prayerful Stephen Van Rensselaer [*q.v.*] blocked that plan by voting for Adams. Van Buren's early bitterness towards Adams was probably caused by the latter's offer of the ministerial post in London to Clinton. In the Senate he voted yea on the tariff bills of 1824 and 1828, guided partisan opposition, served on the finance committee and as chairman of the judiciary committee. He opposed the sending of envoys to the Panama conference, offering the explanation that he was opposed to all forms of international alliances. In his speeches on internal improvements (*Register of Debates in Congress*, vol. II, 1826, 19 Cong., 1 Sess., cols. 20–21, 619, 717–18), he laid down a policy of opposition to which he steadfastly adhered. Congress, he said, had no constitutional right to construct commercial roads and canals within states. His practical objections to the program of his political rivals were strengthened by the consideration that most of the projects would deflect trade from the Erie Canal and New York. So adept was he in politics that he was reëlected senator (1827) with the aid of Clinton's friends. By this time, however, he was turning to Jackson, and took the liberty of telling Jackson to refrain from answering defamatory pamphlets. He read such pamphlets and planned the answers, advising editors here and there what to say about campaign issues. After pronouncing a touching eulogium upon Clinton, who died in 1828, he ran for governor of New York in order that a "Bucktail" state administration would be in control after he should become Jackson's secretary of state. He resigned the governorship to enter the cabinet after making to the legislature several recommendations, one of which—the enactment of a safety-fund banking law, as suggested by Joshua Forman [*q.v.*]—was adopted. He returned to Washington society, of which he was enamoured, and became at once the most influential member of the Jackson cabinet.

As secretary of state he favored the introduction of his New York political spoils system into the federal administration. Approached on the subject, he replied: "We give no reasons for our removals" (Lynch, p. 325). Being a widower, he pleased the President by his friendly course towards Peggy Eaton (see sketch of Margaret O'Neale). He helped Jackson write his famous toast, "Our Federal Union—It must be preserved" (*Autobiography*, p. 414). So completely did he win the President's confidence that Jackson said that Van Buren was "one of the most frank men" he had known, "a *true man* with no guile" (*Jackson Correspondence*, IV, 260). Before the end of 1830 Jackson proposed to Van Buren that they run on the same ticket, he to resign after a year and leave Van Buren to carry on his policies (*Autobiography*, pp. 506–07). This Van Buren refused to do and persuaded the President that it was best for him to resign as secretary of state so that the cabinet could be reorganized. His resignation (Apr. 11, 1831) brought about that of other members and enabled Jackson to eliminate Calhoun's supporters, while his prompt appointment as minister to Great Britain, ostensibly taking him out of politics, showed that he was still in Jackson's confidence (*Ibid.*, pp. 403–08; Bassett, *Life of Jackson*, II, 522–25, 532). Although Van Buren seems deliberately to have kept himself ignorant of the Jackson-Calhoun quarrel (Bassett, II, 514–15), he was accused of causing it, and had heaped upon his head such opprobrious terms as "Flying Dutchman," "Red Fox of Kinderhook," and "Little Magician."

His unusual tact stood him in good stead as secretary of state. He maneuvered Jackson into appointing young energetic ministers, soon established order and confidence in his department, and quieted the fears of the foreign diplomatic corps, who expected trouble with the frontier President. He settled the old dispute over the West Indian trade between Great Britain and the United States, secured an agreement with France by which that country ultimately and reluctantly paid claims for compensation for injuries inflicted upon American commerce during the Napoleonic wars, negotiated a treaty with Turkey providing for free access to the Black Sea and a most favored nations clause, and tried to buy Texas from Mexico, arguing that it was a necessity for the development of the Mississippi Valley and that Mexico would finally lose it through revolution if she did not sell to the United States. Jackson's Maysville Road veto was largely the work of Van Buren, who drafted the message (*Autobiography*, pp. 315–22; Bassett, *Life of Jackson*, II, pp. 484–96), and he supported Jackson in his other important domestic policies. In August 1831 he was on his way to London as minister to Great Britain, but in January 1832 his appointment was rejected by the deciding vote of Vice-President Calhoun. He then took his son John with him to travel in France and in Holland.

His return, purposely timed to follow his nomination for vice-president in May 1832, was celebrated extensively in New York City. His graciousness, his courtesy toward even his bitterest foes, and his charming conversation made him a favored guest at such celebrations as the New York Democrats could provide. In the course of the presidential campaign he aided Jackson in defeating a bill to recharter the Bank of the United States and opposed the theories of nullification, as he did internal improvements at national expense, but he intentionally remained vague on the tariff. Contrary to some opinions, he did not disagree with Jackson over the removal of the government's deposits in the Bank, but he did hesitate about the time of their removal (*Jackson Correspondence*, V, 179–82, 183–84). When Jackson appealed to him to have the New York Assembly issue a public defense of his message on nullification, Van Buren wrote the report of the joint committee, endeavoring to show the soundness of the party on the state-rights question, while supporting the President against the nullifiers (*Documents of the Senate of . . . New York . . . 1833*, 1833, no. 34; *Autobiography*, pp. 548–53; *Jackson Correspondence*, IV, 504–08).

Elected vice-president in 1832 as Jackson's running mate, he proved to be an able and fair presiding officer of the Senate. Not once did he lose the confidence of Jackson. It has been remarked that toward his chief he had a "perfect bedside manner" (J. F. Jameson, Preface to *Jackson Correspondence*, Vol. IV, p. v). Accepted by his party as Jackson's protégé, he was nominated for the presidency by a convention held in Baltimore in May 1835, Richard M. Johnson [*q.v.*] being nominated for vice-president.

His platform was enunciated in the letters he wrote during the campaign, especially in the able letter of Aug. 8, 1836, to Sherrod Williams (*Niles' Weekly Register,* Sept. 10, 1836, pp. 26–30). It was clear that he opposed the distribution of the surplus in the treasury and the improvement of rivers above ports of entry, and that he would not recharter the Bank under any consideration. He had supported Tallmadge's resolution on the Missouri Compromise calling for the non-extension of slavery and had signed a call for a meeting in Albany to protest against the extension of slavery (1820), but in 1831 he had announced himself as a stanch advocate of the right of slave-owning states to control slavery within their respective boundaries. He had advised Governor Marcy in 1835 to condemn the activities of the Garrison abolitionists (message of Jan. 5, 1836), and in 1836, in the Senate, he had given a casting vote in favor of the bill barring abolitionist propaganda from the mails (*Register of Debates,* 24 Cong., 1 Sess., Col. 1675; see also T. H. Benton, *Thirty Years' View,* I, 587–88).

In the election of 1836 there were Democratic defections in the South to Hugh L. White [*q.v.*] and to Willie P. Mangum [*q.v.*], who received the vote of South Carolina; and votes were cast for two Whig candidates, William Henry Harrison and Daniel Webster [*qq.v.*]; but Van Buren had a large electoral majority over the field. As president, he filled the vacancy in the Department of War by appointing Joel R. Poinsett [*q.v.*], and retained all the other members of Jackson's cabinet. In his optimistic inaugural address (Richardson, *post,* III, 313–20), which concluded with a tribute to his predecessor, he urged the preservation of American democracy as a world experiment. His desire to hold together the northern and southern wings of his party was manifested in his avowed opposition to the abolition of slavery in the District of Columbia against the wishes of the slave states, and to any interference with slavery in the states where it existed. Throughout his administration he was plagued by abolitionist agitators and those who would silence them, but his chief problems were economic. The panic of 1837 soon burst upon him. In spite of the fury of clamor against it, he held steadfastly to Jackson's specie circular, and in his message to the special session of Congress (Sept. 4, 1837, Richardson, III, 324–46) he properly said that the panic was the result of over-action in business and over-expansion of credit. Adamant in his determination to divorce the "money power" from the federal government, and distrustful of the "pet banks"

as well as of a central institution, he urged that an independent treasury be established. His recommendations that the installment of the surplus scheduled for distribution to the states in October be withheld, and that treasury notes be temporarily issued to meet the pressing needs of the government, were adopted, but the first independent treasury bill failed of passage. Not until 1840 was Van Buren able to secure the necessary legislation, with some compromise in regard to specie payments, and this was repealed by the Whigs in 1841. The independent treasury was not effectually established until 1846. It has generally been regarded as distinctly creditable to Van Buren's foresight, but at the time of his official advocacy of it he alienated conservative, or bank, Democrats, especially in New York and Virginia, while he was denounced by the Whigs for his "heartlessness" in not undertaking measures of relief and particularly for his failure to resort to paper money. He followed his lifelong policy of refusing to answer villifiers, believing always that "the sober second thought of the people" would uphold him.

Though he was embarrassed by American sympathy with the Canadian rebellion of 1837, and the seizure by Canadian authorities in American waters of the insurgent vessel *Caroline,* his successful effort to preserve peace between Great Britain and the United States was patriotic and commendable, notwithstanding the accusations of the opposing factions that his officials were "the tools of Victoria." His wise policy of conciliation, however, cost him political support along the northern border, as it did also in Maine, in connection with the continued controversy over the northeastern boundary. He refused to annex independent Texas because he wanted no war with Mexico and at heart was opposed to the further extension of slavery. Throughout his administration he and his able cabinet were plagued with the terrible depression, to which crop failures contributed. Calhoun's cooperation, Blair's influential *Globe,* and Jackson's fidelity could not overcome such obstacles. As president, Van Buren had been far more than a wily politician, but perhaps no amount of courage, patriotism, and ability would have availed to carry through an effective program or to gain popular approval in such troublous times. "Little Van" was a "used up man" in the "hard-cider" campaign of 1840. The Whigs, evading issues and appealing to emotions, triumphantly elected William Henry Harrison [*q.v.*] over the decorous President, with an electoral vote of 234 to 60, and a popular plurality of nearly 150,000. Van Buren even lost New York.

He greeted Whigs and Democrats alike at the White House and shattered precedent by calling on President-elect Harrison at Gadsby's. After the inauguration, he retired to the old William Van Ness farm at Kinderhook which he had bought; he now repaired it extensively and called it "Lindenwald." He presently found occasion to deny a statement that he would not again run for the presidency, but he also informed the public that he would take no step to secure another nomination. He made a tour of the West and Southwest, stopping at "Ashland" to see Clay, and at "The Hermitage" to pay his respects to Jackson (1842). Many Democrats throughout the North and West rallied to his support. He answered quite frankly, against the advice of informed friends, many inquiries as to his views on political issues. In the well-known "Hammet letter" (Washington *Globe,* Apr. 27, 1844), published on the same day as Clay's "Raleigh letter," he courageously said that the annexation of Texas would mean war with Mexico and that he saw no need for immediate action, but that he would yield to the popular decision at the polls. This stand probably lost him the Democratic nomination (McCormac, *Polk,* pp. 224–30). His opponents published a year-old letter of Jackson favoring annexation, and succeeded in getting the two-thirds rule adopted by the Democratic convention at Baltimore (1844). Van Buren withdrew his name for the sake of party harmony and James K. Polk [*q.v.*] was nominated. His principles, except on annexation, were adopted in the platform. His followers expected recognition, but President Polk soon let it be known that they were not in favor. He offered Van Buren the London mission purposely to exile him, but Van Buren could not be shelved so easily.

The discontent engendered by his defeat at Baltimore, accentuated by bitter factional strife within the party in New York, turned half the Democrats of the state against the administration. The introduction of the Wilmot Proviso in 1846 provided a rallying point for this discontent and the latent anti-slavery feeling that had been steadily increasing. The next year the "Barnburners" seceded from the state convention, and, meeting at Herkimer, adopted a platform, drafted by Van Buren's son John [*q.v.*], opposing the extension of slavery to the territories to be acquired from Mexico. Van Buren himself drew up a similar address, which, after revision by his son and Samuel J. Tilden, was issued in February 1848 as the address of "Barnburner" Democrats in the legislature. Both "Barnburners" and "Hunkers" sent delegates to the National Democratic Convention of 1848, but the former at length withdrew. At a convention at Utica in June they nominated Van Buren for the presidency, paving the way for a general convention later. At Buffalo, in August, a gathering of anti-slavery men from all parties, organized the Free-soil party, on a platform of opposition to the extension of slavery into the territories. Van Buren, already nominated by the best organized group in the convention, was chosen to head the ticket. He had become convinced, perhaps at the convention of 1844, that northern Democrats had yielded to the "slavocracy" long enough, but accepted the nomination reluctantly, preferring to remain a farmer and to write his memoirs. The Free-soilers helped to defeat Cass by splitting the ticket. For a while Van Buren was popular with the New York Free-soilers, but he alienated them when he supported the compromise measures of 1850. He returned to the Democratic fold in 1852, assured by the elder Blair that he could trust Pierce, but he soon found that his trust was misplaced. He was indignant at the "half baked politicians" who repealed the Missouri Compromise (1854). He hoped the Union would be saved by the election of Buchanan, who promised a peaceful settlement of the Kansas question. Shocked deeply by the Civil War, he found his only solace in his confidence in Abraham Lincoln and refused to be associated with Buchanan, whom he now despised, in holding an ex-president's meeting (suggested by Franklin Pierce) to decide on some course relative to the cause of the Union. After months of suffering with asthma, he died in the summer, despondent over the situation of the Union armies. Funeral services were held in the Dutch Reformed Church of which he had been a faithful member. He left a manuscript, published by his sons under the title, *Inquiry into the Origin and Course of Political Parties in the United States* (1867). His uncompleted autobiography was edited by J. C. Fitzpatrick and published as "The Autobiography of Martin Van Buren" (*Annual Report of the American Historical Association for the Year 1918,* Vol. II, 1920).

[Elizabeth H. West, *Calendar of the Papers of Martin Van Buren* (1910), is an excellent guide to the voluminous Van Buren MSS. in the lib. of Cong., acquired to the time of its compilation; there is valuable material about him in that repository in the papers of various persons who were associated with him; and there is a collection of his letters in the N. Y. State Lib., at Albany. Valuable printed collections are C. Z. Lincoln, *State of N. Y. Messages from the Governors* (1909), vol. III, pp. 230–59; J. D. Richardson, *A Compilation of the Messages and Papers of the Presidents,* vol. III (1896); William McDonald, "The Jackson and Van Buren Papers," in *Proc. Am. Antiquarian Soc.,* vol. XVIII (1908) ; Van Buren—Bancroft correspondence, in *Mass. Hist. Soc. Proc.*, vol. XLII (1909) ; J. S. Bassett, ed., *Correspondence of Andrew Jackson* (6 vols., 1926–33). Among biographies may be cited W. M. Holland, *The Life and Political Opinions of Martin Van Buren* (1835) ; W. L. Mackenzie, *The Life and Times of Martin Van Buren* (1846), a bitter attack but contains letters ; W. A. Butler, *Martin Van Buren: Lawyer, Statesman and Man* (1862) ; George Bancroft, *Martin Van Buren to the End of His Public Career* (1889), to 1841, written for the campaign of 1844 ; E. M. Shepard, *Martin Van Buren* (1888) ; D. T. Lynch, *An Epoch and a Man: Martin Van Buren* (1929). For particular phases see J. S. Bassett, "Martin Van Buren," in S. F. Bemis, ed., *The American Secretaries of State and Their Diplomacy*, vol. IV (1928) ; J. D. Hammond, *The History of Political Parties in the State of N. Y.* (2 vols., 1842) ; D. S. Alexander, *A Political History of the State of N. Y.*, vols. I, II (1906) ; D. R. Fox, *The Decline of Aristocracy in the Politics of N. Y.* (1919) ; William Trimble, "Diverging Tendencies in N. Y. Democracy in the Period of the Locofocos," in *Am. Hist. Rev.*, Apr. 1919 ; H. D. A. Donovan, *The Barnburners* (1925) ; T. H. Benton, *Thirty Years' View* (2 vols., 1856) ; R. H. Gillet, *The Life and Times of Silas Wright* (2 vols., 1874) ; J. S. Bassett, *The Life of Andrew Jackson* (1911) ; E. I. McCormac, *James K. Polk* (1922) ; C. G. Bowers, *The Party Battles of the Jackson Period* (1922) ; R. C. McGrane, *The Panic of 1837* (1924) ; W. E. Smith, *The Francis Preston Blair Family in Politics* (2 vols., 1933) ; F. J. Turner, *The United States: 1830–1850* (1935). For genealogy and local materials, see Harriet C. W. Van Buren Peckham, *History of Cornelis Maessen Van Buren . . . and His Descendants* (1913) ; E. A. Collier, *A History of Old Kinderhook* (1914). For obituaries see *Evening Post* (N. Y.), July 24, 1862 ; *N. Y. Times, N. Y. Tribune*, July 25, 1862.]   W. E. S—h.

VAN BUREN, WILLIAM HOLME (Apr. 4, 1819–Mar. 25, 1883), physician, surgeon, and teacher of medicine and surgery, was born at Philadelphia, Pa., the son of Abraham Van Beuren, a merchant of Philadelphia, and his second wife, Sarah Holme. He dropped the "e" from the first syllable of his name, although his father used the longer form. His grandfather, Abraham Van Beuren, and his great-grandfather, John Van Beuren, were both physicians, and his great-great-grandfather was Johannes Van Beuren [*q.v.*]. He entered Yale College as a sophomore in the class of 1838, but was required to leave during his junior year because of a student prank. He subsequently entered the medical school of the University of Pennsylvania, from which he was graduated with the degree of M.D. in 1840. Yale later recognized his work by giving him honorary degrees. Immediately after his graduation he entered the army as an assistant surgeon, ranking first in the competitive examination which gave him admission, and served in Florida and on the Canadian frontier. He resigned from the army in 1845, and settled in New York City, where he soon built up a large practice, and became a member of the surgical staff of Bellevue Hospital. From 1851 to 1852 he was professor of genito-urinary organs and venereal diseases in the Medical Department of the Uni-

versity of the City of New York. From 1852 to 1866 he was professor of anatomy. He was appointed professor of surgery in Bellevue Hospital Medical College in 1866 and retained this position until his death. This hospital was originally the medical department of the New York City almshouse, of which Johannes Van Beuren, was the first director. He was one of the visiting surgeons of the New York Hospital from 1852 to 1865, afterwards one of its consulting surgeons, and in 1876 was made president of its medical board. He was also for many years on the consulting staff of the Bellevue, Women's, Presbyterian, and other hospitals. In 1859 he was elected vice-president of the New York Academy of Medicine.

During the Civil War he was a member of the standing Executive Committee of the United States Sanitary Commission, which received and distributed during the war $5,000,000 in money and $15,000,000 in supplies. He declined an appointment as surgeon-general of the United States Army. At the close of the war he suffered a serious illness from which he finally recovered. He traveled for some time in Europe, and upon his return gave up most of his visiting practice and devoted himself to consultations, literary work, and to the preparation of his lectures. In collaboration with C. E. Isaacs, he translated Bernard and Huette's *Illustrated Manual of Operative Surgery and Surgical Anatomy* (1852) and C. B. Morel's *Compendium of Human Histology* (1861). He also published *Contributions to Practical Surgery* (1865), *Lectures Upon Diseases of the Rectum* (1870), which went through many editions, and, with E. L. Keyes, published *A Practical Treatise on the Surgical Diseases of the Genito-Urinary Organs, Including Syphilis* (1874). A bibliography of his works is included in the *Index-Catalogue of the Library of the Surgeon-General's Office, United States Army*, volume XV (1894). He was married on Nov. 8, 1842, to Louisa Dunmore Mott, eldest daughter of the well-known surgeon, Valentine Mott [*q.v.*]. They had three children, of whom two daughters survived him.

[H. A. Kelly, W. L. Burrage, *Am. Medic. Biogs.* (1920) ; William Jones, "The Van Beuren Family of New York and New Jersey," *N. Y. Geneal. and Biog. Record*, Jan. 1932 ; a memorial address by E. L. Keyes, printed in the *N. Y. Medic. Jour.*, Apr. 14, 1883 ; R. J. Carlisle, *An Account of Bellevue Hospital* (1893) ; *Obit. Records of Grads. of Yale Univ., 1880–90* (1890) ; *N. Y. Times, N. Y. Evening Post*, Mar. 26, 1883.]   W. J.

VANCE, AP MORGAN (May 24, 1854–Dec. 9, 1915), orthopedic surgeon, was born in Nashville, Tenn., the son of Morgan Brown and Susan Preston (Thompson) Vance. He attended rural schools in Tennessee and the public schools and Moss Academy at New Albany, Ind., to which place the family moved in 1868. Entering the medical department of the University of Louisville in 1876, he was graduated in 1878. Through association with Dr. David W. Yandell [q.v.], one of the foremost surgeons of the city, he was influenced to undertake a thorough study of anatomy and a career in surgery. After graduation he obtained a resident internship in the Hospital for Ruptured and Crippled Children in New York City. Having a natural mechanical bent, he devised and improved apparatus for crippled limbs and diseased spines, which with little change are in current use; this work he continued throughout his career.

Returning to Louisville in 1881, he elected to confine his practice to surgery and became the first exclusive practitioner of this specialty in Kentucky. This departure from established custom caused criticism, which, however, soon died out. While his chief interest was in orthopedic surgery, this branch was too limited a specialty for the Louisville of that period, and he accepted whatever surgery came his way. For years he had the largest operating practice in Louisville. His greatest contribution to surgery was his improvement of the operation of osteotomy for the correction of deformity of long bones of the extremities. He advocated and perfected a bloodless subcutaneous operation by means of a small chisel inserted through a minute incision of the skin ("Femoral Osteotomy," *New York Medical Journal,* Dec. 1, 1888). He also improved the procedure of tenotomy for the treatment of congenital clubfoot. The ingenuity and manual dexterity that enabled him to produce orthopedic apparatus made him an outstanding surgical technician. His skill, together with accurate judgment of indications for operation, brought unusual success to his surgical practice. He adopted asepsis from its inception and was an early advocate of operative treatment for appendicitis. Though frequently offered teaching positions, he refused them in order to devote his time to clinical practice. He did, however, exert a powerful influence upon the surgical thought of the city through the internes of the hospital with which he was connected. He was the medical representative upon the commission which built the Louisville City Hospital and was responsible for its plans and scope; he was the prime mover in the organization and construction of the Children's Free Hospital; and served them both as attending surgeon, as he did, also, the hospital of SS. Mary and Elizabeth. For

thirty-five years he was surgeon to the Masonic Widows and Orphans Home.

He was active in every movement which involved the local profession and a constant attendant upon the meetings of the county and state societies, both of which he served as president. He was a member of the Southern Surgical and Gynecological Association, the American Association of Gynecology and Obstetrics, and the American Orthopedic Association, and was a fellow of the American College of Surgeons. His writings were confined to journal articles, mainly on the subject of orthopedic surgery. An invalidism from nephritis limited his activities for two years before his death, which occurred at his home in Louisville. His memory is kept alive by a ward bearing his name, endowed by popular subscription, in the Children's Free Hospital, for which he had done so much in his lifetime. He was married in 1885 to Mary Josephine Huntoon of Louisville, daughter of Dr. B. B. Huntoon, superintendent of the Kentucky Institute for the Blind; they had eight children.

[*Am. Jour. of Obstetrics,* Mar. 1917; *Jour. Am. Medic. Asso.,* Dec. 18, 1915; *Ky. Medic. Jour.,* Apr. 1, 1916; *Courier-Journal* (Louisville), Dec. 10, 1915; *Evening Post* (Louisville), Dec. 9, 1915; H. A. Kelly and W. L. Burrage, *Am. Medic. Biogs.* (1920).]

J. M. P—n.

VANCE, ZEBULON BAIRD (May 13, 1830–Apr. 14, 1894), governor of North Carolina, senator, son of David Vance, a farmer and country merchant, and Mira Margaret Baird, was born in Buncombe County, N. C. After attending the neighborhood schools, he went to Washington College, Tenn. (1843–44), but withdrew upon the death of his father, who left a widow and eight children. Later, he studied law at the University of North Carolina (1851–52). He received his county-court license in 1852, settled at Asheville, and was immediately elected county solicitor. In 1853 he was admitted to practice in the superior court. He was never a close student of the law and such success as he won at the bar was as an advocate. With the crude, unlettered farmers of his mountain circuit from whom the jurors were drawn, ready wit, broad humor, quick repartee, and boisterous eloquence were indispensable to success, and in the use of these weapons Vance was unsurpassed.

Politics, not the law, was his major interest. Having been reared in "devotion to the Federal Union" (application for pardon, June 3, 1865), he began his political career as a Henry Clay Whig. Upon the dissolution of the Whig party, he declined to follow some of his fellow Whigs into the Democratic party, which he believed to be saturated with a "bitter spirit of disunion," and aligned himself with the newly organized American party. He served one term (1854) in the North Carolina House of Commons. Elected to the 35th and 36th congresses, he served from Dec. 7, 1858, to Mar. 3, 1861. His congressional career was characterized by support of Union measures and opposition to the disunion sentiment then arising in the South. He was elected to the 37th Congress but was prevented from taking his seat by the secession of North Carolina.

In the presidential election of 1860, Vance supported the Bell and Everett ticket. He came out of the campaign with a reputation as a masterly stump speaker. Though upholding the constitutional right of secession, before April 1861 he opposed the exercise of the right for any cause then existing but favored calling a state convention as a means of "demanding terms of the Northern people" and of making "our voices heard among the Southern states whose course is rapidly inoculating the people with dogmas which we cannot approve" (letter of Jan. 9, 1861, in *Raleigh Register,* Jan. 16, 1861). The convention was defeated by popular vote but Vance continued his campaign against secession until Lincoln's call for troops. Thereupon he promptly reversed his position and urged North Carolina to support the other Southern states. On May 20, a state convention, called by the legislature, adopted an ordinance of secession. In the meantime, Vance had organized at Asheville (May 4) a company of "Rough and Ready Guards" of which he was elected captain. During the summer of 1861 he was on active duty with his company along the North Carolina coast. In August, he was elected colonel of the 26th North Carolina Regiment and led it with conspicuous gallantry in the New Bern campaign and in the Seven Days' battle near Richmond.

In the state election of 1862, the Confederate administration, which had become unpopular in North Carolina, furnished the chief issues. For governor, the Confederate party, as the Democrats then called themselves, nominated William Johnston, an "original secessionist"; the Conservatives, composed chiefly of old-line Union Whigs, led by W. W. Holden [*q.v.*], editor of the *North Carolina Standard* and a caustic critic of the Davis administration, selected Vance. Accepting the nomination, Vance pledged himself to "the prosecution of the war at all hazards and to the utmost extremity" (letter of acceptance, June 16, 1862, Dowd, *post,* p. 67). Despite this positive statement, the *Raleigh Register,* organ of the Confederate party, denounced his action as disloyal, dubbed him "the Yankee candidate,"

and warned the people that the North would accept his election as "an indisputable sign that the Union sentiment is in the ascendancy in the heart of the Southern Confederacy" (quoted in S. A. Ashe, *History of North Carolina,* II, 1925, p. 738). He won by an unprecedented majority, was inaugurated Sept. 8, and in his inaugural address committed his administration to a vigorous war policy. Unfortunately the Richmond government chose to accept the Confederate party's misrepresentation of Vance's position and thus laid the basis for most of the controversies it had with him during his two administrations.

In his efforts to keep the North Carolina regiments recruited to their full strength, to equip and provision them, and to sustain the morale of the civilian population, Vance was handicapped by the critical, if not hostile, attitude of the Confederate administration. Its officials charged him with deliberately obstructing the enforcement of the conscription acts. Vance certainly thought them "harsh and odious," and probably unconstitutional, and insisted that it was for the courts, not the conscription officers, to determine that question. He refused to permit the conscription of state officials and demanded that military officers respect the writ of *habeas corpus* when issued by a proper court. Afterwards he made it his "proudest boast" that during his administration no man in North Carolina was denied the privilege of the great writ, the right of trial by jury, or the equal protection of the law. He tried in vain to explain to President Davis that his policy was designed to mitigate as far as possible the severities of the law that it might be enforced among an "unwilling people" (Dowd, p. 92). Though critical of their administration of the law, Vance gave the conscription officers his full support in every effort to enforce it that he thought legal. In 1864 he wrote to the President that its enforcement in the state had been "ruthless and unrelenting" (*Ibid.,* pp. 91–93), and the fact that 18,585 North Carolina conscripts were enrolled in the Confederate armies by September 1864 seems to justify his statement (Ashe, *History of North Carolina,* II, 776).

By 1863 the North Carolina mountains were filled with evaders of conscription and soldiers from practically every Confederate state. To the Confederate authorities these men were "deserters" and deserved no consideration; to Vance, they were "absentees" who should be "persuaded" to return to their duty. Accordingly, in January by proclamation he offered a pardon to all North Carolina soldiers who should return to their regiments by a stated date. His proclamation, reported a colonel, "has brought in a great many stragglers, deserters, or other absentees that never would have otherwise come in" (*Ibid.*, II, 807). Vance himself wrote in a private letter: "Deserters are pouring thro' [Raleigh] in hundreds, really, to their colors" (To E. J. Hale, Oct. 26, 1863, Hale Papers).

To supplement the inadequate resources of the state, Vance procured from the legislature of 1862–63 an appropriation of $2,324,000 for the purchase of cotton and naval stores to be exchanged for supplies abroad, sent agents to England to make purchases, and organized a fleet of swift steamers to run the blockade into the port of Wilmington. They were distributed chiefly to North Carolina soldiers and civilians, but "large quantities were [also] turned over to the Confederate Government for the troops for other states." In a single shipment in 1863, for instance, Vance sent 14,000 uniforms to Longstreet's army in Tennessee (Vance, *The Last Days of the War in North Carolina,* 1885, pp. 28–29. For the best account of these operations see D. H. Hill, *North Carolina in the War Between the States,* 1926, vol. I, ch. x). The Confederate government disapproved of Vance's blockade-running operations and offered "downright opposition" to them (Vance to Seddon, Jan. 7, 1864, in Dowd, *post,* pp. 89–90). Nevertheless, these operations not only supplied the soldiers but also caught the imagination of the people and greatly strengthened their morale.

By 1863, Holden had become convinced that the struggle for Southern independence was hopeless and inaugurated a campaign for peace and the restoration of the Union. At first he advocated peace through negotiations by the Confederate government with the United States government, but failing to move President Davis, he shifted his position to a demand for peace by separate state action. The movement received widespread support and Holden counted on its popularity to force Vance to take the leadership. But Vance proved unexpectedly independent, declared his inflexible opposition to the scheme, and on it broke with Holden. Thereupon Holden announced his candidacy for governor in 1864. The issue, he declared, was simply peace or war. Accepting the issue as thus defined, Vance threw himself into the campaign with all his vigor. Hitherto Holden's pen had been the most effective political weapon in the state; it was now matched by one which proved even more powerful—the oratory of Vance. Vance was elected by an overwhelming majority, and thus held the great mass of North Carolinians to the support of a cause which most of them felt to be contrary to their real interests. In 1865, certain Confederate congressmen and senators, unable to persuade President Davis to open peace negotiations with the United States government, agreed upon a plan of peace by separate state action and selected North Carolina to lead the way. At their request, William A. Graham [*q.v.*] laid their plan before Vance, but Vance flatly refused to have anything to do with it. If other states were whipped, he said, let them say so; as for himself, he declined to have his state "lead the roll of infamy" (Vance to Mrs. Spencer, Apr. 27, 1866, in Cornelia P. Spencer Papers).

When Sherman approached Raleigh in April 1865, Vance attempted to negotiate with him with a view to procuring his recognition of the state government. Failing, and being erroneously informed that Sherman intended to arrest him as a political prisoner, Vance left Raleigh, Apr. 12, for Charlotte to consult with President Davis as to his future course. After an unsatisfactory conference, he determined to proceed without further regard for the Confederate authorities (Dowd, p. 486). Accordingly, on May 2 at Greensboro, he surrendered to General Schofield, who directed him to join his family at Statesville and there await further orders. Arrested by order of President Johnson on his thirty-fifth birthday, he was sent to Washington, and imprisoned in the Old Capitol Prison. He was held there until July 6, when he was released on parole. No reason was ever officially assigned for his arrest or his release.

Returning to North Carolina, Vance formed a law partnership in Charlotte. On June 3, 1865, while in prison, in compliance with the President's amnesty proclamation of May 29, he filed his application for a pardon, which was finally granted Mar. 11, 1867. Again free to enter politics, he was elected in 1870 to the United States Senate, but after two years of vain effort to have his disabilities under the Fourteenth Amendment removed, he surrendered his certificate of election to the legislature on Jan. 20, 1872. Soon thereafter Congress removed his disabilities. At the next session of the legislature (1872–73), he was the Democratic nominee for the Senate but was defeated by another Democrat through a combination of bolting Democrats and the Republican members.

In 1876 the Democrats girded themselves to overthrow the Republican régime and undo the work of Reconstruction, and selected Vance as their candidate for governor. The Republicans nominated Judge Thomas Settle (1831–1888), who challenged Vance to a joint debate. In Settle, Vance found the ablest opponent he had ever met on the stump; but in all that makes up a great popular orator Vance was much his superior. He was elected and inaugurated Jan. 1, 1877. His administration was distinguished by a revival of railroad enterprises; the stimulus it gave to agriculture and industry; the enlargement and improvement of public schools and charitable institutions for both races; the repudiation of the fraudulent Reconstruction state bonds and the adjustment of the state's legal debt on a basis acceptable to its creditors. It marked the beginning of a new era in North Carolina.

Vance served only two of the four years of his term. In 1879 he was again elected to the United States Senate and took his seat on Mar. 18. Re-elected in 1885 and in 1891, he served in the Senate until his death. His senatorial career added both to his fame and to his hold on his constituents. He was a prodigious worker, a diligent student of public problems, and an able debater. An important function of Southern senators in those years was to serve as mediators between the victorious North and the defeated South. In this work few senators were so effective as Vance. His colleagues, with whom he was very popular, soon learned that while devoted to the interests of the South, he nursed no bitterness toward the North. To the North, he was a defender and interpreter of, but never an apologist for, the South; upon the South, he urged the duty of genuine acceptance of the verdict of the war and unfeigned loyalty to the restored Union.

It was Vance's misfortune throughout most of his senatorial career to be cast in the rôle of a minority senator, whether the Republicans or the Democrats were in power. He was a tariff-for-revenue man and for many years was the minority leader on the finance committee. Upon him, in 1890, fell the chief burden of opposition in the Senate to the McKinley Tariff Bill. He was a determined opponent of the internal revenue system, not only because it adversely affected the whiskey and tobacco industries of his state but also because it was notoriously a source of frauds and political corruption. During Cleveland's two administrations, he broke with the President on civil service reform and the money question. He thought the civil service act unconstitutional and as an ardent party man was indignant that the President treated his recommendations as to federal appointments in North Carolina with but scant respect. His last speech in the Senate was in opposition to the repeal of the Sherman Silver Act. He was a great opposition senator, but his name is not connected with any piece of constructive legislation.

Vance's close application to his work undermined his health and impaired one of his eyes. An operation for its removal in 1891 left him almost a nervous wreck. He vainly sought rest and health in foreign travel. In 1894 his physician ordered a complete rest in Florida. Two weeks after his return to Washington he died at his home in that city. He was buried in Asheville. By his first wife, Harriet N. Espy, of North Carolina, to whom he was married on Aug. 3, 1853, Vance had four sons. She died in 1878 and in 1880 he married Mrs. Florence Steele Martin, of Kentucky, who survived him. They had no children.

Vance was fond of books and read widely in history and biography. His most important addresses and essays are: *The Duties of Defeat* (1866); "Address . . . before the Southern Historical Society" in 1875 (*Our Living and Our Dead*, vol. III, no. 5, Nov. 1875; also *Southern Historical Society*, vol. XIV, 1886); *The Last Days of the War in North Carolina* (1885, reprinted in Dowd, *post*); the chapter, "Reconstruction in North Carolina," in H. A. Herbert, ed., *Why the Solid South* (1890). Many of his addresses were autobiographical in their character. His most popular lecture, "The Scattered Nation," dealing with the history of the Jews, was delivered in almost every important city in the United States. Besides its reprint in Dowd (*post*) and in Shurter, *Oratory of the South* (1908), it has been published in separate editions (1904, 1916).

[None of the numerous biographical sketches of Vance is adequate. The best is contained in *The Ceremonies Attending the Unveiling of the Bronze Statue of Zebulon B. Vance . . . and the Address of Richard H. Battle . . . 1900* (n.d.), the address being reprinted in abridged form in S. A. Ashe, ed., *Biog. Hist. of North Carolina*, vol. VI (1907), pp. 477–95. The most pretentious biography, Clement Dowd, *Life of Zebulon B. Vance* (1897), is valuable primarily for the letters and speeches of Vance reprinted therein. Important unpublished sources are: Vance Letterbook, 1862–65 (2 vols.); Executive Papers: Zebulon B. Vance, 1862–65 (36 boxes); Vance Letterbook, 1877–79; Zebulon B. Vance Papers, 1827–1902 (18 vols.); Cornelia P. Spencer Papers, 1859–1903 (2 vols.); and E. J. Hale Papers, 1850–67 (3 vols.), all in possession of the N. C. Hist. Commission at Raleigh. For a different interpretation of Vance's war policies see A. B. Moore, *Conscription and Conflict in the Confederacy* (1924), and F. L. Owsley, *State Rights in the Confederacy* (1925).]   R. D. W. C.

VAN CORTLANDT, OLOFF STEVENSZEN (1600–Apr. 5, 1684), prominent merchant in New Amsterdam and New York City, was born probably in the Netherlands, and apparently spent his youth entirely in the Dutch Republic. No special significance need be attached to the Scandinavian origin of his name and that of his father, Steven, or Stevens. Oloff

Stevenszen seems to have lived near Wijk bij Duurstede, in the province of Utrecht (see *Records of the Reformed Dutch Church, post*). Since he afterwards adopted the surname "Van Cortlandt" (1643), it has been plausibly surmised that he hailed from a very small village called Cortlandt, which existed at that time near Wijk bij Duurstede. He emigrated in the *Haering* (*Herring*), serving in the capacity of a soldier employed by the Dutch West India Company, and arrived in New Amsterdam in March 1638. On July 1, 1640, he was appointed commissioner of cargoes. In 1641 he began the purchase of real estate; in 1643 he is mentioned as a public storekeeper; in 1645 he was one of the Eight Men, and in 1650 he presided over the Nine Men. He held the office of city treasurer in 1657, 1659, 1660, 1661, and 1664; and he was burgomaster (mayor) from 1655 to 1660, and again in 1662 and 1663. In 1663 he was one of the commissioners sent to Hartford to treat on the Connecticut boundary. He served as deacon in the Reformed Church as early as 1646, while the more honorable office of elder was conferred upon him in or before 1670. He was a member of various committees in the city and the colony from 1647 to 1664, and, when in 1664 New Amsterdam became New York, he was chosen to negotiate with the English. Under the new government he acted as alderman in 1665, 1667, 1670, and 1672. In 1667 he was deputy mayor.

During the last ten years of his life he was rated as the fourth richest person in the colony (O'Callaghan, *Documents, post,* II, 699–700). Part of his wealth he owed to his wife, Anneken Loockermans, a native of Turnhout in the Spanish Netherlands (now Belgium), whom he married on Feb. 26, 1642. Van Cortlandt dealt in miscellaneous merchandise, owned a brewery on Brewer (or Brouwer) Street, and helped finance various commercial ventures. He was a hard-headed business man. When he saw fit, he did not hesitate to oppose such personages as the Rev. Evarardus Bogardus and Governor Stuyvesant [*qq.v.*]; and on one occasion at least he refused to permit the tax collector, Paulus van der Beeck, to visit his wine cellar (*The Records of New Amsterdam, post,* II, 234). The progenitor of one of the most prominent families in the American colonies, he was the father of seven children, of whom the eldest, Stephanus [*q.v.*], and the youngest, Jacobus, achieved especial distinction. His daughter Maria, who married Jeremias Van Rensselaer, was present at his death; he still appeared in good health and died "while in his prayers" (*Correspondence of Maria Van Rensselaer, post,* p. 173). In addition to his interesting coat of arms, there are two memorials which attest his opulence and sagacity. One is Van Cortlandt Manor, near Croton, built by his son Stephanus; the other, Van Cortlandt Park, at the northern extremity of New York City, is a symbol of the wealth in real estate amassed by him and his son Jacobus.

[L. E. De Forest, *The Van Cortlandt Family* (1930), with excellent bibliog.; *Records of the Reformed Dutch Church in New Amsterdam and New York, Marriages* (1890), ed. by S. S. Purple; *The Records of New Amsterdam from 1653 to 1674* (7 vols., 1897), ed. by Berthold Fernow; E. B. O'Callaghan, ed., *Calendar of Hist. MSS.*, vols. I–II (1865–66), and *Docs. Rel. to the Col. Hist. of N. Y.*, vols. I–II (1856–58); A. J. F. van Laer, ed., *N. Y. State Lib., Van Rensselaer Bowier MSS.* (1908), *Correspondence of Jeremias Van Rensselaer* (1932), *Correspondence of Maria Van Rensselaer, 1669–1689* (1935).]

A. H.

VAN CORTLANDT, PHILIP (Aug. 21, 1749–Nov. 5, 1831), Revolutionary officer, member of Congress, was the eldest son of Pierre [*q.v.*] and Joanna (Livingston) Van Cortlandt. He was born in New York City a few months before his parents established their residence at the manor-house near Croton. As a boy he attended a small school which his father maintained on the estate. At the age of fifteen he was sent to Coldenham Academy, where he spent a term of nine months studying mathematics, surveying, and bookkeeping. This concluded his formal schooling, but he gained practical experience in surveying by working with Nathaniel Merritt, one of his father's employees. Until the outbreak of the Revolutionary War he was engaged in surveying and disposing of tracts of land which had once been part of the manor of Cortlandt, and in operating several gristmills for his father.

During the year 1775 he made the transition from the position of the moderate Whigs to that of the revolutionary radicals. He was a member of the Provincial Convention, which met at the Exchange in New York City on Apr. 20, 1775, and the following month was chosen as one of Westchester County's representatives in the First Provincial Congress. On June 18 he accepted a commission as lieutenant-colonel of the 4th New York Regiment, but severe illness prevented him from participating in Montgomery's expedition against Montreal. After serving on Washington's staff for a short time, he received a commission as colonel of the reorganized 2nd New York and joined his regiment at Trenton on the day following the battle. He was assigned to duty at Peekskill, started a march to the relief of Fort Stanwix (August 1777), but was ordered back east to assist Gates's army at Saratoga. Rejoining Washington's forces, he was at

Valley Forge, was detached temporarily from his command to supervise the encampment in the spring of 1778, and then returned to his regiment in Ulster County, where he was stationed until April 1779. His effective cooperation with the Sullivan-Clinton expedition won him high praise. He was a member of the court martial which heard charges preferred by Pennsylvania authorities against Benedict Arnold, and he felt that Arnold should have been dismissed from the service. In the spring of 1780 he was sent to Fort Edward and later in the year was transferred to the post at Schenectady, where the 2nd, 4th, and 5th New York regiments were consolidated under his command. In June 1781 Washington ordered him to join the Continental forces on the lower Hudson in time to take an active part in the campaign which culminated in the surrender of Cornwallis. He was brevetted brigadier-general in 1783 for his conspicuous bravery and resourcefulness at Yorktown.

He was elected a delegate to the Poughkeepsie convention in 1788 and joined with the Federalists in voting to ratify the Federal Constitution. His subsequent political activity, however, reflected his conversion to Anti-Federalist principles. He served twice in the state Assembly (1788, 1790) and in the state Senate from 1791 to 1793. In December of the latter year he took his seat in the House of Representatives, beginning a period of service in Congress which continued for sixteen years. During his legislative career he seldom spoke on any measure before the House, but he was punctilious in the performance of his committee and other duties. The record of his votes indicates that he soon joined the Jeffersonian faction and that, when the Republican party came into power, he proved to be a reliable partisan who voted for party measures as a matter of course. In his sixtieth year he withdrew from politics and spent the remainder of his life managing his extensive real-estate holdings. The manor-house became his residence after his father's death in 1814. Although he had never married, he carried on the tradition of generous hospitality which had been established at Croton by his grandfather, Philip. Public affairs took little of his time, but he emerged from his retirement in 1824 to honor Lafayette, accompanying his friend on a large part of the country-wide tour. He died at the manor-house on Nov. 5, 1831, and was buried in Hillside Cemetery, Peekskill.

[An autobiog. fragment found in Van Cortlandt's papers was printed in *Mag. of Am. Hist.*, May 1878. See also L. E. De Forest, *The Van Cortlandt Family* (1930); Helen L. B. Parmelee, in *N. Y. Geneal. and Biog. Record*, July 1874; J. T. Scharf, *Hist. of West-*

chester County, vol. II (1886), pp. 423–36; E. A. Werner, *Civil List . . . of N. Y.* (1889); T. H. Benton, *Abridgement of the Debates of Cong.*, vols. I–IV (1857); John Schuyler, *Institution of the Order of the Cincinnati* (1886), pp. 319–21, on Van Cortlandt's death. A portrait by A. U. Wertmuller, painted in 1795, is in the coll. of Thomas B. Clarke of New York.]

J.A.K.

VAN CORTLANDT, PIERRE (Jan. 10, 1721–May 1, 1814), first lieutenant-governor of the State of New York, born at New York City, was the youngest son of Philip and Catharine (De Peyster) Van Cortlandt, and a grandson of Stephanus Van Cortlandt [*q.v.*]. Little is known concerning his youth beyond the fact that he spent considerable time with his brothers at the manor-house near Croton. On May 28, 1748, he married his second cousin, Joanna Livingston, whose father, Gilbert, had been heir to a large part of the property of Robert Livingston [*q.v.*], first lord of Livingston manor. He established his new home on Stone Street, New York City, where his first son, Philip [*q.v.*], was born, but he moved in September 1749 to Croton and occupied the remodelled manor-house which he had just inherited under the terms of his father's will. There he became deeply interested in the management of his farms and mills, and found great enjoyment in hunting and fishing. His home was famous even beyond the borders of the province for its generous hospitality.

Although he accepted a commission in the provincial militia, and marched to the relief of Albany during the French and Indian War, his public career did not begin until 1768, when he was elected to the seat in the Assembly which had originally been assigned to the manor of Cortlandt. In the Assembly he was inclined to follow the leadership of the Livingstons. He was no defender of the royal prerogative and the "court party" of the De Lanceys received scant support from him, but the intensification of the quarrel with Great Britain caused him, like many other moderate Whigs, to hesitate. The Loyalists sent Governor Tryon in the autumn of 1774 to urge upon him the honors and emoluments which would be his if he refused to join the "rebels"; he declined, however, to give the governor any assurances. On Oct. 19, 1775, he accepted a commission from the provincial congress as colonel of the 3rd Regiment of Westchester militia. He was a member of the second, third, and fourth provincial congresses, became an energetic leader of the Committee of Safety in 1776, and served as president of the Council of Safety during its brief existence in 1777. He presided over the sessions of the convention which drafted New York's first constitution and, with the establishment of the new state government (1777), became lieutenant-governor, a position to which he was periodically reëlected for eighteen years. Although he was a loyal follower of George Clinton, 1739–1812 [*q.v.*], in politics, his partisanship was never offensive, and he was universally praised for the dignity and impartiality with which he conducted the sessions of the state Senate. His continuous and vigorous service in public office was an important factor in enabling New York to play an effective part in the struggle for independence.

Pleading illness in 1795, Van Cortlandt withdrew from public life. His retirement ended his service on the board of regents of the University of the State of New York, to which he had been named in 1784. The remaining nineteen years of his life were devoted to the affairs of his Croton estate. The many visitors to the manor-house found him a tall, patriarchal gentleman, affable and courteous in the manner of the old school of landed aristocrats. He was deeply religious. Although a member of the Dutch Reformed Church, he manifested an increasing interest in the work of the Methodists. Bishop Francis Asbury, Freeborn Garrettson, Woolman Hickson, and other Methodist leaders were frequently guests in his home. He gave the land and subscribed to the building fund for the local Methodist meeting-house, and set aside each year after 1805 a certain grove on his estate for Methodist camp-meetings which he was eager to attend. He died at the manor-house in his ninety-fourth year and was buried in the family cemetery on the estate.

[See L. E. De Forest, *The Van Cortlandt Family* (1930); J. B. Wakeley, in *Ladies' Repository*, Dec. 1866, pp. 705–10; *Journals of the Provincial Cong. . . . of N. Y.* (1842); E. A. Werner, *Civil List . . . of N. Y.* (1889); Robert Bolton, *A Hist. of the County of Westchester* (2 vols., 1848); J. T. Scharf, *Hist. of Westchester County* (1886), vol. II, pp. 423–36; death notice in *N. Y. Gazette & General Advertiser*, May 12, 1814. There is an excellent portrait by John Wesley Jarvis in the possession of Miss Anne S. Van Cortlandt at the manor-house.]   J.A.K.

VAN CORTLANDT, STEPHANUS (May 7, 1643–Nov. 25, 1700), merchant and colonial official, eldest son of Oloff Stevenszen Van Cortlandt [*q.v.*] and Annetje (or Anneken) Loockermans, was born in his father's substantial house on Brouwer Street, New Amsterdam. His formal education was acquired in the school established by the Dutch Church. Under his father's astute guidance, however, he quickly became proficient in commercial affairs. Before he was twenty-one, he was executing commissions for Jan Baptist Van Rensselaer of Amsterdam and exchanging wine, duffels, and blankets

for the beaver skins which his brother-in-law, Jeremias Van Rensselaer, sent down the Hudson from Albany. These mercantile ventures were not interrupted by the English conquest of New Netherland, for Stephanus soon found favor with the new officials, who were not above conniving with him in importing goods contrary to the Acts of Trade (O'Callaghan, *Documents, post,* III, 307–08). He had already acquired a considerable estate when he married (Sept. 10, 1671) Gertrude, daughter of Philip P. Schuyler of Albany.

Van Cortlandt's public career was long and notable. Commissioned an ensign of militia in Kings County in 1668, he was regularly promoted until he reached the rank of colonel. Sir Edmund Andros [*q.v.*] summoned him (1674) to membership in the governor's council, and the instructions of every governor from Dongan to Bellomont contained his name as a councilor. In 1677 he became, by appointment from Governor Andros, the first native-born mayor of the city of New York, a position to which he was again appointed in 1686 and 1687. When the Dominion of New England was created he was named as one of the forty-two councilors to serve under Andros. This close association with the scheme of James II to establish centralized royal control in the northern colonies placed him in an embarrassing position when news reached New York that the "glorious revolution" had driven the king from his throne. As a ranking provincial councilor and mayor of the city of New York, Van Cortlandt endeavored for a time to restrain the rebellious groups which accepted the leadership of Capt. Jacob Leisler [*q.v.*], but he was not sufficiently resourceful to maintain public confidence in the integrity of the provincial government. Leisler maliciously accused him of being "papist," defied his authority as a councilor, and finally compelled him to flee for his life. During his enforced absence from his home he wrote plaintively to Andros, then in England, concerning his many misfortunes. With an eye to the future he urged his friend to present his case to Auditor General Blathwayt in order that he might "get here the Collectors place or at least that commission off auditor with a certaine sallary may bee confirmed unto me" (*Ibid.,* III, 650). His opportunity for revenge came when he was designated a member of the council under the new governor, Henry Sloughter. Supported by Frederick Philipse and Nicholas Bayard [*qq.v.*], he vigorously pushed the prosecution of Leisler on charges of treason and persuaded the governor, who was inclined to hesitate, that the condemned man should be executed at once. However timorous he had been in dealing with Leisler, the rebel, he did not lack assurance in disposing of Leisler, the condemned.

Throughout his career Van Cortlandt was closely associated with the amorphous jurisprudence of the provincial courts. After 1677 he presided at intervals over the mayor's court in the city of New York. Occasionally he was a member of the admiralty courts *ad hoc,* which antedated the creation by the British government in 1697 of the vice admiralty for the dominions. For several years (1688–91) he was a judge of the court of oyer and terminer which sat in Kings County, and he served as councilor during the period when the governor's council constituted a court of chancery. When the supreme court of the province was established by the judiciary act of 1691, he was named an associate justice, serving until his elevation to the post of chief justice, which occurred less than a month before his death.

The royal governors constantly summoned him to administrative as well as judicial posts. Under Gov. Benjamin Fletcher he became an important adviser on Indian relations, accompanying the governor in 1693 to the conference at Albany with sachems of the Five Nations which was designed to preserve the Iroquois alliance during King William's War. In 1698 he was appointed commissioner of customs and collector of revenues in recognition of the services which he had rendered a decade earlier in handling the provincial revenues for Gov. Thomas Dongan [*q.v.*]. But he failed to satisfy Lord Bellomont [*q.v.*], who wrote in 1700 to the Board of Trade that the new collector "gives a just account of all the money that comes to his hands, but he is grown very crazy and infirm, and is a very timorous man. In a word he has never yet made any seizure since his being Collector and I believe never would if he were 50 years to come, in that post" (*Ibid.,* IV, 721). The governor might have softened these harsh words had he been aware that at the very moment he sent off the report his receiver of revenues had been stricken by a fatal illness.

Like most of the provincial councilors of his generation, Stephanus Van Cortlandt used his official position to secure large grants of land. In 1677 Governor Andros issued a general license authorizing him to purchase from the Indians such tracts as he might desire. Apparently the first purchase under the license was made in 1683 and included the region on the east bank of the Hudson "at the entering of the highlands just over against Haverstraw." Several years

later he received from Governor Dongan a patent for the lands immediately north of his original purchase. These two tracts, somewhat extended by additional negotiations with the Indians in 1695, were erected into the manor of Cortlandt by a royal patent, dated June 17, 1697, which endowed the manor lord with the usual legal rights and emoluments and the special privilege, included in only two other grants, of sending a representative to the provincial assembly. Van Cortlandt never resided upon his manor. He used the manor-house, which was a fort-like structure, as a hunting-lodge, trading-post, and office for the transaction of such manorial business as concerned the Indians who remained within its borders. He was the last as well as the first lord of his manor, for in disposing of his property he followed the Dutch rather than the English custom. By the terms of his will his eldest son, John, was to receive the region of Verplanck's Point, while the remainder of his real estate was to be divided equally, after the death of his widow, among his eleven children. The manor lands, which according to the survey of 1732 included 87,713 acres, were not finally divided among the legal heirs until 1753.

[L. E. De Forest, *The Van Cortlandt Family* (1930); *A Jour. Kept by Coll. Stephen Courtland & Coll. Nich. Beyard* (1693); *Correspondence of Jeremias Van Rensselaer, 1651–1674* (1932), ed. by A. J. F. van Laer; E. B. O'Callaghan, ed., *Docs. Rel. to the Col. Hist. of . . . N. Y.,* vols. III–IV (1853–54), *Calendar of Hist. MSS.,* vol. II (1866), and *Documentary Hist. of the State of N. Y.,* vols. I, II (1849); *N. Y. Hist. Soc. Colls., Publication Fund Ser.,* vol. I (1868); J. R. Brodhead, *Hist. of the State of N. Y.,* vol. II (1871); G. W. Schuyler, *Colonial New York* (2 vols., 1885); Mariana G. Van Rensselaer, *Hist. of the City of N. Y. in the Seventeenth Century* (2 vols., 1909); E. F. De Lancey, *Origin and Hist. of Manors in the Province of N. Y.* (1886), reprinted from J. T. Scharf, *Hist. of Westchester County, N. Y.* (1886), vol. I, pp. 31–160.]   J. A. K.

VAN CURLER, ARENT (1620–July 1667), colonist, was born at Nykerk, in the Netherlands, and was baptized Feb. 6, 1620. According to one account he was the son of Hendrik, and according to another, of Joachim van Curler (*Van Rensselaer Bowier Manuscripts, post,* p. 78, note 34); he was a grand-nephew of Kiliaen van Rensselaer, the first patroon of Rensselaerswyck on the upper Hudson in New Netherland. In his eighteenth year he came to New Netherland as assistant to the commissary of Rensselaerswyck; later he was secretary and bookkeeper. In 1641 he received the title of *commis* and assumed full representative authority in government and trade, with some judicial powers. The tenant farmers of Rensselaerswyck, unskilled in New World agriculture, were supplied by the patroon with houses, capital and all the facilities of production. In addition to duties connected with these allotments, the *commis* had responsibilities relating to the breeding of horses and cattle, the care of a growing fur trade, and the fostering of an export trade along the Atlantic coast.

Exact accounts of all transactions were to be sent to the patroons. A sharp reminder from Amsterdam that reports were deficient and in arrears (*Van Rensselaer Bowier Manuscripts*, pp. 658–68) brought from Van Curler the letter of June 16, 1643 (O'Callaghan, *History, post,* I, 456–65), in which some of the difficulties attending the experiment of absentee farming in the wilds of New Netherland were pointed out. Van Curler complained that Adriaen van der Donck [*q.v.*], officer of justice and *schout*, labored to undermine him, and betrayed the patroon's interests. Relief came when Van der Donck removed to his estate by the Harlem River. In 1644 Van Curler married Anthonia Slachboom, widow of Jonas Bronck; the next year he visited Holland. From the second patroon, Johannes van Rensselaer, he obtained the lease of a farm four miles north of the present Albany. Desiring a more congenial field for his ambitions, Van Curler in 1661 procured from Director Petrus Stuyvesant [*q.v.*] a license to purchase the Indian flat, Schonowe, on the Mohawk, to which in the following year he removed. The settlement planted there became Schenectady.

Van Curler gained an enduring influence over the neighboring Indian tribes. He interposed with success to save Father Isaac Jogues [*q.v.*] and his companions from death at the hands of the Mohawks. In 1660 he took part in the treaty which terminated the first Esopus war. At this period the relations of the French in Canada with their southern neighbors did not forbid exchanges of good will. In the winter of 1666, when Governor De Courcelle, in an ill-considered expedition into the Mohawk country, faced starvation with his force, Van Curler headed a movement to supply them with provisions. A year later De Tracy, the Canadian lieutenant-general, sent Van Curler an invitation to visit him in Canada. Accompanied by several Indians, Van Curler set forth by the way of Lake Champlain. Embarking in a small boat, he was overtaken by a sudden gale and was drowned. Perou Bay, the scene of the disaster, was long known as Corlaer's Bay. A more impressive memorial was the name, Corlaer, which the Indians thereafter bestowed on the English governors of New York in commemoration of Van Curler's courage and human understanding. A

memorial tablet was dedicated in Schenectady in 1909.

[For sources, see A. J. F. van Laer, in *Yearbook of the Dutch Settlers Soc. of Albany*, vol. III (1928); *N. Y. State Lib.: Van Rensselaer Bowier MSS.* (1908), translated and ed. by A. J. F. van Laer; E. B. O'Callaghan, *Docs. Rel. to the Colonial Hist. . . . of N. Y.*, vol. III (1853), and *Hist. of New Netherland* (2nd ed., 1855); Jonathan Pearson, *A Hist. of the Schenectady Patent* (1883); *Minutes of the Court of Rensselaerswyck, 1648–1652* (1922), translated and ed. by A. J. F. van Laer. A journal ascribed to Van Curler is printed in *Ann. Report Am. Hist. Asso. . . . 1895* (1896), but according to A. J. F. van Laer (*Van Rensselaer Bowier MSS.*, p. 271) it cannot be Van Curler's.]

R. E. D.

VAN DAM, RIP (c. 1660–June 10, 1749), merchant, colonial politician, was born in Fort Orange (Albany, N. Y.), of a Dutch family living in New Netherland before the English conquest. His parents were Claas Ripse van Dam, a carpenter, and Maria Bords. Early in life Rip voyaged to Jamaica in command of the sloop *Catharine*. He subsequently embarked in trade, and at the age of thirty was listed among the merchants of New York City. He was also concerned in ship building on the North River. In 1693 he was elected a member of the board of aldermen, a station which he filled for three successive years, but he was not conspicuously active in politics until 1702. In that year the seizure and condemnation of some of the vessels in which he had investments, under Acting Governor Nanfan, head of the Leisler party, aroused his antagonism to the popular element of his day as well as to the unpopular navigation acts. Van Dam's resentment embraced the lieutenant-governor, the collector who seized the ships, and the chief justice who condemned them, and he sent petitions attacking these officers to the King, but the trouble subsided later the same year with the accession of Queen Anne to the throne, the arrival of Lord Cornbury [*q.v.*] as Nanfan's successor, and the elevation of Van Dam to the Council.

Van Dam was a councilor for more than thirty years. During most of this time he took no prominent part in controversy, though in 1713 there was friction between Gov. Robert Hunter [*q.v.*] and the Council; two years later the legislature approved an act for appointing a London agent to take notice of measures in Parliament injurious to the colony; and Hunter's successor, Gov. William Burnet [*q.v.*], had trouble with the Assembly. Meanwhile Van Dam built houses, supplied provisions for the troops, furnished money for the colonial treasury, and filled contracts for repairs and improvements to the royal fort. He also invested in forest land, being interested in large patents in the Hudson River region and the Mohawk region.

In 1731, by the death of Gov. John Montgomerie, Van Dam as senior member and president of the Council became the executive head of the province. For thirteen months he exercised the powers of the office and received the salary. Then Gov. William Cosby [q.v.] arrived, and demanded an equal division of the emoluments, by virtue of an order from the King. When Van Dam refused, inasmuch as Cosby's receipts from the governorship while still in England had been three times as great as the disputed salary (Smith, *post*, II, 4–7), the Governor sued in "the Equity side of the Exchequer." Cosby's report of his grievances to the home government (*Documents, post,* VI, 8) described Van Dam as pleading that no such court as the Equity side of the Exchequer existed, that the judges' commissions were void, and that "no Supream or other Court . . . had any being, Jurisdiction, or authority by prescription" (*Ibid.,* p. 11). Van Dam's plea was overruled; but he continued the war with formal charges, alleging that Cosby had failed to fortify the port against the designs of the French. Cosby complained to London, and the Lords of Trade recommended Van Dam's dismissal from the Council. He was suspended by Cosby on Nov. 24, 1735. He failed to recognize this action as removal, however, or George Clarke [q.v.] as the new president of the Council, and appointed municipal officers for New York City after Cosby's death in March 1736, whereupon Clarke issued a proclamation of warning against these appointments. The threat of civil war was dispersed when dispatches from England brought recognition of Clarke as president; his appointment as lieutenant-governor soon followed, and Van Dam's public career came to an end.

In the struggle for popular rights and against prerogative, Rip Van Dam won leadership with William Smith and James Alexander [qq.v.], two of the ablest men in the colony. Prolonging the fight into the later years of his life, he heard complaints of his senility issuing from quarters where there was more reason to complain of his vigor. As a councilor, he was often called upon to settle the disputes of the Reformed churches and other religious societies, a difficult task in view of the unsettled state of those congregations at that period. A disposition to conciliate and tranquillize marked his efforts in this field.

Van Dam married Sara van der Spiegel in September 1684 and had a number of children, of whom two sons and three daughters reached maturity. One of his grand-daughters became the wife of Robert Livingston, third proprietor of the Manor of Livingston.

[Frederic De Peyster, *Memoir of Rip Van Dam* (1865); E. B. O'Callaghan, *Docs. Rel. to the Col. Hist. of . . . N. Y.,* vols. IV–VI (1853–55); *N. Y. State Lib. . . . Calendar of Council Minutes, 1668–1783* (1902); *Jour. of the Legislative Council of the Colony of N. Y.* (1861); J. G. Wilson, *The Memorial Hist. of the City of N. Y.,* vols. II, IV (1892, 1893), *passim; Ecclesiastical Records: State of N. Y.* (7 vols., 1901–16), ed. by E. T. Corwin; William Smith, *The Hist. of the Late Province of N. Y.* (2 vols., 1829–30); "The Letters and Papers of Cadwallader Colden," *N. Y. Hist. Soc. Colls., Pub. Fund Ser.,* vols. L, LI (1918–19); H. L. Osgood, *The Am. Colonies in the Eighteenth Century* (1924), vol. II; D. T. Valentine, *Manual of the Corporation of the City of N. Y.,* 1864, 1865, the latter containing a reprint of De Peyster's *Memoir* and portraits of Van Dam and his wife; *Calendar of N. Y. Colonial MSS.—Land Papers* (1864); S. S. Purple, *Records of the Reformed Dutch Church in New Amsterdam and N. Y.: Marriages* (1890); Jonathan Pearson, *Contributions to the Geneals. of the First Settlers of Albany* (1872); Van Dam's will in *Colls. N. Y. Hist. Soc., Pub. Fund Ser.,* vol. XXVIII (1896).] R. E. D.

VANDENHOFF, GEORGE (1813–June 16, 1885), actor, lawyer, was born in Liverpool, England, the son of John Vandenhoff, a well-known actor (see *The Dictionary of National Biography*). The family, a few generations back, had come to England from the Netherlands. Vandenhoff was educated at Stonyhurst College and later studied for the law. For a time he was solicitor to the trustees of the Liverpool docks. On Oct. 14, 1839, he made his stage début as Leon in Beaumont and Fletcher's *Rule a Wife and Have a Wife* at Covent Garden, where he also acted in new plays by Leigh Hunt and Sheridan Knowles, and as Mercutio in Madame Vestris' famous revival of *Romeo and Juliet*. In 1842, on Sept. 21, he made his American début at the Park Theatre, New York, as Hamlet, with Henry Placide [q.v.] as Polonius. Of his Hamlet, Porter's *Spirit of the Times,* Sept. 24, 1842, recorded, "Taken as a whole, the character has not been more ably performed in this city for the past six years." Vandenhoff followed Hamlet with Virginius, Macbeth, Benedick, and Claude Melnotte, and then began a tour which included the chief cities of the East and took him as far south as New Orleans. At the Walnut Street Theatre, Philadelphia, he played Rolla to the Elvira of Charlotte Cushman [q.v.]; in Boston, where he acted for five weeks, he added Coriolanus and Hotspur to his list of rôles. He acted in New Orleans in February 1843, visited Richmond (where he acted one night with Hackett), Baltimore, and Philadelphia once more, where he played Mercutio to Charlotte Cushman's Romeo. In May he was back at the Park, and then finished his season in Boston. He had made little money, but many friends, and decided to remain in America indefinitely.

From 1843 to 1853 he lived in New York, acted frequently in most American cities, taught elocution, and gave many public readings of "Shakespeare, Sheridan and the Poets." In October 1843 he was leading man for William C. Macready at the Chestnut Street Theatre, Philadelphia, and he has left interesting records of that actor and his methods. At the Park, in 1844, he supported the elder Booth, and in 1846 he played Faulconbridge in the revival of *King John* made by Mr. and Mrs. Charles Kean. One of his most interesting ventures, however, was at Palmo's Opera House, New York, in the spring of 1845, where he staged an English version of Sophocles' *Antigone,* with Mendelssohn's music and an attempt to reproduce a Greek stage. In January 1853 he returned to England, where he acted first in Liverpool in repertory. On Oct. 25, 1853, he reappeared in London, at the Haymarket, as Hamlet, highly praised by the leading papers. He made his great success, however, in what was for him a new style of part—Captain Cozens in Planché's *Knights of the Round Table,* a racy adventure comedy which ran fifty-four nights.

At the end of the season he resolved to retire as soon as he could. He sailed for Boston, and on Aug. 20, 1855, was married in Trinity Church to Mary MaKeath, an American actress. They acted jointly in the English provinces for a year, and then returned to the United States. Shortly thereafter Vandenhoff carried out his plan to retire. The truth seems to be that he never really cared for stage life. In 1858 he was admitted to the New York bar and resumed the practice of law, but continued his popular public readings. His interesting volume of reminiscences, *Leaves from an Actor's Note Book,* was published in 1860. He had already written (1858) a social satire in verse, and in 1861 published *The Art of Elocution* and *Life,* a poem. In 1874 he reappeared in support of Genevieve Ward [*q.v.*] as Wolsey and as Gloster in *Jane Shore.* This was his last stage appearance. He died in Brighton, England, June 16, 1885. Vandenhoff was tall, graceful, scholarly, and somewhat aloof. In his earlier years his acting was of the "new school" of ease and naturalness, but in later years he declared Irving to be "an intellectual machine with the pronunciation and gait of a barbarian." Junius Booth he praised highly, but Lawrence Barrett and John McCullough he considered to have all the faults of the conventional "tragedian." His own book shows him a man of breeding, taste, and good sense.

[The date of birth is from the Cat. of Dramatic Portraits, Harvard Theatre Coll. Other sources include George Vandenhoff, *Leaves from an Actor's Note Book* (1860); G. C. D. Odell, *Annals of the N. Y. Stage,* vols. IV–VII (1928–31); *N. Y. Dramatic Mirror,* Aug. 14, 1886.]
W. P. E.

VAN DEPOELE, CHARLES JOSEPH (Apr. 27, 1846–Mar. 18, 1892), scientist, inventor, pioneer in electric light and traction, was born in Lichtervelde, Belgium, the fourth child of Peter John and Marie Thérèse Coleta (Algoed) van de Poele. Precocious—he fashioned an electric light when he was fifteen years old, in 1861—and inspired in part by his father's work in the East Flanders railway shops, Van Depoele devoted himself early to scientific experiment. After attending a higher school in Poperinghe, he was apprenticed in 1865 to the wood-carving firm of Buisine-Rigot at its shops in Lille and Paris. In Lille he studied at the Imperial Lyceum and continued his preoccupation with electricity. In 1869 he emigrated to America and settled in Detroit, Mich.

In Detroit, Van Depoele became a successful manufacturer of church furniture, but he soon began to concentrate his efforts in the field of electricity. As early as 1870 he exhibited arc lights and as early as 1874 was demonstrating the feasibility of electric traction by both overhead and underground conductors. By 1878, when he was visited by Edison, the old church in which he had finally established his shop, at 28 Pine Street, had become famous. Styled "Detroit's Edison" by the *Detroit Free Press* on Nov. 13, 1878, he proceeded to work towards vibratory regulation for arc lights, and by July 1879, he had demonstrated his improved lights publicly. Early in 1880 the Van Depoele Electric Light Company was formed, and later in the year Van Depoele transferred his experiments in electric traction to the factory of the Detroit Novelty Works at Hamtramck, Mich., where he made tests on a half-mile track. In 1881 the Van Depoele Electric Light Company of Chicago was incorporated; and in 1884, the Van Depoele Electric Manufacturing Company. Meanwhile, in Chicago, Jan. 18, 1883, Van Depoele gave a public demonstration of electric traction, the current being furnished from two wires laid along the track. At the Chicago Inter-State Industrial Exposition early the following September he continued with the first practical demonstration in the world of a spring-pressed under-running trolley. In 1884 and 1885 he was successful in Toronto with both the underground conduit and the overhead systems. On Nov. 14, 1885, his overhead system was put into operation in South Bend, Ind. The *South Bend Tribune* of Nov. 16 ran a proud headline: "South Bend the First

City in the Union to Secure Practical Electric Traction"—and a reporter announced: "The bray of the festive mule must go." In the winter of 1885–86 Van Depoele's system was adopted in Minneapolis, Minn., Montgomery, Ala., and other cities, and by the end of 1886 eight lines had been installed in the United States and Canada. In this year he contributed an article, "Electric Transmission of Power," to the *Telegraphic Journal and Electrical Review* of London (Mar. 5, 1886). Two years later, in March 1888, the Van Depoele system was operating in ten cities, with three other lines under construction—claiming a greater number of lines than all other companies combined (*Senate Miscellaneous Document No. 84*, 50 Cong., 1 Sess.).

In 1888 Van Depoele's electric railway patents were sold to the Thomson-Houston Electric Company of Lynn, Mass., and Van Depoele himself was engaged by that concern as electrician, with American and foreign royalties for his patented railway systems. The sale of the Van Depoele Electric Manufacturing Company followed in 1889, and in this year Van Depoele's telpher and reciprocating patents were assigned to the Thomson-Houston International Company. In November 1891, while planning an electrical exhibit for the World's Columbian Exposition in Chicago, Van Depoele contracted a severe cold, which with resulting complications caused his death after an illness of over four months.

Van Depoele filed in all some 444 applications for patents, of which at least 249 were granted to him under his own name. After his death seventy-two further applications were made, and of these some forty-six were allowed and assigned to the Thomson-Houston Electric Company. Van Depoele's achievements covered a wide variety of electrical inventions and improvements, especially in the field of traction. His little "Giant" generator, patented Sept. 21, 1880, with its smooth regulation of power, was considered one of the best on the market. His first patent on electric railways was granted Oct. 2, 1883; his first on an overhead conductor, Aug. 11, 1885. The patent for his carbon contact or commutator-brush, which he first used in 1882 and which revolutionized motor construction, was taken up Oct. 9, 1888. Other basic patents of prime importance were his alternating-current electric reciprocating engine (1889); his multiple-current pulsating generator (1890); his telpher system (1890), first used in the mines at Streator, Ill., in 1885; his multiple rock-drill (1891); his coal-mining machine (1891); and his gearless electric locomotive (1894). He was experimenting with electric refrigeration before

June 16, 1886, and in the winter of 1889–90 at his residence at 502 Essex Street in Lynn he made several photographs in color. The two most distinctively original of his achievements, however, were the pivoted spring-pressed under-running trolley and the carbon commutator-brush. Of this latter epochal invention alone it has been justly said that the traction industry "would have been indefinitely postponed"—even "impossible" —"without the discovery of the carbon brush" (Rice and Crowther, *post*, p. 600).

Van Depoele was a man of broad culture. Bilingual from the beginning in French and Flemish, he became proficient as well in Dutch, Latin, Greek, English, and other languages. On Nov. 23, 1870, he married Ada Mina, daughter of Cornelius and Cornelia (Weavers) van Hoogstraten of Detroit, and by her he had three sons and four daughters. He became a naturalized American citizen on Apr. 23, 1878. He died in Lynn, Mass., and was buried in St. Mary's Cemetery there. A portrait bust of him, in bronze, by Robert Kraus of Boston, is in the Lynn Public Library.

[Notes, drawings, letters, etc., assembled by Van Depoele's daughter, Romanie Adeline (Van Depoele) Phelan, of Lynn, Mass.; catalogues of the Van Depoele Electric Light and Manufacturing Company, Chicago, Ill.; *The Official Gazette of the U. S. Patent Office*, 1878–98; *The Canadian Patent Office Record*, vol. XVII (1889); *Selected U. S. Patents Relating to Electric Railways Owned or Controlled by the Thomson-Houston Electric Co., Brush Electric Co., and Allied Corporations* (1891); T. C. Martin and J. Wetzler, *The Electric Motor and Its Applications* (1892); *U. S. Circuit Court for the District of Conn.: In Equity, No. 753, Thomson-Houston Electric Co. vs. The Winchester Ave. Railroad Co., et al., Complainant's Proofs* (4 vols., 1895), and report of case in 71 *Federal Reporter*, 192; "The Work of Van Depoele," *Electrical Rev.* (London), June 5, 1896; D. McKillop, "The Father of the Trolley," *Electrical Age*, Dec. 1905; B. G. Lamme, "The Development of the Street Railway Motor in America," *Electric Jour.* (Pittsburgh, Pa.), Oct. 1918; E. W. Rice, Jr., and S. Crowther, "Trials of the Early Electric Trail," *Magazine of Business*, Nov. 1928; *Detroit Free Press*, Mar. 20, 1892.]   C.B.M.

VANDERBILT, CORNELIUS (May 27, 1794–Jan. 4, 1877), steamship and railroad promoter, financier, born at Port Richmond, Staten Island, N. Y. (now part of New York City), was the fourth child and second son of Cornelius and Phebe (Hand) Vander Bilt. His paternal ancestors, who came from Holland and settled on Long Island in the latter half of the seventeenth century, wrote the family name in three words, van der Bilt. The subject of the present sketch preferred to write it Van Derbilt, but during his lifetime other members of the family consolidated the name into one word. His father, a poor man with a large family, did a bit of farming on Staten Island, and some boating and lightering around New York harbor. The blue-eyed, flaxen-haired, boisterous boy Cornelius had no inclination and little opportunity for education, and did not spend a day in school after he was eleven. Already big in body and strong, he became at that age his father's helper. At about thirteen he is said to have superintended the job of lightering a vessel, his father being engaged elsewhere. He had barely reached his sixteenth birthday when, with $100 advanced by his parents, he bought a small sailing vessel called a piragua and began a freight and passenger ferrying business between Staten Island and New York City. On Dec. 19, 1813, when he was only nineteen years old, he married his cousin and neighbor, Sophia Johnson, daughter of his father's sister Eleanor, and set up a home of his own near his birthplace.

The War of 1812 had opened new opportunities for him, and he was busy day and night. Among other important jobs, he had a three months' contract from the government for provisioning the forts in and around New York harbor. Before the war was over, he had several boats under his command. He built a schooner in 1814 for service to Long Island Sound, and, in the following two years, two larger schooners for the coastwise trade. These he sent out—he himself being in command of the largest—not only as cargo boats, but also as traders up the Hudson River and along the coast from New England to Charleston. In 1818 he startled his friends by selling all his sailing vessels and going to work as a captain for Thomas Gibbons [q.v.], owner of a ferry between New Brunswick, on the Raritan estuary, and New York City—an important link in the New York-Philadelphia freight, mail, and passenger route. Gibbons was fighting for life against the steam-navigation monopoly in New York waters which had been granted to Robert Fulton by the New York legislature several years before. Vanderbilt loved a fight; he took Gibbons' one small vessel, put her in better condition, selected a hard-bitten crew and drove them to the limit of endurance, and within a year had turned a losing venture into a profitable one. When he entered Gibbons' service, he removed his family to New Brunswick, took over a rundown tavern by the river-side there, and installed his wife as hotel keeper. She renovated the house and made it famous for good food and service. "Bellona Hall," as it was called, became a favorite stopping place for travelers between New York and Philadelphia. In addition to her duties as chief factotum of the hotel, Mrs. Vanderbilt gave birth to a child about every two years while living in New Brunswick; she had thirteen in all.

Vanderbilt soon induced Gibbons to build a larger and finer steamer, the *Bellona* (1818). Meanwhile, the New York monopoly had brought suit against Gibbons, and for several years there was legal, and sometimes physical, warfare. Only Vanderbilt's lusty, dynamic spirit and resourcefulness kept his employer's line in operation. For months on end New York deputy sheriffs tried to arrest him whenever his boat entered New York waters, but he foiled them in one way or another. He is said to have built a secret compartment on the vessel in which he would hide at such times. Finally, in 1824, the United States Supreme Court ruled that a monopoly such as that granted by the New York legislature was unconstitutional (*Gibbons* vs. *Ogden, 9 Wheaton,* 1). During the eleven years of his service with Gibbons, young Vanderbilt increased and broadened the business enormously. He had built seven more steamers for his employer, some for the New York-New Brunswick-Elizabeth ferries, others to ply a new line on the Delaware.

Vanderbilt had ambitions of his own; and in 1829, having accumulated a considerable nest-egg through his own and his wife's exertions, he resigned from Gibbons' employ in order to enter the steamboat business on his own. Much against the will of his wife, he disposed of "Bellona Hall" and moved her and the eight or nine children to New York City. His first ventures were on the Hudson River, where other concerns were already operating; he inaugurated rate wars with a characteristic zest for conflict. Here, in a competition for the trade between New York and Peekskill, he came into collision, in 1834, with Daniel Drew [q.v.]. The fare between the two points was finally cut to twelve and a half cents, and then Drew sold out to Vanderbilt. The latter now entered the Albany trade, where a more powerful corporation, the Hudson River Association, was functioning. He put two boats on the Albany run and began cutting rates again. In the end his opponents paid him a goodly sum for his agreement to withdraw from competition for ten years. He next established lines on Long Island Sound and on to Providence and Boston. Later he returned to the Hudson River. He is given credit for bringing about a great and rapid advance in the size, comfort, and elegance of steamboats. The "floating palaces" of the 1840's and 1850's would not suffer greatly by comparison with the boats of today in such waters; in many cases they were more luxurious, even if they lacked electric appliances and some other modern conveniences. Vanderbilt found pleasure in making his vessels stanch, fast, handsome, and comfortable. About 1846 he launched on the

Hudson perhaps the finest boat yet seen by New Yorkers; it was named for himself.

Before this time he was undoubtedly a millionaire. He was supposed to have passed the half million mark at the age of forty. But he and his family had so far failed to make any impression upon the exclusive New York society of that day. Cornelius himself was not a figure for the drawing-room or for a luncheon table of fastidious gentlemen. He was apt to be loud, rustic, and coarse in speech, his talk interlarded with profanity and slang of the wharves. He was a big, bumptious, ruthless, tobacco-chewing, hard-headed, hard-swearing, hard-fighting man, yet constructive, courageous, clear-sighted in business matters, broad-visioned for his day, and graced by a certain alluring frankness and faithfulness to a bargain. It is believed that a certain smoldering resentment because of the social cold shoulder turned to him, together with the persuasion of his wife, caused him to build a fine mansion on Staten Island and take his family back there in 1840. But he still wanted to pry open those closed doors on Manhattan, and in 1846, despite his wife's protests, he began building a town house on Washington Place. Scarcely was it ready when Mrs. Vanderbilt was committed to a private sanitarium for insanity, upon his delation, and perhaps because of her tearful yet stubborn refusal to move back to New York. She was released in the spring of 1847, after a few months' confinement, and went obediently to the new home in the city.

The gold rush opened new vistas to Vanderbilt, whom men were now calling "Commodore." Before the end of 1849, traffic to California was beginning to go via Panama, freight and passengers crossing the Isthmus on muleback. Vanderbilt conceived the idea of starting a line of his own via Nicaragua—through the San Juan River to Lake Nicaragua and perhaps thence by canal to the Pacific. At first he called this the American Atlantic & Pacific Ship Canal Company. A trip to England in 1850 in search of capital to finance the venture was fruitless, and he proceeded to develop the route himself. He procured from the Nicaraguan government a charter for himself in the name of the Accessory Transit Company (see *Senate Executive Document No. 68,* 34 Cong., 1 Sess., 1856). He then improved to some extent the channel of the San Juan River, built docks on the east and west coasts of Nicaragua and at Virgin Bay on Lake Nicaragua, and made a fine twelve-mile macadam road from the latter place to his west-coast port. Meanwhile, he was beginning the construction of a fleet of eight new steamers with which he ran lines from New York, and later from New Orleans. His route was two days shorter than that via Panama; he greatly reduced the New York-San Francisco passenger fare and garnered most of the traffic.

He made money so rapidly that in 1853 he announced that he was going to take the first vacation of his life. He built a steam yacht, the *North Star,* sumptuously appointed, and with his entire family, even to sons-in-law and grandchildren, and with several invited guests, including the Rev. Dr. John Overton Choules as chaplain and chronicler, he embarked for a triumphal tour of Europe. Dr. Choules wrote a fulsome history of the voyage, full of unconscious humor, which was published as *The Cruise of the Steam Yacht North Star* (1854). Before going abroad, Vanderbilt resigned the presidency of the Accessory Transit Company, and committed its management to Charles Morgan and Cornelius K. Garrison [*qq.v.*] who, during his absence, manipulated the stock and secured control of the company; but by shrewd buying he won it back in a few months. However, William Walker [*q.v.*], the American filibuster who had seized control of the Nicaraguan government, allied himself with Morgan and Garrison, rescinded the Transit Company's charter on the ground that its terms had been disregarded, and issued a new charter to the rival group. Vanderbilt thereupon aided in bringing about Walker's downfall early in 1857. The doughty "Commodore," now sixty-three, but a harder fighter than ever, had to battle his way through other enemies in Wall Street and Central America, but he triumphed, and the Transit Company was his own again. Scarcely had he brushed aside the last opposition, however, when he approached the Pacific Mail Steamship Company, and the United States Mail Steamship Company, the great carriers via Panama, and offered to abandon the Nicaragua line if they would buy the *North Star* for some $400,000 and pay him $40,000 a month indemnity. They came to his figures reluctantly, but a year later, when he threatened to open the Transit line again, they increased his monthly stipend to $56,000 (*Congressional Globe,* June 9, 1858, 35 Cong., 1 Sess., pp. 2843–44). In the middle fifties he built three vessels, one of which, the *Vanderbilt,* was the largest and finest he had yet constructed, and entered into competition for the Atlantic trade with the Cunard Line and the Collins Line (see sketch of E. K. Collins), even offering to carry the mails to Havre for nothing. He found this an unprofitable venture, however, and at the beginning of the Civil War was glad to sell his Atlantic line for $3,000,000, retaining only the *Vanderbilt*, which he fitted up as a warship and turned over to the government. It has been claimed that he intended only to make a loan of this vessel, but it was interpreted as a gift (Smith, *post*, p. 237). His connection with the expedition of Nathaniel P. Banks [*q.v.*] to New Orleans was less happy, for many of the vessels chartered by him under commission of the government proved unseaworthy. However, his name was expunged from the Senate resolution of censure (*Congressional Globe*, 37 Cong., 3 Sess., Jan. 29, 1863, and *Senate Report 75*, 1863, 37 Cong., 3 Sess.; Myers, *post*, II, 132–37).

Of Vanderbilt's thirteen children, one boy had died young and all of the nine daughters were living. His youngest and favorite child, George, born in 1839, was a soldier in the Civil War and died in 1866 from effects of exposure in the Corinth campaign. His second son, Cornelius Jeremiah, an epileptic, gambler, and ne'er-do-well, had been a great disappointment. The eldest son, William Henry [*q.v.*], he had regarded as being of little force, and had exiled to a farm on Staten Island, though later he became aware of his ability and at last gave him opportunity to use it. This was in connection with railroad enterprises, to which Vanderbilt turned from shipping as he neared seventy. He had begun buying New York & Harlem Railroad stock in 1862 when it was selling at a very low figure. In 1863 he induced the city council to give him permission to extend the line by street-car tracks to the Battery. The stock, which he had already driven up, rose greatly upon public announcement of the ordinance, and even more when Vanderbilt was elected president. Daniel Drew now plotted with members of the council to sell Harlem stock "short," rescind the ordinance, and buy the shares for delivery after the price had dropped to a certain figure. The plot was carried out, but the price dropped much less than was expected, for Vanderbilt bought every share that was offered, and presently it was discovered that the "short" traders had sold more shares than were in existence. The price rapidly rose, and when Vanderbilt forced a settlement, many of the plotters were ruined. He made William vice-president of the Harlem road, and thereafter his son was his first lieutenant.

He next turned his attention to the Harlem's competitor, the Hudson River Railroad, another rundown property. While buying control of the railroad, he sought authority from the legislature to combine the two. Undeterred by his former experience, Drew again plotted, this time with some of the legislators, to sell the stock "short,"

defeat the consolidation bill, hammer down the price, and make a "killing." The former story was repeated: the bill was lost; the price declined considerably but not enough; Vanderbilt, aided by other operators, bought every share offered; the "shorts" discovered that they had agreed to deliver far more shares than were in existence; the price rose greatly; and again Cornelius had revenge on those who had tried to break him. He bided his time on the consolidation of the roads, improving their equipment and service, as he did that of every property he owned, and presently had them on a paying basis. He next sought control of the New York Central Railroad, running from Albany to Buffalo. Its directors countered by forming an alliance with Drew's Hudson River boat line and sending through freight and passengers from Albany to New York by that route. But when the river froze in early winter and the steamboats were stopped, they sought to transfer traffic to the Hudson River road, only to discover that Vanderbilt was halting its trains on the east side of the river, a mile from Albany. Stock in the New York Central declined and Vanderbilt bought quantities of it, finally securing control in 1867. He promptly spent $2,000,000 of his own money in improving the line and buying new rolling stock. He united these two railroads by legislative act in 1869, as the New York Central & Hudson River Railroad, and in 1872 leased the Harlem Railroad to it. He increased the capital stock by $42,000,000 (which was a stock-watering operation of magnitude), but out of three inefficient roads he created a single line, giving uninterrupted service.

In 1868 he sought control of the Erie Railway, a rival line to Buffalo and Chicago. He pursued the same tactics as before, buying every share of stock offered. But this time Drew, Jay Gould, and James Fisk, Jr. [*qq.v.*], who were in control of Erie, outmaneuvered him, throwing 50,000 shares of fraudulent stock into the market, then fleeing to New Jersey to avoid prosecution and bribing the New Jersey legislature to legalize the stock issue. Vanderbilt lost millions by this *coup*, but the plotters had to compromise with him in order to return to New York with impunity, and his loss was greatly reduced. Upon the insistence of his son William that extension of their rail system to Chicago was advisable, in 1873 he bought control of the Lake Shore & Michigan Southern Railway, and two years before his death the Michigan Central Railroad and the Canada Southern Railway. Thus did he create one of the great American systems of transportation. In the last years of his life, his influence on national finance was stabilizing. When the panic of 1873 was at its worst, he announced that the New York Central was paying its millions of dividends as usual, and let contracts for the building of the Grand Central Terminal in New York City, with four tracks leading from it, giving employment to thousands of men. He saw to it, however, that the city paid half the cost of the viaduct and open-cut approaches to the station.

His first wife died in 1868, and on Aug. 21, 1869, he married Frank Armstrong Crawford, a young lady from Mobile, Ala., who survived him when he died on Jan. 4, 1877, after an illness of about eight months. His fortune was estimated at more than $100,000,000, of which he left about $90,000,000 to William and about $7,-500,000 to the latter's four sons; he expressed his contempt for womankind by leaving less than $4,000,000 to be distributed among his own eight daughters (*New York Tribune*, Jan. 9, 1877). His wife received a half million in cash, the New York home, and 2,000 shares of New York Central stock. Vanderbilt bestowed no money philanthropically until late in life, when he gave $1,-000,000 to Vanderbilt University (previously Central University) at Nashville, Tenn., of which he is regarded as the founder, and $50,000 to the Church of the Strangers in New York, of which his friend, the Rev. Charles F. Deems [*q.v.*], was pastor.

[W. A. Croffut, *The Vanderbilts and the Story of Their Fortune* (1886), apparently the source of most of the legends; A. D. H. Smith, *Commodore Vanderbilt. An Epic of American Achievement* (1927), an undocumented popularization; James Parton, *Famous Americans of Recent Times* (1867); "Cornelius Vandergerode, *Certain Rich Men* (1927); "Cornelius Vanderbilt," in *Hunt's Merchants' Mag. and Commercial Rev.*, Jan. 1865; "The Vanderbilt Memorial," in *Nation*, Nov. 18, 1869, a critical contemporary appraisal; B. J. Hendrick, "The Vanderbilt Fortune," in *McClure's Mag.*, Nov. 1908, a good article; E. H. Mott, *Between the Ocean and the Lakes. The Story of Erie* (1899); Gustavus Myers, *Hist. of the Great American Fortunes* (1910), vol. II, biased but documented and valuable; W. O. Scroggs, *Filibusters and Financiers* (1916); John Moody, *The Railroad Builders* (1919); Allan Nevins, *The Emergence of Modern America* (1927); F. C. Hicks, *High Finance in the Sixties* (1929); Matthew Josephson, *The Robber Barons* (1934); J. J. Clute, *Annals of Staten Island* (1877); records of the Moravian Church at New Dorp, Staten Island; scrapbook of clippings on the Cornelius Vanderbilt will, 1877-78, N. Y. Pub. Lib.; Frank Armstrong (Crawford) Vanderbilt and R. L. Crawford, *Laurus Crawfurdiana. Memorials of the Crawford Family* (privately printed, 1833), valuable for second marriage; obituaries in *N. Y. Tribune*, *N. Y. Times*, Jan. 5, 1877.]   A.F.H.

VANDERBILT, CORNELIUS (Nov. 27, 1843–Sept. 12, 1899), financier, philanthropist, son of William Henry [*q.v.*] and Maria Louisa (Kissam) Vanderbilt, and grandson of Cornelius Vanderbilt [*q.v.*], the founder of the for-tune, was born on a farm near New Dorp, Staten Island, N. Y. William Kissam and George Washington Vanderbilt [*qq.v.*] were younger brothers. He first attended the village common school near his home and later private schools in New York City. At the age of sixteen he took a clerkship in the Shoe and Leather Bank. When he left that place four years later to go into the banking house of Kissam Brothers, it is said that he was receiving $50 a month and was living within his income (*New York Times*, Sept. 13, 1899). He had by this time become a favorite of his grandfather, who insisted, however, that he must work his way upward. When he was about twenty-four he was taken by the elder Cornelius into the service of the New York & Harlem Railroad as assistant treasurer. A little later he became treasurer and held that place until 1880, when he was elected vice-president; from 1886 until his death he was president of the road. He was frequently praised by his grandfather for his thoroughness and reliability, and received from him a special legacy of $5,000,000. In 1883 his father resigned his presidencies of the several Vanderbilt railroads, and, under the new arrangement specified by him, Cornelius was elected chairman of the board of directors of the New York Central & Hudson River and Michigan Central Railroads, and president of the Canada Southern Railway. Upon the death of his father in 1885, Cornelius became the head of the Vanderbilt family, and—although the fortune was not held in common—the chief director of its investments. These were profitable, though conservative.

He was the hardest worker of the family. He built a palatial home on Fifth Avenue, and a mansion, "The Breakers," at Newport, R. I., but he had little or no time for society. He was often at his desk in the Grand Central Station Building before any clerk arrived in the morning. A director in many corporations, he took his duties seriously, attending meetings and scanning reports from every corporation minutely. His philanthropic and other activities outside his business were enormous. He was a trustee of the College of Physicians and Surgeons, which his father so greatly aided, and he and his three brothers united in adding the Vanderbilt Clinic to it, while their sister, Mrs. William D. Sloane, gave it a maternity hospital. Vanderbilt was trustee or executive chairman of several other hospitals in New York, a trustee of Columbia University (1891–99), of the General Theological Seminary, and of the new Cathedral of St. John the Divine, one of the board of managers of the Domestic and Foreign Missionary Society of the Protestant Episcopal Church, and for the last twelve years of his life chairman of the executive committee of the Metropolitan Museum of Art. Among his gifts to the Metropolitan was Rosa Bonheur's famous painting, "The Horse Fair," in 1887. He founded the Railroad Branch of the Y. M. C. A. and gave it a handsome clubhouse in New York. He was a warden of St. Bartholomew's Church and contributed generously for ground and buildings for a new parish house. In a single day he often attended meetings at three or four of these institutions. Such strenuous activity undoubtedly shortened his life. His four sons were all students at Yale, and in memory of William Henry, the eldest, who died while a junior there, he presented to the University in 1893 a dormitory then regarded as large and costly. His gifts to Yale are said to have reached a total of $1,500,000. Vanderbilt suffered a slight stroke of paralysis in 1896, and thereupon resigned many of his official posts. He died in New York City of cerebral hemorrhage in 1899. On Feb. 4, 1867, he had married Alice Claypoole Gwynne, daughter of the late Abram E. Gwynne of Cincinnati (*New York Tribune,* Feb. 7, 1867). She survived him, as did three sons, Cornelius, Alfred Gwynne, (lost on the *Lusitania,* 1915), and Reginald; and two daughters, Gertrude, who married Harry Payne Whitney and became a well-known sculptress, and Gladys, who married Count Laszio Szechenyi.

[Seth Low, "Cornelius Vanderbilt," *Columbia Univ. Quart.,* Dec. 1899, pp. 39–43; J. G. Wilson, in *N. Y. Geneal. & Biog. Record,* Oct. 1899, pp. 197–99; F. L. Ford, "The Vanderbilts and the Vanderbilt Millions," *Munsey's Magazine,* Jan. 1900; *Who's Who in America,* 1899–1900; obituaries in *N. Y. Tribune, N. Y. Times,* Sept. 13, 1899. See also bibliographies of the other Vanderbilts.]

A. F. H.

VANDERBILT, GEORGE WASHING-TON (Nov. 14, 1862–Mar. 6, 1914), capitalist, agriculturist, pioneer in forestry, the youngest son of William Henry [*q.v.*] and Maria Louisa (Kissam) Vanderbilt, was born near New Dorp, Staten Island, N. Y. He was educated mostly by private tutors, and spent much of his youth in touring the world with them. He was shy and studious, caring little for finance, though he succeeded in increasing his own fortune materially during his lifetime. He fell in love with the mountains of western North Carolina, and in 1889 began buying land south and southwest of Asheville, eventually acquiring 130,000 acres, it is said, including Mount Pisgah (5,749 feet), one of the most beautiful peaks in the Appalachians. Here he planned the finest country home in America. He had studied architecture, forestry, and landscape gardening in preparation

for it. He worked with the architect, Richard Morris Hunt [*q.v.*], on the plans, and superintended the construction of the building, the final cost of which was reported as $3,000,000. He spent millions more in improving the estate, which he named "Biltmore." Frederick Law Olmsted [*q.v.*] was the landscape gardener. Until the death of his widowed mother in 1896, he lived with her in her New York home. That mansion then reverted to him, but he promptly went to live in his North Carolina château. He married on June 2, 1898, Edith Stuyvesant Dresser of Newport, R. I., who proved a congenial helpmate in all his plans.

He became a scientific farmer and stockbreeder, as well as one of the pioneers in scientific forestry in America. His sales of pedigreed hogs came to be events of importance. One of his Jersey cows broke all records for milk production, and the milk and ice cream from his dairies, sold over a wide area of country, were the finest obtainable. It was said after his death: "The stimulus afforded by his example towards improved agricultural methods in the South is beyond all estimate" (*American Forestry,* June 1914, p. 425). He founded and conducted the Biltmore Nursery, which specialized in trees and plants of the Appalachian region, and at the time of his death was doing a handsome business. He built many miles of roads and trails through his great forest area, making it almost as accessible as a park. Gifford Pinchot was his first superintendent of forests, passing from that place to the head of the United States Division of Forestry in 1898. Vanderbilt founded the Biltmore School of Forestry on his estate, where large numbers of young men received training. He planned and built the model village of Biltmore as a center for the employees on his property. He bought another home in Washington, but spent most of his time in his Carolina mountains, overseeing his numerous operations, studying trees, birds, and animals, or doing research in his large library, which was especially rich in works on nature. He spoke eight languages and had a reading acquaintance with others. Among other benefactions, he built in 1888 and presented to the New York Free Circulating Library (later New York Public Library) its Jackson Square Branch, and gave to Columbia University the ground on which the Teachers College was built. He also built a private museum in New York City, filled it with objects of art which he had collected all over the world, and presented it to the American Fine Arts Society. He offered to sell the major portion of his forest land to the United States for a forest reserve, but the offer was not accepted until after his death, when the government bought a large tract from Mrs. Vanderbilt. He died in Washington, D. C., after an operation for appendicitis. Besides his widow, he left a daughter, Cornelia Stuyvesant.

[O. W. Price, "George W. Vanderbilt, Pioneer in Forestry," *American Forestry*, June 1914; D. A. Willey, "Forest Conservation at Biltmore," *American Homes and Gardens*, July 1909; B. M. Trebor, "Into the Azure of the Blue Ridge," *Travel*, Apr. 1911; Gifford Pinchot, *Biltmore Forest . . . An Account of its Treatment, and the Results of the First Year's Work* (1893); "Biltmore Forest," *Harper's Weekly*, July 28, 1900; *Who's Who in America*, 1912–13; obituaries in *N. Y. Times, N. Y. Tribune, Sun* (N. Y.), Mar. 7, 1914.] A. F. H.

VANDERBILT, WILLIAM HENRY (May 8, 1821–Dec. 8, 1885), financier, railroad operator, son of Cornelius Vanderbilt, 1794–1877 [*q.v.*] and Sophia (Johnson) Vanderbilt, was born at New Brunswick, N. J., where his mother operated a hotel while his father was master of a ferry-boat running thence to New York City. When he was eight years old, his parents removed to New York, and he attended grammar school. He was not physically strong during boyhood and adolescence, a weakness with which his able-bodied and dynamic father could not sympathize. At seventeen he was put to work in a ship-chandler's shop, but about a year later he became a clerk in the banking house of Drew, Robinson & Company, of which one of the partners was Daniel Drew [*q.v.*]. At the age of nineteen William offended his father, now well-nigh a millionaire, by marrying Maria Louisa Kissam, a young woman of refinement and good family, but the daughter of an impecunious Brooklyn clergyman. Cornelius himself had married at nineteen, but he thought it folly for one so weak and footless as William to do the same. William's health declined within a year after his marriage, and, believing that he would never amount to much in business or finance, the father bought a seventy-acre farm for him at New Dorp, Staten Island, and sent him and his wife to it to make their own way. William quietly accepted the situation, and proceeded to make the farm a paying venture. There were born his eight children, four sons and four daughters, all of whom later lived in Fifth Avenue mansions. He increased the size of his farm to 350 acres and handled it so well that its profits rose.

During the depression of 1857 the Staten Island Railroad, a line thirteen miles long, became insolvent, and William soon afterward asked his father's influence in having him appointed receiver. The father, though still doubtful of William's ability, acquiesced, and to his surprise the latter succeeded in rehabilitating the road. He was therefore a railroad executive before his fa-

ther went into that business. When Cornelius acquired control of the New York & Harlem Railroad, he made William vice-president (1864) and gave him a home on Fifth Avenue; and thus, when he was forty-three years old, the son's ability belatedly received parental recognition. The contemptuous ignoring and suppression of it for two-thirds of his lifetime, however, was a bitter drop in his cup; it gave him a somewhat dour exterior, and instilled cynicism into his nature. Soon after receiving the Harlem office, he was also made vice-president of the Hudson River Railroad, the second line acquired by his father. Even though he began to take an efficient hand in railroad affairs, showing great ability in management, in improving track and equipment, in regulating rates and conciliating labor, he was never permitted to become a full executive until his father's failing hand relinquished the reins in the last few months of his life. Then, with less than nine years of life left to him, he rapidly began to expand his activities.

One of his first problems was a contest over his father's will, brought jointly by a scapegrace brother, Cornelius Jeremiah, who had been cut off with $200,000, and two of his eight sisters, who had received only from $300,000 to $500,000 apiece. The bulk of the estate was left to William. The decision of the surrogate in his favor in March 1879 was followed by a secret compromise (*New York Tribune*, Apr. 8, 9, 1879). It was reported that William in settlement had given each of the eight sisters another half million in bonds, and had pacified Cornelius Jeremiah by guaranteeing to him the income from a million dollars.

It was at his insistence that his father had bought control of the Lake Shore & Michigan Southern Railway and the Michigan Central Railroad, and acquired considerable stock in the Canada Southern Railway. William now welded the last-named line into the New York Central network, combining it with the Michigan Central, and became president of all the affiliated corporations. Within three years he had bought control of the Chicago & North-Western Railway and a large interest in the Cleveland, Columbus, Cincinnati & Indianapolis Railway, which paved the way for the later entry of the Vanderbilt lines into Cincinnati and St. Louis. Controlling interest in the rival New York, Chicago & St. Louis Railway (Nickel Plate), opened in 1882, was acquired after that date by the Lake Shore & Michigan Southern. The former road was forced into the hands of receivers in 1885, sold at foreclosure in 1887, and reorganized by the Vanderbilt interests. In 1885 the New York,

West Shore & Buffalo Railway (West Shore), paralleling the line of the New York Central & Hudson River, was leased by Vanderbilt at the instance of J. Pierpont Morgan [*q.v.*]. When the New York Central trainmen and laborers refused to take part in the great railroad strike of 1877, despite a cut in their wages, Vanderbilt distributed $100,000 among them as reward for their loyalty (*New York Tribune,* Aug. 1, 1877). Like his father, he was constructive. He not only greatly improved the railroad lines under his domination, but enormously increased his own fortune.

Following the report on rate discrimination made in 1879 by the committee headed by A. Barton Hepburn [*q.v.*], Vanderbilt, recognizing the unpopularity of unified control, turned over to J. Pierpont Morgan 250,000 shares of his railroad stock for sale in Europe, in order to avoid depressing the American market (*New York Tribune,* Nov. 21, 27, 1879). The sale, which greatly increased the prestige of Morgan and relieved Vanderbilt, also brought much foreign capital into American business. For several years Vanderbilt was a large shareholder and a director of the Western Union Telegraph Company; but in March 1881 he resigned his directorate and sold most of his holdings in the company (*Ibid.,* Mar. 27, 1881). Probably warned by failing health, he resigned all his railroad presidencies in May 1883. Thereafter, he ordered, Vanderbilts should be chairmen of the boards of directors, and the presidents be practical, working executives of somewhat less power. His two older sons, Cornelius and William Kissam [*qq.v.*] were thereupon elected board chairmen of the various Vanderbilt lines.

Soon after his father's death, Vanderbilt erected a mansion on Fifth Avenue which was the talk of the nation, and acquired a gallery of paintings, not to mention sculpture and other items, which was declared to be the finest private collection then in existence. Nevertheless, he remained temperate and simple in personal habits to the end. His sons and daughters were all brought up in the same tradition. He was fond of horses and driving, as his father had been, and was often seen on suburban roads handling the reins of a pair of fast trotters. He was the owner of several racing horses. He made many benefactions during his lifetime. He gave $450,-000 all told to Vanderbilt University, Nashville, Tenn., $50,000 to St. Bartholomew's Episcopal Church, and, in 1884, $500,000 for new buildings to the College of Physicians and Surgeons. When the Khedive of Egypt presented an ancient obelisk to the United States, Vanderbilt paid the expense of *c.* $100,000 for removing it from Egypt and setting it in Central Park, New York (*New York Tribune,* July 21, 1880). In 1884 he insisted upon returning to Mrs. Ulysses S. Grant the deeds to certain real-estate parcels, her husband's swords, medals, works of art, and gifts from foreign governments, all forced by the General upon Vanderbilt in pledge for a loan of $150,000 which he was unable to repay.

It was believed that during the less than nine years of his sole power, William Henry Vanderbilt had nearly or quite doubled the fortune left him by his father. When he died suddenly of cerebral hemorrhage in New York in 1885, it was found that he had bequeathed $10,000,000, half outright and half in trust, to each of his eight children, Cornelius, William K., Frederick W., George W., Mrs. Elliott F. Shepherd, Mrs. William D. Sloane, Mrs. W. Seward Webb, and Mrs. H. McK. Twombly; most of them had already been given mansions. To his eldest son, Cornelius, he gave $2,000,000 more, and $1,-000,000 conditionally to the latter's eldest son, also named Cornelius. More than a million was distributed among various missions, churches, hospitals, the Y. M. C. A., the Metropolitan Museum of Art, and Vanderbilt University. The residue of the fortune was divided between the two eldest sons, Cornelius and William K., subject to the payment of a $200,000 annuity to his widow. To her also he left his home and objects of art; after her death these were to pass to the son George. He had provided elsewhere for the rebuilding of the little Moravian Church at New Dorp, Staten Island, where his father and mother had been parishioners and where he and all his brothers and sisters were christened; and in the cemetery adjoining he had erected a magnificent family mausoleum.

[W. A. Croffut, *The Vanderbilts and the Story of Their Fortune* (1886), with reprint of will; Earl Shinn (Edward Strahan), *Mr. Vanderbilt's House and Collection* (4 vols., 1883–84); also article on the house in *American Architect and Building News,* May 21, 1881; I. K. Morris, *Morris's Memorial History of Staten Island New York* (1898), vol. II; "The Vanderbilt Family of New York," a scrapbook of clippings from the *N. Y. Evening Post,* N. Y. Pub. Lib.; scrapbook of clippings on the Cornelius Vanderbilt will, 1877–78, N. Y. Pub. Lib.; obituaries in *N. Y. Herald, N. Y. Tribune* (two pages), Dec. 9, 1885; *N. Y. Herald,* Dec. 9, 1900, long article with family tree. See also Gustavus Myers, *History of the Great American Fortunes* (1910), vol. II; John Moody, *The Railroad Builders* (1919); Matthew Josephson, *The Robber Barons* (1934); A. D. H. Smith, *Cornelius Vanderbilt* (1927); and other works cited in the bibliography of his father.]

A. F. H.

VANDERBILT, WILLIAM KISSAM (Dec. 12, 1849–July 22, 1920), capitalist, sportsman, second son of William Henry [*q.v.*] and Maria Louisa (Kissam) Vanderbilt and grandson of "Commodore" Cornelius Vanderbilt [*q.v.*], was born on his father's farm on Staten Island, N. Y. He was a brother of Cornelius (1843–1899) and George Washington Vanderbilt [*qq.v.*]. He studied under private tutors for several years, and then was sent for a time to school in Geneva, Switzerland. At nineteen, however, he was set to work in the office of the Hudson River Railroad, of which his grandfather was president and principal owner. He worked his way upward in the railroad offices until in 1877 he was made second vice-president of the New York Central & Hudson River Railroad, in which place he served for six years. In 1883 his father resigned his railroad presidencies, and William Kissam was elected chairman of the board of directors of the Lake Shore & Michigan Southern Railway; he was president (1882–87) of the New York, Chicago & St. Louis Railway, and became chairman of the board in 1887. After the death of his father in 1885, he and his brother Cornelius were the chief managers of the family fortune and investments. As a director in the Vanderbilt railroads and other corporations he served diligently and efficiently, though he was never as fond of business as his brother Cornelius. The latter's partial disablement in 1896 and death in 1899 brought William more actively into the executive work of the Vanderbilt railroads. But the management of such vast properties was irksome to him, and in 1903 he voluntarily permitted the direction of the New York Central system (now comprising nearly 12,000 miles of track) to pass to what was described as the Rockefeller-Morgan-Pennsylvania combination (*New York Tribune*, Mar. 25, 1903). The Vanderbilts were large owners of Pennsylvania Railroad stock, and continued to be dominant in the ownership of the New York Central lines, but thereafter the executive direction was in other hands. Vanderbilt continued, however, as a board member of many railroads until his death, and materially aided in increasing the size of the Vanderbilt fortune.

An enthusiastic yachtsman, he was one of the syndicate which built and sailed the *Defender,* the successful holder of the *America's* cup against a British challenge in 1895 (H. L. Stone, *The America's Cup Races,* 1930). He owned many race horses, being a particularly important figure on the turf in France. He was active in the affairs of the Metropolitan Opera Company and in theatrical matters. He joined with his brothers in founding the Vanderbilt Clinic, and made gifts to the Y. M. C. A. and to Columbia University. During the World War he took an active interest in hospital work and aviation, and contributed towards the relief of war sufferers in Italy. His interest in and benefactions to the Lafayette Escadrille resulted in his being elected honorary president of that organization, and being decorated with the Cross of the Legion of Honor by the French government (*New York Times,* July 23, 1920). He collected a large gallery of fine paintings, which he bequeathed to the Metropolitan Museum of Art. He died in Paris. He married Alva Murray Smith of Mobile, Ala., on Apr. 20, 1875. It is said that in the eighties she fully established the social position of the family, who had hitherto been frowned on by the Astors and Ward McAllister. She divorced Vanderbilt on Mar. 5, 1895, and later married Oliver H. P. Belmont (*New York Tribune,* Mar. 6, 1895, Jan. 12, 1896). Vanderbilt on Apr. 25, 1903, married Mrs. Anna (Harriman) Sands Rutherfurd, daughter of Oliver Harriman (*Ibid.,* Apr. 23, 26, 30, 1903). He left three children, all by his first wife: William K., Jr., Harold S., and Consuelo, who married the Duke of Marlborough.

[R. N. Burnett, "William Kissam Vanderbilt," *Cosmopolitan,* Mar. 1904; B. J. Hendrick, "The Vanderbilt Fortune," in *McClure's Magazine,* Nov. 1908; J. V. Van Pelt, *A Monograph of the William K. Vanderbilt House* (1925); *Who's Who in America,* 1920–21; certificate of first marriage, Dept. of Health, City of N. Y., Borough of Manhattan; obituaries in *N. Y. Times, N. Y. Tribune,* July 23, 1920. See also bibliographies of the other Vanderbilts.]   A. F. H.

VANDERBURGH, WILLIAM HENRY

(*c.* 1798–Oct. 14, 1832), fur trader, was born in Vincennes, Ind., one of the nine children of Henry and Frances (Cornoyer) Vanderburgh. His father, who was a captain in the 5th New York Regiment during the Revolution, moved after the war to Vincennes, where he married and was appointed a judge of the supreme court of Indiana Territory in 1800. William Henry entered the United States Military Academy in 1813, but did not graduate. He soon went West, and in a few years established a reputation as a fur trader with the Missouri Fur Company. During the Leavenworth expedition to the upper Missouri in 1823, as captain of the Missouri Fur Company's volunteers he participated on Aug. 10 in the demonstration against the villages of the Arikaras (*South Dakota Historical Collections,* vol. I, 1902, pp. 196 ff.), made in retaliation for the earlier attack of these Indians upon the trading party led by Gen. William H. Ashley [*q.v.*]. Sometime afterward he left the Missouri Fur Company and became a partner in the powerful American Fur Company, a concern ambitious to gain complete control of the Northwestern fur business.

Vanderburgh soon won the confidence of the company's management, particularly that of Kenneth MacKenzie [q.v.], the autocratic factor of the field headquarters at Fort Union, at the mouth of the Yellowstone. MacKenzie put him in charge of the Rocky Mountain trappers, and his subsequent operations greatly aided the company in eventually achieving its coveted monopoly. Entering the bitter competition for the mountain trade, Vanderburgh proved an indefatigable leader against the partisans of the Rocky Mountain Fur Company, headed by such experienced frontiersmen as James Bridger and Thomas Fitzpatrick [qq.v.]. With his parties he penetrated to the heart of the mountains in 1829–30, suffering great hardships, and on one occasion (1830) fighting a battle with the Blackfoot Indians.

In 1832 he went with his followers to the summer rendezvous of the mountain men at Pierre's Hole, where the employees of companies and the free trappers alike congregated. So successful had he already been in trailing them to some of their best trapping grounds, that Bridger and Fitzpatrick here proposed to him to divide the territory, but Vanderburgh refused. On leaving Pierre's Hole they therefore led him a wild-goose chase. He followed them toward the Three Forks of the Missouri, thus coming unaware into the territory of the hostile Blackfoot. On Oct. 14, 1832, with an advance party of six of his men, he was ambushed by about a hundred Blackfoot warriors on an affluent of the Jefferson River. He and one of his followers, Alexis Pillon, were killed. The remainder of the party retreated, but encountered a company of friendly Flathead and Pend d'Oreille Indians with whom they returned to bury the mutilated body of their unfortunate chief. Able, chivalrous, and energetic, "bearing himself always with the air and quality of a leader" (Chittenden, post, II, 665), Vanderburgh was one of the outstanding figures in that group of hardy adventurers who made the fur-trading epoch of the early Northwest one of the most colorful in American history.

[H. M. Chittenden, *The Am. Fur Trade of the Far West* (2 vols., 1902); Doane Robinson, "Official Correspondence of the Leavenworth Expedition into South Dakota in 1823," *S. Dak. Hist. Colls.*, vol. I (1902); geneal. data from Hazel Whiteleather, Ind. State Lib., Indianapolis.]   J. M. H.

VAN DER DONCK, ADRIAEN (May 7, 1620–c. 1655), colonist, lawyer, was born in the city of Breda in the province of North Brabant. His parents were Cornelis van der Donck and Agatha, daughter of Adriaen van Bergen, a member of a party of Dutch patriots which recovered the castle of Breda from the Spanish in 1590. Van der Donck received his early education in his native city, and about 1638 entered the University of Leyden, where he studied law. Seeking employment, he was brought to the attention of Kiliaen van Rensselaer, patroon of Rensselaerswyck in New Netherland, who was looking for a *schout,* or officer of justice, for his manor. Satisfied of the young man's fitness, Van Rensselaer engaged him; he was commissioned *schout,* May 13, 1641, and arrived at his new post in August of that year. He was given the lease of the farm called "Welys Burg" on Castle Island.

As *schout* he served as sheriff or officer of justice and was in charge of the collection of debts due the patroon from the tenants. Though aristocratic by birth and training, he showed considerable sympathy with the farmers of Rensselaerswyck, declining to press them when they had difficulty in meeting their obligations. In consequence he was accused of laxity in caring for his employer's interests. Van Rensselaer seems also to have expected Van der Donck to exercise a guiding influence over young Arent van Curler [q.v.], the Patroon's grand-nephew, who was *commis* or business agent of the manor. Since the two young men were almost of an age, this situation bred ill feeling which soon grew into enmity. Van Curler complained to the Patroon; the Patroon forbade Van der Donck to carry out a scheme for establishing a colony at Katskill; and during the confused state of affairs following the death of Van Rensselaer in 1643 or 1644, Van der Donck's service as *schout* came to an end. He remained upon his farm at Castle Island, however, until his buildings were destroyed by fire in 1646. Meanwhile, in the summer of 1645 he successfully negotiated a treaty between the Dutch and the Mohawk Indians, and for this service, he was given permission to establish a colony, "Colen Donck," at Nepperhaen on the left bank of the Hudson, opposite the Palisades. Van der Donck was known as the "Jonker" (about the equivalent of esquire), and from this title the settlement on his land derived its present name of Yonkers.

In February 1649, Van der Donck was made secretary of the Board of Nine Men under Petrus Stuyvesant [q.v.]. In this capacity he wrote the famous "Remonstrance" (*Vertoogh van Nieu-Neder-Land,* 1650), setting forth the people's grievances, and he was one of the three sent to The Hague to present it to the States-General. His connection with this act gained him the enmity of Stuyvesant and his secretary Van Tienhoven, who tried in various ways to embarrass him at The Hague. While detained in the Netherlands by the government he finished his legal course at Leyden, received a degree, *Supremus in jure,* Apr. 10, 1653, and was admitted to practice as an advocate before the supreme court of the Netherlands.

During this time he was engaged in writing an account of New Netherland, which was officially recommended to the States-General in May 1653, and in July he was granted a fifteen-year copyright on his work. He had been authorized to prepare a history, but Stuyvesant had refused him access to the official records. Thus his book, *Beschrijvinge van Nieuvv Nederlant,* is, as its title indicates, a description rather than a narrative. It was first published in 1655 at Amsterdam and reprinted in 1656. Van der Donck returned to America late in 1653 with permission to give legal advice, but not to appear before the courts of New Netherland, since there was no lawyer in the colony able to meet him. He died before the end of 1655. In 1645 he had married Mary Doughty, daughter of Francis Doughty, an English minister of New Amsterdam. After his death, his widow married Hugh O'Neale of Maryland.

[E. B. O'Callaghan, *Docs. Rel. to the Col. Hist. . . . of N. Y.,* vols. I, II (1856, 1858); A. J. F. van Laer, *Minutes of the Court of Rensselaerswyck, 1648–1652* (1922), and *N. Y. State Lib.: Van Rensselaer Bowier MSS.* (1908); P. C. Molhuysen, *Bronnen Tot de Geschiedenis der Leidsche Univ.,* III (1918), 70; E. B. O'Callaghan, *Hist. of New Netherland* (2 vols., 1846); J. R. Brodhead, *Hist. of the State of N. Y.* (2 vols., 1846); J. T. Scharf, *Hist. of Westchester County, N. Y.* (1886), I, 66–71.] E.L.W.H.

VANDERGRIFT, JACOB JAY (Apr. 10, 1827–Dec. 26, 1899), river captain, pioneer oil producer, was born in Allegheny, Pa., the son of William and Sophia (Sarver) Vandergrift. He attended private and public schools in Pittsburgh but was thrown on his own resources at an early age and became a cabin boy successively on the river steamboats *Bridgewater* and *Pinta.* Employed subsequently on boats plying the Allegheny River, he attracted the attention of his employers because of his industry and energy, and advanced rapidly. He was the first captain with sufficient courage and determination to utilize the space in front of his boat as well as on the sides in towing barges. Prior to 1853 he was in command of the *Hail Columbia,* one of the finest steamboats on the Wabash River. By 1858 he had purchased part interest in the *Red Fox* and in the *Conestoga.*

Just before the Civil War he went to what is now West Virginia, attracted by newspaper accounts of the oil wells there. The outbreak of the war forced him to sacrifice his investments and leave the state. Going to Oil City, Pa., then

little more than a wilderness, he became a shipper of oil, and later a dealer, making much money through his transactions. About 1868 he formed a partnership with George V. Forman, under the firm name of Vandergrift, Forman & Company, and entered upon extensive operations, laying miles of pipes for facilitating oil transportation from wells to shipping depots. In 1872 John Pitcairn [q.v.] joined the firm, which about that time established the Imperial Refinery, having a daily capacity of two thousand barrels. Although not the builder of the first pipe line, Vandergrift is said to have been the first to make a pipe line profitable. In 1877 the "United Pipe Lines of Vandergrift, Forman & Company" were consolidated with others as "United Pipe Lines," which, in turn, in 1884 was merged into the National Transit Company. Vandergrift and his partner Pitcairn also laid what was probably the first natural gas line of any importance and demonstrated to the manufacturing world the value of gas. Vandergrift subsequently formed gas companies in neighboring West Virginia. In addition to founding the Pittsburgh Petroleum Exchange and the Seaboard National Bank of New York, he was interested in iron and steel production and built the town of Vandergrift, Pa., as a model dwelling place for the employees of his Apollo Iron and Steel Company. He was also a large investor in Pittsburgh real estate, and made his home in that city after 1881.

From his ample fortune he built an orphan home there and aided churches and hospitals. He was twice married: first, Dec. 29, 1853, to Henrietta Morrow of Pittsburgh, who bore him four daughters and five sons; she died in 1881, and on Dec. 4, 1883, he married Frances G. (Anshutz) Hartley. On the morning of the day of his death he went to his office and worked until noon as was his custom. He was buried in Allegheny Cemetery, Pittsburgh.

[Erasmus Wilson, *Standard Hist. of Pittsburgh* (1898); *The Biog. Encyc. of Pa.* (1874); *Encyc. of Contemporary Biog. of Pa.,* vol. I (1889); G. I. Reed and others, *Century Cyc. of Hist. and Biog. of Pa.* (1904, vol. II); *Pittsburg Dispatch,* Dec. 27, 1899.] A.I.

VANDERGRIFT, MARGARET [See JANVIER, MARGARET THOMSON, 1844–1913].

VAN DER KEMP, FRANCIS ADRIAN (May 4, 1752–Sept. 7, 1829), scholar, author, was born in Kampen, Overyssel, in the Netherlands, the son of John Van der Kemp, an army captain, and his wife, Anna Catharina (Leydekker). For several years he was a cadet in an infantry regiment and at the same time cultivated the classical languages. In September 1770 he entered Groningen University, where he devoted himself to linguistic and philosophical studies. At the end of three years he left the institution because his deistical ideas (*Autobiography*, p. 13) and his attachment to a celebrated teacher who was charged with Arminianism made his presence intolerable. He next became a student in a Baptist seminary at Amsterdam, where he engaged in an examination of the Christian religion (*Ibid.*, pp. 18–20), giving his attention to the New Testament apart from dogmatic theology. Satisfied of the truth of the Gospel, he was admitted as candidate for the ministry on Dec. 18, 1775. The following year, Nov. 13, he was installed pastor at Leyden. Disputes with his consistory, principally over a demand for his subscription to a creed, ended in victories for the young preacher.

A burning interest in political agitation earned for Van der Kemp the friendship of the leaders in the Patriot movement, which sought to reduce the power of the Stadtholder and to restrain the House of Orange within constitutional limits. In behalf of this movement he wrote books and pamphlets, often anonymously. When, to shield the printer, he announced his responsibility for a certain publication, he was involved in criminal procedures, which dragged along a year or two and ceased in 1782 with his acquittal. In 1775 the Patriot party found itself in natural sympathy with the American colonies in the uprisings which led to independence, and Van der Kemp publicly advocated the principles which were the foundation of the American cause. With John Adams, who appeared in Amsterdam as American commissioner in the summer of 1780, he formed a friendship to which a correspondence of many years bears witness.

As the political struggle in Holland verged on civil war, the Mennonist pastor became captain of a militia company, withdrawing from the charge of his peaceful congregation. In the first clash of opposing forces, the court party was victor and Van der Kemp was taken prisoner. When, in 1787, the wife of the Stadtholder, a Prussian princess, maneuvered successfully to bring a Prussian army to Amsterdam, only banishment remained for prominent Patriots. Accordingly, the following year Van der Kemp sailed with his family for New York, arriving May 4. The exile's reception by eminent Americans included an invitation to the hospitality of Mount Vernon (Jared Sparks, *The Writings of George Washington*, vol. IX, 1847, pp. 368–69). After six years devoted to experimental agriculture near Kingston, N. Y., he established a home by Oneida Lake on a tract which he named

Kempwyk, near Bernhard's Bay. Here he entered on a life which, if not idyllic, had consolations for ill fortune. He was appointed a justice of the peace, and he organized a society of agriculture and natural history. His impaired fortunes, however, compelled him to seek a new home, and his final residence was in Olden Barneveld (the present Barneveld). Farming, correspondence, discursive studies, and literary work filled up his remaining years. At the solicitation of Gov. DeWitt Clinton, he translated the Dutch colonial records of New York. The resulting twenty-four manuscript volumes were burned in the fire that destroyed the capitol in 1911. Some examples of his miscellaneous writings in Dutch are in American libraries. He was married, May 20, 1782, to Reinira Engelberta Johanna Vos; three children were born to them. In 1903 *Francis Adrian Van der Kemp, 1752–1829: An Autobiography*, with a historical sketch, was published by Helen L. Fairchild.

[The *Autobiog.* contains lists of Van der Kemp's writings in Dutch and English; see also DeWitt Clinton, *Letters on the Natural Hist. and Internal Resources of . . . N. Y.* (1822), pp. 216–19; C. F. Adams, *The Works of John Adams* (10 vols., 1850–56); Crisfield Johnson, *Hist. of Oswego County, N. Y.* (1877); J. C. Churchill, *Landmarks of Oswego County, N. Y.* (1895); *Hist. of Oneida County, N. Y.* (1878).]

R. E. D.

VANDERLYN, JOHN (Oct. 15, 1775–Sept. 23, 1852), historical and portrait painter, was born in Kingston, N. Y., the son of Nicholas and Sarah (Tappen) Vanderlyn, and the grandson of Pieter Vander Lyn (1687–1778), a New York painter of the descendants of early Dutch families in Manhattan (see C. X. Harris, "Pieter Vanderlyn," *New York Historical Society Quarterly Bulletin*, Oct. 1921). John was sent to the Kingston Academy, where he remained until he was sixteen. When not busy at school he worked in the shop of a blacksmith and wagon painter, and, according to Tuckerman's picturesque but uncertain account, it was there that he was met by Aaron Burr [q.v.], who became his chief patron. In 1792 John was taken to New York by his brother Nicholas and introduced to Thomas Barrow, a print-seller, in whose shop he worked for about two years. His first lessons in drawing were taken under Archibald Robertson [q.v.], with whom he studied three years. He painted a few portraits in Kingston, where he returned for a winter, and a few more in New York, and was allowed to copy some of the portraits of Gilbert Stuart [q.v.]. His copy of Stuart's portrait of Aaron Burr was so well done that Burr sent him to Philadelphia to study under Stuart for eight or nine months, employed him on his return to paint his portrait and that of his daughter, Theodosia, and in the autumn of 1796 supplied him with means for a five years' stay in Paris. There he studied under "Mr. Vincent, an eminent painter" (possibly Antoine Paul Vincent). In 1801 he returned to America, and in 1802 painted two pictures of Niagara Falls which were engraved and published in London in 1804.

In the spring of 1803 he returned to Europe. He spent two years in Paris (1803–05), two in Rome (1805–07), where he met and became an intimate friend of Washington Allston [q.v.], and then seven more in Paris (1808–15), traveling widely at intervals. In the second year at Rome he painted his "Marius amid the Ruins of Carthage," which made a great stir. In 1808, at the Paris Salon, it received a gold medal conferred at the behest of Napoleon. It was this success that led the artist to make a stay of seven years in Paris, where he prospered. He made copies after the masterpieces of Raphael, Titian, and Correggio in the Louvre; in 1812 his nude figure, "Ariadne," made a still greater sensation than the "Marius." It was the last of his notable achievements. It was bought and engraved by Asher B. Durand [q.v.], and finally came into the possession of the Pennsylvania Academy of the Fine Arts.

After his return to New York in 1815 Vanderlyn's popularity gradually waned. He painted a number of portraits of eminent men, including four presidents (Monroe, Madison, Jackson, and Taylor), John C. Calhoun, Burr, George Clinton, and Robert R. Livingston. The portrait of Zachary Taylor belongs to the Corcoran Gallery of Art, Washington; those of John A. Sidell, Francis L. Waddell, and a self-portrait are in the Metropolitan Museum, New York; several others are owned by the New York Historical Society. An enmity grew up between Vanderlyn and John Trumbull [q.v.] over the paintings for the rotunda of the Capitol (see Isham, *post*, p. 130), but in 1832 the House of Representatives commissioned Vanderlyn to make a full-length copy of Stuart's Washington. In 1837 he was one of four painters invited to undertake paintings in the rotunda. Going to Paris to paint his "The Landing of Columbus" under this commission, he employed a French artist to assist him, a procedure in which there was nothing unusual. Hostile critics made the most of it, however, and charged him with fraud.

His last years were tragic and embittered. For some twelve years his large panoramas of Paris, Versailles, Athens, and Mexico were exhibited in the New York Rotunda, built for this purpose, in the City Hall Park, New York, but they were costly failures. His affairs went from bad to worse. Worry and poverty crushed his spirit. Finally, in 1852, he reappeared in his native town and borrowed a shilling from an old friend to pay for the transportation of his baggage to the hotel. The following morning he was found dead in his room. He was unmarried. An imposing funeral was given him by the townspeople. His early work is his best, but the "Marius" was vastly overrated and the "Ariadne" is not much more than an accomplished academic study of the nude. Later he leaned too much upon the old Italian masters and thus lost touch with nature; the big historical panel in the Capitol is a typically meretricious example of the so-called grand style. His portraits were somewhat uneven, and only a few of them have any distinction aside from their merits as likenesses.

[There are many references to Vanderlyn in the letters and journals of Aaron Burr. See also Marius Schoonmaker, *The Hist. of Kingston, N. Y.* (1888); William Dunlap, *The Hist. of the Rise and Progress of the Arts of Design in the U. S.* (1918), ed. by F. W. Bayley and C. E. Goodspeed; H. T. Tuckerman, *Book of the Artists* (1867); W. J. Kip, in *Atlantic Monthly*, Feb. 1867; *Putnam's Monthly*, June 1854; C. H. Caffin, *The Story of Am. Painting* (1907); Samuel Isham, *The Hist. of Am. Painting* (1905); Suzanne La Follette, *Art in America* (1929); J. E. Stillwell, *The Hist. of the Burr Portraits* (1928); *Description of the Panorama of the Palace and Gardens of Versailles* (1820); obituaries in *Ulster Republican* (Kingston, N. Y.), Sept. 29, and *Rondout Courier* (Kingston), Oct. 1, 1852; inscription on monument in Wiltwyck Cemetery, Kingston, N. Y.]   W. H. D.

VAN DER STUCKEN, FRANK VALENTIN (Oct. 15, 1858–Aug. 16, 1929), composer, conductor, was born in Fredericksburg, Gillespie County, Tex. He was the son of Jan Frank and Sophia (Schoenewolf) Van der Stucken. His father was of Belgian and his mother of German birth, and after the Civil War the family went to Belgium to live. The lad's musical education was started as soon as he reached Europe, and he was first entered at the Conservatory of Music in Antwerp, where he became a pupil of Pierre Benoît. From 1866 to 1876 he studied violin with Émile Wambach in Brussels, and for the following two years he was a pupil of Reinecke, Grieg, and Langer in Leipzig. By the time he was twenty years of age, he had shown much promise as a composer, and had produced his "Gloria," for chorus and orchestra; his "Te Deum," for solo, chorus and orchestra; and a "Festmarsch" for orchestra. In the season 1881–82, he was *Kapellmeister* for the Stadt Theatre in Breslau. At Breslau he composed his suite on Shakespeare's "Tempest" (1885), "Festzug" (1891), "Pagina d'Amore" (copyright 1891), and a lyric drama, "Vlasda" (copyright 1891). Franz Liszt invited him to Weimar in 1883 to give a concert of his own works under Liszt's patronage. This event occurred in November, and the program included a symphonic prologue to Heine's tragedy, "William Ratcliff."

Van der Stucken's reputation had already extended to the land of his birth, and in 1884 he was invited to succeed Leopold Damrosch [q.v.] as the conductor of the Arion Society, a male chorus in New York City. He held this position until 1895, and in 1892 took the organization on a European tour. Meanwhile, he appeared frequently as an orchestral conductor. During the season 1885–86, he presented a series of "novelty concerts" at Steinway Hall, where he gave the American premiere of Brahm's Third Symphony. Two years later, 1887–88, he gave a series of "symphonic concerts" at Chickering Hall in New York. It was in these concerts that he adopted a policy for which he is perhaps most remembered, the inclusion of a number of "all-American" programs, presenting exclusively the works of American musicians. He was certainly one of the first to offer such programs, and for this he won the undying gratitude of those who urged the cause of American music. In 1889 he gave a program of American compositions at the French International Exhibition. Throughout his whole life he fought for the recognition of American talent at home and abroad.

He was much in demand as a conductor of music festivals. In 1887 he directed a festival in Indianapolis; in 1891, one in Newark; in 1894, another in New York. He left New York in 1895 to live in Cincinnati, Ohio, where he had been offered the conductorship of the Cincinnati Symphony Orchestra and a position as director of the Cincinnati Conservatory of Music. He retained the directorship of the College until 1903, and was conductor of the Cincinnati orchestra until 1907. After the death of Theodore Thomas [q.v.], Van der Stucken was appointed conductor of the Cincinnati May Music Festivals, which he directed regularly from 1906 until 1912. From 1908 he lived mostly in Europe, returning to America for the Cincinnati Festivals (1923, 1925, 1927), and for other events that demanded his attention. He appeared frequently abroad as conductor of the Wagner festival at Antwerp in 1913; in a concert of orchestral works at Copenhagen, 1919; as conductor of a series of Wagner and Gluck concerts in Antwerp during the season 1920–21; and as director of the Ysaye concerts in Brussels, 1921 and 1923. He was decorated with the Order of Leopold and made an Officier de l'Ordre de la Couronne by the king of Belgium. He died in Hamburg, Germany, following a surgical operation, and was survived by his wife, Mary

Vollmer, to whom he had been married in June 1880, and four children. As a composer, Van der Stucken had a fine talent for orchestration; his scores sparkle with subtle effects. His music is seldom heard today, but in his own time it was highly praised. Rupert Hughes said of his songs: "It is always the unexpected that happens, though this unexpected thing almost always proves to be a right thing. Without any sense of strain or bombast he reaches superb climaxes; without eccentricity he is individual . . ." (*American Composers, post,* p. 193). In addition to the works already mentioned, his compositions included "Pax Triumphans" (1902), a symphonic prologue first presented at the Brooklyn, N. Y., Festival in 1900; a festival march, "Louisiana"; a "Festival Hymn" for men's chorus and orchestra; and many shorter works for orchestra, chorus and for solo voice.

[*Who's Who in America,* 1928–29; Henry Hadley, commemorative address on Van der Stucken, published by the American Academy of Arts and Letters, *Acad. Publication,* no. 77 (1932); *Grove's Dict. of Music and Musicians,* 3rd ed., vol. V (1928), and the *Am. Supp.* (1930); *Baker's Biog. Dict. of Musicians* (3rd ed., 1919); Rupert Hughes and Arthur Nelson, *Am. Composers* (revised ed., 1914); J. T. Howard, *Our Am. Music* (1931); *Musical Courier,* Aug. 24, 1929; Olin Downes, "An American Pioneer," *N. Y. Times,* Aug. 25, 1929; *N. Y. Times,* Aug. 20, 21, 1929.] J. T. H.

VANDER VEER, ALBERT (July 10, 1841– Dec. 19, 1929), surgeon, was born in Root, Montgomery County, N. Y., the son of Abram Harris and Sarah (Martin) Vander Veer. His parents were both descendants of early Dutch settlers, the Vander Veers going back to Cornelis Janse Vander Veer who settled in Long Island in 1659. Vander Veer attended the union schools of Palatine, N. Y., and Canojoharie Academy. At the age of eighteen he began his medical studies under Dr. Simeon Snow. In 1861–62 he studied in Albany under Dr. John Swinburne, a surgeon, and attended lectures at the Albany Medical College (later part of Union University). Leaving Albany in 1862 to enlist in the army, he had the distinction of being one of the original hundred commissioned as United States medical cadets. When he was mustered out of service in 1865, he was a surgeon with the rank of major. During the Civil War he was stationed in Washington, D. C., at the hospital of Columbian College (later George Washington University), and there in 1863 he received the degree of M.D. After the war he spent a short time studying at the College of Physicians and Surgeons, New York City.

He returned to Albany in 1866 and on June 5, 1867, married Margaret E. Snow, the daughter of his former teacher, by whom he had six children. His long association with Albany Medical

College began in 1869. He taught anatomy (1869–74), surgery (1876–1914), and served as dean (1897–1904). In 1914 he became professor emeritus of surgery, and in 1915 resigned. In 1874–76 he studied in London, Paris, and Berlin. He was for many years attending surgeon of Albany Hospital (1869–1904) and in 1904 became surgeon in chief. In Albany he was the first to take up the practice of abdominal surgery, and was considered one of the city's most eminent surgeons. He received honorary degrees from several institutions of learning and held office in many societies. He was president of the American Medical Association (1916), the American Surgical Association (1905), the American Association of Obstetricians and Gynecologists, the Medical Society of the State of New York (1885), and the Holland Society of New York (1904). He was decorated with the order of Orange-Nassau by the queen of Holland. He was vice-president of the Albany Institute of Art for thirty years and regent of the University of the State of New York from 1895 to 1927, serving also as vice chancellor (1915–21) and chancellor (1921–22). Forceful and energetic, he devoted himself earnestly to his hospital work, to his practice, and to the societies of which he was a member. Yet he seemed to find time to read extensively and to contribute widely to medical periodicals. In the later years of his life he spent much of his time at his Adirondacks camp, where he farmed on a small scale. A religious man, he was elder of the First Presbyterian Church, Albany, for over forty years. He was survived by three sons, all physicians.

[L. P. De Boer, *The Van der Veer Family* (1913); J. J. Vander Veer, *A Geneal. of . . . the Vander Veer Family in America* (1912); *Who's Who in America,* 1928–29; J. J. Walsh, *Hist. of Medicine in N. Y.* (1919); A. V. Raymond, *Union Univ., Its Hist.* (1907); *Annals of Surgery,* Dec. 1930; F. C. Curtis, in *Albany Medic. Annals,* "Alumni Meeting Number," vol. XL (1930); *Jour. Am. Medic. Asso.,* Dec. 28, 1929; *Trans. Am. Surgical Asso.,* vol. XLVIII (1930); *Surgery, Gynecology, and Obstetrics,* Jan. 1932; obituary in *Knickerbocker Press* (Albany), Dec. 20, 1929; bibliog. of Vander Veer's publications, in *Index-Cat. of the Lib. of the Surgeon-General's Office,* 1 ser., vol. XV (1894), 2 ser., vol. XX (1915).]   G. L. A.

VANDER WEE, JOHN BAPTIST (Feb. 20, 1824–Feb. 24, 1900), known in religion as Brother Alexius, provincial of the Xaverian Brothers, was born in Antwerp, Belgium. Having received considerable schooling in his native city, in 1845 he joined the Congregation of the Brothers of St. Francis Xavier (Xaverian Brothers), the impoverished and somewhat unstable foundation for which Theodore Ryken (Brother Francis Xavier) had obtained a rule only four years previously. Two years later, Oct.

3, 1847, he was professed in the little community of seventeen members. Trained under Ryken in a martyr-like spirit of sacrifice, he became an ideal religious and one of a colony sent in 1848 to establish the first foreign foundation at Bury, England. On the verge of actual starvation, he was forced to remove the colony to Manchester in 1850, where he re-introduced into England May processions and the scapular of Mount Carmel. From this mother-house, the congregation later developed a number of thriving schools in the British Isles. Ill health forced Brother Alexius to return to Bruges, where in 1854 he reorganized St. Francis Xavier's Institute into a popular school for English youths. In 1863 he was in Manchester in charge of the Catholic Collegiate Institute, and in that city assisted in the establishment of an orphange at Mayfield founded by the Duchess of Leeds (the former Louisa Caton of Baltimore, Md.). Apparently his association with her turned his mind toward America, where the Xaverian Brothers had established themselves in Louisville, Ky., in 1854, and in Baltimore in 1866.

In 1872 he left for America, and three years later was named provincial of the Xaverian Brothers in the United States. The Society was desperately poor, its brothers receiving salaries of only $130 a year. It had a small community in Louisville; a few parochial schools; and in Baltimore, St. Mary's Industrial School, an orphanage and home for needy and often wayward boys. With indomitable will and the practice of the severest economies, Brother Alexius labored with remarkable success during twenty-five years of command, though never did he ascribe any credit to himself. With little episcopal assistance and few donations of any consequence, he managed to build, without leaving any indebtedness, Mount St. Joseph's College and Provincial House in Baltimore, St. Xavier's College in Louisville, St. John's Preparatory School in Danvers, Mass.—one of the largest Catholic institutions of its kind—and a college novitiate at Old Point Comfort, Va. He also answered episcopal or pastoral invitations to take over parochial schools or high schools in Lowell, Lawrence, Somerville, and Worcester, Mass.; in Norfolk and Portsmouth, Va.; and in Wheeling, W. Va. Under his régime, St. Mary's Industrial School in Baltimore became one of the largest protectories for boys in the United States and served as a model for Catholic and state institutions for boy training. A humble man, severe in self-discipline yet affable, Brother Alexius was notably successful as an administrator and business man, retaining full control of the community until his rather sudden death from pneumonia. At the end, there was no public funeral or eulogy, but his devoted counselor, Cardinal Gibbons, presided over his funeral before his remains were interred in the Bonnie Brae Cemetery of Baltimore.

[Brother Julian, C.F.X., *Men and Deeds, The Xaverian Brothers in America* (1930); *Mount St. Joseph Collegian*, 5 no. 10; MSS. and chronicles in the archives of Mount St. Joseph Coll.; *Sun* (Baltimore), Feb. 26, 1900; information from an associate, Brother Isidore, C.F.X.]   R. J. P.

VAN DE VELDE, JAMES OLIVER (Apr. 3, 1795–Nov. 13, 1855), Roman Catholic prelate, was born near Termonde, Belgium, of a family of some social and political importance. Schooled in the home of an aunt in Saint-Armand who sheltered a proscribed priest-tutor, the boy was later enrolled in a boarding school at Ghent. Thereafter he taught French and Flemish at Puers and at a college in Mechlin, where he also studied theology in the seminary. Aroused by a patriotic disgust at Belgium's domination by Holland in the forced union decreed by the Congress of Vienna, Van de Velde was studying English and Italian with the object of going either to England or to Italy, when Charles Nerinckx [*q.v.*], in quest of Belgian priests, induced him to accompany him back to America in 1817. At Georgetown College, the young Belgian entered the Society of Jesus, and both taught in the college and followed courses in theology. Ordained by Archbishop Ambrose Maréchal [*q.v.*] on Sept. 25, 1827, he served about four years as chaplain at the Visitation Convent and attended missions in Montgomery County, Md.

In 1831 he was ordered to St. Louis University, where he became vice-president (1833) and president (1840–43). Four years after taking his solemn vows, he represented the vice-province of Missouri in the congregation of procurators of the Society assembled at Rome (1841) and came to know Pope Gregory XVI. As vice-provincial of Missouri (1843–48), he erected several churches, fostered the Jesuit missions of the far West, built an enlarged novitiate for the growing Society, and represented the province at the Sixth Council of Baltimore (1846). In 1848, when he was procurator and socius to the vice-provincial, he was named successor to Bishop William Quarter [*q.v.*] of Chicago, with the command to accept the undesired honor. Consecrated by Archbishop Peter Richard Kenrick at St. Louis (Feb. 11, 1849), Van de Velde undertook the burden, which was aggravated by the apparent hostility of some Irish priests who wanted neither a Jesuit nor a Belgian ordinary, regardless of his decided merits and recognized character as a scholar and self-sacrificing priest. At Chicago his tenure was brief and unhappy, yet he succeeded in reviving religion in the old French settlements as an Irishman could not have done, dedicated several churches, and began seventy, several of which were for the recent German immigrants. His first petition to resign and return to his Society was refused by Rome. In 1852 the Council of Baltimore urged him to retain his see and honored him as its emissary to Rome with the decrees of the Council. Apparently Rome heard his plea, for a year later (July 29, 1853) he was transferred to the quiet diocese of Natchez, although for a time he carried the burden of the dioceses of Chicago and Quincy in addition to his own charge. At Natchez he founded two schools and had started a college when he died suddenly of yellow fever, which he incurred in attending the stricken.

[R. H. Clarke, *Lives of the Deceased Bishops of the Cath. Church in the U. S.*, vol. II (1888), pp. 372–90; J. G. Shea, *Hist. of the Cath. Church in the U. S.*, vol. IV (1892); Francis Janssens, *Sketch of the Cath. Church in Natchez, Miss.* (1886); G. J. Garraghan, *The Catholic Church in Chicago* (1921); J. E. Rothensteiner, *Hist. of the Archdiocese of St. Louis* (1928); *Metropolitan Cath. Almanac* (1856), p. 301; *Cath. Almanac* (1856); Woodstock Letters, vol. X, 1880, p. 121; *N. Y. Freeman's Journal*, Sept. 15, 1849, Nov. 24, Dec. 8, 1855; obituary in *Daily Democratic Press* (Chicago), Nov. 17, 1855.]   R. J. P.

VAN DE WARKER, EDWARD ELY (Nov. 27, 1841–Sept. 5, 1910), gynecologist, was born in West Troy (later Watervliet), N. Y., the son of Martin P. and Lydia Myra (Ely) Van de Warker. His great-grandfather was Martin Van de Warker, who served as a private in the Revolutionary War. His mother was the daughter of John Burgoyne Ely, a descendant of a family of Loyalist sympathies in the Revolution. Van de Warker was first sent to a private school; he later attended Rensselaer Polytechnic Institute, and in 1859 began the study of medicine at Albany Medical College (later part of Union University), where in 1863 he received the degree of M.D. In the same year he became assistant surgeon in the 162nd Regiment, New York Volunteers; later he was surgeon-in-chief, 3rd Brigade, 1st Division, XIX Army Corps, and post surgeon, Winchester, Va., on the staff of Gen. Francis Fessenden. At the close of the Civil War he had attained the rank of major. In 1865 he entered upon the practice of his profession in Troy, N. Y., and on Dec. 23 married Louisa Margaret Gardner of Hancock, Mass., who died in 1868. They had one daughter. Van de Warker moved to Syracuse in 1870 and was married a second time on Nov. 6, 1872, to Helen Augusta Adams of that city. Van de Warker became one of the leading physicians of Syracuse, attained eminence as a surgeon, and was a pioneer in gynecology. As an operator he had few peers. He won immediate recognition for his plastic surgery at the pelvic outlet; he was known to have performed 2,000 laparotomies with relatively few mortalities. He was considered expert in diagnosis as well. He founded and was for many years surgeon-in-chief of the Syracuse Hospital for Women and Children, and served as surgeon to the Central New York Hospital and as consulting surgeon to St. Anne's Maternity Hospital. A founder of the American Gynecological Society, he belonged to many other medical organizations. He acted as president of the Onondaga Medical Society (1878), of the Central New York Medical Association (1885), and of the Syracuse Academy of Medicine; he was chairman of the section of obstetrics, American Medical Association (1887).

A man of wide culture and varied knowledge, his genial temperament made him a delightful companion. He contributed numerous articles to the medical journals of his time, of which the most important were "Mechanical Therapeutics of Versions and Flexions of the Uterus" (*Transactions of the American Gynecological Society*, vol. VII, 1883); "A Gynecological Study of the Oneida Community" (*American Journal of Obstetrics*, Aug. 1884), and "Extra-Uterine Pregnancy and Its Treatment by Electricity" (*Transactions of the American Gynecological Society*, vol. XII, 1888). His interests were not entirely confined to medicine. He was also the author of *Woman's Unfitness for Higher Co-Education* (1903), "Abandoned Canals of the State of New York" (*Popular Science Monthly*, Sept. 1909), and "A Winter Vacation to the Windward Islands" (*Medical News*, Aug. 10, 17, Sept. 17, 1889). Van de Warker retired from active service in 1908 because of failing health and died two years later, survived by the daughter of his second marriage.

[Heman Ely, *Records of the Descendants of Nathaniel Ely* (1885); *Album of the Fellows of the Am. Gynecological Soc., 1876–1900* (1901); H. A. Kelly and W. L. Burrage, *Am. Medic. Biogs.* (1920); *Albany Medic. Annals*, Oct. 1910; *Trans. Am. Gynecological Soc.*, vol. XXXVI (1911); date of death and information concerning Van de Warker's parents from his daughter, Mrs. A. M. Wose; date of birth and information on ancestry from the Empire State Soc. of the Sons of the Am. Revolution.]   **G. L. A.**

VAN DORN, EARL (Sept. 17, 1820–May 8, 1863), Confederate general, was born near Port Gibson, Miss., the descendant of Pieter van Dorn who in the seventeenth century emigrated from Holland to the colony that is now New York. He was the son of Sophia Donelson (Caffery) and Peter Aaron Van Dorn. His father was a graduate of the College of New Jersey (Princeton) in 1795 and removed from New Jersey to Virginia and then to Mississippi, where he was a lawyer and judge of the probate court. His mother was the niece of Mrs. Andrew Jackson. The boy was appointed a cadet of the United States Military Academy at West Point in 1838, was graduated in 1842, and was commissioned in the infantry. In 1843 he married Caroline Godbold of Mt. Vernon, Ala. He was in garrison at Fort Brown, Tex., at the outbreak of the war with Mexico and served in the field with distinction through the war. He was wounded at the city of Mexico. As a first lieutenant, promoted in 1847, he took part in the Seminole hostilities in Florida in 1849–50. In 1855 he was appointed captain in the 2nd (now 5th) Cavalry and until the beginning of the Civil War served with his regiment in Texas and the Indian Territory. In an action with the Comanches near Washita Village he received four wounds, two of them from arrows. He was promoted major in 1860.

He resigned from the army on Jan. 31, 1861, was appointed brigadier-general of Mississippi state troops, and was made major-general to succeed Jefferson Davis. Appointed as colonel of cavalry in the Confederate regular army and assigned to duty in Texas, he received the surrender of most of the Union troops there in April. His appointment as brigadier-general in the provisional army followed, and in September he was appointed major-general. In January 1862 he became commander of the transmississippi district. With a heterogeneous force, partially organized and trained, and hampered rather than helped by a body of wild Indians, he fought and lost the decisive battle of Pea Ridge, Ark., in March. Transferred east of the Mississippi, he operated to thwart the early movements against Vicksburg and in October was defeated by Rosecrans in a severe battle at Corinth, Miss. He was criticized for his conduct, but a court of inquiry found the charges disproved. Upon the arrival of General Pemberton, his senior, to take command, he was put in charge of the cavalry. In a brilliant raid on the Union depots at Holly Springs, Miss., in December, he captured the garrison and destroyed stores of great value, effectively crippling Grant's projected campaign. As he sat at his desk in his headquarters at Spring Hill, Tenn., he was shot and killed by a personal enemy. His death was a serious loss to the service, for he was an excellent cavalry commander. As he was defeated in both the important battles in which he was in chief command, his real merits have been generally overlooked.

[Some letters and papers in Lib. of Cong.; *A Soldier's Honor with Reminiscences of Major-Gen. Earl Van Dorn by his Comrades* (1902), ed. by E. V. D. Miller; G. W. Cullum, *Biog. Register of the Officers and Grads. of the U. S. Military Acad.*, 3rd ed., vol. II (1891); *War of the Rebellion: Official Records (Army)*; R. U. Johnson and C. C. Buel, *Battles and Leaders of the Civil War*, vols. I–II (1887–88); *Confederate Military Hist.* (1899), vol. VII, ed. by C. A. Evans; A. V. D. Honeyman, *The Van Doorn Family* (1909).]
T. M. S.

VAN DYCK, CORNELIUS VAN ALEN (Aug. 13, 1818–Nov. 13, 1895), Arabic scholar, medical missionary, was born at Kinderhook, N. Y., the son of Henry L. and Catherine (Van Alen) Van Dyck. After preparation at Kinderhook Academy, he attended Jefferson Medical College in Philadelphia, graduating in 1839. Appointed a missionary of the American Board of Commissioners for Foreign Missions, he sailed from Boston for Syria in January 1840, and in April reached Beirut. After accompanying William McClure Thomson [*q.v.*] on an extensive tour through northern Syria, he went in July to Jerusalem. In January 1841 he was transferred to Beirut, where he studied Arabic intensively under his lifelong friend Butrus al-Bustāni, the lexicographer, Nasif al-Yaziji, a poet of distinction, and Yusuf al-Asir, a Moslem mufti. A tenacious memory and natural linguistic ability enabled him to acquire rapidly a thorough knowledge of both speech and literature. On Dec. 23, 1842, he married Julia, daughter of Peter Abbott, formerly British consul general in Beirut, and in June of the following year moved to 'Abeih in the Lebanon, where he and Dr. Thomson conducted a high school for boys. During the succeeding six years he prepared Arabic textbooks on geography, navigation, natural history, algebra, geometry, and plane and spherical trigonometry. These books, later revised, long continued in general use. His geography of Syria and neighboring regions, full of apt quotations from classical Arabic travelers and geographers, had an especially wide popularity. Meanwhile he was studying theology, and on Jan. 14, 1846, was ordained by the mission.

Three years later he was transferred to Sidon, his headquarters for extensive medical and preaching tours until November 1857, when he moved to Beirut to continue the translation of the Bible into Arabic which had been begun in 1848 by Eli Smith [*q.v.*]. Working in close cooperation with the ablest native and European scholars, he completed the work in 1865 and at once proceeded to America to supervise the preparation of electrotype plates. During his two

years in New York he also taught Hebrew in Union Theological Seminary. Returning to Beirut in September 1867 he became editor of the mission press of its weekly journal *al-Nashrah*, and, at the same time, professor of pathology in the medical department of the Syrian Protestant College, professor of astronomy in the department of arts and sciences, and director of the astronomical and meteorological observatory. He found time also to carry on medical practice and to write Arabic texts on pathology, chemistry, internal medicine, physical diagnosis, and astronomy. After resigning his professorship in 1883, he practised in the Hospital of St. George until 1893, meanwhile publishing in Arabic eight volumes of science primers, a popular volume on astronomy, and a translation of Mrs. E. R. Charles's *Chronicles of the Schönberg-Cotta Family* (1864). His last work was a translation of Lew Wallace's *Ben Hur*. He was survived by his wife, two sons, and two daughters.

Van Dyck played an important part in the modern renaissance of Arabic literature by showing that it was possible to write correct and idiomatic Arabic in a style so simple as to be readily understood even by the unlearned. Although one of the great pioneer missionary physicians, he is remembered chiefly for his extraordinary mastery of Arabic, and his intimate understanding of the people among whom he worked with so complete a lack of offensive condescension that Lebanese and Syrians adopted him as one of themselves.

[Sources include H. H. Jessup, *Fifty-three Years in Syria* (1910); H. A. Kelly, *A Cyc. of Am. Medic. Biog.* (2 vols., 1912); E. T. Corwin, *A Manual of the Reformed Church in America* (1902); obituary in *Times* (London), Nov. 28, 1895; information furnished by W. T. Van Dyck, of Beirut, Syria, a son. Van Dyck's Arabic publications are listed in Edward Van Dyck, *Iktifā' al-Qanū' bima Huwa Matbū'* (Cairo, 1897), and in J. E. Sarkis, *Mu 'jam al-Matbū' āt al 'Arabīyah w-al-Mu 'arrabah* (Cairo, 1928).]
W. L. W., Jr.

VAN DYKE, HENRY (Nov. 10, 1852–Apr. 10, 1933), poet, preacher, author, university teacher, diplomat, was born in Germantown, Pa., where his father, Henry Jackson van Dyke, was pastor of the First Presbyterian Church. His ancestry in the direct male line was derived from Jan Thomasse van Dyke, the first magistrate of New Utrecht, Long Island, who emigrated to America in 1652. His grandfather was a well-known physician and a graduate of Princeton. His mother, Henrietta Ashmead, belonged to an old and distinguished Germantown family. The elder Van Dyke having accepted a call to Brooklyn the year after his son's birth, most of Henry's boyhood was spent in Brooklyn and New York, where his father was prominent in the councils of the Presbyterian Church. Preparing at the Brooklyn Polytechnic Institute, he took the degree of A.B. at Princeton in 1873 and graduated from the Princeton Theological Seminary in 1877. The following year was spent in study at Berlin and travel abroad. His first pastorate was at the United Congregational Church, Newport, R. I. (1879–83). On Dec. 13, 1881, he was married to Ellen Reid of Baltimore, Md. From 1883 to 1899 he was minister of the Brick Presbyterian Church in New York, returning for brief periods in 1902 and 1911. In 1884 appeared his first book, *The Reality of Religion*; in 1889, *The Poetry of Tennyson,* revised and enlarged in later editions; in 1896, *The Gospel for an Age of Doubt,* being the Lyman Beecher lectures at Yale. Two of his most popular books of outdoor essays belong to this period, *Little Rivers* (1895), *Fisherman's Luck* (1899). His *The Story of the Other Wise Man* (1896) and *The First Christmas Tree* (1897) were first read at the Brick Church as Christmas sermons. In 1899 he accepted a call to Princeton University as Murray Professor of English Literature, the chair having been endowed for him in memory of Dr. James O. Murray [*q.v.*], his predecessor at the Brick Church and at Princeton. In 1900 he moved to Avalon, his Princeton home for the remainder of his life. In the foreword to his collected works (17 vols., 1920–22), he wrote: "This edition is named after the old house where I live. . . . It is a pleasant camp,—this Avalon, with big friendly trees around it, and an ancient garden behind it, and memories of the American Revolution built into its walls and the gray towers of Princeton University just beyond the treetops." The period 1900–1914 was one of abundant literary productivity. In volumes of poems, essays, stories, travel-sketches, and literary criticism, he shared with an ever-widening circle of readers the delights of his fishing-trips to Canada during vacations, his travels abroad, his human interest in people of all sorts and conditions, as well as the fruits of study and meditation in his library among companionable books. Among his stories and romances are *The Ruling Passion* (1901), *The Blue Flower* (1902), *The Unknown Quantity* (1912); among his essays, *Days Off* (1907) and *Out of Doors in the Holy Land* (1908). In 1908–09 he was lecturer at the Sorbonne, the lectures appearing as *The Spirit of America* (1910) and in French as *Le Génie de l'Amérique* (1909).

In 1912 he was elected president of the National Institute of Arts and Letters, and in the following year President Wilson appointed him minister to the Netherlands and Luxembourg

(appointment confirmed, June 27, 1913). Finding it impossible to reconcile his ardent conviction of the right of the allied cause with his duties as minister in a neutral country, he resigned on Sept. 6, 1916. On his way home in 1917 he visited the battle fronts in France, received the degree of D.C.L. at Oxford, and, having volunteered for active service in the United States Navy, he was appointed lieutenant commander in the Chaplain Corps. He was active in arousing public opinion in favor of a vigorous prosecution of the war and in the formation of a league to enforce peace, of which he was one of the original advocates. In 1919 the cross of a commander of the Legion of Honor was conferred on him by the French government. He returned in 1919 to his Princeton professorship, retiring in 1923. He was professor emeritus until his death, and until 1929 he delivered annually a series of university literary lectures to crowded audiences. In 1931 he celebrated his golden wedding. After a brief illness he died Apr. 10, at dawn, in his home at Avalon in his eighty-first year. He was survived by his wife and five of their nine children.

A religious leader whose influence extended far beyond the pale of his own church, an inspiring teacher of college youth, a writer of outdoor essays and short stories in prose of classic purity, of musical verse in the Victorian tradition, a sympathetic interpreter of Tennyson, an influential moulder of public opinion, a fervent patriot, he crowded into a single life an achievement astonishing for its versatility and competence of execution. He was not only an eloquent preacher but an organizer of institutional activities, making the Brick Church a center of civic consciousness and a power in the fight against political corruption. In the doctrinal controversies that shook the Presbyterian Church he was a valiant champion of a positive evangelical Christianity, defending it against a materialistic and rationalistic philosophy on the left and a hard and dogmatic Calvinism on the right. In an address before the New York Presbytery (1890), "Is This Calvinism or Christianity," he repudiated the doctrine of reprobation as "measuring the mind of God by the logic of the seventeenth century"; "The Bible as It Is," in *Historic Presbyterianism* (1893), is a plea for liberty of investigation. His "A Plea for Peace and Work" (1893) was signed by about 235 Presbyterian ministers, and he was a member of the original committee appointed by the moderator of the General Assembly, 1900, to consider the restatement of doctrine. The "Brief Statement of the Reformed Faith" was adopted by an overwhelming vote by the General Assembly of 1902 (see *Outlook,* May 31, 1902, p. 299), and his election as moderator was a recognition of his leadership in the movement for revision. Perhaps his most lasting contribution to his church was his work as chairman of the committee on *The Book of Common Worship,* completed only two years before his death, in which his own deeply devout spirit, his sense of form, his loyalty to the faith of his fathers, and his literary taste contributed to produce a devotional manual rich with the treasures of Christian experience.

Versatility marks the work of Henry van Dyke in the field of letters. His outdoor essays are in the main stream of the American tradition of Thoreau, Burroughs, Muir, though his interest in human character and his deep religious faith, always part of his delight in nature, give them a quality of their own. Of his poem, "God of the Open Air," he said: "It best expresses me." He was an ardent angler, and his skill as a fisherman was excelled only by his skill as a narrator of his fisherman's luck. He was as particular in the choice of the right word as in the choice of the right fly, and he could cast as unerringly in the pools of fancy as in the pools where the brook-trout lurked. The sketches and stories of his French-Canadian guides and friends are among his best. In them he avoids the sentimentality and tendency to preach into which the warmth of his heart and the fervor of his convictions sometimes led him. His *The Story of the Other Wise Man* has been translated into all European and several Oriental languages, and remains his best-known tale. The two volumes of verse in the Avalon edition contain nature lyrics, patriotic songs, hymns, odes, narrative verse, and a Biblical drama. He is always clear and melodious, and, though facile, he had the conscientious craftsman's contempt for slipshod work. Changing standards of taste, the reaction against the Victorians, the rise of a critical realism that challenged the "genteel tradition" have diminished the literary prestige of most of Van Dyke's contemporaries, and from this diminution his own work has not escaped, but when all reservations are made, his place in American letters is secure as master of a lucid style exquisitely adapted to its end.

At the root of his nature was a love of the genuine and simple. The academician in his robes of office, the diplomat in silk hat and black cape, the Oxford D.C.L. in his gown of crimson, he was most at home in his flannel shirt, felt hat, and wading boots, and declared: "The good word of a plain fisherman or hunter is worth more than a D.D. from a learned University." He was devoted to his father, to his brother Paul [*q.v.*], and to his own family, of whose life his daughter Brooke has given a charming picture. In politics a Democrat, he was on intimate terms of friendship with Grover Cleveland and Woodrow Wilson, and he always enjoyed the good fellowship of meetings with literary friends like Mark Twain, James Whitcomb Riley, and Hamilton Mabie. To younger aspirants for literary honors, especially his Princeton students, he gave generous encouragement. The vivid character portrait by Maxwell Struthers Burt in *The Van Dyke Book* (1920 ed.) reveals the impression he made on a discriminating novelist and poet of a younger generation. He called himself an adventurous conservative, and this sums up his essential quality as man and writer.

[*Who's Who in America,* 1932–33; Tertius van Dyke, *Henry Van Dyke, a Biog.* (1935); *The Van Dyke Book* (1905; rev. ed., 1920), ed. by Edwin Mims, with a biog. sketch by Brooke van Dyke; Shepherd Knapp, *A Hist. of the Brick Presbyt. Church in the City of N. Y.* (1909); F. H. Law, *Modern Great Americans* (1926); M. J. Gilley, "Lit. Works of Henry van Dyke," 1923, master's thesis, Columbia Univ.; *Outlook,* May 1, 1897; *Suburban Life,* May 1908; "Book-News," May 1906, pub. by Wanamaker's, Phila.; *Princeton Alumni Weekly,* May 5, 19, July 3, 1933; obituary in *N. Y. Times,* Apr. 11, 1933; personal reminiscences.]

J. D. S.

VAN DYKE, JOHN CHARLES (Apr. 21, 1856–Dec. 5, 1932), art critic and librarian, was born at New Brunswick, N. J., a descendant of Jan Thomasse van Dyke who emigrated from the Netherlands to New Amsterdam in 1652. His father, John Van Dyke, served in Congress and as justice of the supreme court of New Jersey. His mother, Mary Dix Strong, was the daughter of Prof. Theodore Strong [*q.v.*]. The family moved to Minnesota in 1868, and John added to the conventional education which he received from tutors that of a hard-riding and straight-shooting plainsman. After study in the Columbia Law School, he was in 1877 admitted to the bar, but never practised. Returning in 1878 to his native New Brunswick, he served first as assistant librarian of the Gardner A. Sage Library, New Brunswick Theological Seminary, and then (1886) as librarian, a position which he held until his death. From the vantage point of his librarianship, with its relatively easy duties and long vacations, he pursued personal studies in art which bore fruit in numerous books, mostly of a popular and interpretative sort, which were widely read and influential. His criticism was urbane, sensitive, free from eccentricity. In a perhaps excessive avoidance of overstatement it recalls the contemporary literary criticism of William Dean Howells. In

1889 he became a lecturer upon modern art at Rutgers College and from 1891 to 1929 was professor of the history of art. From about 1884 till about 1904 he was the favorite contributor of the *Century Magazine* on artistic subjects, supplying, for example, the brief and excellent comment on Timonthy Cole's masterpieces of reproductive wood-engraving, which were later published in book form as *Old English Masters, with Cole's Engravings* (1902). For his special studies he traveled widely. In the literature of art criticism, he intentionally read little, preferring to stand on his own vivid impressions before the work of art itself. His artistic pilgrimages he varied by travels for the study of natural beauty, and every three or four years produced a book on natural appearances. In his later years the books on nature predominate. Such books as *The Desert* (1901), *The Opal Sea* (1906), *The Mountain* (1916) were hailed by English critics, perhaps because they represented the sober, elegant, and faithful tradition of Gilbert White of Selborne, but in America their quietness obscured their distinguished merits. They are likely, nevertheless, to outlast the art books, which were more nearly attuned to the times.

Perhaps the best of Van Dyke's writing on art is in the twelve little volumes of *New Guides to Old Masters* (1914), in which he resolutely eschewed the merely perfunctory and informational, and set down briefly the personal impressions of the ideal spectator that he was before the pictures. Coming out in 1914, the little books hardly had a reading; they remain a mine of discerning appreciation. His most sensational book, *Rembrandt and His School* (1923), was shaped by his exaggerated faculty of visual discrimination. Possessed of an extraordinary acuteness of vision that tended to be microscopic, he saw immediately, in pictures, features that are generally unnoticed, small repaints, subtle differences of style or handling. Finding many differences in style in the eight hundred or more pictures officially ascribed to Rembrandt, he brought these pictures into stylistic groups most of which seemed to correspond to the score of known pupils and imitators of Rembrandt, thus leaving a residuum of only fifty pictures for the master himself. This invoked a great and unwelcome publicity, and virtually he was scoffed out of court. He stood by his guns, however, and in 1927, in *The Rembrandt Drawings and Etchings,* tried to reduce the list to about a tenth of its traditional proportions. No critic has accepted these puristic views, but many believe that the books brought about a useful ventilation of

the mephitic atmosphere of commercial *expertise*.

Van Dyke was president of the National Institute of Arts and Letters, and a member of the American Academy of Arts and Letters. He was a man of magnificent stature, easily carried, with large gray-blue eyes that belied the habitual fixity of his fine olive mask. He wore his clothes well, said the right word and never too much, and exhibited a native dignity and kindliness. He had the gift of companionship, a perfect rectitude, an elevation of character entirely without pretentiousness. In any group of gentlemen he was a moral and physical ornament. He died in New York City. He was unmarried.

[*Who's Who in America*, 1930–31; W. B. Aitken, *Distinguished Families in America Descended from . . . Jan Thomasse Van Dyke* (1912); J. C. Van Dyke, *The Raritan, Notes on . . . a Family* (1915); *New Brunswick Seminary Bull.*, Mar. 1933; obituary in *N. Y. Times*, Dec. 6, 1932; personal acquaintance.]

F. J. M., Jr.

VAN DYKE, NICHOLAS (Sept. 25, 1738– Feb. 19, 1789), member of the Continental Congress, president of the State of Delaware, was born at New Castle, Del., the son of Nicholas Van Dyke and his wife, Lytie Dirks. He was of the fourth generation in descent from Jan Thomasse Van Dyke who came to New Amsterdam in 1652 from Amsterdam, Holland, and was the third of the family in America to bear the name of Nicholas. The Van Dkyes were a prominent burgher family in Holland and Jan Thomasse was one of the founders of New Utrecht in New Amsterdam. Early in the eighteenth century the family moved to St. George's Hundred in Delaware, where it soon became one of the largest landholders in the province. Of Nicholas' education there seems to be little information available. He was trained for the law, was admitted to practice before the supreme court in Philadelphia in 1765, at the age of twenty-seven, and probably received his training in that city. Soon thereafter he returned to New Castle, in the Lower Counties, where he was a practising lawyer until his death.

Like many of the young lawyers of his day he threw in his lot with the Whigs in 1774, although he remained steadfastly one of the moderate faction. He served on the provincial committee of correspondence, on the committee appointed to solicit funds for the relief of the people of Boston in 1774, and was a member of the New Castle Council of Safety in 1776. In the Delaware constitutional convention of 1776 he was one of the more active delegates, participated in formulating rules for the convention, sat on committees charged with the function of provisioning the state's troops, and assisted in preparing a declaration of rights and in writing the preliminary draft of a constitution. In the first election under the new government he was elected to the Council, the upper legislative house, and, during 1779 served as the speaker of the house. Throughout the war period he held the rank of major in the New Castle County militia, but saw no active service.

On Feb. 22, 1777, during the period in which the moderates controlled the state legislature, Van Dyke was elected to the Continental Congress, and he was returned annually until 1782. The post, however, held few attractions for him, for he was interested primarily in state politics and was ill much of the time. Moreover, he was dissatisfied with the scant provision made by his state for its delegates. Aside from his service on a few minor committees and his signature to the Articles of Confederation, the *Journals* reveal scant participation in the deliberations of Congress, and infrequent attendance. To repeated pleas from his colleagues for more adequate representation from Delaware he paid little heed.

For more than three and a half years during the critical post-war years, from Feb. 1, 1783, until Oct. 27, 1786, he was president of Delaware, having been elected by joint vote of the two legislative houses. His administration witnessed the passage of numerous measures designed to improve commerce and to place the finances of the state on a sound basis. He also dealt with continued agitation on the part of Delaware statesmen to have title to the lands northwest of the Ohio given to the states in common. Following his presidency he again sat in the Council for part of one term. Van Dyke was twice married, first to Elizabeth Nixon and, after her death, to Charlotte Standley. He died in New Castle County, Del., and is buried in the Immanuel Churchyard at New Castle. Nicholas Van Dyke [*q.v.*] was his son.

[W. B. Aitken, *Distinguished Families in America Descended from Wilhelmus Beekman and Jan Thomasse Van Dyke* (1912); H. C. Conrad, *Hist. of the State of Del.* (1908), vols. I, III; J. T. Scharf, *Hist. of Del.* (1888), vol. I; E. C. Burnett, *Letters of Members of the Cont. Cong.*, vols. II–V (1923–31); *Minutes of the Council of the Del. State from 1776 to 1792, Papers of the Hist. Soc. of Del.*, vol. VI (1887); *Proc. of the Convention of the Del. State Held at New-Castle . . . 1776* (reprint, 1927); G. H. Ryden, *Letters To and From Cæsar Rodney* (1933); J. L. Martin, *Martin's Bench and Bar of Phila.* (1883); *Biog. Dir. Am. Cong.* (1928); one volume of Van Dyke's letters and papers, and four volumes of Delaware State papers containing some of his official papers, Library of Congress; *Independent Gazetteer; or, the Chronicle of Freedom* (Philadelphia), Mar. 2, 1789.]   J. H. P.

VAN DYKE, NICHOLAS (Dec. 20, 1770– May 21, 1826), lawyer, United States senator, the son of Nicholas Van Dyke [*q.v.*] and Eliza-

beth Nixon, was born in New Castle, Del. He attended the College of New Jersey and was graduated in the class of 1788. He then read law under the direction of Kensey Johns, a New Castle attorney, and was admitted to the bar in 1792. He established himself in practice in New Castle, and was married to Mary, the daughter of Kensey Johns, his tutor, and his wife, Susannah Galloway. Kensey Johns, 1759–1848 [*q.v.*], was his brother-in-law. Like his father, young Van Dyke's sympathies were from the beginning with the more moderate group in Delaware politics; like him, too, he entered political life, first as a member of the Delaware House of Representatives in 1799 for one term. From 1801 until 1806 he was attorney-general of Delaware. Elected to Congress in 1807 to fill a vacancy, he remained a member of that body until Mar. 3, 1811. Although recognized as a Federalist, he was moderate in his views, and on questions of legislation was invariably guided by his own judgment. Thus he was quite willing to support Jefferson's embargo measure in 1808 but, convinced of the futility of the administration's policy by the beginning of 1809, he demanded a change: "the Emperor of France applauds our magnanimity in abandoning the ocean, and Great Britain laughs at the imbecility of the measure" (*Annals of Congress,* 10 Cong., 2 Sess., 1290). He criticised those who spoke of war with England, but attacked the failure of the President to make specific recommendations for improving the military and naval establishments.

During 1816 Van Dyke was a member of the state Senate, but in the same year he was elected to the United States Senate where he continued in service from March 1817 until his death. As a senator he frequently gave voice to the traditional state-rights sentiments of his father and other Delaware politicians of the Revolutionary and post-Revolutionary period. Although personally opposed to slavery he refused to vote against the admission of Missouri on the ground that Congress had no authority to impose restrictions on slavery, and that slaves had not been freed by the Declaration of Independence. Wherever emancipation had been effected, he asserted, it was by the authority of state laws, and every state had assumed and invariably exercised at its discretion the right of legislation on this class of people (*Annals of Congress,* 16 Cong., 1 Sess., 302). When the Delaware Assembly sent up to Congress a resolution urging the passage of legislation which would prohibit the introduction of slavery into the territory of the United States or into any newly organized states, Van Dyke joined with Representative

Louis McLane [*q.v.*] in an open letter expressing his objections to the sentiments of the resolution. During his senatorship he demonstrated ability as a debater and sat on the committees of claims, pensions, public lands, and military appropriations.

Van Dyke's daughter, Dorcas Montgomery, was married to Charles Irénée, the son of Victor Marie Du Pont [*q.v.*], on Oct. 6, 1824. General Lafayette, a personal friend of Senator Van Dyke, attended the wedding, an outstanding social event, and gave the bride away. Early in the spring of 1826 Van Dyke's health showed signs of rapid decline and he reached his home with difficulty but a short while before his death. He was buried on his farm at St. George's Hundred, but was later reinterred in the Immanuel Churchyard in New Castle. He was widely known for the remarkable ease and elegance of his manner, and the fluency of his speech; he was fond of literature and his taste for architecture was reflected in the construction of several fine houses in New Castle.

[W. B. Aitken, *Distinguished Families in America Descended from Wilhelmus Beekman and Jan Thomasse Van Dyke* (1912); *Biog. and Geneal. Hist. of the State of Del.* (1889); H. C. Conrad, *Hist. of the State of Del.* (1908), vols. I, III; W. T. Read, *Life and Corres. of George Read* (1870); and J. T. Scharf, *Hist. of Del.* (1888), vol. I; Thomas Holcombe, *Hist. of Immanuel Ch.*, New Castle, Del. (1890); *Am. Watchman and Del. Advertiser* (Wilmington), May 23, 1826.]   J. H. P.

VAN DYKE, PAUL (Mar. 25, 1859–Aug. 30, 1933), historian, was born in Brooklyn, N. Y., the son of the Rev. Henry Jackson and Henrietta (Ashmead) van Dyke, and the brother of Henry van Dyke [*q.v.*]. He was graduated from the College of New Jersey (Princeton) in 1881, and from the Princeton Theological Seminary in 1884. He studied at the University of Berlin during 1884–85. After his ordination in 1887 as a Presbyterian minister, he spent ten years in religious work, as pastor at Geneva, N. Y. (1887–89), and at Northampton, Mass. (1892–98), and as instructor in church history at the Princeton Theological Seminary (1889–92). From 1898 until his retirement in 1928 he was professor of modern history in Princeton University. His theological training was reflected in the vigorous moral judgments which marked his teaching and his first books, *The Age of the Renascence* (1897), and *Renascence Portraits* (1905). After the completion of the latter work, he began an exhaustive search in the archives and libraries of Europe for material on the life of Catherine de Medicis. This task was interrupted from July 1917 to July 1919 by war work as secretary of the American University Union at Paris, where his sympathetic help revived many whose lives

and hopes had been shattered. He himself believed this work the most useful of his life, and in his letters from Paris the conviction that the war was a moral crusade finds vehement expression. After the war he continued his interest in the American University Union, serving as director of the continental division at Paris from 1921 to 1923, and again during 1928–29.

His most important work, *Catherine de Medicis* (2 vols., 1922), immediately won international recognition as a definitive history of the religious wars in France. As a biography the work was less successful, in part because of Van Dyke's unwillingness to impose his views on the reader and in part because, although all the elements of the portrait were assembled, the figure of Catherine never clearly emerged. His later biographical studies, *Ignatius Loyola, the Founder of the Jesuits* (1926), and *George Washington, the Son of His Country, 1732–1775* (1931) were less important as scholarly works but more successful as portraits. In 1928 he published *The Story of France from Julius Cæsar to Napoleon III*, which was noteworthy for the vivid descriptions of cultural life in France during the Middle Ages and Renaissance. Among his honorary degrees was that of *Docteur ès Lettres,* granted by the University of Toulouse. He was twice Harvard lecturer at the provincial universities of France, and Louis Liard lecturer at the Sorbonne, Paris. He was an officer of the Legion of Honor.

His slight, delicate figure and gentle manner gave little indication of the vigor of his personality. Although the dogmatism of his earlier years gradually gave place to tolerance, he remained to the end inflexible in devotion to honor and duty. In political and social life he was a Jeffersonian Democrat, and his love both of his own country and of France was intimately connected with his faith in democracy. He died at his summer home at Washington, Conn. He was unmarried.

[*Who's Who in America,* 1930–31; *After Fifty Years, the Record of the Class of 1881, Princeton* (1931); *Biog. Cat. of Princeton Theological Seminary, 1815–1932* (1933); obituary in *N. Y. Times,* Aug. 31, 1933; file in the office of the secretary, Princeton Univ.; papers in the possession of Tertius van Dyke, Princeton; personal acquaintance.]   R. J. S—g.

VANE, Sir HENRY (1613–June 14, 1662), Puritan statesman, for one year governor of Massachusetts Bay, was the eldest of twelve children born to Sir Henry Vane, Knight, and Frances Darcy his wife. A recent biographer claims that his mother was a grand-daughter of Vincent Guicciardini, a descendant of the Florentine historian (Willcock, *post,* p. 351). He was baptized May 26, 1613, at Debden, Essex, which was probably his birthplace, rather than Hadlow, Kent, as is sometimes stated (*Ibid.*, p. 7). He was educated at Westminster School and at sixteen entered Oxford at Magdalen Hall. Since his principles prevented his taking the required oaths, he remained only a brief time and then went to the Continent to study, probably at Leyden, and visited Vienna and Nürnberg. He early became a Puritan and his position in England became uncomfortable. In 1635 he sailed for Massachusetts in the *Abigail*, arriving at Boston on Oct. 6.

He was admitted as a member of the church on Nov. 1 and as a freeman of the colony on Mar. 3 following, and the same day was chosen to serve on the commission for military discipline. Previously, however, he had been made one of three arbiters to whom citizens of Boston had to submit their cases before they could proceed to law (Hosmer, *Vane*, p. 32), and with the Rev. Hugh Peter [*q.v.*] had secured the calling of a meeting at which the two endeavored to reconcile the factions of the former governors John Winthrop and Thomas Dudley [*qq.v.*]. On May 25, 1636, Vane was elected governor of Massachusetts, when he had been in the colony less than eight months and was but twenty-three years old. His first task, carried through successfully, was to establish a series of regulations governing the entrance of ships into the port, and to soothe the feelings and close the mouths of a group of sea captains resentful of the fact that the king's colors were not displayed by the colony—John Endecott [*q.v.*], not long before, having cut the cross from the ensign as idolatrous.

Vane had arrived in Massachusetts just in time to hear the trial of Roger Williams [*q.v.*], with whose views he was in sympathy. On July 26, 1636, as governor, he received word from Williams that the Pequots and Narragansetts were threatening war. In August a punitive expedition under Endecott was sent against the Pequots—a move which was one of the causes of the Pequot War of 1637; but through the magnanimous intercession of the banished Williams the Narragansetts were kept from taking a hostile part, and in October 1636 a treaty was effected at Boston between the English and Miantonomo [*q.v.*], the Narragansett sachem. Shortly afterward a theological storm broke which wrecked Vane's career in America. The arguments of Mrs. Anne Hutchinson [*q.v.*], who laid stress on inner illumination of the spirit, had divided the local clergy into those who preached a "covenant of works" and those who preached a "covenant of grace." Her opponents, claiming that she was teaching a religion which absolved those adhering to it from obedience to law, thus undermining the foundations of the colony, demanded her suppression. Former Gov. John Winthrop [*q.v.*], the Rev. John Wilson [*q.v.*], and most of the other leaders were opposed to her. The Rev. John Cotton [*q.v.*], with whom Vane lived, was at first her supporter, but he eventually joined the majority. Vane, with her brother-in-law, the Rev. John Wheelwright [*q.v.*], stood by her and was bitterly reviled. Disheartened, in December he tendered his resignation as governor, pleading that letters from home necessitated his return to England; but he was persuaded to reconsider and retained the governorship until the end of his term.

The controversy was carried into the election of 1637. Since Vane was strong in Boston, his opponents secured the holding of the election at Newtown, and he was defeated by Winthrop. The next day Boston chose Vane as one of its deputies to the General Court, which promptly quashed the election on the ground of a technical irregularity, but when he was chosen again at a new election he was allowed to take his seat. The struggle was not yet over, however. The General Court on May 17 passed an act prohibiting, under penalties, any newcomer from remaining in the colony more than three weeks without the consent of the magistrates; this move was designed to prevent any addition to the ranks of the Hutchinson party and to allow the incumbent authorities to remain in control. Winthrop circulated an argument in manuscript defending the act and Vane answered him in another, defending civil liberty and religious toleration; both were published, more than a century later, by Thomas Hutchinson [*q.v.*] in *A Collection of Original Papers Relative to the History of the Colony of Massachusetts Bay* (1769) and reprinted in *The Publications of the Prince Society*, vol. II (1865).

Vane sailed for England Aug. 3, 1637. He had not been always wise in his acts as governor, but he was always honest and generous-minded, and his later and more important career in England probably owed much to the lessons in toleration which his experience among the sectarians of New England afforded him. Although he left Massachusetts under the disapproval of the leaders of the colony, he harbored no resentment, and later gladly served the cause of his one-time fellow citizens. When in 1645 he befriended two Massachusetts men in difficulties Winthrop commented: "Sir Henry Vane, . . . though he might have taken occasion against us for some dishonor which he apprehended to have been un-justly put upon him here, yet both now, and at other times he showed himself a true friend to New England, and a man of a noble and gen-erous mind" (*Winthrop's Journal, post,* II, 256). To Roger Williams he was a loyal and a valu-able friend. In 1644 he helped Williams to se-cure the Rhode Island charter, which bore Vane's signature as one of the commissioners for plantations; in 1652 he was instrumental in having rescinded the commission granted the year before to William Coddington [*q.v.*] as proprietary governor of the schismatic colony of Aquidneck; two years later he wrote an af-fectionate letter to the citizens of Rhode Island upbraiding them for the dissensions within the colony.

From the time of his return to England, how-ever, the story of his life belongs in the main to English history (see *Dictionary of National Biography*). In 1639 he was appointed joint treasurer of the navy and in 1640 was knighted by Charles I. On July 1 of that year, at St. Mary's, Lambeth, he married Frances, daughter of Sir Christopher Wray of Ashby in Lincoln-shire; they had thirteen children. Vane was elected to both Short and Long parliaments and was instrumental in securing the condemnation of Strafford and Laud, but had no part in the trial and condemnation of the King. He was a member of all Councils of State. Not in sym-pathy with the Protectorate, after the dissolu-tion of the Long Parliament he retired from public life. Under Richard Cromwell he was once more a member of Parliament, but when the Long Parliament reassembled, he was ex-pelled. Following the Restoration, he was ex-cepted from the act of indemnity, and, after two years in prison was tried for treason, found guilty, and executed on Tower Hill.

[J. K. Hosmer, *The Life of Young Sir Henry Vane* (1888); C. H. Firth, in *Dict. Nat. Biog.*; W. W. Ire-land, *The Life of Sir Henry Vane the Younger* (1905); John Willcock, *Life of Sir Henry Vane the Younger* (1913); H. M. King, *Sir Henry Vane, Jr., Gov. of Mass. and Friend of Roger Williams and R. I.* (1909), uncritical; *Winthrop's Jour.* (2 vols., 1908), ed. by J. K. Hosmer; N. B. Shurtleff, *Records of the Gov. and Company of the Mass. Bay,* vol. I (1853); C. F. Adams, *Three Episodes of Mass. Hist.* (2 vols., 1892).]

J. T. A.

VAN FLEET, WALTER (June 18, 1857– Jan. 26, 1922), horticulturist, physician, was born of Dutch ancestry at Piermont, Rockland County, N. Y., son of Solomon Van Reusselean and Elvira (Du Bois) Van Fleet. His childhood was spent on a small farm in the vicinity of Wat-sontown, Pa., where his father was principal of Watsontown Academy. He developed in boy-hood a keen interest in the growing of plants and at twelve began work in hybridization. Be-coming interested in birds, he published a num-ber of articles on birds in technical and popular periodicals (1876–88), as well as a popular bird book for children. In 1878, under contract as wood chopper with the Collins Railroad Construction Company, he visited the upper tributaries of the Amazon, where an attack of tropical fever near-ly cost him his life. Returning home in the summer of that year, he entered Hahnemann Medical College in Philadelphia, from which he was graduated with the degree of M.D. in 1880, later taking post-graduate work in Jefferson Medical College (1886–87). From 1880 to 1891 he was actively engaged in the practice of medi-cine at Watsontown, Duboistown, and Renovo, Pa., though he made a bird-collecting trip of five months to Nicaragua and the Isthmus of Panama.

While practising medicine he began the syste-matic breeding of the gladiolus and the canna, and in 1891 definitely took up plant-breeding as a vocation. In 1894 he settled at Little Silver, N. J., where for a short time he was managing ed-itor of *Orchard and Garden*. Aside from two years (1897–99) during which he acted as colony physician in the Ruskin Colony at Dickson, Tenn., he devoted the rest of his life to the pro-duction of improved varieties of plants. For a number of years he was associate editor of the *Rural New Yorker* (Oct. 1899–Nov. 1909). In 1909 he became an expert plant-breeder in the federal bureau of plant industry at Chico, Cal., and Washington, D. C. His work in the Depart-ment of Agriculture covered a wide range and included extensive experimentation on the pro-duction of chestnuts resistant to the Asiatic bark blight. Noteworthy new varieties of plants as diverse as azalea, canna, freesia, geranium, gladiolus, Lonicera, rose, pepper, sweet corn, tomato, chestnut, gooseberry, pear, and straw-berry resulted from his work; of these some fifty have been named and commercially dissemi-nated. Van Fleet's outstanding achievements, however, were with the rose. He early recog-nized the need in America for roses of vigorous growth, disease-resistant foliage, and large flow-ers, sufficiently hardy for garden culture through a wide climatic range. He was keenly percep-tive of plant characters, indefatigably industri-ous, and exactingly critical of his productions. A large number of his roses have succeeded un-der varying climatic conditions; this is notably true of the climbing and pillar varieties, Amer-ican Pillar, Dr. W. Van Fleet, Philadelphia, Silver Moon, Alida Lovett, Bess Lovett, Mary Lovett, Mary Wallace, Heart of Gold, Breeze

Hill, and Glenn Dale. The American Pillar and Dr. W. Van Fleet have for some years been recognized as the most generally successful and widely planted climbers in America. Their general good behavior has been an important factor in the recent widespread development of popular interest in rose growing. Among his publications, in addition to his numerous papers on ornithology and horticulture in technical and popular journals and in the *American Rose Annual,* were a series of contributions, "Ruralisms," to the *Rural New Yorker, The Gladiolus* (1911), with Matthew Crawford, *The Cultivation of American Ginseng* (1913), *Golden Seal under Cultivation* (1914), *The Cultivation of Peppermint and Spearmint* (1915), and a brochure on the growing of hardy roses.

Modest and retiring to the point of diffidence, Van Fleet was a most kindly and considerate worker with his associates. At the same time he was outspokenly and incisively critical of the overpraise and misrepresentation of plant novelties indulged in at times by commercial plantsmen. In his editorial work this sometimes led to intense controversy and even to litigation. In 1918 he was awarded the George Robert White medal for eminent services in horticulture by the Massachusetts Horticultural Society; in 1921 he received gold medals from the American Rose Society and the city of Portland, Ore., and a silver medal from the Portland Rose Society, all in recognition of the merit of the Mary Wallace rose. On Aug. 7, 1883, he married Sarah C. Heilman of Watsontown, Pa., who survived him. He died at Miami, Fla.

[*Who's Who in America*, 1920–21; *Official Record, U. S. Dept. of Agriculture,* Feb. 1, 1922; Peter Bisset, in *Am. Florist,* Feb. 18, 1922; C. L. Linz, in *Florists' Exchange,* Feb. 4, 1922; F. L. Mulford, in *Nat. Horticultural Mag.,* Apr. 1929; *Am. Rose Ann.,* 1922; obituary in *Evening Star* (Washington, D. C.), Jan. 28, 1922; records of U. S. Dept. of Agriculture; personal recollections.]   W. A. T.

VAN HISE, CHARLES RICHARD (May 29, 1857–Nov. 19, 1918), geologist, university president, publicist, was born in Fulton, Rock County, Wis., the son of pioneer parents, William Henry and Mary (Goodrich) Van Hise. Prepared at Evansville Academy, he entered the University of Wisconsin in 1874, and after a year's absence in 1877–78, was graduated with the degree of bachelor of metallurgical engineering in 1879. Subsequently he received in course the degrees of B.S. (1880), M.S. (1882), and Ph.D. (1892). He was employed as instructor in metallurgy, 1879–83, assistant professor, 1883–86, and professor, 1886–88; professor of mineralogy, 1888–90; professor of Archaean and ap-

plied geology, 1890–92, and professor of geology, 1892–1903. He was also non-resident professor of structural geology in the University of Chicago from 1892 to 1903, and from 1883 a member of the United States Geological Survey. In April 1903 he was chosen president of the University of Wisconsin; he assumed office in the fall, and was formally inaugurated in June 1904. This position he filled until his death.

Van Hise received his training in geology under Roland Duer Irving [*q.v.*] at a time when the modern science of microscopic petrology was just developing. His first research work of importance was undertaken in collaboration with his instructor and resulted in a paper by the two, "Crystalline Rocks of the Wisconsin Valley," published in *Geology of Wisconsin: Survey of 1873–1879* (vol. IV, 1882). With the termination of the state survey, Irving and Van Hise continued under the United States Geological Survey, and in 1892 Van Hise saw through the press the last product of their joint work, *The Penokee Iron-Bearing Series of Michigan and Wisconsin,* published as Monograph XIX of the federal survey. As planned by Irving this report was to be the first of a series treating each of the important iron-producing districts of the Lake Superior region; after Irving's death the project was carried on by Van Hise as geologist in charge of the Lake Superior division from 1888 to 1900. He was joint author of Survey monographs dealing with the Marquette and Crystal Falls districts and of the special folio of the *Geologic Atlas* dealing with the Menominee iron-bearing district of Michigan; he also supervised the preparation of Survey monographs on four other districts of the region. Meanwhile he published in 1892 a notable series, *Correlation Papers; Archean and Algonkian* (Bulletin 86, United States Geological Survey), and in 1896 "Principles of North American Pre-Cambrian Geology," in the *Sixteenth Annual Report* of the United States Geological Survey. His constant effort to ascertain the fundamental laws governing observed phenomena led him further to *A Treatise on Metamorphism* (Monograph XLVII, United States Geological Survey, 1904), in which he endeavored to show that the changes in rock characteristics take place in accordance with recognized physical and chemical laws. When he accepted the presidency of his University, he necessarily abandoned much of his geological work, but a revision and enlargement of his *Correlation Papers* of 1892, prepared in collaboration with C. K. Leith, appeared in 1909 under the title, *Pre-Cambrian Geology of North America* (Bulletin 360, United States Geological

Survey) and with the same associate in 1911 he brought out *The Geology of the Lake Superior Region* (Monograph LII), the first general treatise on the subject.

As president of the University of Wisconsin, Van Hise exhibited the same breadth of outlook that characterized him as a scientist. Believing that as a state institution its primary duty was to serve the citizens of the commonwealth, he proceeded to develop not only the research activities of the University, but an extension department exceeding in scope any then existing, with numerous means of placing "accumulated knowledge" at the service of Wisconsin citizens. His conviction that it was the duty of the University to give state leadership led him to enter aggressively upon debatable ground, and frequently brought severe, perhaps just, criticism. Nevertheless, under his administration the University increased enormously in material equipment, nearly trebled in enrollment, and excited favorable attention throughout the United States and abroad. Moreover, his conception of the peculiar functions of a state university gained wide recognition and influenced the policies of other institutions.

He served in the capacity of consulting geologist on the Wisconsin Geological and Natural History Survey from 1897 to 1903 and for several years as chairman of the Wisconsin State Conservation Commission appointed in 1908. Late in that year he was called into wider public service as a member of the National Conservation Commission and subsequently contributed to the conservation movement what has been called its most valuable book, *The Conservation of Natural Resources in the United States* (1910). From 1909 he was a trustee of the Carnegie Foundation for the Advancement of Teaching; in 1912 he was a member, and for part of the time chairman, of the board appointed to arbitrate a dispute between the eastern railroads and the Brotherhood of Locomotive Engineers. His contact with problems of the social order set him seeking again for fundamental principles, and in 1912 he published *Concentration and Control; A Solution of the Trust Problem in the United States*. During the World War he gave much time and energy to the work of conservation and allocation of the food supply, preparing for the Food Administration an outline of a series of lectures to be given in colleges and universities, under the title *Conservation and Regulation in the United States during the World War* (2 parts, 1917-18). He was frequently called to Washington for consultation and during August and September 1918 visited France and England

with a party of observers who were guests of the British government. He was an enthusiastic believer in a league of free nations to enforce peace and on Nov. 8, 1918, in Madison, delivered the opening address before a convention of supporters of the project. At the time of his death he was working on a synthesis of his geological and social studies, a treatise on the influence of mineral resources upon the history of civilization, foreshadowed in his address, "The Influence of Applied Geology and the Mining Industry upon the Economic Development of the World," delivered in 1910 before the International Geological Congress at Stockholm (*Compte Rendu,* 1912, pp. 259–61).

Van Hise was the recipient of many academic honors. He was a member of the National Academy of Sciences and other scientific bodies both in the United States and abroad, and in several held office. He was married on Dec. 22, 1881, to Alice Bushnell Ring, who bore him three daughters. He died in Milwaukee, Wis., from meningitis following a nasal operation.

[Biog. sketch (inaccurate in certain details) and addresses by E. A. Birge, T. C. Chamberlin, and Albert Shaw, in *Memorial Service in Honor of Charles Richard Van Hise at the Univ. of Wis.* (1919); J. F. A. Pyre, *Wisconsin* (1920); *Who's Who in America,* 1918–19; C. K. Leith, in *Bull. Geol. Soc. of America,* Mar. 1920, with bibliog.; T. C. Chamberlin, in *Jour. of Geology,* Nov.–Dec., 1918, and in *Memoirs Nat. Acad. Sci.,* vol. XVII (1924), with bibliog.; *Engineering and Mining Jour.,* Dec. 7, 1918; *Science,* Dec. 20, 1918; *School and Society,* Dec. 28, 1918; *Wisconsin State Jour.* (Madison), Nov. 19, 20, 21, 1918; *Milwaukee Sentinel,* Nov. 20, 1918.]

G. P. M.

VAN HOOK, WELLER (May 16, 1862–July 1, 1933), surgeon was born at Greenville, Floyd County, Ind., the son of William Russell and Matilda (Weller) Van Hook. He was graduated from the Louisville, Ky., high school in 1881, from the University of Michigan in 1884, and from the College of Physicians and Surgeons of Chicago (later the medical department of the University of Illinois) in 1885. Following an internship at the Cook County Hospital he took up general practice near Chicago's west side medical center. In 1894 he went abroad and for a year did graduate work in Berlin and Vienna. Upon his return to Chicago he announced the limitation of his practice to surgery.

In 1892 he was appointed professor of principles of surgery at the College of Physicians and Surgeons, and at about the same time he became associated with the Chicago Post-Graduate Medical School as an instructor in clinical surgery. Four years later he transferred to the chair of surgery at Northwestern University Medical School, where he remained until 1908. He was an able teacher and had exceptional operative skill. While he had a general surgical practice he devoted himself especially to the surgery of the genito-urinary tract, in which field he was a pioneer in experimental work. He devised the generally employed method of repair of wounds of the ureter by lateral implantation of the upper segment of the divided tube into the lower; also, a method of implanting the severed ureter directly into the bladder. In April 1896 he published in *Annals of Surgery* his newly devised method of operation for the correction of hypospadias. This method, generally known as the Van Hook-Mayo operation, is equally applicable to the repair of epispadias. In addition to numerous articles in journals, he wrote the chapter "Constitutional Reactions to Wounds and Their Infections" for J. C. Warren and A. P. Gould, *The International Text-Book of Surgery* (1900), and, in collaboration with Dr. A. B. Kanavel, the chapter "Surgery of the Intestines" for W. W. Keen, *Surgery, Its Principles and Practice* (1906–13).

When or how he became a devotee of Theosophy is not recorded. From 1908 until his death he was a constant contributor of essays to *The Theosophist, The Messenger,* and *Reincarnation.* These essays are collected into two volumes, *The Cultural System* (1925) and *The Future Way* (1928). He speaks of them as "a group of essays upon various topics of the divine wisdom." In 1925 he published *Voyages,* a volume of essays concerning which in the "Foreword" he says: "The musings joined together here were written down, for the most part, on a pilgrimage in nineteen hundred and thirteen, to shrines and holy spots in Europe and Asia." His writings are graceful in style, poetic, deeply religious, widely tolerant. Coincident with the growth of his interest in Theosophy and probably as a result thereof, his enthusiasm for professional work and his prestige in the field of surgery waned. Though he continued his surgical practice, the younger generation of the city's medical profession knew him only as a name and his later years were passed in comparative obscurity. He died of a cerebral hemorrhage at his summer home at Coopersville, Mich. On June 16, 1892, he was married at Sweet Springs, Mo., to Anna C. Whaley of St. Louis, Mo.

[*Alumni Record of the Univ. of Ill., Chicago Departments* (1921); *Who's Who in America,* 1912–13, which is authority for dates of birth and marriage; *The Plexus,* June 1899; *Jour. Am. Medic. Asso.,* July 22, 1933; *Hist. of Medicine and Surgery and Physicians and Surgeons of Chicago* (1922); *Chicago Tribune,* July 2, 1933.]   J. M. P—n.

VAN HORN, ROBERT THOMPSON (May 19, 1824–Jan. 3, 1916), representative from

Missouri, journalist, was born in East Mahoning, Indiana County, Pa., the son of Henry and Elizabeth (Thompson) Van Horn. He seems to have been descended from Christian Barentsen Van Horn who emigrated from Holland to New Netherland before 1653. As a boy he attended a subscription school near his birthplace, and by the age of nineteen he had largely mastered the printer's trade. From 1843 to 1855 he worked at his trade in Pennsylvania, New York, and Ohio, and he also studied law. He married Adela H. Cooley of Pomeroy, Ohio, on Dec. 2, 1848. They had four children. In 1855 he removed to Kansas City, Mo., which was his home the rest of his life. He bought the *Kansas City Enterprise,* a weekly, changed its name to the *Western Journal of Commerce,* later the *Kansas City Journal,* and in 1858 he began publishing it as a daily. It was a conservative (Douglas) Democratic paper until 1860, but upon the outbreak of the Civil War it became Unionist and Republican. With certain temporary exceptions he owned and controlled the *Journal* until 1897. Even while in Congress he wrote many of its editorials. His editorials were optimistic, stimulating, and logical. Though his style was a modernized sledge-hammer type, he was, nevertheless, a lucid and vigorous writer. Until the unique journalistic caliber of William Rockhill Nelson [*q.v.*] became manifest in the 1890's, if not thereafter, Van Horn was Kansas City's greatest press agent.

In 1861 he was elected mayor on the Union ticket and took control of the defense of the city. In September he was attached to the 13th Regiment of the Missouri Infantry for the defense of Lexington, Mo., was wounded, surrendered, and exchanged, and then placed as lieutenant-colonel with the 25th Missouri Infantry. His regiment was soon assigned to the Army of the Tennessee, and he took part in the battles of Shiloh and Corinth. In 1863 he returned to Missouri on recruiting assignment but because of his political duties resigned from the service in 1864. From 1863 to 1865 he was a state senator, and he again served as mayor before his senatorship expired. He was a delegate to every Republican national convention from 1864 to 1884 inclusive and was one of the "Immortal 306," who stood by Grant for a third term in 1880. In 1864 he was elected representative to Congress, served three consecutive terms, and later filled that office two more terms, 1881 to 1883 and 1895 to 1897. Because of his ability and whole-hearted work for the development of Kansas City, as well as the influence of the *Journal,* he was usually successful in winning office in a normally Democratic district. His work in Congress was marked by his stanch adherence to conservative Republican policies and by his effective efforts to aid Kansas City in becoming an industrial and railway metropolis.

Through his newspaper editorials and policies, his personal contacts with capitalists, and his state legislative and congressional activities he was able to achieve extraordinary results in making Kansas City the leading railroad center west of Chicago. When Leavenworth and St. Joseph were much larger towns and rivals for bridges and railroads across the Missouri River, he was successful in obtaining the Hannibal Bridge in 1869, and instrumental in bringing a half dozen trunk lines into Kansas City to aid her in outstripping them. He died in Kansas City.

[J. M. Greenwood, *Col. Robert Van Horn* (1905) and in *Mo. Hist. Rev.*, Jan. 1910–Apr. 1910; C. W. Whitney, *Kansas City, Mo.* (1908), vols. I–II; Roy Ellis, *A Civic Hist. of Kansas City* (1930); T. S. Case, *Hist. of Kansas City* (1888); H. C. McDougal, *Recollections* (1910); C. S. Williams, "Christian Barentsen Van Horn and his Descendants" (1911) a typescript in the Lib. of Cong.; *Kansas City Jour.*, Jan. 4, 1916.]

H. E. N.

VAN HORNE, WILLIAM CORNELIUS (Feb. 3, 1843–Sept. 11, 1915), railroad executive, the first of five children of Cornelius Covenhoven Van Horne and his second wife, Mary Minier (Richards), was born in Will County, Ill. On the paternal side, his ancestors were Dutch. His grandfather, Abraham Van Horne, was an officer in the Revolutionary forces and later a minister in the Dutch Reformed Church. On the maternal side, William was of German and French descent. His father, Cornelius, received his education at Union College, Schenectady, studied law, and became active in politics as a Democrat. He moved to Illinois in 1832, and, partly by farming and milling and partly by practising his profession as a lawyer, managed to earn a meager living and to rear his family. It was in these surroundings that William spent the first eight years of his life. There was no school or church in the vicinity and the boy's only schooling, until 1851 when the family moved to Joliet, was that furnished by his mother. When he was three years old he began to make sketches and early showed evidence of ability to draw. In Joliet his father was soon well established and within a year was elected the first mayor of the city. William made the most of his opportunity to attend the public school, to read every book that came his way, and to develop a hobby in collecting rock specimens and studying geology.

The auspicious beginning of the family's life in Joliet was changed when in 1854 the father died. The mother was left practically penniless but managed somehow to keep the family supplied with bread and the children at school. William, who was not an industrious student but had a quick intelligence and a retentive memory, was employed intermittently to deliver telegraph messages and learned to send and receive in the Morse code. At the age of fourteen he was given his first full-time job as telegraph operator, with the Illinois Central Railroad. Later he was engaged in similar capacity by the Michigan Central Railroad. He was the first operator in his district, and one of the earliest in the country, to receive by sound alone and dispense with the use of the recording tape. When the Civil War began he promptly enlisted, but his superintendent secured his release because his services as telegraph operator and general assistant were important to the railroad and because he was the main support of his mother.

In 1862 Van Horne transferred his service to the Chicago & Alton Railroad as ticket agent and operator in Joliet; in 1864, he became train dispatcher for the same railroad in Bloomington; four years later he was appointed superintendent of telegraph and two years afterward superintendent of transportation; in 1872, he became general superintendent of a subsidiary line, the St. Louis, Kansas City & Northern Railway. His success in that position led in 1874 to his appointment as general manager and subsequently as president of the Southern Minnesota Railroad, with offices in La Crosse, Wis. This road, then in its second receivership, was in wretched physical condition and the morale of employees was notoriously low, but under Van Horne the property was soon rehabilitated and the receivership terminated in 1877. He was so successful in this connection that when the road was acquired by another system he was asked in 1879 to return to the Chicago & Alton as its general superintendent. After brief service with his old employers, however, he became general superintendent of the Chicago, Milwaukee & St. Paul.

The size of that system, and its many problems of operation and development of traffic, afforded Van Horne new opportunities for the exercise of his abilities. During his two years as general superintendent he accomplished much in increasing the efficiency of train operation and in reducing operating costs. He had also to assume leadership in competitive struggles with rivals and in connection with one of those encounters (in 1880) he crossed swords with James J. Hill [*q.v.*], when the Chicago, Milwaukee & St. Paul threatened to invade the territory occupied by the nucleus of the present Great Northern. Hill had known of Van Horne's earlier success and was so strongly impressed by the qualities he exhibited in their encounter that he gave Van Horne the great opportunity of his life by recommending him to the directors of the Canadian Pacific Railway as the man most highly qualified to carry out the tremendous task of creating and giving the breath of life to the proposed transcontinental line from Montreal to a terminus on the Pacific Ocean. Van Horne took charge of the work of construction at Winnipeg on Dec. 31, 1881.

The story of the building of the Canadian Pacific is mainly a history of his achievements in overcoming stupendous difficulties. The physical problems and those concerning the relations of the company with its employees were peculiarly his; the problems of finance and relations with the government rested mainly on the shoulders of the directors, but they shared their burdens with him. The project was carried to completion in 1886 and Van Horne, who had served from 1881 to 1884 as general manager, and from 1884 to 1888 as vice-president, was elected president in August 1888. The eleven years of his presidency were marked by further growth in mileage, earning power, and ramification of auxiliary services. Failing health led him to resign on June 12, 1899, and accept election as chairman of the board of directors and member of the executive committee. In these positions, however, he was never active, and in 1910 he withdrew from all official connection with the Canadian Pacific.

The relief from heavy responsibilities in 1899 had quick and beneficial effect upon his health. Leisure he had found distasteful, so he turned to new and distant fields for additional creative work. A visit to Cuba in 1900 fired his imagination with the possibilities of a 350-mile railroad through the eastern provinces of the island. Because of legal complications incident to American occupation, it was not possible to obtain a charter until Cuba had established its own republican government, but, impatient of delay and firm in his faith in the soundness of the project, Van Horne did the unprecedented, accepting temporarily a revocable license in lieu of a charter and proceeding to purchase property for right of way and terminals. By this evidence of confidence in the honor of the Cuban people, by his skill as a diplomat in surmounting obstacles, and by his courteous and aboveboard dealings with the public authorities, he succeeded in winning public approval, and the needed charter was granted very soon after the Republic was organized. On Dec. 1, 1902, the Cuba Railroad was opened for traffic, less than two years from the date of Van Horne's first visit to the island.

His next railroad activity was in Guatemala, where in 1903 he undertook to direct the construction of the last sixty-five miles of a railroad from Puerto Barrios to the city of Guatemala. The completion of the line was delayed by insurrections and the depression of 1907, but the last spike was driven in January 1908. This relatively small enterprise gave Van Horne more trouble per mile of railroad than any other he had undertaken. Coincident with his activities in Cuba and Guatemala, he was a director or officer in several large industrial enterprises, such as the Laurentide Pulp Company, Grand Mère, Quebec; a salt company at Windsor, Ontario; tramway systems in several Canadian cities, as well as in Mexico and Brazil; and the Dominion Coal Company and the Dominion Iron and Steel Company of Cape Breton. He was also a member of the board of the Equitable Life Assurance Society, but knew little of its finance and was horrified by the scandals of 1905 and 1906. With advancing years and impairment of health his activities began to diminish, but in a few things he maintained continued interest. Returning from his last trip to Cuba in June 1915, he was stricken with fever and died in Montreal on Sept. 11 of that year.

In addition to his imposing graystone house in Montreal, Van Horne had a beautiful summer home in St. Andrews, N. B., and a pretentious winter home in Camagüey, Cuba. He took intense interest in designing and supervising the construction of the buildings and grounds, and himself painted some of the mural decorations. His early talent for drawing and painting had been developed as a means of diverting his mind from business cares and his later paintings had artistic merit. For many years he followed his early bent toward paleontology and treasured a large collection of fossils. Other hobbies of his were the collection of paintings and of rare Japanese pottery.

With Van Horne's ability to deal with men, either in directing work or in business transactions, was coupled a strange shyness in formal social gatherings. He declined more than once to accept an invitation from McGill University, of which he was a trustee, to receive an honorary degree. When he retired from the presidency of the Canadian Pacific, his colleagues among railroad executives had made plans for a testimonial dinner in New York as a tribute to him personally and to his substantial contributions to transportation, but Van Horne's dislike of publicity and his aversion to speechmaking blocked their efforts to do him public honor. When knighthood was offered to him, both in 1890 and at the end of 1891, he asked that it be deferred, but finally, in 1894, he accepted royal appointment as an Honorary Knight Commander of the Order of St. Michael and St. George. Prior to 1890 he had become naturalized under the Canadian laws.

In personal characteristics Sir William was of imposing and handsome appearance—tall, massively built, and bearded. Officially he was cold and austere, a leader of the driving type; personally, with friends, he was genial and companionable. He was entertaining as a story-teller, with a tendency in his late years to exaggerate. From those who worked under him he demanded first of all complete loyalty; to them he too was loyal and generous, but he was not noted for his contributions to charity, public institutions, and the like. His wealth was devoted in the main to his family, to his three homes, and to his hobbies.

In March 1867, while a train dispatcher at Bloomington, Ill., he married Lucy Adaline Hurd of Galesburg, Ill., who in 1858, because of her beauty and personal distinction, had been chosen to read the address of welcome when Abraham Lincoln visited Galesburg. Three children were born to them: a son who died in his fifth year and a son and a daughter who with their mother were living when Sir William died.

[The writer, as a youth, was employed by the Canadian Pacific Railway, and occasionally came in contact with Van Horne. The chief source is Walter Vaughan, *The Life and Work of Sir William Van Horne* (1920). See also O. D. Skelton, *The Railway Builders* (1916); J. M. Gibbon, *Steel of Empire* (1935); H. A. Innis, *A Hist. of the Canadian Pacific Railway* (1923); Beckles Willson, *The Life of Lord Strathcona and Mount Royal* (1915), vol. II; J. G. Pyle, *The Life of James J. Hill* (1917), vol. I; *Who's Who in America*, 1914–15; *Montreal Daily Star*, Sept. 13, 1915; *N. Y. Times*, Sept. 12, 1915.]   W. J. C.

VAN ILPENDAM, JAN JANSEN (*c.* 1595–1647), commissary at Fort Nassau on the Delaware, apparently belonged to a well-to-do family of Haarlem, whose name appears on the records of that city as early as 1444. He himself, however, came from Leyden and was probably the Jan Jansen van Ilpendam who in 1616, at Delft, married Judick Hame. In May 1633 he sailed as supercargo on the yacht *Pernambuco* for Brazil, where, in 1635, at the taking of Porto Calvo, he was captured by the Portuguese. Returning to Amsterdam in the summer of 1636 he was appointed on Sept. 4 by the West India Company supercargo on the ship *Rensselaerswyck*, a privately owned vessel, which arrived at Manhattan on Mar. 4 of the following year. He was still at Manhattan on Aug. 5, 1637, when the ship made ready to return to Holland, but seems shortly afterwards to have been appointed commissary at Fort Nassau. In the spring of 1638, Willem

Kieft [*q.v.*], the newly arrived director general of New Netherland, sent Jan Jansen to the South River to protest in due form against the action of Peter Minuit [*q.v.*] in erecting there the arms of the Queen of Sweden; two years later, Van Ilpendam made a similar protest to Peter Ridder, the new Swedish commissioner, but in spite of these protests, his relations with the Swedish remained friendly. He assumed a more aggressive attitude toward the English, however, when, in 1641, some Englishmen of New Haven formed a Delaware Company and through their agents bought lands on both sides of the river, at the Varkens kill and on the Schuylkill. Acting under instructions from Kieft, Van Ilpendam promptly expelled the English from the Schuylkill, and two years later sat as one of the commissioners in a Swedish court of inquiry ordered by Governor Printz to examine the English who continued to trade on the Varkens kill. In 1644, some Boston merchants obtained a charter to trade on the Delaware River and Kieft once more ordered Van Ilpendam to protest against them, instructing him "rather to sink the English ship than to let it pass the fort" (quoted by Johnson, *post*, I, 396). On all these occasions Van Ilpendam seems to have acted with diligence and discretion. In 1645, however, he was accused of fraud and summoned to appear at Manhattan. The case against him was investigated by Cornelis van der Hoykens, the public prosecutor, from whose findings it appeared that Van Ilpendam had "grossly wronged the Company, both in giving more to the Indians than the ordinary rate and in other instances specified in the complaint, affidavits and in his accounts" (*Documents, post*, XII, 26). The Council, thereupon, on Feb. 8, 1646, ordered him with his papers and the fiscal's complaint to be sent to Amsterdam by the first ship, to defend himself before the directors of the Company. He died, apparently, not long after his departure from New Netherland, since on Aug. 16, 1647, his second wife, Catalyntje van Strassel, gave a power of attorney to Jan de Laet for a settlement of his accounts.

["Minutes of the Amsterdam Chamber of the Dutch West India Company, 1635–1636," *N. Y. Geneal. and Biog. Record*, July 1918; N. Y. Colonial MSS. in N. Y. State Lib., see E. B. O'Callaghan, *Calendar of Hist. MSS. . . .* pt. I (1865); *Docs. Rel. to the Col. Hist. of . . . N. Y.*, vols. I (1856), XII (1877); J. R. Brodhead, *Hist. of the State of N. Y* (1853), vol. I; and Amandus Johnson, *The Swedish Settlements on the Delaware* (1911), vol. I.]   A. J. F. v–L.

VAN LENNEP, HENRY JOHN (Mar. 18, 1815–Jan. 11, 1889), missionary and educator, was born at Smyrna in Asiatic Turkey, the son of Adèle Marie (de Heidenstam) and Richard

Van Lennep, both members of European families long resident in the Levant. His parents, acting on the advice of American missionaries, sent him at the age of fifteen to be educated in the United States, where he prepared for college in the Mount Pleasant Institute of Amherst, Mass., and in the Hartford (Conn.) Grammar School. In 1837 he graduated from Amherst College. Since he had decided while in college to become a missionary, he next spent a year at Andover Theological Seminary, then completed his religious training under the direction of Dr. Joel Hawes at Hartford, Conn. On Aug. 27, 1839, he was ordained as a Congregational minister at Amherst. On Nov. 3, he married Emma L., the daughter of Henry Bliss of Springfield, Mass., and later in the same year sailed for Turkey as a missionary of the American Board of Commissioners for Foreign Missions. He was at first stationed at Smyrna, where his wife died on Sept. 7, 1840. After extensive preaching tours through western Turkey and Greece, he visited the United States in 1843 to marry, on Sept. 4, Mary Elizabeth Hawes, the daughter of his former teacher. She died on Sept. 27 of the next year. On his return to Turkey in 1844 he was transferred to Constantinople. During the next ten years he not only carried on regular missionary duties but also taught in the seminary, later Robert College, at Bebek, a suburb of Constantinople, and traveled widely. A visit to Syria and Palestine in 1847 provided the material for his *Bible Lands, Their Modern Customs and Manners Illustrative of Scripture* (1875). Late in 1849 he was in the United States and on Apr. 18, 1850, married Emily Ann Bird, whose father, Isaac Bird, had been a missionary in Syria but had retired to live in Hartford, Conn. William Bird Van Lennep [q.v.] was their son. In 1854 he was transferred from Constantinople to Tokat, a city in north central Anatolia, to establish a mission station and theological seminary. His valuable *Travels in Little-Known Parts of Asia Minor* (2 vols., 1870), illustrated with his own sketches, is based on careful notes taken on journeys during which he visited and described many important archeological remains of the Hittite period. In 1861 he left Tokat and until 1863 was in the United States, but he returned to preach and teach in Smyrna until 1869, when failing eyesight and disagreement with mission policy led to his permanent settlement in the United States.

For three years he taught natural science, Greek, and modern languages in Ingham University at LeRoy, N. Y. He then retired to Great Barrington, Mass., and devoted himself to writing. His familiarity with local customs, mentalities, and languages, together with his lack of condescension toward the people of Turkey, made him an effective preacher and teacher. He used French, Armenian, Greek, and Turkish in addition to English, and he found his recreation in music, archeology, and painting. His *Oriental Album* (1862), a volume of colored representations of near eastern types and costumes, provides evidence of his proficiency as an artist. He died at Great Barrington.

[*The Encyc. of Missions* (1891), vol. II, ed. by E. M. Bliss; *Biog. Record of the Alumni of Amherst College* (1883), ed. by W. L. Montague; *Appletons' Ann. Cyc. . . . 1889* (1890); *N. Y. Tribune*, Jan. 12, 1889; a few letters in L. F. Hawes, *Memoir of Mrs. Mary E. Van Lennep* (1847); MS. "Footsteps of Homer: Niobe of Mt. Sipylus," in Princeton Univ. Lib.; information from son, E. J. Van Lennep, Great Barrington, Mass.]
W. L. W., Jr.

VAN LENNEP, WILLIAM BIRD (Dec. 5, 1853–Jan. 9, 1919), surgeon, was born at Constantinople, Turkey, the son of Emily (Bird) and Henry John Van Lennep [q.v.]. His early education, while living abroad, was entirely under the supervision of his parents. In 1869 the family returned to the United States. Between 1869 and 1872 he attended the Sedgwick School in Great Barrington, Mass. He graduated from Princeton College in 1876. In 1876 and 1877 he studied medicine in a doctor's office in LeRoy, N. Y. In 1880 he graduated from the Hahnemann Medical College of Philadelphia and received the gold medal of the faculty. Following graduation he served an interneship of six months at the New York Homeopathic Charity Hospital, Ward's Island. He then returned to Philadelphia for a short time assisting Dr. Bushrod W. James in practice. From 1882 to 1884 he attended post graduate courses in London, Paris, and Vienna. He settled in Philadelphia upon his return from Europe and devoted himself to the practice of surgery exclusively. On Apr. 28, 1886, he was married to Clara Reeves Hart, the daughter of Thomas Hart of Philadelphia. He taught in the Hahnemann Medical College faculty from 1886 to his death, as professor of surgery after 1895. He was surgeon to the Pennsylvania Homoeopathic Hospital for Children and the Children's Homoeopathic Hospital of Philadelphia, senior surgeon of Hahnemann Hospital of Philadelphia, consulting surgeon of the Camden Homoeopathic Hospital, Woman's Homoeopathic Hospital of Philadelphia, Trenton Homoeopathic Hospital, and the Harper Memorial Hospital. In 1888 he purchased the *Hahnemannian Monthly* from Pemberton Dudley and associated with himself as editor Clarence Bartlett. In 1910 he was elected dean of Hahnemann College. In that office he was instrumental in raising the standards required by modern medicine. He established new laboratories, obtained the Elkins Amphitheatre in the hospital, the amphitheatre in the maternity building, the library and reading room, and many other advancements.

Physically a giant, he was a man of remarkable personality and multiplicity of talents. He was whole-heartedly devoted to Hahnemann, sacrificing all efforts and interests in its behalf. As a teacher he is well remembered by all who sat before him. In all matters pertaining to medical and homeopathic affairs he was consulted frequently by men important in political and medical movements for advancement. He was a member of several medical societies and an active member of the Union League of Philadelphia. During the latter part of 1918, his health broke, and although not regarded as seriously ill, he died suddenly, survived by his wife and daughter.

[T. L. Bradford, *Homoeopathic Bibliog. of the U. S.* (1892) and *Index of the Homoeopathic Medical College of Pa. and the Hahnemann Medical College and Hospital* (1918); W. H. King, *Hist. of Homoeopathy* (1905), vol. IV; *Hahnemannian Monthly,* Jan. 1919; *Philadelphia Inquirer,* Jan. 10, 1919; personal acquaintance.]   C. B—t.

VAN METER, JOHN BLACKFORD (Sept. 6, 1842–Apr. 8, 1930), clergyman and educator, was born in Philadelphia, Pa., his father being Thomas Hurley Van Meter, of Dutch descent, and his mother, Johnetta (Blackford) Van Meter, whose ancestors were English and French. When the boy was about four years old, his father died, and some years later the family removed to Baltimore, Md. Van Meter was graduated in 1859 from the Male Central High School (later Baltimore City College). In recognition of his scholarly and other achievements, several institutions later granted him honorary degrees. On Dec. 19, 1866, he married Lucinda Cassell of Westminster, Md., by whom he had two daughters. For several years he taught in the public schools of Baltimore, and during 1868–69 was principal of the Male Academic and Female Collegiate Institute at Westminster, a Methodist institution. He began preaching in the Methodist Episcopal Church in 1864, and was ordained deacon in 1866 and elder in 1868. He had charge of circuits in Maryland and Pennsylvania (1864–68), and later held pastorates in Washington, D. C., Plainfield, N. J., and Baltimore. For ten years (1872–81) he was chaplain in the United States Navy, being for a time stationed at the naval academy at Annapolis. He resigned the position to take charge of the Huntington Avenue Methodist Episcopal Church in Baltimore.

There he was closely associated with John Franklin Goucher [*q.v.*], pastor of the First Methodist Church, in the founding of the Woman's College of Baltimore (later Goucher College). Though the institution came into existence under the auspices of the Baltimore Conference of the Methodist Episcopal Church, the success of the undertaking was largely due to the efforts of these two men. From 1882 to 1885 Van Meter was a member of the publishing committee of the *Baltimore Methodist,* through which was carried on the campaign for funds for the college. He was a member of all important committees of the Conference connected with its founding and of the board of trustees (1885–88, 1914–30). In 1888, when the college was opened, he was appointed professor of psychology, ethics, and the Bible, the first member of the faculty to be named. In 1914 he was retired with the rank of professor emeritus. He was dean of the college from 1892 to 1910 and acting president from 1911 to 1913. But, as President Goucher was frequently absent for long periods, Van Meter was the real administrator of the institution during much of his connection with it. It was he who largely shaped and maintained the educational policy of the college, a pioneer in the modern educational movement for women in the South, and who placed it among the best colleges of the country. It is a tribute to his zeal and ability that, though the college was practically bankrupt in 1911 when he became acting head, its high scholastic standards were intact. On the intellectual and spiritual ideals of its students he also exerted much influence. He was kindly, delightfully humorous, and so broadly tolerant as to be subjected to criticism for religious heresy. He died in Baltimore.

[*Who's Who in America,* 1918–19; J. T. Ensor, in *Minutes of the Baltimore Conference of the M. E. Church* (1930); pubs. of Goucher Coll.; T. P. Thomas, "Hist. of Goucher Coll." (in preparation); *Sun* (Baltimore), June 2, 1914, and Apr. 9, 1930 (obituary); private information.]   M. W. W.

VAN NAME, ADDISON (Nov. 15, 1835–Sept. 29, 1922), librarian and philologist, was born in Chenango, a few miles from Binghamton, N. Y. His father owned a sawmill and was interested in the shipping on the canal. Prepared for college at the Binghamton Academy and the Phillips Academy at Andover, he graduated from Yale College in 1858 at the head of his class, having won distinction also in various other ways. During one school year, probably in 1858–59 he taught in Perth Amboy, N. J. From July 1859 to January 1861 he was in Europe, spending the first year at the universities of Halle and Tübingen, and the last six months in travel. He passed the year following his return in Binghamton. In July 1861 he was appointed instructor in Hebrew in the theological department. He held this position until 1866. On May 2, 1865, he was licensed to preach by the (Congregational) New Haven West Association but never made any use of the license. In 1865 he was appointed librarian of Yale. He married in Berlin, Prussia, on Aug. 19, 1867, Julia Gibbs, the daughter of Josiah Willard Gibbs, 1790–1861, and the sister of his classmate, Josiah Willard Gibbs, 1839–1903 [qq.v.]. She died Jan. 4, 1916, leaving two sons and a daughter. An article, "Contributions on Creole Grammar," was published in the *American Philological Association Transactions, 1867–70* (1871) ; in 1873 the *Congrès International des Orientalistes: compte rendu de la première session* (vol. I) published his review of a book on the early history of Japan; in the same year the *American Cyclopaedia* published his article on the Arabic language and literature; and in 1875 *Johnson's New Universal Cyclopaedia* had an article from his pen on the Chinese language and literature. He built up the Yale collection of oriental literature until it became one of the best in the United States and gave his own books on the Far East to Yale in 1920. He was librarian of the American Oriental Society from 1873 to 1905, and of the Connecticut Academy of Arts and Sciences from 1865 to 1905. He attended the meeting in 1876 at which the American Library Association was formed, and he was a member of many other bibliothecal, bibliophilic, and bibliographic societies both in this country and abroad. His *Catalogue of the William Loring Andrews Collections of Early Books* (1913) is an excellent description of a number of books gathered to illustrate the first century of printing.

His chief work, however, was as librarian of Yale for forty years. He had an unusual range of interests, a remarkable memory for books, and extraordinarily good judgment in buying. When he took charge of the library it had about 44,500 volumes; when he resigned it had 300,000. This was a marvellous growth at a time when little money was available for books or service, but the most striking thing about this quarter of a million books is not their number but their quality. Becoming librarian emeritus in 1905, he spent some of his leisure years in Europe and his winters usually in Florida. He died in New Haven after a brief illness. On his eightieth birthday the Yale Corporation gave to the library his portrait, painted by W. Sergeant Kendall, the dean of the school of fine arts.

[*Second Biog. Record of the Class of Fifty-Eight, Yale College* (1869), *Fourth . . .* (1897), *Fifth . . .* (1908) ; *Yale Univ. Obituary Record, 1923* (1923) ; *Yale Weekly,* Oct. 6, 1922 ; votes of Yale Corporation ; *New Haven Journal-Courier,* Sept. 30, and Oct. 3, 1922 ; information from family ; personal acquaintance ; statements of appointments at Yale from official records.]   A. K—h.

VAN NESS, WILLIAM PETER (*c.* 1778– Sept. 6, 1826), politician, jurist, was one of the sons of Peter and Elbertie (Hogeboom) Van Ness. The father was a Revolutionary patriot and county judge; two other sons gained some distinction—John P. became a member of Congress, and Cornelius P., governor of Vermont and minister to Spain. William was born at Claverack (later Ghent), Columbia County, N. Y.; he lived for a time in Kinderhook and for a time in Hudson, but for most of his life in New York City. His education was as thorough as the Kinderhook Academy, Columbia College, where he graduated in 1797, and private study in the law office of Edward Livingston [q.v.] could make it. In 1800 he began the practice of law in New York City as the admirer and protégé of Aaron Burr [q.v.]. In February 1801 he went with Burr to Albany, and wrote back to Livingston, his former preceptor, that the Republicans wanted Burr instead of Jefferson for president (*An Examination,* p. 61).

From that day until he became a judge, his political record was as devious as that of any of the New York politicians of the early years of the century when parties were still wavering and undeveloped. Burr admired and trusted him and was in turn worshipped by Van Ness, who became his defender in Peter Irving's *Morning Chronicle,* in politics, and on the dueling field. Van Ness entered with alacrity into the political broils of the Clintons, the Livingstons, and Burr. When James Cheetham [q.v.] published a vicious attack on Burr for his activities in state politics and in the presidential election of 1801, Van Ness replied in a pamphlet entitled *An Examination of the Various Charges Exhibited against Aaron Burr* (1803), signed Aristides—a specimen of invective justifiably compared to the *Letters of Junius.* At the time, no one but Van Buren and Burr, who supplied information on several local and national politicians, seems to have known the identity of the author. Van Ness wrote with such peculiar ferocity and venom that Cheetham's pamphlets appeared almost tame in comparison; Burr was so ably defended that newspapers rang with the unknown author's story of confused truth and fiction.

Breaking, in March 1804, with Van Buren, who, having come of age, chose to enter politics as a Clintonian, Van Ness threw himself more zealously into the political arena to the detriment of his law practice. Believing in duels as a gentlemanly method of ridding the party of its enemies, he played the rôle of second to Burr in the Burr-Hamilton duel (1804), a tragedy which he might have prevented. When the coroner's jury indicted him as accessory in the murder of Hamilton, he fled to Kinderhook and sent pleas for help to Van Buren, with whom he had become reconciled. Through the influence of the latter in the courts and with Governor Daniel D. Tompkins [*q.v.*], Van Ness procured the restoration of his civil rights. He was subsequently associated with Van Buren in several enterprises, including the Bank of Hudson in which they were both directors, but in 1812 clashed with him over a state senatorship, to which Van Buren was elected. In that year President Madison appointed Van Ness a judge in the federal court for the Southern District of New York, a position which he held until his death. In 1811 the New York legislature had requested him, aided by John Woodworth, to codify the laws for public information. The result, *Laws of the State of New York,* with notes, was published in 1813; it was notably successful in method and arrangement. His other works were *Reports of Two Cases in the Prize Court for the New York District* (1814) and *A Concise Narrative of General Jackson's First Invasion of Florida* (1826), published the year of his death. His careless supervision permitted the clerk of his court to embezzle more than $100,000, but the episode had no permanent effect upon his own reputation for business integrity. He was highly respected by his friends for his ability and party loyalty. Apparently he never married.

[J. G. Wilson, *The Memorial Hist. of the City of N. Y.*, vol. III (1893) ; *Names of Persons for Whom Marriage Licenses Were Issued . . . New York* (1860), p. 422; E. A. Collier, *A Hist. of Old Kinderhook* (1914); P. F. Miller, *A Group of Great Lawyers of Columbia County, N. Y.* (1904) ; D. S. Alexander, *A Pol. Hist. of . . . N. Y.*, vol. I (1906); D. T. Lynch, *An Epoch and A Man: Martin Van Buren and His Times* (1929) ; W. L. Mackenzie, *The Life and Times of Martin Van Buren* (1846) ; "Autobiography of Martin Van Buren," ed. by J. C. Fitzpatrick, in *Ann. Report Am. Hist. Asso., 1918,* vol. II (1920) ; Van Buren MSS., in Lib. of Cong.; *Niles' Weekly Register,* Sept. 16, 1826 ; *N. Y. Evening Post,* Sept. 7, 1826.]　　　W. E. S—h.

VAN NEST, ABRAHAM RYNIER (Feb. 16, 1823–June 1, 1892), clergyman of the Reformed Church in America, was born in New York City. He was the son of George Van Nest and Phoebe, daughter of Abraham Van Nest. His first American ancestor was Peter Van Nest who emigrated from the Netherlands in 1647 and settled in Brooklyn. Abraham Rynier graduated from Rutgers College in 1841, and from the New

Brunswick Theological Seminary in 1847. After serving briefly a mission at Greenpoint, Long Island, and the Associate Reformed Church of Newburgh, N. Y., he was from 1848 to 1862 pastor of the Twenty-first Street Reformed Church of New York City.

He then went abroad and for some fifteen years ministered to American residents there. During the year 1863–64 he was in charge of the American Chapel in Paris, and the year following, of the American Chapel at Rome. His most notable service, however, was in Florence (1866–75), where he established a church into which he drew people of diverse religious traditions and modes of life. For it he compiled a liturgical service, which became a model for other churches of a similar character. His sympathies were broad and his evangelical zeal intense; he became affiliated with the Waldenses and later with the Free Church of Italy. His fine personal and intellectual qualities, and his unfailing devotion to good causes, sustained by financial resources of his own, enabled him to accomplish much. Among his other activities, he had a principal part in the founding of the Protestant Orphanage at Florence. After leaving that city he established the American Union Church at Geneva.

Returning to the United States in 1878, he became pastor of the Third Reformed Church of Philadelphia, continuing in this pastorate until impaired health caused his retirement in 1883. For nine years thereafter until his death he was without charge. In 1879 he was president of the General Synod of the Reformed Church in America. He was zealous in furthering the welfare of New Brunswick Theological Seminary, and was a trustee of Rutgers College from 1878 until his death. His publications included occasional sermons and many articles in the religious press. He helped prepare for the press *Lectures on Pastoral Theology* (1853), by James Spencer Cannon, and *Expository Sermons on the Heidelberg Catechism* (2 vols., 1864), by George W. Bethune [*q.v.*], and wrote *Memoir of Rev. Geo. W. Bethune, D.D.* (1867). He died in New York City.

[E. T. Corwin, *Manual of the Reformed Church in America* (1902) ; *Biog. Notices of Grads. of Rutgers Coll.* (1892) ; *Acts and Proc. of the Gen. Synod of the Reformed Church in America,* vol. XVIII (1893); *Christian Intelligencer,* June 8, July 6, 1892.]
　　　　　　　　　　　　　　　　W. H. S. D.

VAN NOSTRAND, DAVID (Dec. 5, 1811– June 14, 1886), publisher, was born in New York City, fifth child of Jacob and Harriet (Rhodes) Van Nostrand. The founder of his family in America was Jacob Jansen, who emigrated from the Netherlands to settle on Long Island in 1638. To avoid confusion with other Jansens, Jacob's children added "van Noorstrandt" to the name, referring to the district of their father's origin, and as generations passed, this became transmuted into Van Nostrand. David's father, a successful merchant in New York City, died leaving eight children when David was only ten years old; but their mother was able to care for them and give them the beginnings of an education. David studied at Union Hall, Jamaica, Long Island, until he was fifteen, when he entered the employ of John P. Haven, a New York publisher and bookseller. Four years later, having saved a little money, he contemplated taking up his studies again; but he had become so valuable to Haven that the latter persuaded him to remain by promising him a partnership upon his coming of age. Van Nostrand accordingly continued with Haven until 1834, when he formed a partnership in a similar enterprise with William Dwight. The panic of 1837 drove the young men out of business, and Van Nostrand accepted the offer of a position from a friend, Lieut. John G. Barnard [q.v.], an army engineer, stationed at New Orleans in charge of the construction of fortifications in Louisiana and Texas.

While he was serving as clerk of accounts and disbursements in Barnard's office, Van Nostrand eagerly studied military engineering and kindred sciences and improved his acquaintance with engineers, scientists, and military men. Returning to New York about 1848, he opened a bookstore at Broadway and John Street. His acquaintance with military and technical men and writings now stood him in good stead; he was solicited by army and navy officers to import foreign books on military and naval science, and soon had built up an excellent trade. The United States Military Academy and other institutions were among his customers. He also ventured into publishing, issuing trade editions, usually enlarged and augmented, of various works, some of which had first been published for the government. In 1864 he took over from George Palmer Putnam [q.v.] the publication of *The Rebellion Record,* edited by Frank Moore [q.v.]; Van Nostrand issued volumes VII–XI (1864–68). In 1869 he installed his own printing plant, moving to more spacious quarters at 23 Murray Street, and established *Van Nostrand's Eclectic Engineering Magazine.* Devoting himself to the publishing of scientific, technical, and military works, he made his concern the largest specialized publishing house in America; and built up an extensive business abroad. He is credited with giving a distinct impulse to scientific investigation in the United States by his importation of foreign treatises, and with en-

couraging American technical men to write by publishing their work. Among the notable works he sponsored were Egbert L. Viele's *Hand-book for Active Service* (1861); Brig. Gen. Silas Casey's *Infantry Tactics* (1862); Henry Jomini's *Life of Napoleon* (2 vols., 1864), translated from the French by Gen. H. W. Halleck; Jomini's *Treatise on Grand Military Operations* (2 vols., 1865); Albert J. Myer's *Manual of Signals* (2nd ed., 1866); James B. Francis' *Lowell Hydraulic Experiments* (2nd ed., 1868); Julius Weisbach's *Manual of Mechanics* (1870); Charles B. Stuart's *Lives and Works of Civil and Military Engineers* (1871); and Squire Whipple's *Elementary and Practical Treatise on Bridge Building* (1872). He continued until his death to publish *Van Nostrand's Engineering Magazine* (the shorter title was adopted in 1878); six months after he died it was merged with the *American Railroad Journal* in the *Railroad and Engineering Journal.*

Van Nostrand was a member of the Union League Club and the St. Nicholas Society, and was one of the founders of the Holland Society of New York. He was twice married: his first wife, a daughter of Rev. Isaac Lewis of New York, died within eighteen months of their marriage; his second, Sarah A. Nichols of New York, survived him. He left no children.

[H. A. Stoutenburgh, *A Doc. Hist. of the Dutch Congregation of Oyster Bay* (1902); B. J. Lossing, *Hist. of N. Y. City* (1884), II, 705; J. C. Derby, *Fifty Years among Authors, Books, and Publishers* (1884); *A Classified Cat. of Am. and Foreign Scientific Books for Sale by David Van Nostrand, Publisher and Importer* (1871); *Van Nostrand's Engineering Mag.,* July, Dec. 1886; *Year Book of the Holland Soc. of N. Y.,* 1886–87; *Union League Club Report,* 1887; *Publisher's Weekly,* June 19, 1886; *N. Y. Times* and *N. Y. Tribune,* June 15, 1886.] A.F.H.

VAN OSDEL, JOHN MILLS (July 31, 1811–Dec. 21, 1891), architect, was born in Baltimore, Md., the eldest of eight children of James H. Van Osdel, said to have been a descendant of Lyman Van Arsdale who emigrated to New York in 1653. Leaving his wife and family in Baltimore, the elder Van Osdel, a carpenter, cabinet maker, and building contractor, went to establish himself in New York. At fourteen, temporarily deprived, through an accident, of the father's support, John undertook to provide for the family by making benches and stools, on an original investment of one board. In New York, where the family soon went, Van Osdel entered into apprenticeship with his father and studied architectural books at the Apprentice Library. At eighteen he embarked in business for himself. In 1831 he married Caroline Gailer of Hudson, N. Y. Returning to Baltimore, he worked at his trade and found time to write one of the numerous carpentry handbooks of the time. In New York, to which he returned in 1836, he reached a turning point in his career—his meeting with William Butler Ogden [*q.v.*], the most prominent citizen of Chicago. Employed by Ogden to plan and erect a large mansion, he established his family in Chicago in 1837, the year of its incorporation as a city. The Ogden house on Ontario and Rush streets, which was burned in the fire of 1871, had a cupola and classic porticoes, occupied with its grounds a full city block, and was perhaps the most imposing dwelling in Illinois at the time. After one more excursion to New York in 1840, where for a short time he is said to have been associate editor of the *American Mechanic,* Van Osdel returned to Chicago and lived there until his death.

When Van Osdel went to Chicago the city contained only thirteen brick buildings; of the remainder more than half were one-story cottages, many of log construction. There were no architects. In 1844, after Van Osdel had spent a year or two in the machinery business and in shipbuilding (he finished two of the first steamboats built in the city), the building-contractors of the town promised to give him their support if he would open an architectural office. In that year six hundred new buildings were put up. In the three years ending in 1859, it is said, Van Osdel earned $32,000 and had to his credit most of the buildings of importance in the rapidly growing city, including the very large Second Presbyterian Church in Gothic, unusual in 1851. During the great fire of 1871, with characteristic resourcefulness, he dug a great pit in which he buried all his plans and records. While the embers were still red he opened a new office and in eighteen months erected 8,000 lineal feet of new buildings. Among them were the Palmer House, the Tremont House, the Oriental and Kendal buildings, and the McCormick and Reaper Blocks. He also designed what were regarded as the three finest residences in Illinois—those of Peter Schuttler in Chicago, Joel A. Matteson in Springfield, and John Wood in Quincy, Ill. His health, not unnaturally, showed signs of strain; in 1873 he spent some time in the Yosemite and the far West and for a year following was in Europe. In 1883 his recollections were published in the *Inland Architect and Builder* (Mar., Apr. 1883). He was trustee of Illinois Industrial University (later the University of Illinois) and was early actively interested in the development of technical training. In politics he was a Garrisonian Abolitionist. He was an active participant in the campaign of 1860, and

published a pamphlet and even wrote a poem on the subject. After the death of his first wife, in 1846 he married Martha McClellan of Kendall County, Ill.; since he had no children by either marriage, he adopted a boy, who died in youth, and three girls.

Van Osdel lived to see the development of skeleton construction, and the passing of his methods of design and construction. His first buildings (notably the second court house, begun in 1851) were in the style of the Greek Revival, as was the Rush Medical College (1844); of his later buildings none rises much above the low level of the taste of the time. A gentleman of the old school, with a charming dignity, wearing by custom a dress coat with brass buttons, he carried gracefully and modestly the honor of being Chicago's first architect.

[A. T. Andreas, *Hist. of Chicago* (3 vols., 1884–86); *Biog. Sketches of the Leading Men of Chicago* (1868), pp. 91–95; *Industrial Chicago* (3 vols., 1891); D. W. Wood, *Chicago and Its Distinguished Citizens* (1881); *Chicago* (1881); obituary in *Chicago Tribune*, Dec. 22, 1891; scrapbook made by Van Osdel's nephew, in the Art Institute of Chicago.]   T.E.T.

VAN QUICKENBORNE, CHARLES FELIX (Jan. 21, 1788–Aug. 17, 1837), Jesuit missionary and educator, was born at Peteghem in East Flanders, where he received his preliminary education. Later he attended a school at Denyze and the seminary at Ghent. After ordination as a Catholic priest in 1812, he taught in a preparatory seminary at Roulers and held a curacy at St. Genoix, near Courtrai. The negotiations between the United States and Great Britain which led to the Treaty of Ghent aroused interest in the former country, and among those who were attracted to the American mission field was Van Quickenborne. On Apr. 14, 1815, he entered the Jesuit novitiate at Rumbeke, and two years later he was assigned to the Maryland mission of the Society of Jesus.

After his arrival in the United States he taught the Scriptures at Georgetown College, conducted religious services in Alexandria, Va., and served as master of novices at Whitemarsh, where he built a stone chapel. He also attended the Catholic congregation at Annapolis, in which place, with the financial aid of the Carrolls, he erected a brick chapel. His religious and charitable services among the poor, and especially among the neglected negroes, challenged such attention that Archbishop Ambrose Maréchal [*q.v.*] described him as a saint. An enthusiastic priest of unbounded zeal and dynamic energy, he was named, in 1823, superior to conduct a Jesuit band of priests, novices, and lay brothers to Missouri.

In a log-cabin at Florissant Van Quickenborne as superior of the Jesuits and as the bishop's vicar general of Upper Louisiana founded the Missouri province of his Society. Soon a church, St. Regis Seminary for Indian boys, a school for Indian girls under the Ladies of the Sacred Heart, and a school at St. Charles gave evidence of his successful labors. In 1828 he established St. Louis College, which in 1832 was incorporated as St. Louis University. A born missionary, as early as 1827 he journeyed into the Osage Indian country, and later visited the Potawatomi, Kickapoo, and other western tribes. In 1836 the first Jesuit mission with a resident priest was founded among the Kickapoo tribesmen, and soon after St. Mary's Mission was established among the Potawatomi Indians near what is now Leavenworth. In the meantime he undertook a series of missionary excursions through Missouri, Illinois, and Iowa, becoming the pioneer of the Catholic faith in Edwardsville, Galena, and Springfield, Ill., and in Keokuk and Dubuque, Iowa. On these excursions he not only preached to the Indians but ministered to the scattered Catholic settlers and laborers in the lead mines. In 1835 and in the year following he was on the site of future Kansas City performing the first recorded baptisms and marriages in that region. He also rendered no small service to the missions of the West by training such Jesuits as Christian Hoecken, Pierre De Smet, and Peter Verhaegen [*qq.v.*]. In order to finance his work and to popularize Jesuit enterprises he gave lectures and collected money in the East. Accounts of the missions which he wrote to his superiors were published in the *Annales de la Propagation de la Foi* from 1826 to 1836. Worn out by his strenuous labors, Van Quickenborne died before he was fifty, while stationed in the missionary parish of Portage des Sioux.

[Scattered information, sometimes conflicting, is supplied by *Catholic Encyc.*; *Records of the Am. Catholic Hist. Soc.*, vol. II (1889), p. 198, vol. XXII (1911), p. 265, vol. XXVII (1916), pp. 99 f.; *Am. Catholic Hist. Researches*, Apr. 1895; J. G. Shea, *Hist. of the Cath. Missions among the Indian Tribes of the U. S.* (1855); *Metropolitan Cath. Almanac* (1838); John Rothensteiner, *Hist. of the Archdiocese of St. Louis* (1928); G. J. Garraghan, *Catholic Beginnings in Kansas City, Mo.* (1920) and *Saint Ferdinand de Florissant* (1923); J. A. Griffin, *The Contribution of Belgium to the Catholic Church in America* (1932).]   R.J.P.

VAN RAALTE, ALBERTUS CHRISTIAAN (Oct. 17, 1811–Nov. 7, 1876), founder of a Dutch settlement in Holland, Mich., was born at Wanneperveen near Zwartsluis, in the Netherlands. His father, the Rev. Albertus van Raalte, and his mother, Christina Caterina Harking, were the parents of sixteen other children. Christiaan was a favored son, and in June 1829 he

matriculated at the University of Leyden, where he studied medicine and then theology. At the University he met Anthony Brummelkamp, who profoundly affected his whole career by inspiring him to religious fervor. When he had completed the theological course, he received a license to preach in the Reformed Church, but he was not formally admitted to the ministry because he refused to subscribe to all the regulations of the Dutch Reformed Church. On Nov. 1, 1834, a new church had been founded, which was named the *Gereformeerde,* instead of the *Hervormde,* Church, and Van Raalte's sympathies were strongly with the seceders because he thought that the established church needed a second reformation. For a time he served as minister in the new church, and in 1844 he removed to Arnhem in order to assist Brummelkamp in training candidates for the ministry in the newly formed denomination. The next year, owing to unfavorable economic conditions prevailing in the Netherlands, a small number of Van Raalte's acquaintances made preparations to emigrate to North America. During a severe illness in the summer of 1846 the thought occurred to him that he should, like a modern Moses, lead his comrades through the wilderness in a foreign country (A. Brummelkamp, Jr., *Levensbeschryving van wijlen Prof. A. Brummelkamp,* Kampen, 1910). Prompt action followed this thought.

In November 1846 he arrived in New York, and about one week later he was cordially received in Albany by Dr. I. N. Wyckoff, who gave him great encouragement. In December he arrived at Detroit, and in the following month he and his companions formulated a plan to found a settlement in western Michigan. On Feb. 9, 1847, accompanied by his wife, Christina Johanna De Moen, to whom he had been married on Mar. 11, 1836, and several men, he arrived at a place that he decided to name Holland, in honor of his native country. Two years later the settlement was visited by Wyckoff, who published a description in *The Christian Intelligencer,* Sept. 20, 1849. Rapidly the number of Dutch settlers increased. Van Raalte was their preacher as well as their physician. In 1867, however, he resigned his position as minister, claiming that, since he had never been ordained, the congregation needed a real minister. He strongly favored the cause of education, and he may be regarded as one of the founders of Hope College and the theological seminary situated at Holland, Mich. He founded *De Hope,* a religious periodical in the Dutch language. He was a born leader, ambitious, industrious, aggressive, broad-minded, patient, undaunted by danger and hardship, but he was afflicted after 1855 by financial worries and bodily disease. At his death he was survived by two sons and five daughters.

[*Album Studiosorum Academiae Luqduno Batavae* (1875); J. A. Wormser, *Een Schat in aarden Vaten,* I, *Het Leven van Albertus Christiaan van Raalte* (1915); H. E. Dosker, *Levensschets van Rev. A. C. v. Raalte* (1893); Anthony Brummelkamp, *Holland in Amerika* (1847); *Zalsmans Jaarboekje* contains numerous articles on Van Raalte; A. J. Pieters, *A Dutch Settlement in Michigan* (1923); J. Van Hinte, *Nederlanders in Amerika* (1928), 2 vols.]   A. H.

VAN RENSSELAER, CORTLANDT (May 26, 1808–July 25, 1860), Presbyterian clergyman, was born in Albany, N. Y., the son of Stephen Van Rensselaer [*q.v.*] by his second wife, Cornelia, daughter of the distinguished jurist William Paterson [*q.v.*]. He grew up with all the advantages that wealth and the high social position of his family afforded. Having received his preliminary education in a boarding school at Hyde Park, conducted by Dr. Benjamin Allen, he entered Yale College in 1823 and was graduated four years later. He then studied law and in 1830 was admitted to the New York bar. Believing, however, that a man of property "is under peculiar obligation to make himself useful," and doubting that it was possible for him to retain proper religious feelings and be "occupied with the ordinary vanities and pursuits of the world" (*Memorial, post,* p. 24), he abandoned law and prepared for the ministry. After spending two years at Princeton Theological Seminary, he completed his course at Union Seminary, Hampden-Sidney, Va., and was ordained to the ministry on Apr. 18, 1835, by the Presbytery of Hanover.

For a time he devoted himself to giving religious instruction to the slaves on Virginia plantations, but increasing opposition to such work soon compelled him to abandon it. On Aug. 2, 1836, he was called by a few Presbyterians in Burlington, N. J., to become their pastor and establish a church. He at once began work and on June 29, 1837, was formally installed. During his comparatively short pastorate, lasting only to May 19, 1840, he developed a vigorous organization and superintended the building of a church edifice. Never again a regular pastor, he maintained a lively interest in the welfare of this congregation for the remainder of his life.

Following his resignation, he ministered to a feeble church in Washington, D. C., for a time and in 1843 was drafted by Princeton Theological Seminary to raise much needed funds. As a result of his solicitations in various parts of the country, he presented the institution with an endowment of $100,000. In February 1846 he was called to the work in which he rendered his most conspicuous service—that of corresponding secretary and chief executive officer of the Presbyterian Board of Education. During the fourteen years he occupied this position he greatly widened the scope of the board's activities. When he assumed office these activities were confined chiefly to furnishing support to candidates for the ministry; under his direction the board furthered the organization of parochial schools, a project in which he was much interested, and the establishment of Presbyterian academies and synodical colleges. He wrote and lectured extensively, originated and edited the *Presbyterian Magazine* (1851–59), and published each year from 1850 until his death a volume of articles, *The Home, the School, and the Church,* on the subject of education. Shortly after his death there was issued, 1861, a collection of his writings, *Essays and Discourses,* which includes a considerable work entitled, "Historical Contributions Relative to the Founders, Principles, and Acts of the Presbyterian Church, with Special Reference to the Division of 1837-8." In 1857 he was elected moderator of the General Assembly (Old School).

He was a man of large frame and everything about him suggested strength and endurance. Seemingly never at rest, he studied and wrote through long hours of travel, and even at business meetings, when his attention was not required, he composed letters or made notes for future use. During his last illness he continued to dictate almost to the end. He was well informed, but not a scholar; an instructive preacher, rather than an effective one. His administrative gifts were marked, and what he lacked in other respects he made up for in perseverance and industry. His devotion to his calling was complete and his services were rendered gratuitously; of his wealth he gave freely to many causes. His death occurred in his fifty-third year at his residence on the Delaware River, Burlington, N. J., and he was buried in the family vault at Albany. On Sept. 13, 1836, he had married Catharine Ledyard Cogswell, by whom he had seven children.

[*Memorial of Cortlandt Van Rensselaer* (1860), containing addresses and articles from the *N. Y. Commercial Advertiser,* July 27, 1860, *World* (N. Y.), Aug. 10, 1860, *N. Y. Observer,* Aug. 2, 1860, and other papers; W. W. Spooner, *Hist. Families of America* (n.d.); Alfred Nevin, *Encyc. of the Presbyterian Church in the U. S. A.* (1884); *Princeton Theological Sem. Biog. Cat.* (1909).]   H. E. S.

VAN RENSSELAER, MARIANA GRISWOLD (Feb. 25, 1851–Jan. 20, 1934), author and art critic, was born in New York City, the daughter of George and Lydia (Alley) Griswold.

She is said to have been a descendant of Matthew Griswold who emigrated to New England in 1639 and settled first in Windsor, Conn., later at Lyme. She was educated chiefly by private tutors at home and by foreign travel, especially in Germany. On Apr. 14, 1873, in Dresden, she married Schuyler Van Rensselaer, an engineer, a descendant of Kiliaen van Rensselaer who was the original holder of the great Van Rensselaer land patent of 1635. They lived in New Brunswick, N. J., her husband's home, until his death in 1884; they had one son, George Griswold, who died tragically in 1892. Going back to New York after her husband's death, Mrs. Van Rensselaer turned to writing and produced a long series of books and articles, chiefly on art and architecture. Her *Book of American Figure Painters* appeared in 1886. In the same year she published a series of reviews, "Art in Phoenicia and Cyprus," in the *American Architect and Building News* (Mar. 20–May 22, 1886), which revealed her surprising scholarship as well as her charm of style. Her other books include *American Etchers* (1886); *Henry Hobson Richardson and His Works* (1888), her most important work on architecture, noteworthy as the first significant monograph on a "modern" American architect; *Six Portraits* (1889), on Italian Renaissance artists; *English Cathedrals* (1892), with illustrations by Joseph Pennell [*q.v.*]; and *Art Out of Doors* (1893), on gardens and landscape architecture. She also produced *Should We Ask for the Suffrage?* (1894), a pamphlet vigorously opposing woman's suffrage; *One Man Who Was Content* (1897), a collection of short stories; *Poems* (1910); and *Many Children* (1921). Her best-known work is her monumental and authoritative *History of the City of New York in the Seventeenth Century* (2 vols., 1909), the research for which had occupied her for years. Largely as a result of its publication she received the honorary degree of Litt.D. from Columbia University in 1910. In 1923 she was awarded the gold medal of the American Academy of Arts and Letters for distinction in literature. Her other activities included serving as an inspector of New York City schools for two years and as president of the Public Education Association of New York (1899–1906). For many years she lived in a fine old house at 9 West Tenth Street, where she died.

Her work is important as the almost perfect expression of a cultural breadth, a cultivated tolerance, and an artistic sensitivity which, united, were characteristic of the finest flowering of nineteenth-century American life. Though not profound, her books are in general sound and, what

is more, delightful reading. Except in the New York *History,* her scholarship lies rather in the tasteful synthesis of existing learning than in any deep research of her own, and therein is its greatest value. She not only expressed the new interest in art that was current in the educated America of the eighties and nineties, but she became one of its chief leaders. Such a book as her *English Cathedrals,* for example, did a great deal to rewaken the public to the beauty of Gothic architecture, as well as to pave the way for many less sound and less well written popularizations to follow. She popularized taste and knowledge in the only true way, by honesty of approach and beauty of style. Her *Richardson* remains a model of appreciative biography, a charming monument to a great man. She was an honorary member of the American Institute of Architects, the American Society of Landscape Architects, and the American Historical Association, and in 1933 was elected a fellow of the New York State Historical Association.

[E. E. Salisbury, *The Griswold Family of Conn.* (1884); *Who's Who in America,* 1934–35; *Who's Who in N. Y.,* 1914; Catherine M. C. Hardie, "Treating More Esp. of Helena Van Rensselaer and Jacob Wendell," MS. in N. Y. Pub. Lib.; obituaries in *N. Y. Herald Tribune* and *N. Y. Times,* Jan. 21, 1934.]
T. F. H.

VAN RENSSELAER, MARTHA (June 21, 1864–May 26, 1932), home economist, was born in Randolph, N. Y. Her father, Henry Killian Van Rensselaer, was a direct descendant of Kiliaen van Rensselaer, first patroon of the manor of Rensselaerswyck. Her mother, Arvilla Owen, was of Welsh ancestry and is said to have been related to Robert Dale Owen [*q.v.*]; she was a remarkable woman who, in spite of the cares of a large family, still found time to reach outside the narrow intellectual boundaries imposed by a restricted income in a little village. In 1884 Martha Van Rensselaer graduated from Chamberlain Institute in Randolph. When she returned there as its preceptress after some years of rich and varied adventure in teaching, she realized one of her childhood dreams. For six years (1894–1900) she served as school commissioner of Cattaraugus County. It was while pursuing this task, which gave her wide and intimate contacts with rural people, that she began to picture the possibilities for the education of country women to which she later devoted herself. In 1900 she was called to Cornell University to organize a service for farm women similar to the extension courses offered farmers. This began with a reading course, centered on the problems of the farm home, in which six thousand readers were enrolled the first year.

Under her direction in 1903 the first credit course in home economics was offered at Cornell; in 1904 the course for farm women was included in the newly created New York State College of Agriculture, and in 1907 a department of home economics was organized at Cornell with Martha Van Rensselaer as lecturer. In 1911 she became professor of home economics, in 1924 director of the School of Home Economics established in 1919 as part of the New York State College of Agriculture, and in 1925 director of the New York State College of Home Economics.

During these years, in which a reading-course for farm homes developed under her direction into a vast extension service available to all the homes of the state and led to the establishment of a college, Martha Van Rensselaer served in many other capacities. She was a member of the executive staff of the United States Food Administration during the World War, home-making editor of the *Delineator* (1920–26), assistant director of the White House conference on child health and protection (1929–32), and chairman of the committee on home-making, housing, and family life of President Hoover's conference on home-building and ownership. She was sent to Belgium on special service for the American Relief Commission and was made chevalier of the Order of the ‘Crown. She received the degree of A.B. at Cornell in 1909. She was president of the American Home Economics Association (1915–16). In 1923 she was chosen as one of the twelve most distinguished women of the United States by a committee appointed by the National League of Women Voters. With Flora Rose and Helen Canon, she published *A Manual of Home-Making* (1919). She lived to see the foundations rise of a magnificent new building that to her characterized the ideal for which she had spent her years at Cornell. She died in 1932 after a long and serious illness which had not been allowed to interfere with her program of living.

[*Who's Who in America*, 1930–31; Cornell Univ., *Twenty-Eighth Ann. Report by President Schurman, 1919–20;* Cornell Univ. Cats.; *Jour. of Home Economics,* Sept. 1932; obituaries in *Ithaca Jour. News,* May 26, *N. Y. Times* and *N. Y. Herald Tribune,* May 27, 1932.]   F. R.

VAN RENSSELAER, NICHOLAS (*c.* Sept. 25, 1636–1678), clergyman, was born in Amsterdam, North Holland, the eighth child of Kiliaen and Anna (van Wely) van Rensselaer. Kiliaen, a wealthy merchant and a director of the West India Company, was the first patroon of the Manor of Rensselaer on the Hudson River in New Netherland. Of Nicholas' early life little is known; while visiting Brussels, he met Charles Stuart, later Charles II, King of England, then an exile on the Continent. Young Van Rensselaer, with fortunate prevision, assured the prince that the Stuarts would be restored to power in England, and that he would ascend the throne of his father. Because of this incident Charles remembered Van Rensselaer when he had forgotten greater Dutch benefactors.

On Oct. 2, 1662, Van Rensselaer was received in the Classis of Amsterdam, and not long after he accompanied Michiel van Gogh, Dutch ambassador, to London as chaplain of the embassy. Charles II in 1664 launched his first war against the Dutch, but when van Gogh returned home the following year, the chaplain remained, and the King gave him a license to preach to the Dutch congregation at Westminster. In addition, Van Rensselaer was ordained a deacon of the Church of England by the Bishop of Salisbury, and was appointed lecturer at St. Margaret's, Lothbury. As a personal mark of regard, Charles gave him a gold snuffbox, which is preserved by the Van Rensselaer family. In 1670 Van Rensselaer was in the Netherlands again, matriculating as a V. D. M.—minister of God's word—at the University of Leyden. He gave his residence as Amsterdam and his age as thirty-three. Two years later he was accepted by the Classis of Amsterdam as an "Expectant for Foreign Churches." These ordinations and appointments were the basis of his claim and preferment in the province of New York.

When Sir Edmund Andros [*q.v.*] came to New York as governor, he was accompanied by Nicholas van Rensselaer, who was recommended to him by the Duke of York for a Dutch pulpit. Andros took great interest in the provincial churches, but, though he had much regard for English orders, he did not look upon Dutch orders with the same respect. One of his first acts was an attempt to induct Van Rensselaer into the church of Albany as colleague of Gideon van Schaats. The Albany consistory resisted, holding that if Van Rensselaer was an Anglican clergyman, then he was not a minister of the Church of Holland. A temporary adjustment of the difficulty was obtained when William Van Nieuwenhuysen, pastor of the Reformed Church of New York, came to Albany as Van Schaats' assistant. Undefeated, Van Rensselaer went to New York with the understood purpose of administering baptism to children. Opposed by Van Nieuwenhuysen, he complained to the governor, and the dispute came before the Council. The proceedings, lasting from Sept. 25 to Oct. 2, 1675, opened with the introduction of Nieuwenhuysen's declaration that he did not look upon

Van Rensselaer as a lawful minister, or his admittance to the Albany pastorate as lawful. After Van Rensselaer's submission of his papers, Van Nieuwenhuysen still insisted that in order to administer the sacraments of the Dutch Church, a minister should have promised "to conduct himself in his services conformably to their Confession, Catechism and Mode of Government." Van Rensselaer accepted these requirements, and was installed in the Albany pastorate. A year later Jacob Leisler [q.v.] and Jacob Milborne declared that Van Rensselaer was not orthodox and Van Rensselaer sued the two for slander. The case finally reached the Governor's Council, and the parties were ordered to be reconciled "by the friendly shaking of hands" (*Minutes of the Court, post,* II, 146–50, 153–55, 162–67).

In 1677 Van Rensselaer was deposed by the governor on the charge of leading a bad life. The authorities to whom reference was made for support of the accusation were Van Nieuwenhuysen and Schaats. It was not unnatural that Van Rensselaer should have been the victim of religious animosity. He had come to America from the most liberal school of learning in Europe, established in memory of the siege of Leyden, and there he may easily have learned to reconcile doctrinal distinctions. Conditions, however, were unpropitious for so broad a mission. Then, too, Charles II, his patron, had lately waged a second war against the Netherlands; moreover, Charles's court, where the young preacher began his ministry, was not esteemed as a school for piety. On Feb. 10, 1675, Van Rensselaer married Alida Schuyler, sister of Peter Schuyler [q.v.]; he had no children. After his death his widow married Robert Livingston [q.v.].

[E. T. Corwin, *Ecclesiastical Records: State of N. Y.* (7 vols., 1901–16); E. B. O'Callaghan, *The Doc. Hist. of the State of N. Y.* (quarto ed.), III (1850), 526–30; E. T. Corwin, *A Manual of the Reformed Church in America ... 1628–1902* (1902); M. K. Van Rensselaer, *The Van Rensselaers of the Manor of Rensselaerswyck* (copr. 1888); Maunsell Van Rensselaer, *Annals of the Van Rensselaers in the U. S.* (1888); N. Y. State Lib. *Van Rensselaer Bowier Manuscripts* (1908) and *Minutes of the Court of Albany, Rensselaerswyck and Schenectady,* vols. II–III (1928–32), tr. and ed. by A. J. F. van Laer; W. W. Spooner, *Historic Families of America* (n.d.).]   R. E. D.

VAN RENSSELAER, SOLOMON (Aug. 6, 1774–Apr. 23, 1852), soldier, congressman, was born in Rensselaer County, N. Y., the son of Henry Kiliaen van Rensselaer, a general in the Revolution, and his wife, Alida (Bradt). He was fifth in descent from Kiliaen van Rensselaer, the first patroon (J. B. Holgate, *American Genealogy,* 1848). In 1792 Solomon entered the United States Army as a cornet of cavalry, and in 1794 served as a captain under Gen. Anthony

Wayne [q.v.] in his campaign against the Indians. He was seriously wounded in the battle of Fallen Timbers, Aug. 20, 1794; was commissioned major in 1799; and was honorably discharged June 15, 1800. He was adjutant general of New York, 1801–09, 1810–11, and 1813–21.

At the opening of the War of 1812 he was assigned to the post of aide-de-camp to his relative, Maj.-Gen. Stephen Van Rensselaer [q.v.], and went with him to the Niagara River. In August 1812, upon receipt of news that Henry Dearborn [q.v.] and Sir George Prevost had arranged an armistice, he negotiated with General Sheaffe a supplementary agreement by which either party might, during the armistice, bring forward troops and supplies on Lake Ontario—an arrangement very advantageous to the United States. When the elder Van Rensselaer resolved to throw his army across the river and seize the British position at Queenstown (Queenston), Solomon was detailed to command the advance party of militia. His part in the attack of Oct. 13, 1812, was successfully carried out. With a force of some three hundred, he gained a foothold on the Canadian shore, and though he suffered several wounds, the troops under his direction scaled the heights above Queenstown and captured a British battery near the summit. Van Rensselaer's wounds necessitated removing him to the American side, and in later years he ascribed the ensuing disaster to his enforced absence from the battlefield— a view of the matter hardly sustained by the facts. In February 1813 the Council of Appointment restored him to the position of adjutant general of the state, and although he campaigned actively for Stephen Van Rensselaer, Federalist candidate for governor against Daniel D. Tompkins [q.v.] in the spring of 1813, he continued in his position and was apparently on excellent terms with Tompkins.

Elected to Congress in 1818 and reëlected in 1820, he opposed the Missouri Compromise. In January 1822 he resigned his seat to accept the postmastership at Albany, to which he had been named over the protest of Vice-President Tompkins, Senator Van Buren, and Senator Rufus King [qq.v.], the first two objecting to having this office assigned to a former Federalist (C. F. Adams, *Memoirs of John Quincy Adams,* vol. V, 1875, pp. 479–82; J. C. Fitzpatrick, "The Autobiography of Martin Van Buren," *Annual Report of the American Historical Association ... 1918,* vol. II, 1920, pp. 125–26). Upon Jackson's election to the Presidency, Van Rensselaer's New York opponents sought to bring about his removal, but Van Rensselaer went to Washington and by calling attention to his honorable wounds in a dramatic interview with Jackson, saved his position (J. W. Forney, *Anecdotes of Public Men,* 1873, 281–83). He was removed, however, by Van Buren in 1839. In the Whig convention at Harrisburg in December 1839, he was a delegate from New York and claimed credit for swinging the delegation from that state to Harrison and thus bringing about his nomination. He was rewarded with restoration to the Albany postmastership in 1841, only to be again removed by Tyler two years later. He sought the same office again from Taylor in 1849, but without success.

As a young man, a penchant for sharp criticism of opponents involved him in a number of personal quarrels, among them an affray with Lieutenant-Governor Tayler of New York in 1807 (see D. R. Fox, *The Decline of Aristocracy in the Politics of New York,* 1919, pp. 104–07) and a near-duel with Peter B. Porter in 1812. In later life he was on cordial terms with some of his former enemies. It is evident that he thought of himself as an ill-rewarded military hero—a rôle for which the chief bases were the gallant but futile assault at Queenstown and the wounds he received there and at Fallen Timbers. In 1836 he published *A Narrative of the Affair of Queenstown in the War of 1812.* He was married, Jan. 17, 1797, to his cousin, Harriet Van Rensselaer, by whom he had several children.

[In addition to sources cited above, see C. Van R. Bonney, *A Legacy of Hist. Gleanings* (2 vols., 1875); *Albany Evening Jour.,* Apr. 24, 1852.]   J. W. P.

VAN RENSSELAER, STEPHEN (Nov. 1, 1764–Jan. 26, 1839), eighth patroon, soldier, congressman, was born in New York, the son of Stephen and Catherine (Livingston) Van Rensselaer, and fifth in direct descent from Kiliaen van Rensselaer, the first patroon. Upon his father's death in 1769, which left the five-year-old child heir to a vast landed estate in Rensselaer and Albany counties, his grandfather, Philip Livingston [*q.v.*], took charge of his education which was begun at Albany and after numerous changes due to the disturbances of wartime was completed at Harvard, where he was graduated in 1782. On June 6, 1783, he married Margaret Schuyler, daughter of Gen. Philip Schuyler [*q.v.*], and in 1785 went to occupy the manor house near Albany. By granting perpetual leases at moderate rentals in kind, he brought more of his estate under cultivation than had any of his predecessors, but he refused to sell any part of his lands outright. He was elected as a Federalist to the New York Assembly in 1789 and 1790, served in the state Senate from 1791 to 1795, and as lieutenant-governor from 1795 to 1801. In

1801 he was the unsuccessful Federalist candidate for governor against George Clinton [*q.v.*]. He sat in the Assembly in several subsequent sessions and in the constitutional conventions of 1801 and 1821.

Meanwhile he had become a major-general in the state militia, and although without active military experience, was called upon by Gov. Daniel D. Tompkins [*q.v.*] in 1812 to take command of the entire northern frontier of the state. He set up his headquarters at Lewiston and by October 1812 had assembled some six thousand troops on the Niagara frontier, but the men lacked discipline and equipment, and their efficiency was further impaired by the refusal of Brig.-Gen. Alexander Smyth [*q.v.*] of the regular army to take orders from or cooperate with Van Rensselaer. Without the support of Smyth, who held his brigade at Buffalo, Van Rensselaer ventured to attack Queenstown (Queenston), Oct. 13, 1812. The advance column secured a foothold on the Canadian shore, but when the remainder of the militia refused to cross the river to their support, they were compelled to surrender, with an aggregate loss of nearly a thousand men. Modern critics hold that the possible advantages to be gained by a successful attack at this point were not sufficient to justify the risk, and that Van Rensselaer was culpable for not having better ascertained the temper of his army (Babcock, *post,* pp. 55–56). Van Rensselaer's correspondence shows that he believed an aggressive stroke was expected by his superiors and that he was both stung and alarmed by criticism of his inaction in the army itself (Solomon Van Rensselaer, *post*). After the defeat he resigned his command and returned to Albany. In the spring of 1813 he again received the Federalist nomination for governor but was defeated by Tompkins.

In 1822 he was elected to Congress to succeed his kinsman Solomon Van Rensselaer [*q.v.*], and retained his seat until 1829. In the choice of the president by the House of Representatives in 1825, he cast the deciding vote in the New York delegation and therefore in the election. He was thought to have pledged his vote to William H. Crawford [*q.v.*], but cast it, on the first ballot, for John Quincy Adams. Van Rensselaer explained to Van Buren that upon taking his seat, being still in doubt how to vote, he had bowed his head in prayer and upon opening his eyes had seen at his feet a ballot bearing Adams' name.

The Patroon's chief services to his state were neither military nor political but economic and educational. An early advocate of a canal to connect the Hudson with the Great Lakes, he was a member of the first canal commission in 1810 and of the second, instituted in 1816, of which from 1825 to his death he was president. In 1820 he was chosen president of the state's first board of agriculture, which he had been instrumental in creating. He bore the expense of a geological survey by Amos Eaton [*q.v.*] of a belt of land following the Erie Canal across New York and thence across New England, with special reference to soil and agricultural possibilities (*A Geological and Agricultural Survey of the District Adjoining the Erie Canal . . . Taken under the Direction of the Hon. Stephen Van Rensselaer,* 1824). In 1824 he established at Troy a school primarily for the training of teachers "for instructing the sons and daughters of farmers and mechanics" in "the application of science to the common purposes of life" (letter of Van Rensselaer's, quoted by Ricketts, *post,* p. 64). The school was incorporated in 1826 as Rensselaer Institute and later became Rensselaer Polytechnic Institute, a pioneer among schools of its kind. He also gave liberally to other educational causes. In 1819 he was elected to the Board of Regents of the University of the State of New York, of which he was chancellor from 1835 to his death. He was president of the Albany Lyceum of Natural History and of the Albany Institute.

Probably the foremost man in the state in point of wealth and social prominence, Van Rensselaer was loved for his simple tastes, democratic behavior, and genial manners. As a landlord he was lenient to a fault (Cheyney, *post,* p. 25) and he refused to subject his tenants to political pressure (Hammond, *post,* I, 161). A genuine aristocrat, he was yet ready to meet the new democracy half way. His integrity was unchallenged, and political opponents held no rancor against him. Van Buren, a member of the opposite party, wrote of him as "that good and true gentleman Patroon Van Rensselaer" ("Autobiography," *post,* p. 514). After the death of his first wife, Margaret Schuyler, who had born him three children, Van Rensselaer married, May 17, 1802, Cornelia, daughter of William Paterson [*q.v.*]. Cortlandt Van Rensselaer [*q.v.*] was one of nine children of this second marriage.

[D. D. Barnard, *A Discourse on the Life, Services and Character of Stephen Van Rensselaer; Delivered before the Albany Inst., Apr. 15, 1839* (1839) ; J. B. Holgate, *Am. Geneal.* (1848) ; Cuyler Reynolds, *Geneal. and Family Hist. of Southern N. Y. and the Hudson River Valley* (1914), vol. I; L. L. Babcock, *The War of 1812 on the Niagara Frontier* (1927) ; Solomon Van Rensselaer, *A Narrative of the Affair of Queenstown in the War of 1812* (1836) ; "Autobiog. of Martin Van Buren," ed. by J. C. Fitzpatrick, *Ann. Report Am. Hist. Asso. . . . 1918,* vol. II (1920) ; Margaret Bayard Smith, *The First Forty Years of Washington Society* (1906), ed. by Gaillard Hunt; P. C. Ricketts, *The Centennial Celebration of Rensselaer Poly. Inst.* (1925); E. P.

Cheney, *The Anti-Rent Agitation in . . . N. Y.* (1887) ; J. D. Hammond, *The Hist. of Pol. Parties in . . . N. Y.* (2 vols., 1842) ; D. R. Fox, *The Decline of Aristocracy in the Politics of N. Y.* (1919) ; *Albany Argus,* Jan. 28, 1839.]
          J. W. P.

VAN SANTVOORD, GEORGE (Dec. 8, 1819–Mar. 6, 1863), jurist, was born in Belleville, N. J., the great-great-grandson of Cornelis Van Santvoord, a Dutch clergyman who emigrated probably from Leyden to Schenectady in 1740, and the son of Staats Van Santvoord, a Dutch Reformed pastor at Belleville who later removed to Schodack, N. Y. A brief and uncongenial experience as a clerk in dry goods stores in Albany and New York preceded the boy's entrance upon advanced studies. He went to the academy at Kinderhook, in 1841 was graduated from Union College in Schenectady, studied law in Kinderhook, and was admitted to the bar in 1844. Shortly thereafter he married Elizabeth, the daughter of Peter Van Schaack and granddaughter of Peter Van Schaak [*q.v.*]. They removed to Lafayette, Ind. In 1845 he delivered a *Eulogy of Andrew Jackson* (1914) at Lafayette, Ind., and in the same year published *Indiana Justice* (1845), a comprehensive manual for justices of the peace in the state. Owing to sickness in his family, he returned to Kinderhook in the autumn of 1846, where he practised law for five years. Again, after a year in New York City, he removed to Troy in 1852 and entered into law partnership with David L. Seymour. Seven years later he formed another partnership with Benjamin H. Hall of the same city, in which he remained until his death. He was twice elected to the New York Assembly, in 1852 from Columbia County (*Albany Argus,* Jan. 29, Mar. 8, 31, 1852) and four years later from Rensselaer, and from 1860 to 1863 he was district attorney of the latter county.

Although widely respected as a member of the bar, his chief contribution was as a writer on legal topics. In an address to the graduating class of the law school of Albany University in 1856, *The Study of the Law as a Science* (1856), he expressed some of his fundamental convictions. He considered law as a science, "laid broad and deep upon those universal principles," and found inspiration in the systematic exposition of the civil law, the introduction of whose liberal principles he felt was necessary to break "the churlish and exclusive spirit of the common law." Thus, a study of the codes appealed to him for their close approximation to the civil law and for the reëvaluation of the classic doctrine of *stare decisis* that they necessitated (pp. 236, 237). In *A Treatise on the Principles of Pleading in Civil Actions under the New-York*

Code of Procedure, first published in 1852, he attempted to provide a systematic body of knowledge of the rules of pleading under the code. His volume was a lucid and valuable contribution, which, for New York lawyers, supplanted to some extent the works of Chitty and other English writers. Along this line also was his *Treatise on the Practice in the Supreme Court of the State of New York in Equity Actions* (2 vols., 1860–62). Perhaps his most widely read volume was his *Sketches of the Lives and Judicial Services of the Chief Justices of the United States* (1854), which stressed the biographical treatment of the occupants of the bench from Jay to Taney and gave comparatively less emphasis to constitutional decisions. Other ventures in the field of biographical writing included a series of articles on the leaders of the French Revolution, which appeared in the *United States Magazine and Democratic Review* (Feb., Apr.–July 1849 and Apr. 1851), and his *Life of Algernon Sidney* (1851), a highly laudatory but useful study, based upon documentary sources and written from the anti-monarchical point of view. He was killed in a railroad accident at East Albany.

[Jonathan Pearson, *Contributions for the Genealogies of the First Settlers of . . . Schenectady* (1873), pp. 236, 237; *Memorial of George Van Santvoord* (1863); *Albany Evening Jour.,* Mar. 6, 1863; copies of *Eulogy, ante,* and *Indiana Justice, ante,* and family information from his son, Seymour Van Santvoord, Troy, N. Y.]

R. B. M.

VAN SCHAACK, HENRY CRUGER (Apr. 2, 1802–Dec. 16, 1887), author, antiquarian, was born in Kinderhook, N. Y., a son of Peter Van Schaack [*q.v.*] by his second wife, Elizabeth Van Alen. His mother was of Dutch stock, tracing descent to Lourens Lourensen, in 1630 a resident of Beverwyck (Albany). Van Schaack's academic education was carefully supervised by his father, who trained him for the practice of law. At twenty-one he was admitted to the bar. After a brief stay at Black Rock, near Buffalo, he moved to Manlius, N. Y., married Adaline Ives (1827), opened a law office, and settled down to the quiet life of a country lawyer.

But the practice of law, though nominally his profession for half a century, soon yielded place to his keen interest in antiquarian pursuits. In 1823 he fell heir to the papers of his uncle Henry Van Schaack, an officer in the French and Indian Wars, an officer of the Crown in Albany, and a Loyalist in the Revolution. In 1832 his father's manuscripts were added to his collection; and there followed in 1833 the papers of his brother-in-law, Maj. John Frey of Palatine Bridge, and those of Matthew Vischer of Albany. Later he acquired many items from the papers of

John Jay. The most interesting of these materials, as well as manuscripts acquired from other sources, by gift as well as by exchange (for he characteristically notes that he never bought an autograph), he arranged in three great folio volumes which he entitled "An Autographic History of the American Revolution: Consisting of Letters and Other Writings of Revolutionary Characters, Illustrated by Engravings and Elucidated by Historic and Biographic Notices in Print." Among the materials thus preserved are letters and other documents written by, or relating to, colonial governors of New York, officers of the Crown, the first officers of the State of New York, and members of the Continental Congress. There are also autographs of forty-four of the signers of the Declaration of Independence, as well as those of the framers of the Constitution, of the presidents and vice-presidents through Andrew Jackson's administration, and of all of the members of the successive cabinets of Washington and John Adams. With these he arranged letters and documents written by lesser figures, as well as quantities of clippings from newspapers and magazines.

From his rich collections Van Schaack drew the material for a biography of his father, *The Life of Peter Van Schaack, LL.D.* (1842)—"the first attempt," wrote C. F. Adams, "to present to the public of the United States a justificatory memoir of one of the Tories in the Revolution" (*North American Review,* July 1842, p. 97). His other publications include *Henry Cruger, the Colleague of Edmund Burke* (1859), *A History of Manlius Village* (1873), *An Old Kinderhook Mansion* (1878), *Captain Thomas Morris in the Country of the Illinois* (1882), and a biography of his uncle, *Memoirs of the Life of Henry Van Schaack* (1892), published posthumously. At Van Schaack's death his manuscript collections were left to three of his fourteen children.

[Sources include E. A. Collier, *A Hist. of Old Kinderhook* (1914); A. J. Vanderpoel, "A Law Library's Treasures," *Chicago Legal News,* Mar. 4, 1882; personal recollections of Robert H. Van Schaack of Evanston, Ill., a grandson; obituary in *Evening Post* (N. Y.), Dec. 19, 1887; prefatory notes in Van Schaack's "Autographic Hist.," now in the possession of the Chicago Hist. Soc. (vol. I), R. H. Van Schaack (vol. II), and Pierrepont Prentice of N. Y. City (vol. III).]

G. V—S.

VAN SCHAACK, PETER (March 1747–Sept. 17, 1832), lawyer, was of Dutch origin, a descendant of Elias (or Claas) van Schaack, three of whose four sons took oath of allegiance to King William III in Albany in 1699. Emanuel, the youngest of these four, was the father of Cornelius Van Schaack, fur-trader, owner of a sloop and of extensive lands near Kinderhook, N. Y., who on Oct. 6, 1728, married Lydia Van Dyck, daughter of Dr. Hendrik Van Dyck and Lydia (Schuyler) of Albany. Their seventh child and fourth son, Peter, was baptized in the Reformed Dutch Protestant Church at Kinderhook, Apr. 24, 1747. Prepared for King's College by the Rev. Richard Charlton, a graduate of Trinity College, Dublin, he became an accomplished Latin scholar and was noted for the purity and elegance of his English, both written and oral. Entering college in 1762, he there became intimately acquainted with Gouverneur Morris, Robert R. Livingston, Egbert Benson, and John Jay [qq.v.]. His friendship with Benson and Jay continued throughout his life. In 1765, while still an undergraduate, he eloped with Elizabeth Cruger, daughter of a wealthy New York merchant, who soon became reconciled with his son-in-law. On graduation in 1766 he ranked at the head of his class and proceeded to study law, first in Albany with his brother-in-law, Peter Silvester, an agent of Sir William Johnson [q.v.], and later in New York with William Smith, 1728–1793 [q.v.], the historian.

In 1769 he was admitted to the bar, and in 1773 was appointed reviser of the statutes of the Colony of New York, in the work of which office he injured his eyesight seriously. The result of his labors, *Laws . . . from the Year 1691 to 1773 Inclusive,* was published in 1774. In May 1774 he became a member of the New York Committee of Fifty-one to correspond with the sister colonies, in November of the Committee of Sixty for executing the association entered into by the Continental Congress, and in the following May, of the Committee of One Hundred. About this time his wife's precarious health and his own failing eyesight led him to return to Kinderhook, where he was promptly elected to the local Committee of Safety. Though he strongly disapproved of the British government's treatment of the colonies and supported such American measures as non-importation and non-consumption, prolonged meditation and consultation of Locke, Grotius, and other writers failed to convince him that it was right to offer armed resistance to the royal government. At the meeting of the Committee of Safety in Albany on May 29, 1776, he therefore refused to pledge himself to take up arms against Great Britain and was expelled from the Committee. Thereupon he attempted to maintain neutrality. (Memoranda outlining his position are printed in Van Schaack, *post*, pp. 54–59 and 71–76.) When summoned to take oath of allegiance to the State of New York at Albany, Jan. 9, 1777, he refused and on Jan. 25 was ordered to Boston, but was called back by order of the Convention, Feb. 3, and permitted to remain on parole at Kinderhook until after his wife's death in April 1778. In June of that year he obtained permission from Gov. George Clinton to go to England for an operation by an oculist, but his further refusal to take oath of allegiance (July 18) subjected him to the penalties of the Banishment Act of June 13, 1778, and in October he sailed for seven years of exile in England.

His voluminous letters, published by his son (H. C. Van Schaack, *post*), give an excellent picture of his life during this period. Through his brother-in-law, Henry Cruger, M.P. for Bristol, he became acquainted with Lord Eldon and other prominent lawyers and consulted with them on professional matters. He attended debates in Parliament to hear Fox, Burke, Sheridan, Pitt, and Mansfield, and traveled fairly extensively in England. In London he renewed his friendship with John Jay. In 1784 the legislature of New York restored him to citizenship and in 1785 he returned to take the oath of allegiance, settling at Kinderhook and building a house there. He was readmitted to the bar (April 1786), is said to have edited a work called *Conductor Generalis* (1786) for use of local magistrates, and engaged extensively in the practice of law until his eyesight failed entirely. Between 1786 and 1828 he gave, it is said, legal instruction to about a hundred young men who came to him as resident pupils. Though he took no active part in politics, he was keenly interested in the adoption of the federal Constitution and sympathized with the Federalist party. On Apr. 27, 1789, he married Elizabeth Van Alen of Kinderhook. Her seven children, besides three children by his first wife, survived when he died at Kinderhook.

[B. F. Butler, in the *Sentinel* (Kinderhook), Sept. 20, 1832; H. C. Van Schaack, *The Life of Peter Van Schaack, LL.D.* (1842), and "An Old Kinderhook Mansion," in *Mag. of Am. Hist.,* Sept. 1878; P. F. Miller, *A Group of Great Lawyers of Columbia County, N. Y.* (1904); E. A. Collier, *A Hist. of Old Kinderhook* (1914); "A Law Library's Treasures," in *Chicago Legal News,* Mar. 4, 1882.]   G. V—S.

VAN SCHAICK, GOOSE (Sept. 5, 1736–July 4, 1789), soldier, was the son of Sybrant Van Schaick, mayor of Albany, N. Y., from 1756 to 1761, and Alida (Roseboom) Van Schaick. He was the descendant of Goosen Gerritse Van Schaick, who was a brewer in Albany in 1649. His own name was often spelled Gosen or Goosen. It is said that he entered upon the campaigns of the French and Indian War at the age of twenty. He served as captain in the New York provincial levies that accompanied Colonel Bradstreet in his successful and decisive campaign of 1758 against Fort Frontenac, and from 1760 to 1762 he served as lieutenant-colonel, first of the 2nd Regiment of New York Provincials and later of the 1st New York Regiment. A patriot at the outbreak of the Revolution, he became a colonel and saw constant service during the war in the defense of the northern and western frontiers of New York.

Soon after being commissioned he was campaigning in Cherry Valley against Joseph Brant; he was sent in 1776 into Tryon County and stationed at Johnstown; he was at Albany to muster the Continental troops at that place to hear the Declaration of Independence read to the populace on July 19, 1776; he was wounded at Ticonderoga on July 6, 1777; and he served at Monmouth under Stirling (see sketch of William Alexander). His most famous exploit, however, was his expedition against the Onondaga in April 1779, when he was serving under Gen. James Clinton. With about 500 men he left Fort Schuyler, invaded the country of the Onondaga, burned their principal settlement together with provisions and stores, slaughtered their cattle, took 32 prisoners and killed a number of the Indians, in six days without the loss of a man. The Continental Congress on May 10, 1779, resolved "that the thanks of Congress be presented to Colonel Van Schaick, and the officers and soldiers under his command" (Heitman, *post*). The 1st Regiment under Van Schaick seems to have been famed for its excellent discipline. Even Van Schaick's vigorous punitive expedition was a preliminary to the better-known campaign of Gen. John Sullivan in the Indian country in the summer of 1779. Gen. James Clinton, who joined Sullivan on this expedition, left Van Schaick in command at Albany. In recognition of his services Van Schaick was made a brevet brigadier-general on Oct. 10, 1783, and he remained in service until November of that year. He had married on Nov. 15, 1770, Maria Ten Broeck, by whom he had six children. He died at Albany.

[N. Y. Sec. of State, *Marriage Licenses* (1860); *N. Y. State Historian, Annual Report . . . 1897*, "Colonial Series," vol. II (1898); *N. Y. Hist. Soc. Colls. . . . 1915*, "Muster and Pay Rolls of . . . the Revolution" (1916); *Public Papers of George Clinton*, vols. I–VII (1899–1904) ed. by Hugh Hastings; F. B. Heitman, *Hist. Register of Officers of the Continental Army* (1914); A. J. Parker, *Landmarks of Albany County* (1897); Jonathan Pearson, *Contributions for the Genealogies of . . . Albany* (1872) and in *Colls. on the Hist. of Albany*, vol. IV (1871), ed. by Joel Munsell; W. W. Campbell, *Annals of Tryon County* (4th ed., 1924); records of the War Department, Washington, D. C.; service in French and Indian War from Peter Nelson, Albany, N. Y.; although date of death often said to be July 4, 1787, he was apparently alive on Sept. 9, 1787, when, according to Munsell, *ante*, II (1867), p. 299, he received title to land in Albany; the date given here is in accord with various authorities.]   E. W. S.

VAN SLYKE, LUCIUS LINCOLN (Jan. 6, 1859–Sept. 30, 1931), agricultural chemist, was born at Centerville, N. Y., the son of William J. and Katherine (Keller) Van Slyke. After preliminary education in the local schools, Van Slyke entered the University of Michigan, where he received the degree of A.B. in 1879, that of A.M. in 1881, and that of Ph.D. in 1882. He was assistant in the chemical laboratory at Michigan (1882–85), professor of chemistry at Oahu College and government chemist of the Hawaiian Islands (1885–88), lecturer in chemistry at the University of Michigan (1888–89), chief chemist at the New York state agricultural experiment station at Geneva, N. Y. (1890–1929), a position which he filled with great distinction, and professor of dairy chemistry in the New York State Agricultural College, Cornell University (1920–29).

As chief chemist it was the duty of Van Slyke to carry on and supervise research in all phases of chemistry connected with agriculture, and to examine feeds, fertilizers, and insecticides in connection with the enforcement of the New York state agricultural laws. He also directed the enactment of helpful legislation for the control of agricultural products, and gave valuable advice in regard to the enforcement of regulations. He will be remembered best, however, for his valuable pioneer work in the field of dairy chemistry. At the time of his appointment to the position at Geneva, the butter and cheese factory system of handling milk, which was firmly established, had given rise to many dairy problems of a purely chemical nature. In connection with these Van Slyke began work on the chemical composition of the constituents of milk and their relation to one another, a subject on which there was very little definite knowledge. The results of his work are classic. Special mention should be made of his researches on milk casein, which had a practical value in the improvement of the art of cheese making and an immense scientific value in contributing to an understanding of the nature and behavior of colloids. Van Slyke wrote easily and forcefully. During his long career he was the author or joint author of more than a hundred and thirty experiment station bulletins and reports, and he was a constant contributor to scientific journals. He was the author of four textbooks: *Modern Methods of Testing Milk and Milk Products* (1906); *The Science and Practice of Cheese Making* (1909), with C. A. Publow; *Fertilizers and Crops* (1912); and *Cheese* (1927), with W. V. Price. He was also a contributor to A. H. Allen's *Commercial Organic Analysis*. In 1897 he was president of the New

York State Dairymen's Association, and in 1901 president of the Association of Official Agricultural Chemists.

Van Slyke was a man of pleasing personality, with a keen interest in civic, social, and religious life. He was for many years elder of the Presbyterian Church of Geneva. He was a tireless and exacting worker, under whom many able chemists received their early training. He was married three times—first to Lucy W. Dexter (June 15, 1882), by whom he had two sons; second to Julia Hanford Upson of Honolulu, H. I. (Apr. 5, 1888), by whom he had one son; and third to Mrs. Hedwig Shaul of Geneva, N. Y. (June 2, 1926), who survived him.

[*Who's Who in America*, 1930–31 ; R. W. Thatcher, in *Jour. of Industrial and Engineering Chemistry*, Nov. 1925 ; L. H. and E. Z. Bailey, *Rus* (1925), p. 681 ; *Experiment Station Record*, Dec. 1931 ; *Jour. Asso. Official Agricultural Chemists*, May 15, 1932 ; obituary in *N. Y. Times*, Oct. 1, 1931 ; information from members of the experiment station staff, Geneva, N. Y., including the spelling of Mrs. Shaul's name.]   H. E. R.

VAN TWILLER, WOUTER (*c.* 1580–*c.* 1656), governor of New Netherland, was born in Gelderland, now a part of the Netherlands, the eldest son of Rijckert and Maria (Van Rensselaer) Van Twiller, the sister of Kiliaen Van Rensselaer, the first patroon, and the aunt of Nicholas Van Rensselaer [*q.v.*]. Wouter Van Twiller was a clerk in the service of the Dutch West India Company at the time he was appointed director-general, or governor, of New Netherland. In 1633 he arrived at New Amsterdam with a company of soldiers from Holland. David Pietersen De Vries [*q.v.*] told interesting anecdotes about this "unfit" person "whom they had made out of a clerk into a governor, who was the sport of the people" (Jameson, *post*, p. 187). Nevertheless, Van Twiller prudently dealt with the English who in 1633 sailed up the Hudson in the *William*, and he permitted them to return peaceably to England. With firm hand he aided the Dutch settlements on the banks of the Connecticut, but he obviously lacked adequate numbers of colonists with which to stem the rapidly rising tide of English immigration.

The animosity of De Vries resulted in a lengthy letter from Van Twiller's uncle in Amsterdam, whose eminence had no doubt played a part in the promotion of the nephew, although Van Rensselaer himself denied it. He had heard, so he said, that Wouter had too often got drunk, was too proud, and not sufficiently interested in religion. More serious was his negligence in keeping books properly and sending reports to Amsterdam. However, he was permitted to retain his position a little longer. One point in his favor had been his aim to imitate his father and his uncle, who had transferred barren wastes in the province of Gelderland into fertile fields and had fattened ill-fed cattle. Unfortunately, the West India Company, influenced by its more wealthy counter-part, the East India Company, misunderstood the potentialities of colonization in North America. What the merchants of Amsterdam wanted was trade in furs and quick profits for themselves, instead of a slower gain through the development of agriculture.

However, Van Twiller strengthened Fort Amsterdam and built a church and a bridge across the creek in the busiest part of town. His uncle's farms on Manhattan were carefully tilled under his care, and he himself developed a tobacco plantation. In 1636 a settlement on Long Island was started, and in 1637 he bought for himself Pagganck, now Governor's Island, and two islands in the East River, now Ward's and Blackwell's. Yet the company in Holland remained ill-pleased, for, in spite of the uncle's warnings, the governor still neglected his books and failed to report regularly. Everardus Bogardus [*q.v.*], moreover, frankly called him "a child of the devil; a consummate villain" (O'Callaghan, *Hist., post,* p. 167). In 1637 Willem Kieft [*q.v.*] was appointed to succeed him. Only the Indians had fully appreciated his good qualities. He had been kind to them and had treated them as equals. For years after his departure, according to the board of accounts (*Documents, post,* I, 151), the Indians were daily calling for the return of Wouter. He was in no hurry to leave either, and he actually bought more land before he departed and obtained from Kieft a lease on Bouwerie No. 1, belonging to the company. Early in 1639 he arrived in the Netherlands, and he immediately proceeded to the headquarters of the company, showing the officials all his books and papers. His uncle reported that the latter were now fully satisfied. Kieft remained his agent in the colony, and after the death of Van Rensselaer, Van Twiller managed his patroonship. In 1649 and 1650 his name appears in various records in New Netherland. He died in 1656 or 1657, survived by his widow, Maria (Momma) Van Twiller.

[E. B. O'Callaghan, *Hist. of New Netherland,* vol. I (1846) and *Calendar of Hist. MSS. in the office of the Sec. of State,* vol. I (1865) ; *Documents Relative to the Colonial Hist. of . . . N. Y.,* esp. vol. I (1856), procured and ed. by J. R. Brodhead and E. B. O'Callaghan ; G. Beernink in *Gelre Vereeniging . . . Werken,* no. 12 (1916) esp. pp. 116, 143, 145 and in *Gelre Vereeniging . . Bijdragen,* XV (1912), esp. pp. 91, 124 ; A. J. F. van Laer, *The Correspondence of Jeremias Van Rensselaer* (1932) and *Van Rensselaer Bowier MSS.* (1908), esp. p. 36 ; *Narratives of New Netherland, 1609–1664* (1909), ed. by J. F. Jameson ; M. G. Van Rensselaer,

Hist. of . . . N. Y. (1909), vol. I; Hist. of . . . N. Y., vol. I (1933), ed. by A. C. Flick.]   A. H.

VAN TYNE, CLAUDE HALSTEAD (Oct. 16, 1869–Mar. 21, 1930), historian, the son of Lawrence M. and Helen (Rosacrans) Van Tyne, was born at Tecumseh, Mich. Starting as a youth in the banking business he rose, while in his early twenties, to the position of cashier in the Iosco County Savings Bank, in northern Michigan. Well launched on a promising career he nevertheless aspired to pursue the profession of a scholar. Accordingly he entered the University of Michigan whence he was graduated in 1896. On June 19 of that year he married Belle Joslyn of Chesaning, Mich. During vacations he had made adventurous bicycle tours, across the Rocky Mountains and in Europe, and later he made a rowing trip down the Danube with his wife. He pursued graduate studies at Heidelberg, Leipzig, and Paris (1897–98), and in 1900 took his Ph.D. degree at the University of Pennsylvania, where he remained as senior fellow in history until January 1903. Then, after six months' work of investigation in Washington in connection with the Carnegie Institution, he came in the autumn of 1903 to the University of Michigan as assistant professor. Three years later, when Prof. A. C. McLaughlin went to the University of Chicago, Van Tyne was promoted to the rank of professor and was made head of the department of American history. In 1911 he became head of the department of history, with which the American group was reunited. Thanks to his consideration for young men, his high standards, and his eye for breeding and culture as well as technical proficiency he succeeded in developing a loyal and scholarly staff.

In spite of his devotion to his research Van Tyne had a strong sense of his academic duties and served on many important committees. A dominating figure in the University, he was also active outside it. During the period 1916–21 he was a member of the board of editors of the *American Historical Review*. Meantime, in 1913–14, he was lecturer in the French provincial universities on the Fondation Harvard pour les relations avec les universitiés Françaises. Some years later he went to India, on the invitation of Sir Frederick Whyte, the first president of the legislative assembly, to estimate the experiments that were being carried on there under the Act of 1919. The resulting observations he embodied in two articles in the *Atlantic Monthly* (July, September 1922) and in a book, *India in Ferment* (1923), which subjected him to some criticism from those who disapproved of British rule. In 1927 he occupied the Sir George Watson chair of American history, literature, and institutions in the British universities, an annual lectureship. The lectures, which were marked by both maturity and charm, were printed under the title, *England and America, Rivals in the American Revolution* (1927).

Van Tyne's scholarly publications were reasonably numerous and of increasingly high quality. Among the earlier ones may be mentioned an edition of *The Letters of Daniel Webster* (1902); a *Guide to the Archives of the Government of the United States in Washington* (1904), compiled for the Carnegie Institution in collaboration with Waldo G. Leland; and *A History of the United States for Schools* (1911), written in collaboration with Prof. A. C. McLaughlin. Within his special field of interest he published several important works. The earliest of these was his dissertation, *The Loyalists in the American Revolution* (1902), an over-ambitious but promising book. Next to appear was *The American Revolution, 1776–1783* (1905), in the American Nation series. At length, after years of research, he published *The Causes of the War of Independence* (1922), the first volume of *A History of the Founding of the American Republic* which he designed as the main work of his life but only half of which he finished. The first volume was valued by his co-workers chiefly as a synthesis of the specialized studies of many investigators, to whom Van Tyne made conscientious acknowledgment. The succeeding volume, *The War of Independence, American Phase* (1929), was widely hailed as a fresh, illuminating, and distinctly readable treatment. The acquisition by William L. Clements of the Shelburne, the Clinton, the Greene, and the Germain papers brought within his reach rich treasures, of which he availed himself. Unhappily his work was cut short by a serious illness in the spring of 1929 and he died Mar. 21, 1930. He was survived by his wife, a daughter, and three sons. In 1930 he received the Henry Russel Award for the most scholarly work produced that year by a member of the University of Michigan faculty, and for his last book he was posthumously awarded a Pulitzer Prize (*New York Times*, May 13, 1930).

Van Tyne was a stimulating though exacting teacher. He was distinguished in appearance, gifted with a whimsical humor, and possessed of a power of apt allusion drawn from rich stores of extensive reading. Very individual in speech and writing, he was vehement in pressing his own opinions and rather inclined to be intolerant of those whose standards differed from his.

[A. L. Cross, in *Michigan Alumnus*, Mar. 29, 1930; memoir prepared by W. G. Leland for publication in *Proc. Am. Academy of Arts and Sciences*; *Who's Who in America*, 1928–29; obituary in *N. Y. Times*, Mar. 22, 1930; *Am. Hist. Review*, July 1930, p. 941; critical reviews of chief works, *Am. Hist. Review*, July 1903, Jan. 1923, Apr. 1930.]   A. L. C.

VANUXEM, LARDNER (July 23, 1792–Jan. 25, 1848), geologist, the son of James and Rebecca (Clarke) Vanuxem, was born in Philadelphia. His father, a native of Dunkirk, France, was a prosperous shipping merchant; his mother was a daughter of Elijah Clarke of New Jersey. Since the son's tastes inclined more to science than to business, he early eschewed the commercial opportunities his father afforded him and, with his parents' approval, went to Paris and entered the École des Mines, where he was graduated in 1819. Returning to the United States, he became professor of chemistry and mineralogy in South Carolina College. During his incumbency he made a geological survey of North Carolina and participated in similar work in South Carolina, publishing his reports in various newspapers and in Robert Mills's *Statistics of South Carolina* (1826).

In November 1827 he resigned his professorship in order to devote himself to geological studies. He examined certain mines in Mexico and a little later was engaged in geologic reconnaissance surveys in New York, Ohio, Kentucky, Tennessee, and Virginia. About 1830 he purchased a farm near Bristol, Pa., and soon afterward married Elizabeth, daughter of John Newbold of Bloomsdale. When the Geological Survey of New York was instituted in 1836, he was assigned to the investigation of the Fourth District, but was soon transferred to the Third. His duties included studies of the extent and limits of the iron and salt bearing formations, and of the relation of the rocks of New York to the "Coal Measures" of Pennsylvania. The results of his work appeared in *Geology of New-York, Part III, Comprising the Survey of the Third Geological District* (1842), upon which his reputation as a scientist largely rests. Prior to this survey no uniform system of nomenclature had been adopted for American geology. The need being imperative, Vanuxem suggested that the geologists of Pennsylvania and Virginia collaborate with those of New York in establishing a common system of names. Out of this cooperation grew the Association of American Geologists and Naturalists, formed in 1840, which in 1847 became the American Association for the Advancement of Science. Later, Vanuxem collaborated with James Hall [q.v.] in arranging the state geological collections in Albany. Having ample means, apparently, he then retired to private life and died in his home at Bristol, Pa.

Vanuxem's investigation of the sedimentaries was excellent work for that period, but his treatment of what he termed the "Primary Class" of crystalline rocks was scant, as was to be expected at a time when petrography had not been developed into an exact science. In some respects he seems to have been in advance of his time, for he showed in the *Geology of New York* a leaning toward views not in harmony with the Mosaic account of the creation, which in his day was considered sacrosanct. Moreover, he appears, perhaps faintly, to have postulated the theory of evolution (p. 27). His intellectual pursuits were varied. He spent much time in the investigation of the Scriptures and left many manuscripts recording his findings and views; he took much interest in new forms of religion, such as Mormonism and Millerism; he made a study of phrenology. He was an early advocate of the emancipation of women from the restrictions then prevailing. The views and actions which his independent thinking led him to adopt caused many to regard him as "a very peculiar man."

[Maximilian La Borde, *Hist. of the S. C. Coll.* (1874); E. L. Green, *A Hist. of the Univ. of S. C.* (1916); H. V. Cubberly, *Bloomsdale: Sketches of the Old-Time Home of the John Newbold Family* (1930); *Jour. of the Elisha Mitchell Scientific Soc.*, July–Dec. 1890; W. J. Youmans, *Pioneers of Sci. in America* (1896); *Am. Jour. of Sci. and Arts*, May 1848; *North Am. and U. S. Gazette* (Phila.), Jan. 28, 1848.]   F. L. G.

VAN VECHTEN, ABRAHAM (Dec. 5, 1762–Jan. 6, 1837), lawyer, was born in Catskill, N. Y., where his great-grandfather had purchased land and settled about 1681. His parents, Teunis Van Vechten and Judikje, daughter of Jacob Ten Broeck, were of Dutch colonial stock. On his paternal side he was a direct descendant of Teunis Dircksen van Vechten, who emigrated with his family from Holland in 1638, settling first at Beaverwyck and later at Greenbush, N. Y. Abraham Van Vechten received his early education at Esopus, attended King's College for a time, and pursued the study of law at Albany in the office of John Lansing [q.v.], an intimate friend. As the first lawyer admitted to practice under the state constitution at the October term of the supreme court in 1785, when new rules were adopted, Van Vechten has frequently been called "the father of the New York bar," although such a title would seem to slight the claims of distinguished colonial predecessors. He opened a law office at Johnstown, N. Y., but, after a brief sojourn, established his permanent practice in Albany.

He soon entered Federalist politics, but at the

start his political career was jeopardized by a remark, attributed to him, to the effect "that the Yankees had already obtain't too much influence in our Government and that it was high time the Dutch people should rally against them." In 1796 he was appointed by Gov. John Jay [*q.v.*] district attorney for the fifth district of the state. Two years later he declined an appointment as associate justice of the state supreme court. He was elected to the state Senate in 1798 and served until 1805, performing valuable services as chairman of the judiciary committee and as a member of the court for the correction of errors. He went on record as opposed to the methods of the Republican promoters of the state bank, fearing competition with the Federalist bank in Albany (D. S. Alexander, *A Political History of the State of New York,* vol. I, 1906, p. 188). During the years 1798–1805 he served, also, as recorder of Albany. In 1805 he was elected to the Assembly from Albany County and remained a member until 1813, ably advocating the Federalist position in opposition to the Embargo (*Ibid.,* pp. 168, 169). In the Federalist victory of 1809 he became attorney-general, only to be turned out by the Clintonians two years later. Again, in 1813, he was made attorney-general, succeeding his friend Thomas Addis Emmet [*q.v.*], and was succeeded in office in 1815 by Martin Van Buren [*q.v.*].

Van Vechten occupied a position of commanding influence at the constitutional convention of 1821, which he attended as a delegate from Albany. He vigorously defended the judiciary from attack, asserting that the convention had been assembled to amend the constitution and that "no man had ever dreamed of its being for the purpose of dismissing officers from our government" (C. Z. Lincoln, *The Constitutional History of New York,* 1906, I, 682–83). He likewise opposed the proposition to vest the impeachment power in a majority of the Assembly as against the two-thirds required under the first constitution (*Ibid.,* IV, 601). Such topics as the freehold qualification for voters, the extension of the elective franchise, and the power and jurisdiction of the court of chancery were also the subjects of addresses which he made.

After the convention he retired from political life and devoted himself intensively to his legal career, where his solid learning, his powers of clear and logical analysis and argument, his unusual gift of eloquence, and his distinguished bearing established him among the leaders of the bar. One biographer claims that Van Vechten served as defense counsel in the celebrated trial of David D. How for the murder of Othello

Church, held at Angelica, N. Y., in 1825 (Proctor, *post,* p. 73), although the record does not substantiate this claim (*cf.* J. D. Lawson, *American State Trials,* vol. VI, 1916, pp. 865–79; Joseph Badger, *Life and Confession of David D. How,* n.d.). The most notable case with which he was associated was that of *Gibbons* vs. *Ogden* (9 *Wheaton,* 1), where he prepared an opinion denying the power of the state legislature to grant a license giving Livingston and Fulton the sole right to navigate the waters of the state. In this position he was fully sustained by Chief Justice Marshall. Owing to illness, Van Vechten took no part in the proceedings before the Supreme Court. In May 1784 he married Catharine, daughter of Philip Pieterse and Anna (Wendell) Schuyler of Albany; they had fifteen children, of whom ten survived infancy.

[Peter Van Vechten, *The Geneal. Records of the Van Vechtens from 1638 to 1896* (1896); Joel Munsell, *The Annals of Albany,* vol. X (1859); S. V. Talcott, *Geneal. Notes of N. Y. and New England Families* (1883); L. B. Proctor, "Abraham Van Vechten, the Father of the Bar of the State of N. Y.," *Albany Law Journal,* July 30, 1898; N. H. Carter and W. L. Stone, *Rec. of the Proc. and Debates of the Convention of 1821 ... N. Y.* (1921); D. R. Fox, *The Decline of Aristocracy in the Politics of N. Y.* (1919); *Albany Argus,* Jan. 9, 1837; Van Vechten's Letterbook (MS.), N. Y. Hist. Soc.]
R. B. M.

VAN WINKLE, PETER GODWIN (Sept. 7, 1808–Apr. 15, 1872), lawyer, United States senator, was the second son of Peter and Phoebe (Godwin) Van Winkle. He was born in New York City, and came from an old Knickerbocker family, the American progenitor of which, Jacob Van Winkle, settled in New Netherland about 1634. What formal education he received was obtained in the primary and secondary schools of his native city. In early manhood he moved to Parkersburg, Va. (now W. Va.), where he began the study of law and in 1835 was admitted to the bar. Although actively engaged in his profession, he was at one time or another recorder of the town, a member of its governing board of trustees, and president of this board—a position equivalent to that of mayor. Beginning in 1852 he served as treasurer and later as president of the Northwestern Virginia Railroad Company, which, in connection with the Baltimore & Ohio Railroad, built and operated a line from Grafton to the Ohio River. He was also for a number of years an attorney and lobbyist for the Baltimore & Ohio.

He was a member of the Virginia constitutional convention of 1850–51, though he seems not to have played a conspicuous rôle in its proceedings. He did, however, take a prominent part in the convention held at Wheeling in June 1861, in which sat representatives from northwestern Virginia. This convention passed an ordinance providing for the reorganization of the government of Virginia on a basis of loyalty to the Union. The government thus created was to supersede that centering at Richmond. Francis H. Pierpont [q.v.] was chosen governor, and Van Winkle was selected as a member of his advisory council. This convention at an adjourned session (in August) also passed an ordinance which provided for the division of Virginia and the creation of what became the state of West Virginia.

A constitutional convention was assembled at Wheeling on Nov. 26, 1861. Van Winkle was one of the leading members of this body, and had much to do with the framing of the constitution. He urged the inclusion in West Virginia of the counties in the extreme eastern section, mainly in order that the Baltimore & Ohio Railroad should be entirely on West Virginia and Maryland soil. When the government of West Virginia was organized, he was a member of the first legislature and had an important part in the legislation enacted by it. In August 1863 he was one of the two chosen United States senators; he drew the long term and so served for six years.

In the Senate his record on routine policies must have impressed the leadership of the Republican party favorably, for he became a member of the important finance committee and chairman of the committee on pensions. His career as a whole, while not a brilliant one, was characterized by exceptional courage and independence of spirit. Though he went along with his party in voting for the Thirteenth and Fifteenth amendments, he refused to follow its leaders on some measures of prime importance. In a rather lengthy speech (Apr. 21, 1864) in opposition to the repeal of the Fugitive Slave Law, he declared himself in favor of turning over the government of the Southern states to the loyal local citizens, though they might formerly have been disloyal, and of withdrawing from that section all federal soldiers as soon as safety should permit. He also opposed the granting of citizenship to the freedmen, believing that the majority of them were not equal to this responsibility. Consistently with this view, he voted against the Fourteenth Amendment in opposition to the wishes of a large majority of his party. His greatest offense against party regularity, however, was his refusal to vote for conviction in the impeachment proceedings against President Johnson. This defiance of the leadership of his party was loudly condemned in West Virginia; the Wheeling *Intelligencer* referred to him as "West Virginia's Betrayer," and de-

clared that there was not a loyal citizen in the state who had not been misrepresented by that vote. With feeling so strong against him, there was no prospect of his being returned to the Senate, and so he did not become a candidate for reelection. Leaving Washington at the end of his term, he spent the three remaining years of his life at Parkersburg. In 1831 he married Juliette, daughter of William P. and Martha Rathbun, of Paramus, Bergen County, N. J., by whom he had several children.

[Daniel Van Winkle, *A Geneal. of the Van Winkle Family* (copr. 1913) ; *Biog. Dir. Am. Cong.* (1928) ; G. W. Atkinson and A. F. Gibbens, *Prominent Men of W. Va.* (1890) ; V. A. Lewis, *How West Va. Was Made* (1909) ; J. C. McGregor, *The Disruption of Va.* (1922) ; *The Jour. of the House of Delegates of the State of W. Va.*, 1 Sess. (1863) ; *Wheeling Daily Intelligencer*, June, Aug. 1861, Nov. 1861–Feb. 1862, May 18, 1868, Apr. 16, 1872 ; *State Journal* (Parkersburg), Apr. 18, 1872 ; T. C. Miller and Hu Maxwell, *W. Va. and Its People* (1913), vol. III.]   O. P. C.

VAN WYCK, CHARLES HENRY (May 10, 1824–Oct. 24, 1895), lawyer, soldier, legislator, the second son of Dr. Theodorus C. and Elizabeth (Mason) Van Wyck, was born at Poughkeepsie, N. Y. He was descended from Cornelius Barentse van Wyck who emigrated to Long Island in 1660. Charles spent his youth at Bloomingburg, Sullivan County, N. Y., at which place his father was a practising physician. He was graduated from Rutgers College, the ranking student of the class of 1843. After graduation he turned to the study of law and was admitted to the bar in 1847. Three years later he was elected district attorney of Sullivan County, and was reëlected to this position for three successive terms (1850–56).

He began politics as a member of the Barnburner wing of the Democratic party, but joined the new Republican movement and represented his district in Congress from Mar. 4, 1859, to Mar. 3, 1863. He recruited the 56th New York Volunteers and commanded the regiment from Sept. 4, 1861, until he was promoted to the rank of brigadier-general, Sept. 27, 1865. He served in the Peninsular and South Carolina campaigns and remained in the army of occupation in South Carolina until August 1865. On Jan. 15, 1866, he was mustered out of the service. He was reëlected to Congress in 1866 and 1868. On the last occasion his election was contested, but he was seated, after a congressional investigation, on Feb. 17, 1870. As congressman he took a leading part in investigations of the New York custom house service and of contracts of the War Department.

In 1857 he acquired lands near Nebraska City, Nebr., and in 1874 removed to that place. He was an active member of the Nebraska constitutional convention of 1875, and was elected to the state Senate for three successive terms (1877, 1879, 1881). In the legislature he was an active advocate of railroad rate legislation and tax relief. As United States senator from 1881 to 1887 he was a strong supporter of tariff reform, railroad regulation, protection of the public lands, and direct popular election of senators. To make possible the last named, he proposed an amendment to the federal Constitution. In the senatorial preferential ballot (provided in the Nebraska constitution) he received an overwhelming plurality for reëlection, but was rejected by the state legislature. He was an active leader of the Farmers' Alliance and of the Populist movement in Nebraska. He would probably have been the Populists' candidate for governor in 1890 but for a peculiar composition of their first convention, for which a personal foe of Van Wyck was responsible. In 1892 he received the nomination but failed of election. In 1894 he was a candidate on the Populist ticket for the state Senate; he was physically unable to make an active campaign, however, and in the election the Republicans were victorious. He was a man of strong and positive personality, an entertaining and eloquent speaker, a genial and generous host, a friend of the masses. He died in Washington and was buried at Milford, Pa., the early home of his wife, Kate Brodhead, whom he married Sept. 15, 1869; she and a daughter survived him.

[Anne Van Wyck, *Descendants of Cornelius Barentse Van Wyck and Anna Polhemus* (1912); J. C. Fisk and W. H. D. Blake, *A Condensed Hist. of the 56th Regiment of N. Y.* (n.d.); M. U. Harmer and J. L. Sellers, "Charles Henry Van Wyck," *Nebr. Hist. Mag.*, Apr.– Dec. 1929; *Omaha Daily Bee*, Oct. 25, 1895; *Nebr. City News*, Oct. 25, 1895; J. S. Morton and Albert Watkins, *Hist. of Nebr.*, vol. III (1913); *Biog. Dir. Am. Cong.* (1928).]   J. L. S.

VANZETTI, BARTOLOMEO (1888–1927) [See Sacco, Nicola, 1891–1927].

VARDAMAN, JAMES KIMBLE (July 26, 1861–June 25, 1930), governor of Mississippi, senator, was born near Edna, Jackson County, Tex., to which his parents, William Sylvester and Mary (Fox) Vardaman, had removed from Mississippi in 1858. After the Civil War, in which the father was a Confederate soldier, the family returned from Texas and settled on a farm in Yalobusha County, Miss. James, the fourth of the six children, after attending the public schools in that county and reading law at Carrollton, was admitted to the bar at the age of twenty-one. He began to practise at Winona, Miss., and there edited in 1883 the Winona *Ad-*

vance. On May 31 of the same year he was married to Anna E. (Burleson) Robinson, a native of Alabama. From 1890 to 1896 he edited the Greenwood *Enterprise*, and in the latter year he established the Greenwood *Commonwealth*, which he edited until 1903. While editing the *Enterprise* he served three terms in the state legislature and in 1894 was speaker of the House. During the Spanish-American War he was captain and later major in the 5th United States Volunteer Infantry, serving in Santiago, Cuba, from August 1898 to May 1899.

In 1895 and 1899 he sought in vain to obtain the nomination for the governorship in the state conventions, which at that time either partially concealed or avoided rifts in the all-powerful Democratic party in Mississippi. When a law was passed in 1902 providing for nominations by party primaries, factionalism within the party became more probable; and it became more necessary for the officeseeker to know the technique of swaying the masses. It was Vardaman's good fortune that a split could be made in the party with more ease than formerly; it was due to his own skill that the party was fractured on class lines. In the next campaign he brought into play his extraordinary power as a political speechmaker. By riding on great eight-wheeled lumber wagons drawn by many yokes of white oxen and by making such declarations as that his first audiences had been "barnyard inhabitants and jackasses," he established his brotherhood with the farmers. He further appealed to the poor white man by asserting that the political dominance of his race was being endangered by the education of the negro. While he doubtless believed this, raising the negro issue may have saved him from being branded as a Populist, even though he was appealing to the economically discontented, many of whom had recently voted the Populist ticket. His interest in the common man seems to have been sincere. With a keen eye for dramatic values in his campaigns, he accentuated his striking appearance by wearing his black hair down to his shoulders and by dressing in immaculate white. He became the idol of the masses, was nominated in the Democratic primary, and was inaugurated governor in January 1904. Though he was charged with extending the spoils system, he made a praiseworthy attack on the system of leasing state convicts to private persons and corporations.

In the summer of 1907, a few months before the close of his administration, he was a candidate for the federal Senate but was defeated in the Democratic primary. To keep from being forgotten while out of office, he began to publish the *Issue,* a weekly political newspaper, at Jackson in 1908. Early in 1910 he again sought a senatorship. The legislature had not been bound by a primary nomination, and after a prolonged, bitter, and corrupt fight, it elected Le Roy Percy. Vardaman charged that the will of the people had been disregarded, and to them he appealed in the 1911 primary and was elected. He entered the Senate on Mar. 4, 1913. There he became conspicuous by strenuously opposing the President's war policies. He was one of the "little group of willful men" who aroused Wilson's indignation by their successful filibuster against the Armed Neutrality Bill, and he was one of the six who voted against the resolution declaring war against Germany. He maintained that the war was injurious to the common people who had put him in office, and for a time many of his constituents agreed with this view. Also, he resented Wilson's refusal to follow his advice on several occasions early in the administration. By the time an enthusiastic support of the war had become the prevailing sentiment in his state, it was too late for Vardaman to withdraw from the opposition with any consistency. He was defeated in 1918 by Pat Harrison, who was aided by a direct appeal from Wilson to the voters of Mississippi. That Vardaman still had a large following was shown when he again ran for the Senate in 1922. Though he was defeated in the second primary, he had received a plurality in the first. Yet he was already so broken in body and mind that most of his speeches had to be made by his friends. Realizing that this was the end, he soon removed to Birmingham, Ala., and there spent his remaining years with his two daughters, who with one of their two brothers and their mother survived him.

[A. S. Coody, *Biog. Sketches of James Kimble Vardaman* (1922); *Vardaman's Attitude toward President Wilson, the Democratic Administration and the American Government* (1918), an opposition pamphlet; *Who's Who in America*, 1930–31; *Biog. Directory Am. Cong.* (1928); *Daily News* (Jackson, Miss.), June 26, 27, 1930; *Commercial-Appeal* and *Evening Appeal* (Memphis, Tenn.), June 26, 1930.]   C. S. S.

VARDILL, JOHN (1749–Jan. 16, 1811), clergyman and British spy, the son of Capt. Thomas and Hannah (Tiebout) Vardill, was baptized on July 5, 1749 (T. A. Wright, *Records of the Reformed Dutch Church . . . New York: Baptisms*, 1902, p. 152). He was born in New York City, where his father, a native of Bermuda, was a ship-owner, and at one time port warden. John graduated from King's College in 1766, and, later, while studying theology, was attached unofficially to the college as a tutor. One of his students was John Parke Custis, stepson of

Washington (W. C. Ford, *Letters of Jonathan Boucher to George Washington*, 1889, p. 45). Vardill was an assistant to Dr. Samuel Clossy, the professor of anatomy; he taught "Languages and other Branches of Science," and was a great favorite of the president, Myles Cooper [*q.v.*]. At the commencement of 1769 he received a master's degree. When he was about to go to England for ordination, the governors of the college voted him a hundred pounds for his services (Minutes, Nov. 11, 1773), and elected him a fellow and professor of natural law (*Ibid.*, Dec. 28, 1773).

In the meantime he had brought himself into public notice as a controversialist, having had a part in writing "A Whip for the American Whig" (Hugh Gaines' *New York Gazette*, Apr. 4, 1768–July 10, 1769), and other essays in connection with the controversy between William Livingston and Thomas Bradbury Chandler [*qq.v.*] over an American episcopate. On Dec. 7, 1772, in the *New York Gazette and the Weekly Mercury* over the signature "Causidicus" he attacked the Rev. John Witherspoon's *Address to the Inhabitants of Jamaica and Other West-India Islands, in Behalf of the College of New-Jersey* (reprinted with Causidicus' attack in William Nelson, *Archives of New Jersey*, 1 ser., vol. XXVIII, 1916, pp. 289–308, 345–59), through which, Vardill claimed, "the Youth of North-America were to be lured by the Charmer's Voice in to the Bosom of Nassau-Hall." He was also the author in 1773, over the signature "Poplicola," of broadcasts against the non-importation agreement and in favor of receiving the tea shipments (see Charles Evans, *American Bibliography*, vol. IV, 1907, p. 385). These appeared in *Rivington's New York Gazetteer.*

He was ordained deacon, Apr. 4, 1774, and priest the following day in the Chapel Royal, St. James's Palace, by Richard Terrick, Bishop of London (Records in the Bishop of London's Registry), and was made M.A. at Oxford, June 28, 1774. On Dec. 6, 1774, following the death of the Rev. John Ogilvie [*q.v.*], he was unanimously elected assistant minister of Trinity Church, New York, although on Dec. 1, he had been attacked anonymously in the *New York Journal* as "a poetaster, the tool of a party, a newswriter, a pamphleteer, a paltry politician, who will forever . . . keep a spirit of dissension among you" (quoted in *Archives of the General Convention, post,* IV, 135). Such of his verses as have survived (manuscripts in New York Historical Society) bear out these accusations, although a rejoinder praising his "universally known and acknowledged" abilities and his "most engaging sweetness of disposition" appeared in the same paper for Dec. 22, 1774. Vardill remained in England, however, to promote the granting of a charter making King's College a university, a project which the Revolution prevented. He continued writing for periodicals in defense of the government, under the name of "Corrolænus," for which he received thanks and promises of patronage. By correspondence he nearly won over to the Crown with promises of judgeships two members of Congress, "but the negotiation was quashed by the unexpected fray at Lexington in April 1775" (Einstein, *post*, p. 412). "In consequence of these and such like services and to give the Loyalists at New York a Proof of the Attention and Rewards which would follow their Zeal and Loyalty" (*Ibid.*, p. 412), he was appointed Regius Professor of Divinity in King's College, with a salary of £200, and the appointment was announced in *Rivington's New York Gazetteer*, Dec. 8, 1774, although the royal warrant was not granted until some time later.

Vardill never returned to America, but spent the years 1775 to 1781 as a spy in the service of the Crown. In a memorial which he addressed to the commissioners on Loyalists claims, Nov. 16, 1783, he recited the precise nature of his services and, while admitting that he had been paid for his services in England, claimed compensation for the salary he had never received from King's College and Trinity Church, New York; the claim was not allowed (Coke, *post*, p. 255). He was given an office at 17 Downing Street, close to that of the Prime Minister, and spent his time mainly in spying on American sympathizers in England. When the Abbé Raynal visited London bearing letters from Franklin in Paris, and when Jonathan Austin came over as Franklin's confidential agent, Vardill found the means to examine their correspondence without their knowledge; on another occasion he induced a New Yorker named Van Zandt, who had come over on business of Congress, with letters from Franklin, to become a British spy. Vardill's greatest feat, however, was in securing the theft, by Joseph Hynson, a seaman in the confidence of Silas Deane [*q.v.*], of the entire confidential correspondence that passed between the American commissioners and the French court from March to October 1777, which corroborated reports of the imminence of French intervention. Within three months of the theft of these papers, Vardill was rewarded by the granting of the royal warrant (Jan. 8, 1778) for his appointment as Regius Professor in New York.

Vardill was in Dublin in 1785 and 1786, but little is known of him until 1791, when he was given the living of Skirbeck, Lincolnshire (*Gentleman's Magazine*, July 1791). He was married and had a daughter.

[Arthur Lowndes, ed., *Archives of the Gen. Convention*, vol. IV (1912); *N. Y. Geneal. and Biog. Record*, Oct. 1894; Lewis Einstein, *Divided Loyalties* (1933); B. F. Stevens's *Facsimiles of Manuscripts in European Archives Relating to America, 1773 to 1783*; D. P. Coke, *The Royal Commission on the Losses and Services of American Loyalists* (1915), ed. by H. E. Egerton; *Gentleman's Mag.*, Jan. 1811.]   M. H. T.

VARE, WILLIAM SCOTT (Dec. 24, 1867–Aug. 7, 1934), contractor, politician, was born on a farm in South Philadelphia, the son of Augustus and Abigail (Stites) Vare. His father was a native of the Isle of Jersey; his mother was of Puritan New England stock. As a boy "he milked the cow, he followed the plow"—according to a campaign ditty current years afterward. The elementary schooling which he received ended when he was twelve, and he went to work in John Wanamaker's store as a cash boy. Later he was employed by his brother George, then a produce merchant, as a huckster, and acquired an intimate acquaintance with the South Philadelphia district and its people which was of much political value to him subsequently. From the time he reached his majority he was closely associated with his brothers George and Edwin. George was recognized as the leader until his death in 1908, then Edwin was in control until he died in 1922, after which time William was sole master of the powerful machine, which, as ward leaders, they had established. They had become contractors and they used their political influence to secure fat commissions from the city, by means of which they acquired considerable private fortunes. On July 29, 1897, William married Ida Morris of Philadelphia.

Apart from this direct connection between business and politics, which often led to denunciation of the brothers as "contractor-bosses," there was nothing to distinguish their earlier course from that of other minor machine leaders. After innumerable factional fights, however, first as allies of Boies Penrose [*q.v.*], and later as opposed to him, they extended their influence from their own wards into neighboring ones, and became known as the "Dukes of South Philadelphia." In 1917 Edwin and William gained control of the Republican organization of the city. Already their support had been a prime factor in the election of Martin G. Brumbaugh to the governorship of Pennsylvania in 1914. At this time Edwin was generally considered a much abler man than William, but the former never attained national prominence, the highest office that he held being that of state senator. Beginning as ward committeeman, William was a member of the Select Council, 1898–1901; recorder of deeds, 1902–12; representative in Congress, Apr. 24, 1912–Jan. 2, 1923, and Mar. 4, 1923–Mar. 3, 1927; state senator, January–November 1923. His only defeat in a popular election, and that by a small majority although Penrose opposed him, occurred in 1911, when he ran for the Philadelphia mayoralty. He was district delegate to each of the national conventions of the Republican party from 1908 to 1920; delegate-at-large in 1924 and 1928, and national committeeman in 1934.

The climax of Vare's career came in the primaries of 1926, when on a light wine and beer platform he defeated George Wharton Pepper and Gifford Pinchot for the Republican nomination to the United States Senate. In the ensuing election he was successful over William B. Wilson, Democratic candidate, by approximately 170,000 votes. Before the election had taken place, however, in accordance with a resolution of May 17, 1926, a special senatorial committee, headed by James A. Reed of Missouri, began a probe into the Pennsylvania primary fight. After a prolonged controversy the Senate, by a vote of 58 to 22, Dec. 6, 1929, rejected Vare on the ground that his primary expenditures were excessive, and that fraud and corruption had been practised. As a matter of fact the expenditures had been less than half those of the faction headed by Pepper, his principal competitor. At the Republican National Convention of 1928, Vare stampeded the Pennsylvania delegation to Hoover (*New York Times,* June 12, 13, 1928), thus contributing largely to the nomination of the latter. No *quid pro quo* came from the White House after the inauguration, much to the disgust of the Philadelphia organization; nevertheless Vare supported Hoover in the campaign of 1932. In 1930, however, he had bolted Pinchot, Republican nominee for governor, in favor of John M. Hemphill, Democratic-Liberal and wet candidate.

In 1928 Vare's health failed but he continued his leadership until ousted by a factional combination two months before his death, which occurred at his summer home in Atlantic City. A member of the Methodist Church, his personal conduct was above reproach. Avowedly a machine leader, he maintained his organization largely by spoils and political charity, gaining popular support by "giving the people something they can see," *i.e.,* lavish expenditure of the city's money on public improvements in South Philadelphia. Throughout his career, however, he opposed child labor and vigorously supported

workmen's compensation, mothers' assistance, and other social reform bills.

[Files of Phila. newspapers from 1900 are replete with articles and editorials, mostly hostile, on the Vares; their activities are defended by the *Sunday Dispatch,* a machine organ. Edwin Vare's career and character are admirably discussed in Harold Zink, *City Bosses in the U. S.* (1930); for a similar discussion of William Vare, see W. L. Whittlesey, "Vare of Philadelphia," in the *Outlook,* Dec. 28, 1927. William Vare's autobiog., *My Forty Years in Politics* (1933), deals with his public record but throws little light on the source of campaign funds or the inside manipulation of the organization; for facts regarding the senatorial investigation, see *Senate Report 1197,* 69 Cong., 2 Sess., pt. 2, *Senate Report 1858,* 70 Cong., 2 Sess., and *Senate Report 47,* 71 Cong., 2 Sess.; other sources include *Biog. Dir. Am. Cong.* (1928); *Who's Who in America,* 1932–33; *Evening Pub. Ledger* (Phila.), Aug. 7, 1934; *N. Y. Times,* Aug. 8, 1934.]   R. C. B.

VARELA Y MORALES, FÉLIX FRANCISCO JOSÉ MARÍA DE LA CONCEPCIÓN (Nov. 20, 1788–Feb. 18, 1853), patriot, educator, and priest, son of Francisco Varela, a Spanish military officer, and Josepha de Morales, was born in Habana, Cuba. After his father's early death, he was trained by a maternal uncle, Bartolomé Morales, governor of Saint Augustine, Fla., who soon sent him to the ancient College and Seminary of San Carlos in Habana. A boy of marked piety with a genius for languages and philosophy, he was ordained a priest (1811) and despite his youth given the chair of philosophy in the college, where he also taught physics and chemistry, Latin, and rhetoric. An educational reformer who would modernize the curriculum, change methods of teaching, and make philosophy a part of common life, Father Varela was not only an inspiring teacher but the author of numerous philosophical brochures and books: *Propositiones Variae ad Tyronum Exercitationem* (1811); *Elenco de las Doctrinas que Enseñaba en Filosofía el P. Varela* (1812); *Institutiones Philosophiae Eclecticae ad Usum Studiosae Juventutis Editae* (1812–14), two parts published in Latin, two in Spanish; *Lección Preliminar del Curso de 1818* (1818); *Apuntes Filosóficos, sobre la Dirección del Espíritu Humano* (Habana, 1818); and *Las Leccíónes de Filosofía* (4 vols., Habana, 1818–20), his most important work. An eclectic in philosophy, he opposed the scholasticism which had dominated Spanish thought for centuries, and followed the eighteenth-century philosophers in substituting for it theories that rested on experience and the use of the reason. In the natural sciences, he depended largely on the laboratory. No pedant, he taught in simple language. As a recreation, he studied music and played the violin or took part in the proceedings of the Royal Patriotic Society of Habana. His oratory, which was notable, was characterized by simplicity, clarity, brevity, and good taste. Upon the establishment of a constitutional monarchy in Spain, Varela gave a course on the new constitution in the college. His lectures drew a large attendance of students and patriots, and his published *Observaciones sobre la Constitución Política de la Monarquía Española* (Habana, 1821) won favor with his liberal countrymen. The following year he was sent to Spain as a delegate to the Cortes in Madrid, where he served on various commissions and drew up a plan of provincial government which would give the Spanish colonies a high degree of local autonomy. Perhaps the first Cuban abolitionist, he also suggested a plan for the gradual abolition of slavery in Cuba.

With the establishment of an absolute monarchy in Spain in 1823, Varela fled to New York (Dec. 17, 1823). Going to Philadelphia, he established *El Habanero,* a literary and political paper, its circulation forbidden in Cuba, to which he contributed articles violent enough to bring danger of assassination (1824–26). About this time he translated into Spanish Thomas Jefferson's *A Manual of Parliamentary Practice* and Humphrey Davy's *Elements of Agricultural Chemistry*. In 1825 he went to New York, where as an assistant at St. Peter's Church he ministered to the Latin peoples. With the aid of Spanish merchants, he bought Christ Church from the Episcopalians (St. James) and served as pastor until 1835, when he was transferred to his final rectorship of the Church of the Transfiguration. He republished in 1827 his *Miscelánea Filosófica* (Habana, 1819), edited the poems of the Cuban, Manuel de Zequeira (1829), and published in two volumes his *Cartas á Elpidio sobre la Impiedad, la Superstición y el Fanatismo* (New York, 1835–38), a defense of Christianity against impiety and false liberalism, a third volume remaining in manuscript. Aroused by nativism, he wrote for the *Truth Teller* (1825) and the *New York Weekly Register and Catholic Diary* (1833), and contributed to *El Mensagero Semanal* (1828–31) of New York and occasionally to the *Revista Bimestre Cubana* (1831) of Habana. For a time he was editor of the *Young Catholics' Magazine,* and in 1841 he joined with Charles C. Pise [*q.v.*] in editing the short-lived *Catholic Expositor and Literary Magazine* (1841–44), for which he wrote a number of apologetic essays marked by learning and fluency.

More than a litterateur and a defender of the faith, Varela was an active priest of boundless zeal for souls and sympathy for the poor and the immigrants. He established one of the first total abstinence societies (*Freeman's Journal,* Mar.

20, 1841), several parochial schools, and a day nursery for the children of laboring women. He did not spare himself in the cholera epidemic. As early as 1829 he was named joint-administrator of the diocese with John Power [*q.v.*], when Bishop John Dubois was in Europe. Ten years later Bishop John Hughes left the same two priests in charge. In 1837 and in 1846 Varela attended the councils of Baltimore as a theologian; from 1839 to his death, he was one of Hughes's vicar-generals. Although he was honored by St. Mary's Seminary with a doctorate in sacred theology (1841), most of his honors came after his death in a living tradition in New York as a worthy priest (*Ibid.,* Feb. 4, 1865) and a growing renown among Cubans as a philosopher and patriot. In 1851 he retired to Saint Augustine, where he died. His old students built a chapel to his memory in the cemetery in Saint Augustine.

[For a discussion of the date of death, often given as Feb. 25, see A. L. Valverde y Maruri, *La Muerte del Padre Varela* (Habana, 1924). See also J. I. Rodriguez, *Vida del Presbítero Don Félix Varela* (1878), and art. in *Am. Cath. Quart. Rev.,* July 1883; Sergio Cuevas Zequeira, *El Padre Varela* (1923); W. F. Blakeslee, *Records Am. Cath. Hist. Soc. of Phila.,* Mar. 1927; J. M. Mestre, *De la Filosofia en la Habana* (1862); J. M. Guardia, in *Revue Philosophique,* Jan. 1892, pp. 51–164; J. T. Smith, *The Cath. Church in N. Y.* (1905), vol. I; J. G. Shea, *A Hist. of the Cath. Church within . . . the U. S.* (1890); *Hunt's Merchants' Mag.,* Sept. 1842; *Truth Teller,* Jan. 23, 1847; *N. Y. Freeman's Jour.,* Mar. 12, 19, 1853; U. S. Cath. Hist. Soc., *Hist. Records and Studies,* vol. II (1900), pp. 47–48; *Ceremonies at the Laying of the Cornerstone of a Chapel . . . St. Augustine, Fla., Dedicated to . . . Félix Varela* (1853). For bibliog. materials, see C. M. Trelles, *Bibliografía Cubana del Siglo XIX* (3 vols., 1911–12).]

R. J. P.

VARICK, JAMES (fl. 1796–1828), one of the founders of the African Methodist Episcopal Zion Church and its first bishop, was born near Newburgh, N. Y., probably about 1750 (see Hood, *post,* p. 162), though a considerably later date has been given (Flood and Hamilton, *post,* p. 687). He first came into notice in 1796 when certain colored members of the Methodist Episcopal Church living in New York secured permission from Bishop Francis Asbury to hold meetings by themselves in the intervals between the services held for them by the white ministers. With several others he hired a house on Cross Street, between Mulberry and Orange streets, and fitted it up as a place of worship. Three years later the congregation organized a church under the laws of the state of New York, which was to be subject to Methodist government and known as the African Methodist Episcopal Zion Church; in 1800 a frame building for its meetings was completed and dedicated. A white minister was regularly appointed to have charge of it, but colored preachers also conducted services.

As a result of a number of causes, in 1820 the church declared its independence. Preliminary action was taken at a meeting of official members, held in Varick's house in July of that year, at which Varick and others were appointed a committee to consider the matter. Subsequently, July 26, 1820, the church adopted resolutions severing the existing connection with the Methodist Episcopal organization. Varick was later appointed chairman of a committee to draw up a Discipline based on that of the Methodists. On Oct. 1, 1820, the church elected Abraham Thompson and Varick, both of whom had long been preachers, elders with the power of performing all the functions of that office until ordained by regularly constituted authorities. Several other churches, including one in Philadelphia, one in New Haven, Conn., and one on Long Island, soon affiliated themselves with Zion Church and on June 21, 1821, a Conference was formed with Varick as district chairman, or presiding elder. Patient efforts to secure ordination from Methodist Episcopal bishops having failed, on July 17, 1822, he and two others, all of whom had previously been made deacons, were ordained elders by three former ministers of the Methodist Church who had withdrawn from the connection. That same year Varick was elected bishop of the African Methodist Episcopal Zion Church and served as such until his death.

Through all the years leading up to the establishment of this denomination, he had been a wise and patient leader. His character was never questioned; he had the confidence of prominent Methodists, and is said to have been an able debater and a forceful preacher. He was married and had three sons and four daughters. After his death, which occurred shortly before the Conference that convened May 15, 1828, Christopher Rush (1777–July 16, 1873), born a North Carolina slave, who had also been influential in Zion Church, succeeded him as bishop.

[Christopher Rush, *A Short Account of the Rise and Progress of the African Methodist Episcopal Church in America* (1843); J. W. Hood, *One Hundred Years of the African Methodist Episcopal Zion Church* (1895); T. L. Flood and J. W. Hamilton, *Lives of Methodist Bishops* (1882); J. M. Buckley, *A Hist. of Methodists in the U. S.* (1896), Am. Church Hist. Ser., vol. V.]
H. E. S.

VARICK, RICHARD (Mar. 25, 1753–July 30, 1831), soldier, was the son of Johannis and Jane (Dey) Varick and a great-grandson of Jan van Varick who came to New York from the Netherlands prior to June 1, 1687, and removed to Hackensack, N. J., about 1712. Richard removed to New York City in 1775 and became a captain

in the first New York regiment in June of that year. Subsequently he became military secretary to Gen. Philip John Schuyler [*q.v.*], and lieutenant-colonel and deputy mustermaster-general of the Northern department. Under the reorganized muster department he was deputy commissary-general of musters until June 1780. In August of that year Benedict Arnold [*q.v.*], commanding at West Point, appointed him his aide. Varick was prostrated on the discovery of Arnold's treason and petitioned Washington for a court of inquiry, which acquitted him with honor.

Despite the verdict, however, Varick found that he was an object of suspicion. He wrote to Washington (Nov. 12, 1780) that he wished to remain in the army but the abolition of the muster department and Arnold's treason had left him stranded, and he petitioned that Washington express to Congress his opinion of Varick. This letter is indorsed "No answer necessary" (Washington Papers, Library of Congress). Not quite half a year later, having obtained the approval of Congress to appoint a confidential secretary and staff of writers to record his letters in books to "preserve them from damage and loss," Washington selected Varick as his recording secretary and turned over to him to arrange, classify, and copy, all the correspondence and records of the headquarters of the Continental Army. In the face of such a display of confidence the whispered slanders against Varick were forever silenced. Varick took quarters in Poughkeepsie and the actual copying began early in 1781; the task was completed in 1783, and the forty-odd volumes of transcripts resulting are a monument to secretarial ability and finished skill. Washington expressed his approbation of the manner in which the work was performed and begged Varick to accept his thanks "for the care and attention" which he had given to the task. "I am fully convinced," he wrote, "that neither the present age or posterity will consider the time and labour which have been employed in accomplishing it, unprofitably spent" (Washington to Varick, Jan. 1, 1784; Washington Papers).

In 1784 Varick became recorder of New York City; in 1786, with Samuel Jones [*q.v.*], he was entrusted with the codification of the New York statutes (*Laws of the State of New-York, Comprising the Constitution and the Acts of the Legislature Since the Revolution*, 2 vols., 1789). Speaker of the New York Assembly in 1787 and 1788, and attorney-general in 1788–89, he became mayor of New York in the latter year and held office until the triumphant Republicans swept out all Federalists in 1801. In 1790 he was appointed with two others to provide new buildings for the state government, which were to be used, temporarily, by the government of the United States. With Alexander Hamilton [q.v.], he attempted, unsuccessfully, to stem the tide of popular disapproval against the Jay treaty in an hysterical public meeting at the city hall in the summer of 1795. In 1817 he was one of the appraisers for the Erie Canal. He was a founder of the American Bible Society and its president from 1828 to 1831, and president of the New York Society of the Cincinnati from 1806 until his death. He died in Jersey City and was buried in the Dutch Reformed Church at Hackensack. On May 8, 1786, he had married Maria, daughter of Isaac and Cornelia (Hoffman) Roosevelt; she survived him by a decade, but they left no children.

[*N. Y. Geneal. and Biog. Record*, Jan. 1877; *Journals of the Continental Congress*; Washington MSS. in Lib. of Cong.; J. G. Wilson, *The Memorial Hist. of the City of N. Y.*, vols. II, III (1892, 1893); F. B. Lee, *N. J. as a Colony and as a State* (1902), vols. III, IV; Martha J. Lamb, *Hist. of the City of N. Y.*, vol. II (1880); E. A. Werner, *Civil List . . . of N. Y.* (1899); C. B. Whittelsey, *The Roosevelt Geneal.* (1902); H. P. Johnston, "Colonel Varick and Arnold's Treason," *Mag. of Am. Hist.*, Nov. 1882; John Schuyler, *Institution of the Soc. of the Cincinnati* (1886); F. B. Heitman, *Hist. Reg. of Officers of the Continental Army* (1893); *N. Y. Evening Post for the Country*, Aug. 5, 1831.]

J. C. F—k.

VARNUM, JAMES MITCHELL (Dec. 17, 1748–Jan. 10, 1789), lawyer, Revolutionary soldier, was born at Dracut, Mass., the eldest son of Maj. Samuel Varnum, a prosperous farmer, and his second wife, Hannah Mitchell. He was a descendant of George Varnum, who came to America about 1635, and a brother of Joseph Bradley Varnum [q.v.]. James was sent to Harvard College, but, probably on account of participation in the student disorders of April 1768, he was expelled. He then entered Rhode Island College (now Brown University), and was graduated with honors in its first class, 1769, defending in his commencement forensic the thesis that America should not become independent. After teaching school for a short time, he decided to study law and entered the office of Oliver Arnold, attorney-general of Rhode Island. He was married on Feb. 8, 1770, to Martha Child, the daughter of Cromwell Child, of Warren, R. I. Varnum made rapid professional advancement after his admission to the bar in 1771, due to his extraordinary mental alertness and powers of concentration. His acquaintance with literary masterpieces from which he quoted fluently and copiously helped him to take advantage of the current mode of courtroom oratory.

His powerful physique led him to become a sturdy advocate of gymnastic exhibitions and military drill. In October 1774 he became a colo-

nel of the Kentish Guards, a troop which later sent thirty-two commissioned officers into the Continental Army; among them was Varnum's close friend Nathanael Greene [q.v.]. In May 1775 Varnum was commissioned colonel of the 1st Regiment, Rhode Island Infantry, which became in 1776 the 9th Continental Infantry. This command served in the siege of Boston and held important positions in the battles of Long Island and White Plains. In December the Rhode Island Assembly appointed Varnum brigadier-general of state militia on the continental establishment. He was commissioned brigadier-general in the Continental Army by General Washington on Feb. 21, 1777, and became active in recruitments and reënlistments. His brigade saw complicated service in 1777; Washington ordered him in November to command Forts Mercer and Mifflin on the Delaware. His gallant, though unsuccessful, defense of these key posts, won him commendation, and during the following winter at Valley Forge the commander-in-chief referred to him as "the light of the camp" (Varnum, *post*, p. 158).

After the evacuation of Philadelphia he was ordered to Rhode Island where he took part in the campaign around Newport. He was then made commander of the department of Rhode Island, Jan. 27, 1779. In order to resume his neglected law practice he resigned from the service in the Continental Army in March 1779, but accepted, the following month, a commission as major-general of Rhode Island militia, a rank that he held until May 1788. He was elected in May 1780 to the Continental Congress and served at intervals until 1787. A contemporary, Thomas Rodney [q.v.], characterized him at this time as "a man about thirty, of florid habit, he has read some little of books, is fond of Speaking and Spouting out everything that his reading has furnished him . . . his temper and councils are very precip[it]ate and but little calculated to be useful in such an Assembly, he is very desirous of enlarging its powers" (*Letters of Members, post*, vol. VI, 1933, p. 19). Varnum's law cases were many and notable. He was an original member of the Society of the Cincinnati, and later succeeded General Greene as president of the Rhode Island branch.

An interest in the Northwest Territory and the Ohio Company of Associates, of which he became a director in August 1787, led to Varnum's acceptance of an appointment as United States judge for the Territory at a time when his health was in a very precarious state. He journeyed on horseback to Marietta, Ohio, arriving on June 5, 1788, and a month later delivered a Fourth of July address that was published by the Ohio

Company in 1788 and is still prized by collectors. He energetically assisted in framing a code of territorial laws—his last official act. He died at Marietta and was buried with great ceremony at the Campus Martius. Later his remains were reinterred in Oak Grove Cemetery. His wife remained in the East and survived him forty-eight years. There were no children.

[J. M. Varnum, *The Varnums of Dracutt in Mass.* (1907); A. B. Gardiner and J. M. Varnum, biographical sketch in *Mag. of Am. Hist.*, Sept. 1887; Wilkins Updike, *Memoirs of the R.-I. Bar* (1842); S. R. Coburn, *Hist. of Dracut, Mass.* (1922); F. B. Heitman, *Hist. Reg. of Officers of the Cont. Army* (1893); *Biog. Dir. Am. Cong.* (1928); *Letters of Members of the Cont. Cong.*, vol. VI (1933) ed. by E. C. Burnett; *Providence Gazette and Country Jour.*, Mar. 7, 1789.]

F. W. C.

VARNUM, JOSEPH BRADLEY (Jan. 29, 1750/51–Sept. 11, 1821), Revolutionary soldier, speaker of the federal House of Representatives, senator from Massachusetts, was born at Dracut, Mass., a son of Samuel and Hannah (Mitchell) Varnum and a brother of James Mitchell Varnum [*q.v.*]. Later assertions by Federalists of Varnum's illiteracy were malicious, but he was largely self-taught and sometimes betrayed a lack of early educational advantages. He was married, on Jan. 26, 1773, to Molly Butler, the daughter of Jacob Butler, of Pelham, N. H., a woman of strong character and marked domesticity, who bore her husband twelve children. They received as a gift from his father 160 acres of land with half a dwelling-house and a barn. Farming remained Varnum's primary and preferred occupation throughout his career, and he was proud, in 1818, of owning 500 acres with "more than ten miles of good stone fence upon it" (*Magazine of American History, post,* p. 408). Observance of the British troops in Boston in 1767 interested Varnum in military tactics, and in 1770 one of two militia companies at Dracut elected him captain. He was replaced in 1774 by an older man though still employed as instructor, and in this capacity he was present at the Battle of Lexington. From January 1776 to April 1787, he was captain of the Dracut Minute-men, and he served in the campaigns against Burgoyne in 1777, at Rhode Island in 1778, and later in suppressing Shays's Rebellion.

He represented Dracut in the Massachusetts lower house, 1780–85, and northern Middlesex County, in the Senate, 1786–95. A mild anti-Federalist, he was sent to the Massachusetts convention to ratify the national Constitution (see his speech on the bill of rights, *Massachusetts Centinel,* Feb. 6, 1788). He was a somewhat irregular candidate for the Second and Third congresses but was nominated regularly in 1794 for the Fourth Congress against Samuel Dexter [*q.v.*], a Federalist. He was elected by a majority of eleven votes, most of his support coming from Dracut and the adjoining towns. The election was protested, because the local board of selectmen, of which Varnum was a member, returned sixty more votes than Dracut was entitled to, but, in accordance with the lax rules of the period, he was exonerated in a Republican Congress of charges of political corruption.

In Congress he favored national defense through the militia as against a standing army, opposed building the *Constitution* and other naval vessels, denounced President John Adams' personal extravagance, and was an early opponent of slavery and the slave trade. He was several times called upon to preside during executive sessions. He benefited from the Jefferson-Randolph dispute when the speaker of the House sided with the latter, and the power of the administration was put behind Varnum in his election to the speakership in the Tenth Congress by one vote. His speakership occurred "in an epoch of commanding mediocrity" (Fuller, *post,* p. 30), and he was reëlected in the Eleventh Congress. A very important adjustment made in his term of office was that of limitation of debate in the House. The speaker, unfortunately for his own standing at home, attached his signature to the Embargo act and brought down upon his head accusations of subserviency to the administration and the South by the New England Federalists (*Salem Gazette,* Jan. 12, 1810). In 1809 he was nominated by the Republicans for lieutenant-governor of Massachusetts, but was defeated.

In 1810, the Massachusetts legislature, deadlocked for several days, finally chose Varnum senator to succeed Timothy Pickering [*q.v.*]. He took his seat in March 1811 and before long was accused by his opponents, and probably justly, of conspiring with the southwestern "war hawks" to bring on the war of 1812. After the declaration of war he and several Democratic representatives were mobbed in Boston (*Boston Gazette,* July 12, 1812). He remained the stanchest New England supporter of "Mr. Madison's war." In 1813 he was president *pro tempore* of the Senate and acting vice-president of the United States. He ran for governor of Massachusetts on a "win the war" platform in 1813, but was badly defeated by Caleb Strong [*q.v.*]. In 1814 he spoke at length in the Senate against Giles's bill for an army of 80,000 men. "The justice of Varnum's criticism could not fairly be questioned," says Henry Adams (*History of the United States,* vol. VIII, 1891, p. 109). At that date he was the only New England war man in Congress.

Still a useful legislator, Varnum served in the Senate until 1817, when he was succeeded by Harrison Gray Otis, 1765–1848 [q.v.]. He re-entered the Massachusetts Senate where he opposed the separation of Maine from Massachusetts. He was a delegate to the state convention to amend the constitution in 1820. Despite his record as a militarist he became a pioneer member of the Massachusetts Peace Society, the predecessor of the American Peace Society. Late in life he revolted from the established Congregational Church and joined the Baptists. He was buried without pomp or ceremony in the Varnum Cemetery at Dracut. He was the author of *An Address Delivered to the Third Division of Massachusetts Militia, at a Revue, in the Plains of Concord*..., printed by William Hilliard in 1800.

[Biography compiled by F. W. Coburn, *Courier-Citizen* (Lowell, Mass.), Aug. 1–Oct. 31, 1933; manuscript "Book of Third Division of the Militia of Mass.," owned by the Town of Dracut; J. M. Varnum, *The Varnums of Dracutt in Mass.* (1907); "Autobiography of General Joseph B. Varnum," *Mag. of Am. Hist.*, Nov. 1888; *Biog. Dir. Am. Cong.* (1928); H. B. Fuller, *The Speakers of the House* (1909); D. S. Alexander, *Hist. and Procedure of the House of Rep.* (1916); Henry Wilson, *Hist. of the Rise and Fall of the Slave Power in America* (1872), vol. I; *Columbian Centinel* (Boston, Mass.), Sept. 15, 1821.]   F. W. C.

VASEY, GEORGE (Feb. 28, 1822–Mar. 4, 1893), botanist, was born near Scarborough, England, of English parents, who removed the year following to Central New York, settling at Oriskany. He was the fourth of ten children and, the family being in humble circumstances, had to quit school at twelve to work in a village store. Already deeply interested in plants, he devoted his spare time to their analysis and was fortunate in making the acquaintance of Dr. P. D. Knieskern, under whose stimulating guidance he became familiar with the rich local flora and was put in touch with John Torrey [q.v.], Asa Gray [q.v.], and other botanists. After graduation from the Oneida Institute he began the study of medicine at the age of twenty-one, attending the Berkshire Medical Institute, Pittsfield, Mass. Toward the last of the year 1846 he married a Miss Scott, of Oriskany, and began the practice of medicine at Dexter, N. Y. In 1848 he removed to northern Illinois, where, at Elgin and Ringwood, he spent eighteen years in professional practice. During this period he continued his botanical studies, collected extensively the unspoiled prairie flora of the region, and extended widely his botanical contacts through correspondence. He helped organize the Illinois Natural History Society and was its first president. Early in 1866 his wife's failing health led him to remove to the southern part of the state, where, however, she soon died. Late in 1867 he married Mrs. John W. Cameron, daughter of Dr. Isaac Barber, of New York.

Fortunately there now came to Vasey the opportunity of devoting himself wholly to botanical pursuits. In the latter half of 1868 he accompanied his friend Maj. John Wesley Powell [q.v.] on an exploring expedition to Colorado, as botanist. Shortly after his return he was made curator of the natural history museum of the State Normal University of Illinois, and in 1870 was associated with Prof. Charles V. Riley [q.v.] in the editorship of the *American Entomologist and Botanist*. On Apr. 1, 1872, he was appointed botanist of the United States Department of Agriculture, in Washington, D. C., and put in charge of the United States National Herbarium, which had been transferred from the Smithsonian Institution in 1868. Up to this time Vasey had published little, and that of a popular nature. The task of organizing thoroughly the National Herbarium, of identifying and arranging the material that had long accumulated, largely from voyages and transcontinental railroad surveys under government auspices, was a difficult undertaking which occupied him closely for several years and was carried through with notable success. His next work of general interest was the preparation of an exhibit of the woods of American forest trees, accompanied by herbarium specimens, for the Centennial Exhibition in Philadelphia. As a guide to this exhibit he published *A Catalogue of the Forest Trees of the United States Which Usually Attain a Height of Sixteen Feet or More* (1876). But grasses now claimed his attention and upon this difficult group, in which he became a distinguished specialist, he published voluminously to the end of his life. Besides papers describing new genera and species from all parts of the United States, his more important publications are: *Agricultural Grasses of the United States* (1884); *A Descriptive Catalogue of the Grasses of the United States* (1885); *Grasses of the Southwest* (2 vols. in 1, 1890–91) and *Grasses of the Pacific Slope* (2 vols. in 1, 1892–93), published also under the title: *Illustrations of North American Grasses* (2 vols., 1891–93); and *Monograph of the Grasses of the United States and British America* (1892). Under his direction, also, experimental studies of grasses and other forage plants suited to arid regions of the West were initiated.

Of gentle dignity and kindly disposition, Vasey was beloved by a wide circle of friends. He died at his home in Washington from acute peritonitis, survived by his wife and six children.

[F. V. Coville, in *Bull. Torrey Bot. Club*, XX, 218–20 (May 10, 1893); W. M. Canby and J. N. Rose, in *Bot. Gaz.*, XVIII, 170–83, with portr. (May 1893); William Frear, in *Agric. Science*, VII, 249–52, with portr. (June 1893); B. L. Robinson, in *Proc. Am. Acad. Arts and Sci.*, XXVIII, 401–03 (1893); *Evening Star* (Washington, D. C.), Mar. 6, 1893; also official sources.]   W. R. M.

VASSALL, JOHN (1625–July ? 1688), colonial entrepreneur, was born in Stepney, Middlesex County, England, the son of William and Anne (King) Vassall and the grandson of John Vassall. His grandfather, probably a religious refugee from France, attained position and security in England, fitted out and commanded two ships against the Spanish Armada, and was later a member of the Virginia Company. His uncle and his father, Samuel and William, were both interested in American colonization, Samuel as a merchant trading extensively with the colonies and as an incorporator of the first Massachusetts company and patentee of large tracts of land, and William as an assistant in the company and an actual settler. In June 1635, at the age of ten, John sailed from England with his father and mother and his five sisters. The family settled first at Roxbury in Massachusetts and the next year at Scituate in the colony of New Plymouth. His father, by reason of his wealth and ability, became influential in both colonies and was involved in the effort to obtain more liberal qualifications for the electorate. In 1646 he returned to England. Two years later he went to Barbados, acquired extensive land holdings, and died there in 1655.

John Vassall remained in Scituate, where he was a member of the militia in 1633 and lieutenant under Cudworth in 1652. He became a captain and later, in Jamaica, was spoken of as "colonel." When Charles II granted Carolina to the Lords Proprietors he, with Henry Vassall, a cousin in London, and some other adventurers proposed to the Lords Proprietors to found a colony. Early in the summer of 1664 the settlers arrived at Cape Fear in what is now the state of North Carolina, and on Nov. 24, 1664, he was appointed surveyor general. He was the leading promoter of the enterprise in the colony, and Henry Vassall was the London agent. Holding out as inducements the promise of land, freedom of religion, and the right to vote, they encouraged settlers from New England, the West Indies, and Europe to join them, but the colony was unsuccessful. In these circumstances he wrote to John Leverett, 1616–1679 [q.v.], asking for aid; and in May 1667 the colony of Massachusetts Bay voted to send relief to Cape Fear. On Oct. 6 of that year he was at Nansemond in Virginia and wrote to Sir John Colleton of the breaking up of this Clarendon County settlement. He seems to have remained there some time trying to obtain redress of grievances against the Lords Proprietors. On Mar. 2, 1672, he was reported as having arrived in Jamaica, where he settled in St. Elizabeth's Parish with his wife, Anne (Lewis) Vassall. He maintained his connections with the mainland colonies throughout his life, interested in the carrying trade among them, the West Indies, and Europe. By his will, proved in Jamaica on July 6, 1688, he provided for the education of his son Samuel at Harvard College. Another son, Leonard, lived most of his life in Boston and died there. His great-grandson, John Vassall, built the "Craigie-Longfellow" house in Cambridge and was living there when the Revolution broke out. He, a Loyalist like many others of the family, went to England.

The vast family estates in the United States were confiscated, and the family name has left no mark on later republican history. Some of John Vassall's fortune, however, was inherited by Elizabeth Vassall Fox, a great-great-granddaughter, the wife of the third Lord Holland, who became a political hostess in London and made "Holland House" the center for the Whig party that was to revolutionize England's own political and social system.

[Samuel Deane, *Hist. Scituate, Mass.* (1831), pp. 366–70; James Sprunt, *Chronicles of the Cape Fear River* (1914); *Mass. Hist. Soc. Colls.*, 2 ser., vol. IV (1816) and 3 ser., vol. VIII (1843), p. 267; *New England Hist. and Geneal. Register*, Jan. 1863; *The Colonial Records of N. C.*, I (1886); *Records of the . . . Mass. Bay*, vol. IV, pt. 2 (1854), ed. by N. B. Shurtleff; *Great Britain Public Record Office. Calendar of State Papers, Colonial Series. Am. and West Ind., 1661–1668* (1880); *Ibid. . . . 1669–1674* (1889); *Ibid. . . . 1675–1676* with addenda (1893); *Ibid. . . . 1677–1680* (1896); Lib. of Cong. Transcripts of Public Record Office Papers, and British Museum Additional MSS.; C. M. Calder, *John Vassall and His Descendants* (1921); F. A. Crisp, *Visitation of England and Wales*, "Notes," vol. XIII (1919); C. K. Shipton, *Biog. Sketches of those who Attended Harvard College in the Classes 1690–1700* (1933); for members of family *Dict. Nat. Biog.* and Thomas Bridgman, *Memorials of . . . King's Chapel Burial Ground* (1853), with text of inscription on monument to Samuel Vassall (1586–1667), which implies incorrectly that the later Vassalls in America were descended from Samuel rather than from his brother William.]   K. E. C.

VASSAR, MATTHEW (Apr. 29, 1792–June 23, 1868), brewer and merchant, founder of Vassar College, was born at East Tuddingham, County of Norfolk, England. According to family tradition, the name was originally spelled Vasseur and the great-grandfather was a French refugee. James Vassar, Matthew Vassar's father, and his wife, Anne (Bennett) Vassar, and his brother Thomas, emigrated to America and settled in Dutchess County, N. Y., in 1796. Finding the local barley did not brew good ale, the brother Thomas returned to Norfolk and obtained English barley-corn for American planting. From this time, the brewing improved, and soon the family moved in from the countryside to the brewery in Poughkeepsie. The boy Matthew ran away from home at the age of thirteen and earned his own way for three years at a farm and country store, and then returned to Poughkeepsie in 1808. On Mar. 7, 1813, he was married to Catherine Valentine, who died in 1863, leaving no children. In 1811 the brewery was burned, and Matthew began an independent brewing business. In addition to his brewery, he engaged in other enterprises, and financed his nephew in the colonization of land in central Michigan. This resulted in the founding of the town of Vassar, named after him. Another venture was a whaling industry. He owned a whaling dock in Poughkeepsie and was part-owner of a whaling fleet. In 1845 he went to Europe, and, in his autobiography, he stated that he visited Guy's Hospital in London, "the founder of which a family relative," and "seeing this Institution first suggested the idea of devoting a portion of my Estate to some Charitable purpose" (*post,* p. 33). His niece, Lydia Booth, was the proprietress of a school for girls in Poughkeepsie, which was later sold to Milo P. Jewett [*q.v.*]. The business of the purchase brought Jewett in contact with Vassar; and the plan of a college for women was the result. Vassar's earlier intention had been the founding of a hospital, later realized by the gift of his two nephews in 1882 to Vassar Brothers Hospital.

His native prudence and sagacity stood him in good stead in the founding of his college, but it is curious to observe that his plans for the intellectual program of his college were better laid than those for its material welfare. The enormous building that he erected in 1861–65 was ill-suited to a woman's college; but the program of studies under the first active president, John Howard Raymond [*q.v.*], was fully abreast of the times and challenged comparison with the best colleges for men. Throughout the four years, 1861–65, Vassar advertised his venture extensively; and the result was an enrollment that crowded his building to capacity from the start and produced a worldwide interest in the venture. A number of women's colleges had been founded before 1865, and several coeducational institutions were open, but Vassar's advertising first brought the idea of higher education for women forcibly to the attention of the modern world, and within ten years the battle had been fought and won. It was proved that mental activity in the abstruse branches of learning did not injure woman's health, and that there were many women eager for intellectual life. The English colleges for women and many other colleges in America were the result of this demonstration. Coeducation soon became the practice from coast to coast in state-supported institutions. The opening of universities on the European continent followed not long afterward.

Vassar's early board of trustees included Samuel F. B. Morse and Henry Ward Beecher, and his correspondence on education with such men as Henry Barnard was voluminous. His private library shows that he also owned works by Herbert Spencer and John Stuart Mill. Indeed, his thought ran ahead of his day; and he was less interested in demonstrating that woman's mind was equal to man's than he was in developing a curriculum suited to the needs of women in the modern world. His hopes in this direction were frustrated by the apparent necessity of the demonstration of mental equality; and the curricula of the early women's colleges therefore closely resembled those for men. His belief in woman's suffrage and his faith in woman's capacity, however, strongly affected the life of the early students. The development of the social sciences and the application of studies to American life led many early graduates into fields of social work. He never had any formal schooling. His turns of speech and poor spelling, together with his occupation as a brewer, developed a misunderstanding of the real genius of the man. This has since been corrected by the publication of his autobiography and letters, and by other records continually coming to light showing his broad vision and steady faith in his enterprise. Many of his sayings stamp him as one of the genuinely original Americans in the second half-century of the republic. He died of a heart seizure, while reading his letter of resignation from the board of trustees at the college. His gifts during his life to the institution amounted to over $800,000. His two nephews, whom he had interested in the venture, increased this to a million and a quarter by their gifts.

[*The Autobiog. and Letters of Matthew Vassar* (1916), ed. by E. H. Haight; J. M. Taylor and E. H. Haight, *Vassar* (1915); MSS., records, maps, etc., in the possession of Vassar College.]   H. N. M.

VATTEMARE, NICOLAS MARIE ALEXANDRE (Nov. 8, 1796–Apr. 7, 1864), founder of a system of international exchanges, ventriloquist, and impersonator, was born in Paris, the son of an advocate. He spent brief periods in a seminary and in a hospital as a student. In Germany, where he had been sent in 1814 with a group of Prussian prisoners, he began the use of his natural gift of ventriloquism and as "Monsieur Alexandre" soon became one of the popular entertainers of the day. He appeared in London in 1822 under the management of W. T. Moncrieff, in whose *Rogueries of Nicholas* he was a great success. His brief appearance in the United States began at the Park Theatre in New York City, Oct. 28, 1839.

Impressed by the number of duplicate books and art objects in libraries and museums which he visited, he had evolved the idea of a system of exchange and had won some support for it in Europe. Early in 1840 he sent Congress a memorial on the subject which received favorable action (*House Doc. 50, 26* Cong., 1 Sess.). Traveling extensively in the United States and Canada, he enlisted the sympathy and aid of prominent people, and returned to France in 1841 with many items for exchange. The expansion of his system and the development of an agency for handling exchanges occupied him until his return to America in 1847. His second memorial to Congress (*Sen. Miscellaneous Doc. 46, 30* Cong., 1 Sess.) and various appeals to state legislatures resulted in his appointment as agent by Congress and a few states to handle their exchanges, and in the granting of some financial aid. After his return to France in 1850, his system continued to flourish for a few years, but it gradually declined in popularity, support was withdrawn, and Vattemare's hope of its permanent establishment failed. Whatever success he attained was due largely to the cooperation given him in America. He seems to have been temperamentally unsuited to carrying out some of his own ideas, which, indeed, were better suited to be the work of an institution than of one man. Some of his suggestions seem impracticable and naïve (see *Proceedings of a Meeting of Citizens of the City of Albany Held Nov. 27, 1847,* 1849, p. 12), but he was interested in moral and social effects as well as in the exchange of material things. In his *Report on the Subject of International Exchanges* (1848), one of his numerous publications, he points out the value of such exchanges in lessening national prejudices and developing good will. He lost no opportunity to urge the establishment of free libraries and museums. It is generally conceded that he was largely instrumental in the founding of the Boston Public Library (H. G. Wadlin, *The Public Library of the City of Boston,* 1911, pp. 1–8, 17–19). He was also responsible for what was known as the American Library in Paris, a collection of American books and documents housed in the Hôtel de Ville, which has since been lost. Evidence that Vattemare count-

ed among his friends many prominent people is to be found in his *Album Cosmopolite* (1837), a collection of letters, miscellaneous autographs, and reproductions. He was a chevalier of the *Légion d'honneur.* The elder of his two sons, Hippolyte, and his son-in-law, C. Moreau, were associated with him in the work of his agency. He died in Paris.

[Vattemare's first name sometimes appears as Nicholas. The chief biog. sources are Hippolyte Vattemare, "Notices of the Life of Alexander Vattemare," *Hist. Mag.,* Dec. 1868; *Memoirs and Anecdotes of Monsieur Alexandre* (1822); J. P. Quincy, in *Proc. Mass. Hist. Soc.,* 2 ser., vol. I (1885); "Strange Career of an Artist," in *Hours at Home,* Oct. 1868; Alphonse Passier, *Les Échanges Internationaux Littéraires et Scientifiques, Leur Histoire . . . 1832–1880* (1880); W. B. Trask, in *New-Eng. Hist. and Geneal. Reg.,* Oct. 1865, pp. 367–69; Elizabeth M. Richards, "Alexandre Vattemare and His System of International Exchanges," 1934, thesis, Columbia Univ.; obituaries in *La Siècle* (Paris), Apr. 11, and *Le Constitutionnel* (Paris), Apr. 12, 1864. Vattemare's papers and records of his agency are in the N. Y. Pub. Lib.; other MSS. are in the Boston Pub. Lib.]   E. M. R.

VAUDREUIL–CAVAGNAL, PIERRE DE RIGAUD, Marquis de (1704–Aug. 4, 1778), the last French governor of Canada, was a native of that colony, third son of Philippe Rigaud, Marquis de Vaudreuil, likewise governor (1703–25), and of Louise Elisabeth de Joybert. As governor's son Pierre was brought up in mild luxury and early entered the army, rising in 1726 to the rank of major. Two years later he accompanied the expedition of the Sieur de Lignery against the Fox Indians in what is now Wisconsin. Then known as the Sieur de Cavagnal, he appears to have acted as commissary and was sent to announce the news of the failure of the expedition to the governor (*Collections of the State Historical Society of Wisconsin,* vol. XVII, 1906, p. 31). In 1730 young Vaudreuil was awarded the cross of the order of St. Louis, the most coveted honor in the army, and in 1733 was appointed governor of Trois Rivières, the third largest settlement in New France. Ten years later he was chosen for the governorship of the colony of Louisiana, succeeding Jean Baptiste Le Moyne, Sieur de Bienville [*q.v.*], and arriving at New Orleans early in 1743. His appointment pleased the colonists, for he had a hereditary reputation for liberality and kindness. His administration did not belie his name; he held a small court, noted for its brilliancy; his good breeding and geniality pleased the populace, and his administration of ten years was so successful that it was long remembered. He carried through one Indian expedition against the Chickasaw, but he had no large problems to meet and left New Orleans in May 1753 on receipt of the news of his promotion to the governorship of Canada. The annals and official papers of Vaudreuil's administration of Louisiana were captured by the British somewhere on the high seas during the transport between Louisiana and France.

After a sojourn at Paris and the court of Versailles, Vaudreuil was commissioned governor of New France, where he arrived on June 23, 1755, to take up the duties of his office. He found the colony on the brink of war with England. On his arrival he was received with pleasure both by the colonists, the tribesmen, and the French officers. He was a native Canadian, had had a successful experience as governor of Louisiana, and it was anticipated that his defense of Canada would prove notable. Notable it was, but not in the expected ways. Vaudreuil had an exaggerated opinion of his military prowess; he was weak and vacillating, and allowed himself to be drawn into the corrupt ring that surrounded the intendant Bigot. He refused to support the plans of Montcalm, who was sent to conduct the war for France; he is even held responsible for the defeat on the Plains of Abraham, Sept. 13, 1759, since he countermanded Montcalm's order for a guard to prevent the English approach. After the death of Montcalm, Vaudreuil retreated to Montreal, where the following summer he was besieged and on Sept. 8, 1760, capitulated. By this last act as governor Vaudreuil ruined the French cause in Canada. He withdrew to France, arriving in December 1760, and soon after was arrested and thrown into the Bastille. At his trial the next year he was acquitted of dishonesty, although his reputation for intelligence suffered. He was granted a pension and continued to live in Paris, a lonely, discredited figure, until his death. The marquise, older than he, died in 1764; they had no children, but collateral descendants preserved his memory and his portraits. His papers were burned in 1870 to keep them from falling into the hands of the invading Germans.

The almost unanimous testimony of historians of the time is that Vaudreuil was contributory to the fall of New France; that he was jealous of better soldiers than himself; that he talked more than was prudent; and that, while not actually dishonest, he granted monopolies to his relatives and failed to check the corruption that went on around him. His officers said, "The Marquis de Vaudreuil has sold the country" (Doughty, *post*, III, 306). His chief virtue was his patriotic devotion to his native land, and his championship of Canadians and Indian allies in the last days of the rule of France in America.

[For the date of death, see *Report Concerning Canadian Archives . . . 1905* (1906), vol. I, p. 434. See also Charles Gayarré, *Hist. of La.* (1903), vol. II, pp. 17–35; G. M. Wrong, *The Rise and Fall of New France* (1928), vol. II; A. G. Doughty, *The Siege of Quebec* (6 vols., Quebec, 1901), which contains a number of Vaudreuil's letters; Francis Parkman, *Montcalm and Wolfe* (1884), vol. I, p. 366; Adam Shortt, ed., *Docs. Relating to Canadian Currency . . . during the French Period* (1925), vol. II, pp. 831–35, n. Vaudreuil's Louisiana papers are among the Loudoun papers in the Huntington Lib., San Marino, Cal.]   L. P. K.

VAUGHAN, BENJAMIN (Apr. 30, 1751–Dec. 8, 1835), diplomat, political economist, and agriculturist, was born in Jamaica, the eldest of eleven children of Samuel Vaughan, a London merchant, and Sarah, daughter of Benjamin Hallowell of Boston. He was sent to Newcome's school at Hackney, and then, with his brother William, was placed under the care of Joseph Priestley [*q.v.*] in the Dissenters' Academy at Warrington. He next studied at Cambridge, though his Unitarian principles disqualified him for formal matriculation and a degree, and then proceeded to study law in the Inner Temple.

During the period of the American Revolution, Vaughan engaged in propagandist activities for the Americans. Politically he was drawn to the Earl of Shelburne, who frequently employed him in confidential matters. From 1776 to 1779 he collected and edited, with Franklin's assistance, the *Political, Miscellaneous and Philosophical Pieces . . . Written by Benj. Franklin* (London, 1779). Vaughan's edition is particularly valuable; not only are his notes prime source material, but it "is the only edition of Franklin's writings (other than his scientific) which was printed during his lifetime . . . and contains an 'errata' made by him for it" (P. L. Ford, *Franklin Bibliography*, 1889, p. 161). In 1780–81 Vaughan studied medicine in Edinburgh, where he made friends with Adam Smith and Dugald Stewart. Family tradition states that he turned to medicine to win his wife, Sarah Manning, whom he married June 30, 1781, for her father, William Manning, a prominent London merchant, refused his consent until Vaughan could earn a living. Instead of practising medicine, however, Vaughan became a partner in his father-in-law's business.

Vaughan's most important work was done in connection with the Anglo-American peace negotiations of 1782. In March, when the Whigs came into power, he suggested Richard Oswald to Shelburne as a fitter person to negotiate with the Americans for "a permanent and affectionate peace" than the "bargaining" diplomats and in July was himself sent to Paris to counteract Charles James Fox's false declaration that the government was insincere. Vaughan was uniquely fitted for this mission; he knew Shelburne intimately, was a close friend of Franklin, and was connected with Henry Laurens [*q.v.*] by marriage. In September John Jay [*q.v.*] prevailed upon him to return to London as a counteragent to Rayneval, whom Jay believed to be sacrificing American to French and Spanish interests. Vaughan's services in promoting confidence between the American commissioners and Shelburne and in reconciling conflicting opinions were valuable, but the unofficial nature and the delicacy of these services precluded any answer to Fox's charges of "a secret agent" and double dealing.

During the next decade Vaughan was busily occupied with political matters and the doctrine of free trade. In 1789 he published *A Treatise on International Trade*. He was ardently sympathetic with the French Revolution and contributed to the *Morning Chronicle,* under the *nom-de-plume* of "A Calm Observer," a series of letters on the dangers of the Russo-Prusso-Austrian alliance. These appeared in book form as *Letters on the Subject of the Concert of Princes and the Dismemberment of Poland and France* (London, 1793). In 1792 he entered Parliament for Calne, but apparently spoke only on Wilberforce's annual bills for the abolition of the slave trade. His English career was abruptly terminated by his flight to France in consequence of an investigation by the Cabinet of the activities of Revolutionary enthusiasts in England (May 8, 1794). In Paris he was imprisoned at the Carmelite Monastery, but owing, probably, to the good offices of Robespierre, he was released after a month and retired to Switzerland.

In 1796 he followed his family and brothers, one of whom was Charles Vaughan [*q.v.*], to America and settled on the family lands at Hallowell, Me. He retired from active politics, but corresponded with the first six Presidents and in 1828 forwarded to John Quincy Adams copies of his papers relative to the definition of the Maine boundary in 1782–83. He did much quietly for his adopted country. He belonged to many scientific and literary societies, was one of the founders of the Maine Historical Society, and carried on numerous experiments in agriculture, reports on some of which he communicated to the Massachusetts Agricultural Society under the signature of "A Kennebec Farmer." Harvard bestowed the degree of LL.D. on him in 1807 and Bowdoin in 1812. His library, said to have been the largest in New England with the exception of Harvard's, was divided, portions going to Harvard, Bowdoin, and the Augusta Insane Hospital. Besides the above-mentioned

books, Vaughan published a second collection of Franklin's works in London, 1793, and assisted Marshall in the 1806 edition. In 1800 he produced *The Rural Socrates or an Account of a Celebrated Philosophical Farmer Lately Living in Switzerland and Known by the Name of Kliyogg,* an enlarged and emended edition of Arthur Young's translation of the work of Hans Kaspar Hirzel. Letters to his brother, John Vaughan, were read before the American Philosophical Society in 1825, and published under the title "On the Grous of North America," in *Early Proceedings of the American Philosophical Society . . . 1744 to 1838* (1884). The copy in the Huntington Library of *An Abridgement of the Second Edition of a Work, Written by Dr. Currie, of Liverpool in England, on the Use of Water in Diseases of the Human Frame . . . with Occasional Remarks* (Augusta, 1799), bears a manuscript note on the title-page, "By Benjamin Vaughan." Vaughan was extraordinarily modest. He never published anything under his own name and consequently much of his work remains unidentified.

One of his striking traits was his genius for friendship. He knew and corresponded with most of the eminent liberal thinkers of his time. Franklin undertook his autobiography at Vaughan's and Abel James's solicitation. Vaughan was a loved member of the group of radicals associated with Priestley, John Horne Tooke, Bentham, Romilly, and Dumont. John Adams even confided to him in 1783 his suspicions of Franklin's Gallophilism. He corresponded with Talleyrand and Robespierre, and was invited to attend the First Constitutional Assembly. Though a Federalist, he maintained a cordial correspondence with Jefferson. Vaughan's wife died in 1834, and his own death occurred in Hallowell the year following; they had three sons and four daughters.

[Vaughan requested that no biography of him be written. The most comprehensive account of his career is G. S. Rowell, "Benjamin Vaughan," *Mag. of Hist.,* Mar. 1916; see also William Vaughan, *Tracts on Docks and Commerce* (London, 1839); R. H. Gardiner, "Memoir of Benjamin Vaughan, M.D. and LL.D.," *Maine Hist. Soc. Colls.,* 1 ser., VI (1859); J. H. Sheppard, "Reminiscences and Geneal. of the Vaughan Family," *New England Hist. and Geneal. Reg.,* Oct. 1865; Wm. W. Vaughan, *Hallowell Memories* (1931); E. H. Nason, *Old Hallowell on the Kennebec* (1909); Nehemiah Cleaveland, *Hist. of Bowdoin Coll.* (1882); Lord Fitzmaurice, *Life of William, Earl of Shelburne,* vol. III (1876); *Papiers de Barthélemy* (6 vols., 1886–1910), vols. IV and V; H. C. Bolton, *Scientific Correspondence of Joseph Priestley* (1892); *Kennebec Journal* (Augusta, Me.), Dec. 16, 1835. Most of Vaughan's private letters to Shelburne are in the possession of the present Marquis of Lansdowne; some letters and many papers are in the Shelburne Papers in the William L. Clements Lib., Univ. of Mich.; of the MSS. left by Vaughan at his death many were destroyed by a fire in the house of his son-in-law; some are in the Pa. Hist. Soc., and others are in possession of the family. The Adams copies of Vaughan's papers on the peace negotiation of 1782–83 are still among the Adams Papers; nine of the letters in this lot were published in *Proc. Mass. Hist. Soc.*, 2 ser. XVII (1903).]

E. V.

VAUGHAN, CHARLES (June 30, 1759–May 15, 1839), merchant, promoter of attempts to develop the Kennebec Valley in Maine, was born in London, England. His father, Samuel Vaughan, was a prosperous London merchant interested in colonial trade; he owned a plantation in Jamaica and had dealings with Boston, where he met Sarah Hallowell, who became his wife. Charles, their son, was brought up on the Jamaican plantation, where his more celebrated brother Benjamin [q.v.] was born. Moving to New England in 1785, Charles spent the rest of his life there, marrying about 1790 in Boston, Frances Western Apthorp, whose sister had recently married Charles Bulfinch [q.v.]. The Vaughans had two sons and two daughters who survived childhood.

Soon after his arrival in New England Vaughan entered upon a long and prominent connection with the "Kennebec Purchase" in Maine. His maternal grandfather, Benjamin Hallowell, had been one of the "Proprietors of the Kennebec Purchase," popularly known as the "Plymouth Company," incorporated in 1753 to take over a region some thirty-one miles wide along the Kennebec, originally a grant to some of the Plymouth settlers. With over-optimistic zeal, Vaughan plunged into two costly developments. At Hallowell, just below Augusta, with a view to establishing a great center at the head of navigation of the Kennebec, he constructed houses, stores, and mills, set up a printing press, built one of the most up-to-date gristmills in the region and a brewery which, it is said, turned out a greater amount of malt liquor than any other in New England. More visionary was his effort to establish a seaport at Jones Eddy near the mouth of the Kennebec, four miles below Bath. He built wharves, warehouses, and a wet dock for masts, which were an important export; he also maintained an agent there to chart the port and transact the expected business. In 1790 he visited England to develop trade connections for his new enterprises. The Jones Eddy project was a complete failure, however. It had an excellent location, being much more accessible than Wiscasset on the Sheepscott, to which exports from the Kennebec had to be carried through a narrow river; but tradition proved stronger than geographical advantage. Wiscasset remained the chief port of the region until after 1812, and, in spite of Vaughan's efforts,

Bath rather than Jones Eddy became the official port of entry. Long before Vaughan's death, only the rotting wharves remained as relics of his venture.

Returning from England in 1791, he established himself as a merchant in Boston, sending Kennebec products on the first leg of the old triangle which included the West Indies and England. He was an incorporator of the Boston Library Society, the Massachusetts Society for Promoting Agriculture, the Massachusetts Society for the Aid of Immigrants, and of Hallowell Academy. In 1793, with Bulfinch and William Scollay, he was a promoter of Boston's first block of brick houses, the Franklin or Tontine Crescent. A year later he withdrew from the venture, and when it led to Bulfinch's bankruptcy in 1796 Bulfinch conveyed his equity to Vaughan (Bulfinch, *post*, p. 98; Place, *post*, pp. 56–59, 72). Two years later Vaughan himself was drawn into bankruptcy by his numerous ventures. His brother Benjamin, who had settled at Hallowell, bought in the ancestral lands on the Kennebec and Charles retained only his Hallowell house, to which he retired for the remainder of his life. He continued as agent for the non-resident owners in the Purchase, prosecuting squatters with a vigor that occasionally involved shooting. With his characteristic energy and enthusiasm he devoted himself to the development of Maine agriculture, and is credited with important developments in farming and stock-raising, through the importation and improvement of animals, seeds, and fruit trees. "Spared the pain of protracted weakness and infirmity," Vaughan died at eighty at Hallowell.

[*Me. Hist. Soc. Colls.*, 1 ser. II (1847), 291, IV (1856), 43–48, V (1857), 331, VI (1859), 89, VII (1876), 278–81, 286; 2 ser. IV (1893), 210; *New England Hist. and Geneal. Reg.*, Oct. 1865; James Sullivan, *The Hist. of the District of Me.* (1795); E. S. Bulfinch, *The Life and Letters of Charles Bulfinch* (1896); C. A. Place, *Charles Bulfinch, Architect and Citizen* (1925); W. W. Vaughan, *Hallowell Memories* (1931); William Vaughan, *Memoir of William Vaughan* (1839); *Boston Transcript*, May 20, 1839; *The Age* (Augusta, Me.), May 21, 1839.]

R. G. A.

VAUGHAN, DANIEL (*c.* 1818–Apr. 6, 1879), astronomer, mathematician, chemist, physiologist, was born at Glenomara, near Killaloe, County Clare, Ireland, one of several children of John Vaughan (or Vaughn). He was first taught by a private tutor and later attended Killaloe Classical Academy, under the care of his uncle Daniel, a priest. It was intended that he should study for the priesthood, but in 1840 he set out for the United States, where he looked for greater freedom in pursuit of studies involving the higher mathematics. He traveled in Virginia and other southern states, and in 1842 was engaged as tutor by a Colonel Stamp in Bourbon County, Ky. Soon a neighborhood school was arranged where the classics, physical geography, astronomy, geology, and advanced mathematics were taught. Stamp's large library was a great attraction to Vaughan, who later walked to Cincinnati, one hundred miles and back again, to obtain the newest scientific books. His own library, gathered from 1842 on, contained the works of Tycho Brahe, Kepler, Laplace, Humboldt, and other European scientists. He had decided linguistic ability, and, after tutoring for two or three years, he accepted the chair of Greek in a college at Bardstown, Ky., which gave him more time for his strictly scientific studies. In 1850 he removed to Cincinnati. There he lectured on chemistry at the Eclectic Medical Institute, and published an article on "Chemical Researches in Animal and Vegetable Physiology" in the *Eclectic Medical Journal* (December 1850). For a number of years he was much in demand as a lecturer on astronomy and other scientific subjects before teachers' institutes, schools, academies, and colleges in the surrounding region. He became a member of the American Association for the Advancement of Science in 1851, and prepared for it an article on "Chemical Action of Feeble Currents of Electricity" (*Proceedings,* vol. V, 1851) and one on "Solar Light" (*Ibid.,* vol. VI, 1852). His work in experimental physiology later brought him a fellowship in the Association.

In 1852, after seven months' study of the problem of the rings of Saturn, he wrote a paper on "The Stability of Satellites Revolving in Small Orbits" (*Ibid.,* vol. X, 1857); in discussing the disintegration of any near satellites by the tremendous tidal action of Saturn he anticipated by many years the demonstration made by J. E. Keeler [*q.v.*] of the nature of the rings of Saturn. In 1854 he published *The Destiny of the Solar System,* lectures delivered in Cincinnati, and wrote on "Researches in Meteoric Astronomy" (*Report . . . of the British Association for the Advancement of Science,* 1855). Six other papers, which led to much correspondence with European scientists, were published in the *London, Edinburgh, and Dublin Philosophical Magazine* between May 1858 and December 1861. In 1858 appeared *Popular Physical Astronomy,* a collection of his lectures, which reveals the high quality of his astronomical researches. From 1860 to 1872 he held the chair of chemistry at the Cincinnati College of Medicine and Surgery, reading a notable valedictory address at the time of his resignation. After this, for a time, he

continued to lecture in Kentucky. When he returned to Cincinnati, his meager income gave his friends anxiety, for he would not ask help. His writing brought him very little, and his lectures became less frequent. At last he disappeared and was forgotten. In April 1879 he was found prostrated by pulmonary hemorrhages and near death from starvation in a wretched tenement room. On Apr. 6, after receiving the last rites of the Roman Catholic Church, he died.

Vaughan was tall, slender, and fine-featured, and wore a long chin beard. Timid and never self-assertive, he was very gentle and patient in his scientific explanations. He never married. His room at the medical college was his laboratory, study, and living-room. A constant reader, he was a familiar figure at the public library on Vine Street, where he quietly sat and read, often with his woolen shawl about him. Since his death he has been almost forgotten, yet, without connection with observatories or astronomers, without a telescope, so far as is known, he grasped many of the profoundest problems of physical astronomy and through sheer mathematical genius was able to offer remarkably brilliant solutions.

[See Otto Juettner, *Daniel Drake and His Followers* (1909), with portrait; J. U. Lloyd, *Etidorpha* (7th ed., 1897), with portrait; *Pop. Sci. Monthly,* May, Aug., Nov. 1879; and obituary in *Cincinnati Commercial,* Apr. 7, 1879. There is a bronze bust of Vaughan in the Cincinnati Pub. Lib. on Vine St.] D–L. S.

VAUGHAN, VICTOR CLARENCE (Oct. 27, 1851–Nov. 21, 1929), biochemist, hygienist, medical teacher and administrator, investigator of disease, was born near Mount Airy, Randolph County, Mo., the eldest of five children of John and Adeline (Dameron) Vaughan. His paternal grandfather, Sampson Vaughan, emigrated from Wales to North Carolina about 1810; his maternal forebears were of the Du Puy and Dameron families of Virginia. In 1872 Vaughan received the degree of B.S. from Mount Pleasant College, Huntsville, Mo., where he was student-instructor in Latin and chemistry. After two more years of teaching at Mount Pleasant, he went to the University of Michigan. There in 1875 he received the degree of M.S.; in 1876, that of Ph.D.; and in 1878, that of M.D. In the meantime he lectured to medical students on physiological chemistry (1875–83). On Aug. 16, 1877, he married a childhood friend, Dora Catherine Taylor; he and his wife had five sons, four of whom became physicians. His positions at Michigan included those of professor of physiological chemistry, and associate professor of therapeutics and materia medica (1883–87), director of the hygienic laboratory (1887–1909), professor of hygiene and physiological chemistry (1887–1921), and dean of the medical school (1891–1921). As a junior member of the faculty of the medical school he initiated a policy of strengthening its personnel through additions determined solely by merit; later he was largely responsible for increases in the length of the medical course and in requirements for entrance; when he became dean in 1891 he not only built up what was perhaps the ablest faculty in the country but secured increased clinical facilities, developed the medical library, and gave vigorous encouragement to graduate work. As a result of his efforts the medical school at Michigan had a prominent place in the national movement to elevate and standardize American medical education about the beginning of the twentieth century.

As late as 1880 Vaughan discredited the ubiquity of bacterial agents as causes of infectious disease. In 1888, however, he and F. G. Novy went to Berlin to study bacteriology and hygiene in the laboratory of Robert Koch. They returned within the year to preside over the first laboratory in the United States for the systematic teaching of bacteriology to students and physicians. There Vaughan and successive groups of carefully chosen assistants investigated the bacteriology and treatment of tuberculosis, typhoid fever, and summer diarrhoea. Vaughan published much on disease that was provocative of thought, but even more important than his own discoveries was the stimulus his teaching and example provided many younger workers. His work upon ptomaines with Novy led to biochemical investigations of food poisons and had a beneficial effect upon the development of methods of food preservation. Their *Cellular Toxins* (1902) was preceded by three expanding editions of a book on ptomaines, leucomaines, and bacterial proteins. Vaughan's *Protein Split Products* (1913), written with two of his sons, contains valuable ideas upon protein fever; it was followed by *Infection and Immunity* (1915) and *Protein Poisons* (1917), the Herter lectures for 1916. Vaughan early developed the interest in public health and in popular education in preventive medicine for which he is best known. For many years he was an active member of the Michigan state board of health (1883–95, 1901–18); in 1885 he received one of the Lomb prizes for his *Healthy Homes and Foods for the Working Classes* (1886); and under the supervision of George Miller Sternberg [*q.v.*] of the American Public Health Association he carried on experimental work on disinfectants. In 1898, when he served as a major in the Spanish-American War, he was appointed a member of the com-

mission headed by Walter Reed [*q.v.*] to study the cause and prevention of typhoid fever, then epidemic in military camps. After the death of the two other members of the commission, it fell to Vaughan to complete the classic *Report on the Origin and Spread of Typhoid Fever in the U. S. Military Camps* (2 vols., 1904). Some years later, with H. F. Vaughan and G. T. Palmer, he published *Epidemiology and Public Health* (2 vols., 1922–23).

He published several other books and upwards of two hundred articles, carried on private practice for many years, became a medico-legal expert in toxicology with a national reputation, and was the founder of *Physician and Surgeon* (1879), of which he was managing editor for some time, and the *Journal of Laboratory and Clinical Medicine* (1915). He was president of the American Medical Association (1914–15) and of the American Tuberculosis Association (1920), and a member of numerous scientific and other learned societies in the United States and abroad. In 1921–22 and 1925–26 he was chairman of the division of medical sciences of the National Research Council. Throughout the World War he served in the office of the surgeon-general and on the executive committee of the general medical board of the Council of National Defense, rising to the rank of colonel. He later received a Distinguished Service Medal for his work in epidemiology and was made knight of the Legion of Honor by the French government. He was a tireless worker, placid, genial, and unhurried, but capable of an incisive and indomitable opposition when obstruction threatened what seemed the true road of progress. With students his popularity was great and his influence immense. His informal autobiography, *A Doctor's Memories* (1926), gives a vivid and pleasing picture of a man whose honesty and sincerity won confidence and friendship wherever he went. He died in Richmond, Va., where he had been living for two years.

[In addition to Vaughan's *A Doctor's Memories* (1926), see *Who's Who in America,* 1928–29; *Cat. of Grads. . . . Univ. of Mich.* (1923); *Jour. of Laboratory and Clinical Medicine,* June 1930, a memorial number with a full bibliog.; *Am. Men of Sci.* (4th ed., 1927), ed. by J. M. and Jaques Cattell; C. H. McIntyre, in *Builders of Am. Medicine* (1932); obituary in *Richmond Times-Dispatch,* Nov. 22, 1929.]   H. S—l.

VAUX, CALVERT (Dec. 20, 1824–Nov. 19, 1895), landscape architect, was born in London, England, the son of Dr. Calvert Bowyer and Emily (Brickwood) Vaux. Having received his early education at the Merchant Taylors' School in London, to which he was admitted in December 1833, he entered the office of Lewis N. Cottingham, a well-known architect of the time, as an articled pupil. In the summer of 1850 Andrew Jackson Downing [*q.v.*] visited England for the purpose of securing the services of a trained architect to assist him in his growing practice and chose Vaux (see A. J. Downing, *Rural Essays,* 1853, p. xlvi). Until Downing's untimely death in 1852 Vaux worked with him at their joint office at Newburgh on the Hudson, and assisted in the design of the grounds about the Capitol and the Smithsonian Institution at Washington. About 1857 he removed to New York City, where he lived for the rest of his life. In the same year he published his only book, *Villas and Cottages: a Series of Designs Prepared for Execution in the United States,* which contains a record of his early architectural work. It was revised in 1864 and reprinted in 1867.

In 1857, in collaboration with Frederick Law Olmsted [*q.v.*], Vaux submitted a design for Central Park, New York. Upon the acceptance of their plan, submitted under the signature of "Greensward," the two were put in charge of its execution, Olmsted as architect in chief, and Vaux as consulting architect. (A full account of their difficulties is to be found in Olmsted and Kimball, *post,* vol. II). For a number of years the two were associated in private practice, Vaux supplying the knowledge of architecture which Olmsted lacked. Their work includes Prospect Park in Brooklyn, Morningside Park and Riverside Park in New York City, the South Park in Chicago, the state reservation at Niagara Falls, and a suburban village at Riverside, near Chicago. For many years Vaux was landscape architect to the department of public parks of New York City (1881–83, 1888–95). It has been said of him that nothing "could have induced him to degrade his art or misuse the reputation which secured his employment, by consenting to modify his criticism, or give the sanction of his name to a plan he could not approve. He was a modest and unassuming gentleman, a most genial companion, a loyal and incorruptible public servant . . ." (Howland, *post,* p. 19). On Nov. 19, 1895, he was drowned in Gravesend Bay. He was survived by two sons and two daughters. His wife, Mary Swan McEntee, daughter of James S. McEntee of Rondout, N. Y., whom he married on May 4, 1854, died in 1892.

[C. J. Robinson, ed., *A Reg. of the Scholars . . . Merchant Taylors' School . . . 1562 to 1874,* vol. II (1883), p. 256; F. L. Olmsted, Jr., and Theodora Kimball, eds., *Frederick Law Olmsted* (2 vols., 1922–28); *Memories of Samuel Parsons,* ed. by Mabel Parsons; Samuel Parsons, Jr., in *Trans. Am. Soc. Landscape Architects . . . 1908* (n.d.); E. H. Hall, in *Sixteenth Ann. Report . . . Am. Scenic and Hist. Preservation Soc.* (1911); "Calvert Vaux, Designer of Parks," *Park International,* Sept. 1920. H. E. Howland, in *Reports . . . of the Century Asso. for the Year 1895* (1896);

obituaries in *Garden and Forest,* Nov. 27, *Evening Post* (N. Y.), Nov. 21, and *N. Y. Tribune,* Nov. 22, 1895; unpub. data in the possession of Vaux's daughter, Mrs. G. L. Hendrickson.]

K. McN.

VAUX, RICHARD (Dec. 19, 1816–Mar. 22, 1895), lawyer, public official, penologist, was born in Philadelphia, Pa., the son of Roberts [*q.v.*] and Margaret (Wistar) Vaux. He received his early education at the Friends' Select School and under private tutors. After studying in the office of William Morris Meredith [*q.v.*], secretary of the treasury under Zachary Taylor, he was admitted to the bar, Apr. 15, 1837, at the age of twenty. Shortly thereafter he went abroad and carried with him dispatches from the American minister in London, Andrew Stevenson [*q.v.*]. Vaux remained in London for a year, serving meanwhile as secretary of the legation *ad interim,* and later as private secretary to the minister. He was not inclined to enter upon a diplomatic career, however, although the opportunity presented itself.

Returning to Philadelphia in 1839, he found that he had been nominated by the Democrats for a seat in the Pennsylvania House of Representatives. Although he failed of election, this event marked the beginning of a long political career, during which he held both local and federal offices. In 1840 he was a delegate to the Democratic state convention and in 1842 he lost the election for mayor of Philadelphia by a few hundred votes. He was appointed an inspector of the Eastern Penitentiary and a member of the board of controllers of the city public schools. From 1841 to 1847 he served as Recorder, a judicial office, and during his incumbency none of his decisions was reversed on appeal. After two more defeats as a candidate for mayor, 1845 and 1854, he was finally elected in 1856. He immediately undertook administrative reorganization and helped to make the changes necessitated by the consolidation of the city in 1854. In 1859 he became a member of the board of directors of Girard College and from 1862 to 1865 served as president of the board. During this period he was instrumental in introducing vocational and technological training into the college curriculum. In 1872 he was defeated for congressman-at-large. Years later, however, he served out the unexpired term of Congressman Samuel J. Randall, May 20, 1890–Mar. 3, 1891, but he was defeated as candidate to succeed himself, in the next election. He rose to the position of Grand Master of the Pennsylvania Grand Lodge of Masons; was president of the Philadelphia Club (1888–94); and was identified with the Historical Society of Pennsylvania and the American Philosophical Society. On Mar. 12, 1840, he married Mary, daughter of Jacob Shoemaker and Sarah (Morris) Waln; a son and four daughters, with his wife, survived him.

His chief interest undoubtedly lay in the field of penology. He served for fifty-three years (1839–92), as one of the governing board of the Eastern Penitentiary, which his father had helped to plan and manage, and for forty years (1852–92) as president of the board. There was no wavering in his complete faith in the system of separate confinement, the defense of which he undertook on all suitable occasions. He published *Short Talks on Crime-Cause and Convict Punishment* (1882) and *Brief Sketch of the Origin and History of the State Penitentiary for the Eastern District of Pennsylvania, at Philadelphia* (1872). He was an orator of ability, whose somewhat archaic and dignified language harmonized well with his physical appearance and made him especially acceptable on commemorative occasions. He brought about the wearing of gowns by the judiciary of Philadelphia, and it is said that the Law Association finally adopted the custom "with no enthusiasm, and mainly to secure relief from Mr. Vaux's importunity" (R. D. Coxe, *Legal Philadelphia*, 1908, p. 183).

[R. W. Davids, *The Wistar Family* (1896); G. P. Donehoo, *Pennsylvania: A Hist.* (1926), vol. IX; *U. S. Mag. and Democratic Rev.*, Aug. 1847; J. W. Jordan, *Colonial Families of Phila.* (1911), vol. I; J. H. Martin, *Martin's Bench and Bar of Phila.* (1883); E. P. Oberholtzer, *Phila.: A Hist. of the City and Its People* (n.d.), vol. IV; *Biog. Dir. Am. Cong.* (1928); H. E. Barnes, *The Evolution of Penology in Pa.* (1927); *Abstract of the Proc. of the Grand Lodge . . . of Free and Accepted Masons of Pa.* (1896); *Press* (Phila.), Mar. 23, 1895; *Pennsylvanian* (Phila.), Mar. 14, 1840, for marriage notice.]   T. S—n.

VAUX, ROBERTS (Jan. 21, 1786–Jan. 7, 1836), philanthropist, was a descendant of a French family the members of which left their homeland in the seventeenth century and settled in Sussex, England. His father, Richard, son of George Vaux, a London physician, emigrated to Philadelphia in his early youth and died there in 1790 at the age of thirty-nine, leaving two children, Roberts and Susannah, and his wife, Ann (Roberts), who was a descendant of one of William Penn's friends and companions, Hugh Roberts. Both the parents were Quakers. Roberts Vaux received his schooling at the Friends' Academy in Philadelphia, and at eighteen entered the employ of a highly respected merchant, John Cooke. Upon reaching his majority he set up a business of his own, which he carried on for a few years. The death of his sister in 1814 created in him an emotional crisis which resulted in his resolving to retire from active business and devote his life to the service of his fellow

men. The same year, Nov. 30, he married Margaret Wistar, daughter of Thomas Wistar; she bore him two sons, one of whom was Richard [*q.v.*].

In a short time Vaux became associated with almost every worthy public and private activity for social welfare in his community. He took a leading part in the creation of a free public school system and was the first president of the board of controllers of the public schools of Philadelphia, serving in that capacity from 1818 to 1831. Profoundly interested in prison problems, he was one of the officers of the Philadelphia Society for Alleviating the Miseries of Public Prisons, which his father-in-law nad helped to found. He prepared most of its memorials to the legislature and stanchly defended the system of separate confinement of prisoners. In 1821 he was appointed to the commission which planned the Eastern Penitentiary, and it was he who drafted the legislation for its administration. Until his death he took an active interest in the work of this institution. Out of an address which he delivered before the Prison Society grew the movement for the establishment, in 1826, of a house of refuge for juvenile delinquents. His most eloquent and persuasive writing was in exposition and defense of penal reforms; among them may be mentioned *Notices of the Original, and Successive Efforts, to Improve the Discipline of the Prison at Philadelphia, and to Reform the Criminal Code of Pennsylvania: with a Few Observations on the Penitentiary System* (1826); and *Reply to Two Letters of William Roscoe, Esquire, of Liverpool, on the Penitentiary System of Pennsylvania* (1827).

Penology was but one of his many interests, however: he was a manager of the Pennsylvania Hospital; as a member of the building committee and later as a manager, he had an active part in the creation of the Frankford Asylum for the Insane; he assisted in the founding of an institution for the instruction of the blind and another for the deaf and dumb. An ardent advocate of temperance, he served as president of the Pennsylvania State Temperance Society, and as vice-president of the United States Temperance Convention. The Philadelphia Saving Fund Society, the Philadelphia Hose Company, and the Apprentices' Library Company numbered him among their founders. He assisted in the organization of the Academy of Natural Sciences, the Linnaean Society, the Franklin Institute, the Athenaeum, and the Historical Society of Pennsylvania; published papers on the locality of Penn's treaty (*Memoirs of the Historical Society of Pennsylvania*, vol. I, pt. 1, 1826); and wrote *Memoirs of the Lives of Benjamin Lay and Ralph*

Sandiford (1815), and *Memoirs of the Life of Anthony Benezet* (1817). Political life apparently attracted him little. He served as a member of the Philadelphia common council (1814–16), but he declined in 1834 a presidential appointment as director of the Bank of the United States, to which he was violently opposed, and had earlier, 1832, declined an appointment as commissioner to treat with the "emigrating Indians west of the Mississippi River." It was only at the insistence of his friends that he accepted, in the fall of 1835, the position of justice of the court of common pleas. He died in Philadelphia less than three months later.

[R. W. Davids, *The Wistar Family* (1896); T. McKean Pettit, "Memoir of Roberts Vaux," *Memoirs of the Hist. Soc. of Pa.*, vol. IV, pt. 1 (1840); Henry Simpson, *The Lives of Eminent Philadelphians Now Deceased* (1859); G. P. Donehoo, *Pennsylvania: A Hist.* (1926), vol. IX; H. E. Barnes, *The Evolution of Penology in Pa.* (1927); J. F. Lewis, *Hist. of the Apprentices' Library of Phila.* (1924); J. M. Willcox, *A Hist. of the Phila. Saving Fund Soc.* (1916); J. J. McCadden, "Educ. in Pa.," manuscript thesis, Teachers Coll., Columbia Univ., and "Roberts Vaux and His Associates in the Pa. Soc. for the Promotion of Public Schools," *Pa. Hist.*, Jan. 1936; death notice in *Poulson's Am. Daily Advertiser* (Phila.), Jan. 8, 1836.]
T. S—n.

VAWTER, CHARLES ERASTUS (June 9, 1841–Oct. 27, 1905), educator, son of John Henderson and Clara (Peck) Vawter, was born in Monroe County, Va. (now W. Va.). His father, a farmer and civil engineer, at the age of sixty joined the Confederate army with his four sons, and all five in time became captains. Charles, who had entered Emory and Henry College in 1858, left upon the outbreak of the war to enlist in the Monroe County Guards, a part of the "Stonewall Brigade." He soon proved himself a leader; he was appointed a captain of sharpshooters in 1862 and served in the field until March 1865, when he was captured and imprisoned in Fort Delaware. Released in June, he returned to Emory and Henry, where he graduated in 1866 and in July of that year married Virginia Longley, daughter of Prof. Edmund Longley. Seven children were born of this union, all of whom survived their father. After teaching for a year, he entered the University of Virginia, graduated in mathematics with distinction, and was elected professor of mathematics and teacher of Hebrew at Emory and Henry. Taking office in 1868, he served this institution for ten years. In 1878 Vawter was selected to build and organize the Miller Manual Labor School of Albemarle County, Va.; the trustees of the school appointed by the county judge, were Col. Charles Scott Venable [*q.v.*] and Prof. Francis Henney Smith, of the University of Virginia, his old friends. This school was founded by a bequest of Samuel Miller of $1,250,000 in Virginia state certificates; Vawter persuaded the legislature to pass an act which preserved its endowment to the school and aided many other schools in Virginia holding similar certificates.

Vawter came to his task with enthusiasm, rich experience, and clear views on education. He was greatly interested in the development of public schools in Virginia and the South and had very definite views of the kind of education the Southern people needed. The Miller School, an institution for orphan boys and girls, established on a farm, with buildings and shops especially erected and equipped, offered him a rare opportunity to realize his ideal of a school that would train the mind and hand together. He made it his life work to build here an industrial school which became a model for all the South and caused him to be recognized as a leader in the new education. He had great influence in promoting the development of industrial education in the public schools throughout the country. He was a member of the state board of education and rendered valuable service in organizing the public schools of Virginia under the constitution of 1902; he served as chairman of the board of trustees of the Normal and Industrial School for girls at Farmville, Va., which became a State Teachers' College; he was also chairman of the board of the Normal and Industrial Institute for Negroes at Petersburg and of the state board of charities and corrections. For a number of years he was rector of the board of trustees of the Virginia Polytechnic Institute, and aided President J. M. McBryde [*q.v.*] in shaping the policies of that institution. He took great interest in the work of the Conference for Education in the South, which he helped to organize in 1898, taking a part in all of their meetings and speaking wherever he could help. He had also a large part in the educational work of the Methodist Episcopal Church (South); he was a trustee of Emory and Henry College, and president for many years of the Virginia Sunday School Association.

[O. F. Morton, *A Hist. of Monroe County, W. Va.* (1916); G. V. Bicknell, *The Vawter Family in America* (1905); *Who's Who in America*, 1903–05; *The Miller Manual Labor School of Albemarle, Crozet, Va.* (1892); reports of the Miller School, 1880–1904; *The Outlook*, Nov. 11, 1905; *Times-Dispatch* (Richmond, Va.), Oct. 28, 1905.]
C. W. D.

VEAZEY, THOMAS WARD (Jan. 31, 1774–July 1, 1842), governor of Maryland, was descended from John Veazey who emigrated from England to Maryland in the latter half of the seventeenth century. In what became Cecil County he acquired a plantation, "Cherry Grove," which remained in the family for many generations. Here was born Thomas Ward, the son of Edward Veazey, a planter who was also high sheriff of Cecil County from 1751 to 1753, and of Elizabeth (De Coursey) of Queen Anne County. After graduating from Washington College, Chestertown, Md., in 1795, Veazey became a planter at "Cherry Grove." He was interested in politics, however, and in 1808 and 1812 was chosen presidential elector, voting for James Madison. In 1811 and again in 1812 he was elected to the Maryland House of Delegates; but he left it to become a lieutenant-colonel of Maryland troops in the War of 1812. From 1833 to 1835 he served on the council of Gov. James Thomas. In January 1836, he was elected on the Whig ticket to succeed Thomas, and was re-elected in the two years following.

His first term was troubled by strife over the state constitution. At that time Maryland was a mere federation of counties and cities in which the majority of the population could be dominated in the legislature by the minority. The state Senate was chosen by an electoral college. In the voting of 1836 for these electors, nineteen Democrats were chosen to represent districts totaling more than 200,000 population, whereas twenty-one Whigs represented less than half that number. Bent upon remedying this state of affairs, the Democratic electors asked the Whigs to agree in advance to choose a majority of men who favored constitutional reform; when the Whig electors refused, the Democrats left for home instead of going into session to elect senators. Veazey met the situation courageously, announcing that the old Senate would continue to function until a new one was legally elected; and he called upon the existing senators to assemble for duty. Public opinion supported the Governor, and the recusant electors returned to Annapolis and cooperated in electing a new Senate. Following up this moral victory, Veazey recommended constitutional reform in his message of Nov. 25, 1836, and the episode resulted in the adoption of a series of amendments amounting practically to a new instrument of government.

His other policies were also, in general, wise and progressive. He urged a registration law to prevent fraud in elections; he stood for sound financial methods; he encouraged internal improvements, especially the completion of the Chesapeake & Ohio Canal and the Baltimore & Ohio Railroad; and he recommended repeatedly the reorganization and expansion of the educational system with the aim of making it general and public. Owner of many slaves, he was hostile

to abolitionist meddling from outside the state, but he favored the work of the American Colonization Society. He was three times married: on Nov. 18, 1794, to Sarah Worrell of Kent County, Md., who died in 1795 leaving an infant daughter who did not survive childhood; on Mar. 29, 1798, to Mary Veazey, a cousin, who bore him five children; and on Sept. 24, 1812, to Mary Wallace of Elkton, Md., who also bore him five children. He spent his last years at "Cherry Grove."

[H. E. Buchholz, *Govs. of Md.* (1908); *Tercentenary Hist. of Md.*, vol. IV (1925); J. T. Scharf, *Hist. of Md.* (3 vols., 1879); G. N. Mackenzie, *Colonial Families of the U. S. A.*, vol. I (1907); G. A. Hanson, *Old Kent, the Eastern Shore of Md.* (1876); George Johnston, *Hist. of Cecil County, Md.* (1881); E. S. Riley, *A Hist. of the Gen. Assembly of Md.* (copr. 1905); legislative journals and documents, 1835–38; *Baltimore Clipper*, July 7, 1842; *Am. and Commercial Daily Advertiser* (Baltimore), July 9, 1842.]   M. W. W.

VEBLEN, THORSTEIN BUNDE (July 30, 1857–Aug. 3, 1929), economist and social theorist, was born in Cato township, Manitowoc County, Wis., the sixth of twelve children of Thomas Anderson and Kari (Bunde) Veblen. His parents had emigrated from Norway in 1847 and had settled on the Wisconsin frontier under conditions of enormous hardship. When Veblen was eight the family moved to Wheeling township in Minnesota, where his father took up a 290-acre farm tract. The boy grew up in a clannish Norwegian community, well insulated against the more mobile life of the Americans around. He learned more of Norwegian speech than of English. At seventeen, because of his father's zeal for education, he was packed into a buggy and deposited at Carleton College, Northfield, Minn., where he spent three years in the preparatory department, and finished the college course in three more, graduating in 1880. He suffered a good deal—a strange "Norskie" boy among Americans, lacking money and social standing, uneasy in the theological atmosphere in which the college was drenched. He had a lazy manner and a biting tongue that infuriated students and faculty alike; the only teacher who saw his promise and whom Veblen liked was John Bates Clark, at whose theory of distribution he was to aim his sharpest shafts years afterward. He read English literature, dabbled in poetry, delivered ironical orations, studied philosophy and economics, trifled with some of the radical doctrines then current, fell in love. After graduation he taught for a year (1880–81) at Monona Academy, Madison, Wis., then, lured by the growing reputation of the Johns Hopkins University, he left for Baltimore to do graduate work. When he failed to get a fellowship he left before the end of the term to study philosophy at Yale with President Noah Porter [*q.v.*] and social theory with William Graham Sumner [*q.v.*]. Both men were impressed with him, and both his essay, "Kant's Critique of Judgment" (*Journal of Speculative Philosophy,* July 1884) and his history of the surplus revenue of 1837 (awarded the John Addison Porter prize in 1884) marked him as a distinctive mind. Yet he had to struggle along, lonely, always in debt, earning his board by teaching in a military academy, regarded as a foreigner and an agnostic. When he took his Ph.D. degree, in philosophy, in 1884, he found that no teaching post was available. Disheartened he went back to his Minnesota farm.

The next seven years were probably the most miserable in Veblen's life. His education among Americans had unfitted him for the narrow life of a Norwegian farmer, yet it had not placed any other way of life within his grasp. He seemed to disintegrate. While he read aimlessly and without stint he kept complaining of his health, railing at the parasitism of business men, mocking the sanctities of a conventional Lutheran community. He tried repeatedly for a teaching position but always without success. On Apr. 10, 1888, he married Ellen May Rolfe, with whom he had had a college romance, and whose connections with a prominent business family held out some hope of employment. But an untoward turn of events shattered even that hope, and Veblen and his wife settled down on a farm in Stacyville, Iowa, waiting for something to turn up. Nothing did. He finally decided to get back to some institution of learning as a graduate student and use that as a fresh point of departure.

In 1891, at the age of thirty-four, he turned up at Cornell University, rustic, anaemic, strange-looking in his corduroys and coonskin cap. J. Laurence Laughlin, who was worlds apart from Veblen and yet saw some of his quality, managed to obtain a special fellowship for him. Veblen's first essay, "Some Neglected Points in the Theory of Socialism" (*Annals of the American Academy of Political and Social Science,* Nov. 1891), contained many of the germs of his later theories. He seemed to spring into sudden maturity. And when Laughlin, called to be the head of the economics department at the new University of Chicago, secured him a teaching fellowship there (1892–93) at $520 a year, Veblen's long quest for some niche in the academic world seemed at last realized. Although he was never regarded with favor by the ruling powers, the next year he became a reader in political economy, then an associate,

in 1896 an instructor, and in 1900 an assistant professor. He dug down into anthropology and psychology and used them to focus a sharp new light upon economic theory. The titles of his essays, generally published in learned journals, reveal the turn of his mind: "The Economic Theory of Woman's Dress," "The Instinct of Workmanship and the Irksomeness of Labor," "The Beginnings of Ownership," "The Barbarian Status of Women," "Why is Economics not an Evolutionary Science?," "The Preconceptions of Economic Science," "Industrial and Pecuniary Employments." His work as managing editor of the university's *Journal of Political Economy* (1896–1905, and in effect earlier) gave his thinking further range and depth. He met, either in the university or nearby, a group of mature minds with which he could match his own: Jacques Loeb [*q.v.*], Franz Boas, James H. Tufts, John Dewey, William I. Thomas, Lester F. Ward [*q.v.*], Albion W. Small [*q.v.*].

His first book, *The Theory of the Leisure Class,* published in 1899 when Veblen was forty-two, gave him prominence overnight. Into it he poured all the acidulous ideas and fantastic terminology that had been simmering in his mind for years. It was a savage attack upon the business class and their pecuniary values, half concealed behind an elaborate screenwork of irony, mystification, and polysyllabic learning. The academic world received it with hostility. The literary men, led by William Dean Howells, were delighted with its merciless exposure of aristocratic attitudes but missed its attack on the business men and the middle class. Veblen now proceeded to a more direct analysis of business, and in 1904 he published *The Theory of Business Enterprise,* based on the material turned up in the *Reports of the Industrial Commission* (19 vols., 1900–02). It contains Veblen's basic economic theory—dealing with the effects of the machine process, the nature of corporate promoting, the use of credit, the distinction between industry and business, and the influence of business ideas and pressures upon law and politics.

It was a decade before Veblen published another book. In the interim he wrote essays on the methodology of economics for the professional journals. In them, in a manner that was exasperating because it was at once summary and elegiac, he rejected not only the prevailing economic doctrines but also the unconscious premises behind them. His life was disturbed by marital difficulties, and when, in 1904, his wife reported one of his relationships to the university authorities it became impossible to remain at Chicago. In 1906 he went as an associate professor to Leland Stanford Junior University at the invitation of President David Starr Jordan. For a time he was reunited with his wife at Palo Alto, but soon the difficulties between them began again, and the two were finally separated. They had no children. Veblen was relatively happy at Stanford. He spent part of his time in a mountain cabin, with a little farm around him. He made friends, had the esteem of the faculty, went his own way. But once more an unconventional relationship with a woman violated the academic mores, and in December 1909 he was forced to leave. He sought a Carnegie grant for an archeological expedition to the Baltic and Cretan regions, and dug deep into the literature of the subject. But the grant was not forthcoming. Finally through the efforts of Herbert J. Davenport he was invited to the University of Missouri, as lecturer, and began his teaching there in 1911. About that time he secured a divorce, and on June 17, 1914, he was married to Anne Fessenden (Bradley); she also had been divorced, and had two daughters. Veblen stayed at Missouri for seven years. It was there that his most famous course, which he had already begun to teach at Chicago—Economic Factors in Civilization—reached its classic form. It was rambling, erudite, omniscient; it swept all history and all cultures. His classroom manner was casual and inarticulate to the point of despair. He cared little about teaching itself, and had no talent for it. But while he was never popular with the run of students he had many disciples and won their unstinted affection. The book which most nearly approximates the content of his principal course is *The Instinct of Workmanship* (1914). It is at once the most searching and most perplexing of all his books, an ambitious book, full of provocative blind alleys. While Veblen himself later called it his only important book (Dorfman, *post*, p. 324) it must be finally set down as a splendid failure. Plunging morass-deep into instinct psychology it emerges with the thesis that the instinct of workmanship, deeply ingrained in man since savage times, has been thwarted throughout history by the piling up of predatory and pecuniary institutions.

After 1914 Veblen's interests turned from topics of professional concern to current issues, and his writing took on a faster tempo and a more strident tone. His tenure at Missouri also became precarious, and finally in 1918 he burned his academic bridges and moved to New York, where he became first an editor of the *Dial* (issue of Oct. 5, 1918) and then, in 1919, a member of the faculty of the New School for Social Research. To this period belong his more revolu-

tionary writings. Much of Veblen's appeal up to that time had lain in the fact that his most savage attacks on the social system had been in the blandest manner. He had combined his uncompromising idol-smashing with all the intellectual qualities of the liberal mind—detachment, subtlety, complexity, understatement, irony. His *Imperial Germany and the Industrial Revolution* (1915), has a bareness of structure not found in his earlier books, although it was still ambiguous enough to suffer the supreme irony of having George Creel's Committee on Public Information use it as grist for the propaganda mills, while the Post Office Department held it up as subversive doctrine. Its thesis was that Germany's strength lay in the fact that she borrowed the industrial techniques from England but instead of borrowing the English democratic procedure she combined them with the unqualified feudal-militaristic institutions congenial to business. In *An Inquiry into the Nature of Peace* (1917) Veblen made his meaning clearer by describing patriotism and business enterprise as useless to the community at large, and analyzing them as the principal obstructions to a lasting peace. In *The Higher Learning in America* (1918) he levelled so bitter and direct an attack on the "conduct of universities by business men" that on reading an earlier draft friends had advised him to withhold it from publication. Every one of Veblen's books was in reality directed to an analysis of business enterprise. In *The Vested Interests and the State of the Industrial Arts* (1919) he came closer to his subject with a savageness of tone that repelled many of his disciples who had been accustomed to his subtler manner. He defined a vested interest as "a marketable right to get something for nothing," pointed out that the aim of business was to maximize profits by restricting or "sabotaging" production, and sharpened his now familiar antithesis between business and industry. During the "red hysteria" of 1919–20 Veblen, writing editorials for the *Dial*, described the passions aroused by the concern for the safety of capitalist institutions as a form of *dementia praecox*, contrasted the aims of Bolshevism with those of the guardians of the "vested interests," and wrote openly of the possibilities of a revolutionary overturn. In his papers collected in *The Engineers and the Price System* (1921) he sketched out a technique of revolution through the organization of a soviet of technicians who would be in a position to take over and carry on the productive processes of the nation. Veblen was no longer hiding his meaning behind elaborate anthropological analogies. His irony was still there, but it was soaked in vitriol.

Veblen's last years were lonely and his life tapered off. For a while he had plans, as the head of a group of technicians, for pushing further the investigation of the revolutionary rôle of engineers. But as with his other plans, nothing came of it: he had no talent for promotion or organization. His investigations for the Food Administration among the I. W. W. for five months in 1918 had met with no official response. His attempts to become part of Wilson's peace conference mission had come to nothing (Dorfman, p. 374). No one would furnish money for a projected trip (1924–25) to England to study British imperialism. On Oct. 7, 1920, his second wife died. He felt tired, ill, rootless. Finally some admiring ladies, solicitous for his health, took him into their home and watched over him. He had reached the stage of being greatly lionized and little understood, and he moved about like a ghost among groups of liberal intellectuals, with his pale sick face, his sharp Van Dyke, his loose-fitting clothes, his shambly gait, his weak voice so infrequently used, his desperate shyness. His last book, *Absentee Ownership and Business Enterprise in Recent Times* (1923), while the best summary of his doctrine, shows some signs of failing powers. In 1925 an offer of the presidency of the American Economic Association, made after considerable opposition from within the organization, was rejected by Veblen because, as he said, "They didn't offer it to me when I needed it" (Dorfman, p. 492). In May 1926 Ellen Rolfe died, and Veblen returned to his cabin near Palo Alto. Here he lived with his step-daughter until his death in 1929, reading aimlessly, worrying incessantly about his losses through investment, watching the movement of events with a dull ache of bitterness and resignation. Six months before the end he said "Naturally there will be other developments right along, but just now communism offers the best course that I can see" (*Ibid.*, p. 500). He died, of heart disease, in Palo Alto, leaving instructions to have his body cremated and the ashes thrown into the sea, and that no memorial of any kind should be raised for him and no biography written.

Veblen's was perhaps the most considerable and creative body of social thought that America has produced. While his thinking does not fall easily into the accepted categories of liberalism and radicalism, he has affected both traditions powerfully. His intellectual attitudes and methods are those of liberalism, especially in his apparatus of disinterestedness and his lack of a

program or of real direction; but his criticism of capitalist society is drastic and, at least in its implications, revolutionary. Nor is it easy to judge of the claim that he represents a strain of thought indigenous to America. He seems to have been relatively unaffected by other American writers. But while his intellectual material was largely European, the deepest sources of his impulses and attitudes lay in the transplanted European stock of the American Northwest and Middle-West, rugged, hard-bitten, agrarian, suspicious of urban finance, vigorously populist. In economic theory his influence was crucial in weakening the hold of neo-classical theory and introducing a more realistic "institutional school." But his most powerful effect was not on academic theory but on economic opinion and policy. He was in no small measure responsible for the trend toward social control in an age dominated by business enterprise.

[Joseph Dorfman, *Thorstein Veblen and His America* (1934), a very full account, supersedes all previous treatments of Veblen and must be drawn upon for all later treatments. Shorter and more interpretive studies are: W. C. Mitchell, introduction to *What Veblen Taught* (1936), a book of selections from Veblen; Lewis Mumford, "Thorstein Veblen," *New Republic*, Aug. 5, 1931; E. S. Bates, "Thorstein Veblen," *Scribner's Mag.*, Dec. 1933; Max Lerner, "Veblen and the Waste Land," *New Freeman*, Feb. 25, 1931; "What is Usable in Veblen?," *New Republic*, May 15, 1935; and "Gateway to Veblen's World," *Nation*, Mar. 11, 1936; John Chamberlain, in *Farewell to Reform* (1932). A complete bibliography of Veblen's writings, arranged chronologically is in Dorfman. For certain personal details see *Bulletin of Yale Univ. Obit. Record of Grads. Deceased during the Year Ending July 1, 1930*; A. A. Veblen, *Veblen Genealogy* (1925), in Lib. of Cong., "autographed from the typed copy"; obituaries in *N. Y. Times, San Francisco Chronicle*, Aug. 6, 1929.]

M. L.

VEDDER, ELIHU (Feb. 26, 1836–Jan. 29, 1923), figure and mural painter, illustrator, born in New York, was the son of Elihu and Elizabeth Vedder, and a descendant of Harmon Albertse Vedder (*c.* 1637–*c.* 1715), an early Dutch settler in Schenectady, N. Y. He spent much of his boyhood in Schenectady, with several trips to Cuba, where his father was engaged in business. For a time he attended the Brinkerhoff School in Jamaica, L. I. His artistic talent asserted itself early, and as a boy of twelve he began to study art by himself. For a time he worked under Tompkins H. Matteson [*q.v.*] in Sherburne, N. Y. In 1856 he went to Europe, where he studied under François Edouard Picot in Paris for eight months and then went to Florence to live. Returning to America, he arrived penniless in New York at the outbreak of the Civil War. Serious work met with no success, and he resorted to such pot-boilers as comic valentines, sketches for *Vanity Fair,* and diagrams for dumb-bell exercises for a teacher of calisthenics. During these difficult times, living in a bare room in Beekman Street, he conceived the ideas for his early pictures, "The Fisherman and the Genii," "The Roc's Egg," "The Questioner of the Sphinx," "The Lost Mind," and "The Lair of the Sea-Serpent," but it was not until 1865 that he succeeded in finishing them. In that year he was admitted into the National Academy, became a member of the Society of American Artists, and for a second time went abroad. After spending some time in France, he went early in 1867 to Rome, where he made his home for the rest of his life, though he also had a villa on the island of Capri. He made frequent visits to America, where he held periodical exhibitions of his work, now received with increasing admiration.

The distinctive merit of Vedder's work is its rare imaginative power and thoughtfulness. His workmanship is heavy; his color is not remarkable. He is essentially a painter of abstract ideas rather than visible realities, and he penetrated farther into that realm than any other American painter except Albert Pinkham Ryder [q.v.]. It was in 1884 that he published his series of more than fifty illustrations to the Rubáiyát of Omar Kháyyam, his magnum opus. The character of these drawings, which he called accompaniments, was ponderously beautiful. They had the charm of sweeping rhythmic line that is the preëminent technical merit of his designs, and supplemented the text with genuine insight and deep sympathy. When they were exhibited in Boston in the spring of 1887, they were accompanied by a group of sixteen paintings, the "Cup of Death," the "Soul between Doubt and Faith," the "Fates Gathering in the Stars," and the "Last Man." The originality and solemnity of these motives, in which Vedder gave thrilling hints of an unknown world and intangible realities, made a deep impression. In the last phase of his life as an artist he turned to mural decoration. On the wall of the staircase landing in the Library of Congress, Washington, is his large mosaic "Minerva" (1897), with five wall paintings (1896) which symbolize "Government," "Corrupt Legislation," "Anarchy," "Good Administration," "Peace and Prosperity." In conception they show but little invention, and in imaginative force they fall below the standard set by the easel paintings. They have the dignity befitting their place in a great public building, but they are devoid of charm. The tympanum (1894) which decorates the west wall of the Walker Art Building, Bowdoin College, Brunswick, Me., is a more satisfactory example of Vedder's weighty style. He also

decorated a ceiling (1893) in the C. P. Huntington mansion in New York, the subject being "The Sun with the Four Seasons." Examples of his painting may be seen in the Metropolitan Museum of Art ("The Lost Mind," 1864–65, and "African Sentinel"), the Museum of Fine Arts in Boston ("The Lair of the Sea-Serpent," 1864, "The Questioner of the Sphinx," 1863, "The Fisherman and the Genii," "Lazarus," an Italian landscape, and the portrait of Kate Field), at Wellesley College, and the Carnegie Institute, Pittsburgh, Pa.

Vedder was married to Caroline Beach Rosekrans of Glens Falls, N. Y., July 13, 1869. He died in Rome, survived by one of his three children, a daughter. He published three books: *Miscellaneous Moods in Verse* (1914), *Doubt and Other Things* (1922), and *The Digressions of V* (1910), a rambling and entertaining memoir, without continuity of narrative but full of whimsical and ironic comments on men and things, which gives a faithful portrait of the man himself.

[In addition to *The Digressions of V*, see *Who's Who in America*, 1922–23; Samuel Isham, *The Hist. of Am. Painting* (1905); Suzanne La Follette, in *Art in America* (1929); Pauline King, *Am. Mural Painting* (1902); Herbert Small, *Handbook of the New Lib. of Cong.* (1901); W. H. Bishop, in *Am. Art Rev.*, June, July 1880; W. H. Downes, in *Atlantic Monthly*, June 1887; W. C. Brownell, in *Scribner's Mag.*, Feb. 1895; Elisabeth L. Cary, in *Internat. Studio*, Sept. 1908; Ferris Greenslet, in *Outlook*, Nov. 26, 1910; H. T. Carpenter, in *Bookman*, Apr. 1912; F. J. Mather, Jr., in *Scribner's Mag.*, July 1923; Cat. of the Doll and Richards Gallery, Boston, 1887; obituaries in *Nation*, Feb. 21, 1923, p. 207, and *N. Y. Times*, Jan. 30, 1923.] W. H. D.

VENABLE, CHARLES SCOTT (Apr. 19, 1827–Aug. 11, 1900), mathematician, soldier, and educator, was born at "Longwood," Prince Edward County, Va. A descendant of Abraham Venables, who emigrated from England to Virginia by 1687, he came of a line of country gentlemen, members of the House of Burgesses and the General Assembly, officers in the armies of the Revolution and the War of 1812, builders of Virginia institutions. His father, Nathaniel E. Venable (1791–1846), graduated at Hampden-Sidney College in 1808 and served in the War of 1812; his mother, Mary Embra Scott, was the daughter of Capt. Charles Scott, a Revolutionary officer. Reared in the atmosphere of a cultured home and taught by private tutors, the boy entered Hampden-Sidney at twelve and graduated at fifteen in 1842. From 1843 to 1845 he was a tutor in mathematics in the College, then, after spending a year at the University of Virginia, he became professor in 1846. The year 1847–48 also he spent at the University of Virginia, where altogether he completed the courses in six schools, and in 1852–53 he studied mathematics and astronomy at Berlin and Bonn. He remained at Hampden-Sidney until 1856, when he became professor of natural philosophy at the University of Georgia. In November 1857 he was elected professor of mathematics at South Carolina College (later University of South Carolina). In 1860 he was appointed on a commission to make observations in Labrador on the eclipse of that year.

Entering with spirit into the conflict of 1861 he took part as a lieutenant in the Congaree Rifles in the reduction of Fort Sumter. He then joined the Governor's Guards and fought as a private in the first battle of Manassas. He assisted in the defense of New Orleans and helped in building the fortifications at Vicksburg. When in 1862 Gen. Robert E. Lee was made military adviser to the President of the Confederacy, he selected Venable as one of his aides, with the rank of major; later he became lieutenant-colonel. Venable continued with General Lee to the end at Appomattox and then, following the example of his great leader, took up the work of training young men. He was elected professor of mathematics at the University of Virginia in 1865 and taught there continuously until his retirement.

A dignified and forceful gentleman, with marked talents and wide learning, Venable inspired the admiration and devotion of all. He was affectionate as a father with his students, though stern when necessary. From the beginning he did much for the development of the University. Owing to his initiative, in 1867 new schools were organized for applied chemistry and engineering. As chairman of the faculty (1870–73, 1886–88), he was chiefly responsible for the establishment and endowment of the School of Astronomy, and for the addition of the Schools of Biology and Agriculture, and of Natural History and Geology (Bruce, *post*, IV, 27). He induced the legislature to increase the small annuity of the University from $15,000 to $40,000.

Venable was chairman of the trustees of the Miller Manual Labor School of Albemarle County, Va., and helped to make it one of the foremost industrial schools in the South. Compelled by ill health to retire from active service at the University of Virginia in 1896, he was made emeritus professor. He was married, first, on Jan. 16, 1856, to Margaret Cantey McDowell, daughter of Gov. James McDowell [*q.v.*]; and second, on July 5, 1876, to Mrs. Mary (Southall) Brown, widow of Col. J. Thompson Brown. There were five children by the first marriage

and one child by the second. Francis Preston Venable [*q.v.*] was his son, and one of his daughters married Raleigh Colston Minor [*q.v.*].

Besides a long series of mathematical textbooks for schools and colleges, his only publications were *An Address Delivered before the Society of Alumni of the University of Virginia... July 26, 1858* (1859); *The Campaign from the Wilderness to Petersburg. Address... before the Virginia Division of the Army of Northern Virginia... Oct. 30, 1873* (1879); and "Report of Prof. C. S. Venable on the Total Eclipse of July 18, 1860," in *Report of the Superintendent of the Coast Survey... 1860* (1861).

[Elizabeth M. Venable, *Venables of Virginia* (privately printed, 1925); Richard McIlwaine, *Addresses and Papers* (1908), pp. 60–61; W. M. Thornton, *Charles Scott Venable, A Memorial Address* (1901); P. A. Bruce, *Hist. of the Univ. of Va.* (5 vols., 1920–22); A. L. Long, *Memoirs of Robert E. Lee* (1886); obituary in *Times* (Richmond), Aug. 12, 1900.]   C. W. D.

VENABLE, FRANCIS PRESTON (Nov. 17, 1856–Mar. 17, 1934), professor of chemistry, university president, was born in Prince Edward County, Va. The son of Charles Scott Venable [*q.v.*] and Margaret Cantey (McDowell) Venable, he was reared in the cultural atmosphere of a university community, since his father, after service on the staff of Gen. Robert E. Lee during the Civil War, accepted the chair of mathematics in the University of Virginia. Here Venable was graduated in 1879, having been inspired by the able teaching of Prof. James W. Mallet [*q.v.*] to specialize in chemistry. He taught for a while in the high schools of New Orleans, but ambition was stirred in him and within a year he went to Germany to study at Bonn and Göttingen under such eminent leaders in chemistry as Kekulé, Clausius, and Wallach, receiving the degree of Ph.D. from the University of Göttingen in 1881.

While studying in Germany he was called in 1880 to the chair of chemistry in the University of North Carolina. When he arrived at Chapel Hill he found only a dingy basement, with no equipment, in which to begin his life's work. Undaunted, he utilized to the best advantage the meager funds available in the days of penury which followed the Reconstruction period. Laboratory equipment was improvised and improvements on standard equipment were made. Modest researches were undertaken with the students collaborating, and there developed the healthy combination of teaching and research which characterized the whole of Venable's career. The success of his early efforts led in time to the setting apart of a special building for his work; a fund to purchase a department library was begun; and original researches, chiefly on the atomic weight of zirconium, were accomplished.

In 1883, feeling the need of organized scientific effort on the part of the University faculty and of a medium of publication, Venable joined with Joseph A. Holmes [q.v.], professor of geology, in the organization of the Elisha Mitchell Scientific Society. He was its first president and made frequent contributions to its *Journal* embodying the results of the researches he carried out in cooperation with his students.

In 1900 Venable's qualities of leadership and his grasp of University affairs made him a logical choice for the presidency of the University of North Carolina. During his administration the financial affairs of the University were set in order, athletics were encouraged in the student body, and creative scholarship on the part of the faculty was demanded. The strain of his activities finally proved too great for his health and in 1914 he was persuaded by friends to resign the presidency and resume his professorship. In this decision he was influenced largely by the prospect of returning to the laboratory, to close contact with students, and to his own research. Convinced that his investigation of the atomic weight of zirconium had resulted in too low a number, he now attacked this problem again in cooperation with Prof. J. M. Bell, and found that the atomic weight should be at least a unit higher. The variable results obtained, unexplainable at the time but faithfully recorded in the literature, were shown later by George de Hevesy to be due to the presence of considerable proportions of the element hafnium, then unknown.

In addition to a long list of papers, Venable published a number of books on chemical subjects: *A Course in Qualitative Chemical Analysis* (1883); *A Short History of Chemistry* (1894); *The Development of the Periodic Law* (1896); *Inorganic Chemistry* (1898), in collaboration with J. L. Howe; *The Study of the Atom* (1904); *A Brief Account of Radio-activity* (copr. 1917); *Zirconium and Its Compounds* (1922). He served in 1899 as vice-president of Section C (Chemistry) of the American Association for the Advancement of Science, and in 1905 as president of the American Chemical Society; he was the recipient of honorary degrees from various institutions; but perhaps the honor that touched him most deeply was the designation during his last years of the new laboratory erected on the University campus as Venable Hall.

Venable married Sallie Charlton Manning on Nov. 3, 1884. Toward the close of his life, as the failure of his bodily powers gradually compelled him to retire from classroom and research laboratory, he found consolation in the affectionate regard of his fellows, in the happiness of his home, and in his garden. He was survived by his wife, three daughters, and two sons.

[E. M. Venable, *Venables of Va.* (copr. 1925); *Who's Who in America,* 1932–33; K. P. Battle, *Hist. of the Univ. of N. C.* (2 vols., 1907–12); J. M. Bell, "Francis Preston Venable," *Industrial and Engineering Chemistry,* July 1924, and "Dr. F. P. Venable's Contributions to Chemistry," *Jour. of Chemical Educ.,* June 1930; *Ibid.,* Aug. 1926; *Jour. of the Elisha Mitchell Sci. Soc.,* Dec. 1934; *News and Observer* (Raleigh), Mar. 18, 1934; personal acquaintance.]

C. H. H.

VENABLE, WILLIAM HENRY (Apr. 29, 1836–July 6, 1920), teacher, writer, author of *Beginnings of Literary Culture in the Ohio Valley,* was descended from William Venable who settled near the Delaware River about 1680 and became a Quaker preacher. The third of five children of Quaker parents, William and Hannah (Baird) Venable, William Henry was born in a log cabin on a farm near Waynesville, Ohio. In 1843 the family moved to Ridgeville, a hamlet near Cincinnati, where the boy attended a district school and through the influence of his father began to read Josephus, Plutarch, Shakespeare, *Don Quixote,* and *Lewis and Clark's Journal.* In his late adolescence he began to teach at Sugar Grove; he attended a teachers' institute held at Miami University, and studied for three years, teaching to support himself, at the South-western Normal School, Lebanon, Ohio. In 1860 he went for one year to Vernon, Ind., as principal of the Jennings Academy. He helped to edit the *Indiana School Journal,* and on Dec. 30, 1861, married Mary Ann Vater of Indianapolis, who bore him seven children.

Returning to Cincinnati in 1862, he taught natural science in Chickering Institute for twenty-five years, being proprietor of the school from 1881 to 1886. In 1889 he became teacher of English literature in the Hughes High School; subsequently he taught in the Walnut Hills High School and served as head of the department of English. He helped to develop the educational system of Cincinnati and had some influence in a wider sphere through the textbooks in literature and expression which he compiled, his *School History of the United States* (1872), and his activities in connection with teachers' institutes and associations. Some of his thoughts on education were set forth in a volume of short papers, *Let Him First be a Man, and Other Essays* (1893). He also enjoyed a local reputation as a poet, dealing for the most part with homely themes: "My Catbird," "The School Girl," "Tunes Dan Harrison used to Play." Several volumes of his verse were published during his lifetime, and after his death his son, Emerson Venable, edited *The Poems of William Henry Venable* (1925).

Venable is chiefly remembered, however, for his *Beginnings of Literary Culture in the Ohio Valley* (1891), the result of more than twenty years of interest in the intellectual life of his native region. During that time, in preparing numerous papers for local journals and historical societies, he had assembled through research in libraries and conversations with members of an elder generation a store of information which he was urged to publish. Encouraged by several friends interested in local antiquities, including the publisher Robert Clarke [*q.v.*], he assembled a volume of more than five hundred pages—which he modestly described as "discursive, even desultory . . . a repository of accumulated notes" —and equipped it with an excellent index. Though in no sense a finished treatise, the book is a valuable compilation, and Venable's appreciation of the significance of the material and his scrupulous work in gathering and preserving it entitle him to the gratitude of later students of the field.

[*William Henry Venable: An Appreciation Read before the Cincinnati Schoolmasters Club, Oct. 9, 1920* (1921); *Who's Who in America*, 1918–19; *The Biog. Cyc. and Portrait Gallery . . . of Ohio* (6 vols., 1883–95), vol. IV; *Ohio Centennial Anniv. Celebration at Chillicothe* (1903), ed., by E. O. Randall; *Hist. of Cincinnati and Hamilton County, Ohio* (1894); Emerson Venable, *Poets of Ohio* (1909); *Cincinnati Enquirer*, July 7, 1920; *Commercial Tribune* (Cincinnati), July 7, 1920.]   W. E. S—h.

VERBECK, GUIDO HERMAN FRIDOLIN (Jan. 23, 1830–Mar. 10, 1898), missionary to Japan, was born in the town of Zeist, in the Netherlands, the son of Carl Heinrich Willem and Ann Maria Jacobmina (Kellerman) Verbeek; Guido changed the spelling of the family name. His parents were deeply religious and he was reared under Moravian influence, attending the Moravian Church and school in his native town. At Zeist he learned not only Dutch, but German, English, and French. Later he was a student in the Polytechnic Institute of Utrecht. From his mother he derived a love for poetry and music; he played a number of instruments and sang. In 1852 he emigrated to the United States, going first to Wisconsin, then, in 1853, to Brooklyn, and, soon after—to put into practical use his knowledge of engineering—to Arkansas. Apparently he had thought from time to time of being a missionary, and during a serious illness while in Arkansas he made a definite decision to follow that calling.

Accordingly, in 1855 he entered the Presby-

terian theological seminary at Auburn, N. Y., and was there until 1859. Toward the close of this period he learned that the foreign board of the Dutch Reformed Church was looking for a Dutch-American to send as a missionary to the newly opened Japan, where for centuries the only direct contact with Europe had been through Dutch merchants. He offered himself and was accepted. On Mar. 22, 1859, he was ordained, and on Apr. 18, he married Maria Manion of Philadelphia. They sailed for Japan with the party which initiated the work of his board in that country, and established a home in Nagasaki. The long-standing edicts against Christianity were still prominently displayed throughout Japan and such little missionary work as was possible had to be done inconspicuously, largely through the distribution of literature and through teaching English. Not until 1866 did he baptize the first two converts—men who had come in contact with Christianity through a volume found floating on the water at Nagasaki. In Nagasaki he established a small school, where English was taught by means of the Bible. Before many years, at the request of the government, he took charge of a school for interpreters in Nagasaki, using chiefly the New Testament and the Constitution of the United States as his texts. Students of his, among them Okuma and Soyeshima, later rose to prominence in national affairs. With the overthrow of the Shogunate and the restoration of the Emperor some of his former pupils became influential at Yedo (Tokyo). In 1869, at the invitation of the new administration, he went to Yedo and headed a school which laid the foundations for the Imperial University. His advice was sought by some of the most powerful ministers of state as they endeavored to reorganize Japan. It was partly as the result of his suggestion that the Iwakura mission (1871–73) was sent to America and Europe.

In 1873, after a vacation in Europe and America, Verbeck became attached to the government in a more advisory capacity, and either translated or supervised the translation into Japanese of the Code Napoléon, the constitutions of many of the states of Europe and America, and numerous western laws, legal documents, and treatises on law. At the same time, now that Christianity was officially (1873) tolerated, he taught Bible classes, preached on Sundays, and later taught in a theological seminary. His health being threatened under the pressure of his many duties, he resigned from the government, was decorated by the Emperor, spent some months in the United States resting, and on his return to Japan in

1879 gave himself almost entirely to his missionary duties. For longer or shorter periods he preached, taught in the theological school (later a part of the Meiji Gauin), lectured at the government school for nobles, helped prepare a hymn book and other religious literature in Japanese, and assisted in the translation of the Bible. Modest and unassuming, he was courageous in upholding what he believed to be right. Never robust, he was able by self-discipline and a carefully ordered life to perform an immense amount of work and to conserve his mental powers to the end of his life. He died in Tokyo, survived by five sons and two daughters; one of his sons was William Verbeck [q.v.].

[W. E. Griffis, *Verbeck of Japan* (1900); R. E. Speer, *Servants of the King* (1909); annual reports of the Board of Foreign Missions of the Reformed Protestant Dutch Church (after 1868 the Board of Foreign Missions of the Reformed Church in America); *Gen. Biog. Cat. of Auburn Theological Sem.* (1918); Mrs. W. I. Chamberlain, *Fifty Years in Foreign Fields* (1925); *N. Y. Times*, Mar. 13, 1898, which gives date of death incorrectly.]   K. S. L.

VERBECK, WILLIAM (Jan. 18, 1861–Aug. 24, 1930), educator, inventor, was born in Nagasaki, Japan, son of the Rev. Guido Herman Fridolin Verbeck [q.v.] and Maria (Manion). Until he was seventeen, except for a brief visit to America, he lived in the Orient, receiving his early education from his father. Later he attended the high school in Oakland, Cal., and the California Military Academy. He enlisted in the California National Guard, in which he rose to the rank of major. For a time he was commandant at St. Matthews Hall, San Mateo, Cal. In June 1885, however, he went to New York to market certain inventions which he had perfected, but litigation soon exhausted his resources, and in October of the same year he joined the faculty of the Peekskill Military Academy, Peekskill, N. Y. The following summer, July 28, he married Katharine Jordan of San Mateo, and in the fall became co-principal at Cayuga Lake Military Academy, Aurora, N. Y.

His work at Aurora attracted the attention of the Rt. Rev. Frederick D. Huntington [q.v.], bishop of Central New York, and two years later Verbeck became head of St. Johns School, Manlius, N. Y., now the Manlius School, a diocesan preparatory school founded in 1869. Only twelve students greeted him in the fall of 1888, but, within a year, the number had increased to sixty, and within five years, to double that number. He reorganized the institution, combining the stereotyped military system with English public school methods, following somewhat, particularly with respect to self-govern-

ment, the methods employed by Henry A. Coit [q.v.] of St. Paul's School. Discarding both the autocratic English prefect system and cold, austere military authority, he secured his ends by developing *esprit de corps* and school loyalty. Successful in an extraordinary degree, notwithstanding financial difficulties and fires that all but destroyed the plant, he built up a school which at the time of his death numbered about three hundred boys. His ability was widely recognized. He was elected a member of the National Institute of Social Sciences in 1914, was president of the Association of Military Colleges and Schools of the United States, 1918–20, and was created a Commander of the Order of the Crown of Italy in 1926.

In New York, also, he served as an officer of the National Guard, and in June 1910, Gov. Charles E. Hughes appointed him adjutant-general. In the federalization of the National Guards of the states thereafter undertaken by the government, it became necessary to reorganize the New York troops into a modern division. Verbeck performed the duty with vigor and ability. His appointment expired Dec. 31, 1912, and he retired from the Guard with rank of brigadier-general. A pioneer in the scout movement, he was one of the first three national scout commissioners of the Boy Scouts of America, 1910–11, a member of the National Council, 1911–16 and, except for a brief interval, an honorary member until his death.

He was endowed with no little mechanical ingenuity, and between Sept. 25, 1883, and June 5, 1917, he was granted six patents; the most of these covered photographic camera mechanisms, and included a folding stereoscope and a panoramic photographic apparatus. He was a capable writer and a ready speaker. Personally magnetic, he had great appeal, especially for boys. He participated in field and track sports, was an expert fencer and swordsman in French and Japanese styles, and was an adept in oriental sword tricks. Versed in jiu jitsu, he could wrestle and box. He was a good horseman, an expert marksman, and an inspiring drill master. His funeral was held in a Japanese garden of his own creation at the school, and he was buried on the site of a proposed new chapel under the inscription: "He rests here where he lived, among the boys he loved." His wife and three sons survived him.

[For Verbeck's educational ideas, see his article, "The Ideal Military School," *The Manlius Bull.*, Dec. 1916; other sources of information include *Who's Who in America*, 1930–31; *N. Y. Herald Tribune*, Aug. 25, 1930; *Manlius Bull.*, Nov. 1930; *Gen. Orders No. 13, Aug. 25, 1930, Adjutant General's Office, N. Y.*; Patent

Office reports; minutes and correspondence of the executive board, Boy Scouts of America; personal acquaintance.]   J. F., Jr.

VERBRUGGHEN, HENRI (Aug. 1, 1873–Nov. 12, 1934), violinist, conductor, was born in Brussels, the son of Henri and Elisa (Derode) Verbrugghen. The father was a well-to-do manufacturer, and he intended that his only son should become a surgeon. From early childhood the lad was musical, and after studying under Jeno Hubay at the Brussels Conservatoire he made a public appearance at the age of eight. He then studied with Eugène Ysaye and a year later made such a success when he played before the Cercle Littéraire et Musicale that Ysaye persuaded the boy's parents that he should follow a musical career. In 1888 Verbrugghen went to London with Ysaye, where he played in orchestras under Sir George Henschel, Sir Frederic Cowen, and Sir Henry Wood. Three years later he went to Glasgow to become concert-master in the Scottish Orchestra recently founded by Henschel. In 1894 he spent a year in Paris as concert-master of the Lamoureux Orchestra, but in 1895 he resumed his position in Glasgow, with the added appointment of assistant conductor. During the next few years he acted successively as teacher of violin at the Royal Irish Academy of Music in Dublin, and as an orchestral conductor in Colwyn and Llandudno, Wales. In 1902 he organized the Verbrugghen String Quartet, and from 1902 to 1905 he conducted the Promenade Concerts in Queens Hall, London. After this engagement he returned once more to Glasgow, where he had been appointed head of the departments of orchestra, opera, and chamber-music at the Athenaeum. In 1911 he succeeded Henry Coward as conductor of the Glasgow Choral Union.

In 1915 an official committee from New South Wales visited Europe in search of a musician to become head of the state conservatory at Sydney, Australia. Verbrugghen was chosen from 400 applicants, and he held the position for seven years, acting also as conductor of a symphony orchestra in Sydney. During the season of 1922–23 he came to America. When he appeared as one of five guest conductors with the Minneapolis Symphony Orchestra, his conducting made such an impression on the audiences and the sponsors of the orchestra that he was offered a three-year contract as permanent conductor. Verbrugghen remained as director until the season of 1931–32, but after the first concert of that season he collapsed at rehearsal, and ill health prevented his resuming his duties. After a period of rest and convalescence he was able to ac-

cept (1933) the chairmanship of the music department at Carleton College, Northfield, Minn., a position he held at the time of his death in Northfield. In April 1930 Verbrugghen was made an officer of the Belgian Crown by King Albert, and the order was formally bestowed at one of his concerts. He was married, Sept. 21, 1898, to Alice Gordon Beaumont of London. He was survived by his wife and four of their six children.

[*Who's Who in America,* 1934–35; *Baker's Biog. Dict. of Musicians* (3rd ed., 1919), ed. by Alfred Remy; obituaries in *Minneapolis Tribune, N. Y. Times,* and *N. Y. Herald Tribune,* Nov. 13, 1934; *Musical Courier,* Nov. 17, 1934; *Musical America,* Nov. 25, 1934.]

       J. T. H.

VERENDRYE, PIERRE GAULTIER DE VARENNES, Sieur de la [See LA VERENDRYE, PIERRE GAULTIER DE VARENNES, SIEUR DE, 1685–1749.]

VERHAEGEN, PETER JOSEPH (June 21, 1800–July 21, 1868), Jesuit educator and provincial, was born at Haecht in Flanders of a family of some prominence. In 1821 he came to Philadelphia with a number of Belgian youths, all of whom were inclined to the priesthood, and in October entered the novitiate of the Jesuits at Whitemarsh, Md. Two years later he accompanied the band of Jesuits led by Charles Van Quickenborne [q.v.] to Florissant in Missouri. Early in 1825 he was raised to the priesthood at the Seminary of the Barrens, in Perry County, Mo. After the Jesuits had taken over the academy opened by Bishop Louis G. du Bourg [q.v.] in St. Louis and had erected new buildings, Van Quickenborne, in 1829, named Verhaegen rector. Within a short time the institution had 150 students. The faculty came to include Pierre De Smet [q.v.], J. A. Elet, James Oliver Van de Velde [q.v.], and other enthusiastic Belgian priests and scholars, and the prestige of the college increased rapidly. In 1832 Verhaegen obtained an act incorporating it as St. Louis University. Four years later he became superior of the Indian missions, which he described in a significant article, "The Indian Missions of the United States under the Care of the Missouri Province of the Society of Jesus" (*Annals of the Propagation of the Faith,* London, 1841); this article did much to stimulate interest in western missions in the East and in Europe.

In 1844 Father Verhaegen became provincial of the Maryland Province of the Society of Jesus. When the Jesuits assumed control of St. Joseph's College at Bardstown, Ky., in 1847, Verhaegen became its president, inspiring new life into what had been a declining institution. Three years later he became pastor at St. Charles, Mo., where he served until his death except for occasional intervals when he served as professor of moral and dogmatic theology at St. Louis University or was absent on lecture and missionary tours.

Verhaegen was considered one of the best-educated Jesuits in the whole province, and he was an able linguist, a sound philosopher, an inspiring teacher, and a preacher whose learned discourses evidenced wide reading. A man of dynamic energy, he proved a capable organizer and administrator of men, schools, and missions. There were few in his day who better understood the management of Indians and the spirit of the pioneer West.

[*Catholic Encyc.*, XIII, 363; John Rothensteiner, *Hist. of the Archdiocese of St. Louis* (2 vols., 1928); J. J. Conway, *Hist. Sketch of the Church and Parish of St. Charles Borromeo* (1892); B. J. Webb, *The Centenary of Catholicity in Ky.* (1884), *Records of the Am. Cath. Hist. Soc. of Phila.*, Sept. 1908, June 1909; W. H. Hill, *Hist. Sketch of the St. Louis Univ.* (1879); *Memorial Vol. of the Diamond Jubilee of St. Louis University* (1904); J. A. Griffin, *The Contribution of Belgium to the Catholic Church in America* (1932).]

R. J. P.

VERMILYE, KATE JORDAN[See JORDAN, KATE, 1862–1926].

VERNON, SAMUEL (Dec. 6, 1683–Dec. 5, 1737), silversmith, was born at Narragansett, R. I., the son of Daniel Vernon who had been born in London of a wealthy merchant's family. Heavy losses in the great London fire of 1666 may have been the cause of his coming to America about that time. Daniel was a man of good cultural background and that he was a man of standing in his community is witnessed by his marriage at Narragansett, on Sept. 22, 1679, to Ann Dyre, the widowed daughter of Edward Hutchinson, the younger, and grand-daughter of the famous Anne Hutchinson [*q.v.*]. Further witness to his standing is the list of local public offices he filled.

Nothing is known of the early years of Samuel Vernon and of his professional training, but the high quality of his work is evidence of a good apprenticeship. As he was second cousin to Edward Winslow, 1669–1753 [*q.v.*], of Boston, one of the most able of colonial silversmiths, there is a possibility that he served his apprenticeship in the Winslow workshop. Whatever his training, Samuel Vernon stands at the head of the list of producers of beautiful silver in early Rhode Island. This silver is notable not only for its craftsmanship but also for the variety of design and the novelty of many of the pieces. Several of his productions are found in the Victoria and Albert Museum in London. His mark was his initials in Roman capitals over a *fleur-*

de-lis, the whole within a heart. His shop was in Newport. In 1715 he engraved the plates for the first indented bills of credit of the first bank established by the Colony of Rhode Island and Providence Plantations. He received two hundred pounds for the work and the plates were used for various issues up to the year 1737.

He served as assistant in the Rhode Island General Court from 1729 until his death, and also as a judge of the superior court of judicature. In 1730 he became a member of a committee "to have a care and oversight of the people and goods that should be suspected to come from Boston" where some smallpox had appeared. He was married, on Apr. 10, 1707, to Elizabeth Fleet of Long Island who bore him eight children and who preceded him in death. William Vernon [*q.v.*] was his son.

[See Harrison Ellery, "The Vernon Family and Arms," *New-Eng. Hist. and Geneal. Reg.*, July 1879; the Ellery genealogy and *The Diary of Thomas Vernon, a Loyalist, R. I. Hist. Tracts*, no. 13 (1881); C. L. Avery, *Early Am. Silver* (1930); E. R. Potter, S. S. Rider, *Some Account of the Bills of Credit or Paper Money of R. I., R. I. Hist, Tracts*, no. 8 (1880); *Records of the Colony of R. I. and Providence Plantations*, vol. IV (1859). William Davis Miller of Kingston, R. I., has made the most thorough study of Vernon and his silver, but the results of his study have not yet been published.]

K. A. K.

VERNON, WILLIAM (Jan. 17, 1719–Dec. 22, 1806), merchant, member of the Continental Navy Board, was born in Newport, R. I., the youngest of the eight children of Samuel Vernon [*q.v.*] and Elizabeth (Fleet) Vernon. He was married to Judith, the daughter of Philip Harwood. She bore him three sons before her death in 1762. He built up a considerable fortune during the "golden age" of Newport commerce, the four decades preceding the Revolution. In partnership with his brother Samuel he was active in trading along all three sides of the old Newport commercial triangle—rum to Africa, slaves to the West Indies, and molasses back to Newport. The firm's letter books throw considerable light on this trade. In 1756, for instance, William and the Redwoods (Abraham Redwood [*q.v.*]), accepted a note from two Guinea Coast traders for 4,353 gallons of rum, payable in good slaves at the rate of 115 gallons each for man-slaves and ninety-five gallons for women. The firm also engaged in privateering, and in King George's War owned the very successful *Duke of Marlborough* as well as having an interest in others (see Chapin, *post*). William owned a splendid mansion that became British and French headquarters during the Revolution, and in 1774 had five negroes in his household.

The Vernon family divided during the Revolution, Thomas becoming one of the most active of the many Newport Loyalists while William and his other brothers were active on the side of the patriots. In 1773 the Assembly had named William and two others to petition the king about the cod fisheries; in 1774 he was one of the local Committee of Correspondence; and in 1775 he was one of a committee appointed to collect facts concerning British depredations, his own brig, the *Royal Charlotte,* having been seized by Capt. James Wallace of H.M.S. *Rose* and condemned in Boston. By 1776 the British occupation caused Vernon to leave Newport for the remainder of the war.

On Apr. 19, 1777, the Continental Congress appointed James Warren [*q.v.*], of Plymouth, John Deshon, of New London, and Vernon to serve as the "Navy Board of the Eastern Department" or "Eastern Navy Board." This group, which sat at Boston with Vernon as chairman, was authorized "to have the Superintendence of all Naval and Marine Affairs of the United States of America within the four Eastern States under the direction of the Marine Committee . . .," —later under the Board of Admiralty (*Rhode Island Historical Society Publications,* VIII, 208–10; Paullin, *post,* pp. xxvii, 148). They were to have charge of the building, manning, and fitting for sea of all naval vessels, providing the necessary materials and stores, to keep registers of personnel, and order courts martial. A similar group for the "Middle Department" sat at Philadelphia. Vernon did invaluable work for the infant American navy in this capacity, and his correspondence reveals the extreme difficulties common to all those who were involved with money and supplies for the American cause. He advanced large sums from his own fortune for the purpose and wrote in 1778 that although the enemy had at least £12,000 sterling of his property in addition to his Newport real estate, it "never broke my rest a moment" (*Rhode Island Historical Tracts,* no. 13, p. 136).

Returning to Newport after the Revolution, he resumed his local importance. He was a wide reader, spoke several languages and corresponded with many of the notable men of his day. Always public spirited, he was an incorporator and second president of the Redwood Library, an overseer of the poor, and a benefactor of the College of New Jersey, now Princeton University.

[Two volumes of papers of the business firm of Varnum, in Newport Historical Society; *The Diary of Thomas Vernon, A Loyalist, R. I. Hist. Tracts,* no. 13 (1881); H. W. Preston, *R. I. and the Sea* (1932); H. M. Chapin, *R. I. Privateers in King George's War* (1926); G. C. Mason, *Newport Illustrated* (1875); "Papers of William Vernon and the Navy Board," *R. I. Hist. Soc. Pubs.,* n.s., vol. VIII (1900); C. O. Paullin, *Out-Letters of the Continental Marine Committee*

and Board of Admiralty (1914), vol. I; *Records of the Colony of R. I. and Providence Plantations,* vol. VII (1862); *Providence Gazette* (Providence, R. I.), Jan. 3, 1807.]   R. G. A.

VEROT, JEAN MARCEL PIERRE AUGUSTE (May 23, 1805–June 10, 1876), Roman Catholic prelate, was born in Le Puy, France, where he received a classical education before going to Saint-Sulpice in Paris for philosophy and theology. As a Sulpician, he was ordained by Archbishop de Quelen of Paris (Sept. 20, 1828) and sent to Baltimore, Md. (1830), where he taught for a number of years in St. Mary's College and Seminary. A catechism which was widely used, several manuscripts on philosophy, theology, and scripture, a few articles in Abram Ryan's *Pacificator,* and pastorals in his later years comprised his total literary output. As pastor at Ellicott's Mills, Sykesville, Clarksville, and Doughoregan manor (1854–58), he took a personal interest in the poor and in the slave population. In 1857 Archbishop John Joseph Hughes [*q.v.*] sought his services as superior of his provincial seminary at Troy, N. Y., but about this time he was named vicar-apostolic of Florida, and on Apr. 25, 1858, he was consecrated as titular bishop of Danaba by Archbishop F. P. Kenrick in the Baltimore cathedral.

At that time Florida had only three or four priests and as many dilapidated churches, established in the Spanish régime. Verot was virtually a missionary who faced torturous visitations in which he revived the faith of Spaniards and half-breeds, preached to the Indians, and built chapels and stations in outlying settlements. He enlarged churches at Fernandina, replaced a church at Tallahassee, established schools for boys and girls in Saint Augustine, brought the Sisters of Mercy from Hartford, Conn., and introduced a number of priests and nuns, as well as a colony of Brothers of the Christian Schools, from Europe. In his pastoral letters and in northern visits he encouraged Catholic colonists to come to Florida, and was one of the first to make known the opportunities there for emigrants from the North and from Europe. Deeply impressed with the Spanish tradition, he repaired the ancient cathedral of Saint Augustine with the native cochina shell, excavated the foundations of the ruined Nuestra Señora de la Leche and restored the Spanish chapel, and enlarged the church at Key West. In 1861, in a sermon on slavery, *A Tract for the Times: Slavery and Abolition,* he outlined the attitude of the Church, which condemned the slave trade, imposed a code of rights and duties of masters and slaves, and sustained the property rights of masters in their negroes. The publication of this sermon, widely quoted in the press, was suppressed in Baltimore by Secretary Seward. The first year of the Civil War saw Verot transferred to the see at Savannah, with Florida continued under his care. The war brought ruin and devastation. Churches and religious institutions were pillaged and destroyed, sometimes wantonly, by Federal troops, as at Jacksonville, Dalton, and Saint John's Bar. Verot was especially disliked as a rebel-bishop, yet he attended Andersonville, did all that was possible for northern prisoners, and furnished nuns as nurses in the military hospitals. With peace came the labors of physical and social reconstruction. Verot made begging journeys throughout the North. Churches were rebuilt and restored; colored benevolent societies were established at Saint Augustine; schools were fostered; the Ursulines burned out at Columbia established an academy at Macon, while the Sisters of Mercy erected a school at Columbus; and the Sisters of Charity at Savannah welcomed Jefferson Davis' penniless children.

At the Vatican Council in 1870 Verot was the *enfant terrible* who spoke frequently in the negative on the question of papal infallibility, urged corrections in the breviary, suggested that for propriety's sake clerics be forbidden to hunt and kill game, and advised that instead of condemning obscure errors of German idealists it would be better to condemn any theory that negroes have no souls. On July 13, he was one of the eighty-eight who voted *non placet* on the question of papal infallibility. He was one of fifty-five bishops who signed a letter to the pope explaining their policy of remaining away from the final ballot (July 18) rather than scandalize by openly and publicly voting *non placet* on the definition of the dogma. On its passage, as a loyal Catholic, Verot gave his formal adherence to the doctrine. During the sessions, Saint Augustine was made a see. Verot disinterestedly accepted Florida, and on his return installed Bishop Ignatius Persico in the superior diocese of Savannah. To the end, he labored courageously and successfully in his impoverished state.

[R. H. Clarke, *Lives of the Deceased Bishops of the Cath. Church in the U. S.*, vol. III (1888), pp. 94–107; J. G. Shea, *Hist. of the Cath. Church in the U. S.*, vol. IV (1892); Cuthbert Butler, *The Vatican Council* (1930); F. J. Zwierlein, *The Life . . . of Bishop McQuaid* (1926), vol. II; *Sadliers' Cath. Directory* (1877); *Records Am. Cath. Hist. Soc.*, June 1900; *N. Y. Freeman's Jour.*, May 22, July 10, Nov. 27, 1858, June 24, July 8, 1876; obituary in *Daily Fla. Union* (Jacksonville), June 13, 1876.]   R. J. P.

VERPLANCK, GULIAN CROMMELIN (Aug. 6, 1786–Mar. 18, 1870), author, congressman, was born in New York City, the son of

Daniel Crommelin and Elizabeth (Johnson) Verplanck. He was a descendant of Abraham Verplanck who settled in New Amsterdam about 1635; his uncle, for whom he was named, his father, a judge and congressman, and his grandfather, William Samuel Johnson [*q.v.*], were all Federalists of note in New York. His mother died when he was three years old and his grandmothers directed his early education. He was graduated at Columbia in 1801 and then read law under Josiah Ogden Hoffman [*q.v.*]; in 1807 he was admitted to the bar. On Oct. 2, 1811, he married Mary Elizabeth Fenno, a sister of Hoffman's wife and the grand-daughter of John Fenno [*q.v.*]; two sons were born to them.

Verplanck was a Federalist, but by 1808 Federalism in New York was at a low ebb. Imitating the Democratic-Republicans, who had sometime before organized their Tammany Society, Verplanck, with Isaac Sebring and Richard Varick, founded in New York the Washington Benevolent Society to perpetuate Federalism, and this society became the model of others formed elsewhere. It was of service in restoring the prestige of the Federalists in 1809, but it was soon deprived of Verplanck's presence and aid. While defending a student threatened with loss of his diploma, Verplanck became a principal with Hugh Maxwell [*q.v.*] in the Columbia College commencement riot of 1811. De Witt Clinton presided over the resulting trial and, seeking Federalist support, he fined Verplanck $200 (see *The Trial of Gulian C. Verplanck, Hugh Maxwell and Others . . .*, 1821). This event resulted in a pamphlet and press war that lasted nearly a decade. Among the pamphlets was one by Verplanck, *A Fable for Statesmen and Politicians* (1815), to which Clinton replied in *An Account of Abimelech Coody* (1815), which was bitterly personal. In 1815 Verplanck went to Europe and spent two years in travel, vainly trying to save his wife's life. During the trip he acutely observed political matters and the English judicial system. On his return he and Charles King [*q.v.*] founded the *New York American,* in which appeared seven poetical satires by Verplanck aimed at Clinton and his administration. These have a caustic erudition that class them among the best ever written in English; later they were published as *The State Triumvirate, A Political Tale, and the Epistles of Brevet-Major Pindar Puff* (1819). From 1821 to 1824 he was a professor in the General Theological Seminary of the Episcopal Church, in New York, and published *Essays on the Nature and Uses of the Various Evidences of Revealed Religion* (1824), a work comprised chiefly of philosophical considerations and only secondarily of textual criticism. It condemns the *a priori* method and is based upon inductive reasoning and legal principles of evidence, which Verplanck, the lawyer, applied to revelation. It is one of the earliest works in America influenced by the Scottish school of common-sense philosophy and it represents a conservative deistic approach.

Verplanck was elected to the New York Assembly in 1820, 1821, and 1822, where educational measures were his chief interest. In 1824 he was elected, largely because of his opposition to the high tariff, to the House of Representatives, of which he remained a member. He was placed upon the Ways and Means Committee and was its chairman from 1831 to 1833. It was the Verplanck tariff bill that was under consideration when Clay introduced his famous tariff compromise. Verplanck was chiefly instrumental in 1831 in obtaining a law improving the copyrights of authors; for this achievement he was tendered a dinner by the *literati* of New York, at which he delivered an address on "The Law of Literary Property" (published in *Discourses and Addresses*). He supported Jackson in 1828, but would not follow him in his opposition to the Bank, and he was not renominated. Now estranged from the Democrats, he headed the assembly nominations and though defeated, he ran as Whig candidate for mayor of New York in 1834. He lost in a close contest, but it was New York's first direct mayoralty election and the earliest in which the name Whig was prominent. The same year he refused to consider the nomination for governor because he was opposed to any association with the anti-Masonic group. He passed most of his remaining life on the family estate in Fishkill, though he served in the New York Senate from 1838 to 1841. The Senate was then the court for the correction of errors, which reviewed the decisions of the court of chancery, and Verplanck wrote many elaborate opinions, frequently carrying the court with him when he differed with the Chancellor. Some of the most valuable changes in the state constitution made by the conventions of 1846 and 1868 are said to have been suggested by Verplanck's speech in the Senate in 1839 (*Speech . . . in the Senate of New York on the Several Bills and Resolutions for the Amendment of the Law and the Reform of the Judiciary System,* 1839).

In 1847 he published *Shakespeare's Plays: with His Life,* in three volumes, with woodcuts by H. W. Hewet, an edition important as an illustration of the development of wood engraving, and as the second serious attempt of American Shakespearean scholarship to use the latest Eng-

lish researches, especially those of J. P. Collier, in connection with the original editions. With Robert C. Sands and William Cullen Bryant [*q.v.*] he edited the *Talisman,* an annual, 1828–30. Some of his essays are collected in *Discourses and Addresses on Subjects of American History, Arts, and Literature* (1833). He belonged to many societies and was a member of the board of regents of the University of the State of New York, 1826–1870, and president of the Board of the Commissioners of Emigration, 1848–70.

[W. E. Ver Planck, *The Hist. of Abraham Isaacse Ver Planck and His Male Descendants in America* (1892); C. H. Hart, *A Discourse on the Life and Services of the Late Gulian Crommelin Verplanck* (1870), pub. also in *N. Y. Geneal. and Biog. Record,* Oct. 1870; *Gulian C. Verplanck* (1870), pub. also in *Proc. Century Asso. in Honor of the Memory of Gulian C. Verplanck* (1870); W. C. Bryant, *A Discourse on the Life, Character, and Writings of Gulian Crommelin Verplanck* (1870); D. R. Fox, *The Decline of Aristocracy in the Politics of N. Y.* (1919); L. B. Mason, "The Political Career of Gulian Crommelin Verplanck," MS. in the Columbia Univ. Lib.; *N. Y. Times,* Mar. 19, 1870.]

L. B. M.

VERRILL, ADDISON EMERY (Feb. 9, 1839–Dec. 10, 1926), zoölogist, was born at Greenwood, Me., the second son of George Washington and Lucy (Hillborn) Verrill. On his father's side he was a descendant of Samuel Verrill who was in Gloucester, Mass., in 1727; on his mother's, of early Pennsylvania Quakers. He was prepared for college at the Norway Liberal Institute in Norway, Me., where his family lived after 1853, and in 1859 entered Harvard College. There he was Agassiz's assistant in the Museum of Comparative Zoölogy from 1860 to 1864, two years after his graduation from the Lawrence Scientific School with the degree of B.S. As an undergraduate he spent several summers with Alpheus Hyatt and Nathaniel S. Shaler [*qq.v.*] in field work in Maine, Labrador, and on the islands of Anticosti and Grand Manan. In 1864 he was called to Yale University as professor of zoölogy; in 1907 he retired as professor emeritus. For a number of years (1870–94) he also taught geology in the Sheffield Scientific School, and for two years (1868–70) acted as professor of entomology and comparative anatomy at the University of Wisconsin. On June 15, 1865, he was married to Flora Louisa Smith of Norway, Me., sister of his associate, Prof. Sidney I. Smith. In 1873 appeared his *Report upon the Invertebrate Animals of Vineyard Sound and Adjacent Waters,* the first extensive ecological study of the marine invertebrates of the southern New England coast, for many years a standard reference work. For sixteen years (1871–87) he was in charge of the scientific work of the United States Commission of Fish and Fisheries in southern New England. In connection with this he devised a cradle sieve, a rake dredge, and a rope tangle for collecting starfishes in oyster beds, the latter of which has great value in commercial oyster-growing (see C. D. Sigsbee, *Deep-Sea Sounding and Dredging,* 1880, pp. 163–68). His scientific studies were interrupted for several years by his work in preparing zoölogical definitions for the revised edition of *Webster's International Dictionary* (1890). During the ensuing years he investigated the invertebrate life of the northern New England coast, the Gulf Stream, the Pacific coast of Central America, the Bermudas, and the West Indies. Everywhere he turned, his discerning eyes found new types of animal life which others had overlooked; he once estimated that he had discovered a thousand undescribed forms. Much of his most important work appeared after his retirement in 1907 at the age of sixty-eight; at eighty-five, still sturdy and vigorous, he extended his studies to the Hawaiian Islands and during the next two years discovered many new species. At last, however, his remarkable vitality was exhausted, and toward the end of his eighty-eighth year he died at Santa Barbara, Cal., survived by four of his six children.

His publications over a period of sixty-four years covered a wide range, but the majority deal with marine invertebrates, among them sponges, corals, sea-stars, worms, mollusks, *Crustacea,* and representatives of other groups. Some of these were comprehensive monographs which are still standards of reference. His most successful work was probably that on corals and coelenterates (including studies of the *Actinaria* and *Alcyonaria* of the Canadian Arctic expeditions, 1922), where he not only described new species and worked out a sound system of classification but made careful observations on mode of life. Other notable work includes his *Monograph of the Shallow-Water Starfishes of the North Pacific Coast* (1914), *Report on the Starfishes of the West Indies, Florida, and Brazil* (1915), and several valuable unpublished reports, among them one on the higher *Crustacea* of Connecticut, and another on the deep-sea *Alcyonaria* of the Blake expedition, which Verrill considered in many respects his most important work. His *Bermuda Islands* (2 vols., 1901–07), which deals with the history, geology, botany, and zoölogy of Bermuda, attests the breadth of his knowledge in diverse fields. In addition to his notable achievements in the classification of marine invertebrates, he built up a large zoölogical collection in the Peabody Museum at Yale, of which he was curator for forty-

three years (1867–1910), and served as associate editor of the *American Journal of Science* for fifty years (1869–1920). He was an early member of the National Academy of Sciences and of many other American and foreign learned societies, and for some years was president of the Connecticut Academy of Arts and Sciences.

Tall, with thick, wavy hair, and piercing blue eyes, he is remembered as a man with a marvelous memory, an encyclopedic mind, and an uncanny aptitude for close discrimination. He had great skill in drawing, producing with little effort vivid sketches of even the most intricate structures. In contrast with Hyatt, whose bent was philosophical, and Shaler, with a gift for generalization and popularization, Verrill was the patient, painstaking investigator, capable of giving a vast accumulation of details clarity and order, and of making the most minute distinctions salient. Standing a little aside from the main course of biological investigation as it developed in his lifetime, Verrill held firmly to a belief in the value of taxonomical work as a basis for other scientific investigations. He himself would never have been satisfied with a knowledge of animals under laboratory conditions alone. It is perhaps partly as a consequence of this that his true position as one of the greatest systematic zoölogists of America has not yet been fully recognized.

[*Geneal. and Family Hist. . . . of Conn.* (1911), vol. I, ed. by W. R. Cutter, etc.; *Who's Who in America,* 1926–27; W. R. Coe, in *Nat. Acad. of Sci. . . . Biog. Memoirs,* vol. XIV (1932), with full bibliog., in *Am. Jour. of Sci.,* May 1927, in *Sci.,* July 8, 1927, and in *Yale Alumni Weekly,* June 10, 1927; G. D. Smith, in *Yale Sci. Monthly,* Mar. 1907; Edwin Linton, in *Sci.,* May 21, 1915; obituary in *New Haven Jour.-Courier,* Dec. 11, 1926.]   W. R. C.

VERWYST, CHRYSOSTOM ADRIAN (Nov. 23, 1841–June 23, 1925), missionary and Indian linguist, was a native of the town of Uden, North Brabant, the Netherlands. His family was induced to emigrate to the United States by the representations of the Rev. Theodore J. Van den Broek, a Dominican missionary who had worked in the West with Samuel Charles Mazzuchelli [*q.v.*]. In 1848, after Van den Broek's visit, a considerable group removed from the Netherlands and formed a settlement in Brown County, Wis. The Verwyst family, consisting of father, mother, and four sons, landed at Boston after a voyage of fifty-five days in a sailing vessel and remained there several years. By 1855 they had earned enough money to make the journey to Wisconsin and join their kinsmen in the settlement called "Franciscus Bosch," where they bought sixty acres of land and built a log cabin. It took the combined efforts of father and sons four years to clear thirty of the sixty acres.

In 1859 Verwyst decided to enter the priesthood and began his studies with the local priest; the next year he was admitted to St. Francis Seminary, near Milwaukee, where he remained as a student five years. He was drafted for the Union army in 1863 and, though he was not a citizen, was obliged to buy his exemption. After this experience he did not take out his citizen's papers for about fifteen years. Ordained on Nov. 5, 1865, he was first stationed for three years in Waupaca County, with headquarters at New London; in 1868 he was transferred to Hudson, and officiated in Saint Croix and Pierce counties for four years; in 1872 he became resident priest for six years at Seneca, Crawford County, where he built a church and parsonage. He was sent next to minister to the Indians and whatever white groups might be found in the Lake Superior region. After four years of a wandering ministry he determined to enter the Franciscan order. Following his novitiate, when he took the name Chrysostom, he was sent in 1883 to Bayfield, Wis., where a Franciscan monastery was established. There Verwyst spent the remainder of a long and useful life, except for a short sojourn in Missouri and California (1897–1900) for the improvement of his health, and a period of twelve years (1900–12) at Ashland, Wis.

A specialist in the Chippewa language, in 1901 he published at Harbor Springs, Mich., *Chippewa Exercises: Being a Practical Introduction into the Study of the Chippewa Language*. He also prepared two articles for the State Historical Society of Wisconsin: "Geographical Names in Wisconsin, Minnesota, and Michigan Having a Chippewa Origin" (*Collections*, vol. XII, 1892, pp. 390–98) and "Historic Sites on Chequamegon Bay" (*Collections*, vol. XIII, 1895, pp. 426–40). His study of the *Missionary Labors of Fathers Marquette, Ménard and Allouez in the Lake Superior Region* was published in Chicago in 1886 and his *Life and Labors of Rt. Rev. Father Frederic Baraga* at Milwaukee in 1900. He published for a time a monthly Chippewa magazine entitled *Anishinabe Enamaid*, and in 1907 put out *Katolik gagikwemasinaigan mi sa Katolik enamiad gegikimind*. In 1915 the fiftieth anniversary of his ordination was celebrated at Bayfield. A stalwart figure, with soft brown eyes, and a scholar's habit, he was a man without guile, open and aboveboard, cheerful and gentle, beloved alike of white men and Indians.

[Sources include Verwyst's own account of his life, "Reminiscences of a Pioneer Missionary," *Proc. Wis.* *State Hist. Soc. . . . . 1916* (1917), pp. 148–85; necrology in *Official Cath. Directory, 1926*; personal acquaintance.]   L. P. K.

VERY, JONES (Aug. 28, 1813–May 8, 1880), mystic sonneteer and transcendentalist, was born in Salem, Mass., eldest of six children of a union of cousins, Jones and Lydia (Very) Very. His earliest American ancestor, the widow Bridget Very, settled in Salem about 1634, and her descendants, several of whom fought in the Revolution, farmed and followed the sea for six generations. The elder Jones privateered in the War of 1812, was briefly imprisoned in Halifax, N. S., and returned to be master until his death (Dec. 22, 1824) of the Boston barque *Aurelia*. On this ship young Jones accompanied his father in 1823 to Kronstadt, Russia, and in 1824 to New Orleans, where he attended grammar school while the ship was lading. After his father's death the youth continued his education until 1827, when he began work as errand boy for a Salem auctioneer. The normal child now became a grave adolescent, turned by circumstances from the family sea-going tradition. Sporadically tutored for four years by a friendly Salem pundit, J. F. Worcester, Very in 1832 became assistant in the Fisk Latin School of Henry Kemble Oliver [*q.v.*]. There he fulfilled three semesters of collegiate requirements, and earned future tuition expenses. He entered Harvard in February 1834 as a second-term sophomore. His unusual maturity and studious habits brought him few friends, but he was regularly a speaker at college "exhibitions," won both junior and senior Bowdoin Prizes, and was graduated in 1836 with second honors. That autumn his undergraduate record netted him an appointment as Greek tutor to the freshmen, enabling him to study simultaneously at the Harvard Divinity School.

This marked the beginning of Very's two most important years. Hitherto mildly Unitarian, he was soon overtaken by a species of religious exaltation. By September 1837, convinced that he must set down allegedly audible pronouncements of the Holy Ghost, he began to compose religious sonnets with remarkable celerity, and was even moved to tears when the Rev. Henry Ware questioned the veracity of his visions. All his work, he constantly insisted, was "communicated" to him. In Salem that December, Elizabeth Palmer Peabody [*q.v.*] heard him read his Bowdoin Prize essay, "Epic Poetry." Knowing the Verys well, she helpfully suggested to Emerson that Jones lecture at the Lyceum in Concord. When Very met him in early April 1838 Emerson was enthusiastic, and

Jones, inspired, returned to Cambridge to write another essay, this time on Shakespeare, which he sent to Emerson in August. Among his colleagues, however, Very's spiritual intoxication had brought his sanity in question. Requested to withdraw, he attended his last faculty meeting, Sept. 10, 1838, and a week later entered McLean Asylum, Somerville, remaining until Oct. 17. Having successfully preached his doctrine of "willess existence" to the inmates, Jones devoted the remainder of the autumn to the attempted conversion of Emerson. Among the transcendentalists he enjoyed some popularity; and men who talked earnestly with him doubted rumors of his insanity. James Freeman Clarke's pronouncement, "Monomania? . . . Monosania!," was bolstered by Emerson's "Profoundly sane!" Very believed in complete, unquestioning submission to the will of God, and seemed the answer to Emerson's recent plea for a "newborn bard of the Holy Ghost." When Clarke in March and April 1839 published twenty-seven of Very's sonnets in his *Western Messenger,* impetus was given to the preparation, under Emerson's aegis, of a book of Very's prose and verse, *Essays and Poems.* Published in September 1839, the verses were called by W. H. Channing "an oracle of God"; by William Cullen Bryant, "among the finest in the language"; and Emerson, who planned to send copies to Carlyle and Wordsworth, thought they bore "an unquestionable stamp of grandeur." Hawthorne, who disliked Very, none the less called him "a poet whose voice is scarcely heard . . . by reason of its depth." Less notice was given Very's prose essays, "Epic Poetry," "Hamlet," and "Shakespeare," though the latter, partly a result of conversations with his friend Edward Tyrrell Channing [*q.v.*], reveals the core of Very's belief. Through some of the poems runs a vague undercurrent of human warmth, but their philosophy contains the worst elements of Asiatic quietism. Emerson rightly regarded Very's doctrine as too other-worldly, utterly lacking in the Yankee vigor which would have stiffened and saved it. The poems are characterized by clarity and simplicity; but color is inordinately subdued, ideas few, and humor absent. They are distinguished only by sincere religious emotion.

By April 1840 this fervor had faded sufficiently for Emerson to recognize its underlying philosophic negativity. The friendship waned. Very returned to Salem to write increasingly mediocre verse. Lacking a degree in divinity, he was licensed to preach (1843) by the Cambridge Association, and held temporary pastorates in Eastport, Maine, and North Beverly, Mass. But he was too shy to preach well, and at forty-five had virtually retired. He was tall, slender, and hollow-cheeked. He lived with his sisters, doing occasional genealogical research for the Essex Institute, contributing to newspapers. He called himself a "failure," and lived out forty years of anticlimax in his provincial haven, with his mind and hopes directed toward that other world to which he had formerly enjoyed at least a visionary access.

[Two editions of Very's work were posthumously published: *Poems* (1883), with a valuable intro. memoir by Wm. P. Andrews; and *Poems and Essays* (1886), containing some six hundred poems, ed. by J. F. Clarke. Biog. material is best set forth in Emerson's journals and letters; *Essex Inst. Hist. Colls.,* vols. I–II (1859–60); *Bull. Essex Inst.,* Jan., Feb., Mar. 1881; G. W. Cooke, *An Hist. and Biog. Intro. to Accompany the Dial* (2 vols., 1902); Rose H. Lathrop, *Memories of Hawthorne* (1897); F. B. Sanborn and W. T. Harris, *A. Bronson Alcott* (2 vols., 1893); Records of the Harvard College Faculty, vol. XI, 1829–40; obituary in *Salem Observer,* May 15, 1880. Critical estimates are to be found in the *Dial,* vol. II, no. 1, vol. III, no. 1; Albert Ritter, *Jones Very, der Dichter des Christentums* (Leipzig, 1903); Gamaliel Bradford, *Biog. and the Human Heart* (1932); and P. P. Burns, "Jones Very," *Howard Coll. Studies,* June 1922.]   C.H.B.

VERY, LYDIA LOUISA ANN (Nov. 2, 1823–Sept. 10, 1901), author, was born in Salem, Mass., the youngest child of Capt. Jones and Lydia (Very) Very, and a sister of Jones Very [*q.v.*]. Shortly after Captain Very's death in 1824, the family moved from Lydia's birthplace, at Boston and Essex Streets, to 154 Federal St., where Lydia remained throughout her life. Educated in the Salem public schools and at the classical school conducted by Henry Kemble Oliver [*q.v.*], she began in 1846 a period of about thirty years of primary teaching. When her brother Washington opened his private school in 1847, she relinquished her initial charge in order to join him. But he died in 1853; the school lapsed; and until her retirement in 1878, she taught the lower grades at Bowditch Grammar School. Never married, she lived with her mother, her sister Frances, and her brothers, Jones and Washington. Short, plump, brown-haired, energetic, she was the hardest worker of her Unitarian family, and its most ardent humanitarian.

This uneventful career was punctuated in 1856 by the appearance of *Poems,* a small volume of verse, printed at Andover, Mass. More deeply influenced by her friend Elizabeth Palmer Peabody [*q.v.*] than by her brother Jones's mysticism, she centered her interest in children, animals, and flowers. Her poetry shows no transcendentalism, though she must certainly have been exposed to it; and her view of nature, if fresh and hearty, is entirely orthodox. Except for occasional contributions to the *Salem Gazette* and the *Boston Transcript,* she published nothing more for thirty years. After the death of Jones in 1880, however, lacking another vocation, she returned to literature. First fruit of this regeneration was *Poems and Prose Writings* (1890), a copiously augmented reprint of her earlier volume, together with some essays on Salem scenery which show her less skilful in prose than in verse. Receiving a copy of this, the aged Whittier wrote in 1891, "I heartily thank thee for sending me the volume, and am truly thy friend." Her sister died in 1895. Lonely but undaunted, she persuaded a Boston publisher to bring out three books in 1898. Some skill in drawing enabled her to illustrate them herself. Her *Sayings and Doings among the Insects and Flowers,* first published at Salem in 1897, tells sixteen nature-stories with charming simplicity, and one of them, "The Town Pump," contains gentle satire on Salem selectmen. The novels are unfortunately third-rate; *The Better Path, or Sylph, the Organ-grinder's Daughter* (1898) moralizes sentimentally, *A Strange Disclosure* (1898) is an undistinguished tale of New England small-town life, and *A Strange Recluse* (Salem, 1899) tells of a wealthy London clubman who casts bread upon the waters and gets it back sodden with romance. Her last work, *An Old-fashioned Garden, and Walks and Musings Therein* (1900), far surpasses the novels. An anecdotal review, in simplest language, of her quiet life, it tells of the garden, childhood sports, pets; of her "Thoreau Field Club," formed to seek arbutus along Salem turnpike; of the evil effects on nature of advancing industry. The book ends with a salute to earth, the last lyrical expression of optimism from a sane, industrious spinster, who died in the early morning of Sept. 10, 1901.

[Jones Very, "The Very Family," *Essex Inst. Hist. Colls.,* vols. I–II (1859–60); *Vital Records of Salem, Mass.,* vol. II (1918); Salem town records for 1901; *Who's Who in America,* 1899–1900; Sidney Perley, *The Poets of Essex County* (1889); *Salem Gazette,* Feb. 22, 1889; *Boston Transcript,* Feb. 21, 1890, and Sept. 10, 1901 (obituary); obituary in *Salem News,* Sept. 10, 1901; letter from J. G. Whittier on Lydia Very's poems, 1891, in colls. of the Essex Inst.]

C. H. B.

VESEY, DENMARK (*c.* 1767–July 2, 1822), mulatto rebel, because of his intelligence and beauty became at the age of fourteen the protégé of one Captain Vesey, a slaver of Charleston, S. C., trading from St. Thomas to Santo Domingo. The name "Télémaque" that his owner gave him was corrupted to "Denmark." At Cap Français (now Cape Haytien) the boy was sold to another, but later was returned as subject to epi-

lepsy and for the next twenty years sailed with his master as a faithful slave. In 1800, having drawn $1,500 in the East Bay Street Lottery, Charleston, he purchased his freedom for $600 and set up for himself as a carpenter. Active and powerful, he accumulated a considerable estate, and was the reputed autocrat of several wives and a numerous progeny. Without particular grievances on his own account, he resented his children's inheritance of slavery from their mothers, and, stimulated by events in Santo Domingo, he laid the foundation, 1818–22, for his uprising. Admitted to the Second Presbyterian Church in 1817, he joined the African Methodist congregation when they built their church, and acquired great influence through classes organized ostensibly for religious instruction. He was literate and quoted Scripture with powerful effect, identifying the negroes with the Israelites; and he interpreted the debate on the Missouri Compromise to mean that negroes were held by their masters in defiance of law. Exempt from slave restrictions, he carried his message to the plantations from the Santee to the Euhaws, a belt of more than a hundred miles. Meetings were held at Vesey's house, 20 Bull Street, where contributions were taken for arms; a blacksmith was set to making daggers, pikes, and bayonets, and a white barber to fashioning wigs and whiskers of European hair. The plans of the conspirators are not clear, but probably after taking the city they would have been guided by circumstances. Betrayed by a negro, they advanced the date for the uprising to Sunday night, June 16, but such effective precautions had been taken that the conspiracy collapsed.

Next day a court of two magistrates and five freeholders, customary in South Carolina since colonial times in cases involving slaves or persons of color, convened as both judge and jury, and, having laid down the customary rule of evidence that testimony of two should establish guilt, proceeded to the trial of the suspects. Carefully chosen men of integrity comprised the court, but when the *Charleston Courier* (June 21, 1822) published a communication on the "Melancholy Effect of Popular Excitement," citing the death of an innocent negro some years earlier as the result of a joke, the court protested against the insinuation of disrespect and drew a rebuke from Judge William Johnson [*q.v.*], apparently the author of the original communication (*Charleston Courier,* June 29, 1822). After a three days' search Vesey was taken on the night of June 22 at the house of one of his wives. He had counsel and ably defended himself, cross-examining witnesses with skill, but on the testimony of informers, some of whom thus saved themselves, he was condemned to be hanged (notice of execution, *Ibid.*, July 3, 1822). Of the negroes brought to trial, thirty-five were hanged, thirty-four were sent out of the state, and sixty-one were acquitted. Four whites, at least three of whom were foreign-born, were tried in the court of sessions for misdemeanor, and fined and imprisoned.

The true extent of the conspiracy will never be known, for Vesey and his aides died without making revelations. In the face of the intense excitement that prevailed, it was considered remarkable that the customary machinery of the law functioned and that no unusual punishments were inflicted. The local newspapers kept quiet about the insurrection and referred only briefly to the trials.

[A summary is in W. G. Simms, *The Hist. of S. C.* (1840), appendix; a sketch of Vesey is in *An Account of the Late Intended Insurrection among a Portion of the Blacks of this City. Published by the Authority of the Corporation of Charleston* (1822); the same sketch is repeated in *An Official Report of the Trials of Sundry Negroes Charged with an Attempt to Raise an Insurrection in the State of South Carolina* (1822), by L. H. Kennedy and Thomas Parker; see also Achates (Thomas Pinckney?), *Reflections, Occasioned by the Late Disturbances in Charleston* (1822); T. W. Higginson, "Denmark Vesey," *Atlantic Monthly*, June 1861; A. H. Grimké, *Right on the Scaffold, or, The Martyrs of 1822* (1901).]   A. K. G.

VESEY, TÉLÉMAQUE [See VESEY, DENMARK, *c.* 1767–1822].

VESEY, WILLIAM (Aug. 10, 1674–July 11, 1746), Anglican clergyman, rector of Trinity Church in New York City, was born in Braintree, Mass., the son of William and Mary Vesey. His father was evidently a farmer and a Jacobite, for in 1699 Governor Bellomont wrote that he had been sentenced to stand in the pillory for "desperate words" against the king (O'Callaghan, *Documents, post*, IV, 534–35). Vesey was graduated at Harvard College in 1693, the year the New York Assembly passed the Ministerial Act, which Gov. Benjamin Fletcher interpreted as establishing the Church of England in the colony. Following graduation, Vesey preached on Long Island for about two years and then went to Boston to assist at King's Chapel. On Nov. 2, 1696, he was called to New York on condition that he go to London for ordination according to the liturgy of the Church of England. With a loan of £95 from the wardens and vestrymen he departed in November 1696; received an honorary degree of M.A. from Merton College, Oxford; was ordained priest, Aug. 2, 1697, by the Bishop of London; and on Dec. 25, having returned to New York, was inducted

by Fletcher into the parish of Trinity Church, which had meanwhile been granted a charter of incorporation.

Fletcher's successful efforts to have the law interpreted in favor of the Church of England brought Vesey into many controversies with the royal governors, who held widely divergent views concerning the rights vested in Trinity and its rector. Disagreements, beginning under Richard, Lord Bellomont [*q.v.*], over the King's (later Queen's) Farm and other land grants; struggles over the payment of the rector's salary; differences with Gov. Robert Hunter [*q.v.*] concerning the rights of the Presbyterians in Jamaica and the use of the fort chapel for services, brought stormy times for Vesey, whose extreme conservatism and positive ideas about the church made him resist determinedly and often none too tactfully any attempt to infringe on what he regarded as his prerogatives. So bitter did feeling become between Vesey and Hunter, who accused the former of being a Jacobite, that Vesey left for England in 1714 to lay his case before the Bishop of London. His exoneration appears to have been complete, for he not only remained rector of Trinity but became the Bishop's commissary in New York and New Jersey, in both of which capacities he served until his death. His last years were more peaceful, though he was violently opposed to Whitefield's preaching in New York.

Vesey enjoyed the respect and confidence of his parishioners, among whom were many of the most prominent citizens politically, financially, and socially. He cooperated with the Society for the Propagation of the Gospel in Foreign Parts in providing missionaries and teachers for the poor, and in establishing a charity school in connection with Trinity; he was also the trustee of many bequests for the city's poor, and in his own will left £50 for that purpose. He preached at various missions throughout his district and at his death had twenty-two congregations in his charge. Vesey and Rector streets in New York City were named for him. His widow, Mary, daughter of Lawrence Reade, whom he married in 1698, became the wife of Judge Daniel Horsmanden [*q.v.*].

[Morgan Dix, *A Hist. of the Parish of Trinity Church in the City of N. Y.*, vol. I (1898); J. G. Wilson, *Centennial Hist. of the Protestant Episcopal Church in the Diocese of N. Y.* (1886); E. B. O'Callaghan, *Documents Relative to the Colonial Hist. of the State of N. Y.*, vols. IV (1854), V (1855), and *The Documentary Hist. of the State of N. Y.*, vol. III (1850); E. T. Corwin, *Ecclesiastical Records: State of N. Y.*, vols. II–IV (1901–02); C. K. Shipton, *Sibley's Harvard Grads., Vol. IV, 1690–1700* (1933); "The Case of William Atwood," in *N. Y. Hist. Soc. Colls.*, Pub. Fund Ser., vol. XIII (1881).]   E. L. J.

VEST, GEORGE GRAHAM (Dec. 6, 1830–Aug. 9, 1904), representative and senator in the Confederate Congress and United States senator from Missouri, was born at Frankfort, Ky., the son of John Jay and Harriet (Graham) Vest. He graduated from Centre College in 1848, and from the law department of Transylvania University in 1853. The following year he went to Pettis County, Mo., and began the practice of law at Georgetown; in 1856 he moved to Boonville, Cooper County.

In 1860 he was presidential elector on the Douglas ticket, and that year was elected to the Missouri House of Representatives, where he was made chairman of the committee on federal relations. He was the author of the "Vest Resolutions" denouncing coercion of the South, and in large part formulated the stinging legislative report condemning the seizure of Camp Jackson by the Federal forces under Nathaniel Lyon [*q.v.*]. Probably he was the author also of the "Ordinance of Secession" adopted by the Southern wing of the Missouri legislature at Neosho in the fall of 1861. This assembly chose him as a representative in the Confederate Congress, where he served from February 1862 until January 1865, resigning to accept a seat in the Confederate Senate.

After the fall of the Confederacy Vest returned to Missouri, where he resumed the practice of law, first at Sedalia, and later at Boonville. In 1877 he moved to Kansas City, and two years later was elected as a Democrat to the United States Senate, of which he was a member until Mar. 3, 1903. As a delegate to the Democratic convention held at Baltimore in 1872, he worked for the temporary Democratic-Liberal Republican coalition and for the nomination of Horace Greeley [*q.v.*]. His senatorial career, in the main, was characterized by a disinclination to recognize new developments and new issues in American life; he adhered largely to bygone principles and precedents. Credit must be accorded to him, however, for his outstanding opposition to the high protective tariff measures of his day. He steered the Wilson Tariff Bill through the Senate, and, although the Gorman amendments added a greater degree of protection than he wished, he nevertheless made the leading speech in its defense. When Spain was ceding Puerto Rico and the Philippines to the United States, Vest was one of the leading exponents of the theory that it was unconstitutional to "acquire territory to be held and governed permanently as colonies." In 1900 the *Chicago Journal* pronounced Vest "that great big little fellow . . . with a tremendous intellect in a body

so small and emaciated," and went on to assert that he was "still half the brains of the Democratic side of the Senate" (quoted in the *Boonville Weekly Advertiser,* Feb. 24, 1900).

He was a lawyer of the highest ability, and was at his best in pleading before a jury. His jury oration entitled "Tribute to a Dog" not only won him the case in which it was used, but has ever since been accounted a masterpiece of its kind. As a stump speaker few could equal him in wit or in power to sway the emotions of an audience. In 1854 he married Sallie E. Sneed of Danville, Ky. He died in Sweet Springs, Mo., and was buried in St. Louis; his wife and two children survived him.

[*Pictorial and Geneal. Record of Greene County (Mo., 1893)*; H. L. Conard, *Encyc. of the Hist. of Mo.* (1901), vol. VI; A. J. D. Stewart, *The Hist. of the Bench and Bar of Mo.* (1898); A. E. Trabue, *A Corner in Celebrities* (1923); J. P. Boyd, *Vital Questions of the Day* (1894); E. M. C. French, *Senator Vest, Champion of the Dog* (1930); *Biog. Dir. Am. Cong.* (1928); *Who's Who in America, 1903–05*; *Kansas City Jour.,* Aug. 10, 1904; *St. Louis Globe-Democrat,* Aug. 10, 11, 1904.]   H. E. N.

VETCH, SAMUEL (Dec. 9, 1668–Apr. 30, 1732), soldier, trader, who formulated the first adequate plan for the expulsion of the French from North America, was born at Edinburgh, Scotland. The second son of William Veitch (*sic*) and Marion Fairly, he spent his boyhood uneasily in northern England while his hunted, proscribed father preached for Presbyterianism and conspired against Episcopacy and Toryism on both sides of the Border. In his teens he received some higher education in the Netherlands. After the accession of William and Mary, his Whig connection and his own ability gained him a commission in a Scottish regiment. In 1698, as a captain in the forces of William Paterson's "Company of Scotland Trading to Africa and the Indies," he went out to Darien (Central America) and was made a member of the colonial council. He came to disapprove of Paterson and his ill-calculated venture, however, and when the colonists fled to New York in 1699, he accompanied them and remained in that province.

His handsome, commanding presence, his wide experience, and his natural gifts soon commended him to the Scots of his own generation and clannish spirit. Robert Livingston [*q.v.*] of Albany, secretary of Indian affairs, whose daughter Margaret Vetch married on Dec. 20, 1700, was a son of the Rev. John Livingston who had persuaded William Veitch to abandon the study of medicine for the Presbyterian ministry. Vetch was soon deep in the Albany Indian trade, which by extension included illegal trade overland with the French at Montreal. About 1702 he moved to Boston, where he engaged in maritime commerce with Acadia and Canada. This commerce was contrary to the British trade laws, and was resented by the colonists, especially settlers on the border, who were suffering from French and Indian attacks. In 1701 Vetch's sloop *Mary* was condemned for illicit trading, but it was subsequently restored to him. In 1705 Gov. Joseph Dudley [*q.v.*], whose confidence he had gained, sent him with others to Quebec to negotiate a truce with the Governor of Canada and arrange for an exchange of prisoners, but the terms proposed by the Canadian authorities were not accepted by Massachusetts. Vetch, however, who claimed that certain concessions had been granted him as a reward for his services, improved the opportunity to trade profitably with the French and Indians of Acadia, to whom he furnished arms and ammunition. Public opinion in Massachusetts became aroused, and in 1706 Vetch with five others was tried by the General Court and fined. The next year he carried his case to England, where the Privy Council, ruling that the General Court of Massachusetts, being a legislative body, had no power to try cases and impose sentences, ordered a retrial by the Suffolk County Court. Vetch, safe in England, escaped retrial, and only one of the other defendants was convicted.

Meanwhile, Vetch had won favor and made his most distinctive contribution to colonial history by proposing a plan for conquering the French in America which included the Albany scheme of 1690 and New England's designs on Acadia and Newfoundland ("Canada Survey'd," *Calendar of State Papers, Colonial Series, America and West Indies, 1708–09*, pp. 41–51). His proposals for an attack on Montreal by way of Lake Champlain and a complete investment of Quebec by land and sea were well calculated to succeed. Thereafter Acadia, Newfoundland, and even the Spanish colonies could be attended to. An acquiescent, optimistic Whig ministry in March 1709 dispatched Vetch to carry out the enterprise, empowering him to enlist colonial assistance from Pennsylvania northward. A fleet, bearing a commander-in-chief, munitions, and five regiments, was to follow in April. Col. Francis Nicholson [*q.v.*] accompanied Vetch as a volunteer.

Bad weather delayed their arrival at Boston until Apr. 30, but colonial enthusiasm vied with Vetch's impatient energy, and although Quaker Pennsylvania and New Jersey failed him, within two months he had three well-trained New England regiments and their transports waiting at Boston, while the land expedition commanded by Nicholson was ready with its boats at Wood Creek on Lake Champlain. Vetch had engineered the best cooperative colonial efforts up to that time, only to have it wasted when his expected British auxiliary was diverted to Portugal. Even then the colonial leaders decided to attack Port Royal, in Acadia, but the naval commanders at the northern ports refused to assist and the scheme was dropped. Deeply discouraged, the colonies sent Nicholson, Col. Peter Schuyler [*q.v.*], and five Iroquois chiefs to implore Queen Anne for remuneration and for aid the next year. With British aid arriving late in 1710, the easy conquest of Port Royal and Acadia (called thereafter Annapolis Royal and Nova Scotia) was effected and Vetch, although Nicholson had commanded, received the promised military governorship. In 1711, at the insistence of Massachusetts, he took part in the expedition against Canada which a Tory ministry entrusted to Rear Admiral Sir Hovenden Walker and General "Jack" Hill. He generously did his best to help by piloting and advice, but Walker's ludicrous fears and ineptitude brought the expedition to disastrous failure at the mouth of the St. Lawrence.

Vetch's subsequent career was unhappy. Completely ignored in England, he spent his own and his friends' resources in maintaining Annapolis for the British Crown. His former protégé, Nicholson, who secured the civil governorship of Nova Scotia, harried him unmercifully at Annapolis and Boston and would have utterly ruined him but for the death of Queen Anne and the return of the Whigs to power. Vetch fled to England in 1714, and secured the civil governorship in January 1715, only to lose it in 1717 while still engaged in a vain effort to clear up his affairs. Tempted by several unfulfilled ministerial promises of remunerative employment, he remained in England and died in 1732 a prisoner in king's bench for debt.

[*Sloane MS. 3607* (letter-book, 1711–13), British Museum; MSS. of the Canada Expedition, Huntington Lib., San Marino, Cal.; papers in the possession of Mrs. R. W. Kelley, Mrs. J. L. Redmond, and J. R. Speyers, Esq., of New York, and of Dr. J. C. Webster, Shediac, N. B.; H. L. Osgood, *The Am. Colonies in the Eighteenth Century* (1924), vols. I, II; *Hist. of the State of N. Y.* (1933), ed. by A. C. Flick, vol. II; *Calendar of State Papers, Colonial Ser., America and West Indies, 1706–15* (6 vols., 1916–28); Thomas M'Crie, *Memoirs of Mr. William Veitch and George Brysson* (1825); Everett Kimball, *The Public Life of Joseph Dudley* (1911); George Patterson, "Hon. Samuel Vetch, First English Governor of Nova Scotia," *Nova Scotia Hist. Soc. Coll.*, vol. IV (1885); J. C. Webster, *Samuel Vetch* (privately printed, Shediac, N. B., 1929); sketch by R. H. Vetch, in *Dict. Nat. Biog.*; E. B. O'Callaghan, *Docs. Rel. to the Col. Hist. of . . . N. Y.*, vols. IV, IX (1854–55). Portraits of

Vetch, his wife and daughter, are in the possession of Mrs. R. W. Kelley and J. R. Speyers.]   J. B. B.

VETHAKE, HENRY (1792–Dec. 16, 1866), teacher, economist, was born in Essequibo County, British Guiana, and was brought to the United States by his parents at the age of four. Graduating at Columbia College in 1808, he subsequently taught mathematics and geography there; he also studied law. In 1813 he became professor of mathematics and natural philosophy at Queen's College (now Rutgers University). He moved rapidly from one institution to another, going to the College of New Jersey in 1817, to Dickinson College in 1821, and returning to the College of New Jersey in 1829 as professor of natural philosophy. In 1832 he became professor in the University of the City of New York, which he left in about three years to become president—for eighteen months—of Washington College, Lexington, Va. Here he also occupied the chair of intellectual and moral philosophy. His longest period of academic service was at the University of Pennsylvania, where he was professor of mathematics and philosophy (1836–55) and of philosophy (1855–59), vice-provost (1845–55), and provost (1855–59). He was not successful in administrative work. In 1859 he was appointed professor of mathematics in the Polytechnic College, Philadelphia, where he remained until his death. On Apr. 15, 1831, he was elected a member of the American Philosophical Society.

Vethake's political economy was thoroughly orthodox. Despite his hopeful American environment, where rapid progress was being made in all departments of economic life, and notwithstanding his residence in Philadelphia, which was the home of the budding nationalist school, he was obsessed with the notion of diminishing returns. He was opposed to practically every form of governmental interference in economic life, and constantly betrayed the current European fear that the capitalist would be inconvenienced for humanitarian objects. He affords a good illustration of the transfer of classical economic inhibitions to the new continent. His *Introductory Lecture on Political Economy* (1831), devoted mainly to a defense of the science, then unfamiliar in this country, may be read today with profit. One of the earliest in a long line of scholars proficient in the mathematical and natural sciences who expounded political economy, he appreciated the limitations and at the same time the difficulties of social studies. By the time he published *The Principles of Political Economy* (1838, 1844), he had broadened his concept of wealth to include services, and

that of capital to embrace knowledge and skills, but this natural introduction to a liberal treatment of the whole subject was denied in the subsequent chapters. His acceptance of the wage-fund theory, *i.e.*, that wages were paid out of a predetermined allocation by capitalist employers, led him to declare, in the way so familiar in British economic writing of the period, that "no advantage can be derived, by the receivers of wages, from the trades' unions" (p. 327), and that: "Although . . . the action of the trades' unions can hardly be stigmatized as of a *dishonest* character, . . . such action is, nevertheless, a violation to a certain extent of the rights of property. And if these rights may be once violated by the trades' unions, they may be again and again violated by them; and the apprehension of this taking place would constitute a check to the accumulation of capital with its usual rapidity; inducing, in consequence, a fall of wages below the usual rate" (p. 330). He was opposed to the statutory shortening of hours for all but children, and held that the leisure time provided the worker might tend to "deteriorate instead of improving his condition, by being spent . . . in dissipation and vice . . ." (p. 335). He refused to condemn the production of commodities by convicts, was wary of even private charity, and could tolerate public works to relieve the unemployed only if wages on them were below the going rate. However, he came close to approving the absorption of economic rent in taxes. He edited, and published in 1840, J. R. McCulloch's *A Dictionary, Practical, Theoretical, and Historical, of Commerce and Commercial Navigation,* with additional articles, mostly embracing American material, and was the editor, and in large part the author, of *Encyclopædia Americana, Supplementary Volume* (1848); this last named, while in the main prepared from secondary sources, showed his wide range of knowledge and ability to cull essential data. He contributed to a number of periodicals, writing always with great taste and clarity. He was married in 1836.

[S. A. Allibone, *A Critical Dict. of English Lit.,* vol. III (1871); J. L. Chamberlain, *Universities and Their Sons: Univ. of Pa.,* vol. I (1901); H. M. Lippincott, *The Univ. of Pa.* (1919); *Washington and Lee Univ. . . . Hist. Papers,* no. 6 (1904); *Pub. Ledger* (Phila.), Dec. 18, 1866.]   B. M.

VEZIN, HERMANN (Mar. 2, 1829–June 12, 1910), actor, was born in Philadelphia, Pa., the son of Emilie (Kalinsky) and Charles Henri Vezin, a merchant of French ancestry. He was graduated from the University of Pennsylvania in 1847 with the degree of A.B., and in 1850 received the degree of M.A. In the same year he went to England, bent upon becoming an actor in spite of the traditional parental opposition, and made his first appearance in that country at the Theatre Royal in York. After various provincial engagements, during which he rose from the playing of minor rôles to the acting of such leading characters as Richelieu, Sir Edward Mortimer, Claude Melnotte, and Young Norval, he made his London début in 1852. Except for a brief professional tour of the United States in 1857–58, he remained on the British stage for the rest of his long life, sometimes in support of stars, sometimes at the head of his own companies, and sometimes in the direction of theatres. He acted with Fechter, Samuel Phelps, Henry Irving, and in 1878 played Dr. Primrose in support of Ellen Terry in W. G. Wills's successful play, *Olivia,* dramatized from *The Vicar of Wakefield.* In 1863 he married Jane Elizabeth Thompson, who as Mrs. Charles Young had made a reputation as an actress both in Australia and in England, and he acted in many plays with her between their marriage and her death in 1902. In 1889 he was called upon by Irving to appear as Macbeth at the Lyceum Theatre in his stead in an emergency, receiving high praise from him and substantial acknowledgment in the form of a diamond ring and a check for £120.

Not imposing in stature, Vezin was described by Sir J. Forbes-Robertson as a "bright and dapper little man, then (1874) at the height of his popularity," and as "learned and dictatorial on the art of acting" (*A Player, post,* pp. 226 and 116). He was scholarly and intellectual in his impersonations rather than thrilling and inspiring, and had a somewhat hard and formal delivery. Yet so excellent an authority as Henry Morley declares in his *Journal of a London Playgoer* (1866, p. 326) that he was "a quietly good actor, who can rightly speak blank verse and give true but enforced expression to a poet's thought." During his long career he acted many hundred characters in every type of play, among the most important being Sir Giles Overreach in *A New Way to Pay Old Debts,* Hamlet, Ford in *The Merry Wives of Windsor* (with Phelps as Falstaff), Jaques in *As You Like It* (with Mr. and Mrs. Kendal), Dan'l Druce, James Harebell in *The Man o'Airlie,* and Lesurques and Dubosc in *The Courier of Lyons.* His appearances on the stage during his later years were only occasional, his time being occupied in giving lessons to stage aspirants, and in appearing at recitals and readings. His last acting was as Old Rowley in Sir Herbert Tree's production of *The School for Scandal* at His Majesty's Theatre in April 1909. He had been active on the British stage for nearly sixty years, and had been a resident of London, where he died, for the greater part of that period. He had a son who also became an actor.

[C. E. Pascoe, *The Dramatic List* (1879); Dutton Cook, *Nights at the Play* (2 vols., 1883); W. M. Phelps and John Forbes-Robertson, *The Life and Life-Work of Samuel Phelps* (1886); H. B. Baker, *The London Stage . . . from 1576 to 1888* (2 vols., 1889); Clement Scott and Cecil Howard, *The Life and Reminiscences of E. L. Blanchard* (2 vols., 1891); Erskine Reid and Herbert Compton, *The Dramatic Peerage* (1892); John Hollingshead, *Gaiety Chronicles* (1898); Bampton Hunt, ed., *The Green Room Book* (1906); Johnston Forbes-Robertson, *A Player under Three Reigns* (1925); *Stage* (London), June 16, 1910; *Athenaeum* (London), June 18, 1910; *N. Y. Dramatic Mirror,* Jan. 1, June 18, 1910; obituary in *Times* (London), June 14, 1910.]   E. F. E.

VIBBARD, CHAUNCEY (Nov. 11, 1811–June 5, 1891), railroad executive, congressman, capitalist, was born in Galway, N. Y. His father, Timothy Vibbard, Jr., was a descendant of a French family of the island of Jersey; his mother, Abigail (Nash), was of pioneer English stock. Chauncey attended the common schools of Galway and Mott's Academy for Boys in Albany, completing his course at fifteen. He became a clerk in a wholesale grocery store in Albany, and later clerk in a wholesale dry-goods house in New York City, then for some two years was a book-keeper in Montgomery, Ala. Late in 1836 he returned to his native state and was appointed chief clerk of the Utica & Schenectady Railroad, opened to traffic in that year. Here at last was work to his taste. He quickly mastered a maze of details, and made himself so necessary to the company that by 1849 he was general superintendent of the road; he had also become a stockholder.

An able organizer with considerable vision, Vibbard drew up with his own hand the first railroad time-table followed in the state and pledged his word to the public that, barring extraordinary difficulties, the trains should run as scheduled—an almost unheard-of thing at that time. He increased the comfort of passenger travel, and sought every appliance that would make for speed, safety, and efficiency. He saw that railroad conditions between Buffalo and Albany were essentially absurd: no less than ten little railroads functioned over portions of the distance; delays, inconvenience, and unnecessary costs were inevitable. He urged over a long period that these roads be consolidated, and at length the idea was taken up by Erastus Corning [*q.v.*], president of the Utica & Schenectady, with the result that in 1853 all the roads were welded into one line known as the New York Central, with a capital of $23,085,600. From

1853 to 1865 Vibbard was general superintendent of the consolidated line; he reorganized the system and made it a smoothly working machine. Meanwhile, by wise investments, he built up a considerable private fortune. He was for several years the principal owner of a large liquor concern in New York (dealing mostly with the South), which went out of business because of the Civil War.

In 1861 he was sent as a Democrat to Congress. In 1862 he was appointed director and superintendent of military railroads. He refused a renomination to Congress, although he could easily have been reëlected. In 1864 he supported McClellan's candidacy for the Presidency. In 1865 he resigned his position with the New York Central to devote his time to private business interests, though he continued as a large holder of railroad stocks. He was a partner in Vibbard & Foote, extensive dealers in railroad supplies, and was one of the owners of the Day Line of steamboats between New York and Albany. He served three years as president of the Family Fund Insurance Company, was one of the original stockholders in New York's first elevated railway, and was a director of the Central Branch Union Pacific Railroad. In his later years he was interested in developing railways in the southern United States and in Central and South America. His wife, Mary A. (Vedder) of Milton, N. Y., died in 1884, and Vibbard himself died in Macon, Ga., in 1891, leaving a daughter and two sons.

[Obituaries in *World* (N. Y.), *N. Y. Herald, N. Y. Times,* June 6, 1891; *N. Y. Tribune,* June 7, 1891; F. W. Stevens, *The Beginnings of the New York Central Railroad* (1926); annual reports of the N. Y. Central R.R., 1854–65; *Biog. Dir. Am. Cong.* (1928).]

A.F.H.

VICK, JAMES (Nov. 23, 1818–May 16, 1882), seedsman, florist, and publisher, was born at Chichester, near Portsmouth, England, son of James and Elizabeth (Prime) Vick. In his boyhood he was a friend of Charles Dickens and their friendship continued in after years. In 1833 he came to the United States with his parents, settling first in New York City. Here he learned the printer's trade and worked for a time on the *Knickerbocker Magazine.* His case in the composing room adjoined that of Horace Greeley, who remained his lifelong friend. In 1837 he removed to Rochester, N. Y., and worked as a compositor in several newspaper offices. During a printer's strike the leading journeymen started a paper called the *Workingman's Advocate,* which in a few months passed into the hands of Vick and one or two others, who soon sold it to Henry O'Reilly [*q.v.*]. About this time Vick published Frederick Douglass' paper, the *North Star.*

Being passionately fond of flowers, in his leisure time he cultivated a garden and developed a taste for agriculture and horticulture. In 1848 he began to import seeds from abroad. Over the signature of "Young Digger" he contributed articles to the *Genesee Farmer,* published in Rochester. These brought him into contact with the management of the paper and in 1850 he was made one of the editors, the others being Daniel Lee and Patrick Barry [*q.v.*]. After the death of Andrew J. Downing [*q.v.*], editor of the *Horticulturist,* Vick purchased that magazine from Luther Tucker [*q.v.*] and published it in Rochester from 1853 to 1855 with Barry as editor. From 1857 to 1862 he was editor of the *Rural New Yorker,* also published in Rochester. It was while connected with this journal that he began the seed business which was destined to bring him a world-wide reputation.

The seeds which he had imported from abroad he planted in a little garden on Union Street, and gradually increased his stock; later he had gardens elsewhere. Soon he was sending out so many seeds that he had to begin to charge for them. They were sent by mail in answer to mail orders accompanied by cash. By 1862 his business had so increased that for the remainder of his life he gave it his whole attention. He employed a force of 150, and often the firm received 3,000 letters a day; in some seasons he spent $30,000 for postage. The circulation of his *Floral Guide,* or annual catalogue, reached 200,000 copies. In 1878 he founded *Vick's Monthly Magazine,* later known as *Vick's Illustrated Monthly Magazine* and under other titles, which he himself edited.

With the establishment of his business, seeds were placed within easy reach and a new era in the culture of flowers began in the United States. For about twenty years his name was a household word and he was more widely known than any other seed merchant at home or abroad. In various ways he exercised great influence on the horticulture of the country. He made some notable advances in the cross breeding of garden flowers, among his creations being the white double phlox, fringed petunia, white gladiolus, "the sunrise" amaranthus, and the Japan cockscomb. Vick's gardens in the blooming season were a great attraction to visitors and did much to beautify Rochester. His name is commemorated there in Vick Park, and Portsmouth Terrace was named after his birthplace. In all his dealings he maintained the highest character for honesty, integrity, and liberality, and he was always ready to help in any good work. He served as secretary of the American Pomological Society (1862–64), and was a corresponding member of the Royal Horticultural Society. For twenty-five years he was superintendent of the Sunday school connected with the First Methodist Episcopal Church. He died of pneumonia and was buried in Mount Hope Cemetery, Rochester. On July 5, 1842, he married Mary Elizabeth, daughter of John and Susan Seelye, of Rochester, who with four sons and three daughters survived him.

[*Rochester Democrat and Chronicle* and *Rochester Morning Herald*, May 17, 1882; *Vick's Monthly Magazine*, June 1882; *Rural New Yorker*, May 27, 1882; *Thirteenth Ann. Report of the Secretary of the State Hort. Soc. of Mich.* (1884); *Proc. Western N. Y. Horticultural Soc.*, 1883; J. M. Parker, *Rochester: A Story Historical* (1884); *Rochester Hist. Soc. Pubs.*, vol. VI (1927); J. F. Hart, *The Industries of the City of Rochester* (1888).]   C. R. B.

VICTOR, FRANCES FULLER (May 23, 1826–Nov. 14, 1902), author, historian, was born in Rome Township, Oneida County, N. Y., of New England stock, the eldest of the five daughters of Lucy (Williams) Fuller and her husband, whose name is said to have been Adonijah. When she was thirteen years old her family moved to Ohio. Frances and her sister Metta Victoria wrote verse for newspapers while still in their teens and, having attended a girls' school at Wooster, went to New York to seek literary careers. Friends of Alice and Phoebe Cary, they belonged to the coterie that buzzed around that impresario of "female poets," Rufus Wilmot Griswold [*q.v.*]. He is said to have edited their joint volume, *Poems of Sentiment and Imagination, with Dramatic and Descriptive Pieces* (1851). Frances returned home to assist her sick parents, is said to have married a Jackson Barritt of Pontiac, Mich., in 1853, and forgot her literary aspirations. In 1862 she married a naval engineer, Henry Clay Victor, whose brother, Orville James Victor [*q.v.*], had married Metta Victoria. The next year her husband was ordered to duty at San Francisco, and she followed him. Stimulated by a new environment and by the necessity, in that greenback era, of supplementing her husband's salary, she began again to write and contributed to various San Francisco and Sacramento newspapers. In 1865 the Victors moved to Oregon. Mrs. Victor conceived a strong enthusiasm for the Pacific Northwest and, by systematic travel and study, collection of documentary material, and interviews with old inhabitants, became the most competent authority on the region and its history. Her first books on it were *The River of the West* (1870) and *All Over Oregon and Washington* (1872). The first is chiefly an account, largely autobi-

ographical, of Joseph L. Meek, the second a handbook of the region. After her husband perished in the wreck of the *Pacific*, Nov. 4, 1875, Mrs. Victor lived by her writing. She was a member for eleven years of Hubert Howe Bancroft's staff and wrote part of the *History of the Northwest Coast* (2 vols., 1884) and the whole of the *History of Oregon* (2 vols., 1886–88), the *History of Washington, Idaho, and Montana* (1890), the *History of Nevada, Colorado, and Wyoming* (1890), and volumes VI and VII of the *History of California* (1890), besides contributing biographical sketches to other portions of the work. She had a pleasing style, strove for accuracy and fairness, and usually attained them. Her historical work is still regarded with respect. After her work with Bancroft was completed she was for a time in narrow circumstances and sold toilet articles from door to door in Salem, Ore. Later a small pension and her earnings kept her in modest comfort. Among her other separate publications are: *The New Penelope* (1877), a volume of short stories and verse; *Atlantis Arisen: or, Talks of a Tourist about Oregon and Washington* (1891); *The Early Indian Wars of Oregon* (1894); and *Poems* (1900). She was able to work cheerfully to the last. She died unexpectedly in a Portland boarding house in her seventy-seventh year.

[H. H. Bancroft, *Literary Industries* (1890); Alfred Powers, *Hist. of Oregon Lit.* (1935); Joseph Gaston, *The Centennial Hist. of Ore.* (4 vols., 1912); W. A. Morris, "The Origin and Authorship of the Bancroft Pacific States Pubs.," *Quart. Ore. Hist. Soc.*, Dec. 1903; *Morning Oregonian* (Portland), Nov. 15, 1902 (obituary), Nov. 16 (editorial and article).] G. H. G.

VICTOR, ORVILLE JAMES (Oct. 23, 1827–Mar. 14, 1910), author, publisher, was born at Sandusky, Ohio, of German and English stock, the son, it is said, of Henry and Gertrude (Nash) Victor. After completing a four-year course in the Norwalk Academy, he read law in the office of Charles B. Squire of Sandusky, contributed verse and prose to several magazines, and in 1852 became assistant editor, under Henry David Cooke [*q.v.*], of the *Daily Register*. In July 1856 he married Metta Victoria Fuller (Mar. 2, 1831–June 26, 1885), who was at that time a more important literary personage than he was.

From his marriage almost to the close of his long life Victor was associated with various New York publishing houses that specialized in the production of cheap, popular books and magazines. For a number of years he was the chief editor of Erastus F. Beadle's enterprises. He was the editor, at various times, of such magazines as the *Cosmopolitan Art Journal*, the *United States Journal, Beadle's Magazine of To-day*, the

Western World, the *Saturday Journal*, and the *Banner Weekly*. His own works include: *The History, Civil, Political, and Military, of the Southern Rebellion* . . . (4 vols., 1861–68); issued originally in monthly parts; *The American Rebellion: Some Facts and Reflections for the Consideration of the English People* (London, 1861); *Incidents and Anecdotes of the War* (1862); *History of American Conspiracies* (1863); and paper-backed biographies of Winfield Scott, Anthony Wayne, John Paul Jones, Ethan Allen, Israel Putnam, Giuseppe Garibaldi, and Abraham Lincoln. These biographies were part of the Dime Biographical Library, one of the many "Libraries" that Victor edited. His work, in general, is that of a competent, industrious, and undistinguished publisher's drudge.

In 1860, however, he made history and conferred a memorable boon on his compatriots by inventing the American dime novel. He himself signed none of the hundreds of such novels published by the firms of Beadle & Company and Beadle & Adams, but he first conceived the idea, worked out the details, and taught a corps of writers to produce the kind of story he wanted. Among the authors that he engaged and trained were Augustine Joseph Hickey Duganne [*q.v.*], Mary A. Denison, Edward Sylvester Ellis [*q.v.*], Ann Sophia Stephens [*q.v.*], and his own wife. She produced at least one masterpiece of the kind, *Maum Guinea and Her Plantation Children*, published during the early part of the Civil War. The Beadle dime novels were simple, brisk, wholesome stories of adventure, usually in a Western or Southwestern setting, and were sold by the million to Northern soldiers. Their success provoked competition, and competition brought with it sensationalism. Victor lived to see the *genre* that he had devised fall into disrepute and dwindle to insignificance. His home for many years was at Hohokus, N. J., where, during his wife's lifetime, he liked to entertain his literary friends. He died there in his eighty-third year.

[*Who's Who in America*, 1901–02; C. M. Harvey, "The Dime Novel in Am. Life," *Atlantic Monthly*, July 1907; *N. Y. Tribune*, Mar. 17, 1910; E. L. Pearson, *Dime Novels* (1929).]   G. H. G.

VIEL, FRANÇOIS ÉTIENNE BERNARD ALEXANDRE (Oct. 31, 1736–Dec. 16, 1821), priest and Latin scholar, was born in New Orleans, La. His father, Dr. Bernard Alexandre Viel, a native of France, emigrated to Louisiana and was among the first surgeons to practise in the colony. His mother was Marie Macarthy, part Irish and part Creole. In 1747 Dr. Viel took his eleven-year-old son to France and placed him in the Royal Academy of Juilly conducted by the Oratorian brotherhood. He proved a splendid student and soon led his classes. For nine years he never left the institution even for holidays. Exposed to such continuous religious influence it was almost inevitable that, after his graduation, he should join the Oratorians. He was the first native-born Louisianian to take holy orders. He was sent as an instructor to Soissons, then to Mans, and finally in 1760 returned to his alma mater, the Academy of Juilly, where he taught the humanities and rhetoric until in 1776 he was appointed *grand préfet* of the college. When the French Revolution destroyed all the Oratorian institutions of learning and scattered the order in 1792, Abbé Viel returned to Louisiana and became the parish priest of the Attakapas, where for twenty years he served his simple agricultural flock, earning their love and affection. In 1812 he was recalled to France to aid in the reestablishment of his order, and for five years taught at Juilly until he suffered a slight stroke. When he recovered he was permitted to devote the rest of his life to the useless but learned avocation to which he was fanatically attached—the translation into Latin verse of the works of great French authors. He was a Latin scholar of the utmost distinction.

When he fled from Paris in 1792 he left with a friend a manuscript he had just completed, a rhymed version in Latin of Fénelon's *Télémaque* (1797). Six of his former pupils discovered it and, to do him honor, paid for its publication in 1808. Four years later when Viel returned to Paris he corrected this edition and in 1814 brought out a second one. He called it *Telemachiada* and dedicated it to his six ex-students who had made the first edition possible. Altogether he did five volumes of translations of the works of various authors, one of which, *Le Voyage de la Grande Chartreuse* (1782), ran into seven editions. His rendering of these French masterpieces into Latin verse was so beautiful in its accuracy and richness that the poet Barthélemy, who had been his pupil, wrote a poem in which he spoke of

"Viel qui de Fénelon virgilisa la prose."

The abbé died on Dec. 16, 1821, at the College of Juilly, where he had spent the best part of his life, first in acquiring and then in disseminating learning.

[E. L. Tinker, *Les Écrits de Langue Française au XIXe Siècle* (1932); Alfred Mercier, in *Comptes-Rendus de l'Athénée Louisianais*, July 1890; Gustave Devron, *Ibid.*, July 1899, with a portrait; Charles Hamel, *Histoire de l'Abbaye et du Collège de Juilly* (Paris, 1868); Charles Richomme, *Histoire de l'Université de Paris* (Paris, 1840); obituary in *Journal des Débats* (Paris), Dec. 20, 1821.]   E. L. T.

VIELE, AERNOUT CORNELISSEN

(1640–c. 1704), interpreter and negotiator with the Indians, was born in New Amsterdam, probably the son of Cornelis Volkertszen and Maria (du Trieux) Viele. His father was an emigrant from Holland, an inn-keeper and trader, and apparently prosperous. The boy was baptized on May 27, 1640. He was a resident of Albany as early as 1659, and the year following he joined in a petition to forbid white men trading within the Indian country. He married Gerritje Gerritse Vermeulen, the step-daughter of Arent Janse Timmerman, probably in 1663. Twelve years later he was a recognized interpreter between the red men and the white, and this service he performed in 1682 at Albany at a conference between the Five Nations and commissioners from Maryland. At this period he had acquired command of the Iroquois dialects, with a degree of skill in the studied features of Indian oratory. Public speaking among the Indians was a formal art, which the envoys of the Canadian governors, and some at least of the French missionaries, cultivated and which their rivals for the affections of the Indians could not afford to neglect. Viele had need of every resource when as the deputy of Gov. Thomas Dongan [q.v.] he harangued an Onondaga audience, in opposition to Charles Le Moyne and the eloquent Jesuit, Father Lamberville, and planted the arms of the Duke of York in the Onondaga Castle. A few years later he led a large party of men, advance agents of New York trade, into the Ottawa country north of the Great Lakes. They were captured by the vigilant French, and he was taken to Quebec, from which he returned home, escaping apparently, after an imprisonment of four months.

From 1688 to 1690 he was living for considerable periods with the Onondaga, who were in those years enjoying their ascendancy among the Iroquois. While he was on one of these missions, it would seem, the Schenectady massacre occurred. Five of his family, his eldest daughter, her two children, a daughter-in-law, and a grandson, perished. His son, Aernout, was carried away, but escaped after three years of captivity. These events gave an added motive to his efforts to protect the New York border. In 1691 he was enrolled as a fusilier. He supported Lieut.-Gov. Jacob Leisler [q.v.] in the civil strife that rent the colony and was appointed resident general agent by him. Governor Fletcher kept him employed at the Onondaga outpost, from which he reported danger signals when Frontenac was stirring. Governor Bellomont (see sketch of Richard Coote, Earl of Bellomont) continued the settled Indian policy after the peace between France and England at Ryswick; and Viele, who was then living on Long Island, was soon on guard again at Onondaga Castle. His journal, from Apr. 14 to May 7, 1699, gives the details of his journey and transactions (*Documents, post,* vol. IV, pp. 560–62).

A second trading adventure is recorded. For two years he was journeying in the country of the Shawnee to the southward of the province. In regions nearer home he acquired property. From Indians on the Hudson he received land in the region soon to be comprised by Dutchess County. Later, the Mohawk gave him title to a tract on the river near Schenectady. He was prominently connected with the Reformed Dutch Church in Albany. After 1704 his name falls out of the records, which seems a fair indication that he was dead.

[*Documents Relative to the Colonial Hist. of . . . N. Y.,* vols. III (1853), IV (1854), IX (1855), procured and ed. by J. R. Brodhead and E. B. O'Callaghan; *Calendar of Hist. MSS. in the office of the Sec. of State,* vol. I (1865), ed. by E. B. O'Callaghan; *Minutes of the Court of Albany, Rensselaerswyck, and Schenectady,* vol. III (1932), trans. and ed. by A. J. F. van Laer; Jonathan Pearson, *A Hist. of the Schenectady Patent* (1883) and *Contributions for the Geneal. of the First Settlers of Albany* (1872); *Viele Records* (1913) and *Sketches of . . . Knickerbacker-Viele* (1916), ed. by K. K. Viele.]   R. E. D.

VIELE, EGBERT LUDOVICUS (June 17,

1825–Apr. 22, 1902), engineer, was born at Waterford, N. Y., the son of John Ludovicus and Kathlyne Knickerbacker Viele. The founder of his family in America, Cornelis Volkertszen, father of Aernout Cornelissen Viele [q.v.], was a tavern keeper in New Amsterdam as early as 1639. John Ludovicus Viele was a state senator, a judge of the court of errors, and a regent of the University of the State of New York. Egbert attended the common schools of Lansingburg, graduated with honors at the Albany Academy, and began the study of law. In 1843, however, he secured appointment to the United States Military Academy, where he graduated in 1847. He was sent at once to join an infantry regiment fighting in the Mexican War, and after the peace he saw service on the southwestern frontier. On June 3, 1850, he married Teresa Griffin, who bore him eight children.

In 1853 he resigned his commission, returned to New York, and opened an office as a civil engineer. From 1854 to 1856 he was employed by the state of New Jersey, and in the latter year became chief engineer of the projected Central Park in New York City. He made preliminary surveys and submitted a plan for the development of the park, but after a reorganization of the park commission in the following year his design was superseded by that of Frederick Law Olmsted and Calvert Vaux [*qq.v.*], and his services were discontinued. In 1860 he was engineer of Prospect Park, Brooklyn.

While engineer of Central Park Viele began a study of the original topography of Manhattan Island, and later repeatedly called attention to the necessity for recognizing the natural drainage system of the island in planning streets and sewers. In 1865 he published a pamphlet, *The Topography and Hydrology of New York,* urging sanitation from the point of view of the engineer. He thus had a part in the movement which resulted in the Metropolitan Health Law of 1866. His *Topographical Atlas of the City of New York,* published by Julius Bien [*q.v.*] in 1874, "showing the original water courses and made land," was of much value to the erectors of large buildings.

Meanwhile, in the first year of the Civil War, Viele's *Hand-book for Active Service* (1861) was published in New York and also (in two parts) in Richmond, Va. Viele became a captain of engineers in the 7th New York Militia, served in the defenses of Washington, and on Aug. 17, 1861, was made a brigadier-general of volunteers. He was second in command of the Port Royal expedition, participated in the capture of Fort Pulaski and the taking of Norfolk, Va., was military governor of Norfolk from May to October 1862, and was then put in charge of the draft in northern Ohio. In 1863 he resigned and resumed his engineering practice in New York. About 1868 he promulgated a plan for the "Arcade" underground railway, a presage of the subways which came much later. He served as a commissioner of parks for New York City in 1883–84, and in 1885–87 as a Democratic representative in Congress. In that body he did much to further the building of the Harlem Ship Canal. He then returned to private life and to his practice. About 1895, while visiting England, he spoke before a committee of the House of Lords upon American municipal administration. As a member of the International Congress of History, he gave the closing address at The Hague Congress in 1898. He was an early member and a vice-president of the American Geographical Society, president of the Aztec Society, and a trustee of the Holland Society of New York. His first marriage was terminated by divorce in 1872 and shortly afterward he married Juliette H. Dana. Two sons and two daughters survived him; the elder son, Herman Knickerbocker Vielé, studied civil engineering with his father and later became an artist; the young-

er, Egbert Ludovicus, Jr., was taken by his mother to France and there attained distinction as a poet, under the name Francis Vielé-Griffin.

[Viele apparently used no accent in his signature; his son H. K. Vielé, in "Gen. Egbert L. Vielé," *N. Y. Geneal. and Biog. Record,* Jan. 1903, uses the accent and spells the middle name Lodovickus, while Viele's daughter, Kathlyne Knickerbacker Viele, in *Viele 1659–1909* (1909) and *Viele Records* (1913), uses the forms adopted in this sketch. See also *Who's Who in America,* 1901–02; G. W. Cullum, *Biog. Reg. Officers and Grads. U. S. Mil. Acad.* (3rd ed., 1891), vol. II; *Thirty-third Ann. Reunion Asso. Grads. U. S. Mil. Acad.* (1902); *Year Book of the Holland Soc. of N. Y.* (1903); *Biog. Dir. Am. Cong.* (1928); *Bull. Am. Geog. Soc.,* Apr. 1902; C. C. Cook, *A Description of the N. Y. Central Park* (1869); *Army and Navy Jour.,* Apr. 26, 1902; *N. Y. Tribune,* Apr. 23, 1902.]   A. F. H.

VIGNAUD, HENRY (Nov. 27, 1830–Sept. 16, 1922), journalist, diplomat, historian, christened Jean Hélidore, was born in New Orleans, La., the eldest of the six children of Jean Lucien and Clémence (Godefroy) Vignaud. His paternal grandparents, born in Provence, came with their parents to Louisiana in the eighteenth century. He was educated in the schools of New Orleans, in which, 1852–56, he was also a teacher. His career as a journalist commenced with articles for the newspapers of New Orleans; from 1857 to 1860 he edited a weekly paper at Thibodaux, La., *L'Union de LaFourche,* and in 1860–61 he was editor of a weekly review devoted to French culture, *La Renaissance Louisianaise.* He also tried his hand at drama and is said (Cordier, *post*) to have had two plays produced at the French theatre of New Orleans.

With the outbreak of the Civil War he became a captain in the 6th Louisiana Regiment but was made prisoner in 1862, when New Orleans was captured. Escaping, he reached Paris and never returned to the United States. In Paris he entered the service of the Confederate mission under John Slidell [*q.v.*]. His duties seem to have been chiefly journalistic and he wrote for the *Index,* the Confederate organ published in London, and for the *Mémorial Diplomatique,* a Paris weekly, winning the praise of Henry Hotze, in charge of Confederate propaganda (*Official Records of the Union and Confederate Navies,* 2 ser. III, 1178). Of the latter paper he became the regular musical and dramatic critic, and also, 1867–75, the *administrateur.*

Vignaud's diplomatic career in the Confederate mission was brief, but in 1869 he was appointed to a secretaryship in the Roumanian legation at Paris, and in 1872 he served as translator for the United States in the presentation of the *Alabama* claims for the Geneva arbitration (F. W. Hackett, *Reminiscences of the Geneva Tribunal,* 1911, pp. 106, 125 n.). On Dec. 14, 1875, recommended by Elihu B. Washburne (E. B. Washburne, *Recollections of a Minister to France*, 1887, II, 324), he was appointed second secretary of the United States legation in Paris, and on Apr. 11, 1885, was promoted to be first secretary. For thirty-four years he was the indispensable member of the Paris mission, frequently acting as chargé d'affaires, and serving always with distinction. His dispatches, *e.g.*, those of October 1884, relating to the good offices of the United States in the Franco-Chinese War, display a very high degree of understanding and diplomatic skill. He enjoyed the complete confidence of his own as well as of the French government and was often called upon for special services, as, for example, to be umpire in the arbitration, 1905, of French claims against Haiti. On Mar. 31, 1909, at the age of seventy-eight, he resigned his position as secretary of the embassy, but was appointed honorary counselor. Public recognition of his long service came from the American colony in Paris and from the Department of State (*New York Herald*, Paris, May 9, 1909), from the French government, which promoted him to the rank of Grand Officier in the Legion of Honor, and from Tulane University, which conferred upon him the degree of LL.D.

Vignaud's distinction as a historian was achieved after the age of seventy. He had earlier worked at histories of America, which he left in manuscript as *"ouvrages sans valeur"* (Cordier, *post*), but his special interest in Columbus grew out of his close association with Henry Harrisse and with the Peruvian scholar Manuel Gonzalez de la Rosa, and the publications of the Columbian anniversary of 1892. Convinced by De la Rosa that the famous letter of Toscanelli of 1474 was not genuine, he presented a paper on the subject, as also did De la Rosa, at the Congress of Americanists of 1900 (*Congrès International des Américanistes, XIIᵉ Session*, 1902, pp. 11–62). Two volumes followed: *La Lettre et la Carte de Toscanelli* (1901) and, somewhat revised and enlarged, *Toscanelli and Columbus* (1902), after which Vignaud brought out three volumes on Columbus and one on Amerigo Vespucci: *Études critiques sur la vie de Colomb avant ses découvertes* (1905); *Histoire critique de la grande entreprise de Christophe Colomb* (2 vols., 1911); and *Améric Vespuce, 1451–1512* (1917). At the age of ninety-one he summarized his views on Columbus in a small book, *Le vrai Christophe Colomb et la Légende* (1921).

Vignaud's conclusions respecting Columbus may be briefly stated as follows: Columbus was born in 1451, of humble origins; he did not go to sea as a boy, but was a weaver, like his father; he did not go to Portugal until 1476, never made a voyage to Iceland, had no letter from Toscanelli suggesting that the Indies could be reached by the west, and did not set out in 1492 to find the Indies, but to discover islands and lands to the west, which in fact he found. These views, contradicting many points of the accepted Columbus tradition, aroused a controversy that is not yet ended. It is probably fair to say that, while his findings have deserved and received the most careful attention, they have not been generally accepted.

Vignaud also displayed a broad interest in the whole range of studies of aboriginal America and of the earliest European contacts with the new world. His address of Nov. 4, 1913, as president of the Société des Américanistes de Paris (*Journal . . . des Américanistes de Paris*, n.s. XI, 1 ff.) is a masterly analysis of the problems of this field of research, and his numerous contributions, for the most part published in the *Journal . . . des Américanistes* (n.s., vols. I–XIV, 1903–22), indicate the scope of his scholarship. His work was recognized by the award of numerous honors and prizes, and by election as a foreign corresponding member of the Institut de France.

Vignaud was married in 1879 to Louise Compte of Paris, who survived him a few years. They had no children, and made their home in Bagneux, a southern suburb of Paris, where their ancient and comfortable house was the scene of Vignaud's historical labors and of a hospitality freely extended, especially to American scholars. His library of many thousand books, pamphlets, and maps, is now the property of the University of Michigan. Among his papers was an unfinished history of cartography in approximately 650,000 words. He was of medium height and build, wiry and energetic. His kindly and keen features, with roughly trimmed beard, his animation, and his personal characteristics were French. He was perfectly bilingual, speaking and writing both French and English with distinction. He combined versatility of interest with powers of intense application and mastery of details, and possessed a boundless capacity for work.

[*Who's Who in America*, 1922–23; short sketches of Vignaud by Henri Cordier, one of his most intimate friends, in *Jour. . . . des Américanistes de Paris*, n.s. XV (1923), 1–17, with excellent portrait, geneal. table, and bibliog.; by E. A. Parsons, *La. Hist. Quart.*, Jan. 1922; and by Stoddard Dewey, in *Ex Libris* (Am. Lib. in Paris), June 1924, with photographs of Vignaud in his library and in his garden; *Le Mémorial Diplomatique* (Paris), 1863–75, containing many signed articles by Vignaud and his musical and dramatic criticisms; Vignaud's correspondence in U. S. Dept. of State, Diplomatic Archives, Despatches, France, 1875–1909 ; review of Vignaud's historical work by Henri Froidevaux in *France-Amérique*, Oct. 1921 ; dates of appointments from Dept. of State ; obituary in *N. Y. Times*, Sept. 19, 1922, and editorial, Sept. 20 ; personal recollections of conversations and visits, 1907–14.]   W. G. Le—d.

VIGO, JOSEPH MARIA FRANCESCO (Dec. 3, 1747–Mar. 22, 1836), soldier, merchant, was born in Mondovì, Piedmont, now a part of Italy, the son of Matheo and Maria Magdalena (Iugalibus) Vigo. While a youthful member of a Spanish regiment, he was sent to New Orleans and there became interested in the fur trade. He soon received his discharge, became a very successful trader, and gained at the same time great influence with the French settlers and with the Indians. In 1772 he had reached out as far as the new post at St. Louis, where he established his headquarters and ultimately formed a secret partnership with Fernando de Leyba, the Spanish lieutenant governor at St. Louis.

When George Rogers Clark [*q.v.*] made an expedition, on behalf of Virginia, for the protection of the early American settlers in the northwest country, Vigo became interested in the American cause. Twice he journeyed to Kaskaskia from St. Louis to give assistance to Clark. The last time, on Jan. 29, 1779, was after his return from Vincennes, where he had gone at the instance of Clark to aid the American commandant. Imprisoned by the British, he was later released as a Spanish citizen, and he very promptly carried information and financial aid to Clark. There at Kaskaskia was inaugurated that memorable campaign which ended the British influence in the northwest territory and fixed the claims of the Americans to the northwest country. Clark was sadly in need of assistance, having only Virginia colonial money that was of no value with the French inhabitants. Francis Vigo, as he was usually called in America, threw his fortune into the balance and rendered assistance so valuable that he shares with Clark the responsibility for this conquest. When Virginia later ceded all this territory to the confederation of American states, she made the condition that the United States should assume and pay all expenses and indebtedness incurred by her in maintaining defense of the same ; but Vigo was not repaid in his lifetime. He gave freely of his time, influence, and fortune, to the American cause, but he spent his declining years in comparative want. When an old man he sold his family silver to buy food. Nearly one hundred years passed before the federal Supreme Court ordered his claims to be paid, and his heirs received about $50,000.

Vigo removed from St. Louis to Vincennes before 1783 and soon became a naturalized citizen of the United States. After the Revolution he rendered conspicuous service, both civil and military. He was executor in the will of Governor De Leyba, dated at St. Louis on June 10, 1780. Sometime before 1783 he married Elizabeth Shannon, the daughter of Clark's quartermaster. She died on Mar. 20, 1818, leaving no descendants. Vigo lived during his last years on a farm near Vincennes, but spent much of his time at the home of his old friend William Henry Harrison [*q.v.*]. For many years he was a practising member of the Roman Catholic Church but in his later days he fell away from that faith. He died without receiving the last rites of the Church and was buried in the Protestant Cemetery. In the city of Vincennes, where he died and was buried, a street bears his name. There are a county and township in Indiana named for him, and great tribute was paid to him at the dedication of the memorial to George Rogers Clark.

[Bruno Roselli, *Vigo: A Forgotten Builder of the American Republic* (1933) ; J. J. Thompson, "Penalties of Patriotism, Vigo," in *Jour. of the Ill. State Hist. Soc.*, Jan. 1917 ; Dorothy Riker, "Francis Vigo," in *Ind. Mag. of Hist.*, Mar. 1930 ; "Governors Messages and Letters. Messages and Letters of Wm. H. Harrison," *Ind. Hist. Coll.* (1922), vol. I, ed. by Logan Esarey ; B. J. Griswold, *Fort Wayne* (1927) ; W. H. English, *Conquest of the Country Northwest of the River Ohio* (2 vols., 1896) ; C. C. Baldwin, "A Centennial Law Suit," in *Western Reserve and Northern Hist. Soc.*, Tract 35, Dec. 1876 ; 91 *U. S. Reports*, 326 ; *House Reports 13*, 25 Cong., 3 Sess. (1838) ; *House Report 525*, 27 Cong., 2 Sess. (1842) ; *House Report 216*, 30 Cong., 1 Sess. (1848) ; Voorhis Memorial Coll., George Rogers Clark Papers, Mo. Hist. Soc. Lib. Mo. ; Burton Coll. Public Lib., Detroit, Mich. ; Draper Coll., Wis. State Hist. Soc. Lib., Madison, Wis. ; Vigo Papers, D. A. R. Chapter, Vincennes. For law suit of heir see sketch of John Law.]   S. M. D.

VILAS, WILLIAM FREEMAN (July 9, 1840–Aug. 27, 1908), lawyer, cabinet member, senator from Wisconsin, was the son of Judge Levi Baker Vilas and Esther Green (Smilie) Vilas, and a descendant of Peter Vilas (1704–1756), an emigrant from England. Brought by his parents from his birthplace, Chelsea, Orange County, Vt., to Madison, Wis., in 1851, he was graduated at the University of Wisconsin in 1858, and at the Law School of the University of Albany (N. Y.), in 1860. He was admitted to the bar in Madison in 1860, but before he became heavily involved in legal practice he went to war with the 23rd Wisconsin volunteer regiment, rising to the rank of lieutenant-colonel. Mustered out, he returned to Madison and gained immediate distinction in his profession. He served the state, 1875–78, as reviser of statutes (*Revised Statutes of the State of Wisconsin*, 1878) and assisted in reëditing the first twenty volumes of *Wisconsin Reports* (published 1875–76). He became a professor of law (1868–85, 1889–92) and a regent (1881–85, 1898–1905) of the University of Wisconsin, a worker on many non-political bodies and commissions, and in 1885 a member of the Wisconsin legislature.

At the home-coming banquet for General Grant given by the Society of the Army of the Tennessee in the old Palmer House in Chicago, Nov. 13, 1879, Vilas made the successful speech of an evening too full of oratory (*Milwaukee Sentinel,* Nov. 14, 1879). He was established by this as the most prominent Democratic orator in Wisconsin, and he contested thereafter with General Edward S. Bragg [*q.v.*] for the reality of party leadership. In 1884 he was permanent chairman of the convention that nominated Cleveland for the presidency, and served as chairman of the committee that notified the nominee. Cleveland appointed him postmaster-general and relied upon him as a counselor and friend. In 1887 the President and his young wife were entertained at the handsome Vilas mansion in Madison (*Wisconsin State Journal,* Oct. 7, 1887; *New York Herald,* Oct. 8, 1887). As postmaster-general (Mar. 6, 1885–Jan. 16, 1888), Vilas was useful because of an intimate knowledge of the West and an unusual degree of executive ability; but he issued a circular warning postal employees against "offensive partisanship" that evoked a scolding from civil service reformers (*Wisconsin Magazine of History,* Sept. 1932, p. 5). In 1888, when L. Q. C. Lamar [*q.v.*] was elevated to the Supreme Court, Vilas was shifted to the Department of the Interior. Here his special abilities had even greater value since the business of the department was largely in the West and since the arbitrary accumulation of unrelated bureaus in the department gave skill in administration a chance to show itself He knew, perhaps, too much for his comfort. Part of his fortune was based upon speculations in land and lumber, and these aroused intermittent attacks from his political opponents in Wisconsin (*Wisconsin State Journal,* Jan. 18, 1893; *Milwaukee Sentinel,* Oct. 22, 1894). Upon the termination of the Democratic administration in 1889 he returned to Madison. In 1891 he was elected by the Democratic legislature to succeed John C. Spooner [*q.v.*] in the United States Senate. He was defeated by Spooner six years later and retired to private life. A trusted friend of Cleveland, Vilas adhered to the gold standard, fought Bryan in the convention at Chicago, and was chairman of the committee that drafted the platform of the "Gold Democrats" at Indianapolis in September 1896.

For the rest of his life he was an onlooker in politics, with Republicans dominating his state, and a new order rising to power in the LaFollette group. He was the first citizen of Madison, after the death of General Lucius Fairchild [*q.v.*], and was active in the rebuilding of the University of Wisconsin under Presidents Thomas C. Chamberlin, Charles Kendall Adams, and Charles R. Van Hise [*qq.v.*]. Under the influence of Van Hise he provided, by a carefully drafted will, that his large estate should go to the University after the death of his wife and the one daughter who survived him. He was married on Jan. 3, 1866, to Anna Matilda Fox.

[Vilas' papers, as yet sealed, are in the custody of the State Hist. Soc. of Wis., and may be expected to provide abundant materials for the history of business in the Northwest. His widow procured the private printing of *Selected Addresses and Orations of William F. Vilas* (1912), with a brief biographical sketch. There are sketches of his life in 137 *Wisconsin Reports,* xxxi-liii; and in *Proc. State Hist. Soc. of Wis.* (1909), pp. 155–64, by B. W. Jones; and there are excellent obituaries in *Milwaukee Journal,* Aug. 27, 1908; and *Milwaukee Sentinel,* Aug. 28, 1908. See also C. H. Vilas, *A Genealogy of the Descendants of Peter Vilas* (1875); R. G. Thwaites, *The University of Wisconsin* (1900).]

F. L. P.

VILLAGRÁ, GASPAR PÉREZ de (*c.* 1555–*c.* 1620), officer of the expedition of Juan de Oñate [*q.v.*] to New Mexico in 1598, author of an epic poem on New Mexico, was born probably between 1551 and 1555 in Puebla de los Angeles, Spain, the son of Hernán Pérez de Villagrá and a descendant of the illustrious Pérez family of the town of Villagrá. Apparently he was graduated from the University of Salamanca with the degree of bachelor of letters, but it is unknown when and why he traveled to America. He is first heard of when he enlisted in and lent his services to the Oñate expedition in 1596. Over his own protests he was appointed *procurador general,* captain of cavalry, and member of the council of war. Of his services on that undertaking it has been said: "As a faithful vassal of his king he . . . did not spare himself but contributed money and risked his life. Frequently in a single year he traveled more than 1,500 leagues; at other times he fought heroically, as at the siege of the *peñol* of Ácoma . . . But he was indefatigable: hunger, thirst, long journeys, countless dangers, downpours, scorching heat, and cold snows he experienced with resignation" (from the Spanish of González Obregón, *post,* I, vi). These experiences earned for him appointments as *juez asesor* in ecclesiastical affairs (1598) and *factor* of the royal treasury in New Mexico. In 1599 he went back to Mexico for a year to report on New Mexico and enlist more soldiers. In 1603 he received for himself and his descendants the title of *hijos dalgo del solar*; between 1603 and 1605 he was made captain of the Tepehaunes Indians and given charge of the *alcaldía mayor* of Guaneceví, Durango.

In 1608 or 1609 Villagrá returned to Spain. In 1610 his *Historia de la Nueva Mexico,* an epic poem of thirty-four cantos, was published at Alcalá de Henares. The poem summarizes the earlier expedition to New Mexico and gives in detail the events of the Oñate expedition until the suppression of the revolt at Ácoma in 1599. Although it has little to recommend it as a literary composition, it has "the distinction of being the first published history of any American commonwealth" (Hodge, *post,* p. 17). In 1613 Villagrá asked permission to return to New Spain to meet charges of cruelty in punishing deserters; he was sentenced to banishment from New Mexico for six years and from Mexico city for two, and was ordered to pay the costs of the trial. He went back to Spain in the same year. In 1620 he was appointed by the king *alcalde mayor* of Zapotitlan, Guatemala, and was on his way to America to assume his new duties when he died suddenly at sea. He was survived by his wife, Catalina de Soto, a son, and a daughter who married a grandnephew of Montezuma. He is described by companions as heavy-set and of small stature, bald but with a heavy gray beard tinged with red.

[The best sources for information on Villagrá's life are *"Documentos Relativos á Gaspar Villagrá,"* in *Historia de la Nueva Mexico por el Gaspar de Villagrá* (2 vols., 1900), ed. by Luis González Obregón, and *Hist. of N. Mex.* (1933), a translation of Villagrá's hist. by Gilberto Espinosa, with intro. and notes by F. W. Hodge. See also J. G. Shea, "The First Epic of Our Country," *U. S. Cath. Hist. Mag.,* Apr. 1887; and H. R. Wagner, *The Spanish Southwest* (1924).]
C. W. H.

VILLARD, FANNY GARRISON [See VILLARD, HELEN FRANCES GARRISON, 1844–1928].

VILLARD, HELEN FRANCES GARRISON (Dec. 16, 1844–July 5, 1928), reformer, was born in Boston, Mass., the fourth child of the abolitionist William Lloyd Garrison [*q.v.*] and Helen Eliza (Benson) Garrison. "We shall demand for her the rights of a human being, though she be a female," wrote her militant father some weeks later. Named for her mother and paternal grandmother, Fanny (as she was always called) grew up a healthy, beautiful child, in a home surcharged with the exciting atmosphere of the greatest reform movement in American history. Educated in the Winthrop School, Boston, she spent her early years in close contact with the abolition struggle. After the Civil War, on Jan. 3, 1866, she married Henry Villard [*q.v.*], Washington correspondent of the *Chicago Daily Tribune*. After an extended visit to Europe (July 1866–June 1, 1868), the young couple settled in Boston, where a daughter was born to them in 1868, and a son in 1870. During another visit to Germany in 1872 a second son was born. In 1876 the Villards established their home in New York, and in 1879 acquired a summer estate at Dobbs Ferry, N. Y., where their fourth child, a son, was born and died. During all these years Mrs. Villard's life was centered in her family and in the career of her husband, which involved much travel in the United States and abroad and another prolonged visit to Germany (1883–86).

The death of her husband in November 1900 marked the beginning of her public career. Possessed of wealth and leisure and her father's crusading spirit, she found she could make an excellent platform appearance and command a loyal following. With intense and widely extended activity, she now gave herself to philanthropy and social reform. In the great tradition of her father, she participated in the militant work of the National Association for the Advancement of Colored People, serving as a member of its advisory committee. Always a woman suffragist, she labored indefatigably until victory came with the passage of the Nineteenth Amendment in 1920. For many years (1897–1922) she headed the Diet Kitchen Association, which under her leadership first established public milk stations for infants and children in New York City. In her last years she devoted her best energies to the cause of peace, which she interpreted, as did her father, in terms of absolute non-resistance. At the close of the World War she gathered about her a determined group of pacifists and in October 1919 founded the Women's Peace Society, which she led as president until her death. In 1921, at the Conference of the Women's International League for Peace and Freedom, in Vienna, she presented resolutions calling for "non-resistance under all circumstances . . . immediate, universal, and complete disarmament, . . . absolute freedom of trade the world over" (*Report of the 3rd International Congress of Women,* 1921, p. 150). She died in her eighty-fourth year and was buried at her home at Dobbs Ferry.

Fanny Garrison Villard was a woman of infinite charm and grace. Her inward serenity of mind and sweetness of temper matched the outward beauty of her person. Her exquisite refinement was salted by a high sense of humor and an intense absorption in current affairs. Her gentleness and culture as wife and mother revealed themselves in later years as the adornments of a courage and rock-like resolution which were the central elements of her character. Her father lived in her again. No one who saw the spectacle will forget her marching up Fifth Avenue in her old age at the head of the women's peace parade, her white head, crowned with its little black bonnet, nodding its defiance at the hostile but admiring crowds. A lady in personal bearing and social caste, she was democratic to the core, an ardent lover of mankind, and a passionate and valiant idealist.

[W. P. and F. J. Garrison, *William Lloyd Garrison* (4 vols., 1885–89); *Memoirs of Henry Villard* (2 vols., 1904); *Luncheon Given by Women's Peace Society in Celebration of Mrs. Henry Villard's 80th Birthday* (1924), pamphlet, with addresses; personal statement, with data, by Oswald Garrison Villard, *N. Y. Times,* July 6, 1928.]   J. H. H.

VILLARD, HENRY (Apr. 10, 1835–Nov. 12, 1900), journalist, railway promoter, financier, whose name was originally Ferdinand Heinrich Gustav Hilgard, was born in Speyer, Rhenish Bavaria, the son of Gustav Leonhard Hilgard and Katharina Antonia Elisabeth (Pfeiffer) Hilgard. He came from an important family, his father being a jurist who rose to the supreme court of Bavaria, while two of his uncles were leaders in the revolution of 1848 in Rhenish Bavaria. Young Heinrich's sympathy with their republican sentiments estranged him from his father and the boy was sent for a time to a military school at Phalsbourg in Lorraine. He graduated from the Gymnasium in Speyer, and attended the universities of Munich and Würzburg for a time, but disagreed again with his father and emigrated to America. Fearing that his father would have him returned to Germany and placed in the army, he adopted the name Villard, which had been borne by one of his schoolmates at Phalsbourg. Upon landing at New York in October 1853, he proceeded to the West by easy stages, spent some time in Cincinnati and Chicago, and eventually arrived at the home of relatives in Belleville, Ill. During the year 1855–56 he successively read law, peddled books, sold real estate, and edited a small-town newspaper, but made little progress along any line except the mastery of the English language.

Increasing facility in the use of his adopted tongue served to equip him for the field of journalism which was to occupy his attention largely for the next decade. In 1858 he served as a special correspondent for the *Staats-Zeitung* of New York, observed and reported the Lincoln-Douglas debates for that paper, began a personal friendship with Lincoln, and collected his Lincoln stories, which have since been widely quoted.

Service with this German-American paper, however, he regarded merely as preliminary to his real objective—a regular berth with the English-language press. Late in 1858 reports of the discovery of gold in the Pike's Peak country so aroused his adventurous spirit that he conceived a plan for a journey to the Rocky Mountains in the rôle of a correspondent, made a connection with the *Cincinnati Commercial,* and in the spring of 1859 set out across the Plains. His sojourn of some months in the mining camps not only enabled him to make the acquaintance of several noteworthy men, including Horace Greeley, but provided him with the materials for a guidebook for immigrants which he published in 1860 under the title *The Past and Present of the Pike's Peak Gold Regions,* a very accurate account of the natural resources of Colorado and a rather extraordinary achievement for a young man of twenty-five who seven years before had not known a word of English.

As correspondent for the *Commercial* he covered the Republican National Convention at Chicago in 1860, and he served in a similar capacity for that paper, as well as for the *Daily Missouri Democrat* of St. Louis and the *New York Tribune* during the ensuing campaign. With the election of Lincoln, he was selected by the *New York Herald* as its correspondent at Springfield, Ill. Here he remained until the departure of Lincoln for Washington, supplying his paper with regular dispatches, which the *Herald* was forced to share with other members of the New York Associated Press. Since at the same time Villard corresponded freely with Western papers, a considerable portion of the political news which the country read during those memorable weeks was supplied by the young immigrant who had not yet turned his twenty-sixth birthday.

With the outbreak of the Civil War, he supported the Union cause and became a war correspondent, first for the *New York Herald,* and later for the *New York Tribune,* accompanying the Union armies in Virginia and the West until late in November 1863, when ill health forced him to abandon field work for a time. The following year, in conjunction with the Washington representative of the *Chicago Daily Tribune,* he organized a news agency to compete with the New York Associated Press, and represented his agency with the Army of the Potomac in the campaign of 1864 in Virginia. Upon the conclusion of the war, he served as a correspondent in the United States and Europe until the autumn of 1868, when he became secretary of the American Social Science Association, with headquarters in Boston. This work, in addition to bringing him into the movement for civil service reform, enabled him to study and investigate public and corporate financing, including that of railways and banks, and thus indirectly prepared him for the most notable phase of his career—that of railway promoter and financier.

In 1871, to restore his failing health, he went to Germany and then to Switzerland. In Germany again, in the winter of 1873, he was brought into contact with a protective committee for the bondholders of the Oregon & California Railroad Company. He became a member of the committee, and the following year was sent to Oregon as their representative, to investigate and recommend as to the future policy to be employed by the bondholders. He perfected a plan for the harmonious operation of the Oregon & California Railroad, the Oregon Central Railroad, and the Oregon Steamship Company, which owned a fleet of steamers plying between Portland and San Francisco; in 1876 he became president of the first and last named companies. Meanwhile he had joined a committee for the protection of the bondholders of the Kansas Pacific Railway, and when in 1876 this company became financially embarrassed he was named a receiver for the road, a position which forced him to match his wits with such redoubtable foes as Jay Gould and Sidney Dillon [qq.v.] of the Union Pacific. It was in connection with this company that he achieved his first important financial success and laid the foundation of his later fortune.

Villard's real love, however, was the Oregon country. On his first visit to the region he had been very favorably impressed with its possibilities and there gradually developed in his mind the idea of building a railway empire in the Far Northwest. Perceiving the great strategic value of the south bank of the Columbia River as a railway route, he purchased the Oregon Steam Navigation Company from Simeon Gannett Reed [q.v.] and his associates in 1879, organized the Oregon Railway & Navigation Company, and proceeded to construct a railway eastward from Portland along that route. His plan was to make this line the Pacific Coast outlet for any northern transcontinental railway which might be built, and to concentrate the trade of the Northwest in Portland. As he progressed with his plans, however, he clashed with the Northern Pacific, then recovering from the financial disasters of the seventies, whose objective was Puget Sound. Appreciating the great advantage which the superior harbor of the Sound would give the Northern Pacific over his own road with terminus at Portland, Villard re-

solved to prevent the completion of the rival road. When his offer of running rights over his line to tidewater was refused, he decided to purchase a controlling interest in the Northern Pacific. After quietly buying the stock of the Company to the limit of his resources (December 1880–January 1881), he appealed to his friends and supporters for assistance. Issuing a confidential circular to about fifty persons, he asked them to subscribe toward a fund of eight million dollars, the precise purpose of which was not then revealed. It is eloquent testimony to the confidence which he inspired in men that, besides the sum first requested, an additional twelve million dollars was eventually subscribed. This transaction, commonly known as the "Blind Pool," remains one of the notable achievements in the annals of railway finance.

With the means thus secured he established his control of the Northern Pacific; he organized a holding company—the Oregon & Transcontinental—to harmonize the interests of his various railway properties; on Sept. 15, 1881, he became president of the Northern Pacific, and completed the line in 1883. Since he also controlled the Oregon & California Railroad, and had recently organized the Oregon Improvement Company for the development of the natural resources of the region, he now dominated every important agency of transportation in that part of the country. His triumph, however, was of short duration. Because of a combination of circumstances, including faulty estimates of construction costs, the Northern Pacific, upon its completion, was confronted with a huge deficit which forced the resignation of Villard from the presidency early in 1884. From 1884 to 1886 he was in Germany, recovering from a nervous breakdown; in the latter year he returned to New York as agent of the Deutsche Bank. With the aid of German capital he saved the Oregon & Transcontinental in September 1887, and reëntered the board of the Northern Pacific in 1888, where, for the next two years, he strove earnestly, but unsuccessfully, to effect an adjustment of the clashing interests of the various cities and transportation companies of the Pacific Northwest. His failure in this effort was attended by his retirement from the Oregon Railway & Navigation Company, though after a brief interval he continued as chairman of the board of the Northern Pacific until 1893, when his railway career came to an end.

Meanwhile Villard was displaying his versatility by activities along other lines. His early realization of the possibilities of the electrical industry prompted him to extend financial assistance to Thomas A. Edison and to found the

Edison General Electric Company in 1889. In 1881 he inaugurated, under the direction of Raphael Pumpelly [*q.v.*], the Northern Transcontinental Survey, an examination of the Northern Pacific land grant of genuine scientific value. Nor had his activity as a financier dulled his earlier interest in journalism. When, through his financial successes with the Kansas Pacific and the Oregon Railway & Navigation Company, he became a man of wealth, his thoughts quickly turned to the possibility of controlling a journal of independence and fearlessness, and of such high editorial standards as to compel attention from the entire country. Accordingly, in 1881, he acquired a controlling interest in the New York *Evening Post,* placed Horace White, E. L. Godkin, and Carl Schurz [*qq.v.*] in charge of the editorial department, and, as a guarantee of independence on the part of the paper, promptly abdicated the right of influencing its editorial policy.

During the years 1879 to 1883 Villard was probably the most important railway promoter in the United States. In those years he was frankly aiming at a monopoly of transportation facilities in the Pacific Northwest; yet he showed no disposition to take unfair advantage of such a position, or to victimize the people of the region. Although alert to the protection of his interests against rival companies, he displayed fairness, moderation, and breadth of view in dealing with the cities on the Coast. On Jan. 3, 1866, Villard married the only daughter of William Lloyd Garrison [*q.v.*]. In 1879 he established a home at Dobbs Ferry, N. Y., where in his sixty-sixth year he died. He was survived by his wife, Helen Frances Garrison Villard [*q.v.*], with a daughter and two sons.

[Villard MSS., Widener Library, Harvard Univ.; *Heinrich Hilgard Villard: Jugend Erinnerungen, 1835–1853* (1902); *Memoirs of Henry Villard* (2 vols., 1904); Villard's *The Past and Present of the Pike's Peak Gold Regions* (1860), repr. (1932) with introduction and notes by Le Roy R. Hafen; E. V. Smalley, *Hist. of the Northern Pacific R.R.* (1883); Allan Nevins, *The Evening Post* (1922); J. B. Hedges, *Henry Villard and the Railways of the Northwest* (1930); *N. Y. Times,* Nov. 13, 1900.]   J.B.H.

VILLERÉ, JACQUES PHILIPPE (Apr. 28, 1761–Mar. 7, 1830), first Creole governor of the state of Louisiana, was born in the parish of St. John the Baptist, near New Orleans, La., the son of Joseph Roy Villeré, naval secretary of Louisiana under Louis XV, and of Louise Marguerite de la Chaise, grand-daughter of one of the treasurers of the colony. His father was executed by the Spanish authorities under Alexander O'Reilly [*q.v.*] in 1769, after the revolt of the French inhabitants against the Spanish

governor, Antonio de Ulloa [*q.v.*], and the boy was educated in France at royal expense as reparation for the death of his father. He served for a time as lieutenant of artillery in Santo Domingo, resigning to return to Louisiana where in 1784 he married Jeanne Henriette Fazende. In time he became one of the leading sugar planters of the vicinity of New Orleans. In his plantation residence the British established headquarters in 1815 just prior to the battle of New Orleans, while Villeré was serving as a major-general of Louisiana militia.

Meanwhile he had been a member of the convention which in 1812 framed the first constitution for the state of Louisiana, and unsuccessful candidate for the governorship in the election of that year. He was elected governor in 1816, and served four years. The second governor of the state and the first Creole to hold that position, he used his office to diminish the friction between the French element of the population and the United States authorities, but was criticized for neglecting his fellow Creoles in matters of patronage. In opposition to certain views of the contemporary medical fraternity, he advanced the opinion that yellow fever was not due directly to climate, observing that Louisiana prisoners, segregated from the city, did not become victims of the disease (*Journal of the House ... Fifth Legislature of ... Louisiana,* 1820, pp. 6–7). He exerted an administrative influence for better educational facilities, but his term in the governorship was on the whole uneventful—"quiet, prosperous and healing." In the last year of his administration he announced the entire extinguishment of the state debt and the existence of a current surplus of $40,000 in the treasury. He was honored in death with a military funeral. He was a man of vigor with an interest in practical and public affairs, and direct descendants bearing his name have continued to play important rôles in the affairs of New Orleans.

[Alcée Fortier, *Louisiana* (1914), vol. II, and *A Hist. of La.* (1904), vols. II, III; H. E. Chambers, *A Hist. of La.* (1925); Arthur Meynier, Jr., *Meynier's Louisiana Biogs.* (1882); *L'Abeille* (New Orleans), Mar. 9, 1830; records of St. Louis Cathedral, New Orleans, Book X, p. 113.]   H.C.N.

VINCENNES, FRANÇOIS MARIE BISSOT, Sieur de (June 17, 1700–Mar. 25, 1736), founder of the Indiana city bearing his name, was born at Montreal, the headquarters for western traders, the son of Jean Baptiste Bissot, Sieur de Vincennes [*q.v.*] and Marguerite Forestier) Bissot. His godfather was François Margane, Sieur de la Valterie. Hence he frequently signed himself Margane, which confused early writers with the belief that he was not a son of Jean Baptiste Bissot, Sieur de Vincennes. While merely a lad the younger Vincennes accompanied his father to his western post, and after his death remained for several years in command at Ke-ki-onga, the Miami village on the site of Fort Wayne. In 1722 he was commissioned ensign in the colonial army. Meanwhile, the several tribes of the Miami began moving down the Wabash River, and Vincennes accompanied the Ouiatenon and built a fort near Lafayette, Ind., where he commanded for about four years. The Piankashaw Miami passed still farther down the Wabash, building villages on the White River, then within the jurisdiction of Louisiana, rather than of Canada. For some time the authorities of the former colony had been attempting to establish a post on the lower Wabash, and now persuaded Vincennes to ally himself with French Louisiana. Some time in 1731 or 1732 Vincennes complied with the request of the governor of Louisiana and built a fort on the site that now bears his name. In two letters written by him from that post in 1733 (Roy, *post*, pp. 92–93) he described his fort, the Indians he controlled, and the commerce for which his post was well situated. He also mentioned the war with the Chickasaw, which was to bring about his tragic death.

Louisiana was at this time engaged in a desperate struggle with the Indians on the Mississippi, especially with the Chickasaw, who harbored the refugee Natchez and traded with the English of Carolina. The governor of Louisiana, Jean Baptiste le Moyne, Sieur de Bienville [*q.v.*], in the spring of 1736 gathered all his resources; from Illinois and the Wabash he summoned the French officers and traders to a rendezvous somewhere near the site of Memphis. Vincennes from his post joined Pierre D'Artaguiette of Illinois, and together they advanced down the Mississippi to the designated place. But Bienville was detained, and the Indians from the upper posts grew impatient and hastened their officers into a premature attack. They were seriously defeated; and Vincennes, a Jesuit priest, and seventeen other young Frenchmen were dragged to the Chickasaw village on the headwaters of Tombigbee River in the present state of Mississippi and there tortured and burned at the stake. The day of the defeat was Palm Sunday of 1736, although dated two months later by many authorities. Vincennes not only built a post on the Wabash, but he assisted Louisiana in its struggle to maintain the Mississippi Valley for France. His fort was an outpost, and of him it is said "his name will be perpetuated as

long as the Wabash flows by the dwellings of civilized man" (Bancroft, *post*, p. 368).

[P. G. Roy, "Sieur de Vincennes Identified," in *Ind. Hist. Soc. Pub.*, VII (1918), no. 1; George Bancroft, *Hist. of the U. S.*, vol. III (1840); C. W. Alvord, *The Illinois Country* (1920); P. C. Phillips, "Vincennes in its Relation to French Colonial Policy," in *Ind. Mag. of Hist.*, Dec. 1921; G. J. Garraghan, *Chapters of Frontier Hist.* (1934).]

                                          L. P. K.

VINCENNES, JEAN BAPTISTE BISSOT, Sieur de (Jan. 19, 1668–1719), explorer and French officer in the Mississippi Valley, was the son of François and Marie (Couillard) Bissot, the former a Norman from Pont-Audemer, who emigrated to New France before 1639. In 1672 François was granted the seigniory of Vincennes, on the southern bank of the St. Lawrence River, opposite Quebec, where he had already established a mill and a tannery. The seigniory was to pass to his sons (*Bulletin, post,* Mar. 1919, p. 65). At his death in 1673 his son-in-law, Louis Jolliet, became the guardian of the boys. He placed Jean Baptiste in the seminary at Quebec, where Jolliet himself had been educated. The lad, now Sieur de Vincennes, remained at school for four years, 1676 to 1680, then, as "he was not fit for the ecclesiastical estate," he was dismissed and in 1687 went to France. There, through the patronage of his godfather, the former intendant, Jean Talon, Vincennes obtained a commission as ensign in the marine, the branch of the army that was stationed in New France. In 1696 he married Marguerite Forestier, the daughter of the chief surgeon of New France. François Marie Bissot, Sieur de Vincennes [*q.v.*], was their son.

Just when Vincennes first visited the West does not appear, for when Governor Frontenac in 1696 sent him to command among the Miami Indians he was already well known to them and much beloved. In 1698 he accompanied Henry de Tonty to the West, leaving the party during its voyage on Lake Michigan to proceed to St. Joseph River, where the Miami dwelt (*Early Narratives of the Northwest*, 1917, ed. by L. P. Kellogg, pp. 342, 345). From this time until his death Vincennes continued to live among these Indians and to carry on trade with them. In 1705 he was suspended from his position in the army, because he exported brandy for trade; but later he was pardoned, because he had rescued Iroquois prisoners and assisted in maintaining the peace of 1701. Meanwhile the Miami tribe had removed from St. Joseph River to the present Maumee, where a great village called Ke-ki-onga was built on the site of Fort Wayne, Ind. This was Vincennes' headquarters, and there he lived and died. In 1712 he went to the aid of

Dubuisson of Detroit, who was involved in a contest with the Fox Indians at that post. After their defeat Vincennes was sent to carry the news to Quebec, but he returned to his command the same autumn. His services in preventing the Miami from going over to the British were so important that thirty years after his death his name and influence were invoked to bring the Miami back to the French alliance. For twenty years he was the principal personage among the Miami and cooperated with other officers in maintaining French power in the West.

[P. G. Roy, "Sieur de Vincennes Identified," in *Ind. Hist. Soc. Pub.*, VII (1918); J. D. Dunn, "Who was our Sieur de Vincennes," in *Ind. Mag. of Hist.*, June 1916; B. J. Griswold, *The Pictorial Hist. of Fort Wayne* (1917), vol. I; *Bulletin des Recherches Historiques*, Mar. 1919, Apr. 1900.]   L.P.K.

VINCENT, FRANK (Apr. 2, 1848–June 19, 1916), traveler, author, and collector, was born in Brooklyn, N. Y., the son of Harriet (Barns) and Frank Vincent, a member of the drygoods firm of Vincent, Clark & Company, in New York City. His father had an estate at Tarrytown-on-the-Hudson and sent his son to the Peekskill Military Academy and, in 1866, to Yale College. Lack of health caused him to leave college at the end of his second term and another attempt in 1867 proved equally abortive; but Yale conferred upon him, in 1875, an honorary degree of M.A., and he was later, in 1905, enrolled with his old class, 1870, as a graduate member.

Undiscouraged by the apparent failure of his formal education, he resolved (*Biographical Record, post*, pp. 352–53) to "survey the entire field of literature, science, and art . . . in famous standard and epoch-making books"; and to make a systematic tour of the most interesting parts of the world" and to write of the less frequented and less known countries. These ambitions he later considered fulfilled. He claimed, in the fifteen years from 1871 to 1886, to have traveled 355,000 miles "over the entire world" and alone to have crossed Lapland and to have penetrated 1,000 miles into Brazil, where he discovered the double cataract of the Iguaçú. In those days, few Americans ventured beyond the usual European tour, and Vincent was acclaimed a Marco Polo, while his lucid and lively, though careless, style was admired by Longfellow and others of the New England school. Probably it is the first of his books that has remained the most readable, *The Land of the White Elephant* (1874), describing his adventures in 1871–72 in Cambodia, Siam, and Burma, entertainingly illustrated with numerous maps, plans, and engravings. With sketchbook in hand, camera and diary also, armed with letters to the influential, he wandered Hero-

dotus-like, ceaselessly asking questions, setting down wonders and facts, hobnobbing with kings, premiers, high priests, or exploring fearlessly and with good-natured acceptance of hardship. It was not only the culinary arts and more obvious customs that he recorded; native ideas and emotions found in him a sympathetic, though superficial, interpreter. If there is absence of the scientific spirit in sifting his information, the impression left on the reader is all the more vivid.

From these lands, chiefly from Cambodia, he brought home a collection of antiquities and more recent art objects in bronze, lacquer, stone, and painted wood, including fragments of Buddha statues, about 1,000 years old, from the great temple of Nagkon Wat. These he gave, in 1885, to the Metropolitan Museum of Art in New York, and thus became a patron (now known as fellow-in-perpetuity). For over twenty years, he wrote successfully for publication. Among his books were *Norsk, Lapp, and Finn* (1881); *Around and About South America* (1890); *In and Out of Central America* (1890); and *Actual Africa* (1895). He edited *The Plant World* (1897) and *The Animal World* (1898) for Appletons' Home Reading Books Series.

His personality was eager, almost aggressive. On June 3, 1909, when sixty-one, he married a distant cousin, Harriet Stillman Vincent of Brooklyn. They had no children. They made their home in New York City, but he died in Woodstock, N. Y., and was buried in Sleepy Hollow Cemetery at Tarrytown. He had become an honorary member of some twenty-six scientific and literary societies and the recipient of nine decorations from sovereigns and foreign governments on four continents.

[*Obituary Record of Yale University . . . 1916* (1916); *The Biog. Record of the Class of 1870 Yale College* (1911); *Metropolitan Museum of Art, Annual Reports . . . 1871 to 1894* (reprint 1895); files of the museum; *Who's Who in America*, 1912–13; Vincent's own books, esp. the prefaces; date of death from *N. Y. Times*, June 21, 1916.]   F.B.H.

VINCENT, JOHN HEYL (Feb. 23, 1832–May 9, 1920), bishop of the Methodist Episcopal Church, educational leader, was born in Tuscaloosa, Ala. His father, John Himrod Vincent, a Pennsylvanian, was of Huguenot ancestry, a descendant of Levi Vincent, born in France, who died in New Jersey in 1763; his mother, Mary Raser, was the daughter of a Philadelphia sea-captain. In 1837 the Vincents returned to the vicinity of Lewisburg, Pa. The father was farmer, trader, miller, postmaster, and Methodist Sunday School superintendent. Young Vincent attended local schools, worked in a store, and was principal of an academy. He had early determined to be a minister, however, and in 1850 was licensed as an exhorter and local preacher. As such he traveled Luzerne Circuit, carrying a translation of Dante among the pious books in his saddle-bags. At his mother's death in 1852 he went to relatives in Newark, N. J., where he studied briefly in the Wesleyan Institute. The next year he joined the New Jersey Conference of the Methodist Episcopal Church on trial, was ordained deacon in 1855, and elder in 1857.

Transferring to the Rock River Conference, in Illinois, he held pastorates in Joliet, Mount Morris, Galena, and Rockford. At Galena, U. S. Grant, then undistinguished, was an inconspicuous member of his congregation, and the two became life-long friends. Vincent's progressive ideas in religious education early began to attract attention. To fit himself for better teaching service he visited the Holy Land in 1862–63. His promotion to Trinity Church, Chicago, in 1864 gave him his opportunity for leadership. The work of the American Sunday School in those days was confined to one hour a week, in which Scripture verses were memorized and dull lessons recited from "Question Books." Vincent and his progressive associates saw that there could be little improvement without better trained teachers, and no effective training until there was uniformity of subject and teaching material. Accordingly he advocated and was largely instrumental in introducing uniform lessons into the Chicago schools. This innovation made possible, in 1864, a Union Sunday School Institute for the Northwest, with a regular publication, the *Northwestern Sunday School Teachers' Quarterly,* which, he said later, "met a want and kindled a fire." The next year this journal became a monthly, the *Sunday School Teacher* (Chicago), and in 1866 its pages contained a specimen of a new system of study in leaflet form, a revolutionary departure, which led within a few years to uniform lessons for all Protestant denominations in the United States and ultimately, for the entire Protestant world. In 1866 the Methodist Episcopal Church plucked Vincent out of the pastorate and his local leadership and placed him in New York as general agent of its Sunday School Union, and in 1868 elected him editor of Sunday School literature and corresponding secretary of the Sunday School Union. In that office he served for twenty years. He soon became the recognized leader of the American Sunday School movement. He edited the *Sunday School Journal* and the *Berean Lessons,* which won enormous popularity, and he directed the teacher-training activities which his energy had set up all over the country.

His idea of holding a protracted national training institute bore fruit in 1874 in a Sunday School teachers' assembly, which met for two weeks in August at Fair Point on Lake Chautauqua in western New York. The location of this summer school he discussed with his friend Lewis Miller [*q.v.*] of Akron, Ohio, a Methodist Sunday School superintendent, an enthusiastic promoter of religious education. On Miller's advice it was located in the camp-meeting grove. The two men admirably supplemented each other, Miller functioning as president and Vincent as superintendent of instruction. From this small beginning developed the so-called Chautauqua movement, a system of popular education. Beginning as a summer tent-school for Sunday School teachers, the assembly developed rapidly into a summer resort, for study and lectures. In 1878 Vincent presented a plan for a course of prescribed reading, extending through four years, with examinations and a diploma, designed to afford multitudes of belated students what he called "the college outlook"—a glimpse of literature, science, and religion. This "Chautauqua Literary and Scientific Circle" (C. L. S. C.) was immediately and immensely popular, local "circles" springing up in hundreds of places. It marked the beginning of directed home study and correspondence schools in America, and the summer classes at Chautauqua were the forerunner of summer schools under college auspices. The Chautauqua platform presented to immense audiences the most eminent scholars, lecturers, reformers, and publicists, and found an extension in similar "daughter assemblies" and later in thousands of local "Chautauquas," in which popular programs, entertaining, instructive, and "uplifting," were given for brief periods in halls or tents.

From 1878 to 1888 Vincent's career was crowded with activity: he planned the Chautauqua summer programs and directed them; edited the Sunday School literature for his Church, which attained a circulation of millions of copies; founded in 1885 the Oxford League for Methodist young people; and filled countless speaking engagements, traveling with an expert stenographer, making Pullman sections his workshops, and employing every labor-saving device available. In 1888, however, the General Conference elected him bishop. He could no longer give his major attention to Chautauqua and the Sunday School, but the old fire burned in him, and in his contacts with the younger ministers he continually gave expression to his cherished ideals. The religious views of his early days had been modified by his reading of Horace Bushnell and Robertson of Brighton, and he became the advocate of intellectual and spiritual culture, for education rather than emotion, for a more sane evangelism, and for a type of religion which should pervade the whole of life. The Itinerants' Club, which he fathered, was the Sunday School Institute idea applied to the Methodist ministry. It introduced the young minister to helpful books, suggested improved methods of parish work and saner types of evangelism. His official residences were at Buffalo, N. Y. (1888–92), Topeka, Kan. (1892–1900), and after 1900, when he was placed in charge of Methodist work in Europe, at Zurich, Switzerland. In 1904, at the age of seventy-two, he was retired. His last years, spent in Indianapolis and Chicago, were devoted to reading, writing, and lecturing along the lines in which he had won eminence. He married, Nov. 10, 1858, Elizabeth Dusenbury of Portville, N. Y., by whom he had one son, George Edgar Vincent.

Bishop Vincent was above medium height, gracious in manner, with a rich and flexible voice. As a lecturer on education, morals, and the training of children, he excelled. He was tolerant in temper, liberal for his time in his theology, giving the hospitality of the Chautauqua platform to such leaders as Edward Everett Hale, Charles William Eliot, and Lyman Abbott [qq.v.]. He was the first Methodist to be invited to Harvard as University preacher. His influence was always exerted in behalf of moderate denominational self-assertion and interdenominational comity. His books included: *Sunday School Institutes and Normal Classes* (1872); *The Modern Sunday School* (1887); *The Chautauqua Movement* (1886); *Our Own Church* (1890); *The Revival and After the Revival* (1883); *A Study in Pedagogy* (1890).

[Autobiog. in *Northwestern Christian Advocate*, Apr. 6–Nov. 2, 1910; L. H. Vincent, *John Heyl Vincent* (1925); J. L. Hurlbut, *The Story of Chautauqua* (1921); Ellwood Hendrick, *Lewis Miller* (1925); H. M. Hamill, "Hist. of the Teacher-Training Movement," *World-Wide Sunday-School Work* (1910); Boyd Vincent, *Our Family of Vincents* (1924); *Chicago Daily Tribune*, May 10, 1920.]   J. R. J.

VINCENT, MARVIN RICHARDSON (Sept. 11, 1834–Aug. 18, 1922), clergyman and theological professor, was born in Poughkeepsie, N. Y., the son of Leonard M. and Nancy M. (Richardson) Vincent; his father and his maternal grandfather, Marvin Richardson, were Methodist ministers. Admitted to Columbia College in 1850, he became a pupil of Charles Anthon and Henry Drisler [qq.v.], whose instruction in the classics laid the foundation for his life-long interest in the study of words. Graduating with the degree of A.B. in 1854, he taught

for eight years, first in the Columbia Grammar School (1854–58) and next, as professor of Latin, in the Troy Methodist University (1858–62).

For a year, 1862–63, he served as acting pastor of the Pacific Street Methodist Episcopal Church, Brooklyn, but, changing his denominational convictions, he was ordained by the Presbytery of Troy on June 18, 1863. For the next ten years he was pastor of the First Presbyterian Church of Troy, during which period he became widely known as a scholarly preacher. From 1873 to 1887 he was pastor of the Church of the Covenant, New York. In the latter year he was called by the board of directors of the Union Theological Seminary, New York—of which he had been a member since 1873—to the chair of Sacred Literature in succession to Edward Robinson, W. G. T. Shedd, and Philip Schaff [qq.v.]. This call he accepted with a "goodly amount of diffidence," and for twenty-nine years gave instruction in the literature of the New Testament. During most of these years he was also a trustee of Columbia (1889–1913). When failing health compelled him in 1916 to become professor emeritus, he retired to Forest Hills, L. I., where six years later death came to him as a not unwelcome visitor. In 1858, he married Hulda F. Seagrave of Providence, R. I.

By the time he came to Union Seminary, Vincent had reached the conviction that the Bible portrays "the historical development of God in man"; that its value centers in "the Incarnate Word [who] is the final interpreter of the written word"; and that its authority "as a rule of faith and practice must be tested by His spirit, example and teaching." Disinclined to controversy but believing in the "right to prosecute the free investigation of the Scriptures within the church," he supported the cause of his colleague, Charles A. Briggs [q.v.], when the latter was tried for heresy before the Presbytery of New York.

Vincent's pen was active and versatile. Apart from numerous sermons, addresses and pamphlets, he published *In the Shadow of the Pyrenees* (1883), a travel book; *The Age of Hildebrand* (1896), in Ten Epochs of Church History; and in 1904 a metrical version of Dante's *Inferno*. To the study of the New Testament he contributed *A History of the Textual Criticism of the New Testament* (1899), *A Critical and Exegetical Commentary on the Epistles to the Philippians and to Philemon* (1897), which is marked by sound judgment and clarity of presentation; and *Word Studies in the New Testament* (4 vols., 1887–1900). The last-named substantial work is not a commentary but a study of the vocabulary of the Greek New Testament, designed to serve the needs of students of the English Bible. The impulse to the *Studies* was received when, as professor at Troy University, he collaborated with his colleague Charlton T. Lewis [*q.v.*] in translating in two volumes (1860–62) John Albert Bengel's *Gnomon Novi Testamenti*. Accomplished as a New Testament scholar, competent in theology, and endowed with the gifts of charming manners, humor, and good fellowship, Vincent was an admirable example of a culture at once Christian and Greek.

[*Union Theol. Sem. Bull.*, Jan. 1923; obituary of Leonard M. Vincent, in *Minutes of the Ann. Conferences of the Methodist Episcopal Church*, 1893; *Gen. Cat. Union Theol. Sem.* (1926); *Who's Who in America*, 1922–23; *N. Y. Times*, Aug. 19, 1922; personal acquaintance.]   J. E. F.

VINCENT, MARY ANN (Sept. 18, 1818–Sept. 4, 1887), actress, followed her profession continuously from the age of sixteen until within four days of her death. She was born in Portsmouth, England, the daughter of an attaché of the Royal Navy named John Farlow, who died when she was only two years old. After the death of her mother two years later, she was brought up by her grandmother. Acquaintance with members of a theatrical troupe aroused her interest in the stage at an early age, and in April 1835 she made her début at a theatre in Cowes, Isle of Wight, as a chambermaid in *The Review, or the Wags of Windsor*. Her second rôle was a much more important one, that of Volante in John Tobin's then popular comedy, *The Honeymoon*. She remained at the theatre in Cowes until the end of the season. In August of the same year she was married to James R. Vincent, an actor nine years her senior, and thereafter, throughout her entire career, she was known both on and off the stage as Mrs. J. R. Vincent. After acting here and there in the provincial theatres of Great Britain, she and her husband accepted an engagement at the National Theatre in Boston, arriving in that city on Nov. 7, 1846, and making their first appearance on Nov. 11 in *Popping the Question,* as Miss Biffin and Mr. Primrose. Mrs. Vincent remained at the National Theatre for two years after the death of her husband on June 11, 1850. Her marriage in 1854 to John Wilson, an actor, was unhappy, and after a separation it ended in divorce twelve years later.

Going to the Boston Museum on May 10, 1852, as Mrs. Pontifex in *Naval Engagements,* she was uninterruptedly, with the exception of the season of 1861–62, a member of its stock company for more than thirty-five years. A list of the characters she acted there is virtually the repertory of that theatre from season to season. She became its leading comedienne, and later its leading old lady, playing a range of parts as varied as those of Nancy Sikes in *Oliver Twist,* Mrs. Malaprop in *The Rivals,* Mrs. Candour in *The School for Scandal,* Maria in *Twelfth Night,* Goneril in *King Lear,* and Queen Gertrude in *Hamlet,* as well as many parts in the ephemeral plays of the day. The total number of these characters acted by her was well over four hundred, and the number of her performances on the stage of the Boston Museum extends far into the thousands. On Thursday, Sept. 1, 1887, she suffered a stroke of apoplexy at her home after having acted Mrs. Keziah Beekman in *The Dominie's Daughter* the previous evening, and died early Sunday morning. She was buried from St. Paul's Church, Boston, of which she was a communicant, and her remains were interred in Mount Auburn Cemetery in Cambridge.

In the eyes of Boston Mrs. Vincent was more than an actress. Her name was a household word, even among the many who never went to a theatre. With William Warren [*q.v.*], the leading comedian of the Boston Museum for many years, she was a Boston institution. An associate recalls "the jolly, chubby, little figure, the bobbing curls, the inimitable, tripping walk, and the gasping pleasant voice, all suggestive of mirth and merriment" (Ryan, *post*, p. 44). She was hospitable and charitable, fond of animals, and but for the solicitude of her friends she would have spent almost every cent she earned in helping the poor and friendless. Her fiftieth year on the stage was commemorated at the Museum on Apr. 25, 1885, with afternoon and evening performances in which she appeared as Mrs. Hardcastle in *She Stoops to Conquer* and as Mrs. Malaprop in *The Rivals*. The Vincent Memorial Hospital in Boston was founded in her memory, being opened in 1891 with ceremonies presided over by Bishop Phillips Brooks [*q.v.*]; the Vincent Club of young society women, named in her honor, adds to the funds for its support by the giving of annual amateur theatricals.

[J. B. Richardson, *Mrs. James R. Vincent, A Memorial Address* (1911); Catherine M. Reignolds-Winslow, *Yesterday with Actors* (1887); G. P. Baker, in *Famous American Actors of Today* (1896), ed. by F. E. McKay and C. E. L. Wingate; E. H. Sothern, *The Melancholy Tale of "Me"* (1916); Kate Ryan, *Old Boston Museum Days* (1915); *Boston Herald*, Apr. 19, 26, and *Boston Daily Globe*, Apr. 26, 1885; *Boston Transcript*, Apr. 27, 1885, and Sept. 6, 1887; *Boston Times*, Sept. 11, 1887; *Theatre*, Nov. 7, 1887.]
E. F. E.

VINTON, ALEXANDER HAMILTON (May 2, 1807–Apr. 26, 1881), clergyman of the Protestant Episcopal Church, was born in Providence, R. I., son of David and Mary (Atwell) Vinton, and probably a descendant of John Vinton who settled in Lynn, Mass., some time before 1648. Alexander was one of five brothers, three of whom graduated from West Point and entered the army, though later Francis [q.v.] became an Episcopal clergyman. Alexander received a classical education and spent three years in Brown University. He then went to Yale, and graduated from the medical department with the degree of M.D. in 1828. For the next four years he practised his profession in Pomfret, Conn. Although reputed to have been something of a sceptic in his early days, he became convinced of the truth of Christianity and in 1834 turned from medicine to the ministry. After spending a short time in the General Theological Seminary, New York, he was ordained deacon by Bishop Benjamin T. Onderdonk on June 28, 1835, and the following year advanced to the priesthood by Bishop Alexander V. Griswold. In the meantime he had had charge of a church in Portland, Me., for a few months, and then returned to his native city to become rector of Grace Church. Here he remained until 1842, when he was called to St. Paul's Church, Boston. Among his parishioners was young Phillips Brooks, upon whom Vinton made a deep impression. Brooks said of him later, his "vigorous mind and great acquirements and commanding character and earnest eloquence, made him a most influential power and gave a noble dignity to the life of the church in Boston" (Tiffany, *post,* p. 544). In the contest over the bishopric of Pennsylvania in 1845, which resulted in the election of Alonzo Potter [q.v.], Vinton was one of the candidates put forward for that office. In 1851 he was made a member of the Massachusetts board of education. Leaving St. Paul's in 1858, he was rector of Holy Trinity, Philadelphia, until 1861, of St. Mark's, New York, until 1869, and then, returning to Boston, of Emmanuel Church until 1877. Thereafter, he made his home in Pomfret, Conn., serving, however, as lecturer at the Cambridge Divinity School.

In his day, Vinton ranked among the leading preachers of the Episcopal Church. In appearance and voice he had the physical basis for oratory. "As an imposing and manly representation of the clerical profession, he was imaged in bronze upon the Soldiers Monument on Boston Common, in the act of blessing the troops on their departure for the war" (Allen, *post,* I, 45). He was a low churchman and was prominent in the evangelical group. He emphasized the need of conversion, was a diligent pastor, and defended the faith with earnestness and logical acumen.

He was one of the signers of the "Muhlenberg Memorial," addressed to the House of Bishops in 1853. When the first American Church Congress was held in 1870, Vinton was chosen to act as president. Collections of his sermons appeared in 1855 and 1867, and many other sermons and addresses were published separately. He was married on Oct. 15, 1835 to Eleanor Stockbridge, daughter of Ebenezer Thompson of Providence, by whom he had six children. His death, from pneumonia, occurred in Philadelphia, where he had gone to take part in the consecration of the Church of the Holy Trinity.

[J. A. Vinton, *The Vinton Memorial* (1858); *Obit. Record Grads. Yale Univ.,* 1881; H. B. Huntington, *A Hist. of Grace Church in Providence, R. I.* (1931); A. V. G. Allen, *Life and Letters of Phillips Brooks* (2 vols., 1900); C. C. Tiffany, *A Hist. of the Protestant Episcopal Church in the U. S. A.* (1895); *Boston Daily Advertiser,* Apr. 27, 1881.]   H. E. S.

VINTON, FRANCIS (Aug, 29, 1809–Sept. 29, 1872), soldier, Protestant Episcopal clergyman, was born in Providence, R. I., the son of David Vinton, a goldsmith and merchant, and Mary (Atwell) Vinton. His first paternal ancestor in America was probably John Vinton who in 1648 was a resident of Lynn, Mass. Two of Francis' brothers, John Rogers and David Hammond, had graduated from the United States Military Academy, and in his seventeenth year, July 1, 1826, Francis entered that institution. In 1830 he graduated, ranking fourth in a class of forty-two, and was commissioned second lieutenant, 3rd Artillery. From 1830 to 1832 he served in garrison at Fort Independence, Mass., and while there began to study law at Harvard. He was on topographical and engineering duty from July 17, 1832, to September 1833, when he was sent to Fort Constitution, N. H. While here, January 1834, he was admitted to the bar. In 1836 he saw active service in the Creek Nation. He was on recruiting duty, when, Aug. 31, 1836, he resigned from the army with the intention of following his brother, Alexander Hamilton Vinton [q.v.], into the ministry.

After studying at the General Theological Seminary, New York, he was ordained to the diaconate by Bishop A. V. Griswold at St. John's Church, Providence, Sept. 30, 1838; the following March he was advanced to the priesthood. On Oct. 8, 1838, he married Maria Bowen, daughter of John Whipple of Providence; she died in childbirth on June 6, 1840, and on Nov. 3 of the following year he married Elizabeth Mason, daughter of Commodore Oliver Hazard Perry [q.v.], by whom he had seven children. For a time he had under his care his nephew, Francis Laurens Vinton [q.v.]. His first parish was at

Wakefield, R. I., where he built a church with funds collected largely in Providence and New York. He then went to St. Stephen's, Providence, where again he built a church. At Easter, 1841, he became rector of Trinity Church, Newport, R. I. Called to Emmanuel Church, Brooklyn, in 1844, he began a pastorate of eleven years, during which he rose to prominence in his denomination. Facing discouraging conditions in his parish, by unwearied labors and the influence of his own character and spirit he built up a strong church, which was merged with Grace Church and established in a new edifice on Brooklyn Heights. In 1846 he was called to All Saints, New York, and in 1847 he was asked to become associate rector of Trinity Church, New Haven, Conn., with right of succession; on June 3, 1848, he was elected bishop of Indiana; but all these positions he declined. In the memorable contests over the bishopric of New York in 1852 and 1854 Vinton both times came within a few votes of election as provisional bishop. Becoming assistant minister of Trinity Parish, New York, in 1855, he was assigned to Saint Paul's Chapel, and four years later transferred to Trinity Church, where the eloquence of his preaching attracted large congregations. In 1869 he became first professor of ecclesiastical polity and canon law in the General Theological Seminary, which position he held until his death.

Vinton's fluency of utterance, his exceptional command of language, and his grace of manner brought him an enviable reputation as a public speaker; he was also a clear thinker and a logical debater, conspicuous in the councils of the Church. An ardent evangelical, he carried on his ministry with fervor and enthusiasm. An extreme low churchman in the beginning, he made in practice, if not in dogma, a considerable advance toward the high church position. His military and legal training were an aid to him. He had a high estimate of authority, was well disciplined, prompt, and direct, with, however, a tendency to peremptoriness which sometimes offended. His preparation for the bar was an excellent background for his work in canon law. A number of his sermons and addresses were printed, but his chief publication was *A Manual Commentary of the General Canon Law and the Constitution of the Protestant Episcopal Church in the United States* (1870). After ten months of failing health, he died at his home in Brooklyn.

[J. A. Vinton, *The Vinton Memorial* (1858); G. W. Cullum, *Biog. Reg. Officers and Grads. U. S. Mil. Acad.* (3rd ed., 1891), vol. I; G. C. Mason, *Annals of Trinity Church, Newport, R. I.*, 2 ser. (1894); *Fourth Ann. Reunion Asso. Grads. U. S. Mil. Acad.* (1873); *Francis*

Vinton; Priest and Doctor (1873); *Sun* (N. Y.), Sept. 30, 1872.]
H. E. S.

VINTON, FRANCIS LAURENS (June 1, 1835–Oct. 6, 1879), Union soldier, mining engineer, was born at Fort Preble, Portland Harbor, Me., the son of an army officer, John Rogers Vinton, and Lucretia Dutton (Parker). His mother died in 1838, and his father was killed at the siege of Vera Cruz in 1847. Thereafter, until 1851, when he was appointed to the United States Military Academy by President Fillmore, the boy was cared for by his uncle, Francis Vinton [q.v.], who had left the army for the Protestant Episcopal ministry.

Vinton graduated at West Point tenth in his class in 1856 but resigned within a few months and proceeded to France, where he entered the École des Mines. After four years of study he returned to the United States, where he at once obtained a position as instructor in mechanical drawing at Cooper Union, New York City. In February 1861, he left to head an expedition to explore the mineral resources of Honduras, but had barely started before the news of the outbreak of the Civil War caused him to return to the United States. He was commissioned captain in the 16th United States Infantry on Aug. 5, 1861, and was soon given permission to raise a regiment, of which he was made colonel on Oct. 31, 1861. He commanded this regiment, the 43rd New York, with skill and distinction in the various battles of the Virginia peninsular campaign (March–August 1862). After September 1862 he commanded a brigade in the VI Corps (Army of the Potomac) until he was wounded in the battle of Fredericksburg, Dec. 13, 1862, so severely that he was never able to rejoin his command. Appointed a brigadier-general of volunteers on Mar. 13, 1863, he resigned less than two months later.

In the following year, when the School of Mines of Columbia College opened its doors, Vinton was selected by Thomas Egleston [q.v.], whom he had known at the École des Mines, to fill the chair of civil and mining engineering. A man of great personal charm and extremely popular with his students, he taught such subjects as mechanical drawing and elementary civil engineering with great skill, but his presentation of mining was necessarily confined to European practice, since he had had no contact with mining in America. To a man who had successfully commanded a brigade of soldiers in combat this must have seemed a task which offered but little scope for his real capacity. After thirteen years in the chair he resigned and went to Denver, Colo., where he established himself as a consulting mining engineer. Here, in addition to engineering employment, he found congenial work as Colorado correspondent of the *Engineering and Mining Journal* of New York, to which, during the next two years, he contributed well written and beautifully illustrated articles. On a professional trip to Leadville, Col., then coming to the height of its glory, he became infected with erysipelas and died within a few days, at the age of forty-four. His impressive funeral services were chiefly a recognition of the distinction of his military career, but were attended by the most prominent mining men of the state.

[*N. Y. Herald,* Oct. 7, 1879; G.W. Cullum, *Biog. Reg. Officers and Grads. U. S. Mil. Acad.* (3rd ed., 1891), vol. II; *Engineering and Mining Jour.,* Oct. 11, 25, 1879; *Eleventh Ann. Reunion Asso. Grads U. S. Mil. Acad.* (1880); J. A. Vinton, *The Vinton Memorial* (1858); *Army and Navy Jour.,* Oct. 11, 1879.]
T. T. R.

VINTON, FREDERIC (Oct. 9, 1817–Jan. 1, 1890), librarian, was born in Boston, Mass., the son of Josiah and Betsey S. (Giles) Vinton and a descendant of John Vinton, of Huguenot stock, who was a resident of Lynn, Mass., as early as 1648. Prepared for college at the academies of Weymouth and Braintree, Frederic was graduated at Amherst in the class of 1837. Intending to enter the ministry, he studied at the Andover Theological Seminary and at Yale, 1840–42. Although he was never ordained, he was in charge of a church in St. Louis from 1843 to 1845. His health failing, he returned to the East and taught at Nantucket and at Eastport, Me., from 1845 to 1851. In the latter year he was engaged by his brother, Alfred Vinton, a prominent citizen of St. Louis, to catalogue his large private library, and Frederic's studies in connection with this catalogue determined his future career. This manuscript catalogue, now in the Library of Princeton University, contains, in an extensive preface, a discussion of the principles of classification which antedates any other printed in America.

After another year of teaching in South Boston, Vinton was appointed, in 1856, assistant librarian of the Boston Public Library, under its first librarian, Edward Capen, whom he aided in the preparation of the printed catalogues issued in 1858, 1861, and 1865. He was largely responsible for the classification of the Bates Hall collection. In 1865 he became first assistant librarian of the Library of Congress, under Ainsworth Rand Spofford [*q.v.*], where he was engaged in the preparation of the *Catalogue of the Library of Congress: Index of Subjects* published in 1869, and the annual volumes of the alphabetical catalogue from 1867 to 1872. In

1873 he became the first full-time librarian of the College of New Jersey (now Princeton University). The Chancellor Green Library Building had just been completed, and his first task was the classification and the arrangement of the collection of about 18,000 volumes. Under his intelligent and forceful management, the library grew rapidly and at the time of his death in 1890 numbered 70,000 volumes. The years from 1877 to 1884 he spent in the preparation of the *Subject-Catalogue of the Library of the College of New Jersey at Princeton* (1884), one of the most scholarly and useful publications of the sort up to that time. Despite his infirm health, he was a man of great energy and devotion to his profession and he was one of the small group who founded the American Library Association in 1876. To the *Princeton Review* and other journals he contributed articles dealing with books, libraries, and missions.

Vinton married, Sept. 13, 1843, Phoebe Clisby, daughter of Seth and Elizabeth Clisby of Nantucket; she died Feb. 23, 1855, and on June 1, 1857, he married Mary B. Curry, daughter of Cadwallader Curry of Eastport, Me., who survived him. The four children of his first marriage died in infancy; two children were born to his second wife, who survived him.

[S. R. Winans in *Princeton Coll. Bull.,* Apr. 1890, with a list of Vinton's writings; J. A. Vinton, *The Vinton Memorial* (1858); manuscript records of Amherst Coll. Alumni Council, of the Boston Pub. Lib., and of the Lib. of Cong.; Vinton's annual reports (MSS.) in Princeton Univ. Lib.; *Amherst Coll. Biog. Record* (1927); *Obit. Record Grads. Amherst Coll.,* 1883; *Library Jour.,* June 1890; *N. Y. Times,* Jan. 2, 1890.]
J. T. C.

VINTON, FREDERIC PORTER (Jan. 29, 1846–May 20, 1911), portrait painter, was the son of William Henry and Sarah Ward (Goodhue) Vinton. He was born at Bangor, Me., but was taken by his parents to Chicago when he was ten, and his education was begun in the public schools of that city. After five years the family returned to New England, and the boy obtained a place as clerk for the Boston firm of Gardner Brewer & Company, and was later employed by C. F. Hovey & Company until about 1864. By this time he had fully determined to be a painter, his choice being confirmed by the sympathy and advice of William Morris Hunt [*q.v.*]. He entered the drawing class of the Lowell Institute, took anatomy lessons from Dr. William Rimmer [*q.v.*], and drew from casts in the Athenæum gallery. In order to raise funds for European study he then worked for ten years in two Boston banks, in the meanwhile contributing art criticisms to the *Boston Advertiser*. In 1875, having laid up $1000, he went to Paris and entered the atelier of Léon Bonnat. The following year he went to Munich with Frank Duveneck [*q.v.*] and studied for a year in the Academy there, but he did not care for Munich methods and returned to Paris to study for a time under Jean Paul Laurens. He was the only American in Laurens' studio. Here he painted his first Salon picture, "A Gypsy Girl," now owned by the city of Lowell, Mass.

In 1878 Vinton returned to Boston, took a studio in Winter Street, and painted the vigorous portrait of Thomas G. Appleton which was his first great success. Many sitters came to him and he was soon ranked among the foremost American portrait painters. For thirty-three years he was busily occupied in Boston, producing some three hundred portraits. He had for sitters such men as Charles Francis Adams, Wendell Phillips, Francis Parkman, Gen. Charles Devens, Senator George F. Hoar, William D. Howells, and others equally prominent. Few portraits of men made by Americans are as fine as his best examples, such, for instance, as his "Dr. Samuel A. Green," in the Groton (Mass.) Library. In 1882 he went to Spain with William M. Chase [*q.v.*] and made ten fine copies of the masterpieces of Velasquez in Madrid, which were exhibited in Boston and elsewhere on his return. In June 1883 he married Annie M. Pierce of Newport, R. I. He was at that time occupying Hunt's old studio in Park Square, Boston, but in 1892 he bought a house in Newbury Street and constructed a pair of handsome and well lighted studios on the top floor. There he lived and worked until his death. He had no children.

In November 1911 a memorial exhibition of his work was opened in the Museum of Fine Arts, Boston. It contained 124 paintings, of which one half were portraits, and the rest landscapes, genre pieces, and copies after Velasquez. Vinton was a confirmed realist who ennobled his prose by his breadth of style and dignity. He believed that nothing but truth will endure, and in his practice he endeavored to live up to that difficult standard. He was a National Academician and a member of the National Institute of Arts and Letters.

[Biog. and appreciation by Arlo Bates, in *Memorial Exhibition of the Works of F. P. Vinton* (Museum of Fine Arts, Boston, 1911); *Who's Who in America*, 1910–11; *Boston Transcript*, May 20, 24, 1911; *Boston Daily Advertiser*, Nov. 12, 1878; *Atlantic Monthly*, June 1875; F. T. Robinson, *Living New England Artists* (1888); *Am. Art News*, June 17, 1911; *Cat. of Paintings* (Museum of Fine Arts, Boston, 1921).]

W. H. D.

VINTON, SAMUEL FINLEY (Sept. 25, 1792–May 11, 1862), lawyer and congressman, a descendant of John Vinton whose name appears in the records of Lynn, Mass., in 1648, and the eldest of seven children of Abiathar and Sarah (Day) Vinton, was born in South Hadley, Mass. His father was a farmer; his grandfather, also named Abiathar, was a soldier in the Revolutionary War. Young Vinton prepared for college with the aid of his local pastor, entered Williams in 1808, taught school at intervals to meet expenses, and graduated with the class of 1814. He read law under the direction of Stephen Titus Hosmer, subsequently chief justice of the supreme court of Connecticut, was admitted to the Connecticut bar in 1816, and a few months later commenced practice in Gallipolis, Ohio, a village of French *émigrés*. Here, in 1824, he married Romaine Madeleine Bureau, who died in 1831, having borne him two children. He rose rapidly in public esteem as an advocate. In 1822 he was elected to Congress and continued to serve until Mar. 3, 1837. At this time he had declined to be a candidate for reëlection, but in 1842 he yielded to the demands of the Whigs, and served again as congressman from 1843 to 1851. He was at various times a member of the committees on public lands, roads and canals, and the judiciary; he was made chairman of the Committee of Ways and Means during the war with Mexico, after he had declined the nomination for speaker of the House.

Vinton's first speech in Congress, in May 1824, was on a resolution which he offered with a view to the protection of the lives of passengers on steamboats navigating the Ohio and Mississippi rivers. As a remedy for the unprofitable management of the school lands in Ohio, he introduced and successfully promoted the passage of a bill to authorize that state to sell those lands and invest the proceeds in a trust fund, a precedent which was subsequently followed in other states. When in February 1828 a bill for the appropriation of funds for the Indian service, and particularly for the removal of Indians from lands east of the Mississippi to a reservation west of that river, was before Congress, Vinton, for the purpose of preventing any disadvantage to either slave states or free states, moved and made a memorable speech in support of an amendment which provided that no Indians living north of 36° 30' should be aided in removing south of that line, nor any Indians living south of it be aided in removing north of it. Vinton spoke frequently, but usually briefly and effectively, on such subjects as the survey and sale of public lands so as to prevent speculation, the Cumberland Road and other internal improvements, the tariff (favoring protection), and the apportionment of representatives. He opposed the annexation of Texas, and opposed a direct tax for the prosecution of the war with Mexico. On Feb. 12, 1849, he reported from the Committee of Ways and Means the bill providing for the establishment of the Department of the Interior, which became a law nineteen days later. Vinton was the unsuccessful Whig candidate for election as governor of Ohio in 1851. He served for one year, 1853–54, as president of the Cleveland & Toledo Railroad, and then returned permanently to Washington, D. C. In April 1862 he was appointed by President Lincoln as one of three commissioners to appraise emancipated slaves within the District, but he died less than a month later. Sarah Madeleine Vinton Dahlgren [q.v.] was his daughter.

[J. A. Vinton, *The Vinton Memorial* (1858); (S.) M. V. Dahlgren, "Samuel Finley Vinton, a Biog. Sketch," *Ohio Archæol. and Hist. Soc. Pubs.*, vol. IV (1895); "Memoir of the Hon. Samuel F. Vinton," *Am. Rev.*, Sept. 1848; Calvin Durfee, *Williams Biog. Annals* (1871); *Biog. Dir. Am. Cong.* (1928); *Daily Nat. Intelligencer* (Washington, D. C.), May 12, 1862.]

N. D. M.

VISSCHER, WILLIAM LIGHTFOOT (Nov. 25, 1842–Feb. 10, 1924), journalist, actor, was born in Owingsville, Ky., the son of Frederick and Elizabeth Walker (Lightfoot) Visscher. He was a descendant of Harmen Visscher, who emigrated from Hoorn in the Netherlands before 1644 and settled in Beverwyck (later Albany). He was educated at Bath Seminary, Owingsville, and Stevenson's Academy, Danville, Ky., and left his studies to enlist in the Union forces as a member of the 24th Kentucky Volunteers. He was mustered out at Covington, Ky., after serving about three years as hospital steward. In 1865 he became private secretary and amanuensis to George Dennison Prentice [q.v.], editor of the *Louisville Daily Journal,* and in 1868 received the degree of LL.B. from the University of Louisville. In the seventies he went west and for most of the rest of his life was occupied in newspaper work, first in Saint Joseph and Kansas City, Mo., later as editorial writer for some of the most important journals in the West, including the San Francisco *Daily Mail* in the late seventies, the *Cheyenne Daily Sun* (1883–85), the Denver *Great West* (1885–86), the Portland *Morning Oregonian* (1889), and the Tacoma *Globe* in the nineties. After about 1895 he lived in Chicago, where he was a special contributor to the *Herald* and other papers.

He wrote much journalistic verse (*Black Mammy,* 1886; *Blue Grass Ballads,* 1900; *Poems of the South,* 1911) and some plays, sketches, and indifferent novels (*Fetch Over the Canoe,* 1908; *Amos Hudson's Motto,* 1905), and had consid-

erable success on the lecture platform and on the stage. Early in the century he played leading parts in New York in Opie Read's *The Jucklins* and *The Starbucks.* In *Ten Wise Men and Some More* (1909) he recorded reminiscences of his pioneer and journalistic friends, among whom were such well-known figures as Col. W. F. Cody ("Buffalo Bill"), Eugene Field, Bill Nye, and Franklin K. Lane. His best-remembered work, *A Thrilling and Truthful History of the Pony Express* (1908), is a vivid account of the system of swift communication between East and West before the coming of the transcontinental railroads. He also wrote the last chapter of the 1917 edition of Cody's *Buffalo Bill's Own Story.* He married on Mar. 16, 1876, Emma Mason (d. 1896) of Pittsfield, Ill., by whom he had one child, a daughter. He died in Chicago of a heart attack. He is described as short of stature, broad-shouldered and vigorous, with bright, twinkling eyes and a carefree manner.

[S. V. Talcott, *Visscher* (1883); *Who's Who in America,* 1922–23; Opie Read, *I Remember* (1930), pp. 204–13; publisher's note, in *Poems of the South,* pp. ii–iii; obituary in *Chicago Daily Tribune,* Feb. 11, 1924; unpublished memoir by Viva G. V. Weber, Visscher's daughter.]

J. C. F–h.

VITALE, FERRUCCIO (Feb. 5, 1875–Feb. 26, 1933), landscape architect, was born at Florence, Italy, the son of Lazzaro and the Countess Giuseppina (Barbaro) Vitale. He was educated at the Classical School of Florence, and at the Royal Military Academy of Modena from which he was graduated in 1893. As a commissioned officer in the Italian army he was sent to Washington in 1898 and made military attaché to the Italian embassy. Later that same year he was sent to the Philippines as a military observer. Not long afterward he resigned his commission in the Italian army and devoted himself to landscape architecture. For generations many of his ancestors on his mother's side had been students of the fine arts at the University of Padua and patrons of art in Venice; his father was an architect of distinction and brilliance. With this background, after several years of practice in his father's architectural office and further study in Florence, Turin, and Paris, Ferruccio Vitale entered upon his profession.

In 1904 he returned to the United States and in association with George F. Pentecost, Jr., established an office in New York for the practice of landscape architecture. That same year he was admitted to membership in the American Society of Landscape Architects, and four years later he was elected to fellowship in the society. His practice was extensive, embracing not only the design of many private estates but also the planning of towns and suburbs. For Washington, D. C., he designed Meridian Hill Park. Although he did not become a naturalized American citizen until 1921, he contributed notable service during the World War as a member of the town planning division of the United States Housing Corporation, working at Dayton, Ohio, and at Watertown, N. Y. On Sept. 24, 1927, President Coolidge named him a member of the National Commission of Fine Arts to succeed James L. Greenleaf of New York whose term had expired. He served on this Commission until 1931, when because of ill health he was forced to resign. At the time of his death he was a member of the architectural commission of the Century of Progress exposition at Chicago.

Throughout his whole professional life Vitale worked unceasingly to bring about a closer collaboration among the arts and to strengthen the position of landscape architecture as one of the fine arts. As a member of the board of trustees of the American Academy in Rome and as a member of its executive committee he rendered valuable service to this end. It was in great measure through his efforts that there was established in 1915 the first fellowship in landscape architecture at the American Academy in Rome. He was also instrumental in the founding of the second and third Academy fellowships. He was one of the founders and a trustee of the Foundation for Architecture and Landscape Architecture at Lake Forest, Ill. He was a member of the Architectural League of New York and winner of its gold medal in 1920. He was a past president of the New York Chapter of the American Society of Landscape Architects and was elected an honorary member of the American Institute of Architects in 1927. On May 29, 1910, he married Rosamond Flower Rothery of Wellesley, Mass., who with two daughters survived him.

[Unpublished data in possession of Mrs. Ferruccio Vitale; "Ferruccio Vitale: a Minute on His Life and Service Prepared for the New York Chapter of the American Society of Landscape Architects," in *Landscape Architecture*, July 1933; *Who's Who in America*, 1930–31; *N. Y. Times*, Feb. 27, 1933.]   K. McN.

VIZCAÍNO, SEBASTIÁN (*c.* 1550–*c.* 1628), merchant-explorer, was born in Spain, probably the son of Antonio Vizcaíno of the town of Corcho, a commoner. Vizcaíno is said to have served in the royal army in Portugal in 1567. He went to Mexico about 1585 and, becoming interested in the very profitable China trade, made at least one voyage to Manila between 1586 and 1589. He was a passenger on the unlucky galleon *Santa Ana* when it was taken off Lower California and burned by Thomas Cavendish in November 1587, and lost a good part of his fortune. In

1593 a company which he had organized for the exploration of the Gulf of California, reputedly rich in pearls, received a commission from the viceroy of New Spain, and in 1594 an expedition was sent out under the command of one Pérez del Castillo, who bungled it badly and returned to face criminal action. Apparently no blame was attached to Vizcaíno, for the following year his company was given a new contract, and in June 1596 he sailed from Acapulco with three ships and 230 men. The expedition was entirely fruitless, though Vizcaíno asserted that he had reached latitude 29° 30′, and by the following December he was back at Acapulco. After many delays and long negotiations, a new voyage was undertaken in 1602 to explore the outer coast of California as far as Cape Mendocino, locate good harbors that might be used as refuges for the Manila galleons, and find the supposed Strait of Anian, through which the English and French were rumored to have reached the Pacific.

A full complement of men, experienced navigators to advise the *general*, Vizcaíno, two cosmographers, and a company of missionaries left Acapulco in three good vessels on May 5, 1602. Vizcaíno explored the difficult coast of Lower California in the teeth of the heavy northwest gale that prevails on that coast almost the year round and reached San Diego Bay in November. After resting and refitting he sailed northward again and on Dec. 15 discovered Monterey Bay, which he called "the best harbor that could be desired." Vizcaíno had encountered all the hardships of the northern passage—head winds, fog, thirst, hunger, and scurvy—and had so many disabled men that he sent one of his vessels back with them. With the two remaining vessels he pushed on up the coast to Cape Mendocino, which he reached on Jan. 12, 1603, missing San Francisco Bay in the bad weather. At Cape Mendocino his expedition was found to be so badly battered that there were not enough hands to man the sails, and he decided to return. On Feb. 18, 1603, he reached Mazatlán. This expedition, the first to make a scientific exploration of the west coast, furnished the first maps of that dangerous coast, did much to explode the myth of the Northwest Passage, and discovered Monterey Bay.

Vizcaíno strongly recommended the establishment of a port at Monterey for the protection and refitting of the Manila galleons. Winning some support, he went to Spain to plead his case before the Council of the Indies and received a royal decree establishing the port of Monterey with him in charge (1607). Meanwhile, however, a new viceroy in New Spain, the marquis of Montesclaros, opposed the plan on the grounds of expense and expediency, and the undertaking was abandoned for a hundred and sixty years. By way of compensation Vizcaíno was put in command of an expedition to discover the fabulous islands, "Rica de Oro" and "Rica de Plata," which were supposed to lie in the neighborhood of Japan. The expedition sailed in 1611, established the non-existence of the islands, made an ineffectual attempt to promote relations with Japan, and returned to Mexico in January 1614. In 1615 Vizcaíno was in the New Spanish province of Avalos, where he enlisted a force to defend the coast against Dutch attack. Beyond that date nothing is known of him. He had married, sometime before 1589, a woman of some property and in 1596 had one son.

[*Colección de Documentos Inéditos,* vol. VIII (Madrid, 1867), ed. by Louis Torres de Mendoza; Francisco Garrasco y Guisasola, *Documentos Referentes al Reconocimiento de las Costas de las Californias* (Madrid, 1882); *Hist. Soc. of Southern Cal. Pubs.,* vol. II, pt. 1 (1891); H. R. Wagner, *Spanish Voyages to the Northwest Coast of America in the Sixteenth Cent.* (1929); George Davidson, *The Discovery of San Francisco Bay* (1907); H. E. Bolton, *Spanish Exploration in the Southwest* (1916); C. E. Chapman, in *Southwestern Hist. Quart.,* Apr. 1920; Juan de Torquemada, *The Voyage of Sebastian Vizcaino to the Coast of Cal.* (1933), translated from Torquemada's *Monarquía Indiana* (Madrid, 1615); Martín Fernández de Navarrete, *Colección de los Viages . . . que Hicieron los Españoles desde Fines del Siglo XV* (Madrid, 5 vols., 1825–37).]
L. B. S—n.

VOGRICH, MAX WILHELM KARL (Jan. 24, 1852–June 10, 1916), pianist, composer, editor, was born in Hermannstadt (Nagy-Szeben), Transylvania, the son of Tobias Wogritsch and Therese (Schäffer) Wogritsch. He started his career as a musical prodigy, and at the age of five began to study piano. At the age of seven he made his first public appearance. From 1866 to 1869 he was a pupil at the Leipzig Conservatory, studied piano with Ignaz Moscheles, Ernst Wenzel, and Carl Reinecke, and theory and composition with Moritz Hauptmann, Ernst Richter, and Reinecke, and then started in earnest on his career as a pianist. He toured Europe, Mexico, and South America from 1870 to 1878, and then came to the United States for the first time. He gave several recitals in New York, and toured the country as accompanist to the celebrated violinist August Wilhelmj. He was also associated with Eduard Reményi, for George P. Upton [*q.v.*], in his *Musical Memories* (1908, p. 63), mentions Vogrich as Reményi's "*protégé,* a young musician of extraordinary talent, who has since become a lost Pleiad." The young Vogrich was, however, not entirely lost, for, although he did not continue to appear publicly as a pianist, and left America to live in Australia from 1882 to 1886, he returned to New York in 1886 and

stayed there for sixteen years, busying himself with composition and music editing. From 1902 to 1908 he lived in Weimar, and in 1908 moved to London, where he stayed until the outbreak of the World War in 1914. He spent the last two years of his life in New York City, acting during this time as adviser to the music publishing firm of G. Schirmer.

Vogrich was a prolific composer, and many of his works were widely used in their day. He composed three operas, all to his own librettos: "Vanda," produced in Florence, 1875; König Arthur," Leipzig, 1893; and "Der Buddha," Weimar, 1904. He was the composer of incidental music to Ernst von Wildenbruch's "Die Lieder des Euripides" (copyright, 1905), and of a dramatic scene, "The Highland Widow." His oratorio, "The Captivity" (copyright, 1890), was performed at the Metropolitan Opera House, New York, in 1891, and his "Memento Mori" (1910), for violin and orchestra, was played in Berlin in 1912 and in New York the season preceding his death. His violin concerto, "E pur si muove" (1913), was dedicated to Mischa Elman, who performed it in Berlin in 1913 and in New York in 1917. Others of his works were: two cantatas, "The Diver" (copyright, 1888), and "Der junge König und die Schäferin" (copyright, 1890); a "Missa Solemnis"; two symphonies, in E minor and A minor; an Andante and Intermezzo for violin and orchestra; a concerto in E minor for piano; as well as many pieces for piano, and for violin and piano, songs, and shorter choruses.

A year before his death Vogrich came into newspaper prominence when he sued the estate of the widow of Theodore Havemeyer, the sugar magnate, for thirty thousand dollars. Vogrich claimed that Mrs. Havemeyer had promised to bequeath him this sum, and when the will was published he was the beneficiary of only ten thousand dollars. It was currently understood in musical circles that Vogrich had been Havemeyer's protégé. When Havemeyer was living, Vogrich had charge of the music in his household, and had benefited so largely from Havemeyer's generosity that he was enabled to give up his routine work in New York and settle in Europe where he could devote himself entirely to composition. He died following a surgical operation, and was survived by his wife, Alice Rees, formerly an English singer, whom he had met in Australia.

[Books on American music give scanty recognition to Vogrich. L. C. Elson omits him entirely in *The Hist. of Am. Music* (revised ed., 1915); in Rupert Hughes and Arthur Elson, *Am. Composers* (revised ed., 1914), his name is included in a list; and J. T. Howard, in *Our American Music* (1913), gives him only a brief paragraph. The articles in *Grove's Dict. of Music and Musicians, Am. Supp.* (1930), and in *Baker's Biog. Dict. of Musicians* (1919) are more detailed. For information about the suit against the Havemeyer estate see the *N. Y. Times,* Oct. 12, 1915. An extensive obituary notice appeared in the *Musical Courier,* June 15, 1916, and a shorter one in the *N. Y. Times,* June 11, 1916.]   J.T.H.

VOLCK, ADALBERT JOHN (Apr. 14, 1828–Mar. 26, 1912), caricaturist, dentist, was born in Augsburg, Bavaria, one of two sons of Andrew von Volzeck, a prominent manufacturer and land owner. He studied at the Polytechnic Institute, Nürnberg, and perhaps at the University of Munich, participated in the march on Berlin in 1848, and was forced to flee because of his revolutionary sympathies. In 1849, penniless and without friends, he landed in America, where he lived first in St. Louis, Mo., and then joined the gold rush. In 1851 he was recommended to Dr. Chapin A. Harris [*q.v.*], one of the founders of the Baltimore College of Dental Surgery, for appointment as an instructor. In 1852, having studied as well as taught, he received the degree of D.D.S. He was married on July 6, 1852, to Letitia Roberta Alleyn of Baltimore, Md., by whom he had two sons and three daughters. He was a charter member of the Maryland State Dental Association, one of the first users of porcelain in the filling of teeth, and a founder of the Association of Dental Surgeons. He was instrumental during the Civil War in getting medicine into the South.

During the war, in an effort to combat the activities of Thomas Nast [*q.v.*], Northern caricaturist, Volck made a series of caricatures favorable to the South under the pseudonym of V. Blada. Notable among these are drawings of Lincoln and Gen. Benjamin F. Butler as "Don Quixote and Sancho Panza," of Lincoln passing through Baltimore on his way to his inauguration, and of Gov. Thomas Hicks of Maryland as "Judas." The most important and best known collection of his work is *Confederate War Etchings* (n.d.), which contains twenty-nine plates; a volume of *Sketches from the Civil War in North America* (1863) bears a London imprint, possibly false. Volck was responsible for the illustrations in *Bombastes Furioso Buncombe* (1862) and the *American Cyclops* (1868) of James Fairfax McLaughlin. He also illustrated *A Popular Life of General Robert E. Lee* (1872), by Emily V. Mason. He is said to have drawn the head of Jefferson Davis for the ten-cent stamp of the Confederacy, but it is probably the work of his brother, Frederick Volck, a sculptor. His caricatures of General Butler, by whose orders he had been incarcerated in Fort McHenry in 1861, were used to defeat Butler when

he was a candidate for the governorship of Massachusetts. After the war his interest in political satire, for which he had a marked natural gift, seems to have died. His portrait in oils of Robert E. Lee (1870) is in the Valentine Museum, Richmond, Va. About 1880 he became interested in working in bronze and silver. His most interesting achievements are a bas-relief of Basil L. Gildersleeve [*q.v.*], a shield in memory of the Confederate women in the Confederate Museum in Richmond, and a large bowl presented in 1897 to Mayor Alcaeus Hooper of Baltimore. In the seventies he was one of the founders of the famous Wednesday Club of Baltimore, and he made many illustrations for its theatrical productions and musical soirées, besides carving for the main lounge of the clubhouse a tremendous wooden mantel. Later he was the founder of the Charcoal Club. He died in Baltimore, survived by two daughters and a son.

[Sources include Meredith Janvier, *Baltimore in the Eighties and Nineties* (1933); G. C. Keidel, in *Argus* (Catonsville, Md.), Oct. 2–Nov. 20, 1915; Murat Halstead, in *Cosmopolitan,* Aug. 1890; *Mag. of Hist.,* extra number 60, 1917, which reprints much of Volck's work; Albert Shaw, *Abraham Lincoln, His Path to the Presidency* (1929) and *Abraham Lincoln, the Year of His Election* (1929); Frank Weitenkampf, *Am. Graphic Art* (1912); C. W. Drepperd, *Early Am. Prints* (1930); August Dietz, *The Postal Service of the Confederate States of America* (1929); A. H. Starke, *Sidney Lanier* (1933); *Sun* (Baltimore), Mar. 27 (obituary) and Mar. 31, 1912, Feb. 4, 1917; minute books of Md. State Dental Asso. and Asso. of Dental Surgeons; information from Henrietta Volck Falkinburg, Volck's daughter. Many of Volck's caricatures are in the possession of the Peabody and Pratt libraries, Baltimore, Md.]

          G.M.A.

VOLK, LEONARD WELLS (Nov. 7, 1828–Aug. 19, 1895), sculptor, son of Garret and Elizabeth (Gesner) Volk, was born at Wellstown (later Wells), N. Y., one of a family of twelve. On his mother's side he was a direct descendant of Anneke Jans Bogardus. He spent his boyhood on a farm and attended district schools in Avon and Palmyra, N. Y., and in Berkshire County, Mass. At sixteen he began to learn marble carving in his father's shop at Pittsfield, Mass. He practised his craft at Bethany, Batavia, and Buffalo, N. Y., and in the autumn of 1848 went to St. Louis, Mo., where a year later he began his self-taught studies in drawing and modeling. Early works were a copy in marble of Joel T. Hart's bust of Henry Clay, and a portrait of Father Theobald Mathew (1850). Archbishop Kenrick of St. Louis gave him his first order, high-relief portraits for a mausoleum. On April 22, 1852, he married Emily Clarissa, daughter of Dr. Jonathan King Barlow of Bethany, and settled for a year in Galena, Ill. There he met his wife's cousin, Stephen A. Douglas [q.v.], who became deeply interested in his career. Volk returned to St. Louis and thence went to Rock Island, Ill., and engaged in business. In 1855, supplied with funds by Douglas, Volk left his wife and child in Pittsfield, and went to Rome. When he returned to the United States in 1857, he opened a studio in Chicago and at once became a leader in art movements there. He organized the first art exhibition held there (1859); he was one of the founders of the Chicago Academy of Design (1867) and its president for some time. Taking advantage of the Lincoln-Douglas debates (1858), he made close studies from life of both contestants. Direct results of these are the colossal Douglas monument at Chicago, statues of Lincoln and Douglas in the Illinois State Capitol, Springfield (1876), a marble statue and a marble bust of Lincoln (1860). The bust, exhibited in Paris in 1867, was placed in the building of the Chicago Historical Society, where it was destroyed in the great fire of 1871; the original model was preserved. Other important works are the statuary for the soldiers' monument at Girard, Pa., said to be the first of its kind in the country; the soldiers' monument at Rock Island, Ill.; a bronze statue of Gen. James Shields, in Statuary Hall, Washington, D. C. (1893); and a statue of Lincoln at Rochester, N. Y. In 1880 Volk published a small book, *History of the Douglas Monument at Chicago.*

Although Volk attempted ideal figures (such as his Faith and Ione), his talent lay rather in faithful portraiture. Among his many authentic studies of his contemporaries are those of Elihu B. Washburne, Zachariah Chandler, James H. McVicker, J. Young Scammon, and David Davis. He was probably the only sculptor to study Lincoln closely and advantageously from life, and his life-mask and casts of Lincoln's hands are invaluable historic mementos. He approached his art by the avenue of the marble carver's craft, and it is to his credit that he was untouched by the pseudo-classicism he saw in Italy during his three visits there. Shortly after his wife's death in the spring of 1895, he died at Osceola, Wis., where he was accustomed to spend the summers. He was survived by a son, who became eminent as a painter, and a daughter.

[*Biog. Sketches of the Leading Men of Chicago* (1868); Lorado Taft, *The Hist. of Am. Sculpture* (1903); C. E. Fairman, *Art and Artists of the Capitol of the U. S.* (1927); obituary in *Chicago Tribune,* Aug. 20, 1895; biog. statement, signed by Volk, in N. Y. Pub. Lib.; information from Volk's grandson, Jerome D. Volk of Lovell, Me.]   A. A.

VON HOLST, HERMANN EDUARD [See Holst, Hermann Eduard von, 1841–1904].

VONNOH, ROBERT WILLIAM (Sept. 17, 1858–Dec. 28, 1933), painter, born at Hartford, Conn., was the son of William and Frederika (Haug) Vonnoh. The family moved in Robert's boyhood to Boston, where he attended the public schools. At the age of fourteen, admiring another boy's drawings, he decided to be an artist, and his mother permitted him to enter a lithographer's shop. In 1877 he entered the recently established Massachusetts Normal Art School (later the Massachusetts School of Art), from which he was graduated in 1879. Meanwhile he taught in the Boston Free Evening Drawing School in Roxbury and at Thayer Academy, South Braintree. With money he had saved he went to Paris in 1881 and became a pupil of Boulanger and Lefebvre at the Académie Julian, but an unfortunate investment of his fund brought him home after two years. During 1883–85 he was principal of the East Boston Evening Drawing School; during 1884–85 he taught at the Cowles Art School, and in 1886–87 at the school of drawing and painting in the Boston Museum of Fine Arts. He married, July 7, 1886, Grace D. Farrell. Four years of study at Paris followed. In 1891 Vonnoh took an instructorship at the Pennsylvania Academy of the Fine Arts, Philadelphia, which he held through 1894, and entered upon a professional career in which he painted upwards of 500 portraits, many of them of great distinction. Many of his pupils, among them W. J. Glackens and Maxfield Parrish, became well-known artists. He later returned to the Pennsylvania Academy for two more years as instructor (1918–20).

Vonnoh's point of view as a creative painter was succinctly set forth in his article, "The Relation of Art to Existence" (*Arts and Decoration,* Sept. 1922). Pleading vigorously for vocational training, this amounted to a well-written diatribe against the forms of literary education prevalent in colleges and schools. The author asserted that "it is not so important to know how to read and write if one must know it at the expense of genuinely productive work. . . . Literary education teaches children how to tell others to do things that they themselves cannot do" (p. 329). Vonnoh himself was a man of great personal charm and cultivation, with marked linguistic ability. He maintained studios at New York and Los Angeles, and he was one of the founders of the summer art colony at Lyme, Conn. His second marriage, Sept. 17, 1899, was to Bessie O. Potter, American sculptor. The two had the distinction of being the only man and wife who were members of the National Academy of Design.

Winning as painter many prizes and honorable mentions, Vonnoh was represented in his lifetime at the Metropolitan Museum, New York, by "La Mère Adèle"; by portraits of S. Weir Mitchell at the College of Physicians, Philadelphia; the "Family of Woodrow Wilson," at the White House; Col. Lucius Hudson Holt, at the United States Military Academy, West Point; Gov. Hiram Bingham, in the Connecticut State House; Charles Francis Adams, in the Massachusetts Historical Society, and many others. One of his latest works, painted *con amore* at the request of the alumni association, was the likeness of Walter Smith, English-born founder of the Normal Art School. At the presentation of this work, during the semi-centennial celebration of the school in December 1925, the artist gave personal reminiscences of his days as an art student in Boston. A published list of his honors then showed that as early as 1884 he won the gold medal of the Massachusetts Charitable Mechanics' Association, and that he was awarded bronze medals at the Paris expositions of 1889 and 1900, a gold medal at the Panama-Pacific Exposition (1915), and the Proctor portrait prize of the National Academy of Design (1904). Vonnoh's portraits were strong and serious, never daring or experimental. He painted many landscapes, some of them of great charm. Always interested in problems of craftsmanship, he made his own frames, which were thoroughly consistent with the tonality of his pictures. Failing eye-sight from 1925 onward brought to a rather somber close a career that had been remarkably productive and fortunate. Vonnoh's last years were spent at Gréz-sur-Loing, France; he died at Nice from a heart attack. He was survived by his wife.

[*Who's Who in America*, 1928–29; *Am. Art News*, Dec. 30, 1905; "Vonnoh's Half Century," *Internat. Studio*, June 1923; *Bull. Mass. School of Art*, Jan.–Feb., Apr.–May 1926; Cat. of La. Purchase Exposition, 1904; obituaries in *Art News*, Jan. 6, 1934, and *N. Y. Times*, Dec. 29, 1933; information from Bessie Potter Vonnoh.]   **F. W. C.**

VON RUCK, KARL (July 10, 1849–Nov. 5, 1922), physician, the son of George and Clara von Ruck, was born in Constantinople, Turkey, where his father, a native of Stuttgart, was stationed in the German diplomatic service. He attended the University of Stuttgart, where he obtained the degree of B.S. in 1867. Then studying medicine at the University of Tübingen, he was graduated M.D. there in 1877. After further study in England and at the University of Michigan he received the degree of M.D. from the University of Michigan in 1879. He practised his profession at Norwalk, Ohio, first as a general practitioner, then developing a surgical practice, and later settling upon the specialty of tuberculosis. From the beginning of his medical studies he was interested in this disease from contact at Tübingen with Felix von Niemeyer, an important clinician of the time. Also during a period of study in Berlin in 1882 he was present at the meeting there when Robert Koch announced the discovery of the tubercle bacillus.

To further his specialized work he removed to North Carolina and took over a sanitorium at Sulphur Springs near Asheville. Its destruction by fire shortly thereafter caused his removal to Asheville and the founding of Winyah Sanitorium at that place in 1888. This was one of the earliest private sanatoria for tubercular patients and made for him a comfortable fortune. In 1895 he organized the Von Ruck Research Laboratory for Tuberculosis, where after two years of immunological investigation he produced a modification of Koch's first tuberculin, a watery extract of the tubercle bacillus. He was an early advocate of the complement-fixation test for the diagnosis of tuberculosis and for its use in the quantitative estimate of immunity to the disease. Application of his laboratory research to the clinical material of the sanitorium resulted in 1912 in his anti-tuberculosis vaccine. This vaccine was used widely in the treatment of tuberculous patients, although designed primarily for the protective immunization of children and others exposed to tuberculous infection. This pioneer work in tuberculosis subjected him to much criticism and ridicule, which, to a man of his strong convictions and intolerance of opposition, was doubly galling. Though he was throughout his career in constant controversy with his fellow-workers in the tuberculosis field, his work and many of his ideas have been generally accepted. About 1913 he turned over the management of Winyah Sanitorium to his son, in order to concentrate on research. In collaboration with his son, Silvio Von Ruck, he published *Studies in Immunization against Tuberculosis* in 1916. He married Delia Moore of Ottawa County, Ohio, on Dec. 25, 1872. The death of his only son, Silvio, and of his only grandchild, Silvia, almost simultaneously of pneumonia in 1918 was a crushing blow, followed by the death of his wife in 1921. He died of nephritis the next year.

[H. J. Achard, "Karl von Ruck," *Am. Rev. of Tuberculosis*, Jan. 1923; *Am. Jour. of Clinical Med.*, Dec. 1922; *Jour. of the Am. Med. Assn.*, Nov. 11, 1922; *N. Y. Times*, Nov. 7, 1922; Stuttgart given as birthplace in *Who's Who in America*, 1922–23, but Achard, *ante*, gives Constantinople on authority of Von Ruck's verbal statement to him.]   **J. M. P—n.**

VON TEUFFEL, BLANCHE WILLIS HOWARD [See HOWARD, BLANCHE WILLIS, 1847–1898].

VOORHEES, DANIEL WOLSEY (Sept. 26, 1827–Apr. 10, 1897), senator from Indiana, was born in Butler County, Ohio, the descendant of Steven Coerte Van Voorhees, an emigrant from Holland about 1660, and the son of Stephen and Rachel (Elliott) Voorhees. Taken to Indiana when two months old, he was brought up on a farm in Fountain County, and, though he early evinced more of a taste for books than for manual labor, he always considered himself as belonging to the farming class. In 1849 he was graduated from Indiana Asbury (now De Pauw) University and then read law. On July 18, 1850, he was married to Anna Hardesty of Greencastle, Ind. They had four children. Admitted to the bar in 1851, in 1853 he became prosecuting attorney for the circuit court. In 1857 he removed to Terre Haute, which became his permanent home. After his defeat for Congress in 1856, President Buchanan appointed him federal district attorney for Indiana. Elected to Congress, he served in the House of Representatives from Mar. 4, 1861, to Feb. 26, 1866, when his election was successfully contested by Henry D. Washburn. He was one of the most virulent of those Democrats whose criticisms were heard throughout the war period. To him abolitionism and secession were equally hateful; and he bewailed the breaches of the Constitution and the tyranny of the war government in terms of unmeasured opprobrium. He was, however, by no means an irreconcilable partisan. He voted for the bill to make Grant a lieutenant-general and was one of eight Democratic absentees when the Thirteenth Amendment passed the House. He introduced the resolution—which so alarmed the extreme Republicans—unqualifiedly indorsing President Johnson's Reconstruction policy.

From 1869 to 1873 he was again in the House of Representatives, in 1877 was appointed to the Senate and served from Nov. 6, 1877, to Mar. 3, 1897. In his twenty years as senator he attained the eminence attached to long service and oratorical ability (for his speeches see *Speeches*, 1875, comp. by C. S. Voorhees, and *Forty Years of Oratory*, 2 vols., 1898). His views on financial questions were typical of his party and state and rested on the desire for a large and freely circulating currency, on the belief that protection bore hardly on the farmers, and on a distrust of New England and the "money power." With the passage of time, however, his attitude became less strictly agrarian, and he supported President Cleveland in the various questions that divided the Democratic party. As chairman of the committee on finance, he led the fight for the repeal of the Sherman silver purchase act during the extra session of 1893, and in the following year he was the nominal manager in the Senate for the Wilson tariff bill.

Large and tall, with fair hair and "dark-grey hazel" eyes, he won the sobriquet of "Tall Sycamore of the Wabash" and was unrivalled in the middle West as a stump speaker and forensic orator. Two of his best known achievements as a lawyer were his defense of John E. Cook, one of John Brown's associates in the Harpers Ferry tragedy, and his defense of Mary Harris of Washington, D. C., for murder. He was generous and sympathetic to a fault. Though too ready to lend his aid to those seeking money from the government, yet he did not, himself, profit by his government positions and was also generous with his own money. He died poor in spite of a lucrative practice. He was influential in the building of the present Library of Congress. He died in Washington, and his funeral services were in St. John's Episcopal Church. He was buried in Terre Haute.

[Biog. sketches by A. B. Carlton, in *Speeches, ante*; and by T. B. Long, in *Forty Years of Oratory, ante*; W. W. Thornton, in *Green Bag*, Aug. 1902; H. D. Jordan, in *Miss. Valley Hist. Rev.*, Mar. 1920; J. G. Blaine, *Twenty Years of Congress* (2 vols., 1884–86); Hugh McCulloch, *Men and Measures of Half a Century* (1888); the inconclusive evidence for his connection with the Knights of the Golden Circle during the Civil War in F. G. Stidger, *Treason Hist. of the Order of Sons of Liberty . . .* (1903); E. W. Van Voorhis, *A Geneal. of the Van Voorhees Family* (1888); *Evening Star* (Washington, D. C.), Apr. 10, 1897.]   H.D.J.

VOORHEES, EDWARD BURNETT (June 22, 1856–June 6, 1911), agriculturist, was born at Minebrook, Somerset County, N. J., the son of John and Sarah (Dilley) Voorhees. He was a descendant of Steven Coerte Van Voorhees who emigrated from the Netherlands and settled on Long Island in 1660. At twenty-one Edward entered Rutgers College, where he was graduated with the degree of A.B. in 1881. The following year he spent as assistant to Prof. Wilbur O. Atwater [*q.v.*] at Wesleyan University, Middletown, Conn. In 1883 George H. Cook [*q.v.*], then director of the New Jersey State Experiment Station, offered him the position of assistant chemist, which he accepted. On Oct. 18 of the same year he married Anna E. Amerman, by whom he had two daughters and five sons. In 1888 he was promoted to chief chemist, and in 1890 he became, also, professor of agriculture at Rutgers, in which position he served until his death. Consciously or unconsciously Dr. Cook had prepared his assistant to fill the place which by Cook's death in 1889 was suddenly left vacant, but it was not until 1893 that Voorhees was appointed thereto. In 1896 he was made director of the College Station as well, and for some fifteen years he arranged the work of the two stations so that the College Station pursued fundamental research while the State Station set into practical application and made available to the farmers of New Jersey the scientific findings.

Voorhees was president of the Association of Official Agricultural Chemists (1893–94), secretary-treasurer of the Association of American Agricultural Colleges and Experiment Stations (1897–1903), and president in 1904, vice-president of the State Board of Agriculture (1893 to 1901), and its president (1901–11). He lent his influence to the fight against tuberculosis in cattle, was president for a short time of the state tuberculosis commission, and for a year was head of the New Jersey Microscopical Society. In the summer of 1904 he visited the experiment stations of England, Scotland, Ireland, Belgium, France, and Italy and brought home much valuable information. In 1898 he published *Fertilizers,* which was immediately accepted as a standard college textbook and went through thirteen editions; for use in secondary schools, he wrote *First Principles of Agriculture* (1896). He collaborated with Herbert Myrick in preparing *The Book of Corn* (1903); in 1907 he published *Forage Crops for Soiling, Silage, Hay and Pasture.* Besides these books, he wrote numerous articles for scientific journals.

Perhaps the founding of short agricultural courses for farmers was Voorhees' most useful work. He had rare ability as a teacher, not only of students, but of the thousands of farmers with whom he spent much of his time, lecturing to them, listening to their problems, and advising them. He always emphasized his one great precept, "improve the land." Under his management the experiment farm carried out extensive field tests with respect to top-dressing of meadows, special crop fertilizers, spraying of orchards, control of strawberry weevil, egg production, milk sanitation, and many other problems. Lectures and demonstrations explained to the farmers of the state the principles underlying the failure or success of these experiments. As a result of such leadership there came a more intensive specialization of agriculture, improved farming practice, and larger returns for the effort expended. His skill in choosing able men to collaborate with him insured continuation of the work when his own labor was finished.

[E. W. Van Voorhis, *A Geneal. of the Van Voorhees Family in America* (1888); J. McK. Cattell, *Am. Men of Sci.* (2nd ed., 1910); *Who's Who in America,* 1910–11; *U. S. Dept. of Agric., Experiment Station Record,* Aug. 1911; *Proc. of the Thirty-second Ann. Meeting of the Soc. for the Promotion of Agricultural Sci.* (1912); C. R. Woodward and I. N. Waller, *New Jersey's Agricultural Experiment Station* (1932); *Thirty-ninth Ann. Report of the State Board of Agriculture* (Trenton, 1912); *Trenton True American,* June 8, 1911.]

L. G.

VOORHEES, PHILIP FALKERSON (1792–Feb. 23, 1862), naval officer, was born in New Brunswick, N. J. He entered the navy as a midshipman, Nov. 15, 1809, and fought through the War of 1812, participating in the capture of the *Macedonian* by the *United States,* and of the *Epervier* by the *Peacock.* For his services in the latter engagement he was awarded a silver medal by Congress (J. F. Loubat, *The Medallic History of the United States,* vol. I, 1878, p. 198). His life was uneventful for many years except for a Mediterranean cruise in the *North Carolina* (1825–27). In 1831 he sailed again for the Mediterranean commanding the *John Adams* bearing dispatches for David Porter [*q.v.*], chargé d'affaires at Constantinople. He returned to the United States in 1834, and for the next seven years resided at Annapolis, Md., where he married Anne Randall, May 12, 1835; by this marriage he had two children.

On July 15, 1842, Voorhees, who by this time had risen to the rank of captain, again sailed for the Mediterranean commanding the frigate *Congress,* and the next year was ordered to join the Brazil squadron under Commodore Daniel Turner [*q.v.*]. On Sept. 28, 1844, he assisted in rescuing H.M.S. *Gorgon* which was stranded in the Rio de la Plata. The following day while off Montevideo, a schooner from Buenos Aires, the *Sancala,* fired on an American brig, the *Rosalba,* lying near the *Congress.* For this action Voorhees captured the *Sancala* and the whole Argentine squadron which was blockading Montevideo. The squadron was released after an apology but the *Sancala* was retained. Voorhees also refused to allow the blockade to be enforced against American vessels. Commodore Turner finally released the *Sancala,* though he considered Voorhees' action justifiable. The following spring Voorhees returned home, reaching Annapolis, Mar. 12, 1845.

On June 2 he was court-martialed for his action against the Argentine squadron and sentenced to reprimand and suspension for three years. Again, on June 24, he was court-martialed on a series of trivial charges, chief of which was disobedience to an order of Commodore Turner. He was found guilty on two specifications and suspended for eighteen months. George Bancroft [*q.v.*], secretary of the navy, dissatisfied with the findings of the court, ordered it to review its proceedings. The court re-convened, Aug. 5–8, 1845, and ordered Voorhees "To be dismissed from the service of the United States"; but President Polk mitigated his sentence to suspension from duty for five years. On Jan. 7, 1847, the President removed the suspension, and in 1849 Voorhees was ordered to take command of the East India squadron "in manifestation of his complete rehabilitation in honor as well as in rank" (*Official Opinions of the Attorneys General of the United States,* vol. VI, 1856, p. 202).

In 1855 he was placed by the naval retiring board on the reserved list on furlough pay. Voorhees appealed from the decision of the board, but the decision was sustained. Voorhees applied for a review of his case and President Buchanan referred the matter to the attorney-general who rendered a decision highly favorable to Voorhees, deeming him to be the victim of many blunders and misunderstandings. He was then placed on the reserve list with leave pay. He presented a memorial to Congress in December 1860 asking for restoration to active service, but nothing came of it. Though Voorhees was guilty of an error in judgment in capturing the Argentine squadron, his motives were admirable. Even the court that sentenced him to dismissal praised his "Uniform character, previous to these occurrences, for integrity, his gallant services as an officer, and his long continuance in the naval service, without reproach or dereliction of duty" (*Ibid.,* p. 202). His remaining years were passed quietly in Annapolis.

[*American and Commercial Advertiser* (Baltimore), Feb. 26, 1862; *Sun* (Baltimore), Feb. 25, 1862; J. B. Moore, *The Works of James Buchanan,* vol. VI (1909); *Defence of Philip F. Voorhees . . . before a Gen. Naval Court Martial* (1845); *Defence of Philip F. Voorhees before the Court of Inquiry* (1857); *Memorial of Capt. Philip F. Voorhees to the Senate and House* (1860); J. B. Moore, *A Digest of International Law,* vol. I (1906), pp. 178–82; *Niles' National Reg.,* Dec. 14, 1844, Feb. 22, Mar. 22, June 14, 1845; M. M. Quaife, *The Diary of James K. Polk,* vol. I (1910), pp. 41–43; log of U.S.S. *Congress,* Sept. 28–29, 1844 (MS.), Navy Dept.; letters to and from Voorhees, and transcript of service, Navy Dept.; information from Randall family, Annapolis, and from records of births and marriages, St. Anne's Episcopal Church, Annapolis.]   L. H. B.

VOORSANGER, JACOB (Nov. 13, 1852–Apr. 27, 1908), rabbi, was born in the Netherlands, at Amsterdam, the son of Wolf and Alicia (Pekel) Voorsanger. He was educated at the Jewish theological seminary of his native city, receiving the degree of rabbi in 1872. After spending a time in London, he came to the United States in 1873, and on Aug. 24 married, at Cincinnati, Eva Corper, by whom he had eight children. He occupied pulpits in Philadelphia (1873–76), Washington, D. C. (1876–77),

Providence, R. I. (1877–78), and Houston, Tex. (1878–86). In 1886 he became assistant to Elkan Cohn at the Temple Emanu-El, San Francisco, and from 1889 to his death served as its rabbi. Largely through his efforts, the University of California created a Semitic department in 1894, and from that time on he was professor of Semitic languages and literature, giving generously of his time and efforts, and collecting funds for the library. He also officiated as chaplain and special lecturer at the Leland Stanford Junior University.

In his day, Voorsanger was the foremost rabbi of the Pacific Coast. He spoke English fluently and without foreign accent, and commanded a direct and terse style. He belonged to the reform school of Judaism, but he had an inherent love of Jewish tradition which held him back from the radical reform tendencies in vogue in America in the last quarter of the nineteenth century. Though with the reform Judaism of his day he opposed the ideology of Zionism, he was interested in Palestine, visiting the country a few years before his death, and on his return writing a sympathetic series of articles appealing for the support of Jewish Palestinian institutions.

Voorsanger was a gifted journalist. He was editor of *The Jewish South,* of Houston, Tex., from 1881 to 1883, and *The Sabbath Visitor,* of Cincinnati, from 1883 to 1886. In 1895 he founded the weekly magazine *Emanu-El,* which he developed into the leading Jewish paper on the Pacific Coast, continuing as its editor till his death. He was the author of *The Chronicles of Emanu-El* (1900), a valuable contribution to the history of San Francisco Jewry, and was a contributing editor of *The Jewish Encyclopedia.* In 1913 Rabbi Martin A. Meyer edited a volume of Voorsanger's sermons, under the title *Sermons and Addresses by Jacob Voorsanger.*

Communal activities occupied a prominent place in his many-sided interests. He was a governor of the Hebrew Union College, a founder and vice-president of the California Red Cross Society, the first president of the Manila Library Association, and a member of the Hebrew Veterans of the Spanish-American War. It is claimed that in the San Francisco earthquake and conflagration of 1906, he was the first public man to organize immediate relief measures. Within one hour after the shock, while buildings were still tottering and flames were raging, he began to marshal men and food, and within four hours the mayor made him chairman of relief. He was a man of imposing stature and a born organizer and leader. Of broad sympathies and forceful personality, he worked with voice and pen for humanitarian causes. His companionable, democratic ways won him friendship and respect. His erudition, eloquence, ready pen, and public spirit made him a strong civic and religious force.

[*The Jewish Encyc.,* XII (1912), 451; *The Am. Jewish Year Book, 5664* (1903); *Year Book of the Central Conference of Am. Rabbis,* vol. XVIII (1908); *Who's Who in America,* 1906–07; *Hebrew Union Coll. Jubilee Volume* (1925); *The Am. Hebrew* (N. Y.), May 1, 1908; *Emanu-El* (San Francisco), May 1–June 26, 1908; *Jewish Tribune* (Portland, Ore.), May 1, 1908; *Am. Israelite* (Cincinnati, Ohio), Apr. 30, May 4, 1908; *Bulletin* (San Francisco), Apr. 28 and 30, 1908; name of wife from Voorsanger's son, Dr. Elkan Voorsanger.]   D. de S. P.

VOSE, GEORGE LEONARD (Apr. 19, 1831–Mar. 30, 1910), engineer, educator, born at Augusta, Me., was the son of Hon. Richard Hampton Vose, prominent in the legal and political life of that state, and of Harriet Green (Chandler) of Boston. He was a descendant of Robert Vose of Lancashire, England, who emigrated to Dorchester, Mass., some time prior to 1654. In 1848, after high-school training at Augusta and at Salem, Mass., Vose entered the office of Samuel Nott, a prominent civil engineer of Boston. Subsequently he studied for a time in the Lawrence Scientific School at Harvard. In 1850 he began his professional work in the field of railroad engineering, and for some ten years was widely engaged upon railroad location and construction in various parts of the United States and Canada.

In the mean time he published *Handbook of Railroad Construction* (1857), one of the earliest works on the subject to appear in the United States. Three years later he withdrew from the practical activities in which he had been engaged and gave his attention chiefly to writing and teaching. From 1860 to 1864 he was associate editor of the *American Railway Times,* Boston. In 1866 he removed from Salem, Mass., where he was then living, to Paris, Me. Here he concerned himself with various professional matters and prepared his *Manual for Railroad Engineers and Engineering Students* (2 vols., 1873), which went through several editions. In 1872 he was appointed professor of civil engineering at Bowdoin College, Brunswick, Me. His students included a considerable number who later became prominent in the engineering profession, among them Robert E. Peary and George E. Waring [*qq.v.*]. In 1881 Vose was called to the Massachusetts Institute of Technology as professor of civil engineering, where he remained for five years. The active interest which he took in the Boston Society of Civil Engineers led to his election as its president in 1884, in which capacity he served until 1887. His later years were passed at his home in Maine, ill health preventing him from engaging in much professional work. He died at Brunswick, in the seventy-ninth year of his age.

His years of practical experience, together with a rare gift of awakening the keen interest of his students in the subject he taught, made him an exceptionally successful instructor. His books gave him a wide reputation. In addition to the works already mentioned and various articles in periodicals, he was the author of *Orographic Geology* (1866); *A Graphic Method for Solving Certain Algebraic Problems* (1875); *An Elementary Course of Geometrical Drawing* (1878); *A Sketch of the Life and Works of Loammi Baldwin* (1885); *Bridge Disasters in America* (1887). On Nov. 9, 1854, in Bethel, Me., he married Abba Valentine Thompson, daughter of Rev. Zenas Thompson; she died in 1870 and on Apr. 16, 1872, he married Charlotte Buxton Andrews. He had four daughters and a son.

[*Jour. of the Asso. of Engineering Societies,* Feb. 1911; E. F. Vose, *Robert Vose and His Descendants* (1932); W. B. Lapham and S. P. Maxim, *Hist. of Paris, Me.* (1884); *Daily Kennebec Jour.,* Mar. 31, 1910.]   H. K. B—s.

VOUGHT, CHANCE MILTON (Feb. 26, 1890–July 25, 1930), aircraft designer and manufacturer, was born in New York City, the son of George Washington and Annie Eliza (Colley) Vought. He attended the public schools of New York City, the Pratt Institute, Brooklyn, and New York University, where he specialized in the study of internal combustion engines. Subsequently he enrolled at the University of Pennsylvania, but left in 1910 without graduating and became consulting engineer for Harold F. McCormick of Chicago. For three years he was associated with McCormick in experimental developments. Ambitious, daring, and of strong mechanical bent, Vought learned to fly at the age of twenty, under the instruction of the Wright brothers. He became a finished and skilful, though not a professional, pilot, and continued to fly actively until 1917.

From 1912 onwards his career was exclusively devoted to aeronautics. His first aviation appointment was that of consulting engineer for the Aero Club of Illinois. In 1914 he became editor of the pioneer aviation weekly, *Aero & Hydro.* Later in that year, in association with the Mayo Radiator Works in New Haven, Conn., he designed and constructed an advanced training plane, used by the British during the World War. This airplane laid the foundation of his reputation as a designer. In 1916, as chief engineer of the Wright Company, Dayton, Ohio, he produced the famous Vought-Wright Model V military biplane. In 1917, soon after the Wright-Martin Aircraft Company merger, Vought launched out for himself in the Lewis & Vought Corporation, which was financed by Birdseye B. Lewis. During the war he served as consulting engineer to the bureau of aircraft production in Washington, and to the Engineering Division of the Army Air Corps at McCook Field, Dayton.

The early days of the Lewis & Vought Corporation in Long Island City were perhaps the most interesting, as they were the most critical of Chance Vought's career. Possessing a remarkable charm of manner and at home in any society, he was idolized by his small group of a dozen workmen. Neither by education nor instinct was he a plodding, finished calculator. He had, however, an intuitive, artistic sense for clean, streamlined airplanes, combined with practical ability and a thorough knowledge of the structure and uses of aircraft, particularly as regards naval requirements. An indefatigable worker, he developed new designs practically alone, and knew how to realize his drawings in the shop, working at times with his own hands. He had a keen business sense, and could hasten a government payment when necessary to meet the payroll of his small concern. The Lewis & Vought Corporation and its successor, the Chance Vought Corporation, rapidly became the outstanding constructors of the two-place advanced training plane known as the Vought VE-7 (1919). Even in the period of the box-like aircraft, Vought designs had been singularly attractive in appearance, and as design improved, Vought airplanes continued in the forefront. The Vought UO-1 (1922–25) convertible observation airplane, specially designed for use from battleships and cruisers and for operations on aircraft carriers, solved the difficult problem of catapulting a heavy and fully equipped plane. The FU-1 single-seat high-altitude supercharged fighter (1925) was but little less noteworthy. The Vought O2U Corsair was a famous single-float seaplane, convertible into a landplane for catapulting and deck landing. This type, as a stock naval seaplane, set four world's records for speed and altitude. Vought worked above all for tactical flexibility in naval aircraft, developed his types by wise evolution, and maintained unsurpassable standards of workmanship. The operations of the Chance Vought Corporation were highly successful and in 1930 it employed 700 men as compared with the initial dozen.

In February 1929 Vought joined with the Pratt & Whitney Aircraft Company of Hartford and the Boeing Airplane Company in forming the vast United Aircraft & Transport Corporation, securing thereby an excellent return for his interests. He was very active on the directorate of the United, and continued as president and consulting engineer of the Chance Vought unit until his death. During his busy career he found time to write many papers and articles for technical journals on aircraft design, construction, and performance, and to be active in the Aircraft Committee of the Society of Automotive Engineers. He was a member of many clubs, loved New York, the theatre, and American life. He died in the Southampton Hospital, Southampton, Long Island, of septicemia, leaving his large personal fortune to his wife, Ena (Lewis) Vought, daughter of Birdseye B. Lewis, whom he married Dec. 4, 1920, and to their two children. His wife had been closely associated with him in his work, and had personally assisted him in the shop in the earlier stages of his career.

[E. E. Wilson, "Chance Milton Vought," lecture before Am. Soc. of Mechanical Engineers, Jan. 22, 1931; "Chance M. Vought Dies at Southampton," *U. S. Air Services,* Sept. 1930; "America's Aircraft Builders and Their Products," *Sportsman Pilot,* Oct. 1929; *N. Y. Times,* July 26, 1930.]   A. K—n.

VROOM, PETER DUMONT (Dec. 12, 1791–Nov. 18, 1873), lawyer, congressman, governor and chancellor of New Jersey, was born in Hillsboro Township, Somerset County, N. J., the son of Col. Peter Dumont and Elsie (Bogert) Vroom. The male line was Dutch, the first Vroom to come to America being Cornelius Petersen Coursen of Langeraer, the Netherlands, who arrived on Long Island about 1638, but the original stock is said to have been French Huguenot. The name Vroom (or de Vroom) was first taken by Hendrick, son of Cornelius Petersen; otherwise the family retained the name of Coursen (or Corsen). The elder Peter Vroom (1745–1831) rose by successive degrees from the rank of lieutenant to that of lieutenant-colonel in the 2nd Battalion of the Somerset, N. J., militia in the Revolutionary War. Subsequently he was sheriff of Somerset County, county clerk, member of the General Assembly (1790–98, and 1813) and of the Legislative Council (1798–1804); he was also a justice of the peace and judge of the court of common pleas.

Vroom received his preparatory education at the Somerville Academy, Somerville, N. J., and was graduated from Columbia College, New York City, in 1808. He read law under George McDonald at Somerville and was admitted to the New Jersey bar as attorney in 1813 and as counsellor in 1816 and became sergeant-at-law in 1828. He practised successively at Schooleys Mountain (1813), Hackettstown (1814–16),

Flemington (1817–21), and Somerville, where he remained about twenty years. While at Flemington he married, May 21, 1817, Ann V. D. Dumont of Somerset County. Although he had been a Federalist, in 1824 he became a strong supporter of Andrew Jackson. He served as a member of the New Jersey Assembly in 1826, 1827, and 1829. In 1829 he was elected to the combined office of governor and chancellor of the state. He served until 1832 (when he was defeated by Samuel L. Southard, a Whig) and again from 1833 to 1836. The equity opinions he rendered as chancellor were so sound that "for the most part, they stood unquestioned" for many years after (Whitehead, *post*, p. 382). In 1837 he was appointed by President Van Buren one of three commissioners to adjust land-reserve claims in Mississippi under a treaty with the Choctaw Indians (appointment confirmed, Mar. 8, 1837). He was elected to Congress in 1838 but, owing to irregularities in some of the returns, was not commissioned. After what is known as the "Broad Seal War," the courts established that he was elected by a clear majority, and he was seated, serving in the House of Representatives from Mar. 4, 1839, to Mar. 3, 1841.

At the end of his term he removed permanently to Trenton. After the death of his first wife he married, Nov. 4, 1840, Maria Matilda Wall, daughter of Gen. Garret D. and Maria (Rhea) Wall of Burlington, N. J. In 1844 he was a delegate to the convention that framed the constitution of New Jersey. In 1848 he was associated with Henry Woodhull Green, William Lewis Dayton [*qq.v.*] and Stacy G. Potts in framing statutes to comply with the new constitution. He declined an appointment as chief justice of the state supreme court, but in 1854 accepted appointment (confirmed Feb. 9, 1854) by President Pierce as minister to the court of Prussia. He was in Berlin until 1857, when he was recalled at his own request. In Prussia he handled well the difficult question of the right of Germans, naturalized as American citizens but living in Prussia, to claim exemption from the compulsory military law of their native country.

In 1860 Vroom was placed upon the Breckinridge and Lane Democratic electoral ticket. He was opposed, however, to the secession movement and was a member of the futile peace conference which met at Washington, Feb. 4, 1861. He supported George Brinton McClellan for president in 1864, and in 1868 was an elector on the Seymour and Blair presidential ticket. In 1865 he took the place of his son, John P. Vroom, who died that year, as law reporter of the New Jersey supreme court and served until 1873. He

was one of the commissioners of the sinking fund of the state from 1864 until his death. He was vice-president of the American Colonization Society and the American Bible Society, and was long a ruling elder of the Reformed Dutch Church at Somerville. Of vigorous constitution, a hard worker at all times, he practised his profession with undiminished powers until a short time before his death, which occurred in Trenton.

[*Biog. Dir. Am. Cong.* (1928); L. Q. C. Elmer, in *N. J. Hist. Soc. Colls.*, vol. VII (1872); J. P. Snell and Franklin Ellis, *Hist. of Hunterdon and Somerset Counties* (1881); Abraham Messler, *Centennial Hist. of Somerset County* (1878), and *Sermons . . . on the . . . Death of the Hon. Peter D. Vroom* (1874); John Whitehead, *Judicial and Civil Hist. of N. J.* (1897); *Biog. Encyc. of N. J.* (1877); *Our Home*, Dec. 1873; obituary in *Daily State Gazette* (Trenton, N. J.), Nov. 19, 1873.]   A. V—D. H.

WABASHA (*c.* 1773–*c.* 1855), chief of the Mdewakanton Sioux occupying the region south of the Minnesota River, was born probably in the vicinity of the present Winona, Minn. The name, also spelled Wapasha, was borne by a succession of chiefs, of whom this one was perhaps the best known. His father, the first historical bearer of the name, was born about 1718, was closely allied to the British before and during the Revolution, and died about 1799. The second Wabasha, known also as La Feuille and The Leaf, first came into prominence through his conferences with Zebulon M. Pike, on the upper Mississippi, in the fall of 1805. He sided with the Americans in their difficulties with the Winnebagos, Menominees, and Sauks. During the War of 1812, though he never openly broke with the British, he seems to have favored the Americans. At any rate the British suspected him and actually tried his son-in-law, Rolette, by court-martial for collusion with the Americans. He was a conspicuous and forceful figure in the great council of Aug. 5–19, 1825, at Prairie du Chien, between representatives of the federal government and the tribes of the central north. In the Sauk War of 1832 (see sketch of Black Hawk) he supported the Americans, and it was probably a band of his warriors who fell upon the remnants of Black Hawk's band on the Iowa side of the Mississippi. On his death he was succeeded by his nephew, perhaps his son, Wabasha, often known as Joseph Wabasha, under whom his people were removed to the upper Minnesota. The latter, at his death on Apr. 23, 1876, was succeeded by his son, the fourth Wabasha, also known as Joseph Wabasha, who for many years was chief of the Santee Sioux on the Niobrara reservation in Nebraska, and was a citizen of the United States.

The second Wabasha, in spite of John Shaw's statement that he was exceptionally tall (*post*, p.

214), appears to have been of less than medium stature. That he was impressive in bearing was, however, the common testimony of all who met him; and there is equal agreement that he had notable abilities and high character. Pike wrote of him with great respect, and Stephen H. Long, who visited him in 1817, noted that he was considered one of the most honest and honorable of any of the Indians, and endeavored to inculcate into the minds of his people the sentiments and principles adopted by himself (*post*, p. 17). Keating (*post*, I, 258) recorded his reputation for wisdom, prudence, and skill in oratory, and Beltrami, the Italian traveler (*post*, II, 181), asserted that he needed only "an embroidered coat, a large portfolio . . . and spectacles" to have all the appearance of a great statesman.

[*Handbook of Am. Indians*, pt. 2 (1910), ed. by F. W. Hodge; "Jour. of Stephen W. Kearney," *Mo. Hist. Soc. Colls.*, vol. III (1908); S. H. Long, "Voyage in a Six-oared Skiff . . . in 1817," *Minn. Hist. Soc. Colls.*, vol. II (1860), esp. pp. 17, 21; W. H. Keating, *Narrative of an Expedition . . . Under Stephen H. Long* (1825), I, 257–58; J. C. Beltrami, *A Pilgrimage in Europe and America* (1828), II, 181; John Shaw, "Sketches of Indian Chiefs and Pioneers of the North-West," *Wis. Hist. Soc. Colls.*, X (1888), 214; C. C. Willson, "The Successive Chiefs Named Wabasha," *Minn. Hist. Soc. Colls.*, vols. II (1860) and XII (1908).]

W. J. G.

WACHSMUTH, CHARLES (Sept. 13, 1829–Feb. 7, 1896), paleontologist, was born in the city of Hanover, Germany, the only son of Christian Wachsmuth, a lawyer and member of the Frankfurt Parliament of 1848. Although the boy was in feeble health almost from the hour of his birth, his father decided to prepare him for the law, but he was obliged to give up his studies, and, upon advice of his physician, entered a mercantile house in Hamburg. In 1852 he was sent to New York as an agent of the company, and about two years later he went west, and settled in Burlington, Iowa, where he entered the grocery business. In the meanwhile, in an effort to regain his health in the out-of-doors, he devoted his leisure to the collecting of fossils.

In 1865 the business prospered so that he was able to retire and to devote all of his time to collecting and studying—a pursuit that he enjoyed with signal success to his very last day. He acquired large collections of the rare crinoids and a special library on the subject which attracted the attention of scientists the world over. Louis Agassiz [*q.v.*], on one of his western lecturing tours, visited him, became very enthusiastic over the acquirements, and in 1873 purchased the material for the Museum of Comparative Zoölogy at Cambridge. He induced Wachsmuth to go to Cambridge with him, where he could continue his studies to greater advantage, and

Wachsmuth worked with Agassiz until the latter's death in December of that year. Returning once more to Burlington he began to make a new collection, but with very different and much enlarged ideas from those that he had previously held. He soon made the acquaintance of a young lawyer, Frank Springer [*q.v.*], who had a strong interest in crinoids, and the friendship of the two men developed into a partnership that lasted through life.

The joint plan of Springer and Wachsmuth was a pretentious one. It involved the personal critical examination of all the collections of crinoids throughout the world, and a complete revision of everything ever described. This stupendous undertaking occupied fifty years, the work being carried on by Springer alone for twenty years after Wachsmuth's death. The resulting monumental monograph, *North American Crinoidea Camerata*, superbly illustrated, was dedicated to Agassiz and appeared in 1897 as volumes XX and XXI of the *Memoirs of the Museum of Comparative Zoölogy*. Usually associated with Springer, Wachsmuth published numerous other memoirs on the morphology of the crinoids. Some of the most important appeared in the *Proceedings of the American Academy of Natural Sciences* in Philadelphia: "Transition Forms in Crinoids" (3 ser., vol. VIII, 1879), "Revision of the Palæocrinoidea" (3 ser., vols., IX, XI, XV, XVI, 1880–87), "The Summit Plates in Blastoids, Crinoids, and Cystids" (3 ser., vol. XVII, 1888), "Discovery of the Ventral Structure of Taxocrinus and Haplocrinus" (3 ser., vol. XVIII, 1889), and "The Perisomic Plates of Crinoids" (3 ser., vol. XX, 1891). His "Notes on the Internal and External Structure of Paleozoic Crinoids" appeared in the *American Journal of Science and Art*, August 1877. A complete bibliography of his publications is to be found in the *American Geologist, post*. After Wachsmuth's death, several monographs left unfinished were completed by Springer.

Widely honored by his fellow scientists, Wachsmuth was elected member of many learned societies both at home and abroad, and throughout life carried on an extensive correspondence with most of the savants in his field the world over. His wife, Bernandina Lorenz, also of Hanover, to whom he had been married in 1855, survived him. He was interred at Aspen Grove Cemetery, Burlington.

[Personal acquaintance of the author; C. R. Keyes, "Biographical Sketch of Charles Wachsmuth," *Am. Geologist*, Mar. 1896, and "Memorial of Charles Wachsmuth," *Proc. Iowa Acad. Sci.*, vol. IV (1897); Samuel Calvin, "Memoir of Charles Wachsmuth," *Bull. Geo-*

logical Soc. of America, vol. VIII (1897), Apr. 30, 1897.]   C.R.K.

WACKER, CHARLES HENRY (Aug. 29, 1856–Oct. 31, 1929), brewer, executive, city planner, was the only child of Frederick Wacker, a German emigrant who settled in Chicago in 1854, and his wife, Catharine Hummel. He was educated in the schools of Chicago and studied one year at Lake Forest Academy. He started in business as an office boy, 1872–76, in the firm of Carl C. Moeller & Company, grain commissioners, and then toured Europe and Africa for three years, spending some time studying in Stuttgart and Geneva. Returning to his position in 1879, he remained there until the following year when his father took him into partnership in the malting business to form the firm of F. Wacker & Son which in 1882 became Wacker & Birk Brewing and Malting Company. From 1884 until 1901 he was president of this firm, and, from 1895 to 1901, he was also president of the McAvoy Brewing Company, with which it was consolidated in 1889. In 1901 he turned his attention to real estate and, from 1902 to 1928, he was president of the Chicago Heights Land Association.

His interest in civic affairs was given an impetus by his connection with the World's Columbian Exposition in Chicago in 1893 as a member of the board of directors and of various committees. He became an enthusiastic supporter and eventually the leader of a movement, started by the Merchants and Commercial Clubs, to beautify the city of Chicago. He was vice-chairman of the Merchants Club's Committee from 1907 to 1909, and its chairman for a short time in 1909. In 1909 Mayor Busse and the City Council created the Chicago Plan Commission to improve and beautify Chicago's "loop" and lake front, and appointed Wacker chairman. He held this position until Nov. 4, 1926, when he resigned because of illness. In appreciation of his remarkable work and untiring efforts in sponsoring and developing the Chicago Plan, the City Council renamed South Water Street, the double-decked drive along the river, which Wacker had been most influential in securing as a part of the Plan, Wacker Drive.

He was made secretary of the Chicago Zoning Commission in 1920, was president of the Chicago Relief and Aid Society, and, when it merged with the Chicago Bureau of Charities to form the United Charities of Chicago, became (1909–12) the first president of that body. He was a director of many important companies, and a member of a great many social clubs, German clubs, and singing societies. In 1921 he was awarded a medal of honor by the Société des Architectes Français. Some of his articles and addresses on the Chicago Plan were published; among them are *An S-O-S to the Public Spirited Citizens of Chicago* (1924), and articles in the *American City*, October 1909, and in *Art and Archæology*, September-October 1921. He was twice married, first to Ottilie Marie Glade on May 10, 1887, and, after her death, to Ella G. Todtmann, Mar. 19, 1919. By the first marriage there were two sons and a daughter, who, with his second wife, survived him.

[*Who's Who in America*, 1928–29; *Who's Who in Chicago*, 1926; A. T. Andreas, *Hist. of Chicago*, vol. III (1886); *A Biog. Hist. with Portraits of Prominent Men of the Great West* (1894); *One Hundred Years of Brewing* (1903); W. D. Moody, *Wacker's Manual of the Plan of Chicago* (1911); D. H. Burnham and E. H. Bennett, *Plan of Chicago Prepared Under the Direction of the Commercial Club* (1909); *Chicago Daily Tribune*, Nov. 1, 1929.]   J.K.W.

WADDEL, JAMES (July 1739–Sept. 17, 1805), clergyman, was born in Newry, Ireland, the son of Thomas Waddel. His parents emigrated in the fall of 1739 and settled on White Clay Creek in south-eastern Pennsylvania. He was educated in the "log college" of Samuel Finley [*q.v.*] at Nottingham, Pa., and served as a tutor there. Later, while preparing himself for the ministry, he taught in the academy of Robert Smith at Pequea in Lancaster County, Pa., and in the classical school of John Todd of Louisa, Va. As a young man in Virginia he was much influenced by the charm and evangelical zeal of Samuel Davies [*q.v.*]. Licensed to preach by the Presbytery of Hanover on Apr. 2, 1761, and ordained at a meeting of the presbytery held in Prince Edward County on June 16 and 17, 1762, he received calls from congregations both in Virginia and in Pennsylvania. On Oct. 7, 1762, he accepted a call from a congregation in Northumberland and Lancaster counties of the Northern Neck of Virginia. During the first year there he was assisted in reviving the fervor of his congregation by the forceful preaching of George Whitefield [*q.v.*]. As a nonconformist preacher he was naturally subject to attack by the Anglican clergy. In all such encounters he seems to have borne himself well. The magistrate had become very lax in the enforcement of the laws in regard to dissenters, and they permitted him to take the qualifying oaths six months after his acceptance of his first charge in Virginia. There is no record of his ever being oppressed by the law. In 1768 he married Mary, the daughter of James Gordon of Lancaster County, Va. One of their ten children married Archibald Alexander [*q.v.*] and became the mother of Joseph A. and Samuel D. Alexander [*qq.v.*]. In 1776 or 1777 he accepted a call from the Tinkling Spring congregation in Augusta County and in 1778 removed with his family to the Shenandoah Valley. Later he was pastor of the two congregations of Tinkling Spring and Staunton. In 1785 he removed east of the Blue Ridge to a plantation he called "Belle Grove," not far from the town of Gordonsville and lived there for the rest of his life. He established a group of churches in Orange, Louisa, and Albemarle counties and preached regularly in the Hopewell church near Gordonsville, in the Brick church near Orange Court House, and in the old meeting house on the Rockfish Gap road about five miles from Charlottesville.

In person he was tall and very thin. His eyes were light blue, his complexion fair, his face and forehead long and narrow. His manner was gentle. He spoke with animation but never ranted. His voice was low, sweet, and very distinct. Although he permitted his daughters to learn the minuet, he was a stanch defender of the Calvinistic theology and a determined opponent of the philosophical deism then dominant in the South. His ministry helped to establish the cordial understanding between the Virginia squirearchy and the Presbyterian Church. His eyesight had never been good and in 1787 he became blind. In 1798 he underwent an operation for cataract, as a result of which he recovered his sight for a time. During the eleven years of his blindness he continued to preach as before, or perhaps with increased effectiveness. He died at his home.

[W. B. Sprague, *Annals of the Am. Pulpit,* vol. III (1858); W. H. Foote, *Sketches of Virginia* (1 Ser., 1850); William Wirt, *The Letters of the British Spy* (1803), letter VII; J. W. Alexander, *Memoir of the Rev. James Waddel* (1880), reprinted from *Watchman of the South* in 1844; J. R. Graham, *The Planting of the Presbyterian Church in Northern Virginia* (1904); Arista Hoge, *The First Presbyterian Church, Staunton, Va.* (1908). He spelled his name with one l and pronounced it "waddle." Many of his descendants spell it with two ll's and pronounce it with accent on last syllable.]   T. C. J., Jr.

WADDEL, JOHN NEWTON (Apr. 2, 1812–Jan. 9, 1895), clergyman and educator, was born at Willington, S. C., the son of Elizabeth Woodson (Pleasants) and Moses Waddel [*q.v.*]. He pronounced his surname as did his father. He is reputed to have said that he had "waddeled" through life thus far and could "waddle" on to the end. He received his early education in a neighborhood school and in a grammar school at Athens, Ga. He graduated from Franklin College (the University of Georgia) in 1829. Upon graduation he taught for several years in his father's old academy at Willington. On Nov. 27, 1832, he was married to Martha A. Robertson. They had eight children. In 1837 he removed to

Alabama and from there to Mississippi, where, in 1842, he established the Montrose Academy which became an educational center of that part of Mississippi. Being made a charter member of the board of trustees, he took a leading part in the founding of the University of Mississippi at Oxford. On Oct. 23, 1843, he was ordained to the Presbyterian ministry and supplied a group of churches in and around Montrose. From 1848 to 1857 he taught ancient languages in the University of Mississippi and during this period also supplied the Presbyterian Church at Oxford. There his wife died in 1851, and on Aug. 24, 1854, he was married to Mary A. Werden of Berkshire County, Mass., who died in 1862 after some years of invalidism. In 1857 he resigned to go to the Presbyterian Synodical College at La Grange, Tenn., to teach ancient languages and in 1860 became president of that institution. When the Federal army occupied La Grange in December 1862 he received official orders to discontinue his labors as a minister in that place. Thereupon he slipped through the Federal lines and later became a chaplain in the Confederate army. Later still he was placed in charge of all the chaplains connected with the army of Joseph E. Johnston. In the meantime he had taken a leading part in the organization of the first General Assembly of the Southern Presbyterian Church at Augusta, Ga., in December 1861 and was stated clerk of that body from 1861 to 1865. In 1868 he was elected moderator of the General Assembly, the highest office in the gift of his church. At the close of the Civil War he became chancellor of the University of Mississippi and shortly afterward, on Jan. 31, 1866, was married to his third wife, Harriet (Godden) Snedecor. As chancellor he made a tour of the leading colleges and universities of America, seeking for his own university the best thing that could be found in the leading institutions of this country. In 1874 he resigned the chancellorship. From 1874 to 1879 he was secretary of education for the Southern Presbyterian Church, with headquarters in Memphis. From 1879 to 1888 he was chancellor of the Southwestern Presbyterian University at Clarksville, Tenn.

He wrote numerous articles for the religious papers and reviews, a short history of the University of Mississippi, *Historical Discourse . . . on the . . . University of Mississippi* (1873), and *Memorials of Academic Life: Being an Historical Sketch of the Waddel Family* (1891). He was a faithful minister of the Gospel, but he was preëminently an educator whether in the academy, in the university, or in the pulpit. There must be assigned to him an honorable place among the leading educators in the entire South during the time in which he lived. He died in Birmingham, Ala.

[Diary in Lib. of Cong.; Memorial in Minutes of Nashville Presbytery, Apr. 1895, pp. 12–15, Hist. Foundation of Presbyterian and Reformed Churches, Montreat, N. C.; *Memorials of Acad. Life, ante*; *Hist. Cat. of the Univ. of Miss.* (1910); H. A. White, *Southern Presbyterian Leaders* (1911), with picture incorrectly labelled as of James Waddell; *Birmingham Age-Herald*, Jan. 10, 1895; information from great-grand-daughter, Elizabeth H. West, Lubbock, Texas.]

W. L. L.

WADDEL, MOSES (July 29, 1770–July 21, 1840), teacher and clergyman, was born in Rowan, now Iredell County, N. C., the son of William and Sarah (Morrow) Waddel, who emigrated from County Down, Ireland, and settled in Rowan County, N. C., in 1767. His surname was accented on the first syllable. He got his elementary schooling in a neighborhood school and received advanced instruction at Clio's Nursery, established by James Hall [*q.v.*] in 1778. Completing his school education there in 1784, he began to teach pupils in the neighborhood of his home. In 1788 he removed with his parents to Greene County, Ga., and there opened a school. He graduated from Hampton-Sydney College in 1791 and later studied theology under Virginia clergymen. After receiving his license in May 1792, he preached for a time in the vicinity of Charleston, S. C., but soon removed to Columbia County, Ga., and established a school near Appling. While living there, he preached at the Calhoun settlement across the Savannah River, some fifty miles away, in Abbeville District, S. C. There he met and in 1795 married Catherine, the sister of his most distinguished pupil, John C. Calhoun [*q.v.*]. She lived slightly more than a year after their marriage. In 1800 he married Elizabeth Woodson Pleasants of Halifax County, Va., and in 1801 removed to Vienna, a town on the South Carolina side of the Savannah, and opened another school. John Newton Waddel [*q.v.*] was their son.

In 1804 he removed to Willington, a community about six miles south of Vienna, and there opened the school that gained and maintained a widespread reputation. The first school house was a two-room log cabin. In 1809 four recitation rooms and a chapel were built. The students studied in log and brick huts about the school house and boarded with neighboring farmers. A monitorial form of student government, which was headed by the master, made for strict discipline. Although some of his pupils thought him cruel and severe, he had an unusual capacity for stimulating in boys a desire to learn. A. B. Longstreet, in his *Master William Mitten,* described

his Willington teacher as a man of "about five feet nine inches; of stout muscular frame, and a little inclined to corpulency. . . . His head was uncommonly large, and covered with a thick coat of dark hair. . . . His eyes were gray, and overshadowed by thick, heavy eye-brows, . . . [and] his *tout ensemble* was . . . extremely austere" (*post*, p. 108). At Willington, between 1804 and 1819, Waddel taught most of those four thousand students that in various places received instruction from him. In addition to large numbers of clergymen, he trained many senators, governors, congressmen, judges, and lawyers. His most distinguished pupils were John C. Calhoun, William H. Crawford, Hugh S. Legaré, George McDuffie, A. B. Longstreet, and James L. Petigru [*qq.v.*].

In 1818 he published a most tedious religious tract, *Memoirs of the Life of Miss Caroline Elizabeth Smelt,* which, however, went through several editions. In 1819 he became president of Franklin College (the University of Georgia). He is usually given the credit for building up the student body there and stimulating its religious life. Retiring in 1829, he lived in Willington until 1836, when he returned to Athens following a paralytic stroke.

[Notes, letters, diary, and memoir in Lib. of Cong.; J. N. Waddel, *Memorials of Academic Life* (1891); A. B. Longstreet, *Master William Mitten* (1864), esp. chap. VIII and *Eulogy on the Life and Services of the Late Rev. Moses Waddel, D.D.* (1841); Colyer Meriwether, "History of Higher Education in South Carolina," *United States Bureau of Education, Circular of Information*, no. 3 (1888), pp. 211–35; George Howe, *Hist. of the Presbyterian Church in S. C.*, vol. II (1883); W. B. Sprague, *Annals of the American Pulpit*, vol. IV (1858); *Writings of Hugh S. Legaré*, vol. I (1846), ed. by M. S. Legaré Buffen; W. J. Grayson, *James Louis Petigru, A Biog. Sketch* (1866); R. M. Lyon, "Moses Waddel and the Willington Academy," *N. C. Hist. Rev.*, July 1931; *Abbeville Press and Banner* (S. C.), July 7, 28, 1887; information from grand-daughter, Elizabeth H. West, Lubbock, Texas.]

R. M. L.

WADDELL, ALFRED MOORE (Sept. 16, 1834–Mar. 17, 1912), congressman and author, was born at Hillsboro, N. C., the son of Hugh and Susan (Moore) Waddell and the great-grandson of Hugh Waddell, Francis Nash, and Alfred Moore [*qq.v.*]. He was educated at the Bingham School and Caldwell Institute in Hillsboro and at the University of North Carolina, 1851–53. After studying law with Frederick Nash [*q.v.*], John L. Bailey, William H. Battle [*q.v.*], and Samuel F. Phillips, he was admitted to the bar in 1855 and in the following spring settled in Wilmington, his permanent residence, excepting a year, 1882–83, as a newspaper editor in Charlotte. His chief joy and distinction, however, were in public service, oratory, and historical authorship rather than in the practice of law.

He was clerk and master in equity of New Hanover County, 1858–61. Stanchly conservative and unionist, he supported the American presidential ticket in 1856, opposed the growing secession movement, purchased and edited a unionist newspaper, the *Wilmington Herald*, in 1860–61, and went with the North Carolina delegation to the Constitutional Union National Convention in 1860 as an alternate. During the Civil War he served first as adjutant and in 1863–64 as lieutenant-colonel of the 41st North Carolina regiment (3rd Cavalry), from which he resigned on account of impaired health.

He accepted the results of the war and favored a conservative readjustment of the Southern régime, advocating limited negro suffrage in an address to negroes in Wilmington in the summer of 1865 (*Sentinel*, Raleigh, Aug. 8, 1865). After three years of radical Reconstruction and the outrages of the Kirk-Holden war in 1870 the Conservative party attacked the Republican-negro régime in the campaign of 1870. First elected to Congress that year, he served by reelection until 1879. In Congress he spoke eloquently and with wide acclaim in temperate defense of the South, in deprecation of partisanship and sectionalism, and for the honor, character, and solidarity of the American union. He opposed the Ku Klux Act of 1871 as unnecessary, unconstitutional, and partisan, though he voted for congressional investigations of alleged Southern outrages, served reluctantly on the joint select investigating committee of 1871, and signed the minority report. As chairman of the House committee on the postoffice and post-roads, 1877–79, he sought improvements in the postal service and the establishment of postal savings banks. Democratic overconfidence and inactivity and a wide distribution of his limited negro suffrage speech caused his defeat in 1878. He was a delegate to the Democratic national conventions of 1880 and 1896, and an elector-at-large in 1888.

His fine stage presence, genial personality, and polished eloquence placed him in great demand in North Carolina and other states for commencement, patriotic, historical, and political addresses. For five months in 1880 he canvassed Vermont, Maine, and New York for the Democratic ticket. Pride in his state and his distinguished lineage stimulated him to historical authorship. *A Colonial Officer and His Times, 1754–1773. A Biographical Sketch of Gen. Hugh Waddell of North Carolina* (1890), *Some Memories of My Life* (1908), *A History of New Hanover County and the Lower Cape Fear Region, 1723–1800*, vol. I (1909), and several addresses possess descriptive strength and substantial worth, if not the

highest scholarship. Ordinarily dignified and reserved, he was in critical times a bold, courageous leader. He made fervent speeches in the bitter "White Supremacy" campaign of 1898, redeemed the state from the abuses of Republican-Populist-negro rule, and he was the chief leader of the white citizenship in Wilmington that on Nov. 9–10 forcibly rid the city of a negro newspaper, offending whites and negroes, and a corrupt and unpopular government, and precipitated a bloody race riot. Elected mayor, he quickly restored peace and order and until 1905 gave to the city a dignified, clean, and peaceful government. He was an Episcopalian and a Mason. He was married three times: to Julia Savage in 1857, to Ellen Savage, her sister, in 1878, and in 1896 to Gabrielle deRosset, who with two children of his first wife survived him.

[*Some Memories of My Life, ante*; *Who's Who in America*, 1912–13; James Sprunt, *Chronicles of the Cape Fear River* (1914); J. G. deR. Hamilton, *N. C. since 1860* (1919) and *Reconstruction in N. C.* (1906); *Morning Star* (Wilmington), Mar. 19, 1912.]

A. R. N.

WADDELL, HUGH (1734?–Apr. 9, 1773), soldier, was born in Lisburn, County Down, Ireland, the son of Hugh and Isabella (Brown) Waddell. He spent several years of his boyhood in Boston, Mass., whither his father had fled after a fatal duel. After the death of his father, who had returned to Ireland and found himself propertyless there, young Waddell emigrated to North Carolina. In 1754, soon after his arrival, he went as a lieutenant with the regiment of James Innes to help Virginia drive the French from the Ohio and was promoted to be a captain, although mismanagement caused the troops to be disbanded in the summer without active service. In the winter of 1754–55, he was clerk of the council of the new governor, Arthur Dobbs [*q.v.*], who had been a friend of his father in Ireland. In 1755 Dobbs ordered him to protect the frontier from the Cherokee and Catawba. In Rowan County near present-day Statesville, he built Fort Dobbs, authorized by the Assembly of 1755, a substantial three-story blockhouse of oak logs, and commanded its garrison until late in 1757. With Virginia commissioners he negotiated an offensive-defensive alliance with the Cherokee and Catawba in 1756. "Finding him in his person and character every way qualified ... as he was young, active and resolute," Governor Dobbs sent him as major in command of three companies to aid the expedition of John Forbes [*q.v.*] against Fort Duquesne in 1758; and in this successful campaign he "had great honour done him being employed on all reconnoitring parties, and dressed and acted as an Indian . . ." (*Colonial Records, post,* VI, 282). Indian outrages on the frontier in 1759 caused Dobbs to send him as colonel in command of two companies, with authority to summon the militia of the frontier counties and cooperate with South Carolina or Virginia; and in February 1760 with great gallantry, he defended Fort Dobbs against an Indian night attack. In 1762 he married Mary, the daughter of Roger Haynes of "Castle Haynes" near Wilmington, and settled at "Bellefont," Bladen County.

His military renown as the foremost soldier in the colony before the Revolution, his marriage, and his character and ability brought wealth, social prestige, and political influence. He owned land in Rowan, Anson, Bladen, and New Hanover counties and had mercantile interests with his brother-in-law, John Burgwin, at Wilmington and in the back country. He was a justice of the peace in Rowan and Bladen and intermittently represented each in the colonial assembly—the former in 1757, 1758, 1759, and 1760; the latter in 1762, 1766, 1767, and 1771. He visited England and Ireland in 1768. He was one of the chief leaders of the "inhabitants in arms" who at Brunswick on Feb. 19–21, 1766, defied the new royal governor, William Tryon, and offered successful armed resistance to the enforcement of the Stamp Act. Nevertheless, his relations with Tryon were close. He commanded the armed escort of the governor on his visit to the Cherokee in 1767 and in 1771 volunteered his services for the military suppression of the Regulators in the back country, who were violently resisting excessive taxes, exorbitant fees, and dishonest local government. As general and commander in chief under the governor, he was ordered to raise troops in the west and join the eastern forces headed by the governor. Intercepted by armed Regulators near Salisbury, he was unable to take part in the battle of Alamance on May 16, but soon thereafter he marched with troops to pacify the western counties. Dobbs in 1762 and Tryon in 1771 recommended him for appointment to the council. He died from an illness of several months' duration and was buried at "Castle Haynes."

[*The Colonial Records of N. C.,* vols. V–IX (1887–90); *The State Records of N. C.,* vol. XXII (1907); A. M. Waddell, *A Colonial Officer and his Times . . . A Biog. Sketch of Gen. Hugh Waddell* (1890).]

A. R. N.

WADDELL, JAMES IREDELL (July 13, 1824–Mar. 15, 1886), Confederate naval officer, was born at Pittsboro, Chatham County, N. C., the son of Francis Nash and Elizabeth Davis (Moore) Waddell, and the great-grandson of Hugh Waddell [*q.v.*]. He was reared by his pa-

ternal grandparents and became a midshipman of the United States Navy on Sept. 10, 1841. On May 27, 1842, he was seriously wounded in a duel with Midshipman Archibald H. Waring. The episode gave him a limp for life and cost him eleven months of active duty. Until the outbreak of the Civil War his most vigorous service afloat was his Mexican War tour of duty from Feb. 21 to Oct. 6, 1846, aboard the *Somers,* active off Vera Cruz. At the end of the Mexican War he was married to Ann S. Iglehart, of Annapolis, Md., in 1848. Promotion to the rank of passed midshipman became effective on Aug. 10, 1847, in the middle of a two-year assignment for instruction at the naval school at Annapolis, later the Naval Academy. His promotion to the rank of lieutenant on Sept. 15, 1855, came in the course of a three-year cruise to Brazil aboard the *Germantown.* A short voyage in 1857 to Central America aboard the storeship *Release* brought him some favorable mention for courage in connection with an epidemic of yellow fever that appeared just after leaving Aspinwall. Afterward, until July 11, 1859, he taught navigation in the Naval Academy. During this period one of his students described him as a handsome, well proportioned man, slightly over six feet tall and weighing about two hundred pounds—a "splendid specimen of manhood" of "noble bearing . . . gracious . . . courtly . . . radiant with kindness" (*North Carolina Booklet, post,* p. 128).

When he returned from duty in the Orient in 1862 he resigned, and his name was stricken from the rolls Jan. 18. Secretly entering the Confederacy by way of Baltimore, he was commissioned a lieutenant in the Confederate States Navy on Mar. 27, 1862. He saw Farragut's fleet capture New Orleans. Hardly a month later he served with the Drewry's Bluff batteries in the repulse of the James River flotilla supporting McClellan's Peninsular campaign. Similar battery duty at Charleston, until March 1863, ended his services within the Confederacy. He went to Paris for duty aboard some vessel acquired by James D. Bulloch [*q.v.*]. On Oct. 19, 1864, near Funchal, Madeira, he took command of the new fast Indiaman, *Sea King,* and transformed her into the Confederate *Shenandoah.* Under orders to concentrate upon the untouched New England whaling fleets in the Pacific, he reached Melbourne on Jan. 25, 1865. Several prizes were burned and bonded on this initial leg of the cruise. A defective propeller shaft and bearing demanded that the *Shenandoah* be dry-docked. After a general overhauling of the ship and some brief legal difficulties over alleged recruiting among neutrals the ship left Melbourne on Feb. 18. In extricating himself from these charges, Waddell made good use of the international law he had read while teaching at Annapolis. Though Confederate officers claimed then, and with apparent sincerity long afterward, that the charges were groundless, forty-two welcome "stowaways" appeared on deck just out from Melbourne. More surprising to this generation is that Waddell, always short-handed, procured American recruits from the crews of nearly all his prizes—even from those that carried newspapers telling of Lee's surrender at Appomattox. His course from Melbourne is best traced by his prizes. Four whalers at Ascension Island were captured on Apr. 1; the Sea of Okhotsk yielded one in May—over a month after Appomattox. The Bering Sea in a week, June 21–28, afforded twenty-four or twenty-five. Three were used as cartels; the remainder burned. A newspaper aboard one of the first Bering Sea prizes told of Lee's defeat, but it also carried Davis' Danville Proclamation declaring that the war would be continued with renewed vigor. Seamen from the prizes continued to enlist in the Confederate navy; and Waddell continued his search. No additional sails were sighted until Aug. 2, when the *Shenandoah* fell in with the British merchantman *Barracouta,* roughly a thousand miles west of Acapulco, Mexico, and thirteen days from San Francisco. She reported the complete collapse of the Confederacy.

In such circumstances the *Shenandoah* had no standing in maritime law to protect her against Seward's claim that such Confederate ships were pirates. The dangers of landing in the nearest port of the United States were obvious. Waddell disregarded all advice to beach his ship and let each man shift for himself or seek the nearest British colonial port. With fine courage and magnificent seamanship he laid a course for England by the way of Cape Horn. On Nov. 6, flying the only Confederate flag that ever went around the world, the *Shenandoah* stood in to Liverpool—some 17,000 miles without speaking a ship. The "piratical" officers remained in England until after amnesty was offered. In 1875 Waddell became a captain for the Pacific Mail Company. Two years later he wrecked the *San Francisco* on an uncharted reef, but no passengers were lost. He died in Annapolis while commanding the Maryland state flotilla for policing the oyster beds. He was survived by his widow but no children.

[*War of the Rebellion: Official Records* (Navy); personnel records, Naval Records Office, Washington, D. C.; S. A. Ashe, "Capt. J. I. Waddell, *N. C. Booklet,* vol. XIII (1913); J. T. Mason, "The Last of the Confederate Cruisers," *Century Mag.,* Aug. 1898; J. D. Bulloch, *The Secret Service of the Confederate States in Europe* (1883), vol. II; W. C. Whittle, "The Cruise of the Shenandoah," *Southern Hist. Soc. Papers,* vol. XXXV (1907), reprinted from *Portsmouth Star,* Mar. 13–Apr. 3, 1907; John Grimball, "Career of the Shenandoah," *Ibid.,* vol. XXV (1897), reprinted from the *News* (Charleston, S. C.), Feb. 3, 1895; C. E. Hunt, "The Shenandoah," *Mag. of Hist. with Notes and Queries,* extra no. 12 (1910) for charges against the integrity of Waddell; *Sun* (Baltimore), Mar. 16, 17, 1886.]
J. D. H—l.

WADE, BENJAMIN FRANKLIN (Oct. 27, 1800–Mar. 2, 1878), senator from Ohio, the tenth of eleven children of James and Mary (Upham) Wade, was a native of Feeding Hills, a hamlet near Springfield, Mass. His father traced his descent from Jonathan Wade of County Norfolk, England, who emigrated in 1632 and became an honored citizen of Medford, Massachusetts Bay Colony. His mother was the daughter of a Baptist clergyman of West Springfield. Decius S. Wade [*q.v.*] was his nephew. Reared amidst the poverty and hardships of a New England farm, Wade received little education in childhood, save that acquired from his mother and at a local school in the winter months. With his parents he moved in 1821 to the frontier community of Andover, Ohio, where two of his brothers had gone a year earlier. For the next few years he was by turns a farmer, drover, laborer, medical student, and school teacher in Ohio and New York state, but about 1825 he settled down to the study of law in Canfield, Ohio, and in 1827 or 1828 was admitted to the bar. Diffidence in public speaking threatened his ambitions at the outset, but perseverance gradually made him a vigorous advocate, and partnerships with Joshua R. Giddings [*q.v.*] in 1831 and Rufus P. Ranney [*q.v.*] in 1838 brought him a wide and successful practice in northeastern Ohio. On May 19, 1841, he was married to Caroline M. Rosekrans of Ashtabula and they took up their residence in Jefferson, Ohio, his place of practice. She bore him two sons, James F. and Henry P. Wade, and with them survived him.

Once established in the law, Wade turned his attention to politics and public office. After a term (1835–37) as prosecuting attorney of Ashtabula County he was elected to the state Senate in 1837. There he identified himself with the anti-slavery element; his outspoken opposition to a more stringent fugitive-slave law in Ohio is said to have been responsible for his failure to be reëlected in 1839. But he was returned to the Senate for a second term in 1841 and was chosen by the legislature in 1847 to sit as president-judge of the third judicial circuit. His forceful and business-like methods on the bench, together with his rising popularity, commended him to the Whigs in the legislature and in 1851, apparently without effort on his part, he was elected to the United States Senate. Twice re-elected as a Republican, he served until Mar. 3, 1869.

Wade's entrance into the Senate in the early fifties was eventful in the history of slavery and the Union. Rough in manner, coarse and vituperative in speech, yet intensely patriotic, he speedily became a leader of the anti-slavery group in Congress. At heart an abolitionist, he supported a move in 1852 to repeal the Fugitive-slave Law (*Congressional Globe,* 32 Cong., 1 Sess., p. 2371) and denounced the Kansas-Nebraska Bill (*Ibid.,* 33 Cong., 1 Sess., pp. 337–40). He also opposed the several efforts to win Kansas for slavery and almost every other measure or device for the promotion or protection of the system. When the controversy in the Senate became intensely personal and Wade was much involved, he entered into a secret compact (1858) with Simon Cameron and Zachariah Chandler [*qq.v.*] whereby they pledged themselves to make their own the cause of any Republican senator receiving gross personal abuse, and to "carry the quarrel into a coffin" (Riddle, *post,* pp. 215–16). He was an ardent supporter of the proposed homestead legislation of the period, saying in 1859 that it was "a question of land to the landless," while the bill to buy Cuba was "a question of niggers to the niggerless" (*Congressional Globe,* 35 Cong., 2 Sess., p. 1354). During the secession crisis of 1860–61 he took his stand on the Republican platform of 1860, and as a member of the Senate Committee of Thirteen voted against the Crittenden proposals (*Senate Report No. 288,* 36 Cong., 2 Sess.), holding that the time for compromise had passed.

With the outbreak of war, Wade became one of the most belligerent men in Congress, demanding swift and decisive military action. Personally a fearless man, he played a dramatic part in momentarily stemming a portion of the Union retreat from Bull Run (July 21, 1861). When the army was reorganized he pressed vigorously for another forward movement, and when McClellan delayed, Wade became one of his sharpest critics. With Senators Chandler and J. W. Grimes he was instrumental in setting up the Committee on the Conduct of the War. From the moment of its creation the Committee, under Wade's chairmanship, became a violently partisan machine, suspicious of the loyalty of those who ventured to dissent from its wishes and bent upon an unrelenting prosecution of the war. Its members worked in close cooperation with Secretary of War Stanton, a kindred spirit whom Wade had urged for that office, but they were generally critical of the President. Like other

Radical Republicans in Congress, Wade seemed temperamentally incapable of understanding Lincoln and deplored his cautious and conservative policies. He himself favored drastic punitive measures against the South, including legislation for the confiscation of the property of the Confederate leaders and the emancipation of their slaves (*Congressional Globe,* 37 Cong., 2 Sess., p. 3375; Edward McPherson, *The Political History of the United States . . . during the Great Rebellion* (1864, pp. 196 ff.). He was not overburdened with constitutional scruples where measures that he favored were concerned. At the same time he decried the President's "dictatorship" and found Lincoln's clement reconstruction policy, announced on Dec. 8, 1863, particularly obnoxious. When he and Henry Winter Davis [*q.v.*] attempted to counteract it by a severe congressional plan, embodied in the Wade-Davis bill, and Lincoln checked this by a "pocket-veto," announcing his reasons in a proclamation (July 8, 1864), their indignation was unbounded. The resultant Wade-Davis Manifesto (Aug. 5), a fierce blast, condemned the President's "executive usurpation" as a "studied outrage on the legislative authority" and insisted that in matters of reconstruction Congress was "paramount and must be respected" (Appletons' *American Annual Cyclopaedia . . . 1864,* 1865, pp. 307–10). Previously Wade had joined with others in indorsing the Pomeroy circular, designed to replace Lincoln with Salmon P. Chase (G. F. Milton, *The Age of Hate,* 1930, p. 28), but when that project collapsed and the Manifesto aroused a storm of disapproval in Ohio, he gave his support to Lincoln in the closing weeks of the election contest in 1864. But he continued to resist the President's reconstruction policy, characterizing it as "absurd, monarchical, and anti-American" (*Congressional Globe,* 38 Cong., 2 Sess., p. 1128).

The accession of Johnson to the presidency in April 1865 was hailed by Wade and his faction as a godsend, and they hastened to make overtures to him in behalf of their own measures. When to their surprise he took over Lincoln's policy, Wade dubbed him either "a knave or a fool," and contended that to admit the Southern states on the presidential plan was "nothing less than political suicide" (H. K. Beale, *The Critical Year,* 1930, pp. 49, 314). From December 1865 onward, along with Charles Sumner, Thaddeus Stevens, and other vindictive leaders, he waged a persistent campaign against Johnson, pressing for the enactment of the congressional program, including the Civil Rights, Military Reconstruction, and Tenure of Office bills. At the opening of the session in December 1865 Wade promptly introduced a bill for the enfranchisement of negroes in the District of Columbia (*Congressional Globe*, 39 Cong., 1 Sess., p. 1), and supported negro suffrage in the campaign of 1866, although he was willing to readmit the Southern states if they ratified the fourteenth amendment within a reasonable time (*Ibid.*, 39 Cong., 2 Sess., p. 124). His methods during the period leave the impression that he, like Stevens, was ready to resort to almost any extremity in order to carry through the congressional policies or gain a point.

The Radicals succeeded in having Wade elected president *pro tempore* of the Senate when that office became vacant (Mar. 2, 1867). According to the statute then in force, he would have succeeded to the presidency in the event of Johnson's removal. But it appears that the prospect of Wade's succession really became an embarrassment to them, for many of the conservatives felt that he would be no improvement and might prove less satisfactory than Johnson (*Diary of Gideon Welles,* 1911, vol. III, 293; Oberholtzer, *post,* II, 134n.). Wade himself voted for Johnson's conviction despite the fact that he was an interested party. So expectant was he of success that he began the selection of his cabinet before the impeachment trial was concluded (Adam Badeau, *Grant in Peace,* 1887, pp. 136–37; C. G. Bowers, *The Tragic Era,* 1929, pp. 188–89). Thwarted in his presidential ambitions by Johnson's acquittal, and having failed of reëlection to the Senate, Wade sought the second place on the ticket with Grant in 1868. However, after leading on the first four ballots in the Republican convention, he lost the nomination to Schuyler Colfax.

Upon his retirement from the Senate in 1869 Wade resumed the practice of law in Ohio. He became general counsel for the Northern Pacific Railroad and served for a time as one of the government directors of the Union Pacific. In 1871 Grant appointed him a member of the commission of investigation which visited Santo Domingo and recommended its annexation (*Report of the Commission of Inquiry to Santo Domingo,* 1871). Seven years later he died in Jefferson, Ohio.

[The chief documentary sources for Wade's public career are the *Cong. Globe* and the "Report of the Joint Committee on the Conduct of the War," *Senate Report No. 108,* 37 Cong., 3 Sess., (3 vols., 1863); *Senate Report No. 142,* 38 Cong., 2 Sess., (3 vols., 1865). A. G. Riddle, *The Life of Benjamin F. Wade* (1886), is too brief and uncritical to be of much historical value. Short sketches of Wade's life are to be found in L. P. Brockett, *Men of Our Day* (1872), pp. 240–62, a contemporary eulogistic account; *The Biog. Cyclopædia and Portrait Gallery . . . of . . . Ohio,* vol. I (1883), 293–94; *Biog. Dir. Am. Cong.* (1928); *N. Y. Herald* and *N. Y. Times,* Mar. 3, 1878. J. F. Rhodes, *Hist. of the U. S.* (9 vols., 1893–1922); and E. P. Oberholtzer,

A Hist. of the U. S. since the Civil War (4 vols., 1917–31) contain numerous references to Wade, as do the biographies of his political contemporaries. D. M. DeWitt, *The Impeachment and Trial of Andrew Johnson* (1903) is useful for the post-war period. This work, like the more recent studies of the war and reconstruction eras, is hostile to Wade and his faction.]

A. H. M.

WADE, DECIUS SPEAR (Jan. 23, 1835–Aug. 3, 1905), Montana jurist, was born near Andover, Ashtabula County, Ohio, the son of Charles H. and Juliet (Spear) Wade. Charles Wade was a farmer, and the son worked on the farm with but little schooling until he was sixteen years old. Then he began to teach school in winter and to attend the academy at Kingsville, Ohio, in summer. He also studied law in the office of his uncle, Benjamin F. Wade [*q.v.*]. In 1857 he was admitted to practice and established himself in Jefferson, Ohio. He was elected probate judge of Ashtabula County in 1860. The next year he volunteered for three months' service in the Federal army and was made lieutenant, but apparently he soon left the army to resume his duties as judge. On June 3, 1863, he married an English girl named Bernice Galpin, by whom he had one daughter. He served as probate judge till 1867 and then practised law for two years. In 1871 he was appointed chief justice of Montana by President Grant; he was reappointed every four years until the expiration of his fourth term in 1887.

When Wade went to Montana the supreme court judges also acted as district judges, and each of them traveled extensively by stagecoach and on horseback. No decisions of the supreme court were published before 1868, and few precedents had been established. The statutes were vague, and the customs of the miners' courts were the generally accepted law. Litigation, which was extensive, for the most part involved mining claims and water rights in an arid country where the English common law did not seem to apply. Decisions had to be reached by the formation of new principles or by the application of old rules to new conditions. In the case of *Robertson* vs. *Smith* (1 *Montana Reports,* 410) Wade's decision in the district court, based on the miners' law, was affirmed by Knowles in the supreme court. In 1872 Congress passed a law opening mineral deposits in public lands and defining in a general way the rights to quartz claims but leaving much to be determined by the courts. Terms had to be defined and rules made governing ambiguous situations. In a long series of cases Wade and Associate Justice Hiram Knowles formulated the mining and irrigation law for Montana. In the first six volumes of the *Montana Reports* almost half of the decisions were Wade's, and few of them were reversed on appeal. In fourteen out of seventeen cases taken to the United States Supreme Court, his opinions were affirmed. When Wade retired from the bench in 1887 he entered into partnership with Edwin Warren Toole [q.v.] and William Wallace. In 1889 he was appointed a member of a commission to draft a code supplanting the conflicting and confusing laws of the territory. It was adopted by the legislature in 1895, and *The Codes and Statutes of Montana* (2 vols.) was published in the same year. Wade wrote the four chapters on the bench and bar in Montana which appear in Joaquin Miller's *An Illustrated History of Montana* (2 vols., 1894) and a number of newspaper articles on Montana history. He was also the author of a novel, *Clare Lincoln* (1876). He lived and practised in Helena until 1895, when he returned to Ohio. He died in Ohio near Andover.

[See Joaquin Miller, *An Illustrated History of Montana* (2 vols., 1894), which contains a biog. sketch and summaries of important cases; C. P. Connelly, in *Mag. of Western Hist.*, May 1891; Theodore Brantley, in *Contributions to the Hist. Soc. of Mont.*, vol. IV (1903); *Ohio Law Bull.*, Oct. 9, 1905; *Proc. Mont. Bar Asso. . . . 1914* (n.d.), pp. 316–21; obituaries in *Anaconda Standard*, from which the date of death is taken, and *Helena Independent*, Aug. 5, 1905.]   P. C. P.

WADE, JEPTHA HOMER (Aug. 11, 1811–Aug. 9, 1890), financier, was one of the founders of the American commercial telegraph system. He was born in Romulus, Seneca County, N. Y., the son of Jeptha and Sarah (Allen) Wade and a descendant of Benjamin Wade, a clothier, who was living in Elizabeth, N. J., in 1675. The elder Jeptha Wade, a surveyor and civil engineer, died in 1813, and about this time or later the family moved to Seneca Falls. The boy learned the carpenter's trade, and as a young man operated a small sash and blind factory. Interest in art, however, led him to study painting with Randall Palmer, a local portrait painter, and for five or six years after 1837 he traveled through New York, Louisiana, and Michigan as an itinerant painter of portraits. While at Adrian, Mich., he learned of the invention of the daguerreotype and purchased a camera to widen his field of portraiture.

The news of the success of the telegraph in 1844 led him to study the possibilities of the invention of Morse and in 1847 he contracted to build a telegraph line from Detroit to Jackson—"a frail, one-wire affair." Other lines, which came to be known as the Wade Lines, followed in rapid succession—from Detroit to Milwaukee, from Detroit to Buffalo by way of Cleveland, from Cleveland to Cincinnati and St. Louis. Meanwhile Royal E. House, Henry O'Reilly,

Ezra Cornell [qq.v.], and other men were building up individual systems and in the early fifties competition became furious. In 1854 the lines of Wade and House were consolidated, with Wade as the general agent, controlling a network over the Old Northwest. Similar consolidations of other systems were taking place at the same time, and in 1856 most of the western lines were combined in the Western Union Telegraph Company, with Anson Stager [q.v.], formerly of the O'Reilly lines, as general superintendent and Wade as general agent. Within a few years Wade pushed on into the Far West, organizing the California State Telegraph Company and the Pacific Telegraph Company to connect St. Louis with San Francisco. A line to Salt Lake City from the West was completed in October 1861, putting out of business the firm operating the pony express and preparing the way for the transcontinental railroad and the daily mail. Wade was promoted from the position of general agent to that of managing director, and in 1866 became president of the enlarged Western Union, but illness in 1867 caused him to give up the responsibilities of that office.

About 1856 he had established his residence in Cleveland, and thenceforth was closely identified with Cleveland business. In 1867 he took a leading part in the organization of the Citizens' Savings & Loan Association and became its president, and later he held the same office with the National Bank of Commerce. He was also actively interested in railroad building and management and served on the boards of directors of most of the lines entering Cleveland. He was sinking-fund commissioner, a member of the public park commission, and a director of the Cleveland workhouse board, and also a member of the National Garfield Monument Association. In 1882 he gave Wade Park, a tract of seventy-five acres of land, to the city of Cleveland, and other philanthropies evidenced his generous public spirit. A part of the site of the Western Reserve University was one of his gifts.

Wade was twice married: on Oct. 15, 1832, to Rebecca Loueza Facer, who died Nov. 30, 1836, and on Sept. 5, 1837 to Susan M. Fleming, who died in August 1889. In physique Wade was slightly over six feet tall and powerfully built. In his personal characteristics he was modest and easily approached, genial and an interesting conversationalist. He never lost his interest in painting and music.

[S. C. Wade, *The Wade Geneal.* (1900); J. H. Kennedy, in *Mag. of Western Hist.*, Oct. 1885; H. F. Biggar, *Loiterings in Europe* (Cleveland, 1908); J. D. Reid, *The Telegraph in America* (1879); *Cleveland Past and Present* (1869); *A Hist. of Cleveland and Its Environs*, vols. I, II (1918); *Cleveland Weekly Leader*

and Herald, Aug. 16, 1890, reprinting article from the
Sunday Leader, Aug. 10, 1890.]   E. J. B.

WADE, MARTIN JOSEPH (Oct. 20, 1861–
Apr. 16, 1931), Iowa jurist, was the son of Irish
immigrant parents, Michael and Mary (Breen)
Wade, who, soon after their marriage at Worcester, Mass., settled at Burlington, Vt., where
Martin was born. Having spent his later boyhood in Butler County, Iowa, he attended St.
Joseph's College at Dubuque. In 1886 he received
the degree of LL.B. from the University of Iowa
and began to practise law in partnership with
C. S. Ranck at Iowa City. His marriage to Mary
Gertrude McGovern of Iowa City on Apr. 4,
1888, was the culmination of a college romance.
Having a penchant for teaching, Wade began
lecturing on torts in the law college of the University of Iowa in 1890; during the following
year he was an instructor in law; and from 1892
to 1894 served as professor of law, giving courses
in as many as five subjects. An unexpected appointment to fill a vacancy on the bench of the
local district court in December 1893 changed
the course of his career, though he remained on
the faculty of the university as professor of medical jurisprudence from 1894 to 1903. As a result
of that experience he published in 1909 *A Selection of Cases on Malpractice of Physicians, Surgeons and Dentists.* In 1894 he was elected to
his position as judge in the eighth district without opposition, and in 1898 was reëlected for
four years. If the selection of Wade as president
of the Iowa State Bar Association in 1897 was
an indication of his professional standing, his
election to Congress in 1902, the only Democrat
in the Iowa delegation, was probably due to his
political sagacity. Though he served only one
term as United States representative (1903–05),
this sojourn in Washington introduced him to
national politics. From 1907 to 1914 he was a
member of the Democratic National Committee,
and during the campaign of 1908 he was on the
executive committee.

In March 1915 he left a thriving law practice
in the firm of Wade, Dutcher, and Davis, which
he had organized in 1905, to become United
States district judge for the southern district of
Iowa (appointment confirmed, Mar. 3, 1915).
Admirably qualified for the position by temperament, legal training, courage, and a deep sense of
justice, he conducted his court with impressive
dignity and in strict adherence to his conception
of righteousness. Always intensely patriotic, he
brought to the bench an aggressive loyalty to the
American system of government. The Constitution, he thought, was inspired. Good citizenship
was his principal obsession. He was tireless in

explaining the government to aliens and declared
that his naturalization work was of prime importance. His remarks upon sentencing Kate
Richards O'Hare for obstructing enlistment during the World War (*O'Hare* vs. *United States,
253 Federal Reporter,* 538) were typical of his
patriotic fervor. He regarded militant pacifists
and socialists as public enemies. In hundreds of
prohibition enforcement cases he lectured boot-
leggers about respect for law. Wade fathered the
Iowa statute of 1921 requiring that the principles
of republican government and the meaning of the
Constitution must be taught in the public schools.
With W. F. Russell he published *The Short Constitution* (copyright 1920), which purported to
be "talks" by a judge on constitutional rights and
was intended to be the first in a series of volumes
on "elementary Americanism." He also conceived of teaching good citizenship by the "case
method" and prepared some brief *Lessons in
Americanism* (copyright 1920) that were to be
syndicated to newspapers, and, with W. H. Bate-
son, *The Constitution through Problems* (copyright 1931). Though none of these projects attained popularity, he never lost his enthusiasm
for patriotic uplift. He spent the last four years
of his life in California and died in Los Angeles,
survived by his wife and his two daughters.

[*Who's Who in America,* 1930–31; *Biog. Dir. Am.
Cong.* (1928); C. R. Aurner, *Leading Events in John-
son County, Iowa, Hist.,* vol. II (1913); Cats. of the
Univ. of Iowa; *Iowa Official Registers; Proc. Iowa
State Bar Asso.,* vol. XXXVII (1931); obituaries in
Iowa Jour. of Hist. and Politics, July 1931, *Iowa City
Press-Citizen,* Apr. 16, and *Des Moines Reg.,* Apr. 17,
1931.]   J. E. B.

WADSWORTH, JAMES (Apr. 20, 1768–
June 7, 1844), community builder, pioneer in public school education, was born in Durham, Conn.,
the youngest of the three sons of John Noyes and
Esther (Parsons) Wadsworth, and a descendant
of William Wadsworth, who settled in Cambridge, Mass., about 1632 and accompanied
Thomas Hooker to Hartford, Conn., in 1636.
James graduated from Yale College in 1787 and
spent the winter of that and the following year
in teaching at Montreal, Canada. His father had
died while the son was in college, leaving a fair
estate to his children. At the suggestion of a
relative, Jeremiah Wadsworth [*q.v.*] of Hartford, Conn., who had secured holdings in the
Phelps and Gorham Purchase in western New
York, James and his brother William bought a
portion of his land there and became agents for
the remainder.

The property acquired by them was on the east
bank of the Genesee River, in what are now the
townships of Geneseo and Avon. In the summer
of 1790 they started on their journey from Dur-

ham to their wilderness possessions, William with an oxcart, a few men, and a slave woman, traveling overland; James, in charge of household effects and provisions, taking the water route to Canandaigua. They established themselves a little below the present town of Geneseo, and as time went on prospered remarkably. They constantly extended their cultivated land, raised corn, hemp, which they manufactured into rope, and some tobacco; maintained herds of cattle, bred mules, and in later years prosecuted wool-growing on a large scale. Their operations both as agriculturists and land agents ultimately brought them substantial returns, with which they increased their own holdings until they were among the largest land owners of cultivated areas.

Their influence in developing the Genesee country was unparalleled. William was the practical man of affairs, James the thinker, planner, and counselor. Most of the agency work fell to him. From February 1796 to November 1798 he was in Europe, with the cooperation of Robert Morris, Aaron Burr, DeWitt Clinton, and others, interesting foreign capitalists in American investments. He was a student of political economy and the physical sciences, and sought through the application of the latter to improve agricultural methods. With a view to instructing others along these lines, he frequently arranged for the insertion of articles in newspapers and agricultural periodicals, and for the preparation of pamphlets on scientific subjects. These he was in the habit of distributing gratuitously. His chief interest, in fact, outside his business affairs, was in public education. No one in the state was more energetic in efforts to improve the common-school system. He urged the establishment of county academies for the better training of schoolmasters; was instrumental in securing the enactment of legislation authorizing the sending of *Lectures on School-Keeping* by Samuel Read Hall [*q.v.*] to the trustees of each school district; and sought to interest persons in preparing suitable textbooks, setting aside $30,000 for that purpose, a part of which was to be offered in premiums for the best treatises on prescribed subjects, and the remainder to be expended in stereotyping the works selected. Through his tireless efforts the school district library system was finally established in New York State. When certain educational papers were started he contributed liberally to their support, and frequently bore the entire expense of large editions containing special articles. He gave freely toward the erection of schoolhouses and churches, and toward the maintenance of lec-

ture courses on scientific subjects. For the town of Geneseo he built and endowed a public library, and it is reputed to have been in part through his influence that his friend John Jacob Astor, 1763–1848 [*q.v.*], provided for the founding of the Astor Library in New York City.

On Oct. 1, 1804, he married Naomi, daughter of Samuel and Jerusha (Wolcott) Wolcott of East Windsor, Conn. At his death, in Geneseo, he left two sons and two daughters. One of the sons was James S. Wadsworth [*q.v.*].

[F. B. Dexter, *Biog. Sketches Grads. Yale Coll.*, vol. IV (1907); H. R. Stiles, *The Hist. and Geneals. of Ancient Windsor, Conn.* (2nd ed., vol. II, 1892); Samuel Wolcott, *Memorial of Henry Wolcott . . . and Some of His Descendants* (1881); Orsamus Turner, *Hist. of the Pioneer Settlement of Phelps and Gorham's Purchase* (1851); L. L. Doty, *A Hist. of Livingston County, N. Y.* (1876); Henry Barnard, *Am. Jour. of Education*, Sept. 1858; H. G. Pearson, *James S. Wadsworth of Geneseo* (1913); James Renwick, in *Monthly Journal of Agriculture*, Oct. 1846; *Albany Evening Journal*, June 10, 1844.]
　　　　　　　　　　　　　　　　　　　　H. E. S.

WADSWORTH, JAMES SAMUEL (Oct. 30, 1807–May 8, 1864), Union soldier, was the son of James Wadsworth [*q.v.*] and his wife, Naomi, daughter of Samuel Wolcott of East Windsor, Conn. Born at Geneseo, N. Y., at a time when the hardships of the first settlement there were over, Wadsworth grew up among pioneer surroundings, but as the prospective heir to a great landed estate. He spent two years at Harvard, without graduating, studied law, and was admitted to the bar, but did not practise, his legal education having been intended only to prepare him for the management of his properties. On May 11, 1834, he married Mary Craig Wharton, daughter of John Wharton, a Quaker merchant of Philadelphia. His position in the community and his own sense of public duty made him active in politics throughout his life, although he had no ambition for office. At first a Democrat, his strong anti-slavery sentiments made him join in organizing the Free-Soil party, which merged with the Republican party in 1856. He was a delegate to the unofficial "peace conference" in Washington in February 1861.

From the outbreak of the Civil War his life and fortune were unreservedly at the service of the country. "It always seemed to me," wrote his friend John Lothrop Motley, "that he was the truest and the most thoroughly loyal American I ever knew" (Pearson, *post*, p. 34). But he was no candidate for high military rank. The governor of New York, on the understanding that he could name two major generals of volunteers, offered an appointment to Wadsworth, who advised the selection of a regular army officer instead, and accepted only when this was found impossible. "I am better than a worse man," was his sagacious comment, and he was frankly gratified when the grant of power to the governor was refused. He went to the front, however, and offered his services as an aide to Gen. Irvin McDowell, a gift accepted with hesitation, for a middle-aged gentleman of national reputation would not seem to be either physically or mentally suitable for an orderly officer. But he proved at the battle of Bull Run that both in hard riding and in intelligent obedience he could match the youngest of the staff. On Aug. 9, 1861, he was commissioned brigadier-general of volunteers. The appointment, which was partly political, was intended to conciliate Republicans of Democratic antecedents. Wadsworth accepted it after considering in his usual detached fashion what the effect on the public service might be. He was, indeed, much better qualified than most of the non-professional general officers. Though destitute of military training like the rest, he had the habit of command, rarer among Union than among Confederate volunteers, and his civil occupations had fitted him peculiarly well for the care of his men in the field. A military education would not have shown him how to organize a system of supply by ox team, as he did when his brigade was camped in the Virginia mud near Arlington during the first winter of the war and mule-drawn wagons could not get through. He was fortunate in not being required to command a large force in action until he had been nearly two years in service and the men under him were seasoned veterans. When the Army of the Potomac moved to the peninsula in the spring of 1862, he was left in command of the defenses of Washington. Doubtful of getting service in the field, he accepted the Republican nomination for governor of New York but was defeated at the election. In December 1862, after the battle of Fredericksburg, he took command of the 1st Division, I Corps. It had a small part in the battle of Chancellorsville and a very great one at Gettysburg. On the first day of the battle, in spite of terrific loss, it held the Confederates in check while the rest of the army was hastening to the battlefield. On the second and third days it held Culp's Hill, on the right of the Union line. In the reorganization of the army for the 1864 campaign, Wadsworth received the 4th Division of the V Corps, made up largely of regiments from his old command. After nearly succeeding in breaking through the Confederate center on the second day (May 6) of the battle of the Wilderness, it was outflanked and driven back. Wadsworth had already had two horses shot under him; his third was unmanageable, and the Confederate line was close upon him before he could

turn. He was shot in the head, and the enemy's advance passed over his body. He died two days later in a Confederate field hospital. He was survived by his wife and their six children.

[C. C. Baldwin, *Wadsworth* (copr. 1882); H. G. Pearson, *James S. Wadsworth of Geneseo* (1913), an adequate biog., with ample citations of authorities; L. F. Allen, *Memorial of the Late Gen. James S. Wadsworth* (1865); *Proc. Century Asso. in Honor of . . . Brig. Gen. James S. Wadsworth* (1865); *War of the Rebellion: Official Records* (Army); *Battles and Leaders of the Civil War* (4 vols., 1887–88); N. Y. Monuments Commission, *In Memoriam, James Samuel Wadsworth* (1916); Morris Schaff, *The Battle of the Wilderness* (1910); obituary in *N. Y. Times,* May 11, 1864.]   T. M. S.

WADSWORTH, JEREMIAH (July 12, 1743–Apr. 30, 1804), Revolutionary soldier and congressman, was born in Hartford, Conn., the son of the Rev. Daniel Wadsworth, pastor of the First Church of Christ, and Abigail Talcott, the daughter of Gov. Joseph Talcott [*q.v.*]. William Wadsworth, the first American ancestor of the family, came to America from England about 1632. Jeremiah was four years of age when his father died and he was placed in charge of his uncle, Matthew Talcott, a ship-owner of Middletown. At the age of eighteen, in the hope of improving his health, he embarked as a common sailor aboard one of his uncle's vessels, followed the sea for about ten years and rose to the rank of captain. On Sept. 29, 1767, he was married to Mehitable Russell, the daughter of the Rev. William Russell, of Middletown; they had three children.

His early championship of colonial rights combined with his knowledge of mercantile affairs induced the legislature, in April 1775, to appoint him commissary to the Revolutionary forces raised in Connecticut. On June 18, 1777, the Continental Congress elected him deputy commissary-general of purchases, and he served until his resignation the following August. Upon the retirement of Joseph Trumbull [*q.v.*] as commissary-general, he was appointed, in April 1778, to fill the post and remained until he resigned on Dec. 4, 1779. Despite scarcity of funds and lack of cooperation on the part of state authorities, he kept the Continental Army so well provisioned that Washington wrote, "since his appointment our supplies of provision have been good and ample" (W. C. Ford, *The Writings of George Washington,* VII, 1890, p. 141). At the request of Rochambeau he served as commissary also to the French troops in America until the close of the war, and in the summer of 1783 he went to Paris in order to submit a report of his transactions. Proceeding to England and Ireland in March 1784, he invested the considerable balance remaining to his credit in merchandise that he disposed of profitably upon his return to America.

He was a member of the state convention called in 1788 to consider the ratification of the federal Constitution, and voted in its favor, possibly for financial as well as political reasons since he held public paper that was bound to appreciate in value upon adoption of a new frame of government. He was elected a Federalist to Congress in 1787 and 1788, but attended only in 1788. He was a strong advocate of assumption, a policy in which he appears to have had a large speculative interest (*The Journal of William Maclay*, new edition, 1927, pp. 174, 231, 323). In 1795 he was elected to the state legislature and to the executive council, remaining a member of the latter body by annual election until 1801.

His business interests were varied and important. He was a founder of the Bank of North America in Philadelphia and of the Hartford Bank, a director of the United States Bank, president of the Bank of New York, and one of the promoters of the Hartford Manufacturing Company, established in 1788, "the first purely wool-manufacturing concern founded on a strictly business basis, and the first in which power machinery was employed" (A. H. Cole, *The American Wool Manufacture*, 1926, I, 64). He established in 1794 the first partnership for insurance in Connecticut. He introduced fine breeds of cattle from abroad and engaged in experiments with a view to improving agriculture. Honorary degrees were awarded to him by Yale and Dartmouth colleges for his interest in the promotion of literary institutions. He died at Hartford and was laid to rest in the Ancient Burying Ground.

[Manuscript letters and papers in the Conn. Hist. Soc., Hartford, and the N. Y. Hist. Soc., New York City; R. R. Hinman, *A Hist. Coll. from Official Records . . . of the Part Sustained by Conn. during . . . the Revolution* (1842); H. A. Wadsworth, *Two Hundred and Fifty Years of the Wadsworth Family in America* (1883); *Diary of Rev. Daniel Wadsworth* (1894); S. V. Talcott, *Talcott Pedigree in England and America* (1876); C. J. Hoadly, *The Pub. Records of the Colony of Conn.*, vols. XIV (1887), XV (1890); *Record of Conn. Men . . . During the . . . Revolution* (1889), ed. by H. P. Johnston; W. B. Weeden, *Econ. and Social Hist. of New England* (1890), vol. II; C. J. Hoadly, *The Pub. Records of the State of Conn.*, vols. I (1894), II (1895), III (1922); W. C. Ford, *Jours. of the Cont. Cong.*, vols. VIII–XXIV (1904–34); *Conn. as a Colony and as a State* (4 vols., 1904), ed. by Forrest Morgan; G. L. Clark, *A Hist. of Conn.* (1914); E. C. Burnett, *Letters of Members of the Cont. Cong.* (7 vols., 1921–34); *Conn. Courant* (Hartford), May 2, 1804.]

E. E. C.

WADSWORTH, PELEG (May 6, 1748–Nov. 12, 1829), Revolutionary general and member of Congress, was born in Duxbury, Mass., the son of Deacon Peleg Wadsworth and his wife, Lusanna Sampson. He was descended from an Englishman, Christopher Wadsworth, who settled in Duxbury in 1632. After graduating from Harvard College in 1769, he kept a private school in Plymouth and prepared pupils for college and for the army. In 1774 he was elected captain of a company of minute-men and member of the committee of correspondence for Plymouth County. When the news of the battle of Lexington arrived, he marched, Apr. 20, 1775, to Marshfield to stand off a British regiment, but before any fighting occurred the red-coats retired. Shortly afterwards he accompanied Col. Theophilus Cotton's regiment to Roxbury, and as engineer under the orders of John Thomas [*q.v.*] laid out the American lines at that place and at Dorchester Heights. He also investigated the problem of erecting defenses at Cape Cod.

On Feb. 13, 1776, he was appointed aide-de-camp to Artemas Ward [*q.v.*] and served in that capacity until Apr. 23, 1776, when Ward was forced to resign because of failing health. The same year he saw service under Washington in New York and on Long Island, and in 1778 under Sullivan in Rhode Island. On Aug. 25, 1778, he was appointed adjutant-general, and on July 7, 1779, brigadier-general of the Massachusetts militia. Amid these activities he found time to serve on the board of war of Massachusetts and, for a term (May 28, 1777–May 1, 1778), as representative from Duxbury in the legislature. In 1779 he was second in command of an expedition dispatched by the authorities of Massachusetts under Solomon Lovell and Dudley Saltonstall [*q.v.*] to expel the British from Fort George (Castine, Me.). The attempt failed and the Americans retreated after sustaining serious losses in men and matériel. A committee of inquiry appointed by the legislature of Massachusetts honorably acquitted Wadsworth of responsibility for the disaster. In March 1780 he was placed in command of the eastern department with headquarters at Thomaston, Me. On the night of Feb. 18, 1781, a party of British raided his dwelling and carried him off to Fort George where he remained captive until June 18, when he managed to effect his escape with a companion by cutting a hole in the roof of his prison by means of a gimlet obtained from a barber at the fort.

After the war he removed to Falmouth (Portland), Me., where for several years he was engaged in trade and politics. He served as selectman, as representative in Congress from 1793 to 1807, and as chairman of a committee to consider the separation of the district of Maine from Massachusetts. In 1806 he removed to Oxford County where he had purchased 7800 acres of land and where he procured the incorporation of the town of Hiram. Here he spent the remainder of his days, living like a patriarch in a commodious frame house, "Wadsworth Hall," which served as church, court, school, and drilling place for the community. Lumbering, farming, and civic affairs engaged his attention. He lies buried in the family graveyard on his estate. On June 18, 1772, he was married to Elizabeth Bartlett, of Plymouth, by whom he had eleven children. A daughter, Zilpah, became the wife of Stephen Longfellow, and was the mother of Henry Wadsworth Longfellow and Samuel Longfellow [qq.v.]. Henry Wadsworth Longfellow, during his youth, lived in a brick house (the first in Portland), built by the General in 1785 and 1786, and known today as the "Wadsworth-Longfellow House." Peleg's son, Henry, became a naval officer and lost his life in the Tripolitan War. After him the poet was named.

[Papers and personal belongings of Wadsworth are in "Wadsworth Hall" and the "Wadsworth-Longfellow House." He wrote a series of autobiographical letters to his children which were edited by H. L. Bradley and published in 1903 under the title, *A Story About a Little Good Boy.* Consult also: W. D. Williamson, *The Hist. of the State of Me.* (1832), vol. II; F. H. Underwood, *The Life of Henry Wadsworth Longfellow* (1882); H. A. Wadsworth, *Two Hundred and Fifty Years of the Wadsworth Family in America* (1883); Levi Bartlett, *Geneal. . . . of the Bartlett Family* (1876); *Coll. and Proc. of the Me. Hist. Soc.,* 2 ser., vols. I (1890), II (1891), V (1894), VI (1895), X (1899), XVI (1913), XVII (1913), XVIII (1914), XIX (1914); *Mass. Soldiers and Sailors of the Revolutionary War,* vol. XVI (1907); Nathan Goold, *The Wadsworth-Longfellow House* (1908); E. K. Gould, *Storming the Heights* (1932); *Biog. Dir. Am. Cong.* (1928); *Portland Advertiser,* Dec. 1, 1829.]   E. E. C.

WAGGAMAN, MARY TERESA McKEE (Sept. 21, 1846–July 30, 1931), writer, was born in Baltimore, Md., the daughter of John and Esther (Cottrell) McKee. Her father, a native of Ireland, joined the gold rush to California in 1849, acquired a fortune, and became a ship-broker in New York. Her mother, the daughter of an Anglican clergyman, died when Mary was six years of age. The child was brought up in Mount de Sales Convent, Catonsville, Md. At the outbreak of the Civil War her father took her to New York to live in the home of friends, in whose well-filled library she spent much of the next two years attempting to supplement her education. In the autumn of 1863, when her father, a Southern sympathizer, was seized and imprisoned for several months at Fort Lafayette, New York, she became one of a group of ardent Southern sympathizers in the Northern city. In the spring of 1864 she returned to the convent to be valedictorian of her graduating class. After her father was released from prison upon Lincoln's orders, she accompanied him to Liverpool, where they joined other exiles who were attempting to send supplies through the blockade to the depleted South. At the close of the Civil War they returned, broken in fortune, and took up their residence in Baltimore. There in 1870 she married Dr. Samuel J. Waggaman (d. 1913), who later became a professor in the National College of Pharmacy, Washington, D. C., where shortly after their marriage they established their home. They had eleven children, six of whom survived their mother.

She began writing during her school days. When twenty-five years of age she published a poem, "The Legend of the Mistletoe," in *Harper's New Monthly Magazine* (January 1872). When her eldest son became a communicant and she could find no story which would properly inculcate lessons of piety, she wrote *Little Comrades, A First Communion Story* (1894) for her own children. Its enthusiastic reception by Catholic children led her to write others, and for thirty-five years she contributed short stories and serials, and infrequently poems, to Catholic periodicals. Among her earlier serials subsequently published in book form were *Tom's Luck-Pot* (1897), *Little Missy* (1900), and *Corinne's Vow* (1902); and among the later ones, *The Secret of Pocomoke* (1914), *Grapes of Thorns* (1917), and *The Finding of Tony* (1919). At the age of seventy-seven she wrote a winning story (published in *The Columbiad,* 1923) in a contest of over 3,000 contestants. Shortly before her death, at the age of eighty-five, she completed a final serial story. In 1903 she published *Carroll Dare,* a novel of colonial Maryland and revolutionary France, and the next year *Strong-Arm of Avalon* (1904), her only other venture into historical fiction. After her death an autobiographical article, "An American Bastile," describing her Civil War experiences, was published in the *Ave Maria* (May 28, June 4, 1932). In her later writing she was primarily concerned that her stories should strengthen the religious faith and loyalty of young Catholic readers. To this aim she sacrificed realism, variety, and literary distinction. Her characters, however, never become priggish or pretentious; her plots are inventive; and her style easy, natural, and straightforward.

[*N. Y. Times,* Aug. 1, 1931; *Evening Star* (Washington, D. C.), July 31, 1931; *Baltimore Catholic Review,* Aug. 7, 1931; *Catholic World,* Sept. 1931; *Commonweal,* Aug. 26, 1931; communications from Mrs. Waggaman's daughter, Mrs. Charles P. Neill, Washington, D. C.]   V. L. S.

WAGNER, CLINTON (Oct. 28, 1837–Nov. 25, 1914), laryngologist, was born in Baltimore, Md., of a German-American family whose ancestor, Basil Wagner, was said to have received, in 1667, a grant of land from the Crown in the province of Frederick, afterwards Carroll County, Md. His mother, of Welsh descent, *née* Peters, was born in Baltimore in 1806. He attended St. James College, Hagerstown, Md., then entered upon the study of medicine in Baltimore, and received the degree of M.D., at the University of Maryland in 1859. He entered the Medical Corps of the United States army, the first of twenty-eight applicants, served at Fort Leavenworth, Kan., and later at San Antonio Arsenal, Tex., where his command was surrendered to the Confederates by David E. Twiggs [*q.v.*] at the opening of the Civil War. Wagner, loyal to the Union, was given a position of much responsibility by the Surgeon-General Hammond of the army and after several promotions became medical director of the regular, or Second Division, V Corps, of the Army of the Potomac, ranking as brevet lieutenant-colonel. He established numerous field hospitals and organized on the Mississippi River the first floating hospital in Western waters. He was many times at the front during severe engagements and risked great personal perils. One of the most notable was at Gettysburg, where he established a field hospital near Little Round Top, the site of which is now marked by a monument bearing his name. He continued in the Medical Corps of the army after the war, but resigned in 1869 and went abroad to study laryngology in London, Vienna, Berlin, and Paris. After two years he returned to New York City and established himself as a specialist. His brilliant qualities as a teacher and as a practitioner soon attracted attention; he established the Metropolitan Throat Hospital and Dispensary, modeled after the London Throat Hospital of Golden Square, and rivaling the best institutions of its kind abroad. It soon became famous among students in the United States as the first special hospital and school of instruction of graduates in laryngology and rhinology.

Wagner devised many new instruments and surgical methods, and his long experience as a general surgeon and his extraordinary technical skill enabled him to perform with success major operations upon the throat and neck that few specialists were in the habit of undertaking. He was the best master of thyrotomy of his time. In a pioneer thesis, *Habitual Mouth-Breathing* (1881), he called attention to mouth-breathing in its relation to medicine. Many of his most valuable contributions were published in the *Transactions of the American Laryngological Association* from 1879 to 1893. In 1882 he was among the first to enter upon the organization of the New York Post-Graduate Medical School

and Hospital, where he became its first professor of laryngology and rhinology. An important achievement of his career was the founding of the New York Laryngological Society in 1873, nearly fifteen years before a similar organization was founded in Europe and five years before the organization of the American Laryngological Association, which grew out of the New York society. In 1914 Wagner became an honorary fellow of the national Association.

In the midst of a brilliant and prosperous professional career, he retired from active practice in New York. For several years he resided at Colorado Springs and other well-known health resorts of the Southwest. Later he spent much time abroad, published practical studies of many popular sanitaria, and acquired an unusually wide and accurate knowledge of climatology. He was a man of untiring energy and indomitable courage; no difficulty seemed to him unsurmountable, and no danger too great. As a pioneer in American laryngology he stands in the foremost rank. He was married on Aug. 28, 1882, to Elizabeth Vaughan of London, who survived him. They were detained abroad at the outbreak of the World War and made their residence at Geneva, Switzerland, where he died.

[Personal acquaintance; *Who's Who in America,* 1901–02; F. J. Stockman, biographical article in H. A. Kelly, W. L. Burrage, *Am. Medic. Biog.* (1920); memoir by D. B. Delavan, *Trans. Am. Laryngological Asso.*, vol. XXXV (1915); and obituary notice in *Medic. Record,* Dec. 5, 1914; *N. Y. Times,* Nov. 26, 1914.]   D. B. D.

WAGNER, WEBSTER (Oct. 2, 1817–Jan. 13, 1882), manufacturer of sleeping-cars, was born at Palatine Bridge, N. Y., the son of John and Elizabeth (Strayer) Wagner, both of German descent, whose families had settled in the Mohawk Valley at an early date. After obtaining an ordinary education and working on his father's farm, Wagner learned the wagon-making trade from an older brother and engaged in that business with him. Since the venture was not successful, in 1843 Wagner became station master of the New York Central Railroad in Palatine Bridge, holding the position for upwards of fifteen years and adding to his duties those of freight agent. Struck with the possibilities in special cars for the use of the night-travelling public and being a skilled craftsman in wood, he undertook the design of a sleeping-car. By 1858, with the financial help of Commodore Vanderbilt, he had completed four sleeping-cars and put them into operation on the New York Central Railroad. These cars had a single tier of berths, and the bedding was packed away by day in a closet at the end of the car. While they were crude affairs, they immediately became popular. Wagner thereupon organized the New York Central Sleeping Car Company at Palatine Bridge to manufacture his cars, which were used exclusively on the New York Central Railroad and its various branches. By 1865 he had evolved a more comfortable coach or drawing-room car, and in that year the New York Central Sleeping Car Company was reorganized as the Wagner Palace Car Company to manufacture both sleeping and drawing-room cars. The drawing-room car, which was put into service in the late summer of 1867, became as popular as the sleeping-car; both yielded fortunes to Wagner and his associates. About 1870 Wagner contracted with George M. Pullman [q.v.] to use the latter's newly patented folding upper berth, and hinged back and seat cushions for the lower berth, with the distinct understanding that the Wagner Company would use cars containing the Pullman inventions only on the lines of the New York Central Railroad. In 1875, however, when the Pullman Company's contract with the Michigan Central Railroad expired, Wagner secured the contract to run his cars over that road, thus making a through connection for the Vanderbilt lines between New York and Chicago. As a result of this breach of contract, the Pullman Company brought an infringement suit against Wagner's company for a million dollars' damages; the suit was still in process at the time of Wagner's death.

Wagner was also very active in New York state politics. He was elected assemblyman by the Republicans of Montgomery County in 1870, and in the following year was elected senator from the eighteenth district. Thereafter he continued in the state Senate until his death, having been reëlected without opposition at the end of each two-year term. As a delegate to the Republican National Convention in Chicago in 1880, he was extremely active in securing the nomination of President Garfield, being strongly opposed to the third-term aspirations of General Grant. He was married to Susan Davis of Palatine Bridge, and at the time of his death, which occurred in a train collision on the New York Central Railroad at Spuyten Duyvil, N. Y., he was survived by his widow and five children.

[Joseph Husband, *The Story of the Pullman Car* (1917); *Proc. of the Senate and Assembly of the State of New York in Relation to the Death of the Hon. Webster Wagner* (1882); *N. Y. Tribune, N. Y. Times,* Jan. 15, 17, 1882; *Sun* (N. Y.), Jan. 16, 1882.]

C. W. M.

WAGNER, WILLIAM (Jan. 15, 1796–Jan. 17, 1885), merchant, philanthropist, was born in Philadelphia, Pa., the youngest child of John Wagner, a cloth merchant and importer, and his

wife Mary (Ritz) Baker Wagner, a daughter of Christian Ritz. William graduated from the Philadelphia Academy in 1808. Four years later he was placed in the counting house of a relative, but soon afterward was entered as an apprentice to Stephen Girard [q.v.]. He continued his studies in Latin, French, and mathematics, attracting the favorable attention of his master, and in 1814 Girard placed the youth in charge of a convoy of goods to be stored in Reading, Pa., in the fear that the British might reach Philadelphia. Two years later, Wagner was made assistant supercargo of Girard's ship, *Helvetius,* sailing on a two-year voyage to the Far East. As a boy he had begun to collect specimens of ores and minerals, and during this voyage he managed to gather a large collection of minerals, shells, plants, and organic remains, the nucleus of a museum which became the foundation of the Wagner Free Institute of Science.

Upon his return to Philadelphia in 1818 he retired from Girard's employ and engaged in business on his own account. He married Caroline M. Say, daughter of Dr. Benjamin Say [q.v.], on Jan. 1, 1824. In 1833 he attempted to mine anthracite coal in Schuylkill County, with heavy financial loss, but seven years more of successful commercial pursuits permitted him to retire from business, in 1840, to devote himself to studies in geology and mineralogy. His first wife having died, he married Louisa Binney in March 1841, and after a two-year tour of Europe bought a large property known as "Elm Grove," in the suburbs of Philadelphia, where he lived until his death.

In the residence he built on this land Wagner arranged a museum for his collections, and in 1847 began to give free lectures on geology, mineralogy, and conchology. After a few seasons his house was found to be too small to accommodate the audiences that desired admittance, but in 1852 he obtained permission to use part of Commissioners Hall, in the District of Spring Garden; and in 1854, when that district was absorbed into the city of Philadelphia, he received permission from the city government for continued use of the building, which was then unoccupied.

The opportunity thus offered he seized upon to establish his cherished project—a free institute of science. He gathered around him a distinguished faculty, all of whom served gratuitously. Wagner himself occupied the chair of geology, mineralogy, and mining. The legislature of Pennsylvania granted a charter for the Wagner Free Institute of Science, and its first season was inaugurated May 21, 1855. The lecture room was always filled to overflowing. When in 1859 the Philadelphia city government desired possession of the building, a new building was at once projected, and on June 2, 1860, on property owned by Wagner, the cornerstone was laid. The structure was completed in 1864, but was not occupied for lectures until the end of the Civil War. Dedicated May 11, 1865, the Wagner Free Institute of Science, together with an ample endowment for the continuance of the work, was turned over by its founder to a board of trustees. It had been incorporated Mar. 30, 1864, and by the act of incorporation was empowered to confer degrees.

Wagner died in Philadelphia some twenty years later, and was buried in a tomb in the institution he had founded. He had "struggled for more than three-score years to found his Free Institute of Science, and not only worked and waited . . . but denied himself many of the luxuries, if not what many persons would deem the necessaries, of life" (Westbrook, *post,* pp. 19–20). His wife also gave her encouragement and even her private patrimony to the establishment of the Institute. Wagner's greatest interest in science lay in the field of paleontology, and his best-known contribution to the subject was a paper he read before the Academy of Natural Sciences, Philadelphia, in January 1838 (*Journal,* vol. VIII, 1839). In H. G. Bronn's *Handbuch einer Geschichte der Natur* (Stuttgart, 1848), Wagner's name was applied to several fossil specimens which he seems to have described for the first time.

[R. B. Westbrook, *In Memoriam: William Wagner* (1885); Henry Leffman, Joseph Willcox, and Sydney Skidmore, in *Founder's Week Memorial Volume* (Phila,. 1909); W. H. Dall, "Notes on the Paleontological Publications of Prof. William Wagner," *Trans. Wagner Free Inst. of Sci.,* vol. V (1898); J. T. Scharf and Thompson Westcott, *Hist. of Phila.* (1884), vol. II; J. W. Jordan, *Colonial Families of Phila.* (1911), vol. II; *Phila. Press,* Jan. 19, 1885; *Public Ledger* (Phila.), Jan. 19, 1885.]   J. J.

WAHL, WILLIAM HENRY (Dec. 14, 1848– Mar. 23, 1909), scientific journalist, metallurgist, the son of John H. and Caroline R. Wahl, was born in Philadelphia, Pa. After graduating from Dickinson College, Carlisle, Pa., in 1867 with the degree of A.B., he entered the University of Heidelberg, Germany, where in 1869 he received the degree of Ph.D. In 1870 he was employed upon the *Journal of the Franklin Institute,* and in 1871, when he became secretary of the Institute, he also became editor of the *Journal.* He held both positions until 1874. He collaborated with Prof. Spencer F. Baird [*q.v.*] of the Smithsonian Institution in compiling the *Annual Record of Science and Industry* for the

years 1873–78, was an instructor in the physical sciences at the Academy of the Protestant Episcopal Church, Philadelphia (1871–73), and later taught physics and physical geography at the Philadelphia Central High School (1873–74). From 1875 to 1876 he acted as editor of the department of arts, sciences, and patents of the *American Exchange and Review.* In 1876 he became editor of the *Polytechnic Review,* which in 1879 was merged with the *Engineering and Mining Journal.* From 1880 to 1895 he was a member of the staff of the *Manufacturer and Builder of New York.* It was, however, as secretary of the Franklin Institute and editor of its *Journal* from 1882 to the time of his death that Wahl achieved distinction. During a critical period of several years in which the existence of the Institute was seriously jeopardized, he maintained the normal work of the organization, himself receiving a compensation so small as to be wholly incommensurate with his labors. Under his editorship the *Journal,* which had been for the most part a reprint of current scientific material, became a valuable source of original information. Nor were his literary activities confined to the congenial task of editing the *Journal.* He translated and edited a number of books relating to chemistry, metallurgy, and general science, and wrote a *Report on the Light Petroleum Oils Considered as to their Safety or Danger* (1873), and with W. H. Greene, "A New Process for the Manufacture of Manganese on the Commercial Scale" (*Journal of the Franklin Institute,* March 1893), and "A New Method of Reducing Metallic Oxides" (*Ibid.,* June 1893).

Among his contributions to practical and applied science, the most important was the discovery and application of aluminum as an energetic oxidizing agent for the creation of high temperatures in metallurgical operations, the basis of what is known as the "thermit process." This was the outgrowth of an attempt to smelt or produce metallic manganese and chromium free from carbon. In order to make a receptacle or crucible containing no carbon and sufficiently refractory to withstand very high temperatures, graphite crucibles were lined with magnesite, a highly refractory magnesium mineral. Since the temperatures obtained with ordinary coke or coal fires were insufficient to produce the reducing temperature and reaction desired, powdered or granulated metallic aluminum was mixed with the charge. The aluminum was capable of removing and appropriating the oxygen of the manganese monoxide, thus setting free the manganese, and the heat liberated by the reaction was sufficient to bring to an intense heat and liquefy the contents of the crucible. Similar results were obtained with chromite or chromic oxide, one of the most refractory minerals known. Though these processes were subsequently patented, Wahl never obtained any monetary benefit from them.

On Sept. 9, 1874, he married Julia Lowther of Seafield, County Mayo, Ireland, and after her death made her sister, Mary B. Lowther, his wife. He resigned his office as secretary of the Franklin Institute on Jan. 13, 1909. On the following Mar. 23 he died, survived by his wife. He devised his entire fortune of about eighty thousand dollars to the Franklin Institute.

[*Who's Who in America*, 1908–09; *Jour. of the Franklin Inst.*, June 1909; F. L. Garrison, in *Trans. Am. Inst. Mining Engineers*, vol. XXI (1893), p. 887; *Am. Men of Sci.* (1906), ed. by J. M. Cattell; obituary in *Pub. Ledger*, Mar. 24, 1909.]   F. L. G.

WAIDNER, CHARLES WILLIAM (Mar. 6, 1873–Mar. 10, 1922), physicist, was born in the suburbs of Baltimore, Md., the son of Charles W. Waidner of Baltimore and Sophia (List) Waidner, born in Germany, who was brought to America at the age of one year, her father having left the year previous on account of participation in the Revolution of 1848. Waidner's education was obtained in the public schools and Friends High School, Baltimore, and at the Johns Hopkins University, where he secured "Proficiency in Electrical Engineering" in 1892 and the degrees of A.B. (1896) and Ph.D. (1898). Here he came under the influence of Prof. Henry A. Rowland [*q.v.*] and the inspiration of Rowland's immediate associates at a time of exceptional progress in the field of physics. In 1897–98 he held a fellowship, and in the following year an assistantship in physics. In 1899 he was appointed to the faculty of Williams College, Williamstown, Mass.

After two academic years at Williams College, Waidner was appointed, Aug. 1, 1901, to the staff of the National Bureau of Standards, newly organized under Samuel Wesley Stratton [*q.v.*], becoming the first chief of the Section, later the Division, of Heat and Thermometry. The immediate problem confronting his section was the establishment of a standard scale of temperature, and his work to this end, in collaboration with Dr. George K. Burgess, led eventually to the adoption of the International Temperature Scale. The quality and scope of their studies soon brought the Bureau of Standards recognition as one of the leaders in pyrometric research. After the temperature scale had been established, attention could be given to problems involving the application of temperature measurements, such

as precise calorimetry, the thermodynamic properties of refrigerants, physical constants and properties of materials. During the World War, the division was in charge of work on engines for aviation. All these and other subjects are treated in the publications of the Division of Heat and Thermometry (since 1923 the Division of Heat and Power).

Waidner's outstanding characteristics were his clear views and accurate thinking on scientific matters, and his devotion to the welfare and progress of those with whom he was associated. The creative thought and sympathetic inspiration of the chief contributed largely to many important pieces of work of his division which do not bear his name, and perhaps his greatest contribution to science is to be found in the work of the men whom he trained and inspired. During the entire period of his active service to the government, he was a member of the editorial committee which passed on all scientific papers prepared by the staff of the National Bureau of Standards. To him this meant much more than a perfunctory reading of all papers. It meant a critical study of every one of them to make sure that the institution which was to such an extent his scientific offspring should not publish any statement or opinion which was open to either doubt or misunderstanding. He was also for some time chairman of the personnel committee of the Bureau. Completely absorbed in his work he seldom rested and never took a vacation unless his immediate health required it. He was appointed chief physicist of the Bureau of Standards in 1921 but died early in the following year, leaving no near relatives.

[Sources include *Who's Who in America*, 1920–21; *Am. Men of Sci.* (3rd ed., 1921); *Jour. Washington Acad. of Sci.*, Apr. 19, 1922; *Science*, Apr. 14, 1922; G. A. Weber, *The Bureau of Standards: Its Hist., Activities, and Organization* (1925); *Evening Star* (Washington), Mar. 11, 1922; *Washington Post* and *Sun* (Baltimore), Mar. 12, 1922; records of the National Bureau of Standards; personal acquaintance. A bound collection of Waidner's papers, many of which were published in the *Jour. of Research* of the Bureau of Standards, is deposited in the library of that institution.]   H. C. D.

WAILES, BENJAMIN LEONARD COVINGTON (Aug. 1, 1797–Nov. 16, 1862), scientist and planter, was born in Columbia County, Ga. He was the eldest of the nine children of Levin and Eleanor (Davis) Wailes, who were both natives of Prince George's County, Md. In 1807 the family moved to the Mississippi Territory where Wailes received his education in Jefferson College at Washington, Mississippi Territory, and in the field, surveying with his father. From 1814 to 1820 he was engaged in surveying and in clerical work at land offices in the old southwest; for a time, he was also assistant to the Choctaw agent and attended the treaty conferences of 1818 and 1820 with the Choctaws. He became locally known as an authority on the geography of their country. On Mar. 30, 1820, he was married to his distant cousin, Rebecca Susanna Magruder Covington, daughter of Brigadier-General Leonard Covington. They lived first near and then in the village of Washington, and ten children were born to them. Though Wailes was register of the land office at Washington from 1826 to 1835, his chief vocation was cotton planting. Eventually he managed, in addition to a small establishment at Washington, two plantations in Warren County which belonged in the family, and in all controlled about 150 slaves.

He is chiefly remembered, however, for his interest in the natural phenomena of the region in which he lived, its soil, rocks, fossils and shells, and the plant and animal life. For many years he collected specimens in all these fields and, in addition to stocking his own cabinet, helped build collections at Jefferson College, at the University of Mississippi, and at the state capitol. His interests brought him in contact with John J. Audubon, Joseph Henry, Joseph Leidy, J. Louis Agassiz, and Benjamin Silliman, 1779–1864 [qq.v.]. To most of these, as well as to other scientists and to the Smithsonian Institution, he supplied information and specimens of the natural history of his region. In 1852 he was appointed assistant professor of agriculture and geological sciences in the University of Mississippi, and in this capacity performed the field work for a projected survey of the state. He entered with zeal upon this task. Later, the writing of the report unexpectedly devolved upon him. His *Report on the Agriculture and Geology of Mississippi* (1854) was written under too much pressure and covered too many fields of knowledge to remain a distinguished contribution to any one of them; nevertheless, judged as a pioneer work, it was well done. Today it is chiefly valuable to the student of agricultural history.

After the completion of this work, the history of his region became an increasingly absorbing interest to Wailes, and in November 1858 he organized a state historical society of which he was the first and only president. Though this died at the end of a year, a number of valuable documents were collected and preserved, and several worth-while studies were made. Wailes wrote a short life of General Covington, which was privately printed in 1928 under the title *Memoir of Leonard Covington*. In history as in

natural science he was more interested in collecting information than in interpreting it and he was generous in furnishing information about the history of his locality to such men as James Parton, Charles Lanman, and Peter Force [qq.v.]. He served for nearly forty years as a trustee of Jefferson College and was president of the board at the time of his death. Except for serving in the state legislature in 1825 and 1826 he eschewed politics, but as a Whig he chafed at the rising power of the Democrats and he watched with apprehension their movement toward secession.

[The chief sources are a thirty-six volume manuscript diary kept by Wailes during the last ten years of his life, and numerous loose manuscript papers divided between The Mississippi Department of Archives and History and a grand-daughter, Mrs. Charles B. Brandon, of Natchez. Volumes I–IV and X–XIII of the diary are in the Archives; volumes V–IX and XIV–XXXVI, in the possession of Mrs. Brandon. See also, B. L. C. Wailes, *Memoir of Leonard Covington* (1928); *Miss. Hist. Soc. Pubs.*, vol. V (1902); James Parton, *Life of Andrew Jackson* (1860), vols. I, II.]

C. S. S.

WAINWRIGHT, JONATHAN MAYHEW (Feb. 24, 1792–Sept. 21, 1854), bishop of the Protestant Episcopal Church, was born at Liverpool, England, the son of Peter Wainwright, an English merchant, and Elizabeth, daughter of the Rev. Jonathan Mayhew [q.v.] of Boston. His father had come to Boston, Mass., shortly after the American Revolution, but prior to Jonathan's birth had returned to England, where he remained until the boy was about eleven years old. Jonathan spent several years at a Church of England school, and after the return of his parents to the United States, he attended an academy in Sandwich, Mass., where he prepared for Harvard. He was graduated at that institution in 1812, and from 1815 to 1817 was instructor there in rhetoric and oratory.

Meanwhile he studied theology, under the care of the rector of Trinity Church, Boston, and on Apr. 13, 1817, was ordained deacon in St. John's Church, Providence, R. I. Having been called to Christ Church, Hartford, Conn., he was admitted to the priesthood there on Aug. 16, 1817. In 1819 he became assistant minister at Trinity Church, New York, but in January 1821 assumed the rectorship of Grace Church, where he served for thirteen years. In 1834 he reluctantly left New York to assume the rectorship of Trinity Church, Boston, to which position he was called partly because his pacific character and Massachusetts background made his presence in the diocese peculiarly desirable at a time when it was sadly divided. Early in 1838, however, he welcomed the opportunity to return to New York as assistant minister at Trinity, in charge of the congregation of St. John's Chapel. During the temporary absence of the rector, Dr. William Berrian, Wainwright was placed in charge of Trinity Parish as assistant rector.

Although not inclined to controversy and considerate of the opinions of others, he nevertheless became involved with the Rev. Dr. George Potts, a Presbyterian divine, in what proved to be one of the celebrated disputations of the day. Rufus Choate had made the assertion that the Pilgrim Fathers had founded a "state without a king and a church without a bishop." Wainwright retorted that "there cannot be a church, without a bishop." The newspaper letters through which the controversy was conducted were later published under the title: *Can There Be a Church Without a Bishop? Controversy Between Rev. Drs. Wainwright and Potts . . . Letters Originally Published in the Commercial Advertiser* (1844). In 1852 he was a delegate to the third jubilee anniversary of the Society for the Propagation of the Gospel in Foreign Parts, held in Westminster Abbey, London. Oxford honored him with the degree of D.C.L.

Upon his return to the United States, he was chosen provisional bishop of New York. His consecration service, Nov. 10, 1852, marks the first time a bishop of the English Church participated in consecrating a prelate on American soil. Wainwright's election terminated a protracted controversy within the diocese caused by doctrinal differences and the suspension of Bishop Benjamin T. Onderdonk [*q.v.*]. Uniting firmness with conciliation and impartiality, Wainwright soon brought harmony into the long-distracted diocese. He was a man whose intellectual, moral, and physical qualities were well balanced. In person he was of striking appearance, well proportioned, and of benevolent countenance. A dignified courtesy, ripeness of learning, a sanguine temperament, and strong social inclinations gained him much popularity.

A devoted advocate of higher education, he was one of the founders in 1829 and a member of the original council of the University of the City of New York (later New York University), incorporated to afford a liberal and non-sectarian school of higher learning. At first active in the enterprise, he withdrew his name as a candidate for chancellor, and later became inactive, probably because of a growing conviction that the university would not be entirely non-sectarian, and would prove a rival to Columbia College, of which he was long a trustee. He was one of the first members of the examining board of Trinity College, Hartford, Conn., and was for several years secretary to the board of trustees of the General Theological Seminary in New York. As a writer he was indefatigable, publishing sermons, addresses, and a number of books. He was the chief working member of the committee which prepared the standard edition of the *Book of Common Prayer,* and he supervised the American edition of the *Illustrated Prayer Book* (1843). His publications include: *A Collection of Psalm, Hymn, and Chant Tunes, Adapted to the Service of the Episcopal Church* (1823); *The Pathways and Abiding-Places of Our Lord Illustrated in the Journal of a Tour Through the Land of Promise* (1851); *The Land of Bondage, its Ancient Monuments and Present Condition; Being the Journal of a Tour in Egypt* (1852). Worn out by untiring labors and ceaseless devotion to his office, he died in New York City in his sixty-third year. On Aug. 10, 1818, he married Amelia Maria, daughter of Timothy Phelps, of New Haven, Conn. She and eight of their fourteen children survived him, one of whom was Jonathan Mayhew Wainwright, 1821–1863 [*q.v.*]. In 1856 *A Memorial Volume: Thirty-four Sermons by the Rt. Rev. Jonathan Mayhew Wainwright, D.D., D.C.L.,* was published under the editorship of his widow, with a biographical memoir by the Rt. Rev. George W. Doane.

[J. N. Norton, *Life of Bishop Wainwright* (1858); J. G. Wilson, *The Centennial Hist. of the Protestant Episcopal Church in the Diocese of N. Y., 1785–1885* (1886); W. B. Sprague, *Annals of the Am. Pulpit,* vol. V (1859); Morgan Dix, *A Hist. of the Parish of Trinity Church in the City of N. Y.,* vols. III, IV (1905–06); *Contributions to the Hist. of Christ Church, Hartford,* vol. I (1895); W. R. Stewart, *Grace Church and Old N. Y.* (copr. 1924); T. F. Jones, *N. Y. Univ.* (1933); *N. Y. Daily Times,* Oct. 2, Nov. 11, 1852, Sept. 22, 25, 1854; information from Hon. J. Mayhew Wainwright of New York City.] L. C. M. H.

WAINWRIGHT, JONATHAN MAYHEW (July 21, 1821–Jan. 1, 1863), naval officer, was born in New York City, the son of Jonathan Mayhew Wainwright [*q.v.*] and Amelia Maria (Phelps) Wainwright. On June 13, 1837, he was appointed midshipman and soon thereafter was ordered to the sloop *Porpoise* employed in the survey of harbors south of the Chesapeake. After a cruise in the East Indies on board the *John Adams* (1838–40), he was attached to the *Macedonian* and made a voyage to the West Indies. He next spent several months at the naval school at Philadelphia preliminary to an examination for passed midshipman, to which grade he was promoted from June 29, 1843. A period of duty with the depot of charts and instruments in Washington was followed by a cruise in the East Indies on board the *Columbia* (1845–46). After promotion to a lieutenancy from Sept. 17, 1850, he served in the Mediterranean on board the *San Jacinto* (1851–

53). Duties at several receiving ships were interrupted in 1856–57 when he was with the *Merrimack* on special service and in 1858–59 when he was with the *Saratoga* of the Home Squadron. At the outbreak of the Civil War he was on waiting orders.

His first active duty in the war was that of a lieutenant on board the *Minnesota* of the Atlantic Blockading Squadron, April–July 1861. On Jan. 18, 1862, he was given command of the *Harriet Lane,* the flagship of the mortar flotilla of the West Gulf Blockading Squadron, and a month later he seized, off the coast of Florida, the Confederate vessel *Joanna Ward* and sent her as a prize to New York. When on Apr. 24 Farragut ran past Forts Jackson and St. Philip on the lower Mississippi, the mortar flotilla supported the movement. Wainwright took a position within five hundred yards of Fort Jackson and kept up a continuous fire. As commander of the flagship of the flotilla he had a prominent part in the operations of Commander David Dixon Porter [*q.v.*] that culminated in the surrender of the forts and the Confederate naval forces. He was commended by Porter for his coolness and bravery. In October with the *Harriet Lane* he participated in the capture of Galveston. On Jan. 1, 1863, when the Confederates recaptured this port his ship was attacked by the *Bayou City* and the *Neptune,* and was carried by boarding. Bravely fighting a superior force, Wainwright was killed instantly by a musket ball through the head after receiving three wounds in the head and three in the left thigh. He was buried at Galveston. After the war his body was sent to New York and was interred near that of his father in the cemetery of Trinity Church.

In December 1844 he was married to Maria Page of Clarke County, Va., who died on Dec. 22, 1854. Jonathan Mayhew Wainwright, the eldest of the four children that survived him, entered the navy and was killed in 1870 in an engagement with pirates; a second son rose to be a major in the army, and a daughter, Marie, became a well-known actress.

[See O. S. Phelps and A. T. Servin, *The Phelps Family of America* (2 vols., 1899), which gives the date of birth as July 27; R. C. M. Page, *Geneal. of the Page Family in Va.* (1883); Record of Officers, Bureau of Navigation, 1832–63; *Navy Reg.,* 1838–63; *War of the Rebellion: Official Records* (*Navy*), 1 ser., vols. XVIII–XIX, XXIV; D. D. Porter, *The Naval Hist. of the Civil War* (1886); *Am. Ann. Cyc.,* 1864; Veterans' Administration, Civil War Records; obituary in *N. Y. Tribune,* Jan. 12, 1863. Some information has been supplied by a grandson of Wainwright.]   C. O. P.

WAINWRIGHT, RICHARD (Jan. 5, 1817– Aug. 10, 1862), naval officer, was born in Charlestown, Mass., the son of Lieutenant-

Colonel Robert Dewar and Maria Montresor (Auchmuty) Wainwright, and a descendant of Richard Wainwright who was a planter in South Carolina in the early eighteenth century. His father (1781–1841), an officer of the United States Marine Corps, is noted for his suppression of a mutiny in the Massachusetts state prison in 1824, an authentic record of which for many years formed one of the standard selections in school readers. Wainwright entered the navy as a midshipman on May 11, 1831, and after some preliminary training in his profession at Norfolk made a cruise in the Mediterranean (1833–36). He prepared at the Norfolk naval school for his examination for the grade of passed midshipman, a rank to which he was promoted from June 15, 1837. After a period of service at the Washington navy yard he was ordered to duty with the United States Coast Survey. In September 1841 he was promoted lieutenant. From 1842 to 1845 he was with the *Vincennes* of the Home Squadron, and from 1846 to 1847 with the *Columbia* of the Brazil Squadron. In 1848 he returned to the Coast Survey, serving there until 1856, part of the time as commander of the *J. Y. Mason.* After a period of service with the *Merrimack* of the Pacific Squadron (1857–60), he was assigned to ordnance duty at the Washington navy yard, where he was stationed in 1861. He was promoted commander from Apr. 24 of that year. In October he commanded the sailors at Fort Ellsworth near Alexandria, and in November he conveyed a detachment of seamen to Cairo, Ill. On the last day of the year he was detached from the navy yard and ordered to command the *Hartford,* the flagship of Flag Officer D. G. Farragut [*q.v.*], preparing for service on the lower Mississippi. On Apr. 24, 1862, when the fleet passed Forts St. Philip and Jackson, the flagship was subjected to a galling fire from the forts and was set on fire by a fire raft, being with difficulty saved from the flames. On the following day, when it was steaming up the river, shots were exchanged with the batteries on shore. The flagship arrived off New Orleans much riddled, with a loss of thirteen men. Later when she passed and repassed the batteries at Vicksburg she gave a good account of herself. On July 15 below Vicksburg she engaged the enemy's ram *Arkansas* and suffered a loss of nine men. In all of the operations of the squadron Wainwright until the last days of July had a distinguished part. He then suffered an attack of remittent fever which proved fatal within two weeks. His death occurred on board his vessel at Donaldsville, La.

On Mar. 1, 1849, he was married to Sally

Franklin Bache, a great-grand-daughter of Benjamin Franklin and a grand-daughter of Richard Bache and Alexander J. Dallas [*qq.v.*]. Richard Wainwright [*q.v.*] was the eldest of his four surviving children.

[Annette Townsend, *The Auchmuty Family in Scotland and America* (1932); Record of Officers, Bureau of Navigation, 1832–63; *Navy Reg.*, 1817–62; Pension Records, Veterans' Administration; *War of the Rebellion: Official Records (Navy)*, vols. IV, XVIII–XIX, XXII; R. S. Collum, *Hist. of the U. S. Marine Corps* (1890); obituary in *Evening Star* (Washington, D. C.), Aug. 19, 1862; letter from Richard Wainwright, Jr., Sept. 22, 1933.]   C.O.P.

WAINWRIGHT, RICHARD (Dec. 17, 1849–Mar. 6, 1926), naval officer, was born in Washington, D. C., the son of Richard Wainwright [*q.v.*] and Sally Franklin (Bache) Wainwright. As a youth he attended private schools in Washington. In 1864 he received from President Lincoln on the recommendation of Admiral Farragut an appointment at large to the United States Naval Academy, then at Newport, R. I. On his graduation in 1868 he joined the *Jamestown* of the Pacific Fleet, and two years later was promoted master. From 1870 to 1873 he was with the *Colorado,* the flagship of the Asiatic Fleet. His marriage to Evelyn Wotherspoon of New York City, Sept. 11, 1873, occurred a few days before he received his lieutenancy. After periods of service with the bureau of equipment, the hydrographic office, and the United States Coast Survey, he was with the Asiatic Fleet (1877–80). While he was absent from the United States, the U.S.S. *Huron* was wrecked off Hatteras, and a naval court of inquiry headed by Admiral David Dixon Porter placed the blame on the dead officers, among whom were several of Wainwright's friends. On his return home Wainwright made an intensive study of the case and proved that the wreck was caused by erroneous data furnished to the officers by an expert in Washington. As a result of his findings the court was reconvened, its verdict reversed, and the officers exculpated.

From 1880 to 1884 Wainwright was on special duty with the bureau of navigation. From 1884 to 1887 he was with the *Tennessee* and *Galena* of the North Atlantic station, part of the time as secretary to the commander-in-chief. He was steel inspector (1887–88), instructor at the United States Naval Academy (1888–90), on special duty with the *Alert* (1890–93), on duty at the hydrographic office (1893–96), and chief of the intelligence office (1896–97). When in November 1897 he left the last-named position to go to the battleship *Maine,* his services were commended by Theodore Roosevelt, then assistant secretary of the navy. In the meantime,

September 1894, he had been commissioned lieutenant commander. As executive officer of the *Maine* he was next in command to Admiral C. D. Sigsbee [*q.v.*] when that vessel was sunk in Havana harbor, Feb. 15, 1898. Soon thereafter he was attached to the tender *Fern* as the navy's representative in the recovery of the bodies and in the examination of the hull for evidence of the cause of the disaster. On his return to Washington he applied for sea duty and was chosen to command the *Gloucester,* formerly the pleasure yacht *Corsair* of J. Pierpont Morgan, a small frail naval vessel, without armor and with an inferior battery. It was intended to protect her with armor, but on Wainwright's protest this was not done, and he was able to sail without delay and arrive in Cuban waters in time to participate in the battle of Santiago Bay, July 3, 1898. When the Spaniards steamed out of the harbor, he fearlessly attacked at close range the destroyers *Furor* and *Pluton,* each the superior of the *Gloucester,* and after a brief engagement sank one and beached the other, killing or wounding two-thirds of their officers and men. He next turned his attention to the burning Spanish flagship *Infanta Maria Teresa* and rescued some two hundred officers and men, including Cervera, the Spanish admiral. He also rescued part of the crew of the *Almirante Oquendo.* Later in July he participated in the naval operation off Puerto Rico, entering the harbor of Guanica under circumstances that added to his reputation for courage and initiative. For his eminent and conspicuous conduct in the battle of Santiago he was advanced by Congress ten numbers in rank. A loving cup was presented to him by the citizens of Gloucester, Mass., and a sword by the people of Washington, D. C. John Davis Long [*q.v.*], secretary of the navy, wrote that his action with the two Spanish destroyers was "one of the most intrepid and brilliant heroisms in all naval history" (Long, *post,* II, 34).

Wainwright was made a commander from Mar. 3, 1899; a captain from Aug. 10, 1903; and a rear-admiral from July 11, 1908. From 1899 until 1902 he was at the Naval Academy, during the latter part of the period as its superintendent. He commanded the *Newark* (1902–04), the *Louisiana* (1907–08), the second division of the Atlantic Fleet (1908–09), and the third division of the same (1909–10). His last duty was as aid for operations to the secretary of the navy. He was retired as rear-admiral on Dec. 17, 1911. Both before and after his retirement he contributed articles to naval periodicals, chiefly to the *Proceedings of the United States Naval Institute.* These include "Fleet Tactics"

(*Proceedings of the United States Naval Institute,* vol. XVI, 1890), "The Battle of the Sea of Japan" (*Ibid.,* vol. XXXI, 1905), and "The General Board" (*Ibid.,* vol. XLVIII, 1922). He was joint editor with R. M. Thompson of *Confidential Correspondence of Gustavus Vasa Fox* (2 vols., 1918–20). Wainwright made his home in Washington, D. C. He left two children, one of whom was a naval officer. He was of average height, slender and erect.

[Annette Townsend, *The Auchmuty Family* (1932); Record of Officers, Bureau of Navigation, 1864–93; *Navy Register,* 1865–1926; *Who's Who in America,* 1924–25; J. D. Long, *The New Am. Navy* (2 vols., 1903); R. W. Neeser, *Statistical and Chron. Hist. of the U. S. Navy* (1909); E. S. Maclay, *Hist. of the U. S. Navy,* vol. III (1902); *Army and Navy Reg.,* Mar. 20, 1926; *Army and Navy Jour.,* Mar. 13, 1926; *Proc. U. S. Naval Inst.,* vol. LII (1926); obituary in *Evening Star* (Washington, D. C.), Mar. 7, 1926.]

C. O. P.

WAIT, SAMUEL (Dec. 19, 1789–July 28, 1867), college president, was born in White Creek, Washington County, N. Y., the son of Joseph and Martha Wait, farmers, and the grandson of Elder William Wait. Schoolmates in the neighborhood remembered him as physically well developed, persevering in his studies, companionable. In 1809 he joined the Baptist Church at Middletown, Vt., where his family had moved after residing in nearby Granville, N. Y., and Tinmouth, Vt. He became pastor at Sharon, Mass., in 1816, and was ordained there in 1818. On June 17, 1818, at Sharon, he was married to Sarah, the daughter of Deacon Jonathan Merriam. While studying, in 1813, at Salem Academy, Washington County, N. Y., he had become convinced that a preacher must have "strength to meet the infidel on his own ground, and this strength at this day must be derived from study" (Brewer, *post,* p. 4). Accordingly he became a theological student in Philadelphia and then a student and tutor, 1822–26, in Columbian College (now George Washington University, Washington, D. C.), which the organized Baptists were endeavoring to establish. Columbian College probably could not award degrees at that early date but because of his work he received the A.M. degree from Waterville College, Me., in 1825.

A trip southward with President William Staughton [*q.v.*] in search of funds for Columbian College in 1826–27 resulted in his acceptance of a pastorate at New Bern, N. C., in 1827. Deeply impressed with the sad condition of the Baptists, he participated actively in the organization of the North Carolina Baptist state convention in 1830, and when no other acceptable person would serve, he became its general agent.

He toured the state in a covered wagon for two years, 1830–32, at a salary of about a dollar a day, out of which he supported the wife and child who accompanied him, and effectively educated the Baptists in cooperation. When the state convention determined to establish an institution for educating ministers Wait was again called into service, and he toured the state for one more year, spreading the news and collecting funds and serviceable articles. In February 1834, Wake Forest Manual Labour Institute was opened, and Wait, as the principal, accepted a varied assortment of boys as pupils. A farm house served for classrooms; former slave cabins as dormitories; a tent as dining-hall. He also directed them in working the community farm that was to help support the school and the pupils. A competent faculty was gradually assembled, the manual labor aspect abandoned, and a new building erected. In 1838 the Institute became Wake Forest College, and Wait was its president until 1846; thereafter he was president of the board of trustees. Without reputation for eloquence or great scholarship, he laid well the foundations of the school among a very plain but aspiring people. Between 1850 and 1860 he wrote "Origin and Early History of Wake Forest College," published in the *Wake Forest Student.* After a happy pastorate at Yanceyville he was president of Oxford Female College from 1851 to 1856. His last years were spent in Wake Forest at the home of his only child.

[Manuscript diary, 1826–27, letters, 1829–60, and scrapbook, in Wake Forest College Library; J. B. Brewer, "Life and Labors of Elder Samuel Wait, D.D.," *N. C. Bapt. Hist. Soc. Papers,* vol. I, no. 1, Oct. 1906; W. L. Wait, "The Early Life of Doctor Samuel Wait," *Wake Forest Student,* Apr. 1885; William Cathcart, *The Bapt. Encyc.* (1881); G. W. Paschal, "History of Wake Forest College," *Wake Forest Bull.,* Nov. 1924–July 1927, and *Hist. of Wake Forest Coll.* (1935); *Biblical Recorder,* July 31, 1867.]

C. C. P.

WAIT, WILLIAM (Feb. 2, 1821–Dec. 29, 1880), lawyer and writer on law, was born at Ephratah, N. Y., the son of William and Polly (Vail) Wait, both members of the Society of Friends. After the death of his father in 1825, he was reared at the home of his mother's parents at Vail Mills, near Broadalbin, N. Y. He was educated at the district school and apprenticed to a local shoemaker. He began the study of law while engaged in his trade, by which he supported his mother and three sisters, but finally finished his legal education in the office of Daniel Cady [*q.v.*], who had become interested in him. In 1846 he was admitted to the bar and in 1848 was elected prosecuting attorney of Fulton County, N. Y. A subsequent fifteen years of practice in Johnstown, the county seat of Fulton County, failed to earn for him more than a local reputation as a lawyer of average ability. In 1865, however, after several years of arduous labor, he published in two large volumes his first treatise, *The Law and Practice in Civil Actions.* Written to discharge what Blackstone had termed a lawyer's duty to his profession, this work on practice, pleading, and evidence in civil actions and proceedings brought in the lower New York courts became a *vade mecum* for the local magistrates and legal practitioners. Code procedure in New York was then in a confused stage of transition from the common-law forms, and a well-indexed manual on actions and defenses with practical forms and precedents was gratefully received by the legal profession. By this treatise, which was subsequently expanded and passed through eight editions, Wait's reputation was made. He abandoned active practice and zealously devoted himself to his legal writings.

His topical *Digest of New York Reports* (5 vols., 1869–77), though not a great work, was extremely useful to contemporary lawyers, especially those who lacked access to original reports. His next publication, *The Code of Civil Procedure of the State of New York* (1870), which embodied recent statutory provisions, was republished five times between 1871 and 1877. In 1872 he produced one of the earliest manuals for quick search, *A Table of Cases Affirmed, Reversed, or Cited,* for the state of New York. Its usefulness in saving lawyers many hours of search and in enabling them to avoid the citation of decisions subsequently reversed or restricted was instantly acclaimed. A contemporary's assertion that "every State in the Union ought to have a similar work executed" (*American Law Review,* Jan. 1873, p. 336) has found fruition in *Shepard's Citations,* a growing refinement and elaboration on Wait's first effort in this field. About the same time Wait prepared a thorough and reliable work on New York practice, *The Practice at Law, in Equity, and in Special Proceedings in All the Courts of Record in the State of New York* (7 vols., 1872–80). Revised by later writers to include subsequent statutes and decisions, *Wait's Practice at Law* continues to be a standard authority on New York adjective law. It was followed in 1875 by his edition of Herbert Broom's *Commentaries on the Laws of England,* a work based largely on Blackstone's *Commentaries.* Wait's last important work was *A Treatise upon Some of the General Principles of the Law . . . Including . . . Actions and Defenses* (7 vols., 1877–79), a topical digest of the general principles of law. Beginning with such topics as "Actions" and "Agency" and continu-

ing through "Wills," every legal subject was concisely digested. Each point represented the actual holding of an American or English decision. These volumes were in reality a *corpus juris* for lawyers and students of that day. The painstaking care with which he conducted his legal research resulted in overwork and physical exhaustion, and after an illness of only a few months he died of consumption at his home in Johnstown. In 1850 he married Margaret E. Stewart (d. 1853), by whom he had one daughter. In 1858 he married Caroline Van Alen of Kinderhook, N. Y. They had three daughters and two sons. Wait's books had brought him a fortune of $100,000, which he left to his wife and the four children who survived him.

[Information on Wait's parentage, early life, and marriages has been supplied by his son, William Wait of Peekskill, N. Y. Other information is from Fulton County records; obituaries in *N. Y. Times* and *Albany Evening Jour.,* Dec. 30, 1880, the latter reprinted in *Albany Law Jour.,* Jan. 8, 1881; and book reviews in *Central Law Jour.,* Feb. 16, 1877, and *Albany Law Jour.,* Aug. 20, 1870, Mar. 4 and Oct. 21, 1871, May 4 and Oct. 5, 1872, Jan. 15, 1876, Mar. 17, 1877, and Jan. 11, 1879.]

V. L. W.

WAIT, WILLIAM BELL (Mar. 25, 1839–Oct. 25, 1916), educator of the blind, inventor, was born at Amsterdam, N. Y., the son of Christopher Brown and Betsey Grinnell (Bell) Wait and a descendant of Thomas Wait who came to America from England in 1634. He was graduated from Albany Normal College in 1859 and became a teacher in the New-York Institution for the Blind, where he remained two years, with the exception of three months when he was in the army during the Civil War. Reënlistment was refused because of nearsightedness, so he studied law and was admitted to the bar in 1862. The field of teaching attracted him, however, and he became superintendent of the public schools in Kingston, N. Y. He had barely entered upon his duties when he was called, in October 1863, to become the superintendent of the New-York Institution for the Blind in New York City and from this time until his death, a period of more than fifty-three years, he was continuously employed in its service. From 1905 on he was emeritus principal.

Programs and aims for the education of the blind were in the 1860's strongly influenced by sentiment, and for many years the Institution for the Blind had been designated a charity; its inmates included children and some adults, former pupils who stayed on in the shelter of the Institution, occupied as teachers of the oncoming children or as workers in the mechanical department. An air of dependency permeated the group. Wait began quickly to dispel this pall, and the

Institution gradually took on a strictly educational aspect. Wait conceived it his duty to exalt the pedagogical purpose of the Institution and to subordinate or altogether abandon the eleemosynary. In 1912 he was instrumental in having the name of the school changed to The New York Institute for the Education of the Blind. In his annual report for 1866, he first published the results of his studies concerning improved methods for printing literature in tangible form. Two years later, in his report, he presented a horizontal point system, a variant of that set up in 1829 by Louis Braille of Paris. He gave increasingly greater attention to the perfecting of this punctographic means of publishing, which came to be known as the New York Point System, and was successful in promoting its adoption until it was used by a large majority of readers in America. To him belongs greatest credit for increasing the opportunities of the blind to study textbooks and to read the classics in literature in a form adapted to their needs and without the intermediary of a reader. In 1878 another system, known as American Braille, was promoted and there ensued a war of the "points" that ended in a compromise—a system quite different from either—which became effective after Wait's death.

For the printing of books in the New York Point System he invented the stereograph, a plate embossing machine, and for the use of blind writers a smaller apparatus called the kleidograph simulating the typewriter. These inventions and his other services to the blind in the production of literature won for him in 1900 the John Scott Medal of the Franklin Institute of Philadelphia. He also devised a musical notation in the horizontal point system. In 1871 he was one of the founders of the American Association of Instructors of the Blind and for forty years a dominant power in the organization. Through its agency he bore a large part in determining the character of the training for young blind people of the United States. His most important articles appeared in its *Proceedings* (see *Index*, 1922). Among his published works are: *Elements of Harmonic Notation* (1888); *The New York Point System* (1893); *Phases of Punctography* (1913); *The Uniform Type Question* (1915); *New Aspects of the Uniform Type Folly* (1916). He was an indomitable leader in advancing education of the blind to the status of a profession, a promoter of pedagogical ideals and practices, a foe of sentimentalism in dealing with the blind, and a doughty champion of their right to intellectual development. On Oct. 27, 1863, he was married to Phebe Jane Babcock,

who became one of the pioneers among women physicians in New York City. She died in 1904, and two of their four children survived him.

[*Who's Who in America*, 1916–17; J. C. Wait, *Family Records of the Descendants of Thomas Wait* (1904); *New England Hist. and Geneal. Reg.*, Oct. 1919; *Outlook for the Blind*, Oct. 1916; *Am. Asso. of Instructors of the Blind, Twenty-Fourth Biennial Convention* (1918); *N. Y. Times*, Oct. 26, 1916.]

E. M. V—C.

WAITE, MORRISON REMICK (Nov. 29, 1816–Mar. 23, 1888), chief justice of the United States, was born in Lyme, Conn., whither his great-great-grandfather, Thomas Wait, had moved from Sudbury, Mass., about the beginning of the eighteenth century. It is said that his family was connected with Thomas Wayte, one of the signers of the death warrant of Charles I (*Harper's New Monthly Magazine,* February 1876, p. 315). Waite's father, Henry Matson Waite, was chief justice of Connecticut and his grandfather, Remick Waite, served for many years as justice of the peace. His mother was Maria (Selden) Waite, grand-daughter of Col. Samuel Selden, the story of whose distinguished services in the Revolution became a family heritage. Waite was graduated at Yale College in 1837 in the class with William M. Evarts. In October 1838 he entered the law office of Samuel M. Young, Maumee City, Ohio, and in 1839 he was admitted to practice. In 1850 the firm moved to Toledo. Young soon retired and Waite was joined by his younger brother, Richard. By this time Waite's law practice had assumed large proportions, and in the ten years from 1851 to 1861 he argued thirty-one cases before the Ohio supreme court. His legal work, at first, was largely confined to financial adjustments, foreclosures of mortgages, untangling of titles, and such matters. In the law of real estate and the status of legal titles he became a recognized authority. It was this training which made him indispensable to the railroad interests.

Waite took an active part locally in the campaign which resulted in the election of William Henry Harrison to the presidency. At twenty-nine he was an unsuccessful candidate for Congress. In 1849 he was elected to the state legislature where he served one term. In 1862 he ran as an independent Republican candidate for Congress and was again defeated. During the Civil War, he was the leader in practically every meeting and movement in his locality whose aim was the promotion of the Union cause (Waggoner, *post*). In 1863 he was offered by the governor of Ohio an appointment to the state supreme court, but he refused it. He did, however, become a close and trusted adviser of the governor.

In 1871 Waite was appointed by President Grant to serve with Caleb Cushing and William M. Evarts [*qq.v.*] as American counsel in the Geneva Arbitration. He contributed five of the thirteen chapters of the American *Argument,* in which he set forth clearly and simply the facts regarding the building, escape, and depredations of the Southern cruisers, the use of British ports as bases of operations for Confederate officers, and lack of "due diligence" on the part of the British government (Hackett, *post,* p. 124). Waite also replied "in excellent tone and temper" (*Ibid.,* p. 306) to Sir Roundell Palmer's argument upon the special question of the supply of coal in British ports to Confederate cruisers. "Sir Roundell Palmer was overwhelmed" (Jones, *post,* p. 259).

On his return from Geneva he was elected to the Ohio constitutional convention of 1873, and became its president. He contributed considerably to the work of the convention, especially to the debates on the judiciary. On Jan. 20, 1874, during a session of the convention, a messenger brought news that, on the previous day, Waite had been nominated chief justice of the United States. The appointment came as a general surprise. He had had no previous judicial experience and had never practised before the court over which he was called to preside. Beyond his service in the Geneva Arbitration, his reputation was not extensive. These facts and the character of Grant's other nominations caused some apprehension. The nomination, however, was well received by the bar of the country. Waite was confirmed unanimously by the Senate on Jan. 21.

He immediately assumed a large share of the work of the Court, writing the opinion in the first case to be argued after he went on the bench (*Tappan* vs. *Merchants' National Bank,* 86 *United States,* 490). In the fourteen years of his chief justiceship he gave the opinion of the Court in more than a thousand cases. His opinions covered a wide range. There were problems growing out of the war yet to be decided. Much of the radical reconstruction legislation was still on the statute books. The war amendments were yet to be construed. The development of the Western states, transcontinental railroads, the agrarian movements, the control of public utilities and rates, the relation of states to the liquor traffic brought new and grave problems before the Court. In all these matters Waite contributed substantially.

The doctrine of the Slaughterhouse Cases was soon reaffirmed by Waite in *Minor* vs. *Happersett* (88 *United States,* 162). Upholding the right of a state to deny the vote to women, he held that suffrage was not a privilege of United States citizenship and that the Fourteenth Amendment did not add to the privileges and immunities of citizens. In *McCready* vs. *Virginia* (94 *United States,* 391) he held that the right to plant or take oysters in the waters of a state was not a right pertaining to United States citizenship, and that it might be denied persons not citizens of the state. In *United States* vs. *Reese* (92 *United States,* 214) Waite demolished the Radical Reconstruction plan of protecting the negro by direct federal action, holding sections three and four of the Civil Rights Act of May 31, 1870, unconstitutional. In *United States* vs. *Cruikshank* (92 *United States,* 542) he held that the Fourteenth Amendment did not authorize Congress to legislate affirmatively for the protection of civil rights and did not add to the rights of one citizen against another.

In the famous case of *Munn* vs. *Illinois* (94 *United States,* 113) he upheld the power of a state to regulate the charges of grain elevators and public warehouses—businesses that were "clothed with a public interest." In other Granger cases the Court upheld state laws fixing maximum rates for passengers and freight on all railroads operating within the state. By its action in these cases the Court profoundly affected the course of American social and economic development (Warren, *post,* II, 581). The due process clause was narrowly interpreted, while the power of the states was necessarily enlarged. In *Peik* vs. *Chicago & Northwestern Railway Company* (94 *United States,* 164), Waite held that until Congress acted, a state regulation of railroads was valid, "even though it may indirectly affect those without," but this position was reversed in the case of *Wabash, St. Louis & Pacific Railway Company* vs. *Illinois* (118 *United States,* 557), with Waite dissenting.

The wide scope of authority left the states, together with the dictum that "for protection against abuses by the legislatures, the people must resort to the polls, not to the court" (94 *United States,* 113), has created the impression that Waite recognized practically no limits to the police power under the due process or any other clause. However, it was Waite himself who laid the foundation for the modern interpretation of due process, as a limitation on state power. His statements in *Railroad Company* vs. *Richmond* (96 *United States,* 521) that "appropriate regulation of . . . property is not 'taking' property," and in *Spring Valley Water Works* vs. *Schottler* (110 *United States,* 347) that reasonable "regulations do not deprive a person of his property without due process of law," were followed by a dictum in the Sinking Fund Cases: "The United States . . . equally with the States . . . are prohibited from depriving persons or corporations of property without due process of law" (99 *United States, 718–19*). Then came his famous dictum in *Stone* vs. *Farmers' Loan and Trust Company:* "From what has been said it is not to be inferred that this power . . . of regulation is itself without limit. . . . [It] is not a power to destroy. . . . The State cannot . . . do that which . . . amounts to a taking of private property . . . without due process of law" (116 *United States,* 331). Upon these dicta rested the decision of the rate cases, in 1890 after Waite's death (134 *United States,* 418), which made the Court the final judge in matters of rates.

Waite's interpretation of the contract clause constitutes another major contribution to constitutional development. Under the reserved power to alter or amend charters, the states were permitted wide discretion in interfering with rates of charge (*Ruggles* vs. *Illinois,* 108 *United States, 526; Spring Valley Water Works* vs. *Schottler,* 110 *United States,* 347). In *Stone* vs. *Farmers' Loan and Trust Company* (116 *United States,* 307) the chief justice held that although a charter had specifically provided that the company might fix charges, this fact did not imply that a railroad commission could not also fix rates. In 1879, in *Stone* vs. *Mississippi* he held that certain police powers, over lotteries in this case, could not be contracted away. "No legislature can bargain away the public health or the public morals" (101 *United States,* 819).

These decisions not only modified profoundly the decision of doctrine of vested rights as established in the Dartmouth College case but they also indicated Waite's willingness to allow the states to exercise wide regulatory power over corporate enterprises in matters pertaining to the "public interest." The authority of the state was always presumed. This principle of wide state power is seen in a number of cases involving suability of states. In *Louisiana* vs. *Jumel* (107 *United States,* 711) he held that a suit against a state officer was a suit against the state itself when the result was to compel the state specifically to perform a contract. In *New Hampshire* vs. *Louisiana* (108 *United States,* 76) he held that a suit by a state on behalf of its citizens against another state was in violation of the Eleventh Amendment. When the Court finally found a way to break down this harsh rule of non-suability, Waite did not lend his support. He was on the side of the minority in the case of *United States* vs. *Lee* (106 *United States,*

196) when the Court held that a suit in ejectment against federal officers in control of the "Arlington" estate of the Lee family was not a suit against the United States but against agents of the government acting unconstitutionally.

In the interpretation of the commerce clause he held in *Hall* vs. *De Cuir* (95 *United States,* 485) that a state provision against race discriminations in interstate conveyances was an undue interference with the power of Congress. In *Pensacola Telegraph Company* vs. *Western Union* (96 *United States,* 1) he held an act of Florida, which attempted to confer an exclusive franchise upon a corporation, unconstitutional as an interference with an act passed by Congress, under its power to regulate commerce. Commerce was broadened to include the transfer of intangibles, such as telegraphic communications. In *Western Union Telegraph Company* vs. *Texas* (105 *United States,* 460) he held invalid a Texas act which placed a specific tax on each message sent out of the state.

Waite scanned closely the claims of individuals as against the state, even interpreting the bill of rights strictly. In *Reynolds* vs. *United States* (98 *United States,* 145) he upheld an act of Congress forbidding polygamy in the territories, interpreting freedom of religion as pertaining to belief not action contrary to law. In *Boyd* vs. *United States* (116 *United States,* 616) he concurred in the decision that a federal act requiring defendants in revenue cases to produce private papers or else the allegations of the government attorney would be taken as confessed, was unconstitutional because it forced one to testify against himself. But he disagreed that this act amounted to an unreasonable search and seizure. He dissented in *Kring* vs. *Missouri* (107 *United States,* 221), interpreting the *ex post facto* clause narrowly.

In the application of international law several important cases were decided by Waite. In *Wildenhus's Case* (120 *United States,* 1), he upheld the authority of the State of New Jersey in taking jurisdiction over the crew of a Belgian merchant vessel in a New Jersey port when a murder was committed aboard the vessel. In doing so he upheld the doctrine that local authorities have jurisdiction over matters which are of such a nature as to disturb the peace of the port. In *United States* vs. *Arjona* (120 *United States,* 479) he upheld the power of Congress to punish for the counterfeiting of foreign securities on the basis of the "necessary and proper" clause. The commerce clause was also suggested as authority for this power. In *United States* vs. *Rauscher* (119 *United States,* 407) he dissented from the decision that a fugitive extradited from England could be tried only for the crime for which he was extradited.

As Justice Miller said, Waite's "style was eminently judicial, terse, vigorous, and clear," and his administrative duties were discharged "with eminent skill, courtesy, and tact" (126 *United States*, 610–11). In 1875 he refused to allow his name to be considered for the presidential nomination the following year, believing it very improper to make the Supreme Court bench a stepping stone to political office. In civic affairs, however, he was active throughout his life. He was a trustee of the Peabody Education Fund for the fourteen years preceding his death, and was one of the members of the Yale Corporation from 1882 until his death. He was a vestryman in the Protestant Episcopal Church and a constant attendant at services. He was married on Sept. 21, 1840, to his second cousin, Amelia C. Warner of Lyme. They had five children, one of whom died in infancy. Waite was impressive in appearance. He was of medium height and heavy-set, but gave the appearance of a much taller man. He was in good health until five days before his death, when he caught cold, which developed into pneumonia. He was survived by his widow, two sons, and a daughter.

[Sketches of Waite appear in 126 *U. S. Reports*, 585–612; *Ohio State Bar Asso. Proc.... 1888* (1888), pp. 173–88; F. R. Jones, in *Green Bag*, June 1902, pp. 257–62; H. L. Carson, *The Hist. of the Supreme Court of the U. S.* (1902), vol. II; B. R. Cowen, in W. D. Lewis, ed., *Great American Lawyers*, vol. VII (1909); A. P. Stokes, *Memorials of Eminent Yale Men* (2 vols., 1914); Charles Warren, *The Supreme Court in U. S. History* (1928), vol. II. His opinions are in 86–126 *U. S.* See also J. T. Wait, "Henry Matson Waite," in *New-Eng. Hist. and Geneal. Register*, Apr. 1870, pp. 101–05, containing genealogy; Clark Waggoner, ed., *Hist. of the City of Toledo* (1888); F. W. Hackett, *Reminiscences of the Geneva Tribunal of Arbitration* (1911); J. B. Uhle, "The Opinions of Chief Justice Waite," *Current Comment*, May 15, 1890; obituaries in *Chicago Legal News, N. Y. Times*, Mar. 24, 1888. Through the courtesy of members of the family, the author has had access to private letters of Waite, his wife, and his father, scrapbooks of newspaper clippings, his personal expense book, and other records.]   B. R. T.

WAKELEY, JOSEPH BURTON (Feb. 18, 1809–Apr. 27, 1875), Methodist Episcopal clergyman and author, was born in Danbury, Conn., the son of James and Rebecca (Cooke) Wakeley. Although some secondary sources give Beaumont as his middle name, the entry recording his birth in the Danbury vital records gives Burton; on the title pages of his books his name commonly appears as J. B. Wakeley. He attended the district school of his native town and early showed eagerness to learn and an exceptional memory. His father, a hatter by trade and a man of excellent sense and wide reading, determined,

if possible, to give the boy a college education. He also encouraged him to practise oratory and to attend courts and other places where speakers of ability might be heard. Business reverses prevented Joseph from going to college, and except for his district school training his formal education was limited to a term in an academy at Fairfield, Conn., and another at Seabury Academy, Stamford. Fascinated by tales of the sea, he shipped as a cabin boy on a vessel bound to Liverpool from New York, but finding that he must serve grog he left the vessel before it sailed. A brig upon which he next secured a position was nearly wrecked when a few days out of port, and put back into Chesapeake Bay for repairs. Cured of his desire to be a sailor, he returned to Danbury, learned the hatter's trade, and finally went into business for himself. In July 1831 he married Jane McCord of Sing Sing (Ossining), N. Y. His parents were Congregationalists, but Joseph joined the Methodist Church.

His talents were such that he felt he could devote his life to some higher service than that of making hats, and his friends were of the same opinion. Methodist officials saw in him the possibilities of an effective preacher, and in May 1833 he joined the New York Conference of the Methodist Episcopal Church on trial; in 1835 he was ordained deacon, and in May 1837, elder. During his ministry of forty-two years he held many appointments, serving, among others, churches in New York, Trenton, Newark, Jersey City, Poughkeepsie, and Yonkers. From 1866 to 1868 he was presiding elder of the Poughkeepsie district, and from 1868 to 1872, of the Newbury district. He overcame many of the defects in his early education by hard study, and the oratorical training of his youth stood him in good stead, so that he did not suffer greatly by comparison when speaking on the same platform with Henry Ward Beecher, John B. Gough, and Horace Greeley. He was a large-hearted, humane person, of exuberant spirits, with a keen sense of humor and a copious stock of anecdotes at his command, interested in people and in the practical problems of life. To the temperance movement and later to the prohibition movement he gave vigorous support, publishing in 1875 *The American Temperance Cyclopædia of History, Biography, Anecdote, and Illustration.*

Outside of his regular duties, his chief interest was in antiquarian research, and it is for his contributions to the history of early Methodism that he is chiefly remembered. Among his published works were *The Heroes of Methodism* (1856); *Lost Chapters Recovered from the Early*

History of American Methodism (1858); *Anec-dotes of the Wesleys: Illustrative of Their Char-acter and Personal History* (1869); *The Bold Frontier Preacher: A Portraiture of Rev. Wil-liam Cravens, of Virginia* (1869); *The Prince of Pulpit Orators: A Portraiture of Rev. George Whitefield* (1871). He was also the editor of Henry Boehm's *Reminiscences, Historical and Biographical, of Sixty-four Years in the Min-istry* (1865). Wakeley died at the home of a friend in New York City after a few days' illness and was buried at Sing Sing.

[W. E. Ketcham, "Memoir of J. B. Wakeley, D.D.," in Wakeley's *Lost Chapters Recovered from the Early Hist. of Am. Methodism* (ed. copr. 1889); *Minutes of the New York Conference of the M. E. Church* (1876); John M'Clintock and James Strong, *Cyc. of Biblical, Theological, and Ecclesiastical Literature*, vol. X (1881); *Christian Advocate*, May 6, 1875; *N. Y. Times*, Apr. 29, 1875; vital records of Danbury, Conn., in Conn. State Lib.]   H.E.S.

WALCOT, CHARLES MELTON (*c.* 1816–May 15, 1868), actor and dramatist, was born in London, England, received a public school edu-cation, and was then trained as an architect. He is said to have emigrated to Charleston, S. C., probably in 1837, and to have become treasurer of the Charleston Theatre. Natural inclination and a singing voice carried him to the stage. He married about this time Miss Powell, an actress, and evidently went touring, for his son Charles Melton [*q.v.*], was born in Boston in 1840. The first record of Walcot in New York is at the Military Garden, June 28, 1842, when he played Wormwood in *The Lottery Ticket* and later other rôles. The next season found him at Mitchell's famous Olympic, where he remained, with few interruptions, for the next seven years, and built up a substantial reputation both as an ec-centric comedian and a dramatic actor. Those were busy days for any actor, especially in a stock company where the bills were changed sometimes almost every night and each bill num-bered more than one play or skit. For the first two or three years Walcot was seldom off the program. He was the first to play Don César de Bazan in America, at the Olympic, Dec. 9, 1844. More interesting to a later age, no doubt, would be Walcot's own farces, or burlesques, in the composition of which he seems to have been adept. On Jan. 1, 1844, at the Olympic, was produced *The Imp of the Elements, or The Lake of the Dismal Swamp.* Much more successful were his *Don Giovanni in Gotham* and its suc-cessor, *The Don Not Done, or Giovanni from Texas* (Olympic, Mar. 25, 1844), described as "an original musical, fantastical, local extrava-ganza." On Mar. 27 came his *Old Friends and New Faces,* in which Mrs. Walcot played four

rôles. On Apr. 8 Mitchell had the temerity to produce *The Marriage of Figaro,* "with the overture and music selected chiefly from Mo-zart's operas." Walcot sang Figaro, but how much of Mozart's music he selected to render we do not know. There are many evidences that he fancied himself as a vocalist. To finish that sea-son, he had a brief try at summer management at Vauxhall Gardens. He appeared at the Arch Street Theatre, Philadelphia, Oct. 29, 1847, as Sir Harcourt Courtly in Dion Boucicault's *London Assurance,* and at various times acted other rôles in standard comedy, including those of Charles Surface and Bob Acres. Among the rôles, other than burlesque, in which he was esteemed seem to have been those of Bert Lav-ater in Planché's drama of that name, and Red-law in an adaptation of Dickens' *The Haunted Man.* In 1852 he was engaged by J. W. Wallack, and except for a brief excursion abroad and a briefer experiment in stage management in Bal-timore (1853) he played chiefly at Wallack's until 1859.

Ireland (*post,* p. 400) says he was "one of the very best light and eccentric comedians who ever trod our stage." Earlier criticisms found fault sometimes with his exaggerated methods and facial contortions. It was generally conceded that he was an "honest, upright and kind-hearted man." Existing portraits show a sensitive face beneath an unusually high, bald, and domelike forehead, with side hair combed forward and slight side whiskers, almost the portrait of a pleasant clergyman rather than an actor. Many of his burlesques were topical, and hence were a part of the mid-century movement, both in Eng-land and America, to free the stage of "classical" shackles and bring it closer to contemporary life. Though his plays are quite forgotten, Walcot evidently had no inconsiderable share in this movement. After leaving Wallack's, he acted less and less, chiefly because his voice was fail-ing him, and he died at a son's home in Philadel-phia in May 1868.

[The date of Walcot's birth is given sometimes as Sept. 20, 1815. He is said to have been the son of Thomas B. Melton and to have been named Charles Walcot Melton. His wife's name is given by some writers as Anne. Sources include J. N. Ireland, *Records of the N. Y. Stage* (2 vols., 1867); T. A. Brown, *Hist. of the Am. Stage* (1870); G. C. D. Odell, *Annals of the N. Y. Stage* (7 vols., 1927–31); Frederic Boase, *Modern Eng. Biog.* (3 vols., 1892–1901); Theatre Coll., Harvard College Lib.; obituary in *Am. Ann. Cyc.,* 1868.]   W.P.E.

WALCOT, CHARLES MELTON (July 1, 1840–Jan. 1, 1921), actor, was born in Boston, Mass., the son of Charles Melton Walcot [*q.v.*] and his wife. He made his first appearance on

Walcot

Walcott

the stage in Charleston, S. C., in 1858 under the name of Brown but soon resumed his own name. Like many youthful stock actors, he began with old men's parts. In 1859 he played at the National Theatre, Cincinnati, in 1860–61 at Richmond, Va., and in 1861–62 at the Winter Garden, New York, where he had character parts. He then appeared (1862–63) with Laura Keene [q.v.] at her theatre in *Old Heads and Young Hearts* and other plays. On May 31, 1863, he married Isabella Nickinson, a young actress of sixteen, and thereafter until her death they always appeared together. In 1864 Walcot played Horatio during the famous hundred-night run of Booth's *Hamlet* in New York. Three years later the Walcots moved to Philadelphia, where they remained, chiefly at the Walnut Street Theatre, for a number of years. In 1872, however, Walcot supported Charlotte Cushman [q.v.] and played Fagin to Lucille Western's Nancy Sikes. He later played at McVicker's, Chicago, and at the Madison Square and Palmer's in New York, and toured the entire country in Bronson Howard's *The Banker's Daughter* (1879). In 1887 the Walcots joined Daniel Frohman's famous Lyceum Stock Company in New York. There they enjoyed a period of long runs, with light work, great public favor, and the opportunity for domestic stability and social life. In an interview published in the *New York Dramatic Mirror*, Apr. 18, 1896, Walcot contrasted conditions in the nineties with those of his youth, when he had to be able to support visiting stars in their repertoires, alternating, for example, Iago and Othello with Booth on successive nights, and getting up new plays constantly. His rôles at the Lyceum included those of dignified or comic middle-aged or elderly men in plays like *The Wife,* by H. C. de Mille and David Belasco (1887), and *The Princess and the Butterfly* (1897) and *Trelawney of the Wells* (1898) by Pinero; he also appeared in Pinero's *Lady Bountiful,* in a revival of *Old Heads and Young Hearts,* and many of the other Lyceum plays.

After the turn of the century his parts grew fewer, for the last of the stock companies had vanished. Early in the century he supported Otis Skinner for two years in *The Duel.* In 1908 he acted with John Barrymore, in 1909–10 with Henrietta Crosman. In the Empire Theatre revival of *Trelawney of the Wells,* January 1911, he again took his rôle of Sir William Gower. He was then seventy-one. His wife had died (June 2, 1906), and he sorely missed the companionship which had characterized both their domestic and artistic life. He spent his last years

inactively in his home in New York, where he died. In appearance he somewhat resembled his father, though his forehead was less doming and his face and aspect ruddier. In his Lyceum days he often wore a moustache, and offstage could have passed for a genial though dignified British squire. His dramatic schooling under such players as Laura Keene, Edwin Booth, and Charlotte Cushman had been thorough, and he had profited by it, adding to natural gifts as a comedian the skill to touch any required stop. In method he bridged a gap between the older, broad romantic acting and the new realistic method, and in his best years, at the Lyceum, he brought to the nascent new drama, with intelligent adaptability, the authority of the "old school." Much the same could be said of Mrs. Walcot. They were both greatly loved by the public.

[G. C. D. Odell, *Annals of the N. Y. Stage,* vol. VII (1931); Daniel Frohman, *Memories of a Manager* (1911); Harvard Theatre Coll., which contains letters from Walcot; death notices in *N. Y. Times, N. Y. Herald,* Jan. 4, 1921.]

W. P. E.

WALCOTT, CHARLES DOOLITTLE (Mar. 31, 1850–Feb. 9, 1927), paleontologist and administrator, youngest of four children of Charles Doolittle and Mary (Lane) Walcott, was born at New York Mills, Oneida County, N. Y. He was a descendant of William Walcott who emigrated from England to Salem, Mass., in 1637. Since his father died when Charles was a child, he was early thrown upon his own resources, and his education was limited to that provided by the public schools and the Utica Academy. His systematic training ceased altogether in 1868. He worked for two years as a clerk in a hardware store, meanwhile showing a growing interest in natural history, which manifested itself mainly in the collection of fossils and minerals. In 1871 he turned definitely toward a geological career. Going to Trenton Falls, N. Y., he associated himself with W. P. Rust, a farmer, under an arrangement that gave him his board and lodgings with a certain part of his time for study. There he formed a collection of Trenton fossils sufficient to attract the attention of Prof. J. L. R. Agassiz [q.v.] of Harvard. It was arranged that he should enter upon a course of study under Agassiz's supervision, but Agassiz's death prevented the carrying out of the plan. In 1876 Walcott entered the employ of James Hall, 1811–1898 [q.v.], state geologist of New York, at Albany. In July 1879 he was appointed a field assistant with the newly organized United States Geological Survey under the direction of Clarence King [q.v.]. He remained with the survey under the régime of King and

327

J. W. Powell [*q.v.*], gradually advancing in position. Until 1879 his work had been mainly directed to a study of the Cambrian formations of the New England states and areas east of the Mississippi. His first assignment under King was in the Grand Canyon region of Colorado and Utah. In 1882 he collaborated with Arnold Hague [*q.v.*] in a survey of the Eureka mining district of Nevada, gradually assuming administrative duties as well, until in 1893 he was promoted to the position of geologist in charge. On the retirement of Powell in 1894 he was selected as his successor and remained in that position until 1907. As director of the survey, Walcott simply became head of a body of scientific men already organized, of whom he had, through association, a thorough working knowledge. It remained for him to develop and strengthen the organization on lines already laid down, and this he did most effectively through affiliation with state organizations and professors in the various universities. He also took up the work of reclamation begun by Powell and had a very active part in the work which led eventually to the establishment of the Forest Service and the Bureau of Mines. At the time of his resignation in 1907 the annual appropriations for the support of the survey had more than tripled, while the personnel, both in number and efficiency, exceeded that of any similar existing organization.

But Walcott was not more interested in administration than in paleontology, and the demands of so large and growing an organization he found irksome. When in 1907 he was offered the secretaryship of the Smithsonian Institution he welcomed it as a possible relief from some of his most wearisome administrative burdens. That his hopes in this direction were not to be fully realized was early apparent. The growing activities of the National Museum, the Zoölogical Park, and other governmental bureaus administered by the institution, together with those of the Smithsonian proper, all demanded time and attention. Further, owing to his official position and proved executive ability, he was involved in many other projects. He exerted great influence in the founding of the Freer Gallery, and was active in the founding and organization of the Carnegie Institution, the National Research Council, and the National Advisory Committee for Aeronautics, over which he presided until his death. He was secretary and chairman of the executive committee of the board of trustees of the Carnegie Institution, and treasurer (1899–1902), vice-president (1907–17), and president (1917–23) of the National Academy of Sciences. The World War brought other duties. Later he

took an active part in inaugurating the air-mail service, in organizing work in surveying and mapping by aerial photography, and in drafting the air commerce act of 1926. In the meantime the institution over which he presided was threatened with decline to secondary rank through the shrinking value of its endowment and the vastly larger endowments of institutions newly organized. Plans to check this decline were set in motion a short time before Walcott's death.

The demands made upon him were certainly sufficient to warrant a complete abandonment of all personal scientific work. Yet season after season he found time for field work, mainly in the Canadian Rockies, returning each year enthusiastic over new materials and discoveries, but in later years lacking in stamina for his manifold duties. He did extensive work on the Cambrian field of geology and wrote some notable papers on the organization of the trilobite. His first paleontological paper, "Description of a New Species of Trilobite," appeared in the *Cincinnati Quarterly Journal of Science* in July 1875; his last, *Pre-Devonian Paleozoic Formations of the Cordilleran Province of Canada* (1928), some time after his death. Of the upwards of 222 titles in his bibliography, 110 dealt with the Cambrian formations. Of his faunal studies, the most comprehensive is said to be "The Fauna of the Lower Cambrian or *Olenellus* Zone" (*Tenth Annual Report of the United States Geological Survey*, pt. I, 1890); his most monumental work is his *Cambrian Brachiopoda* (2 vols., 1912), Monograph 51 of the United States Geological Survey. The most striking of his field discoveries was that of the Middle Cambrian Burgess shale of British Columbia, with its undreamed-of wealth of fossil invertebrate remains still retaining recognizable impressions of their softer parts. From these beds alone he had at the time of his death described seventy genera of fossil forms, and a hundred and thirty species (Schuchert, *post*, p. 457).

Walcott was a man of large frame, tall, erect, and impressive in appearance; in his younger days he wore a full reddish beard. He was reserved, dignified, and calm, with a slight stiffness of manner that at first gave an impression of coldness. In the midst of the most distracting administrative duties he could always find immediate relief in scientific research. He was a member of the leading scientific societies in Europe and America and received a number of honorary degrees, among them that of Sc.D. from Cambridge University in 1909 and that of Ph.D. from Kongelige Frederiks Universitet, Norway, in 1911. He was awarded the Bigsby Medal of the Geological Society of London in 1895, and its Wollaston Medal in 1918; the Hayden Medal of the Academy of Natural Sciences of Philadelphia in 1905; the Gaudry Medal of the Société Géologique de France in 1917, and the Mary Clark Thompson Medal of the National Academy of Sciences in 1921. On June 22, 1888, he married Helena Burrows Stevens, by whom he had three sons and a daughter. After the death of his first wife in a railroad accident in 1911, he married Mary Morris Vaux (June 30, 1914), who survived him.

[The best material on Walcott is contained in N. H. Darton, "Memorial of Charles Doolittle Walcott," *Bull. Geological Soc. of America*, Mar. 1928, with bibliog. See also F. A. Virkus, *The Abridged Compendium of Am. Geneal.*, vol. II (1926); *Who's Who in America*, 1926–27; "Charles Doolittle Walcott . . . Memorial Meeting," *Smithsonian. Miscellaneous Colls.*, vol. LXXX, no. 12 (1928); G. O. Smith, *Charles Doolittle Walcott* (1927), reprinted from *Am. Jour. of Sci.*, July 1927; Charles Schuchert, in *Report of the Nat. Acad. of Sci.* (1928), reprinted from *Sci.*, May 13, 1927; T. C. Chamberlain, in *Jour. of Geology*, Oct.–Nov. 1927; "Eminent Living Geologists," *Geological Mag.* (London), Jan. 1919; obituary in *Evening Star* (Washington, D. C.), Feb. 9, 1927.]　　　　　G. P. M.

WALCOTT, HENRY PICKERING (Dec. 23, 1838–Nov. 11, 1932), physician and public health administrator, was born in Hopkinton, Mass., the son of Samuel Baker and Martha (Pickman) Walcott. Following his graduation at Harvard College in 1858, Walcott studied medicine under Morrill and Jeffries Wyman [*qq.v.*] and took his degree of M.D. in 1861 at Bowdoin College, Brunswick, Me. He went to Europe in June 1861 to further his medical studies in Vienna and Berlin, returning to America in November 1862. Subsequently he began to practise in Cambridge, Mass., at first as assistant to his former teacher, Dr. Morrill Wyman. After service on the Cambridge school committee and as city physician, he was appointed in 1882 a member of the State Board of Health, Lunacy, and Charity. The public health movement was vaguely coming into being and the pioneer efforts of Lemuel Shattuck [*q.v.*] were bearing fruit. Four years of membership were followed by twenty-nine years as chairman.

Walcott's first task was the reorganization of the badly maintained Tewksbury State Almshouse. This accomplished, he next, in 1886, widened the influence of the Board of Health by giving it advisory power regarding public water supplies, drainage, sewerage, and the protection of the purity of inland waters. By assuming only advisory capacity and never mandatory powers, he upheld the town and local authorities and never usurped any of their jealously-guarded rights. That he succeeded well is evident, for

the decisions of the Board were almost invariably accepted without question by the towns. Subsequently the Board of Health of which he was chairman recommended and planned the Metropolitan Sewerage Commission to coördinate the work of many communities near Boston. A special commission of which he was chairman in 1893 recommended the building of the Charles River Basin in Boston, a public health measure of first importance. Finally, he planned and saw executed in 1895 the metropolitan water supply system for Boston. He also established an antitoxin laboratory, under the direction of Theobald Smith, for the manufacture of diphtheria antitoxin for free distribution in the state.

In addition to his chairmanship of the Board of Health, Walcott was chairman of the Metropolitan Water and Sewerage Board and was president of the American Public Health Association, of the Massachusetts Medical Society, the Massachusetts Horticultural Society and the American Academy of Arts and Sciences. For many years he was a trustee of the Carnegie Institution of Washington, chairman of the trustees of the Massachusetts General Hospital and, in 1912, he served as president of the Fifteenth International Congress on Hygiene and Demography in Washington. He was an honorary fellow of the Royal Sanitary Institute of Great Britain. He was one of the incorporators of the Cambridge Hospital in 1872 and served as its president for twenty-five years. In 1890, while serving as Overseer, he was made a member of the Board of President and Fellows of Harvard College, and acting president in 1900 and again in 1905.

Besides tributes to Charles W. Eliot and Reginald H. Fitz [*qq.v.*] in *Proceedings of the Massachusetts Historical Society*, vols. LII and LX (1919, 1927), and a memoir of Morrill Wyman [*q.v.*], printed in *Sons of the Puritans* (1908), Walcott wrote an essay on Alexander Agassiz [*q.v.*] which he delivered before the American Academy of Arts and Sciences (*Proceedings*, vol. XLVIII, 1913). Otherwise his writing was practically confined to the annual reports of the Board of Health. In them one finds the germinal ideas of most of the public health movement in America. Building on the sound foundations laid by Lemuel Shattuck, Walcott erected a structure of wide usefulness to his local community, and helped to make public health the concern of all civilized peoples. He was the most important man in the field in his day. On May 31, 1865, he was married to Charlotte Elizabeth, daughter of Reuben Richards of Boston. His wife died in 1879. Of the three children, one died as a baby, one became a cotton merchant and the other a judge, lawyer, and bank president. He was intimate with the leading Bostonians in science and in literature; among them were William James, Charles W. Eliot, Alexander Agassiz, Nathaniel S. Shaler, and Charles Sprague Sargent [*qq.v.*]. He was one of the most beloved and honored figures in Boston during his many years of service to the commonwealth. He retired, except for his connections with Harvard University, fifteen years before his death. He died in his ninety-fourth year in Cambridge, Mass., partially deaf, wholly blind for the previous five years but with intellect, wit, and good spirits unimpaired.

[His chief contributions to public health are contained in George C. Whipple, *State Sanitation* (2 vols., 1917), dedicated to Walcott. See also: A. S. Walcott, *The Walcott Book* (1925); *New England Jour. Med.*, Nov. 17 and Dec. 1, 1932; X. Henry Goodnough, *Ibid.*, Nov. 9, 1933; M. J. Rosenau, in *Summarized Proc. Am. Acad. of Arts and Sci.*, vols. LXXXII–LXXXVI (1934); *Who's Who in America*, 1932–33; *Report of the Class of 1858, Harvard Coll.*, 1868, 1888, 1898; *Boston Evening Transcript*, Nov. 11, 1932; *Boston Herald, N. Y. Times*, Nov. 12, 1932.]   H. R. V.

WALDEN, JACOB TREADWELL (Apr. 25, 1830–May 21, 1918), Protestant Episcopal clergyman and author, the son of Jacob Treadwell and Beulah Hoffman (Willett) Walden, was born at Walden, Orange County, N. Y., a town founded by his father. During most of his life the son was known simply as Treadwell Walden. After studying at St. James' College, Maryland, and at St. Paul's College, Long Island, in 1850 he entered the General Theological Seminary, New York. Graduating in 1853, he was ordained deacon by Bishop J. M. Wainwright, July 2, 1854, in Trinity Church, New York. In January 1855 he became assistant at Trinity Church, Newark, in February 1856 was put in charge of it, and there was ordained priest by Bishop G. W. Doane on May 19 of that year. In September 1857 he became rector of Christ Church, Norwich, Conn. While here he published *The Sunday School Prayer Book* (copr. 1862), a collection marked by more attention to the nature of children and by less rigorous theology than was common in most similar books of the period. In March 1863 he went to St. Clement's Church, Philadelphia, for which he secured the erection of a parish house and other improvements. He served on the committee appointed by the United States Sanitary Commission to investigate the treatment of Union prisoners, and is said to have drafted its report (*Narrative of Privations and Sufferings of U. S. Officers and Soldiers while Prisoners of War*, 1864). St. Clement's was involved in financial difficulties, how-

ever, and in 1868, conscious of his vestry's lack of confidence, Walden resigned.

In February 1870 he was called to St. Paul's Church, Indianapolis. He at once took a prominent part in the church life of the city and the affairs of the diocese of Indiana. In 1871 he published *Our English Bible and Its Ancestors*, a series of parish lectures on the history of the English version and the need for a revision. In the appendix he argued that the New Testament word *metanoia* means "change of attitude" rather than "repentance for sin," a subject to which he was to return in future publications. Although his work in Indianapolis seems to have been successful, he left in 1872, and in the next year became rector of St. Paul's, Boston. Compelled by ill health to resign in May 1876, for some years he lived and occasionally officiated in or near New York. Meanwhile, the essay on *metanoia* had appeared as an article in the *American Church Review* (July 1881), and in his *An Undeveloped Chapter in the Life of Christ* (1882). In 1882 he was called to St. Paul's, Minneapolis.

Three years later he retired from the active ministry and subsequently spent several years in England. After his return in 1889 he divided his time between Boston, Mass., and Wonalancet, N. H. In 1896 an enlarged treatment of his favorite subject was published as *The Great Meaning of Metanoia*. Walden's place in the development of the Episcopal Church lies in the part he played in the humanizing and liberalizing movement by which the broad church group grew out of the older evangelical. He was twice married: first, in 1858, to Elizabeth Leighton Law, of Norwich, Conn., who died in 1883; and second, in 1885, to Grace Gordon of Boston. He was survived by two sons by his first wife. Walden died in Boston.

[*Who's Who in America*, 1916–17; *Living Church*, June 1, 1918; *The Living Church Annual and Churchman's Almanac* (1919); *Boston Transcript*, May 21, 1918; records of the dioceses with which Walden was connected, and of St. Clement's, Phila.] E. R. H., Jr.

WALDEN, JOHN MORGAN (Feb. 11, 1831–Jan. 21, 1914), bishop of the Methodist Episcopal Church, was born near Lebanon, Ohio, the son of Jesse and Matilda (Morgan) Walden, who moved to Hamilton County in 1832. He was of Virginian ancestry, his great-grandfather Walden having moved from Culpeper County to Kentucky in 1770, and his grandfather, Benjamin, to Ohio in 1802. After the death of his mother in 1833 John went to live with relatives near Cincinnati. He attended a local school until 1844, when he went to work. Becoming a wanderer, he found employment as a carpenter, in a country store and postoffice, and in connection with theatrical performances. A carpenter for whom he worked interested him in Thomas Paine's writings, and he became a skeptic. He read extensively in Scott and Goldsmith and wrote romantic stories over the name of Ned Law for the Hamilton, Ohio, *Telegraph* (1849–53). After attending Farmers' College, College Hill, Ohio, in 1849, he taught for a year in Miami County, where he was converted by a Methodist circuit rider. Returning to Farmers' College he was graduated in 1852 and for two years was a teacher there.

In 1854 he went to Fairfield, Ill., where he published the *Independent Press,* opposing in his editorials the liquor traffic and "squatter sovereignty." The Illinoisans starved him out by refusing to support his paper, and in 1855 he returned to Ohio, where he reported for the *Cincinnati Commercial.* So deeply interested in the Kansas troubles did he become while reporting the National Democratic Convention of 1856 that he went to Kansas, where he established the Quindaro *Chindowan,* a free-soil organ. He was a delegate to five free-state conventions, including the Leavenworth constitutional convention (1858). That same year he campaigned over half the Territory, opposing the Lecompton constitution.

On Sept. 8, 1858, he was admitted on trial to the Cincinnati Conference of the Methodist Episcopal Church. The first two years of his ministry were spent on circuits, and on July 3, 1859, he married Martha Young of Cheviot, Ohio. In 1860 he was admitted to the Conference in full connection and sent to the York Street Church, Cincinnati. While he was here the Civil War began, and he became very active and raised two regiments to defend the city against threatening attack. After service in connection with the Ladies' Home Mission in Cincinnati (1862–64) and as corresponding secretary of the Western Freedmen's Aid Commission and of the Methodist Freedmen's Aid Society, he became in 1867 presiding elder of the East Cincinnati District. The following year he was chosen an assistant agent of the Western Methodist Book Concern. His penchant for statistics and organization, his business ability, and his sympathetic cooperation with preachers made the Concern a financial success.

At the General Conference of 1884 he was elected bishop. In his official capacity he presided at some time over every Conference in the United States and inspected Methodist missionary work in Mexico, South America, Europe, China, and Japan, doing much to shape the mis-

sionary policy of his Church. He was a delegate to the Ecumenical Conferences in London, 1881, Washington, 1891, and Toronto, 1911. With respect to church organization he insisted upon strict adherence to the written law, but otherwise he was liberal in his views. He was noted for his wit and for his optimistic spirit. He was happiest when, attired in a white slouch hat and linen duster, he started out for a day's recreation with fish bait in his pocket. His wife and three of his five children survived him. In recognition of his work for the colored race the name of Central Tennessee College, in Nashville, was changed in 1900 to Walden University.

[D. H. Moore, *John Morgan Walden* (1915); *Biog. Cyc. and Portrait Gallery . . . of the State of Ohio,* vol. V (n.d.); *The Biog. Encyc. of Ohio of the Nineteenth Century* (1876); H. C. Jennings, "Bishop John Morgan Walden," *Jour. of the Twenty-seventh Delegated Gen. Conference of the Methodist Episcopal Church* (1916); C. T. Greve, *Centennial Hist. of Cincinnati and Representative Citizens* (1904), vol. II; *Who's Who in America,* 1912–13; *Cincinnati Enquirer,* Jan. 22, and *Cincinnati Times-Star,* Jan. 28, 1914; Walden Papers, in possession of Mrs. S. O. Royal.]   W. E. S—h.

WALDERNE, RICHARD (*c.* 1615–June 1689), pioneer, soldier, was born at Alchester in Warwickshire, England, the eighth child and seventh son of William and Catharine (Raven) Walderne. He was baptized on Jan. 6, 1615 (*New England Historical and Genealogical Register,* January 1854, p. 78). After a preliminary visit "to see the country" (1635–37), he emigrated to New England about 1640, settling at Dover, N. H. With him he brought a wife, of whom nothing is known beyond the tradition (Bodge, *post,* p. 293) that she was "a Gentlewoman of a very good family (whose parents were very unwilling She Should come away)." Having acquired large tracts of land at Cochecho (part of the present Dover) and Penacook (now Concord), Walderne became principally engaged in lumbering and trade with the Indians. He filled at various times practically all of the important local offices, both administrative and judicial, and served almost without interruption from 1654 to 1674 and again in 1677 as a representative to the General Court at Boston, in which body he was several times chosen speaker (Scales, *post,* pp. 202f.).

Especially delegated in 1662 to deal with the Quaker "menace" at Dover, Walderne zealously discharged his duty by sentencing three "vagabond" women of the sect to be whipped at the cart's tail through thirteen towns to the end of the Bay Colony's jurisdiction (Bouton, *post,* I, 243). His achievements as major of the Norfolk County militia were inconspicuous except on one occasion when, by a "contrivement" akin to treachery, he managed to take without bloodshed some two hundred hostile Indians, who had sought refuge by mingling with the pacified tribes of New Hampshire. Some six or seven of these captives were later hanged and most of the remainder sold into slavery (Belknap, *post*, I, 142f.; Bouton, I, 357–60; Bodge, p. 306). The incident was remembered bitterly by the local tribes, and when with the resumption of general hostilities Cochecho was raided on the night of June 27–28, 1689, the Major was singled out by them for special torture before being put to death (Scales, pp. 219f.).

Upon the establishment of a separate provincial government for New Hampshire in 1680, Walderne was appointed one of the President's Council; and after the death of President Cutt in 1681 he became acting president until the arrival of Cranfield. His extensive land holdings and prominent position in the colony marked him naturally as the one first to be sued by Robert Mason in the attempt of the latter to make good his hereditary claims. Walderne refused to defend himself at the trial or produce evidence of his title, for he declared that the jury were personally interested and hence incapable of doing justice. Judgment was given against him and a fine imposed for the "mutinous and seditious words" with which he had addressed the court (Bouton, p. 514, note). Walderne was twice married; the second time, to Anne Scammon, sister of Richard Scammon of local fame (*New England Historical and Genealogical Register*, January 1854, p. 65, note; January 1855, pp. 55f.). His descendants continued for generations to occupy a distinguished place in New Hampshire political affairs.

[For sources see John Scales, *Hist. Memoranda Concerning Persons and Places in Old Dover, N. H., Collected by Rev. Dr. Alonzo Hall Quint, and Others* (1900); S. D. Bell, in *N. H. Hist. Soc. Colls.*, vol. VIII (1866); G. M. Bodge, *Soldiers in King Philip's War* (3rd ed., 1906); Nathaniel Bouton, *Provincial Papers, Documents and Records Relating to the Province of N. H.*, vol. I (1867), vol. II (1868). The account of the seizure of the Indians at Cochecho was first given in Jeremy Belknap, *The Hist. of N. H.* (3 vols., 1784–92) and was based upon tradition; but some corroborative evidence appears in the *Provincial Papers* and a critical discussion of the incident is to be found in Bodge.]
G. P. B.

WALDO, DAVID (Apr. 30, 1802–May 20, 1878), physician, Santa Fé trader, banker, was the son of Jedediah and Polly (Porter) Waldo and a descendant of Cornelius Waldo who settled in Ipswich, Mass., as early as 1647. He was born in Clarksburg, Harrison County, Va. (now W. Va.), and in his early youth engaged in rafting logs down the Ohio River. In 1820 he moved to Gasconade County, Mo., where he prospered, and served in various county offices. He was

also major of the militia. Determining to attend medical college, he set about cutting pine logs in order to finance his education. Binding his logs into a large raft he floated them down the Gasconade, Missouri, and Mississippi rivers, and delivered them to Laveille and Morton at St. Louis for the sum of $500. He pursued his medical studies at Transylvania University, Lexington, Ky.

Waldo began to practise medicine in Gasconade County, but soon moved to Osceola, then to Independence, Mo., and finally to Taos, in what is now the state of New Mexico. On May 5, 1829, he received his third degree in Masonry from Missouri Lodge No. 1, but he subsequently returned to Taos; he became a citizen of Mexico in 1830, and an *ayuntamiento* of Taos. He is supposed to have become interested in commerce as early as 1827 and he finally gave up his practice to enter the Santa Fé trade, in which he continued for over thirty years. He amassed a great fortune before the Mexican War, and returned to Missouri, where he subsequently became captain of Company A in the regiment commanded by Alexander William Doniphan [*q.v.*]. One of his brothers was killed at Mora in 1847. After the war, Waldo returned to Independence, Mo., and on Mar. 27, 1849, married Eliza Jane Norris, born June 25, 1822, at Mount Sterling, Ky. They had five children.

Of several fortunes acquired in the overland trade, Waldo lost two—one by a storm when trading in Chihuahua, and the other by reason of a fire which destroyed his large train of merchandise intended for trade with Fort Laramie. It is said that his sustained energy, perseverance, and indomitable will gave him a force quite irresistible. He had quick perception and sound judgment, was honest and fair in all his dealings, and was generally liked and respected. He owned and enjoyed a large and valuable library and spoke French and Spanish with facility. During the Mexican War he rendered useful service in translating documents captured from the Mexicans by American troops. An ardent Mason, he gave a valuable lot in Taos to Bent Lodge No. 204, on June 15, 1860. After his retirement from the overland trade he made contracts with the United States government for carrying provisions to the army at distant points and carrying mail to Santa Fé. The latter part of his life was devoted largely to banking. He died in Independence, Mo.

[*Waldo MSS.*, Mo. Hist. Soc., St. Louis; Waldo Lincoln, *Geneal. of the Waldo Family* (1902), vol. I; *Missouri Grand Lodge Bull.* (St. Louis), Apr. 1925; W. E. Connelley, *Doniphan's Expedition* (1907); *Hist. of Franklin, Jefferson, Washington, Crawford and Gasconade Counties, Mo.* (1888); *House Report No. 284,*

34 Cong., 1 Sess.; *Down the Santa Fé Trail and into Mexico: The Diary of Susan Shelby Magoffin* (1926), ed. by Stella M. Drumm; R. E. Twitchell, *The Leading Facts of New Mexican Hist.* (5 vols., 1911–17), vols. II, V.]

                             S. M. D.

WALDO, SAMUEL (1695–May 23, 1759), Boston merchant, capitalist, and politician, was a grandson of Cornelius Waldo who was living in Ipswich, Mass., as early as 1647, and the eldest surviving child among the twelve born to Jonathan and Hannah (Mason) Waldo of Boston. He was baptized in the First Church of that city on Dec. 22, 1695. According to tradition, he went to the Boston Latin School, which his sons later attended. He began business as a merchant on capital advanced by his father; and in 1722 married Lucy, daughter of Major Francis and Sarah (Whipple) Wainwright of Ipswich. Their children were Samuel, Jr., Lucy, Hannah, Francis, Sarah, and Ralph. Waldo imported miscellaneous merchandise such as "choice Irish duck, fine Florence wine, negro slaves, and Irish butter" which he sold from his home on Queen Street. He also dealt in rum, fish, and lumber. As an official mast-agent, he collaborated with Thomas Westbrook of Falmouth (Portland, Me.) in getting out white pines for the British navy. One product of his activities in this line was the famous colonial lawsuit of *Frost* vs. *Leighton* (see *American Historical Review*, January 1897). It was Waldo who employed Leighton to cut timber on Frost's farm, and Waldo's lawyer who defended him.

Land speculation on a great scale was Waldo's chief interest, and his career is significant mainly for his unwearied efforts to develop his wild lands on the coast of Maine between the Muscongus and Penobscot rivers. In 1729, when Col. David Dunbar established himself at Pemaquid on the Maine coast and began to bring in settlers, the Muscongus proprietors chose Waldo to go to England and press their claims against Dunbar. Waldo remained abroad two years, until the Privy Council handed down a verdict which gave him victory. He now became the chief proprietor of the Muscongus grant, henceforth called the Waldo patent, and started to settle the region and to manufacture lime and iron. At the same time he entered on large plans with Thomas Westbrook for industries on the Stroudwater River in Falmouth. Strong opposition to his settlement projects arose, however, and doubts as to validity of his title to the eastern lands were circulated. To meet this attack Waldo published in 1736 a pamphlet entitled *A Defence of the Title . . . to a Tract of Land . . . Commonly Called Muscongus Lands,* setting forth proofs of his legal ownership. Blaming Gov. Jonathan

Belcher [*q.v.*] for his difficulties, he returned to England in 1738 and for three years was a leader in the conspiracy to oust the governor. Belcher's successor, commissioned in 1741, was Waldo's permanent attorney, William Shirley [*q.v.*].

About this time financial difficulties beset Waldo. One of the means he adopted for extricating himself was to bring about in 1743 a foreclosure against his former partner, Thomas Westbrook, as a result of which he acquired all of Westbrook's properties. With a friend in the governor's chair, he also resumed operations in Maine, only to have them blocked by King George's War. In the Louisburg campaign of 1745 he served as a brigadier-general, second in command of the Massachusetts forces. An unsigned portrait of Waldo with the harbor and fort of Louisburg in the background, now in the Walker Art Gallery at Bowdoin College, was painted at this period, presumably in 1749 and probably by the artist Robert Feke [*q.v.*], rather than by John Smibert, to whom it has sometimes been attributed (H. W. Foote, *Robert Feke, Colonial Painter,* 1930, pp. 72–73, 198–200). The picture shows Waldo as an elegant military officer, tall and portly. In the 1750's he again renewed his land schemes and advertised abroad for settlers, chiefly in Scotland, Ireland, and Germany. By this time he and Governor Shirley had become bitter enemies as the result of a dispute over certain military fees which Waldo claimed and the Governor refused to sanction. In 1757 Shirley was replaced by Thomas Pownall [*q.v.*], and in the spring of 1759 the new governor conducted an expedition down to the Penobscot River and there built a fort. Waldo, now sixty-three years old, accompanied the party; on May 23, while walking about near the present city of Bangor, he fell dead of apoplexy. He was buried at the new fort, but in 1760 his body was removed to King's Chapel Burial Ground, Boston. Today his association with Maine is perpetuated in several names such as Waldoboro, Waldo County, Brigadier's Island, and Mount Waldo.

[Knox MSS., Mass. Hist. Soc., vol. L; "The Belcher Papers," *Mass. Hist. Soc. Colls.,* 6 ser., VI–VII (1893–94); *Correspondence of William Shirley* (2 vols., 1912), ed. by C. H. Lincoln; G. A. Wood, *William Shirley, Gov. of Mass.,* vol. I (1920); Court Files (Suffolk) of the Supreme Judicial Court, Boston, 1737–1740/41; Thomas Hutchinson, *Hist. of the Province of Mass. Bay,* vol. II (1765); Waldo Lincoln, *Geneal. of the Waldo Family* (1902), vol. I; *New-Eng. Hist. and Geneal. Reg.,* July 1874; Jennison Papers, Am. Antiquarian Soc.; *Me. Hist. Soc. Colls.,* 1 ser. IX (1887), 2 ser. XI (1908).]

                             A. C. F.

WALDO, SAMUEL LOVETT (Apr. 6, 1783–Feb. 16, 1861), portrait painter, was born at Windham, Conn., one of eight children of Zacheus Waldo and Esther (Stevens) Waldo. His father, a farmer, was a descendant of Cornelius Waldo who emigrated to New England about 1647. Waldo was educated in the country schools and at the age of sixteen was allowed to go to Hartford to take drawing lessons of an obscure portrait painter named Stewart, who was an indifferent instructor. Having sold a picture for fifteen dollars, the young student presently (1803) took a studio in Hartford, but he met with scant success and was obliged to supplement his slender income by painting signs. In Litchfield, Conn., where he painted several portraits he met the Hon. John Rutledge of South Carolina, who invited him to go to Charleston. There he met with pronounced success and remained about three years. By 1806 he had laid aside enough money to go to England, with letters to Benjamin West and John Singleton Copley [*qq.v.*] in London. According to Dunlap, he painted a few portraits in London at five guineas each, "but had not employment enough to pay expenses" (*post*, II, 357). He was married at Liverpool or Chester on Apr. 8, 1808, to Josephine Elza Wood, who died in 1825.

Returning to America in January 1809, he settled in New York. There for more than fifty years he worked diligently as a portrait painter, after 1820 in partnership with William Jewett [*q.v.*], one of his pupils. In 1826 he was one of the thirty founders of the National Academy of Design and in 1847 became an associate. The firm of Waldo and Jewett prospered, and numerous excellent if somewhat literal likenesses were executed by the two painters in collaboration. It is probable that Waldo painted the heads and hands, while his assistant painted the backgrounds and costumes. Examples of their work in public collections include the portrait of G. W. Parke Custis of Arlington, Va., in the Corcoran Gallery, Washington; a sketch from life of Gen. Andrew Jackson (1817), and "Old Pat, the Independent Beggar," with several other canvases, including a self-portrait and a portrait of his second wife, in the Metropolitan Museum, New York; the portrait of Mrs. William Steele, in the City Art Museum of St. Louis, Mo.; the likeness of Peter Remsen owned by the New York Historical Society; several portraits of former mayors of New York in the City Hall; the portrait of President James Madison in the possession of the Century Association, New York; and two portraits of John Trumbull. Thomas B. Clarke acquired his portrait of R. G. Livingston de Peyster (1828), a prominent New York merchant, that of Rebecca Sanford

Barlow (1810), and a portrait of a lady which has been warmly praised for its freshness of color and admirable modeling. Isham aptly describes the work of Waldo and Jewett as "scores of heads . . . of dignified, benevolent gentlemen, with white hair and white chokers, or of ladies in wonderful caps and shawls" (*post*, p. 141) and praises their "quiet and unaggressive" painting for its technical merit. Other critics were not so indulgent; one of them calls Waldo "really a commercial face maker," who was "competent but never inspired" (Mather, *post*, p. 26). After the death of his first wife, Waldo married Deliverance Mapes on May 8, 1826, in New York City. He died in New York in 1861, at the age of seventy-seven.

[Waldo Lincoln, *Geneal. of the Waldo Family* (1902); vital records, Windham, Conn.; William Dunlap, *A Hist. . . . of the Arts of Design in the U. S. A.* (3 vols., 1918), ed. by F. W. Bayley and C. E. Goodspeed; Samuel Isham, *The Hist. of Am. Painting* (1905); F. F. Sherman, in *Art in America*, Feb. 1930; F. J. Mather, C. R. Morey, and W. J. Henderson, *The Am. Spirit in Art* (1927); H. W. French, *Art and Artists in Conn.* (1879); *Art News*, Jan. 24, 1931; cats. of T. B. Clark Coll., 1899 and 1928, and of Corcoran Gall. of Art, 1908; death notice in *N. Y. Herald*, Feb. 18, 1861.]
W. H. D.

WALDO, SAMUEL PUTNAM (Mar. 12, 1779–Feb. 23, 1826), author, was born at Pomfret, Conn., the third child of Samuel and Mary (Putnam) Waldo, a grandson of Gen. Israel Putnam [*q.v.*], and a descendant of Cornelius Waldo who was living in Ipswich, Mass., as early as 1647. Of his boyhood the records are meager. His writings give evidence of his early reading and taste for literature, and according to his own statement (*Biographical Sketches . . . of Naval Heroes*, p. 283), he was in Boston in 1797 at the launching of the U.S.S. *Constitution*. There is no record of his attendance at college or service in the War of 1812, but he speaks of travel in the South and of having visited Jefferson at Monticello in 1813 (*Ibid.*, p. 388). He studied law and practised at East Windsor, Conn., from about 1805 to 1816. In the next year he began his literary career by writing out and publishing at Hartford Capt. Archibald Robbins' oral narrative of his shipwreck and slavery in Africa in 1815–17. This work went through eleven editions in one year. Though the title, *Journal Comprising an Account of the Loss of the Brig Commerce . . . by Archibald Robbins,* gives no hint of Waldo's part in its composition, he identified himself in later works as its "compiler."

Of the popular writings he published in the next five years, the first was *The Tour of James Monroe, President of the United States, through the Northern and Eastern States in 1817* (1818), later editions of which included also an account of President Monroe's summer travel in 1818 and a sketch of his life. Waldo's *Memoirs of Andrew Jackson, Major General . . . and Commander in Chief of the Division of the South* (1818) passed quickly through five editions, and at least two reprints appeared in 1828, one as "by a citizen of Massachusetts" and another as "by a citizen of Hagerstown, Md." Like his other books, it met a contemporary interest but has slight historical value, leaning heavily on *The Life of Andrew Jackson* published by John H. Eaton [*q.v.*] in 1817. Waldo had, however, some acquaintance with naval officers, had access to General Putnam's books and papers, and, according to his own statement (Preface to *Biographical Sketches . . . of Naval Heroes*), had collected "records, pamphlets, newspapers, and even hand-bills" of the Revolutionary period. Hence somewhat more value is attached to the *Life and Character of Stephen Decatur* (1821) and to his last book, *Biographical Sketches of Distinguished American Naval Heroes in the War of the Revolution* (1823). In the preface to the latter volume he remarked that he had sold 80,000 copies of his works in the preceding four years but "added nothing to his pecuniary means." In 1819 he established at Hartford the *Rural Magazine and Farmers' Monthly Museum,* but published only five numbers, February–July (file in the Library of Congress). In a postscript to the last number he stated that "the work has been solely furnished by the Editor, except a few original poems." He also wrote "A Brief Sketch of the Indictment, Trial, and Conviction of Stephen and Jesse Boorn for the Murder of Russell Colvin" which appeared as the third part of a book on this sensational trial—*Mystery Developed, or Russell Colvin (Supposed to be Murdered) in Full Life . . .* (1820). Though his writings show some reading and range of interests, they have otherwise little distinction. His biographical formula was a pound of rhetoric to an ounce of fact, and he was much inclined to dilate on the blessings of his country, free from the "poverty, crime, or social disorders" of other lands. He was unmarried. His death at Hartford in early middle age is said to have been hastened by the death of his betrothed.

[Waldo Lincoln, *Geneal. of the Waldo Family* (1902), vol. I; J. D. Hall, *Geneal. and Biog. of the Waldos in America* (1883); J. H. Trumbull, *Memorial Hist. of Hartford County, Conn.* (1886), vol. I; Pomfret (Conn.) Vital Records, Conn. State Lib.; *Connecticut Observer* (Hartford), Mar. 6, 1826.]   A. W—t.

WALDRON, RICHARD [See WALDERNE, RICHARD, 1615–1689].

WALES, JAMES ALBERT (Aug. 30, 1852–Dec. 6, 1886), cartoonist, was born in Clyde,

Ohio, the son of William Washington and Martha (Dimm) Wales. After attending school in Sandusky he went to Toledo to study wood engraving. Later he went to the engraving shop of Bogart & Stillman in Cincinnati, where he found another Ohio boy, William Allen Rogers [*q.v.*], also trying to learn to draw. He drew political cartoons on the presidential campaign of 1872 for the *Cleveland Leader* and in 1873 went to New York, where some of his early work was done for *Wild Oats* and *Frank Leslie's Illustrated Newspaper*. In the fall of 1875, with Frank Hegger, the portrait photographer, he went to London. He drew for *Judy*, the *Illustrated Sporting and Dramatic News,* and the *London Illustrated News,* tried for a position on the staff of *Vanity Fair,* and made a trip to Paris, where he spent most of his time studying the best drawings in the Louvre. On his return to New York he worked for *Frank Leslie's* for a time. In 1877 he joined the staff of the English edition of *Puck,* established by Joseph Keppler [*q.v.*] and Adolph Schwarzmann. On Mar. 25, 1878, he married Claudia Marshall Cooper, a first cousin of Richard Harding Davis [*q.v.*].

Beginning with Feb. 12, 1879, Wales started in *Puck* a series of full-page political portraits under the general title of "Puck's Pantheon." Incisive, sardonic, they were well drawn and quite comparable to the best work being done. These drawings definitely established his reputation. Soon afterwards he was doing front and back covers and double-page spreads for *Puck* on social and political subjects. Characteristic examples are those on the Chinese question (Mar. 12, 1879), "A Suggestion for the Next St. Paddy's Day Parade" (Mar. 19, 1879), and "The Irish Idea of a 'Christian Burial'" (May 7, 1879). Less dramatically vindictive in political satire than Thomas Nast [*q.v.*], but more of a realist than Keppler, he had a decided and recognized gift for portraiture. Rogers spoke enthusiastically of his work. When the *Judge* was started by W. J. Arkell, Oct. 29, 1881, as a political rival to *Puck,* Wales took a prominent part in it, but in June 1885, becoming dissatisfied with the paper's policy, he returned to *Puck.* He died suddenly in his thirty-fifth year from a heart attack and was buried at Clyde. He was survived by his wife and two sons. He was tall and ruddy-faced, with a silky turned-up moustache and wore pince-nez. There is little question that if he had lived he would have been recognized as one of the foremost American caricaturists.

[Frank Weitenkampf, *Am. Graphic Art* (1924); W. A. Rogers, *A World Worth While* (1922); obituaries in *N. Y. Times, N. Y. Tribune, World* (N. Y.), Dec. 7,

1886, *New Yorker Staats-Zeitung,* Dec. 8, and *Mail and Express* (N. Y.), Dec. 9; *Journalist,* Dec. 18, 1886; information from J. A. Wales, Jr., E. P. Allen, and S. H. Horgan.]   W. P.

WALES, LEONARD EUGENE (Nov. 26, 1823–Feb. 8, 1897), judge, was born at Wilmington, Del., the son of John and Ann (Patten) Wales, and a descendant of Nathaniel Wales who came with his father, Nathaniel, from Yorkshire, England, to Boston in 1635. John Wales was prominent in public life in Delaware, and from 1849 to 1851 served as United States senator. Leonard completed his preparatory studies at the Hopkins Grammar School, New Haven, Conn., and then entered Yale, where he was graduated in 1845. Having studied law in his father's office in Wilmington, he was admitted to the bar on May 8, 1848. For the ensuing two years he gave much of his time to editorial work on the *Delaware State Journal,* organ of the Whig party, to which the Wales family adhered. In May 1849 he was appointed clerk of the United States circuit and district courts for Delaware and served as such until 1864. In 1853 and 1854 he was city solicitor of Wilmington, and in 1856 he took an active part in organizing the Republican party in Delaware. Upon President Lincoln's call for volunteers in 1861, Wales was among the first in the state to respond. He was commissioned a second lieutenant in Company E, 1st Delaware Volunteers, which was stationed along the line of the Philadelphia, Wilmington & Baltimore Railroad, south of the Susquehanna River. After the expiration of his three months' term of enlistment, he returned to civil life, but in May 1863 he was appointed a member of the Delaware board of enrollment, which administered the national draft law.

In September 1864 Gov. William Cannon appointed him as associate justice (for New Castle County) of the Delaware superior court. Entering upon his duties Oct. 1, 1864, he held the office for nearly a score of years, functioning not only as a *nisi prius* judge and in the orphans' court but also, in accordance with the Delaware system, sitting *en banc* as a member of the court of general sessions of the peace and jail delivery, of the court of oyer and terminer, and of the court of errors and appeals. Upon assuming judicial station he ceased to participate in partisan politics but continued certain quasi-public activities. He was especially interested in the work of the Historical Society of Delaware and served for a number of years as its president. True to ancestral traditions, he promoted various educational enterprises, being a founder of

the West End Reading-Room in Wilmington and of the Ferris Reform School.

On Mar. 10, 1884, upon nomination of President Arthur, Wales was confirmed as United States judge for the district of Delaware, and was sworn in four days later. Subsequently, for about three years, he took over the work of the judge of the New Jersey district, who had become incapacitated. It is said that only in a single instance were any of his decisions reversed upon appeal to a higher tribunal (*Report of the . . . American Bar Association, post,* p. 532). His reported opinions indicate learning, logical reasoning, and clarity of expression. After the establishment of the circuit courts of appeal in 1891, he was regularly called to sit with its judges when they held sessions in his circuit. He continued performing his duties almost to the last, dying in his native city after less than a week's illness. He was never married.

[C. M. R. Carter, *John Redington . . . with Notes on the Wales Family* (1909); *Obit. Record Grads. Yale Univ., 1890–1900* (1900); *Hist. and Biog. Encyc. of Del.* (1882); 3–6 *Houston's Del. Reports; Report of the . . . Am. Bar Asso.* (1897); "Leonard Eugene Wales" (1898), in *Hist. and Biog. Papers of the Hist. Soc. of Del.,* vol. III; *Every Evening: Wilmington Daily Commercial,* Feb. 9, 1897.]   C. S. L.

WALKE, HENRY (Dec. 24, 1808–Mar. 8, 1896), naval officer, was born on his father's plantation, "The Ferry," in Princess Anne County, Va., the son of Anthony and Susan (Carmichael) Walke, and a descendant of Thomas Walke who came from Barbados to Virginia in 1662. His father, a graduate of Yale College and former diplomatic agent to Algiers, settled with his family at Chillicothe, Ohio, in 1811. Henry attended the local academy, and on Feb. 1, 1827, entered the navy as a midshipman. During his early cruising he was at sea in two hurricanes, one in the *Natchez* in 1827, and another in the *Ontario* in 1829 in which he showed characteristic courage by leading men aloft to furl a topsail. He was made a lieutenant in 1839, sailed around the world in the *Boston,* 1840–43, and in the Mexican War was executive of the bomb-brig *Vesuvius,* participating in operations against Vera Cruz, Alvarado, Tuxpan, and Tabasco. Just before the Civil War he commanded the storeship *Supply* at Pensacola, and after the seizure of the Pensacola Navy Yard by the South, on Jan. 12, 1861, he entered under a flag of truce and took its garrison and non-combatants to New York. Though obviously justifiable, this action involved leaving his station and violation of orders. He was court-martialed, but the sentence "to be admonished" was very lightly imposed.

In September 1861, he joined Commodore

Foote's flotilla on the upper Mississippi, and served during the next two years with great energy and distinction. Commanding the gunboat *Tyler* in the autumn of 1861, he was frequently under fire in reconnaissance work, and on Nov. 7 with the *Tyler* and *Lexington* effectively covered transport and troop movements in Grant's operation against Belmont. He was shifted to the *Carondelet* in January 1862 and participated in the attack on Fort Henry, Tennessee River, on Feb. 6. Without returning to the base at Cairo, he then proceeded in advance to the next point of attack, Fort Donelson, Cumberland River, and on Feb. 13 carried on alone a six-hour bombardment that, in his opinion, did more damage than the attack of the four ironclads, including his own, next day. His most celebrated exploit was the subsequent running of the batteries at Island No. 10, an operation which he alone favored in the preliminary council, eagerly volunteered for, and, after thorough preparation, executed successfully on the stormy night of Apr. 4. This was "one of the most daring and dramatic events of the war" (A. T. Mahan, *The Gulf and Inland Waters,* 1883, p. 34). The *Carondelet,* with the *Pittsburg* under Egbert Thompson [*q.v.*], rendered invaluable service in covering the army's passage of the river below. The personnel of both vessels received official thanks, and General Pope wrote warmly of Walke's "thorough and brilliant" cooperation (*War of the Rebellion: Official Records, Navy,* XXII, 724). The *Carondelet* was also conspicuous in engagements with the Confederate flotilla above Fort Pillow, May 10, at Memphis, June 6, and in the hard running fight with the ram *Arkansas* in the Yazoo River, July 15.

Walke became a captain, though only after reconsidered action, on July 16, 1862. In command of the new ironclad *Lafayette,* February–August 1863, he fought under Porter in the passing of the Vicksburg batteries on Apr. 16, the five-hour action at Grand Gulf, Apr. 29, and subsequent operations until the fall of Vicksburg. From September 1863 to August 1865 he commanded the *Sacramento* in the Atlantic in pursuit of Confederate raiders, and held the *Rappahannock* blockaded at Calais for fifteen months. He was made commodore in 1866; commanded the Mound City Naval Station, 1868–69; became rear admiral in 1870; and retired in 1871. His home thereafter was in Brooklyn, N. Y. He was thrice married, to Sara J. Aim, Jane Ellen Burges, and Julia Reed, the last of whom with two sons and two daughters survived him. His skill in painting, which he cultivated in later years, is evidenced by a number of pictures, in-

cluding the sketches that illustrate his *Naval Scenes and Reminiscences of the Civil War* (1877). This book, while historically valuable, is contentious in tone, emphasizing his war service, which he felt was inadequately recognized in his post-war assignments. He asserted in an appeal to President Grant that he had "fought more for his country than any other officer in the navy" (Personnel Files, Navy Library). The statement seems almost justified by his gunboat record and his eager exploitation of every opportunity for fighting.

[Sources cited in the text; *Officers of the Army and Navy (Regular) Who Served in the Civil War* (1892), ed. by W. H. Powell, Edward Shippen; L. R. Hamersly, *The Records of Living Officers of the U. S. Navy . . .* (4th ed., 1890); "The Walke Family of Lower Norfolk County," *Va. Mag. of Hist. and Biog.,* Oct. 1897; *Court Martial of Commander Henry Walke, U. S. N.,* (1861); obits. in *Mil. Order of Loyal Legion of U. S., Commandery . . . of N. Y., Circular no. 2,* series of 1896–99; *N. Y. Herald,* Mar. 7, 9, 1896.]   A. W—t.

WALKER, ALEXANDER (Oct. 13, 1818–Jan. 24, 1893), journalist and author, was born in Fredericksburg, Va., the son of Alexander and Susan Walker. His father was a merchant. The boy attended Fredericksburg Academy, and, after a brief experience teaching school, entered the University of Virginia in 1836. Here he studied ancient languages, mathematics, and natural philosophy. He was out the next year, but returned to study law during the session of 1838–39. In 1840 he opened a law office in New Orleans, during the heat of the Harrison-Van Buren campaign. He at once offered his services to the Democratic leaders and made many speeches in the campaign. He was later a member of nearly all the ante-bellum Democratic conventions. Indeed, his interest in politics and journalism prevented his law practice from becoming extensive. He became one of the managers of the *Jeffersonian* of New Orleans, the chief Democratic organ of the state. In 1842 he married Mary Elizabeth McFarlane, daughter of Dr. James S. McFarlane, head of the Marine Hospital in New Orleans. By appointment of Governor Johnson, he was judge of the city court in New Orleans from 1846 to 1850.

Walker was a firm believer in "manifest destiny" and heartily sympathized with those who were seeking to unite all the countries of the continent into one nation. In 1845 he urged the annexation of Texas; he was one of the supporters of the noted filibuster, William Walker [*q.v.*], and in 1851 he was a backer of the disastrous expedition of Gen. Narciso Lopez to Cuba. During the Mexican War he was connected with the *New Orleans Daily Delta.* In 1852 the *Delta* office published his *City Digest.*

His unsigned account of the yellow fever epidemic in New Orleans appeared in *Harper's Magazine* in November 1853. From 1855 to 1857 he edited the *Cincinnati Enquirer,* then the leading Democratic paper in the West. In 1856 he published *Jackson and New Orleans,* a very full account of the achievements of Jackson and the American army in 1814–15. Four years later he added a chapter to this book and changed its title to *The Life of Andrew Jackson* (1860); in this form it was reissued in 1866 and again in 1890. From Cincinnati he went to Washington, D. C., but after a short stay returned in 1858 to New Orleans and the *Daily Delta.*

He was a member of the Louisiana secession convention in 1861 and was subsequently with Gen. Albert Sidney Johnston's army in Tennessee; he wrote a graphic account of the battle of Shiloh, which appeared in the *Delta* and in H. C. Clarke's *Diary of the War for Separation* (1862). When New Orleans was captured he was sent for a short time as a prisoner to Ship Island. After the surrender of Lee at Appomattox he returned to New Orleans. With Henry J. Labatt he compiled a work called *The Bankrupt Law* (1867). He edited the *New Orleans Times* until its suspension by Judge E. H. Durell [*q.v.*] during the controversy between Henry Clay Warmoth and P. B. S. Pinchback [*qq.v.*] over the governorship in 1872; he then helped establish the *Herald,* which was merged with the *Daily Picayune* in 1874. He continued to edit the *Picayune* until 1875. Thereafter, although not again an editor, he was a frequent contributor to the daily press. He wrote on New Orleans duels, on the Myra Clark Gaines case, and on other matters of local history and tradition. In 1884 he contributed to the *Times-Democrat* a series of articles on General Butler in New Orleans. He wrote zestfully, with a fluent style. Journalism was his chief interest, his social inclinations enabling him to get a peculiarly rich satisfaction out of newspaper experiences. He died, survived by two sons, at the home of the younger, in Fort Smith, Ark.

[*Univ. of Va. alumni records; Univ. of Va. . . . with Biog. Sketches* (1904); obituaries in the *Daily Picayune* and *Times-Democrat,* both of New Orleans, Jan. 25, 1893; information from the librarian of the Wallace Library, Fredericksburg, Va.]   R. P. M.

WALKER, AMASA (May 4, 1799–Oct. 29, 1875), business man, economist, congressman, was born in Woodstock, Conn., the son of Walter and Priscilla (Carpenter) Walker, and a descendant of Samuel Walker of Lynn, Mass., who came to New England about 1630. His childhood was spent in Brookfield, Mass., to which place his parents moved not long after his birth.

Here he attended the district school and worked on the farm—or for the card manufacturers of Leicester at seventy-five cents a week—until he was fifteen years old, when he became a clerk in a country store. During the next six years he varied this employment by farm work, by teaching, and by an attempt to prepare for Amherst College which failed because of his frail health. At twenty-one, with a partner, he purchased a store in West Brookfield, but three years later sold his share in the small business and became an agent for the Methuen Manufacturing Company. His next move carried him to Boston, where in 1825 he established a boot-and-shoe store with Charles G. Carleton, whose sister Emeline he married on July 6, 1826. Her death occurred two years later, and on June 23, 1834, he married Hannah Ambrose of Concord, N. H. To this marriage three children were born.

While he was extending his business southward and westward from Boston, Walker's attention was drawn to the railroad as the coming means of transportation. In a series of articles published in the *Boston Daily Advertiser and Patriot* in 1835, under the signature "South Market Street," he urged the building of a railroad to connect Boston and Albany; he was also one of a committee to visit Albany in order to induce the citizens of that city to build their end of such a road. Four years later, on a trip to the West, he presented to audiences in St. Louis and Alton, Ill., the desirability of a railroad connecting Boston with the Mississippi River, but his suggestion that the time would come when a man might travel from Boston to St. Louis eating and sleeping on the train provoked only mirth.

In 1840, being now provided with a modest livelihood despite heavy losses in the panic of 1837, he retired from business, partly because of ill health but also because he wished to devote his time to study and to public service. The first months after his retirement were spent in Florida in search of health, but for the most part the years which followed were crowded with activities. In 1842 he visited Oberlin College, which he had helped to found, and for seven years thereafter, at irregular intervals and without remuneration, he lectured at Oberlin on political economy. From 1853 to 1860 he was an examiner in political economy at Harvard, and from 1860 to 1869 he lectured at Amherst College.

Walker's special interest in the field of economics was the monetary system, to which he had turned his attention after the panic of 1837. In 1857 he published in *Hunt's Merchants' Maga-*

zine and Commercial Review a series of articles on the subject, which also appeared in pamphlet form as *The Nature and Uses of Money and Mixed Currency* (1857). The panic of 1857 gave him an opportunity to put his opinions to practical test. When the business men of Boston agreed to maintain specie payment in that city Walker argued that it could not be done for more than two weeks and that the tightening of credit necessitated by the effort would result in the ruin of many business houses. His proposal that the suspension should take place at once met with shocked opposition; but twelve days later, after a number of failures, suspension was forced upon the Boston banks. The publicity which this episode gained brought him much into demand as a speaker on currency problems. His most considerable publication, *The Science of Wealth: A Manual of Political Economy* (1866), was widely read and in 1876 was quoted by Walker's son, Francis Amasa Walker [*q.v.*], in his better-known work, *The Wages Question* (pp. 141, 231). Amasa Walker's qualifications for the authorship of his treatise he described as "a practical knowledge of business and banking affairs generally, and a most earnest and persistent search for the truth in all matters appertaining to my favorite science" (*Science of Wealth*), p. ix).

In politics, Walker was successively a Clay protectionist, a member of the Anti-Masonic party, a Democrat, a Free-Soiler, and a Republican. In 1848 he was elected to the Massachusetts House of Representatives and was the candidate of Free-Soilers and Democrats for speaker. The next autumn he entered the state Senate. In 1851 and 1852 he was secretary of state of Massachusetts, and the following year he served as chairman of the committee on suffrage of the constitutional convention of the state. In 1859 he was chosen for a second term in the state House of Representatives, where he assisted in revising the Massachusetts banking laws. Elected as a Republican to fill a vacancy in Congress (Dec. 1, 1862–Mar. 3, 1863), he joined in the monetary debates of that body and throughout the remainder of his life, both in his private correspondence and in articles in periodicals, he frequently expressed his views on monetary questions, especially his belief in the need for contraction of the currency.

During the years after his retirement from business Walker lived in the Brookfield residence which had belonged to his father. He was president of the Boston Temperance Society in 1839; ten years earlier he had been a founder and the first secretary of the Boston Lyceum. Though warmly attached to the anti-slavery cause, he insisted that reform must be accomplished by constitutional means. His heart was also enlisted in the cause of world peace and as vice-president he attended the International Peace Congress held in England in 1844 and the Paris Congress of 1849.

[Holmes Ammidown, *Hist. Colls.* (1874), vol. II; F. A. Walker, *Memoir of Hon. Amasa Walker, LL.D.* (1888), repr. from *New-Eng. Hist. and Geneal. Reg.*, Apr. 1888; *New-Eng. Hist. and Geneal. Reg.*, Jan. 1898; J. P. Munroe, *A Life of Francis Amasa Walker* (1923); D. H. Hurd, *Hist. of Worcester County, Mass.* (1889); *Biog. Dir. Am. Cong.* (1928); *Boston Transcript*, Oct. 29, 1875; Hugh McCulloch Papers, vol. III, Lib. of Cong.]   E. D.

WALKER, ASA (Nov. 13, 1845–Mar. 7, 1916), naval officer, son of Asa T. and Louisa (Morrell) Walker, was born in Portsmouth, N. H. He entered the United States Naval Academy, then temporarily located at Newport, R. I., Nov. 27, 1862. The following summer as a midshipman on the *Macedonian* he cruised for four months off the coast of Spain and northern Africa in vain pursuit of the Confederate cruiser *Alabama,* which was never sighted. In 1866 he was graduated and was sent on a voyage to the East Indies on the *Sacramento,* which was wrecked in the Bay of Bengal, June 19, 1867, at the mouth of the Sambalding River but without loss of life. Walker's subsequent service included a number of long voyages in Asiatic waters, where he acquired a wide reputation for his skill as a navigator. In 1883 he sailed as navigating officer of the *Trenton,* which had just been fitted out with a complete installation of electric lights, probably the first warship in the world to be so equipped. He spent four tours of duty at the Naval Academy, as assistant in mathematics (1873–74, 1879–83), head of the department of astronomy, navigation, and surveying (1886–90), and head of the department of mathematics (1893–97). His *Navigation* (1888) was used as a textbook at the Naval Academy for many years.

On May 23, 1897, Walker, then a commander, was given command of the *Concord.* On this vessel he transported a heavy load of ammunition from Mare Island to Dewey's squadron off Yokohama, joining him on Feb. 9, 1898, and participating in all the further movements of the fleet. When Commodore Dewey arrived off the coast of Luzon, Philippine Islands, Walker in the *Concord,* supported by the *Boston,* proceeded at full speed and reconnoitered Subig Bay. On Apr. 30 Walker reported that there were no Spanish ships in the vicinity, and on the morning of May 1 Dewey in his flagship, the *Olympia,* steamed into Manila Bay with his fleet. The *Concord* was the fifth in line. In the battle which followed, the *Concord* shelled and destroyed the Spanish transport, *Mindanao*. Walker also assisted in the later operations leading up to the capture of the city of Manila. Throughout the campaign Dewey reposed the fullest confidence in Walker's skill and judgment. On June 10, 1898, he was advanced nine numbers in grade "for eminent and conspicuous conduct" in the battle of Manila Bay.

Walker was promoted to the rank of captain in 1899, and was given duty at the Naval War College (1899–1900) and on the naval examining board (1900–05), as a member of the naval general board. Finally he was made superintendent of the Naval Observatory (1906–07), his last service. He was commissioned rear admiral in 1906, and was retired for age, Nov. 13, 1907. His remaining years were passed quietly at his home at Annapolis, Md. He lived to become the last surviving commander who fought under Dewey at Manila Bay. Walker married Ruth Leavitt Brooks of Portsmouth, N. H., on Dec. 16, 1867. By her he had a daughter who died in childhood and a son. His wife died, Jan. 31, 1877, and on June 11, 1890, he married Arabella W. Grant of Frankfort, Ky., who died in 1927.

[*Who's Who in America*, 1914–15; *Autobiog. of George Dewey* (1913); "The Battle of Manila Bay," *Century Mag.*, Aug. 1898; *Army and Navy Jour.*, Aug. 24, 1867, Mar. 11, 1916; ann. registers, and materials in the superintendent's office, U. S. Naval Acad.; archives in office of naval records, U. S. Navy Dept.; obituaries in *Evening Capital* (Annapolis, Md.), and *Sun* (Baltimore), Mar. 8, 1916; information concerning the family from Dr. W. D. Walker, Walker's son.]

L. H. B.

WALKER, MADAME C. J. [See WALKER, SARAH BREEDLOVE, 1865–1919].

WALKER, DAVID (Sept. 28, 1785–June 28, 1830), negro leader, was born in Wilmington, N. C., of a free mother and a slave father. His status was that of a free man and in his youth he traveled widely in the South. At an early age he acquired a deep and bitter sympathy with the enslaved members of his race and in his wide reading, particularly in historical works, he sought parallels to the American negro's situation in the enslavement and oppression of ancient peoples. Some time before 1827 he went to Boston where he established a second-hand clothing business on Brattle Street. In 1829 there appeared the work for which he is best known, an octavo pamphlet of seventy-six pages entitled *Walker's Appeal in four articles together with a Preamble to the Colored Citizens of the World, but in particular and very expressly to those of the United States of America*. The text of the appeal was a closely reasoned, eloquent and occasionally rhetorical argument against slavery.

The author called upon the colored people to rise against their oppressors and to resort to whatever violence might be necessary, but, at the same time, he counseled forgiveness of the past if the slaveholders would let their victims go.

The *Appeal* was calculated to stir up the suppressed race to mob and race violence by its forceful, primitive, emotional tone, but, on the other hand it contained a religious and prophetic vein that pled with the slaveholders to repent of their sins while there was still time, since the wrath of God must surely overwhelm them otherwise. Many anti-slavery leaders and free negroes rejected Walker's policy of violence and he circulated his pamphlets at his own expense. His courage and sincerity could possibly have served his cause more effectively had he adopted other tactics, but his course at least testifies to the strength of these two characteristics. A second edition of the pamphlet appeared in 1830 and penetrated the South to spread consternation there among the slaveholders, especially in the seaboard slave states, where incoming ships were searched for it. In a single day after a copy was discovered in Georgia the legislature rushed through a law that made "the circulation of pamphlets of evil tendency among our domestics" a capital offense. A price was set on Walker's head in the South, and the mayor of Savannah wrote with reference to the possible punishment of the author to the mayor of Boston, Harrison Gray Otis [*q.v.*]. The latter replied in a letter (Feb. 10, 1830), a copy of which he sent also to William B. Giles [*q.v.*], governor of Virginia, in which he condemned the tendency of the pamphlet but stated that the author had not made himself amenable to the laws of Massachusetts. True to his expressed intention Walker published a third, revised, and still more militant edition of the pamphlet in March 1830. Three months later he died. It was rumored and widely believed that his death was due to poisoning, but this has never been proved.

In 1828 he was married in Boston to a woman referred to simply as "Miss Eliza ——" in H. H. Garnet's *Walker's Appeal, With a Brief Sketch of His Life* (1848). The only child of the marriage, Edwin G. Walker, born posthumously, was elected in 1866 to the House of Represetatives of the Massachusetts legislature.

[John Daniels, *In Freedom's Birthplace* (1914); *William Lloyd Garrison, 1805–1879, The Story of His Life*, vol. I (1885); G. W. Williams, *Hist. of the Negro Race in America* (1883), vol. II; S. J. May, *Some Recollections of Our Antislavery Conflict* (1869); *Richmond Enquirer* (Richmond, Va.), Feb. 18, 1830.]

M. G.

WALKER, DAVID (Feb. 19, 1806–Sept. 30, 1879), jurist, son of Jacob Wythe and Nancy

(Hawkins) Walker, was born in what is now Todd County, Ky. His father's ancestors are said to have come to Virginia from Staffordshire, England, about 1650. David was an apt pupil; he began the study of Latin when he was seven, and soon thereafter was reading the classics.

Admitted to the bar in Kentucky in 1829, he went to Little Rock, Ark., in 1830, and shortly afterward settled in Fayetteville. From 1833 to 1835 he served as prosecuting attorney. He was a member of the convention of 1836 which drew up the first state constitution, and there worked to prevent unfair apportionment, advocating that the number of free white males be adopted as the basis of apportionment in order that the slaveholding counties might not dominate the state. In 1840 he was elected to the state Senate as a Whig. Four years later he was nominated for Congress, but was defeated by the matchless campaigner, Archibald Yell [*q.v.*]. In November 1848, much to his surprise, while on a visit to Kentucky, Walker was elected associate justice of the supreme court of Arkansas by a Democratic legislature over so prominent a Democrat as Elbert H. English [*q.v.*]. In the presidential election of 1860 he canvassed the state for the Bell and Everett ticket. The following year he was elected to the state convention called to consider the matter of secession. He was made president of the convention and was largely instrumental in preventing secession at that time. When, however, following the bombardment of Fort Sumter, the convention reassembled and voted for secession, Walker appealed to the five opponents to make the vote unanimous. Some raiding Federal soldiers arrested him in 1862, but he was released on taking the oath of allegiance. He served as chief justice of the Arkansas supreme court from 1866 until the state government was reorganized under the Reconstruction Act. Upon the overthrow of the Carpet-bag régime (1874) he was elected associate justice of the supreme court and served until 1878, when he resigned on account of failing health.

He was interested in the economic development of the state and went to Boston in 1870 in an effort to secure a railroad for northern Arkansas. Gov. Augustus H. Garland [*q.v.*] appointed him delegate to the Centennial Exposition in Philadelphia, where he delivered an address setting forth the natural resources and attractions of his state. His bearing was so dignified and reserved that many thought him unapproachable; yet he had numerous intimate friends. He started fourteen young men on their professional careers by boarding them and teaching them law. He was charitable, giving freely of his store to those in want, particularly in the short harvest year of 1874. In 1833 he married Jane Lewis Washington of Kentucky, who bore him six sons, two of whom died in infancy, and two daughters. David Shelby Walker [*q.v.*] was his cousin.

[*Jour. of the Proc. of the Convention Met to Form a Constitution . . . for the People of Ark.* (1836); *Jour. of Both Sessions of the Convention of the State of Ark.* (1861); *Jour. of the House of Representatives . . . of Ark.* (1848); *Ark. Reports,* 1848–54, 1866–68, 1874–78; John Hallum, *Biog. and Pictorial Hist. of Ark.* (1887); Fay Hempstead, *A Pictorial Hist. of Ark.* (1890) and *Hist. Rev. of Ark.* (1911); *Va. Mag. of Hist. and Biog.,* Apr. 1897; D. Y. Thomas, *Ark. in War and Reconstruction, 1861–1874* (1926); *Ark. Gazette* (Little Rock), Oct. 3, 1879; information from Miss Sue Walker, a grand-daughter.]   D. Y. T.

WALKER, DAVID SHELBY (May 2, 1815–July 20, 1891), jurist, governor of Florida, was born near Russellville, Logan County, Ky., the son of David and Mary (Barbour) Walker. His forebears had come to Kentucky from Virginia and had soon risen to prominence in public life. His father represented Fayette County in the Kentucky legislature (1793–96), fought in the War of 1812, and was a member of the federal House of Representatives from 1817 until his death in 1820. David's mother died when he was about six years of age, after which time he lived with his sister at La Grange, Oldham County, Ky., and was educated in private schools. In 1837 he removed to Tallahassee, Fla., where his brother George was living and also his kinsman, Gov. Richard K. Call [*q.v.*]. Here he studied law in his brother's office, was admitted to the bar, and began the practice of his profession.

With the powerful support of Governor Call, Walker began his political career by representing the seventh district in the first state Senate in 1845, resigning before the completion of his term. In 1848 he was elected mayor of Tallahassee; in 1848–49 he was a representative of Leon County in the state House of Representatives; and in 1850 he was appointed register of public lands and as such became *ex-officio* superintendent of schools, which positions he held until 1859 (Rerick, *post,* I, 221). He was an able and energetic superintendent and is considered the founder of the public-school system of Florida because of his influence in securing the passage of the basic law of 1853 (*Ibid.,* I, 226). Upon the collapse of the Whig party he affiliated with the American party and was its candidate for governor in 1856 (*Ibid.,* II, 230). Although defeated he polled a large vote because of his record as superintendent, and because he advocated lowering the price of public lands. In 1859 he was chosen associate justice of the Florida supreme court (*Ibid.,* II, 89).

Walker opposed the secession of Florida and

during the Civil War devoted himself to his judicial duties. In November 1865 he was elected governor without opposition under the Johnson reconstruction régime, and was inaugurated Dec. 20. He was in ill health and his administration was a troubled one because of numerous conflicts with the commander of the Federal forces in the state. He opposed the bringing of immigrants to Florida on the ground that the negroes had the right to furnish the labor supply, and he advised against the ratification of the Fourteenth Amendment (*Journal of the Senate of the Fourteenth General Assembly of . . . Florida,* 1865). The initiation of the congressional plan of reconstruction in 1867 brought his administration to an end. He was nominated for Congress by the Democrats in August 1868, but declined (Davis, *post,* p. 538). Resuming the practice of law in Tallahassee, he continued in private life until 1879 when, with the end of the Carpet-bag government, he was chosen a judge of the second judicial circuit, which position he held until his death. Throughout his public career he enjoyed a very great measure of popularity, and, notwithstanding the brevity of his term, he is classed as one of the best of the Florida governors. During the last years of his life he made a reputation as an able jurist. Though successful as a lawyer, he died comparatively poor because of his lavish charity. He was twice married: first, May 22, 1842, to Philoclea, daughter of Col. Robert W. Alston, who died May 7, 1868, and second, to Elizabeth Duncan. Of his first marriage there were born three sons and one daughter; of his second, one daughter, all of whom survived him. He was buried in the Episcopal cemetery at Tallahassee. David Walker [*q.v.*] was a cousin.

[Sources include J. A. Groves, *The Alstons and Allstons of North and South Carolina* (1901), incorrect as to date of marriage; R. H. Rerick, *Memoirs of Fla.* (2 vols., 1902); W. W. Davis, *The Civil War and Reconstruction in Fla.* (1913); *Florida Times-Union* (Jacksonville), July 21, 22, 1891; information as to certain facts from Walker's grand-daughter, Evelyn Cockrell, Thomasville, Ga., and from a grand-nephew, C. B. Gwynn, Tallahassee, Fla.; Register of marriages, St. John's Church, Tallahassee; Walker's reports as superintendent of schools, in the journals of the legislature, 1854–58.]   R. S. C.

WALKER, FRANCIS AMASA (July 2, 1840–Jan. 5, 1897), educator, economist, statistician, the son of Amasa Walker [*q.v.*] and Hannah (Ambrose) Walker, was born in Boston. His father's activities as a political economist, patron of education, and persistent advocate of social reforms insured the boy a stimulating home environment and a social direction of thought. Francis matriculated at Amherst College at fifteen, but lost one year because of weak eyes. After obtaining the A.B. degree in 1860,

he spent nine years in such varied activities as studying law (1860–61) in the Worcester office of Charles Devens and George F. Hoar [*qq.v.*], fighting in the Civil War (August 1861–January 1865), teaching Latin and Greek at Williston Seminary in Easthampton (1865–68), and writing editorials for Samuel Bowles's *Springfield Daily Republican* (January 1868–January 1869). He married, on Aug. 16, 1865, Exene Stoughton of Gill, Mass. They had seven children, five sons and two daughters.

The war brought opportunity to shoulder responsibilities beyond his years as an assistant adjutant-general. He rose from private to brevet brigadier-general (Mar. 13, 1865), and despite wounds, imprisonment at Libby, and permanent impairment of health, he closed his military career with an idealized concept of human relationships in warfare. His own *History of the Second Army Corps in the Army of the Potomac* (1886) scarcely mentions him; but his subsequent career showed that his experiences as a young officer had made him, by the age of twenty-four, a mature man possessed of poise and judgment, with a strong sense of the importance of discipline and keen insight into human nature. At the same time he emerged with a fun-loving temperament, although he was capable of truly Jovian wrath, and a personal charm which amounted to genuine magnetism.

In 1866 David A. Wells [*q.v.*] became special commissioner of the revenue and in January 1869 Walker was appointed, first, a special deputy under Wells and, next, chief of the Bureau of Statistics. He reorganized the Bureau along scientific lines, introducing some foreign improvements, and established his reputation as a statistician. He struggled to free the Bureau from dependence upon politics and special interests. In superintending the census of 1870 Walker had to work under the act of 1850, which gave him inadequate authority and in practice substituted party patronage for intelligence as the guiding principle of census-taking. The effect upon the figures, for the South particularly, was disastrous, as Walker was the first to admit. But a decade later, as superintendent of the tenth census (1879–81), working under a new law (1879), he appointed his own staff of enumerators. The scope of this inquiry extended to twenty-two quarto volumes—almost an encyclopedia of population, products, and resources. The work was enthusiastically praised, also bitterly criticized. However, it "immediately established in Europe the reputation of General Walker as a statistician of the highest order" (Dewey, *post,* p. 168). Walker strongly urged that the census bureau be given a permanent organization allowing uninterrupted maintenance of needed services and more skilled enumeration. When funds for Walker's retention as superintendent of the census of 1870 had failed, Grant had made him commissioner of Indian affairs (November 1871–December 1872) in order that he might continue his supervision of the census without pay. He prosecuted his labors on the census, contributing to a *Statistical Atlas of the United States* (1874), and injected common sense and honesty into the administration of Indian affairs (Wright, *post*, pp. 267–68). In 1874 he published *The Indian Question.*

Walker's thorough statistical investigations, together with service as chief of the bureau of awards at the Centennial Exposition in Philadelphia (1876), gave him a tremendous fund of information on the economic and social situation in the United States. The political situation he knew all too well from his necessary contacts with politicians. This equipment, added to his training and natural endowments, helped to make him notable as an economist, educator, and public administrator. As professor of political economy and history in the Sheffield Scientific School of Yale (1873–81) and as president of Massachusetts Institute of Technology (November 1881–January 1897) Walker dared to be a pioneer, abandoning old ideas for new, and stoutly defending his innovations in the comparatively fresh fields of economics and education.

His unceasing demand for a fresh consideration of principles powerfully stimulated the development of economics, and, because of his special combination of humanitarian sympathy with practical realism, he laid significant emphasis on human factors in industry. He became a foremost figure in a new inductive and historical school of economics. Of first importance was his attack upon the wages-fund theory; he showed that wages were not wholly dependent upon the amount of pre-existing capital, but also and more particularly upon the current productivity of labor. Thereafter, economists who did not abandon the theory materially modified it. According to his theory of distribution, which aroused sharp controversy, interest was regulated by a general principle of supply and demand, the profits of the entrepreneur were like rent, and the laborer was left "as the residual claimant to the remaining portion of the product" (J. L. Laughlin, in *Journal of Political Economy,* March 1897, p. 30; see diagram in Walker, *Political Economy,* 1888, p. 254; and critical discussion of his treatment of the entrepreneur in L. H. Haney, *History of Economic Thought,* 1920, p.

613). Competition he firmly believed in as the fundamental basis of economic life. However, he recognized that perfect competition is not attained in practice.

In his fight for the independence of economic thought, Walker's bitterest battle concerned money. He defined money to include banknotes, and everything serving as a medium of exchange. He asserted that the government had the right to declare irredeemable paper legal tender, adding however that governments were not yet wise enough to avoid over-issue, and effectively exposing the inflation fallacy. His adherence to international bimetallism Walker proclaimed when a delegate to the International Monetary Conference of 1878 and he held to the doctrine ever afterward. He declined to go as a delegate to the abortive Brussels Conference of 1892, and as a member of a commission to Europe in 1897, but he remained unflagging in his zeal, preaching everywhere the necessity for broadening the base of the world's money by international agreement for the use of silver with gold. Bryan's claim that the United States could do this alone, Walker strongly denied. He sensed early the sectional animosity which was to rage over the election of 1896, pleaded for tolerance and understanding between creditors and debtors, and tried desperately to offset the free-coinage movement by organizing business men behind international bimetallism. He failed, and suffered denunciation and misrepresentation for his pains.

In his discussion of economic conditions Walker showed to what ridiculous pass the blind acceptance of *laissez-faire* led its worshippers. He advocated a limited reduction of hours of labor from fourteen to ten or eleven for increased efficiency, but he doubted whether an eight-hour law could be applied safely throughout industry and he thought unemployment due chiefly to the effects of world-wide division of labor. Immigration gave him great concern, as causing recourse to such violent laborers' weapons as the boycott, picketing, and sabotage, which he supposed native workmen would not employ. The decreasing native birthrate he ascribed to the "competitive shock" of immigration. Relations between labor and capital seemed to him, in 1888, to have reached an equilibrium which could not be disturbed without threatening public welfare. A classic example of his controversies on economic principles was that with Prof. S. M. MacVane of Harvard, over the wages-fund theory (*Quarterly Journal of Economics,* April 1887, pp. 265–88; April 1888, pp. 263–96).

Walker is said to have become "unquestionably the most prominent and the best known of American writers" in the economic field (F. W. Taussig, quoted in *Springfield Daily Republican*, Jan. 6, 1897, p. 7). His influence extended into England (markedly), Italy, and France, but not far into Germany. As a theoretic economist perhaps he stood higher abroad than at home, where in his lifetime he was considered greater as a statistician and administrator. This was due to three main facts: his public duties deprived him of time for deep study of the economic writings that appeared in his later years; he espoused currency doctrines distasteful to his section and profession in the United States; and he had an innate sense of fairness in controversy which, in spite of his exuberance of speech, made men say they were luckier to have him to disagree with than some men to agree with. This last characteristic was well illustrated in his position on protection. He was a free-trader, partly because he realized that protectionism was incompatible with internationalism; yet the free-traders attacked him because he conceded that the protectionists had established a claim to a hearing. Similarly, cotton, woolen, worsted, and silk manufacturers urged him for membership upon the tariff commission of 1882, while lumber protectionists objected.

Walker's crowning work was in the field of education. He shouldered the burden of technical education at a difficult time and won for it public recognition. He increased the enrollment of Massachusetts Institute of Technology from 302 to 1198, and its buildings from one to four, adding much expensive laboratory equipment and five new departmental courses. Most important, "he knew young men, he rejoiced in young men, and his knowledge was power over them and power in them" (Tyler, *post*, p. 64). He had vigor and enthusiasm left over for the advancing of strenuous educational reforms. College subjects should be pursued seriously, he thought, as a valued occupation rather than as an excuse for prolongation of childhood. From the first, the laboratory method should be employed as much as possible, in order to maintain interest and a sense of responsibility in pupils of mechanical trend as well as in those of retentive memory. Technical schools should give grounding in history and political science to broaden pupils' understanding beyond their special fields; and these schools should maintain separate identities in order to free them from arrogant attitudes on the part of classical associates. He stood out against absorption of the Institute by Harvard. So loyal was he that he declined several more lucrative openings in other institutions. By his ardent advocacy of educational reforms he spread democratic doctrines of learning and teaching far beyond the walls of Massachusetts Institute of Technology, serving on school committees, on boards of education, and as college trustee. He set the Institute on a solid basis of permanent usefulness.

Upon his death the *Springfield Daily Republican* (Jan. 6, 1897) said that "in him the sense of life abounded." This vitality, coupled with unselfishness and loyalty, gave him special usefulness as an active public citizen. He continually served his community upon time-taking committees and commissions, and he served many groups and causes removed from Boston; a partial list of his affiliations fills nearly five pages in his biography. Such service is too pervasive to be measured accurately.

Walker lectured widely at colleges and universities, and before special groups such as the National Academy of Science (vice-president, 1891–97), the American Economic Association (president, 1885–92), and the American Statistical Association (president, 1882–97). Leading periodicals published these lectures or comments upon them if they were controversial. His most significant conclusions appeared in book form, the chief being *The Wages Question* (1876); *Money* (1878); *Money in Its Relation to Trade and Industry* (1879); *Land and its Rent* (1883); *Political Economy* (1883), a textbook of many editions and revisions; and *International Bimetallism* (1896). To this output were added his reports as president of M.I.T. and in other official capacities and a continuous stream of magazine and newspaper articles, letters, and rejoinders, covering a wide field of public affairs. His *Discussions in Economics and Statistics* (2 vols., 1899), were edited by D. R. Dewey; and his *Discussions in Education* (1899) by J. P. Munroe.

[J. P. Munroe, *A Life of Francis Amasa Walker* (1923), contains a bibliography of his writings and reported addresses. See also D. R. Dewey, "Francis A. Walker as a Public Man," *Rev. of Reviews*, Feb. 1897; J. L. Laughlin, "Francis Amasa Walker," *Jour. of Pol. Economy*, Mar. 1897; H. W. Tyler, "The Educational Work of Francis A. Walker," *Educational Review*, June 1897; C. D. Wright, "Francis Amasa Walker," *Quart. Pubs. Am. Statistical Asso.*, June 1897; *Mass. Inst. of Technology. Meetings Held in Commemoration of . . . Francis Amasa Walker* (1897); Silvanus Hayward, "Gen. Francis A. Walker," *New-Eng. Hist. and Geneal. Register*, Jan. 1898. A few letters have been salvaged by the family and occasional items may be found in the MSS. of W. B. Allison, E. Atkinson, W. E. Chandler, Manton Marble, and John Sherman. Perhaps the best newspaper obituaries appeared in the *Boston Herald* and *Springfield Daily Republican*, Jan. 6, 1897.]

J. P. N.

WALKER, GILBERT CARLTON (Aug. 1, 1832–May 11, 1885), congressman, governor of Virginia, was born in Cuba, Allegany County,

N. Y. (*Binghamton Daily Republican*, May 12, 1885). Self-confident and well prepared in a Binghamton school, he entered Williams College in 1851 but soon withdrew and entered Hamilton College, Clinton, N. Y., where he graduated in 1854. After studying law privately he settled to its practice in 1855, in Owego, Tioga County, N. Y. Two years later he married Olive Evans of Binghamton. From 1859 to 1864 he practised in Chicago. He participated actively in politics but failed of election as district attorney in Tioga County and as corporation counsel in Chicago, for both of which offices the Democrats had nominated him. Like many others, during the Civil War he changed from Douglas Democrat to Unionist.

Early in 1865 he moved to Norfolk, Va., hoping that the climate of that region would be helpful in his fight against tuberculosis, the disease which eventually caused his death. In Norfolk business enterprises engaged him, notably the Exchange National Bank of which he was organizer and president. Soon, however, natural inclination and the advantage of being a Carpet-bagger took him into Reconstruction politics. Though defeated for the Virginia constitutional convention of 1867, he was of great service to the state—through influential friendships in Washington—in having the new constitution adopted without its most radical and most objectionable provision, that disfranchising all who having held office under the United States had aided the "rebellion." Important native business men and politicians, including William Mahone [*q.v.*], arranged for his nomination for the governorship by the "True Republican" faction and for the retirement of the "Bourbon," or Democratic, candidate in favor of him as a "Conservative." In 1869, accordingly, he canvassed the state against Gen. H. H. Wells, the candidate of the "Radicals," or Republicans, and of certain important railroad interests. Men noted that Walker was handsome, dignified in public, affable in private, a ready and pleasing speaker though not an orator, and "not a Yanky; he don't look like one" (letter cited in Blake, *post*, p. 107 n.). The immediate outcome was the restoration of Virginia to the Union under "Conservative" auspices, for which he was long acclaimed "savior of the state." As governor for somewhat over four years (1869–74), Walker advocated strict enforcement of law and order and scrupulous compliance with the spirit of the new national enactments with respect to the civil and political equality of the freedmen. This stand brought him further credit and applause. He proposed also the funding of the state's huge debt upon terms very hard for the state and the transfer of the state's very large interests in transportation companies to private hands for what they would bring; and both policies became law through his management of the negro vote in the legislature (Pearson, *post*, ch. 3). It was currently believed that in both these transactions he profited personally (Blake, p. 136 n.), and his fiscal schemes almost immediately proved unworkable. Moreover, Capitol gossip long had it that he was given to reckless dissipation. Nevertheless, he was representative in Congress from the Richmond district for two terms (1875–79). He then returned to his native state, where he was once more lawyer, politician, and promoter, first in Binghamton, and after 1881 in New York City, where he died. He was buried in the lot owned by his father-in-law in Spring Forest Cemetery, Binghamton.

[H. J. Eckenrode, *The Political Hist. of Va. during the Reconstruction* (1904); C. C. Pearson, *The Readjuster Movement in Va.* (1917); N. M. Blake, *William Mahone* (1935); *Biog. Dir. Am. Cong.* (1928); *Messages and Official Papers of Hon. G. C. Walker, Gov. of Va.* (1871), copy in Va. State Lib.; obituaries in *The State* (Richmond), *Richmond Dispatch*, *Binghamton Daily Republican*, and *N. Y. Times*, May 12, 1885; memoranda from Binghamton Public Library.]

C. C. P.

WALKER, HENRY OLIVER (May 14, 1843–Jan. 14, 1929), portrait, figure, and mural painter, son of Thomas Oliver and Sarah Lucy Walker, was born in Boston, Mass. After a common-school education he engaged in commercial pursuits until 1879, when he made the inevitable flight to Paris. He studied for three years as a pupil of Léon Bonnat, and then returned to Boston and opened a studio. A successful exhibition in 1883 served to make his work known; thereafter he was busily employed in portrait painting. Soon he turned his attention to ideal figure subjects, and made his first essays in decorative work. About 1889 he moved to New York. On Apr. 19, 1888, he was married to Laura Margaret, daughter of John P. Marquand. They established their home at Lakewood, N. J.; in later years they had summer homes at Cornish, N. H., and Belmont, Mass. In New York Walker continued to paint portraits, but he also produced some excellent ideal pictures, and he now had opportunities to make mural decorations, a specialty in which he soon made his mark. Among his ideal paintings are "Boy and Muse," in the William T. Evans collection; "Narcissus," in the Boston Museum of Fine Arts; "Girl and Kitten," in the Thomas B. Clarke collection; and "A Morning Vision," in the Metropolitan Museum, New York. The "Portrait of Mrs. Evans and Son," which came to the National Gallery of Art with the other works from the Evans collection, is noteworthy.

His mural decorations for public buildings must be placed first among his achievements. His Library of Congress paintings, "Joy and Memory" and "Lyric Poetry" (one large tympanum and six small tympani in one of the corridors), are among the most decorative and poetic of the many mural works in the library. The two historical paintings in the Massachusetts State House, the "Pilgrims on the Mayflower" and "John Eliot Preaching to the Indians," in the nature of the case are less interesting from a decorative point of view, and less personal and spontaneous than the Washington work. The large square panel in the Appellate Court House, New York, is a handsome allegory entitled "The Wisdom of the Law," with eleven figures, well composed and pleasing in color, but the symbolism is somewhat far-fetched. The motive of the lunette in the Minnesota Capitol is "Yesterday, Today and Tomorrow." Other murals by Walker are in the Essex County Court House, Newark, N. J. Walker was a member of the National Academy (1902), the National Society of Mural Painters, and of numerous other societies. He won many prizes and medals. He died in Belmont, Mass., in his eighty-sixth year.

[*Who's Who in America,* 1910–11 ; Pauline King, *Am. Mural Painting* (1902) ; Herbert Small, *Handbook of the New Lib. of Cong.* (1901) ; *Am. Art Ann.,* 1923–24; cats. of the Thomas B. Clarke coll., 1899, and the W. T. Evans coll., 1901; obituaries in *Am. Art Ann.,* 1929, and *N. Y. Times,* Jan. 15, 1929.]   W. H. D.

WALKER, JAMES (Aug. 16, 1794–Dec. 23, 1874), clergyman and college president, was born in what was a part of Woburn, now Burlington, Mass., the son of James Walker, commissioned major-general by President Adams in 1798, and of Lucy (Johnson) Walker, a descendant of Edward Johnson, 1598–1672 [*q.v.*]. Prepared for college at the school at Groton, Mass., afterward Lawrence Academy, he graduated from Harvard College in 1814. After assisting Benjamin Abbot at Phillips Exeter Academy for a year, he studied divinity at Cambridge under Henry Ware and received his license to preach on May 15, 1817. He accepted the call of the Harvard Church in Charlestown and was ordained on Apr. 15, 1818. In the controversy between the Trinitarians and Unitarians he immediately became a leader among the "liberals." He was an organizer of the American Unitarian Association in 1825, and he contributed to the *American Unitarian Tracts* and to *The Christian Examiner,* which he edited from 1831 to 1839. On Dec. 21, 1829, he married Catherine

Bartlett, the daughter of George Bartlett of Charlestown. They had no children. In July 1839 he resigned his pulpit to become Alford Professor of Natural Religion, Moral Philosophy and Civil Polity at Harvard. In 1853 he became president of the university. His administration was competent but uneventful; when he intended to retire in 1858 the faculty unanimously requested that he remain, on the grounds of public duty. In 1860 he resigned on the plea of advancing years.

Though a theological liberal in the 1820's, he was temperamentally conservative and cautious. He kept clear of all reform agitations, regarded Theodore Parker as a "phenomenon," and made it a rule never to preach about anything until people in the omnibus had stopped talking about it. He was an erudite but not original mind. His pamphlet, "Philosophy of Man's Spiritual Nature in Regard to the Foundations of Faith," in the *American Unitarian Tracts* (1 Ser., No. 87, 1834) was eagerly seized upon by young Transcendentalists for its assertion "that, to a rightly constituted and fully developed soul, moral and spiritual truth will be revealed with a degree of intuitive clearness, and certainty, equal at least to that of the objects of sense" (p. 19). However, in such a passage he was simply repelling scepticism by the argument that innate faculties exist in the soul for the apprehension of spiritual truth; he was following implicitly the lead of the Scotch Realists, from whom he derived almost his entire thought. In 1849 he edited Dugald Stewart's *Philosophy of the Active and Moral Powers* and in 1850 Thomas Reid's *Essays on the Intellectual Powers of Man.* Drawing upon these sources, he became the preeminent expounder of the metaphysics of early nineteenth century Unitarianism, of a common-sense rationalism combined with a simple piety and a lofty ethical tone. Thoroughly provincial, he traveled out of New England only twice, to deliver ordination sermons in Baltimore and in Cincinnati. He was devoid of esthetic interests, his sermons are closely knit but sententious. His contemporaries sometimes complained that he lacked decision, which they attributed to his faculty for seeing all sides of all questions; but he won their affection and respect by his apparent sincerity, his dialectical powers, his great physical vitality, above all by his handsome and commanding presence, which they thought similar to Webster's. His last years he spent in Cambridge, an honored and dignified figure. He published *Sermons Preached in the Chapel of Harvard College* in 1861, and another collection was issued after his death, *Reason, Faith, and*

Duty (1876). He left his library and $15,000 to Harvard.

[*Addresses at the Inauguration of the Rev. James Walker* (1853); W. O. White, "Introduction," to *Reason, Faith, and Duty, ante*; Joseph Lovering, "Memoir," *Amer. Acad. of Arts and Sciences Proc.*, vol. X (1875), pp. 485–95; H. W. Foote, *The Wisdom from Above, Sermon Preached at King's Chapel, Sunday, Jan. 3, 1875* (1875); *Mass. Hist. Soc. Proc.*, 1 Ser., vol. XIII (1875), 2 Ser., vol. VI (1891); C. A. Bartol, "The Great Man and the Little Child," *Unitarian Review*, Feb. 1875; *Hist. of the Harvard Church in Charlestown, 1815–1879* (1879), pp. 164–207 for bibliography of Walker's publications; *Services at the Dedication of a Mural Monument to James Walker* (1884); *Boston Evening Transcript*, Dec. 28, 1874; *Boston Daily Advertiser*, Dec. 26, 1874; the manuscript catalogue of Walker's library, Widener Lib., Harvard University.]
P. M.

WALKER, JAMES BARR (July 29, 1805–Mar. 6, 1887), clergyman, editor, and author of theological works, was born in Philadelphia, the son of James and Margaret (Barr) Walker; his father died before the child's birth. In his infancy his mother moved with her family to a frontier farm near Pittsburgh, and, after a little schooling, James was apprenticed to learn printing. Subsequently, finding no employment in Pittsburgh, he walked to Philadelphia and obtained work in printing-shops there; later he was similarly employed in New York City, and for a time he taught school at New Durham, N. J. On business for an uncle he went to Ravenna, Ohio, where he bought a half-interest in the *Western Courier* and began the practice of law. In the late twenties, apparently, he entered Western Reserve College, then at Hudson, Ohio, where he had an intense religious experience and was fired by Theodore D. Weld [*q.v.*] with abolitionist enthusiasm. Leaving college after about a year to become an agent for the American Bible Society, he traveled over western Ohio, which was then just being settled. On June 6, 1833, he married Rebecca, daughter of Thomas Randall of Bridgewater, Mass. For the two years following he conducted a religious paper at Hudson, but opposition to his anti-slavery views caused him to sell it. After a little theological study he was ordained, Sept. 21, 1837, by the Presbytery of Portage, and became pastor of the Presbyterian Church at Akron, Ohio, which he served for two years.

In 1839 he moved to Cincinnati, to publish the book which gave him fame, *The Philosophy of the Plan of Salvation*. It was issued in 1841, anonymously, and by 1855, when it appeared in a fifth enlarged edition, still anonymously, it had sold over twenty thousand copies, was being extensively used as a textbook in the United States, and had been published in England and Scotland and translated into French, German, Italian,

Welsh, and Hindustani. The book held its position until the 1870's, the later printings bearing Walker's name. The appeal of this treatise on Christian apologetics lay in its original method and in its clear, untechnical language.

In 1840 Walker established in Cincinnati a religious paper, *The Watchman of the Valley*. His anti-slavery views and his Oberlin theology aroused hostility, but despite advice to leave the city he continued the paper until 1842. He then became pastor of the Congregational Church in Mansfield, Ohio, which, composed chiefly of abolitionists and temperance reformers, flourished under his leadership. In 1846 he organized in Chicago another religious paper, *The Herald of the Prairies*. After managing this for four years he was recalled to the Mansfield Church and served it until 1857, leaving to take charge of the Congregational Church of Sandusky, Ohio.

Having accumulated independent means, in 1863 he left Sandusky to live at Mansfield. From 1859 to 1865 he was a lecturer in Chicago Theological Seminary. For a Christian college in a Christian community, on the Oberlin model, he bought a large tract in Benzie County, Mich., and after two years spent in preparation for the enterprise, he took up his residence at Benzonia, where for five years he lived in frontier conditions. He was a member of the Michigan Senate in the session of 1865. Because of financial mismanagement he left the community, giving his lands for educational purposes. In 1870 he became professor of intellectual and moral philosophy and belles-lettres in Wheaton College, Wheaton, Ill., and in 1871, pastor of the Congregational Church there. At Wheaton he lived until his death, serving the church until 1880 and teaching until 1884. His first wife died in 1875 and on Apr. 3, 1876, he married Mary A. (Myrtle) Weamer, widow of Capt. George Weamer of Norwalk, Ohio. He had no children, but reared in his home thirteen orphans. He published several other theological books, which sold largely but were not as popular as his first, and in 1881, *Experiences of Pioneer Life in the Early Settlements and Cities of the West*, an autobiography.

[In addition to the *Experiences*, see W. L. Chaffin, *A Biog. Hist. of Robert Randall and His Descendants* (1919); *Congregational Year-Book* (1888); *Advance* (Chicago), Mar. 17, 1887; *Congregationalist* (Boston), Mar. 17, 1887; *Chicago Tribune*, Mar. 9, 1887.]
R. H. N.

WALKER, JOHN BRISBEN (Sept. 10, 1847–July 7, 1931), publisher, was born at the country home of his parents, John and Anna (Krepps) Walker, on the Monongahela River near Pittsburgh, Pa. After attending Gonzaga

College in Washington, D. C., he entered Georgetown College, but left after two years to accept in 1865 an appointment to the United States Military Academy at West Point. In 1868, having resigned from the Military Academy, he accompanied the new minister, John Ross Browne [*q.v.*], to China, where he served as a military adviser during the reorganization of the Chinese military service. Returning to America in 1870, he engaged in the manufacture of iron in the Kanawha Valley in West Virginia, and in four or five years estimated his holdings at half a million dollars. He was engaged in the construction of a large blast furnace when he lost all his property in the financial panic of the seventies. Turning to journalism, he wrote a series of articles on the mineral industries for Murat Halstead's *Cincinnati Commercial* which led to his appointment as the managing editor of the *Pittsburgh Telegraph* in 1876 and three months later to a similar position on the *Washington Chronicle*. In 1879, the *Chronicle* having been discontinued, Walker purchased sixteen hundred acres of land near Denver, Colo., and developed a highly successful alfalfa ranch. He also bought and reclaimed over five hundred lots of bottom land in Denver. Selling both the ranch and the Denver lots at a large profit, he returned to the East and in 1889 bought the expiring *Cosmopolitan Magazine* from Joseph N. Hallock. In five years he had increased the circulation from 16,000 to 400,000 and had made the *Cosmopolitan* one of a great triumvirate of inexpensive but good American illustrated magazines. He quickly followed the example of McClure in going to fifteen cents in 1893, and two years later joined Frank A. Munsey and McClure at the ten-cent level. The *Cosmopolitan* was one of the pioneers in bringing the popular magazine into close touch with current affairs. Walker was both publisher and editor, though he was aided for varying periods by such distinguished associates as W. D. Howells, H. H. Boyesen, A. S. Hardy [*q.v.*], and others. He was the first president of the American Periodical Publishers' Association. In 1905 he sold the *Cosmopolitan* to W. R. Hearst.

Walker's was a restless and adventurous mind, continually entertaining new projects. In December 1895 he sent Hobart C. Chatfield-Taylor to Spain to feel out officials on the possibility of the United States buying the independence of Cuba for $100,000,000. In 1897 he founded and for several years maintained Cosmopolitan University, a free correspondence school with a nominal matriculation fee. He urged a credit system based on convertible bonds to prevent panics

(1897), a national clearing house (1899), and a parcels post (1903). He was an enthusiast in regard to aviation, automobiles, and good roads, and in 1896 he offered a prize for the automobile showing the greatest speed, simplicity and ease of operation, and safety, and the lowest cost on a run from City Hall Park, New York, to Irvington, the contest being won by a Duryea Motor Wagon which made the 16½ miles in 65 minutes. Two years later he bought out the Stanley Automobile Company and began the manufacture of Locomobile steam cars at a factory he built at Philipse Manor, on the Hudson. He was the first president of the Automobile Manufacturers' Association, organized a national highway commission, and invented and manufactured the automatic road crowner, a machine for removing moisture from clay and thus preventing winter freezing.

After the outbreak of the World War, he became active in the Friends of Peace and Justice, which was interested in preventing the entrance of the United States into the conflict, and he was chairman of their national convention in Chicago in 1915. Besides the *Cosmopolitan,* he was for several years publisher of the *Twentieth Century Home* (later the *Twentieth Century*), a women's monthly, and *Your Affairs,* a pacifist monthly. He was the author of many articles and pamphlets on political and economic questions, and of "A Modern Swiss Family Robinson," published serially in the *Cosmopolitan* (October 1904–May 1905). He was married three times: to Emily Strother, daughter of D. H. Strother [*q.v.*], by whom he had eight children and from whom he was divorced; to Ethel Richmond, by whom he had four children; and to Iris Calderhead, who with nine of his children survived him. Walker was a man of versatile talents, dynamic energy, both mental and physical, and a disinterested passion for social justice.

[See *Who's Who in America,* 1920–21; "Notes on Some American Mag. Editors," *Bookman,* Dec. 1900; "The Napoleon of the Mags.," *N. Y. Herald,* Sept. 3, 1893; C. H. Towne, *Adventures in Editing* (1926); files of *Cosmopolitan Mag.,* 1889–1905, which throws much light on Walker's activities; obituaries in *N. Y. Times* and *N. Y. Herald Tribune,* July 8, 1931. Information has been supplied by Iris Calderhead Walker.]

F. L. M.

WALKER, JOHN GRIMES (Mar. 20, 1835–Sept. 15, 1907), naval officer, was born at Hillsboro, N. H., son of Alden Walker, a merchant and cotton manufacturer, and Susan (Grimes) Walker. He was a descendant of Philip Walker who was brought to Rehoboth, Mass., by his mother previous to 1643. After his mother's death in 1846 he lived with his uncle Gov. James W. Grimes [*q.v.*] of Iowa, and by his aid secured an appointment as midshipman, Oct. 5, 1850. Through his uncle's subsequent service as United States senator, 1859–69, and chairman of the Senate naval committee, 1864–69, Walker also gained political contacts and influence of value in his later years. Following a long Pacific cruise in the *Falmouth* he attended the Naval Academy for a year, graduating in June 1856, at the head of his class. He then cruised in the Brazil Squadron and in 1859–60 was an instructor in mathematics at the Naval Academy.

In the Civil War, after serving briefly in the *Connecticut,* he became first lieutenant, Nov. 2, 1861, of the steamer *Winona,* West Gulf Squadron, was wounded slightly in the passage of the forts below New Orleans, and participated in Farragut's advance to Vicksburg. He was made lieutenant commander July 16, 1862, and given command of the small ironclad *Baron De Kalb* of Admiral D. D. Porter's Mississippi Squadron. In the *De Kalb* he led the brilliant gunboat attack on Arkansas Post, Jan. 10–11, 1863, for which he received special mention (*Official Records of the Union and Confederate Navies,* I ser., XXIV, 118). He was afterward greatly relied upon by Porter as one of his ablest younger officers. He took part in four subsequent expeditions up the Yazoo River, during the last of which, in June, he commanded five vessels which destroyed shipping and stores valued at $2,000,-000. He temporarily commanded a naval battery ashore in the siege of Vicksburg, and after its fall he had charge of the naval units in a joint expedition against Yazoo City, during which the *De Kalb* was sunk, July 13, 1863, by a torpedo. After leave in the North he commanded the *Saco,* January 1864–January 1865, and subsequently the *Shawmut,* under Porter on the Atlantic coast blockade. He was advanced five numbers for distinguished war service and was promoted, July 25, 1866, to commander.

Notable in his later career were his three years on the staff of Admiral Porter at the Naval Academy, 1866–69; his secretaryship of the lighthouse board, 1873–78; a period of two years' leave, 1879–81, during which he gained valuable experience through administrative work with the Chicago, Burlington, & Quincy Railway; and his long duty, 1881–89, as chief of the Bureau of Navigation. In this position, and up to his retirement, he was generally recognized as the most influential officer in the navy, simple in manners, with Yankee humor and nasal twang, but of excellent judgment, progressive ideas, and keen knowledge of human nature. Admiral Albert Gleaves (*Life and Letters of Rear Admiral Stephen B. Luce . . .,* 1925, p. 172) speaks of him as "politically the most powerful man in the service" and "one of the ablest administrators and executives the Department has ever had." He was made commodore Feb. 12, 1889, and given command of the Squadron of Evolution, which, late in 1891, during strained relations with Chile, was sent to the South Atlantic. Here he commanded the station till September 1892, and then till June 1893 the North Atlantic station. From April to August 1894, during the establishment of the Hawaiian Republic and agitation for its annexation, he was entrusted with the North Pacific command, and his reports, favorable to recognition of the republic and emphasizing the need of American naval vessels in the Islands, had considerable influence on congressional and public opinion.

He retired for age on Mar. 20, 1897, but in July following President McKinley appointed him to the Nicaragua Canal Commission, and in June 1899 he became president of the new Isthmian Canal Commission to study both the Nicaragua and Panama routes. The commission's report in November 1902 favored the Nicaragua route, but after negotiations with the French Panama Company, in which Walker took a prominent part, and a reduction of the company's price on its rights and property from $109,000,000 to $40,000,000, the commission shifted in favor of Panama. He remained head of the commission until the final transfer of the French rights in May 1904, and was again head of the reorganized commission which administered the Canal Zone and operations till Apr. 1, 1905, when the whole commission resigned to permit more unified control. After his final retirement Walker made his home in Washington. He died from heart failure near Ogunquit, Me., during a summer visit to that vicinity. His body was cremated and the ashes interred at Arlington. He was married, Sept. 12, 1866, to Rebecca, daughter of Henry G. Pickering of Boston, and had two sons and four daughters.

[J. B. R. Walker, *Memorial of the Walkers of the Old Plymouth Colony* (1861); William Salter, *The Life of James W. Grimes* (1876); James Barnes, "Rear Admiral John G. Walker," *Review of Reviews* (N. Y.), Sept. 1897; J. G. Walker, "The Engineer in Naval Warfare," *North Am. Rev.,* Dec. 1890; Report and Letters to the Navy Department relating to the Sandwich Islands, *Sen. Ex. Doc. 16,* 53 Cong., 3 Sess.; statement before the committee on interoceanic canals, *Sen. Doc. 253,* 57 Cong., 1 Sess.; *Report of the Isthmian Canal Commission 1899–1901, Rear Admiral John G. Walker . . . President* (2 vols., 1901–02); *Army and Navy Jour.,* Sept. 21, 28, 1907; *Washington Post,* Sept. 17, 1907; official papers, letters, etc., in the Navy Department and in the possession of the Walker family.]   A. W—t.

WALKER, JONATHAN HOGE (July 20, 1754–Jan. 1824), jurist, was born near Hogestown, Cumberland County, Pa., the son of William and Elizabeth (Hoge) Walker and the grandson of William Walker who fought under the Duke of Marlborough and emigrated to Pennsylvania about 1710. His maternal grandfather, John Hoge, a large landholder, was the founder of Hogestown and the uncle of Moses Hoge [q.v.]. His father was a prosperous farmer and during the French and Indian War saw service as a subaltern. During the Revolution Jonathan accompanied several expeditions against the Indians in western Pennsylvania, from which experiences he developed an interest in the transmontane section of the state and a desire to live there. In his late twenties he entered Dickinson College and graduated there with the first class in 1787. Then he read law in the office of Stephen Duncan, at Carlisle, whose daughter Lucretia (or Lucy) he married. In the spring of 1790 he was admitted to the bar of Northumberland County. Shortly thereafter he set himself up in practice at Northumberland, one of the first resident attorneys in that frontier village. In his political affiliations he was a Jeffersonian, though surprisingly mild in temper for one who lived in the democratic hotbeds of Carlisle and Northumberland and fraternized with such radical souls as Robert Whitehill and Thomas Cooper [qq.v.]. His Republicanism won him, on Mar. 1, 1806, an appointment from Gov. Thomas McKean as president judge of the 4th Pennsylvania district, comprising the counties of Center, Mifflin, Huntingdon, and Bedford. During the same year he removed to Bellefonte, where he lived until 1810, when he established himself in Bedford. When in 1818 Congress created western Pennsylvania as a separate judicial district, President Monroe appointed him federal judge for the district. He held his first court at Pittsburgh in December 1818, and he removed to Pittsburgh the following year. In 1818 he made an address to the people of the district, which was characteristic of him in its expressions of feeling and sense of his duties and responsibilities as a judge.

He was a very large man, more than six feet tall and of heavy build. As a judge he commanded the confidence of the people for impartial decisions. He was an excellent scholar and carried with him through life the taste and appreciation for the classics that he acquired in college. He died in Natchez, Miss., while visiting his eldest son. His second son was Robert J. Walker [q.v.]

[Hist. of that Part of the Susquehanna and Juniata Valleys Embraced in . . . Mifflin, Juniata . . . Snyder (1886), esp. vol. I, p. 463; H. C. Bell, Hist. of Northumberland County, Pa. (1891); J. W. F. White, "The Judiciary of Allegheny County," in Pa. Mag. of Hist. and Biog., July 1883; W. H. Egle, Pa. Genealogies; Scotch-Irish and German (1886); J. H. Tyler, The Family of Hoge (1927), ed. by J. F. Hoge.]

J. H. P.

WALKER, JOSEPH REDDEFORD (Dec. 13, 1798–Oct. 27, 1876), trapper-explorer, guide, was born probably in Virginia, shortly before his parents moved to Roane County, Tenn. In 1819 he moved to the neighborhood of Independence, Mo., and in the following year was with a party of trappers that entered New Mexico only to be expelled by the Spanish authorities. For the greater part of the next twelve years he operated from Independence as a trader and trapper, serving for a time as sheriff of Jackson County. He was one of the imposing company led by Benjamin Bonneville [q.v.] which on May 1, 1832, left Fort Osage for the mountains. In July of the following year, at the Green River rendezvous, Bonneville sent him, with about fifty men, on an exploration westward. Walker led his men to Great Salt Lake, then to the Humboldt River, and on to what has since been known as Walker Lake. From there they scaled the Sierra Nevada and after a long and difficult passage in which they narrowly escaped with their lives descended the western slope, reaching Monterey in November. So far as it is known, they were the first whites to cross the Sierra from the east and were also, it is generally maintained, the first to see the Yosemite Valley. Starting on his return in February 1834, Walker crossed the Sierra farther to the south by the gap since known as Walkers Pass and reached the Great Basin, rejoining Bonneville on Bear River, in the present Utah, in the early summer. Henceforth he was "Captain" Walker.

For the next nine years he seems to have remained in the mountains, living from time to time among the Shoshones, though he is recorded as having reached Los Angeles on a horse-buying venture in 1841. In August 1843, at Fort Bridger, he joined Joseph B. Chiles's company of emigrants, and later led a part of it, by way of Walkers Pass, to the coast. Returning with a cavalcade of horses, he overtook J. C. Frémont's second expedition, homeward bound, at Las Vegas de Santa Clara and accompanied it to Bent's Fort. He guided Frémont's third expedition (1845–46) to California, but returned to the Rockies before the beginning of the conquest. In April 1847 he was again in Jackson County, where he remained for nearly two years, but contrived to reach California among the first of the Forty-niners. For a time he sold cattle at the mines, and was later the leader of various prospecting parties. In 1861 he led a company to

Arizona and in the following year discovered a number of rich placers on the future site of Prescott. At the age of sixty-nine, though still vigorous, he brought his wanderings to a close and made his home with his nephew, James T. Walker, in Ignacio Valley, Contra Costa County, Cal., where he remained until his death.

Walker was more than six feet tall and of large frame. According to Washington Irving he was "brave in spirit, though mild in manners" (*The Adventures of Captain Bonneville*, 1850, p. 30). He was truthful, honest, and exceptionally modest regarding his exploits. His restless energy and insatiable curiosity carried him over vast stretches of territory, and none of the "mountain men" had a better knowledge of the geography of the West. He came of an adventurous family. Of his brothers, Joel P. has the distinction of having headed the first family of avowed emigrants to reach Oregon (1840), Samuel S. died on his way to California in 1849, Isaac appears to have been killed by Mormons in Arizona, and John to have fallen at the Alamo in 1836.

[D. S. Watson, *West Wind, the Life Story of Joseph Reddeford Walker* (1934); H. H. Bancroft, *Hist. of Cal.*, vol. III (1885), pp. 389–92, vol. V (1886), pp. 765–66; R. G. Thwaites, *Early Western Travels*, vols. XXVIII (1906), XXX (1906); H. M. Chittenden, *The Am. Fur Trade of the Far West* (1902), vol. I; F. N. Fletcher, *Early Nev., the Period of Exploration* (1929); *Hist. of Contra Costa County, Cal.* (1882); *Adventures of Zenas Leonard* (1904), ed. by W. F. Wagner; information from Francis P. Farquhar, San Francisco.]   W. J. G.

WALKER, LEROY POPE (Feb. 7, 1817–Aug. 22, 1884), Confederate secretary of war, was born and died in Huntsville, Ala. His father, John Williams Walker, a native of Virginia, was president of the first constitutional convention of Alabama (1819), and one of the first two United States senators from that state; his mother was Maria, daughter of Leroy Pope. Walker entered the University of Alabama in the class of 1835 but left college in his junior year; later he studied law at the University of Virginia and under Arthur F. Hopkins [*q.v.*] at Huntsville, Ala. Admitted to the bar in 1837, he began practice in Mississippi but after a year returned to Alabama, settling first at Bellefonte and later at Moulton. He served as state solicitor and in 1843 was elected to the lower house of the legislature from Lawrence County. From 1847 to 1850 he represented Lauderdale County and served as speaker. In the latter year he was a delegate to the Nashville Convention, and in the fall, having been elected a judge of the circuit court, he moved back to Huntsville. Three years later he resigned and returned to the legislature. Active in Democratic politics and effec-

tive on the stump, he was chosen presidential elector for the state at large in 1848, 1852, and 1856.

By 1860 Walker was definitely identified with the secessionist wing of his party. He was chairman of the Alabama delegation to the Democratic convention at Charleston, and as such announced the withdrawal of the delegation; he was also a delegate to the Richmond convention, and supported John C. Breckinridge [*q.v.*] in his campaign. The Alabama secession convention sent Walker as special commissioner to Tennessee in an effort to induce that state to secede, and he was received by the legislature, which he addressed. On Feb. 21, 1861, President Jefferson Davis made him secretary of war in his first cabinet. The appointment was determined by political expediency rather than by Walker's fitness for that office, since Davis wished to unite all the states and leading interests of the South in support of his administration, and Walker had been recommended by William L. Yancey [*q.v.*]. Walker was utterly inexperienced in administration, and the tremendous and, in many cases, impossible tasks that confronted him as secretary weighed upon him heavily. Criticism in Congress convinced both Walker and Davis that the former should resign, and he was offered a foreign mission which he declined. He planned to run for the Senate if Clement C. Clay [*q.v.*] retired, and in the meantime desired a military appointment. On Sept. 16, 1861, he resigned with his health seriously impaired, and the following day Davis appointed him brigadier-general. He served in the Department of Alabama and West Florida, and was in command, first at Mobile, and later at Montgomery. His efforts to secure an assignment to active duty failing, he resigned Mar. 31, 1862. He was appointed the following year judge of a military court and served in that capacity until 1865.

After the war Walker resumed the practice of his profession in Huntsville. He served as president of the constitutional convention of 1875 and was delegate at large to the Democratic national conventions of 1876 and 1884. Widely known and popular in the state, respected for his learning, wisdom, and character, an able lawyer with a large, important, and profitable practice, he exerted an influence in Alabama out of all proportion to his activity in public affairs. He was twice married: first, to a Miss Hopkins of Mississippi; second, in July 1850, to Eliza Dickson Pickett, daughter of Judge William Dickson Pickett and Eliza Goddard (Whitman) Pickett of Montgomery.

[Sources include C. A. Evans, *Confederate Mil. Hist.* (1899), vol. I; *Jour. of the Cong. of the Confederate*

States of America, vol. I (1904) ; J. B. Jones, *A Rebel War Clerk's Diary* (1866), I, 37–39 ; T. W. Palmer, *A Reg. of the Officers and Students of the Univ. of Ala.* (1901) ; "The Cabinet at Montgomery," *Harper's Weekly*, June 1, 1861 ; *Daily Reg.* (Mobile), Aug. 23, 1884 ; information as to certain facts from members of the family. Walker's official letter-book (Feb. 21–Sept. 15, 1861) is in the Confederate States of America material in MSS. Div., Lib. of Cong.]

J. G. deR. H.

WALKER, MARY EDWARDS (Nov. 26, 1832–Feb. 21, 1919), physician, woman's rights advocate, was born in Oswego, N. Y., the daughter of Alvah and Vesta (Whitcomb) Walker. Among her ancestors was the "Widow Walker," one of the early settlers of Plymouth Colony, who came to America before 1643. Her early education was obtained in the school conducted by her father, mother, and sisters on the family farm near Oswego. From her father, who in addition to teaching was a farmer and physician, she acquired an ambition to study medicine, in disregard of the prejudices which in the 1840's and 1850's looked with scandalized disapproval on attempts by women to invade any of the professions except teaching. Overcoming all the many obstacles in her path she succeeded in completing her studies and in 1855 received her physician's certificate from the Syracuse Medical College. She began to practise at Columbus, Ohio, but soon removed to Rome, N. Y. In neither place did she find the services of a woman doctor in great demand.

While teaching school in New York City at the age of sixteen, she began to pursue those objectives known as "woman's rights." She discarded skirts for full trousers, partly concealed by long flapping coats. For the first three years of the Civil War she was a nurse in the Union army. Between March and August 1864, she appears to have served as a spy while nominally attached to the 52nd Ohio Infantry in the capacity of contract surgeon. On Oct. 5, 1864, she was commissioned and assigned to duty as an assistant surgeon. In the army she dressed like her brother officers, trousers with gold stripes, felt hat encircled with a gold cord, and an officer's greatcoat. Her jacket was cut like a blouse and fitted loosely at the neck.

Following her resignation from the army in June 1865, she worked for a short time on a New York newspaper—one of the first women in America to be so employed—and then set herself up as a practising physician in Washington, D. C. She continued wearing men's attire, a frock coat and striped trousers by day, and full evening dress when on the lecture platform or at evening social gatherings. She wore her hair in curls, in order, so she said, that "everybody

would know that I was a woman." Her wearing of trousers brought her many vexations. Not only did boys rotten-egg her and men make her the butt for sardonic or ribald humor—"Bill" Nye (Edgar W. Nye [*q.v.*]) called her a "self-made man"—but her own sex also disapproved of her. Women made faces at her in the streets and in a myriad other ways manifested their dislike for her labors in their behalf. Several times she was arrested for "masquerading in men's clothes"—occasions which she welcomed because of the opportunities they provided for displaying the permission said to have been given her by Congress to wear trousers. That Congress ever gave such permission is open to question. The *Congressional Records* do not yield any information on this point.

While in Washington she took part in the agitation for the popular election of United States senators and other similar reforms, and gave play to her genuine talent as an inventor. She is credited with devising the inside neckband on men's shirts which protects the skin from the collar button, and the return post-card sent out with registered mail. Most of her zeal, however, went into the improvement of woman's lot. In 1897 she founded a colony for women only called "Adamless Eden." She was a believer in spiritualism and possessed a highly individualistic literary style for which she found outlet in two books : *Hit* (1871), and *Unmasked, or the Science of Immorality* (1878). Her genuinely fine and kindly soul took great pride in the bronze medal given her by Congress for her war service, although the medal was stricken from the list by the Board of Medal Awards, on Feb. 15, 1917, because the occasion for its giving was not of record in the War Department archives. A fall on the Capitol steps at Washington in 1917 was the indirect cause of her death near Oswego two years later. She was never married.

[A biography of Dr. Walker by Mrs. C. M. Poynter of Omaha, Nebr., is in preparation. See records in the War Dept., Washington, D. C. ; *Who's Who in America*, 1918–19 ; J. B. R. Walker, *Memorial of the Walkers of the Old Plymouth Colony* (1861) ; *Lineage Book, Nat. Soc., D.A.R.*, vol. CIX (1929) ; *Personal Recollections of the War of the Rebellion*, ed. by A. N. Blakeman, vol. IV (1912) ; *Literary Digest*, Mar. 15, 1919 ; *Washington Post, N. Y. Times*, Feb. 23, 1919.]

W. E. S—a.

WALKER, PINKNEY HOUSTON (June 18, 1815–Feb. 7, 1885), jurist, son of Joseph G. Walker, a Kentucky lawyer, and Martha (Scott), was born on a farm in Adair County, Ky. He was of Scotch-Irish descent, his first American ancestor, John Walker, having come to America from Ireland between 1726 and 1730. Attending country school in winter, helping his father on the farm in summer, and working in a village store occupied most of Pinkney's time as a youth until he was nineteen years of age, when he went to live in Rushville, Ill. After four years in a store there, he attended an academy at Macomb for several months and then entered upon the study of law in the office of his uncle, Cyrus Walker. Admitted to the bar in 1839, he practised in Macomb, at first in partnership with Thomas Morrison and later with his uncle. In 1848 he returned to Rushville where, after practising five years, most of the time in partnership with Robert S. Blackwell, he was elected to the circuit bench to fill a vacancy. He was reëlected in 1855, but resigned early in 1858 to accept an appointment tendered by Gov. William H. Bissell [q.v.], as justice of the supreme court of Illinois. In June of that year he was elected to that position and also in 1867 and 1876, serving continuously until his death. From 1864 to 1867 and in 1874–75 he was chief justice.

Among Walker's most important opinions may be mentioned *Carroll* vs. *East St. Louis, 67 Ill.,* 568 (1873) and *Starkweather* vs. *American Bible Society, 72 Ill.,* 50 (1874), in which he pointed out the danger involved in the use of a corporation as a legal device for holding land in perpetuity; and *Ruggles* vs. *People, 91 Ill., 256* (1878), in which he held that a grant by the state to a railroad company of a power to fix rates did not bar subsequent legislative regulation of rates under the police power. He concurred in the opinion in *Munn* vs. *Illinois, 69 Ill.,* 80, upholding the power of the state to regulate and fix maximum rates of charge in grain elevators. Walker's opinions were neither brilliant nor scholarly, but were characterized by practicality, cogency of reasoning, and clarity of expression. He was a prodigious worker. Especially was he incessant in his endeavors to keep the supreme court docket clear, a no small undertaking during his first twelve years as a judge when there were but three justices on the bench. On one occasion, between the second week in November (the close of the September term) and the first of the following January, he wrote sixty-two opinions, and during his judicial career, approximately 3,000—said to be the largest number ever written by a judge in the United States. His integrity and fairness were uniformly recognized by associates on the bench and by lawyers who practised before him. Though a Democrat in politics, his appointment to the supreme bench was at the hands of a Republican governor, and his three elections came from a normally Republican district.

Physically, Walker was of a large and powerful frame and until the last years of his life possessed such rugged health that during all his years as judge he never missed a session of the court. He was a lover of books, and read much in the field of science and philosophy. He was known for his many acts of generosity and kindness, and as a judge was patient and considerate, especially with young and inexperienced members of the bar. On June 2, 1840, he married Susan McCroskey, a native of Adair County, Ky. To them nine children were born, five of whom, two sons and three daughters, survived their father.

[E. S. White, *Geneal. of the Descendants of John Walker* (1902); *The Biog. Encyc. of Ill. of the Nineteenth Century* (1875); ¸. M. Palmer, *The Bench and Bar of Ill.* (1899), vol. I; *Chicago Legal News,* Feb. 14, 21, 1885, May 11, 1889; "In Memoriam, Pinkney H. Walker," 113 *Ill. Reports,* 13–28; J. E. Babb, "The Supreme Court of Ill.," *The Green Bag,* May 1891; *Proc. Ill. State Bar Asso.* (1886); *Chicago Tribune,* Feb. 9, 1885.]   G. W. G.

WALKER, REUBEN LINDSAY (May 29, 1827–June 7, 1890), Confederate soldier, civil engineer, was born in Logan, Albemarle County, Va., the son of Meriwether Lewis and Maria (Lindsay) Walker and a great-grandson of Thomas Walker [q.v.]. After graduating from the Virginia Military Institute in 1845, Reuben practised his profession of civil engineering and later engaged in farming in New Kent County, Va. He was married in 1848 to Maria Eskridge of Staunton, Va., and after her death, in 1857 to Sally Elam, daughter of Dr. Albert Elam of Chesterfield County and grand-daughter of Gov. James Pleasants [q.v.] of Virginia.

At the beginning of the Civil War Walker was made captain of the Purcell Battery and was hurried off to Aquia Creek, Va. During the following four years he served without a day's leave of absence. He arrived at Manassas in time to shell the retreating enemy and during the remainder of 1861 was with his battery in Virginia. In March 1862 he was promoted major and served as chief of artillery for A. P. Hill's division. Though ill in Richmond during the Seven Days' Battle, he was connected with Hill's command until the end of the war. At Fredericksburg, Hill reported that Lieutenant-Colonel Walker directed the fire from his guns "with admirable coolness and precision," and he was cited in numerous other battle reports. Shortly after Fredericksburg he was promoted colonel, and became chief of artillery when Hill was made commander of the III Army Corps. He commanded sixty-three guns at Gettysburg and was in the remaining hard-fought campaigns in Virginia. In February 1865 he was appointed brigadier-general of artillery.

Walker was not a dashing artilleryman like Alexander, Chew, and Pegram, nor was he as intellectual as Long or Alexander; but he showed an engineer's knowledge and appreciation of topography and was unexcelled in the Confederate artillery as an organizer. He was also outstanding for his courage and dogged devotion to duty, his physical hardihood, and his noble appearance. Six feet four inches in height and of massive frame, with long dark hair, sweeping moustache and imperial beard, and a superb horseman, he was one of the most striking figures in Lee's army.

After the war he engaged in farming. In 1872 he moved to Selma, Ala., and until 1874 was superintendent of the Marine & Selma Railroad. Returning to Virginia in 1876, he was employed by the Richmond & Danville Railroad until 1877. Later he was superintendent of the Richmond street railways and served as construction engineer for the Richmond & Alleghany Railroad. He superintended the building of the women's department of the Virginia State Penitentiary and in 1884 was appointed superintendent of construction of the Texas State Capitol, residing in Austin until 1888. Before his appointment there had been much scandal in connection with the management of this project, and Walker was put in charge because of his integrity, faithfulness, and efficiency. He died on his Virginia farm at the confluence of the Rivanna and the James. While a Confederate soldier he had fought in sixty-three battles and engagements and in his later years he grew sensitive to the query, "Why General, not wounded in the war?" Drawing himself up to his giant's height and squaring his great shoulders he would reply, "No, sir, and it was not my fault" (Wise, *post*, pp. 753–54). His wife and eight children survived him.

[*War of the Rebellion: Official Records (Army)*; J. C. Wise, *The Long Arm of Lee* (2 vols., 1915); C. A. Evans, *Confed. Mil. Hist.* (1899), vol. III; R. C. M. Page, *Geneal. of the Page Family in Virginia* (1893); C. G. Chamberlayne, *Ham Chamberlayne—Virginian* (1932); *Richmond Dispatch*, June 8, 1890; information from the Walker family.]   R. D. M.

WALKER, ROBERT FRANKLIN (Nov. 29, 1850–Nov. 19, 1930), Missouri jurist, was born at Florence, Morgan County, Mo., of Scottish and Virginian ancestry through his father, Belford Stephenson Walker, and of Welsh ancestry through his mother, Abigail (Evans) Walker. His parents, both natives of Delaware County, Ohio, moved to Morgan County, Mo., at an early age. Walker graduated from the

University of Missouri with the degree of B.S. in 1873, and from the same institution received that of M.S. in 1877. After teaching school and studying law in Missouri and in Texas, he was admitted to the Missouri bar in 1876, and at Versailles, the county seat of Morgan County, began a distinguished professional career of fifty-four years, thirty-five of which were in public service.

As prosecuting attorney of Morgan County (1877–85), assistant attorney-general of Missouri (1885–89), and attorney-general (1893–97), Walker became thoroughly familiar with the substantive and procedural law of crimes. A Cleveland Democrat in 1896, he publicly supported the Palmer and Buckner national ticket, thus bringing to an end, seemingly, his political career. In 1897 he gave up his residence in Versailles and moved his law office to St. Louis, where he soon became known as a safe, industrious, and successful lawyer in private practice. In 1912, when the animosities of 1896 were forgotten, Walker was elected as a regular Democrat to the supreme court of Missouri for a term of ten years, and reëlected in 1922. His death occurred at Jefferson City thirteen months before the expiration of his second term.

Walker's judicial actions and opinions are recorded in 247–326 *Missouri Reports*. The opinions exhibit adequate learning, a realistic grasp of modern social conditions, a desire to make law fit in with those conditions, jealousy in guarding the individual right from encroachment by the police power, and a rhetorical grace above the average in American legal literature. His most important work was in criminal appeals. Without trying to overrule earlier cases, he intentionally and tactfully accomplished much in the gradual mitigation of the older Missouri doctrine that all error presumes prejudice against the defendant in criminal appeals. Toward the end of his life he was able to say: "Where it is disclosed by the record that the accused had a fair trial there is an increasing and commendable tendency on the part of appellate courts, not to disturb a verdict of guilty for mere technicalities" (*State* vs. *Cutter*, 318 *Mo.*, 687).

Although it was not generally known in his lifetime, Walker was a writer of poetry, always simple in style and generally humorous or satiric in tone. Some of his shorter and lighter verses, written while he was a member of the supreme court, were published anonymously in the "Just-a-Minute" column of the *St. Louis Post-Dispatch* (oral statement from Clark McAdams, editor, September 1933). In 1927 Walker caused to be printed an uncopyrighted book of 180 pages, entitled *Random Rhymes by R. E. Klaw-fera*. When reversed the pseudonym becomes Ar Ef Walker. This book is now valuable because much of it relates to the personal, gossipy, or seamy side of Missouri political history. One of the poems, "Bill and John," is a bitter and merited denunciation of two eminent and successful corporation lobbyists. Walker was twice married; first, Sept. 20, 1877, to Nannie A. Wright of Fayette, Mo., who died in 1892; second, Sept. 28, 1896, to Mrs. Geneva C. Percy of Brooklyn, New York. A daughter and a son, children of the first wife, survived him.

[A. J. D. Stewart, *The Hist. of the Bench and Bar of Mo.* (1898); *The Book of St. Louisans* (2nd ed., 1912); *Who's Who in America*, 1930–31; *Mo. Bar Jour.*, Dec. 1930; 326 *Mo. Reports* (1931); *A Sheaf of Memories* (n.d.), addresses by Walker before the Old Settlers Asso. of Morgan County; *St. Louis Post-Dispatch*, Nov. 20, 1930; letters from daughter and from registrar, Univ. of Mo.; newspaper clippings and other data in Mo. Hist. Soc., St. Louis.]   T. W.

WALKER, ROBERT JOHN (July 19, 1801–Nov. 11, 1869), whose name is sometimes given as Robert James and most often as Robert J. Walker, United States senator, secretary of the treasury, governor of Kansas Territory, was born in Northumberland, Pa., the son of Jonathan Hoge Walker [*q.v.*] and his wife Lucretia (or Lucy) Duncan. Prepared for college at town schools and by private tutors, Robert attended the University of Pennsylvania, where he graduated first in his class in 1819. Money had to be borrowed for his board and tuition from his landlord, the Rev. Samuel B. Wylie; it was repaid in a few years by young Walker himself. He was admitted to the bar in Pittsburgh in 1821. Walker at once plunged into politics. In the fall of 1823 he was one of the sponsors of a meeting of the Republicans of Allegheny County to nominate Andrew Jackson for the presidency, and wrote the address which called on the party in Pennsylvania to support him at a state convention. The Harrisburg convention of 1824 marked the success of this movement, and Walker's speech was adopted as the address of the convention. Subsequently, a laudatory biographer said: "Thus at the early age of twenty-two, we find Mr. Walker the acknowledged leader of the democracy of ... Pennsylvania." (*United States Magazine and Democratic Review*, Feb. 1845, p. 157).

None the less, in 1826 he moved to Natchez, Miss. Thither he had been preceded by his brother Duncan, with whom he entered into a lucrative law practice. But Walker's associations were mainly with the more eager and speculative spirits of those flush times. His speculations

in plantations, slave, and wild lands were magnificent, involving a debt of several hundred thousand dollars. At the same time he always posed as the friend of the squatter and small farmer. Though known as a Jackson man, Walker did not at first take conspicuous part in politics. In 1834, however, he was taken up by the Democratic managers of the state as almost the only available man able to cope in debate with the redoubtable and eccentric Senator George Poindexter [*q.v.*]. Walker's successful campaign for the Senate was carefully managed by an inner ring of which William M. Gwin was the most important member. It was marked by the introduction of a type of stump speaking and sectional appeal which was new in Mississippi. The great stroke of this campaign of 1835, however, was the procurement of an "original letter" from Andrew Jackson, expressing confidence in the candidate. Some have questioned the authenticity of this letter (Claiborne, *post*, p. 416), but it was conspicuously useful to Walker for some years, serving as a sort of certificate of respectability when he was accused of being too intimate with banks and bankers.

Walker took his seat in the Senate on Feb. 22, 1836. He was one of the most ardent of the southwestern group, and rarely missed an opportunity to speak in favor of the claims of new states to public lands, in favor of preëmption and lower prices, and against distribution of the surplus, the protective tariff, and abolitionism. He won an early notoriety by seeking a quarrel with Clay; and, being an eager and indefatigable worker, he soon won a place for himself. He was conspicuous in the debates on the complicated matters connected with the surplus revenues and the "American system"; and his friends gave him credit for the permanent preëmption law of 1841. He was a powerful supporter of the independent treasury plan. He was reëlected to the Senate for the term beginning Mar. 4, 1841, over Seargent S. Prentiss [*q.v.*]. He was definitely identified with the anti-bank and repudiating party in Mississippi.

Walker's service as a senator is chiefly memorable for his activities in connection with the annexation of Texas. By temper, by conviction, and by interest he was an expansionist. His resolution of Jan. 11, 1837, calling for recognition of the independence of Texas was with difficulty put through the Senate, but his efforts won great applause in Texas. His opportunity came only with the presidency of John Tyler. It is doubtful whether he inspired Tyler's bank vetoes, but it is certain that he was one of the President's foremost allies in the efforts of 1843–45 to add Texas to the Union. In January 1844 he wrote to Andrew Jackson that the Senate would ratify a treaty of annexation, and urged him to put pressure on Houston to secure one. A published letter of his, dated Jan. 8, 1844 (*Letter of Mr. Walker of Mississippi, Relative to the Annexation of Texas,* 1844), was very widely circulated and served as the major weapon in the campaign to prepare public opinion for the expected treaty. It contained an elaborate argument that annexation would help toward the ultimate extinction of slavery, but the claim has been made that this was omitted from the version of the letter circulated in the South (G. L. Prentiss, *A Memoir of S. S. Prentiss,* 1855, II, 336). When Tyler's treaty of annexation came to the Senate, Walker was the leader in defending it; many factors, however, combined to bring about its decisive defeat.

Meanwhile, the Democratic party was engaged in the difficult task of selecting a presidential candidate. Walker appears to have been at the center of the manipulations which resulted in the rejection of Martin Van Buren and the nomination of James K. Polk [*qq.v.*]. There is some indication that it was on his initiative that Van Buren's letter (published Apr. 27, 1844), which declared against immediate annexation, was solicited. Walker, long the leader of the annexationists, was too shrewd a politician to play the game of Tyler or Calhoun; his rôle, then, was that of leader of an insurgent group, working to defeat Van Buren and secure an annexationist candidate who would divide the embittered factions as little as possible. This group, potently aided by Thomas Ritchie of Virginia, was successful at the Baltimore convention. In the campaign of 1844 Walker also served as head of the Democratic campaign committee in Washington. In this capacity he was betrayed by over-eagerness, for he circulated a pamphlet, *The South in Danger* (1844), which was so violent in its attempts to identify the Whigs with abolitionism that the Whigs reprinted it for use in the North.

Walker's last service to Texas was in February 1845, when he drafted the compromise resolutions which finally resolved the deadlock in the Senate over annexation. Meanwhile, Polk was being subjected to pressure to give him an important place in the cabinet. Dallas and the westerners favored him for the state department, but Polk finally made him secretary of the treasury. The appointment was clearly a concession to Lewis Cass and the western Democrats, though Andrew Jackson wrote to Polk on May 2, 1845, that Walker, because of his financial associations, was the only one of the cabinet of whom

he disapproved (J. S. Bassett, ed., *Correspondence of Andrew Jackson,* VI, 1933, p. 405).

During his four years as secretary, Walker, despite bad health, was indefatigable. His first concern was to secure the establishment of the independent or "constitutional" treasury system for the handling of public monies; until this was obtained he felt that the country had its "hand in the Lions mouth." Far more of his energy, however, was devoted to the revision of the tariff, a matter in which he saw eye to eye with the President. His well-known report of 1845 on the state of the finances, which at once became a classic of free-trade literature, set forth with emphasis the constitutional, economic, and social arguments in favor of a tariff for revenue only (*House Document No. 6,* 29 Cong., 1 Sess.). It smells a little of the study but remains a very able state paper; and at the time it was utilized in the current controversy in England as well as in the United States. The tariff bill of 1846, largely framed by Walker, was put through as an administration measure with difficulty and with the aid of personal lobbying by him. It was, however, a moderate protective rather than a free-trade measure, and from Walker's point of view it was mutilated by the omission of duties on tea and coffee.

The financing of the Mexican War was carried out simply and successfully. Walker had close personal relations with the powerful Washington firm of Corcoran and Riggs, and although it is possible that certain financiers enjoyed the use of government funds longer than was proper, the public borrowings were made on favorable terms and without scandal (*Diary of Polk,* III, 140 ff.). Walker initiated two administrative changes of importance. On his urgent recommendation, provision was made for the establishment of a warehousing system for the handling of imports (9 *United States Statutes at Large,* 53), such as has remained in use ever since. His last public report was a study of this system, based especially on the data obtained by commissioners whom he had sent to England (*Report of the Secretary of the Treasury on the Warehousing System* (*Senate Executive Document No. 32,* 30 Cong., 2 Sess.). He was also mainly responsible for the creation of the Department of the Interior in 1849. The bill for its organization was drawn by him as a direct result of his administrative experience, and was carried through the Senate by Jefferson Davis assisted by Daniel Webster. Polk signed the bill though he did not approve of it.

Walker constantly urged in the cabinet the acquisition of all the territory the United States could get—which, by the autumn of 1847, meant all of Mexico. His views were well known, and when he was joined by Buchanan and Vice-President Dallas, anti-slavery northerners expressed great alarm. Polk was not to be stampeded by any pressure from official advisers, and had at least the tacit support of all his cabinet save Walker and Buchanan in his final decision to submit the Trist treaty to the Senate (February 1848). It was said, but cannot be proved, that Walker lobbyed behind Polk's back for the rejection of the treaty. At any rate, a few months later Walker and the President were talking cordially about the possible annexation of Yucatan, while it was the Secretary of the Treasury who suggested $100,000,000 as the sum which might be, and was, offered for Cuba.

When he went out of office in 1849, Walker made no attempt to resume participation in state politics. Until 1857 he lived as a private citizen in Washington, attending to his extensive speculative interests—lands in Mississippi, Louisiana, and Wisconsin, projects for a Pacific railroad, a quicksilver mine in California; practising in the Supreme Court; and, in 1851–52, making a long stay in England to sell the securities of the Illinois Central Railroad. In 1853 he was offered and accepted the mission to China, but there was disagreement or misunderstanding about it and he resigned, feeling that President Pierce had abused him badly. Walker's influence was rated highly by politicians behind the scenes, and in 1856 he was again brought into active politics as a supporter of Buchanan's presidential ambitions. After the election he was regarded as a strong candidate for the State Department; but there was strong objection from the South. His appointment as governor of Kansas Territory (March 1857) was made with the concurrence of all Democratic factions, and both Buchanan and Douglas had to urge him to accept the position. But Kansas, though the grave of governors, offered a great opportunity to a man confident in his own powers, and it seems likely that Walker saw the governorship as a stepping-stone to the Senate and the presidency (F. W. Seward, *Seward at Washington,* 1891, II, 299).

Walker's understanding with Buchanan was explicit that the *bona fide* residents of Kansas should choose their "social institutions" by fair voting, and he stood steadily by the implications of this pledge. His inaugural address, however, was not read or approved by the cabinet. Designed as an appeal to the patriotism and self-interest of the Kansans, and containing the "isothermal" thesis that climatic conditions would be the ultimate determinant of the location of

slavery, it aroused a storm of protest in the South. *"We are betrayed,"* wrote a fire-eater at once (Harmon, *post,* p. 9). Walker suddenly became a liability to the administration. This was because of his attempts to conciliate the free-state party in Kansas by promising with reiterated emphasis that he would do his utmost, with the support of the administration at Washington, to enable a majority of the people in Kansas to rule. Walker's ambition was to bring a pacified and Democratic state into the Union, and he was convinced that it would be a free state. He failed to accomplish this, less because of certain blunders he made than because of the failure of the administration to support him. But he did prevent recurrence of civil war. Finally, when he failed to persuade the President that the so-called ratification of the Lecompton Constitution was unacceptable, in December 1857 he resigned in a letter which was a pamphlet. He subsequently took some part in the agitation against the Lecompton Constitution.

Walker was at heart a Free-Soiler as early as 1849 and is said to have freed his slaves in 1838. The outbreak of the Civil War, accordingly, found him an eager Unionist, though still very much a Democrat, and in the spring of 1861 he was speaking at Union meetings. In 1862 he and F. P. Stanton became proprietors of and frequent contributors to the very loyal *Continental Monthly,* which lasted until the end of 1864. From April 1863 to the latter part of 1864 he undertook a financial mission in Europe which he himself later summarized by saying that while abroad he had "caused to be taken and bought" 250 millions of Federal bonds (*National Intelligencer,* Nov. 12, 1869). His prestige in England, both because of his treasury report of 1845 and his governorship of Kansas, was considerable, and he made use of it not only in favor of the Union bonds but also in the publication of a series of pamphlets showing, not very candidly, how slavery, Jefferson Davis, and the repudiation of debts were almost synonymous terms.

Walker's subsequent activities were obscure but characteristic. His law business had long been concerned chiefly with the prosecution of claims. He seems to have been concerned with a minor phase of the peace parleys at Montreal in 1864–65 (Dunbar Rowland, ed., *Jefferson Davis . . . His Letters, Papers and Speeches,* 1923, VII, 327, n. 1); he acted as lobbyist of the Russian minister and Seward in putting the Alaska purchase bill through Congress; and during his last illness he penned an article urging the advantages which would come to Nova Scotia were it to submit to annexation to the

United States (*Washington Chronicle,* Apr. 23, 1869). He died in Washington on Nov. 11, 1869.

Walker was "a mere whiffet of a man, stooping and diminutive, with a wheezy voice and expressionless face" (Claiborne, p. 415); he weighed less than a hundred pounds. Though his health was bad and he may have been epileptic (McCormac, *post,* p. 529, n. 88), he was a particularly energetic and busy person who greatly impressed his associates by his encyclopedic knowledge. At one of the busiest periods of his life he was engaged, as a labor of love, on a "history of republics." His marriage on Apr. 4, 1825, to Mary Blechynden Bache, a great-granddaughter of Benjamin Franklin, grand-daughter of A. J. Dallas, and daughter of Richard Bache of Texas, seems to have been happy; there were eight children of whom five survived him.

[Materials concerning Walker are widely scattered. Among accounts of his life are W. E. Dodd, *Robert J. Walker, Imperialist* (1914), a short sketch; H. D. Jordan, "A Politician of Expansion: Robert J. Walker," *Miss. Valley Hist. Rev.,* Dec. 1932; G. J. Leftwich, articles in *Green Bag,* Mar. 1903; and *Pubs. Miss. Hist. Soc.,* VI, 1902, pp. 359–71; *U. S. Mag. and Democratic Rev.,* Feb. 1845, pp. 157–64; J. F. H. Claiborne, *Mississippi,* vol. I (1880); H. S. Foote, *Casket of Reminiscences* (1874); J. W. Forney, *Anecdotes of Public Men* (1873), pp. 117–30; obituary in *National Republican* (Washington, D. C.), Nov. 12, 1869; and, in particular, death notice and article in Washington *Daily Morning Chronicle,* Nov. 12, 1869. For important aspects of his career, see G. W. Brown, *Reminiscences of Gov. R. J. Walker* (1902); W. A. Dunning, "Paying for Alaska," *Pol. Science Quart.,* Sept. 1912; H. B. Learned, "The Establishment of the Secretaryship of the Interior," *Am. Hist. Rev.,* July 1911; and "The Sequence of Appointments to Polk's original Cabinet," *Ibid.,* Oct. 1924; E. I. McCormac, *James K. Polk* (1922); A. B. Morris, "Robert J. Walker in the Kansas Struggle" (MS., 1916); M. M. Quaife, ed., *The Diary of James K. Polk* (4 vols., 1910); J. E. Winston, "Robert J. Walker, Annexationist," *Texas Rev.,* Apr. 1917; "Mississippi and the Independence of Texas," *Southwestern Hist. Quart.,* July 1917; and "The Lost Commission," *Miss. Valley Hist. Rev.,* Sept. 1918; *Trans. Kan. State Hist. Soc., 1889–96* (1896), containing documents of Walker's administration as governor; G. D. Harmon, "President James Buchanan's Betrayal of Governor Robert J. Walker of Kansas," *Pa. Mag. Hist. and Biography,* Jan. 1929; A. E. Taylor, "Walker's Financial Mission to London," *Jour. of Economic and Business Hist.,* Feb. 1931. Various MS. collections of his contemporaries in the Lib. of Cong. and the Hist. Soc. of Pa. are important.]

H. D. J.

WALKER, SARAH BREEDLOVE (Dec. 23, 1867–May 25, 1919), pioneer negro business woman, known throughout her later life as Madam C. J. Walker, was born in Delta, La. Her parents were Owen and Minerva Breedlove, poor negro farmers, and her childhood was evidently one of great poverty and hardship, for at the age of six she was orphaned and placed in the care of an older sister. She was married in Vicksburg at the age of fourteen to C. J. Walker and at twenty she was left a widow with a small

daughter to support. She removed to St. Louis, Mo., where she worked as a washerwoman, and reared and educated her daughter. She herself studied in the public night schools of that city. In 1905 she hit upon the formula of a preparation for improving the appearance of the hair of the negro. She experimented on herself and her family with such success that she became convinced of the commercial possibilities of her product, and after a year spent in preliminary work in Denver, Colo., she traveled for two years to promote the preparation. In that time her mail-order business grew to such dimensions that an office was necessary and she settled in Pittsburgh in 1908, staying just long enough to establish a branch there in charge of her daughter. She then resumed her traveling. In 1910 she settled in Indianapolis, Ind., where she founded the Madam C. J. Walker laboratories for the manufacture of various cosmetics and a training school for her agents and beauty culturists. At the height of her career she had about two thousand agents selling her preparations and did a business of more than $50,000 annually. One of her most original ideas was to organize these agents into clubs for business, social, and philanthropic purposes and to bring delegates together in three-day conventions at regular intervals. She stimulated their activities and gave them prestige in their respective communities by offering cash prizes to the clubs that did the largest amount of philanthropic or educational work among colored people.

When she died in May 1919 she was the sole owner and the president of the Madam C. J. Walker Manufacturing Company; she also owned town houses in New York and Indianapolis, and a conventionally handsome and luxurious country estate, "Villa Lewaro," at Irvington-on-the-Hudson. By the terms of her will one-third of her fortune of more than a million dollars went to her daughter and the remaining two-thirds to educational institutions and charities. Throughout her life too she retained a great simplicity and kindliness of character, was always easily approachable and genuinely interested in all movements for the education or uplifting of her race. The methods she taught and the use of her application were popularized by the "straightening" feature on which she capitalized to create a nationwide and even international market. Healthy by-products were the diffusing of the knowledge and practice of personal hygiene among all classes of colored people and the opening up of business careers as agents and beauty culturists for negro women. It is probably true, as an editorial in the *Crisis* of July

1919 stated, that in her lifetime Madam Walker "revolutionized the personal habits and appearance of millions of human beings." She died at her home in Irvington.

[Personal letter from F. B. Ransom, attorney for Madam Walker during her life and for the Sarah B. Walker estate; conversations with Dr. W. E. B. Du Bois, W. E. Pickens, and other personal friends; *Who's Who of the Colored Race*, 1915; *The Madam C. J. Walker Beauty Manual* (1928); *Crisis*, July 1919; *Indianapolis News*, and *N. Y. Times*, May 26, 1919.]

M. G.

WALKER, SEARS COOK (Mar. 23, 1805–Jan. 30, 1853), mathematician and astronomer, was born in Wilmington, Mass., the son of Benjamin Walker and Susanna (Cook) Walker, and a brother of Timothy Walker [*q.v.*]. The devotion of his mother guarded his childhood after the death of his father in 1811, and directed his education in preparation for entrance into Harvard College. For a decade after his graduation in 1825, he taught school near Boston and in Philadelphia, whither he removed in 1827. During this period he acquired an astronomical clock, a twenty-inch transit instrument, and a small Dollond telescope; and from about 1836, when he gave up his school to become actuary to the Pennsylvania Company for Insurance on Lives and Granting Annuities, his leisure hours were devoted to astronomical observation and study. In 1837 he founded one of the first astronomical observatories in the United States in connection with the Philadelphia High School and imported from Munich superior instruments of observation.

He then began to make extensive contributions to the *Proceedings and Transactions of the American Philosophical Society* and to astronomical journals, concerning the observations made at his observatory and including a large body of observations of occultations of stars by the moon; as early as 1834 he had prepared parallactic tables which greatly reduced the time required to compute the phases of an occultation. But he made his recognized entrance into the ranks of scientific investigators, on Jan. 15, 1841, when he read a brilliant memoir on "Researches Concerning the Periodical Meteors of August and November," before the American Philosophical Society (*Transactions,* new series, vol. VIII, 1843). In 1845 he accepted a position in the astronomical staff of the United States Naval Observatory in Washington, D. C., and in 1847 advanced the prestige of this newly founded institution by his announcement, on Feb. 2, 1847, that the planet Neptune, which had been discovered on Sept. 23, 1846, was identical with a star seen twice by Lalande in May 1795, and

which had been referred to as fixed star No. 26266 in Lalande's catalogue. His researches in this relation enabled him to determine the orbit of Neptune thus early after its discovery.

From 1847 until his death, Walker was in charge of the computations of geographical longitude in the United States Coast Survey. His discussion of the largest collection of observations of moon culminations and occultations ever made in America, undertaken with the object of determining the longitude of a central datum point for American surveys, led to the conclusion that longitudes deduced from moon culminations could not be reconciled with those from occultations. His examination of the theory of these observations, in the course of seeking for an explanation of the discrepancies which his discussion had revealed, led him to break sharply with traditions of long standing and gave weight and finality to his conclusion that the new electric telegraph furnished the best means for determining the difference of longitude from place to place, and hence the longitude of any certain place from a prime meridian. The telegraphing of transits of stars was original with him, as was also the application of the graphic registration of time-results to the registry of time-observations for general astronomical purposes. This system came to be known as the American method. On Oct. 10, 1846, the transit of a star was telegraphed by the Naval Observatory to Philadelphia. As Walker stated before the American Association for the Advancement of Science, "this was the first practical application of the method of star-signals, which is [destined] sooner or later to perfect the geography of the globe" (*Proceedings,* vol. II, 1850, p. 184). This was the last of those researches, justly regarded as models of practical application of some of the most refined processes of analysis, which have afforded him a place of prominence among American astronomers.

Impaired mental health soon caused him to cease his labors, and, under the care of his sister, Susan, who had been the center of his home in Washington, he traveled to Cincinnati, Ohio, to pass his last days in the family circle of his elder brother. He was buried near Cincinnati. His "Researches Relative to the Planet Neptune" is to be found in the *Smithsonian Contributions to Knowledge,* vol. II (1851); his "Ephemeris of the Planet Neptune," in the same, vol. II, Appendices 1 to 3, and in vol. III (1852), Appendix 1. Occasional writings appeared in the *Proceedings of the American Philosophical Society,* and the *Astronomical Journal,* Apr. 20, 1850, to Apr. 11, 1851.

[*Wilmington Records of Births, Marriages, and Deaths* (1898); B. A. Gould, Jr., "An Address in Commemoration of Sears Cook Walker," *Trans. Am. Asso. Advancement of Sci.*, vol. VIII (1855); *Ann. Report, Superintendent of the Coast Survey*, 1846, 1848, 1850, 1851, 1853 (1846–54); *Astronom. Jour.*, Mar. 15, 1853; *Cincinnati Daily Enquirer*, Feb. 1, 1853.]

G. W. L.

WALKER, THOMAS (Jan. 25, 1715–Nov. 9, 1794), physician, soldier, and explorer, the second son of Thomas and Susanna (Peachy) Walker, was born in King and Queen County, Va. His ancestors are supposed to have emigrated from Staffordshire, England, to tidewater Virginia in the middle of the seventeenth century; and he is believed to have received his education at the College of William and Mary, but there is uncertainty in both cases. Certain it is that his father died in his youth and that he went to live in Williamsburg with his sister, Mary Peachy, who had married the senior Dr. George Gilmer. Here he acquired a knowledge of medicine and later removed to Fredericksburg where he practised for some years, acquiring eminence in the field of surgery. His pupil, William Baynham [*q.v.*], bore witness to the excellence of his training. He also kept a general store and carried on importing and exporting operations. In 1741 he was married to Mildred Thornton, the widow of Nicholas Meriwether and a relative of George Washington. Through this union he acquired about 11,000 acres of land in the present Albemarle County, known as the "Castle Hill" estate. This was the foundation of his fortune. His trading operations probably carried him to the valley of Virginia, for soon he had valuable connections in that section.

In 1748 he made one of a company of prominent western land speculators who explored the southern end of the Virginia valley and staked out rich claims for themselves under a grant made to one of the associates. A large tract surrounding the present town of Abingdon came into Walker's possession in this manner. In 1749 the Loyal Land Company was organized on the basis of a grant of 800,000 acres from the Council of Virginia, and Walker became its chief agent. In 1750 he led a party of explorers westward to spy out their lands. The journal he kept on this occasion is well known and marks him as the first white man to have made a recorded expedition to the Kentucky country. Unfortunately for his associates, he failed to reach the green meadows of the blue grass country. In 1752 he made his first appearance in the Virginia House of Burgesses, but during the same year he was commissioned deputy surveyor of Augusta County and relinquished his seat (*Jour-*

nals of the House of Burgesses of Virginia, 1752–1758, H. R. McIlwaine, ed., 1909, pp. vii–ix). In 1755 he became commissary-general to the Virginia troops serving under George Washington in the French war, and was present at the memorable defeat of Braddock. Charges were brought against him in the House of Burgesses in 1759 by Thomas Johnson of Louisa County that his commissary accounts were irregular. He was absolved from the charges of fraud, but it appears that he had contracted a secret partnership in the supply business with Andrew Lewis [*q.v.*], an associate in land speculations and a commander of the troops Walker supplied (*Journals of the House of Burgesses of Virginia, 1758–61*, 1908, pp. 88–90).

In 1756 Walker was back in the House of Burgesses, this time as a member from the frontier county of Hampshire, which he continued to represent until 1761. The place of his residence during the years since 1748 is something of a mystery. It is certain that he carried on business operations in Louisa as early as 1754, and it is likely that the commissary business took him to Hampshire, which lies across the Potomac from the strategic point of Cumberland, Md. Though not necessarily the case, it is probably true that he resided in these respective counties during the years he represented them in the legislature. In 1761 he sat for the first time for Albemarle County; in 1763 he was a commissioner to sell lots in Charlottesville, the new county seat (Edgar Woods, *Albemarle County in Virginia*, 1932), and in 1765 he built the homestead on the "Castle Hill" estate. From this time forward he made his home at "Castle Hill," where he was a neighbor of Peter Jefferson, and later acted as guardian for his son Thomas. In 1768 Walker represented Virginia at the important Indian treaty at Fort Stanwix. The next year he signed the non-importation agreement and thereafter took an important part in the revolutionary movement. In 1775 he was named one of a commission to negotiate with the Ohio Indians at Pittsburgh, and in 1776 was a member of the Virginia Committee of Safety. When the state government was organized in that year, he became a member of the executive council (*Journals of the Council of the State of Virginia*, H. R. McIlwaine, ed., vol. I, 1932). In 1779 he headed the Virginia commission which extended the North Carolina-Virginia boundary to the westward. Daniel Smith [*q.v.*] was also a member of the commission. Having completed this service, he was again a member of the Council but declined reappointment in 1781 (*Official Letters of the Governors of the State of Virginia,*

H. R. McIlwaine, ed., 3 vols., 1926–29). The following year he ended his public career by representing Albemarle in the House of Delegates. Here he served on a committee appointed to vindicate Virginia's claim to western lands. His first wife died on Nov. 16, 1778, and some time thereafter he married her cousin, Elizabeth Thornton. By his first wife he had twelve children, most of whom married into prominent Virginian families and two of whom, John and Francis, attained distinction, the former serving as United States senator and the latter as a member of the federal House of Representatives. Francis W. Gilmer [q.v.] was his grandson; Reuben L. Walker [q.v.] was a great-grandson; and a grand-daughter, Judith P. Walker, married William C. Rives [q.v.].

Thomas Walker is typical of that company of bold spirits who explored and exploited the early frontier, being a man of action rather than of ideas. He died at the age of seventy-nine and was buried at "Castle Hill."

[*Jour. of an Exploration in the Spring of the Year 1750, by Dr. Thomas Walker* (1888), with a sketch of the life of Walker by a descendant, Dr. William C. Rives, of Washington, D. C., who possesses Walker's correspondence and papers; *First Explorations of Ky.* (1898), edited by J. S. Johnston, The Filson Club Publications, no. 13; Archibald Henderson, "Dr. Thomas Walker and the Loyal Company of Virginia," *Proc. Am. Antiquarian Soc.*, n.s., vol. XLI (1932); A. W. Burns, "Daniel Boone's Predecessor in Kentucky" (mimeograph copy in Lib. of Cong.); *Christopher Gist's Jours.* (1893), edited by W. M. Darlington; Philip Slaughter, *Memoir of Col. Joshua Fry* (1880?); T. P. Abernethy, *Western Lands and the Revolution* (to be published); W. B. Blanton, *Med. in Va. in the Eighteenth Century* (1931); *Va. Gazette and Gen. Advertiser* (Richmond), Nov. 12, 1794.]   T.P.A.

WALKER, THOMAS BARLOW (Feb. 1, 1840–July 28, 1928), lumber magnate and art collector, was born in Xenia, Ohio, the son of Platt Bayliss and Anstis (Barlow) Walker. His father died in Missouri on his way to the California gold fields in 1849 and six years later the widowed mother and her children moved to Berea, Ohio, where Walker supplemented his early schooling with an occasional term at Baldwin University. Working to help support the family and to finance his education, he sold grindstones for Fletcher Hulet, traveling for the purpose all over the Northwest. On Dec. 9, 1863, he married Hulet's daughter, Harriet, and with her took up his permanent residence in Minneapolis.

Until the late sixties Walker was employed as surveyor, an occupation which revealed to him the value of the pine stands of northern Minnesota. His knowledge, together with money furnished by Minneapolis men, made possible the firm of Butler, Mills & Walker, which invested heavily in pine lands, especially through the purchase of Chippewa Half-Breed Scrip, which was supposedly non-transferable. A federal investigation of these purchases exonerated Walker and other purchasers from blame on the specific point designated by Congress, but the report stated that the "testimony reveals a reckless carelessness in making large purchases, and we think, on the part of many of the claimants, guilty participation in an ingenious device to evade the orders of the Government" (Report of the Jones Commission, *post*, p. 12). Walker escaped disaster in the panic of 1873 by disposing of most of his holdings before the crash, but subsequently, with new partners from time to time, he extended his timber holdings until he was the largest operator in Minnesota. Eventually the Walker lumber interests were concentrated in the family, largely through the Red River Lumber Company. In the late eighties Walker and his sons began to invest in California lands, seeking "enough timber to enable the mills to run permanently with the timber supply always growing" (*Minneapolis Times*, May 3, 1905). Lumbering, sale of cut-over ore lands, real-estate deals in and about Minneapolis, and various other ventures made Walker a millionaire many times over. By the early years of the twentieth century he had practically withdrawn from active business, to devote most of his time to civic and philanthropic enterprises and especially to his growing art collection.

Walker's interest in art started with the purchase of a portrait of Washington by Rembrandt Peale [q.v.], and by 1880 he had to build a special room to house his acquisitions. Subsequently additions were made to his home to form the Walker Art Gallery, which was opened to the public. He was one of the founders of the Minneapolis Society of Fine Arts and was its president from 1888 to 1893, but was unwilling to merge his treasures with those of the Society and finally built an edifice to house his paintings, jewelry, stones, pottery, jade, and glass. This collection was of uneven merit, many trivial and bizarre objects being mingled with those of unquestioned significance. In 1925 he organized the Walker Foundation, a corporation to administer the gallery and collections, and two years later gave the Foundation a permanent endowment. In 1915 he contributed "Memories of the Early Life and Development of Minnesota," to the *Collections of the Minnesota Historical Society* (vol. XV).

He was a conservative Republican, impatient of the vagaries of "reformers" (see letter to *Min-*

neapolis Tribune, Sept. 13, 1907). In 1895 he published *A Review of Our Tariff Rates from 1821 to 1895.* He supported actively the Young Men's Christian Association, the Methodist Episcopal Church, of which he was a member, the Minneapolis Public Libary, which he had helped to found, and many other philanthropic enterprises. At his death he was survived by five sons and a daughter.

[*Who's Who in America,* 1926–27; *Sketches of the Life of the Honorable T. B. Walker* (1907), comp. by P. B. Walker; Report of the Jones Commission, *Sen. Ex. Doc. 33,* 43 Cong., 1 Sess.; M. N. Orfield, *Federal Land Grants to the States with Special Reference to Minnesota* (1915); W. W. Folwell, *A Hist. of Minn.,* esp. IV (1930), 465 ff.; *Minneapolis Daily Times,* July 30, 1903; R. I. Holcombe and W. H. Bingham, *Compendium of Hist. and Biog. of Minneapolis and Hennepin County* (1914); M. D. Shutter, *Hist. of Minneapolis* (1923); *Minneapolis Journal,* July 28, 1928, and *passim.*]
L. B. S—e.

WALKER, TIMOTHY (July 27, 1705–Sept. 1, 1782), Congregational clergyman, was born in Woburn, Mass., one of the twelve children of Capt. Samuel Walker and his wife, Judith Howard. Nine of these children died within two months in 1738, victims of diphtheria. Timothy was graduated from Harvard College in 1725. In March 1730, before he was twenty-five, he was called to the first parish to be established in Penacook (later Rumford and still later Concord), N. H. Before he was installed, he made an agreement that if through extreme old age he should be unable to carry on the whole work of the ministry his salary should be reduced; but as sole minister of Concord he continued till the day of his death.

The township of Penacook had been granted in 1726 by Massachusetts to one hundred selected settlers from Andover and Haverhill. It lay within the district designated as the shire of Bow by New Hampshire, and its boundary lines were not clearly established. In 1727 the entire Bow district was granted by New Hampshire to a group of absentee proprietors. Thirteen years later the Crown made a settlement whereby the township was thrown into New Hampshire, and the Massachusetts pioneers were threatened with dispossession. Walker, as agent for the Rumford proprietors, made three trips to England in 1753, 1755, and 1762, in order to appeal directly to the King in Council, and finally, in behalf of the settlers and original landholders, won a favorable decision from the Crown. This judgment, that a change of provincial boundaries did not affect titles to private property, is important in the history of Colonial land tenure.

Walker's house was the town's chief mansion during the first half-century of its development. His diaries, of which only fragments remain,

were kept from the time of his ordination in 1730 until his death in 1782 and are valuable in recreating the picture of life in a pioneer village. Edited by J. B. Walker, they were published in 1889 under the title, *Diaries of Rev. Timothy Walker.* In the fifty-two years of his ministry Walker preached every Sabbath but one. Often he took his gun into the pulpit with him. In theology he was a moderate Calvinist, accepting the Half-way Covenant. While the town had no legal government, it was necessary for him to depend on voluntary contributions from his parishioners; in 1750 his salary had become so meager that the people, through Walker's son-in-law, petitioned the governor for a permanent subsidy, stating that the loss of "a gentleman of unspotted character and universally beloved by us" would be irreparable (Lyford, *post,* I, 189–90). His will shows that he had accumulated very little property; he preferred to labor along with his flock for the necessities of life. He may best be styled as a farmer-preacher, insisting upon the duties of practical religion, and rarely entering into the religious controversies of his century. Two controversial sermons of his were published, however. The first, *The Way to Try All Pretended Apostles* (1743). The former was preached in January 1742. George Whitefield's "pretended" evangelical powers had stirred Walker, with many others, to protest. In this sermon he gave a vivid characterization of the evangelists: "by their Gesture, their Tone, their Delivery, of avowing so much of transport they endeavour what they can to depress and darken the Understanding, and to warm the Imagination, and to alarm the Affections, and when once these are set up to tyrannize over the Understanding, the Mind is thereby rendered susceptible of any Impressions, and so men become moulded into any Form which their enthusiastic or designing Leaders would have them." Later, in 1771, when Hezekiah Smith [*q.v.*], a Baptist evangelist from Haverhill, came to preach at Concord, Walker attacked him in a sermon entitled *Those Who Have the Form of Godliness* (1772), so vehement that two men left the meeting house and turned Baptist. Testimony to the strength of his influence is furnished by the fact that the peripatetic Whitefield let Concord severely alone.

During his active career Walker was able to keep up an interest in the classics and maintain general admiration from family and friends. On Nov. 12, 1730, he had married Sarah Burbeen of Woburn, who bore him five children. His daughter, Sarah, became the wife of Benjamin Rolfe, second in distinction among the Concord inhabitants, and after Rolfe's death, married Benjamin Thompson [*q.v.*], later Count Rumford.

[Samuel Sewall, *The Hist. of Woburn* (1868); *Woburn Records*, pts. I, III (1890, 1891); Nathaniel Bouton, *The Hist. of Concord* (1856); J. O. Lyford, *Hist. of Concord, N. H.* (2 vols., 1896); *Concord Town Records, 1732–1820* (1894); *N. H. State Papers*, vol. XXIV (1894), ed. by A. S. Batchellor.]   E. H. D.

WALKER, TIMOTHY (Dec. 1, 1802–Jan. 15, 1856), writer on legal subjects, jurist, teacher, was born in Wilmington, Middlesex County, Mass., the son of Benjamin Walker, a farmer, and Susanna (Cook) Walker, and a brother of Sears Cook Walker [*q.v.*]. He was sixth in direct descent from Elder William Brewster [*q.v.*] of the *Mayflower*. Until he was sixteen he worked on his father's farm with scarcely any schooling, but in 1822, having succeeded in preparing himself for college, he entered Harvard. In 1826 he was graduated as first scholar. The following three years he taught mathematics in the Round Hill School, Northampton, Mass., conducted by George Bancroft [*q.v.*]. During this time he contributed to the *North American Review*, delivered lectures on natural science, published *Elements of Geometry* (1829), and attended law lectures given by Judge Samuel Howe [*q.v.*]. In the fall of 1829 he entered the Harvard Law School, where he remained one year, coming under the instruction of Justice Joseph Story [*q.v.*] and his colleagues. Early in August 1830 he arrived in Cincinnati, Ohio, and entered the law office of Storer and Fox as a student.

After being admitted to the bar in 1831 he began the practice of law. Two years later with Judge John C. Wright, who had been a judge of the supreme court of Ohio and a member of Congress, he organized what was a private law school, with a few students and without the power to confer degrees. In 1835 it became a part of Cincinnati College, founded in 1818, and until 1867 was known as the Law School of Cincinnati College; in 1896 it became a part of the University of Cincinnati. In 1842 he accepted an appointment as judge of the court of common pleas of Hamilton County to fill a vacancy, and in 1843 became the editor of the *Western Law Journal*. When in 1855 Ohio was divided into two federal judicial districts he was appointed to draw up rules of practice for the circuit and district courts of the southern district. He had published an argument in favor of codification as early as 1835 and continued for the rest of his life to work for simplification of the rules of pleading and practice, and for changes in the laws having to do with crime and with the status of married women. Most of the reforms he ad-

vocated he saw before his death incorporated into the laws of Ohio. His most important contribution to the law, however, and his greatest achievement, was a series of lectures delivered in the law school he founded, published as *Introduction to American Law* (1837). "While pursuing my legal studies," he writes, "I found myself much in the condition of a mariner without chart or compass. I experienced at every step the want of a first book upon the law of this country. ... In a word, I came to the conclusion that fewer facilities have been provided for studying the elementary principles of American Jurisprudence, than perhaps for any other branch of useful knowledge" (*Introduction*, p. v). The book received instant recognition by the legal profession and went through eleven editions, the last published in 1905.

On Aug. 1, 1855, Walker was thrown violently from his carriage. Returning to his office before complete recovery, he contracted a heavy cold which settled on his lungs and in the following January caused his death at his home in Walnut Hills, Cincinnati. A contemporary legal magazine commented on "the vigor and clearness of his mind, the absolute precision of his ideas, his quickness and his conciseness . . ." and on the fact that he "never did a discourteous or an unfair thing" (*Monthly Law Reporter*, Apr. 1856, pp. 708–09). He was married on Mar. 11, 1840, to Ella Page Wood, by whom he had three sons and two daughters.

[See A. G. W. Carter, *The Old Court House* (1880), pp. 122–24; C. T. Marshall, *A Hist. of the Courts and Lawyers of Ohio* (1934), vols. I, III; H. P. Farnham, ed., *Ohio Jurisprudence*, vol. I (1928), p. cvi; Clara L. de Chambrun, *The Making of Nicholas Longworth* (1933), which contains part of Walker's diary; and obituaries in *Cincinnati Gazette* and *Cincinnati Daily Enquirer*, Jan. 16, 1856.]   A. H. T.

WALKER, WILLIAM (May 8, 1824–Sept. 12, 1860), adventurer, was born in Nashville, Tenn. His father, James Walker, was a native of Scotland who settled in Nashville in 1820 and married Mary Norvell of Kentucky. William, the eldest of four children, enjoyed unusual educational advantages for a young man of his time and environment. After graduating from the University of Nashville in 1838, he studied medicine at the University of Pennsylvania, where he received the degree of M.D. in 1843. He continued his medical studies in Paris for a year and then spent a year in European travel. Finding the practice of medicine distasteful, he next studied law and in due course was admitted to the bar in New Orleans. As his clients were few, Walker soon turned to journalism, and in 1848 became one of the editors and proprietors of the New Orleans *Daily Crescent*. His newspaper did not prosper, and in 1850 he joined the great migration then under way to California.

After another brief experience in journalism in San Francisco, Walker removed to Marysville, Cal., where he devoted his energies to law and politics. His three years as editor and lawyer among the pioneers of California involved him in several duels and once brought him a jail sentence for contempt of court. In 1853 he became interested in "colonizing" the Mexican states of Sonora and Lower California with American settlers. After failing to obtain the sanction of the Mexican authorities for his plans, he organized an armed expedition on his own account, and in October of that year sailed from San Francisco on the pretext that certain Mexicans had urged him to come and protect them from the Apache Indians, who were then committing depredations in Northwestern Mexico. After landing, Nov. 3, at La Paz, Walker proclaimed Lower California an independent republic, with himself as president. On Jan. 18 following he annexed—on paper—the neighboring state of Sonora. Meantime, since the federal authorities in San Francisco prevented the departure of supplies and reinforcements, Walker and his followers were threatened with starvation. Constantly beset by hostile Mexicans, they retreated northward into the United States and surrendered to a military force stationed at the border. Walker and his chief associates were brought to trial in San Francisco for violating the neutrality laws, but Walker was acquitted by a sympathetic jury, and the fines imposed on his associates were never paid.

In 1855 Walker fitted out an expedition of "emigrants" to Nicaragua, whither he had been invited by the leader of a revolutionary faction then badly in need of outside aid. He landed in Nicaragua with fifty-seven followers and at once joined in the fighting. With the help of the Accessory Transit Company, an American transportation concern operating between Atlantic ports and San Francisco by way of Nicaragua, he captured Granada, then the capital, and brought the revolution to an end. Under the peace agreement he became commander-in-chief of the army, which he proceeded to recruit with Americans brought to Nicaragua free of charge by the Transit Company. He was now virtually master of the state. In May 1856, the new régime was recognized by the United States, and in July Walker had himself inaugurated as president.

Walker cherished grandiose schemes of uniting the small Central American republics into a military empire. He planned an interoceanic canal which would bind his government to the European powers by the strong ties of commerce, and he proposed to develop the agricultural resources of Central America by reintroducing African slavery. He did not contemplate annexation to the United States, as many American historians have assumed, but repeatedly disavowed such a purpose. All these plans came to nothing, however, for he made the two-fold mistake of taking sides in a struggle between two groups of capitalists in New York for control of the Accessory Transit Company and joining forces with what proved to be the weaker of the two. Claiming that the Company's derelictions had voided its charter, Walker seized its ships and other property in Nicaragua and turned them over to the favored group, to whom he issued a new charter. The opposition was headed by Cornelius Vanderbilt [q.v.], a relentless and none too scrupulous fighter, who resolved upon Walker's destruction. Vanderbilt dispatched agents to Central America to aid a recently formed coalition of neighboring republics in expelling Walker from Nicaragua. Through their operations Walker was soon cut off from reinforcements from the United States and was closely besieged by allied forces from Honduras, El Salvador, Guatemala, and Costa Rica. On May 1, 1857, he surrendered to Commander Charles Henry Davis [q.v.], of the United States Navy, who had intervened to prevent further bloodshed.

After returning to the United States, Walker was soon busy with preparations for a second expedition to Nicaragua, of which he claimed still to be the lawful president. In November he eluded the federal authorities and sailed from Mobile, but shortly after landing near Grey Town he and his followers were arrested by Commodore Hiram Paulding [q.v.] of the United States Navy and sent back to the United States. Nearly three years passed before Walker again succeeded in reaching Central America. In August 1860 he landed in Honduras, evading American and British naval forces stationed off the coast of Nicaragua to prevent his landing there. He planned to proceed into Nicaragua by land, but while on his way along the coast he was arrested, Sept. 3, by Capt. Norvell Salmon of the British navy and turned over to the Honduran authorities. He was condemned to death by a court martial and died by the fusillade at Trujillo on Sept. 12.

Walker's personal appearance revealed none of the characteristics which have caused him to be designated as the greatest of American filibusters. Below medium height, weighing but little over a hundred pounds, homely and extremely shy and reticent, he evoked wonder and incredulity from those who first saw him after hearing of his exploits. But from all accounts, when once aroused he seemed a wholly different man, and this may explain his ability to maintain iron discipline and something like personal devotion among his heterogeneous and often wild and desperate followers. His legal and journalistic experience made him a fluent and lucid writer, and his story of his career, *The War in Nicaragua* (1860), published a few months before his last expedition, is a remarkably accurate and impersonal narrative.

[Walker's own story is the best source. Other works include: W. O. Scroggs, *Filibusters and Financiers* (1916); Lorenzo Montúfar y Rivera Maestre, *Walker en Centro-América* (Guatemala, 1887); J. J. Roche, *By-ways of War* (1901); M. P. Allen, *William Walker, Filibuster* (1932); *Evening Post* (N. Y.), Sept. 21, 24, 28, 1860.]   W. O. S.

WALKER, WILLIAM HENRY TALBOT (Nov. 26, 1816–July 22, 1864), soldier, was born in Augusta, Ga., a descendant of a family which had moved to that state from Charles City County, Va., in the late eighteenth century. His father, Freeman Walker, was the first mayor of Augusta and a senator from Georgia; his mother was Mary Washington (Creswell) of Wilkes County, Ga., a niece of Gov. Matthew Talbot of Georgia. After attending school in Augusta, William entered the United States Military Academy and was graduated in 1837, number forty-six in a class of fifty. He was commissioned second lieutenant of the 6th Infantry and before the end of the year saw active service in the Florida Indian War. At the battle of Okeechobee, Dec. 25, 1837, he was thrice severely wounded and was brevetted first lieutenant for gallant conduct. On Oct. 31, 1838, he resigned from the army, but was reappointed Nov. 18, 1840, and rejoined his regiment, serving through the Florida war. On Nov. 7, 1845, he was promoted captain. He then served in the Mexican War and was brevetted major, Aug. 20, 1847, for heroic conduct at Contreras, and lieutenant-colonel, Sept. 8, 1847, for similar gallantry at Molino del Rey. In the latter battle he was desperately wounded and for a long time it was feared that he would die. The state of Georgia presented him with a sword of honor in 1849. After the Mexican War, he was on sick leave and recruiting service from 1847 to 1852, and deputy governor of the military asylum at East Pascagoula, Miss., from 1852 to 1854. In the latter year he became commandant of cadets and instructor in military tactics at West Point, serving as such until 1856, and being promoted in 1855 to major. For a brief time he was on frontier duty in Minnesota, and then on sick leave until 1860.

Though Walker sincerely regretted the conflict between the North and the South, he resigned his commission in the United States Army Dec. 20, 1860. One of the most experienced officers who entered the Confederate service, he would probably have attained greater fame had he not been in such poor physical condition. He was appointed major-general of Georgia volunteers on Apr. 25, 1861, and on May 25 was made brigadier-general in the Confederate army. During the next five months he served at Pensacola, Fla., and as a brigade commander in northern Virginia. On Oct. 29, 1861, he resigned his commission, ostensibly because of ill-health, and unquestionably he had been reported as sick in Richmond two months before. Nevertheless, in November he was appointed major-general of Georgia state troops and Gen. Alexander R. Lawton [q.v.], Confederate commander at Savannah, wrote Secretary of War Benjamin, "that the feelings with which he [Walker] has now left the Confederate service, fomented by the temper which Governor Brown has (in the past at least) exhibited toward the War Department, might cause great embarrassment here, if he is permitted to assume command under state authority" (*War of the Rebellion: Official Records, Army,* 1 ser. VI, 307).

Walker reëntered the Confederate service on Mar. 2, 1863, as a brigadier-general. On May 18, Gen. J. E. Johnston [q.v.] reported to Jefferson Davis that Walker was the only officer in his western command competent to head a division, and obtained his appointment, Jan. 25, 1864, as major-general. He commanded a division in Mississippi, and after the fall of Vicksburg was ordered to Georgia in time for the battle of Chickamauga. In this battle he was in command of the reserves. Later, in his official report, he criticized Gen. D. H. Hill [q.v.] for disintegrating the reserves in their attack and declared that if he could have made his own dispositions he felt "satisfied that the enemy's left would have been carried much easier than it was, and many a gallant man been saved, and his retreat intercepted" (*Ibid.,* 1 ser. XXX, pt. 2, p. 242). Walker served with the Army of Tennessee during the campaign in northern Georgia. He was killed in a sortie from Atlanta while in front of his division and his body left in the Union lines. It was later recovered, however, and interred in the old family burial ground at Summerville, Ga., now a part of Augusta. He married Mary Townsend of Albany, N. Y., and had two sons and two daughters.

[*War of the Rebellion: Official Records (Army)*; C. A. Evans, *Confederate Mil. Hist.* (1899), esp. vol. VI; G. W. Cullum, *Biog. Reg. Officers and Grads. U. S. Mil. Acad.*, vol. I (1879); M. J. Wright, *Gen. Officers of the Confederate Army* (1911); W. A. Clark, *A Lost Arcadia or the Story of My Old Community* (1909); W. J. Northen, *Men of Mark in Ga.*, vol. III (1911); information as to certain facts from William Robinson and W. H. T. Walker, Jr., Augusta.]   R. D. M.

WALKER, WILLIAM JOHNSON (Mar. 15, 1790–Apr. 2, 1865), physician, financier, and philanthropist, was born in Charlestown, Mass., the son of Maj. Timothy Walker, merchant and shrewd investor in real estate, and of Abigail (Johnson) Walker, lineal descendant of Edward Johnson [*q.v.*], author of the *Wonderworking Providence of Sion's Savior in New England.* From Phillips Academy at Andover, Walker went to Harvard, zealously studied Latin and geometry, and graduated in 1810. Immediately he began to study medicine and received the degree of M.D. from Harvard College in 1813. His subsequent training abroad, under Laennec, Corvisart, and Sir Astley Cooper, taught him to use the percussion method in diagnosing chest and abdominal ailments. In 1816 he returned to Charlestown, where on Apr. 16 he married Eliza Hurd, and began to practise medicine. Despite his imperious will and extreme independence, fundamental kindliness made his professional career eminently successful. He was appointed physician and surgeon to the State Prison and consulting surgeon to the Massachusetts General Hospital. Not the least of his accomplishments was the inspiring instruction of several young men who became famous doctors, among others, Morrill Wyman [*q.v.*]. As orator before the Massachusetts Medical Society in 1845 he presented *An Essay on the Treatment of Compound and Complicated Fractures,* published that same year, based on detailed records of his cases and on wide reading. Advocating extremely high professional standards, he emphasized the necessity of cleanliness in all operations and dressings. Shortly thereafter he retired from his practice to accumulate a large fortune in railroad and manufacturing stocks in order, as he later wrote to President Stearns of Amherst, "that I may contribute to education."

In 1861, Walker left his family for a boarding house in Newport, R. I., to devote the remainder of his life to well-planned philanthropy. In 1860 he had offered Harvard a sum of approximately $130,000, for reforming the Medical School. His plan called for more laboratory and clinical work, at the expense of the prevalent deadening lecture system. The Harvard Corporation refused the gift because he demanded an entirely new faculty acceptable to himself.

Thereupon Walker changed his will, originally in favor of Harvard exclusively, so as to divide his wealth, after leaving $260,000 to his family and forty women friends, among Amherst, Tufts, the Massachusetts Institute of Technology, and the Boston Society of Natural History. During the year 1861, Walker endowed at Amherst and Tufts professorships in mathematics, to be filled by young men of proved ability. At Amherst he provided for tutorial instruction in mathematics for classes chosen according to their ability and interest in the subject. The pedagogical theories of the Rev. Thomas Hill [*q.v.*], added to his own medical experience, led him to urge that all students in geometry make their own figures and scales, teaching themselves by eye and hand, before the logical demonstrations. His practical and experimental aims in education were again emphasized in his ideas for field trips in connection with his gift to Williams College of a building for the study of natural history. The scientific and industrial outlook of the projected Massachusetts Institute of Technology, and his regard for William Barton Rogers [*q.v.*], its chief founder, caused him to provide, in 1863, about two-thirds of the fund of $100,000 demanded in the charter before the Institute could begin operations.

In the midst of his planning, Walker died suddenly of a self-diagnosed heart disease. His will brought his total contributions to American education to about $1,250,000.

[A sketch of Walker by President W. A. Stearns of Amherst in a speech delivered at the laying of the cornerstone of Walker Hall on June 10, 1868 (pamphlet, Amherst), and a letter of Walker to the Trustees of Tufts College (MS., at Tufts) present valuable information. Other bits appear in T. F. Harrington, *The Harvard Medic. School* (1905), vol. III; W. S. Tyler, *Hist. of Amherst Coll.* (1873); J. P. Munroe, "The Mass. Inst. of Technology," *New England Mag.*, Oct. 1902; E. S. Rogers, *Life and Letters of Wm. Barton Rogers* (1896), vol. II; *Medic. Communications of the Mass. Medic. Soc.*, vol. X, no. 5 (1865); T. B. Wyman, *Geneals. and Estates of Charlestown* (1879); *Boston Transcript*, Apr. 7, 1865.]   A. A. L.

WALKER, WILLISTON (July 1, 1860–Mar. 9, 1922), church historian, born in Portland, Me., came of clerical New England stock. His father, George Leon Walker, was a distinguished Congregational minister. His Christian name was the family name of his mother, Maria Williston. He received the degree of A.B. from Amherst College in 1883, and graduated from the Hartford Theological Seminary in 1886. On June 1 of that year he married Alice Mather, by whom he had two daughters. With his bride he went to Europe for further study and received the degree of Ph.D. at Leipzig in 1888.

Appointed associate professor of history in

Byrn Mawr College, as successor to Woodrow Wilson, he served in that capacity until 1889. From the latter year until 1892 he was associate professor of church history at the Hartford Theological Seminary and from 1892 to 1901 professor of Germanic and Western Church history in the same institution. In 1901 Yale University called him to succeed George Park Fisher [*q.v.*], as Titus Street Professor of Ecclesiastical History, which position he held for the remainder of his life. From 1896 on he acted as a trustee of Amherst College, and beginning in 1901, as secretary of the corporation. For the school year 1916–17 he served as acting dean of the Yale Graduate School, and as provost of the University from 1919 until his death. As first incumbent of this office he contributed to the efficiency of the administration of the university by the coördination of departments. He was president of the American Society of Church History and of the New Haven Colony Historical Society, and was a member of several other organizations, particularly those concerned with the history of the colonial period.

His interest was ever unflagging in the work of the Church and especially in that of the Congregational body. In 1913 he served on the committee of nineteen which drafted a new constitution for the denomination, and in 1919 he was a member of the commission on Christian unity between the Congregational and Episcopalian bodies. His concern for Christian unity and for Christian missions is evidenced by the following publications: *The Validity of Congregational Ordination* (1898), Dudleian Lecture at Harvard University; "The War and Church Unity" in *Religion and the War* (1918), by members of the faculty of the School of Religion, Yale University; *Approaches Towards Church Unity* (1919), edited in collaboration with Newman Smyth [*q.v.*]; *Twenty Years of Work, a Paper Presented on the 20th Annual Meeting of the Woman's Congregational Home Missionary Union of Connecticut* (1905).

As a lecturer on church history Walker was possessed of singular charm. The story of the Church in his hands unrolled as a colorful panorama of stirring deeds. His writing was characterized by sobriety, balance of arrangement, and judgment, thoroughness, and accuracy. His major contributions to historical scholarships lay in the field of Congregational history in New England, on which he published three books: *The Creeds and Platforms of Congregationalism* (1893); *A History of the Congregational Churches in the United States* (1894), in the American Church History series; *Ten New*

England Leaders (1901); and several articles. Outside of the colonial period his best two works from the scholarly standpoint are his doctoral dissertation, *On the Increase of Royal Power in France under Philip Augustus* (Leipzig, 1888) and *John Calvin* (1906, French translation, Geneva, 1909). On the order of textbooks are: *The Reformation* (1900), and *A History of the Christian Church* (1918). His *Great Men of the Christian Church* (1908) contains a series of popular brief biographies.

[*Yale Alumni Weekly*, Mar. 17, 1922; *Yale Divinity News*, Mar. 1922; R. S. Fletcher and M. O. Young, *Amherst Coll.: Biog. Record* (1927); C. M. Geer, *The Hartford Theological Sem.* (1934); *Congregationalist*, Mar. 23, 1922; *Proc. Am. Antiquarian Soc.*, Apr. 1922; *Who's Who in America*, 1920–21; *New Haven Jour.-Courier*, Mar. 10, 1922.]   R. H. B.

WALLACE, CHARLES WILLIAM (Feb. 6, 1865–Aug. 7, 1932), educator and Shakespearean investigator, was born at Hopkins, Mo., the son of Thomas Dickey and Olive (McEwen) Wallace. His father, a farmer and county judge, was a descendant of Thomas Wallace, who emigrated from Ireland in 1726 and settled in New Hampshire. Wallace was educated in public schools, took the degree of B.S. at Western Normal College, Shenandoah, Iowa, in 1885, and received the degree of A.B. at the University of Nebraska in 1898. He had graduate work at Nebraska (1900–02), at the University of Chicago, and at various German universities (1904–06). He received the degree of Ph.D. from the University of Freiburg in Breisgau in 1906. His pedagogical experience included teaching in country schools, in normal schools in Iowa and Nebraska, and the principalship of a preparatory school to the University of Nebraska (1897–1900) which he founded. He was assistant instructor in English at the University of Nebraska (1901–03), instructor, adjunct professor, and assistant professor in successive years, associate professor (1907–12), and professor of English dramatic literature (1912), a title he retained until his death. He is best known for his researches in Shakespeare and the Tudor drama, which he carried on from 1907 to 1916. He and his wife examined in England, they reported, over five million original records, finding many documents of interest and importance, several groups of which Wallace published. During 1916 and 1917 he lectured on Shakespeare before learned societies and universities throughout the United States.

In 1918 he went to Wichita Falls, Tex., on an extended leave of absence. He had long interested himself in oil geology, and he entered the venturesome oil industry late in life as an independent operator with the object of obtaining funds for the scholarly investigations to which he was devoted. His first successful developments were in Wichita County; in 1922 he bought rights in Archer County and later made further purchases, obtaining large holdings in a region previously thought dry. He personally directed drilling operations, and his ventures brought large returns. He died of cancer in Wichita Falls in 1932. At the time of his death he was working on a collection of records pertaining to Shakespeare and the English stage which he had planned for years to publish. His wife, Hulda Alfreda (Berggren) Wallace of Wahoo, Neb., whom he married on June 14, 1893, was associated with him in study at the University of Nebraska, in his London researches, and even in his management of his oil fields. She lacked his advanced academic training but was a rapid and accurate worker, much the quicker worker, indeed, of the two. They were a remarkably devoted married pair, and Wallace never failed to pay tribute to her assistance.

Wallace's publications include *Spider-Webs in Verse* (1892), *Globe Theatre Apparel* (1909) and *Keysar vs. Burbage and Others* (1910), both printed privately in London, *The Evolution of the English Drama up to Shakespeare* (Berlin, 1912), and a series of articles in *University Studies of the University of Nebraska*: "The Newly-Discovered Shakespeare Documents" (vol. V, 1905), "The Children of the Chapel at Blackfriars, 1597–1603" (vol. VIII, 1908), "Three London Theatres of Shakespeare's Time" (vol. IX, 1909), "Shakespeare and His London Associates" (vol. X, 1910), and "The First London Theatre" (vol. XIII, 1913). He also wrote "Gervase Markham, Dramatist" (*Jahrbuch der Deutschen Shakespeare-Gesellschaft*, 1910), "New Shakespeare Discoveries" (*Harper's Magazine*, Mar. 1910), "Shakspere's Money Interest in the Globe Theatre" (*Century Magazine*, Aug. 1910), "Shakspere and the Blackfriars" (*Ibid.*, Sept. 1910), "The Swan Theatre and the Earl of Pembroke's Servants" (*Englische Studien*, vol. XLIII, pt. III, 1911), and a series of important articles in the London *Times*, Sept. 12, 1906 (letter), Oct. 2 and 4, 1909, Mar. 28, 1913, Apr. 30 and May 1, 1914, and May 8 and 15, 1915. His discoveries were of undoubted value, but, since all were not published and since other scholars have now worked in his field, it is hard justly to estimate their importance. He was the finder of a new signature of Shakespeare and of much new material that threw light on the intricate history of the Tudor

stage. He himself felt that because of this material the entire dramatic literature of the period needed reëditing and the history of the drama rewriting. The zeal, industry, and the surprising success of the Wallace quests were unmistakable, but Wallace's absorption in his work seems to have destroyed his perspective, for he anticipated results disproportionate even to what he had already accomplished.

[Sources include *Who's Who in America*, 1932–33; obituary in *Nebr. State Jour.*, Aug. 8, 1932; personal acquaintance; and information from Mrs. Wallace. See also G. G. Greenwood, *The Vindication of Shakespeare* (London, 1911), which contains criticism of Wallace's work.]
L. P.

WALLACE, DAVID (Apr. 24, 1799–Sept. 4, 1859), governor of Indiana, congressman, a great-grandson of Andrew Wallace who emigrated from Scotland with his widowed mother in 1724, was born in Pennsylvania, the son of Andrew and Eleanor (Jones) Wallace, the latter believed to be a niece of John Paul Jones. While David was still a child the family moved to Ohio, first to Troy and then to Cincinnati. After having been engaged in mercantile pursuits, Andrew Wallace acquired the *Liberty Hall Gazette and Cincinnati Mercury*, which he published for some two years, and then moved to Brookville, Ind., where he kept a tavern. During the War of 1812 he served as a quartermaster to Gen. William Henry Harrison.

David, the eldest of seven brothers, thus grew up on what was then the Western frontier. When about fifteen, he was sent to New Orleans to enter business and stayed there for perhaps a year. He then obtained an appointment to the United States Military Academy, largely through the interest of General Harrison. After graduating in his class of 1821, he remained at West Point for a time as a teacher of mathematics. On June 1, 1822 he resigned his commission, returned to Brookville, and entered the office of an attorney to study law. He was admitted to the bar in 1824 and soon had a lucrative business, being reputed one of the most brilliant young men in the state. Before long he was equally prominent in politics. A devoted admirer of Henry Clay, he ultimately became one of the Whig leaders of Indiana. Meanwhile, 1828–30, he represented Franklin County in the lower house of the legislature; in 1831 and again in 1834, he was elected lieutenant-governor. An ardent advocate of state banking, he did much to bring about the adoption of the charter of the State Bank of Indiana.

In the early summer of 1832 he moved to Covington, Ind., and when elected governor in 1837, to Indianapolis, where he made his home for the rest of his life. He ran for governor on a platform of public improvements, which he enthusiastically sponsored; unfortunately, however, the state lost millions through procuring loans from Eastern speculators. This loss, together with the effects of the financial depression of the time, left the state burdened with debt and unfinished improvements. The resentment of the public was so great that Wallace's friends decided it was unwise to renominate him for governor in 1840. He was elected to Congress in that year, however, and served on the ways and means committee during the sessions of 1841 and 1842. Though the Whig party was somewhat weak at the time, Wallace would probably have been reëlected to Congress in 1842 had his Democratic rival not succeeded in discrediting him for his really enlightened support of a measure that was unpopular because of its supposed extravagance, namely, the appropriation of $30,-000 to Samuel F. B. Morse [q.v.] to enable him to perfect the telegraph.

Wallace resumed the practice of law in Indianapolis. He was a member of the state constitutional convention of 1850, and in 1856 was elected judge of the court of common pleas, on which he served with distinction until his death. He was married twice: first, to Esther French Test, by whom he had four sons, one of whom was Gen. Lewis Wallace [q.v.] ; second, to Zerelda G. Sanders, by whom he had two daughters and a son. At the time of his death, the Indianapolis bar paid him marked tribute for his high character as a courteous and urbane gentleman, a talented and eloquent advocate, especially in criminal cases, and a judge with wide legal knowledge, who was ever kindly but possessed an inflexible sense of justice.

[G. S. Wallace, *Wallace: Geneal. Data* (1927); *Lew Wallace, An Autobiog.* (2 vols., 1906); *Proc. of the Indianapolis Bar upon the Occasion of the Death of Hon. David Wallace* (1859); N. M. Woods, *The Woods-McAfee Memorial* (1905); J. P. Dunn, *Greater Indianapolis* (1910), vol. II; *A Biog. Hist. of Eminent and Self-Made Men of the State of Ind.* (1880), vol. II; W. W. Woollen, *Biog. and Hist. Sketches of Early Ind.* (1883); G. W. Cullum, *Biog. Reg. Officers and Grads. U. S. Mil. Acad.* (3rd ed., 1891), vol. I; C. W. Taylor, *Biog. Sketches and Review of the Bench and Bar of Ind.* (1895); *Biog. Dir. Am. Cong.* (1928); R. L. Rusk, *The Lit. of the Middle Western Frontier* (1926), I, 137, n.]　　　　　　　A.L.L.

WALLACE, HENRY (Mar. 19, 1836–Feb. 22, 1916), editor and writer on agricultural subjects, was born near West Newton, Pa., the son of Martha (Ross) and John Wallace, a farmer who had emigrated from Ireland in 1832. From 1855 to 1857 he attended Geneva Hall, a preparatory school in Logan County, Ohio, and in 1859 graduated from Jefferson College, now Wash-

ington and Jefferson College, in Pennsylvania. From 1860 to 1861 he studied at the theological seminary at Allegheny, now Pittsburgh Theological Seminary, and from 1861 to 1863 at the theological seminary at Monmouth, Ill. Meanwhile he taught for a year, 1859–60, in Columbia College in Kentucky and in an academy at West Newton during the summer of 1861. He was licensed to preach by the United Presbyterian presbytery of Monmouth on Apr. 9, 1862, and was ordained on Apr. 1, of the next year. On Sept. 10, 1863, he married Nannie Cantwell, of Kenton, Ohio, who died in 1909. They had five children.

He was pastor of the United Presbyterian Church in Rock Island, Ill., and Davenport, Iowa, from 1863 to 1871 and in Morning Sun, Iowa, from 1871 to 1876. Failing health compelled him to give up the ministry in 1877, when he removed to Winterset, Iowa, to take up farming and recover his health. Tuberculosis had taken the other members of his family, and he was the sole survivor. He was the agricultural editor of the *Madisonian* for a year, and he was then dismissed by the editor for his reflections on "the unwillingness of politicians to forward the agricultural interests" (*Own Story, post,* III, p. 20). Then buying a half interest in the *Winterset Chronicle,* he increased the number of its subscribers from 400 to 1400. He became the contributing editor of the *Iowa Homestead* at ten dollars a week, and served in this capacity for twelve years, becoming part owner of this journal. In 1895, with his two sons, Henry Cantwell Wallace [q.v.] and John P. Wallace, he bought *Wallaces' Farm and Dairy,* later *Wallaces' Farmer,* and was the editor of this journal until his death.

A man of strong physique, tall, well-proportioned, and commanding, he possessed a keen intellect and stood high in the estimation of his fellowmen, whether farmers, churchmen, or politicians. He combined agricultural journalism and religion so successfully that *Wallaces' Farmer* became one of the leading agricultural periodicals. It was read not only for its treatment of farm problems but also for its sermons. In 1908 he was appointed by President Theodore Roosevelt as a member of the Country Life Commission; in 1910 he was elected president of the National Conservation Congress; in 1911 he was chairman of the national committee on the men and religion movement; and in 1913 he was appointed with James Wilson to investigate agricultural conditions in Great Britain (see report, *Agricultural Conditions in Great Britain and Ireland,* n. d.). He was an able public speaker and an influential leader in political and religious movements, a champion of railroad regulation and of agricultural education. He was a prolific writer on agricultural subjects and was the author of *The Doctrines of the Plymouth Brethren* (1878), *Clover Culture* (1892), *Uncle Henry's Letters to the Farm Boy* (1897), *Clover Farming* (1898), *Trusts and How to Deal with Them* (1899), *The Skim Milk Calf* (1900), and *Letters to the Farm Folks* (1915). After his death three small volumes of his *Uncle Henry's Own Story of his Life* (1917–19) were published.

[*Uncle Henry's Own Story, ante*; *Tributes to Henry Wallace* (1919); *Who's Who in America*, 1916–17; *Annals of Iowa*, Oct. 1921; *Biog. and Hist. Cat. of Washington and Jefferson College* (1902); *Iowa State Register* (Des Moines), Feb. 23, 24, 1916; *N. Y. Times*, Feb. 23, 1916; information from Henry Agard Wallace, his grandson.]   L. B. S—t.

WALLACE, HENRY CANTWELL (May 11, 1866–Oct. 25, 1924), agricultural journalist and secretary of agriculture, was born in Rock Island, Ill., the son of Nannie (Cantwell) and Henry Wallace [*q.v.*]. He attended the city schools and helped his father on the farm, at the same time learning the printer's trade in the newspaper offices in Winterset. From 1885 to 1887 he attended the Iowa State Agricultural College, now the Iowa State College of Agriculture. He then rented one of his father's farms and was married, on Nov. 24, 1885, to Carrie May Broadhead of Muscatine, Iowa. They had six children, among them Henry Agard Wallace. Returning to the Iowa State Agricultural College in 1891, he graduated in 1892. James Wilson [*q.v.*], recognizing the importance of dairying, obtained the appointment of Wallace as assistant professor of agriculture in dairying. In 1894 he became part owner and publisher, with Charles F. Curtiss, of the *Farm and Dairy*, published at Ames, Iowa. In a few months he, his father, and his brother, John P. Wallace, became the owners and decided to move it to Des Moines. The name was changed to *Wallaces' Farm and Dairy* and later to *Wallaces' Farmer*. Henry C. Wallace became associate editor and, on the death of his father, editor. He held to the policies of his father in editing this journal, one of the leading agricultural periodicals in the United States. The editorial columns dealt with a variety of agricultural topics and the leading problems of the time, both domestic and foreign. He exerted a large influence through various farm organizations, among which may be mentioned especially the Cornbelt Meat Producers Association, of which he was the secretary for fourteen years. He labored for the equalization of railroad rates for farm products and became

a recognized leader of national movements for the advancement of agricultural interests. During the World War he bitterly opposed the food administration policy of Herbert Hoover.

When the Republicans returned to power in 1921 on a platform promising farm relief, Harding appointed him as secretary of agriculture and, reappointed by Coolidge, he served in this capacity until his death. He opposed the transfer of all marketing functions to the Department of Commerce. He urged that the Department of Agriculture should not only assist the farmer in increasing the efficiency of production but that it should also develop improved systems of marketing. The adjustment of production to the needs of consumption was emphasized as a proper function of the department. A champion of conservation, he fought for the retention of the forest service, which Secretary Fall attempted to have transferred to the Department of the Interior. He had an important part in framing agricultural legislation. He supported the principles of the McNary-Haugen Bill. He reorganized the department into more unified and effectively correlated bureaus, established the bureau of agricultural economics and the bureau of home economics, and inaugurated the radio service for market reports. He was a zealous advocate of education, being concerned primarily with the improvement of the rural schools, the establishment of courses in agriculture in the high schools, and the advancement of the agricultural colleges along scientific and practical lines. After his death, *Our Debt and Duty to the Farmer* (1925) was published with a last chapter written jointly by Nils A. Olsen and Henry A. Wallace. A United Presbyterian by training and profession, he was an active churchman and a loyal supporter of Y. M. C. A. work, with which he was officially connected in various capacities. His funeral services were held at the White House, and he was buried at Des Moines.

[L. H. Pammel, *Henry Cantwell Wallace* (n.d.) in Prominent Men I Have Met Series; L. S. Ivins and A. E. Winship, *Fifty Famous Farmers* (1924), pp. 401–07; E. R. Harlan, *A Narrative Hist. of the People of Iowa* (1931), vol. III; *Who's Who in America*, 1924–25; Herman Steen, "H. C. Wallace," *Prairie Farmer*, Mar. 5, 1921; *N. Y. Times*, Oct. 26, 28, 30, 1924; *Des Moines Register*, Oct. 26, 1924.]   L. B. S—t.

WALLACE, HORACE BINNEY (Feb. 26, 1817–Dec. 16, 1852), literary, art, and legal critic, brother of John William Wallace [*q.v.*], was born in Philadelphia, Pa., the son of John Bradford and Susan (Binney) Wallace, and a lineal descendant of John Wallace, who came to Newport, R. I., from Scotland in 1742. His father was a lawyer and a member of the state legislature, and his mother was prominent in Philadelphia society. His schooling began under a "venerable woman" in Burlington, N. J., the home of his paternal grandparents and the summer home of his parents. In 1822, his father's land interests took the family to Meadville, on the fringe of the wilderness, where his training was continued by his father and the Rev. William Lucas. Before his fifteenth year, he had revealed an unusual gift for higher mathematics, and when he entered the University of Pennsylvania in 1830, he soon placed himself at the head of his class. After two years, he transferred to the College of New Jersey at Princeton, where he took the degree of A.B. in 1835. His interest in science led him to enter the office of Thomas Harris, M.D., and to study for one term in the Medical School of the University of Pennsylvania, but surgery had no attraction for him and he undertook instead a special course in chemistry under Dr. Robert Hare [q.v.]. He then entered his father's office to study law until the death of the latter in 1837, when he transferred to the office of Charles Chauncey, and was admitted to the bar of Philadelphia in the spring of 1840. He never practised, but devoted his attention to legal and literary commentary. When his mother died on July 9, 1849, he went to Europe for twelve months to study the arts, particularly church architecture. Failing health prompted him to go abroad again on Nov. 13, 1852, and he died suddenly, presumably a suicide, in Paris, where he had gone for medical treatment. He was buried in the cemetery at Montmartre, but was reinterred in St. Peter's churchyard, Philadelphia, on Mar. 4, 1853. He never married.

While still in college, Wallace began to write anonymously for the periodicals, and presumably published a number of stories and essays which even his contemporaries failed to identify. His modesty led him to withhold his name from his only novel, *Stanley, or the Recollections of a Man of the World* (2 vols., 1838). After his return from his first trip abroad, he came to the attention of Rufus W. Griswold [q.v.], editor of *Graham's Magazine,* who dedicated his *Prose Writers of America* (1847) to him as the most promising young writer of his acquaintance. Various works attributed to Griswold have been, in part, credited also to Wallace, among which are *Napoleon and the Marshals of the Empire* (2 vols., 1848) and a pamphlet, *The Military and Civil Life of George Washington* (1849).

His legal writings, the only ones which he published under his own name, consist of detailed and critical commentaries on *A Selection of Leading Cases in Various Branches of the Law,* by

John William Smith (2 vols., 1844), and on *A Selection of Leading Cases in Equity,* by Frederick Thomas White and Owen Davies Tudor (2 vols. in 3, 1849-51). He and his collaborator, J. I. Clark Hare [q.v.], supplied numerous examples and extended comment on American cases paralleling the English ones cited by the original authors. Together they also published *Select Decisions of American Courts* (2 vols., 1847), a purely American compilation on the same plan, which was revised in 1857 under the title *American Leading Cases.* In all this work, Wallace demonstrated an analytical legal mind and a clear style.

After his death, his literary miscellanies, most of them unfinished essays of philosophical nature, were collected in two volumes, *Art, Scenery, and Philosophy in Europe* (1855), and *Literary Criticisms and Other Papers* (1856), containing some of his best writing. Auguste Comte recognized him as his leading American disciple and compared his mind to that of Jefferson (Preface to *Système de Politique Positive,* Paris, 1853, III, xvii), and Wallace, in an essay in *Art, Scenery, and Philosophy* (p. 332), acknowledges his master's discovery that "mental and moral subjects are capable of being embraced and analyzed by science." His essays on Michael Angelo, Leonardo, and Raphael show esthetic as well as scientific perception, two faculties which he clearly distinguished in his own thought. Those on his contemporaries, G. P. Morris [q.v.], later abridged as a preface to Morris' *Poems* (1860), and R. W. Griswold [q.v.], have not the same philosophical detachment. His early grasp of positivism places him as a promising figure in the transition stages of nineteenth-century thought, but his modesty in publication and his premature death make it difficult to estimate his true weight.

[*"Memoir," and "Obituary" by Horace Binney, in Wallace's *Art, Scenery, and Philosophy in Europe* (1855); J. A. Phelps, *The Wallace Family in America* (1914).]   R. Er. S.

WALLACE, HUGH CAMPBELL (Feb. 10, 1863–Jan. 1, 1931), financier, politician, diplomat, was the son of Thomas Bates Wallace, a merchant of Lexington, Mo., and his second wife, Lucy (*née* Briscoe), widow of Frank P. Gaines. His ancestor William Wallace emigrated as a child with relatives from Northern Ireland in 1724 to Pennsylvania and later moved to Virginia. Hugh Wallace's success in business and politics was foreshadowed by his energy, shrewdness, and business acumen as a schoolboy in Lexington. He was a born trader; he always seemed to have a job; he was hardly grown when he made a business trip to Texas and New Mexico. At twenty-two he was appointed receiver of public moneys in Salt Lake City by President Cleveland, and held office from 1885 to 1887, when he resigned to join his older brother in Tacoma, Wash. They organized a bank, and Hugh also engaged in extensive real estate and commercial activities. He was closely identified with the development of Tacoma and throughout his life retained an important interest in the city's financial affairs. He organized a steamship line to Alaska during the Klondike gold rush, and acquired an interest in Alaskan gold mines. He became one of the most influential financiers of the Northwest.

While visiting President Cleveland in Washington, D. C., he met Mildred Fuller, daughter of Chief Justice Melville W. Fuller, and married her on Jan. 5, 1891. Two of their three children died in infancy. He never ran for public office, though he was offered nominations for governor and United States senator in the state of Washington, and he held only two political appointments in his life. Friendly, eloquent, keen-witted and clear-headed, convincing in his sincerity, of unquestioned integrity, he was early in the councils of the Democratic leaders of the Northwest. He was elected to the Democratic National Committee in 1892 and 1896, resigned in 1896, and was elected again for a four-year term in 1916. He was a delegate-at-large from Washington to Democratic national conventions from 1896 to 1912, and took a prominent part in the presidential campaigns of 1892, 1912, and 1916. Following Wilson's election Wallace refused the secretaryship of war but became an intimate member of the President's unofficial family, a trusted adviser, particularly in regard to Western politics. After the United States entered the World War he made unofficial confidential visits to England, France, and Italy for President Wilson.

On Feb. 27, 1919, the President appointed him ambassador to France. During the difficult postwar days Wallace worked tirelessly to keep French friendship for the United States unbroken, so wholeheartedly and so ably that among the many harsh things said in the press of both countries, little or no criticism of Wallace appeared. Following the withdrawal of the American delegation to the Peace Conference he was appointed American representative on the Supreme Council and the Conference of Ambassadors at Paris, and although empowered to act only as observer and not as active participant, his influence was considerable. He signed for the United States the treaty concerning the Ar-

chipelago of Spitzbergen (Feb. 9, 1920), and the Treaty of Trianon (June 4, 1920). He resigned on Mar. 4, 1921, but at President Harding's request remained at his post until the arrival of his successor in July. The French government bestowed on him the Grand Cross of the Legion of Honor, and during the rest of his life he spent much of his time in France, where he had established many warm friendships. In 1927 he was named American representative in the International Academy of Diplomacy, organized under French auspices. In 1930 he became president of the Foch National Memorial, Incorporated. During and following his term as ambassador he assembled a valuable library of works dealing with the history of the Franco-American relations, which he presented to the United States government for the American embassy in Paris shortly before his death. He died of heart disease at his home in Washington, D. C., after a long illness.

[F. W. Dawson, *The Speeches of the Hon. Hugh C. Wallace . . . 1919–21* (copr. 1921); Beckles Willson, *America's Ambassadors to France* (1928); *Who's Who in America,* 1930–31; W. H. Miller, *Hist. and Geneals. of the Families of Miller, Woods, Harris, Wallace . . . and Brown,* pt. V (1907); G. S. Wallace, *Wallace: Geneal. Data* (1927); *N. Y. Times,* Jan. 2, 1931 (see also *N. Y. Times Index* for preceding years); *Tacoma Daily Ledger,* Jan. 2, 3, 1931; *Washington Post,* Feb. 16, 1919; *Lit. Digest,* Mar. 29, 1919; *Current Opinion,* Apr. 1919.]   I. L. T.

WALLACE, JOHN FINDLEY (Sept. 10, 1852–July 3, 1921), civil engineer and railroad executive, was born at Fall River, Mass., the son of the Rev. David Alexander and Martha (Findley) Wallace. His family moved to Boston in 1854 and subsequently to Monmouth, Ill., where on Jan. 1, 1857, his father took office as the first president of Monmouth College. Here the son was enrolled as a student during the years 1865–71, but he refused to take certain subjects required for a degree and consequently did not graduate. He married Sarah E. Ulmer on Sept. 11, 1871. To help pay his college expenses he worked as a rodman on the Carthage & Burlington Railroad in 1869, and as a draftsman for the Rockford, Rock Island & St. Louis in 1870. His first permanent position was that of assistant engineer in the employ of the United States (1871–76), working on improvements in the upper Mississippi, particularly on surveys of the Rock Island rapids and for a ship canal at Keokuk, Iowa. During the next few years he engaged in private practice at Monmouth, but served also as city engineer and county surveyor.

From 1878 to 1881 he was chief engineer and superintendent of the Peoria & Farmington Railroad and from 1881 to 1883, of the Central

Iowa Railway in Illinois; these five years were spent largely in supervising construction between Peoria and Keithsburg. He was chief engineer and master of transportation of the Central Iowa between Oskaloosa and Peoria from 1883 to 1886; in 1886–87 he was engaged in surveys and construction for the Northern Pacific in Wyoming, and in 1887–89 was bridge engineer for the Atchison, Topeka & Santa Fé. He then re-entered consulting practice in association with E. L. Corthell [q.v.] and during the next two years was concerned with bridges over the Mississippi River at St. Louis and New Orleans, and the entrance of the Santa Fé, the Chicago & Alton, and the Illinois Central railroads into Chicago. He was also for a time resident manager of the Chicago, Madison & Northern. In 1891 he began a thirteen-year connection with the Illinois Central, rising through various offices to that of general manager in 1901. His work included the elevation of the Chicago tracks, the provision of facilities to handle the crowds visiting the World's Columbian Exposition, and the construction of terminals at Chicago, New Orleans, and Memphis.

Wallace became interested in Panama through a visit to the Isthmus in December 1896. He was suggested for membership on the first Canal Commission, but failed to receive an appointment. In June 1904, however, he was made the first chief engineer of the Canal, in which position he served for about a year. He favored the sea-level plan, but the type had not yet been determined by Congress; most of his work, therefore, was of a preliminary nature, although some actual excavation was begun. When the Canal Commission was reorganized in April 1905, with Theodore P. Shonts [q.v.] as chairman, Wallace was made a member, retaining also the position of chief engineer; he continued, however, to feel hampered by the lack of authority and by conflicting instructions and in June 1905, attracted by an offer from a private concern, he resigned. The Secretary of War, William H. Taft [q.v.], objected strongly to his resignation, and a bitter controversy, involving a senatorial investigation, ensued (*Senate Document 401*, 59 Cong., 2 Sess.). Wallace defended his administration in a series of articles in the *Engineering Magazine* (September-November 1905, March 1906), and subsequently contributed an article, "Panama and the Canal Zone," to *America Across the Seas* (1909), by Hamilton Wright and others.

After his withdrawal from the Canal project, he was connected with a large variety of enterprises. He was president and chairman of the board of Westinghouse, Church, Kerr & Company (1916–18), member of the executive committee of the Taylor-Wharton Iron & Steel Company (1915–21), and chairman of the board of the Southern Oil & Transport Corporation (1917–21), and was employed as a consultant by many other concerns. He became chairman of the Chicago Railway Terminal Commission in 1914. Professional honors accorded him included election as first president of the Western Society of Engineers in 1896, as first president of the American Railway Engineering and Maintenance-of-Way Association in 1899, and as president of the American Society of Civil Engineers in 1900. He died in Washington, D. C., whither he had been called to testify before the Senate Committee on interstate commerce.

[Printed sources include: *Who's Who in America*, 1920–21; James Wallace, *Wallace-Bruce and Closely Related Families* (1930); *Railway Age*, July 9, 1921; W. F. Johnson, *Four Centuries of the Panama Canal* (1906), pp. 286–315; brief autobiog. in *Sen. Doc. 401*, 59 Cong., 2 Sess., I, 543 ff.; "First Ann. Report of the Isthmian Canal Commission," *House Doc. 226*, 58 Cong., 3 Sess.; "Ann. Report of the Isthmian Canal Commission ... Dec. 1, 1905," *Sen. Doc. 127*, 59 Cong., 1 Sess.; *Outlook*, May 6, July 8, 1905, June 24, 1911; *World's Work*, Apr. 1907; *Chicago Tribune* and *Evening Star* (Washington, D. C.), July 4, 1921. The Wallace collection in the N. Y. Pub. Lib. includes many of his professional reports and a number of volumes of "Personal Memoranda."]   R. E. R.

WALLACE, JOHN HANKINS (Aug. 16, 1822–May 2, 1903), originator of the *American Trotting Register,* was born on a farm in Allegheny County, Pa., the son of Robert and Elizabeth (Hankins) Wallace. His father was descended from Scotch-Irish ancestors who emigrated to Pennsylvania early in the eighteenth century; his maternal grandmother, from Edward Riggs who emigrated to Boston in 1633. As a boy John Wallace was more interested in books than in farming, and excessive application to his studies when attending Frankfort Springs Academy resulted in impaired health. Urged to live in the open, he went to Iowa in 1845 and on a farm at Muscatine, speedily regained his health.

Here he began studies in the breeding and pedigrees of cattle. The region, however, was one in which the breeding of horses, especially light-harness horses, was carried on extensively, and he soon transferred his attention to equine genealogies. There then existed no reliable stud book devoted to the American thoroughbred, and none whatever of trotting horses. Accordingly, Wallace spent several years in compiling such a work, and in 1867 published in New York the first volume of *Wallace's American Stud Book*. It was not a financial success, but as an appendix he had included pedigrees of trotting horses. The interest which these aroused led him to abandon all other pursuits and make trotting horses and their pedigrees his life-study. In 1871 he brought out the first volume of *Wallace's American Trotting Register,* and in 1874 the second volume. In the meantime he had returned to Pennsylvania and in 1875 he removed to New York City, which was thereafter his home. In that year he began publishing *Wallace's Monthly,* a magazine devoted to the interests of the trotting horse. In 1886 he brought out the first volume of *Wallace's Year-Book of Trotting and Pacing,* an annual compendium of statistics. After publishing nine volumes of the *Trotting Register* and six of the *Year Book,* he sold his publications in 1891 for the sum of $130,000 and retired to private life. Six years later he published *The Horse of America* (1897), in which he presented the result of much valuable investigation together with a defense of his career and his theories of horse breeding. Interested also in his own ancestry, he published *Genealogy of the Riggs Family* (1901) and *Genealogy of the Wallace Family* (1902). He was twice married: first, on October 2, 1845, to Ellen Ewing of Uniontown, Pa.; she died in 1891, and on May 3, 1893, he married Ellen Wallace Veech, his first wife's niece.

When Wallace began his studies there was no recognized trotting breed of American horses. In 1876 he organized in New York the National Association of Trotting Horse Breeders, and two years later, under his auspices, the Trotting Standard was devised and in 1879 adopted to govern all registration in the *Trotting Register.* The enormous stimulation of light-harness horse breeding in America and the world-wide fame of the American trotter were direct outcomes of these achievements. When in 1891 he sold out his publications over 16,000 different trotting stallions had been registered as standard and more than twice that many mares. In 1933 over 70,000 stallions and at least 150,000 mares had been registered. Single specimens of the breed have sold as high as $125,000, and American standard blood has become dominant in all parts of the world. To Wallace more than to any other one person these results are attributable.

[Biog. sketch appended to Wallace's *The Horse of America* (1897); *Wallace's Mo.,* Aug. 1878; *Horse Rev.,* May 11, 18, 1903; B. F. Gue, *Hist. of Iowa* (1903), vol. IV; *N. Y. Herald,* May 3, 1903; *Sun* (N. Y.), May 4, 1903; personal acquaintance.]   J. L. H.

WALLACE, JOHN WILLIAM (Feb. 17, 1815–Jan. 12, 1884), legal scholar and author, was born in Philadelphia, which was his home for the most of his life. His father, John Bradford Wallace, grandson of William Bradford, 1721/22–1791 [*q.v.*], the "patriot printer," stood

high as a lawyer among the members of a very distinguished bar; his mother, Susan (Binney) Wallace, according to her brother Horace Binney [*q.v.*] possessed "the most uniformly . . . bright and vivid mind" that he had ever known (Flanders, *post,* p. xviii). Wallace was educated by his parents and at the University of Pennsylvania, where he graduated in 1833. He studied law with his father and John Sergeant [*q.v.*], and was admitted to the bar on Oct. 27, 1836. With his abilities and distinguished connections he would have found easy the way to professional honors, but he never engaged in active legal practice. In 1841 he became librarian and treasurer of the Law Association of Philadelphia. He contributed the American notes to the third volume of *Cases, Chiefly Relating to the Criminal and Presentment Law, Reserved for Consideration,* known as "British Crown Cases Reserved" (6 vols., Philadelphia, 1839–53). Pursuing his duties as librarian in his enthusiastic and scholarly way, he published anonymously in the *American Law Magazine* (January 1844) a contribution which was republished as *The Reporters, Chronologically Arranged: with Occasional Remarks upon Their Respective Merits* (1844). By this book, with revised and enlarged editions (1845, 1855, and 1882), full of professional learning lightly carried, his memory lives among legal scholars.

In 1844 he became a standing master in chancery of the supreme court of Pennsylvania. The first of three volumes of his reports of *Cases in the Circuit Court of the United States for the Third Circuit,* covering the years 1842–62, appeared in 1849, the others in 1854 and 1871. In 1850 he visited England and Scotland and met great barristers and judges of the day. After the death of his brother Horace Binney Wallace [*q.v.*], he took the latter's place as coeditor with J. I. Clark Hare [*q.v.*] of J. W. Smith's *Selection of Leading Cases on Various Branches of the Law* and *American Leading Cases,* collaborating in the preparation of three editions of the first and two of the second. From 1857 to 1860 he was again abroad, mainly in Italy, and upon his return resigned his librarianship, Nov. 26, 1860, though he continued until Dec. 3, 1864, to serve as treasurer of the Law Association. On Mar. 21, 1863, he had become the reporter of the Supreme Court of the United States, from which office he resigned on Oct. 9, 1875. The twenty-three volumes of *Wallace's Reports* cover a period of great importance in the Court's history (December 1863–October 1874) and are of the highest quality.

After being for twenty-four years a member of

the Historical Society of Pennsylvania, Wallace became its president, Apr. 13, 1868, and served as such until his death. Among his publications, in addition to those mentioned above, were: *The Want of Uniformity in the Commercial Law between the Different States of Our Union* (1851); *Pennsylvania as a Borrower . . . Her Ancient Credit: Her Subsequent Disgrace: Her . . . Future* (1863); *An Address Delivered at the Celebration by the New York Historical Society, May 20, 1863, of the Two Hundredth Birth Day of Mr. William Bradford* (1863); *A Discourse Pronounced on the Inauguration of the New Hall, March 11, 1872, of the Historical Society of Pennsylvania* (1872); *An Address of Welcome, from the Librarians of Philadelphia, to the Congress of Librarians of the United States* (1876); "Early Printing in Philadelphia" (*Pennsylvania Magazine of History and Biography*, vol. IV, 1880, pp. 432–44); *An Old Philadelphian, Colonel William Bradford, the Patriot Printer of 1776: Sketches of His Life* (privately printed, 1882; published, 1884).

Wallace was a devout Roman Catholic. He was a man of positive opinions, likes, and dislikes, but reserved in expression. His manners were marked by a courtesy that had become old-fashioned. His attainments were both wide and profound in law, history, and belles-lettres, and also in other unusual fields such as the art of printing, and all his publications were characterized by literary quality. He married (June 15, 1853) Dorothea Francis Willing, who survived him, as did his only child, a daughter.

[Prefaces to 1 *Wallace* and *The Reporters*; Henry Flanders, in *Pa. Mag. of Hist. and Biog.*, VIII (1884), v–xliv; C. J. F. Binney, *Geneal. of the Binney Family* (1886); *Univ. of Pa. Biog. Cat.* (1894); *Phila. Press*, Jan. 14, 1884; *Legal Intelligencer* (Phila.), Jan. 18, 1884.]   F. S. P.

WALLACE, LEWIS (Apr. 10, 1827–Feb. 15, 1905), lawyer, soldier, diplomat, author, commonly known as "Lew" Wallace, was born at Brookville, Ind., the son of David [*q.v.*] and Esther French (Test) Wallace. His mother, to whom he was deeply attached, died during his boyhood. He early displayed a love of adventure; his father tried to keep him in school, but the boy was irked by ordinary tasks and preferred to draw caricatures or to play truant. As he grew older, however, he carried his books to the woods as often as his gun and rod. When his father was elected governor of Indiana in 1837 and the family moved to Indianapolis, Lew's zest for reading was stimulated by the advantages of the state library. Before he was sixteen he began to support himself by copying records in the county clerk's office. About the same time,

Prescott's *Conquest of Mexico* made such a deep impression upon him that he determined to write upon the theme. Thus *The Fair God* of later years had its inception. In 1844–45 he reported the proceedings of the Indiana House of Representatives for the *Indianapolis Daily Journal*, and soon afterwards began the study of law in his father's office. When the Mexican War began, he raised a company of which he became second lieutenant and which was assigned to the 1st Indiana Infantry. His services in Mexico gave him experience without involving him in the dangers of any serious engagement.

He campaigned against Taylor in 1848 and edited a Free-Soil paper, chiefly because of resentment against Taylor's treatment of the Indiana regiments. Following the campaign he became a Democrat. Admitted to the bar in 1849 he began practice in Indianapolis. Soon he moved to Covington, and in 1850 and 1852 was elected prosecuting attorney. In 1853 he changed his residence to Crawfordsville, and in 1856 was elected to the state Senate. There he advocated a reform in divorce laws and in 1859 proposed the popular election of United States senators. In the summer of 1856 he had organized a military company at Crawfordsville which he drilled so efficiently that most of its members became officers in the Civil War.

After Fort Sumter was fired upon, Gov. O. P. Morton [*q.v.*] made him adjutant-general of the state. Within a week he had 130 companies in camp, seventy more than the state quota, and was made colonel of the 11th Regiment. Soon at the front, he helped to capture Romney, on the South Branch of the Potomac, and to evict the enemy from Harpers Ferry. An excellent disciplinarian and popular with his men, he was promoted rapidly. On Sept. 3, 1861, he was made a brigadier-general and on Mar. 21, 1862, after his service at the capture of Fort Donelson, Tenn., a major-general. Unfortunately, he incurred the ill will of General Halleck, who twice removed him from command; the first time he was restored by President Lincoln, the second time, by General Grant. In November 1862, he was president of the military commission that investigated the operations of the army under Maj.-Gen. D. C. Buell [*q.v.*]. The following year he saved Cincinnati from capture by Gen. E. Kirby-Smith [*q.v.*], after which event the President gave him command of the Middle Division and VIII Army Corps, with headquarters at Baltimore. With 5,800 men, part of them inexperienced, he held a force of 28,000 under Gen. Jubal A. Early [*q.v.*] at the Monocacy, July 9, 1864. Though defeated, he probably saved Washington from capture, and was highly commended by Grant in his *Memoirs* (*post,* II, 306). He served on the court martial which tried the assassins of Lincoln, and was president of the court that tried and convicted Henry Wirz [*q.v.*], commandant of Andersonville Prison.

At the close of the war he undertook to procure munitions and to raise a corps of veterans for the Mexican liberals, and spent some time in Mexico. Returning to Crawfordsville, he practised law, and in 1870 was an unsuccessful candidate for Congress on the Republican ticket. In 1878 he was appointed governor of New Mexico, serving until 1881, when President Garfield appointed him minister to Turkey. There he lived for four years, 1881–85, winning the confidence of the Sultan to an unusual degree. In 1890 he declined an offer of the mission to Brazil tendered by President Harrison.

Wallace is best known, however, as a man of letters. In 1873 he published *The Fair God,* a story of the conquest of Mexico, which won him wide recognition. The fame thus attained was greatly enhanced by *Ben Hur; A Tale of the Christ* (1880), of which 300,000 copies were sold within ten years. It was translated into a number of foreign languages, including Arabic and Chinese, and was successfully dramatized. The extraordinary success of this work was largely due to the fact that the greatest figure in history was with the deepest reverence brought into a strong story dramatically told. Among his other publications were *The Life of Benjamin Harrison* (1888), written for campaign purposes; *The Boyhood of Christ* (1888); *The Prince of India* (1893), inspired by his stay in Constantinople; and *The Wooing of Malkatoon* (1898), a poem, with which was included *Commodus,* a tragedy, written many years earlier. In 1906 appeared *Lew Wallace, An Autobiography,* which Wallace had brought down only to 1864, but which was sketchily completed by his wife and Mary H. Krout.

On May 6, 1852, he married Susan Arnold (Dec. 25, 1830–Oct. 1, 1907), born in Crawfordsville, the daughter of Col. Isaac C. and Maria Aken Elston. Fifty years later he called her "a composite of genius, common-sense, and all best womanly qualities" (*Autobiography,* I, 209). She was a frequent contributor to newspapers and periodicals, and one of her poems, "The Patter of Little Feet," had wide popularity. Other publications by her include *The Storied Sea* (1883); *Ginèvra: or The Old Oak Chest* (1887); *The Land of the Pueblos* (1888); and *The Repose in Egypt* (1888).

Wallace's poise and urbanity marked him as a man of the world, yet he was simple in taste and democratic in ideals. For politics he had no aptitude; the law he did not like; the military life challenged his adventurous spirit but could not hold him after his country had no special use for his services; art, music, and literature were his most vital and permanent interests. Many a young person had reason to remember the gracious hospitality of his study, built as "a pleasure-house for my soul." Never a church member, he believed in the divinity of Christ. His last years were serene. He lectured frequently and received unstinted praise. He died at Crawfordsville, and five years after his death his statue was unveiled in the Capitol at Washington as representative of the state of Indiana.

[In addition to the *Autobiog.,* see *Commemorative Biog. Record of Prominent and Representative Men of Indianapolis and Vicinity* (1908); J. P. Dunn, *Greater Indianapolis* (1910), vol. II; M. H. Krout, "Personal Record of Lew Wallace," *Harper's Weekly,* Mar. 18, 1905; Meredith Nicholson, in *Review of Reviews,* Apr. 1905; *N. Y. Tribune, Indianapolis Star, Indianapolis News* and *Daily Sentinel* (Indianapolis), Feb. 16, 1905; *Senate Doc. 503,* 61 Cong., 2 Sess.; *War of the Rebellion: Official Records* (*Army*); *Personal Memoirs of U. S. Grant* (2 vols., 1885–86).]   A. L. L.

WALLACE, WILLIAM (Mar. 16, 1825–May 20, 1904), inventor, manufacturer, was born in Manchester, England, the second son of Thomas and Agnes Wallace. At the age of seven he emigrated with his parents to the United States, and for nine years the family moved about from place to place, stopping wherever the father could find work at his trade of wire drawing. Meanwhile, Wallace obtained a little common-school education. In 1841 his parents finally settled in Derby, Conn., and with his father and two brothers he went to work for the Howe Manufacturing Company. Here he remained until 1848, when he and his brothers went into the wire-drawing business with their father under the firm name of Wallace & Sons; two years later they established their plant at the newly founded industrial town of Ansonia, Conn.

In 1853 the business was incorporated, and from that time until his retirement in 1896, Wallace was active in the organization, becoming president on the death of his father. He built up a large business, rolling copper and brass and drawing wire, and by 1880 Wallace & Sons was the largest establishment of its kind in the Connecticut Valley. Throughout this long period Wallace personally supervised most of the mechanical affairs, mapping out work, laying out new buildings, installing equipment, and devising many of the special tools and machines used in the factory.

Becoming interested in electricity, he installed

a well-equipped laboratory in his home, and established personal contacts with the electrical pioneers of the United States. The results of his studies and experiments became manifest about 1874, when he constructed dynamo-electric machinery at his plant. In this enterprise he had the cooperation of the well-known electrician Moses G. Farmer [q.v.]. In 1875 and 1876 a number of dynamos employing armatures of the Siemens, Gramme, Pacinotti, and multi-polar types were constructed. One of these, the Wallace-Farmer dynamo, based on Farmer's patent of 1872, was used at the Centennial Exhibition at Philadelphia in 1876, and was the only one employed for illuminating the exposition buildings and grounds. Wallace's company began the manufacture of this type of machine for the market early in 1875, adapting it later for arc lighting in connection with Wallace's plate-carbon arc lamp, patented Dec. 18, 1877, and believed to be the first commercial arc light made in the United States. Wallace was the first to demonstrate the operation of arc lights in series. In 1876 he developed a low-tension dynamo for the Western Union Telegraph Company to take the place of batteries. In conjunction with his brother Thomas, he constructed also an enormous electro-disposition plant at Ansonia for the purpose of copper-plating the steel wire used by the Postal Telegraph Company in the installation of the harmonic telegraph system developed by Elisha Gray [q.v.]. In this plant thirty-one huge Wallace plating dynamos were used and over one hundred miles of steel wire at a time were copper plated. Wallace spent large sums of money in public exhibitions, with a view to bringing the possibilities of the dynamo to public attention; but with the beginning of the establishment of the electrical industry in the United States in the 1880's, he retired from the field and confined his attention to rolling copper and brass.

Wallace was a lovable man, genial and agreeable in manner and always willing to assist others in every possible way. After the purchase of his organization by the Coe Brass Company in 1896, he took up his residence in Washington, D. C. On Sept. 15, 1849, he married Sarah Mills at Birmingham, Conn.; he was survived by a son and a daughter.

[Trans. Am. Soc. of Mechanical Engineers, vol. XXV (1904); W. J. Hammer, "William Wallace and His Contributions to the Electrical Industry," Electrical Engineer, Feb. 1–22, 1893; Electrical World and Engineer, June 4, 1904; W. G. Lathrop, The Brass Industry in the U. S. (1926); Samuel Orcutt and Ambrose Beardsley, The Hist. of the Old Town of Derby, Conn. (1880); Washington Post, May 21, 1904.]
C. W. M.

WALLACE, WILLIAM ALEXANDER ANDERSON (Apr. 3, 1817–Jan. 7, 1899), frontiersman, Texas ranger, popularly known as "Bigfoot" Wallace, was born near Lexington, Va., the son of Andrew and Jane (Blair) Wallace. His family were of colonial stock and Scottish origin. Wallace went to Texas in 1837 to avenge the massacre of a brother and a cousin at Goliad in March of the previous year, drifted inland from Galveston, and settled down to the life of a farmer. In 1840 he enlisted as a private in a company of rangers under John Coffee Hays [q.v.] whose duty it was to protect the frontier country around San Antonio from hostile Indians and lawless whites. In the course of this service he fought in the battle on the Salado— an incident in Woll's invasion of Texas in 1842 —and later in that year, after Woll's retreat to Mexico, in the futile Mier expedition which ended for Wallace with nearly two years in Mexican prisons. On Sept. 28, 1845, about a year after his release, he enlisted as first sergeant in Capt. R. A. Gillespie's Texas Mounted Rangers and on June 29, 1846, one day after the company was mustered out, he reënlisted in Gillespie's company, then a part of Hays's 1st Regiment, Texas Mounted Rifle Volunteers. With this organization he served in the Mexican War, being honorably discharged as first lieutenant in September 1846. In 1850 he was himself designated by Governor Bell to raise a company of volunteers for frontier service.

The recital of his more formal military service is by no means the whole story of his Indian warfare. Time and time again in the course of his fifty active years he had to leave his Medina River farm with a hastily gathered band of neighbors to protect life and property from Indian raiders. In particular, a contract he entered into in 1850 to carry the mail between San Antonio and El Paso brought its share of Indian conflict. Five hundred of the six hundred miles to be traversed lay in entirely unsettled country, much of which was infested with hostile Indians; the trip took a month. On only one occasion, however, when careless camp guards let the Comanches steal his mules, did he fail to deliver the mail in El Paso on schedule time. He had no sympathy with the Civil War and took no part in it, save to protect the noncombatants on the frontier whose men were away in the army.

In his prime Wallace stood six feet two inches in his moccasins and weighed 240 pounds. He never lost a tooth; he never wore glasses. His outdoor life, especially his Indian warfare, developed exceptional quickness of eye and hand. Despite his limited schooling he was for a frontiersman well read. He was greatly admired and beloved for his prowess, his generosity, his geniality, and his story-telling ability and although he was not so able a leader as Hays, Ben McCulloch, or Lawrence S. Ross [qq.v.], he became a folk-hero of Texas. Never married, he lived alone for the most part until his early seventies, when the palsy which he attributed to his Mexican prison experience forced him to live with friends who could give him needed physical care. He died, near Devine, Tex., of pneumonia. Texas rewarded his public service with a gift of 1280 acres of public land, and honored him after death by removing his body from its first burial place at Devine to the State Cemetery at Austin.

[Record book of P. H. Bell, no. 77, Tex. State Lib.; Tex. Land Office records; Laws of Tex. (Special, Mar. 30, 1888, General, Feb. 20, 1899); records of Adj.-General's Office, War Dept., Washington; two letters of Wallace privately owned (photostats, Univ. of Tex. Lib.); *Frontier Times*, May and July 1926, April 1928, June 1931; *Dallas Morning News*, Oct. 5, 1898, Sept. 15, 1929; *Daily Express* (San Antonio), Jan. 8, 1899; sundry narratives to be used with caution, the most popular being J. C. Duval, *The Adventures of Big-Foot Wallace* (1870) and the most convincing, A. J. Sowell, *Rangers and Pioneers of Texas* (1884) and *Early Settlers and Indian Fighters of Southwest Texas* (1900), containing a sketch which is practically the same as Sowell's *Life of Bigfoot Wallace* (1899), with an additional paragraph on the last illness, death, and burial of Wallace; G. S. Wallace, *Wallace: Geneal. Data* (1927).]   E. H. W.

WALLACE, WILLIAM JAMES (Apr. 14, 1837–Mar. 11, 1917), jurist, was born in Syracuse, N. Y., the son of Elisha Fuller and Lydia (Wheelwright) Wallace. He obtained his secondary education in the private schools of Syracuse and his academic legal training in Hamilton College, obtaining the degree of LL.B. from that institution in 1857. He was admitted to the bar of the state of New York, and began practice in Canastota, but he soon moved to Syracuse, where sometime later he became a member of the firm of Ruger, Wallace & Jenney.

In 1873 Wallace was elected mayor of Syracuse. In the succeeding year he was appointed, by President Grant, United States district judge for the northern district of New York. When, in 1882, the position of judge of the second circuit court fell vacant, Wallace was promoted to that bench. At that time there was but one judge for the whole circuit, which was, in the magnitude of its business, the most important in the United States. Wallace himself stated that "the business of the Federal Courts in this city [New York] alone which devolved upon the circuit judge was, in my deliberate judgment, as extensive, as important, and as various as was allotted to any single judge in this country or in

England to undertake" (*Dinner in Honor of Judge . . . Wallace, post*, pp. 18–19). The pressure was somewhat relieved by Act of Congress on Mar. 3, 1887, curtailing the jurisdiction of the circuit courts and providing for an additional circuit judge. That act was, in turn, followed by the act creating the circuit courts of appeal. On the establishment of these latter courts, Wallace was appointed presiding judge for the circuit, in which office he remained until his retirement in 1907 when he resumed active practice with the firm of Wallace, Butler & Brown.

During his long tenure Wallace earned for himself the respect of the legal world by the caliber of his decisions, which were characterized by Mr. Justice Lurton as having "enriched for all time the judicial literature of his country" (*Ibid.*, p. 29). Further evidence of the respect in which he was held is furnished by his nomination in 1897 by the Republican party for the important position of chief judge of the court of appeals of New York (though he was not elected). While to a later day his views may seem ultra-conservative, they were probably not more so than those held in general by a federal bench not noted for its liberalism.

Wallace was twice married: first to Josephine Robbins of Brooklyn, N. Y., who died in 1874, and second, in April 1878, to Alice Wheelwright. The latter also predeceased him so that on his death, which occurred in Jacksonville, Fla., he was survived only by an adopted daughter.

[*The Dinner in Honor of Judge William J. Wallace on His Retirement from the Bench given by Members of the Bar of the State of N. Y.* (1907); J. L. Bishop, in *N. Y. County Lawyers' Asso., Year Book*, 1917; *Who's Who in America*, 1916–17; C. E. Fitch, *Encyc. of Biog. of N. Y.* (1916), IV, 345; *N. Y. Times*, Mar. 13, 1917; *Albany Evening Journal*, Mar. 12, 1917.]   L. M. S.

WALLACE, WILLIAM ROSS (1819–May 5, 1881), poet, was born probably in Lexington or in Paris, Ky. He is said to have been the son of a Presbyterian minister and was presumably of the Highland Scotch stock of the Pennsylvania and Virginia frontier. It is probable that he is the William Wallace of Paris, Ky., and later of Hanover, Ind., who appears as a student at Hanover College in 1833–35. He is said also to have lived in Bloomington, Ind. His first printed poem was *The Battle of Tippecanoe* (Cincinnati, 1837). He returned to Lexington to study law, and practised his profession in New York City from 1841 until his death. He was twice married and had three children, a daughter by his first wife, and a son and daughter by his second. His second wife was a Miss Riker, whom he is said to have married in October 1856 (*New York Times, post*).

During the first two decades of his residence in New York Wallace seems to have been more occupied with literature than with legal affairs. He became a frequent contributor to *Harper's Magazine* and *Harper's Weekly, Godey's Lady's Book,* the *New York Ledger,* the *Celtic Monthly,* the *Journal of Commerce,* and the *Louisville Daily Journal,* and his best known lyrics, odes, and love songs were collected as *Meditations in America, and Other Poems* (1851). A longer work, *Alban the Pirate* (1848), a poetical romance "intended to illustrate the influence of certain prejudices of society and principles of law upon individual character and destiny" (Griswold, *post,* p. 551), met with little success. The outbreak of the Civil War stirred Wallace to write a number of fervently patriotic songs, among them "The Sword of Bunker Hill" and "Keep Step with the Music of the Union" (1861) and "The Liberty Bell" (1862), which were set to music and became widely popular. After the war he seems to have published little or nothing. He moved on terms of easy intimacy with such local "literati" as Samuel Woodworth, George P. Morris, and Thomas Dunn English [*qq.v.*], and was a close friend of Edgar Allan Poe after the latter's return to New York in 1844. He was responsible for inducing Poe to have his daguerreotype taken by M. B. Brady in 1848. After Poe's death he defended his memory against the aspersions of John Neal [*q.v.*]. He is said to have been "not unlike Poe in both temperament and habits. He was not a little like him in physique—in brightness of the eye, and in a superb courtliness of manner. He had the same, or a similar, irresolute will; but he was a delightful companion to meet if you met him at the right time" (Benton, *post,* pp. 732–33).

William Cullen Bryant commended Wallace for his "splendor of imagination" and "affluence of poetic diction," George D. Prentice [*q.v.*] pronounced him "the greatest lyrical poet of the country," and Poe, taking Wallace as his text, vigorously belabored the New England group for their failure to recognize any merit but their own (*The Works of Edgar Allan Poe, post*). Nevertheless only a few of Wallace's poems, and those chiefly his militant patriotic songs, have survived as anthology pieces. Though every one knows

> "And the hand that rocks the cradle
> Is the hand that rules the world,"

the name of the writer is seldom connected with the familiar quotation. The lyrics that were praised by contemporaries for their general resemblance to the poetry of Shelley and Keats have been forgotten by posterity for the same reason.

["Wallace's Poëms," *U. S. Democratic Rev.,* Dec. 1857; R. W. Griswold, *The Poets and Poetry of America* (1873); Joel Benton, in *Forum,* Feb. 1897; E. C. Stedman and G. E. Woodberry, eds., *The Works of Edgar Allan Poe,* vol. VIII, p. 280; Mary E. Phillips, *Edgar Allan Poe* (2 vols., 1926); Hervey Allen, *Israfel* (2 vols., 1926); H. S. Mott, *The New York of Yesterday* (1908); G. E. Woodberry, *The Life of Edgar Allan Poe* (2 vols., 1909); records of Hanover Coll., Hanover, Ind.; obituaries in *N. Y. Times* and *N. Y. Herald,* May 7, 1881.]
G. F. W.

WALLACK, HENRY JOHN (1790–Aug. 30, 1870), actor, was born in London, England, and was the eldest child of William H. and Elizabeth (Field) Granger Wallack. His father was of Jewish ancestry. The family were all theatrical; Mrs. Wallack had for a time been David Garrick's leading woman, and the best traditions of the eighteenth-century English stage were bred into her descendants. Her four children by Wallack—Henry John, James Willliam [*q.v.*], Mary, and Elizabeth—all became actors, and all save Elizabeth spent some time in the United States. After an uneventful early training, Henry Wallack had by his twenty-eighth year become so noted an actor in England that he was engaged for a long American contract, and made his début in Baltimore in 1819. He brought with him his wife, the former Fanny Jones, a dancer of great beauty and charm, who appeared whenever opportunity offered for her talent. After long stays in Baltimore, Philadelphia, and Washington, Wallack first played in New York in May 1821 at the Anthony Street Theatre. Notices of this first engagement show that he appeared in such rôles as those of Brutus, Octavian, Rob Roy, Coriolanus, Captain Bertram in *Fraternal Discord,* and Gambia in the opera, *The Slave.* The *New York Mirror* (June 5, 1824) said of him, "Few men . . . possess so noble a person or a more intelligent and beautiful countenance; the expression of his eye is quick and full of meaning—his movements are easy and correct—his voice mellow and musical." After the birth of her daughter Fanny in 1822, Mrs. Wallack became a dramatic actress and was attached to the Park Theatre for ten years. She was the mother of Wallack's three children—James William [*q.v.*], Julia (Mrs. Hoskins), and Fanny (Mrs. Charles Moorhouse), all well-known actors.

After an extended tour of the country, Wallack became leading man of the Chatham Garden Theatre in 1824. He returned to England in 1828–32 and 1834–36, acting in the latter period as stage manager and leading actor at Covent Garden. His wife obtained a divorce about 1833, and about a year later Wallack married Miss

Turpin, a singer. When his brother James opened the National Theatre in New York in September 1837, Henry was his stage manager, and acted important rôles. In the autumn of 1839 he appeared opposite Edwin Forrest [*q.v.*] in several parts, such as Iago to Forrest's Othello. On Nov. 25 of that year he and his second wife began a long engagement at the New Chatham Theatre. On Dec. 23 Wallack's two daughters made their débuts there with their father in *The Hunchback*. Fanny was an actress of unusual talent; Julia spent most of her time thereafter in opera. In the summer of 1840 Wallack returned to England, where in 1843 he rented Covent Garden for a short and disastrous season. He appeared again in America, as Sir Peter Teazle in *The School for Scandal,* in September 1847 when the Wallacks opened the Broadway Theatre, and throughout that season his daughter Fanny was leading lady there. Wallack spent most of his latter years in the United States, dying in New York at the age of eighty. One of his last appearances was as Falstaff in 1858. His second wife died in 1879. He played a tremendous and varied repertoire during his lifetime, his parts ranging from the chief Shakespearean heroes to Rolla in *Pizarro,* Fagin in *Oliver Twist,* and Anthony Absolute in *The Rivals.*

[G. C. D. Odell, *Annals of the N. Y. Stage* (6 vols., 1927–31); J. N. Ireland, *Records of the N. Y. Stage* (2 vols., 1866–67); M. J. Moses, in *Theatre,* May 1905; C. H. Haswell, *Reminiscences of an Octogenarian* (1896); article on J. W. Wallack, in *Dict. of Nat. Biog.;* Robinson Locke Dramatic Coll., and coll. of newspaper clippings on the Wallacks, N. Y. Pub. Lib.]

A. F. H.

WALLACK, JAMES WILLIAM (*c.* 1795–Dec. 25, 1864), actor, son of William H. and Elizabeth (Field) Granger Wallack, and brother of Henry John Wallack [*q.v.*], was born in London, England. He made his first appearance at the age of four at the Royal Circus in a fairyland pantomime. His father wished him to follow a naval career, but young Wallack was so unhappy at the prospect, so eager to be an actor that the father relented. At twelve the boy appeared with the troupe of the Academic Theatre in London, where plays were given with casts of children. His vigorous and capable performance attracted the notice, it is said, of Richard Brinsley Sheridan, the dramatist, who obtained for him a place in the company of the Drury Lane Theatre. There Master Wallack rose in favor, and when the house was burned in February 1809, he went to the Royal Hibernian Theatre, Dublin. In October 1812 he returned to the rebuilt Theatre Royal, Drury Lane, and at about seventeen played Laertes to the Hamlet of Robert William

Elliston. During the next six years he scored in such parts as Benedick, Petruchio, and Mercutio. Lord Byron, one of the governing board of the theatre in 1815–16, is said to have been his close friend. In 1817 he married Susan Johnstone, daughter of John Johnstone, a popular singer.

On Sept. 7, 1818, he made his American début before an enthusiastic audience at the Park Street Theatre, New York, as Macbeth. James H. Hackett [*q.v.*], a contemporary, describes him as of distinguished figure and bearing, with abundant dark hair, sparkling eyes, and finely cut features (*Notes and Comments, post,* p. 120). His acting was of the school of Kemble. All accounts mention his rich and sonorous voice, clear articulation, quick and vigorous movement, revealing a nervous, exuberant vitality. He played in Boston and other American cities, even as far south as Savannah, in Shakespearean rôles and as Don César de Bazan, Captain Bertram in *Fraternal Discord,* Massaroni in *The Brigand,* and Don Felix in *The Wonder.* After a season in England (1820) he returned to America and in New York played Hamlet, Rolla, Macbeth, Richard III, and Romeo. An injury to his leg in a stage-coach accident made him slightly lame for the rest of his life. He returned to England in 1823 to become stage manager at Drury Lane under Elliston. In 1827 he played Iago there to the Othello of Edmund Kean, with whom he acted also as Edgar, Malcolm, Macduff, Faulconbridge, and Richmond.

The autumn of 1828 brought him again to America. When he played at the Arch Street Theatre in Philadelphia, the competition of Edwin Forrest at the Walnut and Thomas Abthorpe Cooper [*qq.v.*] at the Chestnut resulted in his being paid $200 nightly, a very high salary for the period. From 1834 to 1836 he was again in England, but his American engagements were becoming more and more important, and in 1836 he offered $1,000 for a satisfactory play by an American writer. Nathaniel P. Willis' *Tortesa the Usurer,* first produced in April 1839, is believed to have been the one accepted. On Sept. 1, 1837, he assumed the management of the National Theatre in New York, the first of four Wallack theatres, with his brother Henry as stage manager. When the house was burned on Sept. 23, 1839, he took over Niblo's Garden for a time. After tours in America, England, and Ireland, he appeared in London in 1843 as leading actor and stage manager of the Princess Theatre, where he achieved one of his greatest successes as Don César de Bazan. In 1844 he was again at the Park, New York. He is said to have crossed the Atlantic thirty-five times.

Early in 1851 he appeared at the Haymarket, London, as actor and stage manager. But his wife's death that year brought on an illness and greatly saddened him. Upon his recovery, he appeared for the last time in England at St. Pierre in J. S. Knowles's *The Wife*. Back in New York in 1852, he took over Brougham's Lyceum at Broadway and Broome Streets, and, with his sons John Lester [*q.v.*] as stage manager and Charles as treasurer, opened it in September with *The Way to Get Married*. There for nine years the second of the Wallack theatres flourished, with the manager himself playing many and varied parts—his implacable Shylock, his gentle Sir Edward Mortimer in Colman's *The Iron Chest*, his whimsical Jaques of *As You Like It*, his Martin Heywood in Jerrold's *The Rent Day*, his Petruchio, Mortimer, Erasmus Bookworm, Dick Dashall, and many others. To Wallack's thoroughness as stage manager Edward A. Sothern [*q.v.*] attributed much of his success (*Birds of a Feather, post*, p. 57). A grand benefit was given him on the afternoon and evening of May 29, 1855, at the Academy of Music, Forrest, E. L. Davenport [*q.v.*], and others of America's foremost actors taking part. In 1861 he and Lester opened the new Wallack's Theatre at Broadway and Thirteenth Street. Wallack had ceased acting by this time, but at the close of the season in 1862 he spoke a few words, his last public appearance. His health declined rapidly thereafter until his death on Christmas Day, 1864. Though the admirable versatility of Wallack's acting is considered by one critic to have been in a sense a hindrance to him (Odell, *post*, II, 529), he remains the most distinguished member of a notable family whose history for over fifty years was inseparably linked with that of the New York stage.

[See *A Sketch of the Life of James William Wallack (Senior)* (1865); M. J. Moses, *Famous Actor-Families in America* (1906), which has a discussion of the date of birth, and article in *Theatre*, May 1905; William Oxberry, *Oxberry's Dramatic Biog.*, vol. V (1826); John Genest, *Some Account of the English Stage* (1832); T. A. Brown, *A Hist. of the N. Y. Stage* (3 vols., 1903); G. C. D. Odell, *Annals of the N. Y. Stage*, vol. II (1927); Lester Wallack, *Memories of Fifty Years* (1889); A. C. Dayton, *Last Days of Knickerbocker Life in N. Y.* (1897 ed.); W. C. Russell, *Representative Actors* (1872); F. G. De Fontaine, *Birds of a Feather . . . Talks with Sothern* (1878); J. H. Hackett, *Notes and Comments* (1863); *Wilkes' Spirit of the Times*, Mar. 8, 1862; Robinson Locke Dramatic Coll. and other clippings, N. Y. Pub. Lib.; obituaries in *N. Y. Tribune*, Dec. 26, and *N. Y. Herald*, Dec 27, 1864.]
A.F.H.

WALLACK, JAMES WILLIAM (Feb. 24, 1818–May 24, 1873), actor, son of Henry John [*q.v.*] and Fanny (Jones) Wallack, was born in London, England, but was brought to America in 1819 for a stay of several years. At the age of four he made his first stage appearance in Philadelphia, playing the part of Cora's child with his uncle, James William Wallack [*q.v.*], in *Pizarro*. When the latter seized him with well-simulated anger, he spoiled the scene by screaming and begging "Uncle Jim" not to hurt him, while the house rocked with laughter. He attended private schools in New York and in England. At fourteen he became call boy at the Bowery Theatre, New York, where he also played small parts. At seventeen, after several seasons with provincial touring companies in England, he joined his father, then stage manager at Covent Garden Theatre, London. Two years later he was engaged for the National Theatre, New York, and there in three years rose from "walking gentleman" to leading juvenile. When his uncle, the elder James William, opened there in 1837 in *The Rivals*, young James played Fag. Later he was engaged for the Bowery Theatre, and soon began playing leads in tragedy and comedy. Sometime before 1844 he was married at New Orleans to Mrs. Ann Duff (Waring) Sefton, a notable tragic actress, who thereafter appeared with him in many plays. His two children by her both died young. He played Othello at the Haymarket, London (1851), Macbeth in Philadelphia (1852), and later toured America with great success. In 1853 and 1855 he made two losing ventures as a manager in London and Paris. Thereafter he remained in the United States, where his earnings were large.

He was at his best in tragedy or romantic and somber drama, especially in parts where a rugged physique and a deep, powerful, but flexible voice could be displayed to advantage. Macbeth, Othello, Hotspur, Iago, Richard III, and Leon de Bourbon in *The Man in the Iron Mask* were favorite parts with his public, and he is declared to have been the only American who made a success with Byron's *Werner*. In 1861 he and Mrs. Wallack for a few weeks played with Edwin L. Davenport [*q.v.*], and then for three years divided honors in a Shakespearean repertoire. In 1865 he joined the stock company of his cousin Lester Wallack [*q.v.*] at the latter's theatre in New York. On Dec. 27, 1867, he appeared for the first time in the rôle of Fagin in *Oliver Twist*. He was not anxious to play the part, studied it carelessly, did little rehearsing, and went to the theatre with only a vague notion of what he was going to do. But once into the part, his natural genius inspired him, and the character became the talk of New York. Here also he scored heavily in the eccentric character of Johnson in

The Lancashire Lass, one of his phrases, "a party by the name of Johnson," becoming a catchword of the day. At Booth's Theatre in the winter of 1872–73 he made a deep impression as Matthias in *The Bells* and displayed his old versatile genius as Mercutio, Jaques, and other classic characters. But he had contracted tuberculosis and was compelled to retire in mid-season. He died a few months later on a train near Aiken, S. C., whither he had gone in search of health.

[G. C. D. Odell, *Annals of the N. Y. Stage,* vols. V–VII (1927–31); M. J. Moses, *Famous Actor-Families in America* (1906); *The Autobiog. of Joseph Jefferson* (1897); Alfred Ayres, in *Theatre,* May 1902; Robinson Locke Dramatic Coll. and other clippings, N. Y. Pub. Lib.; obituary in *N. Y. Times,* May 25, 1873.]

A.F.H.

WALLACK, JOHN LESTER [See WALLACK, LESTER, 1820–1888].

WALLACK, LESTER (Jan. 1, 1820–Sept. 6, 1888), actor, dramatist, son of James William [*q.v.*] and Susan (Johnstone) Wallack, was born in New York City so near midnight on Dec. 31, 1819, that the exact date was in question. He was christened John Johnstone Wallack. His early education was obtained in private schools in England. At fifteen, at a school at Brighton, he played his first dramatic part, that of Rolla in *Pizarro,* and did well until he spoiled the evening by making his death-fall so close to the footlights that the curtain came down across him, whereupon his fellow-actors dragged him under it by the legs, while the audience roared with laughter. "I hesitated long," says he, "before I made up my mind to become an actor" (*Memories of Fifty Years,* p. 24). His first professional appearance was therefore delayed until he was nearly twenty, when he played Angelo in Willis' play, *Tortesa the Usurer,* with his father in the English provinces. Resolved not to lean on his father's name, he was billed as "Allan Field." A year later he played with his uncle Henry [*q.v.*] at Rochester, near London, under the name of John Lester. For a time he was a member of the Theatre Royal company, Dublin, and in 1844 stage manager and actor at the Theatre Royal, Southampton. In 1845 at the Queen's Theatre, Manchester, he played Benedick to the Beatrice of the beautiful Helen Faucit, and Mercutio to the Romeo of Charlotte Cushman. On the latter's high recommendation he was engaged for the Haymarket, London, but through unfortunate circumstances did not make a very good impression.

An offer of £8 a week in 1847 took him to America, where he made his first appearance at the Broadway Theatre, New York, on Sept. 27 as Sir Charles Coldstream in *Used Up,* a farce.

During that season (under the name of John Wallack Lester) he handled such parts as Captain Absolute, Mercutio, Sir Frederick Blount in Bulwer-Lytton's *Money,* and Osric in *Hamlet.* At the Chatham Theatre in July 1848 he made a sensation as Don César de Bazan; at the Broadway in August he played Cassio to Edwin Forrest's Othello, and in December won another success as Edmond Dantès in *The Count of Monte Cristo.* That year he was secretly married to Emily Mary Millais, sister of Sir John Millais, the artist. During 1849 Wallack presented two of his own plays, *The Three Guardsmen,* with himself as d'Artagnan and his cousin James William [*q.v.*] as Athos, and *The Four Musketeers, or Ten Years After,* both winning great popular acclaim. In September 1850 he entered Burton's company at the Chambers Street Theatre, where he was noted for his Sir Andrew Aguecheek and Charles Surface. When his father took over Brougham's Lyceum in September 1852, Lester was stage manager. Here his numerous parts, mostly comic or romantic, included those of Claude Melnotte, Wildrake, Bassanio, Don Pedro, Orlando, Sir Benjamin Backbite, and Captain Absolute. He also appeared in his own plays, as De Rameau in *Two to One* (1854), Peveril in *First Impressions* (1856), Leon Delmar in *The Veteran* (when, as C. H. Haswell says in his *Reminiscences of an Octogenarian,* 1896, the sacrifice of Lester's beautiful whiskers for this part "excited general lamentation among the young womanhood of the city"), Manuel in *The Romance of a Poor Young Man,* and Wyndham Otis in *Central Park* (1861). The Wallack company included among other famous actors Laura Keene, John Brougham, E. A. Sothern, Henry Placide, and George Holland [*qq.v.*].

When the new Wallack's Theatre was opened at Broadway and Thirteenth Street in 1861, it was Lester who was the real manager. There he appeared for the first time as Lester Wallack and played many new parts: Elliott Grey in his own play, *Rosedale* (1863), Hugh Chalcote in *Ours,* Henry Beauclerc in *Diplomacy* (1878), and Prosper Couramont in *A Scrap of Paper* (1879). Many famous names are found in the company from time to time—the younger James W. Wallack, John Gibbs Gilbert, Edwin L. Davenport [*qq.v.*], Charles Fisher, and Charles J. Mathews, for examples. This house closed in April 1881, and the new Wallack Theatre at Broadway and Thirtieth Street was opened on Jan. 4, 1882. Wallack managed it until 1887, when he retired. On May 21, 1888, one of the most famous of all theatrical benefits was given for him; *Hamlet* was played with Edwin Booth in the lead, Lawrence Barrett as the Ghost, Joseph Jefferson and William J. Florence as the grave-diggers, Helena Modjeska as Ophelia, Gertrude Kellogg as the Queen, Rose Coghlan as the Player Queen, and other well-known players in the supporting parts. Wallack died less than four months later at his home near Stamford, Conn. He was survived by his wife and four children. His reminiscences, *Memories of Fifty Years,* was published in 1889.

[In addition to Wallack's *Memories of Fifty Years* (1889), see M. J. Moses, *Famous Actor-Families in America* (1906) ; Edward Robins, *Twelve Great Actors* (1900) ; *Wilkes' Spirit of the Times,* Apr. 26, 1862; William Stuart, in *Galaxy,* Oct. 1868; W. J. Florence, in *North Am. Rev.,* Oct. 1888; *Critic,* May 26, Sept. 15, 1888; Arthur Wallack, in *Evening Post* (N. Y.), July 23, Dec. 17, 1910; Robinson Locke Dramatic Coll. and other newspaper clippings, N. Y. Pub. Lib.; obituary and editorial in *N. Y. Times,* Sept. 7, 1888.]

A. F. H.

WALLER, EMMA (*c.* 1820–Feb. 28, 1899), actress, was born in England, and after a brief stage career in the provincial theatres of that country traveled to the United States in 1851 with Daniel Wilmarth Waller, to whom she had been married in 1849. Her husband was an actor and is said to have been a native of New York, the son of a merchant named Wilmarth, the transposed name by which he and his wife were known being assumed for professional purposes at the outset of their joint stage career. Although Mr. Waller acted Hamlet and other tragic rôles in New York soon after their arrival, there is no authentic record of his wife's appearance in that city at this time. Going to San Francisco in 1853, they sailed thence for Australia, where at Melbourne Mrs. Waller acted Lady Macbeth. Returning to London, Mrs. Waller made her début at the Drury Lane on Sept. 15, 1856, as Pauline in Bulwer-Lytton's *The Lady of Lyons.* In the diaries of E. L. Blanchard he notes that "as Pauline—she lacked vigour, but was gentle and graceful" (Scott and Howard, *post,* I, 164). If his judgment is correct, she must have grown appreciably in physical and intellectual intensity, for she became one of the leading emotional actresses on the American stage.

Towards the end of 1857 the Wallers returned to the United States, where they thereafter remained. Mrs. Waller made her début at the Walnut Street Theatre in Philadelphia on Oct. 19, 1857, as Ophelia to the Hamlet of Mr. Waller. On the second and third nights of that engagement she acted successively Pauline and Lady Macbeth. She was described as "of stately presence, neither slender nor stout in person, and had an interesting and expressive face" (*New York Dramatic Mirror, post,* p. 17) ; the same

spectator adds that she acted Lady Macbeth with an "intensity of . . . passion" that was "almost painful." Her first appearance in New York was on Apr. 5, 1858, as Marina to her husband's Ferdinand in a new version of John Webster's tragedy, *The Duchess of Malfi.* Thereafter she starred for some twenty years throughout the country, often with Mr. Waller as her principal associate, among her most conspicuous characters being Queen Margaret in *Richard III* and Queen Katharine in *Henry VIII* (both in support of Edwin Booth), Meg Merrilies in *Guy Mannering,* Nelly Brady in Edmund Falconer's *The Peep o'Day,* and Julia in Sheridan Knowles's *The Hunchback.* Though Mrs. Waller was accused of imitating the Meg Merrilies of Charlotte Cushman, she had never seen her in the part, and her Meg was an original assumption of that character. "The weird dignity of her bearing," wrote William Winter, "was impressive beyond words ; there were moments, indeed, when she seemed to be a soul inspired by communion with beings of another world" (*post,* p. 196). She was also one of a number of actresses who seemed to take pleasure in impersonating male Shakespearean characters, among the most noteworthy of these being her interpretations of Hamlet and Iago. She closed her career as an actress in 1878 as Hester Stanhope in a modern play entitled *An Open Verdict.* Afterwards, like many other actors and actresses, she gave public readings from Shakespeare and other dramatists, her last noteworthy public appearance being made at Chickering Hall in New York on Dec. 1, 1881. Mr. Waller died in 1882, and for some years thereafter she taught elocution in New York. Ill health finally compelled her to abandon all active professional work, and she lived in complete retirement at the home of her son in New York, where she died.

[J. N. Ireland, *Records of the N. Y. Stage,* vol. II (1867) ; T. A. Brown, *Hist. of the Am. Stage* (1870) and *A Hist. of the N. Y. Stage* (3 vols., 1903) ; G. C. D. Odell, *Annals of the N. Y. Stage,* vols. VI–VII (1931) ; Clement Scott and Cecil Howard, *The Life and Reminiscences of E. L. Blanchard* (2 vols., 1891) ; William Winter, *The Wallet of Time,* vol. I (1913) ; obituaries in *N. Y. Tribune,* Mar. 2, 1899, *Boston Transcript,* Mar. 11, and *N. Y. Dramatic Mirror,* Mar. 11.]

E. F. E.

WALLER, JOHN LIGHTFOOT (Nov. 23, 1809–Oct. 10, 1854), Baptist clergyman, editor, and denominational leader, was born in Woodford County, Ky., the son of Edmund and Elizabeth (Lightfoot) Waller, and a descendant of Col. John Waller who emigrated to Virginia about 1635. He came of a line of pioneer Baptist preachers : his great-uncle John Waller was incarcerated repeatedly by the Virginia colonial authorities for preaching the Gospel "contrary to law"; his grandfather, William E. Waller, was a useful minister in both Virginia and Kentucky; his father was renowned for his evangelistic zeal and is reported to have baptized 1,500 persons. Scantily rewarded for his ministerial labors, Edmund Waller nevertheless assembled a good library and sent his older sons to school. Upon their return he placed his younger children under their instruction and from his brothers John Lightfoot Waller received his early education. Later he spent fifteen months at the Nicholasville Academy, where he completed the requirements in Latin and Greek for admission to Transylvania University. Unable to attend college, he purchased the textbooks used in Transylvania and, studying at home, finished the required college course. So retentive was his memory and so thorough his knowledge of whatever he read that his father called him his "Theological Encyclopaedia." He taught a select school in Jessamine County from 1828 to 1834; joined the Glen's Creek Baptist Church in 1833; and in August of the following year married Amanda M. Beatty.

The Baptists at this time were numerically the leading religious body in Kentucky. In 1830, however, Alexander Campbell [q.v.] and others caused a division by seeking to restore "original Christianity." Waller ably defended the faith of his fathers in a pamphlet entitled *Letters to a Reformer, Alias Campbellite* (1835), in which he reviewed the history of the so-called "Current Reformation." This won for him the reputation of being a courageous and vigorous writer. Strongly urged by his admirers, he accepted in 1835 the editorship of the *Baptist Banner,* Shelbyville, Ky., then the only Baptist paper in Kentucky. By 1841 the influence of this periodical had been greatly extended through its absorption of the *Pioneer* of Illinois and the *Baptist* of Tennessee. Thereafter it was known as the *Baptist Banner and Western Pioneer.* The Baptist ministry soon recognized in their young lay editor an able champion of their faith and a wise counselor in all their plans. In 1840 Waller was ordained at Louisville, and for a brief period was a country pastor. For two years, 1841–43, he was the general agent of the General Association of Kentucky Baptists, the acceptance of which office occasioned his retirement as editor.

From 1842 to his death, he participated in many public religious debates, vigorously defending the Baptist position against the chosen representatives of the Presbyterians, the Methodists, the Disciples, and the Universalists. Due largely to his capable and militant leadership,

Kentucky Baptists made notable advancement; the college at Georgetown was reorganized, the General Association of Kentucky Baptists was established for missionary ends, the widespread opposition to an educated ministry waned, and Sunday Schools, Bible, missionary, and benevolent societies multiplied. He founded in 1845 the *Western Baptist Review,* a monthly publication, later called the *Christian Repository,* a periodical which was for many years a potent factor in moulding the religious thought of Southern Baptists. In 1849 he was chosen by popular vote as a delegate to the Kentucky constitutional convention. The next year he resumed editorship of the *Baptist Banner and Western Pioneer.* In 1852 he was elected president of the Bible Revision Association, serving in that capacity until his death. His writings include "The History of Kentucky Baptists," in Lewis Collins' *Historical Sketches of Kentucky* (1847) and *Open Communion Shown to be Unscriptural and Deleterious . . . to Which is Added A History of Infant Baptism* (1859). He died in Louisville, and was buried in Frankfort, Ky.

[J. H. Spencer, *A Hist. of Ky. Baptists* (1886), vol. I; W. B. Sprague, *Annals of the Am. Pulpit,* vol. VI (1860); William Cathcart, *The Baptist Encyc.* (1881); *Western Rev.,* 1845–49; *Christian Repository,* 1849–54; *Va. Mag. of Hist. and Biog.,* Jan. 1914; *Tri-Weekly Ky. Yeoman* (Frankfort), Oct. 12, 1854.]

R. W. W.

WALLER, THOMAS MACDONALD (*c.* 1840–Jan. 25, 1924), lawyer, governor of Connecticut, was born in New York, the son of Thomas Christopher Armstrong and Mary his wife, emigrants from Ireland. His parents and a brother died before he was nine years old. For a summer he sold papers in New York and then shipped as a cabin boy on a fishing vessel. In 1849 he was aboard the schooner *Mount Vernon,* which was to sail for California from New London, Conn., but through the interest of a New London merchant, Thomas K. Waller, he elected to remain in the East. Waller adopted him, and upon reaching his majority Armstrong took his benefactor's name. He attended the Bartlett High School in New London, studied law, and in 1861 was admitted to the New London County bar. On Apr. 22 of that year he enlisted in Company E, 2nd Connecticut Volunteers, but on account of trouble with his eyes was discharged the following June. In partnership with a schoolmate, Samuel H. Davis, he then entered upon the practice of law in New London.

His career in Democratic politics began in 1867–68, when he served as representative from New London in the General Assembly. His maiden speech was in advocacy of bridging the

Connecticut River at Saybrook and was based on what was for him a characteristic argument: "You cannot resist the 19th Century." In 1870 and 1871 he was secretary of state, and in 1872 and 1876 was returned to the General Assembly, serving as speaker during his last term. From 1876 to 1883 he was the state's attorney for New London County. In 1883 he was elected governor by a majority of 2,390 in a normally Republican state. In the election of 1885 he received a plurality, but not the constitutional majority required at that time, and his opponent was therefore chosen by a Republican legislature. From 1885 to 1889 he was consul-general at London, England.

After his return he removed his law practice to New York but retained his residence in New London. In New York he formed the firm of Waller, Cook & Wagner, which became identified with public service corporations in the West. As the leader of Connecticut Democrats he seconded the nomination of Grover Cleveland at the Chicago convention in 1884. At the convention of 1896 he uncompromisingly attacked Bryan's free-silver policy and as a protest against his nomination led the Connecticut delegation from the hall. It was in this campaign that Waller rose to his greatest heights. The New York *Sun* had already conferred on him the title of "The Little Giant from Connecticut," for he resembled Stephen Douglas in size, physical vigor, eloquence, and power on the platform. As leader of the "Gold Democrats" in Connecticut he spoke before a hissing gallery at the Grand Opera House in New Haven, and in ten minutes had the crowd in sympathy with him personally, if not with his faction of the party. Although he reconciled the opposing factions after the campaign, his influence in the party was diminishing. After 1900 he took little part in politics, although he was one of the two vice-presidents of the Connecticut constitutional convention of 1902. Thenceforward he was the "Grand Old Man" of Connecticut Democrats.

In New London "Tom" Waller was known as a rough and ready, breezy, democratic individual who had intense personal magnetism and unusual ability as a public speaker. He was mayor of the city from 1873 to 1879. Against considerable opposition he discouraged small-town ways of doing things, and thus laid the foundation for municipal growth. He was also active in real-estate developments, notably that of Ocean Beach, and was an incorporator of the street railway and of the Mechanics Savings Bank. His wife was Charlotte Bishop of New London, by whom he had one daughter and five sons. Waller died at Ocean Beach.

[F. C. Norton, *The Governors of Conn.* (1905); *Encyc. of Conn. Biog.* (1917), vol. IV; W. F. Moore, *Representative Men of Conn.* (1894); Dwight Loomis and J. G. Calhoun, *The Judicial and Civil Hist. of Conn.* (1895); *Who's Who in America,* 1918–19; *New London Day,* Jan. 25, 1924, and following days; *New Haven Journal-Courier,* Jan. 26, 1924.]

W. G. La—d.

WALLIS, SEVERN TEACKLE (Sept. 8, 1816–Apr. 11, 1894), lawyer, author, was born in Baltimore, Md., the second son of Philip and Elizabeth Custis (Teackle) Wallis, both descended from families long settled upon the Eastern Shore of Chesapeake Bay. After attending private schools and St. Mary's College, Baltimore, where he graduated in 1832, he studied law in the office of William Wirt [*q.v.*] and of Judge John Glenn, and in 1837 was admitted to the bar. He was one of the founders of the Maryland Historical Society in 1844, and that same year became a corresponding member of the Royal Academy of History, Madrid; two years later he was admitted a fellow of the Royal Society of Northern Antiquities, Copenhagen. In 1847 he made his first visit to Spain, and in 1849, commissioned by the government to report upon the titles to public lands in Florida, he embarked upon his second visit. Both inspired literary productions. He proved a prolific writer, leaving addresses, verses, and criticisms which, when collected for publication by admiring friends, filled four volumes (*Writings of Severn Teackle Wallis,* Memorial Edition, 1896). He was a frequent contributor to the daily press, and his anonymous articles on current topics were often recognizable from their terseness, pungency, wit, and wealth of illustration.

A Whig in early life, Wallis became a Democrat upon the disintegration of his party, but he was preëminently the reformer, never surrendering his personal independence of opinion. His first appearance as a candidate was in 1847, when he was defeated for the legislature. In 1851 he made an unsuccessful bid for the office of state's attorney, but in 1857 refused the post of district attorney proffered him by President Buchanan. He joined in the reform movement of 1858 in Baltimore, writing an influential address, and the following year was a member of the committee which drew up a series of reform bills adopted by the legislature in 1860; one of these measures was an election law which made possible a reform government for Baltimore. In 1861, after the struggle between the sections had brought open rupture, his sympathies were with the Confederacy, although he did not advocate secession. He was elected against his wishes a delegate to the special Assembly held at Frederick in April 1861, and as chairman of the Committee on Federal Relations of the House of Delegates, he expressed his views in several reports, arguing vigorously against the doctrine of military necessity. This action made him obnoxious to the Washington government, and along with other prominent Marylanders he was arrested in September and suffered imprisonment for fourteen months. His letters to the press in the heated campaign of 1875, when he supported the Reform ticket, are among the choicest of Maryland polemics. Subsequently, despite frail health, he participated actively in the campaigns of 1882 to 1887, in which his thoughtful eloquence was a powerful weapon.

For almost half a century Wallis was regarded as the leader of the Maryland bar. He argued thousands of cases before the state courts and appeared before the United States Supreme Court in many important cases. His eloquence brought him into frequent demand as an occasional speaker. For twenty years he served as provost of the University of Maryland. He was one of the original trustees of Peabody Institute and president of the board during the last year of his life. From 1892 until his death he was president of the Maryland Historical Society. He also served as president of the Civil Service Reform Association of Maryland and the Reform League of Baltimore. Though domestic in his tastes—loving his home, his books, and his friends—he never married.

[C. Sems and E. S. Riley, *The Bench and Bar of Md.* (1901); J. T. Scharf, *Hist. of Baltimore City and County* (1881); *The Biog. Cyc. of Representative Men of Md. and the D. C.* (1879); R. H. Spencer, *Geneal. and Memorial Encyc. of the State of Md.* (1919), vol. II; W. H. Browne, Introduction to Wallis' *Works*, vol. I; Bernard Steiner, "Severn Teackle Wallis," *Sewanee Rev.*, Jan.–Apr. 1907; *Hist. of Baltimore, Md.* (1898); S. C. Chew, *Addresses on Several Occasions* (1906); W. C. Bruce, *Seven Great Baltimore Lawyers* (1931); and J. U. Dennis, "Some Personal Recollections of a Quartet of the Baltimore Bar," *Report of the . . . Md. State Bar Asso.*, 1905; *Proc. Md. Hist. Soc. in Commemoration of . . . Severn Teackle Wallis* (1896); *Sun* (Baltimore), and *Baltimore American*, Apr. 11, 1894; several letters preserved at the Maryland Hist. Soc.]
E. L.

WALN, NICHOLAS (Sept. 19, 1742–Sept. 29, 1813), lawyer, Quaker preacher, was born at Fair Hill, near Philadelphia, Pa., the son of Nicholas and Mary (Shoemaker) Waln and a cousin of Robert Waln, 1765–1836 [*q.v.*]. His great-grandfather, Nicholas Waln, born in the West Riding of Yorkshire, emigrated in the *Welcome* and arrived at New Castle, Del., in 1682. Waln was educated in the William Penn Charter School, and became both a good Latin and German scholar. He was admitted to the bar, Oct. 8,

1762, and had eight cases as a minor in a single term of court. He quickly became a successful lawyer. In 1763–64 he spent a year as a student in the Inns of Court in London. On his return to Philadelphia his fees for a year, on his own testimony, reached the mark of £2000. In February 1772 he experienced a remarkable religious conversion which culminated in a unique public prayer (reported in Joseph Oxley's *Journal of His Life*, 1838, p. 474). He immediately withdrew from the practice of law and gave himself completely to the service of the Society of Friends, of which he was a lifelong member. He was married, May 22, 1771, to Sarah Richardson. They had seven children, only three of whom reached maturity.

In 1783 Waln went on an extensive religious visit of two years to England, visiting the families of the members of the Society of Friends as well as the public meetings in that country. His preaching was marked by unusual power, and he was recognized at home and abroad as one of the most impressive Quaker preachers of that period. In 1795 he paid a similar visit to the Quaker meetings and families in Ireland. He possessed an almost uncanny gift for feeling out the states of mind and conditions of life of persons in his audiences, and acquired, especially during the visit in Ireland, the reputation of being a "prophet." During the period between 1772 and 1813 he exercised a notable influence upon the Society of Friends in Philadelphia, and in his travels he reached most of the centers of Quaker life and thought in America. In 1789 he was appointed clerk (chief official) of the Philadelphia Yearly Meeting, which included the Friends of Pennsylvania and New Jersey. From the year 1777 until 1789 he was clerk of meeting of ministers and elders. He took an important part in the proceedings of the meeting at the critical time of the Revolutionary War in its dealing with the "Free Quakers," who supported the patriotic cause with arms. In this connection he appears as one of the characters in Dr. S. Weir Mitchell's novel, *Hugh Wynne*. Notwithstanding the weight and solemnity of Waln's preaching, he was inclined to humor and was noted for his wit and repartee.

[Mary I. Harrison, *Annals of the Ancestry of Charles Custis Harrison and Ellen Waln Harrison* (1932); R. C. Moon, *The Morris Family of Phila.*, vol. II (1898); J. W. Jordan, *Colonial Families of Phila.* (1911), vol. I; *Quaker Biogs.*, vol. IV (1914); James Bowden, *The Hist. of the Soc. of Friends in America*, vol. II (1854); Isaac Sharpless, *A Hist. of Quaker Government in Pa.* (1898), vol. II; H. D. Eberlein and H. M. Lippincott, *The Colonial Homes of Phila.* (1912); minutes of the Phila. Yearly Meeting, 1789–1813, unpublished; John Smith, "MS. Memorials," vol. III, 1722–77, in Haverford Coll. Lib.; *Friend*, 1848, pp.

53–54, 1904, p. 140; obituary in *Poulson's Am. Daily Advertiser*, Oct. 1, 1813.]   R. M. J.

WALN, ROBERT (Feb. 22, 1765–Jan. 24, 1836), merchant, manufacturer, politician, was born in Philadelphia, Pa., the youngest son of Robert and Rebecca (Coffin) Waln and a great-grandson of Nicholas Waln who settled in Pennsylvania in 1682. He entered his father's counting-house at an early age. Upon his father's death in 1791 he entered into a joint partnership at 57 South Wharves with Jesse Waln, his cousin, who had also been trading in foreign merchandise. Together they built up a thriving business in the West India and English trades, and later concentrated upon the East India and Chinese trades. Their enterprises were on a large scale, Stephen Girard [q.v.] being the only one who exceeded them in their business ventures. On Oct. 10, 1787, Waln married Phebe Lewis, by whom he had nine children. One of his sons was Robert Waln [q.v.].

He was very active in civic and national affairs, especially during the exciting period between the adoption of the Constitution and the War of 1812. He was a member of the Pennsylvania state legislature (1794–98) and of the House of Representatives, where he first filled a vacancy and then served a term from Dec. 3, 1798, to Mar. 3, 1801. Like all substantial shipowners at that time, he was a Federalist and therefore opposed to the ruling party because of the restrictions placed upon shipping. He was one of the Federal leaders who engaged a thousand sailors to protect their political meeting in January 1809 from being interrupted by the Republicans, the result of which was an extensive riot. He also entered into a violent debate with John Rutledge of South Carolina and John Randolph of Virginia, when he presented a petition in the Sixth Congress regarding the slave trade and the Fugitive Slave Law (Simpson, *post*, p. 929). During the War of 1812 he constructed one of the first cotton textile mills at Trenton, N. J. He also had an extensive interest in the Phoenixville iron-works. Because of these two connections, he became an ardent protectionist and became strongly identified with the high tariff acts of 1816, 1824, and 1828. When the famous Boston Report was published exerting a strong influence for free trade, Waln was selected by the Pennsylvania Society for the Encouragement of Manufactures and Arts as best fitted to reply. His report of over one hundred pages, *An Examination of the Boston Report* (1828), was considered as having successfully countered all the assertions made by the free traders. Waln's other offices included those of

vice-president of the Philadelphia chamber of commerce (1809), director of the Philadelphia Insurance Company (1804–13), first president of the Mercantile Library (1821–24), and trustee of the University of Pennsylvania (1829). He was a member of the common council of the city of Philadelphia (1794, 1796) and of the select council (1807, 1809, 1811). He was an orthodox Quaker and actively entered into the controversy against Elias Hicks [q.v.], who was advocating the liberalization of the Quaker rules and regulations. His *Seven Letters to Elias Hicks* (1825) attracted a great deal of attention.

[J. K. Simon, *Biog. of Successful Phila. Merchants* (1864), pp. 129–32; Henry Simpson, *Lives of Eminent Philadelphians* (1859); J. T. Scharf and Thompson Westcott, *Hist. of Phila.* (1884), vol. III, p. 2213; H. M. Lippincott, *Early Phila.* (1917); E. P. Oberholtzer, *Phila., a Hist. of the City*, vol. II (1912); H. D. Eberlein and H. M. Lippincott, *The Colonial Homes of Phila.* (1912); Abraham Ritter, *Phila. and Her Merchants* (1860); letter from James Canby to David Lewis, May 22, 1819, in Ridgway Branch of the Lib. Company of Phila.; *Biog. Dir. Am. Cong.* (1928); J. F. Watson, *Annals of Phila.*, vol. I (1856), vol. III (1879); J. W. Jordan, *Colonial and Revolutionary Families of Pa.* (1911), vol. III, and *Colonial Families of Phila.* (1911), vol. I; obituary in *Poulson's Am. Daily Advertiser*, Jan. 25, 1836.]   H. S. P.

WALN, ROBERT (Oct. 20, 1794–July 4, 1825), author, known as Robert Waln, Jr., son of Robert [q.v.] and Phebe (Lewis) Waln, was born in Philadelphia, Pa., and died unmarried at Providence, R. I., in his thirty-first year. The wealth and social position of his family made it unnecessary for him to earn his living. On the other hand, the traditions of the Society of Friends with whom they had long been affiliated forbade idleness. The young man showed an active interest in the great importing business conducted by Jesse and Robert Waln, his father and father's cousin, with Canton and the East. But literature was his chosen pursuit. His education, obviously liberal, was broadened by extensive and purposeful reading, for which Philadelphia afforded rich opportunities, while at the stately country seat of his father, Waln-Grove, at Frankford, five miles from Philadelphia, was an unusually large and well-equipped library. He maintained an eager interest in current American literary activity, contributed to the periodicals of the times and was conversant with their editors, and developed a special aptitude for criticism and biography. He exemplifies very well a Philadelphia tradition of aristocratic scholarship and belles-lettres.

His first independently published work (February 1819) was a vivid satire on manners in the wealthy inner circle of Philadelphia society: *The Hermit in America on a Visit to Philadelphia. . . . Edited by Peter Atall, Esq.* In March of the same year this had a second edition, in which considerable alterations were made. Early in 1821 appeared a second series of the Hermit's observations. These works are both in prose. In November 1820 Waln had published *Sisyphi Opus, or Touches at the Times,* written in classical couplets, touching on some of the same themes. Another satire, purely literary in subject, also written in couplets, *American Bards,* had been published in August 1820. Part of this, the author said, had been written during a voyage "beyond the Cape of Good Hope." It should not be confused with a contemporary piece of the same title.

During 1823 he published, in quarto numbers, an elaborate work on China, its geography, history, customs, and trade relations. His interest in this subject was definitely related to the family business. Intensive research during many years was supplemented by a four months' residence in Canton from September 1819 to January 1820. The first draft of the manuscript was largely written during the long voyage home. About the same time he took over the editorship of the *Biography of the Signers to the Declaration of Independence* (vols. III–VI, 1823–24), which had been begun by John and James Sanderson. Altogether he edited or wrote some fourteen of the lives. From Waln-Grove in the summer of 1824 he issued proposals for publishing by subscription a *Life of the Marquis de La Fayette,* completing it at the same place in June 1825. His sudden death occurred scarcely three weeks later. In August was published posthumously his *Account of the Asylum for the Insane Established by the Society of Friends, near Frankford, in the Vicinity of Philadelphia.* All these works show a remarkable ability for compiling and verifying facts. His talent is further shown by his lyric poems, which, though few in number, bring the more intimate side of his personality attractively to view. They are to be found chiefly in the little volume containing "Sisyphi Opus." A few remain uncollected from current publications, like the *Atlantic Souvenir.* So also does some of his prose.

[Sources include records of the Phila. Monthly Meeting, Southern District, of the Soc. of Friends, from which the date of birth is taken; colls. of the Geneal. Soc. of Pa., the Hist. Soc. of Pa., and the Ridgway Branch of the Lib. Company of Phila.; Samuel Kettell, *Specimens of Am. Poetry* (1829), vol. III, p. 213; obituary in *Poulson's Am. Daily Advertiser,* July 9, 1825.]   J. C. M.

WALSH, BENJAMIN DANN (Sept. 21, 1808–Nov. 18, 1869), entomologist, was born in Clapton, London, England, the son of Benjamin Walsh. He was of a well-to-do family; one of his brothers became a clergyman and another, editor of the *Field,* London, and author of a standard treatise on the horse. Benjamin was intended for the church, and was educated at Trinity College, Cambridge, where he received the degree of B.A. in 1831, became a fellow in 1833, and in 1834 was awarded the degree of M.A. He resigned the fellowship, however, and declined to follow the study of divinity. For some years he led a literary life, writing for *Blackwood's Magazine,* and in 1837 publishing *The Comedies of Aristophanes, Translated into Corresponding English Metres.* About this time he married Rebecca Finn, and at the age of thirty emigrated to the United States, expecting to settle in Chicago. He finally made his home in Henry County, Ill., near the town of Cambridge, where for thirteen years he engaged in farming. He then moved to the town of Rock Island, where he carried on a successful lumber business for seven years more.

In England he had known and worked with Charles Darwin, who had aroused his interest in natural history. Retiring from business about 1858, he devoted the rest of his life to entomology. He wrote many articles for the agricultural newspapers and published a number of admirable articles in the *Proceedings of the Boston Society of Natural History* and in the *Transactions of the American Entomological Society.* These papers were of very high rank and attracted the attention of scientific men both in America and in Europe. He became, also, one of the editors of a journal started in Philadelphia known as the *Practical Entomologist.* His ability as an incisive writer, his breadth of knowledge, and his power to prophesy accurately the future of economic entomology were extraordinary. He often pointed out what the states and the federal government should do against the certainty that insect ravages would increase. He was the first to show that American farmers were planting their crops in such a way as to facilitate the multiplication of insects, and was one of the first to suggest the introduction of foreign parasites and natural enemies of imported pests. His witty and vigorous invective against charlatanistic suggestions as to remedies attracted great attention. In 1868, with Charles V. Riley [*q.v.*], he founded and edited the *American Entomologist.* His death occurred in the following year as the result of a railway accident near Rock Island.

Walsh's bibliography shows 385 titles of individual record and 478 in co-authorship with Riley. The latter titles, however, are mainly those of short notes and answers to correspondents in the columns of the *American Entomolo-*

gist. His longer scientific papers were sound and in many respects ahead of his time. He was an early adherent of the doctrine of evolution, and in 1864 published a long paper, "On Certain Entomological Speculations of the New England School of Naturalists" (*Proceedings of the Entomological Society of Philadelphia,* vol. III), in which he attacked the anti-evolutionary views of Agassiz and Dana. In 1867 he was appointed state entomologist of Illinois, and assumed the duties of that position, although his appointment was not confirmed until the next biennial session of the legislature. He was the second state entomologist to be appointed, Asa Fitch [*q.v.*] of New York being the first. Walsh's sole report was published in the *Transactions of the Illinois State Horticultural Society* for 1867. His work in entomology made a great impression both on scientific men and on the leading agriculturists, and undoubtedly the influence of this mature, cultivated, and far-seeing man accounts in part for Riley's brilliant career. Walsh's collections and many of his notes were destroyed in the Chicago fire of 1871.

[For sources, see W. W. R. Ball and J. A. Venn, *Admissions to Trinity Coll., Cambridge,* vol. IV (1911); Samuel Henshaw, *Bibliog. of the More Important Contributions to Am. Economic Entomology* (1890); E. A. Tucker, in *Trans. Ill. State Hist. Soc. for 1920* (1921); C. V. Riley, in *Am. Entomologist,* Dec. 1869, Jan. 1870; *Ill. State Jour.* (Springfield), Nov. 23, 1869. The date of birth is that given by Riley; E. A. Tucker gives July 1808; the birthplace is from Ball and Venn.]
L. O. H.

WALSH, BLANCHE (Jan. 4, 1873–Oct. 31, 1915), actress, daughter of Thomas P. and Armenia (Savorie) Walsh, was born on the lower East Side of New York, where her father, popularly known as "Fatty" Walsh, was a well-to-do saloonkeeper and Tammany politician. She spent fifteen months of her girlhood in the living quarters of the Tombs, New York's famous prison, where her father then held the position of warden. She received a common-school education. Her parents (her mother in particular) were inveterate theatre-goers, and Blanche, even when a girl, began to take much interest in amateur acting. In 1888, at the age of fifteen, she made her first professional appearance in a small part in Bartley Campbell's melodrama, *Siberia.* Marie Wainwright, then a famous star, became interested in her and took her into her company in 1889, her first appearance in New York being at the Fifth Avenue Theatre in December, as Olivia in *Twelfth Night.* She was nearly a month short of her seventeenth birthday, but was tall and womanly enough in appearance to play mature parts. She remained with that company three years, playing also Grace Harkaway

in Dion Boucicault's *London Assurance* and Queen Elizabeth in *Amy Robsart.* She often spoke of Miss Wainwright as her chief mentor in dramatic art. In 1892 she "created"—as the profession has it—the rôle of Diana Stockton in Bronson Howard's popular society drama, *Aristocracy,* following this with another success, *The Girl I Left Behind Me.* In January 1895 she went with Nat Goodwin as leading woman, playing in *A Gilded Fool, In Mizzoura, David Garrick, The Nominee, The Gold Mine,* and *Lend Me Five Shillings.* A dramatization of Du Maurier's novel, *Trilby,* was one of the hits of the autumn of 1895. When Virginia Harned, the star in it, was taken ill in 1896, Blanche Walsh assumed her place and completed the season amid much acclaim. She then returned to Goodwin's company and spent the summer with him in Australia, playing her former parts and adding *Gringoire* and Lydia Languish in *The Rivals* to the list.

Returning to New York in the autumn of 1896, she joined A. M. Palmer's stock company, first appearing in *Heartsease.* In January 1897, in *Straight from the Heart,* she played two parts, those of a brother and sister. She was tall and had strongly handsome features which lent themselves fairly well to a not too heavy type of masculine characterization. She once essayed briefly even the part of Romeo. In William Gillette's *Secret Service,* she went with the company to England. After a brief stay as leading woman with Sol Smith Russell in *A Bachelor's Romance,* she appeared with the Empire Theatre Stock Company in the winter of 1898–99. In 1899 she joined Melbourne McDowell, and for two years played the Sardou repertoire in which the late Fanny Davenport [*q.v.*] had long starred—*La Tosca, Fédora, Théodora,* and *Cleopatra.* In 1901–03 there followed *Marcelle, More Than Queen, Joan of the Sword Hand,* and *La Madeleine.* In 1903 she was cast in the greatest success of her career, and did probably her finest piece of acting in the rôle of the unfortunate servant girl, Maslova, in a dramatization of Tolstoy's novel, *Resurrection.* Next came another Tolstoy story, *The Kreutzer Sonata,* which she revived in later years. Among her later plays were *The Woman in the Case, The Straight Road, The Test,* and *The Other Woman.* During the last three years of her life, she appeared in one-act plays in vaudeville. She married Alfred Hickman, actor, when he was playing the part of Little Billee with her in *Trilby* in 1896, divorced him in 1903, and on Nov. 15, 1906, married William M. Travers, also an actor. She died in Cleveland, Ohio, survived by her husband.

[*Who's Who in America*, 1914–15; *The Green Room Book*, 1908, ed. by John Parker; T. A. Brown, *A Hist. of the N. Y. Stage*, vol. III (1903); *Munsey's Mag.*, Jan., Oct. 1900; obituaries in *N. Y. Times, Sun* (N. Y.), *N. Y. Herald*, Nov. 1, 1915; reminiscences by Blanche Walsh in *Theatre*, July 1905; three vols. on Blanche Walsh in the Robinson Locke Dramatic Collection, N. Y. Pub. Lib.]   A. F. H.

WALSH, HENRY COLLINS (Nov. 23, 1863–Apr. 29, 1927), explorer, author, and editor, was born in Florence, Italy, of American parents, and was brought to America at the age of nine. His father, Robert M. Walsh, was the son of Robert Walsh [*q.v.*]; his mother was Margaret Blount Mullen, who came of a prominent Southern family. Walsh attended Georgetown College, Washington, D. C., and in 1888 was awarded the degree of M.A. The following year he published *By the Potomac, and Other Verses*, proceeds from the sale of which were dedicated to the Georgetown building fund. Meanwhile he had begun a journalistic career as a reporter for the *Times* of Philadelphia, going thence to Mansfield, Pa., and subsequently to New York City.

In 1894 he read an advertisement which stated that for $500 a person passengers could join an expedition being organized for Arctic exploration by Dr. Frederick A. Cook. Walsh secured a reduced rate by promising to serve as historian of the voyage, and in 1896 published *The Last Cruise of the Miranda,* an account of a venture which had led to "little discovery and many hardships." Thereafter he traveled extensively through Central America, sojourned in Copán in 1896, and the following year made a trip by caravan through Morocco and sections of the Atlas Mountains. His interest in travel revived in 1911, when he cruised through the West Indies. In 1925 he penetrated farther into Endless Cavern, Newmarket, Va., than any man before him had gone. His experiences were described partly in magazine articles and partly in *The White World* (1902), written in collaboration with other members of the Arctic Club, of which he was one of the organizers, and edited by Rudolf Kersting.

Walsh had a wide editorial and journalistic experience. In 1888 he and his brother, W. S. Walsh, started a literary magazine, *American Notes and Queries*, which they edited from May to October of that year. During the Spanish-American War, he was a correspondent in the field for the *New York Herald* and *Harper's Weekly*. After a period of service on the editorial staff of the *Catholic World*, he became successively co-editor (1902–06) of the *Smart Set*, editor of the *Travel Magazine* (1907–10), member of the staff of the American Press Association (1911–18), and associate editor of the *National Marine* (1919–21). After 1924 he served as vice-president of the Nomad Publishing Company. Walsh helped to organize the Explorers' Club of New York, and served as president of the Nomad Club and of the Adventurers' Club, also of New York. He was known as a fascinating raconteur. Though born a Catholic, he did not continue in that faith and was buried in Westminster Cemetery, Philadelphia, in which city he died, while absent from his home in New York on a visit to his sister. He was unmarried.

[*Who's Who in America*, 1926–27; *Am. Catholic Who's Who*, 1911; *N. Y. Herald Tribune*, Apr. 30, 1927; W. H. Brewer, *The Arctic Club* (1906); records of Georgetown Univ.; information from Katherine Walsh, sister, and F. S. Dellenbaugh.]
                                                    G. N. S.

WALSH, MICHAEL (*c.* 1815–Mar. 17, 1859), politician and editor, was born near Cork, Ireland, and was brought to America in his childhood. His father, Michael Welsh [*sic*], owned a mahogany yard in New York City, and young Mike, as he always called himself, in a turbulent boyhood on the city streets and as a runaway apprentice acquired a realistic knowledge of life among the poor. Learning the printer's trade, he traveled to New Orleans, but in 1839 returned to New York to set up in business for himself. He worked for a time as reporter and Washington correspondent for the *Aurora,* and tried unsuccessfully to found a paper of his own. Proclaiming himself the champion of the "subterranean" democrats ignored by political leaders, he organized young laborers of the city into the Spartan Association, with a view to exemplifying democratic principles by destroying Tammany control of the local Democratic organization. This aim was reached most simply by forcibly removing the enemy from ward meetings, and as the method was soon copied, the organized gang became a new feature in political practice.

In 1843 Walsh founded his own paper, the *Subterranean,* as a means of rousing the working class against the capitalists and politicians who exploited them. His vigorous and denunciatory editorials, for which he sacrificed advertising, pictured vividly the darker side of city life, and at least twice caused his imprisonment for libel. Agreeing with George Henry Evans [*q.v.*] on the ills of society, he accepted the National Reform program, in 1844 merged the *Subterranean* with Evans' *Working Man's Advocate,* and became a frequent speaker at National Reform Conventions; but his bitter and direct attacks on individuals were an embarrassment to

Evans, and the partnership lasted only three months. Walsh then revived the *Subterranean,* conducting it for two years more, and renewed his activity in local politics.

Social reform, however, was losing ground before the anti-slavery issue. As the New York Democrats split over the free-soil controversy, Walsh joined the Hunkers, and denounced the abolitionists who neglected the wage slaves of the North for the cause of the remote negro. He served three uneventful terms in the state Assembly (1846, 1847, 1852), and in 1852 was elected to Congress. There he won some reputation as a ready debater, supported President Pierce's territorial policy, and urged higher pay for enlisted men in the army. He was defeated by John Kelly [*q.v.*] in 1854, in an extremely close election. When Walsh charged fraud in the count, Kelly made the counter accusation that Walsh was the son of an unnaturalized alien and consequently ineligible.

Walsh then visited Europe, reputedly to get contracts from the Russian government for George Steers [*q.v.*], whose shipbuilding skill he had praised in Congress. He returned penniless, and next visited Mexico on a similar mission. Back in New York, discredited by growing intemperance, he made another unsuccessful venture into journalism. After a convivial night, he was found dead in an area-way, with some suspicion of foul play. He was survived by his widow, Catherine Riley or Wiley, and two children.

[*Sketches of the Speeches and Writings of Mike Walsh . . . Compiled by a Committee of the Spartan Association* (1843); M. P. Breen, *Thirty Years of N. Y. Politics* (1899); J. R. Commons, *Hist. of Labour in the U. S.* (1921), I, 527–30; J. F. McLaughlin, *The Life and Times of John Kelly* (1885); M. R. Werner, *Tammany Hall* (1928); *Working Man's Advocate,* 1844–45; *Congressional Globe,* 33 Cong., 1 and 2 Sess.; *N. Y. Herald, N. Y. Times, N. Y. Tribune,* Mar. 18, 19, 1859.]   H. C. B.

WALSH, ROBERT (Aug. 30, 1784–Feb. 7, 1859), journalist and litterateur, son of Robert and Elizabeth (Steel) Walsh, was born in Baltimore, where his father, since his arrival about 1770, had become a substantial merchant. The elder Walsh may have been born in County Longford, Ireland, or in France, and according to tradition, he succeeded to the title of Count Walsh and Baron Shannon. The Steel family was of Pennsylvania Quaker stock. The younger Robert was prepared by the French Sulpicians of St. Mary's Seminary, Baltimore, for Georgetown College, where he delivered an address on the occasion of Washington's visit to the college. In 1806, as soon as St. Mary's Seminary was empowered by the legislature to grant academic de-

grees, both the bachelor's and master's degrees were conferred upon him. In the meantime, he had read law under Robert Goodloe Harper [*q.v.*] and had become an ardent Federalist. A youth of means, he traveled and studied in France and the British Isles for three years, gaining a wide acquaintance in France through his family connections and in London through William Pinkney [*q.v.*], whom for a time he served as a secretary. He contributed to the Parisian press, became an intimate of Canning, some of whose speeches he later edited, and is said to have written the article on military conscription in France which appeared in the *Edinburgh Review* of January 1809.

On his return to America, Walsh settled in Philadelphia, and edited during its last years (1809–10) the *American Register.* On May 8, 1810, he was married by Bishop Michael Egan to Anna Maria, daughter of Jasper Moylan and a niece of Stephen Moylan and of Bishop Moylan of Cork. They had twelve children. For a brief period, Walsh practised law in a cursory way, but his interest was in books, in journalism, and in conducting a salon, which attracted local and visiting scholars and writers. In 1810, he published a brochure entitled *A Letter on the Genius and Dispositions of the French Government,* which was republished in England and favorably noticed in the *Edinburgh Review* and in the *Quarterly Review* (London). When illness compelled Joseph Dennie [*q.v.*] to relinquish in 1811 the active editorship of the *Port Folio,* to which Walsh had contributed, the latter founded the first American quarterly, *The American Review of History and Politics,* which survived only through eight issues because of its Federalist tone and the War of 1812. In 1813 he published *Essay on the Future State of Europe* and *Correspondence Respecting Russia Between Robert Goodloe Harper, Esq., and Robert Walsh, Jun.* In 1817 he founded another *American Register,* which survived for about a year. He wrote biographical sketches for the *Encyclopædia Americana* (1829–33), edited by Francis Lieber, and a life of Franklin for *Delaplaine's Repository of the Lives and Portraits of Distinguished American Characters* (1815). In 1819 he published *An Appeal from the Judgments of Great Britain Respecting the United States of America,* which brought congratulatory notes from Jefferson, John Adams, and John Quincy Adams and a vote of thanks from the Pennsylvania legislature, but occasioned denunciatory notices in British publications. In 1820, Walsh in association with William Fry founded the *National Gazette and Literary Register,* with which he maintained his connection for fifteen years. A successful liberal tri-weekly, it soon became a daily despite its unpopular support of abolition. In the meantime, Walsh edited (1822–23) the *Museum of Foreign Literature and Science,* founded by Eliakim Littell [*q.v.*], and in 1827 established the *American Quarterly Review,* which he conducted for ten years. He also edited with introductory material many volumes of *The Works of the British Poets,* issued first by Mitchell, Ames & White and later by S. F. Bradford of Philadelphia, contributed an article on Madame de Stael to the *Philadelphia Year Book* (1836), and published *Didactics: Social, Literary and Political* (2 vols., 1836), in which he expressed his views on a multiplicity of subjects. Edgar Allan Poe described him as "one of the finest writers, one of the most accomplished scholars, and when not in too great a hurry, one of the most accurate thinkers in the country" (*Southern Literary Messenger,* May 1836, p. 399).

Aside from his literary activity, Walsh won some reputation as an educator, serving as professor of English in the University of Pennsylvania (1818–28), as a trustee (1828–33), and as a manager of Rumford's Military Academy at Mount Airy, Pa. On Jan. 17, 1812, he was elected to membership in the American Philosophical Society. Ill health finally forced his retirement from many of his activities and in 1837 he settled permanently in Paris, where he founded what was probably the first American salon. He contributed some studies to French magazines and was a correspondent of the *National Intelligencer* (Washington) and of the *Journal of Commerce* (New York). For both financial and social reasons, he welcomed an appointment as consul-general in 1844, in which position he served until 1851. He died in Paris and was buried at Versailles. He married as his second wife (J. C. Walsh, *post,* p. 224) a Mrs. Stocker of Philadelphia.

[After the death of Walsh his papers were accidentally destroyed. There are biog. sketches by two descendants, J. C. Walsh, in *Jour. Am. Irish Hist. Soc.,* XXVI (1927), and H. C. Walsh, in *U. S. Cath. Hist. Mag.,* vol. II, no. 7 (1889) ; and by J. R. Dunne, in a master's essay (MS.), submitted at Cath. Univ. (1933). See also J. G. Shea, *Memorial of the First Centenary of Georgetown Coll., D. C.* (1891) ; J. S. Easby-Smith, *Georgetown Univ.* (1907), vol. I ; M. J. Riordan, *Cathedral Records from the Beginning of Catholicity in Baltimore* (1906) ; E. A. and G. L. Duyckinck, *Cyc. of Am. Lit.* (2 vols., 1875) ; R. W. Griswold, *The Prose Writers of America* (1847) ; F. L. Mott, *A Hist. of Am. Mags.* (1930) ; *Memorial Vol. of the Centenary of St. Mary's Seminary . . . Baltimore, Md.* (1891) ; Consular Letters (State Dept.), vol. IX ; *Hist. Mag.,* May 1859 ; *N. Y. Tribune,* Mar. 1, 1859.]   R.J.P.

WALSH, THOMAS (Oct. 14, 1871–Oct. 29, 1928), poet, critic, and editor, was born in Brooklyn, N. Y., eldest of the seven children of Michael Kavanagh and Catherine (Farrell) Walsh. He seems to have inherited some of the traits of his maternal grandfather, John Farrell, who belonged to the gentry of County Longford, Ireland, and, after having been educated for the Catholic priesthood, married, emigrated to the United States in 1848, and achieved a considerable measure of success. Thomas attended St. Francis Xavier College, New York, and then entered Georgetown University, Washington, D. C., where he received the degree of Ph.B. in 1892, and that of Ph.D. in 1899. He also studied at the Columbia law school, New York (1892–95). In 1904 he made the first of seven journeys to Europe and South America, through which he acquired a lasting interest in Spanish and Hispanic civilization. His connection with the literature, art, and scholarship of Spain resulted, as his correspondence shows, in his forming innumerable friendships. He was elected to the Royal Academy of Letters of Seville (1911), to the Hispanic Society of America (1916), and to the Academia Columbiana of Bogota (1920). In 1925 Spain conferred on him the Cross of Isabella the Catholic.

Some of Walsh's early verse was printed at Georgetown in 1892. Later volumes of his poetry appeared under the titles : *The Prison Ships and Other Poems* (1909), *The Pilgrim Kings* (1915), *Gardens Overseas and Other Poems* (1918), *Don Folquet and Other Poems* (1920). Dramatic blank verse and satire in various forms were the media through which his best gifts found expression. Seldom genuinely lyrical, he was often able to weave together subtle thought with unmistakable emotional passion in a manner reminiscent of ancient Celtic art. His achievements as a translator and anthologist are represented in the following : *Eleven Poems of Rubén Darío* (1916), *Hispanic Anthology* (1920), and *The Catholic Anthology* (1927, 1932). In 1930 *Selected Poems of Thomas Walsh,* a memorial volume edited by John Bunker, appeared ; besides a selection from the published volumes, it contains a few original poems and translations not otherwise issued. Among his manuscripts as yet unpublished are : "The Life, Letters and Idylls of Fray Luis de Leon," "The Life of Juana Inez," "The Wives of the Prophets," and "Modern Poets of Spain and South America." Walsh wrote and read several occasional poems, the most notable probably being "Antietam," read before the Society of the Army of the Potomac on the battlefield of Antietam, 1910. He served temporarily as a member of the editorial staff of the *Catholic Encyclopedia,* contributed to Charles

Dudley Warner's *Library of the World's Best Literature* (1896–97) and from 1924 to 1928 was assistant editor of the *Commonweal*, New York. During 1919 he was placed in charge of relief work done by the National Catholic Welfare Conference in Lithuania, Poland, and the Ukraine. He took an active part in the general social life of Brooklyn, to which city he was devoted, and was an ardent supporter of Catholic cultural and philanthropic efforts. During the last years of his life, he was in chronic poor health, an affliction which did not dampen his spirits or curtail his literary output. The scholar, however, gradually supplanted the poet. He contributed literary criticism to the *Saturday Review of Literature* (New York), the *Poetry Review* (London), *Books,* the literary supplement of the *New York Herald Tribune,* the *Catholic World* (New York), and other periodicals. He died suddenly in Brooklyn and was buried in the same city.

His personal influence was remarkable. Until stricken by disease he was an exceptionally handsome man, whose black hair and mobile mouth set off expressive and winning eyes. A resonant voice, doubtless in part responsible for his success as a lecturer, likewise helped to make him "the perfect dinner guest." He was an admirable raconteur, who relied upon wide experience and a mastery of paradoxical speech. During his early years he had given promise of becoming an excellent pianist, and though he never exercised a native talent for painting, he became a discriminating critic of that art. He had a wide circle of friends both at home and abroad, particularly among young artists and literary men, whom he befriended and encouraged. The service he rendered indirectly to Catholic culture will remain of genuine historical importance, and his awareness of Hispanic civilization was virtually unrivalled in his time. He never married.

[Memoirs by John Bunker and appreciations by E. L. Keyes and Michael Williams, in *Selected Poems of Thomas Walsh* (1930); a memoir by L. Walsh, sister, privately distributed; B. R. C. Low, *Brooklyn Bridge* (1933); G. N. Shuster, *The Catholic Spirit in Modern English Lit.* (1922); *Alumni Reg. of Georgetown Univ.* (1924); *The Am. Catholic Who's Who,* 1911; *Who's Who in America,* 1928–29, where date of birth is given incorrectly; *Commonweal,* Nov. 7, 1928; *N. Y. Times,* Oct. 30, 1928.]   G. N. S.

WALSH, THOMAS JAMES (June 12, 1859–Mar. 2, 1933), senator from Montana, was born in Two Rivers, Wis., the son of Felix and Bridget (Comer) Walsh. His parents met and were married after migrating from Ireland to the United States. After obtaining a public-school education, Walsh began to teach at the age of sixteen, and finally became principal of the high school at Sturgeon Bay, Wis. Teaching provided the funds for a law course at the University of Wisconsin, from which in 1884 he received the degree of LL.B. He was largely self-educated; recognizing the gaps in his formal education, he filled them in by his own efforts.

For six years he practised law with his brother, Henry C. Walsh, in Dakota Territory at Redfield (now S. Dak.). On Aug. 15, 1889, he married Elinor C. McClements of Chicago, a school teacher; she died on Aug. 30, 1917. In 1890 he moved to Helena, Mont. In Montana, still in the frontier stage of development, he rapidly attained prominence. His reputation was made chiefly in copper litigation, but he became widely known also as a constitutional lawyer. He refused an offer to become general counsel for the Anaconda Copper Company, which he at times represented and at other times opposed in the courts. In 1906 he was an unsuccessful Democratic candidate for election to the federal House of Representatives, and in 1910 he was defeated for the Senate. Nevertheless he persisted, and in 1912 was elected to the Senate, in which he served from March 1913 until his death.

For nearly ten years after his entrance into public life, Walsh's career in the Senate was one of single-minded although unspectacular devotion to the public welfare, and he was invariably found on the progressive side in debates. He could be depended on to expound lucidly constitutional points at issue, but he was not yet a figure of national importance in the popular mind. He advocated such advanced proposals as woman's suffrage and the child-labor amendment, and was identified with the section of the Clayton Act of 1914 which protected farm organizations and trade unions from suit under the Sherman Anti-Trust Act. A devoted follower of Woodrow Wilson, Walsh upheld the League of Nations, the Treaty of Versailles, and the World Court, and advocated the limitation of armaments. He was a leader in the prolonged fight in 1916 to confirm the nomination of Louis D. Brandeis to the Supreme Court. He denounced the "anti-Red" raids of Attorney-General A. Mitchell Palmer after the war, saying, "I do not think it is any answer at all to the charge that illegal things have been done to say that there are Bolshevists and anarchists in this country. If there are, they are entitled to whatever protection the law affords" (*Congressional Record,* 66 Cong., 3 Sess., p. 150).

On Apr. 29, 1922, the Senate passed a resolution introduced by Robert M. LaFollette [*q.v.*], directing the committee on public lands to investigate the leasing of naval oil reserves in

Wyoming and California, and calling on the secretary of the interior for all pertinent information. Walsh was asked by LaFollette and Senator Kendrick of Wyoming to take charge of the investigation, because they believed that the chairman and other majority members of the committee were unsympathetic with the inquiry. Considerable publicity had attended the LaFollette resolution, but public interest quickly died down and Walsh was left to examine the evidence undisturbed. Eighteen months were spent in a preliminary digest of the material; in October 1923 the first public hearing was called, and the scandal of Teapot Dome and Elk Hills was slowly disclosed to an incredulous public. Walsh considered his rôle in the investigation a routine part of his public duty, but one commentator remarked that "no more magnificent display of a legal drive through a thwarting jungle of facts to incredible but proved conclusions has ever been witnessed in Washington" (William Hard, *Collier's,* Mar. 15, 1924, p. 7). Calm precision of language, unemotional clarity of mind, and definiteness of purpose characterized his conduct of the investigation. Through his efforts all the sordid details of the transactions were uncovered, and the leases were subsequently voided. It is a commentary on the contemporary attitude toward political morality that the most vigorous condemnation by much of the press and the public was reserved for the public servants responsible for bringing the facts to light (Allen, *post,* p. 154). The perspective of time, however, shows that the oil inquiry was Walsh's most valuable public service.

A delegate to every Democratic National Convention from 1908 to 1932, Walsh was chosen permanent chairman in 1924 and again in 1932. His name was presented for the presidential nomination at the convention of 1924, but his maximum strength was 123 votes, on the 102nd ballot. After the long battle between the Smith and the McAdoo forces had ended in the compromise nomination of John W. Davis on the 103rd ballot, Walsh was offered the vice-presidential nomination but declined it. His suave but firm direction of the convention was universally applauded. In 1928 he allowed himself to be mentioned as a pre-convention candidate for the presidential nomination, and unsuccessfully contested the California primary with Smith, but he abandoned his candidacy before the convention opened.

Walsh's activities in the Senate after the Teapot Dome disclosures were consistent with his earlier career. He voted against the McNary-Haugen bill to provide an equalization fee for farm products on the ground that the plan was unconstitutional, despite popular pressure for it in the West. He voted to submit repeal of the Eighteenth Amendment to the states, although he had been a consistent prohibitionist for many years. He opposed confirmation of the appointment of Judge John J. Parker to the Supreme Court because of the nominee's judicial record on sustaining drastic injunctions to uphold "yellow-dog" contracts. A lifelong interest in Irish independence was reflected in Walsh's proposal that the United States bring the problem of Ireland to the attention of the League of Nations in the latter's capacity as an international public forum. He believed that Anglo-American friendship was endangered by the recurrence of trouble in Ireland.

The outstanding physical feature of Walsh during his early years in Washington was a remarkably long, drooping moustache, which later he clipped short. (For a discussion of his physical appearance in his latter years, see *New Republic,* July 2, 1924.) As a boy he had been an enthusiastic baseball player, and he organized the centennial baseball team in Two Rivers in 1876. Later in life he turned for recreation to golf, fishing, and horseback riding. He was a devout member of the Roman Catholic Church, and his private life was characterized by personal dignity and great kindliness.

In 1933, when Walsh was seventy-three, President-elect Roosevelt selected him to be attorney-general. The press praised the choice as one of the most satisfactory for the new cabinet, and one newspaper said "no wise Democratic politician is likely to go to him in his new job looking for special favors. It would be like asking the statue of Civic Virtue for a chew of tobacco" (New York *Sun,* ed., Mar. 1, 1933). On Feb. 25, 1933, Walsh was married in Habana to Señora Maria Nieves Perez Chaumont de Truffin, the widow of a Cuban banker and sugar grower. Starting for Washington for the inauguration, Walsh was ill for several days in Florida, and he died suddenly on a northbound train early on the morning of Mar. 2, 1933. In addition to his widow, he was survived by a daughter of his first marriage. His death unquestionably weakened the incoming administration.

[Among sketches of Walsh the following may be cited: William Hard, in *Collier's,* Mar. 15, 1924; and *Am. Monthly Rev. of Reviews,* Apr. 1928; J. W. Owens, in *New Republic,* July 2, 1924; Charles Michelson, in *N. American Review,* Feb. 1928; "Wherefore Walsh," *Independent,* Apr. 21, 1928; *N. Y. Times,* Feb. 10, 1924; Oct. 13, 1929; Mar. 3, 7, 10, 1933; *N. Y. Herald-Tribune,* Mar. 3, 1933; *News-Week,* Mar. 4, 11, 1933; *Nation,* Mar. 15, 1933. He himself published "The True History of Teapot Dome" in the *Forum,* July 1924. Important official sources are "Leases upon

Naval Oil Reserves," 68 Cong., 1 Sess., *Senate Report No. 794* (3 pts., 1924–25); *Official Report of the Proc. of the Democratic Nat. Convention* (1924, 1928, 1932). More general accounts of value are M. E. Ravage, *The Story of Teapot Dome* (1924); F. L. Allen, *Only Yesterday* (1931); M. R. Werner, *Privileged Characters* (1935); Mark Sullivan, "The Twenties," *Our Times,* vol. VI (1935). Supplementary details of personal information have been given by John Walsh, brother of the Senator.]   L. P. B.

WALTER, ALBERT G. (June 21, 1811–Oct. 14, 1876), surgeon, was born in Germany. He received the degree of doctor of medicine from Königsberg University, and then took a year's graduate work in Berlin, where he was the pupil and assistant of the celebrated Johann Friedrich Dieffenbach, who suggested that he emigrate to America. The ship which carried him was wrecked off the coast of Norway and he lost all his belongings. Making his way to London, he worked for a year to earn sufficient money to continue his passage to America. Meanwhile, he pursued his studies and made the acquaintance of the distinguished English surgeon Sir Astley Cooper, who always remained his firm friend. Upon reaching the United States, he went to Nashville, Tenn., where he remained two years and then, in 1837, removed to Pittsburgh, in which city he lived until his death.

Walter's versatility as a surgeon is revealed by the fact that he was one of the earliest American pioneers in the field of orthopedic surgery, a skilled oculist, and a most resourceful general surgeon. He is reputed to have cut more tendons in one patient than had any other surgeon; his fame as an accident surgeon, also, was nation-wide. His chief claim to distinction, however, is based on his performance of an epoch-making laparotomy for the relief of ruptured bladder, Jan. 12, 1859, the patient making a good recovery. A partial bibliography of his writings records more than forty, the most of which were articles which appeared in various periodicals. Particular mention should be made, however, of his *Conservative Surgery in Its General and Successful Adaptation in Cases of Severe Traumatic Injuries of the Limbs* (1867). He was impressed with the work of Lister and early practised antisepsis, although he argued against the value of carbolic acid and with great enthusiasm set forth the value of pure air. This, he said, "is not only harmless but priceless to man and to the rest of creation whether in a healthy or an afflicted condition. Poison mingled with the air and not pure air is the enemy the surgeon has to contend with ... and the only method of averting injurious effects is the prompt removal of the patient to a place free from all contaminating influences" (*Conservative Surgery*).

His faults were open and glaring: he was intolerant, greatly lacking in consideration for his colleagues, and highly egotistical. On the other hand he was a man of remarkable talent and marvelous industry. He was fond of animals and was the first president, 1874, of the Humane Society of Pittsburgh. It was his love of surgery and his ability to do it well, combined with his driving energy, that made him impatient, blinded him to the rights of his colleagues, and led him to fail to conform to professional etiquette. His criticisms were generally well founded, for surgery in Walter's day was for the most part badly done; but unfortunately they were not tactfully expressed. Had he possessed leadership with tact he might have had the profession solidly behind him, for he is easily the outstanding figure in the medical annals of Pittsburgh, and holds an important place in the surgical history of the United States. In 1846 he married Frances Anne Butler, daughter of Maj. John J. Butler and niece of Dr. Joseph Gazzam, a well-known local practitioner. He left a son and daughter.

[Theodore Diller, *Pioneer Medicine in Western Pa.* (1927); H. A. Kelly, and W. L. Burrage, *Am. Medic. Biogs.* (1920); *Pittsburg Daily Dispatch,* Oct. 16, 1876.]   T. D.

WALTER, THOMAS (Dec. 13, 1696–Jan. 10, 1725), clergyman, defender of "the new way" of singing, was born in Roxbury, Mass., a son of the Rev. Nehemiah Walter, who emigrated with his father to America from Ireland about 1679, and Sarah Mather, a daughter of Increase Mather [*q.v.*]. As a boy he early displayed a retentive memory and quick perceptions. When he entered Harvard College his uncle, the Rev. Cotton Mather [*q.v.*], wrote in his diary (*post,* p. 128): "I have a Nephew now a Student at Cambridge. I would use various Means, both to preserve him from Temptations and prepare him for Services. I would send for him, talk with him, and bestow agreeable Books of Piety upon him." In 1713 Thomas was graduated with the A.M. degree and a reputation for brilliance and conviviality. He was unsuccessfully recommended on Nov. 7, 1716, by Cotton Mather for the chaplaincy of the Castle. His association with young theological radicals of the day, especially his intimate friendship with John Checkley [*q.v.*], gave his orthodox father and uncle many anxious moments, but on Oct. 29, 1718, he was safely ordained as his father's assistant pastor at Roxbury, and his grandfather, Increase Mather, preached the ordination sermon. He was married, on Dec. 25, 1718, to Rebeckah, the daughter of the Rev. Joseph Belcher, of Dedham. Their only daughter survived him.

In 1719 he engaged in public controversy with Checkley. The young Puritan had help in this literary enterprise, out of which grew his *A Choice Dialogue Between John Faustus, a Conjurer, and Jack Tory His Friend* (1720). His uncle recorded (*Diary*, p. 703): "My kinsman at Roxbury, intending an Answer, to a vile, horrid, monstrous Book, newly published among us, I assist him with Materials." The "monstrous book" was Checkley's *A Modest Proof of the Order and Government ... in the Church,* published in 1723. Walter, meantime, was compiling another work which followed closely upon the work of John Tufts [*q.v.*] and which appeared in 1721 with the title: *The Grounds and Rules of Musick Explained; or, an Introduction to the Art of Singing by Note; Fitted to the meanest capacity.* The preface was signed by approving ministers. The tunes were in three parts. Simple as was the musical technique involved, this book stood for an effort, scientifically and artistically conceived, to correct in the New England churches what Walter called "an horrid medley of confused and disorderly sounds." It ran through successive editions, the latest being that of 1764. Another book, *The Sweet Psalmist of Israel,* appeared in 1722. Walter's participation in his uncle's introduction of inoculation for smallpox nearly cost both men their lives. The incident of the throwing of a heavily-loaded bomb into the chamber in which Walter, who had submitted himself to the experiment, was sleeping, is told at length in Cotton Mather's *Diary* (p. 657). The diarist also gives many of the gruesome details of his nephew's consumption which appeared not long after the grenado episode. He died after a lingering illness and was buried in the Roxbury Cemetery in the tomb that contained the remains of the Rev. John Eliot, and later, those of his father.

[The best connected account of Thomas Walter is C. F. Adams, Jr., "Notices of the Walter Family," in *New-England Hist. and Geneal. Reg.,* July 1854. The many references to him in *The Diary of Cotton Mather, Mass. Hist. Soc. Coll.,* 7 ser., vols. VII–VIII (1911–12), are poignantly interesting. For a contemporary account of the grenado incident see *Boston News-Letter,* Nov. 20, 1721. Other data are in *A Report of the Record Commissioners, Containing the Roxbury ... Ch. Records* (1881), and F. S. Drake, *Town of Roxbury* (1905). L. C. Elson, *Hist. of Am. Music* (rev. ed., 1925), briefly evaluates Walter's contribution to musical technique. See also George Hood, *A Hist. of Music in New England* (1846); M. B. Jones, "Bibliographical Notes on Thomas Walter's 'Grounds and Rules of Musick Explained,'" *Proc. Am. Antiquarian Soc.,* vol. XLII (1933); E. H. Pierce, "The Rise and Fall of the 'Fugue-Tune' in America," *Musical Quart.,* Apr. 1930; F. J. Metcalf, "Thomas Walter, the Second Native Compiler," *Choir Herald,* Sept. 1913.]   F. W. C.

WALTER, THOMAS (*c.* 1740–Jan. 17, 1789), is an outstanding figure in early American bot-

any, concerning whose life comparatively little is known. A native of Hampshire, England, he emigrated to eastern South Carolina as a young man, acquired a plantation on the banks of the Santee River, and there passed the remainder of his life. Presumably he devoted much of his time to agriculture, though certainly also, as an avocation, to a laborious study of the vegetation of that then little-known region, a task for which he appears to have been exceedingly well equipped by temperament and liberal education. Here, completely isolated from the scientific world, he prepared in Latin a succinct descriptive treatise summarizing his studies of the flowering plants found within a radius of fifty miles of his home. The manuscript, dated Dec. 30, 1787, was taken to England early in 1788 by his intimate friend John Fraser, on the latter's return from a long botanical tour in Georgia and the Carolinas, and was published in London that year at Fraser's expense. This book, *Flora Caroliniana,* is the sole record of Walter's work. It is classical not only in text but in importance, and is the first tolerably complete account of the flora of any definite portion of eastern North America in which an author used the so-called binomial system of nomenclature. In it Walter described upward of one thousand species of flowering plants from specimens collected by Fraser and himself, these representing some 435 genera. Of the former more than two hundred are described as new; of the genera thirty-two are so indicated, though only four of these are given distinctive names. Walter's herbarium, which is said to have contained originally all the species treated in the *Flora,* was taken to England with the manuscript and remained in the possession of the Fraser family until 1849, when it was presented to the Linnean Society of London. During the interval it had suffered serious injury and loss. It was acquired by the British Museum (Natural History) in 1863 and has since been studied by many American botanists as an aid in interpreting Walter's brief descriptions. Walter is known otherwise chiefly from his joint effort with Fraser to introduce into general cultivation in England a native Carolina grass, *Agrostis perennans,* from which extraordinary results were expected. This venture, interestingly set forth in a rare folio by Fraser (*A Short History of the Agrostis Cornucopiæ: or the New American Grass,* 1789), ended in dismal failure.

Walter was married three times: on Mar. 26, 1769, to Anne Lesesne, of Daniels Island, who died Sept. 11, 1769; on Mar. 20, 1777, to Ann Peyre, who died in December 1780; and later, to

Dorothy Cooper. Two of three daughters by his second marriage and one by his third married and left numerous descendants. He was buried, at his own request, in a small botanical garden which he had established on his plantation. The much-quoted inscription upon his tombstone gives the year of his death erroneously as 1788. Concerning Walter's extraction, early life, and education, and his motive in emigrating to South Carolina, nothing is known, though a good deal may be inferred. He was unquestionably a sound, conservative scholar, indefatigable, modest, and of discriminating judgment, who, though living in the very midst of a singularly bitter local warfare during the Revolutionary period, was able nevertheless to produce a remarkable work of lasting scientific importance.

[For additional data, with numerous source references as to Walter's plantation, marriages, and descendants, *Flora Caroliniana* and herbarium, the visits of botanists to Walter's grave, and the curious longstanding error as to the date of his death, see W. R. Maxon, "Thomas Walter, Botanist," *Smithsonian Misc. Colls.,* vol. XCV, no. 8 (Apr. 1936), pp. 1–6; *The State* (Columbia, S. C.), Apr. 28, 1935; W. C. Coker, "A Visit to the Grave of Thomas Walter," *Jour. of the Elisha Mitchell Sci. Soc.,* Apr. 1910.]　　W. R. M.

WALTER, THOMAS USTICK (Sept. 4, 1804–Oct. 30, 1887), architect, was born in Philadelphia, Pa., the son of Deborah (Wood) and Joseph Saunders Walter. His grandfather, Frederick Jacob Walter, born in Germany, spent his boyhood in Philadelphia as a "redemptioner," and became a prosperous bricklayer. Walter's youth was marked by his apprenticeship to his father, a bricklayer and stone mason, and by his studies under William Strickland [*q.v.*] and others at the Franklin Institute. He became a master bricklayer in 1825. In 1828 he reëntered Strickland's office for over two years of intensive training in architecture and engineering, and in 1830 began his own practice. His first important commission was for the Philadelphia County Prison, usually called Moyamensing, built in the "castellated" manner. The commission for Girard College followed in 1833. Through the influence of Nicholas Biddle the premiated design was abandoned for one of classical derivation. The white marble building was peripteral in plan, with the Corinthian order of the monument of Lysicrates, Athens, as its chief ornamental feature. The interior, following the requirements of the Girard will, was divided into four groined rooms, each fifty feet square, on each of two floors, rising to an attic floor with four domes on pendentives. A roof of marble slabs, basement areas for the control of the temperature of the vestibules, and an arched treatment whereby the entablature could be replaced, block by block,

were additional features of an archeological triumph. Four pendant buildings were placed axially to either side. The echoes in the vaulted rooms made recitations difficult, and the limited number of windows permitted by the style indicated the weakness inherent in the temple form for a modern school. Girard College marked the climax, and at the same time sounded the death knell, of the Greek Revival in America. A trip to Europe in 1838 afforded Walter the opportunity to study the practical arrangements of English and Continental schools, many of which he was able to use at Girard. Between 1843 and 1845 he was concerned with the construction of a breakwater at La Guaira, Venezuela, said to be still in use. He had the misfortune to lose his eldest son and assistant, Joseph S. Walter, from fever during this undertaking.

From 1851 to 1865 Walter was in Washington in charge of the extension of the United States Capitol, adding the wings of the present structure, the dome, and projecting a center extension, revised as late as 1904 by Carrère and Hastings, and still pending (1936). The cornerstone of the wings was laid July 4, 1851, with Daniel Webster as the orator. Walter had been one of four to win premiums for competitive designs for the extension and had been appointed by President Fillmore to prepare plans, which the latter subsequently approved. Charles F. Anderson, who also designed one of the premiated designs, long claimed credit for the wings and may have influenced the placing of the legislative chambers in the wings instead of at the north and south sides as Walter had intended. He also seems to have had influence, through Capt. Montgomery C. Meigs [*q.v.*], who knew his plans, in details of ventilation, acoustics, and heating. Anderson's drawings, however, are now lost, and only in the unlikely event that a drawing among the Walter papers, signed by the Corps of Topographical Engineers (Brown, *post,* plate 140), was designed by Anderson does there appear to be any need of a revision of the generally accepted belief that Walter is chiefly responsible for the wings as built, admirably adapted to their purpose, to the older parts of the building, and to the significance of the structure. The interior details are certainly his. The cast-iron dome designed by Walter extends nearly thirteen feet beyond its base and, despite its magnificent silhouette, needs the proposed center extension to satisfy the eye of the spectator. Walter also urged that the rotunda be rebuilt and the pilasters replaced by columns, in order to give a more apparent support to the dome. Other works of Walter's in Washington include the completion of the Treasury, begun by Robert Mills [*q.v.*], by the addition of the west and south façades, and, after the removal of the State Department, the north façade; the addition of two great wings to Mills's noble reminiscence of the Parthenon, long the Patent Office; the extension of the old Post Office, later the Land Office, from Mills's designs; St. Elizabeth's Hospital; and designs for the State, War, and Navy Building. In the last instance Walter's conception is seen only in the interior, the numerous colonnettes which now adorn the exterior having been added after his retirement. Walter also designed the naval barracks at Brooklyn and at Pensacola while in the government employ.

Walter's work in Philadelphia, done largely before his departure for Washington, includes such admirable adaptations of classical modes to city architecture as the Matthew Newkirk House, long known as St. George's Hall, and the Dundas House, both with Ionic porticoes. He also assisted Nicholas Biddle in his construction of a peripteral design for his home on the Delaware, "Andalusia." He designed the Preston Retreat and Wills Eye Hospital, various churches, banks, and private houses in Philadelphia, court houses at Reading and at West Chester (based on classic temples with Wren towers added), the beautiful Hibernian Hall, Charleston, S. C., and churches and banks at West Chester, Baltimore, and Richmond. After his virtual retirement in 1865 Walter consulted with John McArthur, 1823–1900 [*q.v.*], regarding the tower of the City Hall, Philadelphia, then rising, and was associated with him in the decorative work the building called for.

Throughout his life Walter was an active leader in the Baptist Church. He wrote *A Guide to Workers in Metals and Stone* (1846), and in collaboration with J. Jay Smith contributed to and compiled *Two Hundred Designs for Cottages and Villas* (1846). He helped to organize the American Institute of Architects in 1857, and became its second president in 1876, holding that office until his death. He was long associated with the Franklin Institute in various official positions. His first wife was Mary Ann E. Hancocks, who died during her eleventh confinement; his second wife was Amanda Gardiner, who bore him two children. He was urbane and cultivated, a conscientious worker, an expansive conversationalist, the firm ruler of his home. Universal deference was paid him in his later years in Germantown. He was handsome and of courtly bearing, with a ruddy complexion and leonine white hair in his later years. His portrait as a young man was painted by John Neagle.

[In addition to "Geneal. Sketches," MS. in the Hist. Soc. of Pa., prepared by Walter in 1871, see G. C. Mason, Jr., in *Proc. Am. Inst. of Architects . . . 1888,* vol. XXII (n.d.); "Mr. Nicholas Biddle and the Architecture of Girard Coll.," *Pa. Mag. of Hist. and Biog.,* no. III, vol. XVIII (1894); R. A. Smith, *Phila. As It Is* (1852), Louisa C. Tuthill, *Hist. of Architecture* (1848), pp. 264–66; *Documentary Hist. . . . of the U. S. Capitol* (1904); Glenn Brown, *Hist. of the U. S. Capitol,* vol. II (1903); "Who Was the Architect of the U. S. Capitol Extension?" *Architecture,* July 1917; H. P. Caemmerer, *Washington, The National Capitol* (1932); W. S. Rusk, "Thornton, Latrobe, and Walter and the Classical Influence in Their Works" (in MS.); *Phila. Press,* Oct. 31 (death notice) and Nov. 1, 1887. Many of Walter's letters, notebooks, sketchbooks, drawings, and account books, and the Neagle portrait are owned by Mrs. C. H. Wegemann of Baltimore, Md. Other sketches and drawings are in the possession of Glenn Cook and Walter Cook of Baltimore; the Coll. of Architecture, Cornell Univ.; the Lib. of Cong.; the office of the architect of the Capitol; the office of public buildings and parks, Navy Building; and the office of the supervising architect, Treasury Dept.]

W. S. R.

WALTERS, ALEXANDER (Aug. 1, 1858–Feb. 2, 1917), bishop of the African Methodist Episcopal Zion Church, was born in a room behind the kitchen of the Donohue Hotel in Bardstown, Nelson County, Ky., the sixth of the eight children of Henry Walters and Harriet (Mathers). His mother, a tall, commanding, light-brown woman of more than two hundred and fifty pounds, was a native of Virginia; his father, born in Larue County, Ky., was the son of his white master. Alexander received the little formal education he was fortunate enough to secure in private schools conducted by the colored churches of Bardstown during the period of the Civil War and Reconstruction. Because of his intelligence and piety he was chosen by the local African Methodist Episcopal Zion Church to be educated for the ministry. His school career lasted for a period of approximately ten years, ending about 1875.

In 1876 he joined a crew of waiters and was sent to work in the Bates House in Indianapolis, Ind. In March of the following year he was licensed to preach and was appointed pastor of the newly organized African Methodist Episcopal Zion Church of that city. On Aug. 28, 1877, he married Katie Knox, by whom he had five children. His rise was meteoric; successive pastorates took him to Corydon Circuit, Cloverport Circuit, and Louisville, Ky.; to San Francisco, Cal.; to Chattanooga and Knoxville, Tenn.; and to New York City. In 1888, at the early age of thirty, he assumed the pastorate of one of the largest and most influential of all the churches of his connection, the historic "Mother Zion" of New York. In 1889 he was sent to London, England, as a delegate to the World's Sunday School Convention; later in the year he was appointed general agent of the Book Concern of his denomination. At the General Conference which met at Pittsburgh in May 1892, he was elected to the bishopric of his Church, one of the youngest persons ever chosen for this high office.

Closely akin to Alexander Walters' interest in his Church was his zeal for the welfare of his race. In 1890 he joined with T. Thomas Fortune and others in issuing a call for a meeting to consider an organization for race protection. This meeting, held in Chicago, established the Afro-American League, which in 1898, at Rochester, N. Y., was reorganized as the National Afro-American Council, with Walters as its president. Convinced that the Republican party of his day did not merit the undivided support of his race, he became a Democrat and was chosen president of the National Colored Democratic League. As such he enjoyed a cordial relationship with Woodrow Wilson, who, in a letter to Walters in 1912, promised "to assure my colored fellow-citizens of my earnest wish to see justice done them in every matter, and not mere grudging justice, but justice executed with liberality and cordial good feeling" (Walters, *My Life and Work*, p. 195).

At the time of his death he was a trustee of the United Society of Christian Endeavor, a member of the administrative council of the Federal Council of Churches of Christ in America, a former president of the Pan African Conference, a vice-president of the World Alliance for Promoting International Friendship through the Churches, and a trustee of Livingstone College and of Howard University. His first wife died in 1896, and he was survived by his second wife, Lelia Coleman of Bardstown, Ky., and six children. Tall, light brown, of commanding presence, he undoubtedly owed some of his success to his personal appearance; but he was endowed as well with the gift of fluent speech, and with exceptional organizing ability. A man of deep piety and evangelical fervor, he possessed also a liberal and progressive mind. An autobiography, *My Life and Work* (1917), appeared the year of his death.

[*Minutes of the Gen. Conference of the African Methodist Episcopal Zion Church*, 1892–1916; J. W. Hood, *One Hundred Years of the African Methodist Episcopal Zion Church* (1895); J. T. Haley, *Afro-American Encyc.* (1895); G. C. Clement, *Boards for Life's Buildings* (1924); *Who's Who in America*, 1916–17; *N. Y. Times*, Feb. 3, 1917.]   R. E. C.

WALTERS, HENRY (Sept. 26, 1848–Nov. 30, 1931), capitalist, art collector, was born in Baltimore, Md., the son of William Thompson Walters [*q.v.*] and Ellen (Harper). After attending Loyola College in Baltimore he entered Georgetown University, Washington, where he

was graduated in 1869 and in 1871 received the degree of M.A. He then spent two years in the Lawrence Scientific School of Harvard University, where in 1873 he was awarded the degree of B.S., and two years in study at Paris. His father having already engaged in the linking of Southern railroads, Henry was destined for the same career. He had much more technical knowledge than the elder Walters, however, and carried on much more extensive operations. He had his first experience in the engineering corps of the Valley Railroad in Virginia, then being extended by the Baltimore & Ohio to Lexington; later he was in the operating superintendent's office of the Pittsburgh & Connellsville Railroad.

Joining the staff of the Atlantic Coast Line Railroad, of which his father was the chief organizer, he became in 1889 vice-president and general manager. He participated in the formation of the Atlantic Improvement & Construction Company (later the Atlantic Coast Line Company), a holding company incorporated in 1889 which enabled the Walters, Michael Jenkins, B. F. Newcomer, and other Baltimore men to build up and retain control of the Atlantic Coast Line Railroad and greatly to expand the system. The Petersburg Railroad was purchased by the Richmond & Petersburg Railroad, and in 1900 the Atlantic Coast Line Railroad Company of Virginia was incorporated and became the parent company in consolidations which by the time of his death gave Walters—as chief stockholder, and chairman of the board—control of 10,000 miles of railway. In many of the transactions leading to this result the Safe Deposit & Trust Company, of Baltimore, of the board of directors of which Walters was chairman, took a leading part. Important acquisitions were the Plant system of railroads in Georgia and Florida in 1902, which brought in over 1600 miles of line, and the Louisville & Nashville Railroad, a controlling interest in which was purchased in 1903 for $50,000,000 from J. P. Morgan & Company; Walters became chairman of the board of the Louisville & Nashville. Besides holding directorships in many railroads and several financial institutions, he represented the railroad owners on the staff of the director-general of railroads from 1918 to 1920. At the height of his career he was said to be the richest man in the South.

Art collecting, which with his father had been an avocation, became with Henry Walters a serious study and a ruling passion. From the time that he first went abroad with his father, during the Civil War, he knew painters and sculptors in their studios. Later he returned to Europe annually, usually spending about three months in acquiring objects of art. Besides many paintings and prints, he purchased oriental and occidental ceramics, sculptures in marble, stone, alabaster, metal and wood, jades and jewelry, textiles of all sorts, lacquer, miniatures, watches, illuminated manuscripts, and incunabula; he also acquired a large art library. For L. S. Olschki, *Incunabula Typographica* (1906) he wrote the preface. His largest single purchase was the collection of Don Marcello Massarenti, containing 900 pieces, in 1902. His collections were housed in a new gallery in Baltimore, opened in 1909. In his will he left his galleries with all of their contents to the city of Baltimore, together with one quarter of his estate for an endowment. They were opened under public ownership in 1934. Walters had earlier made other benefactions to Baltimore, among them four public baths. He spent most of his time in New York and had several other homes besides that in Baltimore.

An enthusiastic yachtsman, he owned the steam yacht *Narada,* and was regularly a member of the syndicate which built defenders of the *America's* cup. He was a close friend of Sir Thomas Lipton, the English yachtsman. At the age of seventy-three, Apr. 11, 1922, he married Sarah Wharton (Green) Jones, of Wilmington, N. C., whom he had known since his youth. He was of small stature, though stout in his later years, with rather thin face and high-bridged nose. A quiet, modest man, he was always fending off photographers and avoiding every kind of publicity. Like his father, he was fond of finger rings, which he changed daily. He was an officer of the Legion of Honor of France. Continuing work almost to the end, he died in New York City and was buried in Baltimore.

[*N. Y. Times,* Dec. 1, 8, 1931; *Sun* (Baltimore), Dec. 1, 1931; *Who's Who in America,* 1932–33; *The Walters Coll.* (1927); *First Ann. Report of Trustees of Walters Gallery* (1933).]   B. M.

WALTERS, WILLIAM THOMPSON (May 23, 1820–Nov. 22, 1894), merchant, railroad president, art collector, was born in Liverpool, Pa., the son of Henry and Jane (Thompson) Walters, both of Scotch-Irish descent. The father, a country merchant in comfortable circumstances, impressed by the unexploited mineral resources of western Pennsylvania, sent his son to Philadelphia to be trained as a civil and mining engineer. Returning to his native district, young Walters explored it on foot and horseback. He was first employed at an iron furnace at Farrandsville, then in Lycoming County, where about this time the first iron was made on a commercial scale with coke. Soon

afterwards he entered the employ of Burd Patterson at the Pioneer Furnace, Pottsville, where the practicability of smelting iron with anthracite was demonstrated. In 1841, when the canal along the Susquehanna River from Columbia, Pa., to Havre de Grace, Md., was opened, Walters removed to Baltimore and entered the produce commission business, trading particularly with Pennsylvania. As a result of this business interest, he later became the controlling director in the Baltimore & Susquehanna Railroad (afterwards the Northern Central), connecting Baltimore with the canal. In 1847 he formed a partnership with Charles Harvey in the foreign and domestic liquor trade, in which he continued until 1883, when his expanding interest in railroads absorbed his time.

Walters' commission business, which early shifted from Pennsylvania to Virginia and the Carolinas, was responsible for his important participation in the railroad development of the South. He became intimately acquainted with Southern merchants and planters, making interest on loans to them as well as receiving commissions on the sale of their produce. An investor in a steamship line between Baltimore and Savannah, and in other water routes, he was quick to recognize that the many railroads being built in the South between 1840 and 1860, unconnected though they were, would prove the successful rivals of steamboat transport. Often these little railroads, joining the cities on the fall line and spreading westward from the Southern ports, fell into financial difficulties from lack of coördination and from over-expansion, and before the Civil War, Walters, with a few Baltimore associates, began buying up these "ribbons of rust," and was about to commence their consolidation, centering upon Wilmington and Norfolk, when the war compelled abandonment of such plans. Walters had opportunity to employ his organizing ability two decades later, however, when the Southern roads, physically ruined by the war, were financially wrecked by the depression following 1873. A primary reason for coöperation between the roads was the development of truck farming in eastern North Carolina and Virginia, which required efficient through service. Walters led the cooperative movement through the successive stages of informal agreements, physical connection and formal contracts for handling through traffic, and the holding company, and was ready at the time of his death to begin with outright absorption and consolidation. His first notable achievement was an agreement with Northern roads for the carriage of perishable produce from the Carolinas and Virginia to Philadelphia, New York, and Boston. This was followed by the incorporation in Connecticut, in 1889, of the Atlantic Improvement & Construction Company, a holding company, the name of which was changed a year before Walters' death to the Atlantic Coast Line Company, which under his son Henry Walters [q.v.] was the means of effecting consolidation of roads reaching from Washington to Florida and Gulf ports, and to Memphis and St. Louis.

Walters began buying pictures when a young man, and while resident in Paris from 1861 to 1865—because his active Southern sympathies made him unpopular in Baltimore—he became intimately acquainted with many painters. He attended the Paris expositions of 1867, 1878, and 1889, and that of Vienna in 1873, buying many canvases of contemporary painters, such as Corot, Munkacsy, Millet, Millais, Delacroix, Detaille, Fortuny, Gerôme, and Alma-Tadema. He compiled *Antoine-Louis Barye, from the French of Various Critics* (1885), for which he wrote a preface. His paintings, in addition to an important collection of Eastern ceramics, crowded his Baltimore home and were placed later in two galleries added to his house, which were occasionally opened to the public. These collections were enormously enlarged by his son, who at death bequeathed them, with a new gallery, to the city of Baltimore. Walters was the patron of poor artists, the chief of whom was the sculptor William Henry Rinehart [q.v.], who began life as a stone-cutter in Maryland. Walters was a trustee of the Corcoran Gallery, Washington, and chairman of the art gallery committee of the Peabody Institute, Baltimore. In 1845 he married Ellen Harper of Philadelphia, who died in London in 1862. Walters bred fine stock on his farm near Baltimore, and brought the Percheron horse to America. For Du Huÿs' *The Percheron Horse* (1868) he wrote the preface. He was a small man, with a thin, straight nose, walrus mustache, stubbly beard and hair, and keen eyes. A trait noticeable to his friends was a fondness for trinkets of gold and enamel, of which he gathered a large number.

[F. A. Richardson and W. A. Bennett, *Baltimore Past and Present* (1871); *Biog. Cyc. of Representative Men of Md. and the D. C.* (1879); G. W. Howard, *The Monumental City* (1889); *Sun* (Baltimore), Nov. 23, 1894; *Baltimore American*, Nov. 23, 1894; H. D. Dozier, *A Hist. of the Atlantic Coast Line Railroad* (1920); S. W. Bushnell, *Oriental Ceramic Art; Illustrated by Examples from the Collections of W. T. Walters* (1897); M. J. Lamb, "The Walters Collection of Art Treasures," *Mag. of Am. Hist.*, Apr. 1892; M. Reizenstein, "The Walters Art Gallery," *New England Mag.*, July 1895; R. B. Gruelle, *Notes: Critical and Biog.: Collection of W. T. Walters* (1895).]
                                                    B. M.

WALTHALL, EDWARD CARY (Apr. 4, 1831–Apr. 21, 1898), Confederate general, United States senator, was born in Richmond, Va. His parents, Barrett White and Sally (Wilkinson) Walthall, moved to Holly Springs, Miss., when he was ten years of age, and there he was educated in St. Thomas Hall, at that time a well-known classical school. After reading law for a year with a brother-in-law at Pontotoc, he returned to Holly Springs and continued this study while serving as deputy clerk of the circuit court. In 1852 he was admitted to the bar and began to practise at Coffeeville. In 1856 he was elected attorney for the tenth judicial district of Mississippi and was reëlected three years later.

Upon the outbreak of the Civil War a volunteer company known as the Yalobusha Rifles was organized in Coffeeville and Walthall was elected first lieutenant. In the summer of 1861 he was elected lieutenant-colonel of the 15th Mississippi Infantry to which his company had been attached. When the Confederates were disastrously defeated at Mill Springs, or Fishing Creek, Ky., in January 1862, Walthall was commanding his regiment and displayed unusual bravery and steadiness. Thereafter he was usually placed where these qualities were especially needed and he became noted for his dependability and resourcefulness when outnumbered or when his army was being forced to retreat. On Apr. 11, 1862, he was made colonel of the 29th Mississippi Infantry, which he commanded at Corinth. He served through the campaign in Tennessee and Kentucky preparatory to the fighting about Chattanooga, and he was commissioned brigadier-general on Apr. 23, 1863, to take rank from Dec. 13, 1862. At Chickamauga nearly one-third of his men were killed or wounded in a severe engagement with a force under George H. Thomas [q.v.] against whom Walthall was several times matched. In mid-November 1863, with his brigade reduced to 1,500 men, he was on the defensive in the famous fight on Lookout Mountain which has sometimes been called the "battle above the clouds." The following day the 600 men left in his brigade participated in the battle of Missionary Ridge, and to them fell the task of covering the retreat of the Confederate army. Though Walthall was painfully wounded in the foot, he would not leave his saddle until his men were withdrawn from the field. After participating in the fighting about Atlanta, he was sent with Hood into Tennessee and at Franklin had two horses shot under him. On the retreat from Nashville he was chosen to command the infantry of the rear-guard, cooperating with Forrest's cavalry. On June 10, 1864, he was commissioned major-general, and won a reputation as one of the ablest of the Confederate division commanders.

On his way home at the end of the war he met Lucius Q. C. Lamar [q.v.]; this was the beginning of a lifelong and intimate friendship and of a brief law partnership at Coffeeville. In 1871 Walthall moved to Grenada. He was one of the leaders in the overthrow of the Carpet-bag government in the state, and a delegate to all except one of the National Democratic Conventions from 1868 to 1884. When Lamar was made secretary of the interior, Walthall was appointed to succeed him in the Senate, and by election and reëlection he remained in that body from March 1885 until his death except for a period from January 1894 to March 1895 when ill health caused him to resign. Before he resigned he had already been elected for the term beginning in March 1895, and he then reëntered the Senate. He served as chairman of the committee on military affairs and was a member of the committees on public lands and on the improvement of the Mississippi River. Declining physical strength limited his activities during most of the time he was in the Senate and he seldom participated in debate. Yet he was respected by the members of both parties and wielded a great deal of influence in his own. As a leader of the minority at a time when some sectional animosity remained he displayed the same strength and resourcefulness as when fighting against odds on the battlefield. His influence rested chiefly upon his strong character and his conciliatory manners. The olive branch that had been put forward so dramatically by Lamar in his eulogy of Charles Sumner was carried more quietly but probably with equal effectiveness by Walthall.

He was twice married, first to Sophie Bridges, who died within a year of their marriage in 1856, and then, in 1859, to Mary Lecky Jones, of Mecklenburg County, Va., whose death followed shortly after his. He had no children, but left an adopted daughter. Though his death occurred in Washington, D. C., he was buried at Holly Springs, Miss.

[*Biog. Dir. Am. Cong.* (1928); *Appleton's Ann. Cyc. 1898* (1899); *Biog. and Hist. Memoirs of Miss.* (1891), vol. II; Dunbar Rowland, *Mississippi* (1907), vol. II; Edward Mayes, *Lucius Q. C. Lamar* (1896); *Confed. Mil. Hist.* (1899), vol. VII; E. T. Sykes, "Walthall's Brigade," in *Miss. Hist. Soc. Pubs.*, centenary series, vol. I (1916); *Ibid.*, first series, vols. IV (1901), and XI (1910); Memphis *Commercial Appeal*, Apr. 22–26, 1898; *Washington Post*, Apr. 22, 1898.]   C. S. S.

WALTHER, CARL FERDINAND WILHELM (Oct. 25, 1811–May 7, 1887), Lutheran clergyman, theologian, was born at Langenschursdorf, near Waldenburg, Kingdom of Sax-

ony, the eighth of the twelve children of the local pastor, Gottlob Heinrich Wilhelm Walther, and his wife, Johanna Wilhelmina Zschenderlein. He attended the Gymnasium at Schneeberg, 1821–29, and at the age of eighteen felt himself "born for nothing but music," but under pressure from his father matriculated at the University of Leipzig as a student of theology. During his university years he suffered poverty, illness, and doubts about his salvation, consorted with a group of pietistically inclined students, read deeply in Luther's writings, and sought advice successfully from Martin Stephan, of St. Johannes Church, near Dresden. Stephan, of lowly origin and irregular education, was a popular, orthodox, erratic, widely influential preacher. After Walther completed his studies at Leipzig in 1833, he became a private tutor at Kahla and was ordained in January 1837 as pastor at Bräunsdorf, but in the easy-going, mildly rationalistic atmosphere of the Saxon State Church he was thoroughly unhappy. In September 1838 Stephan, who was in trouble with both the civil and the ecclesiastical authorities, decided to emigrate to the United States and found an independent Christian community. Upwards of 700 people rallied to him, including six clergymen and various candidates for ordination. Among them were Walther, his older brother, Otto Hermann Walther, and several of their friends. The emigrants sailed from Bremerhaven in five ships, one of which was lost at sea. Walther himself landed at New Orleans on Jan. 5, 1839, and proceeded to St. Louis, Mo. Some of the company settled there, but the greater number occupied a tract of 4,440 acres in Perry County, Mo., where Walther became pastor of the settlements called Dresden and Johannesburg.

Shortly after their arrival in Perry County, the emigrants made the belated discovery that Stephan was a libertine and a rascal, deposed him from office, and expelled him from their domain. Out of the confusion following the discovery Walther emerged as the leader of the community. In December 1839 he and three associates—Ottomar Fuerbringer, T. J. Brohm, J. F. Bünger—opened a school in a log cabin at Altenburg. This school was moved to St. Louis in 1850 and named Concordia Theological Seminary. Long before Walther's death it had become the largest Protestant theological seminary in the United States. In 1841 Walther removed to St. Louis to succeed his deceased brother as pastor of the Trinity congregation. On Sept. 21 of that year, at Dresden, Perry County, he married Christiane Emilie Bünger, by whom he had six children. On Sept. 7, 1844, he issued the first number of *Der Lutheraner* as the exponent of strict confessional Lutheranism. This journal was welcomed throughout the Middle West by scattered Lutheran clergymen holding similar convictions and led directly to the organization at Chicago Apr. 26, 1847, of the German Evangelical Lutheran Synod of Missouri, Ohio, and Other States, which is commonly known as the Missouri Synod. Walther was its president, 1847–50 and 1864–78. In 1850 he became professor of theology in Concordia Seminary without relinquishing his position as chief pastor of the four Saxon Lutheran congregations in St. Louis. In 1855 he established a second periodical, *Lehre und Wehre,* more technically theological than *Der Lutheraner* and animated by the same militant orthodoxy. In 1872 the Missouri Synod entered into a loose confederation with several other Middle Western synods that agreed with it in doctrine. Walther was the first president of this Synodical Conference. The Missouri Synod was now the largest body of Lutherans in the United States and was organized and directed with an efficiency comparable to that of the Prussian Army. Walther dominated its every activity.

He did not look the masterful man that he was. He was of medium height, uncommonly slender, and never in robust health. By middle life he was toothless, and hairless above the temples, and as he refused to wear false teeth his goatee was in grotesque proximity to the end of his nose. But his magnetic personality exercised its spell over individuals and crowds alike. He was a winning speaker and a powerful debater; his memory was a veritable concordance to the whole corpus of early Lutheran theology; and his capacity for work was astounding. He took no thought for himself: the sale of his books enriched the synodical treasury; he did not take a penny in royalties, supporting his family on a meager salary. He had a genius for friendship, conducted an extensive correspondence, and was almost immeasurably hospitable. His one interest outside his work was music: he was an excellent organist and had a fine baritone voice. He displayed his greatest power, though not the most admirable side of his character, in theological controversy. Throughout a good part of his career he was engaged in a series of controversies with other theologians on the nature of the church and the ministerial office and on other matters, and in these controversies he evinced not only immense learning and acumen but bitter feeling, intolerance, and an over-weening belief in his own inerrancy. The climax of his career as a polemical theologian was a contro-

versy over the nature of predestination that began as early as 1868, almost disrupted the Synodical Conference, and did not subside till after his death. As a theologian he was not consciously, it would seem, an innovator; he regarded himself as a pupil of Luther and the Lutheran scholastics, reproducing their thought for the use of his own generation. Actually, his was too vigorous a mind to be a mere receptacle for others' thought. His greatness, however, lay in his genius for organization and leadership. His influence has been greater than that of any other American Lutheran clergyman of the nineteenth century.

Of his many publications the most important are: *Die Stimme unserer Kirche in der Frage von Kirche und Amt* (1852); *Die rechte Gestalt einer vom Staate unabhängigen evangelisch-lutherischen Ortsgemeinde* (1863); *Die evangelisch-lutherische Kirche die wahre sichtbare Kirche Gottes auf Erden* (1867); *Amerikanisch-Lutherische Evangelien-Postille* (1871); *Amerikanisch-Lutherische Pastoraltheologie* (1872); *Lutherische Brosamen* (1876); an edition of J. G. Baier's *Compendium Theologiae Positivae* (1879); *Amerikanisch-Lutherische Epistel-Postille* (1882). Since his death many of his prayers, sermons, lectures, occasional addresses, and letters have been published, and some of them have been translated into English.

After the death of his wife, Aug. 23, 1885, he felt his own end approaching, divested himself of many of his duties, but continued to teach and preach until compelled to take to his bed. He died at St. Louis after a long illness and was buried in Concordia Cemetery.

[No bibliography and no adequate biography exist. Of manuscript material the principal depository is Concordia Seminary. Printed works include: Martin Günther, *Dr. C. F. W. Walther: Lebensbild* (1890), from which several other biographies derive; J. F. Köstering, *Auswanderung der sächsischen Lutheraner* (1866); G. A. Schieferdecker, *Geschichte der ersten deutschen lutherischen Ansiedelung in Altenburg, Perry Co., Mo.* (1865); J. Hochstetter, *Geschichte der Ev.-Luth. Missouri Synod* (Dresden, 1885); C. F. W. Walther, *Kurzer Lebenslauf des weiland ehrw. Pastors Joh. Friedr. Bünger* (1882); Wm. Sihler, *Lebenslauf* (2 vols., 1880); Anton Baumstark, *Unsere Wege nach Rom* (Freiburg, 1870); G. J. Fritschel, ed., *Geschichte der Lutherischen Kirche in Amerika*, vol. II (Gütersloh, 1897); *Briefe von C. F. W. Walther* (2 vols., 1915–16, cover period 1841–71); J. L. Gruber, *Erinnerungen an Professor C. F. W. Walther und seine Zeit* (1930); G. Mezger, ed., *Denkstein zum 75en Jubiläum der Missourisynode* (1922); W. H. T. Dau, ed., *Ebenezer: Reviews of the Work of the Missouri Synod* (1922). D. H. Steffens, *Doctor Carl F. W. Walther* (1917); W. G. Polack, *The Story of C. F. W. Walther* (1935). For an obituary, see *St. Louis Globe-Democrat*, May 8, 1887.]

G. H. G.

WALTON, GEORGE (1741–Feb. 2, 1804), signer of the Declaration of Independence, United States senator, the son of Robert Walton and Sally or Mary (Hughes) Walton, was born near

Farmville, Prince Edward County, Va. His grandfather had emigrated to America from England in 1682. He was left an orphan at an early age and grew up in the household of an uncle. He was apprenticed to a carpenter, who, impressed with Walton's character, intelligence, and ambition, gave him a portion of his wages and released him from his apprenticeship so that he could attend a local school. He was, however, largely self-taught. He removed to Savannah, Ga., in 1769 where he studied and was admitted to the bar in 1774. There he became an ardent patriot and joined with others to call a meeting of the patriot party in July 1774. He was a member of the committee on resolutions and also of the committee of correspondence. At a second meeting in August, he played an important part in condemning the British colonial measures and in allying the Georgia group with the Continental patriot party. He was also a member of the group that called and organized the Provincial Congress at the Liberty Pole in 1775. Unanimously chosen secretary of the Provincial Congress, he served on the committees of intelligence, helped to draw up the articles of association, and wrote addresses to the people and to the king. When the Council of Safety was organized he was elected its president.

The Provincial Congress, on Feb. 2, 1776, elected Walton a delegate to the Continental Congress and, with the exception of 1778, when other interests prevented his attending the sessions, and 1779, when he was governor of the state, he served continuously until Sept. 27, 1781. As a member of the important committees on Western Lands, the Treasury Board, Indian Affairs, and the Executive Committee in charge of Federal Affairs in Philadelphia, he evinced zeal, intelligence and ability. He was a strong advocate of independence and a signer of the Declaration. In the debate on the Confederation he urged that Indian trade be made a monopoly and that its control be vested in Congress. He also advocated equal vote for the states. In January 1777, Walton and George Taylor [q.v.] represented the government at Easton, Pa., and negotiated a treaty with the Six Nations. In Georgia he led the conservative Whigs who favored the union of the civil and military authority and opposed the radical Whigs led by Button Gwinnett [q.v.]. His ardent defense of Lachlan McIntosh [q.v.], who killed Gwinnett in a duel in 1777, led him into difficulties, when, as governor of the state in 1779, he forwarded a forged letter to Congress which brought about the transfer of McIntosh from Georgia. For this conduct, the legislature in 1783 censured Walton and or-

dered the attorney-general to bring suit against him, yet on the preceding day it had elected him chief justice of the state. He was commissioned colonel of the 1st Regiment of Georgia Militia on Jan. 9, 1778, and served gallantly at the siege of Savannah, where his leg was broken by a ball. He fell from his horse and was captured by the British who considered their prize so valuable that they asked for a brigadier-general, at least, in exchange. He was finally exchanged for a captain of the navy in September 1779.

When the British overran Georgia in 1779 the patriot government was torn by dissension. One faction chose John Wereat as governor but a more influential group elected Walton, who held office from November 1779 to January 1780. He was returned to Congress in 1780 and protested against the idea of peace on the principle of *uti possidetis*. He was one of the signers of the *Observations upon the Effects of Certain Late Political Suggestions* (1781) in which he favored extending liberal commercial privileges to Spain. The Loyalist assembly of 1780 disqualified Walton from holding any office in the state, but the patriot legislature immediately appointed him commissioner of Augusta and authorized him to lay out the city of Washington, Ga.

In 1783 he was commissioned by the Confederation to go on to Tennessee and negotiate a treaty with the Cherokee Indians. Thereafter he served for six years as chief justice of Georgia. In 1786 he served on a commission to locate the boundary line between Georgia and South Carolina. He was appointed a delegate to the Philadelphia Convention of 1787 but did not attend because of pressing judicial engagements. He attended, however, the Georgia Constitutional convention of 1788, served as a presidential elector in 1789, and was elected governor a second time in 1789. This administration was marked by the establishment of a new constitution, the location of the capital at Augusta, by frontier difficulties, and the pacification of the Creek Indians. He retired to his estate "Meadow Garden" in 1790, but was shortly elected a judge of the superior court of Georgia and served from 1790 to 1792, from 1793 to 1795, and from 1799 until his death. He was appointed in 1795 to fill out the unexpired term of James Jackson in the United States Senate. His term was uneventful but served to ally him with the Federalist Party.

In 1775, Walton was married to Dorothy Camber, who, although she was the daughter of a loyal British subject, was noted for her wholehearted support of the patriot cause. Walton was one of the founders and a trustee of Richmond

Academy, and a member of the committee to locate Franklin College. As a trustee of the University of Georgia he formulated plans to promote higher education in the state. Small of stature, comely in appearance, Walton was haughty, dignified and stern of manner; he was warm in his attachments and bitter in his enmities. His violent temper would brook not the slightest deviation from what he thought his due, but in spite of this characteristic he was respected by the people and honored by election to many public offices. In 1795 he built a new home "College Hill"; here he died, survived by his wife and one of their two sons. He was buried in the Rosney Cemetery but was removed, July 4, 1848, to the monument erected in Augusta to the Georgia signers of the Declaration of Independence.

[L. B. Andrus, "1933 Memoranda . . . in Re Walton Families," 1934, mimeograph copy in the Library of Congress; *Biog. Dir. Am. Cong.* (1928); *Letters of Members of the Cont. Cong.*, vols. I–IV (1921–33), edited by E. C. Burnett; *The Rev. Records of the State of Ga.* (3 vols., 1908), edited by A. D. Candler; *Hist. Colls. of the Ga. Chapters, D. A. R.*, vol. II (1929); *Hist. Colls. Joseph Habersham Chapter, D. A. R.* (2 vols., 1902); C. C. Jones, *Biog. Sketches of the Delegates from Ga. to the Cont. Cong.* (1891), and *Hist. of Ga.* (1883), vol. II; L. L. Knight, *Ga. Roster of the Rev.* (1920); *Men of Mark in Ga.*, vol. I (1907), edited by W. J. Northen; John Sanderson, *Biog. of the Signers to the Declaration of Independence*, vol. IV (1823); Warren Grice, *The Ga. Bench and Bar*, vol. I (1931); *Columbian Museum and Savannah Advertiser*, Feb. 11, 1804.]   F. M. G.

WALWORTH, CLARENCE AUGUSTUS (May 30, 1820–Sept. 19, 1900), Roman Catholic missionary, was born in Plattsburg, N. Y., the fourth of five children of Reuben Hyde Walworth [*q.v.*], for many years chancellor of New York, and his first wife, Maria Ketchum (Averill). At the Albany Academy and at the Sloan School at Williamstown, Clarence prepared for Union College, Schenectady, from which he was graduated in 1838. For three years he read law under capable practitioners of Canandaigua and Albany, and in 1841 was admitted to the bar. As a member of the firm of Chapin & Walworth, he practised law in Rochester for a year, then, somewhat unsettled in mind and soul, he began to study for the ministry of the Protestant Episcopal Church, in which he had been recently confirmed.

For three years he attended the General Theological Seminary, New York City, which was then torn with dissension over Puseyism, Tractarianism, and High-Church thought. After an unsuccessful attempt to establish a monastic foundation in the Adirondacks on the model of the Nashotah Mission in Wisconsin, he joined the Roman Catholic Church in 1845, taking the

names Alban Alphonsus at his confirmation. Despite the grief of his parents, he soon determined to become a priest of the Order of the Most Holy Redeemer (Redemptorists), and with two other young converts, Isaac T. Hecker and James Alphonsus McMaster [*qq.v.*], went to the Redemptorist College of St. Trond in Belgium to continue his theological studies. Here he made his vows, Oct. 15, 1846, and subsequently proceeded for further study to Witten in Holland, where he was known as "Brother *Pourquoi*" because of his inquisitive and critical mind. Ordained a priest, Aug. 27, 1848, by Bishop Paredis of Ruremonde in Dutch Limbourg, he was ordered to the Redemptorist houses at Clapham near London and at Hanley in Worcestershire. For two years he preached on the English missions, relieved the sufferings of Irish famine refugees, and witnessed the crisis associated with the reestablishment of the Catholic hierarchy in England. After the establishment of the Redemptorist province in the United States, he was assigned to the American mission band. Returning to America in 1851, he preached missions throughout the East for seven years and then, with Hecker and three other converts, he was released from his vows by Pius IX and assisted in the foundation of the Congregation of St. Paul the Apostle (Paulists), in 1858. Again he preached missions, with notable effect. Cardinal Gibbons assigned responsibility for his vocation to a mission conducted by Walworth in New Orleans in 1854.

Broken in health by this arduous life, Father Walworth served temporarily as a chaplain to soldiers on Staten Island, then joined the Albany diocese. For thirty-four years, from 1866 until the year of his death, he was pastor at St. Mary's Church, Albany. As a charity worker, a temperance advocate, a crusader against corruption in politics, and an outspoken critic of industrial evils, he challenged attention. Noteworthy among his publications were: *The Gentle Skeptic* (1863); *The Doctrine of Hell* (1873); *Ghosts* (1878), a brochure; *Andiatorocté* (1888); *Reminiscences of Edgar P. Wadhams* (1893); *The Oxford Movement in America* (1895); *The Walworths of America* (1897); and "Reminiscences of a Catholic Crisis in England Fifty Years Ago" (*Catholic World*, June 1899–January 1900). Despite failing sight and hearing, he managed with an amanuensis to contribute articles to periodicals until his last months, when paralysis left him speechless and helpless. At the end, he was buried with religious and civic honors in the family cemetery at Saratoga Springs.

[There is autobiographical material in Walworth's writings mentioned above. See also Ellen H. Walworth, *Life Sketches of Father Walworth* (1907); Walter El-liott, in *Cath. World,* June 1901; *Albany Evening Journal,* Sept. 19, 1900.]   R. J. P.

WALWORTH, JEANNETTE RITCHIE HADERMANN (Feb. 22, 1837–Feb. 4, 1918), writer, was born in Philadelphia, Pa., the fourth daughter of Matilda Norman, a native of Baltimore, and Charles Julius Hadermann von Winsingen, a German political exile. When Jeannette was a child the family moved to Mississippi, where for a time her father taught modern languages at Jefferson College, Washington, Miss., near Natchez. Her education was informal but effective, her father being her chief instructor. At the age of sixteen she became a governess on a Louisiana plantation, and she seems to have remained so occupied until the Civil War.

At the close of the war she went to New Orleans to enter journalism. She wrote a few articles signed "Ann Atom," for the Sunday edition of the *New Orleans Times,* but although they attracted attention they paid nothing. She entrusted her first novel to a New York firm which failed before the book appeared. In 1870, however, her *Forgiven at Last* was published by Lippincott, and it was followed shortly by *Dead Men's Shoes* (1872). These books were written on a plantation in Tensas Parish, La. Encouraged by Samuel R. Crocker of the Boston *Literary World,* she was able to have her next novel, *Against the World,* published in Boston by Shepard & Gill in 1873. In that year she married Major Douglas Walworth, of Natchez, Miss., a widower. The marriage was childless. For the next five years she lived on her husband's plantation in Arkansas, and here wrote *Heavy Yokes* (1876) and *Nobody's Business* (1878). After a stay in Memphis, where she contributed to the *Memphis Appeal* over the name "Mother Goose," she moved with her husband to New York. Here the Major planned to establish a law practice, and Mrs. Walworth hoped to find a more ready market for her books.

For the next sixteen years she was a very productive writer. In April 1884 she contributed "The Natchez Indians—A Lost Tribe" to the *Magazine of American History.* Judge Albion W. Tourgée [*q.v.*] published one of her novels in *The Continent* (June 6–27, 1883), recommending it as a picture of Southern life. Some of her tales appeared in Frank Leslie's periodicals; *Scruples* (1886) came out in the Boston *Beacon* before appearing as a book in Cassell's Rainbow Series; *Lippincott's Magazine* and the *Overland Monthly* also printed her work. A Mormon study, *The Bar Sinister* (1885), was reprinted with

several variations in title; *Southern Silhouettes,* after serial publication in the New York *Evening Post,* appeared as a book in 1887 and was well received. In 1889 she published *History of New York in Words of One Syllable.* About 1888 the Walworths returned to Natchez, where Major Walworth became editor of the *Democrat.* Books by Mrs. Walworth continued to appear until 1898, several being reprinted two or more times. After the death of her husband in 1915, she lived with relatives in New Orleans.

Much of her writing was, in her own opinion, on a sub-literary level. She utilized familiar scenes and conditions as the background for stories which, in plot and character, rarely rose above melodrama. Her style was clear but unimpressive. Her best work, however, *Southern Silhouettes,* a series of post-war sketches, was notably effective. In some of her stories, such as *The New Man at Rossmere* (1886) and *A Little Radical* (1889), she displayed an unusual penetration into the changing social and industrial conditions in the South. She was a shrewd observer and a witty and interesting companion.

[*Literary World* (Boston), Sept. 18, 1886; *Times-Picayune* (New Orleans), Feb. 5, 1918; C. A. Walworth, *The Walworths of America* (1897); information from relatives.]   R. P. M.

WALWORTH, REUBEN HYDE (Oct. 26, 1788–Nov. 28, 1867), jurist, last chancellor of New York, a descendant of William Walworth who came to Connecticut in 1689, was born in Bozrah, Conn., the third son of Benjamin Walworth, a veteran of the Revolution, and Apphia (Hyde) Walworth. When still a child, he went with his family to Hoosick, Rensselaer County, N. Y., where he worked on his father's farm until he was seventeen. He acquired the rudiments of Latin from a half-brother, supplemented his farm work with work in a country store, and then entered the law office of John Russell in Troy. Admitted to the bar in 1809, he removed the following year to Plattsburgh, where he took up practice. Two years later he accepted an appointment as master in chancery and also served as justice of the peace for Clinton County. During the War of 1812 he served as adjutant-general of the state militia, distinguishing himself in the land battles at Plattsburgh, Sept. 6 and 11, 1814. From 1821 to 1823 he represented his district in Congress as a Democrat. He defended Jackson's conduct as governor of Florida and advocated recognition of the Spanish-American states, but in the main his activities in Congress were unimportant (*Annals of Congress,* 17 Cong., 1 Sess., cols. 570, 1141; 2 Sess., cols. 648, 1060). In 1823 he accepted an appointment as circuit judge of the supreme court for the fourth judicial district of New York, which he held until his appointment in 1828 as chancellor.

Coming into office five years after the enforced retirement of James Kent [*q.v.*], and occupying the chancellorship for twenty years, Walworth contributed significantly to the system of New York equity jurisprudence which had been erected by Chancellor Kent. His achievements as a jurist are recorded in the eleven volumes of Paige's and the three volumes of Barbour's *Chancery Reports,* and in the decisions of the court of errors reported by Wendell, Hill, and Denio. In the law of evidence and in equity pleading and practice, Walworth's decisions filled numerous gaps in the New York law (see especially 1–3 *Paige, passim*), and he added materially to the law relating to injunctions (see, for example, 2 *Paige,* 26, 116, 316), to arbitration in equity matters, and the adoption of statutes in the Northwest Territory (7 *Wendell,* 539, 544). Both Kent and Joseph Story [*q.v.*] valued his judicial labors very highly. A large number of appeals were taken from his decisions to the court of errors and in about one-third of these cases his decisions were reversed. In *Gable et al.* vs. *Miller et al.* (10 *Paige,* 627) the court of errors criticized his learned exposition of theological doctrines to determine whether church trustees were diverting property from the purposes for which it was originally intended, holding that his discussion of such matters would lead to controversies throughout the state (2 *Denio,* 548, 549, 553). Walworth did not appear to be especially sensitive about appeals from his decisions, declaring that they "should be allowed in every case not manifestly frivolous," since only thus could the court of chancery be preserved (26 *Wendell,* 155).

Though in private life Walworth was courteous and refined, on the bench he was highly unconventional and frequently harassed counsel with pointed interrogations and biting sarcasm. This habit won him a host of enemies, and when President Tyler sent his name to the Senate in 1844 to fill a Supreme Court vacancy, Thurlow Weed, writing with Whig animus to Senator Crittenden, said: "He is recommended by many distinguished Members of the Bar of the State *merely because they are anxious to get rid of a querulous, disagreeable, unpopular Chancellor.* Indeed so odious is he that our Senate, when a majority of his own political friends were members, voted to abolish the office of Chancellor. Those who recommended him admit and avow that they did so to get him out of his present office" (quoted in Charles Warren, *The Supreme Court in United States History,* vol. II, 1922, p. 389). Weed's suggestion that the matter be tabled in order that a better selection be made was actually followed. The abolition of the court of chancery under the New York constitution of 1846 has been attributed in large measure to the desire of the bar to retire Walworth to private life. Thus, ironically enough, he contributed to one of the most important reforms in nineteenth-century law, the merger of the courts of law and equity.

Upon his retirement from office in 1848 he was the candidate of the Democratic party for governor, but ran third in the election in which Hamilton Fish [*q.v.*] was victorious, his defeat being due in large measure to the defection of the Free-Soilers. He then retired from political life, later declining a place in the cabinet of President Buchanan. At the outbreak of the Civil War he advocated conciliation and was a prominent delegate to the peace convention. Unlike Kent, who made use of his forced retirement to write the *Commentaries,* Walworth turned from judicial labors to write an extensive genealogy of his mother's family, the Hydes, who traced their descent from Mary Chilton, a passenger on the *Mayflower.* This work, *Hyde Genealogy* (2 vols., 1864), he completed at his Saratoga residence, "Pine Grove," the rendezvous of many celebrities, which had been an informal court during his term as chancellor. By his first wife, Maria Ketchum (Averill), whom he married Jan. 6, 1812, Walworth had six children, one of whom was Clarence A. Walworth [*q.v.*]. By his second marriage, Apr. 16, 1851, to Sarah Ellen (Smith) Hardin of Kentucky, widow of John J. Hardin [*q.v.*], he had one son, who died in infancy. He was an active Presbyterian, an incorporator of the American Board of Foreign Missions, a vice-president of the American Bible Society and of the American Tract Society, and president of the American Temperance Union.

[In addition to Walworth's *Hyde Geneal.* (1864), consult C. A. Walworth, *The Walworths of America* (1897), and E. H. Walworth, in *N. Y. Geneal. and Biog. Record,* July 1895. Sharply conflicting estimates of the Chancellor will be found in Irving Browne's sketch, in *Green Bag,* June 1895, and in W. L. Stone's *Reminiscences of Saratoga* (1875). See also John Livingston, *Portraits of Eminent Americans Now Living,* vol. II (1853); D. S. Alexander, *A Political Hist. of the State of N. Y.,* vols. I, II (1906); 49 *Barbour's N. Y. Reports,* 651–58; campaign circular of 1848 (N. Y. Pub. Lib.); *Albany Law Journal,* Sept. 30, 1876.]

R. B. M.

WANAMAKER, JOHN (July 11, 1838–Dec. 12, 1922), merchant, born in a small frame house on the outskirts of Philadelphia, was the eldest of the seven children of Nelson and Elizabeth Deshong (Kochersperger) Wanamaker. He was descended on both sides from early settlers, his father being of German and Scotch ancestry and his mother of French Huguenot. His paternal grandfather, John Wanamaker, and his father operated a brickyard until the competition of larger brickyards caused the former in 1849 to move to a farm near Leesburg, Ind., where Nelson and his family joined him in 1850. After a hard year during which the elder John died, the family returned to Philadelphia. Nelson Wanamaker went back to brickmaking, and John at thirteen became an errand boy for a publishing house at $1.25 a week. He soon shifted to the men's clothing business, gradually advancing to the position of salesman. But in 1857 a breakdown in his health forced him to take an extended trip west. Wanamaker returned, towards the end of the year, to become secretary of the Young Men's Christian Association in Philadelphia at a salary of $1,000 a year. He thus became the first paid Y. M. C. A. secretary in the country (Gibbons, post, I, 41) ; his success in the face of widespread opposition established the value of such an officer. His marriage to Mary Erringer Brown in 1860 crystallized the problem of his future and led him to break finally with paid religious work.

In 1861 Wanamaker and his brother-in-law, Nathan Brown, invested their modest combined capital in a men's clothing business. In ten years Wanamaker and Brown's "Oak Hall" had become the largest retail men's clothing store in the country (Ibid., I, 113). Brown died in 1868, but the store continued under the original name. The following year Wanamaker opened a more fashionable men's store, known as John Wanamaker & Company, at 818–22 Chestnut Street. In 1876 with characteristic showmanship he converted the rambling old freight depot of the Pennsylvania Railroad at Thirteenth and Chestnut Streets into a huge dry goods and men's clothing store, the "Grand Depot," which attracted considerable attention from visitors to the Centennial Exposition. After the fair, Wanamaker tried to get merchants in other lines to lease space in the "Grand Depot," as it was called until 1885. Failing this, he inaugurated on Mar. 12, 1877, his "new kind of store," a collection of specialty shops under one roof (Gibbons, I, 153). This venture precipitated the first serious crisis in his meteoric career, but after a year of uncertainty, success was evident and the store soon became one of the largest department stores in America.

Wanamaker was always master in his establishments, but he knew how to utilize the skill of close associates. The lower Chestnut Street store he delegated to his brothers. He induced Robert C. Ogden [q.v.] to take charge of "Oak Hall" in 1879. Wanamaker's sons, Thomas B. and Lewis Rodman [q.v.], entered the business after completing their college work at the College of New Jersey (Princeton) in 1883 and 1886 respectively. In 1885 Wanamaker promoted Ogden and Thomas B. Wanamaker to a partnership in profits in the "Grand Depot." During Wanamaker's term as postmaster-general Ogden successfully managed the department store. In 1896 Wanamaker bought from the receivers the old store of Alexander T. Stewart [q.v.] in New York City and placed Ogden in charge. Continued growth encouraged Wanamaker in 1902 to begin enlarging both department stores. The panic of 1907 broke when he was in the midst of this building program; again he was almost ruined. The burden on the aging merchant was increased through the retirement of Ogden in 1907 and the illness of his son Thomas, who died in 1908. But again the storm was weathered. In the development of the modern department store, Wanamaker moved consistently with the vanguard and was often a pioneer. He was an inveterate innovator and even a gambler, and his stores were in an eternal flux of change and reconstruction. He did not create the one-price system, but, beginning in 1865, he implemented it by guaranteeing their money back to dissatisfied customers. He was a master of the art of publicity, notably newspaper advertising. His paternalistic attitude towards his employees led him to set up an employee's mutual-benefit association (1881), training classes for clerks, continuation classes for boys and girls which in 1896 became the John Wanamaker Commercial Institute, and other educational and recreational features.

Wanamaker's apparently inexhaustible energy led him into a wide variety of undertakings, to each of which he managed somehow or other to give effective attention. Next to his mercantile activity, the most characteristic feature of his career was his religious work, especially in connection with the Bethany Sunday School (Presbyterian) which he founded in 1858. He was an outstanding lay leader and derived genuine pleasure and relaxation from his religious activities. An early temperance worker, he hailed the passage of the prohibition amendment and fought the relaxation of the Sunday blue laws in Pennsylvania. His vigorous Christianity saw no inconsistency in requiring military drill of the young men in his store or in offering the government trained complements of men from his employ in 1898 and 1917. A consistent Republican,

Wanamaker in 1886 was considered for the nomination for mayor. In 1888 he raised a large campaign fund to aid the election of Benjamin Harrison. For this he was rewarded with the postmaster-generalship (Mar. 5, 1889). The circumstances surrounding his appointment and his use of the spoils system brought down on his head the severe condemnation of the civil-service reformers. As postmaster-general, he instituted several technical improvements, experimented with rural free delivery, and advocated parcels post and postal savings, both of which were adopted much later; he favored government ownership of the telegraph and the newly perfected telephone services. For several years in the nineties, he waged a vigorous but unsuccessful fight against the Quay machine in Pennsylvania. He sought the Republican nomination for the United States Senate in 1896–97, and for the governorship in 1898. On the outbreak of the World War, he at first urged neutrality, but with the sinking of American ships by German submarines he used his widely read store editorials to increase the clamor for American entry on the side of the Allies.

Wanamaker remained active in his business and religious undertakings to the end of his long life. He died at his home at "Lindenhurst," near Philadelphia, on Dec. 12, 1922, after an illness of about three months. His son, Rodman, succeeded him as sole owner and director of the two department stores. Two daughters also survived him. His wife had died in 1920.

[H. A. Gibbons, *John Wanamaker* (2 vols., 1926), laudatory but not uncritical; J. H. Appel, *The Business Biography of John Wanamaker, Founder and Builder* (1930), and *Golden Book of the Wanamaker Stores* (2 vols., 1911–13; obituaries in *Public Ledger* (Philadelphia), *N. Y. Times*, Dec. 13, 1922. For the civil-service reformers' case against Wanamaker, see W. D. Foulke, *Fighting the Spoilsmen* (1919), ch. 4; *Selections from the Correspondence of Theodore Roosevelt and Henry Cabot Lodge, 1884–1918* (1925), vol. I.]   J. J. S.

WANAMAKER, LEWIS RODMAN (Feb. 13, 1863–Mar. 9, 1928), merchant, the second son of John Wanamaker [*q.v.*] and Mary Erringer (Brown), was born in Philadelphia. His father, whose formal education ended before the completion of grade school, believed strongly in the value of a college training for his children. Rodman, like his elder brother Thomas B., was sent to the College of New Jersey (Princeton). He received his A.B. degree in 1886 and after spending a few months in Europe married, on Nov. 4, Fernande Antonia Henry of Philadelphia and entered his father's "Grand Depot" store. In 1888 he was put in charge of the buying office in Paris, where he remained for ten

years. He returned in 1898 to assist his father, whose sphere of activity had been increased in 1896 by the acquisition of the old store of A. T. Stewart in New York City. In 1902 Rodman was made a member of the firm. His rôle in the management of the huge Wanamaker enterprises was expanded considerably with the retirement of Robert C. Ogden [*q.v.*] from the business in 1907 and the death of his brother Thomas in 1908. John Wanamaker's diary and letters reveal the extent to which he relied upon Rodman in the trying financial crisis of 1907, as well as the close personal bond which existed between father and son. The latter became resident manager of the New York store in 1911. On the death of his father in 1922, he became sole owner and director of both the Philadelphia and the New York corporations.

To his father's emphasis on goods of sturdy quality and the satisfaction of customers, Rodman added an emphasis on "art in trade." From his headquarters in Paris he shipped to America a stream of gowns, paintings, antiques, house furnishings, and other *objets d'art* which at first bewildered the members of the firm at home, but soon became an integral part of the business of Wanamaker's, as of other leading department stores. Wanamaker was an important art patron. He was for a long time president of the American Art Association in Paris. For his services in encouraging French art, he was decorated by the French government in 1897 and again in 1907. He gave a collection of works of art to his alma mater. He also made a notable collection of rare musical instruments, which were used in a series of public concerts given in the New York and Philadelphia stores by outstanding artists. He conceived the idea of installing in the grand court of the Philadelphia store the organ which had been used at the Louisiana Purchase Exposition in St. Louis and of constructing for the New York store a magnificent organ which was completed in 1921.

Wanamaker was an early aviation enthusiast, and was particularly interested in demonstrating the feasibility of commercial transatlantic flights. As early as 1914 he financed the construction of two planes for a transatlantic flight. The war interrupted further activity along this line. On July 1, 1927, however, about a month after Lindbergh made his successful flight, Wanamaker's *America,* commanded by Commander Richard Byrd, successfully completed a flight to France, being the first tri-motored plane to make the crossing. Wanamaker financed three expeditions among the Indian tribes of the West. These were led by Dr. Joseph K. Dixon, who in *The Vanish-*

ing Race (1913) recorded the proceedings at the last Council of the Chiefs, witnessed by the second expedition in 1909. The collection of Indian articles gathered by the expeditions was turned over to the United States government. Although he devoted considerable time to public affairs, Rodman Wanamaker never attained the position in public life which his father held. During the World War, he served without pay as special deputy police commissioner in New York City in charge of police reserves. He was also chairman of the mayor's committee to welcome foreign guests and the homecoming troops. In 1923 he gave to the city the perpetually burning light in Madison Square as a memorial to the city's war dead. He served at various times as consular representative in Philadelphia for Paraguay, Uruguay, and the Dominican Republic. In addition to his French decorations, he was honored by the governments of Great Britain, Italy, Belgium, Serbia, and Venezuela.

Wanamaker's first wife died in 1900, having borne him three children, Fernande, John, and Marie Louise. A second marriage, to Violet Cruger on July 27, 1909, ended in a divorce on Nov. 5, 1923. Wanamaker remained in active charge of both stores until his death at Atlantic City on Mar. 9, 1928. His holdings in the stores were placed in charge of a group of trustees to be administered in the interest of his children, all of whom survived him. With his death, the Wanamaker name disappeared from the list of active directors of the stores.

[H. A. Gibbons, *John Wanamaker* (2 vols., 1926); J. H. Appel, *The Business Biography of John Wanamaker, Founder and Builder* (1930); Princeton University, *After Twenty-Five Years. Class Record of 1886. 1886–1911* (n.d.); *Who's Who in America*, 1926–27; obituaries in *N. Y. Times, Public Ledger* (Philadelphia), Mar. 10, 1928.]　　　　　　J. J. S.

WANAMAKER, REUBEN MELVILLE (Aug. 2, 1866–June 18, 1924), jurist, was born in North Jackson, Mahoning County, Ohio. His parents, Daniel and Laura (Schoenberger) Wanamaker, were of Pennsylvania Dutch extraction. He attended the local schools and Ohio Northern University, Ada, Ohio, where his studies were interrupted from time to time by periods of teaching. On Apr. 7, 1890, he married Fannie Jane Snow, daughter of Prof. Freeman Snow. His legal training was received at Ohio Northern and in the offices of Ridenour & Halfhill in Lima. In 1893 he began practice in Akron, in partnership with W. E. Young. Elected prosecuting attorney of Summit County in 1895 and 1897, he became widely known through his successful prosecution of the leaders of an attempted lynching in August 1900. In May 1906 he be-

came a judge of the common-pleas court of Ohio; in 1912 he was elected as a Progressive to the supreme court of Ohio for the term beginning Jan. 1, 1913, and in 1918, as a Republican, was reëlected. Two years later he was defeated by Frank B. Willis for the Republican nomination to the United States Senate. Before the completion of his second term on the supreme bench, as a result of a long-continued nervous breakdown, he took his own life by jumping from a window at Mount Carmel Hospital, Columbus. His wife, a son, and a daughter survived him.

Wanamaker was a unique figure. According to general opinion an extreme radical, he was in fact less radical in thought than in manner of expression and in disregard of the conventional attitudes of a judge. He had little respect for judicial precedent and often supported his opinions by quoting from Lincoln and the Bible rather than by citing decided cases. "My experience upon the bench has taught me that precedents are followed when they square with the judgment desired to be rendered," he declared in a dissenting opinion. "They can with equal fidelity be ignored when they do not square with the judgment desired to be rendered" (102 *Ohio State*, 547). "Case law," he said in an earlier opinion (89 *O. S.*, 388–89), "is fast becoming the great bane of bench and bar. Our old time great thinkers . . . have been succeeded very largely by an industrious . . . army of sleuths, of the type of Sherlock Holmes, hunting some precedent in some case, confidently assured that if the search be long enough . . . some apparently parallel case may be found to justify even the most absurd and ridiculous contention."

At times almost vitriolic in his condemnation of the opinions of his judicial colleagues, he accused them of usurpation of power, juggling of words, sophistry. In spite of his habit of extravagant expression, however, Wanamaker made a real contribution to the jurisprudence of Ohio. At a time when most judicial thinking was somewhat stereotyped and concerned chiefly with the protection of property rights, he struck out boldly for a liberal construction of constitutions and laws in favor of the rights and needs of the common man. "Written constitutions," he said, "were adopted not as a sword against public interest but as a shield to protect the public interest" (93 *O. S.*, 227). Coming to the supreme bench shortly after the adoption (1912) of the constitutional amendment providing for municipal home rule, he fought long and hard in lengthy dissenting opinions for a liberal interpretation of the amendment which would give to the cities complete power of local self-government, including the right, free from any review by the state public utilities commission, to fix rates to be charged by all public utilities.

Never particularly sound in his thinking in regard to constitutional law, he made his greatest contribution in the field of criminal jurisprudence. Here he became the voice of the court in eradicating from the law of Ohio many outworn technicalities. In his opinions the doctrines of included offenses, double jeopardy, *corpus delicti,* and variance between indictment and proof received a new and modern meaning. One of his opinions in this field was to the effect that it is not necessary for the trial court in an indictment for murder to charge assault and battery as an included offense, and in another he declared that there is no material variance between an indictment which charges the stealing of several "rungs" and proof of the stealing of several "rugs." In addition to his work on the bench he did some occasional writing, contributing a number of articles to the *Saturday Evening Post* and in 1918 publishing a book, *The Voice of Lincoln.*

[Wanamaker's opinions, in 87–100 *Ohio State Reports*; "Memorial," 112 *Ohio State Reports*, lxv; C. T. Marshall, *A Hist. of the Courts and Lawyers of Ohio* (1934), vols. III, IV; *Ohio Law Reporter*, June 23, 1924, July 13, 1925; *Columbus Citizen* and *Akron Beacon Journal*, June 18, 1924; *Ohio State Journal* (Columbus), June 19, 1924.]   A. H. T.

WANLESS, WILLIAM JAMES (May 1, 1865–Mar. 3, 1933), medical missionary in India, was born in Charleston, Ontario, Canada, the son of John and Elizabeth Wanless. After education in the schools at Charleston, Mount Forest, and Guelph he engaged in business, but a religious awakening led him to determine to devote his life to medical missionary service. Accordingly he entered the University Medical College, New York City, where he was graduated in 1889. During his student days as one of the early members of the Student Volunteer Movement for Foreign Missions he was active in awakening missionary interest by addresses and by a unique pamphlet, *The Medical Mission, Its Place, Power and Appeal* (1911), which was the forerunner of missionary literature of its type. On Apr. 1, 1889, he was appointed a missionary of the Presbyterian Board of Foreign Missions, and was enabled to sail for India the following fall by special contributions from the Bryn Mawr (Pa.) Presbyterian Church, which supported him during his entire missionary career.

He began work at Sangli with a small dispensary, his equipment being improvised from packing boxes. In 1892, however, he moved to Miraj, where the prime minister of the state, who had been one of his patients, gave land for a hospital, which was erected by gifts from John H. Converse [*q.v.*], president of the Baldwin Locomotive Works. The Maharajah of Kolhapur, also a patient, became a devoted friend and munificent benefactor and was deeply influenced in his anti-caste attitude by the democracy and brotherhood which he saw in the hospital. From the beginning Wanless' skill and ability drew ever increasing patronage and support, and with funds received from his patients and other friends he developed the most extensive and effective medical missionary plant in India. He established, also, in 1897, the first missionary medical school in India and, in 1900, a leper asylum. A tuberculosis sanitarium, which now bears his name, was projected by him and opened for patients in 1931. From all over southern Asia patients came to Miraj, attracted by his fame, and his medical students were to be found throughout India and far up into Mesopotamia. During his superintendency approximately a million patients passed through the hospitals, and he himself performed annually some 6,000 operations. He was as earnest and thorough an evangelist as he was a skilful and efficient physician and surgeon.

Wanless was thrice decorated by the government of India. In 1910 he received the Kaiser-i-Hind Medal, Second Class; in 1920 he was awarded the Kaiser-i-Hind Medal, First Class; and in 1928 he was knighted for his extraordinary service. The only American to receive this last honor previously was J. C. R. Ewing [*q.v.*], who was for forty-three years a missionary in India. In 1928 ill health compelled Wanless to retire to America, but he was called back to India in 1930, where he remained some months, aiding in the establishment of the tuberculosis sanitarium. He was a vigorous personality, overflowing with energy and good cheer. A remarkable testimony to his place in public esteem was a great meeting of representatives of all communities, held in Poona in January 1928, under the chairmanship of the Aga Khan, for the presentation of a farewell address enclosed in a silver casket. Wanless was married twice: on Sept. 5, 1889, to Mary Elizabeth Marshall, who died Aug. 12, 1906; and on Dec. 5, 1907, to Lillian Emery Havens, who survived him. He died in Glendale, Cal. Some account of his activities is given in his book, *An American Doctor at Work in India,* which appeared in 1932.

[In addition to the above mentioned book, see *Who's Who* (British), 1932; *Presbyt. Advance*, Sept. 23, 1915, Mar. 16, 1933; *Presbyt. Mag.*, Sept. 1928; *Missionary*

Rev. of the World, Apr. 1933; *Los Angeles Times,* Mar.
4, 1933.]   R. El. S.

WANTON, JOSEPH (Aug. 15, 1705–July 19, 1780), governor of Rhode Island, son of William and Ruth (Bryant) Wanton, and descended from Edward Wanton who was in Boston, Mass., as early as 1658, was born into a family prominent in Rhode Island affairs. His father was governor of Rhode Island from 1732 to 1734, his father's brother John was governor from 1734 to 1741, while a first cousin, Gideon Wanton, was governor in 1745–46 and 1747–48. Joseph received no formal education, but acquired from his father and other residents of Newport a practical knowledge of ship-building, privateering, and other occupations associated with the sea. Admitted a freeman of the colony in 1728, he became in 1738 a deputy collector of customs at Newport, which position he held for over ten years. From about 1759 until the collapse of the family fortunes in 1780, he engaged, with two of his sons, in general merchandising under the firm name of Joseph & William Wanton. They dealt extensively with the Browns of Providence, from whom they bought quantities of spermaceti candles for resale in America and the West Indies. To the latter islands the firm also exported fish, cheese, lumber, pork, and mutton, and from thence imported molasses and loaf sugar. Business between the Browns and the Wantons declined in 1774, probably because of the royalist leanings of the latter.

Joseph Wanton was first elected governor in April 1769. Since he was both the elected executive of a charter colony and an officer bound to enforce British colonial regulations, he had a difficult time during his six-year tenure. In 1769 he had to deal with the case of the *Liberty,* a British sloop scuttled by a group of Newporters (*Records, post,* VI, 593–94); and in 1772, with Daniel Horsmanden [*q.v.*], Frederick Smythe, and Peter Oliver [*q.v.*], the chief justices of New York, New Jersey, and Massachusetts, and Robert Auchmuty [*q.v.*], judge of the vice-admiralty court at Boston, he was appointed to inquire into the affair of the *Gaspee* (*Ibid.,* VII, 57–192). Throughout these and other disturbances the governor succeeded reasonably well in appearing to enforce order without unduly restraining the patriot cause, with which he partially sympathized. He believed, however, that for the good of all concerned, America should remain a part of the British empire, and consequently, with the outbreak of hostilities at Lexington, he opposed further revolutionary measures. Although re-elected May 3, 1775, for another term, he declined to appear, May 4, to take the oath of office

and the following day declined to sign the commissions of the troops that had been raised. The General Assembly in June suspended him from acting as governor, and on Oct. 31 deposed him (*Records,* VII, 311–99).

Although Wanton lost the confidence of the patriots, he retained their respect and was not personally molested. He remained in Newport until his death in the summer of 1780, taking no further part in public affairs. A man of large build and impressive appearance, he liked expensive clothes and a bountiful table. On Aug. 21, 1729, he had married Mary, daughter of John Winthrop, F.R.S. They had five daughters and three sons. Although he was often spoken of as a wealthy man, little of Wanton's estate survived the Revolution. His liquid assets were invested in the mercantile firm, which suffered reverses during the war, especially after 1779 when the state confiscated the property of his sons Joseph, Jr., and William, who had openly espoused the British cause; a loan of £500 to his son-in-law, William Browne [*q.v.*] of Salem, Mass., later governor of Bermuda, was never repaid. His father had left the Quakers and his mother the Presbyterians at the time of their marriage; their son was an Episcopalian, a member of Trinity Church in Newport. His gubernatorial career resembled that of Thomas Hutchinson of Massachusetts, but the two men differed widely in personal characteristics. Wanton was less intellectual and less ambitious than his renowned contemporary, but he suffered adversity with greater fortitude.

[J. R. Bartlett, *Hist. of the Wanton Family of Newport, R. I.* (1878); *Records of the Colony of Rhode Island,* vols. VI–VII (1861–62), ed. by J. R. Bartlett; Wilkins Updike, *A Hist. of the Episc. Church in Narragansett, R. I.* (3 vols., 1907); G. C. Mason, *Annals of Trinity Church, Newport, R. I.,* 1 ser. (1890); *New Eng. Hist. and Geneal. Reg.,* July 1926; letters and other MSS. in the R. I. state archives, the R. I. Hist. Soc., and the John Carter Brown Library.]   J.M.M.

WARBURG, PAUL MORITZ (Aug. 10, 1868–Jan. 24, 1932), banker, born in Hamburg, was one of the sons of Moritz and Charlotte (Oppenheim) Warburg. His father was a member of the Hamburg banking house of M. M. Warburg & Company, founded in 1798 by his great-grandfather and conducted thereafter by the family. Paul Warburg, after graduating in 1886 from the Gymnasium at Hamburg, began work with a Hamburg exporting firm, afterwards serving in shipping and banking houses, first at London, then at Paris. In 1895 he was admitted as partner in the Warburg firm at Hamburg. In the same year he married Nina J. Loeb, daughter of Solomon Loeb, of Kuhn Loeb & Company, and in 1902, coming to New York, he became a member of that firm. He became an American citizen in 1911.

Warburg had made special study of the central banking organism in the principal European countries, notably Germany, France, and England. In the United States, after the panic of 1907, he joined publicly with those bankers and public men who were urging fundamental reform in the American banking system. His recognized knowledge of the subject brought him in contact with Senator Nelson W. Aldrich [q.v.], under whose auspices, in 1908, Congress was induced to create a national monetary commission, to investigate the question and report on a feasible plan. The tentative plan of legislation submitted by Senator Aldrich in 1911, if not virtually drawn up by Warburg, undoubtedly reflected many of his ideas (Laughlin, post, pp. 15, 16). With its provision for a national reserve association (like a central bank) with branches, the majority of whose managing officers should be chosen by the private banks in the system, Warburg was in entire sympathy.

Congress refused to adopt the proposal and when, in 1913, it enacted the Federal Reserve law, providing for separate regional reserve banks under the supervision of a reserve board appointed by the president, the banking community generally opposed the change. It has been claimed, and denied, that certain fundamental principles that were incorporated in the Aldrich bill through the influence of Warburg were accepted in the new act (E. R. A. Seligman, in Warburg, The Federal Reserve System, II, 8; Willis, post, pp. 523 ff.). At any rate, he accepted the altered administrative provisions. The result of this cordial acquiescence and of Warburg's recognized knowledge of the problem was that he was nominated by President Wilson on June 15, 1914, as one of the five appointed members of the first Federal Reserve Board. The Senate finally approved his nomination on Aug. 7, 1914. Warburg was an exceedingly useful member of the Reserve Board during his four-year term, which covered practically the period of the World War and involved operations of a previously unimagined magnitude by the Reserve System. When his term was about to expire in 1918, the United States was at war with Germany. President Wilson was admittedly disposed to renominate him, but Warburg wrote frankly to the President that insistence on the renomination of a citizen of German birth would expose both the President and the Reserve Board to attack, at a crucial moment. Warburg therefore retired to private life, devoting himself thereafter chiefly to the organiza-

tion and operation of the International Acceptance Bank.

In his capacity as private banker, Warburg came into nation-wide notice in March 1929 because of his plain warning, in his annual report to his shareholders, of the disaster threatened by the wild stock speculation then raging throughout the country. Almost without exception, responsible bankers had refrained from public warnings of the kind. Warburg declared the spectacular rise in market values of company stocks to be "in the majority of cases, quite unrelated to respective increases in plant, property, or earning powers" (Mar. 8, 1929; quoted in The Federal Reserve System, I, 824). He described the great speculation as sustained only "by a colossal volume of loans carrying unabsorbed securities," and predicted that, "if orgies of unrestrained speculation" were not brought under control, "the ultimate collapse is certain not only to affect the speculators themselves, but also to bring about a general depression involving the entire country." When his warning was abundantly fulfilled by the panic of October 1929 on the Stock Exchange, and by the swiftly succeeding aftermath of extreme commercial depression, he condemned emotional predictions of irretrievable ruin as vigorously as he had warned against the delusions of the period of speculation. With the idea that the gold standard was responsible for the entire collapse he had no sympathy whatever. In his analysis of the causes of the depression, he stressed the bad effects of efforts to maintain high prices by "tariff barriers and other artificial expedients, in the face of constantly accelerated mass production" (New York Times, Jan. 25, 1932, p. 5).

Besides being chairman of the International Acceptance Bank, Warburg was chairman of the Manhattan Company, a director of important railroads and corporations, and a trustee or director of several institutions of educational character. From 1921 to 1926 he was a member of the advisory council of the Federal Reserve Board, and he served as chairman of the economic policy commission of the American Bankers' Association. In 1930 he published The Federal Reserve System. Its Origin and Growth (2 vols.). He died at his home in New York City, leaving a son and a daughter.

[Warburg Papers, in private hands; Annual Reports Fed. Reserve Board, 1914–18; Repôrts of annual meetings of Am. Acceptance Council, 1929–31; Annual Reports of chairman to shareholders of International Acceptance Bank, 1921–29; H. P. Willis, The Federal Reserve System (1923); J. L. Laughlin, The Federal Reserve Act. Its Origin and Problems (1933); "Two Bankers on the Depression," New Republic, Jan. 21, 1931; "Paul M. Warburg," Nation, Feb. 3, 1932; Who's Who in America, 1930–31; obituaries in N. Y.

Times Jan. 25, 1932; American Banker, Jan. 26, 1932; information from Warburg's son, James P. Warburg.]
A. D. N.

WARD, AARON MONTGOMERY (Feb. 17, 1843–Dec. 7, 1913), merchant, was born at Chatham, N. J., the son of Sylvester A. and Julia Laura Mary (Green) Ward. During his childhood his parents migrated to Niles, Mich., where he attended public school until he was fourteen. He was then apprenticed to a trade, but left his master to work in a barrel-stave factory at twenty-five cents a day and later became a day laborer in a brickyard. When he was nineteen years old he went to St. Joseph, Mich., to work in a general store for five dollars a month and his board; at the end of three years he was put in charge of the store with a salary of $100 a month. Going to Chicago about 1865, he was employed by Field, Palmer & Leiter for two years and then worked for a short time for the wholesale dry-goods house of Willis, Gregg & Brown. When this firm failed, he became a traveling salesman for Walter M. Smith & Company, dry-goods wholesalers in St. Louis.

It was while he was traveling out of St. Louis that Ward obtained an intimate knowledge of rural conditions which enabled him to make a distinctive contribution to American life. A source of chronic complaint by people living in the country was the small price received for farm produce compared with the high cost of goods bought at retail. Ward conceived the idea of buying in large quantities for cash direct from the manufacturer and selling for cash direct to the farmer. Back in Chicago, working for C. W. Pardridge, a State Street dry-goods firm, he awaited his chance to go into business for himself. He was ready to start when the Chicago fire of 1871 intervened to wipe out practically all his savings. In the spring of 1872, however, he resigned his position and invested all he had saved, $1,600, in the new business. This, with $800 contributed by George R. Thorne, his partner, constituted the total capital.

The partners began their operations in the loft of a livery stable on Kinzie Street between Rush and State streets. Their first stock was a small selection of dry goods, the first catalogue a single price sheet. Ward was a keen judge of merchandise and he bought at prices which enabled him to sell to the consumer in the country at prices he could pay. From the beginning he followed the policy of satisfying the customer or allowing the return of goods. In 1873–74 purchasing agencies of the National Grange bought through him to stock their cooperative retail stores and he thus earned the good will of farmers in Illi-

nois and Iowa. Making accessible to people in rural sections throughout the country a variety of goods which they could not otherwise have enjoyed with their limited purchasing power, his enterprise succeeded from the beginning, and was forced repeatedly to move to larger quarters as sales increased. Since the business was conducted on a cash basis, it survived the panic of 1873. New lines were added after 1874 and an eight-page catalogue replaced the single price sheet. By 1876 the catalogue had 150 pages, with illustrations; by 1888, annual sales had reached one million dollars. With the building of the Ward Tower at Michigan Boulevard and Madison Street in 1900, the successful business and its founder attracted national attention. At the time of his death, annual sales amounted to some $40,000,000, customers were served in all parts of the world, and the staff of employees numbered 6000.

Ward's public spirit was demonstrated by the protracted legal battle he carried on in the Illinois courts to maintain free from all obstruction the park between Michigan Boulevard and the lake shore, now Grant Park, and it is largely owing to his foresight and tenacity that Chicago has a lake frontage which is the heritage, not of a privileged few, but of the mass of the people, for whom Ward seems really to have cared. He retired from active management of the company in 1901, although he still retained the title of president. Since he had no sons, the management of the business passed into the hands of the five sons of his partner, Thorne. Ward spent much time at his large estate, "La Belle Knoll," at Oconomowoc, Wis., where he raised fine horses. He died at Highland Park, Ill.

On Feb. 22, 1872, in the same year in which he started his mail-order business, Ward married Elizabeth J. Cobb of Kalamazoo, whose sister had married his partner. Mrs. Ward was left the large fortune which her husband had received from the earnings of his mail-order business. During her lifetime, and through her will, she dispensed considerable sums to charitable institutions. Her principal benefactions, however, were to Northwestern University, to which institution in 1923 she gave $4,223,000 for a medical and dental school as a memorial to her husband, adding in 1926 $4,300,000 for the enlargement and maintenance of the school. She died July 26, 1926. The Wards had no children, although it was generally believed until after Mrs. Ward's will was probated that Marjorie Ward, an adopted daughter, was their own.

[P. T. Gilbert and C. L. Bryson, Chicago and Its Makers (1929); Who's Who in America, 1912–13;

Dedication of the Montgomery Ward Memorial Building, Northwestern Univ. (1927) ; The Hist. and Progress of Montgomery Ward & Company (1925), published by the company; Northwestern Alumni News,
Nov. 1926; Inter-Ocean (Chicago), Chicago Daily
News, Dec. 8, 1913; Chicago Daily Tribune, Dec. 8,
1913, July 27, 29, 30, 1926; information and corrobora-
tion from officials of Northwestern Univ. and of Montgomery Ward & Company, and from George Merrick,
Esq., Ward's personal attorney].   E. A. D.

WARD, ARTEMAS (Nov. 26, 1727–Oct. 28,
1800), Revolutionary general, was descended
from William Ward, a Puritan, one of the original settlers of Sudbury and Marlborough, Mass.
His father, Nahum Ward, was a founder of
Shrewsbury, where Artemas was born, and his
mother was Martha How, the daughter of Capt.
Daniel How and Elizabeth Kerley. He attended
school in Shrewsbury and was graduated at Harvard College in 1748. After teaching for a brief
period in Groton, he established, in 1750, a general store in Shrewsbury, which he continued to
run until the burden of his official duties forced
him to abandon it. On July 31, 1750, he was
married to Sarah Trowbridge of Groton, a descendant of John Cotton [q.v.], and she became
the mother of his eight children. He was elected
to many town offices including those of assessor,
clerk, selectman, moderator, and treasurer. On
Jan. 21, 1762, he was appointed a justice of the
Worcester county court of common pleas, and
later, in 1775, he became its chief justice.

During the French and Indian War he took
part in Abercromby's ill-starred attack upon Ticonderoga in 1758 and was promoted from the
rank of major to that of colonel in the provincial militia. The hardships of the campaign impaired his health and thereafter he was never
robust. For many years he represented Shrewsbury in the General Court, distinguishing himself by his opposition to royal authority. In
1768 he was one of the "Glorious Ninety-two"
who refused to vote for the rescinding of Samuel Adams' famous "Circular Letter." So obnoxious to Governor Bernard was his conduct
that the latter deprived him of his military commission in 1766, and in 1768 and 1769 vetoed
his election to the council. Hutchinson, succeeding Bernard, reluctantly approved his election
in 1770, and Ward remained a member of the
board until 1774. In the organization of resistance to General Gage as governor, during the
autumn and winter of 1774–75, he played an important rôle, serving as a member of the conventions held in Worcester County to champion
colonial rights and of the First and Second Provincial congresses. When the news of the battle
of Lexington reached Shrewsbury, he lay ill,
but at dawn on the following day, Apr. 20, he
mounted his horse and rode to Cambridge,
where he assumed command of the patriot forces
under authority granted to him by the Second
Provincial Congress. On May 19 he was formally commissioned general and commander-in-
in chief of the Massachusetts troops. During the
following weeks he directed the siege of Boston
and began the conversion of the undisciplined
bands of militia-men into an army. He was
not present at the battle of Bunker Hill because
he believed it to be his duty to remain at his
headquarters in Cambridge, but he designated
the detachments participating in it and issued
the orders he considered necessary.

On June 17 the Continental Congress, which
had chosen Washington for the supreme command of the American forces, selected Ward as
second in command with the rank of major-general. Upon arriving at Cambridge, Washington
assigned to Ward the command of the right
wing. On Mar. 4, 1776, Ward ordered General
Thomas to seize Dorchester Heights, thus forcing the British to evacuate Boston. Shortly
thereafter, on Mar. 22, he tendered his resignation on the ground of failing health. It was accepted by Congress on Apr. 23, but at Washington's request, he remained temporarily in command of the forces left in Massachusetts after
the withdrawal of the main body to New York.
Until relieved by William Heath [q.v.], on Mar.
20, 1777, he devoted his attention chiefly to
strengthening the defenses of Boston.

During the next three years he served on the
Executive Council. From 1780 to 1781 he was
a member of the Continental Congress, and
from 1782 to 1787, barring one year, a member
of the state legislature. He appeared on many
committees of the latter body and was elected
speaker. During Shays's Rebellion he defended the judiciary in a speech before a mob which
had assembled about the steps of the court
house in Worcester. He served as a Federalist in the First and Second congresses
(1791–93, 1793–95), and was assigned to many
committees dealing with military affairs. In
1798 illness compelled him to resign his position
on the bench. He died of paralysis and was
buried in Mountain View Cemetery in Shrewsbury. His homestead, now the property of Harvard University, is kept as a memorial.

Whatever his official position, Ward was conscientious, hard-working, and inflexible in his
opinions. Deeply devoted to the interests of
Massachusetts, he believed that Providence had
set a seal of especial favor upon the state and
that its citizens were the chosen people. His relations with Washington lacked cordiality. He

resented the strictures which Washington passed upon the men of Massachusetts at the outbreak of the Revolution. When Washington visited the state in 1789, he passed Ward's house but the general was not present to greet him.

[Manuscript letters, diaries, and papers of Ward are widely held. Among the principal collections are those of the Massachusetts Historical Society, the Massachusetts State Archives, Boston, and the American Antiquarian Society, Worcester, Mass. Consult also: Peter Force, *Am. Archives*, 4 ser., vols. I–VI (1837–46), 5 ser. (3 vols., 1848–53); A. H. Ward, *Hist. of the Town of Shrewsbury* (1847), and *Ward Family* (1851); Elizabeth Ward, *Old Times in Shrewsbury* (1892); W. T. Davis, *Hist. of the Judiciary of Mass.* (1900); R. Frothingham, *Hist. of the Siege of Boston* (1903); P. H. Epler, *Master Minds at the Commonwealth's Heart* (1909); Charles Martyn, *The Life of Artemas Ward* (1921), and *The William Ward Geneal.* (1925).]   E. E. C.

WARD, ARTEMUS [See BROWNE, CHARLES FARRAR, 1834–1867].

WARD, CYRENUS OSBORNE (Oct. 28, 1831–Mar. 19, 1902), author, editor, labor leader, was the seventh of the ten children born to Justus and Silence (Rolph) Ward; Lester Frank Ward [*q.v.*] was a brother. They were descendants of Andrew Warde who emigrated to Massachusetts and died in Fairfield, Conn., in 1659. Three years after Cyrenus' birth, in western New York, his parents moved to St. Charles, Kane County, Ill., where until 1848 he aided his father in various frontier activities connected with farming, milling, and construction work, becoming meanwhile a skilled mechanic. He traveled extensively in the Middle West, touring as a violinist with a concert company. His leisure was largely devoted to the study of botany, geology, and ancient and modern languages. On Oct. 25, 1857, he married Stella A. Owen of Wysox, Pa., and the following year, in partnership with his wife's brother, built a hub factory at Myersburg, Pa.; later he was connected with other manufacturing enterprises.

He enlisted for the Civil War, but was rejected. In 1864, however, he was appointed machinist in the Brooklyn Navy Yard, and while employed there became deeply interested in labor problems. His pamphlets and speeches attracted the notice of such journalists as Charles A. Dana and Horace Greeley [*qq.v.*] and led in the late sixties to connections with the *Sun* and the *New York Tribune*. He traveled extensively abroad during the years when the international labor movement was being organized, attended several labor conferences, met Karl Marx and other noted labor leaders, and contributed to the *Sun* a series of articles entitled "A Mechanic Abroad" and "Cooperation Abroad." On his

return to America he resumed work as a mechanic and engaged actively in the labor movement as lecturer, writer, and organizer. His ardent support of social reforms and of the political organization of workers made it difficult for him to retain employment, and he finally devoted himself completely to the cause of labor. Establishing his own printing office, in 1878 he published his first book, *A Labor Catechism of Political Economy*. The extensive sale of this work enabled him to extend his activities as lecturer and writer. He also published numerous pamphlets and labor journals, including *The Voice of the People*, a newspaper. In 1878 he became associate editor of *Man*, a journal devoted to progress and reform.

In 1884 he was appointed to a position with the Geological Survey at Washington, and soon thereafter was transferred to the Bureau of Labor, as translator and librarian. He had long been collecting information about the working classes of ancient times, and in 1887 completed the text of the first volume of his most noted work, *A History of the Ancient Working People*—later entitled *The Ancient Lowly*. Failing to secure a publisher, he set up a print shop in his own house, and in 1889, after two years of arduous labor, the first edition appeared. It immediately attracted wide attention both as a work of learning and also as an ardent and sympathetic interpretation of working-class history. Scholars were inclined to question the validity of many of his conclusions regarding the meaning of ancient records, but his use of inscriptions and casual sources and his emphasis on neglected phases of ancient life were recognized as contributing significantly to the study of antiquity. In 1892 and again in 1896 he traveled widely in Europe, studying current conditions and newly discovered inscriptions and sources in preparation for a second volume of the *History*, which he published in 1900. The next year he died in Yuma, Ariz., whither he had gone in quest of health.

In addition to those already mentioned his writings include a drama based on Abraham Lincoln and the Civil War, *The Equilibration of Human Aptitudes and Powers of Adaptation* (1895), and numerous pamphlets, bulletins of the Bureau of Labor, and articles in periodicals. His distinctive traits were versatility combined with great energy and intensity of purpose, idealism, and sympathy for the working people, whom he urged to refrain from violence and to achieve a socialistic state by political methods. He exerted significant influence on the organization of labor, the movement for social reform, and the interpretation and utilization of history for the advancement of working-class aims.

[Manuscript sketch, "Cyrenus Osborne Ward, A Sketch," by F. E. Ward, a son; G. K. Ward, *Andrew Warde and His Descendants, 1597–1910* (1910); L. F. Ward, *Glimpses of the Cosmos* (1913); E. P. Cape, *Lester F. Ward, A Personal Sketch* (1922); preface to 1892 ed. of *A Labor Catechism of Political Economy*; *N. Y. Times,* Mar. 21, 1902; *Evening Star* (Washington), Mar. 21, 1902..   W. B.

WARD, ELIZABETH STUART PHELPS

(Aug. 31, 1844–Jan. 28, 1911), writer, was born in Boston, Mass., the eldest child of Elizabeth (Stuart) and Austin Phelps [*q.v.*] and the descendant of Nathaniel Phelps who emigrated from England with his father in 1630 and died in Northampton, Mass. She was baptized as Mary Gray, but after her mother's death she changed her name. Her father was the son of a Congregational minister whose eminently orthodox career was interrupted by a remarkable case of "house possession," in consequence of which for about seven months strange phenomena were manifested in his parsonage. Turnips thumping from the ceiling to the study table were among the crasser forms. A man of complete veracity, he wrote a record of this peculiar experience; but many years later the manuscript was destroyed by his grandchildren, for reasons now difficult to appreciate. Of the actuality of the manifestations, it should be added, they had no doubts; nor did they offer any explanation. This event in the Phelps family cannot be overlooked; it can hardly be overemphasized in dealing with the work of the grand-daughter, always interested in psychic phenomena. In 1848 Austin Phelps accepted a professorship at the Theological Seminary at Andover, the youthful home of his wife, the fifth child of Moses Stuart [*q.v.*], one of the most redoubtable theologians that even New England has produced. With all the prestige of the most scholarly academic background, with a brilliant mind, nervous temperament, intense susceptibility to artistic and spiritual impressions, Elizabeth (Stuart) Phelps was attuned to exquisite pleasure and exquisite pain. Under the name of "H. Trusta" she published extraordinarily popular religious tales, written in an easy, natural style, lightened by many glints of humor. *A Peep at Number Five* (1851) is a really charming record of a clergyman's home. *The Sunny Side* (1851) reached the astonishing circulation of some 100,000 copies. *The Angel Over the Right Shoulder* (1851), under the thinnest veil of fiction, shows "the difficult reconciliation between genius and domestic life" (*Chapters, post,* p. 12). "The struggle killed her, but she fought till she fell," her daughter recorded years later

(*Ibid.,* p. 15). It was over when that daughter was eight years old, but one of the strongest influences in her life was the memory of her mother; and many of her own tales, especially *The Story of Avis* (1877), deal with similar struggles.

The death of their gifted mother left the care of three small children to their father, already beginning the nervous invalidism that tortured the remainder of his life. Of his devotion to his children, of his ideal fatherhood, of the atmosphere of his home his daughter wrote glowingly in *Austin Phelps* (1891) and *Chapters from a Life* (1896). It was he who influenced her reading, cultivating a taste severe and catholic; it was from him that she received her real education, although she was a day pupil at schools in Andover, where she had sound training in mathematics and sciences, as well as in languages and literatures. Philosophy and theology were inevitable elements in the very fiber of one bred on Andover Hill. In *Chapters from a Life* (Chap. ii) she wrote some pages about the Andover of her youth that deserve to rank among American classics. Although a resident of the academic center of New England theology and the daughter of one of its most fervent exponents, she was trained in a religion of love and hope, "natural, easy, pleasant." "The fear of an ungodlike God never haunted us," she wrote; "in Creeds we were not over-much instructed" (*Austin Phelps, ante,* p. 154). That the religion thus early acquired was satisfying and sustaining her whole later life testified. Although a motherless and often a lonely child, she seems to have grown through a normal girlhood, enlivened by the usual social and intellectual pleasures, plus a superfluity of young men, mostly of the class known as "theologues," whom in her fiction she alternately pitied and patronized, but rarely escaped.

Crashing into all normal life, destroying its balance and its beauty, came the Civil War; and to her it brought personal tragedy. The shock caused by the death of the boy whom she loved proved almost too much for her physical and mental poise, and for several years she was very nearly a recluse. From the grief of that period and the long brooding emerged *The Gates Ajar,* begun in 1864 and published in 1868 (but title page dated 1869). From childhood she had written, and at thirteen she had begun to publish; now she concentrated the technique and facility thus acquired to "comfort some few . . . of the women whose misery crowded the land" (*Chapters, ante,* p. 97). The result was amazing to the author, as, for different reasons, it is to readers today. In a tale almost devoid of incident, by means of conversations loaded with Biblical quotations and their literal interpretations, this orthodox daughter of an ultra-orthodox theological professor swept away the then current conceptions of heaven, substituting a place of light and love, where the dear dead retained their familiar characteristics and all the things that they had loved worthily here. It reads strangely now, because of its subject and its method; but it brought solace to many thousands and became one of the most influential works of fiction ever written by an American. The circulation in this country fell somewhat below 100,000 but was greater in England; and the book was translated into many European languages. Its success made the author "the most astonished girl in North America," she wrote (*Ibid.*, p. 110); she received letters from all over the world; she was extolled, and she was vituperated. Incredible it all seems now; nevertheless it is true. That the time had come for some such revolution in thought in no way detracts from the originality and daring of the author. One result is easily understood. Thereafter whatever she wrote was published and read; but the overwhelming success was never repeated. She wrote better books, but none that touched the popular imagination so vividly or met the popular need so directly. In *Beyond the Gates* (1883), *The Gates Between* (1887), *Within the Gates* (1901), and in several short stories she again attempted eschatology. Both by inheritance and by temperament she was attuned to the psychic; but her deep spiritual reverence, her Yankee common sense, probably also her keen humor kept her from swinging far from her moorings in orthodox religion.

She wrote voluminously, mainly fiction; also she essayed verse, *Poetic Studies* (1875), *Songs of the Silent World* (1884, but title page dated 1885), but never with the success of prose. As few but the greatest have done she understood and expressed the sufferings of gifted and sensitive women, the depths of loneliness, the torture of jangled nerves. This last experience was hers by birthright. Like her father she was a victim of insomnia in some of its most excruciating forms. These nervous disorders made her at times almost a recluse and deprived her of many coveted forms of service. While still young she had written one of her most intense tales, "The Tenth of January," in the *Atlantic Monthly* (March 1868), dealing with the collapse of a factory building. *The Silent Partner* (1871) and many short stories testify to her sympathy with the narrow lives of women in industry. *Doctor Zay* (1882) is one of the first American novels to deal with women in medicine. Indeed the

problem of the adjustment of women to the complications of modern life was never far from her thought. It reached its highest expression in *The Story of Avis* (*ante*), "a woman's book, hoping for small hospitality at the hands of men" (*Chapters, ante*, p. 157).

For many years her summer home was at East Gloucester, Mass., and here she came to know the pathos and the tragedy of the fisher folk. Here too were seared upon her imagination the horrors of intemperance. For three years she was connected with a mission for temperance reform, and in it she had experiences she counted among the richest in her life. The relinquishment of this work on account of illness was to her a great trial; but she passed on her sympathetic understanding of her neighbors in two tales that rank high in American fiction, *The Madonna of the Tubs* (1886) and *Jack, the Fisherman* (1887). Gloucester also furnished the background for *A Singular Life* (1894), although the first chapters deal with Andover and its theological seminary. Andover repudiated her interpretation of its theology, and Gloucester resented her treatment of its morals; but the reading public of New England took the book to its heart as it had done none of hers since *The Gates Ajar*. It is an impassioned, utterly sincere plea for practical religion in the story of a young minister who tried to live like a "Christ-man" in a liquor-drenched town, among hard-working people. The dominant motive in this book is the dominant motive in all the best of her writing, as it was in her life. Outgrowing much of her early creed, losing interest in theology, she centered her thought on the central figure of Christianity and found solution for life's problems in the teaching and example of Jesus Christ. As a result of lifelong familiarity with the Gospels she wrote *The Story of Jesus Christ: an Interpretation* (1897). Into this she put her whole heart, but she had neither the critical acumen nor the scholarship to treat the great subject in an original manner. She valued the book far more highly than did even her most admiring readers.

She was married to Herbert Dickinson Ward [*q.v.*] on Oct. 20, 1888. They had no children. At their new home in Newton Center, Mass., they wrote several books in collaboration. In *The Master of the Magicians* (1890) and *Come Forth* (1890, but title page dated 1891) they worked on Biblical romances, but without marked success. Throughout the remainder of her life she continued to write prolifically. *Austin Phelps* (*ante*), the biography of her father, and *Chapters from a Life* (*ante*), which she refused to term an autobiography, are especially delightful; indeed they may be considered essential for the understanding of academic New England and its intellectual aristocracy. It was hardly possible that so intense a personality as hers should be at all times balanced and tolerant. Frequently in both her style and her treatment one is aware of the excess to which the nervous temperament is prone. Often even her best writing is marred by redundance and exaggeration; but that she was a master of lucid, fluent, poignant English there is no doubt. "Provincial" is a word easy to apply to her, hard to defend. It is true that she usually wrote about the intellectual, oversensitive people of New England; but also it is true that she saw them as human beings, occasionally had glimpses of their naked souls, perceived for herself and helped her reader to perceive the tragedy and the glory of the will to do "the painful right."

[*Austin Phelps* and *Chapters from a Life*, ante; "Memorial of the Author," by Austin Phelps in Elizabeth Stuart Phelps, under pseud. H. Trusta, *The Last Leaf from Sunny Side* (1853); O. S. Phelps and A. T. Servin, *The Phelps Family of America* (1899), vol. II; *Boston Evening Transcript*, Jan. 30, Feb. 4, 1911.]

E. D. H.

WARD, FREDERICK TOWNSEND (Nov. 29, 1831–Sept. 21, 1862), adventurer, was born and reared in Salem, Mass., the son of Elizabeth Colburn (Spencer) and Frederick Gamaliel Ward, a ship's master and later a ship-broker and merchant. He was the descendant of Miles Ward who emigrated from England to Salem about 1639. In boyish games at school his capacity for leadership emerged, and he showed coolness and daring in sailing small boats in the bay. He went to school at home and from 1846 to 1848 at Norwich University in Norwich, Vt., where he acquired the foundations of a good military training. For the next twelve years he roamed far and wide on sea voyages or commercial ventures, interspersed with military service in Tehuantepec, with William Walker in Nicaragua, and with the French in the Crimea. In 1859 he appeared in Shanghai, China, where he took service on a Yangtse River steamer. No remarkable exterior appearance suggested the pent-up energies, the forceful leadership, or the daring that characterized his actions. In the thickest battle he went unarmed, but invariably carried a riding-whip or cane—a custom followed later by Gordon.

The year 1860 marked a crisis in the Taiping Rebellion, when the rebels, barred from Central China, were trying to obtain the rich coast provinces about Shanghai. Anglo-French resistance protected that international port, but officials and merchants outside were frantic. Just at this time he was introduced to Takee, a Chinese merchant, who became a broker between him and the officials and later his paymaster. Ward married Chang Mei, Takee's daughter. They had no children. For a cash payment Ward agreed to recapture Sungkiang. His first following of foreign adventurers failed, but a second expedition of Filipinos with white officers proved successful. Encouraged by this victory, he tried in the same manner to capture Tsingpu; but, unfortunately for him, it was defended by a strong body of Taipings reinforced by a company of adventurers under Savage, an Englishman. In one of the attacks on this city he was wounded, and his force thereupon rested for several months at Sungkiang. Meanwhile he sought for a larger army. Since an adequate foreign legion would be both politically objectionable and costly, he thought that a sufficient army of well-drilled Chinese under foreign officers would be effective and comparatively inexpensive. Official support was gained; but the foreign consuls, particularly the British, opposed his whole project, and he was arrested in May 1861. Asserting Chinese naturalization, he avoided a trial, and he escaped from a British warship on which he was detained. Early in 1862 his new army was ready. Meanwhile a change had taken place in the Franco-British policy: they were combining with the Chinese to clear a thirty mile radius about Shanghai. His command, now called the "Ever Victorious Army," was enthusiastically acclaimed and cooperated effectively in several campaigns with the Anglo-French forces near Shanghai and Ning-po. During the summer more than 4,000 men served under his banner, and Ward himself, with brevet rank as brigadier-general, was cited for bravery in the capture of Tsingpu early in August. His enterprise had justified itself in the teeth of foreign opposition in its beginnings, and of Chinese jealousy of its present successes. Other Chinese armies resented the superior airs of Ward's men; officials worried over the cost of the force; and widespread gossip credited Ward with untoward ambitions, though none of his actions ever revealed such. His loyalty to the United States was shown in his offer, just before his death, of 10,000 taels to the Federal government for carrying on its Civil War. While directing the attack on Tzeki, he received a mortal wound and died the following day. A magnificent state funeral was accorded him at Sungkiang, his headquarters, and a memorial temple was there erected in his honor in which, until recently, regular sacrifices were offered to his spirit.

Henry Andrea Burgevine [*q.v.*], who succeeded to the command, soon lost his position. Charles

George Gordon ("Chinese" Gordon), after an interval, succeeded; and his success was achieved with the instrument forged by Ward, a fact sometimes—unjustly—forgotten.

[Holger Cahill, *A Yankee Adventurer; the Story of Ward and the Taiping Rebellion* (1930); R. S. Rantoul, "Frederick Townsend Ward," *Essex Institute Hist. Colls.,* vol. XLIV (1908); E. A. Powell, *Gentlemen Rovers* (1913); H. B. Morse, *In the Days of the Taipings* (1927); J. W. Foster, *Diplomatic Memoirs* (1909), vol. II; F. W. Williams, *Anson Burlingame* (1912); *Norwich University* (1911), vol. II, ed. by W. A. Ellis; clippings and papers in the Essex Institute, Salem, Mass.]   W.J.H—l.

WARD, GENEVIEVE (Mar. 27, 1838–Aug. 18, 1922), actress, was born in New York City, daughter of Samuel and Lucy (Leigh) Ward, and grand-daughter of Gideon Lee, mayor of the city in 1833, and through her grandmother a descendant of Jonathan Edwards [*q.v.*]. Named Lucy Geneviève Teresa, she later dropped all but the middle name, which she herself wrote with the accent. She was taken abroad by her mother to be educated and at fifteen elected to become a singer. Rossini sent her to a teacher in Florence. but at eighteen her career was interrupted by her unfortunate marriage (Nov. 10, 1856) to a Russian count, Constantine de Guerbel, whom she met in Italy. A civil contract was performed by the American consul at Nice, which the count appeared to regard as sufficient, but the bride and her mother did not, and they set the time for a church ceremony in Paris. The count failed to appear, and Genevieve found herself, like the heroine of the melodrama, "wedded but no wife." Her father was summoned to Europe, and the family pursued the reluctant bridegroom to Warsaw, where they caught him and by the aid of diplomatic intervention compelled a ceremony. Immediately thereafter the three Wards departed, and never saw him again. Genevieve resumed her studies, and made her French début in April 1859, at Paris, as Elvira in *Don Giovanni.* Her English début was at a Philharmonic concert in London in 1861. Her New York début was at the Academy of Music, Nov. 10, 1862, as Violetta in *La Traviata,* under the name of Mme. Guerrabella. Shortly thereafter, during a Cuban tour (where she was hissed for wearing boots and cloak in the rôle of the page in *Ballo in Maschera*), her singing voice failed her, and for the next decade she had no public record. But she was studying for the dramatic stage, and on Oct. 1, 1873, in Manchester, England, she appeared as Lady Macbeth. The *Manchester Guardian* (Oct. 3) was mildly favorable. She continued to practise and play, and in 1875 reached Drury Lane. In 1877 she went to France to study at the Comédie-Française (she was a gifted lin-

guist), and on Feb. 11, in that year, she played Lady Macbeth in French. She returned to England with a considerable "classic" repertoire, and Sept. 2, 1878, made her dramatic début in America, at Booth's Theatre, New York, as Jane Shore. She acted throughout the country the following winter. A Boston critic, writing of her in the *Boston Daily Advertiser,* Apr. 7, 1879, said, "She is of the school of Ristori, and is not so very far behind that admirable performer." The *New York Post* had previously said her acting was "good, but traditional." On her return to England she secured a play which was new, and effective—*Forget-Me-Not,* by Herman Merivale, a play in the school of Dumas *fils* and Sardou, which gave her talents exact scope. She produced this at the Lyceum, London, August 1879, with a young leading man named Johnson Forbes-Robertson, and so great was its success that she subsequently acted it over two thousand times, and in most countries around the globe which possessed an English-language theatre. It boasted the once-famous line, "There would be no place in creation for such women as I, if it were not for such men as you." (For an account of her performance, see Winter, *post,* II, 405 ff.)

For the next two decades she was professionally active in England, America, and Australia. On Mar. 3, 1883, after a second American tour, she produced Legouvé's *Medea,* and also revived *Forget-Me-Not.* Her last American tour was made in 1887. In 1891 she toured to South Africa. She joined Henry Irving's company at the Lyceum in 1893, playing Eleanor in *Becket* (1893), Morgan le Fay in *King Arthur* (1895), Margaret in *Richard III* (1896). In 1897 she ventured out of her traditional repertoire to play Mrs. Borkman in Ibsen's *John Gabriel Borkman* at the Strand. She never visited America again, but lived quietly in England, teaching younger players, with a record of having acted in seventy-seven plays behind her. She reappeared in 1918, with George Alexander at the St. James, because, she said, "of the war strain." That year, with Richard Whiteing, she published *Both Sides of the Curtain,* which contains personal reminiscences. She celebrated her eighty-fourth birthday by appearing as the Queen in *Richard III.* She died the same year in London. She was, in her prime, said to have "broad, ample shoulders and a waist that typifies good health." She was above average height, with a Roman nose, firm chin, dark eyes, heavy brows—a commanding female, in brief, and though graceful, with a well-trained, flexible voice, born for parts of emotional amplitude and intellectual dominance rather than "sex appeal." Her pictures show a strong resemblance to Ristori. In later years her face grew thin, long, and intellectual, like that of Irving. After her early adventure, she never married again.

[*Who's Who in America*, 1912–13; Zadel B. Gustafson, *Genevieve Ward, A Biog. Sketch from Original Material* (1882); Genevieve Ward and Richard Whiteing, *Both Sides of the Curtain* (1918); William Winter, *The Wallet of Time* (2 vols., 1913); obituaries in *Times* (London), and *N. Y. Times*, Aug. 19, 1922; Harvard College Theatre Coll.]   W. P. E.

WARD, GEORGE GRAY (Dec. 30, 1844–June 15, 1922), engineer, was born at Great Hadham, Hertfordshire, England, the eldest of seven children of Benjamin and Esther (Gray) Ward. His early education was obtained in a private school at Cambridge, to which his parents had removed. Fascinated by the telegraph instrument, he obtained permission, when but six years of age, to visit the local telegraph office at the railroad station, and within a year he had become a proficient telegrapher. At eleven he left school, entered the service of the Electric Telegraph Company, and quickly mastered what knowledge was then available of theoretical telegraphy. Eager for wider experience, he joined in 1865 the Egyptian telegraphic service and was stationed at Alexandria for three years. In a cholera epidemic that visited the city, he and two or three others were the only telegraphers to stay on duty in order to maintain communication with the outside world. His services were especially acknowledged by the Viceroy, Ishmael Pasha. In 1867 he married at Cambridge, England, Marianne, the daughter of William Smith. She died in 1918, leaving three children. In 1869 he joined the French Atlantic cable company and was appointed chief operator at St. Pierre and Miquelon. During the laying of the cable to St. Pierre, he was one of six telegraphers selected for the electrical staff on board the steamship *Great Eastern*. At St. Pierre he remained until 1875, when failing health forced a return to England.

The year 1875 marked the end of his active career as a telegrapher; from that time his services were essentially those of an engineer, promoter, and executive. Within a few years he assumed a leading position among cable executives and maintained it for almost forty years. Shortly after his return to England, he accepted the position of general superintendent in the United States of the Direct United States Cable Company then being organized under the direction of Lawrence Oliphant. In cooperation with Oliphant, he built stations and cable lines and made arrangements for an interchange of traffic with other lines. So efficient was his work that he not only broke the existing monopoly of the Anglo-American Telegraph Company but also reduced the charges for cable services and cut by two-thirds the time necessary to receive a reply. The efficiency of the new company was so evident that the Anglo-American proposed a pool in which the Western Union Telegraph Company later joined. When the pool broke up in 1883 he assumed charge of the interests of both the Direct and of the French companies.

When James Gordon Bennett and John William Mackay [*qq.v.*] decided to break the power of the Western Union by establishing a new cable company, in 1884, they offered Ward the general managership of the newly organized Commercial Cable Company. In 1890 he became vice-president and held both positions until his death, as well as gradually assuming directorships in subordinate and affiliated companies. Under his direction at least five cables were thrown across the Atlantic, while he was primarily responsible for the diplomatic and engineering aspects of the work that resulted in the first cable across the Pacific,—laid to Honolulu in 1902, Manila in 1903, and to China and Japan in 1906. He also laid the cable between the United States and Cuba. In laying the Pacific cable, he planted colonists on the Midway Islands. International recognition for his services came in decorations presented by both the German and Japanese emperors. The Commercial Cable Company was largely his creation, made possible by his aggressive leadership, practical experience, and tactful personality. He died in New York City and was buried from the Episcopal Church of the Heavenly Rest, of which he had been vestryman and warden.

[*Telegraph Age*, Jan. 1, 1908; *Telegraph and Telephone Age*, Jan. 16, 1910, July 1, 1922; *Telegraphist*, Jan. 1, 1885; *Who's Who in America*, 1922–23; *N. Y. Times*, June 16, 25, 1922; information from his son, George Gray Ward, New York City.]   H. U. F.

WARD, HENRY AUGUSTUS (Mar. 9, 1834–July 4, 1906), naturalist, was the son of Henry Meigs and Elizabeth (Chapin) Ward, and a descendant of Andrew Warde who died in Connecticut in 1659. In 1807 Levi Ward, Henry's grandfather, moved westward to the Genesee Valley, the final settlement being made at "The Grove," a large farm in present-day Rochester, N. Y. His father's love for books caused him to neglect the farm and drew violent remonstrances from his wife; this domestic atmosphere, resulting from a state of continual impecunity, and an overemphasis on religious matters, made his youth a strenuous and unhappy one. His interest in natural history seems to have first made itself evident when, although too young for formal classes, he succeeded in joining the geological excursions of Dr. Chester Dewey. When his father fled to the West in 1846, the boy was placed with a farmer, who, fortunately, encouraged him to read. In 1849, with some assistance from an uncle, he entered Middlebury Academy, at Wyoming, N. Y. With a rather vague idea of entering the ministry, he then attended Williams College, 1851–52, and exhibited great interest in science and modern languages. At Williams, James Orton [q.v.] became an intimate friend. Insufficiently prepared to meet college requirements he returned to Rochester and through the intervention of another uncle entered Temple Hill Academy in Geneseo where he made the friendship of the family of James S. Wadsworth [q.v.], and it was through their help and his own exertions that he was enabled to begin his life's career—collecting scientific materials.

When Agassiz was to lecture in Rochester in 1854 James Hall, 1811–1898 [q.v.], commended him to the care of Henry Ward. So thoughtful was that care that Agassiz persuaded the Ward family to let Henry continue his studies at Cambridge, Mass., where he studied and worked in Agassiz's museum. In 1854 he was offered an opportunity of studying in the School of Mines in Paris with one of the young Wadsworths who was commended to his care. Until 1859 the two studied and traveled together. When the elder Wadsworth was no longer able to render financial aid, Ward began his collecting trips. He financed himself for several years by selling specimens of fossils to European museums, but he was at last forced to return to America. Obsessed by the idea of a "cabinet of natural history" both as a source of information to students and income for himself, he managed to stimulate an interest in his project on the part of his family and returned to Europe to make additions to his collection. In 1861 he returned to Rochester, was married, on Nov. 8, to Phoebe A. Howell, and accepted the professorship of natural sciences in the University of Rochester where he remained for almost fifteen years.

In 1862 he contracted to supply Vassar College with a "cabinet," and completed the project in two years. He then developed his own collection, expanded into a second building, and began systematically to prepare material for order and sale. This was the beginning of Ward's Natural Science Establishment. He gathered around him a group of men to be trained in science, and in later years many of them (among them Carl E. Akeley, Frederic A. Lucas [qq.v.], William M. Wheeler and William T. Hornaday) occupied high scientific posts. He also continued his trips,

sometimes as appointed officer on some commission, sometimes merely to add to his own materials. He crossed the Atlantic fifty times in these pursuits. Lewis Brooks commissioned him to prepare a collection of natural history for the University of Virginia, and he exhibited at the Centennial Exposition in Philadelphia. In 1887 he discovered an unusual meteorite in Durango, Mexico, and from that time his chief interest centered on meteorites. His general natural history collection shown at the World's Columbian Exposition in 1893, was bought by Marshall Field to become the nucleus of the Field Museum of Natural History.

A second marriage, on Mar. 18, 1897, six years after the death of his first wife, to Mrs. Lydia (Avery) Coonley [see Lydia Arms Avery Coonley Ward], gave him financial backing to further his interest, and the meteorite collection grew. Notable exploits in the assembling of this collection were the securing of a specimen from the Shah of Persia and one from the government of Colombia. All his life a brilliant and pleasing conversationalist he was his own best agent. But Ward not only collected, he studied, and his catalogues of meteorites contain most valuable information as to exact localities—a knowledge necessary in determining whether or not a group is a single fall. His last great collection of meteorites (also in the Field Museum) contains representatives of more falls than any other collection ever made. He had just finished preparations for another expedition across South America, when he was killed by an automobile in Buffalo, N. Y. His death cut short a valuable work of three volumes describing his meteorite collection and dealing with the subject in general. He was cremated and his ashes rest in Mount Hope Cemetery, Rochester, N. Y. He was survived by his widow and the four children of his first wife.

[Who's Who in America, 1906–07; G. K. Ward, Andrew Warde and His Descendants (rev. ed., 1910); G. W. Chapin, The Chapin Book (1924), vol. I; A. H. Strong, Henry A. Ward, Reminiscences and Appreciation, Rochester Hist. Soc. Pubs. (1922); W. T. Hornaday, "The King of Museum Builders," Commercial Travelers Mag., Feb. 1896, and "A Great Museum Builder," Nation, July 12, 1906; O. C. Farrington, obit. article in Science, Aug. 3, 1906; R. H. Ward, "Mammoths and Meteors," Rochester Democrat and Chronicle (Sunday ed.), Sept. 17–Oct. 29, 1933; Ibid., July 5, 1906.]
W.G.

WARD, HENRY DANA (Jan. 13, 1797–Feb. 29, 1884), reformer, Adventist, Episcopal clergyman, seventh of ten children of Thomas Walter and Elizabeth (Denny) Ward, was born at Shrewsbury, Mass. His father, the third son of Gen. Artemas Ward [q.v.], served in the Revolutionary War and later was sheriff of Worcester

County, Mass. Henry Dana Ward was graduated (B.A.) from Harvard in 1816 and received the degree of M.A. in 1819. He married as his first wife Abigail Porter Jones, daughter of Samuel Jones of Lebanon Springs, N. Y. She died Dec. 23, 1837.

Ward's first reform activity to bring him out of obscurity was in the Anti-Masonic movement. In the year 1828 he wrote an appeal to his brother Masons, a kindly yet deadly attack on the order, entitled *Free Masonry: Its Pretensions Exposed in Faithful Extracts of Its Standard Authors; with A Review of Town's Speculative Masonry . . . by a Master Mason.* In the same year he began to publish a monthly, the *Anti-Masonic Review and Magazine,* in New York. He traveled from state to state with religious zeal stirring up opposition to Masonry; he was one of the outstanding agitators present when the Anti-Masonic party was organized in Vermont, Aug. 5, 1829; and he was present at the Massachusetts and New York conventions the same year. The following year he was among the leaders in the Rhode Island convention and associated with such men as Thurlow Weed and William H. Seward in the national organization of the party.

After the recession of the Anti-Masonic movement, Ward became much interested in the Adventist movement led by William Miller [*q.v.*], and in October 1840 was elected chairman of the General Conference of Christians Expecting the Advent of the Lord Jesus Christ, held in Boston. His published address on this occasion shows him to have been a student of both history and theology (*The First Report of the General Conference of Christians . . .* 1841). He did not accept Miller's reckoning as to the date of Christ's expected return to earth—Oct. 22, 1844—and was opposed to the attempt to fix a definite date, but contented himself with the belief that Christ's return in person would be the next event in the fulfillment of prophecy. As time passed he became inactive in the movement, although he apparently remained an Adventist in belief all his life.

In 1844 he was ordained to the Protestant Episcopal ministry by the bishop of Rhode Island, and soon afterward became rector of a small parish in Kanawha County, Va. (now W. Va.), where he ministered for two or three years. In Virginia he married his second wife, Charlotte Galbraith, daughter of Richard and Rebecca (Allen) Galbraith and a member of a Scotch-Irish family from Dublin. Struggling to support a growing family, he moved to New York City about 1848 and established a girls' school. For

about two years in the early fifties he was rector of St. Jude's Church, New York, but most of his time was given to teaching, in New York or Flushing, L. I., until about 1868, when he retired and moved to Philadelphia. Here he lived in a modest fashion until his death. His later days were occupied in religious studies and writing. Among his works were: *The Gospel of the Kingdom* (1870), *The History of the Cross* (1871), and *The Faith of Abraham and of Christ* (1872). Stricken with paralysis while walking on the streets of Philadelphia, he died the same day. He was buried in Shrewsbury, Mass.

Ward had three sons and one daughter; one son died in infancy, the others attained some distinction—Artemas as an advertising man and the publisher of *The Grocer's Encyclopedia* (1911), and Henry Galbraith as a federal judge.

[I. C. Wellcome, *Hist. of the Second Advent Message and Mission* (1874); M. E. Olsen, *A Hist. of the Origin and Progress of Seventh-day Adventists* (1925); Charles McCarthy, "The Antimasonic Party," *Ann. Report of the Am. Hist. Asso. . . . 1902* (1903), vol. I; Charles Martyn, *The William Ward Geneal.* (1925); *Jour. of the Proc. of the One-Hundredth Conv. of the Protestant Episcopal Church in the Diocese of Pa.* (1884); *Phila. Press,* Mar. 1, 1884.]   E. N. D.

WARD, HERBERT DICKINSON (June 30, 1861–June 18, 1932), author and publicist, was born in Waltham, Mass., the only child of Ellen Maria (Dickinson) and William Hayes Ward [*q.v.*], and the descendant of William Ward who emigrated from England about 1638 and settled in Sudbury, Mass. The boy's earliest memories were of Utica, N. Y., and Ripon, Wis., where his father was teaching. About 1868 the family settled in Newark, N. J. His mother, whose health had long been frail, died in 1873, and his father's two unmarried sisters continued to live with the family and direct the household. Under the watchful eyes of parents and aunts the boy was brought up in what he later called the "Spartan Puritan" tradition. Gray's *Elegy,* repeated by his father until the child knew it by heart, was his Mother Goose. At the age of seven he was encouraged to begin the study of Hebrew, while for modern languages he was sent abroad twice for periods of schooling in Germany and Switzerland. A final year at Phillips Academy at Andover prepared him to enter Amherst College, his father's college, where he graduated with the class of 1884. Though he had become a more ardent collector of minerals than candidate for the ministry, he agreed, at his father's insistence, to complete a theological course before deciding on a profession. Accordingly, after a year of teaching at Catawba College, Newton, N. C., he spent two years at Union Theological Seminary and a year at the Theological Seminary at Andover, supporting himself in part by writing Sunday-school lessons and conducting the Biblical research department for the *Independent*. He was licensed to preach but never ordained.

Though a man of unusual cultivation and markedly original views, he never overcame the handicap of being the son of a notable father and the husband of a famous wife. The decisive event of his year at Andover was his meeting there with Elizabeth Stuart Phelps (see sketch of Elizabeth Stuart Phelps Ward), whom he married, despite her seventeen years' advantage in age, on Oct. 20, 1888. The couple lived in Newton Center, Mass., and Ward became active in the literary and social life of Boston. In collaboration with his wife he wrote three novels, *A Lost Hero* (1891), *Come Forth* (1891), and the *Master of the Magicians* (1890), of which the last, an historical romance of ancient Babylon, was chiefly his own work. He also wrote independently several novels and collections of short stories, of which the most important were *A Republic without a President* (1891), *The White Crown* (1894), *The Burglar Who Moved Paradise* (1897), and *The Light of the World* (1901). His friendship with Daniel S. Ford, owner and editor of the *Youth's Companion,* and with Edwin A. Grozier of the *Boston Post* led him to contribute religious articles and editorials to both publications. He joined the staff of the *Post* for a year about 1899; with the *Youth's Companion* he had no official connection. He served as a member of the Massachusetts prison commission from 1891 to 1901. After his wife's death, he made his home chiefly in South Berwick, Me., in a house inherited from his paternal grandmother. He married, on Dec. 27, 1916, Edna J. Jeffress of Edwardsville, Ill., by whom he had one daughter. The last years of his life were occupied with publicity writing and social work. During the "Liberty Loan" drives he was a publicity agent for the federal treasury department, and later he was attached to the Italian embassy at Washington in a similar capacity. After some ten years of virtual retirement he died in the hospital at Portsmouth, N. H.

[Autobiog. material in his article "My Father," *Independent,* Dec. 28, 1918; *Amherst College Biog. Record* (1929); *Amherst Grads. Quart.,* Aug. 1932; *Who's Who in America,* 1924–25; Charles Martyn, *The Wm. Ward Geneal.* (1925), esp. pp. 271, 394; *N. Y. Times,* June 20, 1932.]   G. F. W.

WARD, JAMES EDWARD (Feb. 25, 1836–July 23, 1894), shipowner, was born in New York City, the son of James Otis and Martha T. (Dame) Ward, and a descendant of William Ward who settled in Sudbury, Mass., about 1638. James Otis Ward had moved from his father's farm near Roxbury, Mass., to New York City, where he became a ship chandler on South Street and soon acquired an interest in numerous sailing vessels, thus beginning the long association of the family name with the Cuban trade. He died in 1855, and the following year the business was reorganized in his son's name, as James E. Ward & Company, with Henry P. Booth and Samuel C. Shepherd as silent partners. Ward soon turned over the chandlery business to his younger brother, George Edgar Ward, and the firm, with its offices and piers at the foot of Wall Street on East River, devoted itself to shipping. By 1875, it owned some forty sailing vessels and occasionally also chartered steamers for the Cuban trade. Some of the Ward vessels ran with sufficient regularity to be termed packets, but the principal business was general freighting to Cuba similar to that later developed by Walter D. Munson [*q.v.*]. The chief freight from New York consisted of flour, potatoes, pork products, papers, hardware, and machinery, while the return cargoes, in addition to the all-important sugar, included tobacco and fruit.

The celebrated Ward Line really dates from 1877, when the firm instituted direct passenger and mail service to Havana. Their chief competitors at this time were the lines of Francis Alexandre & Sons and William P. Clyde & Sons, but the latter group soon restricted its activity to the coastal trade. Ward and his associates, in beginning the new enterprise, sold their sailing vessels to pay for the *Niagara* and the *Saratoga,* iron steamships of about 2,300 tons, built for them by John Roach [*q.v.*] at Chester, Pa., and rated as the finest then under the American flag. The *Saratoga* was subsequently sold to Russia for use as a cruiser and Roach built a second vessel of that name in 1878. Continued additions gave the Ward Line the heaviest tonnage among American lines in foreign service. In 1881 it was incorporated, with a capital of $2,300,000, as the New York & Cuba Mail Steam-ship Company; this has remained its official name. Booth was president, W. H. T. Hughes secretary-treasurer, and Ward apparently chairman of the board and guiding spirit.

Serious competition developed in the later eighties. Henry B. Plant [*q.v.*] in 1886 connected Havana with the new railroad to Tampa by a small, fast steamer which secured a mail contract worth $58,000 a year, leaving the Ward Line barely $1,300. Shortly afterwards, the Compañía Transatlantica Española, backed by a heavy Spanish subsidy, entered the New York-Havana run. This was apparently too much for the Alexandre line, which went out of business in 1888, selling a number of steamships to the Ward Line, which also took over its Mexican service to Progreso, Tampico, and Vera Cruz. The new competition resulted in the reduction of freight rates from $5 to $1.60 a ton and first-class passenger rates from $60 to as little as $35, and forced the Ward Line to omit dividends for two years. Ward claimed and gained considerable credit for keeping the American flag afloat in the merchant marine when he could have operated more cheaply with foreign bottoms. He was a strong supporter of the American Shipping and Industrial League, formed to lobby for merchant-marine relief, and the Ward Line, represented by Hughes, was prominent in the hearings which led to the Postal Aid Act, approved Mar. 3, 1891. Under this act the Ward Line received a subsidy of one dollar a mile, or about $200,000 a year.

At Ward's death in 1894 his line had ten iron or steel ships with a total tonnage of about 30,-000. In 1907, it was the largest of the six companies combined in the short-lived holding company of Charles W. Morse [q.v.], and upon Morse's failure, it was combined in 1908 with the Mallory, Clyde and Porto Rico lines in another holding company headed by Henry R. Mallory, but it retained its autonomous identity. Ward had married, Oct. 1, 1857, Harriet A. Morrill, who died in 1885. Of their three children only one daughter reached maturity. Ward died of Bright's disease, at his summer home at Great Neck, L. I., after an illness of several months. His portrait indicates a certain resemblance to Grover Cleveland, with a solid build, black moustache, and a frank, keen expression of the eyes behind rimmed spectacles.

[Charles Martyn, *The William Ward Geneal.* (1925); *Sen. Ex. Doc. 54,* 51 Cong., 1 Sess.; *House Report 1210,* 51 Cong., 1 Sess.; J. H. Morrison, *The Hist. of Am. Steam Navigation* (1903); W. L. Marvin, *The Am. Merchant Marine* (1902); G. M. Jones, *Govt. Aid to Merchant Shipping* (1925); *Wilson's N. Y. City Copartnership Directory,* 1856–84; *The Trow Copartnership and Corporation Directory . . . of N. Y.,* 1885 ff.; obituaries in *N. Y. Daily Tribune, Evening Post* (N. Y.), and *N. Y. Times,* July 24, 1894.]   R. G. A.

WARD, JAMES HARMON (Sept. 25, 1806–June 27, 1861), naval officer and author, was born in Hartford, Conn., the son of James and Ruth (Butler) Ward and the descendant of Andrew Warde, an English emigrant who died in Fairfield, Conn., about 1659. In 1823 he was graduated from the American Literary Scientific and Military Academy at Norwich, Vt., later Norwich University, and on Mar. 4, 1823, was appointed a midshipman in the navy. The following year he sailed on the *Constitution* for the Mediterranean, where he remained for four years.

On his return he entered Washington College (now Trinity) at Hartford, where he spent a year in scientific study. On Apr. 11, 1833, he married Sarah Whittemore. They had three sons. His subsequent service took him to the Mediterranean again, the coast of Africa, and the West Indies. He was one of the most scholarly officers in his service and was a recognized authority on ordnance and naval tactics. In 1844–45 he delivered a popular course of lectures on ordnance at the naval school at Philadelphia, which he published as *An Elementary Course of Instruction on Ordnance and Gunnery* (1845). This book became widely known and exerted a real influence on the improvement of naval science. In 1852 it was officially adopted as a textbook at the Naval Academy at Annapolis. He urged upon the government the necessity of establishing a naval school, and when the naval school, later the Naval Academy, was opened at Annapolis in October 1845 he was appointed to be executive officer, a post soon designated as commandant of midshipmen. He also acted as head of the department of ordnance and gunnery. Detached in 1847, he commanded the *Cumberland,* Matthew C. Perry's flagship on the Mexican coast, during the remainder of the war. In 1856 and 1857, while cruising in the *Jamestown* off the African coast, he wrote *A Manual of Naval Tactics* (1859), a scholarly work that ran into four editions. In 1860 he published a popular treatise on steam, called *Steam for the Million.*

When the Civil War broke out, he, then a commander, was stationed at the Brooklyn Navy Yard. Gideon Welles summoned him to Washington to plan for the rescue of Sumter. He volunteered to command a relief expedition but was finally convinced by General Scott that such an expedition would be futile. He proposed a "flying flotilla" for use on Chesapeake Bay and the Potomac River. His idea was accepted and in May he was given command of a small fleet called the Potomac Flotilla, consisting of three steamers, the *Thomas Freeborn,* the *Reliance,* and the *Resolute,* and three coast survey schooners. On June 1 he silenced the Confederate batteries at Aquia Creek. On June 27, in an attempt to dislodge another battery at Matthias Point, he sent a working party ashore to throw up breastworks. As it was returning to the boats it was attacked by a large hostile force. Covering the embarkation with the guns of his fleet, he was shot in the abdomen as he was in the act of sighting the bowgun of the *Thomas Freeborn.* He died within an hour. His body was taken to Hartford, where it was buried with the rites of the Roman Catholic Church.

[Archives of the Office of Naval Records and Lib., Navy Department; *War of Rebellion: Official Records (Navy)*, 1 ser., vols. IV–VI; *Battles and Leaders of the Civil War*, vol. II (1888); *Diary of Gideon Welles* (1911), vols. I, II; *Norwich Univ.* (1911), vol. II, ed. by W. A. Ellis; J. R. Soley, *Hist. Sketch of the U. S. Naval Acad.* (1876), pp. 62–63; *U. S. Naval Inst. Proc.*, vol. LXI (1935); G. K. Ward, *Andrew Warde and His Descendants* (1910); *N. Y. Tribune,* July 1–3, 1861; *Daily Morning Jour. and Courier* (New Haven), June 29, July 1, 2, 1861; spelling of middle name from grandson, James H. Ward, Berrien Springs, Mich.]

L. H. B.

WARD, JAMES WARNER (June 5, 1816– June 28, 1897), author, librarian, was born at Newark, N. J., son of William and Sara (Warner) Ward. He attended the Boston public schools until he was fourteen, when he began business as a freight checker in a shipping house in Salem, Mass. In 1834 he went to Columbus, Ohio, and opened a school. At nineteen he married Roxanna Wyman Blake, who bore him a son and a daughter. After the death of his wife in 1844, he moved to Cincinnati, where he became a pupil of and later assistant to Prof. John Locke [*q.v.*] of the Medical College of Ohio. In 1851 he was elected professor of general literature and botany in the Ohio Female College, situated in College Hill, seven miles north of Cincinnati. On June 29, 1848, he married Catherine McClyment Lea, daughter of John and Catherine (McClyment) Lea of Cincinnati, and a niece of Henry Charles Lea [*q.v.*], the historian. Ward left the Ohio Female College in 1854 and for a year, in association with Dr. John A. Warder [*q.v.*], edited the *Horticultural Review and Botanical Magazine* in Cincinnati. In 1859 he moved to New York City, where he spent the next fifteen years first as clerk, later as deputy auditor in the customs house. In July 1874 he began a card catalogue of the Grosvenor Library in Buffalo. The library had been given its charter in 1859, was opened in 1870, and by 1874 had a book collection of 17,900; the staff consisted of two, the librarian and his assistant. Ward became librarian on Oct. 1, 1874, and began twenty-one years of efficient service in which he brought the library from its infancy to a position of real eminence. The first modern inventory was taken in 1876, and the gaps in the collections were filled out. Ward was one of the first members of the American Library Association, organized in 1876, and took part in technical discussions as reported in the *Library Journal*. He had active supervision, together with the architect, of the details of construction of the present building of the Grosvenor Library, which in 1895 superseded the rented quarters. At that time the book collection numbered 38,000, a large collection for the day. Ward retired, Jan. 15, 1896,

and spent the winter in Worcester, Mass., and in the South, returning to Buffalo, where he died at his home, June 28, 1897, aged eighty-one years. He was survived by his wife.

Ward took an active interest in music, art, and the natural sciences, especially astronomy, botany, and microscopy. He contributed papers on these subjects to the journals of the day, composed for the voice and organ, and was the author of much poetry. In 1852 he wrote a poem entitled *Woman,* originally prepared for the Young Men's Mercantile Library Association of Cincinnati, which was revised and read for the graduating exercises of the Ohio Female College, July 17, 1852, and published by the college. In 1857 was published a volume of poems, *Home Made Verses and Stories in Rhyme,* which were usually signed "Yorick," and in 1868 *Higher Water,* a parody on *Hiawatha* describing a stream of the Ohio River. Ward is perhaps best known in the world of books as editor of A. W. Sangster's *Niagara River and Falls from Lake Erie to Lake Ontario* (1886), a series of etchings with an accompanying text which includes a poem, "To Niagara," by Ward. He was a member of several microscopical societies and of the Torrey Botanical Club.

[Sources include J. H. and G. H. Lea, *The Ancestry . . . of John Lea* (1906), from which the date of birth is taken; Grosvenor Lib. records; correspondence with Ward's family; early Buffalo and N. Y. directories; surrogate's records, Erie County, N. Y.; *Bull. Torrey Botanical Club,* Nov. 1873; preface to *Woman* (1852); obituaries in *Buffalo Express, Buffalo Evening News,* and *Buffalo Commercial,* June 30, 1897; interviews with friends of Ward.]

A. H. S.

WARD, JOHN ELLIOTT (Oct. 2, 1814– Nov. 29, 1902), lawyer, politician, diplomat, was born at Sunbury, Liberty County, Ga. His father, William Ward, was a member of the Midway colony of Puritans from Massachusetts which settled in Liberty County before the Revolutionary War. Through his mother, Anne (McIntosh) Ward, he was a descendant of John McIntosh Mohr, who led a clan of Scottish Highlanders to Georgia in General Oglethorpe's time. Ward entered Amherst College in 1831, but left because of a prejudice against Georgians existing at that time. He attended law lectures at Harvard, studied under Dr. Matthew Hall McAllister [*q.v.*] in Savannah, and was admitted to the bar by special act of legislature in 1835 before he was twenty-one.

Early in the following year he was appointed solicitor-general for the eastern district of Georgia, and served until 1838 when he became United States district attorney for Georgia. He resigned in 1839 to enter the Georgia legislature, to which he was again elected in 1845 and

1853, serving as speaker in 1853–54. In 1857 he was made president of the state Senate and acting lieutenant-governor. He is credited with being more responsible than any other person for the final breaking down of the traditional prejudices between up-country Georgians and Savannah representatives in the legislature, even though he led the opposition against the popular bank-control measures of Gov. Joseph E. Brown [q.v.]. Meanwhile, in 1852, reluctant to leave an extensive law practice in Savannah, he had declined the offer of appointment to the United States Senate tendered him by Gov. Howell Cobb [q.v.]. In 1854 he was elected mayor of Savannah, and during his term was so successful in dealing with the great yellow-fever epidemic on the one hand, and in carrying out thorough political and police reforms on the other, that he was offered the renomination without opposition; this, however, he declined.

At Cincinnati in 1856 he was president of the National Democratic Convention which nominated Buchanan. In December 1858 President Buchanan appointed him envoy extraordinary and minister plenipotentiary to China, his particular mission being to exchange ratifications of the new American treaty with China and to settle outstanding American claims. Because of his determined refusal to kotow he was unable to effect a direct exchange of ratifications with the emperor. "I kneel only to God and woman," he declared (Martin, post, p. 200). He accomplished his mission, however, in a manner entirely satisfactory to President Buchanan. He also won the hearty appreciation of his European colleagues in China by his intelligent and friendly cooperation, but he was not blind to certain high-handed tactics on the part of some of them, and he denounced the infamous coolie trade which was carried on for foreign firms by American ships.

He left China on Dec. 15, 1860, arriving home in the opening days of the Civil War. Bitterly disappointed at the secession of Georgia, he took no part in the hostilities, and in January 1866 removed to New York City, where he engaged in the private practice of law. In 1902, a few weeks before his death, he returned to Liberty County, where he died at Dorchester in his eighty-ninth year. He married in 1839 Olivia Buckminster Sullivan, daughter of William Sullivan of Boston; eight children were born to them.

[For sources see I. W. Avery, *The Hist. of the State of Ga. from 1850 to 1881* (1881); W. J. Northen, *Men of Mark in Ga.*, vol. II (1910); W. A. P. Martin, *A Cycle of Cathay* (1896); *Who's Who in America*, 1901–02; *Savannah Morning News*, Dec. 1, 1902;

Ward's official correspondence is in archives of the U. S. Dept. of State, Washington, D. C., parts of it having been published in "Correspondence and Dispatches of the Ministers to China," *Sen. Ex. Doc. 30*, 36 Cong., 1 Sess. (1860), and in "Chinese Coolie Trade," *House Ex. Doc. 88*, 36 Cong., 1 Sess. (1860); President Buchanan's third annual message, giving account of Ward's mission to China is in *A Compilation of the Messages and Papers of the Presidents*, vol. VII (1897).]   I. L. T.

WARD, JOHN QUINCY ADAMS (June 29, 1830–May 1, 1910), sculptor, born on the Ward homestead near Urbana, Ohio, was one of the seven children of John Anderson and Eleanor (Macbeth) Ward, and a grandson of Col. William Ward, who in 1805 laid out and named the town of Urbana. His earliest ancestor of American record is said to have been John Ward of Norfolk, England, who landed at Jamestown, Va., in the first half of the seventeenth century. For two centuries thereafter, the Ward family took an important part in conquering the wilderness. As a boy Ward delighted not only in fishing and hunting, but also in making clay images of men on horseback and of the farm animals, often working in the shop of the village potter. The meager education then obtainable in Ohio schools was at times eked out by lessons from private tutors. At the age of sixteen he was put at work on the farm, in tasks he disliked. He milked cows, but he wanted to model horses. Seeing his unfitness for farming, his Presbyterian parents vaguely hoped that he might become a doctor or a minister, and let him study medicine a while. His health suffered. A fortunate visit to his sister in Brooklyn, N. Y., proved the turning-point in his life. In Brooklyn, at nineteen, Ward realized his dearest hope and began work in the studio of Henry Kirke Brown [q.v.]. No better training could have been devised. Student, helper, companion, he remained seven years under a genial, broad-minded master, who in 1854 carved "J. Q. A. Ward, Asst." on the base of an equestrian statue of Washington, a work still deemed one of the best in the country. While with Brown, Ward practised every craft used in sculpture; he worked in clay, plaster, marble, and even in bronze. He helped in the chasing and riveting of the Washington equestrian. "I spent more days inside that horse," he said, "than Jonah did inside the whale." He passed two winters (c. 1857–59) in Washington, D. C., where he made busts of Alexander H. Stephens, Joshua Giddings, Senator John Parker Hale, Hannibal Hamlin. His success in creating small objects to be cast in precious metal was such that in 1861 the Ames Company, founders of Brown's equestrian, engaged him to design and model the costly hilts for the presentation swords then in demand, as well as cane tops, table bells, pistol mountings. That year he opened a studio in New York, the city where he was to live and work for half a century.

Among the first statues to be placed in New York's Central Park, and one of the best to be found there today, was Ward's "Indian Hunter," a lithe figure striding forward with bow and arrows, and holding back an eager dog (1868). This work had been conceived as a statuette in 1857. For further study, Ward spent months among the Indians of the Northwest. In 1861 he modeled his popular statuette, "The Freedman," cast in bronze in 1865, an authentic figure of a negro, seated, looking very quietly at the shackles from which he had been released. From childhood Ward well knew both Indian and negro types. His "Reminiscent Sketch of a Boyhood Friend," printed in the *Times-Citizen* of Urbana, Ohio, in 1908, is a beautifully written tribute to "Uncle Cæsar," a negro. Both "Indian Hunter" and "Freedman" were shown in the Paris Exposition of 1867. When exhibited in New York, the "Hunter" met the approving eye of August Belmont, who at once gave the artist a commission for a bronze statue of his father-in-law, Matthew Calbraith Perry [*q.v.*], unveiled at Newport, R. I., in 1868. Thereafter Ward never lacked commissions. For Boston's Public Gardens he had already made a granite group called the "Good Samaritan," commemorating the first use of ether as anesthetic. The 7th Regiment Memorial, a heroic bronze figure of a Civil War soldier on a high granite pedestal, was signed by Ward in 1869, and was placed in Central Park four years afterward. In 1872 his statue of Gen. John F. Reynolds was unveiled at Gettysburg, Pa. Two years later, at Hartford, Conn., appeared his statue of the Revolutionary hero, Gen. Israel Putnam. In 1870 he made for Central Park a bronze figure of Shakespeare in doublet, hose, and short cloak, a book in his hand, his attitude pensive. All these works showed the sculptor's solidity of structure and his technical mastery; but the finer flowering of his genius was yet to come.

His equestrian monument to Gen. George H. Thomas, "the Rock of Chickamauga," aroused great enthusiasm when unveiled at Washington, D. C., in 1878. There were those who criticized the easy pose, the loose rein, but Ward had made deliberate choice of both as characteristic of Thomas. In 1879 came his statue of William Gilmore Simms, for Charleston, S. C., and two years later, at Spartanburg, S. C., his Gen. Daniel Morgan, picturesque Revolutionary fighter. With two other figures of Revolutionary heroes,

Ward reached the midmost of his career and almost attained the zenith of his art. His statue of the elderly Lafayette, represented as at the period of his historic visit to the United States in 1824–25, was unveiled at Burlington, Vt., in the summer of 1883. In the autumn of the same year, his "Washington" was erected on the steps of the sub-Treasury in Wall Street, near the scene of the first inauguration. It is a quiet, commanding figure, clad in the civilian costume of 1789, enhanced by a cloak which, together with the upright fasces, solidifies a nobly simple composition. Many critics consider this not only the finest work by Ward but also the consummate monumental representation of Washington—this even when bearing in mind Houdon's famous statue.

Ward's "Pilgrim," placed in Central Park by the New England Society (1885), appeared two years before the Saint-Gaudens "Puritan" was unveiled at Springfield, Mass. Contrasts and comparisons naturally occur to mind yet without discredit to either sculptor. If the Bible-clasping Puritan is the more dramatic performance, Ward's well-armed and well-booted Pilgrim in stout buff-leather has its own austere authenticity, unemphasized by melodrama. Again, comparisons are often drawn between Ward's "Horace Greeley," vivid and active in his fringed arm-chair in front of the old Tribune Building, New York (1890), and Saint-Gaudens' equally whiskered "Peter Cooper," enthroned like a Renaissance prince in front of Cooper Union. Each artist created an admirable characterization of his sitter. Ward, both from circumstance and by choice, gave his subject no delightful adventitious architectural adornments.

A more elaborate production is the Gen. James A. Garfield monument in Washington (1887). The bronze figure of Garfield surmounts a stone pedestal adorned by three vigorous male figures in bronze, "Student," "Warrior," "Statesman," symbolizing three phases of Garfield's life. A decade earlier Ward had encircled the cupola of the capitol at Hartford, Conn., with emblematic figures; a decade later he was to contribute a colossal figure of "Poetry" for the rotunda of the Library of Congress. His forte, however, lay in realistic rather than in idealized representation. He preferred masculine themes. Of special importance is his Henry Ward Beecher monument, erected in front of Borough Hall, Brooklyn, N. Y. (1891). The commanding solidity of the preacher's figure in the well-known Inverness overcoat is at once stressed and humanized by a lyric quality, unusual with Ward, seen in the two pedestal compositions; one shows a negro girl placing a palm at Beecher's feet, the other, two children bringing a garland of oak leaves. Other prominent personages in New York life commemorated in bronze statues by Ward were W. E. Dodge, W. H. Fogg, Roscoe Conkling, August Belmont. Among his many portrait busts in bronze or marble are those of Dr. Valentine Mott, Orville H. Dewey, James T. Brady, Col. E. F. Shepard, W. H. Vanderbilt, Abraham Coles, Joseph Drexel, Gov. Horace Fairbanks, George W. Curtis, Alexander Lyman Holley, and William W. Corcoran.

Noted productions of Ward's final decade include the Stock Exchange pediment, New York (1903), the Soldiers and Sailors monument, Syracuse, N. Y. (1907), the General Sheridan equestrian, Albany, N. Y., and the Major General Hancock equestrian, placed in Fairmount Park, Philadelphia, two years after the sculptor's death. In the first and last of these works he had the able collaboration of Paul Bartlett. A lifetime of study, skill, and experience is garnered up in the vast pediment of the Stock Exchange; Ward's design, beautifully in harmony with his own outlook on life, makes Integrity the central motive, irradiating a sculptured world of the various activities dear and necessary to man. As to the details of the Hancock equestrian, Ward and Bartlett were sometimes at friendly variance, but Ward, the better horseman, was usually right. This work filled his mind during his last days: after a colleague chosen to inspect it had brought back a good report, he said, "Now I can go in peace."

In American art he was a unique figure, of a kind that will not occur again. He brought primitive Ohio vigor to sophisticated New York and set it to work there. He was a born leader and organizer, with the true pathfinder's instinct. Made a member of the National Academy of Design in 1863, he became its president in 1874, whereupon, undaunted by an honor never before given to a sculptor, he warned that body against "dropping into a conceited security." "Give the younger man a chance" was a well-known saying of his. No worthy enterprise in art ever lacked his support. On the formation of the National Sculpture Society, he was acclaimed its president. In 1899, when the society and the city in collaboration erected New York's sculptured arch of welcome to Admiral Dewey, he was the head and front of the actual work, spurring the sculptors to their highest endeavor. His own contribution was the so-called quadriga crowning the arch, "Naval Victory" in her sea chariot drawn by six sea horses, a group of brilliant distinction.

Ward's art was peculiarly American. He was the first native sculptor to create, without benefit of foreign training, an impressive body of good work. In youth he had stood awestruck before Powers' "Greek Slave"; arrived at man's estate, he found himself wholly out of sympathy with the mid-Victorian pseudo-classic ideals fostered in Florence and Rome. "Emasculate!" he cried. He traveled in Europe but never lived or worked there. He nevertheless admired the strength and sincerity of the French school of sculpture dominant in the latter part of the nineteenth century. Strength and sincerity were among his own gifts. Every one who met him was impressed by his virility, his integrity, his devotion to art. Numerous organizations, from academies to zoölogical societies, claimed his membership, sought his counsel, and gave him honors. He belonged to the American Academy of Arts and Letters; he was a trustee of the American Academy in Rome and one of the founders of the Metropolitan Museum of Art. His speeches and writings had style. He had his convictions, his prejudices. He was a good friend and, if need arose, a great fighter, one who well knew when, where, and how to show wrath. "Quincy Ward wasn't redheaded for nothing." His strong bodily frame matched his mind. His friends often said that he looked like a less gnarled, less saddened Michelangelo. About 1858 he married Anna, daughter of John and Rebecca (Noyes) Bannan. She died in 1870. His second wife, Julia, daughter of Charles and Julia (Devens) Valentine, lived but a year after their marriage in 1878. In 1906 Ward married Rachel Smith, a widow, daughter of Simon and Jane (Lefevre) Ostrander of Newburg, N. Y. He died at his home in New York, leaving a widow but no children, and is buried at Urbana, where a replica of the Indian Hunter marks his grave.

[Sources are *Who's Who in America*, 1908–09; *Who's Who in N. Y.*, 1909; Lorado Taft, *The Hist. of Am. Sculpture* (1903); C. H. Caffin, *Am. Masters of Sculpture* (1903); G. W. Sheldon, in *Harper's New Monthly Mag.*, June 1878; Russell Sturgis, in *Scribner's Mag.*, Oct. 1902; Edna M. Clark, *Ohio Art and Artists* (1932); Montgomery Schuyler, in *Putnam's Mag.*, Sept. 1909; William Walton, in *International Studio*, June 1910; Adeline Adams, *John Quincy Adams Ward, an Appreciation* (1912); obituaries in *N. Y. Times*, *N. Y. Tribune*, May 2, 1910, editorial in *Times*, May 3; information from Mrs. Ward; personal acquaintance. The name of Ward's first wife is sometimes given as Bauman or Bamman.]   A. A.

WARD, JOSEPH (May 5, 1838–Dec. 11, 1889), pioneer Congregational clergyman and educator of South Dakota, was born at Perry Centre, N. Y., the son of Dr. Jabez and Aurilla (Tufts) Ward, and a descendant of William

Ward who settled at Sudbury, Mass., about 1638. Joseph grew up in a community dominated by New England traditions, and in a home strongly influenced by religion. After attending the public schools of his locality, he tried his hand at teaching and at farming for a time, and then entered Phillips Academy, Andover, where he was graduated in 1861. That same year he matriculated at Brown University. His college course was interrupted by service in the Union army but sickness intervened and sent him back to his studies, although his summer vacations were spent with the United States Christian Commission. He graduated from Brown in 1865 and then spent three years at Andover Theological Seminary, an institution marked by a missionary spirit which did much to determine Ward's subsequent career. On Aug. 12, 1868, he married Sarah Frances Wood.

Accepting a missionary appointment at Yankton, then the capital of Dakota Territory, he was ordained there on Mar. 17, 1869. His activities in behalf of the religious and educational interests of the region were numerous and varied. Under his leadership the Congregational Association of Dakota was formed, and his influence over the Dakota missions was such that he may be regarded as the father of Congregationalism in Dakota. Owing to the fact that Yankton was not then a separate school district and there was no adequate provision for securing funds by taxation, it was practically impossible to maintain common schools. A few years before Ward's arrival, a public school supported by the enterprise of the Yankton women had been started, and to supplement its work Ward opened a private school. It had a larger growth than had been expected and in 1872 was formally converted into the Yankton Academy. Ward continued in charge of it until he began to promote the establishment of a college, at which time the academy was given over to public control and transformed into the Yankton high school, the earliest public high school in Dakota. Yankton College, the first institution of collegiate rank in the upper Mississippi Valley, the founding of which was largely the result of Ward's activities, was chartered Aug. 30, 1881, and the corner stone of its first building laid June 15, 1882. This institution he served as president and professor of mental and moral philosophy until his death.

He played a very conspicuous part in keeping the school lands of the Territory out of the hands of Eastern speculators, and the education law of South Dakota was almost wholly his work. Interested in every humanitarian enterprise, he

was largely instrumental in securing the establishment in 1879 of the Dakota Hospital for the Insane. In the struggle for statehood, also, he played a large part, especially in the formation of the Citizen's Constitutional Association, which brought about the constitutional convention at Sioux Falls in 1883. This convention, formed by direct authority of the people without authorization from the legislature or enabling act of Congress, framed a worthy organic law for the future state.

Spurning all chances for political advancement, Ward in his last years devoted himself to the service of Yankton College. In 1886 he became involved in a theological dispute over the possibility of future probation for those who died ignorant of Christ's teachings. Scornful of "institutional cowardice," he fought on what he considered the side of liberty, despite the fact that it threatened for a time to wreck the college. The storm soon passed and in 1887 Yankton College graduated its first class. A little more than two years later Ward died, the immediate cause of his death being blood poisoning occasioned by diabetes. He was survived by his wife and five children.

[G. H. Durand, *Joseph Ward of Dakota* (1913); W. J. McMurtry, *Yankton Coll.* (1907); Doane Robinson, *Hist. of S. Dak.* (2 vols., 1904); *Eighth Ann. Cat. of Yankton Coll.* (1890); *State of S. Dak.: First Ann. Report of the Supt. of Public Instruction* (1890); *Congregational Year-Book* (1890); *Andover Rev.*, Jan. 1890; *Advance*, Dec. 19, 1889; *Press and Dakotan* (Yankton), Dec. 19, 1889; Charles Martyn, *The William Ward Geneal.* (1925).]   E. I. S.

WARD, LESTER FRANK (June 18, 1841– Apr. 18, 1913), sociologist, was born in Joliet, Ill. His father, Justus Ward, was a mechanic of an inventive turn of mind; his mother, Silence (Rolph), daughter of a clergyman, is said to have been a woman of scholarly tendencies and versatile accomplishments. Frank was the youngest of ten children. During his early years, spent in Illinois and in Buchanan County, Iowa, to which place his parents moved in his boyhood, he lived in close contact with nature under frontier conditions. At the age of seventeen he went to Pennsylvania, where, at Myersburg, his brother, Cyrenus Osborne Ward [*q.v.*], later a labor leader, was then manufacturing wagon hubs. Beginning in 1861, he spent four terms at the Susquehanna Collegiate Institute at Towanda. In August 1862 he enlisted in the Union army and served until November 1864, when he was discharged on account of wounds received at Chancellorsville. On Aug. 13, 1862, just before his enlistment, he had married Elisabeth Carolyn Vought, by whom he had a son who lived less than a year; his wife died in 1872, and on Mar.

6, 1873, he married Rosamond Asenath Simons.

In 1865 he secured a position in the United States Treasury Department at Washington, with which he remained connected until 1881. Meanwhile, he studied at Columbian College (now George Washington University), from which he received the degree of A.B. in 1869, that of LL.B. in 1871, and that of A.M. in 1872. After leaving the Treasury Department he became assistant geologist in the United States Geological Survey. He was appointed geologist in 1883, and paleontologist in 1892. His chief contributions to the natural sciences include "Types of the Laramie Flora" (*Bulletin No. 37, 1887,* United States Geological Survey), *Status of the Mesozoic Floras of the United States* (1905), a monograph of the Survey, and various articles in its *Annual Reports.* The range of his interests was broad and included biology, anthropology, psychology, and sociology. He was an ardent advocate of the evolutionary hypothesis, and enlisted with enthusiasm in the conflict then waging between science and theology.

Valuable as are Ward's studies in the natural sciences, he is best known because of his leadership in the field of American sociology. Though others had written in this field in earlier years, he became the great pioneer of modern and evolutionary sociology in the United States, through the publication in 1883 of *Dynamic Sociology.* This was followed by *The Psychic Factors of Civilization* (1893); *Outlines of Sociology* (1898); *Pure Sociology* (1903); and *Applied Sociology* (copr. 1906). The last two are a restatement of his general teachings. The *Textbook of Sociology* (1905), by J. Q. Dealey and Ward, is mainly a condensation of the *Pure Sociology.*

Ward sought to give a strongly monistic and evolutionary interpretation to social development. Utilizing his broad background in the modern sciences, he vigorously argued that the human mind is a great factor in evolution. Its emotional, willing aspects have produced ambitious aspirations for individual and social improvement, and the intellect, when rightly informed with scientific truth, enables the individual or the social group to plan intelligently for future development. The mind, in other words, becomes "telic," thus enabling mankind to pass from passive to active evolutionary processes, and from natural to human or social evolution. This ability will usher in an age of systematic planning for human progress, an age in which government will stress social welfare and democracy will pass into "sociocracy."

Ward's point of view throughout is strongly democratic and humanitarian. He assumes wide differences in human heredity and racial aptitudes, yet argues that whatever talent or genius may be latent can be called forth by a stimulating social environment and a general education in the sciences, physical and social, with their applications. Even the mediocre, he taught, might be enabled to double or treble their attainments, if given an education suited to their mentality. Education and freedom from economic strain, he argued, are the essential bases for human progress. Governments, therefore, should aim gradually to abolish harsh poverty and to develop wise national systems of general education, suited in one aspect for genius, in another, for ordinary minds.

In 1906, desirous of greater leisure to prepare *Glimpses of the Cosmos* (6 vols., 1913–18), his "mental autobiography," Ward sought and obtained a call to the chair of sociology in Brown University. This chair he held for the remainder of his life. In *Glimpses of the Cosmos* he republished his minor writings in their biographical and historical background. It also contains a summary of what he considered to be his chief contribution to social philosophy.

In maturity Ward was six feet in height, blonde but sunburned from much outdoor life, athletic in build but slightly stoop-shouldered in old age. He enjoyed excellent health almost to the end of his life and even in his later years he was a tireless walker, geologizing and botanizing for his avocation. He lived simply. In manner he was unassuming, somewhat modest and retiring in disposition, but dignified in bearing. Even in his 'teens he was fond of languages. He studied Greek, Latin, and French with little outside help, and, in later years, German. For reading purposes he acquired some acquaintance with other languages, including Russian, Hebrew, and Japanese. He traveled widely over the United States and Europe and in 1903, as president of the Institut International de Sociologie, he presided over the deliberations of that learned body at the Sorbonne, Paris. He died in Washington, D. C.

[In addition to *Glimpses of the Cosmos,* see E. P. Cape, *Lester F. Ward, A Personal Sketch* (1922); H. W. Odum, *Am. Masters of Social Sci.* (copr. 1927); E. P. Kimball, *Sociology and Education: An Analysis of the Theories of Spencer and Ward* (1932); *Who's Who in America,* 1912–13; *The Cyc. of Am. Biogs.,* vol. VII (1903); *Brown Alumni Mo.,* Apr. 1906; *Am. Jour. of Sociology,* July, Sept. 1919; G. K. Ward, *Andrew Warde and His Descendants* (1910); *Evening Tribune* (Providence), Apr. 19, 1913. Ward's manuscript material, books, and letters are in the lib. of Brown University and the Lib. of Cong.; his diary, covering a period of over forty years, was destroyed by his heirs for personal reasons, but an earlier portion was preserved and, edited by B. J. Stern, was published as *Young Ward's Diary* (copr. 1935).]   J. Q. D.

WARD, LYDIA ARMS AVERY COON-LEY (Jan. 31, 1845–Feb. 26, 1924), author, was born at Lynchburg, Va., the daughter of Benjamin Franklin and Susan Howes (Look) Avery. She was a descendant of Christopher Avery who emigrated from England and settled in Salem, Mass., about 1630. Until her marriage in 1867 to John Clark Coonley and for a few years thereafter, her life was spent chiefly in Louisville, Ky. Removing to Chicago in 1873, she soon won a prominent place in the social and cultural life of that city. For nearly a quarter-century her home was a center of "light and leading" for all who were in any way identified with Chicago's higher interests, and for many distinguished visitors to the city as well. "In that home," wrote Jane Addams, "I first unfolded plans for founding a settlement in Chicago, and met with that ready sympathy and understanding which her adventuring and facile mind was always ready to extend to a new cause she believed to be righteous."

Her first husband died in 1882, and on Mar. 18, 1897, she was married to the scientist, Henry Augustus Ward [q.v.]. After about 1909, save for rather frequent periods of travel, she lived at Wyoming, N. Y., in which village the Avery family had maintained an ancestral summer residence for many decades. Here, as previously in Chicago, she kept a kind of "open house" for the world at large and, in particular, for young and struggling workers in the arts. Here, also, she organized an elaborate summer school, liberally attended sessions of which were held in 1914, 1916, and 1917. A beautiful community hall, dedicated in 1902, stands today in the village of Wyoming as a tangible expression of her generosity and public spirit.

Although she was a frequent contributor to various periodicals from about 1878 onward, her first book, *Under the Pines and Other Verses,* did not appear until 1895. This was followed by *Singing Verses for Children* (1897), *Love Songs* (1898), and in 1921 by a collected edition of her poems in three volumes entitled *The Melody of Life, The Melody of Love,* and *The Melody of Childhood.* She also wrote the words for Dr. George F. Root's cantata *Our Flag with the Stars and Stripes* (1896), and for several other musical compositions.

While a few of her poems are reprinted in some of the standard anthologies and have become widely known, her literary work was more of a recreational and ephemeral by-product than the chief concern of a life spent in untiring human service. She was one of those whose peculiar genius finds its most congenial expression in the exercise of direct inspirational influence through personal contact, and in this sphere she made a notable contribution to American life—a contribution which was vicariously reflected in the work of many men and women who became prominent in various cultural activities. She died in Chicago, survived by four of six children by her first husband.

[E. McK. and C. H. J. Avery, *The Groton Avery Clan* (1912); *Chronicles of an American Home* (1930), ed. by W. R. Browne; *Who's Who in America,* 1922–23; *Chicago Tribune,* Feb. 27, 1924.]   W. R. B.

WARD, MARCUS LAWRENCE (Nov. 9, 1812–Apr. 25, 1884), governor of New Jersey, congressman, philanthropist, was the son of Moses and Fanny (Brown) Ward. His paternal ancestor, John Ward, came with his widowed mother from England and settled in 1635 at Wethersfield, Conn.; in 1666 he became one of the founders of Newark, N. J. Here his descendant, Moses Ward, was for many years a successful manufacturer of candles, and here Moses' son Marcus was born. Educated in local private schools, he became a clerk in a variety store in Newark and later entered his father's establishment, becoming in time a partner in the firm of M. Ward & Son. In this connection he became widely known throughout the state and made a private fortune.

From his early years Ward took an interest in everything concerning his native city. He became a director in the National State Bank in Newark in 1846, was long chairman of the executive committee of the New Jersey Historical Society, and aided in the formation of the Newark Library Association and the New Jersey Art Union. In 1856 he first took an active part in politics, embracing with vigor the cause of the newly formed Republican party. Because of his intense anti-slavery convictions, he went to Kansas in 1858 to take part in the struggle against the admission of slavery there, but found too much mob violence for his taste, and soon returned to Newark and his business. In 1860 he was a delegate to the Republican convention at Chicago which nominated Abraham Lincoln for the presidency.

Soon after the outbreak of the Civil War he began to devise means to ameliorate the condition of the families of those New Jersey soldiers who by death or illness had left their wives and children destitute, and also the condition of such soldiers themselves as needed better hospital accommodations than the Government had prepared. With his own funds, and assuming direct oversight of the project, he took possession of a whole floor in the Newark Custom House, employed eight clerks, and there laid plans for carrying out his patriotic and benevolent ideas. He established a kind of free pension bureau, through which he secured soldiers' pay and transmitted it to their families. He founded a soldiers' hospital in his city—The Ward U. S. Hospital, the foundation of the later Soldiers' Home. In 1862 he consented to run as a Republican candidate for governor, but was defeated by the Democrat Joel Parker [q.v.]. He was a delegate in 1864 to the convention at Baltimore that renominated Lincoln; in the same year he became a member of the Republican National Committee, and continued as such until the nomination of General Grant for the presidency. In 1865 he was elected governor of New Jersey by a large majority. During his administration of three years (Jan. 16, 1866–Jan. 18, 1869) he secured the passage of a public-school law, an act eliminating partisanship in the control of the state prison, and other measures of reform. After a few years of retirement he was elected in 1872 representative in Congress from the sixth New Jersey district and served from Mar. 4, 1873, to Mar. 3, 1875. He was renominated in 1874, but was defeated in a Democratic tidal wave. Declining the federal office of commissioner of Indian affairs, he now retired to private life. After two trips to Europe he visited Florida, where he contracted the malarial fever which brought his death.

On June 30, 1840, Ward married Susan, daughter of John and Elizabeth (Longworth) Morris, by whom he had eight children; two sons, with their mother, survived him. The younger son, Marcus L. Ward, Jr., who outlived his brother, put the family fortune to a unique use by establishing at Maplewood, N. J., in memory of his father, the Ward Homestead, with accommodations for 120 bachelors and widowers who have been prominent in the business or social life of New Jersey and are over sixty-five years of age. The Homestead is like a large country club in appearance, and has a large endowment fund.

[M. D. Ogden, *Memorial Cyc. of N. J.*, vol. I (1915); W. H. Shaw, *Hist. of Essex and Hudson Counties, N. J.* (1884), vol. I; *The Biog. Encyc. of N. J. of the Nineteenth Century* (1877); *Proc. N. J. Hist. Soc.*, 2 ser. VIII (1885), IX (1887); John Livingston, *Portraits of Eminent Americans Now Living* (1854), vol. IV; *Harper's Weekly*, Dec. 9, 1865; *Biog. Dir. Am. Cong.* (1928); *N. Y. Times*, Apr. 26, 1884.] A. V–D. H.

WARD, MONTGOMERY [See Ward, Aaron Montgomery, 1843–1913].

WARD, NANCY (fl. 1776–1781), Indian leader, was born among the Cherokee Indians and lived at the Overhill town of Great Echota in what is now Monroe County, Tenn. Her father is believed to have been a British officer and her mother a sister of the Cherokee chief Attakullaculla. Distinguished among the Cherokee by the title of "Beloved Woman" or "Pretty Woman," she enjoyed the right to sit in council and, especially, the right to revoke by her single will any tribal sentence of punishment or death. It is said that she was one of the first to introduce negro slavery and the use of cattle among the Cherokee. An advocate of peace within the tribe and beyond the tribe, she helped the white frontiersmen again and again. At the outbreak of the Revolution it was she who warned the Watauga and Holston settlers in time to save themselves from destruction at the hands of the Indians. She also exercised her right to spare the prisoners captured in the raids and to pardon them even though already condemned and bound to the stake. Later in the war she again reported early news of Indian attack and supplied the Americans with beef cattle from her own large herd. When the Indians were repulsed she sought to intercede for her people, but, although she seems to have been kindly treated, her mission was unsuccessful.

Her part in the unsettled years after the Revolution is obscure, and, although her name was mentioned by Nuttall (*post*, p. 130) as late as 1819, it is not clear that she was still living at that time.

[James Mooney, "Myths of the Cherokee," *Nineteenth Annual Report of the Bureau of Am. Ethnology*, pt. 1 (1900); *Calendar of Va. State Papers*, vol. I (1875); "Southern Frontier Life in Revolutionary Days," *Southern Hist. Asso. Pubs.*, vol. IV (1900), pp. 457–58; Thomas Nuttall, *A Jour. of Travels into the Arkansa Territory . . . 1819* (1821); J. G. M. Ramsey, *The Annals of Tenn.* (1853), reprint with index (1926).] K. E. C.

WARD, NATHANIEL (c. 1578–October 1652), author, clergyman, was born in Haverhill, England, the son of John and Susan Ward. His father was a Puritan minister. In 1596 Nathaniel entered Emmanuel College, Cambridge, where he received the degree of A.B. in 1599 and that of A.M. in 1603. Educated to be a barrister, he practised law for some time in England. A visit to Heidelberg in 1618 and a chance meeting with the great theologian David Pareus changed the course of his career. Pareus persuaded him to enter the ministry and helped him to obtain the post of chaplain to the British merchants at Elbing, Prussia. In 1624 he returned to England, where he was curate of St. James's, Picadilly, London, 1626–28. In the latter year he was pre-

Ward

sented by Sir Nathaniel Rich to the rectory of Stondon Massey, where he preached Puritan doctrine unhindered until 1631. Laud then called him to answer charges of non-conformity, but did not attempt to remove him. In 1633, however, he was dismissed summarily from office, and the following year emigrated to Massachusetts Bay. Going directly to Agawam (Ipswich), he was installed in the church there as a colleague of the Rev. Thomas Parker [q.v.].

Poor health interrupted his work in the pastorate. After his resignation, he was appointed in 1638 by the General Court to assist in the preparation of a legal code for Massachusetts, "the first code of laws to be established in New England." According to John Winthrop these laws, which were enacted in 1641, were "composed by Mr. Nathaniel Ward" (*Winthrop's Journal,* 1908, ed. by J. K. Hosmer, II, 49). Known as the "Body of Liberties," this code was in effect a bill of rights, setting one of the cornerstones in American constitutional history. That the laws were in advance of English common law is attested by the eightieth, which in contrast to the English provision that a man might punish his wife with a "reasonable instrument," explicitly stated: "Everie married woeman shall be free from bodilie correction or stripes by her husbande, unlesse it be in his owne defence upon her assalt."

In 1645 Ward completed *The Simple Cobler of Aggawam in America,* published in England in 1647 under the pseudonym of Theodore de la Guard. Professing to be the reflections of a self-exiled cobbler upon the political and religious dissensions that were racking both England and America, it is really a protest against toleration. The author is strongly opposed to "polypiety" in the church, and in the state he would restore the old order with king, lords, and commons. "My heart has naturally detested foure things," he says; "The standing of the Apocrypha in the Bible; Forrainers dwelling in my Countrey, to crowd our native Subjects into the corners of the Earth; Alchymized Coines; Toleration of divers Religions, or of one Religion in Segregant Shapes." The book is amusingly digressive: there are satirical thrusts at women's fashions and some neatly turned couplets. Throughout there is the prophecy of Presbyterianism. It remains a landmark in American letters, for its homely style, interwoven with apt and erudite metaphor, surpasses in vigor anything in Colonial literature written within the author's lifetime. It quickly went into several editions, each carefully edited and supplemented by Ward.

The year of its publication found him again in England, preaching before the House of Commons on a recapitulation of the themes of the Simple Cobbler. In the same year appeared *A Religious Retreat Sounded to a Religious Army,* an appeal to the army to submit to the will of Parliament, which has been attributed to him, as have two other works—a sermon before Parliament published in 1648, and *Discolliminium* (1650). To save church and country from disaster, to observe tradition and eschew the new, was his purpose. Thomas Fuller observed that Ward had "in a jesting way, in some of his books, delivered much smart truth of the present times" (*The History of the Worthies of England,* edition of 1840, III, 187), while Cotton Mather wrote that "He was the author of many composures full of wit and sense" (*post,* I, 522). From 1648 until his death in 1652, Ward was settled in the ministry at Shenfield, England. Although he belonged more to the old than to the new England, the making of New England's heritage belongs in part to him.

[J. W. Dean, *A Memoir of the Rev. Nathaniel Ward* (1868), containing a bibliography; *The Simple Cobler of Aggawam in America* (1843), ed. by David Pulsifer, Preface; J. and J. A. Venn, *Alumni Cantabrigienses,* pt. 1, vol. IV (1927); Cotton Mather, *Magnalia Christi Americana* (1702; ed. cited, that of 1853); *Mass. Hist. Soc. Colls.,* 3 ser. I (1825), VIII (1843), 4 ser. VII (1865), *New Eng. Hist. and Geneal. Reg.,* July 1864; N. B. Shurtleff, *Records of the Gov. and Company of the Mass. Bay,* vol. I (1853); *Essex Inst. Hist. Colls.,* vol. VI (1864); M. C. Tyler, *A Hist. of Am. Lit. during the Colonial Time* (1897), I, 227–41; V. L. Parrington, *Main Currents in Am. Thought,* vol. I (1927); C. A. Harris, in *Dict. Nat. Biog.*]
E. H. D.

WARD, RICHARD (Apr. 15, 1689–Aug. 21, 1763), colonial governor of Rhode Island, was born in Newport, a few months before the death of his father, Thomas Ward, who had settled in Newport in 1671. Richard's mother was his father's second wife, Amy Smith. The boy grew up in his native town, which was already a center for shipping engaged in the West India trade. On Nov. 2, 1709, he married Mary Tillinghast, and fourteen children were born to them. In spite of his large family, Ward became comfortably prosperous; he was not only a successful merchant but owned considerable land in the fertile Narrangansett Country.

In 1714 he was elected a member of the Rhode Island Assembly, and thereafter served in various public capacities for many years. On May 7, 1740, he was elected deputy governor, and a few months later became governor on the death of Gov. John Wanton. He continued in office three years, but in 1742 declined to run for a third term. His service as governor came during a period of general unrest in Rhode Island. Not only was the colony feeling the effects of the

434

War of the Austrian Succession, but it was agitated over three local issues: the paper money question, a controversy with Massachusetts over the common boundary, and, beginning in 1742, a dispute with the mother country over the right of appointment of a judge of the court of admiralty, a question involving the interpretation of the colonial charter. Ward retired from office before the war had fairly begun and before either of the other questions was settled, yet he had much to do with all of them. A council of war, of which he was a member, was created in January 1741; soldiers were recruited in response to his proclamation; Fort George was enlarged, and the colony sloop, *Tartar,* was made ready to go to sea. With regard to the paper-money question, Ward as a merchant belonged to the conservative group, but he was unable to prevent the establishment of another bank of issue. In regard to the Massachusetts boundary he stoutly supported the Rhode Island claims, and as stoutly protested to England in behalf of the charter rights. His refusal to remain in office was due, possibly, to interest in the war, for he was present at the siege of Louisburg in 1745.

During the rest of his life he lived quietly, and died in 1763, probably little suspecting that separation of the colonies from England would soon occur. His children carried on their father's traditions of public service. Samuel, 1725–1776 [*q.v.*], was governor of Rhode Island for three terms. Thomas and Henry each acted as secretary of the colony, and Henry was a delegate to the Stamp Act Congress, while Samuel's son Samuel, 1756–1832 [*q.v.*], served with distinction in the American Revolution.

[References to Richard Ward are found in the biographies of his son and grandson: "Life of Samuel Ward," in Jared Sparks, *Lib. of Am. Biog.,* 2 ser. IX (1846), and John Ward, *A Memoir of Lieut.-Col. Samuel Ward* (1875). See also S. G. Arnold, *The Hist. of the State of R. I. and Providence Plantations,* vol. II (1860); and J. R. Bartlett, *Records of the Colony of R. I.,* vol. V (1860).]   **M. A.**

WARD, RICHARD HALSTED (June 17, 1837–Oct. 28, 1917), physician and microscopist, was born at Bloomfield, N. J., the son of Israel Currie and Almeda (Hanks) Ward. He was educated at Bloomfield Academy and Williams College, Williamsburg, Mass., and received from the latter institution the degree of A.B. in 1858 and A.M. in 1861. He was graduated in medicine from the College of Physicians and Surgeons in New York in 1862. He was then commissioned an acting assistant-surgeon of volunteers in the Union Army and assigned to duty in a military hospital at Nashville, Tenn., but he was soon compelled to resign on account of

illness. He spent a year in Minnesota regaining his health and in 1863 settled in Troy, N. Y., where he spent the remainder of his busy and useful life. He early associated himself with Dr. Thomas W. Blatchford in the practice of medicine and in the management of the Marshall Infirmary and Sanitarium with its attached hospital for the insane. In this institution he was attending physician, member of the board of governors, and chairman of the medical board. He was appointed instructor in botany at the Rensselaer Polytechnic Institute in 1867 and promoted in 1869 to professor of botany and lecturer in histology and microscopy, continuing these teaching positions until his retirement in 1892. In the midst of a busy career in medical practice and teaching he found opportunity for extensive research in microscopy, with particular reference to its practical application in medicine and natural sciences. He collaborated in experimentation with the early American manufacturers of microscopes and influenced materially the type and mechanism of these instruments. He perfected a number of accessories for the microscope, notably an iris illuminator for the binocular instrument. He was one of the first to demonstrate by the microscope the difference in cellular structure of blood from various animals.

His research in blood structure and in the microscopical study of handwriting caused his services to be widely employed in legal cases involving murder and forgery. He was also a widely known authority upon the question of purity of water supplies and upon adulteration of foods and medicines. From 1871 to 1883 he was in charge of the section on microscopy in *The American Naturalist,* of Salem, Mass., one of the first departments of any American journal to be devoted to this branch of knowledge. He collaborated with the Rev. Alpheus B. Hervey in the American edition of *The Microscope in Botany* (1885), by Wilhelm J. Behrens. In 1889 he published a volume on *Plant Organization,* with a second edition the following year. He contributed numerous articles on topics relating to botany and microscopy to technical journals. In addition to his medical society affiliations he was a member and first president (1879) of the American Society of Microscopists (later the American Microscopical Society), a member of the Boston Society of Natural History, a fellow of the American Association for the Advancement of Science, of the Royal Microscopical Society of London, and of the Belgian Microscopical Society. He was a delegate to the International Medical Congress at Berlin in 1890, and represented the United States at the International Exposition of Microscopy at Antwerp in 1891. He was married, June 10, 1862, to Charlotte Allen Baldwin, of Bloomfield, N. J.; of their four children, a son became a professor of zoölogy at the University of Illinois and later permanent secretary of the American Association for the Advancement of Science. He wrote *Impressions of the Antwerp Microscopical Exposition* (1892), and *Library Expedients in Microscopy* (1900).

[*Who's Who in America*, 1916–17; H. B. Ward, in *Am. Medic. Biog.*, edited by H. A. Kelly, W. L. Burrage; W. B. Atkinson, *Phys. and Surgeons of the U. S.* (1878); *Biog. Record, Officers and Grads., Rensselaer Polytech. Inst.* (1887); *Jour. Am. Medic. Asso.*, Nov. 3, 1917; *N. Y. Times*, Oct. 29, 1917.]   J. M. P—n.

WARD, ROBERT DeCOURCY (Nov. 29, 1867–Nov. 12, 1931), climatologist and teacher, was born in Boston, Mass., a descendant of William Ward who was in Cecil County, Md., in the latter part of the seventeenth century. At the age of six months Robert was taken by his parents, Henry Veazey and Anna Saltonstall (Merrill) Ward, to Dresden, Germany, where his father was consul for Chile at the court of Saxony. There he remained four years. He then spent a year in Switzerland, where his father died, and a year in England. In 1874 he returned to Boston and entered Noble and Greenough's School (then Noble's School), from which he graduated in 1885. In 1889 he received the degree of A.B. at Harvard, *summa cum laude,* and that of A.M. in 1893. As a graduate student he made two meteorological investigations, one on the sea breeze of New England and another on the thunderstorms of New England, both published in the *Annals of the Astronomical Observatory of Harvard College* (vols. XXI, pt. 2, 1890; XXXI, pt. 2, 1893).

The year 1889–90 he spent in Europe, returning to Harvard in September 1890 to become assistant to Prof. W. M. Davis in physical geography and meteorology. In 1893 he became assistant in meteorology; instructor in meteorology in 1895; instructor in climatology in 1896; assistant professor in 1900; and professor in 1910 —the first professor of climatology in the United States. In founding and developing his department, from which able teachers went to many institutions, he did a prodigious amount of work in assembling and putting into logical order all he could find on climatology by others. He strove to make simple what others had left involved, and thus became an exceptionally clear and exact writer. His first book, *Practical Exercises in Elementary Meteorology* (1899), was a product of necessity, nothing of the kind being available for his students. His next book, which appeared

in 1903, a translation of the first volume of Julius von Hann's *Handbuch der Klimatologie* (1897), served an even greater practical use. His *Climate, Considered Especially in Relation to Man* was published in 1908, and a second edition issued in 1918. His best known book, *The Climates of the United States,* appeared in 1925. It embodies the results of a large amount of personal investigation and of much guided research on the part of his students. His last work, completed just before his death, is an extensive treatment of the climatology of North America for the great Köppen-Geiger *Handbuch der Klimatologie.* He also contributed to scientific journals, and to the eleventh, twelfth, and thirteenth editions of the *Encyclopaedia Britannica.* He was editor of the *American Meteorological Journal,* 1892–96, for many years contributing editor of the *Geographical Review,* and editor of "Current Notes on Meteorology" in *Science,* 1896–1908. He was an extensive traveler, visiting all parts of the United States and much of Europe and South America, and making a trip around the world; wherever he went his observations of weather and climate were keen and abundant, and ready for publication immediately upon his return.

He was president of the Association of American Geographers, 1917, and of the American Meteorological Society, 1920–21, and a member of many other societies at home and abroad. In addition to his other academic duties, he was, from 1900, a member of the administrative board of Harvard College, and for many years chairman of the Board of freshman advisers and a member of the committee on admission. In 1927 he was Harvard exchange professor to the Western colleges. He helped to found the Immigration Restriction League in 1894, and took an active and effective part in all its work. His physique was frail, but the responsibilities he effectively assumed would have been heavy burdens for the most robust, and to him were possible only because he was extremely methodical in all he did. He was a delightful companion, full of information or jovial and witty as occasion required. On Apr. 28, 1897, he married Emma Lane of St. Louis, who survived him but a few weeks; they had two sons and two daughters.

[G. A. Hanson, *Old Kent: the Eastern Shore of Md.* (1876); *Who's Who in America*, 1930–31; *Harvard Alumni Bull.*, Nov. 20, 27, 1931; *Harvard Univ. Gazette*, Dec. 19, 1931; *Harvard Crimson*, Nov. 31, 1931; *Annals of the Asso. of Am. Geographers*, Mar. 1932; *Bull. Am. Meteorological Soc.*, Dec. 1931, May 1932; *Geographical Rev.*, Jan. 1932; *Scientific Mo.*, Feb. 1932; *Science*, Feb. 12, 1932; *Proc. Am. Acad. of Arts and Sciences*, vol. LXIX (1935); *Boston Transcript*, Nov. 12, 1931; personal acquaintance.]   W. J. H—s.

WARD, SAMUEL (May 27, 1725–Mar. 26, 1776), colonial governor, member of the Continental Congress, was born in Newport, R. I., one of the fourteen children of Richard Ward [*q.v.*] and Mary (Tillinghast) Ward. Since his father was not only a prosperous merchant, but governor of the colony from 1740 to 1742, the boy grew up in the brilliant society of colonial Newport. He was educated in the grammar school, but was not sent to college because he was destined by his father to be a farmer. In 1745 he married Anne Ray and settled on a farm in Westerly. Five sons and six daughters were born to them.

Ward's election in 1756 as deputy to the Rhode Island Assembly marked the beginning of his public service. For more than a decade thereafter there was a political feud between Ward and Stephen Hopkins [*q.v.*] of Providence, based on personal antipathy, political differences, and, fundamentally, on sectional rivalry. The colony was divided into two hostile camps: the conservative group, the merchants, found a champion in Ward, while the radicals looked to Hopkins. Three times the Ward party triumphed by the election of their leader as governor—in 1762, 1765, and 1766; three times also it met defeat. In 1761 Ward served as chief justice of the colony.

His first term as governor (1762) was uneventful politically, but in his second term (1765), he signed the charter of Rhode Island College (later Brown University), of which he was an original trustee. His second and third terms (1765, 1766) came during the years of agitation over the Stamp Act. His commercial upbringing led him to sympathize with the colonists and, although anxious to maintain law and order, he supported their cause vigorously. He refused to take the oath to submit to, or enforce, the Stamp Act; he denied the request of the collectors of the customs for an extra guard; and he protested to Captain Antrobus of the British vessel *Maidstone* against the impressment of Rhode Islanders into the Royal Navy.

Defeated in 1767 for reëlection, Ward retired to Westerly, but kept in touch with the course of events. He was among the first to hold at his home an indignation meeting over the punishment of Boston after the "Tea Party," and he prepared a series of resolutions which set forth comprehensively the colonial grievances. When the First Continental Congress was called, he and his former adversary Hopkins were chosen delegates. Little is known of the part he played in this assemblage, but he was reëlected to the Second Continental Congress.

In 1776 the sentiment of the Ward family was rapidly crystallizing in favor of independence. Henry Ward, brother of the former governor, was secretary of state of Rhode Island and performed some of the functions of the governor in place of the Loyalist, Joseph Wanton [*q.v.*], and Samuel Ward's son Samuel, 1756–1832 [*q.v.*], with the consent and approbation of his father, received a commission as captain in the 1st Rhode Island Regiment. From the opening of the Second Continental Congress Ward was an active member of the little group of statesmen who were seeking some formula to guide the colonies. Early in the session he was called by Hancock to preside over the Congress when it resolved itself into the Committee of the Whole, and for several months regularly served as chairman at such times. It was his fortune to propose and to help secure the appointment of George Washington as commander-in-chief of the colonial forces. He died of smallpox, contracted in Philadelphia while the Congress was deliberating.

["Life of Samuel Ward," in Jared Sparks, *Lib. of Am. Biog.*, 2 ser. IX (1846); G. S. Kimball, *The Correspondence of the Colonial Governors of R. I.* (2 vols., 1902–03); E. C. Burnett, *Letters of Members of the Continental Congress*, vol. I (1921); J. R. Bartlett, *Records of the Colony of R. I.*, vol. VI (1861); S. G. Arnold, *Hist. of the State of R. I.*, vol. II (1860); MSS. in the possession of descendants in New York City.]

M. A.

WARD, SAMUEL (Nov. 17, 1756–Aug. 16, 1832), soldier, merchant, the second son of Gov. Samuel Ward, 1725–1776 [*q.v.*], and Anne (Ray) Ward, was born in Westerly, R. I. He was a member of one of the early classes of Rhode Island College (later Brown University), where he graduated with honors in 1771. His father and his uncle were both prominent in colonial affairs, and upon the outbreak of the Revolution he was among the first to answer the call to arms.

Commissioned as captain in the 1st Rhode Island Regiment in 1775, he served with distinction in many campaigns. At the siege of Quebec he was taken prisoner (Dec. 31, 1775), and remained in Canada until his release, in August 1776. Promoted to the rank of major in January 1777, he fought with Washington's army at Morristown and in October was with the forces that defeated Burgoyne. In addition he was one of those who endured the hardships of the winter of 1777–78 at Valley Forge. On Apr. 12, 1779, after his regiment had made an attempt to force the British out of Newport, he received the rank of lieutenant-colonel. Meanwhile, on Mar. 8, 1778, he had married his first cousin, Phebe, daughter of William Greene [*q.v.*] and Catherine (Ray) Greene of Warwick, R. I. They had ten children, of whom seven lived to grow up. One of these, Samuel, 1786–1839 [*q.v.*], was the father of Julia (Ward) Howe [*q.v.*].

In 1781 Ward retired from the military service to begin the life of a merchant. Some time after the conclusion of the war he established himself in New York, in the firm of Samuel Ward & Brother. His business interests required frequent traveling, and he sailed all over the world. Making the arduous voyage to Canton, China, in 1788, he was one of the first Americans to visit the Far East, and he was in Paris when Louis XVI was sentenced to death. Though he had no ambition to play as active a part in public life as had his father and grandfather, the tradition of his family, his commercial wisdom, and his scholarly interests caused him to be highly respected. He became a member of the Society of the Cincinnati in 1784, was elected a delegate to the Annapolis Convention in 1786, was president of the New York Marine Insurance Company from 1806 to 1808, and was one of Rhode Island's representatives at the Hartford Convention in 1814. In 1804 he had moved his residence back to Rhode Island, to East Greenwich, and in 1816 he removed to Jamaica, L. I. In 1828, however, he returned to New York City, where he died.

[John Ward, *A Memoir of Lieut.-Col. Samuel Ward* (privately printed, 1875); *Hist. Cat. Brown Univ.* (1905); *N. Y. American,* Aug. 16, 1832.]   M. A.

WARD, SAMUEL (May 1, 1786–Nov. 27, 1839), banker, was born in Warwick, R. I., the fifth son of Samuel Ward, 1756–1832 [*q.v.*], and Phebe (Greene) Ward, the daughter of Gov. William Greene [*q.v.*] of Rhode Island. In 1790, when the boy was four years old, his family moved to New York, where his father engaged in mercantile pursuits with indifferent success. Since the family income was too small to permit of his being sent to college, Ward received only a common-school education and at the age of fourteen began work as a clerk in the prominent banking house of Prime & Sands. In 1808, when he was only twenty-two, he was made a partner and in time he became head of the firm, the name of which was changed to Prime, Ward & King.

Quick to make up his mind and the soul of punctuality, he disliked circumlocution and indecision in others. A believer in the observance of contractual obligations, he was deeply mortified by the suspension of specie payments on May 10, 1837, by the New York banks, an act which he regarded as a blot upon the city's commercial honor. During the ensuing panic several of the American commonwealths repudiated their obligations, and but for the strenuous opposition of Ward the State of New York might have fol-

lowed their example. Repeatedly he called meetings of the leading financiers, and by his persistence induced them to tide the state over the crisis. So great was confidence in the integrity of his firm that he was able in the early part of 1838 to obtain a loan of some five million dollars in gold bars from the Bank of England, which went far towards enabling the New York banks to resume specie payments in May of that year. In 1839 Ward helped found and became president of the Bank of Commerce in New York, the first great financial institution to be incorporated under an act passed by the New York legislature in April 1838 allowing associations of individuals to engage in the banking business. He was recuperating from an attack of gout when during a secondary crisis the Philadelphia banks and those in Southern cities suspended specie payments in October 1839. For a fortnight he fought strenuously and successfully to prevent the New York banks from following suit, but the strain proved too great for his enfeebled constitution and he died towards the close of the following month.

In October 1812 he married Julia Rush Cutler, by whom he had three sons and four daughters. After her death, Nov. 11, 1824, Ward's character underwent a great change. He gave up smoking, became a devout churchgoer, frowned on all fashionable entertainments, and gave freely to good causes. He contributed to the missions and educational institutions of the Protestant Episcopal Church, and in 1830 helped found the University of the City of New York (New York University) of which he was first treasurer. The following year he became the first president of the New York City Temperance Society, and in 1836 he helped finance Stuyvesant Institute, which was intended to be a copy of the Boston Athenæum. A lover of the fine arts, he had a gallery of paintings in his house at the corner of Broadway and Bond Street. His son Samuel, 1814–1884 [*q.v.*], became a well-known figure in political and social circles and demonstrated facility and charm as a writer; of his daughters, Louisa married the sculptor Thomas Crawford [*q.v.*] and became the mother of the novelist Francis Marion Crawford [*q.v.*] while Julia married the humanitarian Samuel Gridley Howe [*q.v.*], had several distinguished children, and as Julia Ward Howe [*q.v.*] became one of the most famous American women of her generation.

[Biog. material appears in John Ward, *Memoir of Lieut.-Col. Samuel Ward* (privately printed, 1875); Charles King, "The Late Samuel Ward," in *The Biog. Annual* (1841); Julia Ward Howe, *Reminiscences 1819–1899* (1899); Laura E. Richards and Maud Howe Elliott, *Julia Ward Howe 1819–1910* (1915); *N. Y. Times and Commercial Intelligencer,* Nov. 30, 1839. There are some MSS. in the N. Y. Pub. Lib.]   H. G. V.

WARD, SAMUEL (Jan. 25, 1814–May 19, 1884), lobbyist, financier, author, was born in New York City, the son of Samuel Ward, 1786–1839 [*q.v.*] and Julia Rush (Cutler) Ward, and elder brother of Julia Ward Howe [*q.v.*]. He attended Round Hill School, Northampton, Mass., presided over by George Bancroft [*q.v.*], and Columbia College, New York, where he received the degree of B.A. in 1831. He then spent some time in Europe—studying in France, where he purchased the library of Lagrange, the mathematician, and in Germany, where he showed equal enthusiasm for student social life and the reigning intellectual fashions. Returning to New York with a reputation for both fashionable and intellectual distinction, he contributed "additions and improvements" to the first American edition (1832) of *An Elementary Treatise on Algebra* by J. R. Young, is credited with reviewing books on Locke and Euler for the *American Quarterly Review* (December 1832, December 1833), and took a prominent part in the social life of the wealthy and leisured class until he entered the banking house of Prime, Ward & King, of which his father was a member. Banking was not to his taste, however, and soon after his father's death in 1839 he withdrew from the firm. Meanwhile, in 1837, he had married Emily, daughter of William B. Astor [*q.v.*]. She died at the birth of their only child, Margaret, and in 1844 Ward married Medora Grymes, daughter of John Randolph Grymes of New Orleans. Two sons, both of whom died young, were born of this marriage, which proved unhappy and resulted in separation.

Lacking the austerity and the financial aptitude of his father, Ward had lost his fortune by 1849 and in that year he joined the gold rush to California. There followed about a decade of adventurous wandering which gave rise to numerous legends. According to his own statements, he mastered every Indian dialect in California in three weeks, conducted a ferry and a billiard parlor, and adapted himself with great success to a rough and primitive environment. In San Francisco he made the acquaintance of young James R. Keene [*q.v.*] and became his confidant; later Keene was able to give his friend invaluable financial advice, which Ward reciprocated by advice and information on social and personal matters. He visited Paraguay and Nicaragua on official or semi-official missions in 1858 and 1862 respectively, and in 1860 published a polemical pamphlet, *Exploits of the Attorney General in California,* "by an early Californian," severely criticizing Jeremiah Sullivan Black

[*q.v.*], attorney general in President Buchanan's cabinet. During the closing years of the Civil War and the administrations of Johnson and Grant he lived in Washington through the sessions of Congress, a lobbyist in the employ of financiers interested in national legislation. His dinners, breakfasts, and other entertainments gained a reputation for elegance, and public officials were eager to be the recipients of his hospitality. He was not only a gourmet, however, but a man of marked social gifts, able to persuade conversationally as well as gastronomically, and was credited with an influence which won him the title "King of the Lobby." In 1865 he published a volume of verse, *Lyrical Recreations,* which he reissued in 1871.

Warm-hearted, charming, generous to the point of prodigality, Ward had an immensely wide acquaintance and was beloved by a considerable circle of intimates. Among these were Seward, Sumner, Garfield, Evarts, Bayard, Ticknor, Thackeray, and William H. Russell, the British war correspondent, whom he accompanied on a tour through the Confederacy in the early weeks of the Civil War. He was a friend and adviser of Longfellow, and in June 1882 contributed a revealing article, "Days with Longfellow," to the *North American Review.* One of his closest friends in New York was William Henry Hurlbert [*q.v.*] of the *World,* who with Ward and the young Earl of Rosebery formed the "Mendacious Club," of three, when Rosebery visited the United States in the early seventies (The Marquess of Crewe, *Lord Rosebery,* 1931, p. 54). These ties of affection were lasting; Ward became "Uncle Sam" to Rosebery, who later characterized him as "the uncle of the human race" (Richards, *post,* p. 115). He was as well known in London as in New York, and was caricatured by "Spy" in *The Vanity Fair Album* (1880). Devoted to all his sisters' children, he was especially close to his brilliant nephew F. Marion Crawford [*q.v.*], and gave much attention during his last years to launching Crawford on his literary career. Death came to him at Pegli, Italy, with nieces and nephews around him, *The Rubaiyat* on the bed beside him, and a copy of Horace under his pillow. Crawford wrote afterward to Julia Ward Howe, "He died as he had lived, full of thought and care for others, combined with a vagueness concerning all points of morality, which would have been terrible in a man less actively good than he was" (Elliott, *My Cousin, post,* p. 18).

[F. Marion Crawford portrayed Ward in the character of Horace Bellingham, in *Dr. Claudius* (1883). Descriptions by his nieces occur in Laura E. Richards, *Stepping Westward* (1931); Maud Howe Elliott, *Three*

Generations (1923) and *My Cousin, F. Marion Craw-ford* (1934) ; and Margaret Terry Chanler, *Roman Spring* (1935). See also Julia Ward Howe, *Reminiscences* (1899) ; Stephen Fiske, *Off-Hand Portraits of Prominent New Yorkers* (1884) ; E. D. Keyes, *Fifty Years' Observation of Men and Events* (1884) ; *Harper's Weekly*, May 31, 1884 ; *Boston Advertiser, Boston Transcript, Boston Post, Springfield Republican, N. Y. Herald*, May 20, 1884. There are some MSS. in the N. Y. Pub. Lib. A biography by Maud Howe Elliott is in preparation.]   S. G.

WARD, SAMUEL RINGGOLD (Oct. 17, 1817–1866?), negro abolitionist, was born of slave parents on the Eastern Shore of Maryland. His parents ran away to Greenwich, N. J., in 1820. Six years later they removed to New York where the boy received an elementary education and became a teacher in colored schools. He was married in 1838 to a Miss Reynolds. His ability as a public speaker attracted the attention of Lewis Tappan [*q.v.*] and others and led to his appointment in 1839 as an agent of the American Anti-Slavery Society from which he was soon transferred to the service of the New York State Anti-Slavery Society. Licensed to preach by the New York Congregational (General) Association in 1839, he subsequently held two pastorates, at South Butler, Wayne County, N. Y., from 1841 to 1843, where his congregation was entirely white, and at Cortland, N. Y., from 1846 to 1851. He resigned the earlier pastorate because of throat trouble and subsequently studied medicine for a few months. He resumed his anti-slavery labors in 1844 with the Liberty Party and spoke in almost every state of the North. In 1851 he removed to Syracuse where, in October of that year, he took an active part in the rescue of the negro fugitive Jerry. Fearing arrest, he fled to Canada where he became an agent of the Anti-Slavery Society of Canada. He organized branches of the society, lectured, and lent assistance to the numerous fugitives in Canada. In April 1853 he was sent to England to secure financial aid for the Canadian effort and with the help of a committee raised the sum of £1,200 in ten months.

He spoke at both the 1853 and 1854 meetings of the British and Foreign Anti-Slavery Society and delivered numerous other addresses during his stay in Great Britain. He attracted the interest of some of the nobility and met many of the leading philanthropists. His *Autobiography of a Fugitive Negro* (London, 1855), records that John Candler, of Chelmsford, a Quaker, presented him with fifty acres of land in the parish of St. George, Jamaica, and he apparently accepted the gift, for about 1855 he went to Jamaica and in Kingston became the pastor of a small body of Baptists. He continued in this post un-til early in 1860 when he left Kingston and settled in St. George Parish. The new venture did not prosper and he died in great poverty in or after 1866. During his pastorate in Kingston he is said to have exercised a powerful influence over the colored population and was the head of a political party which controlled local elections. In 1866 he published in Jamaica his *Reflections Upon the Gordon Rebellion*. Ward's extraordinary oratorical ability is mentioned by a number of his contemporaries. He was frequently advertised during his lecture tours as "the black Daniel Webster."

[See Ward's *Autobiography*; W. J. Wilson, "A Leaf from my Scrap Book . . .," *Autographs for Freedom*, vol. II (1854), ed. by Julia Griffiths; *Jour. of Negro Hist.*, Oct. 1925 ; information from Mr. Frank Cundall, of the Institute of Jamaica, and from Lord Olivier.]
         F. L.

WARD, THOMAS (June 8, 1807–Apr. 13, 1873), poet, playwright, and musician, was born in Newark, N. J., the son of Thomas Ward, a well-to-do and prominent citizen of that city, who was a representative in Congress, 1813–17. In 1823 he studied at the College of New Jersey (later Princeton) and, although official record is wanting, is supposed to have taken the degree of M.D. at Rutgers Medical College, New York City, founded in 1825 under the leadership of David Hosack and S. L. Mitchill [*qq.v.*]. He studied and traveled in Europe for a time, then returned to New York City to practise his profession for two or three years. But he had ample private means, and, finding himself more interested in "skirmishing with the muse" than in practising medicine, he was soon giving all his time to the literary and musical occupations of a wealthy amateur. His earliest book, published anonymously, was *A Month of Freedom, an American Poem* (1837), a descriptive-historical-moral effusion in blank verse concerned with a month's vacation spent traveling to Washington, the Catskills, Lake George, Niagara Falls, and elsewhere. It is full of Romantic clichés and drenched in Byronism, but has occasional felicities. Ward published a series of verse tales in the *Knickerbocker Magazine* under the pseudonym of "Flaccus," and in 1842 these and other fugitive verses were collected and published as *Passaic, a Group of Poems Touching That River: with Other Musings*, by Flaccus. The tales deal with legends of the Passaic Valley, and are somewhat less romantic than the earlier book; they are followed by "Musings" (first published in the *New York American*) and by shorter verses under the headings "Humorous," "Serious," "National," and "Satirical." It is thoroughly uninspired verse, but won some attention at the time. At the close of the Civil War Ward published a slender pamphlet called *War Lyrics* (1865), breathing fiery patriotism but a desire for reconciliation after victory.

Meanwhile he had married (evidently some years before the publication of *Passaic*) and had made his house on Forty-seventh Street just west of Fifth Avenue the scene of production for various amateur operettas performed for charity. For at least two of these Ward wrote both words and music. The earlier, *Flora, or the Gipsy's Frolic* (1858), was first produced by a company of wealthy amateurs at "Land's End," Huntington, L. I., on July 30, 1857. The next year it was published, and undoubtedly it was many times performed in the large hall which Ward constructed during the war to house his amateur theatricals in the Forty-seventh Street mansion. In 1869 was published Ward's second operetta, *The Fair Truant,* first produced there on May 2, 1867. In all it is said that forty or fifty of these entertainments were given between 1862 and 1872, producing some $40,000, all of which was devoted to charitable purposes. In 1860 Ward edited a book entitled *The Road Made Plain to Fortune for the Million.* In 1866 he read an original poem at the bi-centennial celebration of the founding of his native Newark (*Collections of the New Jersey Historical Society,* vol. VI, 1866, Supplement, pp. 59–74). His last literary labor was a centennial address, delivered before the New York Society Library in 1872. Ward had at least one child who grew to maturity, a daughter Kate, who married Theodorus Bailey Woolsey of New York City (*The New York Genealogical and Biographical Record,* vol. IV, 1873, p. 201).

[Besides the sources noted above, see R. W. Griswold, *The Poets and Poetry of America* (1874); E. A. and G. L. Duyckinck, *Cyc. of Am. Lit.,* vol. II (1875), pp. 294–95; C. N. Greenough, ed., *The Works of Edgar Allan Poe,* vol. V, 1914, pp. 242–55; and *N. Y. Times,* Apr. 14 (death notice), 17, 1873. The records of Princeton Univ. and Rutgers Medical Coll. have also been consulted.]   E. M. S.

WARD, THOMAS WREN (Nov. 20, 1786–Mar. 4, 1858), merchant, only son of William and Martha (Procter) Ward of Salem, Mass., and a descendant of Miles Ward, who was in Salem as early as 1639, played an important but unobtrusive part in the commercial life of the United States between 1830 and 1853. Born and reared in Salem, he married Lydia Gray on Nov. 13, 1810, of which union were born eight children. For some years he was a partner in the Boston importing and exporting house of Ropes & Ward. During a vacation trip to England in 1828 he visited his intimate friend, Joshua Bates [*q.v.*], recently admitted to a partnership in Baring Brothers & Company, through which connection, two years later, Ward became the resident American agent of the London house.

As agent (1830–53) for the leading English firm financing the foreign trade of the United States, he held a position of considerable responsibility. The American business of the Barings, almost all of which passed through his hands, annually involved several millions of pounds sterling. He estimated that during his first three years as agent he had granted to American merchants credits, exclusive of bond operations, aggregating $50,000,000. His task was to maintain the personal relationship regarded as significant by English merchant-bankers in all phases of their business with the United States —selecting correspondents, granting credits, arranging for the transfer of shipping documents, collecting debts, negotiating loans, and reporting upon prevailing economic and political conditions. Perhaps Ward's most difficult task was that of attempting to prevent repudiation of bonded indebtedness by the states of Louisiana, Maryland, and Pennsylvania, the securities of which Baring Brothers & Company had sold to English investors.

He exercised a wide range of discretion in managing the affairs of the Barings. It was upon his initiative that Daniel Webster was retained as counsel for the firm, and in an effort to maintain peaceful relations between Great Britain and the United States Ward personally interviewed President Polk in 1845. Although the Barings recognized that his blunt honesty and conservatism caused some more speculative firms, particularly in New York, to regard him with disfavor, they considered him one of the "soundest" men in the United States, and gave him a large share of the credit for the firm's success in weathering the storm of 1837–42. Inasmuch as Baring Brothers & Company was the only one of the seven leading Anglo-American banking houses to pass through the crisis with unimpaired reputation and credit, Ward's accuracy in judging men and conditions must have been extraordinary.

He retired from active business life in 1853. Two of his sons, Samuel G. and John G. Ward, took over the agency, which was managed by the former alone after his brother's death in 1856. From 1828 to 1836 Ward was treasurer of the Boston Athenæum, and from 1830 to 1842 of Harvard. He bequeathed portions of his estate of $650,000 to both institutions as well as to the American Peace Society and the Boston Missionary Society.

[*Essex Inst. Hist. Colls.*, vol. V (1863) ; *Vital Records of Salem, Mass.* (6 vols., 1916–25) ; Baring Papers, Pub. Archives, Ottawa, Ont.; *Quinquennial Cat. Harvard Univ.* (1925) ; Barrett Wendell and others, *The Influence and Hist. of the Boston Athenaeum from 1807 to 1907* (1907) ; J. E. Semmes, *John H. B. Latrobe and His Times, 1803–1891* (1917) ; *Boston Daily Journal*, Mar. 5, 10, 1858.]   R. W. H.

WARD, WILLIAM HAYES (June 25, 1835–Aug. 28, 1916), publicist and orientalist, was born in Abington, Mass. A descendant of William Ward who settled in Sudbury, Mass., about 1638, he came of a family of Congregational ministers, his great-grandfather and grandfather having been pastors of the First Church, Plymouth, N. H., while his father, James Wilson Ward, was for twenty-one years pastor of the First Church, Abington. His mother was Hetta Lord Hayes, oldest daughter of Judge William Allen and Susan (Lord) Hayes of South Berwick, Me. When William was seven years old his mother died, and his care and education devolved largely on his father. Under his guidance William began the study of Hebrew at the age of six and was required to read through a Hebrew version of the Bible between the ages of six and nine; at nine he began the study of Greek and during the next three years was required to read the whole Bible through in Greek; at twelve he began the study of Latin and during the next three years read the Scriptures through again in that tongue. His father's library was rich in theological and philosophical works, which in his early teens William was encouraged to peruse.

For brief periods he attended various schools, a year being spent at Phillips Academy, Andover. At seventeen he entered Amherst College, where he was graduated in 1856. After teaching for a short time he studied at Union Theological Seminary, New York, and subsequently at the Yale Divinity School. For a few months he served as tutor at Beloit College, Wisconsin, and then went to Andover Theological Seminary, where he was graduated in 1859. He was licensed to preach in January of that year, and on Aug. 6 married Ellen Maria Dickinson of Sudbury, Mass., whose acquaintance he had made at Beloit. They had one child, Herbert Dickinson Ward [*q.v.*]. He and his wife offered themselves to the American Board of Commissioners for Foreign Missions, but were rejected because of the latter's delicate health. Accepted by the Congregational Home Missionary Society, however, they served two years at Oskaloosa, Kan., enduring many privations and hardships. Ward then resumed teaching, serving on the staff of Williston Academy, Easthampton, Mass., and on that of the Free Academy, Utica,

N. Y., and from 1865 to 1867 as professor of Latin and natural science at Ripon College, Wisconsin. In 1868 Henry C. Bowen [*q.v.*], proprietor of the *New York Independent,* offered him a position on the editorial staff of that paper, which he accepted, remaining associated therewith until his death. He served as associate editor, 1868–70; as superintending editor, 1870–96; as editor, 1896–1913; and as honorary editor, 1913–16. He continued his Biblical and oriental studies, the results of which appeared frequently in articles in his paper, and in learned journals of the day. In 1914 he moved from his Newark, N. J., residence to the ancestral home of the Hayes Family at South Berwick, Me. A carriage accident in 1915 paralyzed his arms, and from that time his strength failed until his death the following year.

The range of Ward's intellectual interest was wide. Throughout his life he read Latin and Greek at sight; he was well versed in astronomy and botany; to the Semitic languages he turned for his recreation. He devoted his days to editorial duties; his evenings to study. He followed the work of Rawlinson and others in deciphering the Assyrian inscriptions, and until the coming of Prof. David Gordon Lyon to Harvard in 1882 he was perhaps the only man in the United States who could read Assyrian. At its fiftieth anniversary, in 1876, he presented Amherst College with a translation of the Assyrian texts in its possession. Ultimately he limited his work in the oriental field to the study of Assyrian and Babylonian seals, regarding which he became the leading authority in the world. In addition to many articles on the subject, he published, *Cylinders and Other Ancient Oriental Seals in the Library of J. Pierpont Morgan* (1909) and *The Seal Cylinders of Western Asia* (1910), which became standard authorities. In 1879 President Charles Eliot offered him the chair of Semitic languages at Harvard, but, believing himself not sufficiently proficient in the grammar of classical Arabic, and regarding the editorial chair as offering a wider scope for his talents, he declined the offer. In the winter of 1884–85 he led the first American exploring expedition to Babylonia and surveyed various sites with a view of determining the best place for a later expedition to excavate. Guided by his results, the University of Pennsylvania uncovered ancient Nippur in 1888–1900. He was twice president of the American Oriental Society.

Great as was his eminence as an orientalist, it was equally great as a publicist. He possessed insight and sound judgment, wielded a facile pen, and wrote in a direct and simple, but flexible style. He discovered and encouraged budding poets, one of whom was Sidney Lanier, for whose *Poems* (1884) he wrote a memorial sketch. He was liberal in theology, irenic in temper, and possessed of a passion for righteousness in civic and national life. He was active in the organization of the Federal Council of Churches, and gave much time and labor to many other organizations. His last book, *What I Believe and Why* (1915), is as remarkable for its insight and constructive thinking as for the simplicity of its style.

[Charles Martyn, *The William Ward Geneal.* (1925); *Amherst Coll.: Biog. Record of Grads. and Non-Grads.* (1927); *Jour. of the Am. Oriental Soc.*, Dec. 1916; autobiog. material in *Independent*, June 28, 1915, June 19, 1916; *Independent*, Oct. 18, 1915, Sept. 11, 1916, Dec. 28, 1918; *Outlook*, Sept. 6, 1916; *Who's Who in America*, 1912–13; *N. Y. Times*, Aug. 29, 1916.]

G. A. B.

WARDEN, DAVID BAILIE (1772–Oct. 9, 1845), diplomat, author, book-collector, of Scottish ancestry, was born at Ballycastle, near Greyabbey, County Down, Ireland, eldest of three sons of Robert and Elizabeth (Bailie or Baillie) Warden. He received the degree of A.M. from the University of Glasgow in 1797, together with prizes for "the best historical and philosophical account of the Application of the Barometer to the mensuration of Heights" and for general proficiency in natural philosophy. In May 1797 he was licensed to preach by the Presbytery of Bangor. Being an ardent patriot, he became associated with the United Irishmen, accepting a colonel's commission in that organization and acting as a confidential agent. Arrested and offered the choice of standing trial or transporting himself forever from His Majesty's dominions, he emigrated to the United States in 1799. Shortly after his arrival he was offered a professorship of natural philosophy at Union College, Schenectady, N. Y., but was prevented from accepting by a previous agreement to act as principal of Columbia Academy at Kinderhook; on Aug. 1, 1801, he became principal tutor of the Kingston Academy, Ulster County, N. Y.

In 1804 he was admitted to citizenship and went to Paris as a private secretary to Gen. John Armstrong [*q.v.*], just appointed minister to France. In accordance with presidential instructions dated July 22, 1808, Armstrong designated him to act as consul *pro tempore*. In 1810, when Armstrong was succeeded by Joel Barlow [*q.v.*], Warden returned to the United States and secured appointment as consul at Paris and agent for prize causes, but he was removed from office June 10, 1814, ostensibly on the ground that during the interim between the death of Barlow and

the arrival of his successor, William H. Crawford [*q.v.*], Warden had assumed the character of consul general, with which he was not officially invested. Meanwhile he had published *An Enquiry Concerning the Intellectual and Moral Faculties and Literature of Negroes* (1810), translated from the French of B. H. Grégoire; and a treatise, *On the Origin, Nature, Progress, and Influence of Consular Establishments* (1813), which was translated into several different languages and freely quoted by the noted British jurist, Joseph Chitty, in his *Treatise on the Laws of Commerce and Manufactures* (1820).

The remainder of Warden's life was spent in France. In his retirement he never ceased to promote the interests of American citizens to the best of his abilities. He had taken with him collections of American plants, animals, and insects; and he now devoted a great part of his energies to attempts to disseminate information concerning America. To this end he published *A Chorographical and Statistical Description of the District of Columbia* (1816); *A Statistical, Political and Historical Account of the United States of North America* (3 vols., 1819), apparently intended as a complete reference work which should defend the democratic experiment by presenting the facts to speak for themselves; *Chronologie Historique de l'Amérique* (10 vols., 1826–44), published also as *L'Art de Verifier les Dates*, vols. XXXII–XLI; *Bibliotheca Americo-Septentrionalis* (1820), a catalogue of one of his collections of books on America, which collection was purchased by S. A. Eliot and presented to Harvard College in 1823; *Recherches sur les Antiquités de l'Amérique Septentrionale* (1827); and *Bibliotheca Americana* (1831). A second collection which he made of books on America was acquired by the New York State Library in 1840. Both were especially rich in maps and plans of the battles of the American Revolution and in material relating to the Spanish explorations.

Warden was a member of the American Philosophical Society, of the Lyceum of Natural History, New York, and of numerous European societies. Among his correspondents were Thomas Jefferson, John Quincy Adams, Lafayette, Talleyrand, John Howard Payne, Jared Sparks, Nicholas Biddle, John Jacob Astor, Rembrandt Peale, Joseph C. Cabell, Anthony Morris, and Josiah Quincy.

[MSS., Md. Hist. Soc.; *Md. Hist. Mag.*, June–Sept. 1916; *Ulster Jour. of Archæol.*, Feb., Aug. 1907; *Northern Whig* (Belfast), May 12, 1846, Aug. 6, 1906; E. A. Collier, *A Hist. of Old Kinderhook* (1914); *Olde Ulster*, Nov., Dec. 1913; Marius Schoonmaker, *The Hist.*

of Kingston, N. Y. (1888); W. I. Addison, *A Roll of the Graduates of the Univ. of Glasgow* (1898); information as to certain facts from the Misses Alice and Ella Warden of Baltimore, Miss Sophia Warden of Newtownards, County Down, North Ireland, and Dr. W. T. Latimer and Francis Joseph Bigger of the *Ulster Jour. of Archæol.*] H. H. F.

WARDEN, ROBERT BRUCE (Jan. 18, 1824–Dec. 3, 1888), jurist, author, the son of Robert Bruce Augustine and Catherine E. (Lewis) Warden, was born in Bardstown, Ky. In 1840 he began the study of law in Cincinnati. He served for five years as deputy clerk of the court of common pleas of Hamilton County, and in April 1845 was admitted to the bar. Meanwhile, on Oct. 15, 1843, he had married Catharine Eliza Kerdolff of Cincinnati. They had two sons and a daughter of their own and adopted a daughter of Warden's sister.

In 1851 Warden was elected one of the judges of the county court of common pleas and in 1853–55 was reporter of the state supreme court. A trial for murder by poisoning which he observed intimately during this period determined him to undertake a course of study at the Starling Medical College of Columbus; he later lectured at that college on the forensic doctrines of insanity, elaborating his ideas in a volume entitled *A Familiar Forensic View of Man and Law* (1860). Appointed judge of the supreme court of Ohio by Gov. William Medill to fill the vacancy created by the resignation of Chief Justice John A. Corwin, he took office early in 1855, but served on this bench only a few months before a popular election was held by which Joseph R. Swan was chosen to fill the office. Warden resumed the reportership for a time and then returned to practice, forming a partnership in Columbus with Otto Dresel. Toward the end of the Civil War he removed to Cincinnati and in 1873 to Washington, D. C. Here in 1877 he became a member of the board of health of the District of Columbia, by appointment of President Hayes, serving also as attorney of the board until its expiration. He then practised law in Washington for the rest of his life, in partnership with his son, Charles G. Warden.

In 1874 he published *An Account of the Private Life and Public Services of Salmon Portland Chase*. He was also the author of *A Voter's Version of the Life and Character of Stephen Arnold Douglas* (1860); *A System of American Authorities* (1870); *An Essay on the Law of Art* (1878); and *Law for All* (1878).

[W. A. Warden, *The Ancestors, Kin, and Descendants of John Warden and Narcissa (Davis) Warden* (1901); *The Biog. Annals of Ohio*, vol. II (1905); G. I. Reed, *Bench and Bar of Ohio* (1897), I, 24; C. T. Marshall, *A Hist. of the Courts and Lawyers of Ohio* (1934), I, 303–04; *Weekly Law Bulletin*, Dec. 10, 1888; *Cincinnati Commercial Gazette* and *Washington Post*, Dec. 4, 1888.] R. C. M.

WARDER, JOHN ASTON (Jan. 19, 1812–July 14, 1883), physician, horticulturist, forester, was the son of Jeremiah and Ann (Aston) Warder, and a descendant of Willoughby Warder who came to Philadelphia in 1699. John's parents were members of the Society of Friends but he was never strictly orthodox in religion. Born in Philadelphia, he spent his boyhood in the suburbs of that city. His bent for nature study was fostered by his association with such men as John James Audubon, François Michaux, and Thomas Nuttall [qq.v.], who visited his father's home. In 1830 he moved with his parents to a farm near Springfield, Ohio, where he gained experience in agriculture and fruit growing. For his further education he returned to Philadelphia and graduated from the Jefferson Medical College in 1836. The following year he established his residence in Cincinnati, where he maintained his medical practice until 1855, when he moved to a farm near North Bend, Ohio. In 1839 he published *A Practical Treatise on Laryngeal Phthisis . . . and Diseases of the Voice*, a translation of the French treatise by Trousseau and Belloc.

His most notable work, however, was done outside the medical profession. He was greatly interested in various branches of science and was a member of the Cincinnati Astronomical Society, the Western Academy of Natural Sciences, and the Cincinnati Society of Natural History. In the fields of horticulture and forestry he was an industrious and practical worker. He was active in the Ohio Wine Growers' Association; was president of the Ohio Horticultural Society for many years; and served as secretary and as vice-president of the American Pomological Society, to the *Proceedings* of which he contributed articles on horticulture. From 1871 to 1876 he was a member of the Ohio State Board of Agriculture. Through his writings and editorial services, also, he made important contributions to horticulture. From 1850 to 1853 he edited the *Western Horticultural Review*, in which he first described the *Catalpa Speciosa*, not previously recognized as a distinct species. For a year (January–December 1854), with James W. Ward [q.v.], he conducted the *Horticultural Review and Botanical Magazine*. In addition to his editorial work, he contributed articles on systematic pomology and fruit culture to these and other publications, including the *American Journal of Horticulture*. He was one of the authors of the "Report of the Flax and Hemp Commission," prepared for the

United States government in 1865; he edited an edition of Du Breuil's *Vineyard Culture* (1867); and wrote *Hedges and Evergreens: A Complete Manual for the Cultivation, Pruning, and Management of All Plants Suitable for American Hedging* (1858) and *American Pomology: Apples* (1867).

Warder gave almost as much attention to forestry as he did to horticulture. In 1873 he was appointed United States commissioner to the International Exhibition in Vienna, and the official report on forests and forestry was prepared by him (*Report of the Commissioners,* 1876, vol. I). From its founding in 1875 he was president of the American Forestry Association until a few months previous to its absorption, in 1882, by the American Forestry Congress, of which he was one of the organizers. Shortly before his death the United States Department of Agriculture commissioned him to report on the forestry of the Northwestern states. He did much to foster landscape gardening and the beautification of parks and cemeteries. He married, in 1836, Elizabeth Bowne Haines of Philadelphia and was survived by four sons.

[L. H. Bailey, *Cyc. of Am. Horticulture* (1902), vol. IV; Henry Howe, *Hist. Colls. of Ohio* (1902, vol. I); *Commercial Gazette* (Cincinnati), July 18, 1883; H. A. Kelly and W. L. Burrage, *Am. Medic. Biogs.* (1920); *Proc. Am. Pomological Soc.,* 1852–83; *Proc. Am. Forestry Cong.,* 1882; *Am. Jour. of Forestry,* Aug. 1883; *Seventeenth Ann. Report of the Ohio State Horticultural Soc.* (1884); *Reports of the Ohio State Board of Agric.,* 1871–76, 1883.]   R. H. A.

WARDMAN, ERVIN (Dec. 25, 1865–Jan. 13, 1923), journalist, was born in Salt Lake City, Utah, but his parents, George and Mary Virginia (Ervin) Wardman, were from New England. He was educated at Phillips Academy, Exeter, N. H., and at Harvard, where he received the degree of A.B. in 1888. Joining the staff of the *New York Tribune,* he made his mark with his reports of the Johnstown flood (1889), and was soon assistant city editor. In 1895 he left the *Tribune* to become managing editor of the *New York Press,* and the next year was made editor-in-chief, a position he held with distinction until 1916, except for a few months spent at the front during the Spanish-American War, in which he served as a member of Troop A, United States Volunteers, as first lieutenant of the 202nd New York Infantry, and as aide-de-camp to Gen. John R. Brooke [*q.v.*] in the Puerto Rico campaign. After the war he resumed his work of making the *Press* an aggressive and effective organ of liberal Republicanism. It was he who, in the late 1890's, coined the term "yellow journalism" (*New York Tribune,* Jan. 14, 1923). His own editorial style was crisp and hard-hitting, though remarkably well informed. In 1905 a series of outspoken editorials concerning an alleged attempt to bribe state legislators resulted in Wardman's being summoned to Albany to explain the sources of his accusations. These he steadfastly refused to divulge on the score of newspaper ethics; his position was later supported by the courts.

During the last four years of Wardman's editorship of the *Press,* Frank A. Munsey [*q.v.*] was the owner. When Munsey bought the *Sun* in 1916 and merged the *Press* with it, E. P. Mitchell [*q.v.*], editor of the *Sun,* assumed editorship of the combined papers, and Wardman became publisher. This position he retained after Munsey bought the *Herald* in 1920 and merged the *Sun* with it. He continued to contribute editorials, however, and after Mitchell's retirement was again in charge of the editorial page. His ability as a business administrator was as marked as his ability as an editor, and Munsey is reported to have called him the best equipped man for his position in New York. He was a clean-cut New England type, "grim jawed" but with a glint of humor in his eye, and with a magnificent physique apparently untouched by the strain of his indefatigable industry. His interests were wide, but as an editorial writer his chief field was labor economics. He was chairman of the labor committee and a member of the arbitration committee of the Publishers' Association. When the United States entered the World War he originated the Sun Tobacco Fund, through which some $500,000 worth of tobacco was distributed among the soldiers. In spite of his vigorous forthrightness in controversy, he was much liked personally and showed his native generosity by many anonymous charities. When he died suddenly of pneumonia early in 1923 the Newspaper Editors' and Publishers' Association held a special memorial meeting and passed resolutions in which he is described as "a shining example of the truth, honor, independence, and integrity that are at the foundation of good journalism" (*New York Times,* Jan. 18, 1923).

Wardman was twice married: first, May 14, 1902, to Caroline Klink Eyre, of Washington, D. C., who died in 1908; second, Feb. 8, 1910, to Violet Boyer of Barrie, Ontario. He was survived by his second wife and by a son. For some years before his death he lived during most of the year at New Rochelle, N. Y., but maintained a country place at Sherbrooke, Canada. He was the author of one novel, *The Princess Olga,* which appeared in 1906.

[*Who's Who in America,* 1922–23; obituaries in *N. Y. Herald, N. Y. Tribune,* and *N. Y. Times,* Jan. 14, 1923; editorials in *N. Y. Times* and *N. Y. Herald,*

Jan. 15, 1923; *N. Y. Evening Post,* Jan. 15, 18, 1923; *Editor and Publisher,* Nov. 25, 1916; F. M. O'Brien, *The Story of the Sun* (1928).]

E. M. S.

WARE, ASHUR (Feb. 10, 1782–Sept. 10, 1873), editor, jurist, was born in Sherborn, Mass., the third of the five children of Joseph and Grace (Coolidge) Ware, and a descendant of Robert Ware who was in Dedham, Mass., as early as 1642. His father, a farmer who had lost an arm at the battle of White Plains, was in spite of his lack of a formal education an able surveyor, and was frequently called upon to teach in the town schools. He prepared his son for college with the aid of the local minister, and Ashur was graduated at Harvard in 1804. For a time he was assistant to Dr. Benjamin Abbot [q.v.] at Phillips Academy, Exeter, and later tutor in the family of his uncle Henry Ware [q.v.], a well-known Unitarian clergyman of Cambridge. At this period he was attracted toward the ministry, but a close study of doctrines led him to a liberal position, and this fact, since he was not a controversialist by nature, caused him to turn to other fields. From 1807 to 1811 he was tutor in Greek at Harvard, and from 1811 to 1815, professor of Greek. He then studied law in the office of Loammi Baldwin [q.v.] in Cambridge, and with his classmate, Joseph E. Smith of Boston.

He engaged less in legal practice than in politics, however. With Henry Orne he edited in Boston a Democratic paper called the *Yankee.* In 1817 he moved to Portland, in the District of Maine, partly because of the opportunities there for the practice of law, but mainly to edit the *Eastern Argus,* a paper then engaged in promoting the separation of Maine from Massachusetts. His reputation as a writer and orator continued to grow, and he was an active force both in Maine's "home rule" politics and in the Democratic party. When Maine was made a state in 1820, Ware became secretary of state. On Feb. 15, 1822, President Monroe appointed him judge of the United States district court in Maine. In spite of his lack of judicial experience, he made an exceptional record as a judge, and remained on the bench until 1866. American maritime law was still in its infancy and Ware, by close examination of British precedents and a study of French and Roman law in the original languages, became, in the opinion of Justice Story, perhaps the ablest American authority in this field (*Proceedings of the United States District Court, post,* p. 13). His sympathies were often with the seaman and his decisions, not always welcome to the masters and owners of vessels, did much to raise the standard of life aboard ship. His opinions were collected and published in 1839 and 1849, and each publication went through a second edition. He contributed several articles to Bouvier's *Law Dictionary.*

From 1811 to 1844 he was a trustee of Bowdoin College. He served, also, as president of the Androscoggin & Kennebec Railroad Company, and was the first president of the Casco Bank (1825). Of the Maine Historical Society he was one of the incorporators. On June 20, 1831, he married, in Portland, Sarah Morgridge, who died June 30, 1870; they had four children.

[G. F. Talbot, in *Colls. and Proc. Me. Hist. Soc.,* 2 ser. VI (1890), and G. F. Emery, in *Ibid.,* 2 ser. VIII (1897); *Proc. of the U. S. District Court for Me. District; Commemorating the Services and Character of Hon. Ashur Ware* (1873); Abner Morse, *A Geneal. Reg. of the Descendants of the Early Planters of Sherborn, Holliston, and Medway, Mass.* (1855); William Willis, *A Hist. of the Law, the Courts, and the Lawyers of Me.* (1863); *Resolutions of the Cumberland Bar, and Address of U. S. District Attorney George F. Talbot on the Retirement of Judge Ware* (1866); E. F. Ware, *Ware Geneal.* (1901); *Eastern Argus* (Portland), Sept. 11, 1873.]

R. E. M.

WARE, EDMUND ASA (Dec. 22, 1837–Sept. 25, 1885), educator, the son of Asa Blake and Catharine (Slocum) Ware, was born in North Wrentham, Mass. He was a descendant of Robert Ware who came to the colony at Massachusetts Bay from England as early as 1642. He attended the Norwich Free Academy and was graduated from Yale College in 1863. He then spent two years teaching at the Norwich Academy and in 1865 went to Nashville to assist in organizing the schools of that city. In 1866 he went to Georgia under the auspices of the American Missionary Association as superintendent of schools for the Atlanta district. In December of this year he was licensed to preach by the Congregational Church, and in August 1867 was appointed superintendent of education for Georgia by Gen. Oliver O. Howard [q.v.], of the Freedmen's Bureau. On accepting this position Ware resigned his position with the American Missionary Association, but he retained his interest in its religious and educational work. It was from the Association that he obtained the first $25,000 for Atlanta University which, by resolution of its incorporators, should "never exclude loyal refugees and Freedmen" (Adams, *post,* p. 11). Of this institution Ware was one of the founders and the first president.

The University was chartered in 1867 and opened with a preparatory department in 1869. Normal and college departments were added within the next three years. In 1871 President Ware wrote in his report to the American Missionary Association, "two years ago the corner stone of our first building was laid. During the summer the building was completed. . . . A second building was erected last summer. . . . The whole number of pupils for the year has been 158. . . . Some have come from the Association's schools. Some have had little or no schooling. A large number were brought in by last year's pupils who taught during the summer" (*Twenty-fifth Annual Report,* 1871, pp. 39, 40). Ware was fortunate in beginning his task at a time when the altruistic zeal and moral fervor of the Abolition and missionary movements were at their height, but his own idealism and courage were weighty factors in accounting for the success of the University. He and his associates had profound faith in the mental and spiritual capacities of their students. No small part of President Ware's contribution was communicating that faith to the students themselves, and to the white Southerners who surrounded them. Joseph E. Brown, wartime governor of Georgia, signed a unanimous report of the Board of Visitors which stated in part: "At every step of the way we were impressed with the fallacy of the popular idea (which in common with thousands of others the undersigned have hitherto entertained) that members of the African race are not capable of a high grade of intellectual culture" (*Ibid.,* pp. 44, 45). Ware also understood that the students who flocked to Atlanta, ex-slaves or children of slaves, needed not only a school or college but also a home, and every effort was made to create social intercourse on a high level. In this work, he was associated with his Yale classmate, Horace Bumstead [*q.v.*].

Except for one year when illness necessitated his absence Ware retained the presidency and the active direction of the University until his death from heart disease. He was married, on Nov. 10, 1869, to Sarah Jane Twichell, of Plantsville, Conn. She, with their four children, survived him. A son, Edward Twichell Ware, became the third president of Atlanta University.

[E. F. Ware, *Ware Geneal.* (1901); *Hist. of the Class of 1863, Yale Coll.* (1905); *Obit. Record of Grads. of Yale Coll.,* 1886; M. W. Adams, *A Hist. of Atlanta Univ.* (1930); *Am. Missionary,* Nov. 1885; *Atlanta Constitution,* Sept. 26, 1885.]   M. G.

WARE, HENRY (Apr. 1, 1764–July 12, 1845), clergyman, professor of theology, was born in Sherborn, Mass. He was a descendant of Robert Ware who was in Dedham, Mass., as early as 1642, and was the ninth of the ten children of John and Martha (Prentice) Ware. As a boy, he worked on his father's farm and attended the short winter terms of the country school. When he was fifteen his father died and because of the promise Henry had shown, both in mind and character, his elder brothers decided that he should have the advantages of an education. Accordingly, he was put under the care of the parish minister, the Rev. Elijah Brown, who prepared him for college. In 1781 he entered Harvard, where, four years later, he was graduated, valedictorian of his class. He then took charge of the town school in Cambridge, and at the same time began a course of study with a view to preparing himself for the ministry. On his twenty-third birthday, in the town where he had grown up, he preached his first sermon, and on Oct. 24, 1787, he was ordained pastor of the First Parish Church, Hingham, Mass., succeeding in that office Dr. Ebenezer Gay [*q.v.*].

In this, his first and only pastorate, Ware remained eighteen years. On Mar. 31, 1789, he married Mary, daughter of the Rev. Jonas Clark [*q.v.*] of Lexington. His income of $450 a year proving inadequate for a steadily increasing family, he was "obliged to resort to the only means which seemed to be open to a country clergyman for supplying the deficiency of his salary, that of keeping boarders, and taking the charge of boys to fit for college." It proved, he said, "a very laborious and irksome life, and less profitable than it should have been" (Palfrey, *post,* p. 14). In spite of this handicap, he increased in knowledge and influence and rose to a place of distinction in his profession. Like his predecessor, Dr. Gay, he belonged to the liberal, or Unitarian, branch of the Congregational order, and after the death of Prof. David Tappan, Ware was chosen by the liberals on the board of Fellows of Harvard College as their candidate for the Hollis Professorship of Divinity, the opposing candidate being Dr. Jesse Appleton [*q.v.*]. Ware was nominated by the Fellows and, in spite of strong opposition from some of the Overseers, the nomination was confirmed on Feb. 14, 1805, and he was inaugurated on May 14.

This election, which marked a new era in the history of Congregationalism, gave rise to a memorable controversy between members of the liberal and orthodox parties. In its earlier years, Ware's participation in it was slight, but in 1820 he crossed swords with Dr. Leonard Woods, 1774–1854 [*q.v.*], by publishing that year *Letters Addressed to Trinitarians and Calvinists, Occasioned by Dr. Woods' Letters to Unitarians.* Woods made reply, and in 1822 Ware issued *Answer . . . in a Second Series of Letters Addressed to Trinitarians and Calvinists,* to which, the following year, he added, *A Postscript to the Second Series of Letters. . . .* Some one at the time called the argument the "Wood'n Ware Controversy," by which title it came to be generally known. Ware performed the duties of his office with ability and good judgment. In 1811 he began a course of special instruction for men preparing for the ministry, from which developed the divinity school, organized in 1816, with Ware as professor of systematic theology and evidences of Christianity. Twice, when the college was without a president, he served as administrative officer—in 1810 and in 1828–29. Because of the inconvenience resulting from a cataract on one of his eyes, he resigned the Hollis Professorship in 1840, but continued his work in the divinity school. An unsuccessful operation on his eye seriously weakened him. Before he was entirely incapacitated, however, he was able to arrange and publish some of his lectures under the title *An Inquiry into the Foundation, Evidences, and Truths of Religion* (1842). He died at Cambridge in his eighty-second year.

Ware was respected for his mental attainments and even more for the traits of character he exhibited. He was a man of simple tastes, extreme modesty, gentle disposition, and serenity of mind; yet he was fearless in maintaining his convictions. In the classroom he was noted for his candor, his fairness, and his distrust of ardent partisanship. As a preacher, a contemporary states, "he was too logical, sensible, moderate, and unimaginative," to appeal to all classes (A. B. Livermore, quoted in Eliot, *post*, p. 48). A number of his discourses—chiefly ordination and funeral sermons—were printed, among them one on the death of Washington and one on the death of John Adams. His first wife died July 5, 1805, and on Feb. 9, 1807, he married Mary, daughter of James Otis and widow of Benjamin Lincoln, Jr., who died eight days later; on Sept. 18 of the same year, he married Elizabeth, daughter of Nicholas Bowes of Boston. He was the father of nineteen children, ten by his first wife, and nine by the third. Among them were Henry, John, and William Ware [*qq.v.*]. John Fothergill Waterhouse Ware [*q.v.*] was a grandson.

[E. F. Ware, *Ware Geneal.* (1901); J. G. Palfrey, *A Discourse on the Life and Character of the Reverend Henry Ware, D.D., A.A.S.* (1846); W. B. Sprague, *Annals of the Am. Unitarian Pulpit* (1865); S. A. Eliot, *Heralds of a Liberal Faith* (1910), vol. II; Wm. Ware, *Am. Unitarian Biog.*, vol. I (1850); A. P. Peabody, *Harvard Reminiscences* (1888); *Boston Daily Advertiser*, July 16, 1845.]   H. E. S.

WARE, HENRY (Apr. 21, 1794–Sept. 22, 1843), Unitarian clergyman, son of Henry [*q.v.*] and Mary (Clark) Ware and brother of John and William Ware [*qq.v.*], was born in Hingham, Mass., where his father was pastor, and lived there until 1805, when the elder Henry became professor of divinity at Harvard. The son

received his early education in the schools of his native town and under tutors until 1807, in which year he was sent to Phillips Academy, Andover, Mass. The year following he entered Harvard College, from which he graduated in 1812. He was a somewhat frail, serious-minded youth, religiously inclined from childhood, mingling little in the social life of the college, but taking commendable rank as a scholar. From 1812 to 1814 he taught under Benjamin Abbot [*q.v.*] at Phillips Academy, Exeter, N. H., and then returned to Harvard to complete the preparation for the ministry which he had been carrying on privately. He had written some verse and at a public gathering held in 1815 after the signing of the Treaty of Ghent he delivered a poem, subsequently published under the title *A Poem Pronounced ... at the Celebration of Peace* (1815). On Jan. 1, 1817, he was ordained pastor of the Second Church (Unitarian), Boston, and in October of that year was married to Elizabeth Watson Waterhouse, daughter of Dr. Benjamin Waterhouse [*q.v.*] of Cambridge. John Fothergill Waterhouse Ware [*q.v.*] was their son.

Ware's life was comparatively short and ill health continually interfered with his activities. He was below medium height, thin, and stooping, and was careless as to his dress and personal appearance. His manner did not invite approach and few were on terms of intimacy with him. In spite of these handicaps, however, he became one of the leading ministers of New England, and his writings were widely read both in America and abroad. The whole purpose of his life was usefulness rather than high accomplishment, and into the various fields that he entered he put the full measure of his devotion. He succeeded Noah Worcester [*q.v.*] as editor of the *Christian Disciple* (1819–23), and in 1821 contributed articles, signed Artinius, to the *Christian Register*. In 1822 he projected Sunday evening services for those who had no stated places of worship, a missionary endeavor later carried on by the ministry-at-large. An advocate of preaching without manuscript, he published in 1824 *Hints on Extemporaneous Preaching*. He took a prominent part in the establishment of the American Unitarian Association, and was long a member of its executive committee. At the annual Phi Beta Kappa meeting at Harvard, Aug. 26, 1824, made memorable by the presence of Lafayette, he delivered a poem entitled "The Vision of Liberty." In 1823, one of his three children died, and in less than a year, his wife; on June 11, 1827, he married Mary Lovell Pickard (see E. B. Hall, *Memoir of Mary L. Ware*, 1853). To this marriage were born six children, one of whom was William Robert Ware [*q.v.*]. The condition of Ware's health led him to resign his pastorate in 1828, but his parishioners would not consent to a separation and the following year gave him a colleague in the person of Ralph Waldo Emerson. Meanwhile, he had been appointed first professor of pulpit eloquence and pastoral care in the Harvard Divinity School. After a seventeen-month sojourn in Europe, during which he visited Wordsworth, Southey, Maria Edgeworth, and other persons of note, he felt unable to carry on both pastoral and professorial duties and, relinquishing his parish, he moved to Cambridge.

During his career at Harvard, though in the latter part of it he took over much of his father's work, he found time for considerable writing. One of his works, *On the Formation of the Christian Character* (1831), went through some fifteen editions and was republished abroad. To provide young people with books suitable for Sunday reading, he projected "The Sunday Library," for which he wrote the first volume, *The Life of the Saviour* (1833). This also had wide circulation. Other publications included sermons, addresses, reviews, and memoirs of Joseph Priestley, Nathan Parker, and Noah Worcester. After his death *The Works of Henry Ware, Jr., D.D.* (4 vols., 1846–47), edited by Chandler Robbins, appeared. He was one of the organizers and the president of the Cambridge Anti-Slavery Society, and was subjected to severe criticism in the University and the papers for publicly espousing the abolitionist movement. Later his ardor cooled, for the impatience and intolerance of the abolitionists were repellent to one of his nature. Forced by failing strength to resign his professorship in 1842, he retired to Framingham, Mass., where he died in his forty-ninth year. His body was taken to Cambridge and was buried in Mount Auburn Cemetery.

[E. F. Ware, *Ware Geneal.* (1901); John Ware, *Memoir of the Life of Henry Ware, Jr.* (1846); W. B. Sprague, *Annals of the Am. Unitarian Pulpit* (1865); S. A. Eliot, *Heralds of a Liberal Faith,* vol. II (1910); *Proc. Mass. Hist. Soc.,* vol. II (1880); *Christian Examiner,* Nov. 1843, Mar. 1846.]   H. E. S.

WARE, JOHN (Dec. 19, 1795–Apr. 29, 1864), physician, editor, and educator, was born in Hingham, Mass. His father, Rev. Henry Ware, 1764–1845 [*q.v.*], was a minister and Hollis Professor of Theology at Harvard College; his mother was Mary, daughter of Rev. Jonas Clark [*q.v.*] of Lexington, Mass., and grand-daughter of the Rev. Thomas Hancock, also of Lexington. Two of Ware's brothers became ministers, Henry and William [*qq.v.*], while another brother, Charles, was a physician.

John entered Harvard College at the age of thirteen and was graduated in 1813. Three years later he received the degree of M.D. from the Harvard Medical School, and in 1814 began practice in Boston. He was poor, patients were few, and he turned his hand to other things besides medicine. For ten years he practised dentistry, kept school, took private scholars into his home, wrote for magazines, published a novel, gave popular lectures, and edited medical publications. The novel, *Charles Ashton* (1823), was issued anonymously; to the *North American Review* he contributed a poem (November 1817), a story (July 1818), and reviews of medical and scientific books. From 1823 to 1826, with John W. Webster and Daniel Treadwell [*qq.v.*], he issued the short-lived *Boston Journal of Philosophy and the Arts,* and in 1828, with Walter Channing [*q.v.*], edited the *Boston Medical and Surgical Journal.* During the period before recognition came to him as a teacher of medicine, he edited William Smellie's *Philosophy of Natural History* (1824) and William Paley's *Natural Theology* (1829). His chief medical contribution was an essay, *Remarks on the History and Treatment of Delirium Tremens* (1831), the result of the observations of nearly one hundred cases seen in the course of fourteen years. It was the first important work on the subject in America and ranks with Thomas Sutton's classic account of the same disease published in England in 1813.

James Jackson [*q.v.*], then Hersey Professor of the Theory and Practice of Physic at the Harvard Medical School, was the first to recognize Ware's worth as a teacher. He was put upon the staff of the school in 1832 as Jackson's associate, and when Jackson resigned in 1836 Ware succeeded him as Hersey Professor. At the school and the Massachusetts General Hospital Ware did his best work, a worthy successor to Jackson although a man of lesser caliber. In 1847 he published *Discourses on Medical Education and on the Medical Profession,* in which he made a strong appeal for the highest standards of medical education in an effort to combat irregular practitioners. He became interested, also, in the campaign for moral improvement and wrote *Hints to Young Men* (1850), which passed through many subsequent editions. His more strictly scientific papers include "Contributions to the History and Diagnosis of Croup" (*New England Quarterly Journal of Medicine and Surgery,* October 1842), and *On Hemoptysis as a Symptom* (1860). The former was based on observation of 131 cases, which he divided into classes, separating membranous croup or diphtheria from the others. He gave an excellent clinical description of this disease, but the paper was most valuable because of his effort to overcome the extreme type of treatment used at the time by other physicians. His work on hemoptysis, based on 386 cases observed over a period of forty years, pointed out the importance of this symptom in the early diagnosis of phthisis.

He was one of the founders of the Boston Society for Medical Improvement in 1839 and served as president of the Massachusetts Medical Society from 1848 to 1852. The lecture hall in the Boston Medical Library serves as a memorial to him. It contains his portrait as well as a bust by Bela Pratt [q.v.]. Ware's chief literary effort was *Memoir of the Life of Henry Ware, Jr.* (1846). His health failed some years before his death, but he lived to complete his *Philosophy of Natural History* (1860). The closing days of his life were saddened by the death of his son, Maj. Robert Ware, killed in battle in 1864. He was married, first, Apr. 22, 1822, to Helen, daughter of Levi and Desire Thaxter Lincoln of Hingham. She died in 1858, having borne him eight children. His second wife, Mary Green Chandler, of Petersham, Mass., whom he married Feb. 25, 1862, was an author. The death of Ware and his son in the same year was gracefully memorialized by Oliver Wendell Holmes in his poem, "In Memory of John and Robert Ware."

[E. F. Ware, *Ware Geneal.* (1901); *Proc. Am. Acad. Arts and Sci.*, May 24, 1864; T. F. Harrington, *The Harvard Medic. School* (1905); N. I. Bowditch, *A Hist. of the Mass. Gen. Hospital* (1872); J. W. Farlow, *The Hist. of the Boston Medic. Library* (1918); W. L. Burrage, *A Hist. of the Mass. Medic. Soc.* (1923); H. A. Kelly and W. L. Burrage, *Am. Medic. Biogs.* (1920); *Boston Daily Advertiser*, Apr. 30, May 2, 1864; *Boston Medic. and Surgic. Jour.*, May 5, 1864; notes from descendants and papers in the Boston Medical Library.]
H. R. V.

WARE, JOHN FOTHERGILL WATERHOUSE (Aug. 31, 1818–Feb. 26, 1881), Unitarian clergyman, was born in Boston, Mass., the son of Henry Ware, 1794–1843 [q.v.] and Elizabeth Watson (Waterhouse) Ware. William Robert Ware [q.v.] was his half-brother. Prepared for college in Cambridge, John graduated from Harvard in 1838, and would have been class poet, it is said, had not James Russell Lowell been in the same class. Entering the Harvard Divinity School, he finished the course there in 1842, and the following year became pastor of the Unitarian church in Fall River, Mass., remaining there until 1846. His next pastorate, which lasted until 1864, was at Cambridgeport, Mass.

During the Civil War, in an independent civil capacity, he rendered much service to the Union cause and especially to the soldiers themselves, lecturing or giving patriotic talks in various parts of the country, visiting the men in the camps—often in army boots and slouch hat—and preparing tracts, which were published and circulated among the soldiers by the American Unitarian Society. In 1864 he was called to be minister of the First Independent Society of Baltimore. His congregation, made up originally of old Marylanders, was augmented by many new-comers attracted by the quality of his preaching. The two elements did not mix readily, and the more conservative members found Ware's independence and disregard of ministerial conventions not to their liking. Accordingly, after some three years, July 1867, he resigned. Some of his friends then formed a new religious organization, the Church of the Saviour, the services of which were held in the Masonic Temple. So large did the evening attendance become that the use of an opera house was secured, and even this was sometimes over-crowded. In the summer time he held open-air services in Druid Hill Park. He took great interest in the welfare of the freedmen, and had a leading part in establishing schools for colored children, which ultimately were taken over by the city. His activities in this field were carried on in the face of obstacles and at personal risk, necessitating at times his being attended by armed companions. While living in Baltimore he spent his summers at Swampscott, Mass., where he organized a church.

In July 1872 the condition of his health necessitated his returning North, and he became pastor of the Arlington Street Church, Boston, to which he ministered until his death. His preaching was direct and practical, more concerned with the problems of life than with those of theology. His interest was in men rather than in books, and his ruling ambition was to lessen the injustice and unhappiness of the world. A number of his sermons were printed separately and after his death some twenty-seven of them were published in a volume entitled *Wrestling and Waiting* (1882). Two of his books had wide circulation—*The Silent Pastor, or Consolations for the Sick* (1848) and *Home Life: What It Is and What It Needs* (1864). He was married on May 27, 1844, to Caroline Parsons, daughter of Nathan Rice of Cambridge; she died, Sept. 18, 1848, and on Oct. 10 of the following year he married Helen, daughter of Nathan Rice. By his first wife he had two children, and by his second, two. He died in Milton, Mass., after a year of comparative inactivity caused by a coronary affection.

[E. F. Ware, *Ware Geneal.* (1901); *Gen. Cat. of the Divinity School of Harvard Univ.* (1910); S. A. Eliot,

Heralds of a Liberal Faith (1910), vol. III; *Boston Transcript*, Feb. 28, 1881.]　　　　　　　　H. E. S.

WARE, NATHANIEL A. (d. 1854), author, public official, was born according to some accounts in Massachusetts and according to others in South Carolina, where as a young man he taught school and practised law. The date of his birth is also variously given as 1780 and 1789. About 1815 he removed to Natchez, Miss., where he married Sarah (Percy) Ellis, daughter of Capt. Charles Percy, of the British navy, an early settler in Louisiana. She lost her mind at the birth of her younger daughter and spent the remaining years of her life in an institution for the insane. Ware was a major of militia and made money in land speculation. He was the last secretary of the Territory of Mississippi, being appointed June 7, 1815, and serving until October 1817, when the first governor of the state took office. From April 1815 to May 1816, in the absence of the territorial governor, Ware was acting governor. He was the first to sign an address to the cotton planters, merchants, and bankers of the South in 1838, proposing a scheme for paper money based upon cotton, the cotton to be marketed through an agreement with English cotton manufacturers and the Bank of England. The banks had suspended specie payments, and the masses of notes in circulation were rapidly depreciating. In response to the address, a convention was held in Macon in 1839, but the scheme of cotton notes, like many other similar ones, came to nothing. Ware lived at different times in Philadelphia, Cincinnati, and Galveston. He was fond of travel and had a variety of intellectual interests, including botany and geology. His two daughters, born in Mississippi, Catherine Ann Warfield [*q.v.*] and Eleanor Percy Ware Lee, wrote poems and novels.

Ware is best remembered for his *Notes on Political Economy, as Applicable to the United States* (1844), signed "A Southern Planter." The title of the volume suggests the conviction of the nationalist American writers that the dogmas of the classical school of Europe did not suit the economic situation of a new continent with a rapidly increasing population. Ware had doubtless come to know Henry C. Carey [*q.v.*] in Philadelphia; at any rate the works of this leader of the American optimistic school are often echoed in Ware's work. From residence in the North and from his acquaintance with the natural sciences, Ware was much more alert to opportunities for balanced economic development than were other writers in the South. For him there was no rule except public expediency, and governed by this he moved on to the protectionist

position, a course almost unique in a Mississippian of that period. The Malthusian principle of population, he thought, pointed to an undoubted tendency of the birth rate to outrun the means of subsistence, but by no means defined a limit of economic progress. Scientific agriculture, as proved by many instances which he cited, would indefinitely postpone the period of starvation. He grasped, more firmly than some others of his time, the fact that an improved standard of living would in itself lead to a reduced rate of population growth, pride becoming a grateful substitute for poverty in preventing Malthus' forebodings from being realized. The South at the time he wrote was more and more confining itself to staple agriculture, but Ware explained the virtues of a balanced economy, industry and commerce being joined to tillage of the soil.

He is described as "a handsome man . . . his complexion pure and fair as a young girl's, his cheeks freshly colored, his brow white as a lily, —a very venerable-looking man, with long, thin, white locks falling on his neck" (Tardy, *post*, pp. 26–27). He was "full of eccentricities. . . . His domestic trials rendered him bitter and outwardly morose, even to his friends. . . . He was a philosopher of the school of Voltaire, a fine scholar, with a pungent, acrid wit and cold sarcasm . . ." (*Ibid.*). He died near Galveston, Tex., of yellow fever.

[Dunbar Rowland, *Mississippi* (1907), vol. II, and *The Official and Statistical Reg. of the State of Miss., 1924–28* (n.d.); sketch of Catherine Ann Warfield, in M. T. Tardy, *Southland Writers* (1870), vol. I.]

　　　　　　　　B. M.

WARE, WILLIAM (Aug. 3, 1797–Feb. 19, 1852), Unitarian clergyman, writer, was born in Hingham, Mass., the son of Henry Ware, 1764–1845 [*q.v.*], and Mary (Clark) and a brother of Henry and John Ware [*qq.v.*]. When William was about eight years old, his father became Hollis Professor of Divinity at Harvard, and the boy was fitted for college, partly in Cambridge by his cousin, Ashur Ware [*q.v.*], and partly under the Rev. John Allyn of Duxbury. He graduated from Harvard in 1816, and then taught school, first in Hingham and later in Cambridge, at the same time pursuing studies in theology. On Dec. 18, 1821, he was ordained as pastor of the first Unitarian church to be established in New York City. After doing pioneer work there for nearly fifteen years, he resigned in October 1836.

Ware felt, and not without reason, that he was temperamentally unfitted for the work of the ministry. In the latter part of his life, moreover, he was afflicted with epilepsy. Accordingly, after leaving New York he held but two brief pastorates—at Waltham, Mass. (1837–38), and at West Cambridge (1844–45). His principal interests, aside from religion, were in literature and art. In March 1836 he began a series of articles in the *Knickerbocker Magazine,* which he published in 1837 under the title *Letters of Lucius M. Piso from Palmyra, to His Friend Marcus Curtius at Rome.* It portrays with considerable vividness life in the Roman Empire during the later days of Zenobia's reign, and subsequent editions were entitled *Zenobia: or, The Fall of Palmyra: An Historical Romance.* In 1838 he issued a sequel, *Probus: or, Rome in the Third Century,* published afterward under the title *Aurelian: or, Rome in the Third Century.* These works had deserved popularity at home and in England. Becoming proprietor of the *Christian Examiner* in 1839, he edited it from May of that year until January 1844. During this period he wrote *Julian: or, Scenes in Judea* (1841), depicting incidents in the life of Jesus, portions of which had appeared in the *Examiner.* This work, also, went through several editions. In 1848–49 Ware spent more than a year abroad, chiefly in Italy. Upon his return he delivered a course of lectures in several cities, which he published in 1851 under the title, *Sketches of European Capitals.* Another course, which he did not live to deliver, appeared in book form after his death— *Lectures on the Works and Genius of Washington Allston* (1852). He was the author of a memoir of Nathaniel Bacon in Jared Sparks's *Library of American Biography* (2nd ser. vol. III, 1844), and edited *American Unitarian Biography* (2 vols., 1850–51). On June 10, 1823, he was married to Mary, daughter of Dr. Benjamin Waterhouse [*q.v.*] of Cambridge, a sister of the wife of his brother Henry; they had seven children, four of whom survived their father. During the later years of his life he resided in Cambridge, where he died.

[E. F. Ware, *Ware Geneal.* (1901); W. B. Sprague, *Annals of the Am. Unitarian Pulpit* (1865); S. A. Eliot, *Heralds of a Liberal Faith,* vol. II (1910); *Christian Examiner,* May 1852; E. A. and G. L. Duyckinck, *Cyc. of Am. Lit.* (1875); *Boston Transcript,* Feb. 20, 1852.]
H. E. S.

WARE, WILLIAM ROBERT (May 27, 1832–June 9, 1915), architect and educator, the son of Henry Ware, 1794–1843 [*q.v.*], and Mary Lovell (Pickard) Ware, was born in Cambridge, Mass. He was a half-brother of John Fothergill Waterhouse Ware [*q.v.*]. He was educated first in Cambridge, then in Phillips Exeter Academy, and graduated from Harvard College in 1852. From 1852 to 1854 he was a tutor in private families in New York and then returned to Cambridge, where in 1856, after two years in the

Lawrence Scientific School, he received the degree of S.B. He first entered the office of Edward Clarke Cabot [*q.v.*] in Boston and later became one of the first pupils of the atelier which Richard Hunt [*q.v.*] had established in his New York office. In 1860 he began practice with an engineer, E. S. Philbrick. Three years later he formed a partnership with Henry Van Brunt [*q.v.*]. Their office in Boston for many years was among the foremost in the eastern states. Their work includes the First Church, Boston; the former union station, Worcester; the Episcopal Theological School, Cambridge; two dormitories, the alteration of the old university library (in which, for the first time, Henri Labrouste's ideas of stack construction were adapted to American use), and the famous Memorial Hall at Harvard. This work is largely under the influence of Ruskin and his English followers, with much use of picturesque details, horizontal lines, and polychrome masonry. The Memorial Hall has in addition big scale and a commendable simplicity of scheme.

During his early practice Ware had become more and more impressed with the chaotic character of architectural education. The old apprenticeship system had perished, and there was nothing to take its place. Between 1863 and 1865, therefore, he and Van Brunt established an atelier for students in their own office, adding to the customary design and drawing problems a certain amount of systematic instruction in construction, theory, and history. So successful was this experiment that in 1865 Ware was appointed head of a proposed architectural school in the Massachusetts Institute of Technology. In preparation he spent a little over a year in Europe, studying especially the architectural education of France and England. When he returned, he brought with him Eugène Létang to take charge of the work in design in the new school, thus establishing in America for the first time, the École des Beaux Arts system of training in design. In 1881 he was called to New York to found a school of architecture at Columbia University, at first, strangely enough, as a department under the School of Mines. Here he remained until his retirement as professor emeritus in 1903, after a severe breakdown the year before. He made extensive trips to Europe in 1883, and in 1889–90, and in 1903. At Columbia, as at the Massachusetts Institute of Technology, he devised a school which, while borrowing widely from the French system, was in no sense an imitation of it, but a new system, based on American needs and American conditions. The two schools exerted an enormous influence on other and younger schools throughout the country, so that Ware may be called the founder of American architectural education in a very real sense. Meanwhile he had not lost touch with the profession as a whole. Though he dissolved his partnership with Van Brunt when he left Boston, he was a member of the designing board of the Pan-American Exposition of 1900 and designed the buildings for the American School of Classical Studies at Athens. He served as architectural expert and adviser for many important architectural competitions. A member of the American Institute of Architects from 1859 and a fellow from 1864, he was extremely active in Institute matters. He never married. During his last twelve years he lived quietly at Milton, Mass., with his maiden sister Harriet, writing an important series of textbooks.

Ware's importance as an educator lies in his keen appreciation of the special problem of American architectural education. His ideals appear clearly as early as 1865 in a paper read before the Society of Arts of the Massachusetts Institute of Technology, *An Outline of a Course of Architectural Instruction* (1866), and are even clearer in a paper read two years later before the Royal Institute of British Architects, "On the Condition of Architecture and of Architectural Education in the United States" (*Sessional Papers of the Royal Institute of British Architects, 1866–67*). To him the architect was much more than a mere technician; he was also an artist, an exponent of a traditional cultural history, and a member of society as a whole. Thus he felt the French system too limited, too concerned with technique. In his lectures, characterized by a fascinating discursiveness, he emphasized continually the cultural, social, and creative side of architecture. He tried in every way to keep the student's mind broad and curious. For the development of the creative side, he borrowed from France the idea of teaching design by projects to be solved under criticism and by an unusual emphasis on freehand drawing. All of these ideas are still alive, vital parts of the American architectural tradition. To this wise teaching were added the charm and winning simplicity of his own benign personality, so well expressed in his appearance during his later years—his silky white hair and beard, and his gracious and gentle expression. He was the author of many pamphlets and articles in periodicals; *Greek Ornament* (1878); *Modern Perspective* (1883), a classic work; *The American Vignola* (2 vols., 1902–06); and *Shades and Shadows* (1912–13). He was an honorary member of the Royal Institute of British Architects and of the Société Centrale des Architectes Français, and a fellow of the American Academy of Arts and Sciences. There is an excellent portrait of him painted by Brewster Sewall in the Avery Library, Columbia University.

[Emma F. Ware, *The Ware Geneal.* (1901); *Who's Who in America*, 1914–15; Clara T. Evans, biog. in MS. in the Avery Lib., Columbia Univ.; Grace W. Edes, *Annals of the Harvard Class of 1852* (1922); Élie Brault, *Les Architectes par Leurs Oeuvres* (3 vols., 1892–93); *Final Report of the Building Committee . . . Harvard Memorial Fund* (1878); A. D. F. Hamlin, in *Jour. Am. Inst. of Architects*, Sept. obituary in *N. Y. Herald*, June 10, 1915, *Jour. Am. Inst. of Architects*, July 1915, and *Columbia Univ. Quart.*, Sept. 1915.]   T. F. H.

WARFIELD, BENJAMIN BRECKINRIDGE (Nov. 5, 1851–Feb. 16, 1921), clergyman, was born near Lexington, Ky. His father, William Warfield, a breeder of horses and cattle, was descended from Richard Warfield who settled in Maryland in the seventeenth century. His mother was Mary Cabell (Breckinridge) Warfield, the daughter of Robert J. Breckinridge [*q.v.*]. Prepared for college by private study, he graduated from the College of New Jersey (Princeton) in 1871. After a year of European travel, he became an editor of the *Farmer's Home Journal* of Lexington, attending particularly to matters of livestock. In 1876 he graduated from Princeton Theological Seminary. On May 8, 1875, he was licensed to preach by the Presbytery of Ebenezer, which ordained him on Apr. 26, 1879. On Aug. 3, 1876, he was married in Lexington to Annie Pearce Kinkead, who died on Nov. 19, 1915. In 1876, after graduation from Princeton he studied at the University of Leipzig, and the next winter was assistant minister in the First Presbyterian Church of Baltimore. After a year as instructor in New Testament subjects in Western Theological Seminary at Pittsburgh, he became professor in 1879. In 1887 he was called to be professor of theology in Princeton Seminary, in succession to Archibald A. Hodge [*q.v.*]. There he spent the rest of his life, teaching to the day of his death. He was the chief editor of the *Presbyterian and Reformed Review* from 1890 to 1903 and was a frequent contributor, as he was also to its successor the *Princeton Theological Review*. He published some twenty books on Biblical and theological subjects, besides pamphlets and addresses. This production he maintained by indefatigable intense study in New Testament criticism and interpretation, patristics, theology, especially that of the Reformed churches, and considerable fields of church history. By command of modern languages he kept constantly abreast of theological scholarship.

His work as teacher and writer was governed

by his enthusiastic committal to Calvinism, particularly as stated in the Westminster Confession of Faith, in which he saw "the final crystallization of the very essence of evangelical religion" (*The Significance of the Westminster Standards as a Creed* (1898), p. 36). He held unswervingly to the plenary inspiration of the Bible and was deeply persuaded of the truth of the doctrine of original sin. At Princeton he continued without concessions the theological tradition established by the Hodges. A vivacious teacher, expert in hand-to-hand argument, he moulded many students for a generation and thus influenced the thought of the Presbyterian and other churches. In his writings he was critical or interested in particular subjects rather than constructive or systematic. They contain valuable work in historical theology. His books included *An Introduction to the Textual Criticism of the New Testament* (1886), *The Gospel of the Incarnation* (1893), *The Lord of Glory* (1907), *The Plan of Salvation* (1915), and *Counterfeit Miracles* (1918). Under his will ten volumes composed of his most important articles in periodicals and encyclopedias were published, among them *Revelation and Inspiration* (1927), *Studies in Tertullian and Augustine* (1930), *Calvin and Calvinism* (1931), *The Westminster Assembly and Its Work* (1931), *Perfectionism* (2 vols., 1931–32).

[Necrological Report of Alumni Assoc. of Princeton Seminary, in *Princeton Theol. Seminary Bulletin*, August 1921; *Princeton Theol. Review*, April 1921, May 1921; *Who's Who in America*, 1920–21; Alexander Brown, *The Cabells and their Kin* (1895); J. D. Warfield, *The Warfields in Md.* (1898); p. 40; *N. Y. Times*, Feb. 18, 1921; information from his brother, Ethelbert D. Warfield, Chambersburg, Pa.]   R. H. N.

WARFIELD, CATHERINE ANN WARE (June 6, 1816–May 21, 1877), poet and novelist, was born in Natchez, Miss., the daughter of Nathaniel A. Ware [*q.v.*] and Sarah (Percy) Ellis Ware. Her mother lost her mind at the birth of a second daughter in 1820 and lived for the rest of her life away from home. Her father saw to it that his two daughters, Catherine and Eleanor, should benefit from the best possible tutoring at home. Then, possessed of sufficient means to indulge their desire for further study, he took them to Philadelphia, where they had superior cultural advantages and where they developed into shy and somewhat precocious "blue-stockings." In 1833 Catherine married in Cincinnati Robert Elisha Warfield, the first cousin once removed of Benjamin B. Warfield [*q.v.*] and the son of Elisha Warfield of Lexington, Ky., a physician who had made a fortune as a merchant and who was the owner of the noted horse, Lexington.

The young couple lived in Lexington uneventfully until 1844. In that year she published in collaboration with her sister, Eleanor Percy (Ware) Lee, a volume of verse, *The Wife of Leon, and Other Poems, by Two Sisters of the West*. Since this volume was welcomed with approval, the sisters followed it with *The Indian Chamber, and Other Poems* (1846). Both books were much praised at that time but have for the poetry lover of today no charm whatever, the lines being stilted in style and made colorless by the conventional sentimentalizing of the era. In 1857 the Warfields removed to "Beechmoor," their estate in the Pewee Valley near Louisville. There in comparative retirement she turned with great earnestness to the writing of fiction and produced with some rapidity a series of novels, the first of which was the two-volume *The Household of Bouverie* (1860). It was characteristic of her in its intensity of moral vision and purpose, but also, unfortunately, because of its cheerless pedantic style, its insistence upon rigid principles of conduct, and its quest for sensationalism. Almost unreadable today, this narrative of a hiding criminal who lived upon an elixir of gold won a large public and the approval of various literary critics. Subsequent novels were *The Romance of the Green Seal* (1866); *The Romance of Beauseincourt* (1867) later published as *Miriam's Memoirs* (1876); *Miriam Monfort* (1873); *A Double Wedding* (1875); *Hester Howard's Temptation* (1875); *Lady Ernestine* (1876); *Ferne Fleming* (1877); and *The Cardinal's Daughter* (1877). The struggle between North and South inspired her to return to verse, in which she showed her strong Confederate sympathies; some of this poetry was published in Emily V. Mason's *Southern Poems of the War* (1867). Prejudice against Northerners and their manners is also frankly revealed in her novels that appeared during the period of Reconstruction.

As a novelist her importance lies in her priority in the history of Southern letters rather than in any intrinsic value. She was one of the first woman novelists of consequence in the South. Obviously influenced by the Gothic romancers, by Walter Scott and Charlotte Brontë and Mrs. Henry Wood, she lacked their knowledge of life and their stylistic skill so that her stories sink under an overwrought emotional attitude and a ponderous diction. The best are the first one and those that deal with the life of Miriam Montfort.

[Mary Forrest, *Women of the South Distinguished in Literature* (1861); M. T. Tardy, *Southland Writers* (1870), vol. I; J. W. Townsend, *Ky. in Am. Letters* (1913), vol. I; *Lib. of Southern Literature*, vol. XII (1910), ed. by E. A. Alderman and J. C. Harris; "The

Meadows" in E. M. Simpson, *Bluegrass Houses* (1932); J. D. Warfield, *The Warfields of Md.* (1898), pp. 38, 39; Alexander Brown, *The Cabells and their Kin* (1895).]   G. C. K.

WARFIELD, SOLOMON DAVIES (Sept. 4, 1859–Oct. 24, 1927), financier, was born near Mount Washington, Md., the son of Henry Mactier and Anna (Emory) Warfield, and a descendant of Richard Warfield, who came from Berkshire, England, to Maryland in 1662. His father was prominent in the business and political life of Baltimore. After a common-school education, Solomon obtained a clerkship with George P. Frick & Company and later with D. J. Foley Brothers & Company, both of Baltimore. Forced by ill health to go to his grandmother's country home, he indulged his taste for invention and patented a number of devices, including corn cutters and corn silkers, and soon established in Baltimore the Warfield Manufacturing Company to make them.

Becoming active in politics, he organized a club to support Cleveland in 1888 and afterwards founded and became the president of the Jefferson Democratic Association, the largest independent Democratic organization in Maryland. In 1891 he was nominated by the Independent Democrats for mayor of Baltimore and was indorsed by the Republicans, but he was defeated by Ferdinand Latrobe in a close contest. In 1894 Cleveland appointed him postmaster of Baltimore. He gave the office a progressive business administration, extending the service and for the first time using street cars to transport mail. In spite of being a Democrat, he was reappointed by McKinley and served until 1905. While still postmaster he organized and became president of the Continental Trust Company (1898), which was to be the agency of his later extensive financial operations.

His chief interests were in railroads, public utilities, and cotton manufacturing. Railway consolidation in the South was then in progress, and in 1898 Warfield, with John Skelton Williams [*q.v.*] of Richmond, was a member of the organization committee of the Seaboard Air Line Railway. He became a voting trustee, a director, and a member of the executive committee of the company, but withdrew in 1903. The road having fallen into financial difficulties in the panic of 1907, Warfield was made chairman of the receivers, January 1908, and in two years returned the road to its owners without having assessed the stock or scaled down the bonds, its market value having increased meanwhile over twenty-five million dollars. Warfield became chairman of the executive committee of the reorganized

road and at the time of his death was president of the Seaboard, his management and extension of which were of great importance in the development of Florida. Through participation in the sale of the interest of Baltimore City in the Western Maryland Railway Company to the Gould syndicate, he was made a director of the Missouri Pacific. Fearing that the "duck trust" would move the old-established Maryland cotton duck mills to the South, he formed a local syndicate and became chairman of the board of the International Cotton Mills Corporation (1910), controlling many mills in Maryland and elsewhere. This venture, however, never proved successful; its promotional costs were excessive, and the general drift of the heavy goods industry was toward the cotton fields and the South's cheaper labor supply. Beginning in 1903, he formed a syndicate with a capital of eleven million dollars to purchase the United Electric Light & Power Company of Baltimore. His plans were interrupted by the great Baltimore fire of 1904, which destroyed the large building of the Continental Trust Company. He went to work immediately and secured millions of dollars for the rebuilding of the city. The control of the Consolidated Gas Company having passed to New York interests, he formed a syndicate which brought that control back to Baltimore. Later he joined this company and the only remaining independent electric company of the city with the United Electric Light & Power to form the Consolidated Gas, Electric Light & Power Company. He had long wanted to develop the power resources of the Susquehanna River; unable to do so, after the panic of 1907 he brought the McCall's Ferry current to Baltimore by sale of stock in the Consolidated to the Pennsylvania Water & Power Company. By intensive work he negotiated a contract in 1909 with the Standard Oil Company to bring natural gas to Baltimore from West Virginia. A large proportion of the patrons of the Consolidated thought the terms disadvantageous to them, and the board of estimates of the city would not approve the contract. A bill presented to the legislature to permit a popular referendum on whether the board should negotiate for natural gas was also defeated. The Maryland Public Service Commission was set up in 1910 as a consequence of this fight.

In 1910 Warfield retired from the chairmanship of the Consolidated Gas, Electric Light & Power Company to enter more actively into the development of the Seaboard Air Line, unaware of the tremendous strides which electricity was soon to make. He was director in a number of steamship, railroad, coal, and insurance companies. When the railroads were turned back to their stockholders by the government after the World War, he organized and was president of the National Association of Owners of Railroad Securities, and worked out the plan, incorporated into the Transportation Act of 1920, for equating earnings between strong and weak roads. He was a man of great nervous energy and drove both himself and his associates. Dominating and self-centered, secretive and often indirect in method, he was not lacking in social charm. He was unmarried.

[Sun (Baltimore) and Baltimore American, Oct. 25, 1927; D. H. Carroll and T. G. Boggs, Men of Mark in Md., vol. III (1911); M. T. Copeland, The Cotton Manufacturing Industry of the U. S. (1912); J. J. Esch, Address . . . on the Occasion of the Dinner . . . Dec. 13, 1920, Given in Honor of S. Davies Warfield (n.d.); J. D. Warfield, The Warfields of Md. (1898); Who's Who in America, 1926–27.]   B. M.

WARING, GEORGE EDWIN (July 4, 1833–Oct. 29, 1898), agriculturist, sanitary engineer, author, was born at Poundridge, N. Y., the son of George Edwin and Sarah (Burger) Waring and probably a descendant of Jonathan Waring, who came from Tipperary, Ireland, to Huntington, Long Island, in the eighteenth century. George went to school at College Hill, Poughkeepsie, and subsequently studied agricultural chemistry under James J. Mapes [q.v.]. The son of a farmer, he first directed his attention to scientific agriculture. In the winter of 1854–55 he gave lectures to farmers in Maine and Vermont, and for the next two years managed Horace Greeley's farm at Chappaqua, N. Y. In 1857 he was appointed drainage engineer of Central Park, New York City, a position he held four years. When the Civil War began, however, he became major of the Garibaldi Guards. He saw service for a short time with the Army of the Potomac and was then sent to St. Louis to recruit troops under Gen. John Charles Frémont. He raised six companies and early in 1862 was made colonel of the 4th Missouri Cavalry, United States Volunteers. He served until 1864, principally in the southwestern part of Missouri.

After the war Waring assumed management of the Ogden Farm near Newport, and remained there ten years. He then engaged in the sanitary drainage of houses and towns as a professional expert, attaining considerable success. The deplorably insanitary condition of Memphis, Tenn., and a series of yellow fever epidemics which culminated in 1878 in a visitation of that disease which cost 5,150 lives in a population of some 40,000, provided Waring with an opportunity to exhibit the ingenuity and daring which char-

acterized him. Following the recommendations of a committee of the National Board of Health, of which he was a member, he installed a system of sewers which was unique in several particulars, not the least of which was cheapness. The pipes were much smaller than customary, were for house sewage only, without manholes, well ventilated, and were flushed every twenty-four hours by means of automatic flush tanks. The Memphis sewers were long a subject of controversy among engineers and Waring was compelled by his experience to modify his opinion with regard to some of their features.

In 1879 he served as special agent for the Tenth Census, in charge of social statistics of cities. His *Report* on that subject appeared in 1886. Appointed street-cleaning commissioner of New York City by Mayor William L. Strong [q.v.], he took office Jan. 15, 1895, and continued therein until Jan. 1, 1898. Waring found the department inefficient, badly equipped, and riddled with politics. His efforts to improve it at first met with public ridicule, but in a short time he raised the organization to a high plane of efficiency and was warmly applauded by the whole city. He introduced the three-part separation of refuse at the household—garbage, ashes, and rubbish—to facilitate final disposition; he bought new carts and horses; and he put the sweepers in white uniforms—"not," as he said, "to clean dirty streets but to keep clean streets clean"; he insisted on having "a man instead of a voter at the other end of the broom-handle."

In 1898 Waring went to Havana to collect data for a report to the United States government on the measures it was necessary to employ in order to make that city sanitary and free from yellow fever. He contracted yellow fever and died soon after returning to New York City. His report was completed and submitted to President McKinley by his assistant and executor, G. Everett Hill. A memorial service was held in Cooper Union, at which several distinguished persons made addresses. A permanent memorial to him was created when the Chamber of Commerce of the State of New York raised by public subscription $100,000, the interest on which was to be paid to his widow and daughter during their lifetime. At their death the principal was to be turned over to Columbia University to constitute the Waring Memorial Fund for instruction in municipal affairs. He was married three times: first, Feb. 22, 1855, to Euphemia Johnston Blunt; second, Dec. 27, 1865, to Virginia Clark; and third, July 20, 1898, to Mrs. Louise E. Yates, of New Orleans.

Waring was a prolific writer. Among his best-known books and pamphlets are *The Elements of Agriculture* (1854); *The Handybook of Husbandry: A Guide for Farmers, Young and Old* (1870); *Whip and Spur* (1875); *A Farmer's Vacation* (1876); *The Sanitary Drainage of Houses and Towns* (1876); *The Sewerage of Memphis* (London, 1881); *Report of the Department of Street Cleaning of the City of New York for 1895-'96-'97* (1898); *Street Cleaning and the Disposal of a City's Wastes* (1897); as well as two delightful volumes entitled *The Bride of the Rhine* (1878) and *Tyrol and the Skirt of the Alps* (1880). The sketch entitled "The Garibaldi Guard" in *The First Book of the Author's Club: Liber Scriptorum* (1893) was written by Waring.

[R. N. Waring, *A Short Hist. of the Warings* (1898); Albert Shaw, *Life of Col. Geo. E. Waring, Jr.* (1899); *Charities Rev.*, Dec. 1898; *Rev. of Reviews*, (N. Y.), Dec. 1898; *Nation* (N. Y.), Nov. 3, 1898; *N. Y. Tribune*, Oct. 30, Nov. 7, 23, 1898; *N. Y. Times*, Oct. 30, 1898; *Evening Post* (N. Y.), Oct. 29, editorial, Oct. 31, 1898; information as to certain facts from Waring's son, Guy Waring, and from G. E. Hill.]

G. A. S.

WARMAN, CY (June 22, 1855–Apr. 7, 1914), journalist, author, was born near Greenup, Ill., the son of John and Nancy (Askew) Warman. He was educated in the common schools, and for a time was a farmer and wheat broker at Pocahontas, Ill. In 1880 he went to Colorado, where he worked in the railroad yards at Salida, and was successively locomotive fireman and engineer for the Denver & Rio Grande Railroad. Forced by poor health to give up railroading, he went to Denver to enter journalism and in 1888 became editor of the semi-monthly paper *Western Railway*. In 1892 he started a paper called the *Chronicle* at the new silver mines of Creede, Colo. Meanwhile, both as railway worker and as journalist, he had been writing verses inspired by the grandeur of the Colorado mountains. In 1891 one of these pleasant, facile little poems, "The Canyon of the Grand," won a prize, and in 1892 Warman published a slender volume entitled *Mountain Melodies,* thousands of copies of which were sold on the trains of the Denver & Rio Grande. On Sept. 4 of that year Charles A. Dana [*q.v.*], editor of the New York *Sun,* published a group of Warman's verses in his paper. One of these lyrics, "Sweet Marie," was set to music by Raymond Moore and a million copies were sold in six months. Other popular songs followed, for which Warman sometimes wrote the airs himself.

The silver boom at Creede having collapsed, Warman went to New York City in 1893 to enjoy his celebrity. About this time, seeing in *McClure's Magazine* a railroad story by a man who clearly did not know railroading, he offered to ride a thousand miles in a locomotive cab and give his story to the magazine free if it were not "the best ever." He thereupon rode from New York to Chicago in the engineer's cab of a New York Central flyer and dictated the outline of his tale, "A Thousand-Mile Ride on the Engine of the Swiftest Train in the World" (*McClure's Magazine*, January 1894), immediately upon arrival. The resounding success of this story having opened to him the pages of periodicals both American and English, Warman now produced a long series of short stories and novels depicting the romance and adventure of the frontier and in particular of the spanning of the continent by the trail of the "iron horse." These tales, which have the authenticity of first-hand knowledge and yet belong definitely to the romantic tradition of frontier literature, were collected in a series of volumes: *Tales of an Engineer with Rhymes of the Rail* (1895); *The Express Messenger and Other Tales of the Rail* (1897); *Frontier Stories* (1898); *The White Mail* (1899); *Snow on the Headlight; A Story of the Great Burlington Strike* (1899); *Short Rails* (1900); *The Last Spike and Other Railroad Stories* (1906); *Weiga of Temagami and Other Indian Tales* (1908). He published also a history of American railroad enterprise, *The Story of the Railroad* (1898), and another volume of verse, *Songs of Cy Warman* (1911).

Warman stayed only a few months in New York. For two years he traveled in Europe and the Orient, and for two more he lived in Washington, D. C. He then built a house at London, Ont., which was his home for the rest of his days. He was twice married: first, 1879, to Ida Blanch Hays, of St. Jacobs, Ill., who died in 1887; second, May 17, 1892, to Myrtle Marie Jones, the inspiration of the song "Sweet Marie," whom he met at Salida and married at Denver. Warman died in a Chicago hospital.

[*Who's Who in America*, 1914–15; *N. Y. Times, N. Y. Tribune*, and *Sun* (N. Y.), Apr. 8, 1914; *Literary Digest*, Apr. 25, 1914; Eugene Parsons, "Cy Warman, Bard of the Rockies," in *Interludes*, Summer 1931.]

E. M. S.

WARMOTH, HENRY CLAY (May 9, 1842–Sept. 30, 1931), Union soldier, lawyer, governor of Louisiana, was descended from a family of Dutch extraction which had wandered from Virginia through Kentucky and Tennessee to Illinois. Son of Isaac Sanders and Eleanor (Lane) Warmoth, he first saw the light in a log cabin in MacLeansboro, Ill. His formal education was limited to that received in the village schools and to the training which he was able to pick up as a typesetter in a local printing office. After his father became justice of the peace at Fairfield, the reading of his law books and association with members of the bar inspired the youth with ambition to become a lawyer, and at the age of eighteen he was admitted to the bar at Lebanon, Mo. The outbreak of the Civil War the following year found him established as district attorney of the eighteenth judicial district, which post he relinquished in 1862 to join the Union forces as lieutenant-colonel of the 32nd Missouri Volunteers. After the capture of Arkansas Post he was assigned to the staff of Maj.-Gen. John A. McClernand [q.v.] and participated in the battles around Vicksburg, where he was wounded and furloughed. Charged with circulating exaggerations of Union losses, he was dishonorably discharged but was restored through personal appeal to President Lincoln. After the victory of Lookout Mountain and Banks's Texas campaign, he was assigned, in June 1864, as judge of the provost court for the Department of the Gulf, and when this service was ended he found himself, because of consolidations, without a command.

He thereupon opened a law office in New Orleans early in 1865 and soon won a lucrative practice before military commissions and government departments. In November of that year he was elected as "territorial delegate" to Congress by Louisiana Unionists but was denied a seat. In September 1866 he was a delegate to a special convention of Southern loyalists in Philadelphia called to demand protection for the Union men of the South. With a group including former Gov. Andrew J. Hamilton [q.v.] of Texas he made a canvas of the Northern states in behalf of the congressional program of reconstruction. In the Republican state convention of 1868 the sentiment in favor of his nomination for the governorship was so strong that the constitutional limitation on age was removed to permit him to become a candidate. The nomination was not without opposition, for he defeated his negro rival by only two votes, and a colored faction withdrew its support in the subsequent election. Warmoth was successful, however, and was reëlected in 1870. His gubernatorial term (1868–72) was characterized by discontent, turbulence, a wild orgy of speculation in state-aided railroads, a depleted treasury, and bitter strife over the question of negro suffrage. Although he signed the bill which opened the restaurants, schools, and railroad coaches to negroes without discrimination, he later vetoed a more radical measure and declared his purpose to harmonize the interests of races and to secure justice for

both. Probably, as he claimed late in life, corruption and extravagance would have been worse except for his opposition. Nevertheless, toward the close of his administration he was under attack from three quarters: from white conservatives, from radical Republican negroes—who denounced him as a traitor—and from the so-called Custom-House faction of the Republican party. By 1872 he had become utterly unavailable for renomination, and in consequence he actively supported the Democratic ticket. In the violent disturbances resulting from an election which culminated in two governors and two legislatures, he became, naturally, deeply involved. He was impeached by the hostile legislature in December 1872 and the trial dragged on until it was dropped some weeks after his term had expired. Many years later he published his own account of this stormy period, *War, Politics, and Reconstrnction* (1930).

Although after 1872 he retired from active party politics, he participated at intervals in political affairs. In 1876–77 he was a member of the Louisiana legislature; in 1879 he served in the state constitutional convention; in 1888 he again headed the Republican state ticket, but, though he made the strongest campaign of his career, was defeated; in 1896 he went to St. Louis to help nominate McKinley for president. He was appointed collector of customs for New Orleans in 1890 by President Harrison and served until 1893, when Cleveland replaced him by a Democrat.

In 1873 Warmoth engaged in sugar planting at "Magnolia Plantation," just below New Orleans. He helped to organize a sugar refining company, and to build a railroad which greatly advanced the development of the west bank of the lower Mississippi. He contributed significantly to the advancement of sugar-refining until it was no longer possible to compete with the foreign product, whereupon he sold his plantation and retired to live quietly in New Orleans. In 1884 he had made a trip to France and Germany to study the sugar industry and upon his return secured the establishment of an experiment station on his plantation. When the Sugar Planters Organization determined to fight for a higher duty and for a bounty, he was selected to conduct what proved a successful struggle. During his long life after the bitter era of Reconstruction he overcame much of the antagonism against him, and hundreds who had earlier opposed him gathered to do him honor at his funeral. He was survived by his wife, Sallie Durand of Newark, N. J., whom he had married May 30, 1877, and by two sons and a daughter.

[In addition to Warmoth's book, mentioned above, see: *Who's Who in America*, 1916–17; Mrs. E. S. du Fossat, *Biog. Sketches of Louisiana's Govs.* (1885); Arthur Meynier, *Meynier's La. Biogs.*, pt. 1 (1882); J. R. Ficklen, *Hist. of Reconstruction in La., through 1868* (1910); Ella Lonn, *Reconstruction in La. after 1868* (1918); *Times-Picayune* (New Orleans), Oct. 1, 1931.]   E. L.

WARNER, ADONIRAM JUDSON (Jan. 13, 1834–Aug. 12, 1910), soldier, congressman, bimetallist leader, and promoter of industrial enterprises, was a descendant of John Warner, who came to America on board the *Increase* in 1635, soon afterward settled in Hartford, Conn., and later moved to Farmington. Adoniram was born in Wales, Erie County, N. Y., the son of Levi and Hepsibah (Dickinson) Warner. When he was eleven the family went West, settling at Lake Geneva, Wis. Both parents died before he was sixteen· He attended Beloit College for a term, and in 1853 entered New York Central College, at McGrawville. On Apr. 5, 1856, he married a classmate, Susan Elizabeth Butts, by whom he had nine children. After teaching and serving as superintendent of schools in Mifflin County, Pa., he took charge of a school at Mercer.

At the outbreak of the Civil War he was instrumental in organizing the Mercer Rifles, which became Company G of the 10th Pennsylvania Reserves, of which he was made captain. He served in the Army of the Potomac until wounded at Antietam, rising to the rank of colonel. Declared unfit for active service, he was transferred to the Veteran Reserve Corps late in 1863, and stationed at Camp Morton, Indianapolis, being brevetted brigadier-general, Mar. 13, 1865, for gallant and meritorious service during the war. He read law while still in service, and was admitted to the bar of Marion County, Ind., Oct. 2, 1865, but never practised. He resigned from the army Nov. 17, 1865, and soon thereafter went to Marietta, Ohio. He became a member of the firm of Gates, Skinner & Company, operating in the oil fields of southeastern Ohio and West Virginia, and also bought and developed coal lands. To facilitate the marketing of the coal he built two railroads, the Marietta & Cleveland, running from Marietta to Canal Dover, and, some twenty years later, the Walhonding road, serving the district around Cambridge, Ohio. A still later project of his was the U Street trolley line in Washington, D. C.

Soon after the "demonetization" of silver in 1873, convinced of the injustice and folly of the action, Warner placed himself in the forefront of the denunciators. In 1877 he published a tract of ninety-three pages, *The Appreciation of Money: Its Effects on Debts, Industry, and National Wealth*. The following year, after a hotly contested campaign, he won a seat as a Democrat in the Forty-sixth Congress. In each of the three sessions of this Congress he guided a free-coinage bill through the House, but it was as regularly defeated in the Senate. He failed of reëlection to the Forty-seventh Congress, but was elected to the Forty-eighth and the Forty-ninth. The silver agitation had by this time spent its force, and he was not prominent in his second and third terms.

While the silver question was in abeyance, he appears to have carried on correspondence with economists at home and abroad. He attended the First National Silver Convention held in St. Louis in November 1889, and was made its permanent chairman and chairman of a national silver committee. In the latter capacity he called the Second National Silver Convention in 1892, and he became the president of the American Bimetallic League which was there organized. He was now unquestionably the leading figure in the organized silver movement. He supervised the general activity of the League, made speeches, wrote tracts, and conducted three national conventions in 1893 and one in 1894. During the summer of 1895 he made an extended speaking tour with Joseph Sibley [*q.v.*], potential candidate for the presidency of the American Bimetallic Party, which the League was trying to launch. Late in 1895 he acted as the agent for the League in negotiations which led to its consolidation with the National Bimetallic Union and the formation of the American Bimetallic Union, of which he assumed the presidency. Throughout the spring of 1896 the Union, under Warner's supervision, continued its propaganda unabated, and tried to influence the Democrats to nominate Henry Teller [*q.v.*] for the presidency. It gave its full indorsement to Bryan's candidacy, however, and Warner and his associates took an active part in the campaign. In 1899 he delivered an address at a bimetallic conference in Chicago, still maintaining that the only permanent solution to the monetary question lay in bimetalism.

His last years were spent in industrial activities, for the most part in Georgia. He organized the Gainesville Railway Company, which provided the city with a trolley line, and the North Georgia Power Company, which built fifty-three miles of steel towers from Gainesville to Atlanta, the first in the South. The panic of 1907 seriously undermined his companies and he sold out, retiring early in 1910 to Marietta, where he died.

Warner was well over six feet tall and of commanding appearance. As an orator he was not at his best, but he could hold the attention of an audience by his logical, convincing manner. He was essentially a pioneer in spirit, enjoying nothing better than to break ground, but losing interest in a project once it was well launched. His vision was boundless, and he had many ideas which he was unable to carry through. There is no evidence to show that he received any remuneration for his services to the Bimetallic League or Union, other than expenses. He enjoyed an uphill fight, and, convinced of the logic and justice of an enterprise, he was willing to give his whole energy to promoting it.

[C. O. Warner, *Geneal. of the Descendants of Omri Warner and . . . Hist. of Milo Warner and His Family* (1916); *Daily Register-Leader* (Marietta), Apr. 12, 1911; *Daily Times* (Marietta), Aug. 13, 1910; *Cincinnati Enquirer*, Aug. 14, 1910; pamphlets in Wis. Hist. Soc.; Beman Gates, *Letters from Europe, 1868* (1927); J. F. Brennan, *A Biog. Cyc. . . . of Ohio* (1879); *Biog. Dir. Am. Congress* (1928); *Who's Who in America*, 1910–11; MSS. in possession of Warner's daughter.]

M. S.

WARNER, AMOS GRISWOLD (Dec. 21, 1861–Jan. 17, 1900), sociologist, was born at Elkader, Iowa, the posthumous son of Amos Warner, a country physician, who was killed in an accident, and of Esther (Carter) Warner. The latter was a woman of exceptional intelligence and strength of character, actively interested in temperance, woman's suffrage, and other social movements of the day. In 1864 she moved with her four children to Roca, a village near Lincoln, in the Territory of Nebraska. Amos attended country schools until he entered the preparatory department of the University of Nebraska in 1878. Exceptionally well-read, highly intelligent, and full of enthusiasm, he soon became a leader in student affairs. He had an epigrammatic humor which ever afterward gave a pungent flavor to his speaking and writing. He was graduated with the degree of A.B. in 1885.

Entering the Johns Hopkins University for graduate study in economics and the social sciences, he at once attracted attention by his creativeness and his instinct for reality, and was granted a fellowship. Early in 1887 he delivered a speech on social problems at the church attended by John Glenn, the Maryland philanthropist. Through Glenn's influence he was appointed general secretary of the Charity Organization Society of Baltimore, in which position he served while completing his graduate work. In 1888 he received the degree of Ph.D., and that same year, Sept. 5, he married Cora Ellen Fisher, a graduate of the University of Nebraska. In 1889 Warner became associate professor of economics at his alma mater, where his course in the scientific study of industrial corporations was probably the

first in this subject offered in an American university. In February 1891, President Harrison appointed him superintendent of charities for the District of Columbia. The charitable institutions of the District were then in a chaotic condition, but in two years Warner succeeded in organizing an admirable system and in inducing Congress to found a board of children's guardians.

In 1893 he became professor of economics and social science at Leland Stanford Junior University, accepting the position because the institution had just received as a gift the Hopkins Railway Library. He was especially interested in railway problems and visualized a new department which should include not only economic and financial problems but engineering and administrative questions as well. The following year, in addition to a heavy teaching program, he wrote in less than two months *American Charities,* a book of 407 pages, which became a classic in the field of applied sociology, a fourth edition being published in 1930. It was almost the first book of its kind and for many years was accepted as the best.

Warner had inherited enormous vitality and a fairly strong physique, but ten years of research, organizing and administrative labor, and teaching had seriously undermined it. During the Western railway strike of 1893 he was obliged to travel at night on the open deck of a Sacramento River steamer and contracted a violent cold. This developed into tuberculosis, which compelled him to take a leave of absence from Stanford University, in November 1894, and to spend five years in exile in the Southwest. His mental vigor, however, enabled him to continue the social-economic editorials which he had been writing for the *Real Estate Record and Builders Guide* of New York. In 1897, in a brief period of improved health, he returned to Stanford and delivered before the Chapel Union four addresses based on social science, which revealed his broad religious point of view and his spiritual power. These were published after his death under the title *Lay Sermons by Amos Griswold Warner* (1904). Unable to take up teaching again, he returned to the desert and died at Las Cruces, N. Mex., survived by his wife, a son, and a daughter.

In addition to more than a hundred editorials he wrote numerous addresses and articles, many of which are fundamentally valuable in the history of social economics in America. He spoke and wrote clear, vivid, fluent English, enlivened by quaint humor and practical illustrations. He had a pioneering mind, which seized upon essentials. In teaching he was not a drill-master, desiring that his students get ideas and attack practical social problems, rather than depend upon theoretical textbooks. His reputation in the field of applied sociology must rest chiefly on his *American Charities,* which marked the high achievement of his young manhood.

[Biog. prefaces by G. E. Howard to the second (1908) and third (1919) editions of *American Charities,* and to *Lay Sermons*; Edward Ross, in *Charities Rev.,* Mar. 1900; *Who's Who in America,* 1899–1900; family papers in the possession of Warner's daughter, Esther Warner Kellenbarger.] M. R. C.

WARNER, ANNA BARTLETT (Aug. 31, 1827–Jan. 22, 1915), novelist and author of children's books, was the daughter of Henry Whiting and Anna (Bartlett) Warner, and was descended on both sides from old New England families. Her grandfather, Jason Warner, owned a farm in Canaan, N. Y., and served several terms in the state Assembly. Her father was also a lawyer, and was the author of *The Liberties of America* (1853) and several other books. Anna Warner was born in New York City, where the family for some time maintained a residence. Her mother died soon after she was born, and she and her elder sister, Susan [*q.v.*], were brought up by their aunt, Frances L. Warner. Her early summers were spent in the home of her paternal grandfather in Canaan, but in 1836 her father purchased Constitution Island, in the Hudson River near West Point, intending to use a farmhouse on the island as a summer residence. Severe financial reverses, however, in 1837 forced him to give up his city home, and from that time on, for the most part, the family spent both winters and summers at Constitution Island, though the father was often absent on business, and the two daughters made occasional visits to friends. Constitution Island, which they usually called by the older name of Martelaer's Rock, remained the home of both Susan and Anna Warner as long as they lived.

After 1837 the Warner sisters had to learn to economize, and, as they grew older, they sought to aid with the family expenses. When she was in her early twenties, Anna invented a game called "Robinson Crusoe's Farmyard," and she and her sister earned a little money by coloring cards to accompany the game. Under the name of Amy Lothrop she also began writing stories for children, and, after the success of her sister's first novel, *The Wide, Wide World,* in 1851, she attempted a novel, *Dollars and Cents* (1852). Like her sister's *Queechy,* it made use of both childhood memories of Canaan and more recent experiences with poverty. In 1860 she collaborated with her sister in writing *Say and Seal,*

but in general she devoted herself to books for children. Both with her sister and alone she wrote Bible stories, collections of edifying tales for Sunday school libraries, and Sunday school lessons. Such publications as *Mr. Rutherford's Children* (2 vols., 1853–55) and *Wych Hazel* (1876), which the two sisters wrote together, proved profitable to their authors as well as instructive to their readers. Alone Anna wrote *Stories of Vinegar Hill* (6 vols., 1872), *The Fourth Watch* (copyright 1872), and various works on gardens, such as *Gardening by Myself* (1872). Mr. Warner died in 1875 and Susan Warner in 1885. Anna Warner continued to live on Constitution Island, with a servant, and for a few years more continued to write. In 1909 she published a memoir of her sister. She also carried on the Sunday Bible class which her sister had begun for cadets at the United States Military Academy. The sisters took a strong interest in the Academy, at which their uncle, Thomas Warner, was for ten years chaplain and professor. It was their desire that their island should be attached to the property of the academy, and this was made possible by Mrs. Russell Sage shortly before Anna's death, which occurred in 1915 at Highland Falls, N. Y. Both sisters are buried in the government cemetery at West Point.

Except in minor respects it is difficult to distinguish Anna's work from that of her sister. Though she was somewhat less talented than Susan, her novels and stories have similar virtues and defects. Temperamentally more stable than Susan, she relied less on sentiment, but her work has the same sort of piety, and the blend of realism and romanticism is much the same.

[*Who's Who in America,* 1914–15; Olivia E. P. Stokes, *Letters and Memories of Susan and Anna Bartlett Warner* (1925); Anna B. Warner, *Susan Warner* ("*Elizabeth Wetherell*") (1909); "Bibliog. of the Works of Susan Warner and Anna Bartlett Warner," in *Fourth Ann. Report . . . Martelaer's Rock Asso.* (1923); S. A. Allibone, *A Crit. Dict. of Eng. Lit.* (3 vols., 1858–71); obituary in *N. Y. Times,* Jan. 23, 1915.] G. H.

WARNER, ANNE RICHMOND (Oct. 14, 1869–Feb. 1, 1913), writer of fiction, was born in St. Paul, Minn., the daughter of William Penn and Anna Elizabeth (Richmond) Warner. Her father, a lawyer of St. Paul, was a descendant of Andrew Warner, yeoman, who had emigrated from England to Massachusetts by 1632 and lived successively in Cambridge, Hartford, and Hadley. Her mother was a descendant of John Richmond, who also emigrated from England to America about 1630. Anne Warner was educated at home by her mother, who was a wit and a lover of Dickens, and by a French tutor. In the quiet which her father's scholarly habits imposed upon his household the child cultivated a love of reading and self-expression, became an accomplished pianist, rode and drove for recreation, and associated almost wholly with adults. The routine of her girlhood was broken only by occasional trips to Nunda, N. Y., to visit her paternal grandmother. When she was eighteen she married (Sept. 12, 1888) Charles Eltinge French (d. 1912), a flour manufacturer of Minneapolis, twenty-five years her senior. After the death of an infant daughter in 1892 she occupied herself by compiling a genealogical tree for her son, *An American Ancestry* (1894).

An eager curiosity to see the scenes she had read about took her to Europe in 1901. She settled in Tours with her two children and in 1902 published a slender volume, *His Story, Their Letters*. After spending two years in France she returned to America and went to live in St. Paul, but she found it distracting to write there. The next year she settled in Munich, and two years later in Hildesheim, Germany. In 1904 she published *A Woman's Will* and *Susan Clegg and Her Friend Mrs. Lathrop*. The instant popularity won by Susan Clegg's homely humor prompted her to write *Susan Clegg and Her Neighbors' Affairs* (1906), *Susan Clegg and a Man in the House* (1907), *Susan Clegg, Her Friend and Her Neighbors* (1910), and *Susan Clegg and Her Love Affairs* (1916). In 1905 she published *The Rejuvenation of Aunt Mary,* which she later dramatized. From 1904 until her death her stories appeared in profusion in the popular magazines, many of the serials being published later as novels. A collection of the short stories, *An Original Gentleman,* appeared in 1908. She wrote easily and rapidly, a simple incident often suggesting an entire story to her. In her lively wit and humor and in her method of writing lay much both of the charm and the impermanence of her stories, which are slight in plot and characterization but fresh, vivacious, and amusing.

As her popularity in America grew it became more difficult for her to write there, her friendly generosity refusing to repel admirers. She returned every year or two, however, for brief visits. From 1906 until 1910 she spent much of her time in Hildesheim. In 1910 she rented a house in Marnhull, Dorset, England, and settled there to give her daughter Anne (b. 1895), who was her constant companion, a less kaleidoscopic home life. When her son, Charles Eltinge French (b. 1889), was ill in America dur-

ing the summer and fall of 1912, she was unable to go to him because of her aged and helpless father, whom she had brought to her English home. She was distracted by anxiety and grief and unable to write. She died suddenly of a cerebral hemorrhage a short time after her son's death.

[L. C. Warner and Josephine G. Nichols, *The Descendants of Andrew Warner* (1919); Anne R. W. French, *An Am. Ancestry* (1894); *Who's Who in America,* 1912–13; "Chronicle and Comment," *Bookman,* Mar. 1908, May 1909, Apr. 1913; obituaries in *N. Y. Times* and *N. Y. Tribune,* Feb. 4, 1913; information from Mrs. French's daughter, Anne French Burnham of New York City.]   V. L. S.

WARNER, CHARLES DUDLEY (Sept. 12, 1829–Oct. 20, 1900), essayist, editor, novelist, was born in Plainfield, Mass., by four years the elder of the two sons of Justus and Sylvia (Hitchcock) Warner. His father was descended from Andrew Warner, who had emigrated from England to Cambridge, Mass., by 1632; and his mother from Francis Cooke, a *Mayflower* Pilgrim. Justus Warner was a farmer of some two hundred acres in western Massachusetts. To his widow and sons this land was virtually all that he left when he died in 1834— this and the injunction, "Charles must go to college." In 1837 Mrs. Warner took her sons to live with their guardian, Jonas Patch, at Charlemont, Mass., and in 1841 removed to her brother's home, Cazenovia, N. Y. At the Oneida Conference Seminary there Charles prepared for Hamilton College, from which he was graduated with the degree of B.A. in 1851, and began the lifelong friendship with Joseph R. Hawley [*q.v.*] which was later instrumental in turning him from the law to writing. Another permanent friend made now was Daniel Willard Fiske [*q.v.*]. As a Hamilton undergraduate Charles contributed articles to the *Knickerbocker Magazine,* and his commencement oration burgeoned forth in 1851 as his first book, *The Book of Eloquence.* Ill health resulting from the strain of earning much of his schooling sent Warner in 1853–54 to Missouri, where he did railroad surveying. He joined a friend in business in Philadelphia in 1855. On Oct. 8, 1856, he married Susan Lee, daughter of William Elliott Lee of New York City. In 1858 he took the degree of LL.B. at the University of Pennsylvania and began practice in Chicago. Hard times and a distaste for the law, however, in 1860 helped decide him upon becoming assistant to his friend Hawley, editor of the *Evening Press* in Hartford, Conn.

Kept at home by near-sightedness, Warner became editor in 1861 when Hawley went to the

Civil War. After the war Hawley entered politics, and the editorial weight of the *Hartford Courant,* with which the *Press* was consolidated in 1867, fell increasingly upon Warner. He found time, however, to write for the *Press* a series of humorous essays about his three-acre farm. Henry Ward Beecher caused these to be published as a book, and himself wrote the introduction for *My Summer in a Garden* (1871). These essays, wrought in the best vein of Warner's urbane humor, brought him instant reputation. There is in them a touch of Lamb, whom Warner avowedly admired, and whose mellow grace lingers in all of Warner's other essays: *Backlog Studies* (1873), *Baddeck* (1874), *Being a Boy* (1878), *On Horseback* (1888), *As We Were Saying* (1891), *As We Go* (copyright 1893), *The Relation of Literature to Life* (copyright 1896), *The People for Whom Shakespeare Wrote* (1897), and *Fashions in Literature* (1902). In May 1868 he went on the first of five trips to Europe, and a series of travel sketches he sent to the *Courant* appeared in book form in 1872 as *Saunterings.* In 1876 and 1877 came *My Winter on the Nile* and *In the Levant,* much the best of his travel-books. Here emerged a distinct vein of Chaucerian humor: Warner likes man, but tolerantly riddles his humbug and foibles. Writing with an informed sense of the places visited, he gave studied impressions, not factual guidebooks merely. Later he added to the literature of travel *In the Wilderness* (1878), *A Roundabout Journey* (copyright 1883), *Their Pilgrimage* (1887), *Studies in the South and West* (1889), and *Our Italy* (1891).

Fiction was not Warner's *métier,* and his four novels constituted his least successful body of work. In 1873 he collaborated with his friend and neighbor Mark Twain on *The Gilded Age,* an uneven book in which Warner's Missouri days loom disproportionately. Sixteen years later he made fiction the Pegasus on which he rode, more hard than skilfully, his ultimate hobby, the social responsibility of wealth. Gone now was the humane and humorous ease of his essays; in its place was the style of a stern moralist. Three novels, *A Little Journey in the World* (1889), *The Golden House* (1895), and *That Fortune* (1899), depict respectively the amassing, misuse, and loss of a great fortune. The weakness of this trilogy was perceived by Warner's friend William Dean Howells, who wrote, "He had not the novelist's habit of using experience imaginatively, structurally." Two biographies dated 1881 virtually complete his writings: a pleasant one of Washington Irving for the American Men of Letters Series, of which Warner was editor, and

a less satisfactory one of Captain John Smith. Warner always remained identified with the *Hartford Courant.* From 1884 to 1898, however, he was a contributing editor of *Harper's New Monthly Magazine,* and with his brother, George H. Warner, and others he edited the *Library of the World's Best Literature* (1896–97), in thirty volumes.

In his maturity Warner was a member of the Hartford park commission and the Connecticut state commissions on sculpture and prisons, vice-president of the National Prison Association, and president of the American Social Science Association and the National Institute of Arts and Letters. Yet it was Warner the essayist who contributed most to American life and letters. He was here an artist of delicate fiber and sure taste. No less was he of notable personality, chiefly marked by urbanity and friendliness. To Howells he wrote, "There is not much good in life except friends," and with friends in many walks of life he was rewarded. He never gained wealth by his writings, though in his lifetime they were popular. His rewards were yet of the sort in which he delighted. Something of a scholar in appearance—straight and slender, with a rugged, aquiline head, deep blue eyes under shaggy brows, and carefully cultivated gray hair and beard—he was in fact a frequent lecturer at the universities, by whom he was abundantly honored. Delicate health marred his late years, and he spent his winters usually in the South. At Norfolk, Va., in April 1900, facial paralysis gave warning of the end, which came suddenly from heart failure in Hartford on Oct. 20. He was survived by his wife. They had no children. In 1904 appeared *The Complete Writings of Charles Dudley Warner* in fifteen volumes, edited by Thomas R. Lounsbury.

[The best biogs. are Annie A. Fields, *Charles Dudley Warner* (1904), and the sketch by T. R. Lounsbury, in *The Complete Writings of Charles Dudley Warner,* vol. XV (1904). See also L. C. Warner and Josephine G. Nichols, *The Descendants of Andrew Warner*(1919); *Report of the Eighty-Ninth Commencement of Hamilton Coll.* (1901); *Mark Twain's Autobiog.* (2 vols., 1924); obituary and letters in *Hartford Daily Courant,* Oct. 22, 1900. Information for this article has been supplied by Miss Mary Barton of Hartford, a close friend of the Warners.]   J. A. P.

WARNER, FRED MALTBY (July 21, 1865– Apr. 17, 1923), governor of Michigan, was born in Hickling, Nottinghamshire, England, the son of Joseph and Eliza (Wooley) Maltby. His parents emigrated to America when he was three months old, and shortly after, upon the death of his mother, he was adopted by Pascal D'Angelus and Rhoda E. (Bosford) Warner, of Farmington, Mich. After graduation from the Farmington High School, he attended the Michigian State College of Agriculture for one term. He then became a clerk in his foster father's general store. A few years later this establishment was turned over to him and he conducted it successfully for twenty years. On Sept. 19, 1888, he married Martha M. Davis of Farmington. Ambitious, resourceful, friendly, Warner engaged with marked success in various lines of business. In 1889 he built a cheese factory in Farmington, and before long established additional plants in eastern Michigan, ultimately becoming a national figure in the cheese-making industry. He was a progressive farmer on a rather large scale, a vigorous promoter of real estate, and an active banker.

His participation in politics began with membership in the municipal council of his home village at the age of twenty-five. In 1894 he was elected to the state Senate, in which he served until 1898. At that time Hazen S. Pingree [q.v.] was engaged in his famous struggle with the old Republican party machine. Warner remained friendly with the Pingree faction, though he received the potent machine indorsement as candidate for secretary of state—to which office he was elected in 1900 and 1902—and for governor in 1904. His Democratic opponent for the governorship, Woodbridge N. Ferris [q.v.], advocated direct primaries as a means of crushing machine rule. The issue proved popular in a muck-raking era, and Warner, though at first opposed to reform, found it expedient to compromise to the extent of advocating a local option primary law, and won the election. The campaign had converted him, however, to a belief in a general primary law, and he finally forced the legislature to accept such a measure. Once started on a career of reform, he broadened his program, and, accepting the defection of a large number of his followers as a challenge, took the unprecedented step of running for a third successive term. He won the election by the narrowest of margins, and rounded out six years of impressive executive leadership. During his governorship the legislature passed measures for heavier taxation and lower rates on railroads, stricter control of public utilities and insurance companies, conservation of natural resources, encouragement of the dairy industry, food control, factory inspection, and the curbing of stock manipulation.

After his retirement from office at the age of forty-five, he devoted himself to farming and business, retaining, however, a lively interest in politics. From 1920 until the time of his death he was Republican national committeeman from

Michigan. In several respects his career was unique: although he was by background a conservative, experience and power made him more liberal; himself a product of organization politics, he developed into the sturdiest of fighters for reform; ambitious in the field of capitalistic endeavor, he espoused principles designed to curb capitalism. He died in Orlando, Fla., survived by his wife, two sons, and two daughters.

[For sources, reliance must be placed almost entirely upon contemporary newspaper accounts; useful information is to be found in the *Farmington Enterprise*, Apr. 20, 1923, and in the *Detroit News*, Apr. 17, 1923; an impartial estimate of Warner's rôle in Michigan politics may be found in an editorial, *Ibid.*, Apr. 18, 1923; see also, G. N. Fuller, *Messages of the Governors of Mich.* (4 vols., 1925–27); *Mich. Official Directory and Legislative Manual*, 1901–02, 1903–05; and *Who's Who in America*, 1922–23.]   L. G. V–V.

WARNER, HIRAM (Oct. 29, 1802–June 30, 1881), jurist and congressman from Georgia, was born in Williamsburg, Hampshire County, Mass., the descendant of Andrew Warner, an English emigrant who was in Cambridge, then Newtown, Mass., as early as 1632, and the eldest of ten children of Obadiah and Jane (Coffin) Warner. His parents were dependent upon farming for a livelihood and were in moderate circumstances. Their eldest son received, in addition to a common-school training, only one year of high school. This one year was spent under the direction of Mr. Thaxter, who very soon removed to Sparta, Ga., established a school there, and wrote back to young Warner asking him to come to Georgia to help teach in the school. At Sparta and Blountsville, in Georgia, he taught school and read law until he was admitted to the bar in 1824. He began practice in Knoxville, Crawford County, Ga., where he married in 1827 Sarah (Abercrombie) Staples. They had one daughter. From 1828 to 1831 he represented Crawford County in the state legislature. In 1832 he was a delegate to the state's anti-tariff convention, but, becoming dissatisfied with its actions, he withdrew from it. About this time he removed to Talbot County, where he formed a law partnership with George W. B. Towns [q.v.]. In 1833 he was elected by the legislature judge of the newly created Coweta circuit of the superior courts, at that time the highest court in the state. His election was unusual not only on account of his youth, but also because he did not live in the circuit. Shortly afterward, however, he removed into the circuit and settled at Greenville, Meriwether County. He was reëlected at the expiration of his term, but in 1840 he was defeated. He then resumed practice, with his brother Obadiah, and devoted considerable time to farming, at which he was very successful. When the supreme court of Georgia was established in 1845, although a Democrat, he was given a position on the court by a Whig legislature. In 1853 he resigned and returned to general practice. Elected to Congress he served from 1855 to 1857.

In 1860 he was a member of the Georgia secession convention, where he opposed secession bitterly but finally signed the ordinance. During the Civil War he lost much of his property as a result of pillage, and, of course, all his slaves. He was also hanged to a tree and left for dead by a band of Wilson's Federal raiders, because he told them he had no gold and could not therefore divulge its place of hiding. Following the war he again became judge of the Coweta circuit, where he served until 1867, when he was appointed chief justice of the supreme court of Georgia. The "Reconstruction" constitution of 1868 brought about a reorganization of the supreme court, and he was reduced to an associate justice. In January 1872, however, he again became chief justice and remained in that position until 1880, when he resigned. He died in Atlanta and was buried in Meriwether County, near his wife. He was widely read in the law and characterized by abundant common sense and rugged convictions. In politics he was first a Jeffersonian Republican and later a Democrat. Throughout his entire career, however, he stood for the Union against state rights, a manifestation, it is thought, of early training. He opposed nullification but favored the extension of slavery. He was reared a Presbyterian and was a constant reader of the Bible, but he never became a communicant of any church.

[W. J. Northen, *Men of Mark in Ga.*, vol. III (1911); memorial in 68 *Ga. Reports*, 845–55; L. L. Knight, *Reminiscences of Famous Georgians*, vol. II (1908); Geo. White, *Hist. Colls. of Ga.* (1854); *Biog. Directory Am. Cong.* (1928); *The Descendants of Andrew Warner* (1919), ed. by L. C. Warner and J. G. Nichols; *Savannah Morning News*, July 1, 1881; information from H. Warner Martin, Washington, D. C.]
B. F.

WARNER, JAMES CARTWRIGHT (Aug. 20, 1830–July 21, 1895), Tennessee industrialist, eldest son of Jacob L. Warner, native of Virginia, and Elizabeth (Cartwright) Warner, grand-daughter of Robert Cartwright, pioneer of Middle Tennessee, was born in Gallatin, Tenn. With a common-school education and some training from his father in the tailor's trade, he left home at the age of seventeen to seek his fortune in Nashville. He worked as clerk, first in a wholesale grocery and then in the firm of Kirkman & Ellis, hardware merchants, and on Nov. 3, 1852, he was married to Mary Williams, daughter of a Gallatin neighbor. The young couple moved to Chattanooga, where Warner

established a hardware business of his own. He was elected mayor for a term, and was a member of the General Assembly in 1861. Poor health prevented his enlistment in the Confederate army. During the Chattanooga campaign his home was demolished and after the Confederate defeat, Warner and his family as refugees made their way by wagon-train to Nashville.

Like many another Southerner, Warner faced the aftermath of war penniless and in debt. His business ability was recognized, however, and after a brief term as bank cashier he was appointed, in 1868, secretary of the Tennessee Coal & Railroad Company. He now began a significant career of a quarter of a century in developing the mineral resources of the South. The company had been engaged in haphazard coal mining in southeastern Tennessee since the early fifties. Soon promoted to general manger, Warner foresaw coke making as a solution for the company's surplus of slack coal, which in turn might lead to the manufacture of iron with the new fuel. He was not acquainted with the problems of the blast furnace, but after a visit to the iron works near St. Louis, he and his assistant, Col. Alfred M. Shook [q.v.], erected an experimental furnace at Tracy City. The "Fiery Gizzard," as it was called, was too crude to be a commercial success, but the coke experiment led to contracts to supply furnaces in upper Georgia, and to the erection by Warner of the Chattanooga Furnace. In company with ex-Governor Joseph E. Brown [q.v.] of Georgia, he purchased the Rising Fawn iron property in that state in 1874, reorganized the plant on a scientific and paying basis, and sold it in 1882 along with the Chattanooga Furnace for $311,000. This same year Warner was made president of the Tennessee Coal, Iron & Railroad Company, which had recently built its first furnace at Cowan with the most modern equipment. Poor health, which afflicted Warner periodically throughout his life, had forced him to retire from active participation in the company's affairs in 1874, but now, under the new régime of John H. Inman [q.v.] of New York (1882–85), he began a new program of expansion which led to the absorption of a rival English company in the vicinity and eventually to the entry of the Tennessee Company into the Birmingham district.

Warner's most notable achievement was the revival and modernization of the charcoal iron industry in Middle Tennessee. After a thorough investigation of the ore fields of Hickman and neighboring counties, the Warner Iron Company was organized in 1880, composed of Nashville capitalists. Having secured the controlling interest, he had free rein to develop the property along the most improved lines. The fifty-ton hot-blast Warner Furnace, built at a cost of $125,000, set a new precedent in the charcoal iron industry by its efficient operation. Scientific practice was applied all along the line. A charcoal by-product plant was built and three additional furnaces blown in, all of which were sold to the Southern Iron Company in 1889, the Warner Furnace alone being valued at $1,000,000. Warner retained a large interest in the new company, which under A. M. Shook's management experimented successfully in making steel from Tennessee iron, until the panic of 1893 closed the works.

Warner was one of the finer types of the New South's industrial pioneers. Without any formal training, he attacked the varied technical problems of coal and iron with keen perception, and his grasp of financial problems and market trends was perhaps even more remarkable. He accumulated a handsome fortune and his benefactions, performed without publicity, were generous. He had seven sons and one daughter.

[J. B. Killebrew, *Life and Character of James Cartwright Warner* (1897); *Nashville American*, July 22, 23, 1895; Ethel Armes, *The Story of Coal and Iron in Alabama* (1910); Tenn. Commissioner of Labor, *Second Ann. Report* (1892).]   L.J.C.

WARNER, JONATHAN TRUMBULL (Nov. 20, 1807–Apr. 22, 1895), California pioneer, was born in Hadlyme, Conn., a descendant of Andrew Warner who was in Cambridge, Mass., as early as 1632. Jonathan's parents, who were distantly related, were Selden and Dorothy (Selden) Warner. He appears to have been well educated. In the fall of 1830, in ill health, he reached St. Louis, and in the spring of 1831 was hired by Jedediah Smith [*q.v.*] as the clerk of a trading expedition to New Mexico. The party, with the exception of Smith, who was killed by Comanches, reached Santa Fé early in July. Warner then joined David E. Jackson's trading expedition to California, arriving in Los Angeles on Dec. 5. For two years he trapped and hunted. At the end of 1833 he returned to Los Angeles, where he was employed by Abel Stearns [*q.v.*], and in 1836 he opened a store of his own. In the following year he married, at the mission of San Luis Rey, Anita, daughter of William A. Gale of Boston. About this time he changed his given name to Juan José, chiefly because his middle name was not easily pronounced by those who spoke English, and had no Spanish equivalent. In December 1839, he set out on a visit to the East. While in Rochester, N. Y., in August 1840, he delivered a lecture (later published both in England and in America), in which he urged the retention of Oregon, with the acquisition of California, and suggested the practicability of a transcontinental railway.

He was again in California in June 1841. In 1843 he became a Mexican citizen, and on Nov. 28, 1844, received a large grant of land in the Valle de San José, 110 miles southeast of Los Angeles. This was the beginning of what was known as Warner's Ranch, which became famous because of the many notable events occurring on or near it during and immediately after the war with Mexico. Warner was elected to the California Senate from San Diego County in 1850. The following year an Indian uprising drove him and his family from home, but on its suppression they returned. In 1855 he moved to Los Angeles, and in 1858 began publication of a weekly newspaper, the *Southern Vineyard*. In 1860 he was elected to the Assembly. He served for a time as provost marshal of Los Angeles and thereby acquired the courtesy title of colonel. By 1861 all of his ranch property had passed from his hands. He seems, however, to have retained a competency, and his later years were spent in leisurely quiet. He was the joint author (with Benjamin Hayes and J. P. Widney) of *An Historical Sketch of Los Angeles County* (1876). In 1884 he published a pamphlet, *The Warm and the Cold Ages of the Earth in the Northern Latitudes*. He also wrote "Reminiscences of Early California From 1831 to 1846," which was printed in *Annual Publications of the Historical Society of Southern California* (vol. VII, 1909). Toward the end of his life he became totally blind. He died at his home, survived by several children. His wife had died in 1859.

Warner was six feet three in height, a stature that caused him to be familiarly known as Don Juan Largo (Long John). He was dignified, courteous, and friendly. Although essentially a man of peace, he was not without his share in the turbulence of the early days; he seems to have been a member of the vigilance committee of 1836 that put to death a woman and her paramour for an atrocious murder; he had an arm broken in a political row in 1838, and he was twice in serious trouble with the American authorities in the difficult years of 1846–49. Of the American pioneers in the Spanish period he was the most cultivated, and was perhaps the most widely esteemed.

[L. C. Warner and J. G. Nichols, *The Descendants of Andrew Warner* (1919); H. H. Bancroft, *Hist. of Cal.*, vol. V (1886); H. D. Barrows, in *Ann. Pub. of the Hist. Soc. of Southern Cal.*, vol. III (1895); L. A. Williamson, *Ibid.*, vol. XIII (1928); J. J. Hill, *The*

Warner

Warner   Warner

Hist. of Warner's Ranch and Its Environs (1927) ; *An Illustrated Hist. of Los Angeles County, Cal.* (1889).]

W. J. G.

WARNER, JUAN JOSÉ [See WARNER, JONATHAN TRUMBULL, 1807–1895].

WARNER, OLIN LEVI (Apr. 9, 1844–Aug. 14, 1896), sculptor, son of Levi and Sarah B. (Warner) Warner, was born in Suffield, Conn., of New England colonial stock. Levi Warner, an itinerant Methodist minister, moved to Amsterdam, N. Y., in 1846. The boy attended district school until his fifteenth year, meanwhile showing talent in drawing faces and carving little figures from chalk. At the outbreak of the Civil War he wished to enlist as a drummer boy, a desire which faded in the bustle of the family's removal to Brandon, Vt. There he went to school until the age of nineteen. He had never seen statues, but he longed to make them, and, knowing no better, he bought plaster, set it, and from the resulting block whittled a bust of his father. This was at least a likeness, and in a spirit of consecration he resolved to become a sculptor. To earn money for his art education he mastered telegraphy, at which he worked six years, in Albion and Rochester, N. Y., and in Augusta, Ga. With money saved from his earnings, he went abroad at twenty-five years of age. He entered the École des Beaux-Arts, studying under Jouffroy, and becoming acquainted with Alexandre Falguière, Antonin Mercié, and Jean Baptiste Carpeaux. His talent, industry, and courage won the regard of Carpeaux, who took him as workman into his private studio and invited him to remain as assistant. Warner declined this opportunity. Times were troublous. The Empire fell, the Republic was declared. In sympathy with the Republic, he joined the Foreign Legion, mounted guard at the fortifications, and did not resume his studies until after the Commune.

In 1872 he returned to the United States, where he suffered tragic disillusionment. He struggled four years in his New York studio and at his father's farm in Westminster, Mass.; he worked for silver manufacturers and designed bronze gas fixtures. At the Centennial Exhibition of 1876 he exhibited a striking medallion of Edwin Forrest. About this time his portrait bust of Daniel Cottier, the art dealer, was hailed by artists and critics as a delightful work, truly classic in feeling, yet far as possible from pseudo-classic taste. Other busts followed, penetrating yet poetic interpretations of character, without recourse to the "painter-like quality" then becoming popular in sculpture. Among the best of these are portraits of J. Alden Weir, the painter (1880), Maud Morgan, the harpist (1881), William C.

Brownell, the critic, and John Insley Blair. The last, a masterpiece of rich modeling, is owned by the Metropolitan Museum.

Warner, born a Connecticut Yankee, has been called a pilgrim strayed from Hellas. Hellenic serenity pervades his standing figure of "Twilight" (1879), his "Dancing Nymph" (1881), his relief of "Cupid and Psyche" (1882), the noble bronze caryatids of his Skidmore fountain at Portland, Ore. (1888), and his reclining "Diana," about to rise at the approach of Actaeon, a figure which expresses the beautiful moment of transition between repose and action. In 1889–91 he was in the Northwest, where he made valuable portrait studies of such notable Indian chiefs as Joseph [*q.v.*] of the Nez Percés, Vincent and Seltice of the Cœur d'Alenes, Young Chief and Poor Crane of the Cayuses, Lot of the Spokanes, and Moses of the Okinokanes. The Long Island Historical Society owns a number of his Indian heads in terra cotta. His granite drinking fountain (in the manner of the Renaissance and therefore somewhat uncharacteristic of the sculptor) was completed in 1890 and placed in Union Square, New York, but it was later moved to Central Park. Of the two notably fine seated statues by Warner, that of Governor Buckingham, war governor of Connecticut, is in the State Capitol at Hartford, that of William Lloyd Garrison on Commonwealth Avenue, Boston, Mass. In front of the Boston State House is a stately standing figure of Gen. Charles Devens, completed in 1894 and erected in 1898. For the Columbian Exposition of 1893, Warner executed the souvenir half-dollar, colossal heads of famous artists, a statue of Hendrik Hudson, and busts of Governors Clinton and Roswell P. Flower for the New York State building.

He was soon to engage in the more congenial work of designing and modeling two great bronze doors for the Library of Congress, Washington, D. C., the themes being "Oral Tradition" and "Writing." The Tradition door, with its beautiful panels of classically draped figures and its impressive tympanum, had been fully completed before Warner's sudden death as the result of a bicycle accident. For the second door, little that would have satisfied his sensitive spirit had actually been accomplished, and the commission was therefore turned over to Herbert Adams. Warner is well represented in the Metropolitan Museum. He was a member of the National Academy of Design, the Society of American Artists, the National Sculpture Society, and the Architectural League of New York. Because of his high consecration to his art, and his unswerving choice of the monumental rather than the

467

pictorial in sculptural expression at a time when a picturesqueness of sculptural rendering was popularly applauded, his sudden death at the height of his powers was a severe loss to American sculpture. In 1886 he married Sylvia Martinach, daughter of Dr. Eugene Martinach, a New York physician. He was survived by his wife and two daughters.

[W. C. Brownell, in *Scribner's Mag.*, Oct. 1896; "Henry Eckford" (Charles De Kay), in *Century Mag.*, Jan. 1889; C. E. S. Wood, "Famous Indians," *Ibid.*, July 1893; C. H. Caffin, *Am. Masters of Sculpture* (1903); Lorado Taft, *The Hist. of Am. Sculpture* (1903); Suzanne La Follette, *Art in America* (1929); obituaries in *N. Y. Times* and *N. Y. Tribune*, Aug. 15, 1896; private information.]　　　　A. A.

WARNER, SETH (May 6, 1743 o.s.–Dec. 26, 1784), Revolutionary soldier, was born in Roxbury (then Woodbury), Conn., the fourth of ten children of Dr. Benjamin Warner and his wife, Silence Hurd, and a descendant of John Warner, an original settler of Farmington, Conn. He received a common-school education, but as a youth was better known for his skill in woodcraft than his acquaintance with books. In 1763 the family removed to Bennington, and two years later Seth was married to Hester Hurd. Three children were born to them. At that time Vermont was claimed by both New York and New Hampshire. Many of the settlers had received grants of land from Gov. Benning Wentworth of the latter province, but the courts of New York challenged the legality of the grants and sought to oust the occupants. Under the leadership of Warner, Ethan Allen, and others, the people of Vermont resisted, frequently resorting to violence in ejecting surveyors, settlers, and judicial officers representing the authority of New York. On Mar. 9, 1774, Warner was outlawed by the General Assembly of New York and a reward was offered for his apprehension.

These experiences, combined with the atmosphere of frontier life, bred in him a spirit of sturdy independence, and when the Revolution broke out, he ardently espoused the cause of the colonies. He aided Ethan Allen and Benedict Arnold [*qq.v.*] in the surprise of Ticonderoga on May 10, 1775, and himself captured Crown Point on the following day. At a council of officers held there in June, he and Allen were delegated to procure the incorporation of a contingent of the Vermont troops in the Continental service. After appearing in person before the Continental Congress and the legislature of New York, they obtained authorization for the creation of a regiment of Green Mountain Boys, of which Warner was elected lieutenant-colonel commandant on July 26, at a convention of delegates representing the towns in western Vermont. Later in the year he served on the Canadian border under Richard Montgomery [*q.v.*], and, while the latter was besieging St. John's, he defeated (Oct. 31) at Longueuil a relief expedition led by Sir Guy Carleton. After the death of Montgomery and during the retreat of the American forces from Canada in 1776, he was engaged in bringing up the rear and in collecting reënforcements in Vermont. In 1777, when the advance of Burgoyne up Lake Champlain forced the Americans to abandon Ticonderoga, he commanded the rear guard of St. Clair's army and fought a sharp action with the pursuing British at Hubbardton on July 7, as a result of which he retreated to Manchester, where he bent his efforts to rally troops for the defense of Vermont. On Aug. 9, in company with John Stark [*q.v.*], who had come from New Hampshire with a force to aid the Green Mountain Boys, he arrived in Bennington. In the meantime Burgoyne had dispatched an expedition under Colonel Baum to obtain horses and supplies in Vermont. On Aug. 16 the Americans attacked the invaders about five miles northwest of Bennington. Although Warner's movements during the action have been much debated, it is generally agreed that the timely arrival of his regiment in the latter part of the battle turned the tide in favor of the yeomanry of New England. On Mar. 20, 1778, he was appointed brigadier-general by the Vermont Assembly.

While Warner remained in command of his regiment until 1781, he saw little more active service owing to failing health. In the hope of improvement he returned to Roxbury in 1782 where he died. In 1858 his body was transferred from the Old Burying Ground to the Centre Green where a granite shaft commemorates him. He was a man of commanding appearance, more than six feet in height, with kindly though strongly chiseled features. Modest and unassuming, he was not given to advertising his achievements, preferring to let them speak for themselves.

[L. C. Warner and Mrs. J. G. Nichols, *Descendants of Andrew Warner* (1919); Daniel Chipman, *Memoir of Col. Seth Warner* (1848); G. F. Houghton, *Address Delivered before the Legislature of the State of Vermont, Oct. 20, 1848* (1849); E. B. O'Callaghan, *Doc. Hist. of the State of N.-Y.*, vol. IV (1851); Hiland Hall, *Hist. of Vt.* (1868); *Vt. Hist. Soc. Colls.*, vols. I (1870), II (1871); *Records of the Council of Safety and Governor and Council of the State of Vt.*, vols. I–III (1873–75); F. W. Coburn, *Centennial Hist. of the Battle of Bennington* (1877); William Cothren, *Hist. of Ancient Woodbury, Conn.* (3 vols., 1854–79); W. H. Crockett, *Vt., the Green Mountain State*, vols. I–IV (1921); *New-England Hist. and Geneal. Reg.*, Oct. 1880.]　　　　E. E. C.

WARNER, SUSAN BOGERT (July 11, 1819–Mar. 17, 1885), novelist, was born in New York City, the daughter of Henry Whiting and Anna (Bartlett) Warner, and a descendant of William Warner who settled in Ipswich, Mass., in 1637. She was a precocious child, and from an early age she read widely. Both she and her sister Anna Bartlett [q.v.] were devout Presbyterians from their girlhood. Throughout her youth she was subject to periods of extreme melancholy, and all her life she was, like her heroines, given to frequent and copious weeping. In the spring of 1848, when the family's economic situation was far from reassuring, at the suggestion of an aunt she undertook to write a story. The result was *The Wide, Wide World,* on which she worked intermittently until the summer of 1849. During the next few months the novel was rejected by several publishers, but it was finally accepted by George P. Putnam [q.v.] on the recommendation of his mother. It was published at very end of 1850 under the pseudonym of Elizabeth Wetherell and was well received by most of the reviewers. In less than two years there had been thirteen editions in the United States and several editions, both authorized and pirated, in England. It was included in at least one critic's list of the one hundred best novels in English, and it and *Uncle Tom's Cabin* were said to be the two most popular novels written in America in the nineteenth century. Its popularity is all the more striking because there are almost no incidents in the entire novel, which describes the moral and religious development of an orphan in her early teens. A second novel, *Queechy,* begun before the publication of *The Wide, Wide World* and finished in June 1851, was published in 1852, and was almost as popular as its predecessor. This novel also describes the spiritual and intellectual growth of a girl who has to live in comparative poverty on a farm after living in luxury in New York and abroad. In *Queechy,* however, there is a romantic theme, though the hero's romance is subordinated to his religious conversion.

Susan Warner wrote many other books, but none was so popular as her first two. She wrote many stories for children, both with her sister and alone, and a number of novels, among them *Melbourne House* (copyright 1864), *The Old Helmet* (1863), *Daisy* (1868), *Diana* (1877), *My Desire* (1879), *Nobody* (1882), *Stephen, M.D.* (1883), and others. Many of her novels were based on real incidents, and it was her intention to portray real life in her stories. There is a certain amount of realism in all her works, especially in her descriptions of rural customs,

The source of her popularity, however, seems to have been her sensibility, which equaled that of any of the more extravagant English novelists of the later eighteenth century. It was her description of the emotions of her characters— emotions that found expression in tears on almost every page—that compensated in the minds of her readers for the absence of action. To this sensibility was added a strong piety, which was revealed both in the interpretation of character and in direct comments and exhortations. From 1837 to 1885 she spent the greater part of her time on Constitution Island, near West Point. She made occasional visits to New York and Boston, and she was acquainted with some of her literary contemporaries, including Julia Ward Howe and Catharine Maria Sedgwick. She died in Highland Falls, N. Y., in 1885, after an illness of a few days.

[Anna B. Warner, *Susan Warner ("Elizabeth Wetherell")* (1909); Olivia E. P. Stokes, *Letters and Memories of Susan and Anna Bartlett Warner* (1925); "Bibliog. of the Works of Susan Warner and Anna Bartlett Warner," in *Fourth Ann. Report . . . Martelaer's Rock Asso.* (1923); "Religious Fiction," in *Prospective Rev.,* Aug. 1853; Cuyler Reynolds, in *Nat. Mag.,* Oct. 1898; "Tears, Idle Tears," letter to *Critic,* Oct. 29, 1892; S. A. Allibone, *A Crit. Dict. of English Lit.* (3 vols., 1858–71); death notice in *N. Y. Times,* Mar. 19, 1885.]   G.H.

WARNER, WILLIAM (June 11, 1840–Oct. 4, 1916), lawyer, soldier, congressman and United States senator from Missouri, was born in Shullsburg, Lafayette County, Wis., the son of Joseph and Mary (Dorking) Warner. The youngest of a family of twelve children, he was orphaned at the age of six, and until the age of ten he earned a few dimes occasionally at odd jobs around the lead mines of southern Wisconsin. Thereafter he worked for five years in a country store, saving enough money to pay his way through a two-year academy course. He then taught school for about four years, during which time he studied law at night, and between terms took law courses at Lawrence University, Appleton, Wis., and at the University of Michigan. He did not graduate from either institution, but was admitted to the Wisconsin bar at the age of twenty-one. During the Civil War he became first lieutenant, regimental adjutant, and, in 1863, captain of Company B, 33rd Wisconsin Volunteer Infantry. He served with average merit under Grant in Tennessee and Mississippi, and, because of his fine voice, was chosen to read the Declaration of Independence to both armies in the ceremony of the surrender of Vicksburg July 4, 1863. In 1864 he became major in the 44th Wisconsin Volunteers.

At the close of the war he began a successful

career at the bar in Kansas City. He was city attorney in 1867, circuit attorney in 1868, mayor in 1871, and a leading member of the commission which in 1875 formulated a charter for Kansas City. That instrument, with amendments of 1889 and 1908, was in force until the new manager form of municipal government was adopted in 1925. He was United States district attorney for the western district of Missouri from 1882 to 1884, in 1898, and from 1902 to 1905. In 1884 he was elected to the lower house of Congress, and was reëlected in 1888. His success as a politician is further attested by the fact that he served as a delegate to practically every Republican national convention from 1872 to 1904. Twice he served as commander of the Missouri Department, and in 1888 was chosen national commander of the Grand Army of the Republic. Through his congressional and Grand Army influence, he was largely responsible for the establishment of the Soldiers' Home at Leavenworth, Kan. He was the Republican candidate for governor of Missouri in 1892, but was defeated.

In 1905, for the first time since the Reconstruction era, the Missouri legislature was Republican. After a long and bitter struggle between the two leading candidates, Richard C. Kerens [q.v.] and T. K. Niedringhaus, the choice of the Republican caucus, Warner was put forward as a compromise candidate and elected to the United States Senate. His advocacy of numerous pension bills, and his support of the dependent relative pension bill in the face of the President's veto was highly satisfactory to the old-soldier element. The chief occasion on which he aspired to rise above the level of complacent mediocrity was in connection with the Brownsville, Tex., riot of August 1906. Warner indorsed President Roosevelt's severe discipline of the rioting negro soldiers, making the principal speech in behalf of the administration, and cross-examining the witnesses in the senatorial inquiry into that noted incident. After retiring, he was appointed civilian member of the national board of ordnance and fortifications. Although he held the reputation of being decidedly liberal in his religious convictions, practically his entire legal and political career bore the earmarks of conservatism. He was an unusually able lawyer in jury trials. In August 1866 he married Mrs. Sophia (Bullene) Bromley of Kansas City, by whom he had six children.

[The date of birth is that given in *Who's Who in America*, 1916–17; some other sources give the year as 1839. See also C. W. Whitney, *Kansas City, Mo.* (1908), vol. III; A. J. D. Stewart, *The Hist. of the Bench and Bar of Mo.* (1898); W. L. Webb, *Battles and Biogs. of Missourians* (1900); *Mo. Hist. Rev.*, Jan.

1917; *Biog. Dir. Am. Cong.* (1928); *Kansas City Star*, Oct. 4, 1916; *St. Louis Globe-Democrat*, Oct. 5, 1916.]
H. E. N.

WARNER, WORCESTER REED (May 16, 1846–June 25, 1929), manufacturer, telescope builder, was the son of Franklin J. and Vesta Wales (Reed) Warner, and was born on his father's farm near Cummington, Mass. He was a descendant of Andrew Warner who had settled in Cambridge, Mass., by 1632. Until he was nineteen Warner attended a district school in Cummington and showed a decided preference for mathematics, mechanics, and science, but little love of farming. In 1865 he found work in the drafting room of the American Safety Steam and Engine Company, Boston. When the offices of the company were moved to Exeter, N. H., the following spring, Warner went there to work in the shop as well as the drafting room for three years. There he met Ambrose Swasey, who became his close friend, and in the spring of 1869 the two entered the shops of the Pratt & Whitney Company in Hartford, Conn. Within two years both men were promoted to foremen, Warner having charge of the gear-cutting department and Swasey of a department for building machine tools. They both engaged in "contract work," a system which played a large part in developing individual manufacturing talent, and were so successful that in their eleven years with Pratt & Whitney they jointly accumulated $12,000. In 1880 they undertook to establish their own machine manufacturing business in Chicago, Ill., but the difficulty of obtaining skilled mechanics led them to move in 1881 to Cleveland, Ohio, where they established the Warner and Swasey Company to manufacture turret lathes. This enterprise was wonderfully successful from the start, Warner attending to the administration and Swasey to the manufacturing. They designed and built not only turret lathes but also speed lathes, die-sinking machines, and hand gear-cutters, and such intricate mechanisms as range-finders, gun-sights, and field telescopes for the United States government.

From the days of his youth Warner had been an ardent student of astronomy, and his chief avocation was the engineering of telescopes. The building of astronomical instruments was not included in the original manufacturing scheme of Warner and Swasey, but when the trustees of the Lick Observatory called in 1886 for designs for the great 36-inch telescope, the partners submitted a design incorporating the results of Warner's years of study and work. Their design, which provided much heavier mountings than had ever been used before and heavier construction throughout, won the contract, and the telescope was built and installed under Swasey's personal supervision. Their brilliant success brought the partners world-wide renown. The Lick Observatory telescope was followed by the 40-inch Yerkes telescope, the 72-inch telescope for the Dominion of Canada, and the 60-inch telescope for the Argentine national observatory. For twenty years Warner and Swasey conducted their business without any form of written agreement. In 1900, however, the Warner and Swasey Company was incorporated, with Warner serving successively as president and chairman of the board of directors until he retired in 1911 and removed to his estate, Wilson Park, at Tarrytown, N. Y. He devoted the remaining eighteen years of his life to his astronomical studies and to travel.

During his thirty-years' residence in Cleveland, Warner served as director of several banks, as a trustee of Western Reserve University, the Case School of Applied Science, and the Cleveland School of Art, and as president of the Cleveland Chamber of Commerce. He was active in the founding of the American Society of Mechanical Engineers in 1880, and served as a manager in 1890–93 and president in 1896–97. He was a member of the Royal Astronomical Society, the British Astronomical Association, and the American Association for the Advancement of Science, and received several honorary degrees. In 1916 he endowed the Worcester R. Warner collection of oriental art in the Cleveland Museum of Art. On June 26, 1890, he married Cornelia Fraley Blakemore of Philadelphia, Pa. At the time of his unexpected death in Eisenach, Saxe-Weimar, Germany, he was survived by his widow and one of his three children, a daughter.

[*Who's Who in America*, 1928–29 ; L. C. Warner and Josephine G. Nichols, *The Descendants of Andrew Warner* (1919) ; Guy Hubbard, in *Mech. Engineering*, Aug. 1929 ; J. M. and Jaques Cattell, eds., *Am. Men of Sci.* (4th ed., 1927) ; J. W. Roe, *English and Am. Tool Builders* (1926) ; obituary in *N. Y. Times*, June 26, 1929.]
C. W. M.

WARREN, CYRUS MOORS (Jan. 15, 1824–Aug. 13, 1891), chemist, inventor, and manufacturer, was born at Fox Hill, West Dedham, Mass., the eighth of the eleven children of Jesse and Betsey (Jackson) Warren, both parents being of old colonial stock. His father, a descendant of Arthur Warren who emigrated to Massachusetts before 1638, was a blacksmith and the inventor of the swivel or side-hill plough. In 1829 he established a plough factory and foundry at Peru, Vt., and in 1837 moved to Springfield, Vt., where two years later his iron foundry was wholly destroyed by fire, to the complete impoverishment of the family. Cyrus and his next older brother, Samuel, who obtained their first education in country schools, were ambitious of higher learning and pursued their studies privately, supporting themselves meanwhile by teaching school in winter and by farm work in summer. In 1846 Samuel began the manufacture of tarred roofing in Cincinnati and in the following year asked Cyrus to join him. The business succeeded so well that the two brothers were soon enabled to realize their ambition of securing a college education. In 1852 Cyrus, who had married Lydia Ross on Sept. 12, 1849, moved with his family to Cambridge, Mass., to begin the study of chemistry and zoölogy in the Lawrence Scientific School. He made here the acquaintance of Louis Agassiz [*q.v.*], who became his close friend and adviser. After graduating with the degree of B.S. in 1855, he took his family to Europe, where he studied chemistry first at Paris, then at Heidelberg under Robert Bunsen, at Freiberg in Saxony, at Munich under Justus Liebig, at Berlin under Heinrich Rose, and finally at London.

In 1863 he established in Boston a well-equipped private laboratory where he devoted himself to important researches upon the hydrocarbon constituents of tars. Since the Warren brothers were using various tars in their business, Warren's investigations upon the separation of their components by his improved process of "fractional condensation" (see *American Journal of Science,* May 1865) were of great industrial importance. The process was afterwards applied by Warren to a careful study of the complex mixture of hydrocarbons in Pennsylvania petroleum (*Proceedings of the American Academy of Science,* vol. XXVII, 1893) which may be said to mark the beginning of modern exact research in this field. Later, when the brothers turned to the use of Trinidad asphalt as a roofing and paving material, Warren invented processes of purification. The commercial and industrial development of these enterprises led to the establishment of the Warren Chemical and Manufacturing Company in Boston and the Warren-Scharf Asphalt Paving Company in New York, with Warren as president and treasurer. He took out various patents for processes of fractional distillation, and for improvements in asphalt roofing and paving, and devised an improved apparatus for determining vapor densities and an improved process of organic elementary analysis. In 1866–68 he held the chair of organic chemistry in the Massachusetts Institute of Technology, but the demands of his business enterprises obliged him to resign. The long severe strain to which he was subjected during the business depression of the seventies, and the death of his brother and partner, Herbert M. Warren, in 1880, threw additional burdens upon his shoulders that finally caused a weakening in health. He suffered a paralytic stroke in 1888 and three years later died at Manchester, Vt. He and his wife had four daughters and three sons.

Among self-made successful business men, Warren was an unusual type, his energy, persistence, and administrative ability being coupled with a strong capacity for study and scientific research. He always lamented that the exigencies and entanglements of business prevented him from giving exclusive attention to chemical research. He was the author of thirteen scientific papers, published in Poggendorff's *Annalen der Physik,* the *American Journal of Science,* and the *Proceedings* and *Memoirs of the American Academy of Arts and Sciences.* He left bequests for the promotion of science to Harvard University and to the American Academy of Arts and Sciences. A grant from the C. M. Warren Fund of the American Academy assisted Charles Frederic Mabery [*q.v.*] in his classic researches upon the composition of American petroleums.

[B. W. Davis, *The Warren, Jackson, and Allied Families* (1903); *Proc. Am. Acad. of Arts and Sciences . . . May 1891 to May 1892,* vol. XXVII (1893), with bibliog.; Benjamin Silliman, Jr., in *Am. Chemist,* Dec. 1874; death notice in *N. Y. Tribune,* Aug. 15, 1891.]

C. A. B.

WARREN, FRANCIS EMROY (June 20, 1844–Nov. 24, 1929), pioneer of Wyoming, United States senator, was born in Hinsdale, Mass., the son of Joseph Spencer and Cynthia Estella (Abbott) Warren. His first American ancestor was Arthur Warren who emigrated from England about 1635 and in 1638 settled in Weymouth. Francis' early schooling was interrupted because of his family's financial condition, but later his own efforts enabled him to attend Hinsdale Academy. His appointment as manager of his employer's farm before he was eighteen years old is evidence of early developing leadership. At the age of eighteen he joined the 49th Massachusetts Regiment to fight for the Union. Near Port Hudson, La., he was one of a group of volunteers to prepare the ground for an artillery charge. Most of his comrades were killed, but Warren escaped with a scalp wound. He was awarded the Congressional Medal of Honor for "courage above and beyond the call of duty."

Soon after the war, he went West and in 1868 settled in Cheyenne, Wyo., becoming manager of a furniture store. Associating himself with the growing cattle and sheep interests of that section, he became one of the great cattle men of the West, and sheep men of a later day referred to him as the patriarch of their industry. In 1883 he formed the Warren Livestock Company. When the National Wool Growers' Association was reorganized in 1901, he became its president.

As soon as he became a resident of Wyoming he began to take a conspicuous part in public affairs. His first election was to the board of town trustees. He served on the Cheyenne city council, as mayor, as a member of the Territorial Senate, and as treasurer of the Territory. In February 1885 President Arthur appointed him governor. He was removed by President Cleveland in November 1886, but was again appointed by President Harrison in March 1889, serving until Wyoming became a state in July 1890. Elected the state's first governor, he resigned in a few days to become United States senator. In this capacity he served until March 1893. He was reëlected two years later, and continued in that office until his death. He was the last Union soldier to serve in Congress. He was a delegate to five Republican national conventions between 1888 and 1912. Before the World War he was chairman of the Senate committee on military affairs, and after the war, of the committee on appropriations.

Characteristics developed in the simplicity of his New England background combined with those of frontier life to give Warren a strong personality. A splendid physique, tireless energy, willingness to work hard, keen judgment, executive ability, and a capacity for friendship made possible his valuable service. Interest in military affairs was natural for one who appreciated the task of settling the Indian country. The problem of reclamation of arid lands commanded his attention always, and he is called the "Father of Reclamation" (Beard, *post,* II, 27). He was actively helpful in securing the establishment of the Petroleum Field Office of the federal Bureau of Mines at the University of Wyoming in July 1924. No problem of the important appropriations committee was too intricate for him to master. Representing as he did the first equal-suffrage state, he supported the equal-suffrage amendment to the Constitution. Concerning the Eighteenth Amendment he said: "I cannot give my support to the joint resolution, because I believe and I think my State believes the same way, that the police power should be provided by State legislation . . . I have believed and I believe now, that progress can be truly made faster where we go just fast enough in these lines of reform so that our laws are obeyed and administered actively and completely" (*Congressional Record*, 65 Cong., 1 Sess., p. 5652).

Warren began his career amid the raw beginnings of the West, stood with it during its formative struggles, and lived to see its dreams turning into realities. He was twice married: first, Jan. 26, 1876, to Helen Smith of Middlefield, Mass., who died Mar. 28, 1902; second, on June 28, 1911, to Clara Le Baron Morgan. By his first wife he had a son and a daughter, the latter becoming the wife of John J. Pershing.

[Sources include I. L. Foster, *Some Descendants of Arthur Warren* (1911); I. S. Bartlett, *Hist. of Wyo.* (1918); F. B. Beard, *Wyo. from Territorial Days to the Present* (1933); *Progressive Men of the State of Wyo.* (1903); *Biog. Dir. Am. Cong.* (1928); *Who's Who in America,* 1926–27; *Nat. Wool Grower,* Dec. 1929; "The Senate's Nestor Views the Scene," *N. Y. Times,* Aug. 18, 1929; *Wyoming State Tribune* and *Cheyenne State Leader,* Nov. 25, 1929. For report (1913) on "unlawful fencing and inclosure" of public lands by the Warren Livestock Company see *House Report 1335,* 62 Cong., 3 Sess.]　　　　　　H.J.P.

WARREN, GOUVERNEUR KEMBLE (Jan. 8, 1830–Aug. 8, 1882), soldier, engineer, was born in Cold Spring, N. Y., across the Hudson from West Point, the son of Sylvanus Warren, a close personal friend of Washington Irving and a prominent citizen of Putnam County. Fourth of twelve children, the lad was named for Gouverneur Kemble [*q.v.*], proprietor of a foundry at Cold Spring and sometime member of the House of Representatives. After some instruction in his native town and at Kinsley's School across the Hudson, Warren at sixteen was appointed to the United States Military Academy, with the admonition from Kemble: "We expect you to rank, at graduation, not lower than second." Carrying out instructions literally, he finished number two in his class, July 1, 1850, and was appointed brevet second lieutenant in the restricted Corps of Topographical Engineers. During the next four years he served successively as assistant engineer on the survey of the Delta of the Mississippi River, member of the board for the improvement of the canal around the Falls of the Ohio, head of surveys for the improvement of Rock Island and Des Moines Rapids, and, with Capt. A. A. Humphreys [*q.v.*], as compiler of maps and reports of the Pacific Railroad exploration. Promoted second lieutenant, Sept. 1, 1854, he was chief topographical engineer of the Sioux Expedition of 1855, receiving his baptism of fire on Sept. 3, in the battle of the Blue Water. Promoted first lieutenant, July 1, 1856, he was engaged in making maps and reconnaissances of Dakota Territory and Nebraska Territory until August 1859, when he was detailed as assistant professor of mathematics at the Military Academy.

The opening of the Civil War found him still teaching at West Point, but on May 14, 1861, he became lieutenant-colonel of the 5th New York Volunteers, seeing action at Big Bethel Church, June 10, and subsequently aiding in the construction of defenses around Baltimore and Washington. He was promoted colonel of his regiment Aug. 31, and captain of topographical engineers, United States Army, Sept. 9. In the Peninsular campaign of 1862 he was engaged in the siege of Yorktown and commanded a brigade at Pamunky River and Hanover Court House (May 26, 27). He was wounded at Gaines's Mill, June 27, and brevetted lieutenant-colonel, United States Army, for gallant and meritorious service in that battle. Four days later he commanded the force that repulsed Wise's division at Malvern Hill, and the next day participated in the engagement at Harrison's Landing. He took part in the second battle of Bull Run and the skirmish at Centerville (Aug. 30, Sept. 1, 1862), and commanded a brigade in the Maryland campaign and its sequel, from Antietam to Falmouth, Va. (September–November 1862). Promoted brigadier-general of volunteers, Sept. 26, he served at the battle of Fredericksburg in December. As chief topographical engineer of the Army of the Potomac from Feb. 4, 1863, he saw action in May at Orange Pike, Marye Heights, and Salem. He was promoted major-general of volunteers June 3, 1863, and served as chief engineer, Army of the Potomac, from June 8 to Aug. 12, 1863.

It was at Gettysburg (July 1–3, 1863) that he rendered his most distinguished service. On the second day of that vital struggle, sent at his own suggestion by Meade to examine the Union left, he discovered that Little Round Top, the commanding position, was undefended except for a few signalers. He perceived Longstreet's threat and, intercepting some of Sickles' supports and Sykes's troops on the Peach Orchard road, practically commandeered them for the defense of the hill, just in time to keep Little Round Top from falling into the hands of the Confederates. Had this critical point been taken by Longstreet, it is agreed that the whole Union army would have been forced back in disorder and the day lost. Warren was brevetted colonel, United States Army, for his services in this battle, and in 1888 a bronze statue of him was erected to mark the spot where his alertness and energy came into play. Despite a wound received during the defense of Little Round Top, he continued in action, and was subsequently in temporary command of the II Corps from Aug. 12, 1863, to Mar. 24, 1864, participating in a number of engagements, notably that at Bristoe Station. He was placed regularly in command of the V Corps, Mar. 24, 1864, and with this corps participated in the actions of the Wilderness, Spotsylvania, Cold Harbor, and other engagements, as well as the various assaults on Petersburg. He was promoted major, United States Army, June 25, 1864, and brevetted major-general, United States Army, Mar. 13, 1865.

At Five Forks, Apr. 1, 1865, the last decisive battle of the war, his corps, after conflicting orders, arrived with dispatch on the flank of the Confederates and offered to the cavalry's hard-pressed troops the signal aid that clinched the victory, but to the astonishment of his subordinates and others engaged in that critical action, he was summarily relieved of his command by Sheridan, who had been given authority by General Grant. Transferred to command the defenses of Petersburg and the Southside Railroad, he served here during April and the first half of May, then commanded the Department of Mississippi, May 14–30, 1865. On May 27 he resigned his volunteer commission and reverted to the status of major of engineers, United States Army.

During the later sixties he prepared maps and reports of his campaigns and elaborated for publication the results of some of his early explorations. He served as member of the board of engineers to examine the canal at Washington, D. C., as superintending engineer of surveys and improvements of the upper Mississippi, and as member of the commission to examine the Union Pacific Railroad and telegraph lines. He was also in charge of the survey of the battlefield of Gettysburg. For almost a year, in 1869–70, he supervised the building of the Rock Island bridge across the Mississippi, and there through exposure and over-exertion received the impairment to his health which ultimately caused his death. He continued for twelve years more, however, in the river-and-harbor work of the Corps of Engineers—in the upper Mississippi Valley, along the Atlantic Coast, and in the Great Lakes. On Oct. 10, 1878, he was made a member of the advisory council of the Harbor Commission of Rhode Island, and on Mar. 4, 1879, he was promoted a lieutenant-colonel of engineers. Throughout this period he made repeated requests for a board of inquiry to examine into the causes of his ignominious relief at Five Forks, but since the authorities implicated were then in power, his request was not granted until December 1879. The court then appointed not only fully exonerated and applauded him, but cast reflections upon the manner of his relief. Ironically, however, the

findings vindicating him were not published until three months after his death.

Among Warren's published writings were: "Examination of Reports of Various Routes," with Capt. A. A. Humphreys, in *Reports of Explorations and Surveys . . . for a Railroad . . . to the Pacific Ocean,* vol. I (1855); *Memoir to Accompany the Map of the Territory of the United States from the Mississippi River to the Pacific Ocean, Giving a Brief Account of Each of the Exploring Expeditions since A.D. 1800* (1859); *An Account of the Operations of the Fifth Army Corps* (1866); *Report of the Survey of the Upper Mississippi River and Its Tributaries* (1867); *An Essay Concerning Important Physical Features Exhibited in the Valley of the Minnesota River* (1874); *Preliminary Report of Explorations in Nebraska and Dakota in the Years 1855–'56–'57* (1875); *Report on the Transportation Route along the Wisconsin and Fox Rivers . . . between the Mississippi River and Lake Michigan* (1876); *Report on Bridging the Mississippi River between St. Paul, Minn.; and St. Louis, Mo.* (1878). He was a member of a number of scientific organizations, including the American Philosophical Society and the National Academy of Sciences.

Warren was a firm friend, a generous enemy, gentle, sensitive, kind, and stanch. He was passionately fond of flowers. After the death of his father in 1859, he assumed much of the responsibility for the younger members of the family, whose welfare he guarded faithfully and tenderly. On June 17, 1863, he married Emily Forbes Chase of Baltimore, by whom he had a son and a daughter; two years later his sister Emily married his former aide, Washington A. Roebling [q.v.]. Warren died at his home in Newport, R. I., at the age of fifty-two.

[E. G. Taylor, *Gouverneur Kemble Warren* (1932); *The Biog. Cyc. of Representative Men of R. I.* (1881); G. W. Cullum, *Biog. Reg. Officers and Grads. U. S. Mil. Acad.* (3rd ed., 1891), vol. II; H. L. Abbot, in *Nat. Acad. Sci. Biog. Memoirs,* vol. II (1886) and in *Fourteenth Ann. Reunion, Asso. Grads. U. S. Mil. Acad.* (1883); *War of the Rebellion: Official Records (Army); Proceedings, Findings, and Opinions of the Court of Inquiry . . . in the Case of Gouverneur K. Warren* (1883); *Dedication Services at the Unveiling of the Bronze Statue of Maj.-Gen. G. K. Warren at Little Round Top, Gettysburg, Pa.* (1888); *Army and Navy Jour.,* Aug. 12, 1882; *N. Y. Times,* Aug. 9, 1882.]

W. A. G.

WARREN, HENRY CLARKE (Nov. 18, 1854–Jan. 3, 1899), Orientalist, was born in Cambridge, Mass. His ancestors, who were of English stock, came to New England between 1630 and 1640; his father was Samuel Dennis Warren, and his mother, Susan Cornelia Clarke. In his early infancy a fall from a chaise caused a spinal lesion, as the result of which he grew humpbacked, "and," as he expressed it, "ever since I have been excessively delicate and always ailing" (Harvard Class Reports). Though shut off from most of the activities and pleasures of normal children, youths, and men, he was enabled by his intellectual ability and force of character to rise above physical disabilities and to make important contributions to Oriental scholarship. Most of his work was done while he stood at a high desk with two crutches under his arms to take the weight off his spine; and toward the end of his life he worked while kneeling at a chair, resting the weight of his trunk on his elbows. He made light of his physical suffering, buoyed up always by a sense of humor which never failed him. He was most kind-hearted, generous, and modest, and given to unostentatious deeds of charity.

Prepared for college by private instruction, he took his bachelor's degree at Harvard in 1879, and continued his studies at the Johns Hopkins University (1879–84). His work in college, which centered around Latin, Greek, Sanskrit, and philosophy, was distinguished by his keen interest in the history of philosophy. The natural trend of his mind was toward speculative questions, but he also took an active interest in objective scientific matters. At Johns Hopkins he spent much time in the chemical laboratory, and through all his later years read widely in the natural sciences. He began the study of Sanskrit at Harvard under Prof. James B. Greenough, went to Johns Hopkins in order to study with Prof. Charles R. Lanman [q.v.], and continued with Prof. Maurice Bloomfield after Lanman went to Harvard in 1880. In the summer of 1884 he went to England for a short visit to his brother at Oxford. Contact with the Pali scholar, Prof. Rhys Davids, founder of the Pali Text Society, stimulated his interest in Buddhism and led him to devote all his later scholarly effort to Pali and the sacred books of southern Buddhism. He was the first American scholar to attain distinction in the study of Pali. After his father's death in 1888 he tried the climate of southern California, but soon returned to Boston; his close friendship with Lanman led him to establish himself in Cambridge in 1891. Having inherited substantial means from his father, who was the founder of the Warren Paper Company, he made possible the publication of the Harvard Oriental Series, of which thirty-one volumes were issued between 1891 and 1932.

His most important work, *Buddhism in Translations* (Harvard Oriental Series, vol. III, 1896) has been reissued many times. Nearly half of it

was included by President Fliot in the Harvard Classics. The great skill shown in the selection of the passages and in the order of their presentation, and the vigorous English of the translation, give the book a permanent value. Warren did not live to complete his *magnum opus,* a four-volume edition and translation of Buddhaghosa's *Visuddhimagga* or "Way of Purity," a systematic exposition of the doctrine of Pali Buddhism dating from about 400 A.D. The text was nearly ready for publication at his death, and about one third of the translation had been made. After long delay this work is now in process of being completed and edited for the Harvard Oriental Series.

[C. R. Lanman, "A Brief Memorial," appended to Vol. XXX of the Harvard Oriental Series (1921) and to the seventh and eighth issues of Vol. III, Warren's *Buddhism in Translations*; other sketches by Lanman, in *Jour. Royal Asiatic Soc.*, Apr. 1899, and *Jour. Am. Oriental Soc.*, vol. XX, pt. 2 (1899), the latter repr. from *Harvard Grads. Mag.*, Mar. 1899; Harvard Class Reports, Class of 1879, especially the sixth report (1900); C. W. Huntington, *The Warren-Clarke Geneal.* (1894); *Nation* (N. Y.), Jan. 12, 1899; *Boston Transcript,* Jan. 4, 1899.]   W. E. C.

WARREN, HENRY WHITE (Jan. 4, 1831– July 22, 1912), bishop of the Methodist Episcopal Church, son of Mather and Anne Miller (Fairfield) Warren, was born in Williamsburg, Mass.; William Fairfield Warren [q.v.] was a younger brother. Their father ran a farm, owned a mill, and moved buildings when such service was required. Henry early showed character and ability, and at the age of seventeen was supervisor of the village sawmill. A year later he entered Wilbraham Academy, Wilbraham, Mass., where he prepared for college. In 1853 he graduated from Wesleyan University, Middletown, Conn., having taught science for a time, during his course there, at Amenia Seminary, Amenia, N. Y. After his graduation, he was instructor in ancient languages for two years at Wilbraham Academy.

In 1855 he was admitted on trial to the New England Conference of the Methodist Episcopal Church, was ordained deacon in 1857, and elder in 1859. From 1855 to 1870 he was pastor of churches in Worcester, Mass., Boston, Lynn, Westfield, Cambridgeport, and Charlestown. In 1863 he represented Lynn in the Massachusetts House of Representatives. Transferred to the Philadelphia Conference in 1871, he was stationed at the Arch Street Church, Philadelphia, for three years, at the end of which time he was transferred to the New York Conference and appointed to St. John's Church, Brooklyn. In 1877 he returned to his former charge in Philadelphia, with which he remained until 1879, when he became pastor of the Spring Garden Street Church of the same city. In 1880 he was a delegate to the General Conference, and at that session, such had his reputation become throughout the denomination, he was elected bishop.

His episcopal residence for some four years was at Atlanta, Ga., and while there he took an active interest in the establishment of Gammon Theological Seminary, made possible by gifts of Elijah H. Gammon [q.v.] and designed to prepare men of the African race for the Methodist ministry. Later, he resided at University Park, near Denver, Colo. His duties as bishop took him all over the United States and to Europe, the Far East, Mexico, and South America. He gave many lectures and wrote much for various periodicals. His first book was the result of a visit to Europe—*Sights and Insights; or, Knowledge By Travel* (1874). With Eben Tourjée [q.v.] he prepared *The Lesser Hymnal* (1875). From his college days he was much interested in the natural sciences, a fact which led him to write articles and books of a popular nature on scientific subjects. The latter include *Studies of the Stars* (1878), *Recreations in Astronomy* (1879), and *Among the Forces* (1898). He was also the author of *The Bible in the World's Education* (1892).

He was a man of tall, commanding figure, with a high sense of the dignity of his office, which he never violated, though he is said to have had a rich vein of humor. His contemporaries considered him cold and distant. He had a comprehensive mind and in his preaching dealt with the large and fundamental aspects of the Christian religion. He was married on Apr. 6, 1855, to Diantha Lord Kilgore of Bartlett, N. H., who died on June 21, 1867; and on Dec. 27, 1883, to Mrs. Elizabeth (Fraser) Iliff. He interested himself in the affairs of the University of Denver, especially in the establishment of Iliff School of Theology in 1893—later separated from the University—to the endowment of which his wife gave $100,000. One of his recreations was mountain climbing, and he was president, 1877–78, of the Rocky Mountain Club. He died at University Park, survived by his wife, a son, and two daughters.

[*Alumni Record of Wesleyan Univ.* (4th ed., 1911); *Who's Who in America,* 1912–13; *Christian Advocate,* Aug. 1, 1912; *Zion's Herald,* July 31, 1912; *Rocky Mountain News* (Denver), July 24, 1912.]   H. E. S.

WARREN, HOWARD CROSBY (June 12, 1867–Jan. 4, 1934), psychologist, was born at Montclair, N. J., the son of Dorman Theodore and Harriet (Crosby) Warren, and a descendant of Arthur Warren who was resident in Weymouth, Mass., before 1638. At the age of eighteen months he was badly burned and suffered great pain from a succession of operations. The power of endurance which he developed and the emotional restraint which he learned were outstanding traits of his personality. It is not surprising that, under the circumstances, he became introspective at an early age and that, even as a boy, he was interested in religious and psychological problems. Although brought up in a Puritanical household, he was unusually critical of dogmas and taboos, and early developed a dislike for conventional beliefs and explanations, an attitude which marked all of his subsequent thinking. Owing to his bad health, his secondary education was very irregular. He prepared for college under a private tutor and was graduated from the College of New Jersey (later Princeton University) in 1889. A year or two previous to his matriculation, he had become interested in the Darwinian theory, and during his college years he became acquainted with the writings of Spencer, Huxley, Clifford, and Tyndall. It is in this period that we find the source of his unchanging belief in a deterministic interpretation of mental processes and the beginning of his revolt against mysticism. He found the teaching of James McCosh [q.v.] inspiring, but was more attracted by the philosophy of Spencer and the psychology of the British Associationists. An indication of the profound impression made upon him by these British thinkers is the fact that in 1921, after twenty years' work, he published his *History of the Association Psychology.* He also studied the psychology of George T. Ladd and became acquainted with some of the early writings of William James [qq.v.]. In his senior year he was granted the mental science fellowship for graduate work. In 1890 he was appointed instructor in the department of philosophy, and assisted in elementary psychology and logic. After two years of graduate study and teaching at Princeton, where in 1891 he received the degree of M.A., he went to Germany to work in Wilhelm Wundt's laboratory in Leipzig. It was here that he became acquainted with Edward Bradford Titchener [q.v.], with whom he later developed one of the strongest professional intimacies of his life. Later he studied with Hermann Ebbinghaus at Berlin and with Carl Stumpf at Munich. He read Hugo Münsterberg's *Willenshandlung* and was strongly influenced by the psychophysiological aspect of Münsterberg's action theory.

In 1893 he accepted a position as assistant, with the title of demonstrator, in the new psychological laboratory of Princeton. His advance was rapid. In 1896 he became assistant professor, in

1902 professor of experimental psychology, in 1904 director of the psychological laboratory, and in 1914 Stuart Professor of Psychology. On Apr. 5, 1905, he married Catherine Campbell of Attica, Ind. He received the degree of Ph.D. at the Johns Hopkins University in 1917. He worked with courage and persistence toward the formal separation of psychology and philosophy at Princeton, and in 1920 became first chairman of a separate department of psychology. At this time the laboratory was inadequately housed in Nassau Hall. Through his efforts, and in part through his financial support, Eno Hall, a building devoted entirely to psychology, was erected in 1924. In order to have more time for his literary work, he withdrew from the directorship of the laboratory, but remained chairman of the department until 1932.

A few of Warren's numerous papers in scientific journals were on experimental work, but the majority were of a theoretical nature. In 1919 he published his *Human Psychology*. This was followed a few years later by his *Elements of Human Psychology* (1922), which was translated into French in 1923. This textbook was used extensively and made a popular appeal because of its concise description of fundamental facts, its conservatively behavioristic point of view, and the absence of extreme views on the nature of mental processes. Although impressed by John B. Watson's behaviorism, Warren believed strongly in introspection. He admitted the fact of consciousness but was opposed to any form of vitalism. He was a firm believer in a neurological explanation of all mental processes and, in consistency with this view, championed the double aspect of the relation of mind and body in "The Mental and the Physical: the Double-Aspect View" (*Psychological Review,* March 1914), his address as president of the American Psychological Association.

One of Warren's greatest contributions to psychology was the development of the publications of the *Psychological Review.* From 1894 to 1914 he edited or compiled the *Psychological Index,* either alone or in conjunction with other psychologists. In 1901 he was made associate editor and business manager of the publications. He was joint editor of the *Psychological Bulletin* from 1904 to 1934, and editor of the *Psychological Review* from 1916 until his death. He was intensely interested in words and definitions. In 1915 he was appointed chairman of the committee on terminology of the American Psychological Association. When the committee was discharged in 1924 only seventy-nine terms had been defined. Warren therefore determined to edit a comprehensive dictionary of psychology, and most of his time during his last years was occupied with this task. His *Dictionary of Psychology,* published posthumously in 1934, was practically completed when he died. He was survived by his wife. There were no children.

[Mary P. Warren and Emily W. Leavitt, *A Geneal. of One Branch of the Warren Family* (1890) ; *Who's Who in America,* 1932–33 ; Carl Murchison, ed., *A Hist. of Psych. in Autobiog.,* vol. I (1930) ; H. S. Langfeld, in *Am. Jour. of Psych.,* Apr. 1934 ; S. W. Fernberger, in *Psych. Bull.,* Jan. 1934 ; R. S. Woodworth, in *Psych. Rev.,* Mar. 1934 ; obit. in *N. Y. Times,* Jan. 5, 1934.]

H. S. L.

WARREN, ISRAEL PERKINS (Apr. 8, 1814–Oct. 9, 1892), Congregational clergyman, editor, author, was born in Woodbridge, now Bethany, Conn., of colonial ancestry, son of Isaac and Leonora (Perkins) Warren. His father was a shoemaker, and the son, after receiving a common-school education, was apprenticed to a tailor, but because of a conviction that he ought to enter the ministry he was released from his apprenticeship to prepare for college. Owing to limited resources, he studied mainly without instructors, teaching district schools during two winters. After a short period in the academy at Cheshire, Conn., he entered Yale, where he largely supported himself, chiefly by teaching, and graduated in 1838. After a year in charge of the academy at Cromwell, Conn., he studied at Yale Divinity School, 1839–41. He married, Aug. 25, 1841, Jane Stanley Stow, daughter of Thomas and Phebe (Stanley) Stow of Cromwell, Conn.; she died Feb. 26, 1881. They had three children, of whom one son survived his father. From 1841 to 1845 he served the Congregational Church, Granby, Conn., being ordained pastor Apr. 20, 1842 ; he was pastor of the Mount Carmel Church in Hamden, Conn., 1846–51, and of the church in Plymouth, Conn., 1851–56.

Early in his ministry Warren began writing for the religious press, especially the *Religious Herald* and the New York *Evangelist.* In 1856 he became associate secretary of the American Seamen's Friend Society in New York and editor of the *Sailor's Magazine.* He was called in 1859 to be secretary and editor of publications of the American Tract Society at Boston, which was under anti-slavery management. During the nearly eleven years of his supervision the Society issued over 300 bound volumes and about 700 minor publications, also four periodicals. He prepared a Sunday School commentary on the Gospels and Acts, and a spelling-book and readers for the freedmen, and edited a large number of small books and tracts for army use. In the fall of 1865 he journeyed through the South, studying the needs of the colored people.

When in 1870 the Boston society was merged with the American Tract Society in New York, Warren undertook some book publishing in Boston and New York. In 1875 the *Christian Mirror*, a long-established weekly journal published at Portland in the interest of the Congregational churches of Maine, came into the hands of Gov. Nelson Dingley [*q.v.*], who transferred it to Lewiston and invited Warren to take editorial charge. He brought to the task a vigorous mind, varied experience in religious editing, indomitable energy, and keen joy in his work. He introduced marked improvements in the paper, and its subscription list rapidly increased. After eighteen months he purchased it and reëstablished it in Portland, where he was its editor and publisher throughout the rest of his life. On Jan. 2, 1882, he married Sarah (Linden) Cushman of Portland, daughter of John Linden and widow of Henry Cushman; she died in 1885 and on Oct. 6, 1886, he married Juliet Marion Stanley of Winthrop, Me.

Warren's published writings, besides numerous pamphlets, include *The Seaman's Cause* (1858); *The Sisters, a Memoir* (1859); *Sadduceeism* (1860, revised edition, 1867); *The Cross Bearer* (1861); *A Chapter from the Book of Nature* (1863); *The Christian Armor* (1864); *The Cup Bearer* (1865); *Jerusalem, Ancient and Modern* (1873); *The Three Judges* (1873), dealing with the Regicides; *Chauncey Judd* (1874); *Parousia, a Critical Study of the Scripture Doctrines of Christ's Second Coming* (1879; enlarged edition, 1884); *Our Father's Book* (1885); *The Book of Revelation* (1886); and *Stanley Families in America* (1887).

[*Biog. Record of the Class of 1838 in Yale Coll.* (1879) and *Supplement* (1889); *Obit. Record Grads. Yale Univ.*, 1893; *The Congreg. Year-Book*, 1893; *Christian Mirror*, Oct. 15, 29, 1892; *Congregationalist*, Oct. 13, 1892; *Daily Eastern Argus* (Portland, Me.), Oct. 10, 1892.]　　　　　　　　　　　　　E. D. E.

WARREN, JAMES (Sept. 28, 1726–Nov. 28, 1808), Massachusetts political leader, was born at Plymouth, the eldest son of James and Penelope (Winslow) Warren, and a descendant of Richard Warren of the *Mayflower*. Graduated from Harvard College in 1745, he settled as merchant and gentleman farmer in his native town, where after his father's death in 1757 he also assumed the office of sheriff for the county. On Nov. 14, 1754, he married Mercy Otis [*q.v.*] and had by her, in the course of time, five sons.

From 1766 until 1778 he held continuously a seat in the lower house of the Massachusetts General Court and Provincial Congress, where he became strongly identified with the left wing of the patriot party, a close friend and trusted adviser of the two Adamses. His activity before 1775 was not so conspicuous as that of James Otis, John Hancock, Joseph Warren, and Samuel Adams, though in his own community he figured prominently as an organizer of the radicals and served on most of the local revolutionary committees. The assertion that he was first to propose the establishment of committees of correspondence is without adequate foundation of evidence. He wrote in 1775 to John Adams: "I am content to move in a small sphere. I expect no distinction but that of an honest man who has exerted every nerve" (*Warren-Adams Letters, post*, I, 78). After the death of Joseph Warren at Bunker Hill, James Warren filled the important position of president of the Provincial Congress of Massachusetts until the dissolution of that body, when he became speaker of the House of Representatives in the new General Court. He was appointed paymaster general for the Continental Army by the Continental Congress and served while the army was at Cambridge and Boston. From 1776 to 1781 he served on the Navy Board for the Eastern Department. In September 1776 the General Court designated him, as one of the three major-generals of the provincial militia, to lead a force into Rhode Island. But, unwilling to be subordinated to a Continental officer of lesser rank, he pled the excuse of recent illness to have himself relieved, and the following year, to avoid the repetition of such embarrassment, he resigned his commission. His conduct in this instance was utilized by his chief political enemy, John Hancock, to undermine his prestige, with the result that he failed of reëlection to the legislature in 1778. Partisan charges against him of irregularity in his Navy Board dealings (*Ibid.*, II, 121–23) were later thoroughly disproved. In 1779 he regained his seat, but in the following year lost it again; and from that time until after Shays's Rebellion he was passed over by the electorate. In 1776 he had declined appointment as justice of the Supreme Judicial Court of Massachusetts, and in 1780 he refused the position of lieutenant-governor.

An ardent exponent of the principles of democracy and simplicity, Warren could not but deplore the wave of reckless extravagance that followed the war. During the rebellion of 1786, while there is no reason to suppose that he ever sanctioned violence, it was plain that his sympathies were largely on the side of the insurgents. Therefore, when in the reaction of 1787 he again entered the House of Representatives, he was at once selected by the popular majority to occupy the speaker's chair. Very soon his unorthodox stand on the question of currency, as well as his wholesale criticism of the way in which the government had handled the insurrection, alienated many of his former friends, who, since the attainment of independence, had become increasingly conservative. Indeed, some suspected that he had been in actual alliance with the rebels (J. Q. Adams, *Life in a New England Town*, 1903, p. 150). Even John Adams seems to have felt that his attitude towards the uprising was somewhat equivocal (*Warren-Adams Letters*, II, 325 n.). Mrs. Warren, however, wrote to Adams that the General had "borne the unprovoked abuse with the Dignity of conscious rectitude and that Philippic calmness which is never the companion of *Insurgency, Anarchy or Fraud*" (*Ibid.*, II, 312).

More significant was Warren's able and very emphatic agitation against the ratification of the federal Constitution because of its lack of a bill of rights (*Proceedings of the Massachusetts Historical Society, post*, LXIV, 143–64). On this as on almost every other issue he represented the will of the humbler classes. But once more the trimming tactics of Hancock prevailed, and Warren, defeated as candidate for lieutenant-governor, was obliged to retire from the field of active politics to the less strenuous pursuit of scientific farming. In his later years he was a stanch Jeffersonian Democrat. Twice he tried to re-enter the arena by running for a seat in Congress, but without success. John Quincy Adams commented in his diary during this period: "He was formerly a very popular man, but of late years he has thought himself neglected by the people. His mind has been soured, and he became discontented and querulous" (*Life in a New England Town*, p. 150). Yet in three successive years —1792, 1793, 1794—the legislature selected him for membership in the governor's council, and in 1804, at the age of seventy-eight, he received the honor of being chosen one of the presidential electors for Massachusetts (Massachusetts General Court, Senate Journal, Nov. 20, 1804, MS., vol. XXV, p. 199). He died during the night of Nov. 27–28, 1808.

[The principal source is the *Warren-Adams Letters*, 2 vols., being *Mass. Hist. Soc. Colls.*, vols. LXXII, LXXIII (1917, 1925). See also Emily W. Roebling, *Richard Warren of the Mayflower and . . . His Descendants* (1901); Alice Brown, *Mercy Warren* (1896); James Thacher, *Hist. of the Town of Plymouth* (1832); W. T. Davis, *Ancient Landmarks of Plymouth* (1883), pt. II, and *Hist. of the Town of Plymouth* (1885); Charles Warren, "Samuel Adams and the Sans Souci Club in 1785," *Proc. Mass. Hist. Soc.*, vol. LX (1927), and "Elbridge Gerry, James Warren, Mercy Warren and the Ratification of the Federal Constitution in Mass.," *Ibid.*, vol. LXIV (1931); *The Writings of Samuel Adams* (4 vols., 1904–08), ed. by H. A. Cushing; *The Works of John Adams* (10 vols., 1850–56), ed. by C. F. Adams; J. T. Austin, *The Life of Elbridge Gerry*

(*2 vols.*, 1828–29); and obituary in *Columbian Centinel*, Nov. 30, 1808.]
G. P. B.

WARREN, JOHN (July 27, 1753–Apr. 4, 1815), surgeon, was born in Roxbury, Mass., the son of Joseph and Mary (Stevens) Warren, and a descendant of John Warren who arrived in Salem on the *Arbella*, June 12, 1630. Joseph Warren was a farmer in easy circumstances who was killed by a fall from a tree in October 1755. Brought up by an intelligent mother, John, the youngest of four brothers, entered Harvard College at the age of fourteen, supported himself by his own exertions, became a good classical scholar, acquired an interest in anatomy and formed a club for its study, and was graduated with high rank in 1771. For the next two years he studied with his brother Joseph [*q.v.*], twelve years his senior, a successful practitioner in Boston. He then went to Salem, where he associated himself with Dr. Edward Augustus Holyoke [*q.v.*]. Here he added to his knowledge of medicine and began to establish himself in practice. The events of 1773, however, caused him to join the patriots as a surgeon in Colonel Pickering's regiment.

According to tradition, Warren took an active part in the Boston "Tea Party," Dec. 18, 1773. When the hostilities of the Revolution actually began, he was with his regiment, although he did not take an active part in the battle of Lexington. He was on his way from Salem to Boston when he learned of the death of his brother Joseph at the battle of Bunker Hill. Giving up his practice, he volunteered at once for service in the ranks. When Washington arrived in Cambridge in July 1775, the medical department of the army was organized and Warren, though only twenty-two, was appointed senior surgeon of the hospital there established. He was one of the first to enter Boston after the evacuation. In 1776 he was transferred to New York and appointed surgeon of the general hospital on Long Island. Later he saw service with the army at Trenton and also at Princeton.

Returning to Boston in April 1777, he began private practice, although he also served as surgeon to the military hospital. Soon he was the leading surgeon of the city. When smallpox was prevalent, Warren, Isaac Rand, and Lemuel Hayward established, in 1778, a hospital for direct inoculation, where many patients were treated. His main interests, however, were in surgery and particularly in anatomy. Since there was no medical school at the time in Boston, he gave a private course of anatomical lectures at the military hospital in the winter of 1780–81, which were attended by men still in the army, other physicians, and a few students. There still existed popular prejudice against dissection, and the demonstrations were carried on with much privacy. The Boston Medical Society, which was organized by Warren and others in 1780, indorsed the course and asked Warren to continue his lectures each winter. A second course, given publicly, attracted many literary and scientific men, including President Willard of Harvard College. The third series of lectures and anatomical demonstrations was equally popular, and was attended by the entire senior class of Harvard College. It was soon clear, however, that a medical department in connection with the college was needed, and on Sept. 19, 1782, Warren was requested to draw up plans for a course of instruction. When the school was established, Nov. 22, 1782, Warren was chosen professor of anatomy and surgery. Shortly after, Benjamin Waterhouse [q.v.] became professor of the theory and practice of physic and Aaron Dexter, professor of chemistry and materia medica. Warren and Waterhouse were inducted into office Oct. 7, 1783, and the first course of lectures was delivered that year.

As a surgeon, Warren was a bold and skilful operator; he performed one of the first abdominal operations recorded in America and was a pioneer in amputation at the shoulder joint. His general practice also was extensive. He played a prominent part in dealing with the epidemic of yellow fever which visited Boston in 1798. Favorably impressed by cowpox vaccination, which was first demonstrated in the United States by Waterhouse in 1800, he did much to promote the adoption of this method of treatment. His most notable contribution to medical literature was a book entitled *A View of the Mercurial Practice in Febrile Diseases* (1813), in which he refers to the treatment of many types of fever which were common in his day. As the leading physician of Boston, he took part in practically all the important medical events of his time. His interests, moreover, reached outside his profession: he was grand master (1783–84) of the Massachusetts Lodges of Free and Accepted Masons, was one of the founders and a president of the Massachusetts Humane Society, and held membership in the Agricultural Society and the American Academy of Arts and Sciences. The honorary degree of M.D. was conferred upon him by Harvard College in 1786. He was married, Nov. 4, 1777, to Abigail, daughter of John Collins [q.v.], and was the father of seventeen children, the oldest of whom was John Collins Warren [q.v.] and the youngest, Edward Warren, his biographer.

[Edward Warren, *The Life of John Warren* (1874); James Jackson, *An Eulogy on the Character of John Warren* (1815); H. A. Kelly and W. L. Burrage, *Am. Medic. Biogs.* (1920); T. F. Harrington, *The Harvard Medic. School* (1905); S. D. Gross, *Lives of Eminent Am. Physicians and Surgeons of the Nineteenth Century* (1861); James Thacher, *Am. Medic. Biog.* (1828); James Thacher, *A Military Journal* (1823); W. L. Burrage, *A Hist. of the Mass. Medic. Soc.* (1923); S. F. Batchelder, *Harvard Hospital Surgeons of 1775* (1920), repr. from *Harvard Alumni Bulletin*; *Repository* (Boston), Apr. 8, 1815; family papers in the Mass. Hist. Soc. and Boston Medic. Lib.]   H. R. V.

WARREN, JOHN COLLINS (Aug. 1, 1778– May 4, 1856), surgeon, the eldest son of John [q.v.] and Abigail (Collins) Warren, was born in Boston. His early education was supervised by his father. Later he went to the Public Latin School, and in 1797 was graduated at Harvard College, valedictorian of his class and president of the Hasty Pudding Club, of which he had been one of the founders. After a year spent with a private tutor in French, he entered his father's office as an apprentice in medicine. In June 1799, however, he went abroad and in London, Edinburgh, and Paris studied under the best teachers of the day, particularly Astley Cooper of Guy's Hospital, London, and Dubois in Paris.

Returning to Boston in December 1802, he at once entered into partnership with his father. He assisted in the anatomical dissections in preparation for his father's lectures at the Harvard Medical School, gave popular lectures to select groups on anatomy and physiology, organized a private medical society, was one of the original members of the Anthology Club, and in 1808, with James Jackson [q.v.], prepared a *Pharmacopeia* for the Massachusetts Medical Society. In 1809 he became adjunct professor of anatomy and surgery at the Harvard Medical School, and in 1815, on the death of his father, he became full professor, a position which he held with great distinction until 1847, when he was made professor emeritus. From 1816 to 1819 he served as dean. With his close associate, Jackson, he practically revolutionized medical education and practice in Boston. The Harvard Medical School was moved from Cambridge to Boston in 1815, funds were raised for the Massachusetts General Hospital and it was opened in 1821 with Warren as surgeon and Jackson as physician, and the *New-England Journal of Medicine and Surgery* was established in 1812. In all three of these important enterprises Warren and Jackson were the prime movers.

Warren was an able surgeon and by no means a timid operator in spite of the painstaking care with which he handled the knife. Before the days of anesthesia he did amputations, removed cataracts, and was the first surgeon in the United

States to operate for strangulated hernia. In 1837, when nearly sixty years of age, he published his most important book, *Surgical Observations on Tumours with Cases and Operations*, with excellent illustrations, a landmark in the history of this subject. A previous publication, *A Comparative View of the Sensorial and Nervous Systems in Men and Animals* (1822), was a fair account of comparative anatomy, but Warren failed to grasp the importance of the work of the Scotch anatomist Sir Charles Bell. In addition to strictly surgical papers, he wrote numerous memoirs and essays. He is remembered especially for his connection with the first public demonstration of ether anesthesia. On Oct. 16, 1846, at the Massachusetts General Hospital, Warren, then in his seventieth year, operated on a patient under ether anesthesia given by W. T. G. Morton [q.v.]. To Warren, the outstanding surgeon of his day, belongs the credit for allowing his name and position to be used as a sponsor for this courageous and revolutionary experiment. Warren's account of the operation first appeared in the *Boston Medical and Surgical Journal* for Dec. 9, 1846, and subsequently in *Etherization; with Surgical Remarks* (1848).

Warren had many interests and became a leading figure in New England life. He was active from 1827 to his death in temperance reform, serving for that period as president of the Massachusetts Temperance Society. At the age of seventy-five he gave $10,000 to the temperance cause and made provision in his will for another gift. He was prominently connected with the building of Bunker Hill Monument. At his country estate in Brookline he carried on experiments in farming, and was an active member of the Massachusetts Agricultural Society. He promoted physical education, giving addresses and building a city gymnasium, and published *Physical Education and the Preservation of Health* (1845), and *The Preservation of Health* (1854). Both books went through many editions. Towards the close of his life, he became interested in geology and paleontology, serving as president of the Boston Society of Natural History. The skeleton of a mastodon was procured, set up in a private museum, and described by Warren in a superb volume, *The Mastodon Giganteus of North America* (1852, 1855). His many specimens were left to the Harvard Medical School and form the Warren Museum. He was awarded the honorary degree of M.D. by Harvard in 1819. He married first, Nov. 17, 1803, Susan Powell, daughter of Jonathan Mason [q.v.]. She died in 1841 and in October 1843 he married Anne, daughter of Thomas

L. Winthrop. By the first marriage there were six children; John Collins Warren, 1842–1927 [q.v.], was his grandson. The elder Warren prepared *Genealogy of Warren* in 1854.

[Edward Warren, *The Life of John Collins Warren* (1860); H. P. Arnold, *Memoir of John Collins Warren* (1882); *New England Hist. and Geneal. Reg.*, Jan. 1865; H. A. Kelly and W. L. Burrage, *Am. Medic. Biogs.* (1920); *Surgery, Gynecology and Obstetrics*, Jan. 1926; N. I. Bowditch, *A Hist. of the Mass. Gen. Hospital* (2nd ed., 1872); Joseph Palmer, *Necrology of Alumni of Harvard Coll.* (1864); W. L. Burrage, *A Hist. of the Mass. Medic. Soc.* (1923); T. F. Harrington, *The Harvard Medic. School* (1905); *Boston Advertiser*, May 5, 6, and 8, 1856; *Boston Transcript*, May 5, 7, 8, 1856; bibliog. in *Index-Cat. of the Lib. of the Surgeon-General's Office*, vol. XVI (1895); family papers in the Mass. Hist. Soc. and the Boston Medic. Lib.]

H. R. V.

WARREN, JOHN COLLINS (May 4, 1842–Nov. 3, 1927), surgeon, the son of Jonathan Mason and Annie (Crowninshield) Warren, was born in Boston. His great-grandfather, John Warren [q.v.], his grandfather, John Collins Warren [q.v.], and his father were all distinguished surgeons of Boston. Warren prepared for college at the Public Latin School, graduated from Harvard in 1863, and from the Harvard Medical School in 1866. After a course at the Jefferson Medical College in Philadelphia, he spent three years in Europe, principally in London, Edinburgh, Paris, Berlin, and Vienna. Returning to Boston in 1869, he began practice and soon associated himself with the Harvard Medical School and the Massachusetts General Hospital, as his ancestors had done. Passing through all the grades as a teacher of surgery in the Medical School, he became Moseley Professor of Surgery in 1899, and served as such until 1907. In 1908 he was elected an Overseer of Harvard College.

In his profession he was recognized as a surgeon of note and his many published papers were widely read. The first of his publications on surgical pathology was *The Anatomy and Development of Rodent Ulcer* (1872), which won the Boylston Medical Prize. A second book, largely experimental, dealt with *The Healing of Arteries after Ligature in Man and Animals* (1886). His work in this field culminated in a book entitled *Surgical Pathology and Therapeutics* (1895), based on bacteriology, a notable accomplishment. He collaborated with W. W. Keen in the *American Text Book of Surgery* (1892), and edited with A. Pearce Gould, the *International Text-Book of Surgery* (1900). From 1873 to 1880 he was editor of the *Boston Medical and Surgical Journal*. In 1896 he served as president of the American Surgical Association.

Warren's principal interest, however, was in medical progress and medical education. He was largely instrumental in moving the Harvard Medical School to new and larger quarters in 1883 and again in 1906. In raising funds for the buildings taken possession of on the latter occasion, Warren and Henry P. Bowditch [q.v.] took the lead. The money was secured, and a great medical center was established with the School surrounded by hospitals and laboratories. "To Bowditch and Warren belongs the whole credit of the plan, the main credit for its execution" (*Harvard Graduates Magazine, post*, p. 380). For almost a quarter of a century Warren was chairman of the Cancer Commission of Harvard University. The establishment of the Collis P. Huntington Memorial Hospital for Cancer Research, in Boston, stands to Warren's credit alone. He issued a plea for a medical students' dormitory in 1909, and it was added to the medical group before his death. On May 27, 1873, he married Amy, daughter of Gardner Howland and Cora (Lyman) Shaw of Boston. A son, John, became professor of anatomy in the Harvard Medical School and another, Joseph, professor of law in the Harvard Law School.

[*Trans. Am. Surgic. Asso.*, 1928; F. C. Shattuck in *Harvard Grads. Mag.*, Mar. 1928, and in *Proc. Mass. Hist. Soc.*, Nov. 1927; G. H. Monks in *Surgery, Gynecology and Obstetrics*, Oct. 1931; *Reports of the Secretary, Class of 1863, Harvard Coll.*, 1888 and 1913; T. F. Harrington, *The Harvard Medic. School* (1905); *Who's Who in America*, 1926–27; family papers in Mass. Hist. Soc. and Boston Medic. Lib.; *Boston Transcript*, Nov. 4 and 7, 1927.] H. R. V.

WARREN, JOSEPH (June 11, 1741–June 17, 1775), physician, Revolutionary patriot, born at Roxbury, Mass., was the eldest of the four sons of Joseph and Mary (Stevens) Warren of Roxbury and a brother of John Warren [q.v.]. When the boy was fourteen, his father died. In that year, having been prepared at the school in Roxbury, Joseph entered Harvard College, where he distinguished himself as a student. After graduation in 1759 he was appointed master of the Roxbury Grammar School, where he taught for a year. He became a Free Mason in 1761, and in 1769, when his Lodge, St. Andrew's, united with two others to form a Grand Lodge, he was made provincial Grand Master. Deciding to become a physician, he studied under Dr. James Lloyd. On Sept. 6, 1764, he married Elizabeth, only daughter of Richard Hooton of Boston, who brought him a handsome fortune; by this marriage he had two sons and two daughters.

Warren established himself in Boston, where he formed a friendship with John Adams by the somewhat unusual method of inoculating him for smallpox. He was an excellent physician with a good practice, but soon became deeply interested in politics, ardently espoused the Whig cause, and rather neglected his own affairs. After the passage of the Stamp Act he was closely associated with Samuel Adams and made a number of speeches at Faneuil Hall. He also became a frequent contributor to the press, and published an article in the *Boston Gazette*, Feb. 29, 1768, which caused Governor Bernard to attempt to prosecute the printers. He was also active in the political clubs of the day, being a member of the North End Caucus, and of a smaller club consisting of lawyers, clergymen, and popular leaders. At the time of the excitement caused by the seizure of Hancock's sloop *Liberty*, Warren played a prominent part as mediator. From this time he was continuously active in town meetings, appearing in concert with Samuel Adams, John Hancock, and James Otis [q.v.]. In 1770 he was one of the committee named by the town meeting after the Boston "Massacre" to inform Governor Hutchinson that the troops must be removed, and on the anniversary of the "Massacre" in 1772 he delivered an impassioned commemorative address. He continued to act on committees and was a member of the group that was practically the executive committee of the popular party from 1772 until it was superseded by the Committee of Safety, of which he was also a member. He was one of the three men chosen to draw up the report, *A State of the Rights of the Colonists* (1772), contributing the second part, "A List of the Infringements of Those Rights." In 1774 he was head of the Boston delegation to the county convention, was a member of the committee charged with receiving the donations of food from other colonies, took the lead in organizing opposition to the Regulating Act, and drafted the "Suffolk Resolves," which he forwarded to the Continental Congress. He also engaged in a multitude of other public duties.

In 1775 he was active on the most important local committees and on Mar. 6 made his celebrated second oration in commemoration of the "Massacre," an address which stirred Boston deeply. As the crisis approached he decided to abandon his profession and enter the army. For the moment he remained in Boston and on Apr. 18 dispatched William Dawes and Paul Revere [qq.v.] to Lexington to notify Hancock and Adams of their danger. When the fighting began there, Warren rode out to join the Patriots and took an active part. On Aug. 23 he was chosen president *pro tempore* of the Provincial Congress, which office he held until his death; on May 12 he was appointed chairman of the committee to apply to the Continental Congress for recommendation to set up a new civil government in Massachusetts; on May 18 he was again chosen a member of the Committee of Safety, of which he had been a member from the beginning; on the 20th he became head of the committee to organize the army in the colony.

Less than a month later, June 14, the Provincial Congress elected him a major-general; he had first been considered for the post of physician-general, but desired more hazardous service. He passed the night of June 16 attending to public business at Watertown, where the Provincial Congress was in session. It is said that, anxious as he was to drive the British out of Boston, he questioned the wisdom of Israel Putnam [q.v.] in projecting a battle at Bunker Hill, since the provincial forces were scantily supplied with ammunition. On the morning of June 17 he met with the Committee of Safety at Cambridge and in the afternoon of that day, on receipt of news from the front, he went to Bunker Hill, where he could look over the situation. Putnam, whom he met there, offered to take orders from him, but Warren replied that he was there as a volunteer only and asked where he could be most useful. Putnam then sent him to the redoubt on Breed's Hill, but on reaching that place he again refused to assume command, stating that he had not yet received his commission and would take part only as a volunteer. In the heavy fighting which followed, while attempting to rally the militia, he was shot dead by a British soldier.

[The best life is Richard Frothingham, *Life and Times of Joseph Warren* (1865), which includes many letters and documents; in the Preface the author reviews the literature on Warren up to the date of publication. A few letters are published in "Warren-Adams Letters," vol. I, being *Mass. Hist. Soc. Colls.*, vol. LXXII (1917). The family history is traced in J. C. Warren, *Geneal. of Warren* (1854). Warren's orations have been several times printed.]   J. T. A.

WARREN, JOSIAH (c. 1798–Apr. 14, 1874), reformer, philosophical Anarchist, inventor, was born in Boston and is said to have been distantly related to Gen. Joseph Warren. He appears to have had a fair education, and he early became a musician, playing in local bands. At the age of twenty he married, and soon afterward settled in Cincinnati as an orchestra leader and a teacher of music. On Feb. 28, 1821, he was granted a patent for a lard-burning lamp, and soon afterward established a lamp factory, which proved profitable.

After hearing a lecture by Robert Owen, he became an Owenite, sold his factory, and early in 1825 moved with his family to the colony then forming at New Harmony, Ind. He soon found himself an extreme individualist, opposed not only to community of goods but to all forms of government. Gradually he formulated a theory of society embodying the principle of "sovereignty of the individual," a society wherein interchanges of goods and services should be based solely on cost. In 1827 he returned to Cincinnati, and in May, to test his new views, started what he called an "equity store." Two years later, feeling that he had vindicated his theory, he closed the store, without loss or gain. About 1830 he invented a speed press, which he did not patent. Some two years afterwards one of the Hoe presses was constructed on the same principle. In January 1833 he started a journal, *The Peaceful Revolutionist.* His exceptional inventive talent had enabled him to make his own press, type-moulds, type, and stereotype plates, and he did all the writing, composition, and press-work, but the experiment lasted less than a year. Between 1837 and 1840 he invented the cylinder press, self-inking and fed from a continuous roll of paper, first used in printing the *South-Western Sentinel,* of Evansville, Ind., Feb. 28, 1840; but persistent sabotage by the workmen caused him to destroy it. In 1846 he obtained a patent for a process by which stereotype plates could be made cheaply and easily.

After several experiments with "equity stores" and communities, he moved to New York in 1850. Here he met Stephen Pearl Andrews [q.v.], who became his disciple and chief exponent. Early in the 1850's, at a point on Long Island about forty miles from New York City, he established the town of Modern Times, which became noted as a gathering place for many eccentric characters and lasted until about 1862. His later years were spent mainly in Massachusetts. He died, after a lingering illness, at the home of Edward D. Linton, in Charlestown, and his body was interred at Mount Auburn Cemetery.

Warren is described by Moncure D. Conway (*post,* I, 264–68) as a short, thickset man, with a large forehead, and somewhat restless blue eyes. His industry was tireless, though for a propagandist he wrote and spoke little. His first book, *Equitable Commerce,* appeared in 1846, with later editions in 1849 and 1852. In 1863 he published *True Civilization an Immediate Necessity,* and in 1875 Benjamin R. Tucker brought out another work of his, entitled *True Civilization: a Subject of Vital and Serious Interest to All People.* He also published a number of miscellaneous writings, including *Written Music Remodeled, and Invested with the Simplicity of an Exact Science* (1860). The work of Warren, in music, in mechanics, and in social theory, was notably original. He was the founder in America of philosophical Anarchism.

[Sources include William Bailie, *Josiah Warren, the First Am. Anarchist* (1906); G. B. Lockwood, *The New Harmony Movement* (1905); *Boston Globe*, Apr. 15, 1874; M. D. Conway, *Autobiography* (1904); *Fortnightly Rev.*, July 1, 1865. Warren's theories are developed in S. P. Andrews, *The Science of Society* (1851) and *The Basic Outline of Universology* (1872), and are often expounded in the writings of Benjamin R. Tucker.]
W.J.G.

WARREN, MERCY OTIS (Sept. 14, 1728 o.s.–Oct. 19, 1814), historian, poet, dramatist, was born in Barnstable, Mass., the third child of James and Mary (Allyne) Otis, and sister of the more famous James [*q.v.*], who opposed the writs of assistance and the Stamp Act. She was married on Nov. 14, 1754, to James Warren [*q.v.*], by whom she had five sons. They lived for the most part in Plymouth, but in 1781 purchased the Gov. Thomas Hutchinson house in Milton, where they spent ten years. Possessing uncommon talent for literature and politics, and enjoying through both her husband and brother an enviable intimacy with those high in the Revolutionary councils of the province, Mercy Warren became in a manner the poet laureate and later historical apologist for the patriot cause. Her works include several plays, *Poems Dramatic and Miscellaneous* (1790), and a *History of the Rise, Progress, and Termination of the American Revolution* (3 vols., 1805). Two political satires, *The Adulateur,* published in 1773 (reprinted in *Magazine of History,* extra no. 63, pt. 3, 1918), and *The Group* (1775), are deserving of particular mention. Her history is interesting both for the expert knowledge it reveals of public affairs and for its lively and penetrating commentary upon the leading figures of the day, more especially for the caustic analysis of character and motives among the "malignant party" who opposed American freedom. Like her husband, she held strong democratic convictions, and as a consequence dealt severely with men who in her opinion leaned in the "aristocratical" direction.

At a later date she would doubtless have been termed a feminist for her aggressive concern with public affairs and her insistence upon the right of women to have other than domestic interests. To her friend Abigail Adams [*q.v.*] she wrote that while she admitted "the sex" too often gave occasion "by an Eager Pursuit of Trifles" for reflections upon their understanding, yet she believed that if a "discerning & generous Mind should look to the origin of the Error" it would find "that the Deficiency lies not so much in Inferior Contexture of Female Intellects as in the different Education bestow'd on the Sexes" (Brown, *post,* p. 241). John Adams throughout the Revolutionary period was in frequent correspondence with her, and her other active correspondents on political matters included Samuel Adams, James Winthrop, John Dickinson, Thomas Jefferson, Elbridge Gerry, Henry Knox, and Mrs. Macaulay Graham, the English historian. But the younger generation, on coming into power, showed less respect for her political opinions. When in 1809 she attempted to call her nephew, Harrison Gray Otis, 1765–1848 [*q.v.*], to task for his Federalistic opposition to the Embargo, he affectionately invited her not to meddle in what he conceived to be his personal business (*Warren-Adams Letters, post,* II, 361 ff.).

An amusing though rather pathetic episode in Mercy Warren's later life was her quarrel with John Adams. This was precipitated by the publication of her history, in which Adams felt that he had been done injustice. He objected in a letter dated July 11, 1807, to her statements that "his passions and prejudices were sometimes too strong for his sagacity and judgment" (*History,* III, 392), that since his sojourn in England he had shown a leaning toward monarchy, and that "pride of talents and much ambition, were undoubtedly combined" in his character (*Ibid.,* I, 131–32). Correspondence over this issue was carried on with mounting fury for three months until it was terminated by the unanswerable declaration of Mrs. Warren that Adams' opinions were "so marked with passion, absurdity, and inconsistency as to appear more like the ravings of a maniac than the cool *critique* of genius and science" (*Collections of the Massachusetts Historical Society,* 5 ser., vol. IV, *post,* 489). At length, after almost five years, Elbridge Gerry interceded and managed to effect a reconciliation. Loving letters were exchanged and locks of hair as tokens of a peace which remained unbroken until Mercy's death (*Ibid.,* p. 502 ff.; *Warren-Adams Letters,* II, 382–96). But even in the moment of the revival of their friendship, Adams could not repress the somewhat jaundiced observation to Gerry that "History is not the Province of the Ladies" (*Warren-Adams Letters,* II, 380).

[Sources of chief importance are the *Warren-Adams Letters,* 2 vols., being *Mass. Hist. Soc. Colls.,* vols. LXXII, LXXIII (1917, 1925), and "Corres. between John Adams and Mercy Warren," *Mass. Hist. Soc. Colls.,* 5 ser., vol. IV (1878). See also Emily W. Roebling, *Richard Warren of the Mayflower* (1901); Alice Brown, *Mercy Warren* (1896); Annie R. Marble, in *New England Mag.,* Apr. 1903; Charles Warren, "Elbridge Gerry, James Warren, Mercy Warren," *Proc. Mass. Hist. Soc.,* vol. LXIV (1931); M. C. Tyler, *The Lit. Hist. of the Am. Rev.* (2 vols., 1897); W. C. Ford, "Mrs. Warren's 'The Group,'" *Proc. Mass. Hist. Soc.,* vol. LXII (1928) ; and death notice in *Columbian Centinel,* Oct. 22, 1814.]   G. P. B.

WARREN, MINTON (Jan. 29, 1850–Nov. 26, 1907), classical scholar and teacher, was born at Providence, R. I., the son of Samuel Sprague and Ann Elizabeth (Caswel) Warren, a descendant of Richard Warren, a *Mayflower* Pilgrim. He was graduated from the Providence high school in 1866 and from Tufts College in 1870. After a year of teaching at Westport, Mass., he spent the year 1871–72 in graduate study at Yale, under the guidance of William Dwight Whitney, James Hadley, and Thomas R. Lounsbury [*qq.v.*]. He taught then successively at Medford and Waltham (as principal of the high school), and in the autumn of 1876 he went to Germany for further study: first at Leipzig, then at Bonn (under Bücheler), and finally at Strasbourg (under Studemund), where he received the degree of Ph.D. in 1879. His dissertation on the enclitic *ne* in early Latin (presented in part in the *American Journal of Philology,* May 1881) revealed mature scholarship and originality of interpretation; its results have become a part of accepted grammatical doctrine. His acquaintance at Leipzig with two of Ritschl's younger pupils, Georg Götz and Gustav Löwe, bore fruit some years later in the first publication of the St. Gall Glossary. On his return to the United States he was invited to the Johns Hopkins University as associate in Latin. There he inaugurated the Latin Seminary, and in a library well equipped for intensive study in a few chosen fields, in close and personal touch with his students, he worked more in the manner of the director of a laboratory than as an academic teacher of the usual American type. In the conduct of this work he sacrificed, and sacrificed ungrudgingly, his own productivity to his calling as a teacher, not only in time and strength, but also in placing his own ideas and projects at the disposal of his students. During the years 1886–99 twenty-two dissertations are recorded as having been prepared and published under his direction. His own published work is not large in bulk nor does it embrace wide-reaching and novel points of view. But within its range it reveals the orderly erudition and precision which were his characteristics as a scholar, and it won abundant recognition, perhaps more in Europe than at home. His special field of study was early Latin, and he was an acknowledged master in the idiom of Latin comedy. He remained at the Johns Hopkins University as associate professor and professor until 1899, when he accepted a call to Harvard. In 1905 he succeeded George Martin Lane [*q.v.*] as Pope Professor of Latin. He was

active in the founding of the American School of Classical Studies in Rome (later a division of the American Academy in Rome), and was its second director (1896–97) ; he was president of the American Philological Association for the year 1897. He died in Cambridge. He was married on Dec. 29, 1885, to Salomé Machado of Salem, who with a son and a daughter survived him.

Of his publications the more important are: "On Latin Glossaries" (*Transactions of the American Philological Association,* vol. XV, 1885), with complete and first publication of the important glossary in Codex Sangallensis 912; "Epigraphica" (*Harvard Studies in Classical Philology,* vol. XI, 1900) ; "Unpublished Scholia from the Vaticanus (C) of Terence" (*Ibid.,* vol. XII, 1901) ; "On Five New Manuscripts of the Commentary of Donatus on Terence" (*Ibid.,* vol. XVII, 1906) ; "On the *Distinctio Versuum* in the Manuscripts of Terence" (*American Journal of Archaeology,* Jan. 1900) ; "A New Fragment of Apollodorus of Carystus" (*Classical Philology,* Jan. 1906) ; and "The Stele Inscription in the Roman Forum" (*American Journal of Philology,* July, Oct. 1907). Apart from these longer studies almost every number of the *American Journal of Philology* from the beginning in 1880 to 1899 contains some shorter article, note, or book review from his hand.

Warren was a man of vigorous build, and his personality suggested strength. He was a harddriving, forceful, and incisive teacher, impatient of slowness or ineffectiveness, often sharp in merited criticism, but able to inject enthusiasm and emulation into the tasks he imposed. His nature was open and kindly, and for him his pupils, friends, and colleagues entertained a singular warmth of devotion. He was quick to recognize good work, generous in praise of it, and he seemed to take a peculiar pleasure in contributing from his own store to the work of others. Primarily a teacher of teachers, through his own work and that of his many pupils (who for a generation came to be known as "Warren's men") he earned a conspicuous place among American classical scholars and teachers.

[J. H. Wright, in *Harvard Univ. Gazette,* Jan. 10, 1908; C. R. Lanman, in *Harvard Grads.' Mag.,* Mar. 1908; G. J. Laing, *Ibid.,* S. E. Morison, *The Development of Harvard Univ.* (1930) ; Kirby Smith, in *Am. Jour. Philology,* Oct. 1907, and in *Johns Hopkins Alumni Mag.,* Mar. 1918; *Classical Philology,* Apr. 1908; *Classical Jour.,* Jan. 1908, with portrait; *Tufts Coll. Grad.,* vol. V, p. 196; *Harvard Illus. Mag.,* vol. IX (1908), p. 83; obituary in *Boston Transcript,* Nov. 27, 1907.]   G. L. H.

WARREN, Sir PETER (Mar. 10, 1703–July 29, 1752), British naval officer, son of Michael and Catherine (Aylmer) Warren, was born on the Warren estate at Warrenstown, County Meath, Ireland, where his ancestors had settled in 1282. His mother was the daughter of Sir Christopher Aylmer, first baronet of Balrath, and the sister of Matthew, Lord Aylmer, one of the Lords of the Admiralty and commander-in-chief of the fleet. Peter Warren entered the navy as a midshipman at the age of twelve, remaining in British waters until 1718, when he sailed for the West Indies and the North American coast in the *Rose.* On July 7, 1730, he arrived in New York Harbor as a captain, commander of H.M.S. *Solebay,* a 20-gun frigate, and for the next seventeen years his residence was in New York City.

In June 1731 he acquired title to a number of plots in the city and to "Greenwich House" at the bank of the Hudson, with some twenty acres of ground—the first of six parcels which made up the "Warren Farm" of some three hundred acres, now known as Greenwich Village. The following month he married Susannah De Lancey, elder daughter of Stephen and Anne (Van Cortlandt) De Lancey, sister of James and Oliver De Lancey [*qq.v.*], and grand-daughter of Stephanus Van Cortlandt [*q.v.*]. The wedding reception at the De Lancey home was described in the *New-York Gazette* for July 26, 1731. Five years later Warren purchased a tract of 14,000 acres in the Mohawk Valley, of which his nephew, later Sir William Johnson, became manager, and in 1744 he acquired the famous Warren mansion, demolished in 1865, with forty-six acres, the fifth section of the "Warren Farm," which was completed some time later by a gift of four acres from the city. In 1749 he purchased 100 acres on Turtle Bay. His last city home was 59–65 Broadway (Stokes, *post,* I, 348).

Meanwhile he had commanded successively the *Squirrel,* 20 guns (1735–42); the *Launceton,* 40 guns (1742–45); and the *Superbe,* 60 guns. Early in 1745, when at Antigua, he received orders to cooperate with the expedition projected by Gov. William Shirley [*q.v.*] of Massachusetts against Louisbourg on Cape Breton Island, and on Mar. 13 of that year he set sail in the *Superbe,* with the *Launceton* and *Mermaid,* arriving in time to prevent the French supply ship, *Vigilante,* from entering Louisbourg harbor. This vessel and many other rich prizes were captured. On Saturday afternoon, June 15, just before the capitulation of the fortress, he addressed the army, saying that he would rather leave his body at Louisbourg than not take the city (*Louisbourg Journals, post,* p. 26). His knowledge of American conditions, his sense of strategy, and his ability to work with men of various types all con-

tributed to the success of the expedition. He was promoted to be rear admiral of the Blue Aug. 8, 1745; and with Sir William Pepperrell [*q.v.*], continued in joint supervision of the captured post until, much to his disgust, he was appointed governor of Louisbourg and Cape Breton Island. On Oct. 5 he wrote the Duke of Newcastle asking to be appointed governor of New York, and on June 7, 1746, the day of his final departure from Louisbourg, he asked unsuccessfully for the governorship of New Jersey. As some evidence of his popularity in America, the Admiral Warren, a tavern, was opened at 11–15 Wall Street, and Warren Street, New York City, was named after him. He was also a member of the Governor's Council of New York.

On Nov. 30, 1746, he sailed for Spithead in the *Chester,* arriving Dec. 24, to oppose as impracticable the expedition against Canada projected for the following year. Before he had a chance to return, he was sent on an expedition which culminated in the battle of May 3, 1747, with a French squadron off Cape Finisterre—one of the most important British naval victories since the defeat of the Spanish Armada—in which he was the outstanding hero. On May 29 he was knighted, with the Cross of the Bath; on July 1, he was elected to Parliament; on July 15, he was promoted to be vice-admiral of the White. He then changed his residence from New York City to London and summoned his family to join him.

Sir Peter had command of three later expeditions and retired at the close of the war with £200,000 prize money and a promotion to be vice-admiral of the Red, May 12, 1748. In Parliament he was an outstanding exponent of preparedness (*The Parliamentary History of England,* vol. XIV, 1813, pp. 613, 711). He died in Dublin, and was buried at the church at Knockmark, near Warrenstown; subsequently a monument to him, by Roubiliac, was erected in Westminster Abbey. Of his six children, three reached majority: Anne, who married Charles Fitzroy, created Baron Southampton in 1780; Susannah, who married her cousin, Col. William Skinner of Perth Amboy, N. J.; and Charlotte, who married Lord Abingdon, for whom Abingdon Square, New York City, is named.

[Date of birth from Pedigree of Sir Peter Warren, Office of Arms, Dublin Castle; Thomas Warren, *A Hist. and Geneal. of the Warren Family* (1902); F. J. Aylmer, *The Aylmers of Ireland* (1931); *The Naval Chronicle,* vol. XII (1804); Commission and Warrant Books, Official Correspondence and Logs, Pub. Record Office, London; copies of Admiralty in Letters 480, Colonial Office 5.44 and 5.45 in Lib. of Cong.; I. N. P. Stokes, *The Iconography of Manhattan Island* (6 vols., 1915–28); Warren and DePeyster Papers and Deeds and Misc. MSS. in the library of the N. Y. Hist. Soc.; Gage Papers in William L. Clements Lib.; *Louisbourg Journals, 1745* (1932), ed. by L. E. DeForest; J. S. Mc-

Lennan, *Louisbourg from Its Foundation to Its Fall* (1918); H. W. Richmond, *The Navy in the War of 1739–48* (3 vols., 1920); "The Pepperrell Papers," *Mass. Hist. Soc. Colls.*, 6 ser. X (1898); J. K. Laughton, in *Dict. Nat. Biog.*; bibliography under sketch of Sir William Johnson.]   L. H. R., Jr.

WARREN, RICHARD HENRY (Sept. 17, 1859–Dec. 3, 1933), organist, composer, was born in Albany, N. Y., the son of George William Warren and Mary Elizabeth (Pease) Warren. His father was a self-taught musician who from 1846 to 1858 had been organist of St. Peter's Church, in Albany, and at the time of his son's birth was filling a two years' engagement at St. Paul's in the same city. In 1860, when the boy was one year of age, the family moved to Brooklyn, N. Y., where the senior Warren was organist at Holy Trinity Church for ten years. From 1870 until his death in 1902 he played at St. Thomas' Church in New York City. His father was Richard Warren's first teacher. Following this preliminary instruction the boy studied with Peter A. Schnecker, George Wiegand, and John White, and finally went to Europe where he had lessons with Charles Marie Widor. While abroad he was invited to appear as guest organist in many cathedrals and churches. In 1877 he obtained in New York his first position as organist in America, at the Church of St. John the Evangelist, and remained there for two years. During the season 1879–80 he played at the Madison Avenue Reformed Episcopal Church, and then became organist at All Souls Unitarian Church from 1880 to 1886. For the next nineteen years (1886–1905) he was organist at St. Bartholomew's, and from 1907, at the Church of the Ascension. He was active as a musician until 1921, when he retired to his country home at South Chatham, Mass., where he appeared occasionally as a guest organist at the First Congregational Church. In the years of his retirement he had opportunity to enjoy his hobby, the operation of a small printing press.

From 1886 to 1895 he was conductor of the Church Choral Society, an organization founded by the elder J. P. Morgan. As director of this chorus Warren gave first performances of a number of new works, among them Horatio Parker's "Hora Novissima," produced for the first time by the Society in 1893 at the Church of St. Zion and Timothy. In the summer of 1905 he conducted a series of summer orchestra concerts at St. Nicholas Garden, New York. He also appeared as guest conductor with the New York Philharmonic Society and the Philadelphia Symphony. As a composer he produced a considerable volume of church music—anthems and church services. He also composed several operettas; "Ingala" (1880), "All on a Summer's Day" (1882), "Magnolia" (1886), and "The Rightful Heir" (1899). His opera, "Phyllis" (1897) was produced at the Waldorf-Astoria, New York, in 1900. His most ambitious secular work for chorus was the cantata, "Ticonderoga"; he also composed a number of orchestral works. At the time of his death, at South Chatham, Warren was a widower. His wife, Helen Corbin Hurd, to whom he had been married in 1886, died in New York in 1921. They had no children.

[*Who's Who in America*, 1916–17; Rupert Hughes, *Contemporary Am. Composers* (1900); *Grove's Dict. of Music and Musicians, Am. Supp.* (1930); J. Van Brockhoven, "Richard Henry Warren," *Musical Observer*, Oct. 1910; *Boston Herald, N. Y. Times*, Dec. 4, 1933.]   J. T. H.

WARREN, RUSSELL (Aug. 5, 1783–Nov. 16, 1860), architect and engineer, son of Gamaliel and Ruth (Jenckes) Warren, a descendant of Richard Warren of the *Mayflower*, was born in Tiverton, R. I. One of several brothers who gained success as builders and contractors, he won wide recognition as a conspicuous devotee of the Greek Revival. Removing to Bristol, R. I., at the period of an influx of wealth, he was afforded an outlet for his talents in designing luxurious residences for ship captains and merchants, chief among them the stately DeWolf-Colt mansion (1810). One writer remarks of this house by "the master mind of the Bristol Renaissance" that it is rare to find a design so boldly original in conception transgressing so few architectural tenets (*Architectural Review, post*, Mar. 1901, p. 28.) Warren's first wife was Sarah Gladding, daughter of Capt. John Gladding of Bristol, whom he married on Mar. 10, 1805. After her death in 1817, he married her sister Lydia. He served in the Bristol militia and became major. Later, for a long period, he practised in Providence, R. I. He also was in demand in various other cities, his diversified output including churches, banks, public buildings, and residences. Adaptations of the Greek ideal were always dominant, his structures being distinguished for pillared porticoes and classical colonades, and he developed the cupola motive for dwellings with much success. He passed his winters in the South, chiefly at Charleston, S. C., whose structural beauties he enhanced. Possessed also of engineering skill, he threw a bridge over the Great Pedee River, a feat previously attempted without success. The Warren truss, used the world over in steel bridge construction, is said to have been devised by him. He died in Providence at the age of seventy-seven, survived by his wife. He had no children.

Warren's most notable works in Providence

are the Athenaeum, and the Arcade, housing a nest of small shops under a roof of glass. The Arcade, with its thirteen twelve-ton columns of native granite, was in line with others erected in larger cities about 1828. Philip Hone [*q.v.*], who saw it near completion, described it as of "singular beauty" and added that it would be "much more magnificent than the arcades of New York and Philadelphia" (*The Diary of Philip Hone,* 1927, I, 5). In New Bedford, Mass., the Unitarian Church, the Free Public Library, and a group of patrician residences are among Warren's finest productions. The greatest achievement of his career, however, the stone mansion of John Avery Parker, was lost to New Bedford some years ago. Built in 1834 at a cost of $100,-000, and of more than one hundred feet frontage, it was marked by flanking wings connected with the main pavilion by loggie or peristyles. The interior was remarkable for a magnificent circular staircase, twelve mantels of costly marbles, and great silver-handled doors, each a single panel of solid mahogany. Wonderfully impressive from its great size, it was probably the most successful example in America of the application of the Greek temple type to residential purposes.

[See *Vital Record of R. I.,* vols. IV (1893), VI (1894), ed. by J. N. Arnold; geneal. in article on Theodore Warren in *Representative Men . . . of R. I.* (1908), vol. III; death notice in *Providence Daily Jour.,* Nov. 17, 1860; M. A. De Wolfe Howe, *Bristol, R. I., a Town Biog.* (1930); J. W. Dow, *Am. Renaissance* (1904), *An Architectural Monograph on the Bristol Renaissance* (1917), and articles in *Architectural Rev.,* Mar., July 1901, and *House Beautiful,* Oct. 1901; Howard Major, *The Domestic Architecture of the Early Am. Republic* (1926), which has a picture of the Parker house.]   W. M. E.

WARREN, SAMUEL PROWSE (Feb. 18, 1841–Oct. 7, 1915), organist, composer, was born in Montreal, Canada, the son of Samuel Russell and Harriet Proud (Staynor) Warren. He was eighth in descent from Richard Warren, the London merchant who came to America on the *Mayflower.* His father, a native of Rhode Island, became an organ-builder, worked with Thomas Appleton of Boston, and eventually established his own busines in Montreal. Playing among the awesome rows of organ pipes in his father's shop as a child, Samuel developed an ambition to make those pipes sound. He was given piano lessons and at the age of eleven was deemed sufficiently prepared to study the organ. He proved an apt scholar and at twelve made his first public appearance in recital at St. Stephen's Chapel in Montreal. He became organist at the American Presbyterian Church and officiated regularly for eight years. Upon the completion of his academic studies, he went abroad to continue the study of music. He remained in Berlin four years, 1861–64, studying privately with the celebrated organist, Carl August Haupt. Gustav Schumann was his master in piano; Paul Wieprecht, in theory and instrumentation.

He returned to Montreal but chose New York City as the field of his professional activity. He gave his first public recital there in January 1866 and in April was appointed organist of All Souls Unitarian Church, serving until April 1868. He officiated at Grace Episcopal Church, 1868–74, and at Holy Trinity Episcopal Church, 1874–76. He returned to Grace Church, 1876–94, and from 1895 to 1915, presided over the organ at the First Presbyterian Church, East Orange, N. J. The twenty-four years he served at Grace Church were the most fruitful of his career; his masterly series of more than two hundred and thirty recitals proved him to be one of the great organists of the period. His impeccable musicianship was reflected in the liturgical singing of the splendid chorus choir at Grace Church and in the fine choral work of the New York Vocal Union, which he conducted for eight seasons, 1880–88.

Great personal charm, a self-effacing modesty, great mental capacity, and a truly romantic idealism were Warren's outstanding characteristics. He was a superb teacher and a composer with uncompromising standards. His choral settings for the Episcopal service are of high merit. His ripe scholarship is evidenced in his editions of the organ works of Mendelssohn, Guilmant, and Lemens, no less than in his transcriptions for organ of great symphonic works. Several charming songs reveal his poetic gift. Ever intent upon advancing the cause of true musicianship, he participated in the organization in 1896 of the American Guild of Organists, and in 1902 became honorary president of the Guild. He served as a trustee of the American College of Musicians and was a member of the council of the Boston Conservatory of Music. His scholarly interests were reflected in his valuable library of musical literature, one of the finest of American private collections. With a truly bibliophilic ardor, he gathered original manuscripts, rare books, the published works of the great masters, and the representative extant biographical, historical, and theoretical literature of music.

He was married to Emily Augusta Millard, in Montreal, on Jan. 16, 1867. Mrs. Jeanne Josephine Croker became his wife in 1908. By neither marriage had he any children.

[Personal data from Warren's brother-in-law, Norman Robertson, of Walkerton, Ontario; *Who's Who in America,* 1914–15; *Handbook of Am. Music and Musicians* (1886), ed. by F. O. Jones; *A Hundred Years*

of Music in America (1889), ed. by W. S. B. Mathews;
H. E. Krehbiel, *Review of the N. Y. Musical Season*
(5 vols., 1885–90); *Music*, Nov. 1899, and *Musical
America*, Jan. 15, 1916; *New Music Rev.*, Dec. 1915;
Anderson Galleries, *The Musical Library of the late S.
P. Warren* (1916), No. 1240; *Baker's Biog. Dict. of
Musicians* (3rd ed., 1919); W. T. Upton, *Art-Song in
America* (1930); L. C. Elson, *Hist. of Am. Music* (rev.
ed., 1925); *N. Y. Herald*, Oct. 8, 1915.]　　E. C. K.

WARREN, WILLIAM (May 10, 1767–Oct.
19, 1832), actor, manager, was a native of Bath,
England, the son of Philip Warren, a cabinetmaker. Scorning the efforts of his father to
teach him his trade, he made his stage début
with a small provincial company at the age of
seventeen as Young Norval in *Douglas*. Trained
in the rough surroundings of inferior traveling
troupes, he finally emerged from a wandering
life of hardship and slow advancement. At one
time he was in the company of Thomas Jefferson,
the founder of a famous stage family. In 1788,
when he was under engagement with Tate Wilkinson, one of the leading provincial managers
of that day, he had the good fortune to act in
support of Mrs. Siddons. In 1796, upon the invitation of Thomas Wignell [*q.v.*], he set out for
the United States, arriving in the autumn of that
year. He acted in Baltimore, and then in Philadelphia, where he appeared for the first time on
Dec. 5 as Friar Lawrence in *Romeo and Juliet*
and as Bundle in *The Waterman*. A visit with
the Wignell company to New York soon followed, but his associations with the theatre were
almost exclusively, both as actor and manager,
in Baltimore and Philadelphia. For some time
he was in partnership with William Burke Wood
[*q.v.*]. At their theatre in Philadelphia, Edwin
Forrest [*q.v.*] made his début as Young Norval,
with Warren as Old Norval; and both Edmund
Kean and Junius Brutus Booth [*q.v.*] acted under their management when they first came to
America. Warren was essentially a comedian,
especially adept at the acting of old men, but
he was equally capable in tragedy. Joseph N.
Ireland [*q.v.*] calls him "the most perfect 'old
man' of comedy or tragedy then known in America" (*Mrs. Duff*, 1882, p. 19); William Winter
[*q.v.*] speaks of "the weight, dignity and rich
humor" of his Old Dornton and Sir Robert
Bramble, and of his notable Falstaff and Sir
Toby Belch (*The Jeffersonians*, 1881, p. 66).
Few American managers ever carried for so
many years the double burden of management
and the acting of important characters.

After a long period of prosperity, Warren's
last years were filled with sadness because of his
ill health and disappointment because of his
business reverses. In December 1829 he retired
from management and acted only occasionally

thereafter. Returning to the Chestnut Street
Theatre in Philadelphia for a brief engagement,
he made his farewell stage appearance on Nov.
25, 1831, as Sir Robert Bramble in *The Poor
Gentleman*, being scarcely able to finish the part
because of loss of memory. After almost a year
of comparative seclusion, he died in Baltimore,
where he had made his home during his last
months. He was three times married. His first
wife, of whom little is known and who was not
an actress, accompanied him to America and
died not long after. On Aug. 15, 1806, he married Ann Brunton Merry [*q.v.*]. In 1809 he married Esther Fortune, whose elder sister Euphemia was the wife of Joseph Jefferson, 1774–1832
[*q.v.*]. All their six children were connected
with the theatre. Hester, the eldest, became the
wife of Joseph Proctor [*q.v.*], Anna was the
wife of Danford Marble [*q.v.*], the comedian;
Emma was first Mrs. J. B. Price and then Mrs.
David Hanchett, both of her husbands being actors; Mary Ann married John B. Rice, a theatre
manager, later mayor of Chicago and a member
of Congress, and retired from the stage in 1856;
William [*q.v.*] was the celebrated comedian of
the Boston Museum; and Henry, whose daughter, Sarah Isabel, became the second wife of Joseph Jefferson the younger [*q.v.*], was a theatrical manager. Through inherited ability and
intermarriage, the Warrens hold a conspicuous
place in the annals of the American stage.

[*Life and Memoirs of William Warren* (1889); Wil-
liam Dunlap, *Hist. of the Am. Theatre* (1833); Joe
Cowell, *Thirty Years Passed among the Players* (2 pts.
1844–45); F. C. Wemyss, *Twenty-Six Years of the
Life of an Actor and Manager* (1847); W. B. Wood,
Personal Recollections of the Stage (1855); J. N.
Ireland, *Records of the N. Y. Stage* (2 vols., 1866–67);
William Winter, *The Life and Art of Joseph Jefferson*
(1894); biog. of Warren in *Mirror of Taste* (Phila.),
Feb.–May, Dec. 1811; *Phila. Dramatic Mirror*, Aug.
21, 1841; *Boston Herald*, Oct. 22, 1882 (valuable ar-
ticle); editorial in *Am. Sentinel* (Phila.) and obituary
notice in *Nat. Gazette* (Phila.), Oct. 22, 1832.]
　　　　　　　　　　　　　　　　　　E. F. E.

WARREN, WILLIAM (Nov. 17, 1812–Sept.
21, 1888), actor, was born in Philadelphia, Pa.,
but after his boyhood and youth in his native city,
and after some ten years as a strolling player,
he went in 1846 to Boston. He was the son of
William [*q.v.*] and Esther (Fortune) Warren.
His education in the public and private schools
of Philadelphia was brief. He was naturally attracted to the family profession but did not make
his first appearance until Oct. 27, 1832, on the
occasion of a benefit given in aid of the family
at the Arch Street Theatre in Philadelphia, a
few days after the elder Warren's death. He
then acted Young Norval in *Douglas,* the part
and the play in which his father had made his
début in England forty-eight years before. James

E. Murdoch [*q.v.*] describes him as "a youth slight in figure, and looking much like a student of divinity at home for a vacation . . . silent and thoughtful in expression, and very formal in manner" (*The Stage,* 1880, p. 414). Thereafter he was associated with and obtained his professional schooling in migratory troupes, and in resident companies at Pittsburgh, Baltimore, Washington, Philadelphia, Buffalo, and other American theatrical centers. One of these engagements was with a company under the direction of the second Joseph Jefferson [*q.v.*], who recalls him as "a tall handsome young man about twenty-five years of age," with "fine expressive eyes, a graceful figure, and a head of black curly hair." He acted in New York very seldom, first in 1841; during a visit to England in 1845, he made his only appearance on the London stage.

The year 1846 marks his arrival in Boston, where he lived and worked for forty-two years. He was first associated with the Howard Athenaeum, where on Oct. 5 he acted Sir Lucius O'Trigger in *The Rivals,* remaining at that theatre only during a part of one season. Joining the stock company at the Boston Museum on Aug. 23, 1847, he acted there for the first time as Billy Lackaday in *Sweethearts and Wives,* and as Gregory Grizzle in *My Young Wife and Old Umbrella.* He soon became one of Boston's leading citizens, not merely in his capacity as an actor but as a gentleman who ranked in social standing with members of every profession and with the foremost men of business. In his *Autobiography,* Joseph Jefferson notes an occasion when with him as guests at Warren's table were Oliver Wendell Holmes, Henry Wadsworth Longfellow, and Mr. and Mrs. James T. Fields [*qq.v.*]. He had begun his stage career by acting a wide range of characters in comedy, melodrama, and tragedy; but, although not lacking in versatility, he eventually made comedy his especial branch of acting, and it is upon his skill as a comedian that his reputation rests. Despite the fact that, with the exception of one season (1864–65) when he went on tour, he remained in one city, in one theatre, and with one stock company, he became one of the most eminent of American actors. Few visitors came to Boston without going to the Museum especially to see the famous actor, and a favorite revival season after season was a comedy, adapted from an old English play, entitled *Seeing Warren.*

His rôles, nearly six hundred in about 14,000 performances, extend from such Shakespearean comedy characters as Touchstone and Polonius through such eighteenth-century comedy rôles as Bob Acres, Sir Peter Teazle, and Tony Lump-

kin to leading parts in ephemeral productions of new plays. The demand for his repeated impersonation of Jefferson Scattering Batkins in *The Silver Spoon,* by Joseph Stevens Jones [*q.v.*], is typical of the acclaim he received in popular, though dramatically unimportant plays. If there were no part for him in a play that was put into rehearsal, one was written in so that his absence from the cast might not disappoint his admirers, the most conspicuous example of this being the interpolated character of Penetrate Partyside in *Uncle Tom's Cabin.* One of his associates says of his acting that it "belonged to the best French school. . . . The fine art, the fruition of study, the faithfulness in detail, all were there" (Catherine Reignolds-Winslow, *post,* p. 128), and a well-known critic echoes this judgment, adding: "His acting seems the fine flower of careful culture, as well as the free outcome of large intelligence and native genius. His enunciation and pronunciation of English were beyond criticism" (Clapp, *Reminiscences, post,* p. 56).

To celebrate his fiftieth anniversary on the stage, gala performances were given at the Boston Museum on Saturday afternoon and evening, Oct. 27, 1882, when he played successively Dr. Pangloss in *The Heir-at-Law* and Sir Peter Teazle in *The School for Scandal.* A few months later, on May 12, 1883, he bade farewell to the stage and to the Boston public in the character of Old Eccles in *Caste.* He lived thereafter in retirement, surrounded by his Boston friends and visited by many actors when they came to Boston. He died after a brief illness at the house in Bulfinch Place where he had lived many years. A vast assemblage of friends, acquaintances, and others gathered in Trinity Church to pay tribute to his life and memory, and he was buried in Mount Auburn Cemetery, Cambridge, where also lie Edwin Booth, Charlotte Cushman [*qq.v.*], and other eminent members of his profession. He never married. After his death appeared the *Life and Memoirs of William Warren* (1889).

[*Life and Memoirs of William Warren* (1889); Catherine M. Reignolds-Winslow, *Yesterdays with Actors* (1887); *Autobiog. of Joseph Jefferson* (1889); William Winter, *Life and Art of Joseph Jefferson* (1896) and *Vagrant Memories* (1915); H. A. Clapp, *Reminiscences of a Dramatic Critic* (1902); L. C. Davis, in *Atlantic Monthly,* June 1867; H. A. Clapp, *Ibid.,* Dec. 1888; *Boston Herald,* Oct. 22, 1882; *Boston Transcript,* Nov. 30, 1894, May 27, 1911, and Sept. 20, 1913; obituary in *Boston Transcript,* Sept. 21, 1888.]
E. F. E.

WARREN, WILLIAM FAIRFIELD (Mar. 13, 1833–Dec. 6, 1929), Methodist Episcopal clergyman, educator, first president of Boston University, was born in Williamsburg, Mass., the youngest child of Mather Warren, farmer, sawmill owner, and building mover, and Anne

Miller (Fairfield), woman of remarkable ability and piety. He was a descendant of William Warren who emigrated to Boston from England in 1715 and of John Fairfield, an immigrant to Charlestown in 1635. The boy's religious and reflective temperament was fostered in the family circle and both he and his brother, Henry White Warren [*q.v.*], became important figures in the Methodist Episcopal Church. He attended the local schools and East Greenwich (R. I.) Academy. Entering Wesleyan University in 1850, he was graduated three years later. He then opened a private classical school in Mobile, Ala. Returning North in July 1854, he was admitted to the New England Conference on trial in 1855 and supplied a church in Ballardvale, Mass., until 1856, meanwhile studying at the Andover Theological Seminary. During 1856–57 he attended the University of Berlin and the University of Halle, spending his vacations traveling in Italy, Greece, Turkey, Palestine, and Egypt. After his return to the United States he preached at Wilbraham, Mass. (1858–59), and at Bromfield Street Church, Boston (1860–61). He was ordained elder in 1861 and returned to Germany to become professor of systematic theology at Missionsanstalt in Bremen, remaining there until 1866. Articles in the *Methodist Review, Bibliotheca Sacra,* and other periodicals, and several books in German, notably *Systematische Theologie einheitlich behandelt* (Bremen, 1865), a volume intended to be an introduction to a larger work, gave him a reputation in theological circles.

When the Methodist Biblical Institute was moved from Concord, N. H., to Boston in 1867 and renamed the Boston Theological School, he became its president, serving as such until 1873. He was closely associated with the three Boston philanthropists, Isaac Rich, Jacob Sleeper [*qq.v.*], and Lee Claflin in the founding of Boston University and was the guiding spirit in its development. The theological school became its first department. As the university's acting president, 1869–73, and as president, 1873–1903, the work of creating the institution was largely his. His plans, notable in their comprehensiveness, were based upon a fusion of the English emphasis on the humanities grounded in the classics, the German thoroughness in research, and American democracy. Warren maintained that professional and technical schools should exist in comparative independence instead of operating as departments of a single school, and that pure science is better and more economically organized and is kept more vital in connection with schools of applied science. Full three-year

courses in law, in theology, and in medicine were instituted. In 1878 a fourth year was added to the medical course. Advanced schools of oratory and of music were founded, while courses in science and agriculture in cooperation with the Massachusetts Institute of Technology and the Massachusetts Agricultural College took the place of the colleges of science and agriculture of the original plan. The requirements for admission to the college of liberal arts were constantly increased. A college of commerce and navigation was planned but not established until 1913. By 1875 the schools of law, medicine, and theology had a larger enrollment than those of any other American university having these professional departments. Scholarly teachers, most of them with European training, were secured, among them Borden P. Bowne, Henry N. Hudson, and Alexander Graham Bell [*qq.v.*]. In his zeal for international educational opportunities, Warren completed in 1874 arrangements whereby students of the school of all sciences (the university's graduate school) could study at the National University of Athens and the Royal University at Rome. Warren vigorously opposed attempts to shorten the college course to three years as proposed by his contemporary Charles W. Eliot [*q.v.*]. His annual reports and his essays contributed to the *Boston University Year Book,* 1874–1904, left few phases of education untouched. He himself was an active teacher, maintaining his position as professor in the theological school from 1867 to 1920. He was dean of the school from 1871 to 1873, and from 1903 to 1911. His course in comparative religions, a subject in which he was an authority, was a famous one. The school under his leadership also offered lectures by representatives of other denominations, and was the first to require sociology and the study of missions in the course leading to a degree.

Warren was actively interested in educational opportunities for women, and Boston University was the first university in America to open the full circle of professional schools to them. It awarded the degree of Ph.D. to a woman for the first time in America when in 1878 it conferred the degree on Helen McGill (Mrs. Andrew D. White). Warren was an original member of the corporation of Wellesley College and president of the Massachusetts Society for the University Education of Women. His arguments for the admission of girls to the Boston Latin School were factors in the establishment of the Girls' Latin School.

His principal publications were concerned with conceptions of the universe held by the ancients. In this field, besides many articles, he published *The True Key to Ancient Cosmology and Mythical Geography* (1882), *Paradise Found* (1885), which went through eleven subsequent editions, and *The Earliest Cosmologies* (1909). His most famous address, a masterpiece of sustained imagery, was published in 1886 under the title *A Quest for a Perfect Religion,* went through five English editions, and was reprinted in Spanish, Japanese, and Chinese. The World Parliament of Religions in Chicago in 1893 was in a remarkable measure a realization of his dream. In his religion, Warren was devout without a trace of fanaticism, tolerant yet sure of his own beliefs, conservative but a believer in the essential soundness of modern approach to Biblical study. Under his educational leadership, insistent on academic freedom and enlightened scholarship, there were trained by his theological faculty the men who, with others like-minded, led the Methodist Episcopal Church, comparatively untroubled, through the storms caused by Darwin's *Origin of Species,* Spencer's *First Principles,* and the Tübingen school of Biblical criticism.

He married, Apr. 14, 1861, Harriet Cornelia Merrick of Wilbraham, Mass., later the first editor of the *Heathen Woman's Friend* and *Der Heidenfrauen Freund.* She was a woman of rare ability and training in languages, being proficient in Latin, German, French, and Italian. They had one son and three daughters. Warren retained his active interest in current affairs until his death at the age of ninety-six in Brookline, Mass. He was buried in Mount Auburn.

[Boston Theological School, *Reports,* 1867–72; Boston University, *Yearbooks,* 1874–1904; Boston University, *President's Reports,* 1874–1903; *Bostonia,* Apr. 1900, July 1903; *Boston Evening Transcript,* Feb. 9, 1924, Dec. 7, 1929; *Zion's Herald,* Dec. 11, 1929; *Meth. Review,* Mar. 1924; G. G. Bush, *Hist. of Higher Education in Mass.* (1891); D. L. Marsh, *William Fairfield Warren* (1930) and *Eliot and Warren* (1932); *Who's Who in America,* 1928–29; partial bibliog. of Warren's writings in *Alumni Record of Wesleyan Univ.* (1883); manuscript autobiog. notes in Boston Univ. Lib.]   R. E. M.

WARRINGTON, LEWIS (Nov. 3, 1782–Oct. 12, 1851), naval officer, was born at Williamsburg, Va., and as a youth attended the College of William and Mary. Little is known of his parents and what is known of his stepfather is discreditable (*William and Mary Quarterly,* October 1929). On Jan. 6, 1800, he was appointed midshipman. Soon thereafter he joined the *Chesapeake* and cruised in the West Indies during the last year of the naval war with France. Retained on the peace establishment of 1801, he participated in the war with the Barbary corsairs, 1802–07, serving on board the *President,*

Vixen, and *Enterprise.* In 1805 he was promoted lieutenant. After commanding a gunboat at Norfolk, he was attached in 1809 to the *Siren,* under orders to proceed to Europe with dispatches. On his return home he was transferred to the *Essex,* which, after cruising off the American coast, also made a voyage to Europe with dispatches.

His first duty in the War of 1812 was performed as first lieutenant of the *Congress,* one of the ships of the squadron of Commodore John Rodgers [*q.v.*]. Soon after his promotion to the rank of master commandant, July 1813, he took command of the sloop of war *Peacock.* Sailing from New York in March 1814, he encountered off Cape Canaveral, Apr. 29, 1814, the British brig *Epervier,* and after a sharp action of three quarters of an hour forced her to surrender, with a loss ten times that of his own ship. In recognition of this notable victory, Congress presented him with a gold medal and the state of Virginia with a sword. He next made an extensive cruise in which he visited the Grand Banks and the coasts of Ireland, the Shetland and Faroe Islands, and Portugal, taking in all fourteen prizes. In his last cruise during the war he rounded the Cape of Good Hope and crossed the Indian Ocean, capturing several large Indiamen, valuable prizes. Entering the Straits of Sunda, on June 30, 1815, he fell in with the East India Company's cruiser *Nautilus,* 14 guns, which he took after inflicting a loss of fifteen men, including the first lieutenant mortally wounded. Warrington's claim that he had not heard of the treaty of peace is disputed by the purser of the British vessel, who said that he spoke to him of the peace before the fight began.

In 1816 Warrington commanded the *Macedonian* during a voyage to Cartagena and conveyed thither Christopher Hughes [*q.v.*], delegated by the American government to effect the release of American citizens imprisoned by the Spanish. He commanded the *Java,* 1819–20, and the *Guerriere,* 1820–21, of the Mediterranean squadron. After a period of duty at the Norfolk navy yard he commanded the West India squadron which was employed in the suppression of piracy. In 1826–30 and again in 1840–42 he was one of the three commissioners of the navy board, an administrative body in Washington, D. C., charged with the administration of the naval matériel. During the intervening decade he was commandant of the Norfolk navy yard. On the reorganization of the Navy Department in 1842 he became the chief of the bureau of yards and docks. In 1844 he was for a time secretary of the navy *ad interim.* In 1846 he was made chief of the bureau of ordnance, an office that he held until his death. On Mar. 3, 1817, he was married to Margaret Cary King of Norfolk, Va.

[Record of Officers, Bureau of Navigation, 1798–1858; *Navy Reg.*, 1814–51; *Analectic Mag. and Naval Chronicle*, Jan. 1816; A. T. Mahan, *Sea Power in Its Relations to the War of 1812* (1919); Theodore Roosevelt, *Naval War of 1812* (1904); *Daily National Intelligencer* (Washington), Oct. 13, 1851; *Va. Calendar of State Papers*, vol. X (1892); *Va. Hist. Reg.*, Apr. 1852; *Va. Mag. of Hist. and Biog.*, July 1926.]

C. O. P.

WARTHIN, ALDRED SCOTT (Oct. 21, 1866–May 23, 1931), physician, educator, was born in Greensburg, Ind. The son of Edward Mason and Eliza Margaret (Weist) Warthin, he came of English and Pennsylvania Dutch ancestry. His grandfather was one of the first settlers in Decatur County, Ind., where he set up a general store; his maternal grandmother, also, had journeyed to the frontier. With an uncle, a physician interested in the study of nature, he went afield collecting specimens; and to please his invalid mother he took lessons on the piano. Considered a prodigy by his neighbors, he entered the Cincinnati Conservatory of Music and in 1887 gained a teacher's diploma. During the same period he studied at the University of Indiana under David Starr Jordan [*q.v.*], and upon receiving the degree of A.B. in 1888, he turned to science. Already he had taught botany. His decision caused his father to withhold further aid.

Characteristically undaunted, he enrolled in the medical department of the University of Michigan, and, supporting himself by giving music lessons and serving as church organist, graduated with the degree of M.D. in 1891. His potential value to the medical school as a teacher was recognized by the new professor of medicine, George Dock. While assistant (1891) and demonstrator (1892–95), he learned clinical medicine, and in 1893 received the degree of Ph.D. In 1896 he was given charge of the work in pathology, taking over a department without material and replacing a teacher who believed that bacteria had no relation to disease. His intense energy and curiosity, already manifest in several scientific papers, now found scope. To procure material he arranged that all specimens from the clinics be sent to him, and his diagnostic findings soon became a touchstone for the practitioner, a relationship to clinical medicine which broadened throughout his life. At first he did the entire work of the laboratory which he created, technical and intellectual, teaching large classes, doing autopsies and research, instructing graduate students, holding seminars, and

even giving a course in medical history. By 1903 he was professor and director. On June 27, 1900, he married Katharine Angell. They had four children.

Warthin's summers from 1893 to 1900 were spent in the pathological laboratories of Freiburg, Dresden, and Vienna. In Vienna he came upon Dürer's engraving of the knight riding unconcerned past a leering Devil and a bony Death; and ever after the morbid seemed to him thrice morbid because expressive of the human predicament. Working and writing on numerous themes, among them tuberculosis of the placenta, the hemolymph nodes—which he established as physiological entities—the cause of Banti's disease, heredity in cancer, traumatic lipæmia, and mustard gas poisoning, he came to the study of syphilis, and in some forty papers disclosed its responsibility for conditions previously unsuspected. His findings were often disputed, yet it came to be recognized that in general he was but little more positive than the facts.

Warthin's European experiences made him keenly conscious that the contribution of medicine to American civilization was barely begun, and to further it he gave himself to the founding and support of societies and journals. Possessed of a terse, vivid style, he wrote extensively and was in demand as lecturer. He published *Practical Pathology for Students and Physicians* (1897, 1911) and *General Pathology* (1903, 1908), a translation of the German work of Ernst Ziegler. He also edited the *Annals of Clinical Medicine* (1924–31). He became president of several medical organizations, notably the Association of American Physicians (1928). Shortly before his death he wrote "Forty Years as a Clinical Pathologist," which was published posthumously in the *Journal of Laboratory and Clinical Medicine* (July 1931).

That concern for his kind which led Warthin to study syphilis intensively found other expression in *The Creed of a Biologist* (1930). In this volume he held that man need look no further for immortality than to his descendants, nor for a larger task than to better man. Still there would be old age and death, and to discover a right attitude toward these he studied the aging process and collected books and pictures dealing with the "Dance of Death," a collection which he bequeathed to the University of Michigan. His book *Old Age—the Major Involution* (1929) is unsparingly comprehensive. In *The Physician of the Dance of Death* (1931) he comments on pictures which tell of the doctor's surroundings and behavior when Death lays hands on him. Its author did not have to gain this knowledge, for he died of coronary occlusion, deeming it but a trivial asthma.

Warthin was bright-eyed and fresh-colored, quick and strong. He was drastic yet kind, earnest yet cheerful, and most sensitive to beauty. He loved music, gardens, books, and friends. Unpopular in his early years because of a trenchant sincerity, he lived to be widely appreciated without having relinquished it. In 1927 there was published *Contributions to Medical Science Dedicated to Aldred Scott Warthin,* containing scientific papers from members of his thirty-five classes.

[*Jour. of Laboratory and Clinical Medicine,* July 1931; *Annals of Clinical Medicine,* June 1931; *Jour. of Pathology and Bacteriology,* vol. XXXV, no. 1 (1932); *Jour. of Technical Methods and Bull. of the International Asso. of Medical Museums,* no. 13 (1934); *Am. Jour. of Syphilis,* July 1931; *Archives of Pathology,* Aug. 1931; *Am. Jour. of Surgery,* Nov. 1931; *Boletín de la Asociación Médica de Puerto-Rico,* July 1931; J. McK. and Jaques Cattell, *Am. Men of Sci.* (1927); *Who's Who in America,* 1930–31; *Detroit Free Press,* May 24, 1931.]   P. R.

WASHAKIE (*c.* 1804–Feb. 15, 1900), a head chief of the eastern Shoshones, who befriended the white settlers and was a stout ally of the United States government, was born probably in Montana; the year of birth inscribed on his tombstone is 1804. He was of mixed Shoshone and Umatilla blood; the statement sometimes made that he was part white was apparently based on his exceptionally light color. In the 1840's he became chief of the Eastern band of Shoshones, often called Washakie's Band, whose general range was the lower Green River Valley. From his youth he was noted for his friendship with the whites. He was well known to the early trappers and at various times was in the employ of the American and Hudson's Bay companies. The overland emigrants found him and his people of great assistance in helping them across dangerous fords and in recovering their strayed animals, and a paper testifying to these acts was signed by more than 9,000 emigrants. Though his name does not appear in the treaty, he is said to have been in the great council of 1851, which met at Fort Laramie and later at the junction of Horse Creek and the North Platte. In the fall of 1862, unable to restrain a considerable part of his band from joining the Bannocks in plundering the emigrant trains and settlements, he took his loyal followers to Fort Bridger; but on the crushing defeat of the hostiles by Gen. Patrick E. Connor [*q.v.*] in the Bear River fight of Jan. 29, 1863, the band was reunited under his leadership.

In the treaty council of 1868 at Fort Bridger, wherein for the sake of the Union Pacific right-of-way the Green River Valley was given up in exchange for the present Shoshone reservation in the Wind River region, Washakie represented both his own people and the Bannocks. In the Sioux War of 1876 he sent from the reservation eighty-six of his warriors, under two of his sons, to join Gen. George Crook [*q.v.*] in time for the disastrous battle of the Rosebud, June 17, and three weeks later himself arrived with 213 more. Leading a scouting party for Crook, he penetrated the country of the hostiles and brought back definite word of their whereabouts. When Crook started northward to join Alfred H. Terry [*q.v.*], Washakie returned home with most of his followers. His declining years were spent on the reservation in the patriarchal rôle of ruler, guide, and counselor of his people. He died at Fort Washakie. A military funeral was accorded him, and a monument was erected over his grave.

Washakie was tall, with a powerful physique capable of great endurance. He has been likened in face and bearing to both Henry Ward Beecher and Robert Collyer [*qq.v.*]. All testimony agrees as to his high character and his kindly disposition. As a chief he was something of an absolutist, brooking little opposition to his policies; and he was also somewhat vain, with a fondness for showy ceremonials. Much of his life was spent in defensive wars against more powerful tribes, and even in old age he ranked high as a warrior. In his later years he renounced many of the customs of the tribe, including polygamy, and joined the Protestant Episcopal Church. It has been said of him (Wheeler, *post,* p. 217) that no Indian of mountain or plain was more widely or favorably known.

[Grace Raymond Hebard, *Washakie* (1930); F. W. Hodge, *Handbook of Am. Indians North of Mexico* (1910); J. G. Bourke, *On the Border with Crook* (1891); H. W. Wheeler, *Buffalo Days* (1925); *Cheyenne Daily Sun-Leader,* Feb. 20, 1900; manuscript notes from Professor Hebard.]   W. J. G.

WASHBURN, ALBERT HENRY (Apr. 11, 1866–Apr. 2, 1930), lawyer and diplomat, was the only child of Edward and Ann Elizabeth (White) Washburn. He was born in Middleboro, Mass., where his father conducted a small manufacturing business, and with the exception of a short period when the family resided in London, Ont., received his early education in the schools of that town. He then attended Cornell University, earning part of his college expenses by serving as secretary to Andrew D. White [*q.v.*], and was graduated in 1889. He entered the consular service and represented the United States at Magdeburg, Germany, from

1890 to 1893. In the latter year, invited to become private secretary to Henry Cabot Lodge [*q.v.*], he returned to America and acted in this capacity until 1896. Meanwhile he studied law at the University of Virginia and at Georgetown University, receiving the degree of LL.B. from the latter institution in 1895. He maintained a close personal and political association with the Massachusetts senator until the latter's death.

From 1897 to 1901 he was assistant United States attorney for the Massachusetts district, the varied business arising in the port of Boston, including the celebrated trials growing out of the murders on the barkentine *Herbert Fuller,* giving him wide experience in federal practice. From 1901 to 1904 he served as counsel for the Treasury in customs cases, becoming a specialist in the intricate problems involved in tariff legislation and the importing business.

In 1904 he resigned his official post and for the next eighteen years engaged in private practice. On Jan. 11, 1906, he married Florence B. Lincoln of Springfield, Mass., by whom he had one son. His professional standing was recognized by his election in 1917 as the first president of the Association of the Customs Bar. His briefs and arguments in *American Express Company et al.* vs. *United States* (4 *Court of Customs Appeals Reports,* 146), the Discount Cases (6 *Ibid.,* 291; 243 *U. S.,* 97), and *G. S. Nicholas and Co.* vs. *United States* (249 *U. S.,* 34) have been considered as of special significance in the field of customs law. The first of these cases attracted international attention, involving as it did interpretation of the "most favored nation clause," and in 1913 Washburn received a decoration from the Norwegian government in recognition of his services. He was a Republican in politics, active in the Massachusetts organization, and in general conservative in his views on political and social problems. His interest in political and international affairs and his inherent scholarly tastes found expression in occasional popular articles in magazines and reviews as well as in more technical contributions to professional journals. From 1919 to 1921 he served as professor of international law and political science in Dartmouth College.

In 1922 he was appointed minister to Austria by President Harding, the first to represent the United States since the collapse of the old empire in the World War. He continued at this post until 1930. He negotiated and signed a treaty of friendship, commerce, and consular rights, June 19, 1928, and an extradition treaty, Jan. 31, 1930. In 1922–23 he was a member of the commission of jurists that considered amendment of the laws of war at The Hague, and he was president of the mixed commission to adjust differences arising out of provisional commercial agreements and other difficulties between Austria and Jugoslavia, 1923–25. Washburn's reports were highly valued by the Department of State for their keen, illuminating, and objective interpretations of events in central and eastern Europe. He was frequently consulted by the officials of the new republic on the problems and difficulties of its formative years. His services in connection with the financial rehabilitation of the country and the extension of credit to the struggling government under the auspices of the League of Nations were regarded as a decisive contribution to its survival. His death in Vienna on Apr. 2, 1930, was followed by a flood of tributes from the leaders of Austria and neighboring countries in recognition of his constant and always unostentatious helpfulness. He had resigned early the preceding January and the submission of his nomination as ambassador to Japan was pending, when he succumbed, after a few days illness, to an infection resulting from a minor injury.

[*Publications of the Dept. of State: Press Releases,* Jan. 11, Apr. 5, May 17, 1930; *Reg. of the Dept. of State, Jan. 1, 1930* (1930); *Who's Who in America,* 1928–29; *N. Y. Times,* Apr. 3, 4, 6, 1930; *N. Y. Herald Tribune,* Apr. 3, 4, 1930; personal acquaintance, information from friends and colleagues, records in possession of Mrs. Washburn.]   W. A. R.

WASHBURN, CADWALLADER COLDEN (Apr. 22, 1818–May 14, 1882), soldier, congressman, governor of Wisconsin, pioneer industrialist, was one of the seven sons (an eighth died in infancy) of Israel and Martha (Benjamin) Washburn. His ancestry on both sides went back to early Massachusetts Puritans —on the paternal side to John Washburn who settled in Duxbury in 1632—and his two grandfathers, Capt. Israel Washburn and Lieut. Samuel Benjamin, served with distinction in the Revolutionary War. In 1809 Washburn's father, who had left the ancestral home in Raynham, Mass., three years before, bought a farm and a store at Livermore, Androscoggin County, Me. Here he married and brought up his numerous brood of children, which included, besides the boys, three girls. Members of so large a family could not stay for long under the parental roof-tree; hence, in 1839, equipped with what education he could get from the town schools, and deeply impressed by the advice of Reuel Washburn, a lawyer uncle, Cadwallader borrowed enough money to pay his way to the West, and was soon in Davenport, Iowa. Here, and across the Mississippi in Illinois, he taught school, worked in a store, did some surveying, and read law. In 1842 he opened a law office at Mineral Point, Wis., a small town not far from Galena, Ill., where his brother Elihu B. Washburne [*q.v.*] had settled two years before.

The foundation of his great fortune was soon laid. In 1844 he formed a partnership with Cyrus Woodman, an experienced land agent, and gradually abandoned the law for the far more lucrative business of entering public lands for settlers. Before long the partners owned in their own right valuable pine, mineral, and agricultural lands, and for a short time they operated the Mineral Point Bank. After 1855, when the partnership was amicably dissolved, Washburn carried on his now extensive operations alone. Even politics and the Civil War did not interfere seriously with the normal growth of this pioneer fortune. Proud of his honesty, and of the record of his bank, which never suspended specie payments and liquidated by meeting every obligation in full, Washburn rarely won the ill will of his neighbors; but his judgment on business matters was sound, and the opportunities for making money in a rapidly developing country were abundant.

Washburn's excellent reputation, and his early adherence to the principles upon which the Republican party was founded, brought him an unsolicited nomination and election to Congress in 1854. He sat in three successive congresses, in each of which, by an odd coincidence, his brother Israel [*q.v.*] represented a Maine district, and his brother Elihu an Illinois district. The three brothers, to the satisfaction of their respective constituencies, lent one another much aid, particularly on local matters, but the representative from Wisconsin achieved no very great national prominence. His outstanding act was to oppose vigorously a House plan to pacifiy the South by so amending the Constitution as to continue slavery indefinitely; but his participation in the Washington Peace Convention of 1861 showed his desire to prevent war. When war came nevertheless, his record was admirable. He raised the 2nd Wisconsin Volunteer Cavalry, became its colonel, and by the end of 1862 was a major-general. His command saw hard service in most of the campaigns west of the Mississippi River, and participated in the fighting around Vicksburg. When the war ended, he was in charge of the Department of Western Tennessee, with headquarters at Memphis.

After the war, as a rich man and a former major-general of volunteers, Washburn was clearly marked for a political career if he desired it, but politics never absorbed his chief interest. He served two more terms in Congress, 1867–71, as a thoroughly regular Republican, and one term, Jan. 1, 1872, to Dec. 31, 1873, as governor of Wisconsin. He would probably have welcomed a seat in the United States Senate, or a cabinet appointment, but these honors were denied him, and he was content to devote his later years to the operation and expansion of his vast industrial enterprises. His pine lands brought him into the lumber business and his shrewd acquisition of water-power rights at the Falls of St. Anthony (Minneapolis) on the upper Mississippi enabled him to become one of the nation's foremost manufacturers of flour. In 1856 he helped organize the Minneapolis Mill Company, of which his younger brother, William D. Washburn [*q.v.*] became secretary. Some fifteen years later C. C. Washburn was one of the first to adopt the "New Process" of milling, which created a demand for the spring wheat of the Northwest and completely revolutionized the flour industry in the United States. Like his great rival, Charles A. Pillsbury [*q.v.*], he was prompt in substituting rollers for millstones. In 1877 Washburn, Crosby & Company was organized, and two years later reorganized, with Washburn, John Crosby, Charles J. Martin, and William E. Dunwoody [*q.v.*], as partners. Naturally Washburn's wealth drew him into many other lines of business. He was, for example, one of the projectors and builders of the Minneapolis & St. Louis Railroad.

His private life was saddened, though not embittered, by the insanity of his wife, Jeannette Garr, a visitor to the West from New York City, whom he married Jan. 1, 1849. She became an invalid after the birth of their second child in 1852, and although she survived her husband by many years her mind was never restored. Perhaps as an outlet to his feelings, Washburn took much satisfaction in his philanthropies, among which were the Washburn Observatory of the University of Wisconsin, the Public Library at La Crosse (his residence after 1859), and an orphan asylum in Minneapolis. He suffered a stroke of paralysis in 1881, and died a year later at Eureka Springs, Ark.

[A manuscript sketch of C. C. Washburn's life, prepared by his brother Elihu, together with an extensive collection of Washburn and Woodman papers, is in the possession of the State Hist. Soc. of Wis. See also Gaillard Hunt, *Israel, Elihu and Cadwallader Washburn* (1925); David Atwood and others, "In Memoriam: Hon. Cadwallader C. Washburn," *Wis. Hist. Soc. Colls.*, vol. IX (1882); C. W. Butterfield, "Cadwallader C. Washburn," *Northwest Rev.* (Minneapolis), Mar. 1883; *Biog. Hist. of La Crosse, Trempealeau and Buffalo Counties, Wis.* (1892); C. B. Kuhlmann, *The Development of the Flour-Milling Industry in the U. S.* (1929); W. C. Edgar, *The Medal of Gold* (1925); *N. Y. Times*, May 15, 1882; *Republican and Leader* (La Crosse), May 20, 27, 1882.]   J. D. H—s.

WASHBURN, CHARLES GRENFILL (Jan. 28, 1857–May 25, 1928), congressman, manufact rer, writer, was born in Worcester, Mass., the eldest son of Charles Francis and Mary Elizabeth (Whiton) Washburn. His grandfather, Charles, twin brother of Ichabod Washburn [q.v.], was a partner of that pioneer in the wire industry. Charles Francis Washburn's entire business life was devoted to it, and his son, after graduation from the Worcester Polytechnic Institute (1875) and Harvard College (1880), at once started a wire-goods business of his own, in which he retained a controlling interest throughout his life. He soon entered the employ of the Washburn & Moen Manufacturing Company. By private study, however, he fitted himself for admission to the bar in 1887, and two years later became general counsel for that corporation. It was then rapidly developing the new wire-fencing branch of its industry, and Washburn was brought into intimate contact with the problems of corporation management and patent litigation. In 1891 he withdrew from the Washburn & Moen Company and began the practice of patent law in Worcester, but soon became president of a newly organized concern, the Washburn Wire Company. Eight years as president of the great textile firm, S. Slater & Sons, brought to him thorough knowledge of another of New England's major industries.

From 1897 to 1901 he was a member of the Massachusetts legislature, serving two years in each branch. His effective work, especially on the committees on taxation, the judiciary, and rules and banking, led to his being called upon repeatedly for tasks requiring hard work and good judgment. By appointment of Gov. Winthrop Murray Crane [q.v.] in 1902 he became a trustee of the Lyman and Industrial schools. He was a member of the committee on revision of the corporation laws (1902), and chairman of a special commission on street railways (1919). In 1917 he was a delegate-at-large to the convention for revision of the constitution of Massachusetts.

He was elected as a Republican in 1906 to fill a vacancy in the national House of Representatives caused by the death of Rockwood Hoar, and he was reëlected for the Sixtieth and Sixty-first congresses. His principal service was on the committees on insular affairs and patents and copyrights. He was mainly responsible for solving in 1909 the most difficult problem which long blocked the codification of copyright laws, namely the problem of "pirated" music for phonographs. On the floor of the House he spoke seldom, but his broad experience in legislation and in practical business lent weight to his discussion of matters relating to corporations and the tariff. After the final hearings upon the Standard Oil and Tobacco Trust cases in 1911, Chief Justice White sought the judgment of Washburn as a business man of broad experience upon the question of the probable effect of construing the first section of the Sherman Law so that it would forbid only contracts in unreasonable restraint of trade. Washburn strongly approved such a construction. (See his *Address on the Government Control of Corporations and Combinations of Capital*, 1911.) In the final decision all but one of the justices followed the Chief Justice in unequivocally reaffirming the application of "the rule of reason" to the Sherman Law, thus reversing the Court's attitude in the Transmissouri case of 1897.

Bad health during the campaign was largely responsible for Washburn's defeat for reëlection in 1910. An intimate friend of both Roosevelt and Taft, he parted company with the former in 1912 because of his advocacy of the recall of judicial opinions. In 1916 he was a delegate to the Republican National Convention. After his retirement from political life he retained the presidency of the Washburn Company, and from its establishment in 1914 until his death he served as a Class B director of the Federal Reserve Bank in Boston; but his energies were mostly devoted to literary and philanthropic activities.

His *Industrial Worcester* (1917) was an important history of the development of a great industrial center by a man who had had close personal associations with most of the leaders in that movement. His *Theodore Roosevelt: The Logic of His Career* (1916) was considered by Roosevelt himself and by his intimates as the most discerning characterization of him that had been written. At Harvard the classmates, Roosevelt and Washburn, had been students under Henry Cabot Lodge, and in 1924, at the request of Lodge, already stricken with fatal illness, Washburn came to his assistance and edited a most important portion of *Selections from the Correspondence of Theodore Roosevelt and Henry Cabot Lodge, 1884–1918* (1925). Only a few months later, before the Massachusetts Historical Society, Washburn presented a discriminating memoir of Henry Cabot Lodge (*Proceedings*, April 1925). His third biography, *The Life of John W. Weeks* (1928), dealt with a former senator from Massachusetts, an intimate personal and political friend. Washburn gave freely of his means and of his counsel as a trustee of the Worcester Polytechnic Institute and of the Groton School, and he was especially devoted to the service of the American Red Cross and of the Episcopal Church. He was married, Apr. 25, 1889, to Caroline Vinton Slater, by whom he had a son and a daughter.

[G. H. Haynes, *Life of Charles G. Washburn* (1931); *Biog. Directory of the Am. Cong.* (1928); *Who's Who in America*, 1926–27; *Boston Transcript*, May 25, 1928.]

G. H. H.

WASHBURN, EDWARD ABIEL (Apr. 16, 1819–Feb. 2, 1881), Protestant Episcopal clergyman, was born in Boston, Mass., the son of Abiel and Paulina (Tucker) Washburn, and a descendant of John Washburn who settled in Duxbury, Mass., in 1632; the missionary educator, George Washburn [*q.v.*], was a cousin. Edward's father, a merchant of means, was able to give the boy every advantage. He was prepared for college at the Boston Latin School and in 1838 graduated from Harvard with high honors. Reared a Congregationalist, he studied for the ministry at Andover Theological Seminary and at the Yale Divinity School, and was licensed to preach by the Worcester Association of Congregational Ministers in 1842. Reading, reflection, and the influence of friends in the Episcopal Church led him, however, to enter that communion, and on July 12, 1844, he was admitted to the diaconate at Trinity Church, Boston, and on Oct. 9 of the following year, was advanced to the priesthood. After serving as rector of St. Paul's Church, Newburyport, Mass., until 1851, he went abroad for two years, during which time he visited Egypt, Palestine, India, and China. Upon his return he became, in the spring of 1853, rector of St. John's Church, Hartford, Conn., and on June 16 married Frances H. Lindsley of Washington, D. C., by whom he had a daughter. While serving St. John's he also lectured on ecclesiastical polity at the Berkeley Divinity School, Middletown, Conn. In 1862 he was called to St. Mark's, Philadelphia, where he remained three years. From 1865 until his death he was rector of Calvary Church, New York.

Washburn was distinguished by intellectual and moral qualities of a high order. All who knew him paid tribute to his lofty manhood, his spiritual power, and his ministry of honest convictions. He had a rich knowledge of the history, philosophy, and literature of many lands. His mind was predominantly analytical, and he welcomed the modern critical attitude toward the Bible and theology, convinced that it would increase the growth of Christian life. He expressed his beliefs with boldness and in vigorous, eloquent style, though his preaching was of the kind that appeals to the thoughtful rather than to the masses. Next to Phillips Brooks, perhaps, he was in his day the leading representative of broad churchmanship in the Episcopal communion. He was foremost in the little group which established *The Living Church,* a periodical embodying the point of view and spirit of the more liberal churchmen, and it was edited by his assistant at Calvary Church, William Graham Sumner [*q.v.*]. The paper was of too intellectual a character to be popular and survived but a year (1869–70). Washburn was also one of the original members of "The Club," a more or less informal association of clergymen, the greatest achievement of which was its successful leadership of the movement which resulted in the establishment of the Church Congress. He was interested in the work of the Evangelical Alliance, attending its meetings in the United States and abroad, and on two occasions, 1873 and 1879, presenting papers at its sessions. His scholarly attainments found employment in his services as a member of the American New Testament company of the revisers of the Bible, and in his labors on "The Two Epistles of Paul to Timothy," 1869, a translation and enlargement of J. J. van Oosterzee's work, which, with Dr. Edwin Harwood, he prepared for Philip Schaff's edition of John P. Lange's *A Commentary on the Holy Scriptures.* He contributed numerous articles to periodicals and in 1875 published *The Social Law of God,* sermons on the Ten Commandments, which went through six or more editions. After his death other writings of his were collected and issued under the following titles: *Sermons* (1882); *Epochs in Church History and Other Essays* (1883), edited by C. C. Tiffany; *Voices from a Busy Life* (copr. 1883), a volume of poems which show some skill in versification, but little originality in thought or form; and *The Beatitudes and Other Sermons* (1884). He died in New York City in his sixty-second year.

["In Memoriam," in *The Social Law of God* (ed. of 1881); C. C. Tiffany, *A Hist. of the Protestant Episcopal Church in the U. S. A.* (1895), in Am. Church Hist. Series; H. E. Starr, *William Graham Sumner* (1925); *New Eng. Hist. and Geneal. Reg.,* Oct. 1866; *Churchman,* Feb. 12, 1881; *N. Y. Tribune,* Feb. 3, 1881.]

H. E. S.

WASHBURN, EDWARD WIGHT (May 10, 1881–Feb. 6, 1934), chemist and educator, was born in Beatrice, Nebr., one of the four children of William Gilmor and Flora Ella (Wight) Washburn. His ancestors, from Little and Great Washburn, England, settled in New England before 1626. His father moved from Houlton, Me., to the frontier town of Beatrice, where he became a successful dealer in building supplies. Although the interests of the family lay chiefly in commerce, civic betterment, and politics, Washburn chose a career in chemistry. An honor student in his high school (which taught no chemistry), he assembled a crude chemical laboratory where he produced explosions which brought parental orders to stop "all this foolishness." At the University of Nebraska (1899–1901) he met his expenses by selling his thoroughbred pony and by tutoring. For a year he taught in the high school at McCook, Nebr., then, because Nebraska could not give him the training he desired, he went to the Massachusetts Institute of Technology. Here he had as teacher A. A. Noyes, and as associates, G. N. Lewis and R. C. Tolman. He was graduated B.S. in 1905 and Ph.D. in 1908, serving meanwhile as research associate. A rare combination of methodical worker and keen and imaginative thinker, he showed in his graduate research work the promise of his later brilliance. His paper, "The Theory and Practice of the Iodometric Determination of Arsenious Acid" (*Journal of the American Chemical Society*, January 1908), was the fruit of a study particularly significant because it prompted the first thermodynamic treatment of "buffer" solutions, so important in later work on indicators. He made the first accurate measurement of true transference numbers and of the relative hydration of aqueous ions.

In 1908 he went to the University of Illinois as associate in chemistry; two years later he was made assistant professor of physical chemistry, and in 1913, full professor. His accomplishments included the development of a " 'simple system of thermodynamic chemistry' by means of his 'perfect thermodynamic engine,' the measurement of Faraday's constant with the iodine coulometer, and the development of a high precision viscosimeter and of apparatus for the precise measurement of the electrical conductivity of aqueous solutions of electrolytes" (Briggs, *post*, p. 221). In 1915 he published a textbook, *An Introduction to the Principles of Physical Chemistry* (2nd ed., 1921; French translation, 1925). In 1916 he became head of the department of ceramic engineering, and he effectively applied the principles of physical chemistry and thermodynamics to this virgin field until 1922, when he was chosen editor-in-chief of the *International Critical Tables of Numerical Data: Physics, Chemistry and Technology*. For four years he gave himself unsparingly to the exacting labors of preparing the seven volumes of these tables, the first of which appeared in 1926 and the last in 1930, thus making a notable contribution to science and technology.

Assuming the leadership of the division of

chemistry at the National Bureau of Standards in 1926, Washburn infused new life and activity into his department, initiated a program of thermochemical research, instituted and directed an extensive project on petroleum research, was responsible for the isolation of the first crystals of rubber, and found time to make many personal contributions to science. In December 1931 he made his most notable discovery—the fractional electrolysis of water with respect to the isotopes of hydrogen, a discovery which revealed new possibilities in physical, chemical, and biological research. For this achievement he was awarded the Hillebrand prize of the Chemical Society of Washington.

He was the author of approximately a hundred scientific papers; was a member of the National Academy of Sciences, the National Research Council, and numerous professional societies; and carried a tremendous burden of assignments on scientific committees of national and international scope. On June 10, 1910, he married Sophie Wilhelmina de Veer of Boston, by whom he had four children. Washburn's hobbies were the study of world history and genealogy, and his recreations were tennis, bridge, and "twenty questions." He was well informed, and eagerly discussed their own subjects with experts in many fields. Quiet, friendly, yet reserved, by his ability, fairness, and dignity he at once commanded admiration and respect.

[*Am. Men of Science*, 1933; *Who's Who in America*, 1930–31; L. J. Briggs, in *Science*, Mar. 9, 1934; *Bull. Am. Ceramic Soc.*, July 1922; *Industrial and Engineering Chemistry: News Edition*, Feb. 10, 1934; *Nature*, May 12, 1934; *Washington Post*, Feb. 7, 1934; details regarding childhood and ancestry from Washburn's son, William de Veer Washburn; personal acquaintance.]

F. D. R.

WASHBURN, ELIHU BENJAMIN [See WASHBURNE, ELIHU BENJAMIN, 1816–1887].

WASHBURN, EMORY (Feb. 14, 1800–Mar. 18, 1877), governor of Massachusetts, law teacher and writer, was born in Leicester, Mass., son of Joseph and Ruth (Davis) Washburn. He was in the seventh generation from John Washburn who settled in Duxbury in 1632. Emory's father and grandfather were Revolutionary soldiers; the former was deputy sheriff of Worcester County and died in 1807. The boy was educated at Leicester Academy and entered Dartmouth in 1813, where the former pastor of Leicester, Dr. Z. S. Moore [*q.v.*], was professor. In 1815, when Dr. Moore became president of Williams, Washburn transferred to that institution and was graduated in 1817. He studied law with Judge Dewey and then for a year, 1819–20, at the Harvard Law School. He was admitted to the bar in Lenox, Mass., in 1821, and practised in Leicester for seven years, also serving as town clerk. In 1828 he removed to Worcester, where he lived nearly thirty years. He was associated for several years with John Davis [*q.v.*], afterwards governor and senator. Washburn became the acknowledged leader of the bar of western Massachusetts and won an unusually large proportion of his cases. He was always "ready to plod till midnight" in the services of his clients (*Proceedings of the American Antiquarian Society*, Mar. 20, 1877, p. 11). On Nov. 2, 1830, he married Marianne Cornelia Giles, daughter of Nehemiah and Mary (Cowdin) Giles; they had two sons and a daughter.

Washburn represented Leicester in the Massachusetts House of Representatives from May 1826 to May 1828, and made a report favoring a railroad from Boston to Albany, the first railroad in the state. In 1838 he represented Worcester in the House, and in 1841 and 1842 in the Senate, serving as chairman of the judiciary committee. In 1844 he became judge of the court of common pleas (then the trial court of the state) but resigned in 1847 and returned to practice. In 1853 he was nominated for governor by the Whigs. He was then in Europe and knew nothing about the matter until his return. He was elected and served an uneventful year. The Whig party was rapidly disintegrating and he was defeated for reëlection by the Know-Nothing candidate.

On Mar. 17, 1855, he became lecturer in the Harvard Law School and on Feb. 23, 1856, he was appointed to the University Professorship of Law (after 1862 the Bussey Professorship). His subjects were property, criminal law, and domestic relations. He lectured vividly and eloquently, making the dry rules of property live. Undergraduates in the college and professors in other departments used to drop in to his law lectures just to listen to him. In 1860–62 he published *A Treatise on the American Law of Real Property* (2 vols.), which was quickly accepted as the most satisfactory and trustworthy American book on the subject. It was followed by *A Treatise on the American Law of Easements and Servitudes* (1863). Both books went into numerous editions and were greatly valued in their day. When the inauguration of President Eliot was followed by the reorganization of the law school under C. C. Langdell [*q.v.*], Washburn remained as a loyal though somewhat unsympathetic member of the new régime until his resignation Apr. 3, 1876. He was probably the most beloved instructor who ever taught in Harvard Law School. "Every student seemed the especial

object of his solicitous interest. He not only acted as director, confessor, and inspirer of his pupils during their stay in Cambridge, but somehow found time to correspond with them, often for years, after they had scattered through the length and breadth of the land" (Batchelder, *post*, p. 651). His so-called "private office" at the Law School was "deluged with an unending stream of callers, friends, strangers, students, politicians, and clients" (*Ibid.*). He had an even and sunny temper and was the friendliest of men, "as jolly as a boy" (*Boston Transcript*, Mar. 19, 1877).

On his resignation he opened a law office in Cambridge and was elected in November to represent Cambridge in the House of Representatives, where he was made chairman of the judiciary committee. Though he had never been busier or happier, the strain was too great for him and he died in Cambridge a few months later from the effects of pneumonia. His concerns were extremely varied. He was actively interested in prison reform, industrial education, normal schools, schools for the feeble-minded, education in Liberia, and Massachusetts history. His *Sketches of the Judicial History of Massachusetts from 1630 to 1775* (1840) is still of considerable value. He was vice-president of the Massachusetts Historical Society and long active in the American Antiquarian Society.

[A. P. Peabody, in *Proc. Mass. Hist. Soc.*, vol. XVII (1880), with bibliography; Charles Warren, *Hist. of the Harvard Law School* (1908); *The Centennial Hist. of the Harvard Law School* (1918), with bibliography; S. F. Batchelder, "Old Times at the Law School," *Atlantic Monthly*, Nov. 1902; J. C. Washburn, *Geneal. Notes of the Washburn Family* (1898); *Vital Records of Leicester, Mass., to . . . 1849* (1903); *New England Hist. and Geneal. Reg.*, Oct. 1877; *Central Law Jour.*, Mar. 30, 1877; *Am. Law Rev.*, Apr. 1877; *Albany Law Jour.*, Mar. 24, 1877.]

Z. C., Jr.

WASHBURN, GEORGE (Mar. 1, 1833–Feb. 15, 1915), missionary and educator, was born at Middleboro, Mass., the son of Philander Washburn, a manufacturer, and Elizabeth (Homes), and a cousin of Edward Abiel Washburn [*q.v.*]. His ancestor, John Washburn, settled in Duxbury, Mass., in 1632. After attending Pierce Academy in Middleboro and Phillips Academy at Andover, he entered Amherst College in 1851. Graduating in 1855, he spent a year in travel through Europe and the Near East, then entered Andover Theological Seminary. After one year there he went to Constantinople as treasurer of the American Board of Commissioners for Foreign Missions. On Apr. 15, 1859, he married Henrietta Loraine, daughter of Cyrus Hamlin [*q.v.*], president of Robert College. In 1862 he returned to Andover, completed the theological course, and on July 29, 1863, was ordained at Middleboro as a Congregational minister.

Appointed a missionary of the American Board at Constantinople, he also taught at Robert College, which was then located in Bebek, a suburb on the Bosphorus. In the spring of 1868 he left Turkey to devote himself to religious work in New York City but a year later was persuaded by Christopher R. Robert [q.v.] to take charge of the college during President Hamlin's preoccupation with the construction of a building at Rumili Hissar. Organization of a new plan of study, teaching, and administration occupied him until May 1871, when the institution moved to its new quarters, and in June he departed for America. Urged by Hamlin and the trustees, he returned in the autumn to conduct the college while the president was attempting to raise funds in the United States. At first director and professor of philosophy, Washburn became president in 1878. During his twenty-five years in this office the college steadily increased its enrolment, its faculty, its physical plant, its endowment, and its influence among the peoples of the Near East. After 1872 there were many Bulgarian students, a number of whom later became prominent in the political and intellectual life of their country. Both Washburn and Prof. Albert E. Long received immediate information regarding the Bulgarian massacres of 1876 and the first accounts to reach western Europe originated with them. In 1879 both were voted the thanks of the Bulgarian nation by the National Convention. Washburn was later twice decorated by the Bulgarian government and long remained its trusted counselor. During several visits to the United States he secured financial support for the college and was repeatedly consulted on Near Eastern affairs by Secretary Blaine and Secretary Hay and by President Theodore Roosevelt. Using various pseudonyms, he contributed articles on history and current affairs to the *Contemporary Review* and under his own name wrote regularly for American magazines. His valuable study of the geology of the Bosphorus appeared in the *American Journal of Science* (September 1873) and his "Calvert's Supposed Relics of Man in the Miocene of the Dardanelles" was published in the *Proceedings of the American Association for the Advancement of Science* (vol. XXII, pt. 2, 1874).

On Sept. 20, 1903, he resigned the presidency of Robert College, but for another year held his professorship. From 1904 to 1906 he served as treasurer of the college in Boston, then returned for two last years of teaching before settling finally in Boston. Declining appointment as United States ambassador to Turkey because of a conviction that his missionary affiliations made ac-

ceptance unwise, he lectured during 1909 at the Lowell Institute and in the same year published his *Fifty Years in Constantinople*, which is a history of Robert College rather than an autobiography. A man of broad interests and abundant common sense, just and firm in dealing with men, a devout Christian but no proselytizer, Washburn earned the complete confidence of the peoples among whom he worked. As the intimate friend and adviser of Bulgarian, Turkish, British, and American ambassadors and statesmen he exerted an important influence on politics as well as on education in the Near East.

[*Who's Who in America*, 1914–15; *Times* (London), Mar. 18, 1915; F. A. Virkus, *The Abridged Compendium of Am. Geneal.*, I (1925), 644; *Amherst Graduates' Quart.*, June 1915; *Amherst Coll. Biog. Record of Grads. and Non-Grads.* (1927); *Congregational Year-Book* (1915); *Congregationalist*, Feb. 25, 1915; *Boston Transcript*, Feb. 15, 1915; *An Appreciation . . . of the Rev. George Washburn* (1915), printed by the trustees of Robert College; letters and papers in the possession of a grand-daughter, Mrs. Basil D. Hall, Florence, Mass.; information from Dr. C. F. Gates, formerly president of Robert College.]   W. L. W., Jr.

WASHBURN, ICHABOD (Aug. 11, 1798–Dec. 30, 1868) manufacturer, son of Ichabod and Sylvia (Bradford) Washburn, was born at Kingston, Mass. On his father's side he was descended from John Washburn who settled in Duxbury, Mass., in 1632; on his mother's, from Gov. William Bradford. The elder Ichabod, a sea-captain, died when his namesake was an infant, leaving the family in straitened circumstances, and at the age of nine young Washburn was "put out to live" with a chaise and harness maker in Duxbury. He remained with him for five years, learning the trade of harness making, and then returned to his home, where for two years he worked in the cotton mills. He then went to Leicester, Mass., and served a four-year apprenticeship in blacksmithing. Going into business for himself at Millbury, Mass., he began making plows, but soon relinquished this enterprise in order to acquire experience in the more difficult branches of his craft. For a few months he worked in the armory at Millbury, and then found employment with a machinery manufacturer in Worcester, Mass., gaining a knowledge of forging and of finishing all kinds of machinery.

In 1821 he entered into a partnership with W. H. Howard to manufacture lead pipe and machinery used in the production of woolen goods, and the following year he purchased Howard's interest. The demand for the woolen machinery was so great, however, that early in 1823 Washburn gave up making lead pipe and with Benjamin Goddard of Worcester formed the partnership of Washburn & Goddard, manufacturers of machinery for carding and spinning wool. The partners were immediately successful and continued their profitable business for eleven years, eight in Worcester and three in a larger water-power factory in Northville, a suburb. At the end of this period the business had so far outgrown the water-power facilities at Northville that a new site seemed desirable to Washburn; but Goddard preferred to remain where they were, and in 1834 the partnership was amicably dissolved.

Some two years earlier the partners had begun the manufacture of iron wire, of which up to that time little had been made in the United States. The machinery available was crude, capable of drawing but fifty pounds of wire a day, and as a first improvement Washburn devised the wire drawblock. With it the partners increased their production tenfold and were able to build up a substantial branch business of making wire cards. After the partners separated, Washburn continued the manufacture of wire in a new factory in Worcester, directing his whole attention to it until his death and becoming the leader of the industry in the United States. At the suggestion of Jonas Chickering [q.v.] of Boston, he began in 1850 to make steel piano wire and was so successful that thereafter imported wire was discarded. He introduced the galvanized iron telegraph wire so extensively used after 1850, and developed the first continuous method of tempering and hardening wire in 1856. He thus acquired practically the whole of the hoop-skirt wire business, which, at its maximum, amounted to an output of 1,500 tons annually. In operating the many related activities of the business, such as rolling mills, cotton mills to make the cotton for covering crinoline wire, iron and cast-steel furnaces, Washburn at first had the help of his twin brother Charles, but after 1850 his son-in-law, Philip L. Moen was his partner, the main firm being known as I. Washburn & Moen.

Washburn was a devoutly religious man and was deeply interested in the educational facilities of Worcester. Practically the whole of his fortune was bequeathed to religious institutions, to Lincoln (now Washburn) College, Kan., and to the Worcester County Free Institute of Industrial Science (now the Worcester Polytechnic Institute), of which he was an active trustee. He was twice married: first, to Ann Brown of Worcester on Oct. 6, 1823; second, in 1859, to Elizabeth Bancroft Cheever of Hallowell, Me., who survived him. He died in Worcester.

[C. G. Washburn, *Industrial Worcester* (1917); H. T. Cheever, *Autobiog. and Memorials of Ichabod Washburn* (1879); J. W. Roe, *English and American Tool Builders* (1926); *Worcester County Free Institute of Industrial Science: Addresses of Inauguration and*

Dedication . . . Nov. 11, 1868 (1869); *Worcester, Its Past and Present* (1888); *Forty Immortals of Worcester and Its County* (Worcester Bank & Trust Company, 1920); *Worcester Daily Spy*, Dec. 31, 1868.]
C. W. M.

WASHBURN, ISRAEL (June 6, 1813–May 12, 1883), lawyer, congressman, governor of Maine, was a brother of Elihu B. Washburne, Cadwallader C. Washburn, and William D. Washburn [*qq.v.*]. They were born in Livermore, Me., the sons of Israel and Martha (Benjamin) Washburn. Their father sat in the Massachusetts legislature from 1815 to 1819. The failure of his store in 1829 prevented Israel, eldest of eleven children, from attending college, but he studied law with his uncle, Reuel Washburn, and in 1834 was admitted to the bar. He made his home at Orono until 1863, when he moved to Portland. He held several local offices and sat in the Maine legislature in 1842 during the Northeast Boundary dispute. In 1848 he was defeated for Congress but in 1850 was elected, and for the next ten years represented the Penobscot district, first as a Whig and later as a Republican. During part of that time his brothers Cadwallader and Elihu were also in the House, representing Wisconsin and Illinois respectively.

His part in founding the Republican party was his most distinctive work in Washington. On May 9, 1854, the day after the Kansas-Nebraska bill passed the House and ten weeks after the original meeting at Ripon, Wis., he called a meeting of some thirty anti-slavery representatives at the rooms of two Massachusetts congressmen; this group took further steps toward organizing a new party and Washburn is a strong contender for the honor of having been the first to suggest the name "Republican." He used it publicly shortly afterwards in a speech at Bangor. Washburn steadily and strongly opposed the extension of slavery; in 1856 he supported Nathaniel P. Banks [*q.v.*] for the speakership; for a time he was chairman of the committee on ways and means.

On Jan. 1, 1861, he resigned from the House to succeed Lot M. Morrill [*q.v.*] as governor of Maine; later that year he was reëlected. He has been ranked with John A. Andrew and Oliver P. Morton [*qq.v.*] among "the great war governors of the North" (Hamlin, *post*, p. 357), because of his contribution to Maine's excellent war record. Immediately upon the call for volunteers, he summoned the legislature to meet in special session and, though Maine was asked for only two regiments, that body provided for ten, appropriating a million dollars. By 1862, however, recruiting had slackened, and Washburn wrote Lincoln that he would have to resort to drafting to secure "three-year" men. He declined re-nomination for the governorship and in 1863 was appointed collector of the port of Portland. He was several times disappointed in his cherished ambition of a Senate seat, partly through the opposition of James G. Blaine [q.v.]. In 1878, he lost his collectorship, after planning to buy a newspaper to attack the Blaine group. From Mar. 3 of that year until his death he was president of the Rumford Falls & Buckfield Railroad.

Washburn has been described as a "solid, hard-working man of sound knowledge and of rigid integrity" (Hunt, *post*, p. 40). Short, serious, and spectacled, he was less impressive than his brothers in appearance. He was quick-tempered, was a good story-teller, and had a strong love of literature. He wrote *Notes, Historical, Descriptive, and Personal, of Livermore . . . Maine* (1874), read papers on the "North-Eastern Boundary" and on Ether Shepley before the Maine Historical Society (*Collections*, 1 ser., VIII, 1881), and was a frequent contributor to the *Universalist Quarterly*. He was a trustee of Tufts College from its opening in 1852 until his death, declining an offer of the presidency in 1878. On Oct. 24, 1841, he married Mary Maud Webster of Orono, by whom he had two sons and two daughters. She died in 1873 and he married in January 1876 Rebina Napier Brown of Bangor. He died in Philadelphia, whither he had gone for medical treatment, and was buried in Bangor.

[Gaillard Hunt, *Israel, Elihu and Cadwallader Washburn* (1925); *In Memoriam: Israel Washburn, Jr.* (1884); L. C. Hatch, *Me., a Hist.* (3 vols., 1919); Henry Wilson, *Hist. of the Rise and Fall of the Slave Power* (3 vols., 1873–77); J. S. Pike, *First Blows of the Civil War* (1879); C. E. Hamlin, *Life and Times of Hannibal Hamlin* (1899); Francis Curtis, *The Republican Party, a Hist.* (2 vols., 1904); F. A. Shannon, *Organization and Administration of the Union Army* (2 vols., 1928), I, 272; *Biog. Dir. Am. Cong.* (1928); *New Eng. Hist. and Geneal. Reg.*, Jan. 1884; *N. Y. Herald*, May 13, 1883; *Daily Eastern Argus* (Portland), May 14, 1883.]
J.B.P.

WASHBURN, NATHAN (Apr. 22, 1818–Sept. 13, 1903), inventor, manufacturer, was a descendant of John Washburn who settled in Duxbury, Mass., in 1632, and the son of Seth and Catherine (Washburn) Washburn, the latter the daughter of Solomon and Mary Warner Washburn. Nathan was born on his father's farm at Stafford, Tolland County, Conn. In addition to running the farm the elder Washburn owned and operated iron furnaces in Stafford Hollow and Colchester, Conn., and Nathan spent his youth attending school in the winter, and at other seasons working on the farm and puttering around the furnaces. When he was nineteen years old he became a carpenter's apprentice and followed that trade locally for two years.

In 1840 he went to Worcester, Mass., and entered the iron foundry of W. A. Wheeler. After a year there he associated himself with a cousin, Augustus Washburn, and the two engaged in iron foundry work during the succeeding three years in Worcester, Fitchburg, and Ashburnham, Mass., Nathan Washburn showing particular skill in molding, casting, and finishing machine parts. Because of the illness of his partner, he sold out in 1844 and returned to Stafford, where, in association with a friend, he operated a foundry for two years, and then went to Rochester, N. Y. Here he engaged in making castings for cotton and woolen machinery and began supplying the local railroad with iron products. As a result of some investigations which he made relative to the peculiar strains to which pulleys were subjected, he designed an iron pulley so strengthened that it was unaffected by these strains. He next developed an improved railroad car wheel, and on Apr. 3, 1849, patented a cast-iron wheel which in subsequent years came to be known as the "Washburn Chilled Car Wheel." It was much stronger and less likely to break than previous types, for he had discovered a way of cooling cast-iron without cracking it, using in his process charcoal and white sand. As a result, his wheel displaced within a short time every other pattern of wheel.

Selling out his foundry at Rochester in 1849, Washburn returned to Stafford and with E. A. Converse, a woolen manufacturer, organized the partnership of Converse & Washburn for the manufacture of his patented wheel and textile machinery. Converse withdrew in 1854 and Washburn thereafter conducted the business alone. The success of the firm was phenomenal from the start and between 1849 and 1859 mills and foundries were established in Worcester, Mass., in Troy and Schenectady, N. Y., and in Toronto, Canada. The manufacture of iron products for cotton and woolen machinery and the rolling of railroad rails were also undertaken, and by 1857 the concern had an establishment in Worcester covering four acres. During the Civil War it did a large business in the manufacture of gun barrels, Washburn having perfected a new process of puddling pig iron whereby he could produce gun iron superior to that then imported from England. About 1865 he disposed of many of his diversified interests so that he could concentrate his attention in making still further improvements in car wheels. He did, however, become associated with W. C. Barnum and others in the purchase of certain iron ore properties and in operating them. In 1867 he produced a satisfactory steel-tired car wheel at Worcester, and the manufacture and further improvement of this product constituted his major activity for the rest of his life. His wife was Eliza Young of Stafford and at the time of his death, in Stafford Springs, Conn., he was survived by a daughter.

[C. G. Washburn, *Industrial Worcester* (1917); *Commemorative Biog. Record of Tolland and Windham Counties, Conn.* (1903); *Springfield Republican,* Sept. 15, 1903; Patent Office records.]   C. W. M.

WASHBURN, WILLIAM DREW (Jan. 14, 1831–July 29, 1912), representative in Congress, United States senator, mill-owner, son of Israel and Martha (Benjamin) Washburn, was born on a farm in Livermore, Me. Common schools and the academies of Gorham, Paris, and Farmington prepared him for Bowdoin College, where he graduated in 1854. He then studied law with his brother Israel [*q.v.*] in Orono and with John A. Peters [*q.v.*] in Bangor and spent a little time in Washington as a clerk in the House of Representatives.

In 1857 he followed his brothers Cadwallader and Elihu [*qq.v.*] into the West, and settled in Minnesota to practise law. At once he was made secretary and agent of the Minneapolis Mill Company, organized by his brother Cadwallader and others. In 1858 he was elected to the second Minnesota legislature, which never met. From 1861 to 1865 he was federal surveyor-general for Minnesota, living in St. Paul; in 1864 he ran against Ignatius Donnelly [*q.v.*] for the House of Representatives, but was defeated. Upon retiring from his surveyorship in 1865, he once more became agent of the Minneapolis Mill Company, and took up his residence permanently in Minneapolis. In 1867 he was one of those who launched the *Minneapolis Tribune* and in 1871 he sat in the legislature. Lumbering, with a sawmill at Minneapolis and one at Anoka, development of water power, especially on the west side of the Falls of St. Anthony, real-estate deals, and the manufacture of flour were some of his manifold activities. In 1878, after a brief association with his brother in Washburn, Crosby & Company, he founded the milling firm of W. D. Washburn & Company. Elected to the national House of Representatives, partly as the result of a contest between farmers and millers, he served from 1879 to 1885, working especially for the improvement of the upper Mississippi, for control of its floods, and for the improvement of navigation on the Great Lakes. In 1884 many of his interests were consolidated in the Washburn Mill Company. Railroad build-

ing and management, primarily as a factor in the milling industry, also engaged his attention. He was a leader in organizing and promoting the Minneapolis & St. Louis Railroad, and he was the principal projector of the Minneapolis, St. Paul & Sault Ste. Marie Railway Company, of which he was president until 1889.

His election to the United States Senate in that year was a turning point in his life. Upon taking his seat he dropped most of his active connections with his business enterprises, although he remained a director of the Pillsbury-Washburn Flour Mills Company with which the Washburn Mill Company was merged in 1889. His one term in the Senate, however, scarcely gave him time to make himself a power in that body. Defeated in the legislature by Gov. Knute Nelson [*q.v.*] in 1895, through what he was inclined to consider political treachery, he made no further attempts at political advancement but busied himself with business, church, social, and philanthropic interests. He had married Elizabeth Muzzy of Bangor, Apr. 19, 1859, and they had eight children. He was one of the founders of the First Universalist Society of Minneapolis. Not a "mixer," living and acting in what many considered an "aristocratic" manner, he was, while not a negligible political factor, more important as a major figure in the business, financial, and social life of his community.

[E. V. Smalley, *A Hist. of the Republican Party* (1896); *Who's Who in America,* 1912–13; Alonzo Phelps, *Biog. Hist. of the Northwest* (1890); E. W. T. Hyde and William Stoddard, *Hist. of the Great Northwest and its Men of Progress* (1901); Isaac Atwater, *Hist. of the City of Minneapolis* (1893); H. P. Hall's *Observations . . . 1849 to 1904* (1904); W. W. Folwell, *A Hist. of Minn.,* esp. vol. III (1926); C. E. Flandrau, *Encyc. of Biog. of Minn.* (1900); C. B. Kuhlmann, *Development of the Flour-Milling Industry in the U. S.* (1929); W. C. Edgar, *The Medal of Gold* (1925); *Northwestern Miller* (Minneapolis), *passim,* and esp., Jan. 25, 1889 and July 31, 1912; *Minneapolis Morning Tribune,* July 30, 1912.]   L. B. S—e.

WASHBURNE, ELIHU BENJAMIN (Sept. 23, 1816–Oct. 23, 1887), congressman, cabinet member, diplomat, historian, was the third of eleven children born to Israel and Martha (Benjamin) Washburn at Livermore, Me. After the failure of the father's country store in 1829 the large family was forced to rely on a small and not-too-fertile farm for subsistence, and as a result several of the brothers, among them Elihu, were early forced to fend for themselves. Leaving home at the age of fourteen, he added an "e" to his name in imitation of his English forebears and embarked on the road of education and hard work which led him to a position not the least prominent among five brothers—Israel, Cadwallader C., William D. [*qq.v.*], Elihu, and

Charles—notable for their service to state and nation.

A short experience at farm work convinced him that he was not destined for an agricultural career; he disliked his three months of school teaching more than anything he ever turned his hand to; a newspaper publisher to whom he apprenticed himself failed, and while he was working for another printer a hernia incapacitated him for further typesetting. These experiences led him to the decision to study law, and accordingly, after several months in Maine Wesleyan Seminary, Kent's Hill, followed by an apprenticeship in a Boston law office, he entered the Harvard Law School in 1839, where he came under the influence of Joseph Story [q.v.]. Armed with membership in the Massachusetts bar and a few law books, he turned his face westward in 1840, resolved to settle in Iowa Territory.

His brother Cadwallader, who had already settled at Rock Island, Ill., persuaded the newcomer that Illinois was a more favorable location than Iowa, and that the most likely place for a briefless lawyer was the boom town of Galena, where lead mines had recently been opened. Within a month after his arrival Washburne had begun to make a living and some political speeches. He presently formed a connection which was to be of considerable importance, both personally and professionally, with Charles S. Hempstead, the leader of the town's dozen lawyers. The latter, partially paralyzed, needed clerical assistance in his practice and in return threw sundry minor cases to his quasi-partner. This association lasted for a year, after which Washburne practised independently until 1845, when he entered an actual partnership with Hempstead. In this year he married, July 31, one of his benefactor's relatives, Adèle Gratiot, a descendant of the French settlers around St. Louis. Seven children were born to them. Washburne's connection by marriage with Missouri, indirect though it was, commended him to the attention of Thomas Hart Benton [q.v.] on his entry into Congress eight years later, and was of no disadvantage in launching his career.

His moderate earnings from the law were transmuted into a comfortable competence by careful investments in western lands, and he gradually turned his energies into political channels. He became a wheel-horse of the local Whig party, placed Henry Clay in nomination for the presidency at Baltimore in 1844, and ran unsuccessfully for Congress four years later. He was more fortunate in 1852, and in the following year began sixteen years of service in the House which covered the periods of the Civil War and reconstruction. He kept a sharp lookout for the interests of his section (particularly directed toward preventing the misappropriation of public lands to the uses of railroad speculators) and at the same time cast a keen and malevolent eye upon those who would raid the federal treasury. The lobbyist or the known corruptionist fared badly at his hands, and his last long speech in the House (Jan. 6, 1869), on a pension bill, was one of a number of blasts against those who were at the time leading Congress along forbidden paths. For a time he was chairman of the committee on commerce and for two years, chairman of the committee on appropriations, where his efforts to keep down expenses made him the first of a long succession of "watchdogs of the treasury."

Physical disabilities kept him from active military duty during the Civil War but he used his talents in Congress to aid his personal and political friend Lincoln, and to forward the military fortunes of his fellow townsman and protégé, Ulysses S. Grant. He was the sole person to greet Lincoln on his secret arrival in Washington for the inauguration in 1861 (Hunt, post, pp. 229–30). He proposed Grant's name as brigadier-general of volunteers and sponsored the bills by which Grant was made successively lieutenant-general and general. When war gave way to reconstruction, Washburne found himself in the forefront of the Radicals and a member of the Joint Committee on Reconstruction. He turned against Lincoln's successor and when members of the vindictive party "competed with one another in phrasing violent abuse of Andrew Johnson . . . Elihu Washburne deserved one of the prizes" (Ibid., p. 238).

His early sponsorship of Grant continued through the campaign of 1868, when Grant heard the news of his election over telegraph wires run to Washburne's library in Galena. His stanch support was rewarded by appointment as secretary of state in Grant's cabinet, a post which he assumed Mar. 5, 1869, resigned Mar. 10, and vacated Mar. 16. It is probable that this was a courtesy appointment preliminary to his designation, Mar. 17, as minister to France, and designed to give him prestige in the French capital. His connection with the Grant administration remained close and he and Grant were friends until the spring of 1880, when an abortive boom for Washburne ran foul of Grant's own futile aspirations for a third term. Washburne himself immediately adhered to Grant's candidacy, though apparently without great enthusiasm, and remained at least outwardly loyal to his former chief. During the convention he himself received as many as forty-four votes, and it was later contended by his friends that with Grant's support he could have received the nomination which went to Garfield. Be that as it may, Grant vented his disappointment on Washburne and the two never met again.

Meantime he had rendered capable service through very trying times in Europe. As minister to France he witnessed the downfall of the empire of the third Napoleon and, remaining until the autumn of 1877, rounded out the longest term of any American minister to France down to that time. He was the only official representative of a foreign government to remain in Paris throughout the siege and the Commune, and his two volumes of memoirs, *Recollections of a Minister to France, 1869–1877* (1887), constitute a valuable account of those exciting days. In addition to his service to his own country, during the war he made himself useful by looking after the interests of German residents of France.

On his retirement from public life he devoted himself to historical and literary activities, serving as president of the Chicago Historical Society from 1884 to 1887 and publishing, in addition to the *Recollections of a Minister,* several works of some historical value, particularly sketches of early Illinois political figures, prepared for the Chicago Historical Society. For the same society he edited "The Edwards Papers" (*Collections,* vol. III, 1884), a selection from the manuscripts of Gov. Ninian Edwards [*q.v.*] of Illinois.

[Gaillard Hunt, *Israel, Elihu, and Cadwallader Washburn* (1925); J. V. Fuller, "Elihu Benjamin Washburne," in S. F. Bemis, *The Am. Secretaries of State,* vol. VII (1928); G. W. Smith, "Elihu B. Washburne," in *Chicago Hist. Soc. Colls.,* vol. IV (1890); *Encyc. of Biog. of Ill.,* vol. II (1894); *Biog. Dir. Am. Cong.* (1928); *General Grant's Letters to a Friend, 1861–1880* (1897), ed. by J. G. Wilson, being letters to Washburne; *Papers Relating to the Foreign Relations of the U. S.,* 1870–77; *Chicago Tribune,* Oct. 24, 1887; Washburne Papers (101 vols.), MSS. Div., Lib. of Cong.]   L. E. E.

WASHINGTON, BOOKER TALIAFERRO (Apr. 5, 1856–Nov. 14, 1915), negro educational leader, was born on James Burroughs' plantation at Hale's Ford, Franklin County, Va. His father is believed to have been a white man from a neighboring plantation (*Up From Slavery,* p. 2). His mother, Jane Ferguson, was a negro, a cook in the Burroughs family. He speaks gratefully of her "good, hard, common sense" and "high ambitions for her children" (*Ibid.,* p. 28), and recollects her praying that she and her children might be free. The latter

were an elder brother, John, later director of industries at Tuskegee, and a sister, Amanda. They lived in a one-room cabin with a fire-place and "potato-hole" but without wooden floor or glass windows. He never remembered "having slept in a bed until after our family was declared free by the Emancipation Proclamation" (*Ibid.,* p. 5). He tells us that their food was "a piece of bread here and a scrap of meat there. It was a cup of milk at one time, some potatoes at another" (*Ibid.,* p. 9). On Sundays there were two spoonfuls of molasses from the "big house." Failing other breakfast, he ate of the boiled corn prepared for the cows and pigs. Yet, despite the hard conditions, there was on the plantation considerable mutual affection on the part of slaves and master (*Ibid.,* pp. 20–22).

Soon after emancipation they moved to Malden, near Charleston, W. Va., the children walking most of the way. Here his mother secured Webster's "Blue-back Spelling Book," and Booker soon mastered the alphabet, though, he said, "at that time there was not a single member of my race anywhere near us who could read" (*Ibid.,* p. 27). An elementary school for colored children was started, but the boy's wages as a worker in the salt-furnace were needed at home, so he had lessons at night with the teacher. Later he attended regular classes, working five hours before school, returning to furnace or mine in the afternoon. Being asked his name by the teacher, he calmly told him "Booker Washington," believing that bearing such a name would make him "equal to the situation" (*Ibid.,* p. 34). Later he found that his mother had named him "Booker Taliaferro." An important incident of these early days was his overhearing two miners talking about a school for colored people, Hampton Institute. But prior to going there he served a year and a half in the home of Gen. Lewis Ruffner, owner of the salt-furnace and coal mine. Here he soon learned that Mrs. Ruffner "wanted everything kept clean about her, that she wanted things done promptly and systematically" (*Ibid.,* p. 44). Encouraged by her he continued to study evenings and attended school one hour a day. In 1872, at the age of seventeen, he set out for Hampton, about 500 miles distant, with a few dollars and a cheap satchel containing all his belongings. He feared his tramp-like appearance might interfere with his admission to Hampton. But, asked to sweep a room, he found that his lessons in thoroughness at Mrs. Ruffner's stood him in good stead. He swept it three times, dusted it four times. "I guess you will do to enter this institution," was the teacher's verdict (*Ibid.,* p. 53).

He spent three years at Hampton, his tuition being paid by a Northern friend of Gen. Samuel C. Armstrong [*q.v.*], the principal; his board and other expenses he earned as janitor. "Life at Hampton was a constant revelation ... the matter of having meals at regular hours, of eating on a tablecloth, using a napkin, the use of the bathtub and of the toothbrush, as well as the use of sheets upon the bed" (*Ibid.*, p. 58) were new things in his life, and, above all, his "greatest benefit," was contact with General Armstrong. He learned the trade of brick-mason, graduated in 1875, went as a waiter to a summer hotel in Connecticut, then returned to Malden to teach in a colored school where he worked fourteen hours a day. The winter of 1878–79 he spent at Wayland Seminary, Washington, D. C., and afterward gave the "post-graduate address" at Hampton, on "The Force that Wins." This created such a favorable impression that he was called in 1897 to take charge of the Indian dormitory and the night school, and also served as secretary to General Armstrong.

In May 1881 General Armstrong received a letter from George W. Campbell, a banker, merchant, and former slave-holder, and Lewis Adams, a mechanic and ex-slave, both of Tuskegee, Ala., asking for some one to start there a negro normal school, for which they had just secured a charter from the state legislature. Booker Washington was chosen. It is significant that Tuskegee was not established by Northern philanthropy, but was the product of Southern initiative. It opened with forty students "in a dilapidated shanty near the coloured Methodist Church, with the church itself as a sort of assembly-room." Now began incessant labors of thirty-four years. Washington "ate and slept with the people," studying conditions of the Black Belt. Desperately poor and ignorant, they lived mainly on fat pork and cornbread, knew nothing of cleanliness, and raised only cotton. He taught them the dignity of efficient labor, and to "live on the farm off the farm." Teaching, speaking, and traveling in the interest of Tuskegee, he developed his work until when he died the Institute, with its excellent board of trustees on which the white South, the North, and the negro were almost equally represented, had more than a hundred substantial buildings, owned 2000 acres of local land, and had received from Congress 25,000 acres in northern Alabama; had an endowment of nearly $2,000,000 with an annual budget of $290,000; had 1537 students, 197 faculty members, all negroes, and taught thirty-eight trades and professions. He

also started many forms of rural extension work; established the National Negro Business League with its many important ramifications, the National Negro Health Week, and various negro conferences at which the Principal, with his unfailing common sense, resourcefulness, and humor, was at his best. Largely as a result of his labors he could say in 1910, "We have no race problem in Macon County" (*My Larger Education,* p. 308). The high reputation of Tuskegee graduates for character and local leadership became well established.

From 1884, when Washington addressed the National Education Association at Madison, Wis., he was in great demand throughout the country as a public speaker on education and race relations. His addresses were striking for their sincerity, simplicity, and humor; his English was that of the Bible which was his daily study. These addresses, whether before negro teachers, or members of a Southern legislature, or the Harvard alumni body (after he received an honorary degree in 1891), emphasized much the same points: an education fitted for life, the need of keeping close to Nature, and of cultivating the respect of one's neighbors, white and black. It was his epochal speech at the Cotton States and International Exposition at Atlanta, Ga., Sept. 18, 1893, that brought him national recognition as the leader of the negro people, succeeding Frederick Douglass who had just died. His desire "to say something that would cement the friendship of the races" resulted in one of his most famous phrases: "In all things that are purely social we can be as separate as the fingers, yet one as the hand in all things essential to mutual progress" (*Up From Slavery,* pp. 221–22). The effect of the speech, with its advice to Southern white men and negroes alike to "Cast down your buckets where you are," was electric. Clark Howell referred to the address as "one of the most notable speeches, both as to character and as to the warmth of its reception, ever delivered to a Southern audience. The address was a revelation. The whole speech is a platform upon which blacks and whites can stand with full justice to each other" (*Ibid.*, p. 226).

His views were opposed by the negro "intellectuals" who felt he did not sufficiently emphasize political rights, and that his stress on industrial education might result in keeping the negro in virtual bondage. He was more interested in making his race worthy of the franchise, which he himself always exercised without difficulty, than in agitating for it in ways which might inflame public opinion. Looking at the controversy after a generation has passed, we can see that there was truth on both sides, but that as far as the welfare of the masses in the South was concerned, and considering the public opinion of his day, which he wished to influence, he adopted the only policy which could be really effective. Two incidents involving race relations attracted almost as much attention as his Atlanta speech. Of his dining with President Theodore Roosevelt at the White House in the autumn of 1901 he said, "Mr. Roosevelt simply found he could spare the time best during and after the dinner hour for the discussion of matters which both of us were interested in" (*My Larger Education*, p. 177). His own custom was consistent. In the North and in Europe he accepted dinner invitations from white people when he thought they would advance the interests of Tuskegee or of the negro race, but he was extremely modest regarding all the honors shown him by royalty abroad and by leading Americans. The other incident was his call at the apartment of a white family in New York in March 1911, resulting in a misunderstanding which was unfairly played up by some newspapers (see especially the statement of Seth Low, president of the Tuskegee trustees, in *New York Tribune*, Mar. 21, 1911).

He was married three times: first, in 1882, to Fannie N. Smith of Malden, W. Va., a graduate of Hampton, who died in 1884 leaving a daughter; second, in 1885, to Olivia A. Davidson of Ohio, who taught at Tuskegee in the early days and died in 1889 leaving two sons; third, on Oct. 12, 1893, to Margaret James Murray of Mississippi, at the time of their marriage "lady principal" at Tuskegee. He died Nov. 14, 1915, the day after his return home from New York where he had collapsed as a result of over-work. A bronze statue by Charles Keck on the Tuskegee campus shows Washington taking the scales from the eyes of the negro slave. Below are quotations from his speeches, including his characteristic saying, "No man, black or white, from North or South, shall drag me down so low as to make me hate him." Two tributes, from North and South, are sufficient. Theodore Roosevelt said: "As nearly as any man I have ever met, Booker T. Washington lived up to Micah's verse, 'What more doth the Lord require of thee than to do Justice, and love Mercy and walk humbly with thy God'" (quoted in Scott and Stowe, *post*, p. xi). And Henry Watterson [*q.v.*] wrote: "No man, since the war of sections, has exercised such beneficent influence and done such real good for the country—especially to the South" (Stokes, *post*, Appendix VII, p. 78).

He wrote *The Future of the American Negro*

(1899); *Sowing and Reaping* (1900); *Up From Slavery* (1901), which was translated into at least eighteen languages; *Character Building* (1902); *Working with the Hands* (1904); *Putting the Most into Life* (1906); *Frederick Douglass* (1907); *The Negro in Business* (1907); *The Story of the Negro* (1909); *My Larger Education* (1911); and with R. E. Park, *The Man Farthest Down* (1912). He also edited *Tuskegee and its People* (1905).

[His autobiographical works, *Up From Slavery* and *My Larger Education; Booker T. Washington, Builder of a Civilization* (1916), by his secretary, E. J. Scott and Lyman Beecher Stowe; *Selected Speeches of Booker T. Washington* (1932), ed. by his son, E. D. Washington; A. P. Stokes, *Tuskegee Institute: The First Fifty Years* (1931) and "A Brief Biography of Booker Washington Based on Original Sources" (in preparation); obituaries in *N. Y. Times, Montgomery Advertiser*, Nov. 15, 1915, and in other papers.]
A. P. S.

WASHINGTON, BUSHROD (June 5, 1762–Nov. 26, 1829), associate justice of the Supreme Court of the United States, was born in Westmoreland County, Va., the son of John Augustine, brother of Gen. George Washington, and Hannah, daughter of John Bushrod of Bluefield, Va. The Bushrods were one of the first families of Virginia, faithful churchmen, and ardent patriots. After studying under a tutor in the house of Richard Henry Lee, Bushrod entered the College of William and Mary in 1775, graduating therefrom in 1778. Enlisting in the Continental Army as a private, he was present at the surrender of Cornwallis at Yorktown.

After the war he studied law in Philadelphia in the office of James Wilson, whom years later he was to succeed as a member of the Supreme Court of the United States. Admitted to the Virginia bar, he began practice at Alexandria; and in 1787 was elected to the Virginia House of Delegates and a year later to the Virginia State Convention, where he supported Madison and Marshall in their fight for the ratification of the federal Constitution. His growing law practice prompted a removal of his residence from Alexandria to Richmond in 1790, where he received many law students into his office.

To fill the vacancy in the Supreme Court created by the death of James Wilson in 1798, President Adams first turned to John Marshall [*q.v.*], but upon Marshall's declining the honor, tendered the post to Washington, his appointment being confirmed Dec. 20, 1798. At this time the Supreme Court was generally regarded as of little importance in the governmental system. Decisions of consequence had been very few. Declinations of appointments and resignations had been frequent. Joined on the bench within a few years by John Marshall, William Johnson, and other able judges, however, Washington found himself the member of a court whose prestige and power were in the ascendant. To the lot of this group fell the significant rôle of interpreting the Constitution during the critical formative period of the nation's growth, and of formulating the Constitutional theory which was to exert such a vital influence upon future thought and action. Washington's tenure as a justice of the Supreme Court continued until his death, a period of thirty-one years.

He was unacquainted with literature and the arts, but was a devoted and diligent student of the law. By nature mild and conciliatory, yet prompt and firm in decision, he possessed what is generally called a judicial temperament, and as a *nisi prius* judge is said to have been unexcelled. Slow of mind but thorough and clear in reasoning, he rendered a number of opinions influential in the development of American law not only upon Constitutional matters, where he saw eye to eye with Marshall, but also upon admiralty, commercial, and other subjects. Among his notable opinions were those in the following cases: *Marine Insurance Company* vs. *Tucker* (1806), 3 *Cranch,* 357; *Eliason* vs. *Henshaw* (1819), 4 *Wheaton,* 225; *Dartmouth College* vs. *Woodward* (1819), 4 *Wheaton,* 518; *Green* vs. *Biddle* (1823), 8 *Wheaton,* 1; *Thornton* vs. *Wynn* (1827), 12 *Wheaton,* 183; *Ogden* vs. *Saunders* (1827, 12 *Wheaton,* 213; and *Buckner* vs. *Finley* (1829), 2 *Peters,* 586. His courage was such that, sitting as a circuit judge in the case of *United States* vs. *Bright* (24 *Fed. Cas.,* 1232) he did not hesitate to sentence to imprisonment an officer of the state of Pennsylvania for resisting a federal judicial process, though Pennsylvania threatened rebellion if he did.

He was painstaking and methodical in the keeping of his books and accounts and for a period of thirty-five years carefully catalogued and filed away all his letters and papers. To him General Washington devised his library, his public and private papers and letters, as well as the stately "Mount Vernon" with its surrounding 4,000 acres, where, after the death of Martha Washington in 1802, Bushrod made his home. He was also made one of the executors of General Washington's will, and though lacking the business acumen of his distinguished uncle, he was as painstaking in handling the affairs of the estate as he was in respect to his own.

Though Washington favored the abolition of slavery and was in 1816 elected the first president of the American Colonization Society, he was in 1821 made the subject of a bitter attack on humanitarian grounds, for having sold and transported to Louisiana fifty-four "Mount Vernon" slaves, separating many of them from close members of their families. Admitting the substance of the charge, Washington, in a letter published in *Niles' Weekly Register* (Sept. 29, 1821), said: "I do not admit the right of any person to decide for me on this point," and argued that since slaves were property they could legally be made the subject of sale. He contended that insubordination among his slaves and their repeated attempts at escape to the North made their retention unprofitable.

In 1785, Washington married Julia Ann Blackburn, a daughter of Col. Thomas Blackburn of "Rippon Lodge," who had been an aide-de-camp to General Washington during the Revolution. She always accompanied her husband on his rounds as a practitioner and circuit judge. They had no children. In personal appearance Washington was short in stature, sharp-faced, usually negligently dressed, and wore "his dark, unfrosted hair, long and combed back from his forehead" (Warren, *post,* I, 467). He had lost the sight of one eye from over study. An immoderate user of snuff, in later life he frequently had a profusion of the leafy product distributed over his face. He died in Philadelphia and was buried at "Mount Vernon." His wife, prostrated with grief, died while traveling from Philadelphia to "Mount Vernon" to attend his funeral.

[Horace Binney, *Bushrod Washington* (1858); *The Green Bag,* Aug. 1897; *Am. Law Magazine,* July 1845; H. L. Carson, *The Hist. of the Supreme Court of the U. S.* (2 vols., 1902); Charles Warren, *The Supreme Court in U. S. Hist.* (1926), vol. I; E. E. Prussing, *The Estate of George Washington, Deceased* (1927); *Niles' Weekly Reg.,* Sept. 1, 29, 1821; *Tyler's Quart. Hist. and Geneal. Mag.,* July 1922; *Nat. Gazette* (Phila.), Nov. 27, 1829.]   G. W. G.

WASHINGTON, GEORGE (Feb. 11/22, 1732–Dec. 14, 1799), first president of the United States, was born in Westmoreland County, Va., on the estate of his father lying between Bridges Creek and Popes Creek and later known as "Wakefield." The eldest son of Augustine Washington and his second wife, Mary Ball (1708–89), of "Epping Forest," Va., he was descended from Lawrence of Sulgrave, Northampton, England, who was of the fourth generation from John of Whitfield. Four generations later John, son of Lawrence the rector of Purleigh, emigrated to Virginia in 1657–58 and settled in Westmoreland County (Ford, *Writings,* XIV, 331–409; chart opp. p. 319). Augustine Washington was the grandson of John and the son of Lawrence of Bridges Creek, Westmoreland County. He lived in Westmoreland until 1735, when he removed to Little Hunting Creek, on the Potomac. After his homestead there was burned he moved to "Ferry Farm" in King George County, on the Rappahannock nearly opposite Fredericksburg. Augustine died in 1743 and the next half-dozen years of George Washington's life were spent with relatives in Westmoreland and the Chotank region, at "Ferry Farm," and at "Mount Vernon," the home of his elder half-brother Lawrence, who had married Ann Fairfax.

During this period George Washington received the major part of his school training, which totaled seven or eight years. His father and his elder half-brother Lawrence seem to have been his principal, if not his only teachers. The extent of his mother's influence upon Washington cannot be accurately appraised, but from the great respect he accorded her, and the scrupulous manner in which he fulfilled his filial duty, it is justifiable to credit her with a decided influence in the way of discipline and morals. His training in mathematics extended to trigonometry and surveying, which helped develop a natural talent for draftsmanship that found expression in map-making, in designing tabular memoranda, and in giving the pages of his letters an unusual but characteristic pictorial quality. He had a certain appreciation of beauty and a decided appreciation of music and the drama. Early memoranda give an indication of his reading habits and his accounts show purchases of books dealing with military affairs, agriculture, history, and biography, and a fair number of the great novels of the day, such as *Tom Jones, Humphry Clinker,* and *Peregrine Pickle.* He purchased a number of ethical works and ordered and used a bookplate. The quotations that are sprinkled sparingly through his correspondence cover a wide range, and show his familiarity with such authors as Pope and Addison, while his Biblical allusions are varied enough to prove a satisfactory acquaintance with the Book of books. A letter to Lafayette in 1788 (Ford, *Writings,* XI, 265–66) suggests the general outline of his historical and literary knowledge, while his statement to James McHenry in 1797 that he had "not looked into a book" since he came home (*Ibid.,* XIII, 392) adds to the cumulative evidence that he appreciated fully the value of the printed word in his own cultural development. The social intimacy between "Belvoir" and "Mount Vernon," where one of the Fairfax fledglings had nested, brought Washington, at an impressionable age, into contact with the courtly manners and customs of the best English culture. His youthful idealism responded to this stimulus, as it did to the stateliness of the drama,

and the two combined to produce the dignity and poise which were characteristic of his maturity.

Through the Fairfax association developed the first important adventure of his career. When, in 1748, Lord Fairfax sent James Genn, county surveyor of Prince William County, to survey his Shenandoah lands for tenantry, George William Fairfax and George Washington were permitted to go along. The two young men were gone a month, worked hard, and encountered many inconveniences, but gained valuable experience (*Diaries,* I, 3–12). A year later Washington was appointed county surveyor for Culpeper. His duty carried him into wild country where he encountered many hardships, yet his surveys required exactitude and gave him insight into the importance of land ownership. This work was interrupted by the call of duty to accompany Lawrence Washington on his health-seeking voyage to Barbadoes. George was stricken with smallpox on that island and so rendered immune to the disease which raged among the troops he commanded during the Revolutionary War. He returned alone to Virginia to be followed by Lawrence, who died in July 1752, bequeathing the "Mount Vernon" estate in such wise that it shortly became the property of George.

That year he was appointed by Governor Dinwiddie district adjutant for the southern district of Virginia, but was soon transferred to that of the Northern Neck and Eastern Shore. Washington's military ambition, first stimulated by his half-brother's service with Admiral Vernon, was reawakened and increased by his experience in military musters and drills of the Virginia militia. When the French encroached, as was claimed, on the English lands in the Ohio country, he accepted without hesitancy Dinwiddie's appointment (1753) to carry an ultimatum to the trespassers. Though the mission was one of hardship and downright danger, it appealed to Washington as one of honor and possible glory. It certainly was unusual that a colonial governor should appoint a young man of twenty-one to so important a mission, and the exact reasons for the selection are conjectural. Washington was also instructed to strengthen the friendship of the Six Nations with the English. With a party of six frontiersmen, he left Will's Creek in the middle of November 1753 and a week later reached the forks of the Ohio, where he had expected to find the French. But the French had withdrawn for the winter and Washington was faced with a decision between giving up the delivery of the ultimatum, and traveling sixty miles farther into the wintry wilderness to reach the next French post. Before starting on this new journey he endeavored to fulfil the second part of his instructions by holding, at Logstown on the Ohio, a council with such of the chiefs of the Six Nations as he could gather together; but he accomplished little, as the Indians were wary of the English assurances, unbacked by any display of force, when the French were already on the ground with troops and cannon. He found the French at Venango, but the officer there refused to receive his message and directed Washington to the commandant at Fort Le Beouf. Unwilling to return without accomplishing his main mission, he was forced to proceed one hundred miles farther, through winter-clogged swamp-land, nearly to the shores of Lake Erie. After five days of difficult travel he reached the fort and received in writing a polite refusal to pay any attention to Dinwiddie's ultimatum. On the return journey Washington's horses gave out, and with his guide, Christopher Gist, he undertook to walk back to Will's Creek. He was shot at by a prowling French Indian, nearly drowned in crossing the ice-choked Allegheny on an improvised raft, and nearly frozen from exposure (*Diaries,* I, 40–67). His report to Dinwiddie was printed by the Governor as *The Journal of Major George Washington* . . . (1754) and created a stir in England as well as America.

Washington had described a position at the forks of the Ohio (the present location of Pittsburgh) as the best place for an outpost and Dinwiddie dispatched a small force to forestall the French in building a fort there. He commissioned Washington a lieutenant-colonel and ordered him to reinforce the forks with the militia then assembling at Alexandria. These amounted to 150 men and with them on Apr. 2, 1754, Washington marched. He was met on the way by the news that the French had captured the fort. They named it Fort Duquesne. His force was too small for him to attempt to recapture it but Washington, nevertheless, advanced to Red Stone, the Ohio Company's trading post about forty miles from Fort Duquesne, and began a road for the expedition which Dinwiddie was virtually obligated to undertake. At Great Meadows, Pa., on rumors of a French advance, he built an entrenched camp which he called Fort Necessity, and when informed by friendly Indians of the approach of a French scouting party he marched forward to intercept it. Aided by the Indians, he succeeded in surprising and defeating the French (May 27); their leader, Jumonville, was killed. In reprisal the French advanced in force from Fort Duquesne and Washington fell back to Great Meadows; the retreat would have been

continued to Will's Creek, but he feared being overtaken at some less defensible place than Fort Necessity (*Diaries,* I, 101 n.; *Writings,* Bicentennial ed., I, 87). The attack of the French was sustained for ten hours, then they proposed a parley. The terms offered Washington were generous but contained a bit of clever roguery, unnoticed by his translator, which made the signing of them an admission by Washington that Jumonville had been "assassinated." It was part and parcel of the age-old practice of placing the blame for starting a war; it created a stir at the time, but the truth of the matter has long been understood. The tangled condition into which Virginia's military affairs had been brought by Dinwiddie's management made Washington liable to be commanded by junior and inferior officers and, no relief being granted, he resigned near the end of the year 1754.

In 1755 Great Britain sent an expedition of regulars under General Braddock against Fort Duquesne. For reasons not entirely clear, though Washington's knowledge of the country and the influence of Dinwiddie are the probable explanations, Braddock offered Washington the position of aide on his staff. His military ambitions were still alive and this opportunity to serve under a professional soldier appealed to him. The tradition that his advice was scornfully rejected by Braddock is largely a misapplication of the suggestions Washington made later on the Forbes expedition. On the march toward Duquesne he was taken violently ill and left behind, rejoining Braddock only the day before the action at the Monongahela. In that action, weak and debilitated though he was, he strove to carry out Braddock's orders; he had two horses shot under him and four bullets through his coat before every one, along with the fatally wounded general, was swept from the field by the rush of panic-stricken soldiery. With Braddock's death his appointment as aide ended and he returned to "Mount Vernon." Not having resigned his adjutancy of the Northern Neck he issued a call for the militia of his district to be ready for muster and inspection (*Writings,* Bicentennial ed., I, 158). This was the limit of his authority, but to that extent he prepared Virginia for the expected French and Indian invasion of the frontier.

In the fall of 1755 Dinwiddie appointed him colonel and commander in chief of all Virginia forces, thrusting upon him at the age of twenty-three the responsibility of defending 300 miles of mountainous frontier with about 300 men. It was in this savage, frontier warfare (averaging two engagements a month with raiding Indians), that Washington acquired the habit of thinking and acting for the welfare of a people, and the experience of conducting military operations, however poorly, over an extensive expanse of territory. His letters show the depths to which he was stirred by the plight and suffering of the inhabitants, and his strenuous efforts to protect them from the ravages of the Indians. They also show the causes of his partial failure. With too few troops and inadequate supplies, lacking sufficient authority with which to maintain complete discipline, and hampered by an antagonistic governor, he faced difficulties which closely paralleled those that he met in the Revolution. He encountered in 1756, as he had once before, the supercilious arrogance of the British army officer who called in question his right to command because of a pretended difference between a commission signed by the king and one signed by a colonial governor. Washington rode from Winchester to Boston to obtain a settlement of the difficulty, which otherwise might have disrupted Virginia's frontier defense. The journey had an unexpected but important effect in broadening Washington's viewpoint in respect to the people of the other colonies. It was the longest horseback journey he had made up to that time; but there were few Americans, then and for some years later, who were so continuously in the saddle and few who traveled over so large an expanse of the country as did Washington. With the matter of rank settled to his satisfaction, he returned to Virginia and the disheartening duty of defending the frontier. Lacking pay for his men, lacking clothes, shoes, powder, and even food at times, Washington managed nevertheless to protect the frontier so well that fewer inhabitants fell victims to savage fury in Virginia than in the other colonies (*Writings,* Bicentennial ed., II, 11). He continually urged the capture of Fort Duquesne, but with the governor and legislature at loggerheads, Virginia could not raise a force sufficient to undertake it and Washington's efforts to secure cooperation from Maryland and Pennsylvania in the enterprise were unsuccessful. In 1758, however, Great Britain again sent a force of regulars under General John Forbes [*q.v.*] against the post and Washington, with the title of brigadier (there being then two Virginia regiments) was ordered to cooperate. On this expedition Washington suggested an order of march for the British that was remarkably near the modern open-order method of fighting. It was ignored. The fort was abandoned by the French on the near approach of the British (November 1758) and, the main objective of Virginia's frontier defense being thus

accomplished, Washington resigned shortly thereafter.

He married, on Jan. 6, 1759, Martha (Dandridge) Custis, widow of Daniel Parke Custis, and settled down to the life of a gentleman-farmer at "Mount Vernon." Through Mrs. Custis' offspring by her first husband, Washington's strong, natural love of children, nowhere attested better than in his expense accounts, found ample vent. In the death of young "Patsy" Custis (1773), he experienced one of the great emotional shocks of his life. His troubles with "Jacky" Custis brought home to him the difficult problem of the education of youth, and broadened his viewpoint in educational matters. At various times he contributed generously to educational organizations: to Washington College in Maryland, to Liberty Hall (later Washington and Lee) in Virginia, to the Alexandria Academy, to an academy in Kentucky, and to an academy in the Southwestern Territory. He urged the establishment of a national university in the Federal City and provided an endowment for it in his will. The basis of this idea was largely the "indescribable regret" with which he had "seen the youth of the United States migrating to foreign countries, in order to acquire the higher branches of erudition, and to obtain a knowledge of the sciences." His fear that they would imbibe "maxims not congenial with republicanism" was not based on his doubt of republicanism, but on his perception of the danger of sending youth abroad among other political systems before they had "well learned the value of their own" (Ford, *Writings,* XIII, 52).

He had been elected a burgess from Frederick in 1758, after having been defeated in 1755 and 1757, and took his seat in the session of 1759, when he was thanked by the House for his military services. The succeeding fifteen years of Washington's career were uneventful in a public way but undoubtedly were the most enjoyable of his life. They were spent in developing the farming possibilities of the "Mount Vernon" estate, with the variation of trips to Williamsburg to attend the sessions of the legislature, of neighborly visits to Alexandria, Dumfries, and Fredericksburg, of attendance on the Annapolis races and theatre, of fox-hunts and fishing trips. To his taste for theatricals was added an interest in strange animals which were akin to his interest in unusual plants. In his expense accounts one notes payments for seeing a lioness, a tiger, an elk, a camel, and other animals, and once a reference to a sleight of hand performance. Card-games, billiards, boat-racing, in addition to horse-racing, the theatre, dancing, fishing, gunning, and fox-hunting with horse and hounds—all the usual sports and amusements were enjoyed by Washington. His accounts unintentionally show how often he bore the major part of the necessary expenses and how often he made loans to his friends. From these accounts are to be gleaned much information about Washington's personal tastes and fancies. His snuff-taking and pipe-smoking habits were pre-Revolutionary and temporary; but his liking for oysters, watermelons, Madeira wine, and other delicacies was permanent.

But the pleasant, busy life at "Mount Vernon" was not without its annoyances. Many of these were of such nature as to create and gradually strengthen a conviction of the general unfairness of all things British. It was necessary to purchase practically all the supplies needed for "Mount Vernon": farm-implements, tools of all sorts, paint, hardware, even textiles for clothing, needles, and thread. Washington's yearly invoices of goods purchased from Liverpool and London list great quantities of supplies, for he was buying for the annual consumption of a community of village proportions; when the estates of the Custis children were added to those of "Mount Vernon" the combined needs were enormous. The British commercial restrictions imposed needless hardships upon most business transactions and to these were added the sharp practices of the English factors, who were used by every Virginia planter in transacting his yearly business with the English markets. Complaints were easily passed over as the intervening distance and the time necessary for correspondence gave the Virginian little power to enforce redress. By a process of gradual accretion Washington's disappointing experiences in the Braddock and Forbes campaigns were built upon by these commercial annoyances, and a subconscious antagonism was created which even his strong sense of duty and loyalty could not hold in check.

He was successively reëlected as a burgess from Fairfax, faithfully attended the sessions, and shouldered his share of the legislative duties. From 1760 to 1774 he was also a justice of Fairfax, holding court in Alexandria. His experiences in court and as a burgess did much to clarify his view of the handicapping influences of the British colonial system on America. The Stamp Act brought to a focus the developing colonial antagonism and Washington expressed with the logic of common sense the American attitude towards the claims of Parliament. It "hath no more right to put their hands into my pocket, without my consent, than I have to put my hands into yours for money" (*Writings,* Bi-

centennial ed., III, 233). He pointed out the practical difficulties which lay in the path of the enforcement of the act. "Our Courts of Judicature must inevitably be shut up . . . for . . . we have no Money to pay the Stamps . . . and if a stop be put to our judicial proceedings I fancy the Merchants of G. Britain trading to the Colonies will not be among the last to wish for a Repeal of it" (*Ibid.,* II, 426). The British prohibition of colonial paper money was one of the major grievances; with the balance of trade always against them, paper money was a primal necessity to the colonists. A personal matter was the effort to obtain for the officers and men of the old Virginia regiment the bounty land allotted to them for their services in the French and Indian War. Elected their attorney and agent under a prorata agreement as to expenses, Washington pushed the matter to a conclusion, advanced his own funds, some of which he did not get back, and made a hazardous canoe trip with a small party in 1770, down the Ohio and up the Great Kanawha, to locate the land (*Diaries,* I, 401–52). This journey revived his interest in the western territory and increased the knowledge which he had early acquired of its value to the development of the Atlantic seaboard; to an extent, it laid the foundation of his western land policy when president. On this trip Washington killed several buffalo. These animals, it seemed to him, might in the future supply meat for America, so he undertook an experiment with them. At his death, nearly thirty years later, a buffalo cow still remained among the stock animals at "Mount Vernon."

After 1770 the question of British taxes assumed increasing importance in the colonies, and in four short years became the major problem. The device of non-importation was tried, in resistance to British political and economic aggression. Washington strongly supported it, yet prophesied, before 1775, "that more blood will be spilt on this occasion, if the ministry are determined to push matters to extremity, than history has ever yet furnished instances of in the annals of North America" (*Writings,* Bicentennial ed., III, 246). He did not approve of the Boston Tea Party (*Ibid.,* III, 224), while thoroughly in sympathy with the refusal of Massachusetts to submit to the British restrictions. He was one of the burgesses who met in the Raleigh Tavern on May 27, 1774, after the Assembly had been dissolved by the governor, and signed the proceedings of that unauthorized but important meeting, and on July 18 he acted as chairman of a meeting in Alexandria, at which the important Fairfax Resolutions, the work of George Mason [*q.v.*], were adopted. He was next chosen one of Virginia's delegates to the First Continental Congress, 1774, which did little beyond petitioning Great Britain for a redress of grievances. In the interval between that and the Second Congress, Washington was chosen to command the independent militia companies of Frederick, Fairfax, Prince William, Richmond, and Spotsylvania counties and authorized by them to procure equipment, which he did in Philadelphia. The buff and blue uniform chosen by the Fairfax company was the uniform worn by Washington throughout the Revolution, and so has become fixed in the public mind as the Continental Army uniform. At the March session of the Virginia legislature he was elected a delegate to the Second Continental Congress, which convened in Philadelphia May 1775. In that body his most important work was on the committee for drafting the army regulations and planning the defense of New York City. The latter assignment was to exercise a hampering influence upon him later.

His election to command the armies, June 15, 1775, was the result of a compromise between the northern and southern factions which existed, thus early, in Congress. The Massachusetts delegates knew that their only hope was to have the war, which up to then had been centered in the siege of Boston, taken over by the Continental Congress. In bringing about Washington's nomination and unanimous election John and Samuel Adams were the prime movers, and it was natural that Congress should confer the supreme command upon one of its own members when that member was the most prominent southern military character known to it. In his speech of acceptance Washington refused all pay for the arduous employment which he accepted as a duty "at the expense of my domestick ease and happiness" (*Writings,* Bicentennial ed., III, 292). He asked only that he be reimbursed his necessary expenses, of which he kept the account himself with such exactness that after eight years of nerve-wracking warfare his balance was less than a dollar wrong in a total of some £24,-700.

When Washington took command of the army at Cambridge on July 3, 1775, he found it little better than a loosely organized mob of raw New England militia whose terms of service were to expire at the end of that year, or sooner. Earlier than most, Washington gave up as hopeless the idea of an accommodation with Great Britain, and the king's speech in October 1775 confirmed him in his belief that no compromise was to be expected (*Writings,* Bicentennial ed., IV, 321).

The belief which persisted in others of the possibility of an accommodation was a hampering influence that prevented the colonies from exerting their full power in opposition to the British; it was, in large measure, the cause not only of lukewarm support of Washington but also of the growth of downright opposition to him, centering in a clique in Congress. The problems of supply and pay for the troops, which Congress had taken over, became a vexation that grew with the months. Efforts to establish discipline encountered bitter hostility; democratic ideas stood in the way and caused to be construed as a snobbish display of fancied superiority the authority necessary to create an efficient military machine. Opposing disciplinary measures, the New Englanders at the same time criticized Washington for the army's lack of it. Fear of a standing army was another difficulty. Obsessed with this fear, in which the phantom of an accommodation with Great Britain played its part, Congress hesitated to decree long-term enlistments for the troops. Washington stood almost alone in his plea for men who could be held in service long enough to make them seasoned soldiers. At the siege of Boston, he was forced to replace one army by another while holding in check twenty seasoned British regiments, and in the New York campaign the main cause of the so-called retreat through the Jerseys was the inability to collect troops to replace the losses caused by expired enlistments and desertions.

At Cambridge scarcity of powder held Washington back from any major operation until 1776; but when a sufficient quantity was accumulated he seized and fortified Dorchester Heights, a position which threatened Boston with bombardment and placed the British fleet in jeopardy. The city was evacuated Mar. 17, 1776, and with his army of newly enlisted troops Washington marched for New York City, which was the next logical base of operations for the enemy. He had already sent Maj.-Gen. Charles Lee to supervise the work of fortification at that place, so that Washington on his arrival found himself partially committed to a plan of defense mapped out by others. He improved the three months before the British arrived by training his army as well as he could, handicapped by an appalling lack of experienced officers, and in preparing against the inevitable consequences of the decree of Congress that New York must be defended. He had sixteen miles of water-front lines to defend with 10,000 men, and when the British had assembled their whole force in New York Bay they numbered 30,000 trained troops, exclusive of a naval force of over 100 vessels. Any defense worthy of the name, under such conditions, was impossible, yet Washington attempted the impossible from his concept of duty to obey the orders of Congress, and from a disinclination to insist upon his own judgment where he believed his military knowledge and experience inadequate. This hesitancy was more evident throughout the New York campaign than at any other period of the Revolution.

The British tactics in that campaign were far from masterly, though ample to insure success. Howe's choice of Long Island as the point of attack was a safe and sure step. Washington was obliged to divide his force as a result. He sent ten regiments to reinforce Brooklyn, a pitiful few to oppose a veteran force of 30,000; but the main body of Americans had to be held on Manhattan to oppose the attack of the British fleet, which only a strong headwind frustrated. Washington himself crossed over to Brooklyn as soon as it was seen that the British ships could not make way against the wind; but the enemy had already outflanked Sullivan and the tragedy was beyond repair. Howe delayed his assault on the Brooklyn fortifications and, on the night of Aug. 29, Washington moved all the troops over to New York. His arrangements were perfect; the British were kept in ignorance and the retreat was rightly considered a military masterpiece. On Sept. 15, the British landed at Kip's Bay and, despite Washington's presence and desperate attempts to rally his men, they fled in panic and a retreat to Harlem Heights became a necessity. British flanking moves pushed Washington, though not without some sharp skirmishing, back to a strong natural position at White Plains. Howe desisted and returned to New York, on the way gathering in Fort Washington, which had been held against Washington's better judgment but not against his orders.

His report to Congress laid down the general principle on which he was waging the war. "We should on all Occasions avoid a general Action, or put anything to the Risque, unless compelled by a necessity, into which we ought never to be drawn" (*Writings*, Bicentennial ed., VI, 28). Inexperienced troops, always inferior in numbers to the British, made this the only possible course of action until Congress was willing to create a permanent army. The odds against him were heavy. His great need was time: time to make a reluctant Congress realize the necessity of his recommendations; time to raise a permanent army after it was finally authorized; and time to train it to fight after it was raised. Dogged perseverance, a straining to the limit of the scant means in his hands, together with British lethargy, gained him some of the time he needed. He could complain bitterly to his brother that he was "wearied almost to death with the retrograde Motions of things" (*Ibid.*, VI, 246), and could warn Congress in October 1776 that its army was again "upon the eve of its political dissolution" (*Ibid.*, VI, 152). His belief in the moral righteousness of the American struggle for liberty was based on his sense of the injustice and unfairness of the British course. To him rebellion against the king and change of allegiance were matters demanding scrupulous moral honesty. Not until his concept of honor approved the change did he make it; but the step once taken, turning back was for him unthinkable and impossible. As he wrote to his brother: "Under a full persuasion of the justice of our Cause, I cannot ... entertain an Idea that it will finally sink tho' it may remain for sometime under a Cloud" (*Ibid.*, VI, 399). The fortitude with which he met overwhelming difficulties was based upon his faith; defeats to him were merely temporary setbacks and victories merely longer or shorter steps toward final success.

The loss of Fort Lee, on the Jersey shore, resulted from the same misplaced confidence in his generals which had lost Fort Washington, yet both disasters were unrecognized blessings. They freed the Continental Army from responsibility for fixed fortifications, in which it had small chance against the trained British forces, and made it a mobile, maneuvering force which could be handled in accordance with Washington's ideas. The Pennsylvania and Jersey militia failed to answer his appeals and, with a steadily dwindling force, he fell back as the British pushed forword. The so-called retreat through New Jersey was a perfect example of Washington's military principle, for it was a retirement before a superior force of the enemy, conducted so slowly and so cleverly that the British expected to encounter strong opposition at almost every point. His grasp of military science, for all his modest disclaimers, was far above that of any of his generals. His plea at this time to Congress for artillery showed a far-sighted comprehension that few could boast (*Writings*, Bicentennial ed., VI, 280–81).

His calls, while retiring through New Jersey, to Maj.-Gen. Charles Lee [*q.v.*] for reinforcements revealed the first serious military opposition within his own army. Lee delayed marching, apparently with the idea of contesting the supreme command with Washington as soon as the latter's army dissolved or was defeated. The British solved this difficulty by the surprise and capture of Lee, whose troops were promptly marched to Washington's support by the officer next in command. With an army of barely 5,000, Washington reached the Delaware River, swept up all the boats, called in the Princeton rearguard, and crossed into Pennsylvania, where from the west bank he watched the enemy make futile marches up and down the east side, seeking means to cross. The British settled into winter quarters in a series of posts along the Delaware at and near Trenton and in a line across New Jersey to Amboy, confident that the end of the year 1776 would mark the end of the rebel army and of the rebellion. "Short enlistments and a dependence upon militia," Washington felt, would "prove the downfall of our cause" (*Writings,* Bicentennial ed., VI, 347). Yet, under heavy discouragements, he could write to Congress that he conceived "it to be my duty, and it corrisponds [*sic*] with my Inclination, to make head against them [the British] as soon as there shall be the least probability of doing it" (*Ibid.,* VI, 330).

Congress fled to Baltimore, and the protection of Philadelphia forthwith becoming relatively unimportant in Washington's judgment, he fixed his eyes on Morristown, N. J., as the place most threatening to the British arrangements. That place was designated as the rendezvous of the militia and recruits for the army of 1777 and, with the remnant of the army of 1776, on Christmas night Washington crossed the Delaware amid driving ice, crushed the Hessians at Trenton, and dislocated the entire line of British posts along the river. The failure of his two supporting detachments to get across the river postponed the movement to Morristown, of which the Trenton victory was intended to be the first phase. Washington returned to Pennsylvania with nearly a thousand prisoners. A few days sufficed to rest his troops and he again crossed into Jersey, to move northward. Checked by the British reinforcements advancing from New York, he fought the stubborn engagement of the Assunpink, by a forced night march outwitted the enemy, and struck and pierced their line at Princeton. Once he was at Morristown, his position was such a strategic threat to the British that they abandoned their entire New Jersey line and retreated to Brunswick.

Six days before the victory at Trenton he had applied to the Congress, which had fled to Baltimore, for power to handle "every matter that in its nature is self evident," since a necessity of waiting until such things were referred a hundred and thirty or forty miles would in itself defeat the end in view. He had "no lust after power but wish with as much fervency as any Man

upon this wide extended Continent, for an oppertunity [*sic*] of turning the Sword into a plow share" (*Writings,* Bicentennial ed., VI, 402). Congress responded with a grant of powers greater than he had asked and for a term of six months; but when Washington used this authority to compel all citizens who had taken out British protection papers to deliver them up and take the oath of allegiance to the United States, or remove at once within the British lines, he was violently criticized in Congress. It took Washington a year and a half to shake himself free from the entanglements which had been created by the interference and mismanagement of Congress; but from 1777 troops could be enlisted for three years or the war, and in January of that year Washington began to build a permanent military machine that could "bid Defiance to Great Britain, and her foreign Auxiliaries" (*Ibid.,* VII, 199). But the exorbitant bounties offered by the states for home-guard and militia service operated to check enlistments for the Continental Army. Washington was still forced to rely upon the militia for swelling his force to a respectable total at times when the British threatened or actually moved against him. He expressed his opinion of the militia to Congress more than once. If 40,000 men had been kept in constant pay since the commencement of hostilities, and the militia never called out, the expense of the war would not have been nearly so great as it was; when the losses sustained for want of good troops were taken into account the certainty of this was placed beyond a doubt. To this he added his pungent and deft characterization of militia which has seldom been bettered. They "come in you cannot tell how, go, you cannot tell when; and act, you cannot tell where; consume your Provisions, exhaust your Stores, and leave you at last in a critical moment" (*Ibid.,* VI, 403). At Morristown the army grew slowly and slowly acquired discipline. Washington's hope was to "be able to rub along till the new army is raised," but how he was to do it he did not know. "Providence has heretofore saved us in a remarkable manner, and on this we must principally rely" (*Ibid.,* VII, 53). His own efforts to "keep the Life and Soul of this Army together" (*Ibid.,* VII, 225) were barely successful and this accomplishment, as much as anything, measures the power of his personality. Congress, he wrote not without satire, thought that when difficulties were distant from them, it had but to say "Presto begone, and everything is done."

Washington's handling of this small, green, poorly equipped army in the spring of 1777 was remarkable. He managed to keep the enemy from plundering New Jersey at will, checking their forays by vigorous skirmishing which proved costly to the enemy and had a valuable seasoning effect on the Continental troops. It also convinced Howe that the risk of marching across New Jersey again to take Philadelphia was too great and, the capture of that town being a major object with him, Howe set about taking it by sea. He succeeded in puzzling Washington completely, for the logical move was up the Hudson River to cooperate with Burgoyne's advance from Canada, and until Howe finally appeared in Chesapeake Bay Washington was kept in a state of wearing suspense. But, with the suspense dissolved, Washington marched south and on Sept. 11, 1777, met Howe at Brandywine Creek. Here his right wing, under Sullivan, was out-flanked by the British and Washington was forced to retreat. Nevertheless, Washington's proximity, for though defeated he refused to withdraw, and the skirmish at Yellow Springs which was interrupted by a cloud-burst, delayed Howe's entry into Philadelphia two weeks.

The Congress adjourned to Lancaster and then to York, Pa., and again intrusted Washington with dictatorial powers for a six-day period, but he used this authority sparingly. Washington's recognition of the necessity of according first place to the civil power made him always willing to exhaust every means before using the military. He admitted to Congress that "a reluctance to give distress may have restrained me too far," and realizing the "prevalent jealousy of military power" among the people, he avoided every act that would increase it (*Writings,* Bicentennial ed., X, 159). Some months later he wisely used justices of the peace to impress provisions, which through them were obtained without causing a murmur. His method of waging the war admitted of attacking the British only when the possible gain was worth the sacrifice involved. He was cautious always, and with reason, for he was unbelievably handicapped by a paucity of information even where he should have been kept informed. "I am as totally unacquainted with the political state of things, and what is going forward in the great national council, as if I was an alien," he wrote somewhat bitterly to Edmund Randolph "when a competent knowledge of the temper and designs of our allies . . . might . . . have a considerable influence on the operations of our army" (Sparks, *Writings,* VI, 314).

There have been few generals who have had to husband their men and supplies so carefully as did Washington and fewer who have been more ready to expend them on a proper occasion. At Germantown (Oct. 3–4, 1777) Washington

thought the probable gain outbalanced the probable loss and his surprise attack on the British was less a move to regain Philadelphia than to destroy Howe's army. It failed through no fault of plan, but to some extent it contributed to Howe's later resignation, and both Brandywine and Germantown are to be credited with large influence in the decision of France to aid the United States. Valley Forge and the Conway Cabal were to follow these defeats and, at the time the states should have whole-heartedly supported Washington for their own preservation the intrigue to supplant him in command of the army reached its crisis. The victory of Horatio Gates [*q.v.*] at Saratoga on Oct. 17, 1777, furnished Washington's enemies in Congress the opportunity to draw invidious comparisons. The intrigue was at bottom the culmination of the continuous effort of Massachusetts since 1775 to regain control of the war, which would be an accomplished fact with Gates at the head of the army. Opposition to Washington, engineered by this influence, had been steadily growing, for every criticism was cleverly directed to this end. But James Wilkinson [*q.v.*], a bibulous aide of Gates, babbled of a letter from Maj.-Gen. Thomas Conway [*q.v.*] to Gates; Washington wrote a brief note to Conway with no other purpose than to let that gentleman know he was not unaware of Conway's intriguing disposition and this note became the bomb that shattered the secrecy of the cabal. Once in the open, the innate character of the cabal and its purposes roused resentments and antagonisms in Congress which compelled its adherents to abandon the move (in some instances even to deny their connection with the plot) and, lacking congressional support, the military part of the scheme collapsed.

But Washington held no resentments; his eyes were fixed upon the purpose of the war, and, since the cause of the nation had not been harmed by the cabal, he did not allow the episode to interfere with more important things. The criticism of contemporaries occasionally wounded his feelings but signally failed to disturb his steady course; it only marked the critics as men of less vision or, as was sometimes the case, of less honesty. For Washington did not doubt "that the candid part of Mankind, if they are convinc'd of my Integrity, will make proper allowance for my inexperience, and Frailities" (*Writings,* Bicentennial ed., VIII, 295). "We have some among Us, and I dare say Generals," he wrote, "who wish to make themselves popular at the expense of others; or, who think the cause is not to be advanc'd otherwise than by fighting; the peculiar circumstances under which it is to be done, and the consequences which may follow, are objects too trivial for their attention, but as I have one great end in view, I shall, maugre all strokes of this kind, steadily pursue the means which in my judgment, leads to the accomplishment of it" (*Ibid.*). His calm self-restraint allowed him to write to Lafayette, who found himself ensnarled in the Conway coil: "I have no doubt but that every thing happens so for the best . . . and that we . . . shall, in the end, be ultimately happy; when, My Dear Marquis, if you will give me your Company in Virginia, we will laugh at our past difficulties and the folly of others" (*Ibid.*, X, 237). Without such self-control it may be doubted if his success would have been so complete.

The Continental Army emerged from the suffering of Valley Forge better trained, as the result of months of steady drill under Baron von Steuben [*q.v.*], and both the army and the country had been heartened by the news of the alliance with France, in March 1778. Here again Washington's value to the Revolution is manifest for, despite every effort of Congress and its commissioners in Paris and regardless of the French secret aid which had been given for nearly two years, France was not ready openly to assist the Americans until convinced that they would not compromise with Great Britain. The battles of Trenton, Brandywine, and Germantown went far toward convincing France, but the main assurance was the character and purpose of George Washington. Gerard, the French minister, who held long interviews with him, became convinced that Washington's attitude was uncompromising and that the army would, to a man, follow him. This confidence Gerard succeeded in instilling in Vergennes, the French minister of foreign affairs and so, in turn, influencing the French king. The Saratoga victory far from being the deciding element, merely contributed to the convincing effect of Washington's indomitable purpose and honesty of character.

Sir Henry Clinton, succeeding Howe in supreme command in America, abandoned Philadelphia as a consequence of the French Alliance and undertook to march across New Jersey to New York. Washington pursued, and the line of march of the two armies converging, he overtook the British at Monmouth. The resulting conflict (June 28, 1778) not only proved that the Continental Army had developed into a fighting machine of considerable efficiency, but also demonstrated anew Washington's ability as a general. He checked the disorderly and unnecessary retreat of General Lee and turned the confusion into an obstinate and successful holding of a battlefield, from which the British slipped away during the night and made good their retreat to New York City. France's first open aid was D'Estaing's fleet, but his ships, unfortunately, drew too much water to enter New York Bay. The French admiral sailed to attack the British force in Rhode Island, but a storm and the conduct of Maj.-Gen. John Sullivan [*q.v.*] brought this attempt to naught, and created anti-French feeling that required all of Washington's influence and tact to smooth over successfully. D'Estaing sailed for the West Indies and Washington quartered his army for the winter in New Jersey.

Lafayette, who had been with Washington since the summer of 1777, now conceived a plan of returning to France and obtaining a force to conquer Canada. Congress, more attracted by distant glittering schemes than by nearby everyday realities, approved Lafayette's idea, but had the saving sense to send the plan to Washington for an opinion. The calm common sense of his report (*Writings*, Bicentennial ed., XIII, 223–32; see also 254–57) dissolved the dream and showed Congress again that the commander of its armies, despite his keeping his hand scrupulously clear of civil matters, could reason upon them more intelligently than Congress itself. After pointing out the impossibility of collecting the necessary men and supplies, he dwelt upon the consequences of having France and the Indian tribes as neighbors on the north, while Spain would be on the west and south. His analysis was clear even to an obtuse Congress and the plan was laid aside. Lafayette, on his part, met with a refusal from Vergennes to consider the scheme.

The French Alliance, instead of stimulating the Americans to greater effort, operated as a sedative and to Washington's dismay things went from bad to worse. In spite of his urgent pleas to Congress and to the states for supplies and men a disheartening lethargy was displayed everywhere. Unable to move in a major operation, because of lack of troops and supplies (even a lack of powder in August 1779), Washington yet succeeded in sending an expedition into the Indian country under Sullivan, which broke the power of the Six Nations and freed the frontiers from the horrors of Indian warfare. The bright spots in the prevailing gloom were Wayne's victory at Stony Point and "Light-Horse Harry" Lee's capture of Powles Hook. In July 1780 a French army under the Comte de Rochambeau arrived in Rhode Island, the British force there having been withdrawn to New York, but lack of supplies and men prevented real cooperation by

Washington. A conference with Rochambeau at Hartford on Sept. 22, 1780, compelled Washington to lay bare the real situation. The conference could only decide upon a future attack upon New York when the expected second division of the French arrived, or, if this was then impracticable, to transfer the campaign to the South. The situation was described bluntly by Washington: "We have no magazines, nor money to form them; and in a little time we shall have no men. . . . We have lived upon expedients till we can live no longer . . . the history of the war is a history of false hopes and temporary devices, instead of system and œconomy" (Ford, *Writings,* VIII, 468). Another conference with Rochambeau was held in Wethersfield May 21–22, 1781, and the tentative plan of attacking New York without waiting for the expected second French expedition was decided upon. The French marched to the Hudson and joined the American troops; and the combined forces closed in on the British northern defenses of New York City. Then De Grasse arrived with his fleet in the Chesapeake. The siege of the city was abandoned for a move against Cornwallis in Virginia. Leaving a force to threaten New York, Washington, with a detachment of Americans and the whole of the French army, marched southward for a cooperation with De Grasse. The transportation and quartermaster arrangements on this march were all made by Washington. The armies arrived on schedule and the siege of Yorktown progressed steadily to its triumphant conclusion (Oct. 19, 1781) in three short weeks. De Grasse sailed to the West Indies, Rochambeau's army went into winter quarters in Virginia, and Washington led his troops back to the Hudson, making headquarters at Newburgh.

The states now became more supine than before, and Washington's urgent pleas for exertion and his arguments for the necessity of continued effort had small effect. He urged that "unless we strenuously exert ourselves to profit by these successes, we shall not only lose all the solid advantages that might be derived from them, but we shall become contemptible in our own eyes, in the eyes of our enemy, in the opinion of posterity, and even in the estimation of the whole world, which will consider us as a nation unworthy of prosperity, because we know not how to make a right use of it" (Ford, *Writings,* IX, 437). But he was compelled to possess his soul in patience while his countrymen indulged in an orgy of profiteering, even to the extent of carrying on clandestine trade with the British, as they had done at the beginning of the struggle. It was impossible for Washington to stop these things;

they were civil matters to be handled by Congress and the states, but very little was done by either. He was certain the war was not yet over. The king's speech at the opening of Parliament (1782) showed little signs of yielding and the war continued for two dreary years; but no military events of importance took place after Yorktown.

Though the enemy was reduced to inactivity through Washington's efforts, domestic conditions were slowly going from bad to worse. The army, more dissatisfied than ever from neglect and chronic lack of pay, showed an unrest which increased Washington's anxiety daily. The first open display of what was seething underneath came in the shape of a personal letter from Colonel Lewis Nicola [*q.v.*], of the Invalid regiment, who submitted to him a plan for using the army to make Washington a king. The army, at least, would benefit by it and Nicola stated that the idea was prevalent in camp. The proposal shook Washington's soul, for it swept away all that he had so painfully built up during the war, and hinted that the very men on whom he most relied were ready to support him in an apostasy, in a forswearing of honor and principle, for personal power. It was this, more than the idea of a crown, that stunned Washington. He saw his lifework threatened with dissolution through the political and short-sighted muddling of those responsible for the welfare of the army. To find that the men who had followed and trusted him through years of hunger, nakedness, suffering, and bloodshed were now, with victory in sight, ready to fail him, was bitter; and his answer (May 22, 1782) to the proposal was a withering blast which shrivelled the idea of kingship into the ashes of impossibility (Ford, *Writings,* X, 21–24). For a time the dissatisfaction subsided but a few more months saw it rise again in serious form. Anonymous addresses were posted in camp calling on the officers to meet for a discussion of their condition, to address Congress, and to be prepared to take by force, if necessary, what was unjustly denied them. Washington met the situation with a tact, wisdom, and sincerity which neutralized the danger and substituted for overt action further forbearance; and his letter to Congress urging a compliance with the officers' petition put the matter upon personal grounds with unusual emphasis. " 'If, retiring from the field, they [the officers] are to grow old in poverty, wretchedness and contempt; if they are to wade thro' the vile mire of dependency, and owe the miserable remnant of that life to charity, which has hitherto been spent in honor'; then shall I have learned what ingratitude is, then shall I have realized a tale, which will embitter every moment of my future life" (*Ibid.*, X, 181).

Not content with this, he later addressed to the states a circular letter which was largely a plea for justice to the officers and men of the fast-disbanding Continental Army, with which he had ever considered his own military reputation inseparably connected. More than that, it contained some wise advice on civil matters, which ranks it with the Farewell Address, thirteen years later. Now as then he was retiring, as he believed forever, from public service and so felt privileged to speak his mind plainly. In this circular he unconsciously reveals how close to his heart was the national principle for which he had fought, and how earnest his desire that the country prove worthy of the liberty it had gained. Again and again in his letters he showed how important he considered it that the country should take high rank among the nations of the world, and that high rank, he knew, was only to be gained and held by a strong union and by honorable conduct. Four things, he stated, were essential to respectable national existence: (1) "An indissoluble union of the States under one federal head"; (2) "a sacred regard to public justice"; (3) the adoption of a proper national defense; and (4) a spirit of cooperation, and the suppression of local prejudices (Ford, *Writings,* X, 257). He pleaded with the states for the army as he had pleaded with Congress, for the states were really the ultimate powers, and what Congress had promised in the form of half-pay was, he said, the price of the officers' "blood and your independency; it is therefore more than a common debt, it is a debt of honor" (*Ibid.*, X, 262).

There was little of the dramatic in the closing scenes of the war, but Washington intentionally fixed the date for the cessation of hostilities as Apr. 19, 1783, the anniversary of the battle of Lexington. He entered New York, at the head of the troops which still remained in service, as the British evacuated it; he bade farewell to his officers at Fraunces Tavern and set off for Annapolis to resign his commission to Congress. There is some evidence that a slight uneasiness existed in Congress that he might at the last moment decide to become dictator. No such idea could have been entertained by Washington, who resigned "with satisfaction the appointment I accepted with diffidence" (Ford, *Writings,* X, 339). On Christmas eve (1783) he reached "Mount Vernon" and soon afterward could write to a friend: "I feel now, however, as I conceive a wearied traveller must do, who, after treading many a painful step with a heavy burthen on his shoulders, is eased of the latter . . . and from his housetop is looking back, and tracing with an eager eye the meanders by which he escaped the quicksands and mires which lay in his way; and into which none but the all-powerful Guide and Dispenser of human events could have prevented his falling"(*Ibid.*, X, 358). The evidences of Washington's faith in the intervention of Providence in the affairs of man that are scattered through his letters admit of no doubt of his sincerity. Equally apparent are an unusual lack of egoism and a complete absorption in the successful working out of the problem that confronted him.

His financial condition at the close of the war was far from satisfactory. "Mount Vernon," lacking his careful guidance, had deteriorated and now was not even self-supporting. But despite his own financial stringencies, the quiet, unostentatious charity, which is so clearly shown in his accounts, was undiminished; the almost weekly entries of donations to needy applicants continued, and his running accounts were balanced by loss entries in cases of widows and helpless children, and of men who had died in his debt. He had suffered from the depreciation of the Continental currency; amounts owing him from before the war had been liquidated in Continental bills which he had grimly received, because he would not stand accused of repudiating the national money, even though these payments were, on their face, plain subterfuge in debt cancellation. A financial statement of his investments in Continental loan-office certificates, drawn up after the war, shows also that he had loaned every spare dollar to the government in the years of greatest depression and at the times when the outcome of the Revolution was the most doubtful (Washington MSS., 1784, Photostats, Lib. of Cong.).

He had time now (1784) to devote to the idea of opening a route to the western country from tidewater Virginia, by connecting the Potomac and Ohio rivers. This was one of the favorite projects of his life. Before the Revolution, in the Virginia legislature, he was one of the committee appointed to prepare a bill granting authority to form a company for this purpose (J. P. Kennedy, *Journals of the House of Burgesses of Virginia, 1770–1772,* 1906, pp. 292, 297, 304–05). In furtherance of that idea he undertook a horseback journey of observation into the West in the autumn of 1784 (*Diaries,* II, 279–328). He traveled over 650 miles, and returned with knowledge which stood him in good stead later. But his real interest lay in the development of the farms at "Mount Vernon."

His efforts to bring the estate back to a self-supporting condition were discouraging. Slave labor, the only kind available, had proved its inefficiency. No matter how carefully Washington planned, the results went awry because of the clumsy and unintelligent way the work was carried on. Unable either to free his slaves or to develop them into a self-supporting group, he was convinced that the gradual abolition of slavery would prevent much future mischief (P. L. Ford, *The True George Washington,* 1896, p. 154). To gradual abolition, by legislative authority, he pledged his vote. "But," he said, "when slaves, who are happy and contented with their present masters, are tampered with and seduced to leave them; when masters are taken unawares by these practices; when a conduct of this sort begets discontent on one side and resentment on the other; when it happens to fall on a man whose purse will not measure with that of the society [which works to free the slave], and he loses his property for want of means to defend it; it is oppression in such a case, and not humanity in any, because it introduces more evils than it can cure" (Ford, *Writings,* XI, 25–26). Washington had more negroes than he could profitably employ on his farms. "To sell the overplus I cannot, because I am principled against this kind of traffic." Yet he was steadily being pushed toward bankruptcy and may have been saved from it only by his death (*Ibid.,* XIV, 196).

The agreement between Virginia and Maryland in regard to the navigation of the Potomac had led, through meetings at Alexandria and "Mount Vernon," to a call for what is known as the Annapolis Convention, and through this Washington was again to be brought into public life. But at first, in his absorption in the management of "Mount Vernon" and in the affairs of the Potomac Company, this was not clear to him. Life at "Mount Vernon" was pleasantly calm, and his wife's grandchildren filled the measure of his interest. As he wrote to Lafayette: "I have not only retired from all public employments, but I am retiring within myself. . . . Envious of none, I am determined to be pleased with all; and this, my dear friend, being the order for my march, I will move gently down the stream of life, until I sleep with my fathers" (Ford, *Writings,* X, 347). In 1786 this philosophic calm was interrupted by the disturbing news of the rebellion of Daniel Shays [*q.v.*] in Massachusetts, which forced his thoughts again to public affairs. The outbreak added weight to his conviction, which had been steadily growing, that the Articles of Confederation needed revision in the interests of a strong central government. The memories of Valley Forge, of Morristown, of Trenton, of all the instances of needless suffering and difficulty caused by lack of a central power, were vivid, and he wrote vigorously to his friends of the need of strengthening the government and more closely cementing the states. He attended the Federal Convention reluctantly, but as was characteristic when once he decided to do a thing, he gave to the work his full energy and thought. As president of the Convention, possessing the full confidence of every member, he supplied a ground anchor to the proceedings. Much of the confidence afterwards displayed in the Constitution was due to that fact. When its adoption was opposed he admitted that it had imperfections, but maintained that it was the best plan obtainable at that time (*Ibid.,* XI, 205–06; see also a collection of his letters in Max Farrand, ed., *The Records of the Federal Convention,* 1911, vol. III). Since workable machinery was provided for amending the imperfections, his logic was to adopt, and then make the alterations. He saw no choice between this procedure and chaos. In the contest that raged over adoption he expressed two, among many, typically Washingtonian ideas of government. One was that the purpose of the new Constitution was to "establish good order and government and to render the nation happy at home and respected abroad"; and the other, apropos of the theoretical fear of a self-perpetuating president, that "when a people shall have become incapable of governing themselves, and fit for a master, it is of little consequence from what quarter he comes" (Ford, *Writings,* XI, 257). That Washington had completely discarded the idea of monarchy as a just system of government is not open to doubt nor can it be doubted that he was sincere in his belief that the people should govern themselves. He was "sure the mass of citizens in these United States *mean well,* and I firmly believe they will always *act well* whenever they can obtain a right understanding of matters" (*Ibid.,* XIII, 188). Yet it must be admitted that the plan of government which he signed as president of the Federal Convention provided necessary protection for the conservative, property-owning class of citizens and by an elaborate system of counterbalance and check seriously handicapped the common people in exerting much influence upon the course of the government. The explanation of this apparent contradiction lies in the conditions of the time; certainly Washington's justice and honesty are amply proven, and he, less than almost any one else in the Convention, was swayed by considerations of personal property.

Even before the Constitution was adopted, public opinion had fixed on Washington as the first president. He repelled the suggestion when it was made to him and opposed it wherever he decently could. Fame he had never coveted and the purely military ambition of his youth had long since been burned out, as he had gained close acquaintance with the scourge of war. At the age of fifty-six he had no "wish beyond that of living and dying an honest man on my own farm" (Ford, *Writings*, XI, 258). The sense of humor with which he was liberally endowed was usually flavored late in life with a sardonic saltiness, the result of the long, bitter years of the war. "My movements to the chair of government," he wrote, after he had decided to accept and the unanimous election had settled the matter, "will be accompanied by feelings not unlike those of a culprit, who is going to the place of his execution"; for he realized that he was "embarking the voice of the people, and a good name of my own, on this voyage; but what returns will be made for them, Heaven alone can foretell" (*Ibid.*, XI, 379–80). He was sure of his own integrity and firmness, but he could not think with calmness of the possibility of appearing in the light of a bungler and an incompetent. The fortunate outcome of the Revolution, in which he had risked not only his reputation but also his life and fortune, was due, he believed, to the interposition of Providence, and his self-abnegation prevented him from taking credit for the victory. He regarded the Revolution as a great movement of a people and was content with the thought that he had played his part therein with honor. He was as doubtful of his ability to administer the government successfully as he had been of his ability to command the army successfully, and, having already seen the lengths to which partisanship, prejudice, and jealousy could go, he was well aware that this new task would be difficult.

Being unwilling to leave Virginia to become president of the United States with several debts against him, he was compelled to borrow money to clear up local obligations and pay his traveling expenses to the seat of government. He took the oath of office Apr. 30, 1789, on the balcony of the United States Building in New York (the site of the Washington statue, at the old Sub-Treasury building) and delivered his inaugural address in the Senate chamber before both houses of Congress. In it he declined a salary, as he had done when elected commander in chief, but Congress later voted $25,000 annually for the presi-

dent. Washington accepted this amount for defraying the expenses incident to the office, which in his case exceeded it. The realization that the motive of his every action could be subject to a double interpretation and that by his conduct in any instance he might create a precedent, did not tend to lessen the strain upon his fifty-seven years. In the Revolutionary War he had passed through a long siege of emotional repression, which was part of the price he paid for victory, and he was not quite ready to subject his temper to the same sort of strain, if it could be avoided. He was tired; the tinsel and power of high office did not appeal; and his honesty of thought did not permit him to discount the heavy responsibilities of the presidency. Nothing but that same rigorous sense of duty which had carried him through the Revolution could have drawn him again into public life.

Organizing and coordinating the various parts of the governmental machine and appointing the necessary officials occupied the better part of the year 1789; and in this Washington moved with steady caution. As was natural, he thought first of the men whose measure he had taken during the Revolution. Few offers of high place were made without reasonable confidence, or assurance, that they would be accepted and in these offers Washington's personality counted more heavily with the individuals approached than the power or honor that were involved. Even in the minor appointments, Washington moved cautiously. "A single disgust," he wrote, "excited in a particular State, on this account, might perhaps raise a flame of opposition that could not easily, if ever, be extinguished. . . . Perfectly convinced I am, that if injudicious or unpopular measures should be taken by the executive under the new government, with regard to appointments, the government itself would be in the utmost danger of being utterly subverted by those measures" (Ford, *Writings*, XI, 368). When Congress adjourned in September, Washington toured the New England states in an effort to learn for himself the feeling of the people of that region toward the new government. This tour was productive of little other than a warm welcome from the inhabitants and an unnecessary test of official strength between the President of the United States and Gov. John Hancock [*q.v.*] of Massachusetts, in which the latter came off second best, to the great glee of the citizens of Boston.

The pressing domestic problem was that of attaining financial stability for the nation; this necessarily involved the encouragement of manufacturing and commerce. Besides the existence of commercial restrictions, the retention of the western posts by Great Britain constituted the main foreign problem. Nearly every difficulty which developed bitterness during Washington's two administrations seems to have taken its start from a ramification of one or the other of these problems. Divergent theories of government were the basis of the struggle between Hamilton and Jefferson [*qq.v.*] out of which the well-defined Federalist and Republican groups emerged, but personal factors were evident to Washington. In the Revolution he had wasted no time on anything personal and he could not conceive of anything being more important than the question of national independence; so now as president he could not conceive of a personal quarrel being more important than the task of establishing the government on a firm foundation. To him that task was so formidable as to require the aid of every man, and the only parties he recognized, in his singleness of purpose, were those which supported the government, and the group which, for considerations of private advantage, opposed it. Yet for all his uncompromising attitude toward those things which interfered with the development of nationality, his forbearance toward both Jefferson and Hamilton seems that of a wise parent toward wayward sons. He pleaded with both men to compromise, convinced that the country needed their services, and a fair indication of his estimate of both may be gathered from the character of the plea which he made to each (Ford, *Writings*, XII, 174–79).

Methods and means of strengthening the government were in Washington's view debatable, but not the strengthening itself. All during the Revolution he had labored to dissolve local prejudice of every kind, and to substitute for the provincialism he found in the army a national pride and fellowship in being an American. Despite the acknowledgment that he had failed in this, his efforts had borne some fruit as the soldier returned to civil life at the expiration of his term, carrying with him the somewhat broadened view, which he had acquired almost unconsciously and which leavened, to an extent, the ideas of the people among whom he lived. The first displays of military force by the new government proved disastrous. Both Harmar's and St. Clair's expeditions against the Indians failed; but Washington proudly repelled covert suggestions that Great Britain was willing to cooperate against the savages. His purpose was to "keep the United States free from political connexions with *every* other country, to see them independent of *all* and under the influence of

none. In a word, I want an *American* character that the powers of Europe may be convinced we act for *ourselves*, and not for *others*" (Ford, *Writings*, XIII, 119–20).

The display of political partisanship on the part of the Hamilton-Jefferson factions was an influence in Washington's decision to serve a second term, when his overwhelming desire was to spend the remainder of his life in peace and quiet at "Mount Vernon"; but the foreign situation was undoubtedly the main factor in his decision. France's declaration of war on Great Britain stirred up an emotional enthusiasm that was easily developed into criticism of the President's neutrality, and from criticism to opposition to other acts of his administration. Though sympathizing with the French revolutionists at first, Washington was keenly aware of probable developments. As early as 1789 he saw that the disturbance in France was a "revolution . . . of too great magnitude to be effected in so short a space with the loss of so little blood" (Ford, *Writings*, XI, 435), and when the expected excesses began he speedily sickened of the spectacle. He was unopposed in his reëlection, but during his second term he was subjected to the heaviest strains and to villification and abuse which went beyond the bounds of common decency. Washington believed that twenty years of tranquillity would make the United States strong enough to "bid defiance in a just cause to any power whatever" (*Ibid.*, XIII, 151). He could not comprehend an attitude that could place any other problem ahead of this. In this light must be viewed all his decisions, which were strongly Federalist; they were moves designed to strengthen the national government.

The somewhat hysterical criticism of Washington's official formality and dignified, presidential ceremonial was similar to the democratic opposition he had encountered in establishing discipline in the Continental Army. In 1775 discipline was necessary to make the army efficient, in 1789–90 official ceremony was necessary to insure respect for the new government and clothe it with authoritative dignity. Without precedent to guide him, Washington was feeling his way carefully toward a goal which was as clear to him as was the goal of victory in the Revolutionary War. He defined it in his fifth annual message to Congress. "There is a rank due to the United States among nations, which will be withheld if not absolutely lost, by the reputation of weakness" (Ford, *Writings*, XII, 352). His whole course as president was governed by the purpose of obtaining that rank for the United States. The national bank, the excise tax, and the development of the army and navy into permanent, trained organizations, all common-sense projects of value to the nation, yet gave rise to feelings of uneasiness in many honest but provincial-minded men, who in some instances followed the lead of the unscrupulous. The proclamation of neutrality (1793) and the arrival of Genet [q.v.] furnished an exceptional opportunity to embarrass the administration and to demonstrate sympathy for the French. Genet's recall was finally demanded and all the political frenzy that centered around him subsided with unexpected rapidity. The French danger past, there yet remained the British commercial restrictions, while their retention of the western posts and encouragement of the Indians were also matters demanding prompt and careful attention. Wayne's crushing defeat of the savages at Fallen Timbers eliminated the immediate Indian problem in 1794. To attempt a settlement of the other questions Washington appointed John Jay [q.v.] envoy extraordinary to Great Britain.

Domestic trouble of a serious kind arose in Pennsylvania over resistance to the excise tax. This, the so-called Whiskey Rebellion, was a popular defiance of the tax collectors, accompanied by rioting and violence. It demonstrated that the same state indifference to the national welfare, which had increased Washington's difficulties in the Revolution fourfold, was still to be reckoned with, for, the tax being a federal one and the collection of it a federal matter, Pennsylvania's governor virtually ignored the situation. In the face of growing opposition, which seemed to Washington not a mere natural objection to a tax but a movement sponsored by the democratic societies to overthrow the government (Ford, *Writings,* XII, 451–52, 454–55), he was not at all confident of commanding sufficient support to suppress the outbreak of violence, and when the militia responded to his call with heartening alacrity and spirit his relief was great. The rebellion collapsed and the ringleaders were seized. Again Washington displayed that broad understanding which he had manifested in his attitude toward the Loyalists in the Revolution and toward the malcontents of Shays's Rebellion; he felt that the country could not afford to lose such a number of inhabitants by harsh measures of reprisal. In a short time he granted full pardon to all the insurgents who had signed the oath of submission and allegiance to the United States.

In the year 1795, by the Pinckney Treaty, the southern boundary of the United States was established and the coveted navigation of the Mississippi was secured, with port facilities at New Orleans. Offsetting this came the outburst of criticism over the Jay Treaty. Less than a year after the ratification of the treaty it became plain that none of the dire predictions of its opponents had come true; trade was actually improving and before a year was out the hysterical opposition had subsided. The treaty was no more satisfactory to Washington than to its critics (Ford, *Writings,* XIII, 63–66). Even on some of the points which he considered of prime importance it was not as definite as he desired; but he thought it was the best treaty that could be obtained at the time and it did settle the particular matters in controversy with Great Britain which would have made war probable had they remained in controversy much longer. He withstood this storm of opposition as he had withstood others, confident of his integrity of purpose and sure that the honor and welfare of the nation were served; but he likened the bitter attack to a cry against a mad dog, couched in "such exaggerated and indecent terms as could scarcely be applied to a Nero, a notorious defaulter, or even to a common pickpocket" (*Ibid.,* XIII, 76, 231). To the demand of the House of Representatives for the papers relating to Jay's negotiations he firmly refused to yield, being convinced that what the House really wanted was to establish the precedent that its concurrence was necessary in treaty making. His firmness settled the matter and the question has not been raised since.

In his first administration he had mentioned to Jefferson that he "really felt himself growing old, his bodily health less firm, his memory, always bad, becoming worse, and perhaps the other faculties of his mind showing a decay to others of which he was insensible himself" (P. L. Ford, *The Writings of Thomas Jefferson,* I, 1892, p. 175). In 1796 he set about the preparation of an address that would announce to the people his determination to retire from public life. The increasing weight of years admonished him that retirement was as necessary as it would be welcome. Solicitude for the welfare of the nation to which he had given so much of his thought and strength led him to take advantage of the opportunity to give the disinterested advice "of a parting friend, who can possibly have no personal motive to bias his counsels" (Ford, *Writings,* XIII, 285). He knew, however, that in announcing his retirement he risked being charged with a "conviction of fallen popularity, and despair of being re-elected" (*Ibid.,* XIII, 192).

He had assumed the presidency when the United States was little but a name, without power, prestige, or credit; when he retired from office the country was well on the road to international importance. He had given it dignity, as when he rebuked the French minister for presumption in a diplomatic negotiation (1791) and demanded the recall of Genet; he had demonstrated its power by crushing the Indians and suppressing the Whiskey Rebellion; and he had firmly fixed its credit, through Alexander Hamilton. Treaties with Spain and Great Britain had amicably settled the questions of the navigation of the Mississippi and the Florida and eastern boundaries. For the prosperity of the country he had worked unremittingly, and, though he abhorred war, none knew better than he that unpreparedness added to its horrors. In his first annual message to Congress he enunciated the principle: "To be prepared for war is one of the most effectual means of preserving peace" (Ford, *Writings,* XI, 456). The Farewell Address is partly an explanation of his course as president, with main emphasis upon the necessity of a firm union and a strong central government, for which he had labored incessantly the major part of his public life, and which were not in 1796 so taken for granted as they have finally come to be. Respect for the authority of that government and a solemn warning against the spirit of party he made equally important. The activities of political parties which came under Washington's observation were directed, he thought, solely to the subversion of good government, to a usurpation of power for personal ends, and would logically result in the loss of liberty. Morality and education were urged as necessities for a people's happiness, prosperity, and safety; good faith and justice toward all nations, but favors to none, were enjoined, and a warning was given against the insidious wiles of foreign influence. He hoped that these counsels would "be productive of some partial benefit; some occasional good; that they may now and then recur to moderate the fury of party spirit, to warn against the mischiefs of foreign intrigue, to guard against the impostures of pretended patriotism" (*Ibid.,* XIII, 320).

Washington's steadfast fortitude under the most trying difficulties is to be attributed largely to an unusual knowledge of self. No one would have yielded more quickly, he said, to a standard of infallibility in public matters, had there been such a thing; but lacking that, "upright intentions and close investigation" were his guides (Ford, *Writings,* XIII, 105). Dominated by the single idea and purpose of finding out, if possible, what was of greatest benefit to the nation, and bending all his energies toward accomplish-

ing it, Washington could not comprehend acts of opposition to his carefully considered measures as anything other than so many attempts to destroy the government. Brissot de Warville stated that he never saw Washington "divest himself of that coolness by which he is characterized, and become warm, but when speaking of the present state of America" (*Nouveau Voyage dans les États Unis . . . en 1788,* 1791, Vol. II, 269).

Duty, with Washington, became a moral obligation which was not to be evaded even by honorable means; and the barest outline of his spiritual development reveals the heavy sacrifice of personal inclination to that obligation. Resigning his first military commission in 1754, with no expectation of again entering upon a military career, he was unexpectedly appointed an aide by Braddock, and after Braddock's death he was appointed by Dinwiddie to protect the Virginia frontier; resigning again in 1758 to marry Mrs. Custis, he was appointed to command the American armies at the outbreak of the Revolution; resigning at the end of that war, he confidently expected to live the remainder of his life untroubled by public cares; drafted against his will to be president of the United States, he wished to retire in 1793, but was forced by circumstances to remain; retiring in 1797, as he hoped for good, he was again forced to accept command of the army that was being raised in expectation of war with France in 1798. Half his life was spent fulfilling what he conceived to be his duty at the expense of his domestic ease and happiness. He calmly analyzed the opposition to Adams' administration in 1798–99, as hanging upon and clogging the wheels of government, "Torturing every act, by unnatural construction, into a design to violate the Constitution—Introduce Monarchy—& to establish an aristocracy." Yet he was still able to "Hope well, because I have always believed, and trusted, that that Providence which has carried us through a long and painful War with one of the most powerful nations in Europe, will not suffer the discontented among ourselves to produce more than a temporary interruption to the permanent Peace and happiness of this rising Empire" (Ford, *Writings,* XIV, 142–43). President Adams, following popular will, appointed Washington lieutenant-general and commander in chief of the army it seemed necessary to raise. He accepted, with the understanding that he would not take the field until the troops actually were raised and equipped. He insisted on Hamilton's being second in command, and a heated contest of wills between him and Adams ensued. In the end

Adams gave in, but the Provisional Army was not needed and was never personally commanded by Washington. Under pressure of danger to his beloved country the military fire of the Revolution had flamed again, though Washington's steadfast conviction was that war was an unmitigated evil. Changing conditions in France steadily reduced the chance of conflict and Washington once more allotted a greater and greater part of his time to the management of "Mount Vernon." He was not granted opportunity to bring his farms to the point of efficiency he planned, though he had worked out a scheme of rotation of crops in his fields that carried over into the nineteenth century.

His death occurred with startling suddenness. A neglected cold developed into a malignant type of cynache trachealis with which the limited medical knowledge and skill of the time were unable to cope. With his physical strength sapped by mistaken blood-lettings, he fought a losing battle for nearly twenty-four hours. The philosophical calm of his remark that it was "the debt which we all must pay," was only exceeded by the high courage of his declaration, toward the end, "I am not afraid to go" (Ford, *Writings*, XIV, 249). He died at 11:30, Saturday, Dec. 14, 1799. The physical hardships of the Virginia colonial warfare and the later strains of the Revolution had much to do with his final collapse. Though he was a physical giant, over six feet in height and weighing 190 to 200 pounds, with no surplus flesh, he drove himself unsparingly and often beyond his strength; a check-up of the number of letters written daily from headquarters and consideration of the other daily, necessary business justifies the conclusion that, during the Revolutionary War, Washington seldom obtained more than three or four hours of consecutive sleep in any twenty-four.

All contemporaneous descriptions of Washington's appearance agree as to his dignity and impressiveness, many of them enthusiastically so, but Capt. George Mercer, his aide in the Virginia colonial service before Washington obtained world-wide fame, penned a description in 1760 which still remains the best. His frame, Mercer said, gave the impression of great muscular strength. "His bones and joints are large as are his hands and feet . . . rather long arms and legs . . . all the muscles of his face under perfect control, though flexible and expressive of deep feeling when moved by emotion. In conversation he looks you full in the face, is deliberate, deferential and engaging. His voice is agreeable . . . he is a splendid horseman" (P. L.

Ford, *George Washington,* 20 ed., pp. 38–39). An anonymous writer stated that his smile was extraordinarily attractive. His personal charm is attested in many letters of his friends, in the expressed regret of the Virginia colonial officers, on his resignation, at the loss of "such a sincere Friend, and so affable a Companion" (*Writings,* Bicentennial ed., II, 316 n.), in the farewell to his officers, and in the Virginia woman's remark to her friend, that when General Washington becomes "the chatty agreeable Companion, he can be down right impudent sometimes; such impudence, Fanny, as you and I like" (Ford, *George Washington,* 20 ed., p. 110). Add to this the French abbé's note that "The Americans, that cool and sedate people . . . are roused, animated, and inflamed at the very mention of his name" (Abbé C. C. Robin, *New Travels Through North America,* 1783, p. 35), and we have an approximation of the feeling of the people toward him. Leaders of the time, and Washington would have been the last to have denied the value of their assistance, followed and supported him with confidence and enthusiasm: Greene, Sullivan, Wayne in the army; Hamilton, Wolcott, Jay, and Pickering in civil authority. Curiously, the men who opposed him were generally those whose personal ambitions were dependent upon the success of that opposition.

The evolution of Washington's fame until his name was placed high upon the scroll of the world's great, began in 1776–77, when the victories of Trenton and Princeton focused European attention on the hopeless-looking struggle of American backwoodsmen with the most powerful nation in the world. The addition of France to that struggle insured Europe's careful watchfulness of every phase of the conflict and, as Lord John Russell put it, "The success of America was owing, next to the errors of her adversaries, to the conduct and character of General Washington" (*Memorials and Correspondence of Charles James Fox,* Vol. I, 1853, p. 153). Liberty, the basis of the American struggle, was becoming more than an academic definition in European thought and Washington perfectly personified the awakening. As Chateaubriand aptly said (*Travels in America and Italy,* Eng. ed., 1828, vol. I, 106): "He aimed at that which it was his duty to aim at . . . blended his existence with that of his country. . . . The name of Washington will spread with liberty from age to age."

[The miscellaneous Washington MSS. in the Lib. of Cong. are bound in 302 vols., the original letter-books in 35 additional vols., original diaries and account books in over 50 vols., and the contemporaneous Varick

Transcript of Washington's letters during the Revolutionary War in 44 vols. Of Washington letters elsewhere, the Lib. of Cong. possesses 21 boxes and a number of bound volumes of photostats. There are also numerous volumes of copies of miscellaneous Washington records, the originals of some of which cannot now be traced. Numerous letters from and to Washington are in the Continental Congress MSS. in the Lib. of Cong., so that the Washington papers in that library are a more nearly complete collection than that of any other distinguished American. The mass of them is, however, so vast that no comprehensive or complete publication was attempted prior to the Bicentennial ed. of his *Writings*, begun in 1931 (*post*). J. C. Fitzpatrick, *Calendar of the Correspondence of George Washington . . . with the Continental Congress* (1906), and *Calendar of the Correspondence of George Washington . . . with the Officers* (4 vols., 1915), have been published.

W. C. Ford, *The Writings of George Washington* (14 vols., 1889–93) is the most useful edition, but must be supplemented by that of Jared Sparks (12 vols., 1834–37), which contains some hundreds of letters omitted in the Ford ed., and by J. C. Fitzpatrick, ed., *The Diaries of George Washington* (4 vols., 1925). The Sparks ed. suffers from unjustifiable textual alterations and unnoted omissions. Both the Ford and Sparks eds. are being supplanted by *The Writings of George Washington. . . . Prepared under the Direction of the U. S. George Washington Bicentennial Commission* (1931), ed. by J. C. Fitzpatrick, which will probably extend to 30 vols.; it will be the first complete ed. of Washington's letters. Other valuable sources in print are: S. M. Hamilton, *Letters to Washington, 1752–1775* (4 vols., 1898–1902); Jared Sparks, *Correspondence of the Am. Revolution; Being Letters of Eminent Men to George Washington* (4 vols., 1853); *George Washington's Accounts of Expenses while Commander-in-Chief* (Facsim., 1917), with annotations by J. C. Fitzpatrick; *Letters from His Excellency George Washington, to Arthur Young . . . and Sir John Sinclair* (1803 and other eds.); M. D. Conway, *George Washington and Mount Vernon* (1889), mainly agricultural letters to William Pearce and James Anderson (in vol. IV of the *Memoirs of the Long Island Hist. Soc.*); *Letters from George Washington to Tobias Lear . . . from the Collection of Mr. William K. Bixby* (1905). J. D. Richardson, *A Compilation of the Messages and Papers of the Presidents*, vol. I (1896), gives the texts of the important communications to Congress. Washington's travels through the United States are described in J. C. Fitzpatrick, *George Washington, Colonial Traveller, 1732–75* (1927); W. S. Baker, *Itinerary of General George Washington . . . 1775 to 1783* (1892), and *Washington after the Revolution, MDCCLXXXIV–MDCCXCIX* (1898).

Nearly every biographer of Washington has fallen under the spell to which Sparks succumbed and has followed, more or less, the example set by the latter in idealizing the man, though some recent biographies have gone to the other extreme. Mention should be made of M. L. Weems, *A History, of the Life and Death, Virtues, and Exploits, of General George Washington* (1800), though no reliance should be placed on this famous work. Washington Irving, *Life of George Washington* (5 vols., 1855–59) is satisfactory from most viewpoints, though its reliance on Sparks lessens the confidence it would otherwise command; John Marshall, *The Life of George Washington* (5 vols., 1804–07) ranks with Irving, but its Federalist bias during the presidential period should be discounted; Vol. I (1837) of Sparks's ed. of the *Writings* is given over to a life of Washington, the interpretations of which must be used with caution. W. R. Thayer, *George Washington* (1922) is an orthodox life; Woodrow Wilson, *George Washington* (1903), is clear and readable but is also an orthodox interpretation; H. C. Lodge, *George Washington* (2 vols., 1898), is more expansive than Thayer and Wilson, but like them is based upon the partial publications of the *Writings*; Norman Hap-

good, *George Washington* (1901), is a modern treatment of merit; Rupert Hughes, *George Washington* (3 vols., 1926–30) should be used with great caution, but contains bibliographical aids of unusual value; P. L. Ford, *The True George Washington* (1896), republished as *George Washington* (1924), a refreshing study of Washington from various angles, contains a wealth of interesting material which is unnoted as to source and difficult to trace; J. C. Fitzpatrick, *George Washington Himself* (1933), written from his manuscripts, presents many hitherto undeveloped sides of Washington's character. Other recent biographies are S. M. Little, *George Washington* (1929); L. M. Sears, *George Washington* (1932).

G. W. P. Custis, *Recollections and Private Memoirs of Washington* (1861) is the source of most of the unprovable traditions about Washington; B. J. Lossing, *Mount Vernon and Its Associations* (1886), is somewhat more dependable than Custis. The following studies of special phases of Washington's life can be used with confidence: P. L. Haworth, *George Washington, Farmer* (1915), republished as *George Washington, Country Gentleman* (1925); T. G. Frothingham, *Washington, Commander in Chief* (1930); H. L. Ritter, *Washington as a Business Man* (1931); W. C. Ford, *Washington as an Employer and Importer of Labor* (1889); J. H. Penniman, *George Washington as Man of Letters* (1918); P. L. Ford, *Washington and the Theatre* (1899); J. M. Toner, *General Washington as an Inventor* (1892); C. H. Ambler, *George Washington and the West* (1936). J. C. Fitzpatrick, *The George Washington Scandals* (1929), among other things, fixes the authorship of the "Spurious Letters." Stephen Decatur, Jr., *Private Affairs of George Washington from the Records and Accounts of Tobias Lear, 1789–92* (1933), is the cash account of the President's expenses and the only financial record (except the *Accounts of Expenses while Commander-in-Chief, ante*) so far published. H. B. Carrington, *Battles of the American Revolution* (1876) supplies collateral background for the military side; J. C. Fitzpatrick, *The Spirit of the Revolution* (1924) furnishes details of Continental Army headquarters and of Washington's aides; Paul Wilstach, *Mount Vernon* (1930), is useful to any study of Washington's home life. E. E. Prussing, *The Estate of George Washington* (1927), is an able analysis of Washington's fortune. The best genealogy is in volume XIV of Ford's ed. of the *Writings*, which should be supplemented by the material in *Hist. of the U. S. George Washington Bicentennial Celebration, Literature Series* (1932), vol. III. This series also contains many full texts and extracts, carefully compared in most instances with the manuscripts of Washington's letters and state papers.

The number of portraits of Washington is amazing, yet the really reliable portraits are few. Not all the artists who painted or sketched him from life were competent, and their results are heterogeneous and largely mediocre, while the work of those who never saw him can only be classified as efforts of enthusiastic imagination. The Houdon bust, modeled from life at "Mount Vernon," and Gilbert Stuart's Boston Athenæum portrait are beyond just criticism. Other portraits by Stuart, notably the Channing-Gibbs, and some of Trumbull's work, the St. Memin print, and Sharples' best profile also deserve consideration. See Gustav Eisen, *Portraits of Washington* (3 vols., 1932).]

J. C. F—k.

WASHINGTON, HENRY STEPHENS

(Jan. 15, 1867–Jan. 7, 1934), petrologist, son of George and Eleanor Phoebe (Stephens) Washington, was born in Newark and brought up at Locust, N. J. He attended private schools and prepared for college under tutors. Graduated from Yale in 1886, he was a fellow in physics there for the next two years and then spent six years traveling and studying in the West Indies, Europe, Egypt, Algeria, and Asia Minor, in five of these years being enrolled as a member of the American School of Classical Studies at Athens. His interest in archaeology was permanent, and he repeatedly applied chemical and petrographical methods to the study of its special problems.

During this same period, he studied the volcanic islands scattered through the Grecian and Turkish archipelagoes, developing keen interest in the igneous rocks of the earth's crust. He subsequenly visited many other volcanic islands of the eastern Mediterranean and published a series of petrographic papers on their lavas. Two semesters at the University of Leipzig under the great petrographer Zirkel brought him in 1893 the degree of Ph.D., for his researches on the volcanoes of the Kula Basin in Lydia, near Smyrna. On Oct. 25 of that year he married Martha Rose Beckwith, from whom he was divorced about 1914; there were no children.

In 1895 Washington returned to the United States and after a year as assistant in mineralogy at Yale took possession of the old homestead at Locust, N. J., transforming the smokehouse into a laboratory. For the next ten years there came from this isolated source a constant stream of notable contributions to petrology. In 1899 he became associated with Joseph P. Iddings, Louis V. Pirsson [qq.v.], and Whitman Cross in formulating a systematic classification of igneous rocks based primarily upon chemical composition (*Quantitative Classification of Igneous Rocks,* 1903). In 1904 he published *Manual of the Chemical Analysis of Rocks* (4th ed., 1930), which became a standard handbook, used throughout the world. A major and permanent contribution to petrology was his compilation, *Chemical Analyses of Igneous Rocks, Published from 1884 to 1913, Inclusive, with a Critical Discussion of the Character and Use of Analyses* (1917), a revision and enlargement of an earlier work issued in 1903. The 1917 edition contains 8,600 analyses, all of them rated by Washington as "superior," arranged according to the system of classification of which he was co-author. In 1904 he published *The Superior Analyses of Igneous Rocks from Roth's Tabellen, 1869 to 1884,* also grouped according to the new system. These great collections are known to every petrologist in the world.

During the years 1906 to 1912 financial reverses made it necessary for Washington to serve as geological consultant in mining and other enterprises, but in 1912 he accepted a position in the Geophysical Laboratory of the Carnegie Institution of Washington, D. C., and in

this favorable environment resumed his analytical work with redoubled energy. The list of his publications from the Carnegie Institution, including a number of studies prepared in collaboration with others, embraces one hundred titles. As his interest concentrated upon the distinctive characters of igneous rocks of certain regions, he explored Etna and other Italian volcanoes, the older igneous formations of Sardinia, the Deccan Traps of western and central India, and the Hawaiian Islands. Specimens of igneous rocks from Siberia, Eastern China, Iceland, Greenland, and scattered islets of the Atlantic Ocean, the Pribilof Islands in Bering Sea, the Galapagos group, San Felix and San Ambrosio in the South Pacific all yielded information. His "Petrology of the Hawaiian Islands," an important contribution (published in five parts, 1923–26, in the *American Journal of Science*), contained sixty-six new complete analyses made by Washington and his assistants.

His great store of information concerning the chemical and mineral composition of igneous rocks of the globe, surpassing that of any other student of the subject, led him inevitably to make generalizations regarding the rocky crust of the earth. His study, "The Chemistry of the Earth's Crust" (*Journal of the Franklin Institute,* December 1920), republished in the *Annual Report* of the Smithsonian Institution for 1920, was followed by *The Composition of the Earth's Crust* (1924), prepared in collaboration with F. W. Clarke. Many honors came to him: he was chairman (1926–29) of the division of volcanology of the American Geophysical Union, 1926–29, and vice-president (1922–23) of the section on volcanology of the International Geophysical Union, a member of the National Academy of Sciences and the American Philosophical Society, vice-president (1922) of the Geological Society of America, president (1924) of the Mineralogical Society of America, and a member of the Archaeological Institute of America. In 1918–19 he was a scientific attaché at the American embassy in Rome. His work in Italy brought him a decoration from the Italian government, and he held memberships in numerous foreign scientific bodies.

[Printed accounts include: *Who's Who in America,* 1932–33; *Am. Men of Science,* 1933; *Yale Univ. Obit. Record,* 1934; J. V. Lewis, in *Am. Mineralogist,* Mar. 1935; C. N. Fenner, in *Science,* Jan. 19, 1934; *Washington Post,* Jan. 8, 1934. A memoir by Whitman Cross, for the National Academy of Sciences, is in preparation.]
W. C.

WASHINGTON, JOHN MACRAE (October 1797–Dec. 24, 1853), soldier, the second son of Baily and Euphan (Wallace) Washington, was born on his father's estate, "Windsor Forest," in Stafford County, Va. His father was a second cousin of George Washington [*q.v.*]. On Oct. 24, 1814, John became a cadet at the United States Military Academy, where he was graduated July 17, 1817, and appointed third lieutenant of artillery. His first service was in Charleston Harbor, S. C., with the 3rd Artillery, during which he was promoted second lieutenant and appointed battalion quartermaster of artillery, Mar. 20, 1818. In this capacity he served until he was promoted first lieutenant, May 23, 1820, and sent to the Florida frontier.

Under the reorganization of the army, he was transferred to the 4th Artillery, June 1, 1821, and served successively at Savannah Harbor (1821–22), Fort Moultrie (1822–24), and Augusta, Ga. (1824). While at the last station, he was detailed as instructor of mathematics at the artillery school at Fort Monroe, Va., where he remained until 1826. The next year he served at Fort Marion, Fla., and then returned to Fort Monroe as ordnance officer, which post he held until 1833. On May 23, 1830, he was brevetted a captain for ten years' faithful service in one grade (an empty method employed by the government to overcome slow promotion), and on May 30, 1832, was regularly promoted a captain. From 1833 to 1838 he was engaged in the Creek and Florida wars, taking an active part in the battle of Lochahatchee against the Seminoles. During 1838 and 1839, as an assistant quartermaster, he aided Gen. Winfield Scott [*q.v.*] in the delicate task of transporting the Cherokee nation to Oklahoma, and in the prosecution of the Florida War. After duty at the instruction camp, Trenton, N. J., he was again detailed to assist Scott in the even more delicate undertaking of peacefully quelling the Canadian border disturbances, and was at Dearbornville, Mich., Detroit, and Buffalo, N. Y., until 1842. After the success of Scott's mission, he served successively at Fort McHenry, Md., and Carlisle Barracks, Pa., until 1846.

When the Mexican War began he was placed in command of a light battery of eight guns and joined the forces under Gen. John E. Wool [*q.v.*] which made the heroic, bloodless, and successful march through unbroken country from San Antonio, Tex., to Saltillo, Mexico. On the first day of the battle of Buena Vista, Feb. 22, 1847, General Wool placed Washington's battery on the right flank of the army, at the critical pass of La Angostura. Washington's deft and determined management of his command was the chief factor in repelling the vigorous attacks of overwhelming numbers of Mexicans. On the sec-

ond day of the battle, when three regiments of Illinois and Kentucky troops retreated in disorder, he held fast and not only saved the lives of many of the fleeing volunteers, but maintained the key point of the American position by his stanchness and skill. Although six days before this action he had been regularly promoted a major, the news of his commission had not reached him. On Feb. 23, 1847, he was brevetted a lieutenant-colonel for gallant and meritorious conduct in the battle. From June 24 to Dec. 14, 1847, he acted as governor of Saltillo, and during much of the same period was chief of artillery of Wool's division and of the army of occupation. He was then placed in command of the expedition to Santa Fé, and served as civil and military governor of New Mexico from October 1848 until Oct. 23, 1849.

After the cessation of hostilities he served at Fort Constitution, N. H., from 1850 to 1852. In 1853 he embarked with the 3rd Artillery on the steamer *San Francisco,* for transportation to duty on the west coast. In a violent storm off the mouth of the Delaware, he, with three other officers and 178 men, was washed overboard and drowned. In his early career he had married Fanny Macrae, daughter of Dr. Jack Macrae, a nephew of Col. William, brother of Baily Washington. To this union were born three children.

[Sources include F. B. Heitman, *Hist. Reg. and Dict. U. S. Army* (1903); T. H. S. Hamersly, *Complete Regular Army Reg. of the U. S., 1779–1879* (1881); G. W. Cullum, *Biog. Reg. . . . U. S. Mil. Acad.,* vol. I (1879); J. H. Smith, *The War with Mexico* (1919); H. E. Hayden, *Va. Genealogies* (1891); T. A. Washington, *A Geneal. Hist. Beginning with Col. John Washington, the Emigrant . . .* (1891); *Proc. at the Inauguration of the Monument Erected by the Washington Light Infantry to the Memory of Col. William Washington* (1858). The middle name of Washington is that given by the *Va. Mag. of Hist. and Biog.,* Oct. 1914, supported by Heitman; some sources give Marshall.]

W. A. G.

WATERHOUSE, BENJAMIN (Mar. 4, 1754–Oct. 2, 1846), physician and pioneer vaccinator in America, was born at Newport, R. I., one of eleven children of Timothy and Hannah (Proud) Waterhouse. His father, a chair-maker, grandson of Richard Waterhouse who emigrated to Boston in 1669 and later settled in Portsmouth, N. H., is said to have been judge of the court of common pleas and a member of the royal council of the colony. His mother, Quaker-born in Yorkshire, England, was a cousin of Dr. John Fothergill, an eminent practitioner of London. Influenced by a number of learned Scotch physicians practising at Newport and by the reading of medical books in the library of Abraham Redwood [*q.v.*], Waterhouse was soon drawn to medicine. At the age of sixteen he apprenticed himself to Dr. John Halliburton, a surgeon, but he was also taught by Judge Robert Lightfoot, an Oxford graduate, "remarkably well read in Physic." In the portrait of Waterhouse at the age of twenty-two or three, painted by his school friend, Gilbert Stuart, we see a thoughtful student, "pensive but determined-looking and alert," with the "air of a militant Quaker" (Courtney, *post*, p. 2). Early in 1775 he embarked for London, where he made his home for over three years, while attending lectures in medicine, with his kinsman, John Fothergill. During this time he also spent nine months as a medical student in Edinburgh. In 1778 he went to Leyden to acquire, as he later wrote, "a little of the Dutch phlegm" (Waterhouse, *An Essay on Junius,* 1831, p. vi). There he lived with the American ambassador, John Adams, and his two sons. When he matriculated he placed after his name, *Liberae Reipublicae Americanae Foederatae Civis,* an inscription which caused considerable talk, as Waterhouse was the only American student at Leyden and "the British Ambassador at the Court of The Hague domineered the Dutch as if they were English Colonists" (*Ibid.,* p. vi). The Dutch authorities were so cautious that, before he could obtain the *imprimatur* of the university on his inaugural dissertation, *De Sympathia Partium Corporis Humani* (Apr. 19, 1780), he was constrained to add after his name only the word *Americanus.* Waterhouse was an ardent patriot, although never an active participant in political affairs.

Waterhouse returned to America and settled at Newport in June 1782. Upon the establishment of a medical department at Harvard College in 1783, he, one of the best educated physicians in America, accepted the professorship of the theory and practice of physic, and delivered his *Oratio Inauguralis* (not published until 1829) the same year. He was closely associated at first with John Warren [*q.v.*], the professor of anatomy and surgery, and Aaron Dexter, who held the chair of chemistry and materia medica. In 1786 he published the first part of *A Synopsis of a Course of Lectures, on the Theory and Practice of Medicine.* On July 6, 1791, he delivered a discourse at Concord, Mass., on *The Rise, Progress, and Present State of Medicine* (1792) which, with its emphasis on experimental investigation, reveals Waterhouse as a man far in advance of his time.

In 1799, however, came the most important event in his life. In the beginning of this year he received from John Coakley Lettsom, the London physician, a copy of Edward Jenner's *An In-*

quiry into the Causes and Effects of the Variolae Vaccinae (1798). Waterhouse undoubtedly knew of the previous work of another Boston physician, Zabdiel Boylston [*q.v.*], who in 1721 had used inoculations from smallpox pustules to set up a mild form of the disease in an unprotected patient and thus prevent a more serious attack in the future. Since inoculation smallpox was sometimes fatal, the importance of Jenner's cowpox vaccinations lay in the fact that only a mild disease (vaccinia) resulted, although the degree of protection against smallpox was equally great. Waterhouse published a brief account of Jenner's work in the *Columbian Centinel,* Mar. 16, 1799, with the queer title, "Something Curious in the Medical Line," and a few weeks later at a meeting of the American Academy of Arts and Sciences in Boston showed Jenner's book to the members and told of the probable value of the work. After considerable delay, Waterhouse received from England some vaccine in the form of infected threads, and immediately (July 8, 1800) used it on his son, Daniel Oliver Waterhouse, then five years old. As the vaccine pustule went through the various stages described by Jenner, Waterhouse went on to vaccinate another child, a servant boy. The next step was to see if the children were susceptible to smallpox; at Waterhouse's request William Aspinwall [*q.v.*], head of the smallpox hospital in Brookline, inoculated one of the supposedly protected children with smallpox, choosing the servant boy for the experiment. Although the boy's arm became infected with smallpox, there was not the slightest trace of the general disease. Waterhouse, who had followed his own advice and left "the flowery path of speculation" (*The Rise, Progress,* etc., p. 30), wrote of this: "One fact, in such cases, is worth a thousand arguments" (*A Prospect,* etc., 1800, p. 25).

He continued to vaccinate others with cowpox with equally good results. His first report, *A Prospect of Exterminating the Small Pox,* was published within six weeks, Aug. 18, 1800. It contains a clear account of his work, with the logical conclusion that cowpox protected the body from the infection of smallpox. The news of his work soon spread, but unfortunately vaccination was not taken up exclusively by medical men; impure cowpox matter, sometimes mixed with smallpox, was used by "stage-drivers, pedlars, and in one instance the sexton of a church" (*A Prospect,* pt. II, 1802, p. 8). A serious epidemic occurred, a number of people died, and a feeling of resentment against Waterhouse was soon evident. He finally requested (May 31, 1802) the board of health of Boston to make a complete investigation. An experiment with nineteen persons was successfully carried out by a committee of seven outstanding practitioners, including Waterhouse, and the committee concluded that "the cox-pox is a complete security against the small-pox" (*Ibid.*, p. 64). From 1802 on, with the aid of many physicians and public-minded citizens, Waterhouse made vaccination known throughout the neighboring states. President Thomas Jefferson had about two hundred persons vaccinated with vaccine sent him by Waterhouse (*Ibid.*, p. 33). In November 1802 Waterhouse was able to publish part II of *A Prospect,* giving in orderly arrangement the details of his two-year study, and including letters from Jefferson, Benjamin Rush, Jenner, and others. During the next few years he wrote many articles on vaccination for newspapers, particularly the *Columbian Centinel.* It was through his insistence on maintaining the purity of vaccine virus that vaccination was finally placed upon a secure scientific basis in the United States. In 1810 the main facts of his previous publications were abstracted in a pamphlet, *Information Respecting the Origin, Progress, and Efficacy of the Kine Pock Inoculation.* In honor of his work, Waterhouse was made a member of various scientific societies in the United States, Great Britain, and France.

With his most important contribution to medicine accomplished, Waterhouse turned to his other interests. His lecture of Nov. 20, 1804, to the medical students at Harvard College was printed in 1805, *Cautions to Young Persons Concerning Health . . . Shewing the Evil Tendency of the Use of Tobacco . . . with Observations on the Use of Ardent and Vinous Spirits.* This was Waterhouse's most popular book; five editions were published in America, one in London, one in Geneva (in French), and one in Vienna (in German). He felt that the morals of the students of his time had deteriorated, and that the increase in consumption and nervous disorders was the result of intemperance. It probably was a salutary warning at a time when such a caution was needed. In addition to his position in the Harvard Medical School, Waterhouse gave lectures on natural history in general and on mineralogy and botany in particular, first in Rhode Island College (later Brown University) at Providence, R. I. (1784–86), and from 1788 on at Cambridge. A cabinet of mineralogy was sent to him from London by Lettsom and given to Harvard College. His lectures were first published in the *Monthly Anthology* (1804–08), as a pamphlet in 1810, and finally, in part, as *The Botanist* (1811). As early as 1782 he suggested the formation of a humane society in Rhode Island similar to those already active in Europe and in 1785 drew up plans, with Dr. Henry Moyes of Edinburgh, for the Humane Society of the Commonwealth of Massachusetts. After some friction with the other founding members, he gave a discourse, June 8, 1790, on *The Principle of Vitality,* showing the importance of long-continued artificial respiration.

By 1810, however, his relations with his colleagues and the governing board of Harvard College had become strained. The Harvard Medical School at Cambridge lacked clinical facilities; the only patients available for demonstration were in the Boston almshouse, then considered a long distance from Cambridge. Waterhouse was eminently satisfied with his course of didactic lectures at Cambridge and bitterly opposed a move to establish the school in Boston near the contemplated Massachusetts General Hospital, a suggestion made by his more energetic colleague, John Warren. The younger men of the time, particularly John Collins Warren [*q.v.*] and James Jackson, 1777–1867 [*q.v.*], sided with Warren. Waterhouse, "little given to the arts of clinical instruction" (Mumford, *post,* p. 247), endeavored to establish a rival school of medicine in Boston, to be known as the College of Physicians; when this failed, he attempted to damage his colleagues by publishing "false, scandalous, and malicious libels upon the other professors" (*Ibid.*). He was forced to resign in 1812. He had been connected with the United States Marine Hospital since 1808, when he wrote the first *Rules and Orders* for the hospital at Charlestown, Mass., and in 1813 Madison appointed him medical superintendent of all the military posts in New England, a position which he held until 1820. The excellent character of his work can be judged by *A Circular Letter, from Dr. Benjamin Waterhouse, to the Surgeons of the Different Posts* (1817), which concerns the diagnosis and treatment of dysentery.

With an assured income for the time being, Waterhouse turned, except for one publication, *An Essay Concerning Tussis Convulsiva* (1822), towards general literature. An anonymous work is attributed to him, unlike any of his other writtings; the book is a romantic narrative, *A Journal of a Young Man of Massachusetts* (1816), the story of a surgeon captured by the British in the War of 1812 and confined to Dartmoor Prison. There is every evidence that the book was a first-hand account, written by the doctor of a small merchant ship, but Waterhouse may have edited or even augmented the manuscript, as he did with another young man's book published some years later. In 1831 he published *An*

Essay on Junius and his Letters, in which he assigned the authorship of the letters to William Pitt, Earl of Chatham. His last literary undertaking was the editorship of John B. Wyeth's *Oregon* (1833), which he published as a deterrent to western emigrations. Issued when he was nearly eighty, the rather senile moralizing of Waterhouse in this book stands out in marked contrast to the fresh, buoyant narrative of the younger author.

Waterhouse lived in his home on Waterhouse Street, Cambridge, until his death at the age of ninety-two. Burial took place at the Mount Auburn Cemetery. His appearance in younger days may be judged by the Stuart portrait; when he was an older man Holmes noted "his powdered hair and queue, his gold-headed cane, his magisterial air and diction" (*post,* p. 421). He married, first, on June 1, 1788, Elizabeth, the daughter of Andrew and Phoebe (Spooner) Oliver. There were four sons and two daughters. One of the daughters married the younger Henry Ware [*q.v.*]; the other, William Ware [*q.v.*]. Elizabeth Oliver Waterhouse died in 1815, and on Sept. 19, 1819, Waterhouse married Louisa, daughter of Thomas and Judith (Colman) Lee. She survived him, without children, and died in 1863.

[See G. H. Waterhouse, "Descendants of Richard Waterhouse of Portsmouth, N. H.," 3 vols., 1934, typescript in Lib. of Cong. and in New England Historic Genealogical Soc., Boston; *Junius and His Letters* (1831) and *A Prospect of Exterminating the Small-Pox* (2 pts., 1800–02), which contain autobiog. material; T. F. Harrington, *The Harvard Medic. School* (1905), vol. I; H. R. Viets, *A Brief Hist. of Medicine in Mass.* (1930); H. A. Martin, in *N. C. Medic. Jour.,* Jan. 1881; J. G. Mumford, *Surgical Memoirs* (1908); T. J. Pettigrew, *Memoirs of the Life . . . of the Late John Coakley Lettsom* (3 vols., 1817); J. J. Abraham, *Lettsom, His Life and Times* (1933); R. H. Fox, *Dr. John Fothergill and His Friends* (1919); O. W. Holmes, in *Medic. News* (Phila.), Oct. 20, 1883; W. R. Thayer, in *Proc. Mass. Hist. Soc.,* vol. L (1917); vol. LV (1922); W. C. Lane, in *Cambridge Hist. Soc. Pubs.,* vol. IV (1909); W. C. Ford, *Statesman and Friend* (1927); letters and notes in Harvard Coll. Lib., Yale Coll. Lib., Boston Pub. Lib., Boston Medic. Lib., and Mass. Hist. Soc.; town records of Newport, R. I.; *Cambridge Vital Records,* vol. II (1915); "Medic. Lit. of R. I.," *Boston Medic. Intelligencer,* Aug. 3, 1824; *Boston Daily Advertiser, Boston Daily Jour.* (death notice), Oct. 3, 1846. The best accounts of Waterhouse's work on vaccination are by W. M. Welch, in *Proc. Phila. County Medic. Soc.,* vol. VII (1885), and J. W. Courtney, *Benjamin Waterhouse, M.D.* (1926), read before the Fifth Internat. Cong. of the Hist. of Medicine, Geneva, 1926. Family papers in the possession of Mrs. W. R. Thayer of Cambridge, Mass., have also been consulted.]   H.R.V.

WATERHOUSE, FRANK (Aug. 8, 1867– Mar. 20, 1930), capitalist, active in shipping enterprises in the Pacific Northwest, was born in Cheshire, England, the son of Joseph and Mary Elizabeth (Horsfield) Waterhouse. He attended private schools, but at fifteen set out for Amer-

ica, landing in Montreal with fifty dollars in his pocket. He earned a living by hard labor during a good part of the next seven years, working in logging camps and as a hod carrier, and later serving as a constable and deputy sheriff. His wanderings took him into Minnesota and Manitoba. After three years in England, he returned to America, settling in Tacoma, Wash., where in 1893–94 he was a stenographer in the offices of the Northern Pacific Railroad. He then spent a few months selling life insurance, did a record business, and removed to Seattle as a general agent.

In January 1895 he became secretary of the Pacific Navigation Company, which operated a fleet of freight and passenger steamers on Puget Sound, and in May of the same year was appointed general manager. When the rush to the Klondike gold fields began he went to England and organized a company to furnish transportation to the northern British Columbia ports and the Yukon; in 1898 this organization established trading posts on the Yukon. He later purchased the interests of his British associates and formed an American concern, Frank Waterhouse & Company. He introduced the fresh meat business into Alaska and placed the first refrigerator boat on the Yukon.

During the Spanish-American War, he chartered a large fleet of ships for transport service, and nearly all livestock supplies from the Pacific Northwest for the army in the Philippines were shipped in his vessels. He established the first line of steamships to give regular service between Puget Sound and European ports through the Suez Canal, and the first line of freighters from the Sound to Hawaii, New Zealand, Australia, North China, and the Malay Peninsula. During the World War, he engaged in the transportation of military supplies from Seattle to Vladivostok.

Waterhouse had many business interests other than shipping. He organized and was president of Waterhouse & Employes, operating farms in eastern Washington, acquired iron and coal mines, the Arlington Dock Company, and other corporations; and was president of the Yellow and the Seattle taxicab companies. His civic interests were fully as numerous. He was president of the Associated Industries of Seattle, 1919–22, and of the Chamber of Commerce, 1921–22, and chairman of the Seattle chapter of the American Red Cross, 1919–26.

Waterhouse died of heart disease at his home in Seattle. In February 1893 he had married Lucy Dyer Hayden of Tacoma, daughter of John C. Hayden, and he was survived by his widow, one son, and three daughters. Another son, deceased, had been a lieutenant in the Royal (British) Flying Corps in the World War.

[H. K. Hines, *An Illustrated Hist. of the State of Wash.* (1893); *Frank Waterhouse & Company's Pacific Ports* (1914); C. B. Bagley, *Hist. of Seattle* (1916), II, 823; Herbert Hunt and F. C. Kaylor, *Wash. West of the Cascades* (1917), III, 128; C. T. Conover, *Mirrors of Seattle* (1923); C. H. Hanford, *Seattle and Environs* (1924); *Who's Who in America,* 1930–31; *Who's Who in Wash. State,* 1927; *Seattle Daily Times,* Mar. 21, 1930; *Seattle Post-Intelligencer,* Mar. 21 and 23, 1930; *N. Y. Times,* Mar. 21, 1930.]   G. W. F.

WATERHOUSE, SYLVESTER (Sept. 15, 1830–Feb. 12, 1902), educator, publicist, civic leader, was born in Barrington, N. H., the ninth and last child of Dolla (Kingman) and Samuel Ham Waterhouse, a carpenter whose family entered the colonies in 1669 through Richard Waterhouse, tanner and occupant of Pierce's Island near Portsmouth, N. H. A distinguished member of the family was Benjamin Waterhouse [*q.v.*], Harvard medical professor. When he was nine Waterhouse's right leg was amputated as the result of an accident, and while he was still small another injury cost him his left eye. These misfortunes decided him on a life of scholarship. Preparing himself at Phillips Exeter Academy, he entered Dartmouth in March 1851 and the following autumn enrolled in Harvard College, where he distinguished himself in Greek composition and graduated in 1853 with honors. He spent the next two years in the Harvard Law School, from which he received the degree of LL.B. in 1857. He was acting professor of Latin at Antioch College, Yellow Springs, Ohio (1856–57), and instructor in Greek (1857–64), professor of Greek (1864–68), and Collier Professor of Greek (1868–1901) in Washington University, St. Louis, Mo., holding a chair endowed by four of his former students "in grateful recognition" of his "fidelity, learning and ability." An authority on Greek roots, he held this chair until impaired health forced him to retire in 1901 as professor emeritus.

Waterhouse's interests carried him far from the classical subjects he enthusiastically expounded in the classroom. A firm believer in the future of the Middle West, he was an ardent advocate of improving the Mississippi River, attended numerous conventions on river development, and in 1877 was chosen to write an extended memorial to Congress on the subject. He wrote government pamphlets on the cultivation of ramie and jute, and for twenty years urged Southern farmers to diversify their program with these Asiatic crops. He was United States commissioner to the Paris exposition of 1878, honorary commissioner to the New Orleans world's

fair (1884), and Missouri commissioner to the American exposition in London (1887). He was also greatly interested in the proposed Nicaragua canal. He was a member of the Missouri bureau of geology and mines, secretary of the St. Louis board of trade, and secretary of the American Tariff League for Missouri. Upwards of a hundred of his numerous addresses and newspaper articles were published in pamphlets, many in German, French, and Spanish translations. One called *The Resources of Missouri* (1867) was used widely by the state board of immigration to acquaint prospective residents with Missouri. Other pamphlets discussed iron manufacturing, reforestation, trade with Brazil, city parks, western railroads, removal of the national capital, and a barge system on the inland waterways. Waterhouse also wrote on the early history of St. Louis for J. T. Scharf's *History of St. Louis City and County* (2 vols., 1883), and contributed to Hyde and Conard's *Encyclopedia of the History of St. Louis* (4 vols., 1899).

A third serious injury befell him in 1867 when a fall from a carriage brought on a painful spinal trouble. He died of apoplexy following an operation in a St. Louis hospital in his seventy-second year. His body was cremated and the ashes were laid in Pine Hill Cemetery, Dover, N. H. He had never married. He lived frugally in meager quarters, but he left an estate of approximately $172,000, accumulated through sagacious investments. To Washington University he gave $25,000, to be used only when interest had increased the sum to $1,000,000. He made other grants with time stipulations to educational institutions he had attended in the East. His last weeks he spent among his letters, rereading messages from Emerson, Lowell, Longfellow, Agassiz, Wendell Phillips, and other literary personages who were his friends.

[Sources include G. H. Waterhouse, "Descendants of Richard Waterhouse," 3 vols., 1934, typescript in Lib. of Cong.; William Hyde and H. L. Conard, *Encyc. of the Hist. of St. Louis* (1899), vol. IV; James Cox, *Old and New St. Louis* (1894); J. T. Scharf, *Hist. of St. Louis City and County* (2 vols., 1883); M. T. Runnels, *Memorial Sketches . . . Class of 1853, Dartmouth Coll.* (1895); obituaries in *St. Louis Post-Dispatch* and *St. Louis Republic,* Feb. 13, 1902; information from Waterhouse's niece, Mrs. Lilla K. Durgin of Watertown, Mass., and from Dr. G. R. Throop and Philo Stevenson of Washington Univ., where there is a book of clippings about Waterhouse; records of De Paul Hospital, St. Louis; autobiog. notes in lib. of Dartmouth Coll.]   I. D.

WATERMAN, LEWIS EDSON (Nov. 20, 1837–May 1, 1901), inventor, manufacturer, eldest son of Elisha and Amanda Perry (Washburn) Waterman, was born in Decatur, Otsego County, N. Y. He traced his ancestry to Robert Waterman, who emigrated from England to

Plymouth, Mass., about 1636 and later settled in Marshfield. Elisha Waterman was prospering at his trade of wagon-builder when Lewis was born but he died of a fever when the latter was still a small child. The boy obtained no regular schooling until after he was ten years old, but thereafter he devoted as much time as he could to study, even attending the seminary in Charlottesville, N. Y., for a short period when he was fifteen. In 1853 his mother married again, and Waterman accompanied the family to Kankakee County, Ill., where for four years he taught school in the winter and worked as a carpenter in summer. His health would not permit him to continue in manual labor, however, and between 1857 and 1861 he was variously occupied teaching school, selling books, and studying the Pitman system of shorthand. He mastered the subject so thoroughly that during the year before the Civil War he was able to give instruction in it.

Through his experience as a book agent Waterman had discovered that he was an able salesman and in 1862 he gave up teaching to sell life insurance. After some two years he was made the Boston representative of the Aetna Life Insurance Company, in which capacity he continued until 1870, building up a substantial and profitable business. Poor health forced him to give up the Boston agency, and for the next thirteen years he spent much of his time in travel. In 1883 he turned his attention seriously to the perfection of the fountain pen, in which he had been passively interested for several years. A number of fountain pens had been patented previously, but to his mind none of them was satisfactory. He moved to New York City and there began a series of experiments in which he progressed so rapidly that before the year was out he applied for his first patents, which were issued on Feb. 12 and Nov. 4, 1884. His initial improvement was in the ink-feeding device. It consisted mainly of a piece of hard rubber inserted into the open end of the pen barrel and holding the gold pen in position. On the side of this piece of rubber next to the pen was a square groove, in the bottom of which narrow fissures had been made with fine saws; extending from the ink reservoir in the barrel to the nibs of the pen, these fissures automatically controlled the flow of ink. Upon obtaining his patents, Waterman established the Ideal Pen Company in New York to manufacture his pen. Three years later, in 1887, the business had grown to such an extent that it was incorporated as the L. E. Waterman Company, Waterman acting as president and manager until his death. In this capacity he not only successfully directed the manufacturing and selling

branches of his business but also continued to improve the pen, obtaining patents for modifications of his feeding device as well as for improvements of the joints between the nozzle and the barrel and between the cap and the barrel, the most noted being a joint made of disparate cones.

Waterman was twice married: first, June 29, 1858, to Sarah Ann Roberts, in Pittsfield, Ill., and second, Oct. 3, 1872, to Sarah Ellen Varney, in Topsfield, Mass. He died in Brooklyn, N. Y., survived by his widow and by three children of his first marriage, and was buried in Forest Hill Cemetery, Boston, Mass.

[*The Pen Prophet,* Feb. 12, 1905; *Contemporary Am. Biog.,* vol. III (1902); F. D. Waterman, *Waterman Geneal., 1636–1928* (1928); *N. Y. Times,* May 2, 1901; *Brooklyn Eagle,* May 1, 1901; Patent Office records.]

C. W. M.

WATERMAN, ROBERT H. (Mar. 4, 1808–Aug. 9, 1884), sea captain, was born in Hudson, N. Y., a descendant of Robert Waterman who settled in Marshfield, Mass., about 1636, and the son of Thaddeus Waterman, who commanded several New York ships in the early nineteenth century, and of Eliza (Coffin) Waterman. When he was twelve years old, he went to sea as cabin boy on a sailing vessel. In 1829 he was first mate of the crack Black Ball packet ship *Britannia,* sailing between New York and Liverpool under Capt. Charles H. Marshall [*q.v.*]; four years later he was appointed to the command of the *South America,* the finest ship under the Black Ball flag. He retained this command until 1837, when he took over the ship *Natchez,* owned by the New York firm of Howland & Aspinwall, which traded principally with China and the west coast of South America. For several years he continued to command Howland & Aspinwall ships on the run between New York or Boston and Valparaiso and other South American ports.

In 1842 he was sent to China with the *Natchez* and in this trade made a series of remarkable passages. His first two voyages homeward from Canton to New York were made in ninety-two and ninety-four days, respectively, both of which runs were very close to the record, and in 1845 he astounded the maritime world by arriving in New York on Apr. 3, only seventy-eight days from Macao, having established a new world's record. The following year Howland & Aspinwall built the clipper ship *Sea Witch* for him, and in this vessel Waterman established the records which still stand as the best and second best runs between China and any North Atlantic port —seventy-seven days from Macao to New York in 1848, and seventy-four days, fourteen hours from Hong Kong to New York in 1849. In this service, moreover, he had broken every existing record for speed, both in days' runs and over the various sections of the China route. During this period of his life his home was in Fairfield, Conn., where he married, in 1846, Cordelia Sterling, daughter of David Sterling of Bridgeport.

Following his successful voyage of 1849 he made plans to retire from the sea, and after taking the steamship *Northerner* to San Francisco in 1850, bought, in company with Capt. A. A. Ritchie, four leagues of land in Solano County and prepared to settle down. Yielding, however, to the solicitations of the firm of N. L. & G. Griswold of New York, he agreed to take command of their new clipper *Challenge*, then the largest and loftiest clipper ship afloat. Returning to New York, he sailed for San Francisco in the *Challenge* in July 1851. The passage which followed has frequently been cited as the classic instance of a voyage in an American "Hell Ship." It was characterized by numerous acts of insubordination on the part of members of the crew, culminating in an attempt to murder the chief mate and in the deaths, from disease and injury, of nine members of the crew, several of whom were said to have been killed by Waterman himself. On the arrival of the *Challenge* in San Francisco, Oct. 29, 1851, an attempt was made to lynch Waterman, and he was subsequently tried for murder, but was completely exonerated by the testimony of his crew and passengers, who testified that the ship was in deadly peril of seizure by mutineers. Shortly after this incident he was made hull inspector for the government in San Francisco, a position which he held until 1870.

During his life in California, Waterman was regarded as a kindly and sympathetic man and a public benefactor, deeply interested in the welfare of his community. He gave to the city of Fairfield, Cal., the land on which it now stands, naming the place after the town of Fairfield, Conn. About 1859 he built a fine residence a mile from Fairfield, modeling the front of the house to resemble the prow of a ship. He was greatly interested in farming and bred fine strains of poultry and cattle during his later years. He also donated the land for the beautiful Armijo high school and the court house in Fairfield. He died in San Francisco and was buried there, but his body was later removed to Bridgeport, Conn. As a master mariner Waterman made a contribution to the world's sailing records which has probably never been surpassed, and he must be ranked as one of the greatest sea captains of America.

[Unpublished genealogical material relating to the Waterman family, collected by Thurston F. Waterman

of Albany, N. Y.; T. G. Cary, "The Vigilance Committee of San Francisco, 1851" (MS., in Lib. of Cong.); *Hist. of Solano County* (1879); C. C. Cutler, *Greyhounds of the Sea* (1930); files of the *Solano Republican,* 1859–84, *passim*; files of the *Commercial Advertiser* (N. Y.), 1833–52, *passim*; official records of the N. Y. Custom House, 1800–52.]   C. C. C.

WATERMAN, THOMAS WHITNEY (June 28, 1821–Dec. 7, 1898), lawyer, was the fourth of eight children. His paternal grandfather, David Waterman, was an ironmaster of Salisbury, Conn.; his father, Thomas Glasby Waterman (1788–1862), graduated from Yale in 1806, studied law, and in 1813 arrived in Binghamton, N. Y., where he married Pamela, daughter of Gen. Joshua Whitney, promoter for William Bingham [q.v.] in developing the town site. In 1822 Waterman was made district attorney, and in 1828 published *The Justice's Manual.* He sat in the Assembly in 1824 and in the state Senate, 1827–30, taking part in the preparation of *The Revised Statutes of the State of New York* (3 vols., 1829). After 1831 he turned his attention to lumbering, and amassed a comfortable fortune.

Thomas Whitney Waterman entered Yale in 1838. Three years later he was sent abroad for his health and traveled in England and on the Continent. Returning in 1844, he served an apprenticeship in a law office, was admitted to the bar in 1848, and commenced practice in New York City as an associate of his brother-in-law, Judge James W. White. In the following year he published *A Treatise on the Civil Jurisdiction of Justices of the Peace* (1849), a complete revision, rearrangement, and enlargement of the subject earlier treated by his father, to whom this volume was inscribed. In 1851 he published in three volumes *The American Chancery Digest,* including state and federal equity decisions, with an introductory sketch of equity courts and their jurisdiction. It made a favorable impression on his colleagues, and his professional standing was now deemed a sufficient guarantee of the accuracy of his writings.

During the next nine years he edited an American edition (1851) of Joseph Henry Dart's *Compendium of the Law and Practice of Vendors and Purchasers of Real Estate;* a third edition (2 vols., 1852) of R. H. Eden's *Compendium of the Law and Practice of Injunctions;* two editions (1853, 1860) of J. F. Archbold's *Complete Practical Treatise on Criminal Procedure, Pleading, and Evidence;* a new edition (1853) of *The Wisconsin and Iowa Justice,* originally written by his younger brother, Joshua Waterman; a fourth edition (1854) of John Adams' *Treatise on the Principles and Practice of the Action of*

Ejectment; a second edition (1855) of *A Treatise on the Law of New Trials in Cases Civil and Criminal* by David Graham [*q.v.*], to which Waterman added two volumes; a fourth edition (1856) of William Paley's *Treatise on the Law of Principal and Agent*; and *A Digest of the Reported Decisions of the Superior . . . and of the Supreme Court . . . of Connecticut* (1858). His literary work was interrupted in 1861 by the illness of his father, whose death in January 1862 caused him to return to Binghamton to commence active practice, but the publication in 1865 of his American edition of John Tamlyn's *Reports of Cases Decided in the High Court of Chancery* marked the resumption of his legoliterary activities. This work was followed by *A Treatise on the Law of Set-Off, Recoupment, and Counterclaim* (1869), the success of which led the author to abandon practice once more; a second edition (1873) of 6 and 19 *Wendell's Reports* (two other volumes, 18 and 20, of these reports, containing Waterman's notes, were published in 1901); *A Treatise on the Law of Trespass* (2 vols., 1875), which met hostile criticism from those members of the bar who held the law reports to be the only legitimate fountains of legal wisdom; *A Digest of Decisions in Criminal Cases* (1877); and *A Practical Treatise on the Law Relating to the Specific Performance of Contracts* (1881). His last important work, *A Treatise on the Law of Corporations* (2 vols., 1888), was published just before he suffered a stroke of paralysis from which he never fully recovered. His writings were, for the most part, on phases of law which were rapidly changing, and with the appearance of later volumes of reports his digests were soon out-dated; hence his work has not noticeably affected the thought and development of the law of later generations. In 1850 he married a daughter of the Rev. Edward Andrews, pastor of Christ Church in Binghamton. She died in 1871; two daughters survived their father, who died in Binghamton at the age of seventy-seven.

[J. B. Wilkinson, *The Annals of Binghamton* (2nd ed., 1872); F. C. Pierce, *Whitney* (1895); W. S. Lawyer, *Binghamton* (1900); *Albany Law Journal*, Dec. 31, 1898; book reviews in *U. S. Monthly Law Mag.*, Feb. 1851 and *Am. Law Rev.*, Jan. 1870, Apr. 1873, July, Oct. 1875; *Evening Herald* (Syracuse), Dec. 8, 1898; for T. G. Waterman, F. B. Dexter, *Biog. Sketches Grads. Yale Coll.*, vol. VI (1912) and *Binghamton Standard*, Jan. 15, 1862.]   V. L. W.

WATERS, DANIEL (June 20, 1731–Mar. 26, 1816), naval officer, was born at Charlestown, Mass., the tenth child of Adam and Rachel (Draper) Waters, and the great-grandson of Lawrence Waters who came to Charlestown from Lancaster, England, in 1675. Daniel took up seafaring and became a master mariner, making his home first in Charlestown but after 1771 in the adjoining town of Malden. He was one of the Malden minute-men who were engaged with the British on Apr. 19, 1775, and, as one experienced in ordnance, he was shortly afterward requested by the Malden Committee of Safety to prepare the cannon of the town and "enlist a sufficient number of men to make use of them" (Corey, *post*, p. 754). After the American investment of Boston he had charge of a small gunboat in the Charles River and, on Jan. 20, 1776, he was appointed by General Washington to command the schooner *Lee,* one of six vessels under John Manley [*q.v.*]. In the *Lee* he was active in the ensuing warfare on British communications and captured one enemy vessel in February and another on May 10, the *Elizabeth,* laden with merchandise seized in Boston. In early June, aided by the *Warren,* he took an armed troopship with ninety-four Scotch Highlanders on board, and on June 17 he shared with other vessels in the capture of the transports *Howe* and *Annabella* in Nantasket Road.

Upon the recommendation of Washington and others, he was appointed, Mar. 15, 1777, a captain in the Continental Navy. Serving thereafter as a volunteer under Manley in the *Hancock,* he was given command of the frigate *Fox,* but on July 6 both the *Fox* and the *Hancock* were surrendered to superior forces off Halifax. After he was exchanged in 1778, he made a West Indies cruise in the spring of 1779 in the Continental sloop *General Gates.* He then commanded the Massachusetts ship *General Putnam* in the ill-fated expedition against Castine, Me., in which the American ships were destroyed in the mouth of the Penobscot River to prevent their capture. His most famous exploit came at the close of this year when, in the Boston privateer *Thorn* of eighteen six-pounders, he defeated, in a two-hour action on Dec. 25, two enemy privateers of about equal armament but more heavily manned, the *Governor Tryon* and *Sir William Erskine.* The *Tryon* escaped after her surrender. The *Thorn* suffered eighteen killed and injured, and among the wounded was Captain Waters. John Adams wrote of the engagement, "There has not been a more memorable action this war" (Allen, *A Naval History, post,* II, 417). In January 1780 he also captured the *Sparlin* in a forty-minute battle, and brought both the *Erskine* and the *Sparlin* safely into Nantasket Road in February. His last cruise was in the Massachusetts privateer *Friendship,* to which he was appointed in January 1781. After the war he retired to his farm in Malden, where he died. He was married first, in July 1759, to Agnes Smith, by whom he had a daughter; second, on June 8, 1779, to Mary (Wicox) Mortimer, a widow of Boston; and, third, on July 29, 1802, to Sarah Sigourney, of Boston.

[T. B. Wyman, *Genealogies and Estates of Charlestown* (1879), vol. II; D. P. Corey, *Hist. of Malden* (1899); Thomas Clark, *Naval Hist. of the U. S.* (2 vols., 2nd ed., 1814); *Naval Records of the Am. Rev. 1775–88* (1906); *Mass. Soldiers and Sailors of the Revolutionary War*, vol. XVI (1907); G. W. Allen, *Mass. Privateers of the Rev., Mass. Hist. Soc. Colls.*, vol. LXXVII (1927), and *A Naval Hist. of the Am. Rev.* (2 vols., 1913); *Columbian Centinel* (Boston), Mar. 30, 1816.]   A. W—t.

WATERS, WILLIAM EVERETT (Dec. 20, 1856–Aug. 3, 1924), educator, classicist, was born in Winthrop, Me. His father, Jabez Mathews (B.A., Colby, 1843), was a descendant of James Waters who left St. Buttolph, Aldgate, London, in 1630, to settle in Salem, Mass.; his mother, Martha Ellen Webb, traced her lineage to Myles Standish, John and Priscilla Alden, and George Soule, of the *Mayflower* group. Waters attended Woodward High School in Cincinnati, Ohio, and Yale University, where he received the degree of B.A. in 1878. He continued with graduate work at Yale for two years, holding the Clark and the Larned fellowships. After teaching Latin and Greek at Hughes High School in Cincinnati (1880–83), he returned to Yale as tutor in classics. In 1885–86 he engaged in research in classical philology at the University of Berlin under Adolf Kirchoff, Johannes Vahlen, Oldenburg, Albrecht Weber, and Johannes Schmidt, and in 1887 received the degree of Ph.D. at Yale. On June 28, 1888, he married Alma Filia Oyler, daughter of George Washington and Carrie (Pruden) Oyler. He returned to Hughes High School (1887–90), taught Greek at summer sessions of the Chautauqua College of Liberal Arts (1888–90), conducting correspondence courses in Greek under its auspices (1888–95), and served as professor of Greek and comparative philology at the University of Cincinnati (1890–94). After a visit to Greece (1893–94) he accepted the presidency of Wells College, Aurora, N. Y., which he held for six years. In 1900 he joined the group of prominent educators who founded the college entrance examination board and served (1901–02) as assistant secretary. He became associate professor of Greek at New York University in 1901, and from 1902 until his retirement as professor emeritus in 1923 he was professor of Greek there. He made frequent addresses under the free lecture system instituted by the New York board of education, taught Latin at Morris High School, and English, rhetoric, and composition

at the Harlem Evening High School, and was director of a vacation school (1903). After his retirement he was instrumental in raising as a memorial to his predecessor, Dr. Henry Martyn Baird [*q.v.*], an endowment to guarantee to the university permanent membership in the American School of Classical Studies at Athens. He had been elected to the advisory council of this institution in 1904 and remained a member until his death.

Waters was primarily a teacher. Enthusiastic, heedless of the expenditure of time and energy, and responsive always to the interest of his pupils, he was at his best in the classroom. The shyness which he manifested in personal contacts disappeared entirely when he was confronted at one and the same time with a student, a Greek text, and a blackboard. His enthusiasm for literature and philosophy was infectious. He was co-author with William R. Harper of *An Inductive Greek Method* (1888). In 1902 he edited the *Cena Trimalchionis of Petronius Arbiter* and published *Town Life in Ancient Italy*, a translation of Ludwig Friedländer's *Stadtewesen in Italien im Ersten Jahrhundert*. In his latter years he was engaged on a translation of Dio of Prusa for the Loeb Classical Library. He also contributed articles to the *Transactions of the American Philological Association*, the *Pedagogical Journal*, the *Classical Weekly*, and the *New York Evening Post*. He was a member of numerous learned societies. He was a very active member of the West End Presbyterian Church, serving as an elder from 1902 until his death, as superintendent of the Sunday School (1902–05), and as frequent leader of the men's Bible class. He acted as secretary of the class of 1878 at Yale for ten years (1878–88). He took his own life after a year of illness. He was survived by his wife and one son.

[Sources include autobiog. data in *"Vitae"* of the Andiron Club of N. Y. City, vol. I, 1907–23 (unpub. MS.); *Who's Who in America*, 1920–21; *Obit. Record Yale Grads.*, 1925; J. M. Lamberton, *Quarter-Centenary Record, Class of 1878, Yale Univ.* (1905); obit. notices in *Andiron Club Summons*, Mar. 10, 1925; obituary in *N. Y. Herald Tribune*, Aug. 4, 1924; letters from E. O. Waters, Waters' son, E. G. Sihler, and E. D. Perry.]   C. J. K., Jr.

WATIE, STAND (Dec. 12, 1806–Sept. 9, 1871), Indian leader and brigadier-general in the Confederate army, was born near the site of Rome, Ga., the son of a full-blood Cherokee, David Oowatie or Uweti, and a half-blood mother whose baptismal name was Susannah. When twelve years old he was sent to a mission school at Brainard near the line between Tennessee and Georgia. There he learned to speak English and received a fair education. Returning to his home he became a planter and at times assisted his elder brother, Elias Boudinot, *c.* 1803–1839 [*q.v.*], in the publication of the Cherokee newspaper called the *Cherokee Phoenix.* In 1835 he joined Elias Boudinot, his uncle Major Ridge [*q.v.*], and John Ridge, in signing the treaty of New Echota. By this treaty the Cherokee in Georgia agreed to surrender their lands, remove west to what is now Oklahoma, and join the Cherokee West, who had migrated to that region some years earlier. The great majority of the tribe bitterly opposed this treaty, but it was ratified by the United States Senate, and the Cherokee were forced to remove in 1838. The feeling of bitterness against the Ridge and Watie group was intense, however, and in 1839 Major Ridge, John Ridge, and Elias Boudinot were all killed on the same day. Stand Watie himself was marked for slaughter but escaped death and became the leader of the minority, or treaty, party. He was married in 1843 to Sarah C. Bell, a woman of intelligence and strength of character. They had three sons and two daughters, but the sons all died before their father, and both daughters died in 1875. Small in stature, he had great physical strength and endurance. He was an able and fearless soldier and was of frank, candid nature.

At the outbreak of the Civil War the Cherokee sought to remain neutral but at last made a treaty of alliance with the Confederacy. Early in 1861 he raised a company of home guards, of which he became captain. Later in the year he raised the first Cherokee regiment of volunteers known as the "Cherokee Mounted Rifles," and he was made its colonel by the Confederate government. In May 1864 he was raised to the rank of brigadier-general. During the entire war he was very active as a raider and cavalry leader and took part in many engagements in Indian Territory and along its border, including the battles of Wilson's Creek and Pea Ridge. He was one of the last Confederate officers to surrender, not yielding up his sword until June 23, 1865. In 1863 the majority party of the Cherokee had repudiated the alliance with the Confederate States, but he remained loyal to the South and was chosen as principal chief by the Southern wing of the tribe.

After the close of the war he went to Washington as a member of the Southern delegation of the Cherokee, but soon he returned home and resumed the life of planter engaging at times in various business enterprises including tobacco manufacturing.

[Letters and papers in Frank Phillips Coll., and Cherokee Archives, Univ. of Okla.; letters in North-eastern States Teachers' College, Tahlequah, Okla., and in the manuscript colls. of Univ. of Texas; A. H. Abel, *The Slave Holding Indians* (3 vols., 1915–25); M. W. Anderson, *Life of General Stand Watie* (1915); Wiley Britton, *The Civil War on the Border* (2 vols., 1890–99), and *The Union Indian Brigade in the Civil War* (1922); *Nineteenth Ann. Report of the Bureau of Am. Ethnology,* pt. 1 (1900).]   E. E. D.

WATKINS, GEORGE CLAIBORNE (Nov. 25, 1815–Dec. 7, 1872), jurist, son of Maj. Isaac and Marie (Toncre) Watkins, was born at Shelbyville, Ky. He was descended from Thomas Watkins who came from England and settled on Swift Creek in Cumberland (later Powhatan) County, Va., about the middle of the eighteenth century. Following financial reverses, Isaac Watkins moved to Arkansas in 1821, and is said to have built the first tavern and grist mill in Little Rock. After receiving the best educational advantages available in a pioneer settlement, George attended the law school at Litchfield, Conn. Returning to Little Rock in 1837, he formed a law partnership with Chester Ashley, who was the leading lawyer in the state and later United States senator.

On Oct. 16, 1843, Watkins succeeded Robert W. Johnson [*q.v.*] as attorney general. Becoming chief justice of the state supreme court on Nov. 15, 1852, he soon cleared a crowded docket and won a reputation for the disposal of business in an orderly way. The most important decision rendered while he was on the bench was that in the case of *Merrick* vs. *Avery* (14 *Ark.,* 370), 1854, in which, basing his decision on the reasoning in *The Genesee Chief* vs. *Fitzhugh* (19 *U. S.,* 233), he held that the United States had exclusive admiralty jurisdiction over navigable streams. This decision was made some twelve years before a similar ruling by the Supreme Court (*The Hine* vs. *Trevor,* 71 *U. S.,* 555). Shortly before his elevation to the bench he had formed a law partnership with James M. Curran. Upon the death of his partner he resigned, Dec. 31, 1854, in order to meet the obligations of the firm. By close attention to his practice and by judicious investments he accumulated a competence. On Dec. 20, 1862, he was appointed a member of the military court attending the army of Gen. T. H. Holmes [*q.v.*]. He was a zealous supporter of the Confederacy and gave three sons to the army, one of whom rose from a private to the rank of colonel and was killed at Atlanta at the age of twenty-two.

He was married twice: first, in 1841, to Mary Crease, who bore him three sons and two daughters; second, to Sophia, widow of his late partner and daughter of Senator W. S. Fulton, who bore him three daughters. He was a man of slender build, being only five feet, five inches in height, and weighing less than one hundred pounds. His last law partner, U. M. Rose [*q.v.*], said of him: "With an extremely delicate and fragile constitution . . . he possessed strong feelings and a nerve of iron. His reverence for the courts and administration of justice amounted to religion" (Hallum, *post*, p. 227). He died in St. Louis, on his way back from Colorado, where he had gone for the benefit of his health.

[F. N. Watkins, *A Cat. of the Descendants of Thomas Watkins* (1852) ; *War of the Rebellion: Official Records* (*Army*) ; 13–15 *Ark. Reports* ; John Hallum, *Biog. and Pictorial Hist. of Ark.* (1887), pp. 275–78 ; Fay Hempstead, *A Pictorial Hist. of Ark.* (1890), pp. 764–65 ; J. H. Shinn, *Pioneers and Makers of Ark.* (1908), p. 233 ; *Biog. and Hist. Memoirs of Pulaski, Jefferson . . . and Hot Spring Counties, Ark.* (1889), p. 516 ; *Ark. Hist. Asso. Pubs.*, vol. II (1908) ; *Daily Ark. Gazette* (Little Rock), Dec. 8, 10, 1872; *Green Bag*, Sept. 1892.]   D. Y. T.

WATKINS, JOHN ELFRETH (May 17, 1852–Aug. 11, 1903), engineer, curator, was born in Ben Lomond, Va., the son of Francis B. and Mary (Elfreth) Watkins. His father, a physician, was descended from Thomas Watkins who in the War of the Revolution organized a troop of cavalry; his mother, from Timothy Matlack [*q.v.*] of Philadelphia, the "fighting Quaker," who was a delegate to the Continental Congress from 1780 to 1787. After preparing for college at Treemount Seminary, Norristown, Pa., Watkins entered Lafayette College, Easton, Pa., from which he graduated as a civil engineer in 1871. He then joined the staff of the Delaware & Hudson Canal Company as a mining engineer, but continued his studies as a non-resident student of Lafayette and received the degree of M.S. in 1874.

Meanwhile, after a year with the Canal Company, he had entered the employ of the Pennsylvania Railroad Company as an assistant engineer of construction, with headquarters at the Meadow Shops in New Jersey. In 1873 he was disabled for field work by an accident which resulted in the loss of his right leg, and was later assigned to the Amboy division of the Pennsylvania Railroad. Within a few months he was made chief clerk of the Camden & Atlantic Railroad, but before the year was over he was reassigned to the Amboy division of the Pennsylvania system, which position he held until 1886. In 1884 he became associated with the United States National Museum at Washington, D. C., as honorary curator of transportation, and two years later accepted a salaried position, to which he devoted all of his time for the succeeding six years, building up the technological collections pertaining to the transportation industry. In 1892 he resigned from the National Museum

and returned to the Pennsylvania Railroad to prepare that company's exhibit for the World's Columbian Exposition, held in Chicago in 1893. At its close he took charge of the department of industrial arts (a direct outgrowth of the exposition) in the Field Museum, Chicago, but a year later (1895) he returned to Washington as curator of mechanical technology and superintendent of buildings of the National Museum, which positions he held until his death.

In the course of his twenty years' direct and indirect association with the Museum, Watkins became an authority on the history of engineering and the mechanical arts. Among his best known publications were "The Beginnings of Engineering," read before the American Society of Civil Engineers and published in its *Transactions* (vol. XXIV, 1891), *The Development of the American Rail and Track as Illustrated by the Collection in the U. S. National Museum* (1891), and *The Log of the Savannah* (1891), the last two published originally in the annual reports of the Regents of the Smithsonian Institution for 1889 and 1890. His most extensive literary undertaking was a compilation of the history of the Pennsylvania Railroad, 1845–96, the completion of which was interrupted by his death and which was never published. Aside from his official duties he was very active in 1891 in promoting the Patent Centennial Celebration, held in Washington, and was an active member of a number of patriotic and other societies. He was twice married: first, in 1873, to Helen Bryan of Mount Holly, N. J.; second, Jan. 16, 1886, to Margaret Virginia Gwynn of Philadelphia. At the time of his sudden death in New York City he was survived by his widow and five children, three of whom were of the first marriage.

[F. M. Watkins, *A Catalogue of the Descendants of Thomas Watkins* (1852) ; *Who's Who in America*, 1901–02 ; *Ann. Report of the Board of Regents of the Smithsonian Institution . . . 1904: Report of the U. S. Nat. Museum* (1906) ; *Railroad Gazette*, Aug. 28, 1903 ; *Stevens Institute Indicator*, July 1900 ; *Evening Star* (Washington), Aug. 12, 1903.]   C. W. M.

WATSON, ANDREW (Feb. 15, 1834–Dec. 9, 1916), missionary to Egypt, was born in Oliverburn, Perthshire, Scotland, the son of Andrew and Catherine (Roger) Watson. While Andrew was yet a child his father died, and at the age of fourteen he emigrated with his family to the United States. Here, at Lisbon, near Sussex, Wis., he shared in the arduous labor of hewing a farm out of the forest. He had his preparatory education in schools in Wisconsin and graduated from Carroll College in that state in 1857. It was probably while in college that he formed the purpose of becoming a missionary. He attended Princeton Theological Seminary (1858–59) and Allegheny Theological Seminary (1859–60). In preparation for his work as a missionary he took a partial course at Jefferson Medical College (1860–61). On May 15, 1861, he was ordained to the ministry of the United Presbyterian Church and on July 10 was married to Margaret MacVickar of Sussex, Wis. Shortly afterward the newly wedded couple sailed for Egypt as appointees of the foreign mission board of their Church. Here, with the exception of occasional furloughs in America and a few other journeys which took him out of the country, Watson spent more than half a century, sharing in the remarkable development of his Church in the land of his adoption. When he arrived, the Egyptian mission of his board was less than a decade old; at his death there were 13,000 members of his denomination in Egypt.

His first few years were spent at Alexandria; then for several years he resided at Mansûra; from 1873, on, he made his home in Cairo. He shared in many phases of the work of his mission. Acquiring the ability to speak Arabic faultlessly and with great fluency, he came in time to feel that he could express himself more readily in it than in English, and so preferred to preach in it rather than in his mother tongue. He edited a weekly paper in Arabic. For a while he was in charge of a boys' school, and for a brief period he taught in the Assiut Training College. In 1864 he helped found the theological school of his Church which, after several temporary locations, was established at Cairo. From 1869 he taught in it, and from 1892 until his death he was its head. He took a prominent part in obtaining official recognition of the civil and political status of the native Protestant communities in Egypt and for years was his mission's representative in dealing with the Egyptian government. He headed the commission which surveyed the Sudan in preparation for opening of work there. While in the United States, he served in 1890 as the moderator of the United Presbyterian General Assembly, and in 1910 went as a delegate to the World Missionary Conference at Edinburgh. In 1898 he published *The American Mission in Egypt, 1854 to 1896* (2nd ed., 1904). He was widely trusted and loved by the community as a whole, and many of varying social ranks committed to his care the administration of their funds. He was a friend of at least one Coptic Patriarch, of numerous persons connected with the Roman Catholic Church, and of many Moslems. Longing to die in harness,

he was able to keep up his accustomed activities until within a few days of the end of his long life. His death occurred in Cairo, and he was survived by his wife and one son.

[*Necrological Report . . . Princeton Theological Seminary,* 1917; *In Memory of the Rev. Andrew Watson, D.D., LL.D., 1834–1916* (n.d.); *Who's Who in America,* 1916–17; Ann. Reports of the Board of Foreign Missions of the United Presbyterian Church in North America; *Egyptian Gazette* (Alexandria), Dec. 12, 1916; *Missionary Rev. of the World,* Jan. 1917; information from Watson's son, Charles R. Watson.]

K. S. L.

WATSON, DAVID THOMPSON (Jan. 2, 1844–Feb. 24, 1916), lawyer, was born at Washington, Pa., the son of James and Maria (Morgan) Watson. He received his early education in his native town and was graduated at Washington (now Washington and Jefferson) College, with the degree of A.B. in 1864. For a brief period he saw service in the Civil War. Entering the Harvard Law School, he was graduated in 1866 in the same class with Oliver Wendell Holmes, Jr. Two years later he settled at Pittsburgh, where he continued in the active practice of law for nearly a half century, becoming one of Pittsburgh's leading lawyers. For a number of years before his death he was the senior member of the firm of Watson & Freeman. He joined the American Bar Association in 1885 and remained a member for the rest of his life. On June 10, 1889, he married Margaret H. Walker, daughter of William Walker, a Pittsburgh banker.

Watson was retained by the United States Department of Justice as attorney in action brought against the Northern Securities Company in the circuit court, April 1903, to enforce the laws relating to corporate combinations. He was retained, also, by Henry Frick in the litigation between the United States and the Union Pacific Railroad in 1911, and by the Standard Oil Company in several cases. He gained his widest prominence, however, through his connection with the Alaskan Boundary controversy between the United States and Great Britain in 1903. He was the second in rank of the four counsel for the United States, the first being Jacob M. Dickinson [*q.v.*], the third, Hannis Taylor [*q.v.*], and the fourth, Chandler P. Anderson. Watson presented the opening argument in behalf of the United States, following Sir Robert Finlay, who spoke for Great Britain. It was long and able, continuing from Sept. 23 to Sept. 28, inclusive. The report of it fills more than 130 large printed pages. Watson seems never to have held or sought public office. In the multifarious and exacting duties of his profession he found, apparently, all that was needed to engross his attention and satisfy his ambition. He died in Atlantic City, N. J., from heart failure, following an attack of the grippe.

[G. T. Fleming, *Hist. of Pittsburgh and Environs* (1922), vol. III; *Report of the . . . Pa. Bar Asso.*, 1916; *Proc. of the Alaskan Boundary Tribunal* (1904), vol. VI; *Pittsburg Dispatch*, June 11, 1889; *Who's Who in America*, 1914–15; *N. Y. Times*, Feb. 26, 1916.]   C. S. L.

WATSON, ELKANAH (Jan. 22, 1758–Dec. 5, 1842), merchant, canal promoter, and agriculturist, the son of Elkanah and Patience (Marston) Watson, was born at Plymouth, Mass. He was of Pilgrim stock, being sixth in descent, through his mother, from Edward Winslow, third governor of Plymouth Colony; on his father's side he was a descendant of Robert Watson who came to Plymouth about 1632. Young Elkanah received his early education at a grammar school conducted by Alexander Scammell and Peleg Wadsworth [*qq.v.*]. At the age of fifteen he was bound out to John Brown, 1744–1780 [*q.v.*], a prosperous merchant of Providence, R. I. He had already, in 1774, enrolled in a cadet company organized by Colonel Nightingale and in April 1775 asked to be released from his indentures so that he might join the American army besieging Boston. Brown's refusal made him "most melancholy," but Watson was able to serve the patriot cause in other ways, for his employers imported gunpowder for the Continental Army.

In September 1777, when trade in Providence had languished, Watson undertook a dangerous journey to South Carolina to invest funds for the Browns. With more than $50,000 sewed into the linings of his garments he made his adventurous way from Providence to Charleston (some twelve hundred miles) in seventy-seven days. Having safely delivered the funds he, with two companions, set out on a tour of exploration of Georgia and Florida. Dissuaded from entering Florida, they at last turned northward and Watson reached Providence late in April, having visited ten of the original thirteen states.

Watson's apprenticeship was over in January 1779, but a dearth of funds prevented his establishing his own business. He remained in the employ of the Browns and soon embarked for France to carry money and dispatches to Benjamin Franklin [*q.v.*], then one of the American agents in Paris. After a month of Franklin's hospitality he prepared to return to America with valuable papers. Arriving at Nantes he sent his dispatches with the captain of the *Mercury* and opened a mercantile house with a Monsieur Cossoul. The latter took charge of affairs while Watson went to a clerical college at Ancenis to learn French, a study which he continued at Rennes during the winter of 1780–81. He traveled considerably, meeting many interesting characters and greatly enjoying life, while the faithful Cossoul labored at Nantes.

Their business had prospered, the books showing a profit of 40,000 guineas in three years. In 1782 Watson went to England, carrying dispatches from Benjamin Vaughan [*q.v.*] to Lord Shelburne and letters to many influential persons; he opened a London branch of his commercial firm and had his portrait painted by Copley. These glorious days of expansive living were soon curtailed, for the great financial crisis of 1783 threw his several mercantile ventures into the hands of creditors. Liquidation of his affairs required almost a year, after which he embarked upon a tour of the Netherlands (described in *A Tour in Holland in MDCCLXXXIV*, London 1789; Worcester 1790) and of England. Already deeply interested in canals and impressed by their superior convenience and cheapness, he made a special study of the inland waterways of Holland. Upon his return to America late in 1784 he hastened to Mount Vernon to discuss with Washington the feasibility of a system of American canals. He received encouragement, but his early efforts to raise capital were unsuccessful.

In 1785 he laid plans for new commercial enterprises with his old partner Cossoul, who had come to America to join him. Watson was located at Edenton, N. C., and Cossoul established himself in Haiti. Business flourished; Watson's expansive days returned. He purchased a great estate on the Chowan River and became "amply occupied in social convivialities, wandering about the country; in deer hunting and other rural amusements." Again, however, his business collapsed. He sold his plantation, moved north and, after a careful survey of New York state, settled in Albany in 1789. On Mar. 3 of that year he married Rachel Smith, by whom he had three sons and two daughters. Within a comparatively short time he was able to organize the Bank of Albany and was recognized as one of the leading citizens of that community. His enthusiasm for canals had never abated; he incessantly urged his plans upon his influential and wealthy friends. In 1791 three of them, Jeremiah Van Rensselaer, Stephen N. Bayard, and Philip Van Cortlandt, were persuaded to join Watson in a tour of central New York. During this investigation Watson developed a plan for a canal which makes it clear that he was "the first to think his way through New York by water" (Pound, *post*, p. 249). His project was basically sound, but his calculations were extremely faulty. Watson was a prophet whose visions were startlingly accurate, but he often lacked the patience and the talent necessary to their practical achievement. He promoted two canal companies and a stage line from Albany to Schenectady, and in 1798 lobbied successfully for a charter which authorized a company to build a canal around Niagara Falls. He fought for a variety of local improvements, free schools, and turnpike roads. When he fell out with the Dutch directors of the Bank of Albany he was able to secure, through rather dubious means, a charter for the New York State Bank, which he had organized with such success that after four years of operation he was able to retire from active business.

Moving to Pittsfield, Mass., he purchased a large farm and devoted himself to the application of the latest European discoveries in scientific agriculture. He purchased a pair of Merino sheep and imported a special breed of pigs, and, later, an English prize bull, in connection with all of which he carried on energetic publicity campaigns. In 1810, with the enthusiastic aid of some farmer-neighbors, he staged the celebrated "Cattle Show" which preceded the incorporation of the Berkshire Agricultural Society, sponsor of the first county fair in America. It was because of the unflagging efforts of Watson that the county fair early became an American institution. In his later years he corresponded widely upon agricultural subjects, kept in touch with his old friends, traveled extensively, and prepared his autobiography. This volume, left unfinished at his death, was published by his son in 1856 as *Men and Times of the Revolution; or, Memoirs of Elkanah Watson*; a more complete edition appeared the following year. It remains one of the most interesting and intelligent of contemporaneous accounts of the early years of the American Republic. He was the author, also of *History of Agricultural Societies on the Modern Berkshire System* (1820), and *History of the Rise and Progress, and Existing Condition of the Western Canals in the State of New York* (1820). He died in his eighty-fifth year.

[In addition to works cited above, see W. R. Deane, *A Biog. Sketch of Elkanah Watson* (1864); G. A. Worth, *Random Recollections of Albany* (1866); Arthur Pound, *Native Stock* (1931); Robert Troup, *A Vindication of the Claim of Elkanah Watson, Esq., to the Merit of Projecting the Lake Canal Policy* (1821) and *A Letter to the Hon. Brockholst Livingston, Esq., on the Lake Canal Policy of the State of N. Y.* (1822); Jared Van Wagenen, "Elkanah Watson—A Man of Affairs," *New York Hist.*, Oct. 1932; W. C. Neely, *The Agricultural Fair* (1935); *Albany Jour.*, Dec. 12, 1842. Important MSS. are in the Detroit Pub. Lib. and the N. Y. State Lib. at Albany, where the bulk of Watson's private papers are on deposit.]
        F.M.

WATSON, HENRY CLAY (1831–June 24, 1867), newspaper editor, political writer, and author of historical stories for young people, was born in Baltimore, Md. At an early age he went to Philadelphia, and in Philadelphia newspaper offices he received his only education: the printer's trade he learned thoroughly. He was editorially connected with the *North American and United States Gazette* and with the *Philadelphia Evening Journal*. Late in 1861 he went to California, settling in Sacramento, where he became editor of the *Sacramento Daily Union*. In this capacity, he performed successfully duties that today would require the services of several men; he was art critic, book reviewer, news editor, and political writer.

Watson's first book, *Camp-Fires of the Revolution; or the War of Independence* (1850), published in Philadelphia when the author was not yet twenty years old, went through several editions. Like most of his many other works, it is a popular treatment of American history. Of his subsequent publications the more important were *The Old Bell of Independence; or Philadelphia in 1776* (1851), *Nights in a Block-House, or Sketches of Border Life* (1852), *The Yankee Tea-Party; or Boston in 1773* (1852), *Lives of the Presidents of the United States* (1853), *Heroic Women of History* (1853), *Thrilling Adventures of Hunters in the Old World and the New* (1853), and *The Camp-Fires of Napoleon* (copr. 1854). The titles indicate the scope of the work Watson attempted, and the form he most frequently used—the narrative sketch, short, vivid, and dramatic. Although his books are no longer read, they were forerunners of the nineteenth-century type of literature that aimed to present the facts of history in interesting form as a means of popularizing knowledge. Watson was also interested in music, which interest found expression in two compilations: *The Ladies' Glee-Book* (1854) and *The Masonic Musical Manual* (1855).

He died at Sacramento, on Monday, June 24, 1867 (not on July 10, 1869, as is usually stated), at the home of a Mrs. Taylor, with whom he resided. He was buried in the City Cemetery. It is clear that he occupied a position of high importance in the newspaper world of his day and that his political writings exerted no inconsiderable influence; yet, only six years after Watson's death, Newton Booth [*q.v.*] was compelled to "wonder how many there are whose hearts used to be daily stirred by the magic eloquence of his pen, who now ever recall his name" (Crane, *post*, p. 497). Ella S. Cummins, in *The Story of the Files* (p. 83), refers to Watson as "a finished scholar and brilliant writer." His editorials written during the conflict between North and South, were, she says, the "greatest glory" of the *Union*. In the judgment of William H. Mills, editor of the *Union* after it merged with the *Sacramento Record*, Watson's style was "finished, distinguished by lucidity, adapted to political, historical, and national themes, with a full appreciation of their bearing on future events and epochs" (Cummins, p. 84). In the short space of six years he made a definite impress on California journalism. Even if some allowance be made for the uncritical enthusiasm of his associates, the fact remains that no student of the California press has been able to discuss California's contribution to early American journalism without mentioning the brilliant work accomplished by Watson.

[*Sacramento Daily Union*, June 25, 1867; *Daily Alta California* (San Francisco), June 26, 1867; Newton Booth, "A Holiday Excursion with H. C. Watson," first pub. in *Themis* (Sacramento), Dec. 31, 1892, and in L. E. Crane, *Newton Booth of Cal.* (1894); E. S. Cummins, *The Story of the Files* (1893).]   H. S. R—n.

WATSON, HENRY COOD (Nov. 4, 1818– Dec. 2, 1875), editor, music critic, was born in London, the son of John Watson, a musician associated with the Covent Garden Theatre. Like his sisters, who were prominent in oratorio, Watson learned to sing as a child, and when he was about nine years of age he made his début as one of the fairies in "Oberon" at the opera. His teachers were his father, William H. Kearns, and Edward J. Loder, a musician who later married Watson's sister. When his voice broke at adolescence he shipped for a voyage of the Mediterranean, but on his return he settled down to the serious study of music. He also wrote poetry, and did some other literary work.

In 1841 he came to New York, carrying with him letters of introduction to William Cullen Bryant, George P. Morris, Park Benjamin, 1809– 1864, and Horace Greeley [*qq.v.*]. Benjamin immediately engaged him as music critic for a paper he was then editing, the *New World*. In 1843 Watson founded a magazine of his own, the *Musical Chronicle*, which later became the *American Musical Times*. In 1845 he was associated with Charles F. Briggs and Edgar Allan Poe [*qq.v.*] in establishing the short-lived *Broadway Journal*, and he also contributed to various magazines, among them the *Albion*, and the *New Mirror*. In 1855 he became an editor of *Frank Leslie's Illustrated Newspaper*, and in April 1864 appeared the first issue of his own journal,

Watson's Weekly Art Journal which he edited until 1870. In June 1868 it became the *American Art Journal*. From 1863 to 1867 he acted as music critic for the *New York Tribune*.

In addition to his critical and literary work Watson was active as a musician during his entire New York career. He composed many published songs and pieces, and he delivered a number of lectures at the Vocal Institute. In 1852 he published *A Familiar Chat About Musical Instruments*. He was associated with William Vincent Wallace in organizing the Mendelssohn Concert at Castle Garden, and he wrote the libretto for Wallace's opera, "Lurline." In 1842 he was one of the group that founded the Philharmonic Society of New York. He was also one of the organizers of the American Musical Fund Association, and of the Vocal Society which later became the Mendelssohn Union. He is credited with being the first promoter of music trade-journalism (see Dolge, *post*). John Savage [*q.v.*] is quoted as having said that when Watson "wrote on musical art he wrote with consummate knowledge and with a deep sympathy for all that is most elevating, charming and correct in musical thought. As he was an able critic he was a conscientious one, and strove sometimes to achieve by generosity that which could not be encouraged by severity" (Mathews, *post*, p. 380). Watson died in New York City at the home of his sister.

[There is some confusion regarding the date of Watson's birth. Some sources give 1816, some 1818, and, one, 1815. Consult for information Alfred Dolge, *Pianos and their Makers*, vol. I (1911); W. S. B. Mathews, *A Hundred Years of Music in America* (1889); *Grove's Dict. of Music and Musicians*, Am. Supp. (1930); *N. Y. Tribune*, Dec. 3, 1875.]   J. T. H.

WATSON, JAMES CRAIG (Jan. 28, 1838– Nov. 22, 1880), astronomer, was a descendant of Irish ancestors who came to Pennsylvania before the Revolution. His grandfather, James Watson, pioneered in "Upper Canada," prospered and acquired influence, but his father, William Watson, and his wife, Rebecca Bacon, a native of Nova Scotia, met adversity and removed from the farm near Fingal, Ontario (then Canada West), where James, the oldest of their four children, was born, and settled at Ann Arbor, Mich., in 1850. Father and son found factory work. At the age of thirteen the boy had acquired such mechanical skill that an incompetent engineer was discharged, so that he could take his place. While the engine hummed he studied Latin and Greek. He entered high school but he evidenced greater ability than his teacher and quit. At the age of fifteen he entered the University of Michigan and displayed marked ability in the classics, mathematics and mechanics. Under Francis (Franz F.) Brünnow he mastered theoretical and practical astronomy, completing Laplace's *Mécanique Céleste* at the age of seventeen. While still an undergraduate he ground, polished and mounted a four-inch achromatic objective. After graduation in 1857, he became Brünnow's assistant and contributed fifteen papers to astronomical journals before the age of twenty-one. On Brünnow's resignation in 1859 Watson was made professor of astronomy in charge of the observatory, and when the elder man returned the next year, Watson became professor of physics. His astronomical contributions continued to appear; they chiefly dealt with comets and asteroids. His *Popular Treatise on Comets* (1861) exposed many erroneous ideas. He became interested through Gould in the reduction of the Washington Zones, and devoted much time to that work.

In 1863 Brünnow again resigned and Watson was made professor of astronomy and director of the observatory. Three weeks after appointment he discovered "Eurynome," the first asteroid of his twenty-two discoveries. To aid in asteroid work the production of a series of ecliptic star charts was undertaken, and in 1868 he published his *Theoretical Astronomy*, a complete compilation and digest of the theory and method of orbital determination. It was considered an authoritative work and became a textbook in America, Germany, France, and England. In 1869 he began to work with Benjamin Peirce [*q.v.*] on lunar theory. He participated in three eclipse expeditions, to Iowa in 1869, to Sicily in 1870, and to Wyoming in 1878. He had charge of the expedition to observe the transit of Venus in China in 1874. On his return trip he paused in Egypt long enough to assist Egyptian army engineers in establishing a geodetic survey. In 1878 he became interested in Le Verrier's "Vulcan," and announced the discovery of two intramercurial planets at the eclipse in Wyoming, not subsequently verified.

In 1879 he resigned his position at the University of Michigan and became director of the Washburn Observatory of the University of Wisconsin, at Madison. The building and the construction of instruments was there supervised with scrupulous care. He also began a solar observatory and a student observatory at his own expense. Watson was a vigorous man with robust physique; he weighed 240 pounds. But during the course of this work, he became ill from exposure and died very suddenly. His wife, Annette Waite, to whom he had been married in May 1860, survived him. They had no children.

The National Academy of Sciences was made his residuary legatee with provision to prepare and publish tables of the motion of his asteroids. His extraordinary endowments included quickness of perception, mathematical intuition, an excellent memory, keen analytical power, and mechanical ability. He was an accurate and rapid computer, having once determined the elliptic elements of an orbit at a single sitting. He engaged successfully in many business activities. Though active in community affairs he kept quite aloof from society. Somewhat indifferent to public opinion, he was very sensitive of his scientific reputation.

He was a member of the National Academy of Sciences, 1868; the Royal Academy of Sciences of Italy; and the American Philosophical Society. In 1870 he was awarded the Lalande prize by the French Academy of Sciences, and in 1875 was decorated Knight Commander of the Imperial Order of the Medjidich of Turkey and Egypt, 1875. He received many academic distinctions both in America and abroad. His publications, in addition to the works mentioned, include a work on *Tables for the Calculation of Simple or Compound Interest* (1878), and numerous papers in the *American Journal of Science*, Gould's *Astronomical Journal*, Brünnow's *Astronomical Notices*, and *Astronomische Nachrichten*.

[University of Michigan *Memorial Addresses . . . at the Funeral of . . . James Craig Watson* (1882); biographical sketches by A. Winchell, in *Am. Jour. of Sci.*, Jan. 1881, and G. C. Comstock, *Nat. Acad. of Sci., Biog. Memoirs*, vol. III (1895); *Detroit Free Press*, Nov. 24, 1880.]

W. C. R.

WATSON, JAMES MADISON (Feb. 8, 1827–Sept. 29, 1900), writer of textbooks, was born in Onondaga Hill, Onondaga County, N. Y., the son of Simeon and Sally Ann (Wilber) Watson. His early education in the local district school was supplemented by instruction from his father, a Baptist clergyman. In 1839 his family removed to Oswego County, where his schooling was interrupted by periods of work on farms nearby. At seventeen he had saved enough money to enter Mexico Academy, at Mexico, N. Y., but between July 1844 and June 1848 he had only about twelve months in school, since he was obliged to spend most of each year earning his tuition and living expenses. After teaching school in Oswego (1848–50), he entered Falley Seminary, Fulton, N. Y. During the summer of 1851 he sold textbooks. He was assistant teacher at the Chittenango Seminary for about seven months in 1851–52 and principal of the union school at Howlett Hill, April–July 1852. In 1852–53 he read law in Syracuse and Albany, where he was admitted to the bar, Sept. 7, 1853. A visit to New York the same month resulted in his appointment as general book agent for A. S. Barnes & Company, publishers of textbooks. For some years he traveled throughout the country, introducing the Barnes texts in schools and colleges. Observations in many classrooms led him to the conviction that reforms were needed in the teaching of English. His first textbook, *Word Builder* (1855), which emphasized correct pronunciation and use of words in sentences, was widely adopted soon after its publication. Encouraged by its success, he collaborated with Richard Green Parker [*q.v.*] in the production of the National Series of readers and spellers (7 vols., 1857–66). Throughout these years, he lectured before teachers' institutes, and taught occasional classes in elocution and gymnastics. A *Handbook of Calisthenics and Gymnastics* (1863), which appeared in various editions, added considerably to his reputation. On Mar. 31, 1871, he married Emma Hopper, daughter of the Rev. Andrew and Margaret (Inslee) Hopper of Newark, N. J. Resigning about this time as agent for the publishing company, he established his residence in Elizabeth, N. J., where he remained until his death. His Independent Series of readers and spellers, begun in 1868, was completed in ten volumes in 1875.

The income from these texts enabled him to devote his time to civic and church affairs. He was deacon of the Central Baptist Church (1877–1900) and a member of the board of managers of the New Jersey Baptist Convention (1884–97). The churches of Elizabeth, at his recommendation, established the "Red Ribbon Club" for the maintenance of law, order, and temperance, and as president, and editor of its journal, the *Red Ribbon Record* (1885–90), he played a prominent part in the temperance movement. He was president of the Elizabeth board of education (1881–82), and president (1882) and corresponding secretary (1883–98) of the New Jersey Sanitary Association.

[J. M. Watson, "Pantography of My Life," 2 vols., and "Jour. of My Travels in the U. S.," manuscript diaries in the possession of his daughter, Mabel M. Watson of Devon, Pa.; *Who's Who in America*, 1899–1900; F. W. Ricord, *Hist. of Union County, N. J.* (1897), pp. 292–96; obituary in *Elizabeth Daily Jour.*, Sept. 29, 1900.]   R. F. S.

WATSON, JOHN CRITTENDEN (Aug. 24, 1842–Dec. 14, 1923), naval officer, was born at Frankfort, Ky., son of Dr. Edward Howe and Sarah Lee (Crittenden) Watson, grandson of John Jordan Crittenden [*q.v.*], and of ancestry distinguished in both Kentucky and Virginia. After study at Sayre School, Lexington, Ky., he

entered the United States Naval Academy at fourteen and graduated in 1860. Promoted to master, Aug. 31, 1861, he saw his first Civil War service in the sail-frigate *Sabine,* in which duty he was commended for his seamanship in the rescue of a disabled transport (*War of the Rebellion, post,* XII, 243). Afterward, as navigating officer in the *Hartford,* flagship of Admiral David Glasgow Farragut [*q.v.*], he took part in the passing of the forts below New Orleans (Apr. 24, 1862), in the subsequent advance to Vicksburg, and, after promotion to lieutenant (July 16, 1862), in the operations of March 1863 against Port Hudson, Grand Gulf, and Warrington, where he was slightly wounded by a shell fragment. From July 1863 until late in 1864 he was on Farragut's staff as flag lieutenant. Prior to the battle of Mobile Bay he commanded a boat party, July 5, 1864, which destroyed the blockade-runner *Ivanhoe* under the guns of Fort Morgan, and on three nights before the battle he engaged in extremely hazardous boat duty, removing torpedoes from the channel past the fort. Of slight, active build like Farragut, and sharing the latter's fondness for fighting and for reading the Scriptures, he had a devotion for the admiral which was warmly returned. "I am almost as fond of Watson," wrote Farragut to his son, "as yourself" (L. S. Farragut, *The Life of David Glasgow Farragut,* 1879, p. 403). It was Watson who, on the second occasion when this was done in the battle, passed a rope about the admiral to secure him to the mizzen rigging during the fight with the ram *Tennessee.* After the war he went to the European Squadron and was again under Farragut during the latter's European cruise in 1867–68.

Noteworthy in his service prior to the war with Spain were his command of the *Wyoming* (1878–80), which carried the American exhibits to the Paris exposition, his duty as naval representative at the exposition, his command of the new steel cruiser *San Francisco* (1892–94), and his superintendency of the Philadelphia Naval Home (1895–98). He was promoted to captain, Mar. 6, 1887, and to commodore, Nov. 7, 1897. During the Spanish-American War he had command, under W. T. Sampson [*q.v.*], of the North Cuban Blockading Squadron (May 6–June 21, 1898), and from June 27 to Sept. 20 was in command of the "Eastern Squadron" which was organized, though not actually dispatched, to menace the Spanish coast and force the recall from the East of the Spanish reserve squadron under Camara. He was made rear admiral (Mar. 3, 1899), commanded the Mare Island Navy Yard (October 1898–June 1899), and afterward until

October 1900 was in charge of the Asiatic station, succeeding Admiral George Dewey. From then until his retirement (Aug. 24, 1904), he had duty chiefly on the examining and retiring boards, and was also American naval representative at the coronation of Edward VII. Before and after retirement his home was in Washington, D. C., where for many years he was an elder in the Presbyterian Church. He was married, May 29, 1873, to his cousin, Elizabeth Anderson Thornton, daughter of Judge James Dabney Thornton of San Francisco, Cal., and had five sons and two daughters. His burial was in Arlington.

[*Who's Who in America*, 1922–23; *War of the Rebellion: Official Records (Navy)*, vols. XII, XVIII, XXI; W. H. Powell and Edward Shippen, *Officers of the Army and Navy (Regular) . . . in the Civil War* (1892); L. R. Hamersly, *Records of Living Officers of the U. S. Navy* (7th ed., 1902); J. C. Watson, "Farragut and Mobile Bay—Personal Reminiscences," *War Papers*, no. 98 (1916), pub. by Dist. of Columbia Commandery, Military Order of the Loyal Legion; *Army and Navy Jour.*, Dec. 22, 1923; obituary in *Washington Post*, Dec. 15, 1923.]

A. W—t.

WATSON, JOHN FANNING (June 13, 1779–Dec. 23, 1860), antiquarian, publisher, and financier, was the son of William and Lucy (Fanning) Watson, and was born at Batsto, Burlington County, N. J. His ancestors on both sides had emigrated to America from Dublin, Ireland, his father's ancestors settling in Salem, N. J., in 1667, his mother's in Groton, Conn., in 1641. Watson's father was the owner of several vessels, which he sold at the beginning of the Revolution, when he went to sea as a volunteer. After receiving some education Watson was placed in the counting-house of James Vanuxem in Philadelphia, where he remained until he was nineteen. At that time he offended his employers, who were in the French interest, by joining the Macpherson Blues, a military company organized in 1798 when the French difficulties with the United States were acute. He held a clerkship in the United States War Department until 1804, when he resigned to take charge of some business of Gen. James O'Hara [*q.v.*] of Pittsburgh. This took him to New Orleans, and he was later appointed commissary of provisions for the army posts in Louisiana. The death of his father in 1806 led Watson to return to his mother's home in Philadelphia. He at first engaged in business as a merchant, but in 1809 he opened a book store and, along with others in his trade, entered the publishing business. In 1809 he began to publish *Select Reviews of Literature and Spirit of the Foreign Magazines,* which he sold in 1812 and which in 1813 became the *Analectic Magazine.* He also reprinted Dr. Adam Clarke's *Commen-*

taries on the Old and New Testaments. He married Phebe Barron Crowell of Elizabethtown, N. J., said to be a descendant of Oliver Cromwell, in 1812, and two years later retired from the book business to become cashier of the newly organized Bank of Germantown.

While he was a resident of Germantown he took up seriously the work of authorship, directing his efforts to a study of the pioneer days of Pennsylvania and New York. He began in 1820 to collect in a methodical manner the recollections of the "oldest inhabitants" of Philadelphia. For this purpose he prepared a questionnaire, wrote innumerable letters, and traveled considerably, usually on foot. In 1830 he published in a fat volume of eight hundred pages his *Annals of Philadelphia,* in the back of which were his "Olden Time Researches and Reminiscences, of New York City." The work was illustrated by lithographs, many of them drawn from sketches he made from memory for the artist, W. L. Breton, of buildings which had long ceased to exist. (Joseph Jackson, "Iconography of Philadelphia," *Pennsylvania Magazine of History,* Jan. 1935, pp. 64–65.) He related his curious information in an engaging style, and his thoroughness in procuring documentary evidence at a time when this was not critically regarded soon established his work as a local classic, quoted to the present time (1936) because in many instances it is the only source. The *Annals* were reprinted in 1842 and 1856, and several times after Watson's death. In 1832 came his *Historic Tales of Olden Time, Concerning the Early Settlement and Advancement of New-York City and State*; in 1833, *Historic Tales of Olden Time, Concerning the Early Settlement and Progress of Philadelphia and Pennsylvania*; and in 1846, *Annals and Occurrences of New York City and State.* Even before his *Annals* were published, Watson's antiquarian researches awakened an interest in the history of Pennsylvania which culminated in the establishment (1824) of the Historical Society of Pennsylvania. He is said to have persuaded G. W. P. Custis [*q.v.*] to write his *Recollections and Private Memoirs of Washington* (1860), and he was the leader of movements to have the graves of several historical characters properly marked. After serving the Bank of Germantown for thirty-three years, he resigned in 1847 to become treasurer and secretary of the Philadelphia, Germantown & Norristown railroad. In the summer of 1859, upon reaching his eightieth birthday, he retired from business. He died, Dec. 23, 1860, leaving three daughters and two sons, the survivors of seven children.

[See Benjamin Dorr, *A Memoir of John Fanning Watson* (1861); W. P. Hazard, memoir in *Annals of Philadelphia* (1879), which includes some personal researches; B. J. Lossing, in *Harper's Encyc. of U. S. Hist.* (1912), vol. X; obituaries in *Public Ledger* (Phila.), Dec. 25, and *Phila. Daily News*, Dec. 26, 1860. A vol. in MS. of Watson's *Annals* belongs to the Lib. Company of Phila.; another, with a part of his extensive material, is in the Hist. Soc. of Pa.] J. J.

WATSON, JOHN WILLIAM CLARK (Feb. 27, 1808–Sept. 24, 1890), lawyer, senator in the Confederate Congress, was born in Albemarle County, Va., the son of John and Elizabeth (Finch) Watson. His early education was secured in the schools of his county which, though inadequate, enabled him to equip himself for entrance to the law department of the University of Virginia, where he was graduated with the degree of B.L. in 1830. After practising his profession in Abingdon, Va., from 1831 to 1845, he removed to Holly Springs, Miss., where he formed a partnership with J. W. Clapp, a prominent lawyer of that place.

In Mississippi he continued his alignment with the Whig party and was soon regarded as a trusted adviser in its councils. He was a member of the Mississippi state convention of 1851, and concurred in the action of that body denying the right of secession. During the presidential campaign of 1860, he established a newspaper at Holly Springs and placed it under competent editorial charge with the purpose of attempting to stem the tide of disunion. After the election of Lincoln he was defeated by sixteen votes as an anti-secession candidate for the state convention of 1861. He acquiesced in the withdrawal of Mississippi from the Union, however, and accepted various offices in the Confederate government. From Feb. 17, 1864, until the end of the war, he was a senator in the Confederate Congress. He approved the work of the state convention of 1865, of which he was a member, but he opposed giving any aid or comfort to Jefferson Davis, or doing anything to antagonize the victors. He received thirty-three votes for president of the "Black and Tan" convention of 1868, but when it adopted the proscriptive qualifications he resigned and returned to Holly Springs to lead the canvass in northern Mississippi against the constitution, which was rejected. He took an active part in the overthrow of the Ames régime, and in May 1876, was appointed by Gov. John M. Stone [*q.v.*] a judge of the circuit court. As such he was a "terror to evil doers," but in 1882, at the end of his six-year term, he resumed the practice of law. He reached the peak of his legal career in October 1885, when having been appointed by Gov. Robert Lowry to represent Mis-

sissippi before the Supreme Court of the United States in the railroad commission cases, he secured a reversal of the decision of the circuit court of appeals, the Supreme Court ruling that the legislative act, passed in 1884 to regulate rates and to create a railroad commission, was constitutional (116 *U. S.*, 307).

Watson was an uncompromising Puritan in character, an elder in the Presbyterian Church at Holly Springs for more than forty years, and one of the pioneer prohibitionists of the state. He invited Frances E. Willard to Mississippi and paid her traveling expenses when she toured the state crusading for prohibition in January 1882. On Sept. 8, 1831, he married Catherine Davis, sister of Prof. J. A. G. Davis, professor of law at the University of Virginia. To this union were born eight children, only two of whom survived the father; two sons were killed in the Civil War. Watson died at Holly Springs.

[*Biog. and Hist. Memoirs of Miss.* (1891), vol. II; Dunbar Rowland, *Mississippi* (1907), vol. II; Reuben Davis, *Recollections of Miss. and Mississippians* (1889); W. B. Hamilton, "Holly Springs, Miss., in the Year 1878," manuscript thesis in Univ. of Miss. Lib.; J. W. Garner, *Reconstruction in Miss.* (1901); *Proc. Miss. Bar Asso.*, 1891; letters of Watson to W. L. Sharkey, Correspondence of the Governors, Series E. No. 65, Dept. Archives and Hist., Jackson, Miss.; *Jour. of the Cong. of the Confederate States*, vols. IV (1904), V (1905).] P. L. R.

WATSON, SERENO (Dec. 1, 1826–Mar. 9, 1892), botanist, was born at East Windsor Hill, Conn., the tenth of thirteen children of Henry and Julia (Reed) Watson. He was a descendant of Robert Watson who emigrated to America and had settled in Windsor, Conn., by 1639. He was reared on a farm and in 1847 graduated from Yale College, where he displayed an aptitude for the classics. Shy and reticent, he tried teaching, medicine, banking and insurance, editorial work, and farming, with little success. At forty he entered the Sheffield Scientific School to study chemistry and mineralogy, hoping to fit himself for life in California. Reaching San Francisco by the Panama route in April 1867, he soon abandoned hope of farming, and set out to find the exploring expedition led by Clarence King [*q.v.*] and obtain employment in its party, just starting a scientific survey of the Great Basin. King, already annoyed by unpromising applicants for service on this governmental undertaking, was little disposed to favor the middle-aged man, who one July night, dusty and footsore, reached his camp on the Truckee River. However, Watson was permitted to join the party as a volunteer aid, though assigned only menial tasks. Here his varied training, industry, and vigor were much in his favor, and within a month he was receiving a small salary. Soon afterwards, upon the resignation of the botanist of the party, William Whitman Bailey, Watson was commissioned to collect plants and secure data regarding them. Thus, by chance, in his forty-second year he undertook the work in which he was to attain distinction. His collections, which he took to Yale for elaboration, were extensive, well prepared, and accompanied by far more methodical field data than had been taken in earlier governmental surveys. His *Botany* (1871), usually called "Botany of the King Expedition," was the fifth volume in the report of the geological survey, a well-illustrated quarto of five hundred pages. In preparing it, Watson was much aided by Daniel Cady Eaton at Yale, John Torrey at Columbia, and Asa Gray [*qq.v.*] at Harvard. Not only enumerating the plants, it embodied so many keys and group-revisions that it became virtually a flora of the Great Basin and contained phytogeographic matter in advance of its time. Rapidly prepared in finished detail and seen through press by 1871, this impressive work, Watson's maiden effort in scientific publication, gave ample proof that he had found his bent.

Soon afterwards Watson settled in Cambridge, Mass., where in 1873 he became assistant in the Gray Herbarium and the following year its curator, a post he held capably through the rest of his life. Thus settled at Harvard, he undertook the *Botany of California*. Of this great work, the first volume (1876) was collaborative, W. H. Brewer [*q.v.*] of Yale aiding on the *Polypetalae*, and Gray contributing the *Gamopetalae*. The second and even more difficult volume (1880), covering the rest of the flowering plants, ferns, mosses, and hepatics, was prepared chiefly by Watson. This flora, the earliest for its region, greatly influenced subsequent work on the vegetation of the Pacific Slope. In curatorial routine, Watson identified many collections from the western states and Mexico, including the earlier ones of Edward Palmer and C. G. Pringle. Diagnoses of the many new genera and species he encountered were published in eighteen "Contributions to American Botany," appearing chiefly in the *Proceedings of the American Academy of Arts and Sciences,* and including many monographic treatments of difficult groups. To create a guide to the literature of his subject, he spent long evenings compiling his *Bibliographical Index to North American Botany.* The only completed volume was published in 1878 by the Smithsonian Institution. Later he undertook the completion of the *Manual of the Mosses of North America* (1884) begun by Leo Lesquereux and

Thomas Potts James [*qq.v.*], and the continuation of Asa Gray's *Synoptical Flora of North America.* In 1889, aided by John Merle Coulter [*q.v.*], he revised Gray's *Manual of Botany,* extending its range to the one-hundredth meridian. After the King expedition, he did little field work, though for the forestry records of the Tenth Census he made a hurried journey to the Bitter Root Mountains and some other parts of the Northwest. In 1885 he attempted botanical exploration in Guatemala, but was forced by a tropical fever to abandon the undertaking.

Watson was of fine appearance and great dignity, a silent man, who worked steadily, calmly, and with remarkable speed. He remained a bachelor and was something of a recluse; yet to those who ventured to turn to him for aid, he was most kind. He died at Cambridge, of an influenza which caused enlargement of the heart, and was buried by his request in the Harvard Lot at Mount Auburn Cemetery. He was a member of numerous scientific societies both in America and abroad.

[H. R. Stiles, *The Hist. and Genealogies of Ancient Windsor, Conn.* (1891), vol. II ; G. L. Goodale, in *Proc. Am. Acad. of Arts and Sciences,* vol. XXVII (1893), with bibliog. ; *Obit. Record Grads. Yale Univ.* (1892) ; *The Jubilee Anniversary Report . . . Class of 1847, Yale Univ.* (1897), ed. by H. B. Chapin ; J. M. Coulter, in *Botanical Gazette,* May 1892, with portrait ; Walter Deane, in *Bull. Torrey Botanical Club,* Apr. 1892 ; M. B., in *Scientific American,* Apr. 9, 1892, with portrait ; I. Urban, *Berichte der Deutschen Botanischen Gesellschaft,* vol. X (1892) ; obituary in *Boston Transcript,* Mar. 10, 1892 ; Yale alumni records ; personal recollections.]   B. L. R.

WATSON, THOMAS AUGUSTUS (Jan. 18, 1854–Dec. 13, 1934), telephone man and shipbuilder, was born in Salem, Mass., the son of Thomas R. Watson, the foreman in a livery stable, and Mary (Phipps), his wife. The boy went to the public schools of Salem until he was fourteen years old and then went to work. In 1872 he got a job in Boston in the electrical shop of Charles Williams, Jr., at 109 Court Street. A number of inventors had their models made at Williams' shop, and in 1874 Watson did some work for Alexander Graham Bell [*q.v.*], with whom he worked thereafter during all the experimental period of the telephone and the years that followed until it was commercially established. When the first telephone organization was formed in 1877, Watson was given an interest in the business and when Bell went to Europe he became the research and technical head of the Bell Telephone Company.

In the spring of 1881 Watson resigned from the Telephone Company and went to Europe for a year. On Sept. 5, 1882, he married Elizabeth Seaver Kimball of Cohasset, Mass.; they had four children. Soon after his marriage Watson settled in East Braintree, Mass., with the idea of becoming a farmer, but his mechanical inclination asserted itself and with Frank O. Wellington as a partner he opened a machine shop and began to build engines and ships. In 1896 they undertook their first contract for the United States government, the destroyers *Lawrence* and *Macdonough*; these were followed by the lightship for Cape Hatteras and the cruiser *Des Moines*. The increasing size of the ships they were building made it necessary, in spite of hard times, to move down to deeper water and to increase the size of their shipyard. An additional consideration influencing Watson's decision to make this move was the large number of unemployed people to whom the new yard would be able to give work. Interest in these people also brought Watson into public education and for a while into politics, in which he worked for better social conditions. In February 1901, the shipyard was incorporated as the Fore River Ship & Engine Company. Among the vessels it produced were the battleships *Rhode Island, New Jersey,* and *Vermont*; two steel schooners, the seven-masted *Thomas W. Lawson* and the six-masted *William L. Douglas*; and two vessels for the Fall River Line, the *Providence* and the *Boston*. The competition of foreign shipbuilding produced a situation which took the control of the company out of Watson's hands, however, and in 1904 he resigned and retired from business. Admiral Frank T. Bowles then took charge of the further development of the concern until the World War, when the plant was sold to the Bethlehem Steel Company.

When Watson was forty, and recognized as a prominent shipbuilder, he and his wife entered the Massachusetts Institute of Technology as students, taking special courses in geology and literature. In geology he became the respected associate of professional scientists, while in literature he became well known as an interpreter of poetry and drama. He was for some time the president of the Boston Browning Society. For a season he was an actor in the company of Sir Frank Benson in England and he had speaking parts in the Shakespeare Festival at Stratford-on-Avon, Apr. 7–May 6, 1911. He became a proficient student of music and painting. No less did he continue to follow the developments of electrical science and the work of the telephone engineers; nor did his inquiry fail to include problems of philosophy and religion. Ever since as a child he first ventured through the alley from the stable yard out into the world, he found the range of his experience immeasurably ex-hilarating and inspiring; in 1926 he published his autobiography, to which he gave the title *Exploring Life*. He was a fellow of the American Institute of Electrical Engineers, and received three honorary degrees. He died at his winter home at Passagrille Key, Fla.

[Watson's autobiog.; *Who's Who in America*, 1934–35; papers in the Am. Telephone Hist. Lib., 195 Broadway, New York; F. L. Rhodes, *Beginnings of Telephony* (1929); W. C. Langdon, "Thomas A. Watson, 1854–1934," *A. T. & T. Co. Headquarters Bull.*, Dec. 21, 1934, and separately reprinted; *N. Y. Herald Tribune*, Dec. 15, 1934.]   W.C.L.

WATSON, THOMAS EDWARD (Sept. 5, 1856–Sept. 26, 1922), political leader, author, the son of John Smith and Ann Eliza (Maddox) Watson, was born in Columbia County near Thomson, Ga. He was named Edward Thomas, but changed the order in his youth. English Quaker ancestors of his had settled in Georgia by 1768. His grandfather, Thomas M. Watson, a planter, "tall, venerable, imposing" in the eyes of an idolatrous boy, owned forty-five slaves and an estate valued on the tax records at $55,000. With the Civil War, which was associated in the boy's mind with the death of his grandfather and uncle, began the decline of his twice-wounded father to a wretched state of fortune and self-esteem. Romantic and sensitive, yet assertive and ambitious, Thomas confessed much to his diaries and journals, kept a record of his reading, and wrote quantities of verse. He spent two years at Mercer University, a small Baptist college, and two as an impoverished country school teacher. On Oct. 9, 1878, he married Georgia Durham of Thomson, where he now made his home. Two years earlier, having studied law privately, he began his dramatic rise as a criminal lawyer. After eleven years he could estimate his "assets," consisting largely of land, at $30,585. Finding his family in "a miserable shanty skirted by a long marsh," he triumphantly restored them to their old home and administered a public thrashing to the landlord who had mistreated his brother.

In political as in private life Watson assumed the role of agrarian avenger. A rebel and fighter by temperament, he was made by circumstance hostile to the new order and nostalgic for the old. Brought early under the personal influence of Robert Toombs and Alexander H. Stephens [*qq.v.*], he carried over into later movements many of the ideas and something of the spirit of the Confederate agrarians. At twenty-three he directed his first political effort against the state Democratic machine, dominated by capitalist-industrialists, and in his single term (1882) in the state Assembly he maintained this insurgency. As the New South tightened its alliance with the industrial North, and farmers declined in wealth and prestige, Watson's mistrust of Henry W. Grady's message crystallized: such leaders would "betray the South with a Judas kiss." Insisting that the natural ally of the South was the agrarian West, he easily won his race for Congress in 1890 on the Farmers' Alliance platform. Then choosing between fidelity to reform pledges and loyalty to the Democratic party, he boldly announced himself a Populist. His utter fearlessness, his earnestness, and the appealing combination of poet, prophet, and rustic humorist in his nature won a following that was fanatical in its loyalty. Red-headed, scrawny, yet inspiring, Tom Watson became almost the incarnation of the new agrarian revolt in the South.

As the new party's candidate for speaker and its leader in the House, Watson introduced many Alliance reform bills and supported advanced labor legislation. He also introduced the first resolution ever passed providing for free delivery of rural mail (*Congressional Record*, 52 Cong., 2 Sess., pp. 1759–60). In 1891 he founded the *People's Party Paper* and the following year published *The People's Party Campaign Book* (1892), with the subtitle, *Not a Revolt; It Is a Revolution*. Meanwhile, his district had been gerrymandered, and in the bloody and fraudulent election of 1892 his Democratic opponent was declared victor. Undaunted by persecution, he swayed thousands with redoubled denunciations of trusts, capitalist finance, and Democratic policies. The next election, in which he met another defeat, was unquestionably fraudulent and even more bloody, but his fight won praise from radical Populists everywhere. In 1896 he was nominated for the vice-presidency by the national Populist convention before Bryan was chosen to head the ticket. Known as an enemy of fusion with either party, Watson nevertheless accepted the nomination, being assured that only thus could all factions be harmonized, and that the Democrats would withdraw Arthur Sewall [*q.v.*] from their ticket. He campaigned in the West for Bryan, but, contemptuously treated by the Democrats and deserted by Populist fusionists, he admitted that his position was "most humiliating." His small vote was a measure of the demoralization of the Populists that was wrought by fusion.

Embittered by three defeats and what he felt was a betrayal, he retired from public life for eight years and turned to writing. *The Story of France* (1899), a popular history in two large volumes, is a Populist interpretation infused with the author's social philosophy, yet a work of some merit, as is also his *Napoleon: A Sketch of His Life* (1902). His other biographies, *The Life and Times of Thomas Jefferson* (1903) and *The Life and Times of Andrew Jackson* (1912), begun in 1907, are partisan and rambling. *Bethany* (1904) is a sentimental and unorganized novel. Later he published *Life and Speeches of Thos. E. Watson* (1908), *Political and Economic Handbook* (1908), and *Prose Miscellanies* (1912).

As the Populist candidate for president in 1904, Watson polled only 117,183 votes, but gained considerable attention from prominent reformers. In 1905 he founded in New York *Tom Watson's Magazine* (changed to *Watson's Magazine* in 1906), featuring mainly his reform editorials, but also publishing contributions from such authors as Masters, Dreiser, and Gorky. After quarreling with the publishers, he established in Georgia his *Weekly Jeffersonian* and *Watson's Jeffersonian Magazine*. His race for president in 1908 was only a gesture.

New issues now overshadowed the industrialist-agrarian conflict, and Watson, counting forty-four tenants on his broad plantations and estimating his wealth at $258,000, had changed. Old traits of irascibility and vindictiveness gained the upper hand. His politics changed with his character. Shifting his followers from one Democratic faction to the other, he virtually dictated state politics. As bewildered Populists quit his ranks, their places were filled with recruits attracted by his sensational crusades against Catholicism, Socialism, foreign missions, the negro, and Leo M. Frank. Frank, whom Watson had attacked bitterly as an individual and a Jew, was lynched in 1915, after his death sentence for the murder of a girl had been commuted (besides Watson's articles in his magazine and weekly, Sept.–Dec. 1915, see *Augusta Chronicle*, special supplement of Nov. 25, 1915; *New York Times*, Sept. 13, 14, 1915; C. P. Connolly, *The Truth About the Frank Case*, 1915). Then with sudden resurgence of his old spirit Watson arose to denounce American intervention in the World War as "ravenous commercialism," and war-time regimentation as "universal goose-stepping." Until his publications were excluded from the mails and he was temporarily crazed by the death of his two children, he conducted a courageous fight against conscription. Losing his race for Congress in 1918 and the state presidential primary in 1920 by narrow margins, he was overwhelmingly elected to the Senate the latter year on the same platform, the restoration of civil liberties and the defeat of the League of Nations. In the Senate he expressed sympathy for Soviet Russia, organized labor, and oppressed minorities, but his brief senatorial career, ended by his death, while fiery and sensational, was without significant accomplishment.

Some of the pathos and irony of his life may be caught in the "Thomas E. Watson Song," a ballad of "a man of mighty power," who "fought and struggled" and failed. It is still heard in backwoods Georgia.

[Watson MSS., Chapel Hill, N. C., available only by permission of the family; MSS. in possession of family, Thomson, Ga.; J. D. Wade, "Jefferson: New Style," *Am. Mercury*, Nov. 1929; A. M. Arnett, *The Populist Movement in Georgia* (1922); W. W. Brewton, *The Life of Thomas E. Watson* (1926); Daniel De Leon, *Watson on the Gridiron* (1926); obituary in *Atlanta Constitution*, Sept. 22, 1922; "Thomas E. Watson," a Columbia phonograph record.]   V. W.

WATSON, WILLIAM (Jan. 19, 1834–Sept. 30, 1915), engineer, educator, was born at Nantucket, Mass., the son of William and Mary (Macy) Watson. In 1857 he graduated from the Lawrence Scientific School of Harvard University with the degree of S.B. in engineering, having won the Boyden Prize in mathematics, and while serving as instructor in differential and integral calculus, 1857–59, he was awarded a second bachelor's degree, in mathematics, in 1858. Going for graduate study to the University of Jena, he received the degree of Ph.D. there in 1862 and subsequently took a partial course at the École Nationale des Ponts et Chaussées at Paris. While he was in Europe, during the years 1860–63, he collected information on technical instruction which in 1864 was used as a basis in planning the organization of the Massachusetts Institute of Technology. He was appointed to the faculty of the new institution as its first professor of mechanical engineering and descriptive geometry (1865–73) and organized the instruction in these subjects.

In 1867 he visited the Universal Exposition at Paris and took lessons in plaster modeling while there. When he returned to America he brought models illustrating stereotomy, and in his courses introduced for the first time the practice of constructing from the drawings plaster models of the problems which occur in masonry —arches of various kinds, doorways, stairways, domes. While abroad he had also spent some time at Karlsruhe, where he prepared lithographic notes for his lectures on elasticity and resistance of materials. In 1869 he again visited Europe and brought back with him valuable drawings from the Polytechnic School at Karlsruhe as well as a collection of models for instruction in descriptive geometry and mechanism. In

1873 he resigned his professorship in order to devote himself more fully to his studies; in the same year he married Margaret Fiske, daughter of Augustus H. Fiske of Boston, and went as one of the United States commissioners to the Vienna exposition.

He was a member of the American Society of Civil Engineers and of the American Academy of Arts and Sciences (of which he was recording secretary from 1884 until his death). As an active member of the Mathematical and Physical Club, founded in the early eighties, he contributed much in an informal way to further the interests of the instructors in mathematics and physics at Harvard and the Massachusetts Institute of Technology. By his activity in the Society of Arts of the Massachusetts Institute of Technology, which began its work even before the Institute was opened to students and inaugurated the *Technology Quarterly* at a time when technical journals were scarce, he contributed to increase in America the knowledge of recent advances in science and engineering. His published works include: *Papers on Technical Education* (1872); *A Course in Descriptive Geometry* (1873); the chapters on civil engineering and architecture in Vol. III (1876) of the *Reports of the Commissioners of the United States to the International Exhibition Held at Vienna, 1873*, edited by Robert H. Thurston [*q.v.*]; *On the Protection of Life from Casualties in the Use of Machinery* (1880); *A Course in Shades and Shadows* (1889); *Paris Universal Exposition: Civil Engineering, Public Works and Architecture* (1892); *The International Water Transportation Congress, 1893* (1894), and many technical articles.

[*Trans. Am. Soc. Mech. Eng.*, vol. XXXVII (1916); *Technology Rev.*, Nov. 1915; C. R. Cross, in *Proc. Am. Acad. Arts and Sci.*, vol. LII (1917); *Who's Who in America*, 1914–15; *N. Y. Times*, Oct. 1, 1915.]
T. L. D.

WATTERSON, HARVEY MAGEE (Nov. 23, 1811–Oct. 1, 1891), editor and congressman from Tennessee, was born at Beech Grove, Bedford County, Tenn. His father, William S. Watterson, emigrated from Virginia to Tennessee in 1804, served on Andrew Jackson's staff in the War of 1812, accumulated a fortune as a cotton planter, and was a prominent figure in the Tennessee railroad movement at the time of his death in 1851. Harvey Watterson was educated at Cumberland College, Princeton, Ky. He studied law, was admitted to the bar, and began the practice of his profession at Shelbyville, Tenn., in 1830. The next year he was elected to the lower house of the state legislature and by successive reëlections served until 1839 (*Courier-Journal*, *post*). In that year he was elected to the federal House of Representatives and was reëlected in 1841. According to the testimony of his son, Watterson did not take his duties at Washington seriously, but, provided with an excellent income by his father, directed his energies to revelry and occasional escapades of a graver nature, "his principal yokemate in the pleasures and dissipations of those times being Franklin Pierce" (*Marse Henry, post,* I, 26). At the end of his second term in the house he was sent by President Tyler on a diplomatic mission to Buenos Aires to obtain information on the foreign relations of Argentina, commercial matters, and the war then raging with Uruguay. In February 1844 he was nominated chargé, but the Senate in the following June rejected the nomination (S. F. Bemis, *American Secretaries of State and Their Diplomacy,* vol. V, 1928, p. 216).

Returning to Tennessee in 1845, Watterson was at once elected to the state Senate and was made its presiding officer. In September 1849 he became the proprietor of the *Nashville Daily Union,* whose editorship he took over the following year (S. L. Sioussat, "Tennessee, the Compromise of 1850, and the Nashville Convention," *Mississippi Valley Historical Review,* Dec. 1915, p. 235 n.). He remained as editor of the Nashville paper until 1851, when he went to Washington as editor of the *Washington Union.* Watterson had always been a Democrat, but he was opposed to the extension of slavery and retired from the editorship of the *Union* because he could not support the policy of the administration in regard to the repeal of the Missouri Compromise. He retired to private life in Tennessee, refusing the governorship of Oregon, and, in 1857, a nomination to Congress. He supported Stephen A. Douglas [*q.v.*] in the campaign of 1860. He was a member of the secession convention of Tennessee but opposed secession. He remained a Unionist throughout the war, living in retirement on his plantation at Beech Grove. He supported Andrew Johnson [*q.v.*] during his presidency, and for the ten years after the war lived at Washington engaged in the practice of law. After the death of his wife he divided his time between Washington and Louisville, Ky., where his son, Henry Watterson [*q.v.*], was editor of the *Courier-Journal.* At the time of his death he was on the editorial staff of the *Courier-Journal,* in which his writings were signed "An Old Fogy." He was buried in the Cave Hill Cemetery at Louisville.

Watterson married in 1830 Talitha Black, daughter of James Black of Maury County, Tenn. He was a member of the Presbyterian Church. He was sponsored in his political life by Andrew Jackson [*q.v.*], the close friend of his father. In ante-bellum days he was a man of great influence in Tennessee politics and was the recognized leader of the Union wing of the Democratic party in the last decade before the war. He was a vigorous editor and a writer of merit, but his reputation in that line as in others has been obscured by the fame of his son, and only child.

[See obituary in *Courier-Jour.* (Louisville, Ky.), Oct. 2, 1891; Henry Watterson, *"Marse Henry"; an Autobiog.* (2 vols., 1919); *Biog. Dir. Am. Cong.* (1928); and *The South in the Building of the Nation* (1909), vol. XII.]   R. S. C.

WATTERSON, HENRY (Feb. 16, 1840–Dec. 22, 1921), editor and statesman, was born in Washington, D. C., the son of Harvey Magee Watterson [*q.v.*], a member of Congress from Tennessee, and of Talitha Black, also of Tennessee. At that time the "Tennessee dynasty" was in the ascendant. The child, small and sickly, each year made the journey from the capital to the two family homesteads: that of the Wattersons, Beech Grove, in Bedford County, and of the Blacks, Spring Hill, in Maury County, Tenn. A juvenile onlooker in the House, playing at page with the consent of his indulgent father, Watterson was on the floor when John Quincy Adams, then a member, was stricken and carried from his seat to die. He had visited the Hermitage with his father about 1844 and sat on Jackson's knee, and he later met all the other presidents between Jackson and Harding. He died in Harding's time, but he already numbered among his acquaintances Calvin Coolidge, Herbert Hoover, and Franklin D. Roosevelt. His schooling, save for a few terms at the Protestant Episcopal Academy at Philadelphia, was informal; he was the sort of person who readily absorbed education and culture through books and people. The youthful Watterson was for a time looked upon as the possessor of rare talent as a pianist. But a weak left hand and the early failure of sight in his right eye (which later became totally blind) ended his musical studies, although the influence of rhythm upon his journalistic and literary style remained a marked characteristic. As a youth of twelve he played an accompaniment for Adelina Patti, herself aged nine.

By 1856 the family was back in residence in Tennessee, the elder Watterson a strong Union Democrat. The son remained until 1858, when he went East again to engage in newspaper work. After a brief experience working on reportorial assignments for the *New York Times,* Watterson became a reporter for the

Daily States, of Washington—oddly enough holding at the same time "a clerkship, a real 'sinecure' in the Interior Department" (*"Marse Henry,"* I, 59)—and it fell to his lot to report the inauguration of Abraham Lincoln. A Unionist through conviction, although he became a secessionist and Confederate soldier because of sectional sympathies, he was drawn strongly to Lincoln, and some of his best-known writings were devoted to appreciations of the Civil War president. In 1861, for reasons which Watterson thought unsavory (*Ibid.,* p. 81), Secretary of War Simon Cameron [*q.v.*] offered him, through the clerk of the House, J. W. Forney [*q.v.*], a commission as lieutenant-colonel and private secretary. Watterson went home to Tennessee instead, determined to spend his time peacefully in writing until the war cloud was dispelled. He did not think the South could hold out long. But at home he found himself alone. "The boys were all gone to the front, and the girls were . . . all crazy" (*Ibid.,* p. 82). So he joined the Confederate army and, by some loose arrangement not defined, was in and out of it for four years. He was on the staff of Gen. Leonidas Polk [*q.v.*] until he fell ill; then, in his grey jacket, he worked on a Southern propaganda newspaper in Nashville.

After the fall of Nashville he engaged in more desultory soldiering, but he soon found himself appointed editor of the state newspaper at Chattanooga, which he named the *Rebel,* and turned it into the organ of the army. This remarkable journal, copies of which are preserved in Southern archives, was the first medium through which Watterson displayed that color and force of style which were later to make him outstanding among American editors throughout a half-century of active editorship. While editing the *Rebel,* he met his future business partner, Walter N. Haldeman, proprietor of the *Louisville Courier,* who, being a strong Southern sympathizer, had suspended his newspaper and retired behind the Southern lines. Editing the *Rebel,* however, became too precarious as the Union army moved on Atlanta, and, after serving Generals Albert Sidney Johnston and John Bell Hood [*qq.v.*] in various staff capacities, Watterson was offered by the Confederate government an opportunity, if he could reach Liverpool, of selling some cotton to British buyers. The young soldier, after various fantastic adventures with friendly Union officers, found the exits of the country closed, and settled down once more as an editor in Montgomery, Ala.

In 1865 the future "Marse Henry" of editorials and cartoons, the war just over, got an editorial job in Cincinnati on the *Evening Times,* owned by Calvin W. Starbuck. Upon the editor's sudden death Starbuck gave Watterson the place at $75 a week. The *Cincinnati Commercial,* under the inspiration of Murat Halstead [*q.v.*], greeted the young editor's first issue with some telling references to his fresh connection with the Confederate cause. Watterson went to Halstead and asked for quarter, saying that he meant to leave Cincinnati as soon as he could get a grubstake. That visit was the beginning of a friendship and political association which flowered notably through the famous "Quadrilateral" at the Greeley convention in 1872. A brief and successful newspaper venture at Nashville lasted almost through 1866. Watterson married Rebecca Ewing of Nashville on Dec. 20, 1865, and in 1867 took his bride to London. He returned to Nashville to join the staff of the *Republican Banner.* Simultaneously came two offers from Louisville—one from the senescent George Dennison Prentice [*q.v.*] to help edit the *Louisville Daily Journal,* another from Haldeman to become editor of the *Courier,* its publication resumed after the return of its publisher from behind the Southern lines. Watterson proposed consolidation to Haldeman, who declined. He joined the *Journal,* and, after half a year's lively but kindly battle with the *Courier,* the merger was made, and on Nov. 8, 1868, the *Courier-Journal* began its existence.

The *Courier-Journal* was one day old when its young editor began the struggle for the restoration of Southern home rule ("Carpet-Baggery and Peace," *Courier-Journal,* Nov. 9, 1868). Always a foe of slavery, Watterson agitated for the complete bestowal of civil and legal rights upon the negroes in exchange for the return of the South to its homefolk. Carl Schurz and Horace Greeley [*qq.v.*] ranged themselves with the Louisville editor, and, although their cause had a setback in the Greeley-Liberal campaign of 1872, it was won four years later. The Greeley campaign was always held by Watterson to have "shortened the distance across the bloody chasm" (*"Marse Henry,"* I, 266), and it was at the Liberal Republican nominating convention at Cincinnati that he, Schurz, Samuel Bowles, Murat Halstead, and (later) Whitelaw Reid and Horace White [*qq.v.*] formed the Quadrilateral (though they were six, not four), and first met Joseph Pulitzer [*q.v.*], a delegate from Missouri. About 1874 Watterson fixed upon Gov. Samuel Jones Tilden [*q.v.*] as the hope of the party and a reunited country. Carefully and intelligently he began to build up the governor of New York for the presidency, this culminating in the nomination of 1876. To Watterson, Tilden was the "ideal statesman." Except for Lincoln he was the editor's only public hero. During the 1876 campaign Watterson, at Tilden's request, took advantage of a Congressional vacancy through death in the Louisville district and sat, during the summer of 1876 and part of the winter of 1877, in the House as Tilden's floor leader, vociferously watching the contest that ended with the certification of Hayes. It was in this period that the passionate correspondence to the *Courier-Journal* from its Representative-editor in Washington appeared, including the suggestion —so alarming to the Northern press—that "a hundred thousand petitioners . . . ten thousand unarmed Kentuckians" come to the capital to see that justice was done (*Courier-Journal*, Jan. 5, 1877).

After the inauguration of Hayes, the editor returned to his tripod, never again to hold public office, although once he considered being a candidate for the Democratic nomination for governor of Kentucky if that was overwhelmingly desired—which it was not. Never again did he express more than temporary fealty to any Democratic presidential nominee or White House incumbent. He was highly critical of Cleveland and bitterly opposed his third nomination in 1892. The pair never got on, and many were the stories of private reasons for their long estrangement. (See *"Marse Henry,"* II, 116–17, 133–39.) In 1896 the *Courier-Journal* announced it would oppose William Jennings Bryan on the free silver issue. Watterson, on holiday abroad, had no part in the decision. But, learning of it, he cabled back to his partner, Haldeman, the message: "No compromise with dishonor" (*Courier-Journal*, July 13, 1896), and —save for one long editorial, sent from Switzerland—left the conduct of the fight for John B. Palmer and Simon B. Buckner (which meant McKinley) in Kentucky largely to his associate editor, Harrison Robertson. The stand almost destroyed the *Courier-Journal,* so resentful were the Democrats of the state against it, for— chiefly because of its activity—that was the time when, in Robert Ingersoll's phrase, "hell froze over," and Kentucky went Republican. Watterson and Haldeman, working to regain their lost ground, supported William Goebel [*q.v.*] for governor against the Republican nominee in 1898, and by 1900 had managed to figure out a way to support the second nomination of Bryan. In 1908 Watterson allowed Josephus Daniels to use his name as "honorary publicity chairman" in the third Bryan campaign. But he deplored Bryan's appointment as secretary of

state by Woodrow Wilson in 1913 (*Courier-Journal,* Dec. 21, 1912) and assailed him as an impractical dreamer when the Secretary left the cabinet on the war issue.

During the first decade of the twentieth century Watterson's chief national contribution was a series of philippics against "The Man on Horseback," as he called Theodore Roosevelt. Since his editorials were generally carried by telegraph to all newspapers in the country as a matter of news, this crusade became very famous. In the course of it Watterson announced that Roosevelt was unquestionably a paranoiac, determined to assume dictatorship of the country, and urged his family to sequestrate the Colonel. In 1909 he offered to bet the New York *World* a dinner that Roosevelt would quarrel with his chosen successor, Taft, and won the bet easily.

George Harvey [*q.v.*] in 1910 deeply interested Watterson in Woodrow Wilson, behind whom the editor marshaled his forces through the primary contest with Senator James Smith, calling the Governor "the hope of Democracy." But Wilson's blunt admission to Harvey, in answer to a question from the latter, that Harvey's editorial support in *Harper's Weekly* was damaging him with liberals and progressives, offended and alienated the sentimental Watterson, and he attempted to prevent the nomination of Wilson in 1912 (*Courier-Journal,* Feb. 21, 1912). Failing, he became a lukewarm observer and critic, varying from mild to severe, until the issues raised by Charles Evans Hughes and Theodore Roosevelt in 1916 ranged him on Wilson's side. He supported the President enthusiastically that year, and through the war, but he could not accept the idea of the League of Nations, and once more parted company with the President. Charged with being unable to stand by Democratic presidents, he reminded his critics through the *Courier-Journal* that "things have come to a hell of a pass when a man can't wallop his own jackass," an affectedly crude type of retort that, appealing strongly to the humorous sense of the American people, was part of his hold upon his readers.

Many trips abroad and Florida holidays punctuated editorial duties from 1880 on, but invariably Watterson wrote voluminously and frequently from wherever he was. The summer before the World War he was abroad, but he returned after Serajevo to throw himself strongly into an editorial assault against the Central Powers, which he attacked as foes of Christianity. "To hell with the Hohenzollerns and the Hapsburgs," he exclaimed in the *Courier-Jour-*

nal on Sept. 3, 1914, and from then until the armistice, he repeated this stirring objurgation. In 1917 he was awarded the Pulitzer prize for his editorials hailing the declaration of war against the Central Powers by the United States. In August 1918, with two of the three children of his late partner, Haldeman, after litigation with the third growing out of the suppression of a Watterson editorial, the editor sold control of the *Courier-Journal* to Robert W. Bingham, and, after a brief connection as editor emeritus, Watterson, nearly eighty, retired finally to private life, which he spent on his estate, Mansfield, near Louisville, or in Florida and New York City. He showed a mild interest in James M. Cox in the 1920 campaign, but he viewed the triumph of Harding and the anti-Leaguers with serenity. In these years he wrote little, save an occasional letter, with the exception of *"Marse Henry": An Autobiography* (2 vols., 1919), more important for its observations of life and anecdotes of the great than for a real revelation of an astonishing public career. He died at Jacksonville in December 1921, at the age of eighty-one, and was buried in Cave Hill Cemetery in Louisville. During his lifetime he was temporary chairman of several national conventions and author of the resolutions passed by four of these. In these resolutions he put into circulation many resounding phrases which rang from the hustings and were elaborated in his own writings. He was famous and in demand as a public speaker and lecturer. He once in youth wrote a novel, but it is not preserved; for pot-boilers, he collected his lectures as *The Compromises of Life* (1903), and edited a book of *genre* stories by Southern authors, called *Oddities in Southern Life and Character* (1883), a best-seller of its epoch.

His amazing zest for life, his gift for conversation and conviviality, his unusual personal appearance (the fierce blue eye under penthouses of bushy white eyebrows, the flaring mustache and slight goatee, the high, staccato voice combining to make a striking physical type), and his genius for "setting other editors to chattering" about what he wrote—these served to distinguish Watterson among his contemporaries at a time when journalism was personal and editorial writing often had immediate and dynamic effect. Despite the legends, the tipple he liked best was champagne, and, after that, wine and beer; although known as "the Colonel," a term he himself abjured, he did not relish whiskey, and the mint-julep yarns and cartoons were imaginative. He was a prodigious worker, a hard and frequent bon-vivant, a gifted idler when occasion permitted, and—in his home circle—a patriarch.

Never were his famous personality and conversational gifts more glamorous than when he sat on the broad verandahs or in his large library at Mansfield, surrounded by his wife, his children, their children, and an assortment of guests and household pets. It was then that he was wont to say, looking back on a life both full and crowded: "I'm a free nigger at last and will never be anything else, hallelujah!" He died convinced that civilization was facing a crisis that might obliterate it "in seventy years," ascribing this largely to godlessness, for he himself was of undoubting Christian faith, though indifferent to the tenets of the sects. But his pessimism about the future was due partly to the triumph of national prohibition and equal suffrage, championed by those whom for many years he had attacked as "red-nosed angels," "Sillysallies," and "Crazyjanes."

[Sources include *Who's Who in America*, 1920–21; files of the *Courier-Jour.* (Louisville), 1868–1921; Watterson's *The Compromises of Life* (1903), and *"Marse Henry": An Autobiog.* (2 vols., 1919); letters to the author from Watterson; long personal and professional association; obituary in *Courier-Jour.*, Dec. 23, 1921. See also *The Editorials of Henry Watterson* (1923), compiled by Arthur Krock; Royal Cortissoz, *The Life of Whitelaw Reid* (1921); R. S. Baker, *Woodrow Wilson: Life and Letters*, vol. III (1931); W. F. Johnson, *George Harvey* (1929); and *Courier-Jour.*, Mar. 2, 1919, Watterson supplement.]

A. K—k.

WATTERSTON, GEORGE (Oct. 23, 1783– Feb. 4, 1854), librarian, was born on shipboard in New York harbor, the son of David Watterston, master-builder, a native of Jedburgh, Scotland. Eight years later his father, attracted by building operations in the federal city, removed to Washington. For several years thereafter David continued to spell the family name "Watterstone." The boy went to Charlotte Hall School in Maryland. Remembered now chiefly as the first librarian of Congress who was not also clerk of the House of Representatives, he spent four fifths of his life otherwise occupied. Beginning to practise law in Hagerstown, Md., he was later in partnership with Thomas Law in Washington. In 1808 his first novel, *The Lawyer, or Man As He Ought Not to Be*, was published. Thereafter he "never missed an opportunity in any of his books to make a derogatory remark about the law and lawyers" (Kennedy, *post*, p. 5). A comedy, another novel, and two poems followed. He was married on Oct. 26, 1811, to Maria Shanley. They had eight children. In 1813 he was engaged as editor of the *Washington City Gazette*. When the British troops approached the capital in 1814, he marched to meet them at Bladensburg and returned soon to find the capitol in ruins, the library burned, and his own house pillaged.

Next year Thomas Jefferson's collection replaced the burned library, and Watterston was made librarian of Congress. With one messenger he did all the work except selecting additions to the collections, a pleasure retained by the congressional committee. Not until 1827 was he given one assistant. His own salary never exceeded $1,500 per year. Starting in 1815 with 6,500 volumes, the library numbered some 15,000 in 1829. He still had time, along with his library work, to write several more books, almost forgotten now (listed in Kennedy, *post*, pp. 55–57). He also edited at different times and for short periods three local newspapers, held several municipal offices, and was actively interested in politics. On May 28, 1829, Jackson summarily displaced him, a stanch Whig and friend of Henry Clay. For the rest of his life he nursed a grievance and, with Scotch persistence, kept up for years his fruitless efforts at reinstatement. A fortnight after his removal he was on the staff of the *National Journal* in Washington and next year became its editor. For fifteen years he continued to publish guide-books, statistical compends, biographical sketches, text-books, lectures on botany and agriculture. In 1833 he began the movement to build the Washington Monument. He remained as secretary of the Washington National Monument Society from its beginning to his death twenty years later, giving time and energy to every branch of its work. In this closing activity, the longest and most successful of all his efforts, he should have found and doubtless did find the greatest satisfaction of his life. He lived to see the great shaft reach the height of some 150 feet. A few months after his death, construction was entirely stopped and not another stone was laid for nearly a quarter of a century. He died in Washington and is buried in the Congressional Cemetery.

[Papers in the Lib. of Cong.; W. D. Johnston, *Hist. of the Lib. of Cong.* (1904); J. E. Kennedy, *George Watterston, Novelist* (1933); F. L. Harvey, *Hist. of the Washington National Monument* (1903); A. C. Clark, *Greenleaf and Law in the Federal City* (1901); *Daily Union* (Washington, D. C.), Feb. 7, 1854.]

F. W. A.

WATTS, FREDERICK (May 9, 1801–Aug. 17, 1889), commissioner of agriculture, was born in Carlisle, Pa., the son of David and Julian (Miller) Watts and the grandson of Frederick Watts who emigrated from Wales to America in 1760, was an officer in the Revolutionary army, and was afterward brigadier-general of Pennsylvania militia. His father, a graduate of Dick-

inson College, was a successful lawyer in Carlisle. The son also went to Dickinson, where he was a member of the class of 1819, which, however, was never graduated. A few months after he left college in 1819, his father died and during the next two or three years he lived with an uncle, William Miles, on his farm in Erie County. There he acquired a practical knowledge of farming and a taste for farm life that lasted throughout his life. Upon returning to Carlisle he studied law with Andrew Carothers and later formed a partnership with him. In September 1827 he was married to Eliza Cranston, by whom he had three daughters. She died in 1832. In March 1835 he was married to Henrietta Edge, who, with five sons and one daughter, survived him. His ability and character made him a leader in his community for more than fifty years. Active and influential in the affairs of Dickinson College, he was secretary of the board of control from 1824 to 1828 and a member of the board from 1828 to 1833 and again from 1841 to 1844. He was for many years active in the St. John's Episcopal Church. From 1829 to 1845 he reported the cases of the western district of the state supreme court, publishing two volumes of reports with William Rawle, Jr., and Charles B. Penrose and a third volume with Penrose only, then ten volumes, for 1832 to 1840, alone, and nine volumes, for 1841 to 1845 with Henry J. Sergeant. From 1845 to 1871 he was president of the Cumberland Valley Railroad Company, in which he had been interested since its organization and remained a director until his death. In 1849 he was appointed judge of the 9th Judicial District. He served until the judiciary of the state was made elective instead of appointive in 1852, when, as a Whig, he was not elected. He formed a partnership with John Brown Parker and enjoyed a successful practice in Carlisle. In 1869 he retired to one of his farms near Carlisle.

For many years he had been a farmer as well as a lawyer and was well known as one who believed in the application of science to farming. He experimented in farm buildings and equipment and in breeds of livestock, and he encouraged agricultural fairs. In 1840 he had been instrumental in bringing about the trial of the McCormick reaper in Pennsylvania. His prominence as a farmer led to his election as president of the Pennsylvania state agricultural society. He was also the organizer and for many years president of the Cumberland county agricultural society. As president of the state society he was successful in putting through the legislature in 1854 a charter for a Farmers' High School, which developed into the Pennsylvania State College. He was the first president of the board of trustees.

In 1871, at seventy years of age, he was appointed federal commissioner of agriculture by Grant. During his term the division of microscopy was established. He was apparently the first commissioner to give much attention to timber interests and obtained an appropriation for a forestry investigation that was the beginning of the forestry division organized several years later. At his suggestion the weather reporting work of the Smithsonian Institution was transferred to the signal service of the war department; and the Congress made an appropriation to collect and publish meteorological information for the benefit of agriculture. After his retirement on June 30, 1877, as commissioner of agriculture, he returned to Carlisle, where he remained till his death. He was buried in Carlisle.

[T. I. Osmond, *Hon. Frederick Watts* (1930); T. I. Mairs, *Some Pa. Pioneers on Agricultural Science* (1928); C. H. Greathouse, "Hist. Sketch of the U. S. Department of Agriculture," 2nd rev., *U. S. Dept. of Agri. Division of Pubs. Bulletin 3* (1907); *Hist. of Cumberland and Adams County, Pa.* (1886); Alfred Nevin, *Centennial Biog. Men of Mark of Cumberland Valley, Pa.* (1876); *Carlisle Herald*, Aug. 19, 1889, *Philadelphia Inquirer*, Aug. 19, 20, 1889; information from Gilbert Malcolm, Carlisle, Pa.]   C. R. B.

WATTS, THOMAS HILL (Jan. 3, 1819– Sept. 16, 1892), governor of Alabama, attorney-general of the Confederate States of America, was born in Alabama Territory not far from the present town of Greenville in that part of the Creek Indian cession which was later organized into Butler County. He was the son of Prudence (Hill) and John Hughes Watts, a prosperous planter, and the great-great-grandson of Francis Watts, possibly of Welsh and English stock, who was in Prince William County, Va., in 1749. The boy received such training as the schools in his section afforded. He then concluded a bargain with his father to accept money for education in lieu of any further claim upon the family estate. With this money he attended the University of Virginia and graduated in 1839. Returning to Alabama just in time to campaign for Harrison, he attracted attention as a stump-speaker. The following year he was admitted to the bar and on Jan. 10, 1842, married Eliza Brown Allen, who died in 1873 leaving ten children. He practised in Greenville, Ala., until 1847, when he moved his law office to the newly established state capital at Montgomery. From the beginning of his career, he combined work in his profession with political activity. He represented Butler County in the state legislature in the sessions of 1842, 1844, and 1845. In 1849 he

represented Montgomery County in the lower house of the legislature, and in 1853 he was in the state Senate. As the strength of the Whig party waned in Alabama, he, like many of his contemporaries, found temporary refuge in the Know-Nothing party, and he became its unsuccessful candidate for Congress in 1856. He was a strong supporter of the Union, and in the campaign of 1860 he was the leader of the Union forces in the state, campaigning vigorously for Bell and Everett. The election of Lincoln convinced him that the only safety for state rights lay in secession, and he identified himself with the Yancey faction of the Democratic party. He was a member of the Alabama convention of 1861.

Eager for military glory, he organized the 17th Alabama Regiment of which he became colonel. He saw service at Pensacola, Fla., and at Corinth, Miss., and was honorably discharged Apr. 9, 1862, to become attorney-general of the Confederate States. In 1863 he was elected governor of the state of Alabama. He took office in December 1863. Alabama was hard pressed, and much of the governor's time was given to a hopeless attempt to defend the state against northern invaders. He also made a valiant effort to relieve the distress of the people of the state. Considering the encroachment by the Richmond government just as dangerous as encroachment by the Washington government, he opposed such measures as the conscription of state officials and impressment of private property, as violations of the rights of the states. The collapse of the Confederate government ended his administration and destroyed his fortune in land and some 200 slaves. In 1865 he was sent to a Northern prison. His imprisonment was short, and he received a pardon from President Johnson in 1868. Upon his return to Montgomery, he resumed the practice of his profession and prospered again. He continued to be an active worker for the Democratic party and to be interested in the public welfare and in the affairs of the Baptist Church, of which he was a member. In September 1875 he married his second wife, Ellen (Noyes) Jackson. He died in Montgomery.

[Willis Brewer, *Alabama* (1872); *Confederate Military Hist.* (1899), ed. by C. A. Evans, vol. I; E. B. Culver, "Thomas Hill Watts," *Ala. Hist. Soc. Trans.*, vol. IV (1904); W. L. Fleming, *Civil War and Reconstruction in Ala.* (1905); A. B. Moore, *Conscription and Conflict in the Confederacy* (1924); F. L. Owsley, *State Rights in the Confederacy* (1925); J. B. Little, *The Hist. of Butler County, Ala.* (1885); *Univ. of Va.* (1904), vol. I; typescript in Lib. of Cong. of C. B. Heineman, *Watts Families of the Southern States* (1934); *Daily Register* (Mobile), Sept. 17, 1892.]   H. F.

WAUGH, BEVERLY (Oct. 25, 1789–Feb. 9, 1858), bishop of the Methodist Episcopal Church, son of Capt. James and Henrietta (Turley) Waugh, was born in Fairfax County, Va. His father was a veteran of the American Revolution. Waugh received the typical secondary education of the period and his excellent penmanship aided him when very young in securing a position as copyist in a government office in Washington. He early showed business ability and in 1807 became manager of a store in Middleburg, Va. At the age of fifteen he joined the Methodist Episcopal Church, and while at Middleburg became convinced of a call to preach. Abandoning his business career, he was admitted on trial to the Baltimore Conference in 1809 and was ordained deacon in 1811 and elder in 1813. Until 1828 he served as an itinerant in that conference, eleven years being spent in or near the cities of Washington and Baltimore. On Apr. 21, 1812, he married Catharine B. Bushby of Washington.

Waugh was soon recognized as a preacher of more than ordinary ability, and was sent as a delegate to the General Conferences of 1816 and 1820. The question of reform in Methodist polity was then being agitated and Waugh aligned himself with the group desiring to make the Church more democratic by having the presiding elders elected by the annual Conferences rather than appointed by the bishops, as was then the rule. The Baltimore Conference, however, favored the appointive method, and as a result Waugh was not elected to the General Conference of 1824. Ultimately he lost interest in the movement for reform, chiefly because of what he considered the radical and unfair attitude of some of its leaders, and by 1828 he was championing the *status quo*. At the General Conference of 1828, as a member of the committee on the Book Concern, he showed such a knowledge of business affairs that he was elected assistant book agent of the Church. In 1832 he was made the principal book agent. Under his supervision the Book Concern made progress; the indebtedness was cancelled, the output of literature was increased, and a new building was erected. Waugh was already preparing an optimistic quadrennial report for the General Conference of 1836 when, on Feb. 18 of that year, the headquarters of the Book Concern in New York were destroyed by fire, with a loss of over $200,000. Undaunted by this disaster Waugh and others at once began to raise funds for rebuilding. In this work he was engaged when at the General Conference he was elected bishop on the first ballot.

He began his episcopal labors by presiding over the Troy Conference at Pawlet, Vt., on June 22, 1836, and until his death twenty-two years later he never missed holding a Conference assigned to him. It is estimated that during his episcopacy he made twelve thousand appointments and traveled one hundred thousand miles. After 1852 he was the senior bishop. Having as a young preacher opposed what he thought to be the autocracy of the episcopacy, he took extra precautions to insure justice in making appointments. He refused to be influenced in the conduct of his duties by either the pro-slavery or the anti-slavery groups in the Church. Although he was opposed to slavery, he refused to allow the abolitionist leaders at the New England Conference of 1837 to present anti-slavery petitions. He declared that consideration of the slavery issue was not a part of the business of an annual Conference and held that continued agitation on the subject would only lead to the division of the Church. He was "one of the few Southern men who could oppose New England abolitionists and still command their love, though he could not control their sentiments or action" (quoted by Buckley, *post*, II, 161). At the General Conference of 1844 he endeavored to prevent a division of the Church by proposing with Bishops Soule, Hedding, and Morris the postponement of further consideration of the case of Bishop J. O. Andrew [*q.v.*] until the next General Conference. Although a Southerner by birth, Waugh remained with the Methodist Episcopal Church after the schism. He died in Baltimore as a result of exposure at a revival meeting in Carlisle, Pa., and was buried in Mount Olivet Cemetery.

[T. L. Flood and J. W. Hamilton, *Lives of Methodist Bishops* (1882); W. H. Egle, *Pa. Geneals.* (1896); J. E. Armstrong, *Hist. of the Old Baltimore Conference* (1907); *Minutes of the Ann. Conferences of the Methodist Episcopal Church for the Year 1858* (1858); H. C. Jennings, *The Methodist Book Concern* (1924); J. M. Buckley, *A Hist. of Methodism in the U. S.* (2 vols., 1897); C. B. Swaney, *Episcopal Methodism and Slavery* (1926); *Western Christian Advocate*, Feb. 24, 1858; *Sun* (Baltimore), Feb. 10, 1858.]   P. N. G.

WAYLAND, FRANCIS (Mar. 11, 1796–Sept. 30, 1865), clergyman, educator, fourth president of Brown University, was born in New York City, the eldest son of Francis and Sarah (Moore) Wayland, who emigrated from England in 1793. His father, originally a leather merchant, entered the Baptist ministry in 1807, and held pastorates successively in Poughkeepsie, Albany, Troy, and Saratoga Springs. Francis' mother was a woman of superior mind and rare spirit, and to her early training the son owed many of the salient traits of his own character—abhorrence of meanness and wrong, belief in the divine purpose of life, a stern sense of duty, moral courage, and a passion for the truth. At fifteen he entered the sophomore class of Union College, graduating in 1813. He then studied medicine in Troy and during the winter of 1814–15 attended medical lectures in New York. In 1816, however, obeying an inner urge to the ministry, he went to Andover Theological Seminary, where he came under the quickening influence of Moses Stuart [q.v.], an experience that left an indelible impress upon his whole intellectual life.

Forced by want of means to suspend his theological studies, he returned to Union College as tutor in 1817, remaining until 1821, when he was called to the First Baptist Church in Boston, where he soon acquired recognition as a man of force, originality, and broad vision. His sermon on *The Moral Dignity of the Missionary Enterprise* (1823) became almost a classic in the literature of modern missions and exerted a far-reaching influence upon religious thought both in America and in Europe. His two fast-day sermons, *The Duties of an American Citizen* (1825), further enhanced his reputation.

In 1826 he was recalled to Union College, as professor of mathematics and natural philosophy, but hardly had he entered upon his duties when, in February 1827, he became president of Brown University, an office which for twenty-eight years he conducted with such extraordinary energy and crowned with such high and lasting achievement as to make his administration forever memorable in the history of the institution. His dynamic personality was felt from the first moment: discipline was restored, the standard of conduct and study raised, the whole tone of college life altered. Instruction was vitalized by the banishment of the textbook from the classroom and the substitution of the "analytic method," which kept the student on the alert and developed habits of close reasoning and precise statement. The curriculum was augmented by courses in modern languages, history, economics, and the natural sciences; non-resident professors were dispensed with but the faculty was ultimately enlarged; the library was endowed; facilities for study were greatly improved. The funds of the institution were considerably increased and new buildings were added: Manning Hall, through the munificence of Nicholas Brown [q.v.]; Rhode Island Hall, by means of donations from citizens of the state; and a president's house. The University grew in numbers and reputation, and its president attained general recognition as a preëminent figure in education. Great as an administrator, Wayland was perhaps even greater as a teacher. Hundreds of his students testified to the intellectual stimulation received in his classroom, to the corrective effect of his personal counsels, to the inspiration caught from his chapel discourses, and above all to the ennobling influence of his lofty character, which produced upon them all an impression of moral grandeur.

His activities were manifold and his influence reached far. His textbooks in moral philosophy, intellectual philosophy, and political economy were widely used, especially the first, which went through many editions and was translated into several languages. He was instrumental in devising a school system for the city of Providence, and was the author of the plan for free public schools in Rhode Island (1828); he was the first president of the American Institute of Instruction (1830), long time a trustee of Butler Hospital, and a member of the state prison board—as such initiating a thorough reform of the institution. In 1838 he outlined a plan for a national university, as the best object to which to devote the Smithsonian bequest. His example in founding a free library in Wayland, Mass., inspired the act of 1851 empowering towns to support public libraries by taxation.

In 1840 he visited France, England, and Scotland. Upon his return, and possibly as a result of certain reflections upon education abroad, he published his *Thoughts on the Present Collegiate System in the United States* (1842), in which he boldly challenged accepted premises and called for a candid reëxamination of the whole problem of higher education. Disappointed in the response to his appeal, and worn by his arduous labors, in 1849 he tendered his resignation as president; but at the earnest solicitation of the corporation was persuaded to remain, upon the condition, however, of support in a project which had long been maturing in his mind, and which he set forth in his famous *Report on the Condition of the University* (1850). In this *Report,* which was impelled by a democratic and generous conception of higher education as a social agency, he advocated a thorough reorganization of the University, with a view to making its services more widely available and more directly contributory to the needs of society. The proposal was adopted; entrance requirements were made more flexible; new subjects were introduced; a limited elective system was inaugurated. The student enrollment increased materially and $125,000 additional endowment was raised, but the resources of the University were insufficient to carry out the plan in its entirety. It pointed the way, however, which higher education was destined to take, and serves as a lasting monument to Wayland's prophetic vision and progressive spirit.

After his retirement, in 1855, Wayland devoted himself to literary, religious, and philanthropic labors, serving for a time as pastor of the First Baptist Church of Providence, and participating actively in the civic life of the community, in which he was revered for the wisdom of his counsels and the nobility of his character. His views on public questions were marked by candor and deep moral earnestness tempered with the tolerance of a great spirit. His utterance was remarkable for its clarity and sincerity; his addresses and sermons abound in passages of great dignity; and an impressive bearing lent added power to the spoken word. He was twice married: first, Nov. 21, 1825, to Lucy Lane Lincoln, who died in 1834; second, Aug. 1, 1838, to Mrs. Hepsy S. Howard Sage. He had three sons, one of whom was Francis [q.v.].

His published works include, *Elements of Moral Science* (1835), *Elements of Political Economy* (1837), *The Moral Law of Accumulation* (1837), *The Limitations of Human Responsibility* (1838); *Domestic Slavery Considered as a Scriptural Institution* (1845), *The Duty of Obedience to the Civil Magistrate* (1847), *University Sermons* (1849), *A Memoir of the Life and Labors of the Rev. Adoniram Judson, D.D.* (1853), *The Elements of Intellectual Philosophy* (1854), *Notes on the Principles and Practices of Baptist Churches* (1857), *Sermons to the Churches* (1858), *Letters on the Ministry of the Gospel* (1863), *A Memoir of the Christian Labors . . . of Thomas Chalmers* (1864), beside some fifty or more sermons and occasional addresses.

[Francis and H. L. Wayland, *A Memoir of the Life and Labors of Francis Wayland, D.D., LL.D.* (2 vols., 1867); J. O. Murray, *Francis Wayland* (1891); G. I. Chace, *The Virtues and Services of Francis Wayland* (1866); Alexis Caswell, *A Sermon on the Christian Work of Francis Wayland* (1867); *Am. Jour. of Educ.*, Dec. 1863; *New Englander*, Jan. 1866; *Atlantic Mo.*, Jan. 1868; W. C. Bronson, *The Hist. of Brown Univ., 1764–1914* (1914), *N. Y. Times*, Oct. 2, 1865.]

T.C.

WAYLAND, FRANCIS (Aug. 23, 1826–Jan. 9, 1904), lawyer, for thirty years dean of the Yale Law School, was born in Boston, Mass., and died in New Haven, Conn. His father, Francis Wayland [q.v.], was long president of Brown University. His mother, Lucy Lane (Lincoln) of Boston, died when he was seven, and he was brought up by his father and his stepmother. In 1846 he graduated from Brown with the degree of A.B., and after studying law at the Har-

vard Law School and in offices in Providence, R. I., and in Springfield, Mass., he was admitted to the Massachusetts bar. In 1850 he went to Worcester, Mass., and practised there for some seven years. On Oct. 6, 1857, he married Martha Read of New Haven, and soon thereafter removed to that city, where he spent the remainder of his life. He served two terms (1864–65) as judge of probate for the New Haven district, and in 1869 was lieutenant-governor of the state.

At this time the financial state of the Yale Law School was such as to threaten its existence. At the instigation of the local bar association and Yale University, three young members of the bar, Simeon E. Baldwin, William C. Robinson [qq.v.], and Johnson T. Platt, took charge of the school in 1869 and endeavored to renew its life. Soon realizing that busy lawyers like themselves could not successfully direct its activities, they sought for a leader, and at Baldwin's suggestion Wayland was chosen. In 1871 he became instructor in law, a year later professor, and in 1873, dean of the school, in which capacity he served until he retired as professor emeritus in 1903. Wayland was worldly wise, urbane, courteous, well-traveled, with independent means and a wide field of acquaintance. At once he identified the school with himself so fully that thereafter each shared the wide and favorable notice accorded the other. Under his direction the school grew and prospered materially. Whereas in 1873 its faculty consisted of four members, its students numbered twenty-one, its course of study was of two years' duration, and its library contained only 2,000 volumes, in 1903 it had fifteen instructors and a like number of special lecturers, a three-year course, 339 students, and a library of 20,000 volumes. In 1876 a graduate course in law, leading to advanced degrees, was established—the first, it is said, in any English or American law school. As a crowning achievement of his life Wayland personally obtained funds to provide a separate building for the law department and this building, named Hendrie Hall in honor of its chief donor, was fully completed and occupied in 1900.

Though Wayland advanced the material prosperity of the school, he was conservative in his views on legal education. His long deanship occurred at a time when C. C. Langdell [q.v.] at Harvard was making those innovations—including the case method of study, the law faculty of full-time teachers, and the requirement of a college degree before admission as a student—which caused the Harvard Law School to be so long preëminent. Against these radical departures Wayland and his faculty stood out, and ultimately the Yale Law School suffered in prestige. Not until some years after his death and during the administration of his successor, Henry Wade Rogers [*q.v.*], were the changes made which restored the reputation of the institution as a leading American law school.

Wayland was not a great legal scholar. For some years he taught the subject of Evidence and lectured upon English constitutional history, but later he limited himself to the latter subject. For the most part, he confined his activities to the public functions of his office and to his relations with his students. The personal qualities which made him so attractive a civic and public figure were such as to win the affection and admiration of young men. He was "of unusual personal charm, eminently companionable, a born story-teller, with a genius for friendship" (*Outlook*, Jan. 16, 1904, p. 149). Of impressive stature, he was a magnificent figure on horseback, his usual means of conveyance.

Wayland was often called upon to serve as a presiding officer. For some years he was president of the American Social Science Association and thereafter was vice-president and chairman of its jurisprudence department (1876–1902). He was president of the board of directors of the Connecticut State Prison for fourteen years, and for a time of the Connecticut Prison Aid Association; he also served as chairman of the executive committee of the National Prison Congress. He was president of the board of visitors to the United States Military Academy in 1874, vice-president of the board of visitors to the United States Naval Academy at Annapolis in 1880, and trustee (1873–88) and thereafter fellow of Brown University. For twenty-five years he was president of the Organized Charities of New Haven. He was interested in criminology and in prison reform and spoke and wrote much on these subjects. In politics he was an active Republican.

His publications include *A Memoir of the Life and Labors of Francis Wayland, DD., LL.D.* (2 vols., 1867), written in collaboration with his brother H. L. Wayland; *On Certain Defects in Our Method of Making Laws,* presidential address at the meeting of the American Social Science Association, Sept. 5, 1881; *Out-door Relief and Tramps* (1877); *The Pardoning Power: Where Should It Be Lodged and How Should It Be Exercised?* (1884); *On Certain Anomalies in Criminal Jurisprudence* (1885); "Some of the Causes Which Tend to Promote the Increase of Crime in the United States," in *Proceedings of the Annual Congress of the National Prison As-*

sociation . . . Dec. 3–7, 1892 (1893); and other addresses and pamphlets.

[W. C. Robinson, *An Address Commemorative of the Life and Character of Francis Wayland* (1904); L. M. Daggett, "The Yale Law School," *Green Bag*, June 1889; *Report of the President of Yale Univ., 1903–1904* (1904), pp. 150–52; T. S. Woolsey, *Hist. Address in Celebration of the Centennial of the School of Law, Yale Univ., June 16, 1924* (1924); *Yale Alumni Weekly,* Jan. 13, 1904; *Outlook,* Apr. 11, 1903, Jan. 16, 1904; *Who's Who in America*, 1901–02; *New Haven Evening Register*, Jan. 11, 12, 1904.]   C. E. C.

WAYMAN, ALEXANDER WALKER (September 1821–Nov. 30, 1895), bishop of the African Methodist Episcopal Church, was born, a freeman, in Caroline County, Md., the son of Francis and Matilda Wayman. As a boy he worked on a farm with his father, and learned to read by the light of a wood fire. In those days practically his only reading book was the Bible, and his copybooks, the sand and the sides of old buildings. When he was fourteen he was hired out to Benjamin Kerby of Talbot County, whose children taught him all they knew. Returning to Caroline County in 1836, he lived with a James Glanden. Soon afterwards he was converted and joined the Methodist Episcopal Church.

Impelled by the desire to get more education and become a preacher, in 1840 he left home and went to Baltimore, proceeding from there, after a few weeks, to Philadelphia. Here he joined the African Methodist Episcopal Church and was licensed as an exhorter. A Quaker, whose coachman he had become, gave him instruction in English composition. In 1842 he was an assistant on the Princeton, N. J., circuit, taught a small primary school at New Brunswick, and was aided in his efforts to educate himself by students of Rutgers College. The following year he was admitted on trial to the Philadelphia Conference, and after serving two years on the West Chester Circuit was ordained deacon (1845). Subsequent appointments were to Little Wesley Church, Philadelphia, the Salem, N. J., circuit, and Trenton. In 1847 he was ordained elder.

Transferring to the Baltimore Conference in 1848, he became as time went on one of the leaders in his denomination, contributing much to the administration of its affairs and to the extension of its bounds. From 1848 to 1864, with the exception of two years, he was pastor of churches either in Washington or Baltimore. In addition to caring for his own parishes, he organized Ebenezer Church, Georgetown; St. Paul's, South Washington; and Allen Chapel, Good Hope, Md. He was a member of all the General Conferences held during this period and served as assistant secretary. In 1860 he was appointed, with two others, to prepare and publish a new edition of the *Discipline*. At the General Conference of 1864 he was elected bishop. His activities were incessant and his episcopal duties carried him throughout the greater part of the country. At first his labors were largely in the East and South. Soon after the Civil War was over, he inspected the mission work in South Carolina and Georgia, and in 1867 made a tour through these states and Virginia. Subsequently he organized the Virginia, Georgia, and Florida conferences. In 1872 he was assigned supervision of the district that included Indiana, Illinois, Missouri, and California, and thereafter made several journeys to the Pacific Coast. He served as chaplain, Oct. 15, 1874, at the unveiling of the Lincoln Memorial at Springfield, Ill. In the course of his numerous activities he found time to contribute to the historical records of his denomination. His book, entitled *My Recollections of African M. E. Ministers, or Forty Years' Experience in the African Methodist Episcopal Church* (1881), contains much detailed information of value. He also published *Cyclopædia of African Methodism* (1882). He continued his labors well down to the time of his death, which occurred in Baltimore in his seventy-fifth year. He was twice married; his first wife died in 1860; his second, Harriet Ann Elizabeth Wayman, survived him.

[In addition to his *Recollections,* see B. T. Tanner, *An Apology for African Methodism* (1867); R. R. Wright, *Centennial Encyc. of the A. M. E. Ch.* (copr. 1916); *Baltimore American,* Dec. 1, 1895.]

H. E. S.

WAYMOUTH, GEORGE (fl. 1601–1612), navigator, explorer, was a native of Devonshire, England, and had been employed at sea for years, working his way up to a master's rating and attaining some prominence as a navigator. The evidence for the statement that he was sent out in 1593 by the "Russia and Turkey merchants" to discover the Northwest Passage (*Calendar of State Papers, Colonial Series, 1513–1616*, 1862, p. xxxi) is dubious; but he must have been interested in the search, for, on July 24, 1601, the newly formed East India Company discussed a letter received from him "touching his attempte to be made for the discovery of the north west passage to the Est Indies . . ." (Stevens, *post,* p. 182). This company, after long negotiations with the Muscovy Company concerning jurisdiction, decided to ignore the latter and to organize the expedition itself. Waymouth was given £100 "to prepare his instruments and other necessaries" (Stevens, *post,* p. 184), and was promised £500 if he found the passage. He commanded the two ships that sailed, early in

May 1602, from Radcliffe. They passed southern Greenland on June 18 and bore northwestward to Warwicks Foreland and Hudson Strait. There a mutiny, led by John Cartwright, the chaplain, caused the expedition to turn back. The East India Company were naturally disappointed at this early return but the Privy Council cleared the captain of blame. A second expedition was planned but not carried out. Shortly after his return and before his next voyage, Waymouth addressed the king with a manuscript called "The Jewell of Artes" which dealt with navigation, shipbuilding and instruments of war. The treatment of these subjects shows that the author was much better educated than the ordinary sea captain.

On Mar. 5, 1605, he set out as commander of the *Archangel* on a voyage of exploration to Virginia for the Earl of Southampton, the Baron of Wardour, and Sir Ferdinando Gorges. There is reason to believe that this expedition was part of an English Catholic attempt at colonization in America (J. P. Baxter, *Sir Ferdinand Gorges,* 1890, I, 65–67). Sankaty Head, Nantucket, was sighted on May 14, but no landing was made because of the shoals. The *Archangel* stood off to the north and three days later reached Monhegan. For a month the expedition remained near the Georges Islands, trading with the Indians and exploring St. George's River in a shallop that had been brought from England. A cross, which was found by Gilbert in 1607, was set up on one of the islands, now known as Allen Island, and another at the bend of the river near Thomaston, Me. On June 16 Waymouth "waied Anker and quit the Land" (Rosier, *post,* p. 153), carrying with him five captured Indians who later proved useful as pilots to Martin Pring, George Popham [*qq.v.*], and Raleigh Gilbert. In July 1605 the expedition was back in England and the same year appeared an account of it by James Rosier who was employed on the voyage (see Burrage edition, *post*).

In October Waymouth entered into an agreement with Sir John Zouche to assist in planting a colony in Virginia but nothing more was heard of their plans. About that time he prepared a manuscript entitled "Errors and Defects in the usual building of Ships," written, so he asserted, from twenty years' study of mathematics and shipbuilding. In October 1607, James I granted Waymouth a pension of 3s. 4d. *per diem*. In 1609 he engaged in a controversy with Phineas Pett over alleged imperfections in the latter's ships (*Calendar of State Papers, Domestic Series, 1603–1610,* 1857, p. 510). The following year he took part in the siege of Jülich on the Continent, and wrote a manuscript entitled "A Journall Relation of the service at the takeing in of the towne and castle of Gulicke . . ." The last mention of him is the payment of his pension at Easter 1612.

[Henry Stevens, *The Dawn of British Trade to the Eastern Indies, . . . Court Records of the East India Company* (1886); for Waymouth's own account of the voyage of 1602, see Samuel Purchas, *Hakluytus Posthumus or Purchas His Pilgrims* (1906 ed.), vol. XIV, *Hakluyt Society Pubs.*, and Luke Foxe, *North-West Fox* (1635); for the voyage of 1605, *A True Relation of the Most Prosperous Voyage made this present Yeere 1605, by Captaine George Waymouth . . . written by James Rosier* (1605), see edition by H. S. Burrage, *Gorges Soc. Pubs.*, vol. III (1887). See also G. B. Manhart, "The English Search for a Northwest Passage," in *Studies in English Commerce and Exploration in the Reign of Elizabeth* (1924); Thomas Rundall, *Narratives of Voyages Towards the North-West* (1849). "The Jewell of Artes" and "Errors and Defects" have never been printed and are in the British Museum.]   R. J. S—y.

WAYNE, ANTHONY (Jan. 1, 1745–Dec. 15, 1796), soldier, was born at Waynesboro, Pa., the only son of Isaac and Elizabeth (Iddings) Wayne. Isaac Wayne with his father Anthony Wayne, of English ancestry, emigrated from Ireland and about 1724 settled in Chester County, Pa., where he acquired some 500 acres of land and a thriving tannery. At the age of sixteen the boy attended a private academy kept by his uncle, Gilbert Wayne, in Philadelphia, where he is said to have been more proficient in feats of mock warfare, suggested no doubt by the Indian wars in progress, than in his classroom subjects. He learned enough mathematics to qualify as a surveyor, with some further application after he left school two years later. In 1765 he was sent by a Philadelphia land company to supervise the surveying and settlement of 100,000 acres of land in Nova Scotia. On Mar. 25, 1766, after the venture had failed, he returned to Pennsylvania and married Mary Penrose, the daughter of Bartholomew Penrose, a Philadelphia merchant. They had two children. He went to live on his father's estate and took charge of the tannery. In 1774 his father died, and Anthony succeeded to the ownership of a profitable establishment that provided him a very comfortable competence. He was of medium height, had a handsome, well-proportioned face with a slightly aquiline nose and high forehead. His hair was dark, his eyes dark brown and penetrating, giving to his face a very animated appearance.

During the early Revolutionary movement he was chairman of the committee appointed in the county on July 13, 1774, to frame the resolutions of protest against the coercive acts of the British government. He was later made chairman of the county committee appointed to supervise the carrying out of the association drawn up by the first Continental Congress. He represented his county in the provincial assembly that met during 1775. On Jan. 3, 1776, he was appointed by Congress to be colonel of a Chester County regiment engaged in continental service, and as a soldier he served through the war. His youth and lack of formal training in the arts of war prevented him from being on friendly terms with many of his colleagues, and he had personal difficulties with St. Clair, Charles Lee, and James Wilkinson. Contemporaries agreed that he was impetuous, yet Alexander Graydon, who called his manner "fervid," admitted that he could "fight as well as brag" (Stillé, *post*, p. 66). Washington admitted his bravery and his self-possession in battle but feared his impetuousness, when, seventeen years later, he chose him to lead the army against the northwestern Indians. In the spring of 1776 he was sent with the Pennsylvania brigade commanded by Gen. William Thompson to reinforce the faltering Canadian expedition. When the Pennsylvanians met the retreating remnants of Montgomery's army at the mouth of the Sorel River, they were sent down the St. Lawrence to attack what was thought to be the advance guard of the British army at Three Rivers. It turned out to be the main army numbering 3,000, and Wayne, whose regiment was in the front of the attack, found himself sustaining a hot exchange with the enemy in order to cover the retreat of his outnumbered countrymen to Fort Ticonderoga. He was placed in command of the garrison of over two thousand men there and had his first taste of wretched provisioning, of sickness, starvation, and mutiny.

On Feb. 21, 1777, he was appointed to the rank of brigadier-general and was called, on Apr. 12, to join Washington at Morristown, N. J., and to take command of the Pennsylvania line. After a season of training and drill his division took an active part in resisting the British in their campaign against Philadelphia. In the battle of Brandywine on Sept. 11, 1777, he occupied the center of the defense opposing the British at their main point of crossing. He was obliged to retreat when the American right was flanked by Cornwallis, who crossed the creek higher up. When Washington then withdrew to the north of the Schuylkill, he sent Wayne to circle around the rear of the British and to surprise and destroy their baggage train. Wayne, however, was himself surprised and, in the battle of Paoli, Sept. 20, received a drubbing. Being accused of negligence in this action, he demanded a court martial and was acquitted.

Rejoining Washington, he played a conspicuous part in the battle of Germantown, on Oct. 4, leading a spirited and almost victorious attack, but was forced back, when difficulties in the rear turned the victory into confusion and defeat. He wintered with Washington at Valley Forge and led the advance attack against the British at the battle of Monmouth on June 28, 1788.

In a reorganization of the army late in 1778, he was transferred to the command of a separate corps of Continental light infantry. This corps, under his leadership, on July 16, 1779, captured by surprise the garrison at Stony Point, the northernmost British post on the Hudson. Over five hundred prisoners, fifteen cannon, and some valuable stores were taken. For his conduct in this affair Congress ordered a medal to be struck and presented to him. Early in 1780 he led some desultory movements against the British on the lower Hudson, aimed to embarrass their collecting of supplies and cattle and to alleviate the attacks being made on Connecticut. When Arnold attempted to deliver West Point to the British on Sept. 25, 1780, Wayne's prompt movement to that post prevented a British occupation. After the Pennsylvania line mutinied in December 1780, Wayne was instrumental in presenting the soldiers' demands for pay and release to Congress and in getting Congress to redress their grievances. In the Yorktown campaign he was ordered south to serve under Lafayette, who was opposing Cornwallis on the lower James River. When Cornwallis withdrew from Williamsburg, Wayne was ordered to attack part of the British army that was mistakenly supposed to be separated from the rest. With some 800 men he attacked the British army of perhaps 5,000 at Green Spring, Va., on July 6, 1781, and, upon discovering the mistake, he led a charge into the British lines that deceived Cornwallis long enough to permit Wayne to extricate himself with only minor losses.

After the British surrender at Yorktown, Wayne, serving under Gen. Nathanael Greene, was sent to oppose the British, Loyalist, and Indian hostiles in Georgia. He had the tact to divide the Indian opposition by spreading news of the American victory so that, when the Creek irreconcilables attacked his small force in May 1782, he was able to rout them. He negotiated treaties of submission with the Creek and Cherokee in the winter of 1782 and 1783. In 1783 he retired from active service as brevet major-general.

From 1783 to 1792 he was engaged in civil pursuits in which he was less fortunate than in military affairs. The state of Georgia conferred upon him an eight-hundred-acre rice plantation, and he borrowed the necessary capital to work it from Dutch creditors, who subsequently foreclosed on the lands. In politics he was a conservative; he had a militarist's contempt for the radicals who took advantage of the revolt against Great Britain to fashion liberal constitutions like that of Pennsylvania, which he considered "not worth Defending" (Stillé, *post,* p. 71). During the war military affairs were his major consideration; but he said, "let us once be in a Condition to Vanquish these British Rebels and I answer for it that then your present Rulers will give way for better men which will produce better Measures" (*Ibid.*). Accordingly, as a member of the Pennsylvania council of censors in 1783, he favored the calling of a new constitutional convention. He was a representative of Chester County to the Pennsylvania General Assembly in 1784 and 1785. In 1787 he supported the new federal Constitution in the Pennsylvania ratifying convention. He was elected to Congress as a representative from Georgia and served from Mar. 4, 1791, to Mar. 21, 1792, when his seat was declared vacant because of irregularities in the election and in his residence qualification.

After the failure of Harmar and St. Clair to subdue the Indian tribes of the Wabash and Maumee rivers in 1791, Wayne was named by Washington as major-general in command of the rehabilitated American army. He was strongly opposed to the peace maneuvers of 1792 and 1793 but improved his time constructing a reliable military organization at his training camp at Legionville, Pa., and, later, near Fort Washington and Fort Jefferson in the Northwest Territory. On Aug. 20, 1794, he defeated the Indians at Fallen Timbers on the Maumee River near what is now Toledo, Ohio. This victory was the result of several factors. Wayne had far more resources at his command than had Harmar or St. Clair. He did not hazard an autumn campaign after he received news of the final failure of peace negotiations in August 1793. He was fortunate in that the Indians threw away their opportunity to isolate him, when they made a futile attack on Fort Recovery on June 29 and lost many discouraged tribesmen, who went home. He made every effort to avoid offending the British, thus robbing the Indians of the aid they fully expected in the moment of conflict. Finally, when the Indians had assembled at Fallen Timbers to fight, he delayed battle for three days. Therefore, when he attacked, a large part of the Indians were at a distance breaking their three-day fast, and the rest were in a half-starved condition. The complete submission and surrender at Greenville in August 1795 was made possible by Jay's treaty, the British desertion of the Indians, and Wayne's skill in convincing the tribesmen of the hopelessness of their cause without British support. He died at Presque Isle, now Erie, Pa., on his return from the occupation of the post of Detroit.

[Seventy-three vols. MSS. in possession of Hist. Soc. of Pa.; MSS. in Lib. of Cong.; C. J. Stillé, *Major-General Anthony Wayne* (1893), with many letters; S. W. Pennypacker, *Anthony Wayne* (1908), reprinted from *Pa. Mag. of Hist. and Biog.*, July 1908; J. H. Preston, *A Gentleman Rebel* (1930); T. A. Boyd, *Mad Anthony Wayne* (1929); Thomas Wyatt, *Memoirs* (1848), esp. pp. 17–39; Lieutenant Boyer, *A Jour. of Wayne's Campaign* (1866); *Orderly Book of . . . Wayne . . . 1776* (1859); H. B. Dawson, *Battles of the U. S.* (2 vols., 1858) and *The Assault on Stony Point* (1863); J. G. Leach, *Hist. of the Penrose Family* (1903), pp. 33, 38.] R. C. D.

WAYNE, ARTHUR TREZEVANT (Jan. 1, 1863–May 5, 1930), ornithologist, was a descendant of William Wayne who came to South Carolina about the time of the Revolution. He was born in Blackville, S. C., where his parents, Daniel Gabriel and Harriott Julia (Ward) Wayne, had removed to escape the rigors of the siege of Charleston. Returning home after the war, they sent Arthur at the age of six to Miss Charlotte Smith's school. In 1880 he was graduated with honors from the Charleston High School and completed his formal schooling. A collector of bird eggs from early boyhood, in 1874 he came under the influence of Dr. Gabriel Manigault, who encouraged him to collect for the Charleston Museum, where John Dancer taught him bird-skinning so well that it became with him a fine art. Being under the necessity to earn a living, however, he started life as a clerk in the cotton and naval stores firm of Barden & Murdock Company. This proved an unhappy connection for all concerned; highstrung, nervous, and violently impulsive, he was in taste and temperament wholly unsuited to business life. His next venture was equally unsuccessful. In 1883 an experience so fired the boy's enthusiasm that he abandoned all thought of business, for he accompanied William Brewster, 1851–1919 [q.v.], on several field trips near Charleston in an effort to rediscover Swainson's warbler. The following year on Brewster's return they resumed the quest, successfully; and in 1885 Wayne took the first nest and eggs known to science. In the same year, when returning from a brief trip to New York, he met Robert Ridgway [q.v.] in Washington, and formed another friendship of lifelong influence. On June 6, 1889, Wayne was married to Maria Louisa, the daughter of Philip E. and Elizabeth C. Porcher. They had no children. She took from his shoulders so many burdens that her unselfish devotion might be said to have made possible his career.

After a few months at McPhersonville, S. C., where he collected for the market, the young couple returned to the home of the bride's parents. In 1892, accompanied by his wife, he began a series of field trips to Florida, taking many specimens of the ivory-billed woodpecker near Oldtown; in 1893 he collected Carolina paroquet near Kissimmee; and in 1894 he made an unsuccessful search for manatee on Indian River. They lived in a cottage near Mt. Pleasant, S. C., until in 1900 they moved into "Wayne's Place," built for them by Wayne's father. Here for thirty years Wayne gave himself to his work with enthusiasm. He was three times interrupted in his work between 1908 and 1928 by periods of nervous breakdown. In spite of these, his continuity of field work was remarkable, and, although he worked in an area already covered by Audubon and Bachman, he added in forty-five years about one bird a year to the fauna of his state. Two sub-species, Wayne's clapper rail and Wayne's warbler, have been named for him. Among his achievements were the re-discovery of Bachman's warbler in 1901, and his discovery of the breeding grounds of the white ibis in South Carolina in 1922. Besides numerous contributions to the *Auk* and other scientific periodicals, his publications include *Birds of South Carolina*, which appeared in 1910 as the first of the *Contributions from the Charleston Museum*, and *A List of Avian Species for which the Type Locality is South Carolina*, which appeared in 1917 as the third volume of Museum series. He contributed in all 190 papers to scientific journals. In 1928 he was elected fellow of the American Ornithologists' Union.

Small, slight, with nervous brown eyes and dark red hair and mustache, his appearance was not easily forgotten. His remarkable memory and rapid abundance of speech were equally impressive. Second to his passion for ornithology were his pleasure in grand opera and in genealogy. His widow survived him.

[Forty years' personal acquaintance; *Who's Who in America*, 1922–23. Alexander Sprunt's "In Memoriam" in the *Auk*, Jan. 1931, is a eulogy. See also *Auk*, July and Oct. 1930. Wayne's manuscript ornithological journal was purchased by the Charleston Museum with his personal collection of 1800 bird skins. Most of his correspondence was destroyed by Mrs. Wayne in 1930, but his letters from William Brewster are in the library of McGill University, Montreal. An obituary is to be found in the Charleston *News and Courier*, May 6, 1930.] A. K. G.

WAYNE, JAMES MOORE (c. 1790–July 5, 1867), associate justice of the United States Supreme Court, was a native of Savannah, Ga. His father, Richard Wayne, an officer in the British army, had emigrated to South Carolina, where on Sept. 14, 1769, he married Elizabeth Clifford, and thence moved to Savannah. James was the twelfth of thirteen children. He received his early education under the direction of a Mr. Mackay, an Irishman who had graduated at Trinity College, Dublin, and made such progress that he was ready to enter the College of New Jersey (Princeton) at an early age. Here he read promiscuously, took an active part in his literary society, and was graduated in 1808. Returning to Savannah, he took up the study of law under the tutelage of John Y. Noel. Within a few months thereafter his father died and his brother-in-law became his guardian. He was now sent to New Haven, Conn., to study under Judge Chauncey, who put him through a rigorous and systematic discipline in his chosen field. After twenty months, he returned to Savannah and spent five months more in the office of his guardian. In 1810 he began practice in partnership with Samuel M. Bond, and about this time married Mary Johnston Campbell, daughter to Alexander Campbell of Richmond, Va. They had three children.

At the outbreak of the War of 1812, Wayne became an officer of the Georgia Hussars. Near the end of the war, the Georgia legislature passed an act suspending the collection of debts. Wayne, upholding the view which was popular in the Savannah district, opposed this law and was elected to the Georgia House of Representatives, serving 1815-16. He was then elected mayor of Savannah and served two years. After having reformed the financial administration of the city, he returned to private practice in partnership with Richard R. Cuyler, a leader in the local movement for internal improvements. In this movement Wayne took an important part. Having attended an improvement convention in Knoxville, he found the Georgia route to the West slighted, and later, presiding over a convention in his own state, helped to initiate the development of such a route.

In 1824 he became a judge of the superior court of Georgia, resigning in 1829 to become a member of the federal House of Representatives, where he served for three consecutive terms. During this time he supported the administration of President Jackson in practically all its major measures, including the tariff and internal-improvement legislation as well as the Force Bill and the removal of the deposits from the Bank of the United States. Yet he was not a strict-constructionist, for he held that the fed-

eral government had the right to build roads and canals and to charter a bank, although he opposed these measures on grounds of expediency. He took a keen interest in the question of Indian removals and supported Georgia's claim to jurisdiction over the tribes within her borders on the ground that she had acquired this jurisdiction from England and had not surrendered it (*Register of Debates in Congress*, 21 Cong., 1 Sess., p. 1123; May 24, 1830). He served on many important committees and rose to the chairmanship of the Committee on Foreign Relations. Though not an orator, he was a forceful and logical speaker on numerous occasions.

For all these services, President Jackson, on Jan. 9, 1835, appointed him an associate justice of the Supreme Court of the United States. As a member of this tribunal, his opinions in admiralty cases—particularly in that of *Waring* vs. *Clarke* (5 *Howard*, 441)—and in cases involving lands acquired from foreign countries are especially valuable. When the Civil War came on, he took the side of the Union and retained his seat on the bench of the Supreme Court, holding it until his death, from typhoid fever, in Washington, on July 5, 1867. He was the last surviving associate of John Marshall on the bench of the Supreme Court. His remains were taken to Savannah for interment in Laurel Grove Cemetery.

[Wayne's opinions appear in 34–72 *U. S. Reports*. The only good account of his life appeared in John Livingston, *Biog. Sketches of Distinguished Am. Lawyers* (c. 1850; title page missing); this was abridged by George White in *Hist. Colls. of Georgia* (1855). See also "Memoranda," 73 *U. S.*, vii–x; J. G. Bullock, *A Hist. and Geneal. of the Families of Bellinger and De Veaux* (1895), pp. 85–88; A. G. Feather, *The Supreme Court of the U. S.* (1900); H. L. Carson, *The Supreme Court of the U. S.* (1892); Charles Warren, *The Supreme Court in U. S. Hist.* (3 vols., 1922); *Biog. Dir. Am. Cong.* (1928); *Daily National Intelligencer* (Washington), July 6, 1867.]   T.P.A.

WEARE, MESHECH (Jan. 16, 1713–Jan. 14, 1786), colonial leader, Revolutionary patriot, and jurist, was born in Hampton Falls, N. H., the son of Nathaniel Weare and his second wife, Mary Waite. He was a descendant of Nathaniel Weare who had settled in Newbury, Mass., as early as 1638. His father was a judge of the superior court, and Meshech, the youngest son in a family of fourteen children, received a good education and was graduated at Harvard in 1735. On July 20, 1738, he was married to Elizabeth Shaw and after her death, to Mehitable Wainwright, on Dec. 11, 1746. He had two children by his first wife, and eight by his second.

He had expected to enter the ministry but abandoned his intention not long after graduation. For some years he devoted himself to the development and management of his extensive farm property. He also studied law and after 1745 gave steadily increasing attention to public affairs. From 1745 to 1755 he represented Hampton in the legislature, and with occasional interruptions this service continued until the overturn of royal government in 1775. This legislative experience was reinforced by a wide variety of committee service, by three years as speaker, eight as clerk, and by attendance at the Albany Congress in 1754. He was also a justice in the superior court from 1747 to 1775 and a colonel of militia.

He was over sixty years of age when the Revolution began, had many associations with the royalist element and was naturally conservative. His contemporary, Paine Wingate [q.v.], declares that he viewed the revolutionary movement "with caution, and certainly with no prepossession in favor of measures the country was adopting" (post, p. 245). His temperate advice at the early provincial congresses aroused some opposition among the more radical leaders, but when the break with the mother country was irreparable his accession to the Revolutionary cause made him the outstanding civilian figure in his state for the ensuing decade. Between 1776 and 1784 he served as president of the Council which was charged with the executive functions of the state, and in addition was chairman of the important committee of safety. He was, as a result, in contact with both continental and other state authorities and much more than a local leader.

In addition to his executive duties he was chief justice from 1776 to 1782, participated in many constitutional discussions, and exercised widespread influence as a leader of public opinion. In 1784 he was elected president of the state (the title of governor did not come into use for several years). A year later he resigned all offices because of failing health. His contemporaries lay great stress on his equable temper, fairness, shrewdness and honesty, qualities of the utmost value in such a formative period. His extensive correspondence and other papers after various vicissitudes passed into the custody of the New Hampshire and Massachusetts Historical Societies and the Library of Congress. They constitute a valuable source of Revolutionary history.

[Weare's official career can be readily traced in the State Papers of New Hampshire. See especially vol. XXI (1892), which contains a brief sketch by William Plumer. Consult also W. M. Sargent, The Weare Family of Hampton, N. H. (1879); sketch by E. S. Stearns in Warren Brown, Hist. of the Town of Hampton Falls, N. H., vol. I (1900), also privately printed in 1894; Joseph Dow, Hist. of the Town of Hampton, N. H. (1893), vol. II; F. B. Sanborn, "Meshech Weare," Proc. N. H. Hist. Soc., vol. V (1917), pp. 411–13; Paine Wingate, sketch of Weare in Colls. N. H. Hist. Soc., vol. V (1837); C. H. Bell, The Bench and Bar of N. H. (1894); F. M. Colby, "The Governor Weare Estate," Granite Monthly, July 1881.]

W. A. R.

WEATHERFORD, WILLIAM (c. 1780–Mar. 9, 1824), Indian chief, known also as Red Eagle, was born among the Creek Indians. Most of his life he lived on the right bank of the Alabama River within the present limits of Elmore County, a few miles above the site of Montgomery, Ala., and it is usually said that he was born there. Statements concerning his parentage are contradictory; that his mother was a Seminole and his father a "pedlar" of uncertain character, that he was the son of Charles Weatherford, a prosperous Scotch or English trader, and Sehoy, the half-sister of Alexander McGillivray [q.v.]. He had two Indian wives, Mary Moniac, who died in 1804, and Sapoth Thlanie. Actuated to war against the whites by the visit of Tecumseh [q.v.] in 1811, he, nevertheless, did not take up arms until after the battle of Tippecanoe. Then, ignorant that his cause was already hopeless, he led his followers in a war of destruction and won for himself the hatred and malice of the whites. Although they accused him of the utmost limits of personal degradation, they also described him as able, eloquent, and courageous. At the outbreak of the Creek War he was responsible for the massacre at Fort Mims on Aug. 30, 1813, in which some 500 victims were put to death, men, women, and children with indiscriminate cruelty. He was one of the leaders, apparently with Menewa [q.v.] a principal leader, of the Creeks in the disaster at Horseshoe Bend in 1814, when Andrew Jackson [q.v.] defeated about 1000 Indian warriors barricaded in the great bend of the Tallapoosa River. Shortly after the battle he surrendered to Andrew Jackson (for a discussion of the manner of this surrender and a denial of its dramatic character see *Alabama Historical Society Transactions*, II, 1898).

In the remaining years of his life he seems to have accepted the situation and lived fairly prosperously on a plantation among the white people of Monroe County. His personal reputation improved with that adjustment, and no more was heard of his dissolute habits, whether from a reformation of character or from lack of malice is uncertain. In 1817 he married his third wife, Mary Stiggins, a white woman. He bore no important part in the difficulties and anxieties of his doomed people, and, dying before westward removal was actually accomplished, he was buried in the beloved land of his forefathers.

[G. C. Eggleston, *Red Eagle* (1878); J. D. Dreisback, "Weatherford," *Ala. Hist. Reporter*, Mar., Apr. 1884; James Mooney, "Myths of the Cherokee," *Nineteenth Ann. Report of the Bureau of Am. Ethnology*, pt. I (1900); N. H. Claiborne, *Notes on the War in the South* (1819); J. F. H. Claiborne, *Life and Times of Gen. Sam. Dale* (1860); J. H. Eaton, *The Life of Andrew Jackson* (1817), ch. V; A. J. Pickett, *Hist. of Ala.* (1851), vol. II, pp. 267–84, 341–53; H. S. Halbert and T. H. Ball, *The Creek War* (1895).]   K. E. C.

WEAVER, AARON WARD (July 1, 1832–Oct. 2, 1919), naval officer, son of Lieut. William Augustus Weaver of the United States Navy, and Jane (Van Wyck) Weaver, was born in Washington, D. C. On May 10, 1848, he was appointed a midshipman in the navy and ordered to the coast of Brazil, where he served for four years on the sloop *St. Louis* and the frigate *Congress*. In 1853 he entered the United States Naval Academy, studied there for one year, and was graduated in the class of 1854 and commissioned a passed midshipman. He was given his first assignment in the new steam navy on the *Fulton*. In 1856 he was ordered to Coast Survey duty on the steamer *Walker*, and in 1857 was transferred to the steamer *Arctic*. On this vessel, under Commander O. H. Berryman, he assisted in the survey of Trinity Bay, Newfoundland, for the projected Atlantic telegraph cable, and in deep-sea soundings in the Gulf Stream. Late that year he was ordered to the *Marion* and cruised off the coast of Africa on the lookout for slavers. Off the Congo River the *Marion* captured the bark *Ardennes*, and Weaver, then a lieutenant, brought her to New York, arriving in July 1859.

When the Civil War broke out he was ordered to duty on the steam frigate *Susquehanna*. He participated in the capture of Fort Hatteras and Fort Clarke at Hatteras Inlet, N. C., Aug. 28–29, 1861, and of Fort Beauregard and Fort Walker, Port Royal, S. C., Nov. 7, 1861. The following April, before the fall of Fort Pulaski, he had charge of the *Susquehanna's* armed launches, convoying guns up to the army battery at Venus Point. When in May 1862 the *Susquehanna* cooperated with McClellan's operations in the Peninsular campaign, Weaver participated in the engagement with the Confederate batteries at Sewell's Point. That autumn he was given the command of the steam gunboat *Winona* and joined the Mississippi River Squadron. A period of most arduous service patrolling the lower river followed: on Dec. 14, 1862, he engaged a Confederate battery on Profit Island near Port Hudson, his ship being struck twenty-seven times; the following summer the *Winona* shelled and drove off a troop of Texas cavalry which had attacked the town of Plaquemine, La.;

ten days later Weaver with the assistance of two other gunboats routed a large force of Texas cavalry when they attacked Fort Butler, Donaldsonville, La., over one hundred Confederates being killed or wounded. For this service he was commended by Farragut, and by Maj. H. M. Porter of the army. In January 1864 Weaver was ordered to join the South Atlantic Blockading Squadron and captured the blockade runner *Ada*. In June he was transferred to the steamship *Chippewa* and in her participated in the first attack on Fort Fisher. After the battle Admiral Porter gave him the command of the monitor *Mahopac*, and in this vessel he took part in the second bombardment and the capture of the fort. For his part in the action, he was favorably mentioned by Porter and recommended for promotion, and was also mentioned favorably by Commodore William Radford, commander of the ironclad division. Weaver in the *Mahopac* assisted in the capture of Charleston, and participated in the night bombardment of the works near Richmond just prior to the evacuation of the city.

After the war he rose through the grades to the rank of rear admiral (June 27, 1893), his work being of an uneventful routine nature; on Sept. 26, 1893, he was retired. Thereafter he lived quietly in Washington. On Feb. 13, 1864, he married Ida Hyatt of Baltimore.

[L. R. Hamersly, *The Records of Living Officers of the U. S. Navy and Marine Corps* (4th ed., 1890); "Log of the Winona" (MS.), Navy Dept.; U. S. Navy Dept. Office of Naval Records, and Archives; *War of the Rebellion: Official Records* (Navy), 1 ser., vols. XI, XII, XV, XVI, XIX, XX, and (*Army*), 1 ser., XXVI (pt. 1), 202–03; ann. reports of the U. S. Coast Survey, 1856–57; *Who's Who in America*, 1918–19; *Army and Navy Reg.*, Oct. 11, 1919; *Army and Navy Jour.*, Mar. 5, 1864, p. 477; *Evening Star* (Washington), Oct. 3, 1919.]   L. H. B.

WEAVER, JAMES BAIRD (June 12, 1833–Feb. 6, 1912), soldier, congressman, Greenback and Populist candidate for the presidency, was born at Dayton, Ohio, fifth of the thirteen children of Abram and Susan (Imlay) Weaver. His father, a skilled mechanic and millwright, moved in 1835 to a forest-enclosed farm near Cassopolis, Mich., and eight years later to a quarter section of virgin prairie in what soon became Davis County, Iowa. Here on a typical frontier young Weaver grew to manhood. He attended the country schools, and when his father's election to a minor county office took the family to Bloomfield, the county-seat, he had the advantage of the somewhat better schools of that small town. For several years (1847–51) he carried the mail through roadless country and across bridgeless streams, from Bloomfield to Fairfield,

Iowa. In 1853 he accompanied a relative overland to California, and within a few months was cured completely of the gold fever, from which he had suffered since 1848. On his return to Iowa he worked in a store at Bonaparte, and had he consented might have become a partner in the business. By this time, however, he had discovered his aptitude for public speaking, particularly on controversial subjects, and had resolved to become a lawyer. In 1855, after borrowing one hundred dollars at thirty-three and one-third per cent. interest, he entered the Cincinnati Law School. A year later he was graduated and returned to Bloomfield to practise law.

Almost immediately he became absorbed in politics. He had been a Democrat, but, according to his own account, was converted to Free-Soil principles by reading *Uncle Tom's Cabin* and the *New York Tribune*. From 1857 until the outbreak of the Civil War he was active in local Republican circles, and he attended the convention which nominated Lincoln for the presidency, although not as a delegate. When Lincoln called for troops in 1861, Weaver volunteered and was made first lieutenant of the 2nd Iowa Infantry. He was in the thick of the fighting at Fort Donelson, at Shiloh, and at Corinth. On July 25, 1862, probably because his colonel had great confidence in him he was advanced over all the captains of his regiment to the rank of major, and when, during the battle of Corinth, his colonel and lieutenant-colonel were both mortally wounded, he took command. His conduct during this emergency was so gallant that afterwards, with the full approval of the officers who had so recently outranked him, he was commissioned colonel. During the winter of 1863–64, he was stationed at Pulaski, Tenn., where, under orders of a superior officer, he obtained by an assessment upon the inhabitants the means needed to care for some Confederate refugees. Later his political opponents made much more of this incident than the facts warranted. When his term of enlistment expired, in May 1864, he returned to his home in Iowa, and on Mar. 13, 1865, he was brevetted brigadier-general.

Weaver's services to his country and his party launched him upon what would normally have been a successful political career. He failed in 1865 to obtain a nomination for the post of lieutenant-governor, but in 1866 he was elected district attorney of the second Iowa judicial district, and in 1867 he received an appointment as federal assessor of internal revenue for the first district of Iowa, a post which he held until 1873. From this time forward, however, he lost ground with the Republican leaders in his state. He was a devout Methodist, utterly incorruptible, and an ardent prohibitionist; he denounced the extortions of the politically important railways and other predatory corporations; and he objected strenuously to the stand his party was taking on the currency question. Nevertheless, such was his popularity that only the sharpest political trickery prevented him from obtaining the Republican nomination for Congress in 1874, and for governor in 1875. Undoubtedly these defeats, which he believed wholly unmerited, served to undermine his party loyalty, and to drive him towards the "independents," or "Greenbackers," for whose principles he was developing a great affinity. His views on the money question would not at a later date have been regarded as extreme. He was not an advocate of unlimited inflation, nor of debt repudiation, but he held to the quantity theory of money, and opposed what he deemed the systematic efforts of the creditor class to appreciate the purchasing power of the dollar. As a Greenbacker he won a seat in Congress in 1878, ran for president in 1880, was defeated for Congress in 1882, but won again in 1884 and 1886.

When the Farmers' Alliance succeeded the Greenbackers as the chief exponent of soft-money views, Weaver hastened to identify himself with that organization, and he took a leading part in transforming it into the People's, or Populist, party. With but little opposition he was accorded the Populist nomination for the presidency in 1892. Throughout the campaign the magnetism of his personality, enhanced rather than diminished by his whitened hair and his generally patriarchal appearance, was as effective as on the battlefield of Corinth. His commanding presence coupled with the force and fire of his oratory gave him a bearing where a less able speaker would have been laughed off the stage. Only in the South, where falsified accounts of his Pulaski record were deliberately circulated, was he subjected to the discourtesies so commonly accorded to third-party orators. His defeat was inevitable, but he received a popular vote of over a million, and twenty-two votes in the electoral college. His book, *A Call to Action* (1892), published during the campaign, summarized his own political principles and furnished much of the ammunition used by his supporters during the fray.

Weaver's victories in the eighties had been won by the assistance of the Democrats, and after 1892 he was one of the leading advocates of a fusion of all soft-money forces. When in 1896 Bryan captured the Democratic nomination, Weaver strongly favored his nomination by the

Populists also, and helped to bring it about. Fusion, however, rang the deathknell of Populism, and within a few years Weaver found himself, together with most of the Populist leaders, a Democrat, and without a future in politics. With his political career at an end, his neighbors in the town of Colfax, Iowa, where he spent the later years of his life, showed their good will by choosing him to be their mayor. On July 13, 1858, he married Clara Vinson, a school-teacher who had come to Iowa from St. Mary's, Ohio; they were the parents of five girls and two boys. The year of his death, 1912, there was published *Past and Present of Jasper County, Iowa*, in two volumes, bearing his name as editor-in-chief.

[James B. Weaver, Jr., of Des Moines, Iowa, has in his possession "Memoranda with Respect to the Life of James Baird Weaver" (unpublished), prepared by Weaver himself. Substantial extracts from this document, which gives information only down to 1859, are printed in F. E. Haynes, *James Baird Weaver* (1919), a satisfactory account of Weaver's political career, gleaned largely from the newspapers, and from a scrapbook which Weaver kept. See also E. A. Allen, *The Life and Public Services of James Baird Weaver* (1892); H. C. Evans, *The Pioneers and Politics of Davis County, Iowa* (1929); S. D. Dillaye, "Life of Gen. J. B. Weaver" in *Our Presidential Candidates and Political Compendium* (1880); F. E. Haynes, *Third Party Movements Since the Civil War* (1916); J. D. Hicks, *The Populist Revolt* (1931); *Biog. Dir. Am. Cong.* (1928); F. B. Heitman, *Hist. Reg. and Dict. U. S. Army* (1903); *Who's Who in America*, 1910–11; *Register and Leader* (Des Moines), Feb. 7, 8, 9, 1912.]   J. D. H—s.

WEAVER, PHILIP (b. 1791), cotton manufacturer, was a son of John and Ruth (Wilbur) Weaver of North Scituate, R. I., and a descendant of Clement Weaver who was in Weymouth, Mass., by 1643. As early as 1812 Philip went from his home in Coventry, R. I., to work for the Dudley Cotton Manufacturing Company, Dudley, Mass.; in 1815 he was associated with Weaver, Hutchings & Company, for whom he did work on patterns and rollers. Early in 1816 he moved to Spartanburg District, S. C., accompanied by his brothers, John, Wilbur, and Lindsay, as well as William Sheldon, John Clark, Thomas Slack, William Bates, and Thomas Hutchings. He was unhappy in South Carolina, chiefly because he felt that he and his family— he had married Miriam Keene, by whom he had four daughters—were "looked down upon with contempt" because they were "opposed to the abominable practice of slavery" (Wallace, *post*, II, 411); nevertheless, he remained there for a number of years. Between December 1816 and 1820 he and his associates experienced serious difficulties because of shortage of cash; the Spartanburg Judgment Roll lists several judgments against them for both large and small sums. In 1819 Weaver was arrested for non-payment of

one of these claims, but one Thomas Craven went his bail. The Weaver mill was on land owned by Rev. Benjamin Wofford who was at that early date accumulating the fortune with which he later founded Wofford College. In December 1818 he sold to Nathaniel Gist the tract of sixty acres on the Tiger River containing the mill, but Philip and John Weaver continued to operate the mill after the sale. Philip Weaver owned no land in Spartanburg district until Aug. 14, 1819, when John Withers of Columbia sold Weaver & Company 300 acres on the east side of the Tiger.

Whether or not the Weaver mill was the first cotton mill in Spartanburg District has been a matter of controversy. Kohn (*post*) inclines toward the view that the Weavers were first, while Landrum (*post*) is inclined to accept the claim made for George and Leonard Hill. Wallace (*post*) thinks it reasonably clear that the Weavers a little antedated the Hills as manufacturers in Spartanburg. Certainly both the Weaver and Hill mills provided an energetic element in the cotton manufacturing industry in Spartanburg and Greenville counties which undoubtedly laid the foundation for the extensive textile development before 1860.

Philip Weaver left Spartanburg District before 1826 and subsequently settled in Attica, Ind., where shortly before the Civil War he was killed by a runaway horse. His former associates continued in the manufacturing business: John Weaver built a mill nineteen miles from Greenville, on Thompson's Beaver Dam, and operated it until his death several years after the Civil War; Hutchings built and operated several mills in succession with apparent profit, while in the thirties William Bates established the Batesville Cotton Mill.

[L. E. Weaver, *Hist. and Geneal. of a Branch of the Weaver Family* (1928); Yates Snowden, *Hist. of S. C.* (1920), II, 1167; D. D. Wallace, *The Hist. of S. C.* (1934), II, 411, III, 56; August Kohn, *The Cotton Mills of S. C.* (1907); J. B. O. Landrum, *Hist. of Spartanburg County* (1900), pp. 157–65; Philip Weaver's account book, Wofford College Library; S. C. Judgment Rolls, 532, 593, 595; Spartanburg Mesne Conveyance Office, Q 320, R 9, 10, 12, 79; Greenville Mesne Conveyance Office, T 342.]   R. G. S.

WEAVER, WILLIAM DIXON (Aug. 30, 1857–Nov. 2, 1919), electrical engineer, was born in Greensburg, Pa., the son of Caspar and Maria (Massena) Weaver. After completing his elementary education, in 1875 he entered the department of agriculture and mechanic arts in Kentucky University (later the University of Kentucky). A year later he obtained an appointment to the United States Naval Academy, from which he was graduated in 1880 as a cadet engineer. He accompanied the first Greely relief expedition in 1883 on the *Yantic,* made a cruise of the world as an assistant engineer on the *Omaha* (1885–88), and spent two years in the waters of the Orient. During a leave of absence in 1884 he studied electricity and conducted some investigations in the electrical laboratories of the Sorbonne, Paris, and the School of Electrical Engineering, London. While he was stationed at the Brooklyn navy yard (1890) he designed an electrical recorder, used in speed trials, and an apparatus with electrical adjustments for the calibration of steam-engine indicators. Resigning from the navy in 1892, he joined the firm of E. G. Bernard, manufacturers of electrical apparatus in Troy, N. Y., but after a year he gave this up to engage in editorial work. From 1893 to 1896 he was editor of the *Electrical World.* In 1896 he became associated with James H. McGraw in the founding of the *American Electrician* and was the first editor. Three years later McGraw consolidated the *Electrical World* and *Electrical Engineering* and subsequently absorbed the *American Electrician,* publishing all three as the *Electrical World.* Except for a leave of absence during the Spanish-American War, when he served as volunteer chief engineer on the *Glacier,* Weaver continued as editor until his retirement in May 1912.

He was intensely interested in electrical engineering as a profession and in the organization of professional societies. It was he who in 1895 made the suggestion to Andrew Carnegie which later led to the erection of a building in New York for the engineering societies of the United States. To him is due the plan of organization and development of the Society of Illuminating Engineers. He was a founder of the American Electro-Chemical Society and for six years a manager of the American Institute of Electrical Engineers. He was also active in the development of the electrical engineering library, part of the great Engineering Societies' Library in New York. In 1904 he was made treasurer and business manager of the International Electrical Congress held in St. Louis, Mo., and did much to make it successful. In commemoration of his services in the organization and development of the American Institute of Electrical Engineers, a memorial tablet to him was unveiled at the time of the annual meeting, May 16, 1919. His collection of publications on the French Revolution (now at Princeton University), to which he devoted his leisure, was said to be one of the largest in existence on that subject. After retiring to his home in Charlottesville, Va., he was active in civic affairs. On July 26, 1901, in Bremen, Germany, he married Mildred Niebuhr, by whom he had seven children. He died in Charlottesville, survived by his wife and six children.

[*Who's Who in America,* 1920–21; *Navy Registers,* 1881–92; *Electrical World,* Oct. 25, Nov. 1, Nov. 8, 1919; *Electrical Rev.* (Chicago), Nov. 15, 1919; *Proc. Am. Institute of Electrical Engineers,* 1919, vol. XXXVIII (n.d.); *Sci.,* June 4, 1920; *Princeton Alumni Weekly,* Oct. 17, 1923; obituary in *N. Y. Times,* Nov. 3, 1919; names of parents, dates of marriage and death, and other information from Mrs. W. D. Weaver of Charlottesville.]   C. W. M.

WEBB, ALEXANDER STEWART (Feb. 15, 1835–Feb. 12, 1911), soldier, college president, was born in New York, the son of James Watson Webb [*q.v.*] and his first wife, Helen Lispenard Stewart. After training in private schools Webb was appointed a cadet in the United States Military Academy, where he was graduated in 1855 and commissioned second lieutenant of artillery. In this same year he married Anna, daughter of Henry Rutgers Remsen. In 1856 he saw dangerous and exacting duty in Florida during the war against the Seminole Indians. After a year of garrison duty at Fort Independence, Mass., and Fort Snelling, Minn., he returned to the Academy, Nov. 10, 1857, as assistant professor of mathematics.

At the beginning of the Civil War he was commissioned first lieutenant, 2nd Artillery, and returned to duty in the field. Having distinguished himself at Fort Pickens and in the first battle of Bull Run, he was appointed assistant to the chief of artillery of the Army of the Potomac. From March to November 1862 he was inspector general on the staff of Gen. William F. Barry [*q.v.*] and served with distinction in the battles of Yorktown, the Seven Days, and Malvern Hill. At the end of the Peninsula campaign, he was sent to Washington as inspector of artillery in the camp of instruction, but in January 1863 was reassigned to duty in the field as assistant inspector general of the V Corps. Relieved of this duty in May, he assumed command of the 2nd (Philadelphia) Brigade, Second Division, II Corps, which he led at Chancellorsville and at Gettysburg. In the latter action Webb's brigade occupied the Bloody Angle, where it bore the brunt of Pickett's charge and had a decisive part in his repulse. For "distinguished personal gallantry in the battle of Gettysburg" Webb was awarded the Congressional Medal of Honor, Sept. 28, 1891.

After Gettysburg he served continuously, commanding the Second Division, II Corps, until the battle of Spotsylvania Court House (May 1864), where he was severely wounded. After his recovery he did court-martial duty in New York until January 1865, when he became chief-of-staff to General Meade. At the end of six months he was appointed assistant inspector general, Division of the Atlantic, which duty he relinquished in February 1866. From June of that year until October 1868 he was principal assistant professor of history, ethics, and constitutional and international law at the Military Academy, then rejoined his regiment for service in Washington. He was unassigned for a year, and honorably discharged from the army at his own request, Dec. 31, 1870, with the rank of lieutenant-colonel. During his career in the service he occupied every rank to that of major-general, either by appointment or by brevet. The honors that came to him in recognition of personal gallantry indicate his importance as a soldier; he had little experience in leading masses of men or in planning large-scale military activities, but he was an inspiring commander under fire and an intrepid fighter. He enjoyed the highest respect and admiration of his men, who, in later years, delighted to honor him by election to high office in veteran organizations, and after his death took a leading part in causing the State of New York to erect a statue of him at the Bloody Angle.

On July 21, 1869, Webb was elected president of the College of the City of New York, in succession to Horace Webster, also a graduate of West Point, and in accordance with the custom then prevailing was appointed also to the chair of political philosophy. He continued in active service until failing powers forced his retirement on Dec. 1, 1902. Though much admired by faculty and students for his personal qualities, he made no original contribution as an educator. He rigidly maintained the fixed curriculum set by his precedessor, and expended a disproportionate amount of his own time and of that of the faculty on routine matters of administration. During his tenure of the presidency, the College maintained the high standards of scholarship set from the beginning, without significant advancement in the scope of its work, but the picturesqueness of his personality and the dignity of his bearing brought to the life of the institution an impressiveness that in some measure made up for his lack of leadership in scholarly attainment. In 1881 he published *The Peninsula: McClellan's Campaign of 1862.*

After his retirement Webb lived quietly at Riverdale, going to the city only occasionally for patriotic celebrations or to fulfill his duties as a member of the New York Monuments Commission (1895–1911) and member of the council of the Military Service Institution. He died at the end of his seventy-sixth year, survived by four daughters and a son.

[*Who's Who in America,* 1910–11; F. B. Heitman, *Hist. Reg. and Dict. U. S. Army* (1903); *The City College: Memories of Sixty Years* (1907), pp. 107–36; *City College Quart.,* Mar. 1910, Mar., June 1911; *In Memoriam, Alexander Stewart Webb, 1835–1911* (Albany, 1916); *Forty-second Ann. Reunion, Asso. Grads. U. S. Mil. Acad.* (1911); *N. Y. Times,* Feb. 12, 13, 14, 1911.]
D. A. R.

WEBB, CHARLES HENRY (Jan. 24, 1834–May 24, 1905), "John Paul," author, was born at Rouse's Point, N. Y., the son of Nathan and Philena King (Paddock) Webb, and was educated in schools at Champlain, N. Y., and Toronto. At seventeen he went to New York City to try newspaper work. As a result of reading the newly published *Moby Dick,* however, he soon shipped on the whaler *Walter Scott* out of Martha's Vineyard, and spent three and a half years in the South Seas and the Arctic. Upon his return in 1855 he rejoined his family, who had moved to Illinois, and for several years engaged in business with an elder brother at Fulton City. Early in 1859 he began contributing poems, usually humorous, to *Harper's Weekly,* and in 1860 obtained a position on the *New York Times,* for which he wrote "Minor Topics," a column of comment. In 1861 he went to the front as a war correspondent, and was present at Bull Run and in some of the early campaigns in the Shenandoah Valley. His articles appeared sometimes over his initials and sometimes, apparently, over the pseudonym, Leo. An association struck up with another correspondent, Edmund Clarence Stedman [*q.v.*], ripened into a lifelong friendship.

From 1863 to 1866 Webb was in California, at first (1863–64) as a member of the staff of the San Francisco *Evening Bulletin.* Although in later years he vigorously and quite properly objected to being classed as a "California humorist," nevertheless these three years were the time of his greatest literary activity and influence. He soon won leadership in the city's literary circle through his facile pen, warm personality, and ready wit, this last only enhanced by a slight impediment to his speech. He became the close friend of Bret Harte, and later of Mark Twain [*qq.v.*]. All three contributed to the *Californian,* which Webb founded as owner and first editor in May 1864. Webb in addition contributed, usually under his pen-name of Inigo, to the *Golden Era,* the *Sacramento Union,* and the *New York Times.* He also wrote two comedies, *Arrah-na-poke* (a parody of Boucicault's *Arrah-na-poque*) and *Our Friend from Victoria,* both produced in San Francisco. Unfortunately the money which he won by writing, he lost by speculation in mines, so that in 1866 he returned to New York City little the richer.

For the next few years he contributed to *Harper's Monthly,* the *Springfield Republican,* and other papers, published *Liffith Lank* (1866), a parody of Charles Reade's *Griffith Gaunt,* and *St. Twel'mo,* a parody of Augusta Jane Evans' *St. Elmo,* and more surely established his name by becoming the sponsor and publisher of Mark Twain's first book, *The Celebrated Jumping Frog of Calaveras County* (1867). On Oct. 11, 1870, he married Elizabeth W. Shipman of Brooklyn, N. Y. In 1872–73 he engaged in business as a broker and banker, but he was caught in the panic of 1873 and returned to journalism. About this time he began the "John Paul" letters for the *New York Tribune,* collected in 1874 as *John Paul's Book.* This became his best-known volume, and resulted in his being known almost as much by the pseudonym as by his own name. For several years after this time he lived abroad with his family. In 1876 he published *Sea-Weed and What We Seed* and *Parodies: Prose and Verse.* After these volumes, however, his interests turned more to *vers de société* (*Vagrom Verses,* 1889; *With Lead and Line,* 1901). His character, always delightful, mellowed still further with age. He frequently spent his summers in Nantucket, but kept his permanent home in New York City, where he died. In his later life he was greatly interested in invention. He patented an adding machine (1868) and a cartridge-loading machine (1874). In 1893, after nearly a decade of preparatory work, manufacture of his "ribbon adder" was begun, but the financial disasters of that year wrecked the enterprise.

In spite of his decided talents, Webb seems unlikely to be long remembered. His parodies could not survive the writings from which they sprang; *John Paul's Book* invites comparison with Mark Twain's work and suffers accordingly; his verses are clever and graceful, but fail to attain a highly poetic level. He will probably be best known as a "western humorist" for his part in the outburst of literary activity which marked San Francisco in the sixties.

[*Who's Who in America,* 1903–05; E. C. Stedman, in *Critic,* Mar. 1902, with portrait; C. W. Stoddard, in *Pacific Monthly,* Mar. 1908; G. R. Stewart, Jr., *Bret Harte* (1931); obituaries in *Publisher's Weekly,* June 3, 1905; and *N. Y. Times,* May 25, 1905; information from Elizabeth Holder Webb, Webb's daughter.]

G. R. S., Jr.

WEBB, DANIEL (*c.* 1700–Nov. 11, 1773), British general, was an Englishman, probably connected with the Wiltshire Webbs. In March 1721, he purchased an ensigncy in the 1st Foot Guards; in April 1722, he became captain-lieutenant, with the rank of captain, in the same corps; and from 1725 to 1732 he led a company in Grove's regiment of foot. In 1732 he became a captain in the 4th Horse, which under Ligonier developed into one of the finest cavalry regiments in the army (Black Horse, 7th Dragoon Guards). He remained with that corps for twenty years. In 1742 he attained the rank of major and led a squadron at Dettingen and at Fontenoy; a few days after the latter battle, in 1745, he was made lieutenant-colonel and commanded the corps for ten years. Such service brought him favorably to the attention of Cumberland, the captain-general, and he was probably the Webb who in 1754 carried out the thankless task of settling the army accounts with Holland for the previous war. In November 1755, he succeeded Dunbar as colonel of the 48th foot, then in America.

On Cumberland's recommendation, who thought him a "sensible, discreet man as well as a good officer," Webb early in 1756 was selected as third in command in North America under Lord Loudoun and James Abercromby [*qq.v.*]; he was given a temporary commission as commander-in-chief, and sent to New York to supervise preparations for the campaign. Reaching New York only nine days before Abercromby, he never took over officially the chief command. The following August, on the news of the fall of Oswego, Loudoun made him a temporary major-general and sent him up the Mohawk River to make a stand against Montcalm's expected attack on the forts there. Panic-stricken by Indian rumors, Webb on his own initiative destroyed the forts and precipitately retreated. The colonists, suspended, as one of them said, in a "spider's web," made him their chief target of scorn. Their outspoken bitterness combined that winter with a severe attack of the palsy to destroy completely his confidence in his own judgment, yet Loudoun had no one else to leave in command in New York in 1757 when the main army was in Nova Scotia. Distrustful of the provincials, fearful that he had been left without sufficient troops, Webb neglected to strengthen the New York posts or to take any of the measures advised by Loudoun. Of Montcalm's designs on Fort William Henry he had sufficient warning, yet for the six days of the siege in August he lay at Fort Edward, fourteen miles to the south, without attempting relief. Pitt recalled him in December 1757. He was, but probably because of his illness, the most incompetent staff officer who served in America during the Seven Years' War. In 1758, as quartermaster-general, he served in Germany, and in 1760 commanded a brigade at Warbourg. He was promoted major-general in 1759, and lieutenant-general in 1761. He became colonel in

1766 of the 8th Foot and in 1772 of the 14th Dragoons.

[Charles Dalton, *George the First's Army*, vol. II (1912); Army Lists; Richard Cannon, *Hist. Records of the British Army: the Eighth or King's Reg. of Foot* (1844), *the Fourteenth, or the King's Light Dragoons* (1847); *Hist. MSS. Commission, Reports on Various Colls.*, vol. VIII (1913); S. M. Pargellis, *Lord Loudoun in North America* (1933); *War in North America, 1748-1765* (1936).]   S. M. P.

WEBB, GEORGE JAMES (June 24, 1803–Oct. 7, 1887), musician, composer, was born at "Rushmore Lodge," Wiltshire, near Salisbury, England. His father, James Millett Webb, was a landowner with large holdings. His wife was Isabel Ann Archer, and George was their eldest child. The environment of the home was musical; the father was an amateur singer, and the mother a talented musician who gave her son music lessons before he was seven years of age. At a boarding school in Salisbury he studied music with Alexander Lucas, and learned to play the violin and piano. He subsequently decided to make music his profession and studied in Falmouth with an organist of that city. Later he determined to emigrate to America and booked passage for New York, but was persuaded to change his destination by the captain of a ship sailing for Boston. He landed in Boston in 1830, and within a few weeks he was appointed organist of the Old South Church. He soon became associated with Lowell Mason [q.v.] in his educational projects, and was placed in charge of the secular music of the newly organized Boston Academy of Music. He organized an orchestra at the Academy which gave regular concerts for fourteen years—until 1847. In the same year a Musical Fund Society was organized and Webb became conductor of its orchestra until 1852, when he resigned because of other duties, though he remained president of the society until 1855. He was important in the development of music in Boston because he acted as the link between the pioneer efforts of J. C. Gottlieb Graupner, and the future work of Carl Zerrahn [qq.v.] with the orchestra of the Harvard Musical Association.

Meanwhile Webb helped Mason establish a series of Normal Musical Conventions for training teachers in 1836. Attendance at these conventions grew from fourteen in the first year to a thousand in 1849. He collaborated with Mason in compiling song and hymn books—*The Psaltery* (1845); *The National Psalmodist* (1848); and *Cantica Laudis* (1850). Alone he compiled and edited *Scripture Worship* (1834); *The American Glee Book* (1841); and, for the Boston Handel and Haydn Society, of which he was conductor from 1833 to 1836, the *Massachusetts Collection of Psalmody* (1840). He removed to Orange, N. J., about 1870, and lived there for the rest of his life. He occupied himself by giving vocal lessons in New York, and conducting summer normal courses at Binghamton, N. Y. His wife was Caroline Elizabeth Parmella (Haven) Merriam. Of their six children, one daughter became the wife of William Mason, 1829-1908 [q.v.].

As a composer, Webb is known principally for the hymn-tune "Webb." This was originally composed for secular words, " 'Tis dawn, the lark is singing." As a hymn-tune it was first used with the text beginning, "The morning light is breaking," but came to be known almost exclusively as the music for "Stand up, stand up for Jesus." Webb composed many songs, choral works, and a few instrumental pieces, but few of them have survived. George F. Root [q.v.] termed Webb the "most refined and delightful teacher of the English glee and madrigal" he had ever known (Root, *post*, p. 28). His son-in-law, William Mason (*post*, p. 9), described him as "a gentleman of high culture, thoroughly educated in music."

[W. J. Metcalf, *Am. Writers and Compilers of Sacred Music* (1925); J. T. Howard, *Our Am. Music* (1931); G. F. Root, *The Story of a Musical Life* (1891); William Mason, *Memories of a Musical Life* (1901); typescript book by Mary Sturgis Gray, "Webb Descendants of England" (1930), in the possession of members of the family; *N. Y. Tribune*, Oct. 8, 1887.]   J. T. H.

WEBB, JAMES WATSON (Feb. 8, 1802–June 7, 1884), journalist and diplomat, was born at Claverack, N. Y. Through his mother, Catharine Hogeboom, he came of old New York Dutch stock, and through his father, Gen. Samuel Blachley Webb (1753–1807), an aide of Washington, of old Connecticut stock, his first American ancestor being Richard Webb who was admitted freeman in Boston in 1632 and went to Hartford in 1635. Early orphaned, he was educated at Cooperstown, N. Y., under the guardianship of a brother-in-law, but at seventeen ran away to join the army. Appearing in Washington (1819) armed with a letter of identification from Gov. DeWitt Clinton of New York, he persuaded Secretary of War John C. Calhoun to give him a second lieutenant's commission. He was assigned at first to the artillery at Governor's Island, N. Y., but was transferred in 1821 to the 3rd Infantry at Chicago. There, in 1822, he had a notable frontier adventure, when he volunteered to carry to Fort Armstrong on the Mississippi news of a meditated Indian attack on Fort Snelling, Minn., crossing the forests and prairies of Illinois in the depth of winter while trailed by

hostile Indians. As impetuous as he was auda-
cious, Webb fought two duels with fellow-offi-
cers, came near fighting many more, and finally
(1827) resigned from the army in consequence
of one of these embroilments. At this time he
was a first lieutenant; his later title of general
was conferred at the time of his appointment as
minister to Austria (*A Letter . . . to J. Bramley-Moore, post,* p. 5).

On leaving the army young Webb went to
New York City and plunged into a journalistic
career, eventually to become one of the most influential editors in that age of personal journalism. In 1827 he acquired the *Morning Courier,*
and in 1829 acquired and merged with it the
New-York Enquirer, thereafter continuing as
editor and proprietor of the *Morning Courier
and New-York Enquirer* until he sold out to the
World in 1861 and retired from the field. At
first stanchly Jacksonian, he deserted Jackson
in 1832 on the United States Bank issue, and became a chief prop of the Whig party. He was
an anti-abolitionist but a free-soiler, and during
the 1850's urged the preservation of the Union
even at the cost of war. The *Courier and Enquirer* was one of the old sixpenny "blanket
sheets" destined to be starved out by the smaller,
cheaper papers, two of which were founded by
one-time assistants of Webb's, James Gordon
Bennett, the elder, and Henry Jarvis Raymond
[*qq.v.*]. With its chief rival, the *Journal of Commerce,* the *Courier and Enquirer* waged a war
of size which eventually produced folios containing over two thousand square inches of type.
In the 1830's the rivals sent schooners fifty to a
hundred miles to sea in a race for incoming news,
and established pony expresses to hasten the news
from Washington. With the editors of the penny papers Webb later exchanged plentiful invective, until he was called the "best abused" of them
all. He was frequently involved in affairs of
honor growing out of his editorial activities, on
one occasion (1842) escaping prison under the
New York anti-dueling law only by the pardon
of the governor.

At the outbreak of the Civil War Webb sold
his paper and, somewhat to his own surprise,
found himself in the diplomatic service. He had
journeyed to Vienna in 1849–50 under appointment (Jan. 7, 1850), as chargé d'affaires to Austria, only to be greeted with the news that the
Senate had refused to confirm his appointment,
perhaps because of a widespread desire to break
with Austria in protest against the Hungarian
war. He was now (May 31, 1861) made minister to Brazil, and went to his post via France,
where he presented the Union cause to Louis

Napoleon, his friend and correspondent since
their meeting in 1835 while Napoleon was in
exile. Later, through correspondence and another fateful interview (November 1865), Webb
was instrumental in securing a promise of French
withdrawal from Mexico. The record of his
eight strenuous years in Brazil is marked by an
alert patriotism and a bold energy verging on
rashness. He had the satisfaction of seeing the
unfriendly British envoy sent home in disgrace.
He fought tirelessly against the aid extended to
Confederate privateers, protected the interests
of Americans during the Paraguayan War, and
secured the settlement of several long-standing
maritime claims. Retiring from the service in
1869, he traveled in Europe for two years, and
then lived quietly at home, mostly in New York,
until his death. His publications include a number of pamphlets: *To the Officers of the Army*
(1827) on the occasion of his resignation; *Slavery and Its Tendencies* (n.d.), written in 1856;
A Letter . . . to J. Bramley-Moore, Esq., M.P.
(n.d.), on the affair with the British envoy; and
A National Currency (1875). He also wrote
Reminiscences of General Samuel B. Webb
(1882).

Webb was twice married: first (July 1, 1823)
to Helen Lispenard Stewart, daughter of Alexander L. Stewart, who died in 1848; second
(Nov. 9, 1849) to Laura Virginia Cram, daughter of Jacob Cram, millionaire brewer. Of the
eight children born of the first union, five grew
to maturity, the youngest being Alexander
Stewart Webb [*q.v.*], the well-known Civil War
general. There were five sons born of the second
marriage. Webb's tall figure, massive head, and
piercing eyes gave him a dignified, even imposing presence, which he retained until old age, in
spite of a half-century's battle with hereditary
gout.

[In addition to Webb's pamphlets, see for family
data Webb's *Reminiscences of Gen. Samuel B. Webb*
(1882); for the Fort Snelling adventure, dedication to
*Altowan; or, Incidents of Life and Adventure in the
Rocky Mountains* (2 vols., 1846), ed. by Webb; for
charges arising out of the *Carolina* claims, *Gen. J. Watson Webb . . . vs. Hamilton Fish* (1875), and J. B.
Moore, *A Digest of Internat. Law* (1906), vol. VI, pp.
749–50. See also G. H. Andrews, in *Sketches of Men
of Progress* (1870–71), ed. by James Parton; N. A.
Cleven, in *Revista do Instituto Historico e Geographico
Brasileiro . . . Congresso Internacional de Historia da
America* (1925), pp. 293–394; F. E. Stevens, *James
Watson Webb's Trip across Ill. in 1822* (1924); Fred-
eric Hudson, *Journalism in the U. S.* (1873); obituary
in *N. Y. Times,* June 8, 1884. Webb's dispatches from
Brazil were published in *Papers Relating to Foreign
Affairs,* 1862–69.]   E. M. S.

WEBB, JOHN BURKITT (Nov. 22, 1841–
Feb. 17, 1912), engineer, professor of mathematics, inventor, was born in Philadelphia, Pa.,

the son of Charles Roe and Eliza Ann (Greaves) Webb. His grandfather, Burkitt Webb, emigrated from England as a young man and settled in Philadelphia. Webb attended the public schools and the drawing school of the Franklin Institute. For several years, while he worked as clerk in a store, he spent his spare time in the study of mathematics and mechanics, and as a pastime designed and built machinery. About 1860 he formed a small company at Bridgeton, N. J., to make electro-magnetic apparatus for playing organs automatically, but the undertaking was abandoned for lack of capital, and for a year or so Webb was a traveling salesman. In 1863, with his former partner, Oberlin Smith, he organized at Bridgeton the Smith and Webb Manufacturing Company to manufacture special machine tools. The business prospered, but poor health compelled Webb to seek some more healthful climate. Going to Ann Arbor, Mich., he entered the University of Michigan to study civil engineering. After receiving the degree of C.E. in 1871, he was called to the chair of civil engineering which had just been established at the University of Illinois at Urbana. During his eight years there he made a study of the scientific schools of Europe, and after his resignation he spent two full years in advanced studies in mathematics and physics at Heidelberg, Göttingen, Berlin, and Paris. Part of this time was spent in experimental work in electricity in Helmholtz's laboratory in Berlin and in the instrument-maker's shop at the University of Berlin. Webb returned to the United States in 1881 to accept the new chair of applied mathematics at Cornell University, Ithaca, N. Y. During the five years that he held this position he delivered lectures on thermodynamics, mechanisms, drawing and drawing instruments; invented a draft gauge and an inertia-less steam-engine indicator; acted as judge at the International Electrical Exhibition, Philadelphia, in 1884; and published an exhaustive study on "Belting to Connect Shafts Which Are Not Parallel and Do Not Intersect" (Stevens' Indicator, post, p. 160). In 1886 he was called to the chair of mathematics and mechanics at Stevens Institute of Technology, Hoboken, N. J., where he remained until 1908.

In 1888 he invented and brought out his floating dynamometer, a very simple but effective device for measuring the power delivered by dynamos, motors, and the like. In 1892 he perfected his viscous dynamometer and in 1900 the dynamophone, which by a simple telephonic method measured the twist of a transmission shaft carrying power. In addition he wrote many technical papers on advanced mechanics. His lectures on mechanical paradoxes (such as a man's lifting himself by his own boot straps, rolling a barrel up hill by gravity, etc.) were always well received by enthusiastic audiences. Webb believed strongly in graphical methods, and insisted upon precision and accuracy in the work of his students. He was a member of a number of engineering and mathematical societies both in the United States and Europe, and was a vice-president of the American Association for the Advancement of Science (1885). After his retirement he devoted himself to private consulting practice. He married Mary Emeline Gregory, daughter of John Milton Gregory [q.v.], in Urbana, Ill., on Apr. 19, 1876. At the time of his death at his home in Glen Ridge, N. J., he was survived by his widow and six children.

[See Mary E. Cooch, Ancestry and Descendants of Nancy Allyn (Foote) Webb (1910); Who's Who in America, 1912–13, from which the date of marriage is taken; The Semi-Centennial Alumni Record . . . Univ. of Ill. (1918); Stevens Indicator, Apr. 1912; Trans. Am. Soc. Mechanical Engineers, vol. XXXIV (1913); patent office records; obituaries in Pub. Ledger (Phila.) and N. Y. Times, Feb. 19, 1912.]   C. W. M.

WEBB, THOMAS (c. 1724–Dec. 10, 1796), soldier, Methodist preacher, was born in England and became an officer in the British army. He received a quartermaster's commission, Oct. 29, 1754, and was made lieutenant on Nov. 9 of the following year. Sent to America in the campaign against the French, he lost his right eye and was wounded in the right arm on the Plains of Abraham when Wolfe captured Quebec in September 1759. He returned to England and because of his disabilities was retired on a captain's pay. In 1764, under the preaching of John Wesley, he was converted and became a militant Methodist. At a service in Bath, when the appointed preacher failed to appear, Webb was asked to speak in his place and proved so effective a substitute that thereafter he frequently engaged in public exhortation.

About 1766, under appointment as barrackmaster at Albany, he came to America. Soon, having heard that there were Methodists there, he visited New York. His appearance at one of their meetings—in striking military garb and with a sword at his side—awakened some consternation, but when he introduced himself as "a soldier of the cross and a spiritual son of John Wesley" he was warmly welcomed. From that time until his final return to England some sixteen years later he was one of the principal agencies in establishing Methodism in America. He assisted Philip Embury [q.v.] in preaching to the little congregation that gathered in the "rigging loft" on Horse and Cart (later William) Street; he headed the list of subscribers to the fund raised for the building of Wesley Chapel, completed in 1768, advancing, in addition, three hundred pounds as a loan and securing gifts from friends in Philadelphia. His evangelical zeal took him to Long Island, where he awakened considerable religious interest; to Burlington, N. J., where he preached in the marketplace and in the court house and formed a class; to Philadelphia, where he organized another class of a hundred or more; and to Baltimore. He wrote John Wesley urging that he send preachers to America, and during a visit to England in 1772–73 he made strong appeals in behalf of American Methodism. Upon his return in 1773 he was accompanied by Thomas Rankin and George Shadford, sent by Wesley to labor in the colonies.

Wesley, Asbury, and John Adams all bore testimony to the effectiveness of Webb's preaching. Referring to him in his journal under date of Feb. 2, 1773, Wesley remarked that he admired the wisdom of God in raising up various preachers according to the various needs of men. "The Captain," he says, "is all life and fire: Therefore, although he is not deep or regular, yet many who would not hear a better preacher flock together to hear him" (*The Works of the Rev. John Wesley,* 3rd ed., vol. III, 1829, p. 487). John Adams, less concerned about ecclesiastical regularity, unreservedly commended Webb's preaching after listening to him in Philadelphia, Oct. 23, 1774: "In the evening I went to the Methodist meeting, and heard Mr. Webb, the old soldier, who first came to America in the character of quartermaster under General Braddock. He is one of the most fluent, eloquent men I ever heard; he reaches the imagination and touches the passions very well, and expresses himself with great propriety" (C. F. Adams, *The Works of John Adams,* vol. II, 1850, p. 401). Sometime during the Revolution, apparently, Webb returned to England, for he is known to have been there in 1783. He made his home in Bristol and still continued to engage in evangelistic work. Dying suddenly in that city, he was buried in Portland Street Chapel. He was twice married and had two sons, Gilbert and Charles, both of whom came to America after their father's death and settled in Canterbury, Orange County, N. Y.

[W. C. Ford, *British Officers Serving in America, 1754-1774* (1894); J. B. Wakeley, *Lost Chapters Recovered from the Early Hist. of Am. Methodism* (1858); W. B. Sprague, *Annals of Am. Pulpit,* vol. VII (1859); John Atkinson, *The Beginnings of the Wesleyan Movement in America* (1896); H. E. Luccock and Paul Hutchinson, *The Story of Methodism* (copr. 1926); P. N. Garber, *The Romance of Am. Methodism* (1931); *Gentleman's Magazine* (London), Dec. 1796, p. 1117.]   H. E. S.

WEBB, THOMAS SMITH (Oct. 30, 1771– July 6, 1819), Masonic ritualist, patron of music, was born in Boston, Mass., the son of Samuel and Margaret (Smith) Webb, who had emigrated to America from England shortly before Thomas' birth. In his youth he was apprenticed to a printer in Boston, and later he removed to Keene, N. H., where he worked for a number of years at his trade and first became interested in Freemasonry. The first three degrees of ancient craft Masonry were conferred on him in Keene by the Rising Sun Lodge. In 1793 he moved to Albany, N. Y., where he established a paperstaining factory. In 1797, not yet twenty-six years of age, he published a work which was to establish him as a leading Masonic ritualist, *The Freemason's Monitor, or Illustrations of Masonry.* The book had wide circulation, and its first publication was followed by many successive editions, revised and enlarged long after the author's death. He was known as the founder of the American system of chapter and encampment Masonry. He was the presiding officer of a convention of committees which met in Boston in 1797 to form a general grand chapter of Royal Arch Masons. In January 1799, as chairman of a committee, he presented for this group a constitution which was adopted at a meeting in Providence, R. I. This meeting resulted in the formation of the grand encampment of the United States. The original draft of this constitution, with alterations and additions interlined in Webb's handwriting, was placed on file in the archives of the St. John's Commandery, in Providence.

Late in the same year Webb made his home in Providence, and it was there (and later in Boston) that he became active in musical circles and one of the leading patrons of music. In 1809 he joined a group of music lovers brought together by Oliver Shaw [*q.v.*], the blind organist of the First Congregational Church, to form the Psallonian Society, organized "for the purpose of improving themselves in the knowledge and practice of sacred music and inculcating a more correct taste in the choice and performance of it" (Howard, *post,* p. 141). This society lasted until 1832, and in twenty-three years gave thirty-one concerts.

A few years before his death Webb removed to Boston, where he was a member of a group that founded in 1815 one of the oldest and one of the most important musical organizations in America, the Handel and Haydn Society of Boston. In March 1815, Webb, J. C. Gottlieb Graupner [q.v.] and Asa Peabody signed an invitation for a meeting to consider "the expediency of forming a society for cultivating and improving a correct taste in the performance of sacred music, and also to introduce into more general practice the works of Handel, Haydn and other eminent composers" (Howard, *post*, p. 138). Sixteen answered the invitation and in April the society was formed. Webb was elected its first president, and he served more than two years. The first concert of the Society was held in the Stone Chapel in Boston, on Christmas night, 1815.

Webb was married to Mrs. Martha Hopkins, of Boston, in the autumn of 1797. They had five children of whom only two survived the parents. After the death of his first wife, he was married, in 1809, to her sister, who, with their four children, survived him. He was buried with the Masonic rites in Providence.

[C. C. Perkins, *Hist. of the Handel and Haydn Soc.*, vol. I (1883–93); J. T. Howard, *Our Am. Music* (1931); H. W. Rugg, *Hist. of Freemasonry in R. I.* (1895); *Biog. Encyc. of Representative Men of R. I.* (1881); *R. I. Am. and Gen. Advertiser* (Providence), July 20, 1819.]   J. T. H.

WEBB, WILLIAM HENRY (June 19, 1816–Oct. 30, 1899), shipbuilder, was born in New York City, a descendant of Richard Webb, a lowland Scot who settled at Cambridge, Mass., by 1632 and later went to Connecticut. His father, Isaac Webb (1794–1840), was a shipwright who, like Jacob Bell [q.v.] and Stephen Smith, moved from Stamford, Conn., to try his fortune in New York. There the scant mile of yards along the East River from Grand Street to Thirteenth Street contributed more than any other place, except perhaps the Clyde, to the development of shipbuilding between 1807 and 1865. Isaac perfected his art under the able Scot, Henry Eckford [q.v.], and soon developed a prosperous yard of his own. His chief importance lay in his instructing two youths who became the greatest American shipbuilders of their time. One was Donald McKay [q.v.]; the other was his own son William. Isaac wanted William to enter a profession, so he educated him with tutors and sent him to the Columbia College Grammar School. The boy, however, stubbornly insisted on following his father's career. At fifteen he entered upon six years of intensive study of naval architecture and shipbuilding, taking only a week's vacation in that time. He combined in a remarkable way the qualities of naval architect and shipwright. Like J. W. Griffiths [q.v.], he showed bold and successful ingenuity in the designing of vessels. Combined

with this theoretical ability was the practical sense which enabled him to manage a thousand workers and make a fortune in turning out more than a hundred and fifty vessels whose construction was as sound as their design was brilliant. His unusual versatility adapted itself to both sail and steam, wood and iron, merchantmen and warships.

When Webb started building at twenty, New York's transatlantic sailing packets were the finest ships afloat. His first product was the Black Ball packet *Oxford* in 1836, built on a sub-contract from his father. He had built several other vessels, including the packets *New York, Pennsylvania, Ville de Lyons,* and *Duchesse d'Orleans,* before his father's death in 1840, when he became a partner of his father's assistant, Allen. In 1843 Webb started twenty-five years of building in his own name. His yard, extending from Fifth to Seventh Streets on East River, gradually overshadowed the nearby rival establishments of Brown & Bell, Smith & Dimon, W. H. Brown, and the Westervelts. The bald-headed little genius, with his flat nose, close-cropped whiskers, and bulldog expression, always built on contract, which eliminated much of the risk. He continued to build such packets as the *Yorkshire,* the *Guy Mannering,* which was the first three-decker, the *Ocean Monarch, Isaac Wright, Ivanhoe, Yorktown,* and *Isaac Bell.* In 1843 he built the fast pre-clipper *Cohota* for the China trade, followed by the *Panama* and *Montauk.* He ranked high among the builders of regular clippers. His *Celestial,* in 1850, was the first built expressly for the California trade, while his *Sword Fish,* in 1851, made the fourth fastest run to San Francisco. He also built the *Challenge, Comet, Gazelle,* and *Invincible* (1851); *Australia* and *Flying Dutchman* (1852); *Flyaway, Snapdragon,* and *Young America* (1853); *Intrepid,* and *Uncowah* (1856), and *Black Hawk* (1857). While McKay in his specialty of clippers, somewhat overshadowed Webb, eight of the latter's clippers made the San Francisco run in 110 days or less, against seven of McKay's.

Clippers, however, were only one of Webb's varied accomplishments. On a single day, Jan. 21, 1851, he launched a clipper, a Havre packet and a Pacific Mail steamship. He had already built the hulls for eight steamships, the machinery being furnished by nearby "iron works." His only transatlantic liner, apparently, was the *United States* in 1848, but that same year he built for the Pacific Mail Steamship Company the *California* and *Panama,* followed by the *Golden Gate, San Francisco,* and *Yorktown,* three others being built by his brother Eckford on sub-contract. William also built the *Cherokee, Augusta,* and *Knoxville* for lines to Savannah or New Orleans, as well as a powerful Sandy Hook towboat which bore his name.

During the decline of the merchant marine in the later fifties, Webb turned his attention to warships. In 1857 he built the steam revenue cutter *Harriet Lane*. Conceiving the idea of a powerful steam frigate, he was rebuffed at Washington but visited Russia and persisted until he received a $1,125,000 order for the *General Admiral,* launched in 1858. Adapting his yard to iron, he built for the new Italian navy in 1863 the *Re d'Italia* and *Re di Portogallo*. The former, probably the first ironclad warship to cross the Atlantic, was rammed and sunk by the Austrians at Lissa in 1866. Webb was decorated with the Italian order of Saints Maurice and Lazarus. His masterpiece was the strongest and fastest ironclad of the day, the great ram *Dunderberg,* which was laid down for the Union navy, but, not being launched until July 22, 1865, was sold to the French, who renamed her the *Rochambeau*.

Webb retired from shipbuilding in 1869 after building the Sound steamers *Bristol* and *Providence* and the packet *Charles H. Marshall,* but continued for another four years in less successful efforts to operate steamship lines. He had been an original director of the Pacific Mail and a heavy shareholder in the Panama railroad. Now he started a line to rival the Pacific Mail, as well as lines from San Francisco to Australia and New York to Europe. He had been a pioneer in the guano trade and owned considerable New York real estate. At his death he was a director of several New York traction companies and other corporations. About 1870 he published *Plans of Wooden Vessels,* two volumes of plates showing designs of a hundred and fifty ships he had built. Keenly interested in local welfare, Webb was for fourteen years president of the New York City Council for Civic Reform and led the opposition to the Tammany plans of the Aqueduct Commission. Three times he declined a chance to run for mayor. He established and endowed Webb's Academy and Home for Shipbuilders, opened on May 5, 1894. He died in New York. He had married Henrietta A. Hidden in 1843 and was survived by one son, William E. Webb.

[See J. H. Morrison, *Hist. of N. Y. Shipyards* (1909); *Hist. of Am. Steam Navigation* (1903); G. W. Sheldon, "The Old Shipbuilders of N. Y.," *Harper's Mag.,* July 1882; A. H. Clark, *The Clipper Ship Era* (1910); O. T. Howe and F. C. Matthews, *Am. Clipper Ships* (2 vols., 1926–27); C. C. Cutler, *Greyhounds of the Sea* (1931); R. G. Albion, in *New England Quart.,* Oct. 1932, pp. 690–91; James Parton, ed., *Sketches of Men of Progress* (1870–71), pp. 103–12; Henry Hall, ed., *America's Successful Men of Affairs* (1895), I, 703–09; J. H. Mowbray, ed., *Representative Men of N. Y.* (1898), vol. II, pp. 172–74; *Leslie's Hist. of the Greater N. Y.* (1898), vol. III; *Directory of Directors in the City of N. Y.,* 1899; Henry Hall, "Report on the Ship-Building Industry of the U. S.," *House Miscellaneous Docs., 42, 47* Cong., 2 Sess., pt. VIII; *Who's Who in America,* 1899–1900; *N. Y. Herald,* May 6, 1894, and Nov. 1, 1899 (obituary).]
R. G. A.

WEBB, WILLIAM ROBERT (Nov. 11, 1842–Dec. 19, 1926), educator, United States senator, was born near Mount Tirzah, in Person County, N. C., the fifth son of Alexander Smith and Cornelia Adeline (Stanford) Webb, and a grandson of Richard Stanford, congressman from North Carolina (1797–1816). As a child he was given the nickname of "Sawney," which stuck to him through life. His education began in a school conducted by his sixteen-year-old sister, and was continued in the Bingham School at Oaks, N. C. He matriculated at the University of North Carolina in 1860, but he left college in April of the following year to enlist as private in Company H, 15th North Carolina Volunteers. At the battle of Malvern Hill, Va., he was shot three times, receiving a wound in one of his arms that troubled him throughout life. Immediately after the battle he was elected first lieutenant of his company. While recovering from his wounds he reëntered the University of North Carolina but returned to the army early in 1864 as adjutant of Company K, 2nd North Carolina Cavalry. During the Virginia campaign he fought in almost every battle until, three days before Appomattox, he was captured. He was imprisoned first at the Battery, then at Hart's Island, N. Y. On one occasion he escaped, in uniform, and spent a day unmolested sightseeing in New York, but voluntarily returned to prison that night.

After his release he went back to Oaks, N. C. For four years (1866–70) he taught at Horner School, Oxford, N. C., and during that period he completed by correspondence and examination—under the liberal conditions allowed to Confederate soldiers—his work for the degrees of A.B. (1867) and A.M. (1868) at the University of North Carolina. Disgusted with "Carpetbag" and Reconstruction government, he left North Carolina in 1870 for the quieter state of Tennessee, and founded Webb School at Culleoka. Within two weeks the trustees, aghast when he allowed pupils to study out-of-doors, demanded stricter discipline, but Webb refused to "imprison innocent children" and continued his policy of freedom. His, he claimed, was the first "strictly preparatory school" west of the

Alleghanies; all others, he said in a speech delivered at Peabody College, Jan. 29, 1923, regardless of faculty or curriculum, were denominated colleges. He seldom advertised, and printed only a small descriptive circular about the school. He taught only Latin, Greek, mathematics, and English, and used no English grammar. On Apr. 23, 1873, he married Emma Clary of Unionville, Tenn. That year his brother, John M. Webb, whom he later described as "the greatest scholar I have ever seen," joined the faculty. In 1886, when local merchants refused not to sell whiskey to his boys, he moved the school to Bellbuckle, Tenn. The two brothers had $12,000, of which $2,200 went into buildings and $8,000 into books.

Webb was an ardent prohibitionist and a member (1913–26) of the national board of trustees of the Anti-Saloon League of America. In 1896 he campaigned as a Gold Democrat, and served as delegate to the Democratic convention that nominated Palmer and Buckner for president and vice-president respectively. In January 1913 Webb was unanimously elected by the state Senate to fill the unexpired term of the late Senator Robert Love Taylor [q.v.], Newell Sanders, Republican, having previously been appointed by Gov. Ben W. Hooper. As senator he served from Jan. 24 to Mar. 3, 1913, introducing a bill to prohibit desecration of the flag, and making one notable speech in favor of the Webb-Kenyon Bill (named for Representative E. Y. Webb of North Carolina), which prohibited the shipment of liquor into dry states.

He served three times as a lay member of the General Conference of the Methodist Episcopal Church, South. Known as "Old Sawney," the schoolmaster of Tennessee, he was recognized throughout the state as its "first citizen" (*Nashville Banner*, Dec. 20, 1926). He was short and stocky, with gray beard and hair; he wore a black coat that usually had the third button-hole attached to the second button, and a black string tie that was invariably under his left ear. His maxims, like his school, were famous; on his deathbed he sent a characteristic message: "Give the boys my love, and tell them to lead a larger life ... and dont' forget—never do anything that you have to hide." He died at Bellbuckle, Tenn., survived by his wife, four sons, and four daughters.

[Transcripts of letters, speeches, newspaper articles, and documents in possession of W. R. Webb, Jr., principal of Webb School at Bellbuckle, Tenn.; *Biog. Dir. Am. Cong.* (1928); *Alumni Hist. of the Univ. of N. C.* (1924); Randolph Elliott, "Old Sawney's," in *Atlantic Mo.*, Aug. 1920; *Who's Who in America*, 1926–27; *Nashville Banner* and *Nashville Tennessean*, Dec. 20,

1926; E. W. Parks, "Sawney Webb: Tennessee's Schoolmaster," *N. C. Hist. Rev.*, July 1935.]
E. W. P.

WEBBER, CHARLES WILKINS (May 29, 1819–April 1856), author, journalist, explorer, naturalist, and soldier, was born in Russellville, Ky., the first son and second child of Dr. Augustine Webber (1790–1873), who practised medicine for over half a century in southern Kentucky, and Agnes Maria (Tannehill) Webber, said to be the daughter of John Tannehill, a Revolutionary officer in the Continental Army. Educated at home in an informal way, in 1838 Webber went to Texas, then struggling for independence; there he associated himself with John Coffee Hays [q.v.], and other leading members of the Texas Rangers. Later he studied medicine in Kentucky for a short time, and in 1843 entered the Princeton Theological Seminary to prepare for the Presbyterian ministry. In 1844, however, he went to New York to take up journalism. There he renewed acquaintance with John James Audubon [q.v.], whom he had met during a Rocky Mountain tour. The two men became close friends, and Audubon's influence is to be plainly seen in much of Webber's literary work. Webber began his career with articles on Texas adventure for Winchester's *New World*; when it failed, he wrote for the *Literary World*, the *Democratic Review*, the *Sunday Dispatch*, and *Graham's Magazine*, all in New York City. For two years he is said to have been an editor and joint proprietor of the *American Review* (later the *American Whig Review*). In 1849, the year of his marriage in Boston, he organized an expedition to the Colorado and Gila Rivers, which failed when the horses were stolen by Comanche Indians at Corpus Christi, Tex. About six years later he is reported to have obtained from the New York legislature a charter to form a camel company, a project the necessity of which was apparent to those who knew of the difficulties to be met in crossing Western deserts. In 1855 he went to Central America, still eager for excitement. In the winter of the same year he joined the filibustering party commanded by the military adventurer, William Walker [q.v.], and, according to all accounts, was killed at Nicaragua in the battle of Rivas on Apr. 11, 1856.

Webber's principal works are *Old Hicks the Guide, or Adventures ... in Search of a Gold Mine* (1848); *The Gold Mines of the Gila* (1849); *The Hunter-Naturalist* (1851), the first volume of a projected series of seven, of which only two were published; *The Texan Virago ... and Other Tales* (1852); *The Wild*

Girl of Nebraska (1852); *Tales of the Southern Border* (1852); *The Romance of Forest and Prairie Life* (1853); *Spiritual Vampirism* (1853); *Wild Scenes and Song Birds* (1854), volume II of *The Hunter-Naturalist*, illustrated with twenty colored lithographs drawn by Mrs. Webber; *"Sam," or the History of Mystery* (1855), an account of the Jesuits; and *History and Revolutionary Incidents of the Early Settlers of the United States* (1859). A fourteen-page pamphlet, *A Letter to the Country and Whig Party with Regard to the Conduct of the "American Whig Review"* (1847), reveals Webber as no mean master of invective. In it he charges George Hooker Colton (1818–1847) with "falsehood, imbecility, and shameful cowardice," and then dares him to resent his statements.

Webber excelled in descriptions of wild border life; he wrote an easy, rapid, flowing style; his enthusiasm for natural history was real and deep, and his skill in communicating that enthusiasm was his chief strength. His writing reflects a man of strong animal spirits, but one who was able to appreciate the beauty and the poetry, as well as the power and energy, of nature.

[Sources include Webber's own works; E. A. and G. L. Duyckinck, *Cyc. of Am. Lit.* (2 vols., 1855); *New Orleans Medical and Surgical Jour.*, May 1874, for information from Webber's father; private information.]

H. S. R—n.

WEBER, ALBERT (July 8, 1828–June 25, 1879), piano-maker, was born in Bavaria. He was well educated, and became an accomplished musician, particularly as an organist. When he was sixteen years of age he came to America, landing in New York City. He subsequently decided to become a piano manufacturer, and served an apprenticeship with Holden and later with Van Winkle. To earn money for his board he gave music lessons in the evenings, and played the organ in churches on Sundays. Seven years later, when he was twenty-three years of age, he entered business for himself as a piano manufacturer. His first shop was located in the upper stories of a small building at 103 West Broadway, and his complete working force consisted of himself, Edward Stroud, and one case maker. By October 1 the trio completed its first instrument, and by Jan. 1, 1852, five more were ready for sale. In 1857, following a fire which destroyed his shop and equipment, he moved to larger quarters at 155 West Broadway. In 1864 the firm moved again, to the corner of Broome and Crosby Streets, and in 1867 it occupied its own building at 17th Street and 7th Avenue. In 1869 he became a pioneer in the trade by open-

ing warerooms on Fifth Avenue, at 16th Street. From that time his pianos became fashionable, and were known for their high quality.

Weber bore most of the burden of running his business himself. He was in charge of all branches, manufacturing and selling, both wholesale and retail. He was of a social disposition, and spent his evenings at the opera, theatre, and concerts. It was generally believed that he overtaxed his strength, and that overwork was the cause of his death at the age of fifty in New York City. After he died, the business of the Weber Piano Company was carried on by Weber's sons. In 1892 it became the Weber-Wheelock Company, and in 1903, through a merger, it was made a division of the Aeolian, Weber Piano & Pianola Company.

Many anecdotes are told of Weber's brilliance. An accomplished pianist, he would often play to prospective customers, and it is said that "seldom would an intending buyer leave his warerooms without having secured a piano" (Dolge, *post*, p. 298). Unlike Chickering and the Steinways, Weber did not invent or create anything new in piano construction, but he was such a thorough craftsman himself, and such a judge of piano tone, that he knew how to employ the most approved methods of piano-making in use during his career. With V. Wilhelm L. Knabe, the Steinways, and Jonas Chickering [qq.v.], he was one of those who realized the value to piano manufacturers of concerts by pianists, and he often engaged famous soloists to give concerts in leading cities, thus helping to create "a popularity for the piano in proportion to the growth of wealth in the United States" (Dolge, *post*, p. 175). He is credited with having originated the term "baby grand," to designate the short grand piano.

[The most complete account of Weber's career is found in Alfred Dolge, *Pianos and their Makers*, vol. I (1911). Data on Weber and his firm are contained in a pamphlet issued by the Weber-Wheelock Company, *Greater and Lesser New York* (1897). See also Grove's *Dict. of Music and Musicians, Am. Supp.* (1930), and the *N. Y. Tribune*, June 26, 1879.]

J. T. H.

WEBER, GUSTAV CARL ERICH (May 26, 1828–Mar. 21, 1912), physician, was born in Bonn, Germany. His father, Moritz Ignaz Weber, was an anatomist from the University of Landshut who had been called to the chair of anatomy at Bonn; his mother, a von Podowilz, is reported to have had literary attainments. The boy grew up in a home which was frequented by such intellectual leaders of the day as Jean Paul Richter. While studying at the University of Bonn, young Weber came under the suspicion of having been implicated in the revolution of 1848. He transferred his studies to Munich and spent some time with an uncle, an ophthalmologist. He shortly emigrated to America and went to St. Louis, Mo., where in 1849 he continued his medical studies, interesting himself in particular in original anatomical research. Upon his graduation in 1851 from Beaumont Medical College, St. Louis, he returned to the medical centers of Europe, where his father's reputation opened to him the doors of great clinics and classical teachers. He came to the Vienna of Joseph Skoda, Joseph Hyrtl, Ferdinand Hebra, Karl Rokitansky, and Karl Braun, and continued his studies under the tutelage of the latter. From there he went to Amsterdam and thence to Paris to the clinic of Philibert-Joseph Roux.

Apparently the events following the revolution induced Weber to return to America in 1853. He assumed the position of surgeon at a hospital in New York, which had been left vacant by the death of his brother, Edward Weber, but in 1856, his health having also failed, he left for the West. From 1856 to 1863 he held the chair of surgery in the medical department of Western Reserve College, commonly known as Cleveland Medical College. Under his régime the surgical clinic became very popular, and his reputation grew apace. He was appointed surgeon general of Ohio in 1862 and after his resignation served as surgeon of the 129th Ohio Volunteer Infantry until Nov. 1, 1863. In 1864 he organized the staff of the new St. Vincent Charity Hospital, Cleveland, and in the same year the Charity Hospital Medical College, where he was dean and professor of surgery (1864–70). From 1870 to 1881 he was professor of clinical surgery and dean of the medical department of Wooster University (later the College of Wooster), and in 1881 became the dean of a new school, the medical department of Western Reserve University, which was the result of the fusion of most of the faculty of Wooster with that of the medical department of Western Reserve College. In 1894 he returned to the medical department of Wooster University and remained there until 1896. Toward the end of the century he gradually retired from active academic and professional duties. He was appointed American consul at Nürnberg in 1897 by President McKinley and held the position until 1902. On his return to Cleveland in 1903 he suffered an attack of apoplexy which forced him to spend his later years in his country cottage at Willoughby, Ohio, where he died in 1912.

A general practitioner and surgeon whose field was the entire human body, Weber had acquired a training remarkable for its extent and intensity. In the practice of surgery, which was his passion, he developed both great skill and a deservedly high repute. In his lectures he apparently emphasized general principles rather than factual elements, in the manner of the classical European teachers. His style, as far as one can judge from the few articles he published, was elegant and flowing. He was one of the founders and editors of the *Cleveland Medical Gazette,* which first appeared in 1859. His publications include *Address Introductory to the Opening . . . of the Cleveland Medical College Session, 1856–57* (1856) and "A New Method of Arresting Hemorrhage" (*Medical Record,* N. Y., Apr. 24, 1875). He married Ruth Elizabeth Cheney of New York City in 1854, and had by her two children, a son and a daughter.

[*Who's Who in America,* 1900–01; W. H. Humiston, in *Am. Jour. Obstetrics,* Mar. 1913, with portrait; *Jour. Am. Medic. Asso.,* Apr. 6, 1912; J. H. Lowman, in *Cleveland Medic. Jour.,* Apr. 1912; *Ibid.,* May 1912; Martin Stamm, *Ibid.,* June 1912; H. A. Kelly and W. L. Burrage, *Am. Medic. Biogs.* (1920); obituary in *Cleveland Plain Dealer,* Mar. 22, 1912; information on Weber's work in Cleveland from Dr. F. C. Waite, Western Reserve Univ.]   H. S. R—e.

WEBER, HENRY ADAM (July 12, 1845– June 14, 1912), chemist, pure-food reformer, was born in Clinton Township, Franklin County, Ohio, the son of Frederick and Caroline (Tascher) Weber, both natives of the German Palatinate. During his studies at Otterbein College, Westerville, Ohio, in 1861–63 he became interested in chemistry and went to Germany to perfect himself in this science. After studying at Kaiserslautern (1863–66) and at the University of Munich under Justus von Liebig (1866–68), he returned to the United States. Between 1869 and 1874, as chemist of the geological survey of Ohio, he made comprehensive analyses of the minerals and soils of the state. He was professor of chemistry at the University of Illinois from 1874 to 1882. There he planned a new chemical laboratory for the university which was one of the most complete of its kind, and served as chemist of both the state board of agriculture and the state board of health. In the latter capacity he made an exhaustive sanitary examination of the river waters of the state. During this period he first became interested in pure-food legislation. In 1879 he received the degree of Ph.D. from Ohio State University. About this time, in collaboration with Melville A. Scovell [*q.v.*], he began experiments upon the manufacture of sugar from sorghum, patenting a superheat process of clarification that attracted considerable attention. The work led to the establishment of the Champaign Sugar and Glucose Company for the purpose of manufacturing sucrose from sorghum juice and glucose from the starch of sorghum grain (*Transactions of the Department of Agriculture of Illinois,* vols. XVIII–XIX, 1881–82). Weber devoted his time from 1882 to 1884 to the development of this enterprise, but the natural deficiencies of sorghum as a sugar-producing crop, the reduction of the tariff on sugar, and other economic factors caused the general abandonment of the project. From 1884 until the end of his life Weber was professor of agricultural chemistry at the Ohio State University, Columbus, Ohio. He also served as state chemist of Ohio, and chief chemist of the Ohio state dairy and food commission (1884–97), and became recognized as one of the pioneers in the national pure-food movement initiated by Dr. Harvey W. Wiley [*q.v.*]. In 1903 he was appointed, with William Frear, Edward Hopkins Jenkins [*qq.v.*], M. A. Scovell, and H. W. Wiley, a member of the first American committee on food standards, created by Congress. He rendered distinguished service in the movement which led to the passage of the Federal Food and Drugs Act in 1906.

Weber was a member of numerous chemical and scientific societies, and a fellow of the American Association for the Advancement of Science. He was the author of a *Select Course in Qualitative Analysis* (1875) and of numerous bulletins, reports, and articles upon chemical subjects. He died at his home in Columbus, Ohio. He married on Dec. 29, 1870, Rosa Ober of Columbus, Ohio, whom he met in Germany during his student days and who survived him with two daughters.

[*Who's Who in America,* 1910–11; *Semi-Centennial Alumni Record . . . Univ. of Ill.* (1918); obituary in *Ohio State Jour.,* June 15, 1912; information from Weber's nephew, Dr. F. C. Weber.]   C. A. B.

WEBSTER, ALICE JANE CHANDLER (July 24, 1876–June 11, 1916), author, known as Jean Webster, was born in Fredonia, N. Y., the first child of Annie (Moffett) and Charles Luther Webster. Her father, a publisher, was from New England, his wife from the South. Their lineage was British, with a German strain; their American kin included Daniel Boone, Eli Whitney, and Samuel L. Clemens [*qq.v.*]. Jean Webster attended the public schools of Fredonia, finished preparation for college at Lady Jane Grey School, Binghamton, N. Y. (1896), and received the degree of A.B. from Vassar College (1901). She was an able student but a poor speller. Asked by a horrified teacher, "On what authority do you spell thus?"

she retorted, "Webster." Not to enjoy unearned importance, she tried to conceal the fact that she was Mark Twain's grandniece. While a student she was correspondent for a Poughkeepsie newspaper and contributed several stories to *Vassar Miscellany* (vols. XXVIII, XXIX, 1899–1900). Her major studies were English and economics. Visits to institutions for the destitute and the delinquent impressed her imagination permanently and gave direction to her writing.

After college she became an independent writer for magazines. Her first book, *When Patty Went to College* (1903), originally published serially, she had shaped while a student from her experiences at Vassar. The amusing and enlightening Patty series, including *Just Patty* (1911), lead in their field. In her travels, besides a trip around the world (1906–07), she made long sojourns in Italy, where she found the setting for *Jerry Junior* (1907), and for her favorite, *The Wheat Princess* (1905). Her next books, *The Four Pools Mystery* (1908), published anonymously, and *Much Ado About Peter* (1909), were popular. The attraction of an old house (55 West Tenth Street) brought her near to Greenwich Village. Not in revolt, and coveting a whole view of society, she had the recognition of social workers. The inferential thesis of her novels, *Daddy-Long-Legs* (1912) and its sequel *Dear Enemy* (London, 1914), is that under-privileged children, if given the chance, are capable of succeeding in life and of enjoying its beauty. A moving revelation of child-life in an orphanage, timeless in its humor, justice, and lovable make-believe, *Daddy-Long-Legs* made its creator famous as the spokesman for "the small, blue-ginghamed lonely ones of earth." It was memorable for its long run when dramatized, was translated widely, and was finally universalized on the screen by Mary Pickford, who bought the film rights (1918). In writing it Jean Webster is said to have had in mind her close friend and classmate, Adelaide Crapsey [*q.v.*], who may also have been the original of Patty (Mary E. Osborn, *Adelaide Crapsey,* 1933, p. 28). In 1915 she wrote a preface for Adelaide Crapsey's *Verse,* which was also published in *Vassar Miscellany,* March 1915. She was a sane and hopeful realist on her way, it was predicted, to leadership, and was already felt indirectly as a humanitarian. Her literary discipline was diligent and practical; she experienced directly, wrote profusely, and cut ruthlessly.

On Sept. 7, 1915, she was married to Glenn Ford McKinney. She died, June 11, 1916, a day after the birth of her daughter. A room at the Girls' Service League, New York City, and a bed at the county branch of the New York Orthopedic Hospital, near White Plains, were endowed in her memory.

[See *Who's Who in America,* 1916–17; *Woman's Who's Who of America,* 1914–15; Alice Sanford in *Vassar Miscellany,* June 1915; Elizabeth Cutting, in *Vassar Quart.,* Nov. 1916; D. Z. D., in *Century Mag.,* Nov. 1916; Ruth C. Mitchell, *Ibid.* (poem); Francis Hackett, in *New Republic,* Mar. 13, 1915; Channing Pollock, in *Green Book Mag.,* Dec. 1914; *N. Y. Times,* Nov. 9, Dec. 13, 1914, and June 12, 1916 (obituary). Information has been supplied by Annie Moffett Webster, Ethelyn McKinney, Prof. H. E. Mills, and other friends of Jean Webster.]   M. M.

WEBSTER, ARTHUR GORDON (Nov. 28, 1863–May 15, 1923), physicist, was born in Brookline, Mass., the only son of William Edward and Mary Shannon (Davis) Webster. He was a descendant of John Webster who settled in Ipswich, Mass., in 1635. He prepared for college at the high school in Newton, Mass. In 1881 he entered Harvard University, from which he graduated with honors in 1885. In college he showed remarkable linguistic talent, but then and later regarded his study of languages as a diversion, demanding little mental exertion, from his favorite studies of mathematics and physics, which upon occasion he would admit make rather severe demands upon the intellect. After serving one year as instructor in mathematics at Harvard, he went abroad in 1886 for advanced study at the University of Berlin. Four years later he received the degree of Ph.D. from this university, his dissertation, *Versuche über eine Methode zur Bestimmung des Verhältnisses der elektromagnetischen zur elektrostatischen Einheit der Elektricität* (1890), presenting the results of an experimental investigation directed by the great experimentalist, Prof. August Kundt. Returning to America in 1890, Webster accepted a position as docent in physics at Clark University, Worcester, Mass., under Prof. Albert Abraham Michelson [*q.v.*], whom he succeeded as head of the department in 1892. His position at Clark University, at that time a strictly graduate school, afforded him the opportunity to develop a systematic and comprehensive course of lectures on mathematical physics which was unsurpassed in scope and thoroughness by any corresponding course offered elsewhere. He soon acquired a mastery of the art of lucid exposition in his lectures which, with an intuitive appreciation of the difficulties of his students, qualified him as an exceptionally good teacher. In effect, he occupied two distinct positions at Clark University—professor of mathematical physics and professor of experimental physics. As a leader in both subjects he was the inspiration of small groups of devoted students who came to him from year to year from America and abroad.

In the period from 1890 to 1917 his own scientific activities in mathematical physics, were, apart from his lectures, chiefly concerned with expository writing on this subject, the major products of which were two excellent treatises: *The Theory of Electricity and Magnetism* (1897), and *The Dynamics of Particles and of Rigid, Elastic and Fluid Bodies* (1904). Many of his scientific colleagues, while fully recognizing the high merits of his expository writings, were prone to regret that his intense devotion to this phase of his activities should effectively preclude the application of his remarkable mental powers toward the solution of the various outstanding problems of theoretical physics. His activities in experimental physics during this period had mainly to do with the development of various gyroscopic instruments, and with sound investigations, one important product of which was a remarkable instrument for the absolute measurement of the intensity of sound. Throughout this period he was a frequent contributor to scientific magazines of articles dealing with topics that interested him in mechanics, sound, and electricity.

In 1917 Webster was appointed a member of the United States Naval Consulting Board. As his contribution to war work he established a school of ballistics at Clark University, and with his assistants undertook the solution of various important ballistic problems. It was a matter of deep regret to him that he was not assigned to war service abroad, as he felt that his extensive knowledge of foreign languages specially qualified him for such service. After the war he continued his work on ballistics and sound, and on a comprehensive treatise entitled *The Partial Differential Equations of Mathematical Physics.* The book was nearly completed at the time of his death in 1923, and was published in 1927 under the editorship of Dr. S. J. Plimpton. Many honors came to Webster in the course of his career. In 1895 (*Science,* Feb. 15, 1895) he received the Elihu Thomson prize for his paper on "An Experimental Determination of the Periods of Electrical Oscillations." In 1903 he was elected the third president of the American Physical Society, which he had been instrumental in founding in 1899. He was the recipient of various honorary degrees, and was a member of many learned societies both in America and abroad.

Webster was distinguished by a singularly imposing personality. His frank expressions of his views, often in satirical or humorous vein, were invariably interesting and pertinent. He wrote numerous articles presenting popular expositions of scientific subjects or setting forth in trenchant style his opinions on matters of general public interest. In speaking or writing, his use of the English language was impeccable. In the latter years of his life he was subject more and more to moods of depression, so intense at times as to be actually pathological. In such a mood, probably, he ended his own life on the morning of May 15, 1923. He was survived by his wife, Elizabeth Munroe (Townsend) Webster of Syracuse, N. Y., whom he married Oct. 8, 1889, and by a son and two daughters.

[See *Who's Who in America,* 1922–23; *Clark Univ. Lib. Pubs.,* Mar. 1924; E. H. Hall, in *Proc. Am. Acad. of Arts and Sciences,* vol. LXII (1928), and in *Sci.,* July 20, 1923; *Class of 1885, Harvard Coll.* (1825); G. S. Fletcher, in *Physical Rev.,* June 1923; *Harvard Grads. Mag.,* Sept. 1923; obituary in *Boston Transcript,* May 15, 1923. Webster's papers are in the Clark Univ. Lib., Worcester, Mass.]   A. P. W—s.

WEBSTER, DANIEL (Jan. 18, 1782–Oct. 24, 1852), statesman, was born in Salisbury, N. H. He was descended from Thomas Webster, who was brought to Ipswich, Mass., *c.* 1635 as an infant and later removed to the southern New Hampshire frontier. His father, Ebenezer Webster, an unlettered but intrepid colonial, took part in Gen. Jeffrey Amherst's invasion of Canada in 1759 and was allotted some 225 acres of land in the upper Merrimack Valley, where he became a founder and local official in the exposed frontier town of Salisbury. Ebenezer was an early and active revolutionary leader and served with distinction as captain in the militia. He also served capably in the state legislature and participated in the ratification of the federal Constitution as a member of the New Hampshire convention. Later in life Captain Webster, who kept this title even after he had been made a colonel in the state militia, was made a lay judge of the county court of common pleas. Webster's mother, Abigail Eastman, of Welsh stock, was a second wife who, like her predecessor, bore Ebenezer five children; of these Daniel was next to the youngest.

A lad of delicate health, Daniel was spared the heavier tasks which his brothers and sisters shared on the rugged New Hampshire farm. He found opportunity instead for the cultivation of his precocious mind and strongly emotional nature. In the random schools of the neighborhood the boy found that in reading he "generally could perform better" than the teachers in charge but his crude achievements in the irksome task of writing caused his masters to wonder whether after all his fingers were not "destined for the plough-tail" (*Writings and Speeches,* National ed., XVII, 7). His father, however, not satisfied with his clumsy efforts at certain rural tasks, was determined to save him from a life of arduous toil and shortly announced his intention to give Daniel "the advantage of knowledge" that had been denied to himself. Accordingly, in 1796, Captain Webster enrolled his fourteen-year-old son in the Phillips Exeter Academy. The boy was shy and sensitive about his unfashionable attire and clumsy manners, but he made rapid headway with his studies. Only in declamation was he unable to match his fellows: at the weekly public exhibitions, despite careful preparation, he "could never command sufficient resolution" to leave his seat and present his offerings (*Ibid.,* XVII, 10).

In December 1796 Daniel returned with his father to Salisbury without having completed his course. A brief period of school-teaching ended with an arrangement for him to study under the Rev. Samuel Wood of Boscawen, who had offered to prepare him for Dartmouth College. By August 1797 he had achieved fair success in Latin and Greek and in the meantime had satisfied his omnivorous appetite for reading in the village library. With this uncertain equipment he presented himself for admission to Dartmouth at the opening of the regular fall term. Arriving on horseback with baggage and bedding, Webster began a college course that cost him in four years considerably less than two hundred dollars. The swarthy youngster, who was often taken for an Indian, soon acquired the nickname of "Black Dan." He pursued his studies with energy, yet found time for his two youthful enthusiasms, reading and playing. He graduated not far from the top of his class. He dabbled with enthusiasm in poetry and earned part of his board temporarily by contributing to the village newspaper. In contrast with his failure in Exeter days, he was outstanding in one of the college debating societies and developed a reputation as a speaker that led to his being invited by the citizens of Hanover to deliver, at the age of eighteen, the local Fourth of July oration. In this he revealed a florid style and a tendency toward bombast along with the "vigor and glow" that characterized his early oratorical efforts.

Following graduation Webster began the study of law in the office of Thomas W. Thompson of Salisbury. He had no great enthusiasm for the legal profession and seems to have had doubts as to whether he had the "brilliancy, and at the same time penetration and judgment enough, for a great law character" (*Ibid.,* XVII, 92, 95). But he read "Robertson, Vattel, and three volumes of Blackstone," meantime learning the routine of the law office, and began to "feel more at ease" (*Ibid.,* XVII, 100). After some months, however, he gave up these studies to accept a position as teacher in an academy in the small village of Fryeburg, the salary ($350) making it possible for him to aid his father in keeping his elder brother Ezekiel, in college. Offered reappointment at "five or six hundred dollars a year, a house to live in, a piece of land to cultivate" and the probability of a clerkship of the court of common pleas, he was tempted to settle down to spend his days "in a kind of comfortable privacy" (*Ibid.,* XVII, 110). But father and friends advised him to pursue the study of law and with a careful definition of his ideals he returned, in September 1802, to Thompson's office. The embryo lawyer pondered the limitations of his calling. Conceding the power of the law to help "invigorate and unfold the powers of the mind," he tried to offset the hard didactic style of the legal treatise with excursions into history and the classics and made random attempts of his own at expression in verse and rhyme.

He long expected that only a miracle would make it possible to transfer to "the capital of New England." Now, upon the urgent invitation of Ezekiel, who was teaching school there, he went to Boston and had the rare good fortune to be accepted immediately as a clerk by Christopher Gore [*q.v.*], who had just returned from a diplomatic mission abroad. Influenced by the stimulating scholarship of such an employer and his circle of distinguished associates, Webster's fertile mind developed apace. Upon Gore's advice but to his father's surprise and disappointment he declined the profitable clerkship of the court of common pleas which paternal influence had proudly arranged for him. Admitted to the Boston bar in March 1805, he was recalled to Boscawen by a sense of filial obligation. His intention had been to set up an office in Portsmouth, but his father's illness made it a duty "to drop from the firmament of Boston gayety and pleasure, to the level of a rustic village, of silence and of obscurity" (*Ibid.,* XVII, 200).

In September 1807, some little time after his father's death, he transferred his labors to Portsmouth where he remained for nine "very happy years." To this new home he brought his bride, Grace Fletcher, daughter of a New Hampshire clergyman, whom he married on May 29, 1808

(Fuess, *post,* I, 101n.). In his practice of law, the young attorney promptly won distinction. Following the superior court in most of the counties of the state, he found it possible to achieve a practice worth nearly $2,000 a year. He enjoyed the professional rivalry of Jeremiah Mason [*q.v.*], whom he once rated as the greatest lawyer in the country. From their frequent clashes in court he learned the importance of the most careful preparation of his arguments and of the most effective diction. Webster consciously dropped his earlier florid style and sought to achieve the short incisive sentences with which Mason was so masterful. Meantime, the two rivals at the bar became the best of political friends.

During the Portsmouth period Webster was being drawn more and more into politics. Temperamentally a conservative, he had inherited from his father strong Federalist convictions, which were reinforced by other associations, especially by his contacts with the "bigwigs" of Boston. Satisfied that wealth and intelligence should play a dominant rôle in public life, he early reached the conclusion that the Federalist party combined "more than two thirds of the talent, the character, and the property of the nation" (*Writings and Speeches,* XVII, 115). He grew to maturity amid the fear of French revolutionary ideals of democracy and came to picture them as threatening civil war "when American blood shall be made to flow in rivers, by American swords!" (*Ibid.,* XVII, 79). It was this fear that produced his early devotion to "the bonds of our Federal Union." The Jeffersonian victory of 1800 seemed an "earthquake of popular commotion" under a Constitution which he was free to admit left "a wide field for the exertions of democratic intrigue" (*Ibid.,* XVII, 111–12). He therefore labored in his humble way—in Fourth of July orations and in occasional political pamphleteering—to contribute to the revival of Federalism, to arouse those who were disposed to "sit still and sigh at the depravity of the times," while the "contagion of democracy" threatened to "pervade every place and corrupt every generous and manly sentiment" (*Ibid.,* XVII, 158, 175).

He soon became a champion of the shipping interests of New England and of their protection against the retaliatory measures of Great Britain and France in their war for European supremacy. When Jefferson instituted a policy of economic coercion that struck a ruinous blow at the commercial prosperity of New England, Webster contributed a pamphlet, *Considerations on the Embargo Laws* (1808), which effectively voiced the Federalist opposition. By the time that the controversy over neutral rights had led to the outbreak of hostilities with Great Britain, Webster had achieved a recognized place among the Federalists of Portsmouth. In a Fourth of July oration in 1812 he vigorously condemned the administration for having led the nation into an unjustifiable war (*Ibid.*, XV, 583–98). But, unlike the Federalist die-hards who had been for years at least toying with the idea of separating New England from the Union, Webster renounced the idea of resistance or insurrection and took his stand for full freedom of criticism and "the peaceable remedy of election" (*Ibid.*, XV, 594). A month later in his famous "Rockingham Memorial," presented at a Federalist mass meeting in Rockingham County, N. H., he reiterated his anti-war views even more forcefully (*Ibid.*, XV, 599–610).

The enthusiastic reception of this memorial, both by the convention which proceeded to nominate him for Congress and by Federalists generally, launched Webster, with his election in November, upon a national political career. Made a member of the committee on foreign relations, he presented, on June 10, 1813, a series of resolutions calling upon the government to explain the events immediately preceding the outbreak of hostilities and had the satisfaction of making a powerful impression and of seeing his resolutions adopted eleven days later (*Annals of Congress*, 13 Cong., 1 Sess., cols. 149–51, 302–11). Aiming to embarrass the administration as much as possible, he loosed his eloquence against bounties to encourage enlistments and in favor of the repeal of the Embargo Act; in ringing words he proclaimed the constitutional right of the opposition to voice its protests and to utilize full freedom of inquiry. He himself refused to vote taxes in support of the war and denounced the government's draft bill, not only as an "infamous expedient" but as clearly "unconstitutional and illegal" (*Writings and Speeches*, XIV, 55–69). Webster even suggested the expedient of state nullification of a federal law under "the solemn duty of the State Governments to protect their own authority over their own militia, and to interpose between their citizens and arbitrary power" (*Ibid.*, XIV, 68). Since the conscription bill failed, there was no contemporary test of this doctrine. Webster was careful, however, to repudiate any thought of disunion. During the sessions of the Hartford Convention he was busy at Washington and had in the meantime advised the governor of New Hampshire against appointing delegates to a

body that might be unduly influenced by the separatist forces (Curtis, *post*, I, 136).

Reëlected in 1814, Webster became influential in the attempts to make peacetime adjustments to the economic lessons taught in the recent war. Legislation to reëstablish the United States Bank was modified by Calhoun to meet Webster's objections to the lack of adequate safeguards for financial stability and was passed by Congress only to receive a presidential veto. He later voted against the bank bill which did not contain such safeguards but which was signed by the President in April 1816. In the discussions of fiscal policy, including the matter of specie payment for government revenues, Webster revealed an amazing knowledge of and devotion to sound principles of public finance. In the discussion of the tariff he proclaimed himself not an enemy of manufactures, but as opposed to rearing them in hotbeds. His loyalty to the mercantile interests of his section, however, caused him to oppose the high protective duties of the tariff of 1816, especially those originally proposed for cotton, iron, and hemp, which menaced the imports of New England and threatened to add to the cost of ship-building.

In August 1816, midway in his second term in Congress, Webster transferred his residence to Boston, where he sidetracked politics for a law practice that was soon bringing in $15,000 a year. During his last winter at Washington, he had given much of his time to legal work. He was retained before the Supreme Court in three important prize cases and was soon to add to his laurels in the Dartmouth College case. As a result of the complicated operation of party politics in New Hampshire, Webster's alma mater had become a pawn upon the political chess board. A Republican legislature in 1816 enacted a law changing the character of the institution and its governing body, placing it under the thumb of the general court. A suit in which the college trustees sought to defend their rights against the new political forces was carried to the New Hampshire superior court, from which it was appealed to the United States Supreme Court. Webster, after accepting a small fee from the other side, had revealed his sympathies with the college trustees (Fuess, I, 220–21). He had closed the argument for them before the superior court and now for a fee of $1,000, out of which he was to engage an associate, he was placed in charge of the case in the Supreme Court. The notes and briefs of his colleagues furnished most of his materials, but these he carefully overhauled and brilliantly presented (*Writings and Speeches*, X, 194–233). He closed with an appeal in which with consummate pathos he presented the case of the small college which he loved as the case of every college in the land. When on Feb. 2, 1819, the Court in its decision completely upheld the college and its counsel (4 *Wheaton*, 518), Webster became in the opinion of many the foremost lawyer of the time. Three weeks after the Dartmouth College victory he appeared for the Bank of the United States in *McCulloch* vs. *Maryland* (*Writings and Speeches*, XV, 261–67) and received a fee of $2,000 for his services. In three other important cases involving grave constitutional issues that shortly came before the Supreme Court, Webster was to play an important part (*Gibbons* vs. *Ogden, Osborn* vs. *Bank of the United States, Ogden* vs. *Saunders*; Charles Warren, *The Supreme Court in United States History*, 1922, I, 476–88; II, 59, 90, 147–48).

In the midst of a busy law practice Webster could not keep out of the public eye. In December 1819 he opposed the admission of Missouri as a slave state and drafted the memorial of a Boston protest meeting. He made the feature address in favor of free trade at a meeting of New England importers in Faneuil Hall in the autumn of 1820. He was chosen as a presidential elector in the campaign of that year. He played an influential but conservative rôle in the Massachusetts constitutional convention of 1820–21 and helped to hold the democratic forces in check (Fuess, I, 273–80). On Dec. 22, 1820, he delivered at Plymouth a powerful oration in celebration of the two hundredth anniversary of the landing of the Pilgrims. Achieving another great oratorical triumph at the laying of the cornerstone of the Bunker Hill monument on June 17, 1825, he made popular the occasional oratory that was to thrive for decades. He served for a brief period in the Massachusetts House of Representatives in the spring of 1822. In the fall he was drafted to represent Boston in Congress and was promptly made chairman of the judiciary committee when he took his seat in December 1823. A brilliant oration on Greek Independence (Jan. 19, 1824) signalized his return to the national political arena, but he was soon busied with less romantic topics. The tariff question—to him at this time "a tedious, disagreeable subject"—was now to the fore and the financiers, merchants, and ship-builders of Boston expected him to challenge Henry Clay's arguments for protection. Accordingly, on Apr. 1, 2, 1824, Webster attacked the proposed bill and its principles and announced his inability to accord it his vote (*Writings and Speeches*, V, 94–149).

In the preliminaries of the presidential contest of 1824 Webster's private choice was Calhoun; he shared the distrust of New England Federalists for John Quincy Adams. Busied with his own reëlection he avoided any formal commitment, but in the contest in the House he gave his vote to Adams and influenced others in the same direction. Webster had hopes of the mission to Great Britain but Adams showed no inclination to gratify him. Yet, as party lines reshaped themselves under the new administration, Webster became an increasingly loyal supporter. He supported the President's doctrine on internal improvements, pleading for a truly national interest to justify federal aid; he led the futile fight for a revision of the federal judicial system; he made an eloquent appeal for representation in the congress at Panama. Reëlected to Congress almost unanimously, he championed the President in the bitter dispute with Georgia over the Cherokee lands. All the while Webster kept up a busy practice before the Supreme Court and other courts of the country.

In June 1827 he was elected to the United States Senate. The death of Mrs. Webster (Jan. 21, 1828) temporarily destroyed his zest for work and his interest in public affairs. But soon he was in the thick of the fight that accompanied the passage of the tariff act of 1828. The Webster of this period was less satisfied than hitherto with economic theories and more concerned with the realities of life. He had established intimate associations with the Lawrences and Lowells and the mill-owners of his state generally, and had taken a small block of stock when the Merrimack Manufacturing Company was incorporated in 1822 (Fuess, I, 341). The tariff of 1824 had been followed by a vast increase of investment in wool manufacturing and Webster was now (May 9, 1828) frank in stating that nothing was left to New England "but to consider that the government had fixed and determined its own policy; and that policy was *protection*" (*Writings and Speeches*, V, 230). Since the new bill, with all its "abominations," did grant the protection to woolens which the act of 1824 had by implication pledged, he accorded his active support to the measure and helped accomplish its passage. Henceforth, Webster was an aggressive champion of protection.

The months that followed brought bitter disappointments: Adams was defeated for reëlection by Jackson, and Webster's favorite brother, Ezekiel, whom he helped launch a career in New Hampshire politics, died. His energy seemed to ebb and he wondered at times whether he was not growing old. But life took on new meaning following his marriage on Dec. 12, 1829, to Caroline Le Roy, a young and popular representative of New York sophistication, and new and stirring events were ahead. Another month and he was in the thick of the battle against the Calhoun doctrine of nullification. With leonine grace and energy and in the rich tones of his oratory, he met the challenge of Calhoun's mouthpiece, Robert Y. Hayne [*q.v.*]; rising to the height of his forensic abilities in this famous debate of January 1830 (*Ibid.,* V, 248–69; VI, 3–75), he won what his admirers hailed as a brilliant victory over the cause of state rights and nullification. Praising the Union and what it had accomplished and still promised to achieve for the nation, he declared that in origin it preceded the states and insisted that the Constitution was framed by the people, not as a compact but to create a government sovereign within the range of the powers assigned to it, with the Supreme Court as the only proper arbiter of the extent of these powers. Nullification could result only in violence and civil war, he proclaimed; he was for "Liberty *and* Union, now and forever, one and inseparable !" No wonder that, with the plaudits of his audience still ringing in his ears, with the nation-wide fame achieved in this great outburst of eloquence, rosy dreams of the White House continued henceforth to play in Webster's mind.

The tariff problem which had aroused Calhoun and the South still remained. Southern efforts to force a reduction of duties led to the measure of July 1832 in which Webster was concerned primarily with maintaining protection upon woolen cloths. But even the lower duties of this act did not satisfy South Carolina which forced the issue of nullification in the ordinance passed by a convention of that state in November. Webster made clear his intention to support the President in his defiance of the nullifiers and crossed lances with Calhoun in an important debate the following February (*Ibid.,* VI, 181–238). Meantime, against his advice, Clay joined with the anti-tariff leaders in pressing legislation agreeable to the latter; finally in March 1833 the "Compromise Tariff" was enacted. Bitterly disappointed, Webster voted with the opposition. The only satisfaction he could find in the outcome was in the thought that "the events of the winter have tended to strengthen the union of the States, and to uphold the government" (*Ibid.,* XVII, 537). To this end and for the honor of being known as the "Defender of the Constitution," Webster had sacrificed for the time even his lucrative Supreme Court practice.

Politics had developed even new intricacies. The opposition forces of varying views but with common interests in vested rights had combined in the Whig party. Naturally, Webster joined the new coalition. Any temptation toward continued cooperation with Jackson was removed by the latter's war on the Bank of the United States, which Webster supported both on principle and as a profitable client. There was the further fact that Webster, who was as careless in handling his own money as he was profound in his mastery of the principles of public finance, was heavily indebted to the bank for loans extended to him. He had actively advocated the recharter bill and had vigorously condemned Jackson's veto, especially the constitutional grounds that it set forth. Reëlected to the Senate in 1833, Webster regarded Jackson's removal of deposits from the bank as presenting an issue that might lead to the presidential office. He distinguished himself, however, by the constructive quality, in contrast to the personal vituperation of his associates, that marked his reply to Jackson's protest against the resolution of censure which the Senate had adopted. As the election of 1836 drew near the Whigs of the Massachusetts legislature nominated him as their candidate. With other Whig nominees in the field, however, he had few enthusiastic supporters outside of New England and Pennsylvania, despite the friendly visit he had paid to the West in the summer of 1833, and he received only the electoral vote of Massachusetts.

Following this defeat, he gave serious consideration to retirement from active politics, either to recoup his fortune, which had suffered with his law practice, or to improve his presidential chances for 1840. Just at this time, one of the worst for profitable investment, he was acquiring with borrowed money extensive land holdings in Ohio, Indiana, Illinois, Michigan, and Wisconsin. His interests were largely speculative, except that he planned a huge country estate near La Salle, Ill., which was for a time operated by his son, Fletcher. His own personal interests continued in his seaside home at Marshfield where, with the continual lure of "the sea, the sea," he lived in almost feudal ease among devoted retainers and entertained with a lavish hand. Unable to realize upon his ill-timed investments, he was increasingly harassed by his creditors and financial embarrassment haunted him to the end. Only the willingness of his wealthy friends to be levied upon in emergency saved him from actual disgrace.

His Massachusetts followers, however, would not consent to his retirement. After another Western tour—which was a veritable series of ovations—during which the panic of 1837 broke, he returned to the special session of Congress and took a brilliant part in the Whig fight against Van Buren's sub-treasury plan, again breaking lances with Calhoun. The question of slavery and the right of petition brought similar clashes and Webster was impressed with the storm clouds so ominous for the future. In the summer of 1839, following reëlection, he and his family visited England where he hoped to find buyers for his western lands and to acquaint himself still further with the details of the menacing boundary dispute between Maine and Canada. He returned to find that the Whigs had nominated General Harrison for the presidency and he participated in the campaign with all the more zest because he expected it to bring to a close his senatorial career, with retirement to the bar in the event of Van Buren's reëlection and the prospect of a cabinet appointment if Harrison should succeed.

The victorious Harrison made Webster secretary of state, after having paid a tribute to his knowledge of public finance by offering the alternative of appointment to the Treasury Department. On Harrison's death a month later, John Tyler, his successor, retained the cabinet in office. Webster had anticipated the enactment of a series of Whig measures such as those for which Henry Clay made himself the spokesman in the ensuing months (*Writings and Speeches,* XVIII, 100). Soon, however, President Tyler, a Southern Whig of the state-rights school, became involved in a dispute with the Clay following when he successively vetoed the two measures by which the Whigs sought to reëstablish a United States bank. In the split that followed all the members of Tyler's cabinet except Webster resigned. The latter, who was extremely unhappy about these conditions and suspicious of the leadership of Clay, tried to play a conciliatory rôle. He regretted "the violence & injustice" which had "characterized the conduct of the Whig leaders"; he was determined, moreover, not to "throw the great foreign concerns of the country into disorder or danger, by any abrupt party proceeding" (*Ibid.,* XVI, 386; XVIII, 110). He was referring to the complicated negotiations over the Maine boundary which, with consummate skill, tact, and dignity and with the cordial cooperation of the President, he carried on and brought to a successful adjustment in the Webster-Ashburton Treaty of 1842. In this agreement was included an arrangement for joint cruising squadrons to operate off the coast of Africa in the suppression of the slave trade, which was expected to terminate a long-standing controversy over the right of search. His emi-

nently satisfactory discharge of his duties in the State Department included successful negotiations with Portugal, important discussions with Mexico, and the preliminaries to the opening of diplomatic relations with China which led to the commercial treaty negotiated by Caleb Cushing in 1844. Meantime, he rejoiced in the enactment of a Whig tariff (1842) which wiped out what seemed to him the iniquities of the measure of 1833 and returned to the principle of protection.

Webster, who had for some time been under strong Whig pressure to resign, at length with some reluctance (May 8, 1843) left the only office which had ever allowed reasonable satisfaction for his ambition and his talents. He had aspired to a diplomatic mission to England and had tried to juggle events to that end but fate dictated his retirement to private life (Fuess, II, 125–28). Burdened with debt, he returned to meet the heavy demands for his legal services that promised to replenish his exchequer. A seat in the Senate was awaiting his convenience and the returned statesman, convinced that the sober business men and conservatives of Massachusetts had never deserted him, took satisfaction in a reconciliation with his old party associates in which he felt no necessity for offering apologies for his recent independent course. He cooperated cheerfully in support of Clay's candidacy for the presidency in the campaign of 1844 and in the following winter allowed himself to be returned to the Senate.

Devoted to the vested interests of his state— indeed, a virtual pensioner dependent upon their bounty—Webster deemed it his "especial business" as a member of Congress "to look to the preservation of the great industrial interests of the country" from Democratic free-trade propensities (*Writings and Speeches,* XVIII, 231; see also *Ibid.,* IV, 47, XVI, 431–32). All the activities of the protectionists, however, did not prevent the reductions under the Walker Tariff of 1846. Meanwhile, as he had feared, the annexation of Texas had been followed by war with Mexico. Webster had opposed the acquisition of Texas and the resulting extension of slavery and now joined in the Whig policy of condemning the war. He held, however, that supplies should be voted as long as the war was not connected with territorial aggrandizement and that the struggle should be brought to a speedy and successful termination. To this end he gave his second son, Maj. Edward Webster, who died of exposure in service near Mexico city.

Though Webster, impervious to the lure of

empire, introduced resolutions repudiating all thought of the dismemberment of Mexico (*Congressional Globe*, 29 Cong., 2 Sess., p. 422), the war ended in a treaty which gave the United States a vast domain carved out of this neighbor republic. Should the new territory be dedicated to freedom or be thrown open to the westward march of negro slavery, was the inevitable question that arose. Webster had been from the start a strong critic of the peculiar institution of the South as "a great moral and political evil," but had conceded that within the Southern states it was a matter of domestic policy, "a subject within the exclusive control of the States themselves" (*Writings and Speeches*, XVIII, 353; XII, 210). He voted consistently for the Wilmot Proviso, but preferred the "no-territory" basis that would prevent a controversy from arising over slavery. With the triumph of the expansionists he saw nothing in the future but "contention, strife, and agitation" (Fuess, II, 171). Dreams of the presidency still haunted him. In the spring of 1847 he had made a Southern tour in which he was dined and wined until his body and spirits drooped. Even after his recuperation at Marshfield and his return to court for many a strenuous session, he took it for granted, at the age of sixty-six, that people were beginning to say, "He is not the man he was" (*Writings and Speeches,* XVIII, 267). The death of his daughter Julia, who had married Samuel Appleton Appleton, and of his son Edward depressed him even more. Of his children only his son Fletcher survived him. When out of sheer expediency his party turned to a military hero, Gen. Zachary Taylor, he acquiesced in his own repudiation with what grace he could.

In the first winter of the new administration Webster beheld with alarm a serious crisis in the sectional controversy. The abolitionist extremists were advocating a dissolution of the Union and the anti-slavery forces in Congress were bent upon pressing their strength to accomplish the exclusion of slavery from the territories, while Southern leaders, increasingly conscious of the seriousness of the minority status of the South, were developing a sense of Southern nationality and preparing, if need be, to launch a movement for a separate Southern confederacy. Like other conservative statesmen, Webster came to feel that the Union was seriously at stake and was determined to do all in his power to avert the danger. It must not be overlooked that Webster, as the champion of protection, was alarmed to find the continued discussion of the slavery question an obstacle to Whig efforts at tariff revision, causing Southern

Whigs whose rights, property, and feeling had been constantly assailed to argue that they would never "give a single vote for the Tariff until this Slavery business is settled," and that Northern men would have to "take care of their own interests" (*Ibid.,* XVI, 541; XVIII, 391). To Webster the more important public question of the tariff was being sacrificed to the slavery controversy (*Ibid.,* XVIII, 370). He had, therefore, become increasingly annoyed at the militant intransigentism of the anti-slavery forces, especially those who would not believe that "I am an anti slavery man unless I repeat the declaration once a week" (*Ibid.,* XVI, 498). While he believed in the power of Congress legally to exclude slavery from the territories, he had stated as early as 1848 that there was "no longer any important practical question" as to slavery extension (*Ibid.,* XVIII, 283). He therefore rose on Mar. 7, 1850, "to beat down the Northern and the Southern follies, now raging in equal extremes" (*Ibid.,* XVI, 534).

In a well-considered speech he declared himself for Clay's compromise measures and poured oil on troubled waters. He spoke "not as a Massachusetts man, nor as a Northern man, but as an American" (*Ibid.,* X, 57). Slavery was an evil but not so great an evil as disunion. There could be no peaceful secession, he informed the South. On the other hand, he condemned the unnecessary severity of the anti-slavery forces and admitted that Northerners had not lived up to their obligations to return fugitive slaves. Congressional prohibition in the territories was useless since a law of nature had settled "beyond all terms of human enactment, that slavery cannot exist in California or New Mexico" (*Ibid.,* X, 82). To the conservative element of the country Webster's performance seemed "Godlike"; but the anti-slavery men, including those of his own party, could see him only as a fallen star. Nor did he recover their good graces. Webster became, after Taylor's death, secretary of state in Fillmore's cabinet (July 22, 1850). He supported the legislation that substantially covered the ground of Clay's compromise measures and followed with concern the storm that still raged. Even as late as the summer of 1851 the question of secession was being discussed in certain Southern states and Webster felt called upon to write a timely letter denying the right of secession and denouncing it as revolution (*Ibid.,* XVI, 622–23). In the State Department Webster conscientiously and creditably performed the duties of his office, writing the famous "Hülsemann letter" in reproof of the attitude of the Austrian chargé toward American policy in the Hungarian revolution and dealing with more than ordinary diplomatic difficulties with Spain, Mexico, Peru, and Great Britain. His presidential aspirations were again revived in 1852, without serious embarrassment to his relations with Fillmore who was also a candidate. But both men were shelved by the Whigs and, sick in mind and body, Webster repudiated General Scott's nomination and prophesied the downfall of his party.

As the summer progressed, serious illness and suffering stared from his dark countenance. Always fond of the good things of life, he had found since his second marriage increasing opportunity for self-indulgence. Lavish hospitalities, with good food and good drink given and received, made him grow portly though rarely sluggish. Only his active life and early rising kept down the inroads of disease. His annual hay fever became increasingly more distressing. Financial worries pressed down upon him and made him wish at times that he "had been born a miser" (*Ibid.*, XVI, 636). By autumn the inroads of a fatal malady, cirrhosis of the liver, had marked his days and he died on Oct. 24, 1852, murmuring, "I still live."

Two score years in the political arena revealed in Daniel Webster two seemingly contrasting but naturally allied forces. Eloquent champion of the American Union, he was also the special advocate of the new industrial interests then so rapidly forging to the fore in the national economy. In their behalf the leonine Daniel, idol of the "best" people of his state and of his section, sacrificed the popular following that would gladly have rallied to the standard of a great democratic chieftain. The penetrating logic and burning eloquence of his oratory, the masterful and magnetic quality of his personality, contributed little toward bringing to him the support of the toiling masses. Life therefore became for Webster a series of great frustrations. A great constitutional lawyer, he found his equals, or betters, among his eminent contemporaries. His victories in statecraft and diplomacy were never on a par with his soaring ambitions. The presidential office seemed to have been reserved for men of less distinction. Even his personal fortunes failed to bring him the sense of security that often assuages frustration. Withal, however, perhaps no Northerner left so strong an impress upon the political life of this great "middle period," or made a more substantial contribution to the preservation of the Union in the supreme test of the sixties.

[The first attempt at general publication of Webster's works resulted in *The Works of Daniel Webster* (6 vols., 1851), ed. by Edward Everett; and in *The Private Correspondence of Daniel Webster* (2 vols., 1857), ed.

by Fletcher Webster, which included his brief autobiography as written in 1829. Collections of his manuscripts were later made, the most complete being that of the N. H. Hist. Soc. at Concord. The Sanborn collection in New York City is less extensive; the Greenough collection in Washington (Lib. of Cong.) is made up largely of letters received from Webster's correspondents; and the Mass. Hist. Soc. collection is very limited. Important additions, largely of unpublished items selected from the New Hampshire collection, were made available in *The Letters of Daniel Webster* (1902), ed. by C. H. Van Tyne; an effort at publishing his complete works was made in the National ed. under the title, *The Writings and Speeches of Daniel Webster* (18 vols., 1903), ed. by J. W. McIntyre. The earliest biography, prepared with Webster's approval, is S. L. Knapp, *A Memoir of the Life of Daniel Webster* (1831). C. W. March, *Reminiscences of Congress* (1850), later published as *Daniel Webster and His Contemporaries* (1852), is a reminiscent account by a wealthy friend. Immediately following Webster's death, a reminiscent biography appeared in the account of his private secretary, Charles Lanman, *The Private Life of Daniel Webster* (1852), which the family made an attempt to suppress. Other gossipy narratives are Peter Harvey, *Reminiscences and Anecdotes of Daniel Webster* (1877); and the brief "Reminiscences of Daniel Webster" by William Plumer, included in the National ed., XVII, 546–67. Personal recollections give value to the work of his literary executor, G. T. Curtis, *Life of Daniel Webster* (2 vols., 1870). H. C. Lodge, *Daniel Webster* (1883), the first brief formal biography, is colored by the abolitionist tradition and influenced by the highly prejudicial chapter on Webster in James Parton, *Famous Americans of Recent Times* (1867). After a number of rather perfunctory lives came the more penetrating work of S. G. Fisher, *The True Daniel Webster* (1911). Recent biographies, including F. A. Ogg, *Daniel Webster* (1914) and S. H. Adams, *The Godlike Daniel* (1930), have been overshadowed by the excellent and more nearly definitive C. M. Fuess, *Daniel Webster* (2 vols., 1930). Among numerous special works and articles particularly worthy of mention are G. T. Curtis, *The Last Years of Daniel Webster* (1878); E. P. Wheeler, *Daniel Webster, The Expounder of the Constitution* (1905); Gamaliel Bradford, "Daniel Webster," in *As God Made Them* (1929); R. L. Carey, *Daniel Webster as an Economist* (1929); H. D. Foster, "Webster's Seventh of March Speech and the Secession Movement, 1850," in *Am. Hist. Rev.*, Jan. 1922; V. L. Parrington, "Daniel Webster, Realist and Constitutionalist," in *The Romantic Revolution in America* (1927); articles by C. A. Duniway in S. F. Bemis, *The Am. Secretaries of State and Their Diplomacy*, vols. V, VI (1928). There is an excellent bibliography in *The Cambridge Hist. of Am. Literature*, vol. II (1918), pp. 480–88. For an obituary, see *Boston Daily Advertiser*, Oct. 25, 1852.]

A. C. C.

WEBSTER, JEAN [See Webster, Alice Jane Chandler, 1876–1916].

WEBSTER, JOHN WHITE (May 20, 1793–Aug. 30, 1850), university professor, owed his painful notoriety to an appalling crime. He was born in Boston, Mass., the son of Redford and Hannah (White) Webster. His father's success as an apothecary ensured young Webster an academic education, foreign travel, and leisure to deliberate upon a profession. He was graduated from Harvard, M.A., 1811, and M.D., 1815. Completing his medical studies in London, he was entered at Guy's Hospital in 1815 as, successively, surgeon's pupil, physician's pupil, and surgeon's dresser. A visit to St. Michael in the

Azores (1817–18) resulted in his first book and in his marriage, May 16, 1818, to Harriet Fredrica Hickling, daughter of the American vice-consul at St. Michael. They had four daughters. From 1824 to 1849 Webster taught chemistry at Harvard, holding from 1827 onward the Erving professorship of chemistry and mineralogy. In Cambridge his scale of living and hospitality exhausted his inheritance and strained his income. His salary was $1,200 a year, while his lectures at the Massachusetts Medical College brought but a few hundreds more.

In 1842 Webster borrowed $400 from Dr. George Parkman, uncle of the historian, Francis Parkman [q.v.]. In 1847, with but little of this repaid, he gave Parkman his note for $2,432, representing the unpaid balance and a further loan. This was secured by a mortgage of Webster's personal property, including a cabinet of minerals. In 1848, still in distress, he borrowed $1,200 from Robert Gould Shaw, Sr., making over to him the minerals already pledged to Parkman. The latter, hearing of this, became furious; he considered Webster fraudulent, and took care to let him know it. Interviews between the two men became acrimonious. Early on Nov. 23, 1849, Webster called at Parkman's house, and arranged a meeting in his own laboratory at 1:30 P.M. Parkman, at about that hour, was seen approaching the Medical College, on Grove Street, Boston. He was not seen again. His disappearance was a mystery for a week, when Littlefield, janitor of the College, who had become suspicious of Webster's conduct, broke into a vault beneath the laboratory and found some human bones. Other human fragments were found in the furnace and in a tea-chest. As a result of this and of Webster's obviously false statements that he had paid Parkman, Webster was arrested. At the police station he attempted suicide by strychnine. His trial (Mar. 19–Apr. 1, 1850) before Chief Justice Lemuel Shaw [q.v.] is famous for the judge's charge and its definitions of circumstantial evidence. Proof that the remains were really Parkman's depended on the testimony of Dr. Nathan C. Keep, who identified Parkman's false teeth, found in Webster's furnace, as teeth made by himself. Webster's conviction was followed by public protests, founded on the usual ill-informed distrust of circumstantial evidence. Webster sent a plea to the governor, asserting his entire innocence, and in the most solemn and affecting language calling upon God as witness to his truthfulness. Later, however, he made a written confession, basing a new plea, for lesser punishment than death, upon his contention that the crime was not premeditated, but the governor and council could give no credence to any of his statements, and he was hanged, Aug. 30.

As a teacher, Webster was far from brilliant. He wrote *A Description of the Island of St. Michael* (1821), was associate editor of the *Boston Journal of Philosophy and the Arts* (1824–26), compiled *A Manual of Chemistry* (1826), and brought out editions of Andrew Fyfe's *Elements of Chemistry* (1827) and Justus Liebig's *Animal Chemistry or Organic Chemistry* (1841). Indulged as a child and pampered in youth, he developed a petulant and fussy disposition, but his kindly nature was such that for him to commit murder at the age of fifty-six astounded his acquaintances, and gives some weight to his assertion that the act was sudden and unpremeditated. That he had a curiously macabre streak, however, appears from Longfellow's anecdote of a dinner at Webster's home, when the host amazed his guests by lowering the lights, fitting a noose around his own neck, and lolling his head forward, tongue protruding, over a bowl of blazing chemicals, to give a ghastly imitation of a man being hanged (Annie A. Fields, *Memories of a Hostess*, 1922, p. 153).

[Sources include George Bemis, *Report of the Case of John W. Webster* (1850), perhaps the best report of any Am. criminal case; colls. of pamphlets on Webster in Lib. of Cong., Boston and N. Y. Pub. Libs., Boston Athenæum, Am. Antiquarian Soc., and Harvard Coll. Lib.; *Quinquennial Cat. of Harv. Univ.*; *A Vol. of Records . . . Containing Boston Marriages from 1752 to 1809* (1903); information from the superintendent of Guy's Hospital; letter of M. A. De Wolfe Howe, in *Sat. Rev. of Lit.*, Dec. 21, 1929; *Boston Transcript*, Aug. 30, 31, 1850. See also an excellent essay in H. B. Irving, *A Book of Remarkable Criminals* (1918); E. L. Pearson, *Murder at Smutty Nose* (1926), which contains (pp. 323–25) a selected bibliog. of the case; and George Dilnot, *The Trial of Professor . . . Webster* (1928). The date of Webster's marriage and the name of his wife are from Thomas M. Lothrop of Chicago, Ill.; the date of birth is from T. F. Harrington, *The Harvard Medic. School* (1905), vol. III, p. 1453.]

E. L. P.

WEBSTER, JOSEPH DANA (Aug. 25, 1811–Mar. 12, 1876), soldier and engineer, was born at Hampton, N. H., the son of Josiah Webster, a Congregational minister, and Elizabeth (Wright) Webster. He graduated at Dartmouth College in 1832 and studied law, but in 1835 entered the government service as a civil engineer. He was commissioned in the army, July 7, 1838, as a second lieutenant of topographical engineers and was promoted first lieutenant, July 14, 1849, and captain, Mar. 3, 1853. Resigning, Apr. 7, 1854, he settled in Chicago—where he had connections through his marriage in 1844 to a Miss Wright of that city—and acquired a considerable interest in a company manufacturing agricultural implements. In 1855 he was chosen as one of the three members of the Chicago sewerage commission, which was charged both with the construction of an extensive sewer system and with the raising of the level of a great part of the city.

He was appointed major and paymaster in the volunteer army, July 1, 1861, but never performed duty as a paymaster, for he was sent at once to Cairo, Ill., and employed on fortification and other engineering duties until his appointment, Feb. 1, 1862, as colonel, 1st Illinois Light Artillery. Meanwhile, Grant had selected him as his chief of staff; he served with him at Belmont, Forts Henry and Donelson, and Shiloh. His position was not precisely what the title now suggests. The chief of staff, according to Grant's instructions, was to act as his adviser, and also to look after anything not otherwise attended to. He was a general utility man. On the first day at Shiloh, for example, when the Union troops were being forced back on the river, Grant sent Webster to collect artillery for a last stand, if necessary, on the heights above the landing, and here he assembled one hundred guns. Grant repeatedly recommended his promotion. On Dec. 3, 1862, President Lincoln wrote to the secretary of war: "Let Col. James [sic] D. Webster, of Illinois, be appointed a Brigadier General of Volunteers"; but in some way this order was overlooked until Lincoln repeated it. The appointment was not finally made until April 1863, with rank, however, from Nov. 29, 1862. Shortly before, Webster had been put in charge by Grant of all the military railways in the area of his operations. Webster managed them before, during, and after the Vicksburg campaign. He was then designated as Sherman's chief of staff, remaining at the administrative headquarters in Nashville while his commanding general was in the field during the Atlanta campaign and the march to the sea. Thus he was with Thomas at the battle of Nashville. After Sherman reached Savannah the headquarters were transferred, and Webster joined his chief in the Carolinas. He was brevetted major general of volunteers, Mar. 13, 1865, and on Nov. 6 of that year resigned from the army. His entire military service had been passed in close association either with Grant or with Sherman, both of whom had profound confidence in him. Some years after the war, when Gen. William Sooy Smith [q.v.], in personal correspondence with Sherman, complained that statements published by the latter had done him injustice, Sherman proposed that the whole case be submitted to Webster as a competent and impartial judge.

After leaving the army Webster returned to Chicago and spent the rest of his life there. He was assessor of internal revenue from 1869 to 1872, assistant United States treasurer from 1872 to 1875, and collector of internal revenue from 1875 until his death. He was survived by his wife and three children.

[War of the Rebellion: Official Records (Army); F. B. Heitman, Hist. Reg. and Dict. U. S. Army (1903); Biog. Sketches of Ill. Officers (1862); W. T. Sherman, Memoirs (1875); Chicago Daily Tribune, Mar. 13, 1876; unpublished records in the War Dept.]
T. M. S.

WEBSTER, NOAH (Oct. 16, 1758–May 28, 1843), lexicographer, was sixth in descent from John Webster (d. Apr. 5, 1661), an emigrant from England to Newtowne (now Cambridge), Mass., c. 1630–33, who became one of the founders of the colony of Connecticut and, in 1656, its governor. John took up land in the township of Hartford, and it was in the village of West Hartford that the lexicographer was born, the fourth of the five children of Noah Webster (Mar. 25, 1722–Nov. 9, 1813) and his wife Mercy (baptized Oct. 8, 1727–died Oct. 5, 1794), daughter of Eliphalet Steele and great-great-grand-daughter of William Bradford [q.v.], second governor of the Plymouth colony. The elder Noah owned a farm of ninety acres in West Hartford. He served as justice of the peace, as deacon of the parish church (Congregational), and as captain on the "alarm list" of the local militia. He and his wife were married Jan. 12, 1749. Young Noah early showed a bent for books, and his father after some hesitation decided to send him to college. He got his preparatory training from the local minister, the Rev. Nathan Perkins, and from a Mr. Wales, schoolmaster of Hartford. In September 1774 he was admitted to Yale College, and four years later was duly graduated with the degree of B.A., though the elder Noah had to mortgage his farm to meet his son's modest college bills and the War of the American Revolution interfered markedly with academic studies at Yale as elsewhere.

Webster had settled upon a legal career, but his father was unable to help him further and for several years after his graduation from college he earned his living by teaching and clerical work, reading law with various jurists in his spare time. In 1781 he passed his examinations and was admitted to the bar at Hartford, but he did not begin active practice until 1789, and four years later gave up the law for good. The beginnings of his true career go back to 1782 when, while teaching at Goshen, N. Y., he prepared an elementary spelling book, published at Hartford the next year as the first part of *A Grammatical Institute of the English Language.*

The *Institute* was completed with a grammar (1784) and a reader (1785); all three books were written for the use of school children. In preparing the series Webster was moved by patriotic as well as professional and scholarly considerations. He found the schoolbooks then in use deficient on various counts, not least in their neglect of the American scene. The introduction of his speller includes, among other things, a literary Declaration of Independence by which Webster lived and wrought the rest of his days. Later editions of speller and reader gave expression to Webster's patriotic purposes in their very titles: *The American Spelling Book* and *An American Selection of Lessons in Reading and Speaking.* The speller did not differ radically from previous spellers, and at first did not include the orthographical reforms introduced into later editions and now regularly associated with Webster's name, but it was well arranged, gave convenient rules of thumb, and had the clarity and freshness of presentation characteristic of its author. Above all, it was an American product, nicely calculated to meet the particular needs of the American schools of the day, an outgrowth, indeed, of Webster's own experience as a schoolmaster. In length of vogue and volume of sales, however, it surpassed all expectation. The first edition of 5000 copies was exhausted in little more than a year, and in revised editions, under various titles, the book continued to be issued well into the twentieth century. In 1837 Webster estimated that some 15,000,000 copies of his spelling-books had been printed, and by 1890 the number had risen to more than 60,000,000. The wide and long use of Webster's spellers had much to do with the standardization of spelling and, to a less degree, of pronunciation in the United States along lines differing somewhat from those that prevailed in the mother country. Webster's reader did not have the vogue of the speller, although it went through a number of editions. To the edition of 1787 were added, as Webster explained to Franklin, "some American pieces under the discovery, history, wars, geography, economy, commerce, government, &c. of this country . . . in order to call the minds of our youth from ancient fables & modern foreign events, & fix them upon objects immediately interesting, in this country" (Ford, *post,* II, 454). The reader thus became a book patriotic enough to justify the insertion of the word *American* into its title. Webster's grammar, the second part of his *Institute,* was less successful, commercially, than the other parts. The historian, however, reads it with interest and respect as a forerunner (in

theory, at least) of the scientific English grammars of today, based not on rules taken from Latin grammar or pseudo-logical "principles," but on objective study of the actual phenomena of English speech.

Webster had hardly finished compiling his speller when the problem of the copyright presented itself. At that time the federal government had no authority in such a matter, and none of the newly established states had enacted a copyright law. With characteristic courage and energy Webster began, in 1782, an agitation which cost him more time and money than he had anticipated but led to legislative provision of an American copyright. Webster's initiative and leadership in this agitation not only gave him a place in the annals of the day but also brought him into contact with many of the leaders of the young republic and set going the national reputation which he was to achieve. In particular, the copyright agitation took him into politics, and made him an ardent federalist. Forced as he was to promote copyright legislation in thirteen capitals, he became one of the earliest advocates of a strong federal government, and in 1785 printed his views in a pamphlet called *Sketches of American Policy,* a pamphlet which won the interest of Washington and Madison, and, with an earlier series of articles in the *Connecticut Courant* (from Aug. 26, 1783), gave Webster his start as journalist and pamphleteer. Of his other political writings of the decade ought to be mentioned here, if only for its characteristic timeliness, the pamphlet of October 1787, urging the adoption, by the several states, of the newly submitted federal Constitution.

Webster's activities in favor of copyright legislation took him as far south as Charleston, S. C., and involved much travel and long stays in the chief cities of the country. He earned his living during this period in various ways: by ordinary teaching, by holding singing-schools, and by giving public lectures. While in Baltimore, in the summer and fall of 1785, he wrote five papers on the mother tongue, and read them in public with such success that he was "induced to revise and continue reading them in other towns" (Ford, I, 141). This course of popular lectures, with additions and revisions, was published in 1789 under the title, *Dissertations on the English Language.* The added "Essay on a Reformed Mode of Spelling," included in the volume, is of special interest. Webster's lectures in Philadelphia had led to an acquaintance with Benjamin Franklin, and a subsequent correspondence between the two on spelling reform (a subject in which Franklin had long been interested) brought Webster back to Philadelphia in December 1786 for a visit which turned into a stay of ten months. The essay, and Webster's various experiments with a simplified spelling, grew out of this intercourse with Franklin. The boldness and sweep of Webster's original scheme appear plainly enough in a letter, dated Mar. 31, 1786, which he wrote to George Washington. "I am encouraged," he says, "by the prospect of rendering my country some service, to proceed in my design of refining the language & improving our general system of education. Dr. Franklin has extended my views to a very simple plan of reducing the language to perfect regularity" (Ford, I, 110). Franklin's phonetic alphabet, however, simple though it was, proved too radical for adoption by Webster, who for practical reasons gave up counsels of perfection in favor of a "sufficiently regular" orthography, and with the years yielded ground more and more to the traditional spellers, so that in the end little was left of his reforms. But if Webster proved unable to effect any substantial spelling reforms, his spellers and dictionaries, ironically enough, played a great part in strengthening the grasp of orthographical orthodoxy. The American people, ruthlessly schoolmastered year in year out, became rooted and grounded in the faith, and the reforms brought forward by later generations of scholars, with all the backing of the now full-fledged science of linguistics, failed to shake the hold of that traditional spelling which Webster so reluctantly had made his own.

It was during his second stay in Philadelphia, as supervisor of an Episcopal school, that Webster met Rebecca Greenleaf (May 27, 1766–June 25, 1847), daughter of William Greenleaf, a Boston merchant, and his wife Mary (Brown). Webster and Miss Greenleaf were married in Boston on Oct. 26, 1789. They had two sons, one of whom died in infancy, and six daughters. Toward the end of 1787 Webster had settled in New York, as editor of a new venture called the *American Magazine*. The periodical had proved a commercial failure, and in December 1788 Webster had returned to Hartford, where he began his married life and practised law for several years. In 1793, however, he was induced to settle again in New York and take up once more the work of an editor. With the backing of certain prominent Federalists, he launched a daily newspaper, the *Minerva*, and a semi-weekly, the *Herald*, names which in 1797 changed to *Commercial Advertiser* and *Spectator* respectively. His journalistic career lasted ten years, though in 1798 he removed to New Haven and thereafter had less and less to do with the details of management of his newspapers, which, as he tells us, "were established for the purpose of vindicating and supporting the policy of President Washington" (Ford, I, 386) and which became burdensome to him as time elapsed and political conditions changed. In particular, Hamilton's betrayal (as he felt) of President John Adams disheartened Webster and had much to do with his return to his first love, linguistic scholarship. In 1803 he succeeded in disposing of his newspapers and gave up journalism for good. Thenceforth he devoted himself wholeheartedly to what was to prove his chief title to fame, his work as a lexicographer.

A survey of Webster's more important writings up to this turning-point in his life brings out in striking fashion the versatility and productivity of the man. His schoolbooks, such as the three volumes of the *Institute* with their revisions, *The Little Reader's Assistant*, and the series called *Elements of Useful Knowledge*, gave Webster the income which enabled him to retire from journalism and devote himself to study. A popular volume of informal essays was *The Prompter* (1791). The *Dissertations*, mentioned above, were likewise designed for popular reading, but proved a commercial failure. In the economic field, various treatises by Webster moved Lecky to pronounce him "one of the best of the early economists of America" (*A History of England in the Eighteenth Century*, 1882, III, 311). In the medical field Webster wrote, among other things, *A Brief History of Epidemic and Pestilential Diseases* (2 vols., 1799), the standard work on the subject in its day. Of the many political writings, the "Curtius" articles (1795) on the Jay Treaty, the "Aristides" letter to Hamilton (1800), and the *Ten Letters to Dr. Joseph Priestley* (1800) may be mentioned. Webster's edition of John Winthrop's *Journal* (1790) is of special interest as a pioneer work in learned historical publication, while his *Experiments Respecting Dew* (begun in 1790, though not printed until 1809) hold an honorable place among the pioneer American essays in physical science. It has also justly been noted that Webster's activities as statistician and climatologist foreshadowed the work of the census and weather bureaus of later times. These many-sided labors proved an admirable preparation for lexicography, in which the investigator must take all knowledge for his province.

The first fruit of Webster's lexicographical activities was his small work, *A Compendious Dictionary of the English Language* (1806). In its compilation Webster learned the technique of lexicography and tried out ideas of his own, recording, for example, some 5000 words not included in previous dictionaries. Webster however thought of his first dictionary as only preparatory to a larger work, a work upon which he labored steadily for nearly twenty years. Finished in 1825, it came out in two quarto volumes in 1828 under the title, *An American Dictionary of the English Language,* probably the most ambitious publication ever undertaken, up to that time, upon American soil. Financially it proved a disappointment (though not a failure), but its merits at once gave it first place among English dictionaries. It marks, indeed, a definite advance in the science of lexicography. Webster established once for all the practice, already begun in his first dictionary, of freely recording non-literary words, even though he did not push his principles to their logical conclusion and record all words whatsoever, as present practice inclines more and more to do. He justly based his definitions upon the usage of American as well as British writers and speakers, and did not hesitate to record "Americanisms" which he deemed worthy. In defining a word, he proceeded from what he considered its original or primary meaning, and so far as possible derived the other meanings from the primary. In so doing he made many mistakes, because of the deficiencies of current linguistic knowledge, and in some respects he was not abreast with the times, being out of touch, for example, with the comparative and historical linguistic school of his contemporaries Rask, Grimm, and Bopp, but his principles of definition were sound, and the definitions themselves in many cases cannot be bettered today, for Webster was a born definer as well as a man of encyclopedic knowledge. The great weakness of the dictionary lies in its etymologies, which were largely out-of-date before the work came from the press. As a whole, Webster's *American Dictionary* was a scholarly achievement of the first order, richly deserving of its great reputation at home and abroad. His chief contemporary rival in the United States was Joseph Emerson Worcester [*q.v.*], whom he charged with plagiarism, but most of the "War of the Dictionaries" occurred after his own death.

In 1812, Webster removed from New Haven to Amherst, Mass., where he felt he could live more cheaply and with fewer distractions from his scholarly labors. While at Amherst he became interested in local educational needs and helped to found Amherst College. In 1822, however, he returned to New Haven, where he con-

tinued to live the rest of his life, except for a year (1824–25) spent in lexicographical work in France and England, and a winter (1830–31) spent in Washington in successful agitation for a revision of the copyright law. His publications during what may be termed his lexicographical period include, besides five dictionaries with abridgments and revisions, a *Philosophical and Practical Grammar of the English Language* (1807), a revision of the Authorized Version of the English Bible (1833), and various essays and addresses. Webster in early life was something of a freethinker, but in 1808 he became a convert to Calvinistic orthodoxy, and thereafter remained a devout Congregationalist.

[H. E. Scudder, *Noah Webster* (1881); Emily E. F. Ford, *Notes on the Life of Noah Webster,* ed. by Emily E. F. Skeel (2 vols., 1912), including list of writings, vol. II, 523–40, and list of "authorities cited"; H. R. Warfel, *Noah Webster: Schoolmaster to America* (1936); C.–E. A. Winslow, "The Epidemiology of Noah Webster," *Trans. Conn. Academy of Arts and Sciences,* Jan. 1934; F. B. Dexter, *Biog. Sketches of the Grads. of Yale College,* vol. IV (1907); W. H. and M. R. Webster, *History and Genealogy of the Governor John Webster Family* (1915); D. S. Durrie, *Steele Family* (1859); J. E. Greenleaf, *Genealogy of the Greenleaf Family* (1896); obituary in *N. Y. Morning Express,* May 31, 1843; public records; family letters.] K. M.

WEBSTER, PELATIAH (Nov. 24, 1726–Sept. 2, 1795), political economist, was born in Lebanon, Conn., the eldest son of Pelatiah and Joanna (Crowfoot) Smith Webster, and a descendant of John Webster, one of the first settlers of Hartford. After graduation from Yale College in 1746, he studied theology and in June 1749 began to preach in Greenwich, Mass., where on Dec. 20 he was ordained pastor. He married Mrs. Ruth Kellogg of Suffield, Conn., in September 1750 and they had four daughters and a son. His second wife, Rebecca Hunt, whom he married in Boston on Oct. 8, 1785, died in Philadelphia in 1793. In October 1755 Webster left his parish to become a merchant in Philadelphia, and later while maintaining his business, taught for a time in Germantown Academy. In 1765 he visited Charleston, S. C., recording his impressions in a journal (*Publications of the Southern History Association,* vol. II, 1898). On the outbreak of the Revolution his business suffered, and in April 1777, with a cargo of flour and iron bound for Boston, he was seized by the British and held prisoner in Newport for several weeks. The next year he was confined for some time in the Philadelphia jail and much of his property was confiscated, though later all but about £500 was recovered.

Beginning on Oct. 5, 1776, with a letter, in the *Pennsylvania Evening Post* on "the Danger of too much Circulating Cash," he published a succession of studies signed either "A Financier" or "A Citizen of Philadelphia" which were later collected in a volume entitled *Political Essays on the Nature and Operation of Money, Public Finances, and Other Subjects; Published during the American War* (1791). He argued in favor of the support of the war by taxation rather than by loans, a free trade policy, and the curtailment of paper money issues. He has been called "almost the only man of ability and note who held out vigorously against the rag-money party" in Pennsylvania at the time of the issue of bills of credit in 1785 (J. B. McMaster, *A History of the People of the United States*, vol. I, 1883, p. 284). During the struggle in Pennsylvania over the adoption of the Constitution he published *Remarks on the Address of Sixteen Members of the Assembly of Pennsylvania to their Constituents dated September 29, 1787* (1787), in which he cogently demonstrated the specious nature of the objections to the new plan of government, and about the same time he also published *The Weakness of Brutus Exposed: or, Some Remarks in Vindication of the Constitution Proposed by the Late Federal Convention against the Objections and Gloomy Fears of That Writer* (1787), in which he maintained the need for a government with supreme power, "full, definite, established, acknowledged." His faith in a stronger union he had expressed four years before in *A Dissertation on the Political Union and Constitution of the Thirteen United States of North-America* (1783), the pamphlet on which Hannis Taylor [*q.v.*] in the twentieth century rested his claim that Webster was the real author of the Constitution. These exaggerated claims made by Taylor on behalf of Webster have obscured his genuine share in educating the people to the need of a new form of government and his aid in bringing about the adoption of the Constitution, and have also diverted attention from the writings in which he expressed clear and vigorous views on money, credit, taxation, and trade.

[Henry Bronson, "A Historical Account of Connecticut Currency," *New Haven Colony Hist. Soc. Papers*, vol. I (1865); R. R. Hinman, *A Hist. Coll. from Official Records . . . of the Part Sustained by Conn. during the War of the Revolution* (1842); J. B. McMaster and F. D. Stone, *Pa. and the Federal Constitution* (1888); Noah Webster, *A Coll. of Papers on Political, Literary and Moral Subjects* (1843); W. H. and M. R. Webster, *Hist. and Geneal. of the Gov. John Webster Family* (1915); F. B. Dexter, *Biog. Sketches Grads. Yale Coll.*, vol. II (1896); Hannis Taylor, *A Memorial in Behalf of the Architect of Our Federal Constitution* (n.d., c. 1907) and *The Real Authorship of the Constitution of the United States Explained* (1912); E. S. Corwin, "The Pelatiah Webster Myth," in *The Doctrine of Judicial Review* (1914);

Gaillard Hunt, *Pelatiah Webster and the Constitution* (1912), repr. from the *Nation* (N. Y.), Dec. 28, 1911; *Dunlap and Claypoole's Am. Daily Advertiser* (Phila.), Sept. 4, 1795.]   E. D.

WEBSTER–POWELL, ALMA [See POWELL, ALMA WEBSTER, 1874–1930].

WEED, THURLOW (Nov. 15, 1797–Nov. 22, 1882), politician and journalist, the eldest son of Joel and Mary (Ellis) Weed, was born in Greene County, N. Y., where his grandfather, formerly of Stamford, Conn., had settled with his family after the Revolution. Joel Weed, a hard-working but never prosperous farmer, sometimes in jail for debt, moved in 1799 to Catskill, where his son enjoyed a brief schooling. When he was eight years old Thurlow began to earn what he could by odd jobs at the blacksmith's, the printer's, and on Hudson River boats. In 1808 the family moved to Cortland County, and not long afterward to Onondaga, where young Weed was apprenticed to a printer. Several years in various printers' shops in central New York, broken by a few months' militia service in 1813, brought him little pecuniary gain but gave him an unrivalled education in local affairs. In 1817 he became foreman on the Albany *Register,* and tried his hand at writing news paragraphs and editorials in support of DeWitt Clinton's canal policy. On Apr. 26, 1818, he married Catherine Ostrander of Cooperstown.

During the next four years Weed tried to publish Clintonian papers at Norwich and Manlius, and after both had failed he moved on, almost penniless, to Rochester. There he secured a position on the *Rochester Telegraph,* for which he wrote editorials advocating John Quincy Adams for president. Sent to Albany in 1824 to lobby for a bank charter, he promptly set about uniting the friends of Adams and Clay in a common opposition to William H. Crawford, the candidate of Martin Van Buren. He returned to Rochester with the charter, and also with the knowledge that his time and efforts had become essential to his party (*Life, post,* I, 107). Soon he was campaigning through the western counties in behalf of Adams for president and Clinton for governor of New York. Weed himself was elected to the Assembly. Fortune favored him in business as well as in politics, and in 1825 he was able to buy the *Telegraph.*

Throughout the anti-Masonic excitement that followed the disappearance of William Morgan [*q.v.*] in 1826, Weed was an active member of the local Morgan committee, and gave up the *Telegraph* to publish the *Anti-Masonic Enquirer.* As local political organizations were formed, Weed exerted himself to secure candidates who were "sound" on issues other than the Masonic. He held the "infected district" in line for Adams in 1828 and supported National Republicans locally. Leading Anti-Masons raised a fund to establish a paper at Albany, and employed Weed as editor; he was elected to the Assembly in 1829 to make his presence at the capital possible. In February 1830 the first issue of the *Albany Evening Journal* appeared, Weed being reporter, proof-reader, and often compositor, as well as editor, legislator, and political manager. He remained officially an Anti-Mason through 1832, supporting William Wirt [*q.v.*], the party's presidential candidate, but, as before, saw that the nominees for state offices were National Republicans. Most Anti-Masons, he was convinced, were in sympathy with Clay's "American system," and were inevitably opposed to the dominant "Albany Regency," so closely linked, through Van Buren, to President Jackson. He himself ignored the Bank issue, believing it inexpedient to oppose so popular a movement against "moneyed aristocracy." Drilling his party through the unsuccessful campaigns of 1834 and 1836, he was ready for the opportunity offered by the panic and hard times, and helped create the victories that made William H. Seward [*q.v.*] governor in 1838 and Harrison president in 1840.

Weed was now generally regarded as the dictator of his party, and was charged with dominating Seward, to whom he was bound in closest personal friendship. His great influence, however, was exerted in the field of political management. Others formulated the principles and Weed secured the votes. Patronage he regarded as indispensable; he derived "great satisfaction . . . in bringing capable and good men into public service" (*Life, post,* I, 209), the good men being Whigs. Bribery and legislative favors were in his opinion legitimate party instruments, but he was above taking corrupt profits for himself. His paper was a party organ, providing usable facts and arguments, in terse paragraphs, to gain and hold Whigs to the true faith. He shared Seward's humanitarian views but never to the point of endangering the serious business of elections, and while he recognized Horace Greeley's power, he cast a dubious eye on his "isms," especially in the field of social reform. His own anti-slavery sentiments were sincere, but he was more desirous of getting anti-slavery men to accept Whig candidates than of committing the party openly to their cause; for the abolitionists who clamored for a party of their own he had nothing but scorn.

As the fruits of victory vanished with Tyler's accession to the presidency, followed by Seward's defeat in 1842, Weed lost heart, traveled abroad, and even talked of giving up the *Evening Journal.* The campaign of 1844 was not only unsuccessful but ominous of dissensions to come. Too astute to oppose the government in wartime, he directed his efforts to the future of the territories to be acquired, and supported the Wilmot Proviso. With equal astuteness, early in 1846 he recognized Gen. Zachary Taylor's possibilities as a candidate for the presidency, and advised him not to commit himself on controversial questions. Taylor's election, with Fillmore as vice-president and Seward as senator, promised to establish Weed's power firmly, but with Taylor's death the outlook was changed. Fillmore accepted the compromise measures of 1850; Seward, backed by Weed, was their great opponent; and the Whig division was hopeless. Weed, sure of his party's defeat in 1852, went abroad. Thoroughly anti-Nebraska in sentiment, he was slow to join the new Republican party in 1854 until Seward's reëlection to the Senate was assured. He was opposed to Seward's being put forward by the Republicans as a candidate for the presidency in 1856, believing that his chances of election would be better in 1860. His presidential ambitions for Seward were doomed to disappointment, however; and no little of the feeling against Seward in 1860 was due to his long and close connection with Weed, who was highly unacceptable to former Democrats.

Weed was consulted by Lincoln, during the latter's campaign and after, and had considerable influence on appointments, though he was credited with more than he had. In 1861 he went, with Archbishop Hughes and Bishop McIlvaine [*qq.v.*], on an unofficial mission to conciliate English and French opinion after the *Trent* affair. He was willing to accept the Crittenden compromise in 1861, and, distrustful of "ultra abolitionist" influences on Lincoln, would have preferred an untainted and active War Democrat as the Union candidate in 1864, but McClellan's acceptance of the Democratic platform kept Weed in the Republican lines. His influence in New York, badly shaken by Seward's failure in 1860, declined steadily as the Radicals gained strength after Lincoln's death. He had given up the *Evening Journal* and moved to New York City in 1863, where in 1867 he returned to journalism, becoming editor of the *Commercial Advertiser.* Failing health and sight soon compelled him to abandon editorial work, however. Retaining his deep interest in public affairs, he was a frequent contributor to the press on political subjects and was often consulted by political leaders. For some time he had been writing a desultory autobiography. In 1866 his *Letters from Europe and the West Indies* was published. After his death some of his articles on bimetalism were reprinted in *The Silver Dollar of the United States and Its Relations to Bimetallism* (1889).

He was tall and robust, rather awkward in appearance. His charm of manner, unruffled good-nature, and ready generosity drew into the circle of his friends even those political opponents who had suffered most from his vigorous attacks and rough wit. Seward wrote in early years that he had "had no idea that dictators were such amiable creatures" (*Life*, II, 63), and young Henry Adams, meeting Weed in London, won by "his faculty of irresistibly conquering confidence . . . followed him about . . . much like a little dog." He was, thought Adams, "the model of political management and patient address," "a complete American education in himself" (*The Education of Henry Adams*, 1918, p. 146). He died of old age in his eighty-sixth year and was survived by three daughters, his wife and a son having died many years before.

[Weed's "Autobiography" was published by his daughter, Harriet A. Weed, as vol. I of the *Life of Thurlow Weed* (1884); vol. II is a "Memoir" by his grandson, T. W. Barnes. Other sources are: D. S. Alexander, *A Polit. Hist. of the State of N. Y.*, vols. I–III (1906–09); S. D. Brummer, *Polit. Hist. of N. Y. State During . . . the Civil War* (1911); Frederic Bancroft, *The Life of William H. Seward* (2 vols., 1900); F. W. Seward, *Autobiog. of William H. Seward . . .* (1877) and *Seward at Washington* (2 vols., 1891); F. H. Severance, "Millard Fillmore Papers," vol. II, being *Buffalo Hist. Soc. Pubs.*, vol. XI (1907); Horace Greeley, *Recollections of a Busy Life* (1868); Gideon Welles, *Diary* (3 vols., 1911), and *Lincoln and Seward* (1874); *Atlantic Mo.*, Sept. 1883, pp. 411–19; *Mag. of Am. Hist.*, Jan. 1888; *N. Y. Times*, *N. Y. Tribune*, and *Albany Evening Journal*, Nov. 22, 23, 1882.]

H. C. B.

WEEDEN, WILLIAM BABCOCK (Sept. 1, 1834–Mar. 28, 1912), manufacturer and historian, was descended from James Weeden, who settled in Newport, R. I., in 1638. He was born in Bristol, R. I., the son of John Edward and Eliza (Cross) Weeden. His early education was received in the public schools of Westerly, R. I., and at the Connecticut Literary Institute, Suffield, Conn. He was a student at Brown University with the class of 1852, but left before graduation in order to accept employment with Bradford & Taft, wool merchants of Providence. So successful was he in this capacity that, with the dissolution of the partnership about 1864, he became a member of the new firm of Taft, Weeden & Company. Weeden's business activity was interrupted by his service during the Civil War. He first served as a second lieutenant

in the Rhode Island light artillery, but was advanced to a captaincy after the battle of Bull Run. He continued in active service through the Seven Days' Battle, when he resigned his commission and resumed his business connections in Providence. The important phase of his business life began in 1864, when he organized the Weybosset Mills, control of which he retained until their purchase by the American Woolen Company in 1902. These mills were devoted to the large-scale manufacture of cassimeres and worsteds in the Blackstone Valley and in Providence, and raised Weeden to a position of leadership among men of affairs in southern New England.

While probably best known among his contemporaries as a manufacturer, Weeden will undoubtedly be remembered by posterity chiefly as an historian. As a business man he was content to tread the paths worn by his predecessors. As a writer of history he ranks as a pioneer. It was in the seventies that his interest began to turn to public questions and to history. His first literary effort of importance was *The Morality of Prohibitory Liquor Laws* (1875). This was followed by *The Social Law of Labor* (1882), and *Indian Money as a Factor in New England Civilization* (1884), which appeared in the Johns Hopkins University Studies. In the last-named work he began the cultivation of a field which was to engage his attention for many years. His studies resulted in his most important and widely used work, *Economic and Social History of New England* (2 vols., 1890), covering the period from 1620 to 1789. Despite its undeniable defects of arrangement and organization, this work stamps Weeden as one of the handful of men in America who, when history was still politics, dared to embrace a broader and more all-inclusive view of the subject. Like his contemporary, John Bach McMaster [*q.v.*], Weeden was a social historian who sought faithfully to reproduce the life of the people in different periods. Like McMaster, too, he wrote social history of the static sort, as opposed to the dynamic, interpretative variety associated with Frederick Jackson Turner [*q.v.*] and Charles Beard. He wrote numerous other articles and books, the most important of which were *War Government, Federal and State . . . 1861–1865* (1906), and *Early Rhode Island, a Social History of the People* (1910). His activity as a writer of history earned for him membership in such learned organizations as the American Antiquarian Society, the Massachusetts Historical Society, and the Rhode Island Historical Society.

Weeden was married three times: first, on Oct. 12, 1859, to Amy Dexter Owen; second, on

Dec. 5, 1867, to Hannah Raymer Balch, by whom he had seven children; and third, on Apr. 18, 1893, to Jeanie Lippitt, daughter of Henry Lippitt [*q.v.*]. He died in Providence, survived by his wife and six of his seven children.

[*Who's Who in America*, 1910–11; *Alphabetical Index of the Births, Marriages, and Deaths . . . in Providence*, vols. II (1880), XIII (1910); *Proc. R. I. Hist. Soc., 1911–1913* (1913); *Proc. Am. Antiquarian Soc.*, vol. XXII (1912); T. M. Aldrich, *The Hist. of Battery A, 1st Reg., R. I. Light Artillery* (1904); obituary in *Providence Daily Jour.*, Mar. 29, 1912; information from Weeden's widow and W. W. Weeden, a son.]

J. B. H.

WEEKS, EDWIN LORD (1849–Nov. 17, 1903), painter, born in Boston, Mass., was the son of Stephen and Mary (Lord) Weeks, and a descendant of Leonard Weeks, who emigrated from Somersetshire, England, and settled in Portsmouth, N. H., where he received a grant of land, in 1656. Edwin Weeks studied in the public schools of Boston and Newton, but before finishing his course he had an opportunity to go to Paris, where he began his art education at the École des Beaux-Arts under Léon Bonnat and J. L. Gérôme. While his training was still in progress he journeyed to Tangier, Algiers, and Cairo, where he made a number of striking paintings. Some of these early works were hung in the Paris Salon during his novitiate, and the favorable verdict of the critics, together with the approval of his masters, encouraged him to specialize in Oriental subjects. He traveled to Palestine, and did some work in Jerusalem and Damascus, and then ventured on an expedition to India. There during the eighties and nineties he produced an extensive series of brilliant compositions, many of which were exhibited at the Paris Salon. Notable examples included "Jeypore" and "A Hindu Sanctuary at Bombay" (1884); "The Last Voyage, Souvenir of the Ganges, Benares" (1885) and "The Rajah Starting on a Hunt," both in the Metropolitan Museum of Art, New York; "A Rajah of Jodhpore" (1888); "The Golden Temple of Amritsar" (1890); and "The Barbers of Saharanpore" (1895). His "Departure for the Hunt, India" (1884) is in the permanent collection of the Corcoran Gallery of Art, Washington; "The Porter of Bagdad" was bought by the Cercle Volney, Paris; and the "Three Beggars of Cordova" went to the Pennsylvania Academy of the Fine Arts. At the Paris Exposition of 1900 he was represented by "The Awakening of Nourredin," "On the Road to Ispahan," and "Indian Barber." In these paintings Weeks has given to those who are familiar only with the western world "some idea of the sunlight, the color, and the strange, curiously wrought structures of the East," to quote the words of Samuel Isham [*q.v.*], "and his clear, sure interpretation carries conviction of the accuracy of the reproduction" (*post*, p. 408).

He received many honors in many countries, the crowning one being the coveted ribbon of the chevalier of the Legion of Honor which came to him in 1896. He wrote *From the Black Sea through Persia and India* (1896), *Some Episodes of Mountaineering* (1897), and contributed a number of papers to books and magazines. For many years he made his home in Paris, and it was there that his death occurred in the autumn of 1903, when he was fifty-four. The funeral, which was held at the American Church, was attended by leading French and American artists, and many wreaths were sent by artistic societies in France and the United States. The interment was at Billancourt. A collection of 277 of his paintings and sketches was sold at the American Art Galleries, New York, in March 1905.

[Jacob Chapman, *Leonard Weeks . . . and His Descendants* (1889); Helen S. Earle, *Biog. Sketches of Am. Artists* (1915); Samuel Isham, *The Hist. of Am. Painting* (1905); *Boston Daily Advertiser*, Jan. 17, 1876, Feb. 16, 1878; *Am. Art Ann.*, 1905; obituaries in *Boston Transcript*, Nov. 17, and *N. Y. Tribune*, Nov. 18, 1903.]

W. H. D.

WEEKS, JOHN WINGATE (Apr. 11, 1860–July 12, 1926), congressman, senator, secretary of war, was born on a farm near Lancaster, N. H., son of William Dennis and Mary Helen (Fowler) Weeks, and a descendant of Leonard Weeks who emigrated from Somersetshire, England, before 1656 and settled in Greenland, originally part of Portsmouth, N. H. As a boy Weeks attended the local school and by doing the chores on his father's farm laid the foundation for the robust health he enjoyed until in his fifties. At sixteen he taught school for a term and then, in 1877, entered the Naval Academy at Annapolis, where he was graduated four years later. He continued in the navy until 1883, when a general curtailment of personnel forced his discharge. For several years thereafter he worked at surveying in Florida, and while so engaged met and married, Oct. 7, 1885, Martha A. Sinclair, by whom he had two children.

Because the climate of Florida did not agree with his wife, Weeks in 1888 accepted an offer to enter the banking and brokerage business in Boston. The firm of which he became a partner, operating under the name of Hornblower & Weeks, was successful from the start and became in time one of the largest and most respected financial houses in America. Weeks himself acquired a fortune and became a business figure of importance. Love for the navy led him to join the Massachusetts naval militia, and during the Spanish-American War he served with this body in its task of patrolling the Massachusetts coast. The social side of this affiliation Weeks prized greatly—conviviality was an outstanding trait in his nature—and he was never so happy as when attending one of the joyous dinners of the "Wardroom Club," an organization of militia members, which were held on the Boston waterfront in a room modeled after the fashion of wardrooms in naval vessels.

Weeks's first political office, that of alderman-at-large of the city of Newton, Mass., where he made his home, came to him in 1900 unsolicited, as did his election as mayor three years later. His experiences in these offices awakened in him a liking for politics with its human contacts, and consequently when in 1904 friends urged him to stand for Congress he consented. He was elected, gave up his business connections, and remained in the House of Representatives until 1913, when the Massachusetts legislature named him to succeed the retiring Winthrop Murray Crane [q.v.] as United States senator. Weeks's stay in the Senate was limited to one term; in 1918 he was defeated for reëlection by David I. Walsh, Democrat. During the Harding-Cox presidential campaign of 1920 Weeks's service as chief of the New York headquarters of the Republican party won him the regard of Harding, who later named him secretary of war. He continued in this office until October 1925, when ill health compelled him to retire.

In Congress, Weeks was hard-working, conscientious, and an able if not an eloquent speaker. He was tall, heavily and powerfully built, a man who without vanity set a correct appraisal on his superior abilities. His demeanor, simple and kindly, caused him to be universally liked and respected—"the smiling statesman" somebody called him. His political views corresponded in the main to orthodox Republicanism. He was for a high tariff and retention of the Philippines. He preferred the Aldrich currency and banking proposals but, in lieu of them, voted for President Wilson's Federal Reserve Act. He was opposed to the prohibition and woman's suffrage amendments, and probably his vote against the latter had something to do with his defeat in the senatorial election of 1918. As secretary of war he brought large business experience to the solution of the many problems left over from the war administration. In February 1925, when sensational controversy arose concerning the adequacy of the nation's air defenses, he appeared before a House investigating committee and contradicted charges made by William Mitchell, the brigadier-general and assistant chief of the army air service. He died in Lancaster, N. H.

[*Who's Who in America,* 1924–25; *N. Y. Times,* July 12, 13, 1926; *Bankers Mag.,* Sept. 1926; *Boston Transcript,* July 12, 1926; C. G. Washburn, *The Life of John W. Weeks* (1928); *Biog. Dir. Am. Cong.* (1928); Jacob Chapman, *Leonard Weeks . . . and His Descendants* (1889).]   W. E. S—a.

WEEKS, JOSEPH DAME (Dec. 3, 1840–Dec. 26, 1896), technical journalist, statistician, was born at Lowell, Mass., the son of Jonathan and Mary (Dame) Weeks. He was a descendant of Leonard Weeks, who settled in Portsmouth, N. H., in 1656, and of Jacob Heard, New Hampshire Revolutionary soldier. After serving with the United States Christian Commission, 1863–65, Weeks entered Wesleyan University, where he prepared for the Methodist ministry, but he was compelled by a throat disorder soon after graduation in 1869 to abandon the idea of a ministerial career. He spent some time in Iowa working on the *Burlington Hawkeye,* moved to Cincinnati, published a *History of the Knights of Pythias* in 1871, and on Feb. 28 of that year married Mattie J. Fowler, daughter of a Pittsburgh industrialist. In 1872 he became editor of the *American Manufacturer,* published in Pittsburgh, which in 1874 was consolidated with the *Iron World.* Two years later he resigned to become associate editor and manager of the Pittsburgh office of the New York *Iron Age,* but in April 1886, he returned to the *Manufacturer,* of which he had secured control, and continued as its editor until his death. His articles in these journals were regarded as authoritative and were widely quoted.

Deeply interested in the problems of industrial relations, Weeks was instrumental, through the Western Iron Association and the Western Pig Iron Association, in fixing iron prices. He was responsible for the first wage scale offered by the manufacturers to the Amalgamated Association of Iron and Steel Workers; and he subsequently presided over a number of wage conferences, enjoying to an unusual degree the confidence of both sides. His studies of labor relations resulted in a number of publications: *Report on the Practical Operation of Arbitration and Conciliation . . . in England* (1879), *Labor Differences and Their Settlement* (1886), *Industrial Conciliation and Arbitration in New York, Ohio and Pennsylvania* (1881). A firm believer in the protective tariff, he testified before congressional fact-finding committees.

As a scientist, Weeks is credited with conducting the experiments that led to the first use of gas in a puddling furnace. The year before his death he investigated the utilization of by-products in coke manufacture in Germany and urged the example on western Pennsylvania. He made a survey of the iron ores of the James River Valley in Virginia. To the *Transactions* of the American Association of Mining Engineers, of which he was president in 1895, he contributed articles on manganese steel, blast furnaces, fuel problems, natural gas, the Bessemer process.

Appointed a special agent for the census of 1880 he prepared reports on the manufacture of coke and glass and an entire volume on wages in manufacturing industries with supplementary reports on trade societies, strikes, and lockouts. For the census of 1890 he prepared the articles on the mining of petroleum, gas, and manganese, and on the manufacture of refined petroleum, coke, and gas. From 1885 to 1895 he was employed by the department of mineral resources of the United States Geological Survey, contributing annually the articles on coke manufacture, crude petroleum, natural gas, and the production of manganese. To the Pennsylvania bureau of industrial statistics he furnished articles on coke. He was judge of awards in the department of mines and mining at the World's Columbian Exposition, 1893. At the time of his death he was assembling statistics for the Pennsylvania Tax Conference Commission, of which he was chairman, and for the national commission appointed to appraise the property of the Monongahela River Navigation Company. An indefatigable worker, he found time to devote to church, civic, and philanthropic affairs in Pittsburgh and to give advice and assistance to young men in science and industry.

[Jacob Chapman, *Leonard Weeks of Greenland, N. H., and His Descendants* (1889); *Iron Age,* Feb. 3, 1876, Apr. 8, 1886, Dec. 31, 1896; *Am. Manufacturer and Iron World,* Jan. 1, 1897; *Trans. Am. Inst. Mining Engineers,* vol. XXVII (1898); *Am. Manufacturer,* Jan. 2, 1873, Mar. 26, 1874, Feb. 17, 1876, Apr. 9, 1886; *Alumni Record of Wesleyan Univ.* (1883); *Pittsburg Post,* Dec. 27, 1896; information from Wesleyan Univ. Alumni Council.]   M. S.

WEEKS, STEPHEN BEAUREGARD (Feb. 2, 1865–May 3, 1918), North Carolina historian and bibliographer, was born in Pasquotank County, N. C., of English and Huguenot ancestors resident in the locality since the first half of the eighteenth century. Bereft in infancy of his parents, James Elliott Weeks, a planter, and Mary Louisa (Mullen) Weeks, he was reared in the nearby farmhouse of his father's sister and her husband, Robertson Jackson. After attending neighborhood schools and the noted Horner School at Henderson, where he received his first real intellectual impulse, Weeks entered the University of North Carolina in 1882 and was graduated in 1886 with honors. A year later he received the degree of M.A. and in 1888 that of Ph.D. in English, German, and Latin. His compilation of the *Register of Members of the Philanthropic Society* (Raleigh, 1887) strengthened his interest in North Carolina history, which was fixed as the field of his life's work by study under Herbert Baxter Adams [*q.v.*] at the Johns Hopkins University. There after three years' study he received the degree of Ph.D. in 1891. Weeks was twice married: first, on June 12, 1888, to Mary Lee Martin of Chapel Hill, who died in 1891, and second, on June 28, 1893, to Sallie Mangum Leach of Trinity, grand-daughter of Willie Person Mangum [*q.v.*].

He was professor of history and political science at Trinity College (later Duke University) from 1891 until his resignation in 1893 resulting from a faculty quarrel with the president. In the autumn he returned to the Johns Hopkins University as a fellow by courtesy for a year's study and research. Already his skill and industry in research had produced *The Press of North Carolina in the Eighteenth Century* (1891), "The Lost Colony of Roanoke: Its Fate and Survival" (*Papers of the American Historical Association,* Oct. 1891), "The Religious Development in the Province of North Carolina" (*Johns Hopkins University Studies in Historical and Political Science,* May–June 1892), "Church and State in North Carolina" (*Ibid.,* 1893), "General Joseph Martin and the War of the Revolution in the West" (*Annual Report of the American Historical Association,* 1893), and "The History of Negro Suffrage in the South" (*Political Science Quarterly,* December 1894).

From 1894 to 1899 he held a position in the United States Bureau of Education at Washington, performing editorial work on the annual reports of the commissioner and other bureau publications, and carrying on historical research, the chief results of which were "The Beginnings of the Common School System in the South" (*Report of the Commissioner of Education,* 1896–97) and "Confederate Text-books" (*Ibid.,* 1898–99). Additional publications of this period were *A Bibliography of the Historical Literature of North Carolina* (1895), "Libraries and Literature in North Carolina in the Eighteenth Century" (*Annual Report of the American Historical Association,* 1895), "The University of North Carolina in the Civil War" (*Southern Historical Society Papers,* vol. XXIV, 1896), and his largest and best-known work, *Southern Quakers and Slavery* (1896). Weeks was one of the founders of the Southern History Association at Washington in 1896, a member of its administrative council, and a frequent contributor to its *Publications* (1897–1907).

Compelled by impaired health to change his residence, he entered the United States Indian Service in 1899; and, for eight years as teacher and superintendent in Indian schools at Santa Fé, N. M., and San Carlos, Ariz., he waged a successful struggle with disease, enduring with fortitude the interruption of his work and interests. In 1907 he returned to North Carolina, where he was busy for two years with editorial work on the *Biographical History of North Carolina* (8 vols., 1905–17), edited by S. A. Ashe, to which he contributed many signed sketches. Following a two-year principalship of the high school at Trinity, he again accepted a research position in the Bureau of Education at Washington, for which he studied the history of public school education in a number of states. Over a period of years he compiled an index to the North Carolina census of 1790 (*State Records,* vol. XXVI, 1905) and the monumental *Index to the Colonial and State Records of North Carolina* (4 vols., 1909–14), in the last volume of which is an extensive survey of the colonial and state records of North Carolina.

Coördinate with Weeks's interest in historical research and writing was his life-long zeal in collecting North Carolina books, pamphlets, and manuscripts, and in compiling an exhaustive and critical bibliography of North Carolina. After his death at his home in Washington on May 3, 1918, the Weeks collection of Caroliniana, comprising 10,000 books and pamphlets, and the incomplete bibliography were acquired by the University of North Carolina. Weeks was one of the earliest and most productive of the new school of trained North Carolina historians whose primary concern was the objective presentation of the results of scholarly, painstaking investigation of historical sources.

[Sources include *Who's Who in America,* 1916–17; *Alumni Hist. of the Univ. of N. C.* (1924); T. M. Pittman, in *Biog. Hist. of N. C.,* vol. V (1906), ed. by S. A. Ashe; obituary in *News and Observer* (Raleigh, N. C.), May 4, 1918; S. B. Weeks, *The Weeks Coll. of Caroliniana* (1907); information from Weeks's son, Mangum Weeks, and the U. S. Bureau of Education, which has several of Weeks's unpublished MSS.]

A. R. N.

WEEMS, MASON LOCKE (Oct. 11, 1759–May 23, 1825), Episcopal clergyman, book agent, writer, was born at "Marshes Seat," near Herring Bay, Anne Arundel County, Md., nineteenth child of David Weems, and the youngest by his second wife, Esther (Hill) Weems. His father, reputedly of the noble Scottish family of Wemyss, emigrated before 1722 and, with kins-

folk, founded the Weems family, today spread throughout the South. Of Mason before early manhood nothing is definitely known, though there are picturesque legends of varying credibility. In 1783, when abroad, he was in correspondence with John Adams and Benjamin Franklin, then respectively at The Hague and in Paris, concerning the obstacles to ordination, the British law still requiring the oath of allegiance; this, however, being abrogated in August 1784, by Act of Parliament, Weems and Edward Gantt, Jr., were the first candidates to receive Anglican ordination for service in the United States. Ordained deacon, Sept. 5, 1784, by the bishop of Chester, Weems was admitted to the priesthood a week later by the archbishop of Canterbury. Returning to Maryland, he served from 1784 to 1792 in All Hallows and St. Margaret's parishes. In 1791 he began reprinting a series of improving books by Robert Russel, Hugh Blair, Lewis Cornaro, Capt. Henry Wilson, Hannah More, Mrs. Helme, and Henry Brooke.

On July 2, 1795, he was married to Frances Ewell, daughter of Col. Jesse Ewell, and sister of James Ewell [*q.v.*], and settled her amidst her people in Dumfries, Va., where their ten children were born. He thereafter continued and extended his wanderings, which, as a seller of books, and after 1794 as Mathew Carey's agent, led him for thirty-one years up and down the Eastern seaboard from New York City to Savannah, including the nearer hinterland of Pennsylvania. This agency lapsed only during two intervals—first, when he preached in several Virginia parishes, notably at Pohick Church (thereby laying the only basis for his claim: "Formerly Rector of Mt. Vernon Parish," first printed on a book title in 1809), and again later when he "subscriptioneered" for John Marshall's *Washington.* First and last he step-fathered a goodly number of weighty works by Oliver Goldsmith, William Guthrie, William Burkit, James Hervey, Edward W. Montagu, William Coxe, Henry Hunter, and others, besides Carey's edition of the Bible, first suggested by Weems, who while making very large sales continued to offer ideas for embellishing the successive issues. In these as well as in his editings, compilings, writings, and letters, he showed a knowledge of Biblical and general literature which evinced wide and interested reading. He practised as well as proclaimed a passionate faith in the value of "good books," and from his letters alone no impression is clearer than his own belief that by circulating such he was still doing God's work, having merely transferred his activities from the pulpit to a wider mission field.

By 1799, in his *Philanthropist,* and in 1802, in his *True Patriot,* he was preaching a political doctrine which was twin brother to theological universalism. The bent then discovered toward a solvent of pervasive love as a cure-all and end-all for every ill of human existence grew on him, while in his *Hymen's Recruiting Serjeant* (2 pts., *c.* 1799—of which excerpts are found in almanacs of about 1800—he tinctured his senti-mental and vital statistics with magnificent buf-foonery. This empirical chemistry makes a mas-terpiece of what, by a stretch of tolerance, may be called his *magnum opus, The Life and Memo-rable Actions of George Washington* (*c.* 1800), as also his *Life of General Francis Marion* (1809), both being early examples of the sup-posedly ultra-modern fictioned biography. The former (in its first version issued anonymously), although inveighed against by many judicial his-torians or gored to tatters by those of less con-trolled temperament, was the second best-seller of its day, and held its own through over seventy accredited and varying editions, including five in German (1800–1927). In its fifth edition (1806) the hatchet and cherry-tree story first appeared in book form. Both these books, if taken with an adequate supply of salt, may still delight the palate. The *Life of Doctor Benjamin Franklin* (1815), founded largely on the immor-tal autobiography, and the *Life of William Penn* (1822) are not such stimulants to historical bile as their precursors, and are of neither interest nor value. Probably the springs of Weems's fancy had been diverted into his moralizing tracts: *God's Revenge Against Murder* (1807), *God's Revenge Against Gambling* (*c.* 1810), *The Drunkard's Looking Glass* (*c.* 1812), *God's Re-venge Against Adultery* (1815), *God's Revenge Against Duelling* (1820), and the *Bad Wife's Looking Glass* (1823). His letters (1784–1825) compare more than favorably with any in Amer-ican annals, in their self-revelation, spontaneity, mother-wit, and racy English, besides, in their book lists, throwing valuable light on the taste of the reading public of his day. In them, as by common report, we learn that he passed his days in a whirl of febrile excitement, whether without or within, never, until toward the end of his laborious life, flagging in energy or zest. He died at Beaufort, S. C., whence his remains were removed for re-interment at his home, Bel Air, near Dumphries, Va.

[Sources include the diary of William E. Duke, MS. in Md. Diocesan Lib., Baltimore; records of Protestant Episcopal Church Conventions in Md., 1783–93 (pub-lished *c.* 1788–93); William Meade, *Old Churches, Min-isters, and Families of Va.* (2 vols., 1857); obituary in *Reporter* (Warrenton, N. C.), July 8, 1825. See also P. L. Ford and Emily E. F. Skeel, *Mason Locke Weems*

(3 vols., 1928–29), with bibliog.; S. G. Fisher, "The Legendary and Myth-Making Process in Histories of the Am. Rev.," *Proc. Am. Philosophical Soc.,* vol. LI (1912); W. G. Simms, *Views and Reviews in Am. Lit.* (1845); L. C. Wroth, *Parson Weems* (1911); W. B. Norris, in *Nat. Mag.,* Feb. 1910.]   E. E. F. S.

WEIDENMANN, JACOB (Aug. 22, 1829–Feb. 6, 1893), landscape architect, was born at Winterthur, Canton Zurich, Switzerland, the son of Jacob and Elise (Gubbler) Weidenmann. Af-ter a brief apprenticeship in an architect's office at Geneva, he went to the Akademie der Bilden-den Künste, Munich, for his architectural train-ing. After visiting Paris, London, and New York, he found employment as an assistant en-gineer at Panama, but soon proceeded to Callao, and thence to Lima, Peru, where he worked for about a year as engineer and architect. Having become interested in landscape architecture, about 1861 he returned to America, where the profession was still very young. As superin-tendent of parks in Hartford, Conn. (1861–68), he designed Bushnell Park, working closely with the Rev. Horace Bushnell [*q.v.*]. He was one of the promoters as well as the designer of the Cedar Hill Cemetery.

In 1870, soon after he had moved his home and his office to New York City, he published his *Beautifying Country Homes; A Handbook of Landscape Gardening.* He spent nearly two years in a visit to Switzerland about this time. In 1874 he entered into a working agreement with Frederick Law Olmsted [*q.v.*]. With Olm-sted he was engaged on a number of important works, such as the grounds of the Schuylkill reservoir in Philadelphia, and Congress Spring Park, Saratoga. He was also employed upon the Hot Springs reservation in Arkansas, the grounds of the state capitol at Des Moines, Iowa, and those of the state hospital, St. Lawrence, N. Y., and upon many other public and private works, sometimes alone and sometimes in col-laboration with Olmsted. A pioneer in the move-ment for the cemetery in which enclosures are discarded, monuments restricted, and the whole kept in the nature of a park, in 1881 he wrote a two-part article for the *American Architect and Building News* (Sept. 17, 24) which was a plea for the "modern" cemetery, and in 1888 pub-lished *Modern Cemeteries.* It was Weidenmann's intention to compile and publish illustrations of his designs in a volume to be called "American Garden Architecture." He actually prepared for publication many plates, illustrating details, but the work was never completed. Many of the plates are now on file in the New York Public Library. At the time of his death he was laying out Pope Park in Hartford. Of a genial, kindly nature, he kept throughout his life his youthful optimism and his cheerful trust in men. At his death, on Feb. 6, 1893, he was survived by his widow, Anna Marguerite Svàcher, and three daughters.

[Sources include a manuscript biog. by Weidenmann's daughter and other unpublished data in possession of Fine Arts Dept., N. Y. Pub. Lib.; R. F. Wyrick, in *The Cemetery Handbook* (rev. ed., 1932); F. L. Olmsted, Jr., and Theodora Kimball, *Frederick Law Olmsted* (2 vols., 1922–28); G. A. Parker, in *Parks and Recreation*, Oct. 1919, which contains many errors; obituary notice, *Garden and Forest*, Mar. 8, 1893.]

K. McN.

WEIDIG, ADOLF (Nov. 28, 1867–Sept. 23, 1931), composer, teacher, and conductor, was born in Hamburg, Germany, the son of Ferdinand and Hulda (Albrecht) Weidig. His father was a trombonist for thirty-eight years in the City Theatre orchestra at Hamburg. He received his general education in the schools of that city, and began to study violin at the age of twelve with Johannes Jagan, a member of the City Opera orchestra. From 1882 to 1887 he studied in the Hamburg Conservatory with K. L. Bargheer (violin), Hugo Riemann (theory and composition), and J. von Bernuth (piano). When he was sixteen years of age he became a member of the Hamburg Philharmonic Orchestra and played under famous conductors. He entered the Munich Conservatory in 1887 and became a pupil of Rheinberger (harmony, theory, and composition) and Abel (violin), graduating in 1891. In the meantime, 1888, he had composed a string quartet that won for him the Frankfort "Mozart Prize," yielding an annual allowance of 1800 marks for four years. In June 1892, he came to America and settled in Chicago. His abilities as a violinist enabled him at once to enter the Chicago Symphony Orchestra, then the Thomas Orchestra, and he remained a member of the first violin section from 1892 to 1896, when he resigned to devote himself to teaching.

In 1893 he joined the American Conservatory of Music in Chicago, as teacher of violin and theory, and from 1907 till his death he was an associate director of this school. In the course of a few years he became widely known as an original thinker and a distinguished teacher, especially of theory and composition. His scholarly and comprehensive treatise, *Harmonic Material and Its Uses* (1923), was the result of long research and practical experience. His devotion to chamber music led him to become a member (1893–1901) of the string quartet of Theodore Spiering [q.v.], in which he played viola. After 1900 he rarely played the violin in public, but he often appeared as an orchestral conductor, especially of his own compositions.

His compositions cover a wide field and show a fine mastery of all the musical means of expression. Though he was sympathetic to the modern musical idioms and encouraged his students to use them, his own style belonged rather to the conservative wing of modernism. He early displayed creative ability and, while a student at Munich, wrote a Symphony in C Minor and an overture, "Sappho," the latter having been performed by the Thomas Orchestra at the Columbian Exposition in Chicago, 1893. He wrote about twenty-five songs and the songcycle "The Buccaneer" and numerous pieces for piano, for violin and for chorus, three string quartets (in D minor, A, and C minor), a string quintet, a piano trio, a suite for violin and piano, *Opus* 21, Romanza for the cello, *Opus* 14, and Serenade for strings, *Opus* 16. His large orchestral works are: "Semiramis," *Opus* 33 (first performance, 1906), a symphonic fantasy based on a poem by Edwin Markham; "Drei Episoden," *Opus* 38 (1908), based on Clärchen's song from Goethe's *Egmont*; Symphonic Suite in three movements (1914); and "Concert Overture," *Opus* 65 (1919). The Chicago Symphony Orchestra gave first performances of all these except the "Concert Overture" which was played by the Minneapolis Symphony Orchestra with Weidig conducting. In the winter and spring of 1909 Weidig visited Germany and conducted several of his orchestral works, mainly the "Drei Episoden," in Berlin, Hamburg, Frankfort, and Wiesbaden, winning highly favorable citicisms. His compositions are scholarly and brilliantly scored.

On June 29, 1896, he was married to Helen Ridgway, of Hinsdale, Ill., who survived him at the time of his death at Hinsdale. He was a man of genial disposition, of wide information and broad sympathies.

[Information from the family; *Who's Who in America*, 1930–31; *Grove's Dict. of Music and Musicians*, Am. Supp. (1930); *Hugo Riemanns Musik Lexikon* (11th ed., 1929); *Chicago Daily Tribune*, Sept. 24, 1931.]

R. G. C.

WEIDNER, REVERE FRANKLIN (Nov. 22, 1851–Jan. 6, 1915), Lutheran theologian, was born at Center Valley, Pa., the son of William Peter and Eliza Ann (Blank) Weidner. His family was of Pennsylvania German stock, the original American ancestor having been John Weidner, who came to America from the Palatinate in the early part of the eighteenth century. He was graduated from Muhlenberg College, Allentown, Pa., in 1869, and from the Lutheran Theological Seminary, at Mt. Airy, Philadelphia, in 1873. He was ordained the same year. From 1873 to 1878 he was pastor of Grace

Church, Phillipsburg, N. J., and from 1875 to 1877 he spent part of his time teaching in Muhlenberg College. His next pastorate, 1878–82, was at St. Luke's Church, Philadelphia. From 1882 to 1891 he was professor of dogmatics and exegesis in Augustana College and Theological Seminary, Rock Island, Ill. When the Chicago Lutheran Seminary was founded in 1891 in Chicago (now at Maywood, Ill.), he was elected the first president, and acted in this capacity until his death, with the exception of one year as teaching emeritus. Weidner was a great believer in the ecclesiastic future of the West, where he especially learned to know the church life of Lutherans of Swedish antecedents. He believed it his province to train men for the ministry and not to guide the affairs of the organized church. He was rarely found on the general committees or the boards of the church, and found it difficult to sit through the tedious detail of an ecclesiastical assembly.

At the beginning of his teaching career, he leaned heavily on Anglican writers like C. J. Ellicott and J. B. Lightfoot, but later shifted to Lutheran German theologians of the conservative, confessional type. He aimed at bringing the church in America into closer contact with the theological mind of ancient historical seats of Lutheranism. He thought he could reach this goal by writing textbooks on Lutheran theology in English. He became a prodigious compiler. His *Theological Encyclopaedia* (3 vols., 1885–91) is a combination of the work of K. R. Hagenbach and Charles Porterfield Krauth [*q.v.*] on this subject, which he regarded as one of the most important branches taught in a theological seminary. The bibliographies in this work are extended, but scarcely critical. His *Biblical Theology of the New Testament* (2 vols., 1886) works with the findings of B. Weiss. His *A System of Christian Ethics* (1891) is a self-contradictory tome; as all his other works, it is not a logical unity, but an aggregate of notions of various origins.

Weidner visited Europe several times. He observed the curricula of Continental universities, but left no evidence that he understood the prevailing spirit of European university instruction or scholarship, since in his own teaching he stressed textbook, recitation, and bulky assignments. His best effort as a writer of textbooks was *An Introductory New Testament Greek Method* (1889) on which he collaborated with William R. Harper [*q.v.*]. Weidner traveled much in the interests of the Seminary and on lecture tours, working with Dwight L. Moody [*q.v.*], in Northfield, Vt., and with Harper on

Chautauqua programs. He was an excellent preacher, his sermons being of the expository order, rich in applications. He was one of the founders of the *Lutheran Church Review,* but limited his contributions to book reviews. He was high-hearted and straightforward, liked to rule and was at times intolerant. A monument to his executive ability and faith is the Chicago Theological Seminary, the innermost creation of his heart. On July 10, 1873, he was married to Emma Salome Jones of Philadelphia. They had one child. He died in Tangerine, Fla., where he had gone to better his health.

[*Who's Who in America,* 1914–15; H. H. Widener, *The Wideners in America* (1904); *The Luth. World Almanac and Encyc., 1931–33* (1932); biog. sketch by T. E. Schmauk, in *Luth. Ch. Rev.,* Apr. 1915, and by G. P. Lottich, in *Luth. Ch. Work,* Jan. 28, 1915; see also, *Ibid.,* Feb. 11, 1915.]   J. O. E.

WEIGHTMAN, WILLIAM (Sept. 30, 1813–Aug. 25, 1904), chemist, manufacturer, and financier, was born at Waltham, Lincolnshire, England, a son of William Weightman and Anne (Farr) Weightman. When sixteen years of age, he emigrated to America at the suggestion of an uncle, John Farr, who was the founder of the firm of Farr & Kunzi, established at Philadelphia in 1818 to manufacture chemicals. In 1836 the firm became Farr, Powers & Weightman, and after Farr's death in 1847, Powers & Weightman. Under the latter name it attained international recognition among manufacturing chemists. Weightman at first acted as chemist for the firm, but after the death of Powers in 1878 he assumed full charge of the business management as well. He continued in active charge until shortly before his death in 1904. The success of the firm, which was one of the earliest of its kind in America, and the leadership it attained were due largely to the enterprise, ingenuity, and skill of Weightman. The firm early became known for the introduction of new chemicals and the development of processes of manufacture. Weightman was the first to manufacture quinine sulphate, and it was through his efforts that the cheaper alkaloids of cinchona, cinchonidine and cinchonine, became favorably known and widely used as substitutes for quinine at a time when the price of the latter was almost prohibitive. The firm is also credited with having introduced and perfected the manufacture of citric acid in the United States.

As a result of sound management over a period of many years, the business of the firm yielded generous profits, and Weightman amassed a fortune. This was augmented by investments in property so extensive and so profitable that he became the largest real estate owner in Philadelphia and was popularly known as the wealthiest man in Pennsylvania in his time. In addition to being the head of his firm, he was director of the Philadelphia Trust Company, the Northern Trust Company, and the Commercial National Bank. From a professional standpoint, his only interest, other than that manifested in the affairs of his firm, is represented by his connection with the Philadelphia College of Pharmacy, of which he was a member from 1856 until his death. He was a member of the Pennsylvania Historical Society, the Pennsylvania Horticultural Society, and the Franklin Institute. He took no part in social functions or public affairs, but apparently derived his pleasures from his home and his recreation from the cultivation of rare flowering plants at his country home, Ravenhill, in Germantown. On Mar. 17, 1841, he married Louise Stelwagon, by whom he had two sons and a daughter. He died on Aug. 25, 1904, survived by his daughter.

[E. P. Oberholtzer, *Phila., a Hist. of the City and Its People* (1912), vol. III; *Am. Jour. of Pharmacy,* Apr. 1905; *Merck's Report,* July 1927, p. 111; *The First Century of the Am. Coll. of Pharmacy* (1922); obituary in *Pub. Ledger* (Phila.), Aug. 26, 1904.]

A. G. D–M.

WEIL, RICHARD (Oct. 15, 1876–Nov. 19, 1917), physician, medical research worker, was born in New York City, the son of Leopold and Matilda (Tanzer) Weil. His early education was obtained mainly at home and at private schools. Entering Columbia University, where he was graduated A.B. in the class of 1896, he attracted attention by his intellectual versatility, and was offered opportunities for advancement in teaching in several of its departments. He was early attracted to medical research, and with this in mind he devoted much time to biological work. His medical education was obtained at the College of Physicians and Surgeons in New York, where he was graduated in 1900. After a two-year internship in the German Hospital he went to Europe, where he spent a year and a half in the clinics and laboratories of Vienna and Strassburg. In 1904 he returned to New York to practise and to pursue medical investigation.

In 1905 he was appointed demonstrator in pathology at Cornell Medical College, and in 1908, assistant in experimental pathology. Two years later he was promoted to instructor in experimental therapeutics, and in 1911 assistant professor in the same department. In 1915 he was made assistant professor of experimental pathology, which department was merged the next year with that of experimental medicine with Weil at its head. He held this position until his death. From 1904 to 1910 he was adjunct pathologist to the German Hospital. From 1908 to 1913 he was on the staff of the Mount Sinai hospital, and for about the same period served the Montefiore Home. In 1906 he joined the staff of the Huntington Fund for Cancer Research. Working at the Loomis Laboratory, he devoted himself to the field of the serology of cancer and to the general problems of immunity, a field in which he gained an international reputation. In 1910 he devised an exceptionally delicate clinical test for luetic infection, based upon blood hemolysis by cobra venom. Working upon the subject of anaphylaxis, he promulgated the theory that sensitization is essentially cellular in origin and adduced a wealth of demonstration and argument in its support. His most practical contribution to clinical medicine was the method of transfusing citrated blood, which he perfected and employed.

He was a member of the American Society for the Control of Cancer, the American Society of Clinical Investigation, and the Association of American Physicians. He held the office of vice-president of the American Association for Cancer Research and served as president of the Society of Serology and Hemotology and of the American Association of Immunologists. The council of the American Association of Cancer Research charged him with the duty of establishing the *Journal of Cancer Research* in 1915, of which he was managing editor until his death. He was an associate editor of the *Journal of Immunology* and of the *American Review of Tuberculosis.* Beginning in 1899, he contributed over sixty articles to the journal literature of clinical and experimental medicine.

Shortly after the entrance of the United States into the World War in 1917, he offered his services to the government and was commissioned a captain in the medical reserve corps. After a short service at Fort Benjamin Harrison, Ind., he was promoted to the grade of major and assigned as chief of the medical service at the base hospital at Camp Wheeler, Macon, Ga. He died there of pneumonia after little more than a month of service. He was married in 1905 to Minnie, daughter of Isador Strauss of New York, who, with three children, survived him.

[*Jour. of Cancer Research,* Jan. 1918, with list of Weil's writings; *Jour. of Immunology,* Jan. 1918; *Medic. Record* (N. Y.), Nov. 24, 1917; *N. Y. Medic. Jour.,* Nov. 24, 1917; H. A. Kelly and W. L. Burrage, *Am. Medic. Biogs.* (1920); *Science,* Dec. 7, 1917; *Jour. Am. Medic. Asso.,* Dec. 1, 1917; *N. Y. Times,* Nov. 20, 1917; War Dept. records.]   J. M. P–n.

WEIR, JOHN FERGUSON (Aug. 28, 1841–Apr. 8, 1926), artist and teacher, was born at West Point, N. Y., the son of Robert Walter [*q.v.*] and Louisa (Ferguson) Weir. He attended private schools and was tutored by various instructors at the United States Military Academy. He was taught painting by his father and at the National Academy of Design in New York City. Early in the sixties he had a studio of his own in the Tenth Street Studio Building, and was grouped with the "Hudson River School." He married Mary Hannah French, the daughter of the Rev. John W. French, D.D., the chaplain at West Point, on May 17, 1866. His pictures, "The Interior of an Artist's Studio" and "The Gun Foundry," are said to have led to his election as an Associate of the National Academy of Design in 1864 and as an Academician in 1866. During 1868 and 1869 he was in Europe, returning to become the first director of the School of Fine Arts at Yale University, which had been established in 1866. He was professor of painting and design until 1877, and William Leffingwell Professor from 1877 until his retirement in 1913. His masterpiece is probably "Forging the Shaft," owned by the Metropolitan Museum of Art, New York City. He was awarded a bronze medal at the Exposition Universelle in Paris in 1900. Following his retirement Weir and his wife lived in Providence, R. I.

Weir's paintings include *genre,* landscapes, portraits, and flower-pieces. His early studies of industry are the best examples of the first group, "Forging the Shaft" still ranking high among the representations of man in opposition to machinery. "Three Trees," in the Corcoran Gallery in Washington, is a charming landscape, and "East Rock," in the Yale Gallery of Fine Arts, a fine study of rock formation. Many portraits of colleagues are preserved at Yale and the University Club of New York. Admiral Farragut, Elihu Vedder, the painter, and Paul Sabatier, the French savant, likewise sat for portraits. Perhaps the two most notable are those of Weir's cousin, Dr. Robert F. Weir [*q.v.*], at the College of Physicians and Surgeons, New York, and of S. Wells Williams of Yale. "Roses," owned by Nathaniel Vose, Boston, illustrates his flower studies. Always the able craftsman, Weir achieved in his earlier works what a critic of the seventies called "ideal reality." Later his palette took on the lighter tonality of the Impressionist, with a cool green the characteristic note. Weir modelled statues of Benjamin Silliman, the elder (1884), and President Woolsey for sites on the Yale campus, the fountain on the New Haven Green, and the Lafayette plaque on the Pinchot Building, Milford, Pa.

Aside from his art, Weir's activities centered on the development of the Yale School of Fine Arts, where he sought to meet the needs of those who desired both technical and appreciative approaches to the fine arts. The collection of casts, the Alden collection of Belgian woodcarvings, and the Jarves collection of Italian primitives were acquired at his instance, and a chair of architecture was eventually established. A prize scholarship was named in his honor in 1889, and in 1924 the department of architecture was moved into Weir Hall. With a keenly religious nature, Weir sought to clarify spiritual truths in such a manner that they might be discussed as freely as scientific theories; *The Way: the Nature and Means of Revelation* (1889) and *Human Destiny in the Light of Revelation* (1903) were written with this intention. His *John Trumbull* (1901) is still a definitive critique of an early American artist. As a member of the Century Association of New York he delivered an address at the memorial meeting in honor of the artist, Sanford Robinson Gifford [*q.v.*]; he gave the principal address at the fiftieth anniversary of the Yale School of Fine Arts in 1916; and he lectured and wrote extensively on artistic matters throughout his career. Distinguished in his later years by his white hair, moustache, and goatee, his ruddy complexion, and his military step, Weir left a distinct impression on his contemporaries. His appearance is ably suggested in the etching (reproduced in *International Studio,* September 1926) by his brother, J. Alden Weir [*q.v.*]. He was a Scotch mystic, a man of broad culture, and a gracious and charming social being. He and his wife are reported to have lived a romance lasting almost sixty years. He died in Providence, survived by his wife and two daughters, and was buried in New Haven.

[See *Who's Who in America, 1924–25*; *Yale Alumni Weekly,* Apr. 16, 1926, pp. 827, 828; H. T. Tuckerman, *Book of the Artists* (1867); F. J. Mather, *The Am. Spirit in Art* (1927); Samuel Isham, *The Hist. of Am. Painting* (1905); J. L. Chamberlain, ed., *Universities and their Sons* (1899), vol. II, p. 593; obituary in *Providence Jour.,* Apr. 9, 1926. There is a coll. of letters and docs. in the Yale School of Fine Arts, and a coll. of photographs of Weir's works in the N. Y. Pub. Lib. Information has been supplied by Dean E. V. Meeks of the Yale School of Fine Arts, by Mrs. J. D. Perry, Weir's daughter, by W. W. Williams, by A. P. Stokes, and by Irene Weir, Weir's niece, who is preparing a critical biog. of Robert W., John F., and J. Alden Weir. The letters of John F. and J. Alden Weir are being edited by the latter's daughter, Mrs. Mahonri Young.]   W. S. R.

WEIR, JULIAN ALDEN (Aug. 30, 1852– Dec. 8, 1919), painter, was born at West Point, N. Y. His mother was Susan (Bayard); his father, Robert Walter Weir [*q.v.*]. As the youngest of sixteen children he could not have received particular preferment, but he was given every encouragement to further his desire to become an artist. Guided by his father in his early efforts, at eighteen he went to New York to study at the National Academy of Design, and in 1873 he was admitted to the atelier of Gérôme in Paris. In Paris he met Jules Bastien-Lepage, who introduced him to French country life at his home in Damvilliers, journeyed with him to study the Flemish masters in Belgium, and facilitated greatly his *entrée* into the artistic life of Paris. Under Bastien-Lepage's influence Weir began to work directly from nature and to study the great masters of realism, not only in French galleries but in Holland (1874) and Spain (1876), where Velasquez revealed to him a new comprehension of the visible world as manifested in light and values, and furthered his understanding of the work of Manet and Whistler, then being newly acclaimed. His "French Peasant" (1875) shows that at the early age of twenty-three he had an admirable control of his medium and a decided power of visual concentration.

Returning to New York in 1877, he occupied a studio in the Benedict Building, where he painted one of his first pictures to win general recognition—"The Muse of Music" (1882–84), now in the Lotos Club, New York. During trips in Belgium and Holland in 1880–81 with such companions as his brother John [*q.v.*], Bastien-Lepage, and John Twachtman, who was to become a lifelong friend and artistic companion, he purchased for Erwin Davis, the collector, examples of contemporary French masters. It is a tribute to Weir's critical vision and appreciation that he secured the "Woman with a Parrot" and "Boy with a Sword" by Manet and the "Jean d'Arc" by Bastien-Lepage, now in the Metropolitan Museum. At a later time he acquired for Marquand the famous Rembrandt "Portrait of a Man," also in the Metropolitan. About 1883, after nearly ten years of intermittent foreign travel and study, he settled definitely in New York, where he had a studio in the old Tenth Street Building, and became associated with such younger painters as Edwin Abbey, John Twachtman, Theodore Robinson, Albert P. Ryder, William M. Chase [*qq.v.*], and Childe Hassam. His residence abroad had gained him the friendship of J. A. M. Whistler, John Singer Sargent [*qq.v.*], and other painters of international distinction. On Apr. 24, 1883, he married Anna Dwight Baker, daughter of Charles Taintor Baker and Anna Bartlet Dwight, by whom he had three daughters; after his wife's

death he married her sister, Ella Baker, in October 1893.

Spending half the year in the country, alternating between two Connecticut estates, one at Windham, the other at Branchville, Weir passed a tranquil existence in the study of nature, in the companionship of his family and friends, in fishing, hunting, and other rural occupations. Called Julian by his family and intimate friends, but known otherwise as J. Alden Weir, he was universally loved and esteemed. Of impressive appearance, stalwart of build, in feature patterned after the Greek ideal, he was entirely natural, modest, and unaffected in manner. The bust by Olin L. Warner [*q.v.*] is an admirable likeness. In younger life Weir was opposed to the official school of the Academy, and was one of the strong influences in the formation of the Society of American Artists. Later, when the artistic tendency of the two organizations became similar and a consolidation was effected, he resumed exhibiting in the National Academy of Design. He had become a member in 1886, and served as president (1915–17). He was one of the founders in 1898 of Ten American Painters. From 1882 onward he received numerous awards both at home and abroad, one of the latest being the gold medal of the Pennsylvania Academy in 1916 in recognition of his eminent services to American art. He died in New York City of heart failure. A memorial exhibition of his work was held at the Metropolitan Museum of Art in 1924.

In the early period of Weir's painting one sees something of the eclectic. There is little evidence of Gérôme's influence, but "Children Burying a Bird" and other occasional examples show the effect of the naturalistic manner of Bastien-Lepage, not only in a precise realism and a painstaking craftsmanship but also in the predilection for the soft greys and grey-greens which reflect the palette of the French master. Several distinguished portraits, painted in the traditional manner of the studio, exemplify his skilled draftsmanship and highly developed technique, while the studies of his hunting dogs reveal an affectionate understanding and masterful characterization, and the "Still Life with Roses" (illustrated in *Art in America, post*) is set apart by its austere reserve, its imposing design, and the loving and reverential spirit with which it is painted. The French Impressionists and the growing interest in light and color had in the early years of development made a very deep and lasting influence on the style and method of Weir's painting. This became apparent in his show at the American Art Galleries in 1893, where he exhibited in conjunction with Twachtman and the French painters Monet and Besnard. But he was not an Impressionist in the limited sense; his art is more directly related to that of Whistler and to the decorative influence of the Japanese.

His art is decidedly lyrical and intimate. Extremely versatile in the sense that he was a painter of portraits, of *genre,* of still life, and of landscape, using the varied media of oil, water color, pastel, and etching, he nevertheless conceived his pictures within very definite limitations. Never aspiring to the grand manner or the large surface, he was concerned solely with esthetic attributes. His conception was expressed in terms of spatial arrangement, simplification of form, and harmonization of tone, and the very personal way in which he elevated the seemingly commonplace aspect of nature to the realm of highly expressive art. In all his painting there is reflected his own restraint, sincerity, and reasonableness, as well as his subtlety of observation and his delicacy of feeling. He experimented constantly with technique, and his ultimate style is far removed from the early influence of his friend Bastien-Lepage. The color is subdued, marked by neutralized hues of closely related values; the form is manifested by a universal lighting that eliminates strong contrasts; the pigment is applied with short impasto brushwork. The thematic reserve made his style somewhat mannered, but his work has always an unexplainable distinction and charm. Many of his best-known pictures are hung in the Metropolitan Museum, New York, the Art Institute of Chicago, and in the galleries in Washington, D. C.

[See *Who's Who in America,* 1918–19; Weir's semi-autobiog. article on Bastien-Lepage in *Modern French Masters* (1896), ed. by J. C. Van Dyke; Century Asso., *Julian Alden Weir, an Appreciation of His Life and Works* (1921), which contains a list of his works compiled by his daughter; E. H. Blashfield, *Commemorative Tribute to Julian Alden Weir* (1922); Suzanne La Follette, *Art in America* (1929); Samuel Isham, *The Hist. of Am. Painting* (1905); Eliot Clark, in *Art in America,* Aug. 1920; Margery A. Ryerson, *Ibid.,* with list of etchings; H. R. Butler, in *Scribner's Mag.,* Jan. 1916; Duncan Phillips, in *Am. Mag. of Art,* Apr. 1917; Kenyon Cox, in *Burlington Mag.,* May 1909; Frank Weitenkampf, *Am. Graphic Art* (1912); Metropolitan Museum, *Memorial Exhibition of the Works of Julian Alden Weir* (1924); Agnes Zimmerman, *An Essay towards a Catalogue Raisonné of the Etchings . . . of Julian Alden Weir* (1923); obituary in *N. Y. Times,* Dec. 9, 1919, editorial, Dec. 10. Biog. details have been verified by Mrs. Mahonri Young, Weir's daughter.]   E. C.

WEIR, ROBERT FULTON (Feb. 16, 1838–Apr. 6, 1927), surgeon, was the son of James Weir, a prominent pharmacist of New York, and Mary Anne (Shapter) Weir. His grandfather, Robert Walter Weir, was a prosperous merchant, who came to America from Scotland. His mother was of English ancestry. Weir was born in New York City, and his early education was obtained in the public schools. In 1854 he graduated from the College of the City of New York, then the Free Academy, and in 1857 was accorded the M.A. degree from the same institution. During this time he clerked for his father and acquired a considerable knowledge of medicines and their uses, as well as a desire to enter the medical profession. He received the M.D. degree from the College of Physicians and Surgeons, New York, in 1859, having supplemented his courses of study with practical experience in the office of Dr. Gurdon Buck [*q.v.*]. He had also been allowed to make the morning rounds with the house surgeon of the New York Hospital, and for the two years following his graduation, he served as house surgeon there.

In 1861 he entered the United States Army as assistant surgeon and continued in service until the close of the war. His work as the head of one of the largest of the government hospitals, at Frederick, Md., was publicly acknowledged by the surgeon-general. When the war ended, he commenced a general practice in New York City. He was appointed surgeon to St. Luke's Hospital and, from 1873 to 1883, one of the attending surgeons of the new Roosevelt Hospital. From 1876 to 1900 he was attending surgeon to the New York Hospital, but resigned in that year to take charge of the surgical service at the Roosevelt Hospital. From 1870 to 1875 he was professor of surgery at the Woman's Medical College, and in 1883 he became clinical professor of surgery at the College of Physicians and Surgeons and professor from 1892 to 1903. In 1907 he retired completely from public professional life.

Weir was one of the most brilliant surgeons of his time. Dr. W. W. Keen wrote of him: "Weir was a capital operator, careful, judicious and resourceful. I have hardly known a better one. . . . He was indeed a Master Surgeon" (Bradshaw, *post,* p. 508). His operations were often witnessed by many physicians desiring to learn from his technique. Especially notable was his work in connection with surgery of the joints and intestines. He was among the first to recognize duodenal ulcer as an entity. He made an important modification of the Murphy button for its use in gastroenterostomy, and was among the first to adopt Lister's method of antiseptic and aseptic surgery. His contributions to medical literature were many. His thesis at graduation, "Hernia Cerebri," won a prize of $50. In his *Personal Reminiscences* (*post*) are the titles of his papers which describe surgical procedures or operations originated by him. For a list of his many contributions to medical journals, see Shrady (*post*). He served as president of many professional organizations, among them the Practitioners' Society of New York, 1883–84; New York Surgical Society, 1884–85; American Surgical Association, 1899–1900, and the New York Academy of Medicine, 1901–02. He was also a member of the Société de Chirurgie of Paris, and was one of very few to receive an honorary degree from the Royal College of Surgeons in London in 1900.

Forceful, energetic, commanding, Weir gave himself completely to his profession. For hobbies he tried tennis and whist, but felt little enthusiasm for them. His later years were spent for the most part in extensive traveling.

He was twice married: to Maria Washington McPherson of Virginia, on Oct. 2, 1863, and to Mary Badgley Alden of Albany on Nov. 7, 1895. A daughter by his first wife survived him. His portrait by his cousin, John F. Weir [*q.v.*], hangs in the New York Academy of Medicine. Robert Walter Weir [*q.v.*] was his uncle.

[*Who's Who in America*, 1926–27; R. F. Weir, *Pers. Reminiscences of the N. Y. Hospital from 1856 to 1900* (1917); J. J. Walsh, *Hist. of Med. in N. Y.* (1919), vol. V; *Coll. of Physicians and Surgeons, N. Y., A Hist.*, ed. by John Shrady; *Am. Jour. of Surgery*, May 1927; J. H. Bradshaw, article in *Surgery, Gynecology and Obstetrics*, Feb. 1930; *N. Y. Times*, Apr. 7, 1927.]
J. A. H.

WEIR, ROBERT WALTER (June 18, 1803–May 1, 1889), painter and teacher, was born in New Rochelle, N. Y., the son of Mary (Brinkley) and Robert Walter Weir. His father, a native of Paisley, Scotland, settled in New York about 1790, engaged in mercantile and shipping pursuits, and maintained a country-seat in New Rochelle. At ten, as the result of his father's reverses in business, Weir went to work in a cotton factory. He spent the year 1815 in Albany with an uncle, continuing his education there and in New York City, where he made the acquaintance of John Wesley Jarvis [*q.v.*]. In 1817 he entered a mercantile house in the South, and then held a clerical position in New York. For a few months he was instructed by Robert Cook, an English painter in heraldry, between six and eight in the morning, before going to work. In 1821 he turned his entire attention to painting, beginning with a successful copy of a portrait. An early triumph was entitled "Paul Preaching at Athens." He studied anatomy and acquired a knowledge of Italian, and late in 1824, under the patronage of Henry Carey, he

left for Italy, illustrating much of Dante's *Inferno* on the way. In Florence he became a pupil of Pietro Benvenuti, who was frescoing the Pitti Palace, and completed a "Christ and Nicodemus" and an "Angel Relieving Peter" before leaving for Rome a year later. There he lived with Horatio Greenough [*q.v.*], the sculptor, on the Pincian Hill. Returning to America after three years abroad, he opened a studio in New York. He was elected a member of the National Academy of Design in 1829.

In the same year he married Louisa Ferguson. He succeeded Charles Robert Leslie [*q.v.*] in 1834 as instructor in drawing at the United States Military Academy, becoming professor in 1846. Between 1836 and 1840 he was engaged on "The Embarkation of the Pilgrims" for the rotunda of the Capitol, Washington, basing his design on Nathaniel Morton's *New Englands Memoriall* (1669). With the $10,000 he received from this commission he erected a stone church of his own design at Highland Falls, near West Point, the Church of the Holy Innocents, in memory of his two deceased children. Following the death of his wife, Louisa, in 1845 he married Susan Bayard. He had sixteen children, including the two eminent painters, John Ferguson Weir and Julian Alden Weir [*qq.v.*]. He retired after a service of forty-two years in 1876, maintaining a studio in New York until his death. His personality aroused the lasting affection of the generations of students he instructed, among them Grant, Lee, Sherman, and the painter Whistler. His friendliness to his fellow-artists is mentioned a number of times by William Dunlap [*q.v.*], and his ardent churchmanship following his studies for "The Embarkation" by a number of chroniclers. A portrait of Weir by Daniel Huntington [*q.v.*] hangs in the library of the Military Academy.

Weir's works include illustrations, portraits, and "cabinet *genre*." Examples of the first group are the designs for George P. Morris' *The Deserted Bride* (1853) and "The Drawing Book" in the *American Juvenile Keepsake* for 1835; quaint and sentimental they now appear. His portraits include "Red Jacket," the last chief of the Senecas, "General Winfield Scott," now owned by the Metropolitan Museum of Art, and "Governor Throop" and "Mayor Lee," both of the latter in the New York City Hall. His *genre* studies were literary, historical, scenic, and religious in their subject-matter and largely incidental in their interest. The novels of Scott and Cooper, the country of Italy and the Hudson River, the Bible, the Church, and contemporary political history were explored for subjects. On occasion he painted realistically, as in "The Boat Club," or the "Church of the Holy Innocents, Highland Falls." He designed an altarpiece for the Church of the Holy Cross, Troy, N. Y., the allegorical "War" and "Peace" in the old chapel at West Point, and stained-glass windows for Trinity Chapel and Calvary Church, New York City. Many water-colors came from his studio as well, and he was an assiduous collector of fine prints and engravings.

Criticisms of Weir's work follow in a general way the taste of the critic's own generation. For example, the Rev. S. G. Bulfinch in *A Discourse Suggested by Weir's Picture of the Embarkation of the Pilgrims* (1844) speaks of "The Embarkation" as a "living representation of a most memorable scene," and the sculptor Greenough criticizes chiefly the placing of the highlights. H. T. Tuckerman (1867) praises the composition and historicity of the mural, but notes a dryness of tone. On the other hand, he admires the "Flemish authenticity" of the "Child's Evening Prayer." James Jackson Jarves [*q.v.*] is remarkably anticipatory of later criticisms when he says that Weir showed "considerable skill of manipulation and detail, facility of composition, and those composite qualities which make up an accomplished rather than an original man" (*post*, p. 230).

[See William Dunlap, *A Hist. of the Rise and Progress of the Arts of Design in the U. S.* (3 vols., 1918), ed. by F. W. Bayley and C. E. Goodspeed, which contains autobiog. material; H. T. Tuckerman, *Book of the Artists* (1867); J. J. Jarves, *The Art-Idea* (1864); G. W. Cullum, *Biog. Reg. . . . Officers and Grads. U. S. Mil. Acad.*, vol. I (1891), p. 38; cat. of sale of contents of Weir's studio, N. Y., Feb. 19–21, 1891, in N. Y. Pub. Lib.; obituary and death notice in *N. Y. Times*, May 3, 1889. A crit. study of Weir and his two artist sons is being prepared by Irene Weir.]

W. S. R.

WEISENBURG, THEODORE HERMAN (Apr. 10, 1876–Aug. 3, 1934), neurologist, the son of Herman and Sally (Schwartz) Weisenburg, was born in Budapest, Austro-Hungary, and brought to the United States by his parents who settled first in New York City and later in Bethlehem, Pa. He obtained his preliminary education in the public schools of New York and of Bethlehem, and entered the School of Technology of Lehigh University where he studied chemistry for two years. He then matriculated in the School of Medicine at the University of Pennsylvania, and was graduated in 1899 with the M.D. degree. After a short internship at the Lackawanna Hospital, Scranton, Pa., and a longer one as a resident physician at the Philadelphia Hospital (Blockley), in Philadelphia, Pa., he joined the United States Army in January 1901 and served in the Philippines until No-

vember 1902. He returned to Philadelphia and during the succeeding year and a half worked as a general practitioner in that city. He was registrar to the nervous wards of the Philadelphia General Hospital, 1903–04, and assistant neurologist until 1907 when he was appointed a neurologist and consultant to the department for the insane. He was instructor in neurology and neuropathology in the School of Medicine of the University of Pennsylvania from 1904 until 1907 when he was elected professor of neurology in the Medico-Chirurgical College in Philadelphia. After this institution was absorbed by the University of Pennsylvania he was appointed professor of neurology in the Graduate School of Medicine in July 1917. In much of his work he was associated with his close friend, Charles K. Mills [*q.v.*]. He was president of the Philadelphia Neurologic Society in 1908 and of the American Neurological Association in 1918. He took a large part in making successes of the first Anglo-American Congress of Neurology held in London in 1927 and the International Neurological Congress held in Bern in 1931, and at the time of his death he was president of the Association for Research in Nervous and Mental Diseases. He held membership in many professional societies. In 1926 he was made a corresponding member of the Verein für Psychiatrie und Neurologie in Vienna.

During the World War Weisenburg served as contract surgeon and as an executive officer, first in the Military Neuropsychiatric Training School of the Philadelphia Hospital and later as a major in the Medical Corps; he then rose to be chief of the nervous service in General Hospital No. 1 in New York City. His subsequent work as vice dean and professor of neurology of the Graduate School of Medicine of the University of Pennsylvania stands out sharply. In research and in literature the excellence of his work is amply demonstrated in his work "Comprehensive and Analytic Report on the Epidemic of Poliomyelitis in Philadelphia in 1916," published in the *Transactions of the American Neurological Association*, 1918, and in the paper on "Cerebellar Localization and its Symptomatology," read before the Royal Society of Medicine in London in 1927, and published in *Brain*, October 1927. He was a contributor to neurologic and psychiatric journals, but he was best known as the editor-in-chief of the *Archives of Neurology and Psychiatry*, a position he occupied from August 1920 until his death. His final task was a treatise on *Aphasia, a Clinical and Psychological Study* (1935), published posthumously by his collaborator, K. M. McBride. It furnished deductions as to the unified action of the brain in the formation and use of language in contrast with the extreme ideas of precise, cortical localization for the function of speech. During the period of the World War he was editor-in-chief of the *Manual of Neurosurgery,* issued by the Office of the Surgeon-General, Washington, D. C. He was consulting neuropsychiatrist to many hospitals in and near Philadelphia.

On July 4, 1909, Weisenburg was married to Mrs. Constance Van der Veer Field, the daughter of Dr. G. W. and Ann (Van der Veer) Brown. She, with their daughter, survived him. He was buried at Valley Forge, Pa.

[Personal acquaintance; information from the family; manuscript prepared by Weisenburg; institutional records; *Who's Who in America,* 1932–33; J. W. Croskey, *Hist. of Blockley* (1929); Frederick Tilney, obit. art. in *Arch. of Neurology and Psychiatry,* Oct. 1934; J. W. McConnell, in *Jour. of Nervous and Mental Disease,* Nov. 1934; C. A. Patten, in *Am. Jour. of Psychiatry,* Jan. 1935; *N. Y. Times,* Aug. 4, 1934.]

J. W. M.

WEISER, JOHANN CONRAD (Nov. 2, 1696–July 13, 1760), Indian agent, was born near Herrenberg, in Württemberg, Germany, the son of Anna Magdalena (Uebele) and Johann Conrad Weiser. His father was a magistrate of the village of Gross-Aspach and a man of some means. Following the death of his wife, the elder Weiser and eight of his children emigrated to New York in 1710 and settled at Livingston Manor. In 1714 they removed to Schoharie. Conrad spent the winter of 1713–14 with the Iroquois chief Quagnant, when he learned much of the Maqua (Mohawk) tongue and Indian customs. After his return to his family in July, he quarreled with his new step-mother, ran away the following winter, and set up a farm for himself at an Indian village near Schoharie. He served the white people as an interpreter from 1719 to 1729. On Nov. 22, 1720, he was married to Anna Eve Feck by a German Reformed clergyman. They had fifteen children. He removed his family to Tulpehocken, Pa., in 1729 and cultivated a farm, which in thirty years he increased to about a thousand acres.

When he settled at Tulpehocken, he possessed a knowledge of Indian tongues and an appreciation of Indian affairs rivaled by only a few men in the colonies. He renewed his friendship with Shikellamy [*q.v.*], the agent of the Iroquois in Pennsylvania, and for many years they worked together. He early saw the significance of the support of the Six Nations in checking French expansion in the West and convinced James Logan of this by 1730. In 1731 and 1736 he arranged for the conferences at Philadelphia, which resulted in winning the Iroquois to the

interests of the Penns. Weiser and Canasatego, the Onondaga, firmly cemented the Iroquois alliance by the treaty of 1742, although the Delaware were alienated and the Shawnee became suspicious of the Pennsylvanians (*Minutes, post.,* IV, 577–86. This abandonment of Penn's traditional policy was urged by Weiser as vital to the safety of all the colonies, even at the expense of his own. His view was imperial rather than provincial. In 1743 he averted war between the Iroquois and Virginia, and, through his influence, the Lancaster Treaty of 1744 marked a shifting of the direction of Indian affairs from New York to Pennsylvania (*Minutes, post,* IV, 709–37). In King George's War Weiser and the colony of Pennsylvania supported the Six Nations in their efforts to remain neutral and enabled them to resist the efforts of Sir William Johnson [*q.v.*], for whom Weiser had little respect. George Croghan [*q.v.*] and Weiser won over the Western tribes at the treaty of Logstown in 1748, thereby extending Pennsylvania Indian trade to the Mississippi. In 1748 Shikellamy died, and with him went Weiser's commanding position as a backwoods diplomat. He remained one of the best of the interpreters until his death, but Sir William Johnson and George Croghan superseded him in the formulation of policy. He spoke and wrote in German and in English. Several of his hymns, especially "Einweihungs-Lied" (see Weiser, *post,* pp. 401–03), and his Indian reports show literary ability. In his frontier home he maintained a music room furnished with an organ, and in his library, in addition to religious and law books, were the works of Voltaire and Arnholtz. He urged and supported the press of Christopher Sower [*q.v.*] at Germantown.

For a period of years, from 1735 to 1740 or 1741, most of his energies were absorbed in religious activity. Although born a Lutheran, in Tulpehocken he worshipped at the German Reformed Church led by John Peter Miller [*q.v.*] and by 1735 was its chief elder. Under the influence of the religious revival of 1735, Miller and Weiser formed a Baptist group and were baptized by Johann Conrad Beissel [*q.v.*] in May. Following this "religious somersault," Weiser withdrew from the world, grew a beard, and became a "teacher" at Tulpehocken. In August he removed his family to Ephrata and became a member of the cloister under the name of Brother Enoch. His children, Magdalena and Peter, also entered the cloister, but his wife returned to the farm. Weiser now endured fasts and vigils, played the part of evangelist and exhorter, and made at least two proselyting trips to New Jersey.

Beissel and Weiser quarreled, and the latter withdrew from the cloister, being incensed, it is said, among other things at receiving punishment for having four children by his wife during his celibacy. He returned later, however, and was consecrated priest by Beissel in 1740. He was also interested in the Moravian missions to the Indians and made a trip to Onondaga to aid them. In 1742 he was to save Count Zinzendorf's life at one of these missions.

In 1741 he was commissioned justice of the peace for Lancaster County, probably the only German to hold such an office in the colonial period. The following year he was made ranger for northern Lancaster County. At this time he identified himself with the governor's party by exhorting his countrymen to vote against the pacific Quakers in the coming elections. About 1743 he severed his connection with Ephrata, probably with the advice of Henry Melchior Mühlenburg [q.v.], later his son-in-law. He became a naturalized subject of Great Britain in April 1744. His vigorous support of the proprietary party led the Moravians to draw away from him. He joined the Lutheran Church in 1747, and his coreligionists electioneered for him, when he unsuccessfully ran for the Assembly against a Quaker. Upon the erection of Berks County in 1752 he was made a justice of the peace and later served as the first president-judge of the county, from 1752 to 1760. He was also a trustee of the board to educate German youths in Pennsylvania in 1753. He led an expedition on the frontier in the French and Indian War, and he was commissioned colonel in the Berks County regiment. He was one of the commissioners to lay out Reading where he went to live in 1755. There he opened his famous "White Store" and joined the Reformed Church. He lost his health gradually in the last five years of his life. He died on one of his farms, at Womelsdorf.

[Diary and a few papers in Lib. of Cong.; papers in possession of Hist. Soc. of Pa.; J. S. Walton, *Conrad Weiser and the Indian Policy of Pa.* (1900); C. Z. Weiser, *The Life of (John) Conrad Weiser* (1876); J. F. Sachse, *The German Sectarians of Pa.* (2 vols., privately printed, 1899–1900); *Chronicon Ephratense* (1786), tr. by J. M. Hark (1889); H. M. M. Richards, "The Weiser Family," *Pa. German Soc. Proc.*, vol. XXXII (1924); *Minutes of the Provincial Council of Pa.*, vols. IV, V (1851); J. B. Nolan, "Conrad Weiser's Inventory," *Pa. Mag. Hist. and Biog.*, July 1932.]
C. B—h.

WEISS, EHRICH [See HOUDINI, HARRY, 1874–1926].

WEISS, JOHN (June 28, 1818–Mar. 9, 1879), Unitarian minister, author, was born in Boston, the son of John and Mary (Galloupe) Weiss.

His grandfather, also a John Weiss, was a German Jew who had come to the United States as a political refugee and kept a tavern in Germantown, Pa. His father was a barber. Weiss lived his boyhood in Worcester, Mass., attended the public schools and Framingham Academy, and graduated in 1837 from Harvard College. At college he did not stand high in the esteem of the faculty, and was once rusticated, but his temperament—an explosive compound of wit, poetry, and religious idealism—was relished by his classmates. After teaching for a few years, he enrolled in 1840 at the Harvard Divinity School and attended, 1842–43, the University of Heidelberg. He was pastor of the Unitarian Church, Watertown, Mass., where he succeeded Convers Francis, from Oct. 25, 1843, to Oct. 3, 1845, from Mar. 23, 1846, to Dec. 6, 1847, and from June 1862 to June 1869; in the second interval, he was pastor of the First Congregational Society, New Bedford, Dec. 29, 1847, to Jan. 24, 1859. On Apr. 9, 1844, he married Sarah Fiske Jennison of Worcester, who with three sons and two daughters survived him. Impetuous in his enthusiasm, zealous for liberty—which meant open opposition to negro slavery among other things —unpredictably witty, eloquent, and satirical in his sermons, he dazzled, bewildered, and ultimately exasperated his pewholders at Watertown and New Bedford. Unable to find a congenial parish, he was compelled at various times to live on the insecure returns from writing, lecturing, and occasional preaching. He contributed articles, reviews, and poems to several magazines, especially to the *Christian Examiner,* the *Atlantic Monthly, Old and New,* and the *Galaxy,* and was one of the chief supports of Sidney H. Morse's *Radical.* His most substantial achievement was his *Life and Correspondence of Theodore Parker* (1863), which began as a short memoir, undertaken at the suggestion of Joseph Lyman, Parker's literary executor, and grew into a solid, two-volume documentary life of enduring worth. In writing it, however, Weiss incurred the displeasure of Mrs. Parker and of Franklin B. Sanborn, who claimed that Parker had appointed him his biographer. Weiss helped to introduce German literature to New England readers with *The Æsthetic Letters, Essays, and the Philosophical Letters of Schiller, Translated with an Introduction* (1845) and *Goethe's West-Easterly Divan, Translated with Introduction and Notes* (1877). His two original books are *American Religion* (1871) and *Wit, Humor, and Shakespeare: Twelve Essays* (1876), the fullest exhibitions of his high-minded, intensely subjective, somewhat disjointed thought. His conversation, like his sermons and lectures, was a cascade of wit, epigram, and poetic images. He was greatly admired by several of the leaders of his denomination, whose memoirs depict him as a religious genius. He was one of the founders in 1867 of the Free Religious Association. During the last five or six years of his life he lived in Boston, where he died.

[Henry Williams, *Memorials of the Class of 1837 of Harvard Univ.* (1887); *Boston Daily Advertiser*, Mar. 10, 1879; *Christian Register*, Mar. 29, 1879; J. H. Allen, "A Memory of John Weiss," *Unitarian Rev.*, May 1888; C. A. Bartol, "John Weiss," *Ibid.*, Apr. 1879, and "The Genius of Weiss," *Principles and Portraits* (1880); O. B. Frothingham, "John Weiss," *Unitarian Rev.*, May 1888, reprinted in *Recollections and Impressions* (1891); Mrs. J. T. Sargent, *Sketches and Reminiscences of the Radical Club* (1880); *Cat. of the Private Library of the Late John Weiss, to be Sold by Auction* (Boston, 1879); C. L. F. Gohdes, *The Periodicals of Transcendentalism* (1931); M. J. Savage, sketch in S. A. Eliot, ed., *Heralds of a Liberal Faith*, vol. III (1910); F. B. Sanborn, *Recollections of Seventy Years* (1909).]   G. H. G.

WEITZEL, GODFREY (Nov. 1, 1835–Mar. 19, 1884), soldier, engineer, was born in Cincinnati, Ohio, the son of Louis and Susan Weitzel, recent arrivals from the Bavarian Palatinate. After preparatory education in the local schools, he entered the United States Military Academy in 1851, graduated July 1, 1855, as second in a class of thirty-four, and was commissioned brevet second lieutenant of engineers. He became second lieutenant July 27, 1856, and first lieutenant, July 1, 1860.

His first duty was on the fortifications of New Orleans, 1855–59. Subsequently, until January 1861, he was assistant professor of engineering at the Military Academy. During this period his wife died as the result of burns sustained when her dress caught fire. Early in 1861 Weitzel was assigned to the engineer company on duty in Washington, and with this company he took part in the expedition to Pensacola, Fla. (Apr. 19–Sept. 17, 1861), which saved Fort Pickens to the Union. In the fall of the same year he was chief engineer of the fortifications of Cincinnati, then returned to Washington in command of an engineer company. On account of his familiarity with the defenses of New Orleans, in the spring of 1862 he was made chief engineer of General Butler's force, which coöperated with Admiral Farragut in the operations against that place. After the surrender, Apr. 30, he served as assistant military commandant of the city. Made brigadier-general of volunteers on Aug. 29, 1862, he was thereafter continuously engaged in field operations in Louisiana until December 1863. He commanded a brigade and provisional division in the siege of Port Hudson, and in the assaults of May 27 and

June 14, 1863. During this period he became captain in the regular engineer corps, and received the brevets of major and lieutenant-colonel for gallantry at Thibodeaux and Port Hudson.

In May 1864 he assumed command of the Second Division, XVIII Army Corps, in Butler's Army of the James, but was soon detached to become chief engineer of that army. In this capacity he supervised the construction of the defenses of Bermuda Hundred. In August he became brevet major-general of volunteers, and in September returned to troop duty, commanding first the XVIII and later the XXV Army Corps. He received the brevet rank of colonel in the regular service Sept. 29, 1864, for gallantry at the capture of Fort Harrison, Va., and on Nov. 17, 1864, was promoted major-general of volunteers. In December he was second in command to Butler in the first expedition against Fort Fisher, and exercised the active command of the troops sent ashore. During the final operations against Richmond his command occupied the line between the James and the Appomattox rivers, and took possession of the city upon its evacuation, Apr. 3, 1865. For service in this campaign he received the brevets of brigadier-general and major-general in the regular army. General Butler relied greatly upon him, and General Grant spoke of him as a thoroughly competent corps commander (John Russell Young, *Around the World with General Grant*, 1879, II, 304). He had much experience in command of colored troops. When first assigned to this duty, in 1862, he vigorously opposed the idea of arming slaves, and accepted the command under strong protests; but he was successful with these troops, and in 1864 and 1865 all the infantry regiments of his XXV Corps were colored.

After Lee's surrender, in the concentration of troops in Texas incident to the Maximilian episode, Weitzel commanded the Rio Grande district; but the emergency there having been terminated, he was mustered out of the volunteer service Mar. 1, 1866, and returned to duty with the Corps of Engineers, in which he became a major, Aug. 8, 1866. Thereafter until his death he was engaged in the constructive work of his corps, notably in river and harbor improvement. Of the numerous projects with which he was connected, the most important were the ship canals at the falls of the Ohio and at Sault Sainte Marie, Mich., and the lighthouse at Stannard's Rock in Lake Superior. Taking over the first of these enterprises in 1867 after much work had been done, he carried it to completion in 1873. At Sault Sainte Marie he supervised the building of what was at the time the largest lock in the world—515 feet long and eighty wide, with a lift of eighteen feet. The lighthouse, with a tower rising 101 feet above the water, involved the construction below water level of a solid concrete foundation, sixty-two feet in diameter, on top of a rock situated thirty miles from shore. In connection with his various enterprises, Weitzel made and published translations of several German works dealing with hydraulic engineering and canal construction.

He was made a lieutenant-colonel June 23, 1882, and shortly afterward, because of failing health, was transferred from the Great Lakes to less arduous duty at Philadelphia, where he died in his forty-ninth year. He was married, shortly before the close of the Civil War, to Louisa Bogen of Cincinnati, and was survived by his wife and a daughter.

[G. W. Cullum, *Biog. Reg. Officers and Grads. U. S. Mil. Acad.* (3rd ed., 1891), vol. II; *15th Ann. Reunion, Asso. Grads. U. S. Mil. Acad.* (1884); *War of the Rebellion: Official Records* (*Army*); J. F. Brennan, *A Biog. Cyc. and Portrait Gallery . . . of Ohio* (1879); *Cincinnati Past and Present* (1872); *The Biog. Encyc. of Ohio of the Nineteenth Century* (1876); *The Biog. Cyc. and Portrait Gallery . . . of Ohio*, vol. III (1884); Charles Moore, *The Saint Marys Falls Canal* (1907); *Army and Navy Jour.*, Mar. 22, 1884; *Phila. Press*, Mar. 20, 1884.]   O. L. S., Jr.

WELBY, AMELIA BALL COPPUCK (Feb. 3, 1819–May 3, 1852), author, was born in Saint Michaels, Md., the daughter of William and Mary (Shield) Coppuck. Her father served in the War of 1812. Soon after her birth her father, a contracting mason engaged in the building of lighthouses for the federal government, removed with his family to Baltimore. She spent her childhood in this city and received there such formal education as she had. When she was about fourteen the family removed to Kentucky, and Louisville became her home for the remainder of her brief life. She early displayed a facility for writing verse, and by 1837 her poems, signed "Amelia," began to appear in George D. Prentice's *Louisville Daily Journal.* Prentice gave her considerable publicity, praising her "artless melodies" and her personal charm. Her fluent verses, pleasantly touched with melancholy, suited the popular taste, and editors of other papers promptly copied her work, giving it wide circulation. In June 1838 she married George Welby, a young Englishman in business in Louisville. Their home soon became a pleasant literary center, where visitors of distinction were to be met.

During the 1840's her popularity grew. A collected edition of the *Poems* by "Amelia" was published in 1845, bound in crimson and gold, and embellished with a romantic frontispiece

illustrating "The Rainbow," one of her most admired poems. Edition after edition followed, until by 1855 fourteen had appeared. Selections from her work were printed in the anthologies made during the decade by Caroline May, T. B. Read, and R. W. Griswold. An engraving of her portrait, painted by Read, was included in his *Female Poets of America* (1848). Edgar Allan Poe (in "Literati") gave her a high place among the poetical ladies to whom he offered gallant if uncritical praise, especially commending her poem "The Bereaved" for its versification and its admirable unity of effect. Echoes of Drake, Willis, Moore, and Mrs. Hemans filled her poems. Byron she admired extravagantly and to him she addressed some lines entitled "I know Thee Not." Her range of subjects was narrow, but she pleased the general reader by the smoothness and simplicity of her verse, her appeal to the heart, and her images from nature. She died two months after the birth of her only child. She is buried in the Cave Hill Cemetery, Louisville, Ky.

[W. T. Coggeshall, *The Poets and Poetry of the West* (1864); (Cincinnati) *Ladies' Repository*, Nov. 1855; *Louisville Daily Jour.*, May 4, 1852; *Sun* (Baltimore), Jan. 22, 1905; information from the family.]
B. M. S.

WELCH, ADONIJAH STRONG (Apr. 12, 1821–Mar. 14, 1889), educator, was born at East Hampton, Conn., the son of Elizabeth (Strong) and Bliss Welch, a bell founder. On his mother's side he was a descendant of Elder John Strong who emigrated from Plymouth to America in 1630; on his father's, of William Welch (or Welsh) who moved from Nova Scotia and settled in East Hampton about the time of the Revolution. About 1839 he went to Michigan, where he prepared for college at an academy at Romeo. He received the degrees of B.A. (1846) and M.A. (1852) from the University of Michigan. In 1846–47 he studied law and was admitted to the bar, but did not practise. After serving as principal of the union school at Jonesville (1847–49), he joined the gold-rush and remained in California something over a year. On his return he became the first principal (1852–65) of the Michigan State Normal School at Ypsilanti, where he was "largely instrumental in giving form and character to the institution and in determining the direction of its early development" (Putnam, *post*, p. 139). He conducted many teachers' institutes (1852–53), aided in organizing the state teachers' association, and became its first president, and served as trustee of the Michigan Agricultural College. In 1865 he went to Florida for his health. He engaged in business at Pensacola and Jacksonville, and was elected to the United States Senate for a short term (1868–69).

Chosen in 1868 first president of the Iowa State Agricultural College, Ames, Iowa, he served in that capacity from 1869 until failing health obliged him to resign in 1883, and later (1884–89) taught history and psychology. As president of a pioneer college with few buildings, poorly equipped, he worked against many physical handicaps; he himself laid out the campus, locating buildings, drives, walks, groups of trees and shrubbery. From the beginning he defended industrial education as a better preparation for life than the long-established classical course, and supported the right of women to a college education. He based the first two courses, in agriculture and in mechanic arts, on fundamental and applied sciences, and for numerous later developments, as originator of plans and policies, he deserves a share of the credit. He is said to have originated the plan of sending college teachers to conduct farmers' institutes about the state (1870–71), a system later followed in almost every state, and he encouraged systematic experimentation in stock raising and in farm products, which the college began in 1880, seven years before the federal act providing for experiment stations. The class instruction in cooking, conducted by Mrs. Welch in her own kitchen, afterwards developed into the large and widely known division of home economics. In 1883 Welch was sent abroad by the United States commissioner of agriculture to report on agricultural schools in Germany, Belgium, and England.

Welch was a man of great charm, well versed in the classics, in philosophy and history, and in psychology. His publications include *Analysis of the English Sentence* (1855), *Report on the Organization and Management of Seven Agricultural Schools in Germany, Belgium, and England* (1885), *Talks on Psychology Applied to Teaching* (1888), and *The Teachers' Psychology* (1889). Having the gift of ready, persuasive, forcible address, he was in great demand as a speaker before educational and industrial organizations. His written addresses are models of clearness, logical order, and style. He expressed frequently his love of beauty and order, and he was deeply religious. He was married first to Eunice P. Buckingham (d. 1866), daughter of Gen. Catharinus P. Buckingham of Ohio, by whom he had a daughter and two sons, and second in 1868 to Mary (Beaumont) Dudley, daughter of Dr. A. L. Beaumont of Jonesville, Mich. He died in Pasadena, Cal., and was buried at Ames.

[B. W. Dwight, *The Hist. of the Descendants of Elder John Strong*, vol. I (1871), p. 201; *Hist. of Middlesex County, Conn.* (1884), p. 215; Daniel Putnam, *A Hist. of the Mich. State Normal School . . . at Ypsilanti* (1899); B. F. Gue, *Hist. of Iowa* (4 vols., 1903); W. O. Payne, *Hist. of Story County, Iowa* (2 vols., 1911); C. E. Bessey, in *Annals of Iowa*, Apr. 1909; *An Hist. Sketch of the Iowa State College of Agriculture* (pamphlet, 1920); *Aurora* (Ames, Iowa), Apr. 1889; *The Bomb* (Ames, 1897); Mrs. A. B. Shaw, in *Alumnus* (Ames), May 1905; obituaries in *Iowa State Register*, Mar. 15, 22, 1889.]
A.B.N.

WELCH, ASHBEL (Dec. 4, 1809–Sept. 25, 1882), civil engineer, son of Ashbel and Margaret (Dorrance) Welch, was born at Nelson, Madison County, N. Y. When Ashbel was seven years old his parents moved to Deerfield, Oneida County, N. Y., and for the next ten years he attended schools in Utica, completing his education in the winter of 1826 at Albany Academy, where he studied under the immediate direction of Joseph Henry [*q.v.*]. In the summer of 1827 Welch began his engineering career as rodman on the staff of the Lehigh Canal, at Mauch Chunk, Pa., where his older brother was resident engineer, and after three years here he became connected with the Delaware & Raritan Canal, in Trenton, N. J., of which he was made chief engineer in 1835.

During the succeeding twenty-five years he engaged in a variety of engineering work in the transportation field. He made the reconnaissances for and subsequently built the Belvidere Delaware Railroad, which followed the banks of the Delaware River from Trenton northward to Manunka Chunk, near the Delaware Water Gap. In addition to looking after all the engineering work of the Delaware & Raritan Canal, he engaged in a consulting engineering practice covering a varied field of activities. He assisted John Ericsson [*q.v.*], for example, in designing the steamship *Princeton*; he made examinations of coal and iron properties in Virginia; he supervised experiments in gunnery initiated by Commodore R. F. Stockton [*q.v.*] of the United States Navy, and made a trip to Europe in 1844 for the special purpose of superintending the construction of a large, wrought-iron gun. In 1847 he designed and built for the Delaware & Raritan Canal at Bordentown, N. J., a wooden lock, the unusual feature of which was that it was constructed upon a quicksand, and in 1852 he accomplished the unusual feat of enlarging the whole of the Delaware & Raritan Canal in three months. The following year he undertook the work of designing and constructing the Chesapeake & Delaware Canal, but in the course of this arduous task, carried on in connection with his many other engineering activities, he broke down physically and was compelled to give up all active work.

After a rest in Europe in 1854, however, he again took up his consulting engineering work, particularly in connection with New Jersey railroads, being engaged in the construction both of the roads themselves and of terminal facilities. In 1862 he was appointed vice-president of the Camden & Amboy Railroad. In this position he worked ceaselessly to bring about the consolidation of the several competing railroad companies in New Jersey, and, largely through his efforts, in January 1867 final arrangements were made uniting the Delaware & Raritan Canal Company, the Camden & Amboy Railroad & Transportation Company, and the New Jersey Railroad & Transportation Company. Welch was immediately made president of the new organization, known as the United Companies of New Jersey, and was in charge of all administrative matters until December 1871, when the properties were leased to the Pennsylvania Railroad Company.

As early as 1845 Welch, with the assistance of Joseph Henry, began a series of experiments in the application of telegraphy to railroad signaling, and in 1865 presented to the Camden & Amboy Railroad Company a plan for telegraphic safety signals. It was immediately accepted and applied on the railroad between Kensington and New Brunswick, and is generally regarded as the earliest installation of the block signaling system which came into general use in the United States. Welch also carried on investigations looking toward the improvement of railroad rolling stock, particularly car trucks and wheels, and made a study of iron and steel rails, publishing many articles on the subject in technical journals. He was an active member of the American Society of Civil Engineers, serving as vice-president in 1880 and being chosen president the year of his death. On Oct. 25, 1834, he married Mary Hannah Seabrook; four children survived him. He died in Lambertville, N. J.

[W. H. Manning, *The Manning Family of New England* (1902); John Bogart and others, *Ashbel Welch* (1883); *Proc. Am. Soc. Civil Engineers*, vol. IX (1883); *Railroad Gazette*, Sept. 29, 1882; *Railway Age*, Oct. 5, 1882; J. E. Watkins, "The Camden and Amboy Railroad," in *Ceremonies Upon the Completion of the Monument Erected by the Pa. Railroad Company at Bordentown, N. J.* (1891); Waldemar Kaempffert, *A Popular Hist. of Am. Invention* (1924); J. B. Snell, *Hist. of Hunterdon and Somerset Counties, N. J.* (1881); *Press* (Phila.), Sept. 27, 1882.] C. W. M.

WELCH, CHARLES CLARK (June 14, 1830–Feb. 1, 1908), miner, railroad builder, and capitalist, was of English, Scotch, and French descent. Among his ancestors on his father's side were Elder William Brewster of the *Mayflower* and Maj. John Mason of Connecticut. On the maternal side he came of French ancestry, the first American representative being one of the founders of Providence, R. I. His parents, Charles and Pamelia (La Valley or La Valle) Welch, lived on a farm in Jefferson County, N. Y., at the time of their son's birth. On this farm and at the village school young Charles spent his childhood. At the age of fifteen he entered the academy at Watertown, and after receiving some training there he took up teaching. Stories of gold discoveries lured him in 1850 to California, where he engaged for two years in placer and quartz mining in Placer County. Then Australian gold fields beckoned, and he sailed to Sydney. After mining for a year in New South Wales he returned to New York, via Cape Horn.

Presently he moved westward, seeking business opportunities, and settled in Chicago in 1855. The succeeding five years were spent in the real estate and brokerage business. In 1860, lured by mining opportunities, he crossed the plains by stagecoach to Colorado, where he was to make his permanent home. Building on experience, gained in California and Australia, he engaged successfully in gold mining in Gilpin and Boulder counties, operating extensive properties. Then he branched out into other lines. He ran sawmills, operated a tannery and a fire brick plant at Golden, and constructed irrigation ditches. He crossed the plains between Denver and the Missouri River nineteen times during the stagecoach era. Becoming interested in railroads, he was one of the promoters of the Colorado Central Railroad, which was extended west from Golden to the mines and north to a connection with the Union Pacific at Cheyenne. He also built a portion of the Santa Fé line east of Pueblo, Colo. At Louisville, Boulder County, he sank a 200-foot shaft, found a ten-foot vein of coal, and opened and operated the "Welch Mine," which became a large and steady producer. In 1878 he organized an irrigation company and built the Handy Ditch in Larimer County. In the country served by this canal he procured extensive acreage and became a large producer of grain. In 1880 he built the Welch Irrigation Ditch, constructing flumes in Clear Creek Canyon to bring water onto the bench lands northeast of Denver. In 1891 he was one of the promoters of the road that became the electric trolley line between Denver and Golden.

In 1872 Welch was elected to the Colorado territorial legislature from Jefferson County. He introduced the bill for the establishment of the

State School of Mines at Golden and donated the ground for the first building. For many years he served on the board of trustees of the institution. On May 22, 1878, he married Rebecca Jeannette Darrow of Coldwater, Mich., by whom he had two children. He died in Jacksonville, Fla., where he had gone seeking a restoration of health; his body was returned to Colorado for burial.

[*Hist. of Clear Creek and Boulder Valleys, Col.* (1880); W. N. Byers, *Encyc. of Biog. of Col.* (1901); *Sketches of Col.; Being an Analytical Summary and Biog. Hist. of the State of Col.* (1911); W. F. Stone, *Hist. of Col.* (1918), vol. III; *Rocky Mountain News* (Denver), Feb. 2, 1908; E. C. B. Jones, *The Brewster Geneal.* (1908), II, 987.]　　　　L. R. H.

WELCH, JOHN (Oct. 28, 1805–Aug. 5, 1891), congressman, jurist, was born on a farm in Harrison County, Ohio, the son of Thomas and Martha (Daugherty) Welch. His father was of English and his mother of Irish parentage. They were among the early pioneers of Ohio, settling first in Harrison County and moving about 1828 to Athens County. At the age of eighteen, having spent his life until then on the farm, John secured "his time" from his father, and by alternately teaching school to obtain funds and attending classes at Franklin College in New Athens, Ohio, he was able to graduate from that institution in 1828. Traveling some fourteen miles each week to recite, he studied law with Joseph Dana of Athens, but soon broke down physically and for a time ran a sawmill owned by his father. In after years he was fond of telling his grandchildren that he would set the saw and then read Blackstone while it was going through the log. In 1830 he married Martha, daughter of Capt. James Starr; two sons and two daughters were born to this union. In 1833 he was admitted to the bar of Ohio and located for practice at Athens.

Professionally successful from the start, he made a place for himself among such eminent lawyers as Thomas Ewing, Samuel F. Vinton, and Henry Stanbery [*qq.v.*]. After having served from 1841 to 1843 as prosecuting attorney of Athens County, he was elected in 1843 to the Ohio Senate, remaining there for one term of two years. In 1850 he was sent, as a Whig, to the lower house of Congress, where, also, he served but one term, and in 1852 he was a delegate to the national Whig convention that nominated Gen. Winfield Scott for president. From 1862 to 1865 he was a common-pleas judge and while serving as such was appointed by the governor, Feb. 23, 1865, to fill the vacancy on the Ohio supreme court created by the resignation of Judge Rufus P. Ranney [*q.v.*]. In October

1865 he was elected to fill the unexpired term and in October 1867 was elected for a full term. After serving for thirteen years, he returned in 1878 to Athens and resumed the practice of law. In 1887 he published *An Index-Digest to the Reports of Cases Decided in the Courts of Ohio* and later prepared a supplement, which was published after his death. He also wrote a small volume entitled *Mathematical Curiosities* (1883) consisting of new and original rules, puzzles, and an interest table on an entirely new plan— and a number of essays.

His opinions as judge were characterized by their brevity, few being over two or three pages long, and by the almost total absence of any cited cases. They are, however, forcibly stated and clearly reasoned. The positive character of the man is illustrated by the fact that it was his habit, when the court was in consultation, to state his opinion briefly after listening to the other judges, and if they disagreed with him to devote himself to his favorite pastime of solving some mathematical problem while they argued. When the vote was taken his position was already known, for he seldom changed a conclusion he had formed. His mathematical turn of mind made him a particularly valuable member of the court, since much of its time during his presence on the bench was given to the solution of problems of real property, which have in them much that requires the precision of mathematics. Some of his opinions in this field are considered classics, among them that given in the case of *McIntire Administrators et al* vs. *the City of Zanesville* (17 *Ohio State Reports,* 352), wherein he applies the equitable doctrine of "cy-près," holding that where a fund is given by will to the use and support of a "poor school" for the benefit of the poor children of a city in which later a public school system is established, this fund may be used "to buy books and shoes and in rare cases even food" for the poor children attending the public schools. He died in Athens in his eighty-sixth year.

[Welch's opinions are in 16–31 *Ohio State Reports.* Sources include 48 *O. S. R.,* v–vii; *Green Bag,* June 1895; *Proc. Ohio State Bar Asso.,* 1892; *Biog. Cyc. and Portrait Gallery . . . of Ohio,* vol. I (1883); *Biog. Dir. Am. Cong.* (1928); *Athens Jour.,* Aug. 13, 1891.]
　　　　　　　　　　　　　　　　　　　　A. H. T.

WELCH, PHILIP HENRY (Mar. 1, 1849– Feb. 24, 1889), humorist, journalist, was born at Angelica, N. Y., the son of Joseph B. Welch and his wife, Mary (?) Collins. After passing through the public schools at Angelica, he was employed for twelve years by a New York hardware firm, spending two-thirds of his time on the road. He joined his brother in Oil City,

Pa., and from there sent petroleum reports to *Bradstreet's.* Meanwhile he had been married to Margaret Welles Hamilton, daughter of Theodore and Emily (Welles) Hamilton, of Angelica. There were four children. In 1882 Welch went to Rochester, N. Y., to conduct a column called "The Present Hour" in the *Post-Express,* and thereafter he devoted himself consistently to journalistic humor. In 1883 he left Rochester to spend a few months conducting a column called "Accidentally Overheard" in the Philadelphia *Call,* and then (1884) joined the staff of the New York *Sun,* with which he remained until his death. He had found his own particular vehicle in the short humorous dialogue, usually consisting of a single question and answer; into these tiny paragraphs he packed his dry wit and his easy, good-natured satire on the follies of the day. His jokes in the *Sun* seemed to have been referred to as "Queer Wrinkles," but they appeared anonymously and without a column heading. At the same time that he was grinding out his weekly stint for the *Sun,* Welch was sending similar material to *Puck, Life, Judge,* the *Epoch,* the *Times, Drake's Magazine, Harper's Bazaar,* and other periodicals. His jokes were borrowed and stolen all over the country. Week after week the jokes in the San Francisco *Argonaut,* which copied its material from other papers, would be all or nearly all from his pen, though ascribed to many different papers, including some for which Welch had never written in his life. In 1886 Welch was attacked by a cancer in the throat, and was forced to undergo an operation which left his voice impaired. In the summer of 1888 the trouble returned, this time in his chest. A second operation was unsuccessful, and the surgeons did not dare attempt a third. His friends and associates of this time were filled with the deepest admiration of Welch's fortitude and indomitable spirit during these months when he was slowly dying of cancer. He continued to turn off dozens of jokes a week, finally dictating them to his wife when he could no longer write them himself. He died in his fortieth year at his home in Brooklyn and was buried at Angelica.

Through the efforts of Edward Perkins Clark of the *Evening Post* and Alfred Corning Clark, a Welch Memorial Fund was raised to provide for the education of the children. Contributions came from all over the country, ranging in amount from $1 to $10,000; notable contributors were Lowell, Whittier, Mark Twain, and Theodore Roosevelt. During Welch's life he had published only one book, *The Tailor-Made Girl* (1888), a collection of page-length dialogues reprinted from *Puck,* gently satirizing the contemporary well-to-do young lady. As part of the campaign to raise money for the fund, friends now compiled an anthology of his shorter and more characteristic dialogues under the title of *Said in Fun* (1889); illustrations were contributed by most of the well-known humorous illustrators of the day, including W. L. Sheppard, C. D. Gibson, and F. Opper.

[*Journalist,* Jan. 28, 1888; obituaries in *Sun* (N. Y.), *N. Y. Times, N. Y. Tribune,* Feb. 25, 1889; information furnished by Paul H. and Emily H. Welch of New York City, Mary W. Wakely of Angelica, and members of the staff of the *Sun.*]   E. M. S.

WELCH, WILLIAM HENRY (Apr. 8, 1850–Apr. 30, 1934), pathologist, son of William Wickham Welch [*q.v.*] and Emeline (Collin) Welch, was born in Norfolk, Conn., in the house in which both his father and grandfather had lived as physicians for many years. His mother died when he was about six months old, and he was cared for by his grandmother. When he was twelve he was sent to school at the Winchester Institute. There he had as roommate Frederick S. Dennis, also of Norfolk, who became a prominent surgeon in New York and was his lifelong friend. In 1866 he went to Yale, graduating in 1870. After teaching Latin and Greek in a school at Norwich, N. Y., for a year, he entered the College of Physicians and Surgeons of Columbia University but left shortly to spend a year studying chemistry at the Sheffield Scientific School at Yale, where he came under the influence of Oscar H. Allan and George F. Barker [*q.v.*]. In the autumn of 1872 he returned to the College of Physicians and Surgeons to study medicine, and in 1875 was graduated. That spring he went to Europe for several years of study. At Strassburg he had a course in histology with Waldeyer, demonstrations with von Recklinghausen, and some work in chemistry with Hoppe-Seyler. After a summer walking-trip in Switzerland he went to Leipzig, where he worked with Ludwig, and thence, on Ludwig's recommendation, to Breslau to study under Julius Cohnheim, instead of following his original plan of studying under Virchow. There he found himself in a group of men who were later famous —Paul Ehrlich, Carl Weigert, Salomonsen, Albert Neisser, and others. He was there when Robert Koch came to demonstrate to Cohn and Cohnheim his early work on anthrax, which showed the beginning of effective studies of bacteria. After a visit to Vienna, where he was joined by Theophil Mitchell Prudden [*q.v.*], he returned for a time to Strassburg, studying at von Recklinghausen's suggestion inflammation produced in the cornea of the frog. He returned to America by way of Paris and London, hearing Louis-Antoine Ranvier in Paris and Joseph Lister in London.

This first period of study in Germany gave him a clear view of histology, chemistry, physiology, and pathology as they were then being developed there and served as the foundation for his own expanding work in pathology, which he began on his return to New York in the spring of 1878. Dennis, who was beginning his surgical work with Austin Flint and W. T. Lusk [qq.v.], arranged a small laboratory for him at Bellevue Hospital, where he performed the autopsies and taught the students. He lived with Dennis and had some practice in clinical medicine. He refused the invitation of Francis Delafield [q.v.] to teach pathology at the College of Physicians and Surgeons but recommended Prudden, who accepted the place. At the same time he was demonstrator of anatomy, registrar of the Woman's Hospital, and was much occupied in reporting on diagnoses of pathological material.

In 1883 he accepted an invitation to become professor of pathology in the Johns Hopkins University, Baltimore. He spent the year 1884 in Europe studying the new bacteriology under Frobenius and Flugge, pupils of Koch, and then under Koch himself in Berlin. There he found Prudden again and Ehrlich, and the astonishing new horizons suddenly opened before them by the methods and inspiration of Koch stirred his enthusiasm so that from that time on his interest was largely centered in the study of bacteriology. In Baltimore in 1885 he started work with William T. Councilman in rooms in the top of Newell Martin's laboratory of physiology, but a pathological laboratory was soon organized. There a group of men worked under him of whom Welch always spoke with pleasure: Councilman, William S. Halsted [q.v.], G. H. F. Nuttall, Alexander C. Abbott, Franklin P. Mall [q.v.], and B. Meade Bolton. During this time he was especially concerned with the mechanism of the formation of thrombi and with the question of haemorrhagic infarction; the work later led to the publication of his admirable articles on *Thrombosis and Embolism* (1899). He was the inspiration for much brilliant work by the group of his associates. Before the opening of the university hospital, when there was no human material, he found great interest in animal diseases, such as hog cholera and the pleuropneumonia of cattle. Later he devoted himself to the study of diphtheria and pneumonia. He discovered and described in detail the gas-producing bacillus known by his name which was the cause of "gas gangrene" in wounded soldiers

during the World War. With the opening of the hospital in 1889 the selection of men as heads of various departments was greatly influenced by the advice of Welch, who suggested Osler and William Stewart Halsted [qq.v.]. Later, in the same way, for the organization of the school of medicine, which was opened in 1893, he was responsible for the choice of Mall, Abel, and Howell. He himself was the first dean and served in that capacity for several years. In 1896 he established a new type of medical publication, the *Journal of Experimental Medicine,* for the presentation of the results of serious investigation, and was its editor until 1906.

Throughout the earlier years of the Johns Hopkins medical school he was most active in its organization and was perhaps especially influential in determining its character, which was not that familiar at the time in the medical schools of the country. After 1900, though he continued to lecture, his energies were largely devoted to the advance of medical education throughout the country. It was then that the Rockefeller Institute of Medical Research was founded, in a way largely based upon his counsel, and from 1901 to the end of his life he was chairman of the board of scientific directors. From 1906 on, he was associated in a similar advisory capacity with the various activities of the Carnegie Foundation. He was active in many scientific and medical associations. He was president of the Congress of American Physicians and Surgeons (1897), the Association of American Physicians (1901), the American Association for the Advancement of Science (1906), the Association of Pathologists and Bacteriologists (1906), the American Medical Association (1910), and the National Academy of Sciences (1913–16). In addition to his activities in connection with the universities and research foundations in other cities, Welch was deeply interested in those of Baltimore and Maryland, and was long president of the state board of health (1898–1922). In this connection he was frequently consulted by the municipal authorities in matters of public health in the city. He was also a member of the Medico-Chirurgical Faculty of Maryland and its president in 1891. After the entrance of the United States into the World War he served actively with the surgeon-general of the army, visiting many camps and acting as consultant on matters relating to the health of the army; he was made brigadier-general in 1921.

Through all these years his interest in the problems of pathology and bacteriology remained intense. His public addresses, which were many, dealt in general with plans for educational procedures, with broad problems of public health, with the relations of one science to another, and with various periods and personalities in the history of medicine. Some, however, were devoted to topics more closely related to his own field, such as adaptation in pathological processes, morbid conditions caused by the bacillus *aerogenes capsulatus,* and the Huxley lectures on immunity. In 1920 well over three hundred of these were collected in *Papers and Addresses by William Henry Welch,* in three volumes, edited by Walter C. Burket.

Upon the resignation of Ira Remsen [*q.v.*] as president of the Johns Hopkins University in 1912, Welch was appointed chairman of a committee of the faculty and acted virtually as president until President Frank J. Goodnow took office. In 1914 Welch and Wickliffe Rose were asked to advise upon the foundation of a school of hygiene and public health. When the school was opened as part of the Johns Hopkins University in 1918, Welch, who had resigned the Baxley professorship of pathology, was appointed director. The successful development of this school, with its far-reaching influence, through its students, in foreign countries, was brought about by the profound interest of Welch coupled with his skill in the choice of men. In this he was assisted by Dr. W. H. Howell, who later succeeded him as director. In 1925 he published *Public Health in Theory and Practice; an Historical Review.* His work at the school continued until his resignation in 1926. In that year a chair of the history of medicine was endowed by the General Education Board, and Welch entered upon a third career as its occupant. In 1929 the William H. Welch Medical Library, housing the department of the history of medicine, was formally dedicated, with many visitors from abroad taking part in the ceremonies in Welch's honor. Even after his retirement in 1931 Welch continued to work in that department until in the early months of 1933 he became incapacitated by prostatic carcinoma. This confined him to the Johns Hopkins Hospital until his death fourteen months later, on Apr. 30, 1934. He was buried in Norfolk, Conn.

During his later years he made a number of visits to different countries in Europe, among them one in 1905 to sit for the famous Sargent portrait of the "Four Doctors," and another in 1909 to attend university celebrations in Leipzig. His last trip (1927) was for the purpose of purchasing books for the library of the department of the history of medicine. Besides this, at the request of the Rockefeller Foundation, he went in 1915 with Dr. Simon Flexner and Wallace Buttrick [*q.v.*] to China, to study the conditions to be met in the establishment of the Peiping Union Medical College, and later (1921) he went again to Peiping to be present at the formal opening of the school. During his trips to Europe he was always eager to spend some time at a spa such as Carlsbad, and during summers when he did not go abroad he was accustomed to go for a time to Bedford Springs or to Atlantic City, where he could bathe and lie in the sun for long hours. One summer (1931) he spent in Pasadena, where he enjoyed the California climate and saw much of the scientists working there.

Among the numerous portraits of Welch, the best are those of Sargent and Thomas B. Corner. There is also a bronze bust by Konenkov which is an excellent likeness. Further, there exists a moving talking picture in which Welch himself relates the main events of his career. He was short and stout, quite bald in later years, not especially given to niceties in costume. For some years he wore a broad beard, which he later trimmed to a point. He was extremely simple and unaffected in his attitude, and readily approachable. He never married. He lived for all the later years of his life in Baltimore on St. Paul Street, first at 935, then at 807; in each house he occupied the second floor, which was overfilled with books, even the chairs being piled with them. He took his meals at the Maryland Club or at the University Club, of which he was president for many years, and spent a great deal of time in one or the other. On his frequent visits to New York he lived at the University Club, and found it so comfortable that he spent the whole summer of 1932 there, going very often to one of the beaches to swim or lie on the sand, being convinced that long exposure to sunlight maintains health. He was a connoisseur of delicately prepared food and of good cigars, which he smoked constantly, and was a most generous host. He was especially attached to a small group of friends whose conversation in a small room at the club went on for years in a most amusing form. His bodily strength was quite remarkable and his digestive powers extraordinary.

In his relations with the Johns Hopkins University and the medical school there, it was especially his keenness of judgment in any difficult situation and his extraordinary wisdom in organization and in the choice of men that were of great value. His estimate of the results of research was equally penetrating. His interests, however, were by no means confined to medical education. There was no one who seemed so widely read or whose memory could retain in so phenomenal a way every detail of the most miscellaneous reading, in which encyclopedias and the *Dictionary of National Biography* figured largely. All was in order and could be produced at a moment's notice even after many years. His familiarity with the history of music was especially remarkable.

Welch's fame rests upon his service to humanity, and especially to the United States, which such qualities made possible. He grasped at once the significance of the epochal developments in pathology and bacteriology which he witnessed in Europe, and introduced them into America, not only bringing the results of foreign investigations but breathing the whole spirit of this advance into the medicine of America. Later, with great wisdom and foresight, he planned and organized institutions for the promotion of education and investigation throughout the country, an influence felt and treasured in many other countries as well, where aid in these directions was given largely through his advice.

Universities and scientific associations in the United States and abroad conferred a great many honorary degrees and fellowships upon him. He also received a number of medals and decorations, including that of the Legion of Honor. Many banquets were given in his honor: one in 1900 on the twenty-fifth anniversary of his doctorate, when he was presented with a *Festschrift* volume of many papers; another in 1910 on the twenty-fifth anniversary of his professorship; another in 1920 in celebration of his seventieth birthday, with publication of his collected papers and addresses. On his eightieth birthday there were celebrations in many cities, even in Europe and in Asia, and in Washington there was a special meeting at which, among others, President Hoover spoke in his honor.

[See *Who's Who in America*, 1932–33; intro. by Simon Flexner in *Papers and Addresses by William Henry Welch* (3 vols., 1920), ed. by W. C. Burket; *Obit. Record Grads. Yale Univ.*, 1934; *William Henry Welch at Eighty* (1930), ed. by V. O. Freeburg; W. C. Burket, *Bibliog. of William Henry Welch* (1917); Johns Hopkins Univ. Circulars; *Jour. Am. Medic. Asso.*, May 5, 1934; obituaries in *Johns Hopkins Hospital Bull.*, June 1934, and *N. Y. Times*, May 1, 1934; personal letters and notes on conversations with Welch. Dr. Simon Flexner is preparing a biog. of Welch.]

W. G. M.

WELCH, WILLIAM WICKHAM (Dec. 10, 1818–July 30, 1892), physician, was born in Norfolk, Conn. His grandfather, Hopestill Welch, blacksmith in Norfolk, had thirteen children, of whom the third was Benjamin Welch. Benjamin studied medicine under the village doctor, Ephraim Guiteau; married his daughter, Louisa; and practised medicine in Norfolk for sixty years. After the death of his first wife he married Elizabeth Loveland. There were ten children, of whom five sons and three daughters survived. The five sons, all physicians, were Asa G. Welch of Lee, Mass., Benjamin of Litchfield and Salisbury, Conn., James W. of Winsted, Conn., William Wickham of Norfolk, and John Hopestill of New Hartford and Norfolk, Conn. William Wickham Welch, the fourth son, was graduated from the Yale Medical School in 1839 and began the practice of medicine in Norfolk while his father, who died in 1849, was still active. On Nov. 7, 1845, he married Emeline Collin of Hillsdale, N. Y., and by her had a daughter and a son, William Henry [*q.v.*]. His wife died in 1850 when the son was only six months old. On May 2, 1866, he married Emily Sedgwick of Cornwall, Conn., sister of Gen. John Sedgwick [*q.v.*].

His life was devoted to the practice of his profession in Norfolk and the surrounding country. After spending much of the day in his office with patients, he would set out at night in his horse-drawn buggy to visit the sick at whatever distance they lived. He was much in advance of his time in many ways, and very successful in his methods of treatment and the control of nursing. The importance of fresh air impressed him greatly. It is related that when late at night he saw, in passing, the house of one of his patients, windows closed, although he had left orders for abundant fresh air, he would stop his horse, remove the whole window, and carry it home with him. He was especially interested in the treatment of hydrophobia and the bites of venomous reptiles. It does not appear that surgery played any large part in his practice, but he was undoubtedly ready in any emergency. Long after his death his memory continued to be treasured in and about Norfolk. His professional work for fifty years won him the affection of everyone, and he was honored and beloved not only in the sickroom but as a companion and fellow townsman. He was greatly interested in horses and dogs. One or two of his horses were famous, perhaps especially for their endurance throughout his long drives at night. His Dalmatian followed under the buggy until it grew so old that it must be taken on the seat, where it was intolerant of any intrusion.

Welch was a member of the state House of Representatives (1848–50), served in the state Senate in 1851 and 1852, and was elected by the American Party to Congress (1855–57). After that he resumed the practice of medicine but was again a member of the state House of Representatives in 1869 and 1881. He was president of the Norfolk Leather Company, one of the incorporators of the Connecticut-Western Railroad and the Norfolk Savings Bank, and with his brother, John Hopestill, engaged in the knitting business in Norfolk. He died in Norfolk, survived by his wife and children, and was buried in the family plot in the Norfolk cemetery. A drinking fountain for horses was erected in the village in his memory with the inscription, *Fons sum solati talis et ipse fuit.*

[*Obit. Record Yale Grads.,* 1892; Harvey Cushing, in *New England Jour. of Medicine,* May 24, 1934; *Biog. Dir. Am. Cong.* (1928); H. A. Kelly and W. L. Burrage, *Am. Medic. Biogs.* (1920); obituary in *Hartford Courant,* Aug. 2, 1892; information from Dr. W. H. Welch and Senator F. Walcott.] 　W.G.M.

WELD, ARTHUR CYRIL GORDON (Mar. 4, 1862–Oct. 11, 1914), musician, composer, was born at Jamaica Plain, Mass., the son of Stephen Minot Weld and his second wife, Georgianna Hallet. He was a descendant of Thomas Weld [*q.v.*]. After attending Harvard University he went abroad in 1879 to study music. He remained in Europe until 1887, studied composition and orchestration with Becker, Foerster, and Von Comiar-Fiedlitz at Dresden, and with Neumann at Berlin. He was graduated with high honors from the Conservatory of Music in Munich where he was a pupil of Rheinberger, Abel and Levi. During the years in Munich he composed a number of works in the larger forms which were publicly performed in that city. These included a string quartet in C (1885), of which one movement was played in America by the Kneisel Quartet in 1890; a "Romanza" for small orchestra (1886), performed in Boston during the following year; an "Andante" and "Scherzo" for septet (1886); and an orchestral suite, "Italia" (1887), which was subsequently presented at the Worcester Festival (1888) and by the Boston Symphony Orchestra (1890). Other works from this period include a composition for soli, double quartet, chorus and orchestra "Benedictus Dominus Israel"; an "Ode in Time of Peace" for double quartet and organ; four madrigals, and many other songs.

After his return to America Weld lived for a time in Milwaukee, Wis., where he was active as a dramatic critic and conductor of an orchestra. Later he came to New York City to work in a field in which he achieved his greatest distinction, as a conductor of musical comedies and composer of incidental music for the theatre. In November 1900 he conducted the first production of "Florodora," and became general musical director for the productions of Henry W. Savage [*q.v.*]. In this capacity he was well known in theatrical circles, and was made a member of the House Committee of the Lambs' Club, in New York. In 1913 he went to London to conduct performances of the musical comedy "Adele," and in the following year he became personal representative for James K. Hackett [*q.v.*]. He arranged the music for Hackett's performance of *Othello,* and took charge of the musical features of all his plays. He met his death this same year. While driving his automobile in the neighborhood of West Point, N. Y., he was stricken with apoplexy, and died almost immediately. His third wife, Claudia Clarke, a musical comedy actress, was with him in the car.

Weld was a colorful person whose presence lent distinction to many gatherings. According to his obituary notice in the *New York Times* (*post*), he was a "striking looking man and was a commanding figure in the orchestra pit." He always wore a monocle. He had three daughters by his first wife.

[C. W. Fowler, *Hist. of the Weld Family* (1879); H. M. Whitcomb, *Annals . . . of Jamaica Plain* (1897); *Grove's Dict. of Music and Musicians, Am. Supp.* (1930); *Hugo Reimanns Musik Lexikon* (11th ed., 1929); *Boston Evening Transcript, N. Y. Times,* Oct. 12, 1914.] 　J.T.H.

WELD, THEODORE DWIGHT (Nov. 23, 1803–Feb. 3, 1895), abolitionist, was born in Hampton, Conn., the son of Elizabeth (Clark) Weld and the Rev. Ludovicus Weld, a Congregational minister. He was descended from a line of New England clergymen whose progenitor was the Rev. Thomas Weld [*q.v.*], first minister of Roxbury; his ancestry also included Edwardses, Dwights, and Hutchinsons. In Weld's childhood his family moved to western New York, near Utica, where he passed an active, vigorous youth. Here he met Capt. Charles Stuart [*q.v.*], principal of the Utica Academy, a retired British officer, who was to influence profoundly his character and his career. In 1825, when Charles G. Finney [*q.v.*], the Presbyterian revivalist, invaded Utica, Weld and Stuart joined his "holy band" of evangelists, and for two years they preached throughout western New York. Weld labored chiefly among young men; and when he entered Oneida Institute, Whitesboro, N. Y., to prepare for the ministry, scores of them also enrolled. Here he remained for several terms, his expenses being borne by Charles Stuart, who had long considered him "beloved brother, and son, and friend." During vacations Weld labored for the cause of temperance with such effect that by the end of the decade he was accounted the most powerful temperance advocate in the West. Meantime he had met those philanthropists of New York City, led by Arthur and Lewis Tappan [*qq.v.*], who were financing Finney's revival. Attracted by

Weld's talents, they repeatedly urged him to head various reforms which they were backing; but he steadfastly refused to abandon his preparation for the ministry.

In 1829 Charles Stuart went to England to preach the abolition of West Indian slavery. He soon became noted as a lecturer for the British Anti-Slavery Society, and even more as a pamphleteer; but his most eloquent appeals were addressed to Weld. His persuasions were successful. From 1830 on, Weld was consumed with anti-slavery zeal. His first converts to emancipation were the New York philanthropists. In June 1831 the Tappans called a council in New York City, which proposed the immediate organization of an American anti-slavery society on the British model. After Weld's departure, however, the Tappans decided to postpone organization until emancipation in the British West Indies, which was now assured, had become a published triumph. Previously, Weld had urged the New York philanthropists to found a theological seminary in the West to prepare Finney's converts for the ministry. In the fall of 1831 they acceded, and commissioned Weld to find a site for the seminary. On this journey he advocated the anti-slavery cause at every opportunity. In Huntsville, Ala., in 1831, he converted James G. Birney [q.v.], and at Hudson, Ohio, he abolitionized the faculty of Western Reserve College, Elizur Wright, Beriah Green [qq.v.], and the president, Charles Backus Storrs. For the seminary he selected a project already begun, Lane Seminary at Cincinnati, Ohio. The Tappans secured Lyman Beecher [q.v.], most famous preacher of his time, as president, and a notable faculty. Weld supplied the bulk of the students from the converts of Finney's revivals. Among them he organized in 1834 a "debate" on slavery (Barnes, *post,* p. 65), which won not only the students, but also Beecher's children, Harriet and Henry Ward, and several Cincinnatians, among them Gamaliel Bailey [q.v.].

Meanwhile, the New York philanthropists had organized the American Anti-Slavery Society. Unfortunately they adopted the British motto of "immediate emancipation"; and though they defined the motto as "immediate emancipation, gradually accomplished," the public interpreted it as a program of immediate freedom for the slaves. The pamphlet propaganda based upon this motto failed disastrously both North and South, and the society's agents, almost without exception, were silenced by mobs. Weld saved the movement from disaster. Forced out of Lane Seminary by its angry trustees in the fall of 1834,

he trained the ablest of his fellow students and sent them out as agents for the American Anti-Slavery Society. Adopting Finney's methods, they preached emancipation as a revival in benevolence, with a fervor which mobs could not silence. Among them, Henry B. Stanton [q.v.] and James Thome became well known; but thirty-two other "Lane rebels" did their parts in establishing the movement in Ohio, western Pennsylvania and New York, Rhode Island and western Massachusetts. Weld, "eloquent as an angel and powerful as thunder," accomplished more than all the rest combined. Indeed, the anti-slavery areas in the West and the field of Weld's labors largely coincide. Among his converts, Joshua R. Giddings, Edwin M. Stanton [qq.v.], and others were later prominent in politics; while the anti-slavery sentiment among New-School Presbyterians was largely due to his agitation among the ministers.

By 1836 the success of Weld's agents was so apparent that the American Anti-Slavery Society decided to abandon the pamphlet campaign, and devote all its resources toward enlarging his heroic band. Weld himself selected the new agents, to the number of seventy, gathered them in New York, and for weeks gave them a pentecostal training in abolitionism. One of the new agents at this conference was Angelina Grimké [q.v.], daughter of a prominent South Carolina family, whom Weld specially trained in the months that followed. During the next few years the "Seventy" consolidated the anti-slavery movement throughout the North. After the agents' conference, Weld, whose voice was permanently injured, continued to work for the cause. He took over the society's publicity, and initiated a new and successful pamphlet campaign among the converts of the "Seventy," in which the most widely distributed tracts, though published anonymously or under the signatures of other authors, were all from his pen. In addition he directed the national campaign for getting anti-slavery petitions to Congress. On May 14, 1838, he married Angelina Grimké, by whom he had three children.

The last phase of Weld's agency was the most significant of all. Certain of his converts in the House of Representatives, having determined to break with the Whig party on the slavery issue, summoned Weld to Washington to act as their adviser. Here he helped secure the adherence of John Quincy Adams; and when Adams opened their campaign against slavery in the House, Weld served as his assistant in the trial for censure which followed (C. F. Adams, ed., *Memoirs of John Quincy Adams,* vol. XI, 1876, pp. 75–79). For two crucial sessions, 1841–43, he directed the insurgents; and then, an anti-slavery bloc within their party being well established, he withdrew from public life. His influence, however, remained paramount. His lobby at Washington was continued by Lewis Tappan; and its organ, the *National Era,* was edited by Weld's convert, Gamaliel Bailey. In its columns was first published *Uncle Tom's Cabin,* which, as Harriet Beecher Stowe herself declared, was crystallized out of Weld's most famous tract, *American Slavery As It Is* (Barnes, p. 231). Moreover, as the movement spread westward, in almost every district it centered about some convert of Weld or his disciples.

Measured by his influence, Weld was not only the greatest of the abolitionists; he was also one of the greatest figures of his time. His anonymity in history was partly due to his almost morbid modesty. He accepted no office, attended no conventions, published nothing under his own name, and would permit neither his speeches nor his letters to be printed. His achievements as evangelist for Western abolitionism were not recorded in the press, largely because he would not speak in the towns, where Eastern papers then had correspondents. Convinced that the towns were subject to the opinion of their countryside, and that "the springs to touch, in order to win them, *lie in the country*" (Weld-Grimké *Letters, post,* I, 287), Weld and his agents spoke only in the villages and the country districts of the West, away from public notice and the press. After the Civil War, Weld took no part in the controversies among the abolitionists as to their precedence in history, and he refused to let friends write of his own achievements. He survived all of his fellow laborers, dying at the age of ninety-one at Hyde Park, Mass., where he had made his home for thirty-two years.

Weld's chief works are: *The Bible Against Slavery* (1 ed., 1837); "Wythe," *The Power of Congress over Slavery in the District of Columbia* (1 ed., 1836); J. A. Thome and J. H. Kimball, *Emancipation in the West Indies* (1 ed., 1837); *American Slavery As It Is* (1 ed., 1839). With J. A. Thome he prepared *Slavery and the Internal Slave Trade in the United States,* published by the British and Foreign Anti-Slavery Society in 1841.

[This account of Weld's life was pieced together from newspapers, letters and pamphlets of the time. It is more fully presented in G. H. Barnes, *The Antislavery Impulse, 1830–1844* (1933); and G. H. Barnes and D. L. Dumond, eds., *Letters of Theodore Dwight Weld, Angelina Grimké Weld, and Sarah Grimké, 1822–1844* (2 vols., 1934). See also C. H. Birney, *The Grimké Sisters. Sarah and Angelina Grimké* (1885); obituary in *Boston Evening Transcript,* Feb. 4, 1895.]

                                   G. H. B.

WELD, THOMAS (1595–Mar. 23, 1660/61), Puritan divine, colonial agent, whose surname is also spelled Welde, was born in Sudbury, Suffolk, the fourth son of Edmond Weld, a well-to-do mercer, and Amy his wife. Thomas matriculated at Trinity College, Cambridge, and was graduated B.A., 1613/14 and M.A., 1618. Ordained deacon at Peterborough, Mar. 1, 1617/18, and priest the following day, he was successively vicar at Haverhill, Suffolk, and Terling, Essex. As early as Nov. 25, 1630, his nonconformity attracted Laud's attention and on Nov. 24, 1631, the Court of High Commission deposed him "for his contumacy." On June 5, 1632, he arrived in Boston, and a month later became first pastor of the church at Roxbury. In the following November, John Eliot [*q.v.*] was associated with him as teacher.

Weld was a leading minister in the Bay Colony. When the Antinomian controversy arose, he actively attempted to convince the followers of Mrs. Anne Hutchinson [*q.v.*] of their errors, and participated in the trials of the Antinomian leaders. In 1638 he was chosen overseer of Harvard College. With Eliot and Richard Mather [*q.v.*] he prepared the metrical translation of the Psalms known as the "Bay Psalm Book," the first book printed in English America (*The Whole Booke of Psalmes,* 1640). In 1641, with Hugh Peter [*q.v.*] and William Hibbins, he was sent by the General Court to England to seek financial aid for the colony and to further the work of English church reformation. Within a year the agents collected nearly £2000 in money and supplies, although their subsequent efforts were less fruitful. To advertise their mission, Weld and Peter edited and in part wrote *New England's First Fruits* (London, 1643). Meanwhile, in 1642, Hibbins had returned to Boston, and the other agents' energies were dissipated in pious but ill-managed attempts to send homeless children to New England. Soon Peter embarked in parliamentary service, leaving Weld the only active Bay Colony agent. He secured Harvard's first scholarship fund (Davis, *post*), but failed to forestall Roger Williams' attempt to secure a patent to the Narragansett territory. This failure, the agents' activity in English internal affairs, and their diminished colonial collections led to their curt dismissal, Oct. 1, 1645. Strained relations between the Bay Colony and its erstwhile agents continued. The agents secured for specific colonial purposes funds which the General Court frequently misapplied. English donors, suspecting misappropriations, accused Weld and Peter of embezzlement and refused to donate to the New England Company of 1649. Inadequate bookkeeping beclouded the issues. Weld submitted statements to the General Court and the English corporation (*Publications of the Colonial Society of Massachusetts*, vol. XIV, 1913; *New England Historical and Genealogical Register*, April 1885) and prepared for publication "Innocency Cleared," a defense of himself and Peter (*Ibid.*, January 1882). In 1654 the corporation vindicated them (Massachusetts Archives, X, 202–04).

Like Peter, Weld became enmeshed in English affairs. He plotted the sending of Laud to New England in lieu of execution and in December 1643 heatedly upbraided the aged prelate in the Tower for suspending him (Wharton, *post*, pp. 66, 203, 213–14). In 1644, Weld published *An Answer to W. R. . . .*, a defense of New England against William Rathband's attacks. Unable readily to accept the tolerating principles of English Independents, he was induced by Presbyterian plotters to edit with additions Governor Winthrop's manuscript account of New England's Antinomian troubles. The resulting book, *A Short Story of the Rise, Reign, and Ruine of the Antinomians* (1644), by emphasizing Congregational intolerance, jeopardized the Independents' political aspirations and placed Weld in an uncomfortable position, but he recovered his standing by publishing *A Brief Narration of the Practices of the Churches in New England* (London, 1645). He served as rector at Wanlip, Leicester, for a time in 1646, and on Feb. 1, 1649/50 was installed at St. Mary's, Gateshead, Durham, where he actively supported the Commonwealth and in various pamphlets denounced Quakerism, uncovered "Jesuit plots," and opposed Anabaptists. Excluding all but the "elect" from the sacraments, he alienated the majority of his people, and shortly before the Restoration he prudently withdrew from Gateshead. Retiring to London, he signed the Congregational ministers' "Renunciation" of Venner's insurrection in January 1661 and died two months later. His first wife, Margaret Dereseleye, died at Roxbury after bearing four sons; his second, Judith, whom he married at Roxbury, was buried at Gateshead, May 4, 1656; the third, Margaret, survived him.

[W. G. Weld, "The Family of Weld" (MS.), in New Eng. Hist.-Geneal. Soc.; T. W. Davids, *Annals of Evangelical Non-conformity in . . . Essex* (1863), p. 154; S. R. Gardiner, *Reports of Cases in Courts of Star Chamber and High Commission* (1886), p. 260; Henry Wharton, *The Hist. of the Troubles and Tryals . . . of*

William Laud (1695); *Original Letters . . . to Oliver Cromwell* (1743), ed. by John Nickolls; *The Works of George Fox* (1831), III, 143–49, 369–77; Benjamin Hanbury, *Hist. Memorials Relating to the Independents* (3 vols., 1839); A. G. Matthews, *Calamy Revised* (1934); John Winthrop, *The Hist. of New England* (2 vols., 1825–26), ed. by James Savage; N. B. Shurtleff, *Records of the Gov. and Company of the Mass. Bay* (5 vols., 1853–54); *The Hutchinson Papers* (1865), I, 258; David Pulsifer, *Records of the Colony of New Plymouth*, vol. X (1859); *A Report of the Record Commissioners, Containing Roxbury Land and Church Records* (Boston, 1881); *New Eng. Hist. and Geneal. Reg.*, Jan. 1854, Jan., July 1881, Jan. 1882, Oct. 1895, Apr. 1898; Wilberforce Eames, *The Bay Psalm Book* (1903); A. M. Davis, in *Proc. Am. Antiq. Soc.*, n. s., V (1889) and VIII (1893); *Colonial Soc. of Mass. Pubs.*, vols. XIII (1912), XV (1925); *Mass. Hist. Soc. Colls.*, 4 ser. VI (1863), 5 ser. I (1871); *Proc. Mass. Hist. Soc.*, 1 ser. V (1862), VI (1863), 2 ser. VIII (1894), vol. XLII (1909); C. F. Adams, *Antinomianism in Mass. Bay* (1894).]

R. P. S.

WELLER, JOHN B. (Feb. 22, 1812–Aug. 17, 1875), representative and senator in Congress, governor of California, was born in Montgomery, Hamilton County, Ohio. His parents were of German descent and natives of New York State, whence they migrated to Montgomery about 1810. When John was still a youth they moved to Oxford, Butler County, Ohio. After attending public schools and Miami University at Oxford (1825–29), he studied law in the office of Jesse Corwin, brother of Hon. Thomas Corwin [*q.v.*], and in 1832 was admitted to the bar. For several years he served as prosecuting attorney for Butler County.

In 1838 he was elected to the United States House of Representatives as a Democrat, and served three terms (1839–45). At the outbreak of the Mexican War he enlisted as a private in an Ohio regiment, and rose to the rank of colonel. He was the Democratic candidate for governor of Ohio in 1848, but lost the election by a narrow margin. In January 1849 President Polk appointed him chairman of the commission to run the boundary line between the United States and Mexico under the treaty of Guadalupe Hidalgo. Upon his recall by President Taylor in 1850, he removed to California and opened a law office in San Francisco. The following year the California legislature elected him to the United States Senate as a Union Democrat, to succeed John C. Frémont [*q.v.*]. Early in 1857 he was defeated for reëlection by David C. Broderick [*q.v.*], but was nominated for governor by the Lecompton Democrats and elected. The outstanding political event of his administration (1858–60) was the fatal duel between Senator Broderick and David S. Terry [*q.v.*], which grew out of the bitter Broderick-Gwin feud. In December 1860 Weller was appointed minister to Mexico by President Buchanan, but was recalled the next year by President Lincoln

Shortly after the close of the Civil War, he started on a long prospecting tour through Oregon, Idaho, and Utah to Salt Lake City, eventually returning to the Eastern states and residing for a time in Washington. In 1867 he moved to New Orleans and there practised law until his death from smallpox in 1875. He was married four times: his first wife was a sister of M. C. Ryan of Hamilton, Ohio; his second, the daughter of Hon. John A. Bryan; the third, Susan McDowell Taylor, daughter of Hon. William Taylor, a Virginia congressman, and niece of Senator Thomas H. Benton [*q.v.*]; the fourth, Lizzie (Brocklebank) Stanton.

When a member of the House of Representatives, Weller served on the committees on commerce, Indian affairs, and ways and means. He favored the independent treasury bill and defended the Van Buren administration. He opposed the Whig tariff bill of 1842 and advocated lowering of duties for the benefit of agriculture. In 1848, in campaigning for the governorship of Ohio, he denounced the Wilmot Proviso. In the Senate he served on the committees on pensions, and on territories, he spoke frequently in support of Pacific Railroad bills and homestead legislation, and warmly espoused the Kansas-Nebraska bill. Later he favored the admission of Kansas under the Lecompton constitution. He was a pro-slavery Democrat, and voted for Breckinridge in 1860. He had considerable talent for debate, an easy command of language, a good presence, and an agreeable voice.

[*Gen. Cat. . . . Miami Univ., 1809–1909* (1909); *Centennial Hist. of Butler County, Ohio* (1905); O. T. Shuck, *Representative and Leading Men of the Pacific* (1870); T. H. Hittell, *Hist. of Cal.,* vol. IV (1897); W. J. Davis, *Hist. of Pol. Conventions in Cal., 1849–1892* (1893); *Biog. Dir. Am. Cong.* (1928); *Daily Alta California* (San Francisco), Aug. 4, 1857; *New Orleans Times,* Aug. 18, 1875.]   P.O.R.

WELLES, GIDEON (July 1, 1802–Feb. 11, 1878), secretary of the navy, son of Samuel and Ann (Hale) Welles, was born in Glastenbury (now Glastonbury), Conn., on land bought from the Indians by his ancestor, Thomas Welles, governor and first treasurer of Connecticut, who had settled in Hartford in 1636. He attended, 1819–21, the Episcopal Academy at Cheshire, Conn., and, 1823–25, the American Literary, Scientific, and Military Academy at Norwich, Vt. (now Norwich University). From his father he received a comfortable living. He studied law, but by January 1826 had become part-owner and editor of the *Hartford Times,* which, under him, was one of the first papers in New England to declare for Jackson. He resigned the editorship in 1836, but continued to be an impor-

tant contributor to the *Times* until he broke with the editor over the slavery question. In 1826 he was elected to the legislature, being its youngest member, and served there from 1827 to 1835. He led fights against imprisonment for debt, property and religious qualifications on voting, religious tests for witnesses in court, and grants of special privilege by the legislature. He disliked banks. He fathered Connecticut's general incorporation law, which became a model for other states. On June 16, 1835, he married Mary Jane Hale of Lewistown, Pa. They had nine children.

A devoted Jeffersonian democrat who believed in freedom for the individual, strict construction, and state rights, Welles helped organize Jacksonian Democracy in Connecticut and was always depended on by Jackson for advice and support. He was elected state comptroller of public accounts in 1835, 1842, and 1843. Jackson appointed him postmaster of Hartford in 1836, and he served until Harrison removed him in 1841. As chief of the Bureau of Provisions and Clothing for the Navy, 1846–49, he made friendships and acquired experience that were later to prove valuable. He was an unsuccessful Democratic candidate for Congress in 1834 and for the Senate in 1850. On frequent trips to Washington during thirty-five years and on at least five journeys to the West, Welles made a host of friends among important leaders. He seldom forgot a face, a name, or a personality. He was an uncanny judge of men.

He left the Democratic party on the slavery question, and helped organize the Republican party when the Democrats supported the Kansas-Nebraska bill. In 1856 he helped establish the Republican organ, the *Hartford Evening Press,* and became one of its chief political writers. He contributed an important series of articles to the *New York Evening Post* and the *National Intelligencer* in the exciting ante-bellum days. In 1855 William Cullen Bryant spoke of him as "long a valued correspondent of the Evening Post" whose "newspaper style is much better than that of almost any correspondent we have" (W. C. Bryant to Welles, July 17, 1855). He was an unsuccessful candidate for the governorship of Connecticut in 1856, Republican national committeeman and member of the national executive committee from 1856 to 1864, and head of Connecticut's delegation to the Chicago convention. Always a moderate, he deprecated extremists of both sections.

Soon after the election of 1860 Lincoln chose him as the New England member of his cabinet (J. G. Nicolay and John Hay, *Abraham Lin-*

coln: A History, 1890, vol. III, 367), but did not offer him the place until Mar. 3, 1861. As secretary of the navy under Lincoln and Johnson, 1861–69, Welles held that office longer than any previous incumbent. More prophetic than others, he foresaw that the war would be long. With similar foresight he told Chase in 1863 that reconciliation would at best require more than a generation (*Diary,* I, 412). He reorganized his department and created overnight a navy where there was none. What ships there were lay scattered over the world. Many officers joined the Confederate navy. In the Ordnance Bureau only two men remained loyal. Two important navy yards fell into Confederate hands. Welles's administration of the Navy Department was much criticized. Some mistakes he did make. The building of light-draft monitors was a costly blunder that arose from failure to supervise Stimers, whose previous record gave the department excessive confidence in him. The Norfolk navy yard need not have been sacrificed. Welles urged its defense, but the inability of the War Department to send protecting troops, the unwillingness of Lincoln to provoke Virginia into secession, and trust of disloyal subordinates by a loyal though hesitant elderly commandant led to its loss. Welles's orders if carried out would have saved at least the ships and armaments. Welles was accused of slowness and undue deliberation; yet he built an adequate navy from nothing with surprising speed. He was charged with extravagance; yet no other war-time business was conducted so economically. He was criticized for allowing his wife's brother-in-law, George D. Morgan, to collect a handsome commission for purchasing ships; yet the commission was normal, and Morgan drove excellent bargains. Several scandals developed in navy yards, but Welles was the first to investigate and punish offenders. No other department was more free from political favoritism. Doggedly he withstood demands for favors. He refused to yield to the demands of Hale for a navy yard in his district though that senator headed the naval committee (Welles to J. P. Hale, Jan. 12, 1863). "The pretensions and arrogance of Senators become amazing," he exploded (*Diary,* I, 384). "I will not prostitute my trust to their schemes and selfish personal partisanship," he swore (*Ibid.,* I, 327). He urged a new navy yard at Philadelphia in the face of pressure from his own state to locate it at New London. Welles was convinced that the New York press opposed him because he had offended an influential New Yorker when he refused to buy vessels through his agency (*Ibid.,* II, 259–60). His masterly rebukes of naval officers delinquent in duty made him enemies but improved the efficiency of the service. Neither Wilkes's popularity nor Preble's famous name and powerful connections protected them when Welles decided that the good of the service required their removal. He reproved Porter for discourtesy and Phelps for seeking promotion through political pressure. Yet the same vigorous pen defended any officers who deserved it, and his letters of congratulation and praise made the heart glad.

His supervision of naval warfare was creditable. It is hard to determine how much of the credit belonged to him and how much to Gustavus V. Fox [*q.v.*] and to naval officers whom Welles trusted. Welles supervised most matters closely, and intelligently followed experiments in guns, in naval tactics, in new types of ship. He often personally wrote instructions for important engagements. He also knew how to choose reliable advisers and to cooperate with them effectively. Several claim credit for the capture of New Orleans, but Welles certainly contributed greatly to that victory. The failure of Samuel F. du Pont [*q.v.*] at Charleston led to endless disputes and made a bitter enemy of that officer, whom Welles blamed for lack of aggressiveness. "He has a reputation to preserve instead of one to make" (*Diary,* I, 247).

The greatest disputes arose over new ships. The navy had lagged behind France and Great Britain in adopting ironclads, but Welles sponsored their use. Some criticized him for slowness in developing them, others for using them at all. It is significant that in the face of expert and popular skepticism and ridicule Welles studied plans for ironclads as early as March 1861, had Dahlgren report in June on their development in France and Britain, and requested on July 4 and got from Congress a commission to study ironclads and money to build three, if the report was favorable. He conferred in July with the partner of John Ericsson [*q.v.*], saw Ericsson's plans in August, and was so impressed that he rushed Bushnell off to Washington to present them to the Naval Board and curtailed his own vacation in order to speak in their behalf. He signed a contract with Ericsson in September 1861, requested $12,000,000 for ironclads on Dec. 2, and finally got the bill for $10,000,000 passed in the Senate by personal intervention. When, therefore, popular clamor for ironclads burst forth after the battle of the *Monitor* and the *Merrimac* (*Virginia*) on Mar. 7, he was already using for them $10,000,000 obtained while they were still ridiculed. In a letter of Apr. 25, 1862, Ericsson gave the lie to the attack of the *New*

York Herald on Welles and testified that he had cooperated admirably in building the *Monitor.* Welles also developed heavy ordnance, improved steam machinery, and armored cruisers. The much-criticized steam-engine of Benjamin F. Isherwood [*q.v.*] developed speed not equaled until years later. The exigencies of war made him concentrate on monitors useful against an enemy with no navy. As early as December 1862, however, he warned the naval committees that only fast ironclad cruisers could maintain the position of the Union against other naval powers. After the war, he urged enlargement of inadequate navy yards, their modernization to build, repair, and store ironclads, improvement in the selection of naval cadets, and the establishment of a "steam engineering" department at the Naval Academy. Porter, who disliked him, testified that he had "served his country . . . with fidelity and zeal, if not with conspicuous ability" (D. D. Porter, *Incidents and Anecdotes of the Civil War,* 1885, p. 66). Lincoln wrote on July 25, 1863, "Your department has been conducted with admirable success." The blockade was successful; and naval attacks were often brilliantly executed. Welles's navy was an important factor in the crushing of the Confederacy.

Welles's contribution to the general policies of the government was as important as his departmental administration. He was a close observer and critic of the activities of the War Department and always distrusted Stanton (*Diary,* I, 58–69). In many campaigns he cooperated with the army but found it difficult to do so. Seward's interference in the Navy Department at the time of the Sumter expedition and his tendency to meddle and give orders to Welles and his subordinates annoyed Welles. He suspected Seward's motives (*Ibid.,* I, 12, 36, 204–05, *et passim*). Yet when Seward was attacked by congressional enemies Welles loyally supported him. Welles urged the "closing" of Southern ports instead of permitting other nations to recognize Confederate belligerency by blockading them. When the blockade was established he favored rigid enforcement. On July 22, 1861, long before the army acted, Welles ordered naval commanders to give protection to runaway slaves. On Sept. 25 he issued orders to enlist them in the service. In 1862–63 he protested vigorously against Chase's depreciation of the currency (*Ibid.,* I, 147, 167–69, 232, 494). He opposed the admission of West Virginia as unconstitutional. In 1863 he deplored the suspension of *habeas corpus,* the arrest of Vallandigham, and the suppression of the *Chicago Times* (*Ibid.,* I, 321–22, 432–35). He

disliked the excessive use of power involved in freeing the slaves but favored this as a necessary war measure (*Ibid.,* I, 144). In 1863 he had seen that emancipation involved not only moral and political but also industrial and social relations and wondered whether immediate, universal emancipation might not be injurious to master and slave alike (*Ibid.,* I, 403). While others changed ground he contended to the end that the war was not fought against states but against rebellious individuals and that states could not secede (*Ibid.,* I, 414). He backed Lincoln's moderate program and when Johnson became president supported his efforts to restore Southern states. He early urged Johnson to oust his enemies from office and use the patronage to support his policies (*Ibid.,* II, 398, 556). He helped force James Harlan, James Speed, and William Dennison [*qq.v.*] out of the cabinet and warned Johnson against Stanton's duplicity (*Ibid.,* II, 398, 404). He supported the new conservative party movement of 1866. When the Radicals triumphed in 1866 he continued to urge upon them a program of moderation and to defend Southerners against Radical excesses. During the impeachment he gave Johnson vigorous support.

In 1868 he returned to the Democratic fold, in 1872 became a Liberal Republican, and in 1876 not only supported Tilden but also used his still-effective pen to attack the decision of the Electoral Commission. He convincingly maintained that he had stood consistently upon his principles while parties and politicians shifted ground. Between his retirement in 1869 and his death he published articles in the *Galaxy* (Nov.–Dec. 1871; Apr.–May 1872; Dec. 1872; May 1873; Oct., Nov., Dec. 1873; Sept., Oct. 1876; Jan.–Feb., Oct., Nov., Dec. 1877) which remain important historical documents. One of these was expanded and published as *Lincoln and Seward* (1874). His painstaking diary is a storehouse of historical data, though in its published form (*Diary of Gideon Welles,* 3 vols., 1911) there is no indication of the corrections and revisions made in later years by Welles himself (H. K. Beale, in *American Historical Review,* Apr. 1925, pp. 547–52).

Welles had a commanding figure; yet his bounteous white whiskers and wig gave him benignity. To the navy and to Lincoln he was "Father Welles," to Governor Andrew of Massachusetts "that old Mormon deacon." An Episcopalian by faith, he was deeply religious. A New England conscience, a keen sense of duty, and a methodical mind made him a dependable public servant. An unusual memory, interest in people, and capacity for shrewd analysis of character gave him a wide knowledge of politicians; his letters and diary contain remarkable sketches of his contemporaries. Since he was no orator and his editorials were usually unsigned, others gained greater fame, but a vigorous political style and access to leading newspapers gave him far-reaching influence. Throughout the stormy days of the war he maintained poise and calmness that often encouraged but in crises irritated his associates. Realism and unusual common sense prevented too great disappointment on his part when men fell short of his standards. His severer qualities were softened by marked human kindness, loyalty to friends, and a love of amusing anecdote. Never brilliant, he was competent and, above all, faithful and honest. Pronouncing him "a very wise, strong man," Dana said: "There was nothing decorative about him; there was no noise in the street when he went along; but he understood his duty, and did it efficiently, continually, and unvaryingly" (C. A. Dana, *Recollections of the Civil War*, 1898, p. 170).

[MS. diaries, letters, and articles in Lib. of Cong.; obituary by William Faxon in the *Hartford Daily Courant*, Feb. 12, 1878; C. O. Paullin, "A Half Century of Naval Administration in America, 1861–1911," *U. S. Naval Institute Proc.*, vols. XXXVIII, XXXIX (1912–13); C. B. Boynton, *Hist. of the Navy during the Rebellion* (1876–78); F. M. Bennett, *The Steam Navy of the U. S.* (1896); J. P. Baxter, *The Introduction of the Ironclad Warship* (1933); H. K. Beale, *The Critical Year* (1930), for Welles's course under Johnson; Albert Welles, *Hist. of the Welles Family* (1876); J. H. Trumbull, *The Memorial Hist. of Hartford County, Conn.* (2 vols., 1886); H. R. Stiles, *The Hist. of Ancient Wethersfield* (1904), II, 776–77.]

H. K. B—e.

WELLES, NOAH (Sept. 25, 1718–Dec. 31, 1776), Congregational clergyman, was the son of a farmer of Colchester, Conn., for whom he was named, and of Sarah, daughter of Israel and Sarah Wyatt, also of Colchester. At the age of nineteen he entered Yale College, from which he graduated in 1741, remaining there another year as Dean's Scholar. For the next four years he was engaged in teaching, the study of theology, and occasional preaching. A part of this time he was in charge of the Hopkins Grammar School, Hartford, and from 1745 to 1746, tutor at Yale. After having supplied the Congregational church of Stamford, Conn., for several months, he was invited to become its settled pastor, and was ordained and installed there on Dec. 31, 1746. On Sept. 17, 1751, he was married to Abigail, daughter of Rev. Benjamin Woolsey; they had thirteen children.

His pastorate, terminated by his death, covered thirty years to a day. According to the elder Timothy Dwight [*q.v.*], his talents were distinguished, his learning extensive, and his

mind of the imaginative, poetical type. He was "an able preacher; a wise ruler of the church; and an eminently discreet manager of its important concerns" (*Travels in New England and New York*, vol. III, 1822, p. 499). He was prominently mentioned for the presidency of Yale after the resignation of Thomas Clap [*q.v.*] in 1766, and from 1774 till his death he was a fellow of the college. He was a pronounced advocate of resistance to British oppression, setting forth from the pulpit the righteousness and duty of it, both at the time when the Stamp Act was creating excitement and in the opening days of the Revolution. A sermon of his preached before the General Assembly of Connecticut in 1764 and published that year bears the title, *Patriotism Described and Recommended*. He was even more widely known as a defender of the validity of Presbyterian ordination and as an opponent of Episcopacy in the colony. He is now generally credited with being the author of the anonymously published satire, *The Real Advantages Which Ministers and People May Enjoy Especially in the Colonies by Conforming to the Church of England; Truthfully Considered and Impartially Represented in a Letter to a Young Gentleman* (1762). Skillfully and pleasantly written, it was in effect a keen attack upon the English Church and its clergy, and attracted no little attention. In 1763 he published a lengthy address entitled, *The Divine Right of Presbyterian Ordination Asserted, and the Ministerial Authority, Claimed and Exercised in the Established Churches of New England, Vindicated and Proved*. Jeremiah Leaming [*q.v.*], in 1766, published *A Defence of the Episcopal Government . . .*, containing remarks on Welles's address and on one by Charles Chauncy [*q.v.*]. To this Welles replied in *A Vindication of the Validity and Divine Right of Presbyterian Ordination, as Set Forth in Dr. Chauncy's Sermon . . . and Mr. Welle's* [sic] *Discourse, in Answer to the Exceptions of Mr. Jeremiah Leaming* (1767). As a controversialist Welles displayed intellectual vigor, a keen mind, argumentative ability, fairness, and dignity. His death occurred in his fifty-ninth year, and was occasioned by jail fever contracted while he was ministering to British prisoners.

[C. M. Taintor, *Extracts from the Records of Colchester* (1864), p. 106; J. W. Alvord, *Hist. Address Delivered in the First Congregational Church in Stamford, Ct., . . . Dec. 22d, 1841* (1842); E. B. Huntington, *Hist. of Stamford, Conn.* (1868); W. B. Sprague, *Annals Am. Pulpit*, vol. I (1857); F. B. Dexter, *Biog. Sketches Grads. Yale Coll.*, vol. I (1885).]

H. E. S.

WELLES, ROGER (Dec. 7, 1862–Apr. 26, 1932), naval officer and explorer, son of Roger and Mercy Delano (Aiken) Welles, was born in Newington, Conn. He was a direct descendant of Thomas Welles, one of the early governors of Connecticut. In 1880 he was appointed to the United States Naval Academy, graduating in 1884. Three years later he was sent to the North Pacific on the U. S. S. *Thetis,* under Lieut. William H. Emory [*q.v.*], for a cruise in the Arctic and the Bering Sea. On this ship he made three successive voyages into the Polar regions, cruising as far west as Herald Island and Wrangell Land, and as far east as Mackenzie Bay. The last voyage was made under Lieut. Charles H. Stockton [*q.v.*]. During these voyages he acquired considerable knowledge of the Eskimo dialects, and on his return, in collaboration with an interpreter, John W. Kelly, he prepared a pamphlet entitled *English-Eskimo and Eskimo-English Vocabularies* (1890), published by the United States Bureau of Education. In 1891 he was sent as a special representative of the United States for the World's Columbian Exposition to Venezuela and the Guianas, with instructions to explore the Orinoco River. He ascended the river farther than any white man had been before, and brought back an ethnological collection which, with his diary of the journey, is now in the Field Museum, Chicago. For this service he received a certificate and a bronze medal.

During the Spanish-American War Welles acted as executive officer on the converted yacht *Wasp* off the Cuban coast, participating in the battle of Nipe Bay, where the Spanish cruiser *Don Jorge Juan* was sunk. For this service he was given the Atlantic Battle Medal (Nipe Bay). After the war he served on the president's yacht *Mayflower,* attended the Naval War College in 1903–04, and subsequently served three years with the Asiatic Fleet. When the World War broke out, Welles, then a captain, was made director of naval intelligence, a post which he held throughout the war, building up a far-flung censorship personnel. On July 1, 1918, he was given the temporary rank of rear admiral, a promotion made permanent a year later. After the war he commanded successively the first division of the Atlantic Fleet, and the eleventh and fifth naval districts. In September 1925 he was sent abroad as commander of the United States forces in Europe with the *Pittsburgh* as his flagship. He was retired for age on Dec. 7, 1926.

By his own government Welles was awarded the Cuban and Philippine Campaign Medals and the Navy Cross for exceptionally meritorious service in a duty of great responsibility as director of naval intelligence. He was also awarded the Grand Cross of the Order of Naval Merit and Efficiency by the King of Spain, the Second Order of the Rising Sun by the Japanese Government, and was made Grand Officer of the Order of Leopold II by King Albert of Belgium, and Commander of the Legion of Honor by the French Government. He was known in the service as a highly efficient officer and navigator, a strict disciplinarian, but kindly and thoughtful of the welfare of his men, who were devoted to him. On Oct. 17, 1908, he married Harriet Ogden Deen of Staten Island.

[*Am. Ancestry,* vol. IX (1894); Albert Welles, *Hist. of the Welles Family* (1876); *Army and Navy Reg.,* Apr. 30, 1932; Albert Gleaves, *The Life of an Am. Sailor, Rear-Admr. Wm. H. Emory* (1923); *N. Y. Times,* Apr. 27, 1932; *Ann. Report of the Navy Dept. . . . Appendix to the Report of the Chief of the Bureau of Navigation* (1898); transcript of Welles's service record in Bureau of Navigation; information from a brother, L. A. Welles, of N. Y. City.]   L. H. B.

WELLING, JAMES CLARKE (July 14, 1825–Sept. 4, 1894), journalist and educator, was born in Trenton, N. J., the only son of William and Jane (Hill) Welling. He received his elementary education at the Trenton Academy and in 1844 graduated from the College of New Jersey (Princeton). After tutoring in Virginia for two years and reading law, he was made associate principal of the New York Collegiate School in 1848. In 1850 he was married to Genevieve H. Garnett, the daughter of Henry T. Garnett of Westmoreland County, Va. She died two years later, leaving a daughter. In 1850 he was appointed literary editor of the *Daily National Intelligencer* in Washington, D. C. Six years later he became associate editor, with actual control of the paper. His learning, legal training, analytical mind, breadth of culture, forceful pen, and wide acquaintance admirably qualified him for the direction of this journal, which was a leading organ of opinion on the eve of the Civil War and continued as such during most of the conflict itself. His articles on constitutional law in its relation to current difficulties stamped the *Intelligencer* as a conservative Unionist organ. He supported the Bell-Everett ticket in 1860. His editorials on the *Trent* affair and the Monroe Doctrine attracted wide attention. He favored the abolition of slavery but questioned the validity of the Emancipation Proclamation, holding that it should be legalized by constitutional amendment. He joined his friend, Edward Bates [*q.v.*], in declaring trials by military commissions to be irregular, a stand later taken by the Supreme Court. His support of McClellan for the presidency in 1864 proved to be a political blunder for both himself and the *Intelligencer.* He resigned in 1865, went to Europe, and then served for a time as clerk of the federal court of claims. He became president of St. John's College, Annapolis, Md., in 1867. After three years at St. John's, he was made professor of rhetoric and English literature at the College of New Jersey.

He resigned to accept the presidency in 1871 of Columbian College, Washington, D. C., now George Washington University. A close friendship with W. W. Corcoran, the institution's chief benefactor, developed. Their aim was to broaden the scope of the institution's activities so as to make Washington the national educational center. By congressional act of Mar. 3, 1873, the college was incorporated as Columbian University, and, in the following year, it was moved from the suburbs to the heart of the city. Its law and medical faculties were enlarged, and scientific and dental schools, as well as a school of graduate studies, were opened. A movement to amalgamate the then defunct University of Chicago with Columbian and to obtain financial support from John D. Rockefeller did not materialize. In addition to his executive duties, he taught the philosophy of history and international law. His interests were multifarious. He was president of the Cosmos Club in Washington in 1880, of the board of trustees of Corcoran Art Gallery from 1881 to his death, of the Washington Philosophical Society in 1884, and the Anthropological Society of Washington in 1891–1892. He was a regent of the Smithsonian Institution from 1884 to his death and chairman of the executive committee during the last eight years of his life. Some of his writings of this period were collected in *Addresses, Lectures, and Other Papers,* published after his death (1903). In the spring of 1894 he resigned the presidency of Columbian to be effective as of the following October, but he died in Hartford, Conn., in September. He was survived by his second wife, Clementine Louise Dixon, to whom he was married in 1882. They had two children.

[George Washington Univ. Records; "Diary of Edward Bates," *Ann. Report Amer. Hist. Asso. . . . 1930,* vol. IV (1933), ed. by H. K. Beale; *Evening Star* (Washington), Nov. 6, 7, 1871, Sept. 4, 5, 1894; *Hartford Daily Courant* and *N. Y. Times,* Sept. 5, 1894; private information.]   L. J. R.

WELLINGTON, ARTHUR MELLEN (Dec. 20, 1847–May 16, 1895), civil engineer, editor, was born at Waltham, Mass., the son of Oliver Hastings Wellington, a physician, and his wife, Charlotte Kent. Through Benjamin Wellington, who fought at Lexington, Arthur was descended from Roger Wellington, who came to the Massachusetts Bay Colony in 1636. After graduating from the Boston Latin School, Wel-

lington became an articled student of engineering (1863–66) in the office of John B. Henck [q.v.], author of the *Field-Book for Railroad Engineers* (1854). He passed the examination for assistant engineer in the United States Navy, but did not accept an appointment. After completing his apprenticeship he became for a time a surveyor in the park department of Brooklyn, N. Y.; next he had two years' experience in railroad surveying in North Carolina and New York, and in 1870 he joined the Buffalo, New York & Philadelphia Railroad, of which he was soon made principal assistant engineer. After two and a half years in this connection he became locating engineer for the Michigan Central, and later was engineer in charge of the Toledo, Canada Southern & Detroit Railroad.

When the depression of 1873 temporarily halted railroad building, he turned to writing and in 1874 published *Methods for the Computation from Diagrams of Preliminary and Final Estimates of Railway Earthwork,* setting forth methods which he had devised. He also published several shorter articles, among them one which in 1876 he expanded into a series of articles ("Justifiable Expenditure for Improving the Alignment of Railways," *Railroad Gazette,* Sept. 1–Dec. 29, 1876), and in 1877 published in book form under the title, *The Economic Theory of the Location of Railways.* This classic treatise went through a half-dozen editions, becoming the standard monograph on railway location.

In 1878 Wellington became principal assistant engineer for the New York, Pennsylvania & Ohio Railroad and in 1881 went to Mexico as engineer in charge of location and surveys of the Mexican National Railway. Later he became its assistant general manager, remaining until 1884, when he was offered an editorial post on the *Railroad Gazette.* In 1887 he became a part owner and one of the editors of *Engineering News.* While serving as editor, he continued in consulting practice, chiefly in connection with public works such as the elimination of grade crossings at Buffalo and the building of terminals at Toronto. He was a member of the board of engineers of the Nicaragua Canal in 1890, and was adviser to the Massachusetts legislature on street railways in Boston. In 1892 he attempted to develop a new type of thermodynamic engine and in 1893 was consultant on railways in Jamaica. In addition he was an active worker in engineering societies. He married Agnes Bates in 1878, and they had one child, a daughter.

[*N. Y. Tribune,* May 19, 1895; *Proc. Am. Soc. Civil Engineers,* vol. XXI (1895); *Appletons' Cyc. for 1895* (1896).]   T. T. R.

WELLMAN, SAMUEL THOMAS

WELLMAN, SAMUEL THOMAS (Feb. 5, 1847–July 11, 1919), engineer, inventor, was born in Wareham, Mass., the son of Samuel Knowlton and Mary Love (Bessee) Wellman, and a descendant of Thomas Wellman who was in Lynn, Mass., as early as 1640. At the time of Samuel's birth his father was superintendent of the Nashua Iron Company, Nashua, N. H., in which city the boy received his public-school education. Entering Norwich University, Norwich, Vt., he studied engineering for a year and then enlisted in the Union army and served in 1864–65 as a corporal in Company F, 1st New Hampshire Heavy Artillery. On his discharge he returned home and entered the drafting room of the Nashua Iron Company, where his father was still superintendent. Here he worked for two years.

In 1867 his father gave him the task of building, from drawings furnished, a Siemens regenerative gas furnace for the company. Wellman had just completed it when the engineer sent from England by the Siemens Company arrived in Nashua to build the same furnace. The perfection with which the job had been done by young Wellman so amazed the engineer that he forthwith offered Wellman the opportunity of assisting him in erecting other Siemens furnaces. Wellman accepted and during the succeeding six years was engaged in this work in various parts of the country. In Pittsburgh in 1867, at the works of Anderson, Cook & Company, he assisted in starting and operating the first crucible-steel furnace in America. After building two more furnaces for another organization there he spent some time in the offices and steel works of the Siemens agents in Boston, Mass. Then, as a free lance, he constructed for the Bay State Iron Works, South Boston, the first commercially successful open hearth furnace in the United States. Upon the completion of this work he returned to Nashua and built for his father's company an open hearth furnace and rolling mills. In 1873 he went to Cleveland, Ohio, where he designed and built the Otis Steel Works and remained for sixteen years as chief engineer and superintendent.

During this period he began his inventive work in machinery and other equipment for the manufacture of iron and steel, for which he was granted nearly a hundred patents in the course of his life. Two of his inventions brought him worldwide renown. The first, invented in the eighties, was the electric open-hearth charging machine, a device for feeding white-hot steel into open-hearth furnaces; the second, patented Dec. 10, 1895, was an electro-magnet for handling pig iron and scrap steel. In time every open-hearth steel plant of any size throughout the world was equipped with these two devices. In 1890 Wellman with his brother Charles organized the Wellman Steel Company in Cleveland. Six years later they and John W. Seaver formed the Wellman-Seaver Engineering Company, with Wellman as president, and engaged in consulting work, specializing in iron and steel manufacture. Later, this company consolidated with the Webster, Camp & Lane Company of Akron, Ohio, and became the Wellman-Seaver-Morgan Company, of which Wellman was for a time president, and later chairman of the board until his retirement in 1900. He was active in a number of technical and engineering societies both in this country and England, and served as president of the American Society of Mechanical Engineers in 1901. He was married on Sept. 3, 1868, to Julia Almina Ballard of Stoneham, Mass., and at the time of his sudden death at Stratton, Me., he was survived by five children.

[J. W. Wellman, *Descendants of Thomas Wellman* (1918); *Trans. Am. Soc. Mech. Engineers*, vol. XLI (1919); *Iron Age*, July 17, 1919; *The Open Hearth . . . Its Design and Operation* (1920); *Who's Who in America*, 1918–19; *Cleveland Plain Dealer*, July 12, 1919; Patent Office records.]   C. W. M.

WELLMAN, WALTER

WELLMAN, WALTER (Nov. 3, 1858–Jan. 31, 1934), journalist, explorer, aeronaut, was born in Mentor, Ohio. He was the son of Alonzo and Minerva (Graves) Wellman and a descendant of Thomas Wellman who was in Lynn, Mass., as early as 1640. Most of Walter's formal schooling was received in a district school in Michigan. At the age of fourteen he started a weekly newspaper at Sutton, Neb.; at twenty-one he founded the evening *Cincinnati Post,* and from 1884 to 1911 he was the Washington correspondent of the *Chicago Herald* and its successor, the *Record-Herald.*

The first enterprise to bring him wide recognition was a trip to the Bahamas in 1891, in the course of which he located, as he claimed, the exact landing spot of Christopher Columbus (*Chicago Herald,* July 4, 1891), and erected a monument to mark the place on Watling Island, or San Salvador. He was fascinated by the unknown lands of the North; in 1894, journeying by boat and sledge over the ice, he reached a latitude of 81° at a point northeast of Spitzbergen and in 1898–99 he led a similar expedition to Franz-Josef Land, reaching a latitude of 82° north. As a consequence of these expeditions he was commissioned in 1906 by Frank B. Noyes, publisher of the *Chicago Record-Herald,* to attempt a trip to the Arctic regions by air. The airship was built in Paris in the spring of that year (see Wellman's article, "The Polar Air-ship," *National Geographic Magazine,* April 1906) and after some experimental flights was enlarged during the winter of 1906–07. Stormy weather at the base in Spitzbergen delayed trial trips, but on Sept. 2, 1907, Wellman took off for the pole. Continuous and violent squalls nearly wrecked the craft, however, and at last Wellman deflated the ship and returned to Paris, to await a more favorable opportunity. On Aug. 15, 1909, he set out again, with three companions, but after he had covered a distance of only twelve miles the equilibrator broke and he was forced to turn back. He abandoned further attempts to reach the pole by air after the announcement that Robert E. Peary [*q.v.*] had succeeded in doing so on foot.

The most ambitious undertaking of Wellman's career was his attempt to cross the Atlantic by air. The airship *America,* which had been used on previous polar explorations, was rebuilt to a length of 228 feet. It had a lifting capacity of twelve tons and a speed of twenty-five miles an hour. Below the bag of silk and cotton, filled with hydrogen, hung a car of interlaced steel tubing; below the car was a gas tank 150 feet long and two feet in diameter; below the gas tank was a lifeboat with supplies for thirty days, and still lower, an equilibrator which was also a fuel supply, being a string of thirty steel drums filled with gasoline. Prepared for ten days in the air or thirty on the sea, Wellman and five companions took off from Atlantic City, N. J., in a dense fog at eight o'clock in the morning, Oct. 15, 1910. During the flight, for the first time in history wireless messages were sent from land to an airship over water and for several hours messages came back regularly. Trouble was in store, however: one of the motors stalled because of a bad bearing, and the other threatened to set the ship on fire with sparks from the exhaust; the cooling and contraction of the hydrogen at night caused the airship to come to a dangerously low altitude; a northeast wind drove the ship off its course, and it was eventually forced down. The crew was rescued by a steamer some 375 miles off Cape Hatteras, and the *America* drifted away in the wind and was never seen again. Wellman considered the trip a failure, but he had broken the existing world record for time and distance sailing by airship and found himself a hero upon his return to New York. The time in the air was seventy-two hours, and the distance 1,008 miles. In his book *The Aerial Age,* published in 1911, he described the experience fully. It is significant that in all Wellman's dangerous undertakings not a man of his various crews was lost. He was

married twice: first, on Dec. 24, 1878, to Laura McCann of Canton, Ohio, and second, to Belgljat Bergerson of Norway. Four children and his second wife survived him.

[J. W. Wellman, *Descendants of Thomas Wellman* (1918); *Who's Who in America,* 1928–29; *Scientific American,* June 22, 1907, Oct. 1, 29, 1910; *Aeronautics,* Oct., Dec. 1910; *N. Y. Times,* Feb. 1, 1934.]

A. K—n.

WELLONS, WILLIAM BROCK (Nov. 9, 1821–Feb. 16, 1877), clergyman, prominent among the leaders of the Christian Connection in the Southern states, was born near Littleton, Sussex County, Va., the son of Hartwell and Mary W. Wellons. His father was a farmer, and the only formal education William ever received was at winter sessions of country schools. Converted at a camp meeting when he was thirteen years old, he was thereafter governed largely by religious interests. From 1840 to 1845 he taught school, for a part of the time at Airfield, Southampton County, Va. He also conducted religious meetings with such success that in 1845 he was admitted to the Eastern Virginia Conference as a licentiate and in 1846 was ordained a minister of the Christian Connection.

For several years he served as an itinerant, holding revival meetings and organizing churches. While acting as pastor in New Bern, N. C., he married, Apr. 12, 1850, Sarah L. Beasley, a widow. Soon afterward, they removed to Suffolk, Va., which was Wellons' home for the remainder of his life. During these years, he had pastoral oversight of several churches in the vicinity, and was frequently in attendance at conferences and conventions, at which he made his influence strongly felt. In 1854 he was a delegate to the quadrennial Christian Convention held at Cincinnati, and was the Southern member of a committee of three appointed to consider the question of slavery. He was himself a slaveholder and presented a minority report urging that the South be conceded the right to manage its own domestic institutions. The attitude of the majority of the convention was so hostile, however, that finally Wellons announced his withdrawal on behalf of his constituency. Other Southern members followed his example, and in 1856 the General Convention of the Christian Church, South, was organized with Wellons as president. In the meantime, 1855, he had become editor in chief of the *Christian Sun,* the official organ of the Christian Connection in the South, of which he had been an associate editor since 1849, and it was thereafter published in Suffolk. During the Civil War he was forced to discontinue it and remove to Petersburg. At this time he became editor of the *Army and Navy*

Messenger, issued by the Evangelic Tract Society and distributed among Confederate soldiers and sailors. He also did much personal religious work on the field and in hospitals. In 1865 he returned to Suffolk, resumed preaching, labored to reorganize the churches of the neighborhood, and, assuming the financial responsibility himself, began again the publication of the *Christian Sun.* Largely through his influence, the General Convention of the Southern branch of the Christian Connection in 1866 adopted and published a statement of principles and government—an event regarded as significant in the history of the Connection.

Wellons was all his life much interested in education. For some time he conducted a school for young women in his home at Suffolk, and he was instrumental in securing the establishment in 1853 of the Holy Neck Female Seminary in Nansemond County. As a result of a recommendation made by a committee to the Southern Christian Convention in 1870 that normal and theological schools be provided in each of the local Conferences, the Suffolk Collegiate Institute was opened in January 1872 and Wellons was elected principal. As such he served until his death. He took an active part in the temperance movement in Virginia, and during his later years was an advocate of more cooperation on the part of the Christian Connection with other evangelical bodies. He died in his fifty-sixth year of tuberculosis of the lungs.

[E. W. Humphreys, *Memoirs of Deceased Christian Ministers* (1880); P. J. Kernodle, *Lives of Christian Ministers* (copr. 1909); M. T. Morrill, *A Hist. of the Christian Denomination in America* (1912); *Daily Dispatch* (Richmond, Va.), Feb. 17, 1877.]   H. E. S.

WELLS, DAVID AMES (June 17, 1828–Nov. 5, 1898), economist, was born at Springfield, Mass., the son of James and Rebecca (Ames) Wells, and a descendant of Thomas Welles, governor of Connecticut, 1655–59. David graduated from Williams College in 1847, having already become engaged in literary work by assisting in the preparation of *Sketches of Williams College,* published that year. In 1848 he joined the staff of the *Springfield Republican,* in connection with which he displayed mechanical ingenuity by inventing a device for folding paper, to be attached to power presses. He graduated from the Lawrence Scientific School at Cambridge in 1851, where he was a special pupil of Louis Agassiz [*q.v.*]. While at Cambridge he began the publication with George Bliss, in 1850, of *The Annual of Scientific Discovery,* which he continued until 1866. In 1856 he made important improvements in the method of manufacturing textiles. He was a special partner in the publishing firm of G. P. Putnam & Company, 1857–58, and during this period he compiled *The Science of Common Things* (1857) and *Wells's Principles and Applications of Chemistry* (copr. 1858). Later he published *Wells's First Principles of Geology* (1861) and *Wells's Natural Philosophy* (1863), the latter going through fifteen editions.

In 1864 Wells came into wide prominence through the issuance by the Loyalty Publication Company of his first economic work, a pamphlet entitled *Our Burden and Our Strength.* Two hundred thousand copies of this brochure were distributed, and it was translated into French, German, Dutch, and other languages. At that time a lack of confidence in the ability of the United States government ever to discharge its mounting debts had caused the fall of greenbacks and bonds to half their face value. Wells in his pamphlet reassured foreign investors and the people of the North by demonstrating the dynamic character of economic life in the North, with its rapid accumulation of capital and constant introduction of labor-saving devices. Brought by this publication to the attention of Lincoln, Wells was appointed in 1865 chairman of the national revenue commission and in 1866 signed its report making recommendations which became laws. That same year the post of special commissioner of the revenue was created for him, and soon the bureau of statistics was established, of which he put Francis A. Walker [*q.v.*] in charge. The *Reports of the Special Commissioner of the Revenue,* 1866–69, set forth the whole subject of indirect taxes, and recommended the use of stamps in the collection of revenue on liquor and tobacco. In 1867, Wells went to Europe as a member of a commission to investigate costs of industrial production there. As befitted his New England background he was a stanch protectionist, but finding that high wages in America made for efficiency as compared with the backward methods of competing countries, he was converted to free trade, became a member of the Cobden Club, and thereafter for thirty years was a leading advocate of abolition of the tariff. He was a counselor of his close friend, President Garfield, on tariff matters, and later of Grover Cleveland.

The extreme free-trade point of view in Wells's report of 1869 prompted President Grant to abolish the office of special commissioner the following year. Wells, however, was promptly made chairman of the New York state tax commission, and published as one of its reports *Local Taxation* (1871), the earliest really competent study of the subject. His chief problem in New York was to remedy a situation made critical by the increase of the tax burden in that state while contiguous states were attracting capital and enterprise through lenient laws. In 1876 he was named one of the receivers for the Alabama & Chattanooga Railroad, and helped rescue its property. He was one of the trustees of the bondholders who bought in and reorganized the Erie Railway in 1875, and in 1878 he became a member of the board of arbitration of the Associated Railways, deciding on questions of pooling. He took an active interest in politics and was several times a delegate to the Democratic national conventions. He was an unsuccessful candidate for Congress from Connecticut in 1876 and 1890, and he made many speeches in each of Cleveland's campaigns.

Wells wrote a large number of books, pamphlets, and articles, always with a current problem uppermost in his mind. His chief interests were the tariff, the theory of money and the currency question, and taxation. His discussion of all of these took character from his inspection of American economic life, which was marked in his period by progressive lowering of costs of production through the application of science. He, more than others, was the expositor of the nature and consequences of "the machine age." The new economics of production required in his judgment abolition of protective tariffs in order to furnish wide markets, and he was convinced that industrial depressions, with falling prices, were due not to insufficient circulating media, but to sudden and rapid increase in commodities. Some of his most effective writing was in opposition to fiat money or depreciated monetary standards. An excellent example of his work in this field is his *Robinson Crusoe's Money,* issued first in 1876 when resumption was in doubt, and again in 1896 when the "free silver" advocacy was in full swing. Wells was among the earliest to appreciate the importance of what has since been known as "technological unemployment," the displacing of men by machines. He urged the substitution of trained personnel for political hangers-on in tax bodies, sought to bring system into taxation, and was the inveterate foe of the general property tax as applied to intangibles. He accepted the diffusion theory of taxation; his opposition to the faculty theory led him to fight against income taxes. He was an out-and-out apostle of *laissez faire,* and thus missed the later implications of many of the tendencies in American economic life which he discovered and expounded. His writing and speaking was marked by simplicity, candor, and extraordinary facility in the popular adaptation

of statistics. His aptness in illustration was as charming as it was effective; it is evidenced in his *True Story of the Leaden Statuary* (1874). Among his most significant works, beside those mentioned, are *The Relation of the Government to the Telegraph* (1873); *The Cremation Theory of Specie Resumption* (1875); *The Silver Question* (1877); *Why We Trade and How We Trade* (1878); *Our Merchant Marine* (1882); *A Primer of Tariff Reform* (1884); *Practical Economics* (1885); *Recent Economic Changes* (1889); *The Theory and Practice of Taxation* (1900).

Wells died at Norwich, Conn., which had been his residence since 1870. He was married, May 9, 1860, to Mary Sanford Dwight, by whom he had one son; a second wife and a son survived him.

[Albert Welles, *Hist. of the Welles Family* (1876); B. W. Dwight, *The Hist. of the Descendants of John Dwight* (1874); Calvin Durfee, *Williams Biog. Annals* (1871); G. H. Putnam, *Memories of a Publisher* (1915), pp. 35 ff., 357, and *George Palmer Putnam: A Memoir* (1912), pp. 282–8, 346 ff.; *Johns Hopkins Univ. Circulars,* Mar. 1899; *N. Y. Times,* Nov. 6, 8, 1898; E. R. A. Seligman, in *Palgrave's Dict. of Pol. Economy,* vol. III (1926), and in *Encyc. of the Social Sciences,* vol. XV (1935).]   B.M.

WELLS, ERASTUS (Dec. 2, 1823–Oct. 2, 1893), congressman, street railway builder, was born near Sacketts Harbor, Jefferson County, N. Y., the only son among three children of Otis and Mary (Symonds) Wells. Through his farmer father he was descended from Hugh Welles of Essex County, England, who came to America about 1635, and from James Otis [*q.v.*]. With the death of his father his schooling was stopped when he was fourteen years of age. He clerked in stores in nearby Watertown and Lockport until he was twenty and then he emigrated to St. Louis, Mo. Here in 1844 he induced Calvin Case, a prominent business man, to finance an omnibus, said to be the first conveyance of its kind west of the Mississippi. The youthful driver made most of his first trips alone, but gradually the growing community approved the new mode of transportation and additional vehicles were required. He sold his interest in the omnibus line at a good profit and then managed a lead factory and a sawmill for a time. He returned to street transportation and founded the Missouri Railway Company, in 1859. He headed this enterprise until his retirement at the age of sixty, and also promoted a narrow-gauge railway to Florissant, Mo. He served as an official of two banks, and as a director of the Ohio and Mississippi Railroad. He was also president of the Laclede Gas Light Company in St. Louis.

With his business life Wells coupled an active

political career. He was elected to the St. Louis legislative body in 1848 for a one-year term, and returned in 1855 to serve fifteen years as alderman or councilman. During this time he was instrumental in the enactment of ordinances providing for notable improvements in the police, fire protection and water systems. He resigned in 1869 to take a seat as a Democrat in the Forty-first Congress. After holding office four terms, he was defeated in 1876. Two years later he was reëlected, only to retire voluntarily in 1881 because of ill health. His aptitude for committee work, his devotion to the interests of his section, and his friendship with President Grant, whom he had known in St. Louis, combined to make him a respected member despite the minority status of his party. Wells had two outstanding legislative concerns—the improvement of the Mississippi River and the development of the Southwest. He was ahead of his time in regard to both and a number of his bills died in committee. His unreported bill of 1871, dealing with the opening of Oklahoma, antedated that historic event by more than seventeen years. He also worked for appropriations for various Indian Territory tribes in fulfillment of treaty obligations, and sponsored bills for marine hospitals and other government buildings.

Wells was married twice: in 1850 to Isabella Bowman Henry of Jacksonville, Ill., who died in 1877; in 1879 to Mrs. Daniel W. Bell (Eleanor P. Warfield), of Lexington, Ky. By the former he had five children, two of whom matured, the surviving son being Rolla Wells, who was mayor of St. Louis from 1901 to 1909. Following a long illness he died of locomotor ataxia in his seventieth year at his suburban estate, "Wellston," and was buried in Bellefontaine Cemetery.

[Information from Rolla Wells, L. H. Cannon, and Donald Macleay, of St. Louis; Albert Welles, *Hist. of the Welles Family* (1876); Rolla Wells, *Episodes of My Life* (1933); *Biog. Dir. Am. Cong.* (1928); William Hyde and H. L. Conard, *Encyc. of the Hist. of St. Louis* (1899), vol. IV; J. T. Scharf, *Hist. of St. Louis City and County* (1883), vol. I; L. U. Reavis, *St. Louis: Future Great City of the World* (1875); W. B. Stevens, *Centennial Hist. of Mo.* (1921), vol. II; *St. Louis Post-Dispatch*, Oct. 3, *St. Louis Republic*, Oct. 4, 1893.]
I.D.

WELLS, HENRY (Dec. 12, 1805–Dec. 10, 1878), expressman, was born at Thetford, Vt., the son of Shipley Wells, a Presbyterian clergyman who early removed to central New York. The boy worked on a farm and attended school at Fayette. At sixteen he was apprenticed to Jessup & Palmer, tanners and shoemakers at Palmyra. There he met and married Sarah Daggett, who died in Albany on Oct. 13, 1859. In 1861 he married, as his second wife, Mary, the daughter of Henry Prentice of Boston. About 1841 he became agent at Albany for Harnden's express between New York and Albany. In two years he had established Livingston, Wells & Pomeroy's, operating between Albany and Buffalo, and was himself messenger, making a weekly trip on five or six railroads and two stage lines. The company soon abandoned paying two regular fares for transporting messenger and trunk and arranged a kind of commutation, the forerunner of the present intimate relations between railroads and express companies. He carried mail at six cents for a single letter or one dollar for twenty while the government charged from two to four times as much. With James W. Hale, he offered a through service from New York, Boston, and Bangor, Me., vigorously opposed by the post office. The expressmen had the benefit of popular support, roused by penny postage in England, and the government was forced to pass the five-cent postage act of 1845. In 1844 he opened the line between Buffalo and Detroit, Wells & Company, with William G. Fargo [*q.v.*] as messenger. The service, using lake steamers in summer and wagons and stages in winter, rapidly expanded to Chicago, Cincinnati, and St. Louis. In 1846 he sold his interest in the western service and removed from Buffalo to New York to handle the eastern business, now connected with New York and opening offices in London and Paris. In 1850 competition on the route between Albany and Buffalo led to the merger of the three companies, Wells & Company, Butterfield, Wasson & Company, and Livingston, Fargo & Company, into the American Express Company. Wells was president for eighteen years. About this time he removed to Aurora, N. Y.

In 1852, with associates, he organized in New York, Wells, Fargo & Company for business to California. The president was Edwin B. Morgan [*q.v.*], his fellow citizen of Aurora. The usual route to the Pacific coast was by steamship by way of Panama. Adams & Company were already well entrenched in California. The new company began by buying small, independent express lines, and it found its opportunity in the troubled days of 1885, when Adams & Company failed. In 1857 the California service and the business east of the Missouri were linked by the award of the contract for the overland mail to John Butterfield [*q.v.*], who represented the Wells, Fargo interests. The Wells, Fargo interests also took over the pony express for the last months of its service, which was ended by the completion of the telegraph in October 1861. With its overland connections well established, the company prospered until the completion of the transcontinental railroad changed much of the business. In 1868 the Pacific Union Express Company appeared with an exclusive ten-year contract with the railroad and forced Wells, Fargo to expand its capitalization and absorb this company. Similarly, east of the Missouri River, the Merchants Union Express Company was fighting the American Express Company. In 1868 the American and the Merchants Union companies united under the name of American Merchants Union Express Company, after 1873 the American Express Company. At the time of this consolidation Wells retired as president. For the last ten years of his life he traveled a good deal. At his home in Aurora he was president of the First National Bank and first president of the Cayuga Lake Railroad. In 1868 he founded Wells Seminary, now Wells College. He established schools for stammerers in several cities, presumably because he, himself, suffered from an impediment of speech. He died in Glasgow, Scotland, and was buried in Aurora.

From his thirty-fifth to his sixty-fifth year he saw the country grow rapidly and the carrying trades grow equally. In 1841 carrying the express from Albany to Buffalo was almost within the capacity of one man and in 1870 the great American Express Company operated over railroads as far as the Missouri River. The newly opening far West was a fresh opportunity; and in 1871 the country already supported a regular overland stage and mail route. Though his earlier outlook had anticipated expansion toward Europe, he was able to sense his opportunity in the far West of his own country, and he adapted his business to the spread of population over the continent. Something of his own view of the development of the express business can be found in papers he read before the Buffalo Historical Society in June 1863, *The American Express in its Relation to . . . Buffalo* (1864) and before the American Geographical and Statistical Society of Albany on Feb. 4, 1864, *Sketch of the Rise, Progress, and Present Conduct of the Express System* (1864).

[*Wells Fargo Messenger,* Nov. 1912; Jan., May, Oct. 1913, May 1918; W. I. Lowe, *Wells College and its Founders* (1901); A. L. Stimson, *Hist. of the Express Business* (2nd ed., 1858); E. A. Wiltsee, *The Pioneer Miner and the Pack Mule Express* (1931); *Colls. of the Hist. of Albany,* vol. I (1865), ed. by Joel Munsell; *1844. Walker's Buffalo City Directory* (1844), ed. by H. N. Walker; L. R. Hafen, *The Overland Mail* (1926); *Buffalo Courier,* Jan. 2, 1879; *N. Y. Times,* Dec. 11, 12, 27, 1878, Jan. 3, 1879; "Location of Overland Mail," *Missouri Republican* (St. Louis), June 26, 1857.]
                                                    E. H.

WELLS, HORACE (Jan. 21, 1815–Jan. 24, 1848), dentist and anesthetist, a descendant of Joshua Wells who was in Windsor, Conn., as early as 1647, and the eldest child of Horace Wells by his wife Betsy Heath, was born at Hartford, Vt. His parents, who were comfortably situated, gave him a good education in New England church schools and made it possible for him, at the age of nineteen, to go to Boston to study dentistry. In 1836 he moved to Hartford, Conn., where he opened an office, soon acquired a successful dental practice, and in 1838 published a creditable little book entitled *An Essay on Teeth; Comprising a Brief Description of Their Formation, Diseases, and Proper Treatment.* During 1841–42 another young dentist, William T. G. Morton [*q.v.*] of Farmington, Conn., studied dentistry under Wells (J. M. Riggs, in Smith, 1858, *post,* p. 27; also Mrs. Wells, *Ibid.,* p. 29), and they opened a joint office in Boston, but in 1843 the partnership was dissolved and Wells returned to Hartford.

As early as 1840, according to the testimony in 1853 of Dr. Linus P. Brockett [*q.v.*] of Hartford (Smith, 1858, pp. 18–19), Wells was interested in the narcotic effects of nitrous oxide inhalation—which had been known since Humphry Davy's experiments with the gas in 1799—and suggested its use as a means of deadening pain in the extraction of teeth. On Dec. 10, 1844, Gardner Q. Colton [*q.v.*] gave a popular lecture at Hartford to which many were attracted because the lecturer promised to demonstrate the effects of laughing gas. Wells observed that one Samuel A. Cooley, who took the gas, struck his shins and bruised them severely without giving evidence of pain [*cf.* Crawford W. Long]. The day after the lecture, Colton was invited to Wells's office to give him nitrous oxide, and a fellow dentist, John Mankey Riggs [*q.v.*], while Wells was under the influence of the gas, extracted one of his teeth (Dec. 11, 1844) without causing him any pain. Colton taught Wells how to manufacture and to administer the gas and Wells followed up the experiment by extracting teeth from several individuals, none of whom experienced pain. Though familiar with the similar effects of ether, Wells discarded it because he considered nitrous oxide "the least likely to do injury" (Erving, *post,* p. 428). In an interview with Valentine Mott [*q.v.*] of New York, however, he said that he had made use of ether in extractions and voiced his belief that it might be used in major surgical operations (Smith, 1858, p. 81).

Early in 1845 Wells went to Boston with the idea of bringing his use of nitrous oxide before the medical profession. Through his former partner Morton he obtained an opportunity to speak before one of the medical classes of John Collins Warren [q.v.]. He told the class of his experiments and offered to give a demonstration if a subject could be found. A patient was secured and the gas administered, but for some unaccountable reason Wells attempted to extract the tooth before the anesthesia was complete. The man cried out, the students jeered, and Wells was humiliated. He returned to Hartford deeply discouraged.

The first printed statement of Wells's claims to the discovery of anesthesia appeared in the *Hartford Courant* on Dec. 7, 1846, nearly two months after Morton had demonstrated the use of ether, and nearly three weeks after Morton's results had been published by Henry J. Bigelow [q.v.] in the *Boston Medical and Surgical Journal* (Nov. 18, 1846). Early in 1847 Wells went to Paris and while there published a letter, dated Feb. 17, 1847, in *Galignani's Messenger*, stating his claims to priority and declaring that he had used ether as well as nitrous oxide (reprinted in the *Boston Atlas*, Apr. 2, 1847); on May 12, 1847, he published similar claims in the *Boston Medical and Surgical Journal* of anesthesia and in that same year he brought out a pamphlet of twenty-five pages entitled *A History of the Discovery of the Application of Nitrous Oxide Gas, Ether, and Other Vapors, to Surgical Operations,* in which his early experiments and his claims to the discovery of anesthesia were again described at length.

After ether had become recognized, Wells made two or three abortive attempts to prove nitrous oxide a better anesthetic and induced a number of physicians to carry out major surgical operations with laughing gas. Several of these were comparatively successful, but when on Apr. 27, 1848, Henry J. Bigelow finally yielded to the claims of Wells's supporters and at the Massachusetts General Hospital removed a carcinoma of the breast under nitrous oxide, the state of prolonged asphyxia produced by the gas nearly proved fatal, and Bigelow quickly recognized that for protracted operations of this type nitrous oxide was inferior to ether.

By this time, however, Wells was dead. In the winter of 1847–48 he had opened an office in New York, where he hoped to introduce the use of nitrous oxide. He also began to make experiments with chloroform and frequently inhaled it for its exhilarating effect. While under its influence, on Jan. 21, 1848, he created a disturbance for which he was arrested and locked up in the city prison. Here, suffering from discour-

agement and shame and fearing the loss of his reason, he wrote a long letter to the press (*New York Journal of Commerce,* Jan. 25, 1848) and killed himself by slashing his thigh with a razor. He was just thirty-three years old. In personal appearance Wells was tall, heavy-set, and unusually handsome, with high color, curly hair, and pleasant bearing, but he was exceedingly sensitive and shy. On July 9, 1838, he married Elizabeth Wales, by whom he had one son.

[H. R. Stiles, *The Hist. and Geneals. of Ancient Windsor, Conn.,* vol. II (1892); Joseph Wales, *Discovery by the Late Dr. Horace Wells of the Applicability of Nitrous Oxyd Gas, Sulphuric Ether and Other Vapors in Surgical Operations Nearly Two Years Before the Patented Discovery by Drs. Chas. T. Jackson and W. T. G. Morton* (1850; 2nd ed., with additions, 1852); Truman Smith, *An Examination of the Question of Anæsthesia* (1858) and *An Inquiry into the Origin of Modern Anæsthesia* (1867), the former containing sworn testimony and the latter containing a biog. sketch by P. W. Ellsworth; R. M. Hodges, *A Narrative of the Events Connected with the Introduction of Sulphuric Ether into Surgical Use* (1891); James McManus, "The History of Anæsthesia," *Conn. Quart.,* Jan.–Mar. 1895; G. Q. Colton, *A True Hist. of the Discovery of Anæsthesia* (1896); E. A. Wells, "Horace Wells," *Boston Medic. and Surgic. Jour.,* Feb. 5, 1925; H. W. Erving, "The Discoverer of Anæsthesia: Dr. Horace Wells of Hartford," *Yale Jour. of Biol. and Medicine,* May 1933; C. J. Wells, "Horace Wells," *Current Researches in Anesthesia and Analgesia,* July–Aug., Sept.–Oct. 1935, with extensive bibliog.; obituaries in *N. Y. Tribune* and *Boston Transcript,* Jan. 25, 1848, and *Boston Medic. and Surgic. Jour.,* Feb. 2, 1848.]   J.F.F.

WELLS, JAMES MADISON (Jan. 8, 1808– Feb. 28, 1899), governor of Louisiana, seems to have been the grandson of Samuel Levi Wells, a civil engineer who emigrated to America and settled finally about 1760 in Louisiana. His son of the same name and Mary Elizabeth (Calvit) Wells, said to be the grand-daughter of Frederick, sixth Lord Baltimore, became the parents of eight children. The youngest, James, was born at the plantation home, "New Hope," near Alexandria, La. An orphan at the age of eight, he was reared by an aunt until he went away to a Jesuit school at Bardstown, Ky. (St. Joseph's College). He then went to the military school of Alden Partridge [q.v.] at Middletown, Conn., and later read law in Cincinnati, part of the time in the office of Charles Hammond [q.v.]. About 1829 he decided to devote himself to planting and returned to his native parish, where he was very successful until the outbreak of the Civil War. On May 13, 1833, he married Mary Ann Scott. They had fourteen children. He was one of the largest landed planters of Rapides Parish and created a magnificent summer home, "Jessamine Hill," a few miles south of Lecompte. Educated in the North, he had formed strong convictions against the right of secession, to which he clung tenaciously in spite of his large slave holdings and the condemnation of relatives and friends. Indeed, during the Civil War he was often obliged to seek refuge in "Bear Wallow," the unattractive name of his huge hunting preserve near "Jessamine Hill." When the Federals surrounded Port Hudson, he sought protection from their gunboats. He claimed heavy losses because of his Union sympathies and was pressing his claims for damages at the time of his death.

In February 1864 at a special election ordered by Lincoln, he was chosen lieutenant-governor on the ticket with Michael Hahn, whom he succeeded upon the latter's resignation in March 1865. The following November he was elected governor in his own right on the National Democratic ticket. During his administration the legislature conditionally ratified the Thirteenth Amendment but unanimously rejected his recommendation to approve the Fourteenth Amendment. Furthermore, having become converted to negro suffrage, he was so distasteful to a majority that memorials for his impeachment were presented. When Gen. Philip Sheridan appeared in New Orleans as commander of the district, there arose between him and the governor a quarrel over politics that culminated in Sheridan's removal of Wells from office on June 3, 1867. He continued to be prominent in state politics, however, and was chairman of the Louisiana returning board during the disputed election of 1876. He was such a target of Democratic attack in that controversy that he retired permanently from political life to the quiet of his plantation home. He was a man of good education with an active mind, impressive appearance, and courtly manners.

[MSS. on La. Families by G. M. G. Stafford, Alexandria, La.; papers in possession of grand-daughter, Miss Emily Weems, Washington, D. C.; J. R. Ficklen, "Hist. of Reconstruction in La.," *The Johns Hopkins University Studies,* 28 ser., no. 1 (1910); Alcée Fortier, *Hist. of La.* (1904), vol. IV; *The Amer. Annual Cyc. . . . 1864–1867* (1865–1868); *Appletons' Annual Cyc. . . . 1899* (1900); *Daily Picayune* and *Times-Democrat* (New Orleans), Mar. 1, 1899.]   E. L.

WELLS, JOHN (*c.* 1770–Sept. 7, 1823), lawyer, was born in Cherry Valley, Otsego County, N. Y., and spent his early childhood in that frontier region. His grandfather, John Wells, an emigrant from Ireland, had settled there in 1743. The younger John was the son of Capt. Robert Wells, whose wife was a daughter of the Rev. Samuel Dunlop. In the Cherry Valley massacre of 1778, when a mixed band of Loyalist rangers and Indians devastated the countryside, all of the Wells family were murdered with the exception of John, who was attending the grammar school in Schenectady (Howard Swiggett, *War*

out of Niagara, 1933, pp. 152–53). It was many years before Wells recovered from the shock of this tragedy, and when a young man he was dissuaded with difficulty from taking the life of the Indian leader of the raid, who had returned to New York (F. W. Halsey, *The Old New York Frontier,* 1901, p. 323). Until 1783 young Wells remained in Schenectady with an aunt, removing later to New York City and subsequently to the vicinity of Jamaica, Long Island. Having prepared under the Rev. Leonard Cutting and the Rev. Alexander MacWhorter [*q.v.*], he was admitted to the College of New Jersey, where he was graduated in 1788. He then entered upon the study of the law as clerk in a New York law office, and was admitted to the bar as attorney in 1791, and as counselor in 1795.

A Federalist in political sympathies, he revised for publication the collected papers known as *The Federalist,* bringing out the fifth edition in 1802. As editorial associate of William Coleman [*q.v.*] on the Federalist *Evening Post,* he frequently crossed swords with Hamilton's opponent, James Cheetham [*q.v.*] and the opposition sheet known as the *American Citizen.* When William Stephens Smith [*q.v.*], the son-in-law of President John Adams, sued Cheetham for libel in 1805, the defendant, by way of tribute to his opponent's legal talents, employed Wells as counsel. After 1804 he shared with Thomas Addis Emmet [*q.v.*] the bulk of the commercial law practice which had hitherto gone to Hamilton and Burr, and was frequently engaged as special counsel by the city of New York. In the celebrated case of *Gibbons* vs. *Ogden,* involving the right of the state of New York to grant a monopoly of the navigation of its waters by steam, Wells was associated with counsel for Gibbons. He argued unsuccessfully before Kent in 1819 a motion to dissolve the injunction restraining Gibbons from bringing his boat into New York harbor, on the ground that such a grant was unconstitutional since Congress alone had the right to regulate commerce. The court of errors sustained Kent the next year (17 *Johnson,* 488). Wells's death in 1823 prevented his appearing before the Supreme Court when the case was appealed, but in that tribunal, Webster and Wirt, pursuing the same argument, were able to secure a reversal (9 *Wheaton,* 1).

Wells was a man of much ability, and possessed characteristics that made him greatly beloved. Emmet, who had had a wide experience, and was Wells's rival at the bar, said that Wells's argument in *Griswold* vs. *Waddington* was the most able and finished he had ever heard (Johnson, *post,* p. 340). He contracted yellow fever, from which he died, while on a visit of mercy to the poor. In 1796 he married Eliza, daughter of Thomas Lawrence of Newtown, Long Island, and three years after her death in 1812, Sabina Huger of South Carolina. By his first wife he had one son; by the second, two sons and two daughters.

[William Johnson, in 7 *Johnson's Chancery Reports,* 331–43; *Memorial of the Life and Character of John Wells* (1874); *City Hall Reporter* and *N. Y. General Law Mag.,* Oct. 1833; *N. Y. Evening Post,* Sept. 8, 11, 12, 1823; W. W. Campbell, in *Am. Mo. Mag.,* Mar. 1838.]

R. B. M.

WELLS, ROBERT WILLIAM (Nov. 29, 1795–Sept. 22, 1864), jurist, was born at Winchester, Va., the son of Richard Wells. He attended common school in Winchester, and in 1816, upon the recommendation of John George Jackson [*q.v.*], he became a deputy surveyor and served under William Rector in Missouri for one year. Then he began the study of law under the auspices of Jackson. He studied for perhaps a year under Samuel Finley Vinton [*q.v.*], at Gallipolis, Ohio. In 1819 he engaged in surveying and in 1820 began the practice of law in St. Charles, the temporary capital of Missouri. He designed the great seal of the state of Missouri, which was adopted on Jan. 11, 1822 (see own letter, King, *post,* pp. 7–11). He took an official part in the St. Charles Agricultural and Manufacturing Society during 1822, and in 1822 and 1824 was elected to the general assembly as representative from St. Charles County. From 1826 until 1836 he was attorney-general of Missouri. He married Harriet Amanda Rector on Jan. 20, 1830, in Jefferson City. She died on Feb. 3, 1834, leaving three children. In 1831 and again in 1832 he was defeated for representative in Congress. On June 27, 1836, he was appointed federal district judge of Missouri, and upon the division of the state into two districts in 1857 he became judge of the western district, a position he held until his death. One of his opinions, an opinion that the retroactive feature of the bankrupt law was unconstitutional, at the September 1842 term of court, was widely criticized and widely approved. Throughout his career he interested himself in the question of legal change and legal reform. In spite of the long tradition in England and America, he opposed the institution of "trial by jury" in civil cases on the ground that a judge trained in legal theory and processes is more competent to attain truth and justice than were any twelve jurors. In 1845 he was a member and presiding officer of the convention that wrote a new constitution, which was, however, disapproved by the voters. In 1847 he published a book on law reform, *Obser-*

vations on the Pleadings and Practice of the Courts of Justice of Missouri, and a Radical Change Therein Recommended, outlining his plans for simplifying pleading, shortening forms of declaring cases, and combining cases in law and equity. In 1849 he appeared before the Senate in behalf of a proposed bill, which was passed that year. His *Law of the State of Missouri Regulating Pleading and Practise of the Courts of Justice* (1849) contains his notations on this law.

He was also interested in various activities in the state. He served as a member of the first board of curators of the University of Missouri. In the 1840's he was a member of the Democratic central committee. He was president of the Osage River improvement convention of 1843, participated in the organization of the Missouri Historical and Philosophical Society in 1845, and served as one of its vice-presidents for several years thereafter. In 1845 he urged the General Assembly to construct the state's first lunatic asylum. During 1850–55 he was active in the promotion of the plank road and railroad movement. He was a charter member of the Missouri fruit growers' association, organized in 1859, and engaged in farming on a fairly large scale. During the Civil War, although owner of a few slaves, he was a stanch Union man and was president of the emancipation convention of 1862 and of the Missouri state Radical emancipation and Union convention of 1863. He died at Bowling Green, Ky., survived by five of his six children and by his second wife, Eliza (Covington) Wells, to whom he had been married in June 1840. He was buried in Jefferson City, Mo.

[R. T. King, "Robert William Wells," *Mo. Hist. Review,* Jan. 1936; W. V. N. Bay, *Reminiscences of the Bench and Bar of Mo.* (1878); *Proc. and Resolutions in the U. S. Circuit Court on the Death of Hon. Robert W. Wells, U. S. District Judge, Mo., Oct. 3, 1864* (1864); *Mo. Republican* (St. Louis), Sept. 23, 1864.]

R. T. K.

WELLS, SAMUEL ROBERTS (Apr. 4, 1820–Apr. 13, 1875), phrenologist, was born in West Hartford, Conn., the son of Russell Wells of Farmington, Conn., and a descendant of Thomas Welles, who emigrated from England, was living in Hartford in 1636, and became governor of Connecticut. Apprenticed in his youth to the trade of tanner, he practised his trade for some years but was ambitious for medical training. The direction of his life was determined, however, by making the acquaintance of the phrenologists, Lorenzo Niles Fowler and Orson Squire Fowler [*q.v.*], in Boston in 1843. He joined the Fowlers on their lecture tour as an assistant and later accompanied Lorenzo Fowler on lecture tours in the United States, Canada, England, Ireland, and Scotland. On Oct. 13, 1844, he married Charlotte Fowler, the sister of the phrenologists, herself a pioneer phrenologist in America. The same year he became a member of the publishing firm of O. S. & L. N. Fowler, which was then known as Fowlers & Wells. Later the firm became Fowler & Wells. After Lorenzo Fowler removed to England, Wells was the sole proprietor.

Primarily the advocate of phrenology and physiognomy as a means of reading and guiding human character, and as a basis for proper selection in marriage, he also believed in the various other reforms and fads of the period, hydropathy or water cure, temperance, and a vegetarian diet. He taught the utility of shorthand. He advocated improved methods of agriculture, including proper cultivation of the soil, rotation of crops, irrigation, draining, subsoiling, proper fencing, and the proper selection of improved agricultural implements. He was by disposition a business man. Although he undoubtedly believed sincerely in the value of phrenology and its allied methods of character reading, he had an uncritical and unscientific mind. He continued to exploit his beliefs long after they had been discredited. Always ready to listen to new or popular theories, his publishing firm became the voice of much eccentric, trivial, and unsound speculation. He was instrumental, with his wife, in founding and continuing the institute of phrenology. He managed the famous phrenological cabinet in New York City, which for many years drew crowds of curious visitors to have their craniums examined, and to see the remarkable collection of casts. From 1850 to 1862 he edited the old *Water Cure Journal.* He edited the *Illustrated Annual of Phrenology and Physiognomy* from 1865 to 1875. From 1863 to 1875 he edited the more important *American Phrenological Journal and Life Illustrated,* edited earlier by Nelson Sizer [*q.v.*]. The title was changed in 1870 to *Phrenological Journal and Packard's Monthly,* and in 1871 to *Phrenological Journal and Life Illustrated.* He died in New York City.

[Albert Welles, *Hist. of the Welles Family* (1876); *Phrenological Jour.,* Jan. 1885; *N. Y. Tribune,* Apr. 14, 1875.]   E. B. H.

WELLS, WILLIAM CHARLES (May 24, 1757–Sept. 18, 1817), physician and physicist, was born in Charleston, S. C., the second son and fourth child of Robert and Mary Wells. His father was a bookbinder of Dumfries, Scotland, who emigrated to Charleston in 1753 and became a successful printer and bookseller. Wil-

liam grew up near the city waterfront, where he acquired a vocabulary he later regretted, and was sent back to Dumfries to school when ten years of age. Here he remained more than two years, later attended the University of Edinburgh, and finally returned to Charleston in 1771. Displaying an interest in science, he was apprenticed to Alexander Garden, *c.* 1730–1791 [*q.v.*], and remained with him until 1775. Both he and his father were stanch Loyalists, and upon the outbreak of the Revolution both fled to Great Britain, where Wells attended lectures for three years at the medical school of the University of Edinburgh. He then followed the common procedure of going to London, where he did some work under William Hunter and went the rounds at St. Bartholomew's Hospital. In 1779 he served as a surgeon in a Scottish regiment in Dutch service on the Continent, but soon resigned to study for three months at the University of Leyden. He received the M.D. degree at Edinburgh in 1780. The following year, taking advantage of the British capture of Charleston, he returned to America to look after his father's property; but fled to Florida upon the return of the patriot forces to Charleston. He took a printing press with him and claimed to have founded the first weekly newspaper in that colony.

In 1784, Wells once more established himself in London, and continued to practise medicine there for the rest of his life. In 1788 he was made a licentiate of the Royal College of Physicians. He had the advantage of hospital connections, and the support of such influential friends as David Hume and Matthew Baillie. On the other hand, he was handicapped by a disdain for the practising apothecaries (who might have aided him), and by a temperament which made it difficult for people to approach him. He was also hindered by a debt of £600 incurred in his education. Only after ten years of practice did his income equal his expenditures.

Once he had a living income, he began serious investigations in physics and in medicine. He became a member of the Royal Society in 1793, and several of his more significant experiments in physics were published in the *Philosophical Transactions* of that body. In his studies of vision, he claimed to have been the first to experiment with the use of belladonna in the eyes, and refuted the view that the distance vision of near-sighted persons improved with age (*Transactions,* vol. CI, 1811). Between 1790 and 1810, he wrote about twelve papers of minor importance on various disease conditions, which were published in *The Transactions of a Society for the*

Promotion of Medical and Chirurgical Knowledge. His most significant contribution to science was contained in a paper read before the Royal Society in 1813 and published, along with several other papers, in 1818: *Two Essays: One Upon Single Vision with Two Eyes; The Other on Dew . . . and An Account of a Female of the White Race . . . Part of Whose Skin Resembles That of a Negro . . . By the Late W. C. Wells . . . With a Memoir of His Life, Written by Himself.* In this paper, Wells not only assumed that there had been a biological evolution of human species, but clearly explained the principle of a natural selection in the course of a struggle for existence and a consequent survival of the fittest.

Charles Darwin was not familiar with Wells's essay when he first published his *Origin of Species*; but some time between 1861 and 1866 it was called to his attention by Charles L. Brace [*q.v.*]. In the fourth edition (1866) of his great work Darwin inserted into the historical introduction the statement: "In this paper he [Wells] distinctly recognizes the principle of natural selection, and this is the first recognition which has been indicated . . ." Darwin added that Wells applied the principle only to the races of men and not to the animal world in general. A critical reading of the original paper, however, gives the impression that Wells saw its applicability to zoölogy, but stressed only its ethnological implications because this was the matter in hand. In a word, he understood the principle of natural selection as a mechanism of evolution in animal life, but did not realize the whole significance of the theory.

Wells suffered a stroke of apoplexy in 1800, but continued to work strenuously for some years. He was never married. In the spring of 1817 he began to suffer seriously from a disease of the heart, which caused his death. He appears to have had no active religious connections, but was buried in the parish church of St. Brides' in London beside the graves of his parents.

[*Memoir*, noted above; *Dict. of Nat. Biog.* (London); Elisha Bartlett, *A Brief Sketch of the Life, Character, and Writings of W. C. Wells* (1849); *Morning Chronicle* (London), Sept. 20, 1817.]　　R. H. S.

WELLS, WILLIAM HARVEY (Feb. 27, 1812–Jan. 21, 1885), educator, was born in Tolland, Conn., the son of Harvey and Rhoda (Chapman) Wells. He was the descendant of Samuel, the son of Thomas Welles who emigrated from England, settled in Hartford in 1636, and became governor of Connecticut. He worked on his father's farm, attended the district school, spent two terms, 1829–30, at an academy

in Vernon, Conn., and then entered an academy at Tolland. He also taught district school at Vernon. Impaired eyesight forced him to abandon going to college, but he began to teach at the grammar school in East Hartford, Conn. In 1834 he spent eight months in the Teachers' Seminary conducted by the Rev. Samuel R. Hall [*q.v.*] at Andover, Mass. In September 1834 he returned to the grammar school in East Hartford and a year later became principal. In 1836 he was recalled to the Teachers' Seminary at Andover as teacher of English and mathematics, where he taught for eleven years. In 1846 he published his school grammar, of which 90 editions were printed, under various titles, by 1859. In 1847 he was elected principal of the Putnam Free School, Newburyport, Mass.; and, until April 1848, when his new duties began, he assisted Henry Barnard [*q.v.*] in conducting teachers' institutes in Rhode Island and Massachusetts. He was an active institute lecturer in the cause of teacher training, president of the Essex County teachers' association, 1848–49, a founder of the Massachusetts teachers' association, its president, 1851–53, and one of the first editors of the *Massachusetts Teacher*. In 1854 he was appointed principal of the state normal school at Westfield, Mass., a position he held until 1856, when he was elected superintendent of public schools in Chicago, Ill. Shortly after his arrival in Chicago, he organized the first high school in the city, for girls as well as boys. Appreciating the need of qualified teachers, he insisted on the establishment of a training department. He succeeded in obtaining a provision in the new city charter to abolish the district organization; and he established a centralized system under the control of a board of education. As early as 1861 he introduced a graded system of schools, and he prepared for it a course of study which was widely used throughout the country. His book on the *Graded Course of Instruction* (1861) was later embodied in *The Graded School* (1862), which went through many editions. In 1857 he became a member of the board of education of the state of Illinois. He was one of the organizers of a state normal school in Illinois in 1857 and was an active member of its board of trustees, 1857–69. In 1860 he was elected president of the Illinois state teachers' association and in 1863 of the national teachers' association.

Resigning from the superintendency in 1864, he spent the rest of his life in business pursuits. He published in 1878 *Historical Authorship of English Grammar*; and, in 1880, *A Shorter Course in English Grammar and Composition.*

He was married three times: first on July 23, 1840, to Hannah Maria Smith, the daughter of Jonathan Smith, of West Springfield, Mass. She died on May 22, 1842. On May 8, 1843, he married Tabitha Sarah Ordway of Andover, Mass., who died on July 8, 1848. On July 30, 1849, he married Lydia Sophronia Graves, the daughter of Cotton Graves of Sunderland, Mass. He had eleven children.

[*William Harvey Wells . . . In Memoriam* (1887); *Am. Jour. of Educ.,* June 1860; *Jour. of the Proc. of Ill. State Teachers' Assoc. . . . 1868* (1869); A. T. Andreas, *Hist. of Chicago,* vols. II, III (1885–86); H. B. Clark, *The Public Schools of Chicago* (1897); J. W. Cook, *Educational Hist. of Ill.* (1912); John Moses and Joseph Kirkland, *Hist. of Chicago* (1895), vol. II; Albert Welles, *Hist. of the Welles Family* (1876); *Daily Inter Ocean* (Chicago), *Chicago Daily Tribune,* and *Chicago Daily News,* Jan. 22, 1885.]   R. F. S.

WELLS, WILLIAM VINCENT (Jan. 2, 1826–June 1, 1876), writer, was born in Boston, the son of Samuel Adams Wells. He received but slight formal education and at an early age went to sea. For a decade he lived adventurously, visiting many parts of the world, suffering shipwreck five times (see his description, *Pioneer,* July 1855) and rising before the age of twenty to be an officer in the merchant service. He became a member of the Boston and California Joint Stock Mining and Trading Company and in January 1849 sailed as first mate from Boston on the *Edward Everett*. In California he commanded the company's *Pioneer* on what is sometimes erroneously mentioned as the first steamship voyage up the Sacramento River. Upon the break-up of the company soon afterward he mined for two seasons on the Stanislaus and Tuolumne rivers and then spent short periods working as a farmer and as an engineer. Returning to San Francisco, he engaged first in business but about 1853 became a member of the editorial staff of the *Commercial Advertiser*. In the summer of 1854 he sailed as agent of the Honduras Mining and Trading Company to explore the gold-bearing regions in the almost unmapped wilds of eastern Honduras. The record of these seven months of colorful journeying is preserved in his *Explorations and Adventures in Honduras* (1857) and in an article "Adventurers in the Gold Fields of Central America," in *Harper's Magazine* (February 1856). Soon after his return to San Francisco in 1855 he received the appointment as consul for Honduras, an office he held most of the time until 1874. He compiled in about a fortnight, *Walker's Expedition to Nicaragua* (1856), a highly partisan defense of the filibusters' régime. At this time he turned more definitely to journalism, being associated with the *Alta California* and later with the *Daily Times*. He made an expedition to the wilder parts of Oregon which he reported in "Wild Life in Oregon" (*Harper's,* October 1856). In 1858 he joined in the Frazer River gold rush.

By the sixties he had risen to prominence in San Francisco. He had again returned to the editorial staff of the powerful *Alta California,* had gained reputation from his books, and had taken a leading part in the Republican campaign of 1860. In his character he combined love of adventure, conviviality, warmth of friendship, and natural gentility and refinement of manner. He was always a partisan, whether defending his great-grandfather, the Empress Carlotta, the filibusters, or the golden opportunities of Honduras. Although unfortunate in a biographer, these qualities endeared him to his contemporaries. During the Civil War he held the position of cashier and impost clerk in the naval office in San Francisco. During the period of governmental employment he found leisure to work upon his three-volume *Life and Public Services of Samuel Adams* (1865). For this biography of his great-grandfather, he was able to obtain a large number of records preserved in the family, so that his work remains a basic one. In 1865 he accepted an appointment under Emperor Maximilian. He was in Mexico for a short time and conceived a warm-hearted attachment to the imperial régime. He also escaped from official duties long enough to make an "Ascent of Popocatepetl" (*Harper's,* November 1865, and a series of articles in *Overland Monthly,* July–September 1868). He was soon sent to New York City to conduct a bureau aimed to spread throughout the United States propaganda favorable to the empire. He obtained certain concessions in Mexico that promised to make him rich, but the fall of Maximilian put a sudden end to these hopes, and he was forced to return to San Francisco, ill and almost penniless. He was again received upon the staff of the *Daily Times,* but in 1869 he accepted the easier post of clerk for the mayor of the city. With constantly failing strength, he held this appointment until 1874. From this time on, his mind began to be affected, and finally in January 1876 he was admitted to the state asylum for the insane at Napa, where he shortly afterwards died, survived by his widow.

[O. T. Howe, *Argonauts of '49* (1923); Samuel Colville, *Colville's San Francisco Directory, vol. I . . . 1856* (1856); *San Francisco Directory . . . 1868* (1868), comp. by H. G. Langley; *Ibid. . . . 1871* (1871); *San Francisco Directory . . . 1876* (1876), comp. by D. M. Bishop & Co.; *Alta California* (San Francisco), Aug. 21, 1874, June 3, 1876; *Morning Call* (San Francisco), June 3, 1876, June 24, 1883.]   G. R. S., Jr.

WELSH, JOHN (Nov. 9, 1805–Apr. 10, 1886), philanthropist, was born in Philadelphia, Pa., the son of John and Jemima (Maris) Welsh. His father was a successful merchant who trained his sons to follow in his footsteps. While John's brothers established a firm of their own, he became a partner in Dulles, Wilcox & Welsh, dealing in dry goods. After the death of his father in 1854, Welsh joined his brothers in the family West India trade, which was concerned largely with sugar. He married Rebecca B. Miller on Apr. 30, 1829. She died in 1832. On Feb. 6, 1838, he married Mary Lowber. Absorption in business was not complete, and he became interested in Philadelphia affairs. He was a member of the select council from 1855 to 1857 and member and chairman of the city sinking fund commission from 1857 to 1871. He was much interested in developing the Fairmount Park system, and, after successful leadership in the fight to persuade the city government to take on an enlarged plan, he became a member of the Fairmount Park Commission in 1867 and served until his death. He was a vestryman in St. Peter's Protestant Episcopal Church and was very active in the affairs of the Episcopal hospital. Railroads and banks were also within the scope of his interest, and he was president of the North Pennsylvania Railroad. In 1864 he organized a great sanitary fair for war charities in Philadelphia, but his crowning achievement was his management of the finances of the Centennial Exhibition of 1876. This project started under the handicap of much hostility and the gloom of the panic of 1873; its success made his reputation. When the labor was over, his friends gathered a purse of $50,000 to be presented to him to provide a public memorial of his achievement. He was a trustee of the University of Pennsylvania at this time, and he turned over this gift to establish the John Welsh Centennial Professorship of History and English Literature.

After Hayes was elected president, he and Evarts thought that Pennsylvania was entitled to the British mission and let it be known to Senator J. Donald Cameron that, if the Pennsylvanians in Congress could come to some agreement as to a man, he would be appointed. Cameron thereupon commanded an indorsement of his father, Simon Cameron. The very next day a majority of the delegation came to Hayes and said they had been coerced. Hayes was perplexed, but opportunely there came a committee of Philadelphia business men proposing Welsh for the position. Hayes was delighted to have a blameless Pennsylvanian at his disposal and, without consulting Cameron, sent his name to the Senate. Cameron was nonplussed; but Welsh was above reproach, and Hayes had his way (*Diary and Letters of Rutherford Birchard Hayes*, III, 1924, ed. by C. R. Williams, 514–15; *Times*, Philadelphia, Oct. 31, 1877). Welsh spent a part of two years in London. His tall figure and benign countenance framed in large white whiskers made him resemble English nobility, and he was a social success; but he was old and the English climate brought bronchitis each winter. Also he lost a brother and two sisters while away, and in May 1879 he asked to be recalled. His diplomatic experience was confined to paying the British government the $5,-500,000 fisheries award, arranging rather ineptly for an international bimetallic conference, and obtaining the release of an American Fenian from prison.

[*Encyc. of Pa. Biog.*, vol. XII (1919), ed. by J. W. Jordan; J. T. Scharf and Thompson Westcott, *Hist. of Philadelphia* (1884), I; Beckles Willson, *Amer. Ambassadors to England* (1928); *John Welsh Testimonial, Proc. at the Public Celebration of the Endowment of the John Welsh Centennial Professorship of Hist. and English Lit.* (1877); *The Proc. at the Dedication of the John Welsh Memorial . . . 1887* (1887); *Philadelphia Inquirer* and *North American* (Philadelphia), Apr. 12, 1886.]   R. F. N.

WEMYSS, FRANCIS COURTNEY (May 13, 1797–Jan. 5, 1859), actor and manager, was born in London, England, son of an officer in the British navy. His mother, Miss Courtney, was born in Boston, Mass. Young Wemyss was put to school in Edinburgh and then went into business with his mother's brother, Thomas Courtney, Jr., in Dundee. He had, as a schoolboy, done some acting, and when he rebelled at his uncle's discipline, he escaped to the stage. After various experiences with provincial companies, he finally reached London, Apr. 2, 1821. There he was seen by the London agent for the Chestnut Street Theatre, Philadelphia, and engaged. He reached New York in November 1822, and on Dec. 11 made his American début at the Chestnut Street as Vapid in *The Dramatist*. The house was poor and his reception not flattering. But he was delighted with the company, which then included William Warren, William Burke Wood, Henry Wallack, the elder Joseph Jefferson [*qq.v.*], and Mrs. Wood. On Apr. 10, 1823, he married a Miss Strembeck. He made his New York début at the Chatham Garden, Sept. 20, 1824, as Marplot, and in succeeding months played a long list of comedy and farcical rôles. Three years later he was back at the Chestnut Street as stage manager, and in January 1829 he became lessee of that house. Unfortunately he took it over at a time of depression. In his autobiography he records that, with others, he started a fund to aid needy actors, that he often acted two or even three new rôles a night for almost no money at all, and that he once even had to sell lottery tickets to keep his family together. But he had the optimism of his profession, for in 1833 he went three hundred miles by stage to open and manage a new theatre in Pittsburgh. In 1834 he was back in Philadelphia as manager of the Walnut Street house, which he renamed the American Theatre. He paid $4150 a year rent, and the theatre bars paid an additional $3000 to the owners. He also tried management at the Arch Street, Philadelphia, and in Baltimore.

His subsequent fortunes are part of the history of the New York stage. In 1841 he became stage manager of the National Theatre, and on Apr. 29 made his appearance as Belmour in *Is He Jealous?* to the Harriet of Charlotte Cushman [*q.v.*]. Most often, for a decade, he was stage manager, or acting manager, of some theatre (as the Bowery in 1846–47). He was the Duncan to Macready's Macbeth, at the Astor Place Opera House, when the famous riots broke out in May 1849. In September 1849, when Barnum made over his famous "lecture room" into a theatre, Wemyss was the manager. There were regular actors, and also a troop of "Druids, just arrived from Stonehenge." There was also vaudeville, with Wemyss taking part. In 1850–51 he was at the National again, with the younger Joseph Jefferson. Since certain young players were announced as his "pupils" in 1853, he must have been giving lessons. From 1855 to 1857 he was with Laura Keene [*q.v.*], but reduced to such minor parts as Sir Charles Marlow in *She Stoops to Conquer*. He was not listed in the casts of the new plays, and evidently had not adapted his style to changing tastes. Almost his last appearance was as stage manager for a huge benefit performance on Dec. 18, 1858, to raise money to buy "Mount Vernon" for a national shrine. He died in New York Jan. 5, 1859, survived by his wife and children.

Wemyss was neither a conspicuously good actor nor a conspicuously successful manager, yet he became a figure in the early American theatre by virtue of good taste, integrity, and conspicuous devotion to his profession, especially exemplified in his lifelong devotion to the theatrical fund, which he helped to found, and which he administered till his death. He also edited sixteen volumes of the *Acting American Theatre*, with portraits by John Neagle [*q.v.*], and wrote an autobiography, *Twenty-Six Years of the Life of an Actor and Manager* (2 vols., 1847), and *Chronology of the American Stage from 1752 to*

1852 (1852). He was a handsome, affable, courteous man. His portrait by Thomas Sully shows a round, pleasant, jovial face, a high, wide forehead, and a mass of very curly hair.

[In addition to Wemyss' *Twenty-Six Years of the Life of an Actor and Manager* (2 vols., 1847), see G. C. D. Odell, *Annals of the N. Y. Stage* (7 vols., 1927–31); and death notice in *N. Y. Times,* Jan. 6, 1859.]
                                                  W. P. E.

WENDE, ERNEST (July 23, 1853–Feb. 11, 1910), dermatologist, health official, was born at Millgrove, Erie County, N. Y., the eldest son in a family of ten children born to Bernard Philip and Susan (Kirk) Wende; Grover William Wende [*q.v.*] was a younger brother. His father was an enterprising and successful farmer, and Ernest was able to attend school regularly until he graduated from high school. After teaching for two years at Alden, he began the study of medicine at the University of Buffalo but his course was interrupted when he passed an examination for and entered the United States Military Academy at West Point, July 1, 1875. In a year's time, however, he returned to his medical studies, graduating with the degree of M.D. from the University of Buffalo in 1878. For a thesis on influenza, at graduation, he received honorable mention. He practised at Alden for a short time; then attended Columbia University (1881–82) and later the University of Pennsylvania, from which institution he received the degrees of M.D. in 1884 and B.S. in 1885. The next year and a half he spent in Europe, where he studied skin diseases and microscopy at Berlin and Vienna. Returning to Buffalo in 1886, he established himself in practice there. In 1887 he was appointed to the staff of the University of Buffalo as clinical lecturer in dermatology and the following year was made clinical professor; he was also appointed in 1890 professor of botany and microscopy in the Buffalo College of Pharmacy.

In 1892 he received the appointment of health commissioner, which position he held for thirteen years. In this capacity he became nationally known because of the improvements and reforms which he instituted and which were later copied by many other cities. Soon after taking office he investigated the high death rate in infants and found, from bacteriological studies, that the milk became infected because the imperfect construction of the tubes in the then commonly used long-tube nursing bottles afforded a lodging for bacteria. By city ordinance this type of bottle was abolished, in spite of the opposition of druggists and the indifference of others. He also developed methods for the inspection of the source of the city's milk supply; introduced modern ways of handling contagious diseases; instituted systematic examination, both bacteriological and chemical, of the city's water supply; and brought about periodic inspection of the markets, hotels, and restaurants. The death rate was reduced from twenty-four to fourteen per thousand within one year of his taking office.

Wende was a man of original ideas and had a forceful personality. He wielded a powerful influence for good in his community. His interests and accomplishments were varied; he was an amateur ethnologist, archeologist, and botanist; his hobbies included fishing and hunting. In addition to local and state medical societies, he was a member of the American Dermatological Association, the American Microscopical Society, and the Pan-American Medical Congress. He was at one time vice-president of the American Public Health Association, and was a Fellow of the Royal Microscopical Society and of the American Electro-Therapeutic Association. From 1895 until his death he was associate editor of the *Buffalo Medical Journal*. Civic and other interests claimed his attention and he was the active head of the Municipal League for many years. On Aug. 25, 1881, he married Frances Harriett Cutler of Omaha, by whom he had three children.

[*Jour. of Cutaneous Diseases*, May 1910; J. J. Walsh, *Hist. of Medicine in N. Y.* (1919); *Buffalo Medic. Jour.*, Mar. 1910; *Buffalo Morning Express*, Feb. 12, 1910.]   G. M. L.

WENDE, GROVER WILLIAM (Apr. 6, 1867–Feb. 9, 1926), physician, dermatologist, was born in Millgrove, Erie County, N. Y., the son of Bernard Philip and Susan (Kirk) Wende, and a younger brother of Ernest Wende [*q.v.*]. After receiving his preliminary education in public schools, he entered the University of Buffalo, where he was graduated with the degree of M.D. in 1889. The next few years he spent in graduate study, first at the University of Pennsylvania, and later in Prague, Vienna, and Paris. His training included a thorough grounding in the sciences of bacteriology and pathology in their relation to diseases of the skin.

Returning to Buffalo in 1898, he began the practice of dermatology with his brother Ernest. He was soon appointed to the staff of the University of Buffalo and was professor of dermatology there for twenty-seven years. He found time to write a number of scientific articles in a terse, characteristic style. He described many of the rarer skin diseases and became known as an exceedingly accurate observer. Among the better known of his medical contributions were "Porokeratosis with Report of Case" (*Journal of*

Cutaneous and Genito-Urinary Diseases, November 1898); "A Nodular, Terminating in a Ring Eruption—Granuloma Annulare" (*Ibid.*, September 1909); "Nodular Tuberculosis of the Hypoderm" (*Ibid.*, January 1911); "Pellagra as it Occurs in Buffalo and Vicinity" (*Buffalo Medical Journal*, July 1918); "Keratolysis Exfoliativa" (*Journal of Cutaneous Diseases*, March 1919). Both through his writings and through his scientific discussions at various medical congresses Wende became well known and highly regarded. In 1909 he was elected chairman of the section of dermatology and syphilology of the American Medical Association. He was secretary of the American Dermatological Association from 1905 to 1909 and was elected president of that society in 1911. During the World War he was a member of the surgeon general's committee for supervising the treatment of venereal diseases in the army. His activities were not confined to dermatology. He served as president of the Medical Society of the State of New York, and was a member of the American Association of Pathologists and Bacteriologists, the American Association for Cancer Research, the American Society for the Control of Syphilis, and numerous local medical societies.

His private practice grew to large proportions, necessitating the employment of assistants. He was appointed to the staffs of many hospitals, among which were the Erie County, the Buffalo Sisters of Charity, the German, the Buffalo General, the Children's Municipal, and the United States Marine Hospital, all in Buffalo. One of his hobbies was medical photography. He was solid and vigorous both mentally and physically, quiet-spoken, and scholarly. He reached the pinnacle of his profession because of his ability, his thorough training, his agreeable personality, and his striking physique, and also because he was industrious and eminently honest in all dealings with his fellow men. On his way to attend a dinner of physicians he was struck by a street car and died while being conveyed to the hospital. In 1896 he married Mary Graham, daughter of David and Mary (Graham) Tucker.

[*N. Y. State Jour. of Medicine*, Mar. 1, 1926; *Jour. of the Am. Medic. Asso.*, Feb. 20, 1926; J. E. Lane, in *Archives of Dermatology and Syphilology*, Mar. 1926; J. J. Walsh, *Hist. of Medicine in N. Y.* (1919); *Buffalo Morning Express*, Feb. 10, 1926.]   G. M. L.

WENDELL, BARRETT (Aug. 23, 1855–Feb. 8, 1921), teacher and man of letters, was born in Boston, the son of Jacob Wendell, merchant, and Mary Bertodi (Barrett) Wendell. The founder of his family in America was Evert Janse Wendel, who came from East Friesland to New Netherland in 1640. Evert's grandson, Jacob Wendell, great-grandfather of Wendell Phillips and Oliver Wendell Holmes [*qq.v.*], was the first of the family to move to New England. Successful as a merchant in Boston, he was joined there by his nephew John, who was Barrett Wendell's great-great-grandfather. Wendell was privately prepared for Harvard, from which he graduated in 1877, having more widely read, traveled, and exercised his wit (he was among the early contributors to the *Harvard Lampoon*) than most of his classmates. An unsuccessful attack upon the law, which to him was not a congenial subject, left him uncertain about the future. Just then two most fortunate events happened. The first was his marriage, June 1, 1880, to Edith Greenough of Quincy, Mass. Of this marriage there were four children. How much his family meant to Barrett Wendell is delightfully suggested in his letters. The other happy occurrence was his appointment in 1880 to help Prof. Adams Sherman Hill teach English composition to Harvard undergraduates. How successfully he did so appears from the later eminence of many who took his "English 12" and from such testimony as George Pierce Baker's, who says of Wendell's interest in the early numbers of the *Harvard Monthly* (founded 1885): "Nothing ever did so much to give me a sense that an art is greater than any of its servants as Wendell's praise and blame of those successive numbers" (*Harvard Graduates Magazine, post,* p. 575). Another sort of witness to the same skill and interest is Wendell's *English Composition* (1891), which surpassed any other book on the subject. In the same year appeared *Cotton Mather, the Puritan Priest,* in which, through hard study of manuscripts and rare insight, he humanized a perennially important and puzzling character. His *William Shakespere* (1894) proved his sympathetic understanding of the genius of Elizabethan literature. In 1898 Wendell became the first teacher at Harvard to offer American literature as an object of systematic historical and critical study. From that course there emerged *A Literary History of America* (1900), which helped to bring about a reconsideration of certain literary traditions and greatly increased the active study of American letters, both in and outside of the colleges.

By this time Wendell had become a distinguished figure, and in 1902–03 he gave the Clark lectures at Trinity College, Cambridge, England, and published them in 1904 as *The Temper of the Seventeenth Century in English Literature.* Much more notable was his visit to France in 1904–05, when he inaugurated with great success the exchange of professors between France and Harvard founded by James Hazen Hyde. Rarely have circumstances, combined with great gifts as a lecturer, writer, traveler, and friend, enabled any man to interpret two countries to each other as did Barrett Wendell by his Sorbonne lectures on American literature and traditions, and by his remarkable book, *The France of Today* (1907), the insight of which was verified by the World War. This book, perhaps its author's best work, has been translated into French and German. A permanent memorial of his notable visit to the Sorbonne is the classroom there named "La Salle Barrett-Wendell."

Barrett Wendell's other publications of his later middle age—such as *Liberty, Union, and Democracy, the National Ideals of America* (1906), *The Privileged Classes* (1908), and *The Mystery of Education, and Other Academic Performances* (1909)—testify, as do his letters, to the steady enlargement of his field of thought. He was working toward the conclusion that, as he told the American Academy of Arts and Letters in 1917, he could in his later years of teaching do "no better service than by attempting to show how at least things literary can hardly be understood until we try to think of them together" (Lowell, *post,* p. 183). Such was the purpose of his successful course of elementary lectures on comparative literature and his last book, *The Traditions of European Literature, from Homer to Dante* (1920). The author's ill health did not prevent this, or the classroom lectures out of which it grew, from being an important series of broad and stimulating views.

His teaching was remarkable for a variety of qualities: swift and keen generalization, ready control of the background of events and ideas, profuse and well-chosen illustrations, a humble recognition of the mystery of genius, and unforgettable mannerisms permeated by a spirit of absolute sincerity. Skeptical though he was about the validity of certain phases of scholarship, he cared profoundly for what he called "serious criticism," the object of which he defined (*William Shakespere,* p. 1) as "so to increase our sympathetic knowledge of what we study that we may enjoy it with fresh intelligence and appreciation." He had as an undergraduate been deeply influenced by the teaching of James Russell Lowell and he did much to carry on the tradition established by one whom he himself characterized as "a man who . . . found in literature not something gravely mysterious, but only the best record that human beings have made of human life; . . . Here was a man, you grew to feel, who knew literature, and knew the world, and knew you too; ... There came ... a certain feeling of personal affection for him, very rare in any student's experience of even the most faithful teacher" (*Stelligeri and Other Essays Concerning America,* 1893, pp. 211–12). In Barrett Wendell's case it was always the entire person, never the mere teacher, who spoke. Just before his death, in a letter to H. M. Kallen, an intimate friend whose opinions were generally less conservative than his own, Wendell wrote: "After all, the difference between a reactionary and a radical, at heart, is only that the one longs to retain whatever is good and the other to destroy whatever is evil. Neither can be quite right or all wrong" (Howe, *post,* p. 185).

Wendell was a member of the American Academy of Arts and Letters, the Massachusetts Historical Society, and many other societies. He twice received the honorary degree of Doctor of Letters, and in 1920 he was given "le titre honorifique de Docteur de l'Université de Strasbourg."

[M. A. De W. Howe, *Barrett Wendell and His Letters* (1924); *Proc. Mass. Hist. Soc.,* vol. LIV (1921); A. L. Lowell, *Ibid.,* vol. LV (1922); G. P. Baker, in *Harvard Grads. Mag.,* June 1921; J. R. Stanwood, *The Direct Ancestry of the Late Jacob Wendell of Portsmouth, N. H.* (1882); *Who's Who in America,* 1918–19; *Boston Transcript,* Feb. 9, 1921.]   C. N. G.

WENDTE, CHARLES WILLIAM (June 11, 1844–Sept. 9, 1931), Unitarian minister, author, and hymn-writer, was born in Boston, Mass., the son of Carl and Johanna (Ebeling) Wendte. His father, who emigrated to Boston in 1842 from Hanover, Germany, gained a precarious living by painting frescoes in churches. After his death in 1847 the mother supported her two sons by tutoring in German. Wendte attended the Boston public schools, Chauncy Hall, and the gymnasium at Verden, Hanover, and in 1858 became an apprentice in the wholesale woolen house of Blakes and Kinsley. Threatened with tuberculosis, he went to San Francisco in 1861 and by the friendship of Thomas Starr King [*q.v.*] secured a custom-house position. After a period of volunteer militia service he entered the Bank of California, which transferred him in 1865 to Virginia City, Nev. Early association with Theodore Parker [*q.v.*] and his later contact with King turned him to the ministry, and he went East to the Meadville Theological School, Meadville, Pa. (1866–67), then to the Harvard Divinity School (1868–69), from which he was graduated. Wendte became minister successively of the Fourth Unitarian Church in Chicago (1869–75), the Church of the Redeemer (First Unitarian) in Cincinnati, Ohio (1876–82), where his influence upon young Wil-

liam Howard Taft [*q.v.*] and Alexander Johnson, the sociologist, was decisive, and the Channing Memorial Church in Newport, R. I. (1882–85). In 1886 he became a Unitarian missionary supervisor on the west coast, and also served as minister of the First Unitarian Church, Oakland, Cal. (1886), and of Unity Church, Los Angeles (1898). Resigning to recuperate his health, he became minister of the Theodore Parker Memorial Church in Boston (1901–05).

In 1900 Wendte undertook, till 1920, the general secretaryship of the International Council of Liberal Religious Thinkers and Workers. In this capacity he became secretary of the foreign relations department of the American Unitarian Association (1905–15), meanwhile serving (1905–08) as minister of the First Parish, Brighton, Mass. The first meeting of the Council (later the International Association for Liberal Christianity and Religious Freedom) was held in London (1901) attended by seven hundred delegates from over twenty liberal religious movements of the western hemisphere, and from the Brahmo-Somaj, of India. Succeeding congresses were held in Amsterdam (1903), Geneva (1905), Boston (1907), Berlin (1910), and Paris (1913). For the brilliant success of these cosmopolitan gatherings, Wendte labored indefatigably, traveling throughout Europe, as well as in Egypt, Palestine, and Turkey, meeting and conferring with liberal Protestants, Roman Catholics, Jews, Moslems, and Hindus. His enthusiasm for these ecumenical councils of rational, ethical theism was reinforced by unusual linguistic powers, great personal charm and tact, rich theological scholarship, broad tolerance, and a perfect command of executive detail. Of the proceedings and addresses by leading theological scholars and preachers of the western world, Wendte edited *Freedom and Fellowship in Religion* (1907), the *Proceedings* of the Fifth International Congress (1911), and *New Pilgrimages of the Spirit* (1921). Of a similar American organization, the National Federation of Religious Liberals, Wendte served as secretary from 1908 to 1920. He edited the *Proceedings* of the fifth congress in 1915, *The Unity of the Spirit* (1909), *Freedom and the Churches* (1913), and *Religious Liberals in Council* (1913). He was president (1910–14) of the Free Religious Association, and for it published *The Next Step in Religion* (1911), *The Promotion of Sympathy and Goodwill* (1913), and *World Religion and World Brotherhood* (1914). Wendte died without children, Oct. 9, 1931, in Berkeley, Cal., leaving his widow, Abbie Louise

(Grant) Wendte, whom he married Apr. 28, 1896, in Oakland, Cal.

Wendte regarded his biography, *Thomas Starr King, Patriot and Preacher* (1921), as his most permanent and worthy publication, but all his literary output was of high quality. He published four popular hymnals for liberal church schools and a memoir of Charles T. Brooks [*q.v.*], which appeared in Brooks's *Poems* (1885). His last book, *The Transfiguration of Life* (1930), fitly presents his theological convictions, which formed in general an immanental, ethical theism that he early correlated with the evolutionary hypothesis, as well as with the social progressiveness of the nineties—spiritual in purpose, ethical in method. His autobiography, *The Wider Fellowship* (2 vols., 1927), provides a remarkably vivid and factual synopsis of American social and political history, and of worldwide religious liberalism from 1850 to 1925.

[In addition to Wendte's *The Wider Fellowship* (2 vols., 1927), see *Who's Who in America*, 1930–31; *Gen. Cat. of the Divinity School of Harvard Univ.* (1910); J. T. Sutherland, in *Christian Register*, Oct. 8, 1931; and obituary in *San Francisco Chronicle*, Sept. 10, 1931.]   C. H. L—e.

WENLEY, ROBERT MARK (July 19, 1861–Mar. 29, 1929), philosopher, was born in Edinburgh, Scotland, the son of James Adams and Jemima Isabella (Veitch) Wenley. His father, of Norman-French descent and East Anglian origin, was sometime treasurer of the Bank of England and president of the Institute of Bankers of Scotland; his mother, of Lowland Scotch ancestry, was related to the Sibbald and Romanes families. Wenley's traditions were thus strictly of the upper bourgeoisie. He received his early education at a preparatory school in Edinburgh and later at the Park School and a high school in Glasgow, entering the University of Glasgow at the age of fifteen in November 1876. There, at first, he found his studies too easy to require serious attention, and, being very large and strong, he devoted his energies to athletics, gaining prizes in football, rowing, and swimming, but probably laying the foundation for the heart weakness that was ultimately to cause his death. He also seriously injured his right hand in football, making his handwriting almost illegible. During his second year at the university, his work in philosophy awakened doubts of the strict religious Calvinism in which he had been brought up, and he plunged into a course of intensive study on an attempted schedule of four days a week without sleep. The inevitable nervous breakdown came at last, but not until he had been thrice gold medallist in philosophy and once university medallist, and, what was more impor-

tant, had won the close friendship of the Scottish Hegelian, Edward Caird. During this period of heroic study, he was also influenced by, among his other teachers, Lord Kelvin in physics, Jebb and Sonnenschein in the classics, and John Nichol in English literature. He spent fourteen months in Paris, Rome, and Florence, recuperating from his breakdown, after which he returned to Glasgow, where he received the degree of Master of Arts in 1884, followed by those of Doctor of Philosophy in 1895, and Doctor of Science, from the University of Edinburgh, in 1891. He was married to Catherine Dickson Gibson, the daughter of Archibald Gibson, secretary of the Caledonian Railway Company, in April 1889. From 1886 to 1894 he was assistant professor of logic at the University of Glasgow and also, from 1886 to 1895, was in charge of the philosophy department in Queen Margaret College, as well as being degree examiner in mental philosophy, 1888–1891, and becoming dean of the arts faculty in the latter year. He was at various times president of the University Liberal Club, the Students Representative Council, the Students Union, the Theological Society, the Bothwell Literary Association of Edinburgh, and the Dialectic Society of Glasgow. Invited to the University of Michigan in 1896 to succeed John Dewey, he spent the rest of his life there as head of the department of philosophy, with the exception of the years 1925 to 1927, when he was director of the American University Union in London.

Unusually equipped in both scientific and classical scholarship in addition to his command of his own field, a brilliant and powerful lecturer with a mastery of sarcasm and sardonic wit, he was easily the most influential teacher on the Michigan faculty, attracting the ablest students to his classes. A liberal in religion and a Tory in politics he set forth his particular form of Green-Caird-Bosanquet Hegelianism in a series of volumes: *Socrates and Christ* (1889); *Aspects of Pessimism* (1894); *Contemporary Theology and Theism* (1897); *An Outline Introductory to Kant's "Critique of Pure Reason"* (1897); *The Preparation for Christianity in the Ancient World* (1898); *Modern Thought and the Crisis in Belief* (1909); *Kant and His Philosophical Revolution* (1910); *The Anarchist Ideal* (1913); *The Life and Work of George Sylvester Morris* (1917), probably his most valuable book; *Stoicism and its Influence* (1924). He also contributed numerous articles to J. M. Baldwin's *Dictionary of Philosophy and Psychology* (3 vols. in 4, 1901–05) and to James Hastings' *Encyclopedia of Religion and Ethics* (13 vols.,

1908–26), published a history of *The University Extension Movement in Scotland* (1895), and edited *Poetry by John Davidson* (1924).

[Roy Sellars, in *Michigan Alumnus*, Apr. 6, 1929; De Witt Parker, in *University Council and Senate Records*, 1929–32; *Who's Who in America*, 1928–29; *N. Y. Times*, Mar. 30, 1929; personal recollections.]

E. S. B—s.

WENNER, GEORGE UNANGST (May 17, 1844–Nov. 1, 1934), Lutheran clergyman, was born in Bethlehem, Pa., the son of George and Sarah Ann (Unangst) Wenner. After attending public schools and several private academies he was a student at Pennsylvania College (now Gettysburg), 1860–61, at Yale University, 1861–65, where he received the A.B. degree, and at the Union Theological Seminary 1865–68. He was ordained in 1868 by the Evangelical Lutheran Synod of the State of New York, and the same year he became the pastor of Christ Lutheran Church in New York City, the outgrowth of a small group of Lutherans whom he had addressed in a blacksmith's shop on East Fourteenth Street, while a student in 1866. He remained pastor of this church until his death. It is claimed that this pastorate of sixty-six years is the longest on record in the United States. Though he was active in many fields in the church, he considered preaching and pastoral service his life work. He was a devout, sympathetic, genial, and scholarly leader of his people.

He was a pioneer in weekday religious education. In his German parish paper, *Der Sonntags-gast*, of July 1874, he announced the beginning of regular religious instruction for children. This work was probably largely responsible for his almost unparalleled achievement of maintaining a congregation on the Lower East Side in New York City for two-thirds of a century. In November 1905 he read a paper on weekday religious education before the Interchurch Conference (forerunner of the Federal Council of the Churches of Christ in America), which was highly commended. Since then weekday religious education, in addition to catechization, has been a recognized field of church work. As a young minister in 1870, he planned and organized extensive home missionary programs, especially in Greater New York. He sought to promote Lutheran unity by organizing intersynodical ministerial groups, and was one of the leaders in establishing the deaconess work in the General Synod of the Lutheran Church. From 1904 to 1908 he was president of the Synod of New York and New Jersey; from 1908 to 1910 he was president of the Synod of New York.

He was sensitive to proprieties in the services of the church, and became one of the few liturgical scholars that the Lutheran Church in America has produced. Early in the eighties of the last century, he sought by conference and correspondence to develop a Lutheran liturgical consciousness. There were other leaders of like mind and purpose, among them James W. Richard [*q.v.*]. This growing interest in liturgics resulted in the adoption by the General Synod of the Common Service. A lengthy discussion between him and Professor Richard concerning the Lutheran character of certain features of the Common Service promoted liturgical interest and knowledge throughout the Church. Wenner was chairman of the liturgical committee of the General Synod from 1883 until 1915. Later he doubted the historical justification of the Confiteor and Introit in any Lutheran liturgy, and regretted certain extreme liturgical trends in the Lutheran Church. When he died he left the unfinished manuscript of a volume on liturgics.

Though conservatively Lutheran in his theological opinions and in his attitude toward church usages, Wenner's catholic Christian spirit and church statesmanship made him a recognized leader in interdenominational enterprises. He was secretary of the Evangelical Alliance for forty years, and was one of the founders of the Federal Council of the Churches of Christ in America. He was the author of numerous articles of importance, many of which were published in the *Lutheran Quarterly*, and of three books, *Religious Education and the Public Schools* (1907); *The Lutherans of New York* (1918); and *Sixty Years in One Parish* (1928). In the course of his pastorate Wenner baptized more than 8,000 individuals, confirmed 2,140, performed marriage ceremonies for 4,575, and buried 3,291. On Apr. 14, 1880, he was married to Rebecca Pullman. After her death in 1902, he was married, on Feb. 8, 1915, to Mary Wilson Marshall, who died in 1931. He had no children.

[*Who's Who in America*, 1932–33; G. U. Wenner, *Sixty Years in One Pulpit* (1928); *Alumni Record of Gettysburg Coll.* (1932); *Yale Univ. Obit. Record, Year Ending 1935*; G. L. Kieffer, biographical article in the *Lutheran*, Nov. 15, 1934; *N. Y. Times*, Nov. 2, 1934.]

S. G. H.

WENTWORTH, BENNING (July 24, 1696–Oct. 14, 1770), royal governor of New Hampshire, was a great-grandson of Elder William Wentworth, who came to America from Rigsby, England, in 1636, was closely associated with the Rev. John Wheelwright [*q.v.*], and in 1639 settled at Exeter, N. H. Benning was born in Portsmouth, N. H. The eldest son of Lieutenant-Governor John and Sarah (Hunking) Wentworth, he was listed as fifth in his class at Harvard College, where the order was determined by the social standing of the students' families. After his graduation in 1715, he became associated with his uncle Samuel, a merchant in Boston. On Dec. 31, 1719, he married Abigail Ruck, daughter of John Ruck, a prominent merchant; he had three sons, but none survived him. Wentworth was a member of the New Hampshire Assembly for a short time and became a member of the council in 1734. During the years 1734–39 he made several trips to England and Spain.

With his brother-in-law, Theodore Atkinson, he labored to make New Hampshire independent of Massachusetts, and upon achieving that result Wentworth became the first royal governor of the province, serving for the extraordinary period of twenty-five years. Like other colonial governors, and with no more success, he urged the Assembly to grant him a fixed salary in sterling or proclamation money, since New Hampshire was troubled by a depreciating paper currency. Like most of the royal governors of the century he complained frequently that the Assembly was encroaching upon his powers. The House in appointing chaplains, surgeons, and commissaries, in electing committees to handle supplies for the militia, and in limiting the militia's period of service and field of operations invaded his powers as commander-in-chief. He was not a tactful man and as a result of his determination to uphold the royal prerogative in sending writs of election to new towns became involved in a bitter controversy with the Assembly. A deadlock resulted in 1747, but by 1752 both sides were eager for harmony; the representatives from the new towns were admitted by the Assembly, and Wentworth approved the Assembly's choice, Meshech Weare [q.v.], as speaker.

New Hampshire took a prominent part in military expeditions against the French, furnishing one-eighth of the land forces sent against Louisbourg in 1745 and contributing towards the Louisbourg expedition of 1758 and the various attacks on Crown Point; Wentworth received many thanks from the New Hampshire generals for his attention to the troops. During his administration the province grew in wealth and population. In 1761 the Governor made no less than sixty grants of land west and eighteen east of the Connecticut River. With the conclusion of the French and Indian war many soldiers applied for grants in the Connecticut Valley, in territory claimed by both New Hampshire and New York. The resulting controversy was decided by the British government in favor of New York, but the New Hampshire settlers refused to accept the decision and the matter was not settled finally until the formation of the state of Vermont. Although New Hampshire was represented in the Albany Congress of 1754 it was one of the colonies unrepresented at the Stamp Act Congress of 1765, because Wentworth, by proroguing the Assembly, prevented the election of delegates.

Several attempts were made to remove him from the governorship. Complaints were made that he had too many relatives in office, that he had favored them with grants of land, and that he had grown rich through fees and the practice of reserving for himself 500 acres in each township; other complaints dealt with his exercise of the office of surveyor of the King's Woods. The home government said he neglected his correspondence. After some years of this campaign against him John Wentworth [q.v.] in 1765 presented a defense of his uncle to the Marquis of Rockingham, as a result of which Benning was permitted to resign and his nephew was appointed to succeed him both as governor and surveyor of His Majesty's Woods.

After retiring in June 1767, Benning Wentworth resided at Little Harbor with his second wife, Martha Hilton, whom he had married on Mar. 15, 1760. In his last years he was corpulent and much troubled by gout. He died at Little Harbor and was buried in the Wentworth tomb in the graveyard of Queen's Chapel, St. John's Church, Portsmouth. He provided a handsome fortune for his wife, who was the sole heir to his estate. Wentworth was an aristocrat in bearing and manner and showed that he had the courage of his convictions by the way in which he carried out royal instructions. Probably no colonial governor upheld the royal prerogative with more determination. He was a loyal promoter of the Anglican Church and the leader of a powerful social group; his home at Little Harbor was one of the most spacious country houses of colonial America. He left no issue.

[*N. H. Provincial Papers*, vols. V–VII (1871–73), X (1877), XVIII (1890); *Mass. Hist. Soc. Colls.*, 6 ser. (1886–99), IV, VI, VII, IX, X; *New Eng. Hist. and Geneal. Reg.*, July 1888; scattered letters (MSS.) in Lib. of Cong., Mass. Hist. Soc., Newberry Lib. (Chicago), New Haven Hist. Soc., and British Museum; Nathaniel Adams, *Annals of Portsmouth* (1825); Jeremy Belknap, *The Hist. of N. H.*, vol. II (1791); C. W. Brewster, *Rambles About Portsmouth* (1859–69); W. H. Fry, in *N. H. as a Royal Province* (1908); L. S. Mayo, *John Wentworth* (1921); J. N. McClintock, *Hist. of N. H.* (1888); John Wentworth, *The Wentworth Geneal.* (3 vols., 1878); *Boston Gazette*, Oct. 22, 1770.]

I. M. S. W.

WENTWORTH, CECILE de (d. Aug. 28, 1933), painter, was born in New York City, probably between 1853 and 1870. Her maiden name was Smith. The names of her parents do not appear in the accounts of her life, but presumably she belonged to a Catholic family, for she attended the Sacred Heart Convent in New York City. While still a young girl Cecilia, as she was then known, went to Paris to study art, and worked there in the studios of Alexandre Cabanel and Edouard Detaille. In the next few years she met and married Josiah Winslow Wentworth. She appears as an exhibitor in the catalogue of the Paris Salon of 1889 as Mme. C.–E. Wentworth, and for the next thirty years she regularly contributed to that annual exhibition portraits and occasional pictures with religious themes. She was made an *officier d'académie* in Paris in 1894. At the Universal Exposition in Paris in 1900 she received a bronze medal for her painting of Pope Leo XIII, who decorated her with the title of grand commander of the Order of the Holy Sepulchre and gave her the papal title of marchesa. In 1901 the French government conferred upon her the title of chevalier of the Légion d'Honneur, and she became an *officier de l'instruction publique*. She was one of the few women painters to have examples of their work purchased for the Musée National du Luxembourg. She received medals at the National Exhibition at Tours, and at other exhibitions at Lyons and Turin, and had the title of *officier* of the order of Nichau Tftikar conferred upon her by Mohammed EuNacer Bacha-Bey (*Who's Who in America, post*). During the greater portion of her active years she maintained a studio at 15 Avenue des Champs Élysées in Paris, returning for occasional visits to the United States, of which she continued to be a citizen despite her many years' residence abroad. In 1931 her husband, who was also a holder of the papal title of marquis, died in Paris. Soon after that the marquise because of a reduced income removed to the Riviera, where she passed the rest of her life. She lived at Nice in very modest circumstances and at the time of her death there in the municipal hospital on Aug. 28, 1933, it was reported that the American embassy in Paris forwarded money to cover her funeral expenses.

Among her sitters were William Howard Taft, Theodore Roosevelt, Archbishop Michael A. Corrigan, John W. Mackay [*qq.v.*], Cardinal Ferrata, and Queen Alexandra of England. The portrait of Pope Leo XIII in the Vatican Museum in Rome, one of her best known, shows him in an attitude of upright alertness that was extremely characteristic. A portrait of Gen. John J. Pershing is in the Invalides Museum in Paris; one of Maj.-Gen. George B. McClellan is in the Metropolitan Museum in New York. She is further represented by "La Foi" in the Lux-embourg in Paris, and by a portrait of a former president of the Senate in the Senate chamber in Paris. Her portraits are noted for their admirable portrayal of character and a certain spontaneity of facial expression. Though she was one of the most prominent women portrait painters of the latter part of the nineteenth century, she was better known in France than in her native America.

[See *Who's Who in America,* 1920–21; Helen Earle, *Biog. Sketches of Am. Artists* (1916); Marchioness of Wentworth, "Souvenirs of Leo XIII," *Independent,* July 23, 1903; *L'Aristocratie Étrangère en France,* 1899–1901, for Cecile de Wentworth's maiden name and the full name of her husband; obituaries in *Am. Art Annual,* 1933, *Art News,* Sept. 16, 1933, *Figaro* (Paris), Aug. 31, *N. Y. Times* and *N. Y. Evening Post,* Aug 30, 1933.]
                             G. A. C.

WENTWORTH, GEORGE ALBERT (July 31, 1835–May 24, 1906), teacher, author of textbooks in mathematics, was born at Wakefield, N. H., the son of Edmund and Eliza (Lang) Wentworth and a descendant of William Wentworth who emigrated from England in 1636 and signed the "Exeter Combination" three years later. After beginning his education in a district school and the Wakefield Academy, he entered Phillips Exeter Academy in 1852. He remained there for three years, working his way in part but financially assisted by his uncle, Benjamin Lang. In 1855 he entered Harvard College as a sophomore, paying part of his expenses in the next three years by teaching in the neighborhood. Just before graduating in 1858, he was recommended by President James Walker for an instructorship at Phillips Exeter. He was well trained in Latin and Greek, and it was in this field that he began his teaching. In 1859 he was assigned to the department of mathematics, but for some time he continued his teaching of the classics and even gave instruction in other branches. He was married on Aug. 2, 1864, to Emily Johnson Hatch of Covington, Ky., who died on May 1, 1895. For more than thirty years he was at the head of the mathematics department at Exeter, resigning his position in 1891 to devote his full time to the writing of textbooks. For two years, 1883–84 and 1889–90, he was acting principal of the academy and in 1899 was elected a trustee. During his later years he was afflicted with heart trouble and spent considerable time at Bad Nauheim in Germany in search of relief. He died in a heart attack in the railway station at Dover, N. H., survived by two sons and a daughter.

He was an outstanding pupil in his early days at Exeter, being commonly known as "the General," and as a teacher of unusual vigor and dominating power he was a recognized leader, known to the boys as "Bull Wentworth." A multitude of stories and traditions grew up around his name, to be interpreted according to the hearers' own ideals of personality and education. Ignoring all rules of the professional educator, he would often seem to be reading a newspaper while a recitation was in progress but infallibly detected every error in a boy's statement. He coddled no one; he put every boy on his own resources; but his seemingly rough exterior covered a warm heart. His textbooks included his *Elements of Geometry* (1878, with numerous later editions), *Elements of Algebra* (1881), *Practical Arithmetic,* with Thomas Hill (1881), *College Algebra* (1888), and works on trigonometry, surveying, and physics. Not including answer books and teachers' manuals, there were some fifty books copyrighted in his name as sole or joint author, most of them being revisions or elaborations of those mentioned. Of these, the geometry text, which later included both plane and solid geometry, was the most successful. It set a new standard of excellence in the United States and, indeed, abroad. To him, seconded by Edwin Ginn [*q.v.*], his publisher, is largely due the unit page, the condensed step form, and the first notable improvement in America of textbook typography. As a usable geometry it stood supreme for many years. His algebras were noteworthy for the large amount of orderly drill. They were based upon the principles of formal discipline and of learning to do by doing. They furnished the material needed for drill, and they proved of great value to those who were preparing pupils for college entrance examinations. His *Plane Trigonometry* (1882) also marked an advance in scholarship in the secondary school and still more in class-room usability. His *College Algebra,* partly the work of Frank N. Cole, had a great influence for many years on freshman mathematics. Altogether, the schools of the United States owe him much for books that contained a worthy type of mathematics and were at the same time adapted to the needs of the class of schools then dominating the field.

[*Bulletin of The Phillips Exeter Acad.,* Sept. 1906; *Harvard Class of 1858, First Triennial Report* (1861); *Report of the Class of 1858 . . . Fortieth Anniversary* (1898); L. M. Crosbie, *The Phillips Exeter Academy* (1923); F. H. Cunningham, *Familiar Sketches of the Phillips Exeter Academy* (1883); family information and files of his publishers.]   D. E. S.

WENTWORTH, JOHN (Aug. 20, 1737, N.S.– Apr. 8, 1820), last royal governor of New Hampshire, Loyalist, was born in Portsmouth, N. H. His father, Mark Hunking Wentworth, was a wealthy merchant and landowner and his mother, formerly Elizabeth Rindge, belonged to a prominent family of the province. He was descended on his father's side from William Wentworth, who emigrated from England to America some time before 1639; his grandfather, John Wentworth, had served as lieutenant-governor of New Hampshire; his uncle, Benning Wentworth [*q.v.*], held the office of governor for many years following 1741. John was graduated at Harvard College in 1755. He then entered his father's counting-house, and as early as 1759 became one of the proprietors of a township, which was named Wolfeborough, a holding which later absorbed much of his attention.

In 1763 he went to England to represent his father's business interests and his sojourn there profoundly affected his subsequent career. He formed the acquaintance of influential and distinguished Englishmen, among them the Marquis of Rockingham, and he was appointed one of the agents for New Hampshire, serving with Barlow Trecothick, a London merchant. Pursuant to instructions from the provincial Assembly, he used his influence to help secure the repeal of the Stamp Act. Upon the forced resignation of his uncle, Benning Wentworth, he was himself appointed governor of New Hampshire, his commission being dated Aug. 11, 1766. He was also made captain general of the militia and invested with admiralty jurisdiction, and was appointed to the post of surveyor general of His Majesty's Woods in America. He returned to America early in 1767, landing at Charleston, S. C., on Mar. 22. He journeyed northward through the colonies, making certain inspections pertaining to his duties as surveyor, and visiting prominent personages along the way. He took the oath of office as governor at Portsmouth, June 13, 1767.

Wentworth entered upon his new duties possessed of remarkable advantages in the way of family and social prestige, education, knowledge of the world, tact and good sense, and attractive personality. His administration was characterized by energy and a sincere desire to further the welfare of his native province, though it is true that, in accordance with eighteenth-century practice, he saw no impropriety in giving preferment to personal friends and relatives, and appointed to the council several persons related to him by blood or marriage. He displayed great energy in administering the office of surveyor of the King's Woods, making tours of inspection and preventing the private cutting of timber reserved for the Royal Navy. He was especially interested in the development of the interior regions of the province, and was instrumental in securing the division of New Hampshire into five counties.

Grants of land and the organization of towns proceeded rapidly under his jurisdiction. He persuaded the Assembly to appropriate money for a survey, on the basis of which an excellent map of New Hampshire was published in 1784. He initiated a policy of road construction as a part of his program for developing the interior. As captain general he devoted attention to reorganizing the militia. A supporter of sound money, he secured the abolition of paper currency in 1771. He was keenly interested in the establishment of Dartmouth College, granting a charter in 1769 and assisting the project by making grants of land, subscribing to the fund, and personally devoting time and attention to the affairs of the college. He was a member of the original board of trustees. As early as 1768 he had begun the development of his estate at Wolfeborough, where he built a large and pretentious house. On Nov. 11, 1769, he was married to his cousin, Frances (Wentworth), widow of Theodore Atkinson, Jr., former secretary of the province, who was also Wentworth's first cousin. In 1771, one Peter Livius, a disgruntled member of the council, drew up a list of charges against Wentworth and his administration, which was later submitted to the home government. After a period of anxiety, in the course of which he formulated a vigorous refutation of the charges and a defense of his conduct, he was vindicated by the Privy Council in 1773.

It was his misfortune that his administration had opened just as relations between the mother country and the colonies were being subjected to severe strain. As the revolutionary disturbances increased, he found himself in a difficult situation. He was unshaken in his loyalty to the Crown, though he disapproved of certain of its policies. He conducted himself with patience and tact, endeavoring to enforce the laws and to check any revolutionary moves. He was particularly anxious to prevent steps toward cooperation between New Hampshire and the other colonies. Events moved rapidly in 1774 and 1775, however, and with the increasing tension, overt acts against his authority were inevitable. At length he and his family took refuge on a British man-of-war at Portsmouth and in August 1775 he sailed for Boston.

When the British evacuated Boston in March 1776, Wentworth proceeded with them to Halifax, later accompanying the military expedition to New York. In 1778 he went to England. During the war he was exiled by the New Hampshire revolutionary government and most of his property was confiscated. Appointed surveyor to what was left of the King's Woods in

North America in 1783, he took up his post at Halifax. He became lieutenant-governor of Nova Scotia (governor, to all intents and purposes) in 1792, an office which he held until 1808. In 1795 he was made a baronet. As in New Hampshire, he performed his duties as governor with success, his policies being concerned with improvement of transportation, education, and the organization of defense measures. He died at Halifax in his eighty-third year. He had been a devoted American until his exile and he never lost his feeling for his native land and province. Of his children only one, a son, survived infancy.

[Nine letter books of Wentworth, covering 1767–1807, are in the archives of the Province of Nova Scotia, at Halifax; transcripts of three of these, 1767–78, are in the state archives of Concord, N. H.; a number of his letters are in the possession of Dartmouth College. In the transcripts of papers of the Commission of Enquiry into the Losses and Services of American Loyalists, N. Y. Pub. Lib., is a statement by Wentworth. Biog. studies include L. S. Mayo, *John Wentworth* (1921); W. C. Abbott, in *Conflicts with Oblivion* (1924); Lorenzo Sabine, in *Biog. Sketches of Loyalists of the Am. Revolution* (1864). See also Jeremy Belknap, *The Hist. of N. H.* (1812); L. B. Richardson, *Hist. of Dartmouth Coll.* (1932); Frederick Chase, *A Hist. of Dartmouth Coll. and the Town of Hanover* (1891), ed. by J. K. Lord; John Wentworth, *The Wentworth Geneal.* (3 vols., 1878); *Mass. Hist. Soc. Colls.,* 6 ser. IV (1891); *Provincial Papers . . . Relating to . . . N. H.,* vol. VII (1873); *The State of N. H.: Miscellaneous Provincial and State Papers,* vol. XVIII (1890); *Two Reports on the Matter of Complaint of Mr. Livius against Gov. Wentworth* (London, 1773), copy in Dartmouth Coll. Lib.; "Case of Councillor Peter Livius *vs.* Governor John Wentworth—testimony for the defense," in *N. H. Hist. Soc. Colls.,* vol. IX (1889); *Boston Daily Advertiser,* Apr. 22, 1820.]

W. E. S–s.

WENTWORTH, JOHN (Mar. 5, 1815–Oct. 16, 1888), editor, congressman, mayor of Chicago, was born at Sandwich, N. H., son of Paul and Lydia (Cogswell) Wentworth, grandson of John Wentworth of the Continental Congress and of Col. Amos Cogswell of the Continental Army. He was descended from William Wentworth who was in Exeter, N. H., in 1639. John attended public schools and various private academies. He taught school one winter, entered Dartmouth College in 1832, and was graduated in 1836. He then went to Michigan and, finding no place as a school teacher in response to his advertisements in the *Detroit Free Press,* he walked to Ann Arbor and Ypsilanti, and still finding no school, walked back to Detroit, sent his trunk to Chicago by the brig *Manhattan,* took a stage to Michigan City, and walked the lake beach to Chicago, arriving with only thirty dollars. He ate his first meal at the boarding-house of Mrs. Harriet Austin Murphy at Lake and Wells streets on Oct. 25, 1836, and thereafter for forty-nine years, unless absent from Chicago, he celebrated his advent into that city by taking dinner with Mrs. Murphy. Within a month he was in editorial charge of the weekly *Chicago Democrat,* denouncing "wildcat" currency, and entering on activities that resulted in a city charter for Chicago, the election of its first mayor, William B. Ogden [*q.v.*], and the designation of Wentworth as its first official printer. Within three years, at a cost of $2,800, he owned the *Chicago Democrat.* In 1840 he started the *Daily Democrat* and made it for years the leading newspaper of the Northwest. During 1841 he spent some six months in Cambridge, Mass., attending law lectures at Harvard, returned to Chicago, and was soon admitted to the bar.

In 1843, when twenty-eight years of age, he was elected to the House of Representatives of the Twenty-eighth Congress, the youngest member of that body. During his congressional service of 1843–51 and 1853–55 he furthered free homestead legislation, helped to initiate and pass bills for Western railway land grants, a national bonded-warehouse system, harbor construction and improvement, and lighthouse erection, and was the unpaid agent of a number of Mexican War veterans claiming bounties, back pay, and pensions. He was an instigator of the notable National River and Harbor Convention of 1847 in Chicago. An original stockholder of the Chicago & Galena Railroad, he headed its committee which arranged consolidation with the Chicago & Northwestern Railroad. On repeal of the Missouri Compromise he left the Democratic party and joined with those of moderate anti-slavery views who founded the Republican party.

He was elected mayor of Chicago in 1857 on a "Republican Fusion" ticket, and announced he would take no salary. He introduced the first steam fire engine and the first paid fire department of the city. He served one year, declined another term, but in 1860 was again elected. During the Civil War he aggressively supported the Lincoln administration, and as police commissioner threw protection around Clement L. Vallandigham [*q.v.*] for an anti-war speech and then replied in a blunt argument hailed as effective; as police commissioner he frustrated a threatened raid aimed at a wholesale release of Confederate prisoners in Camp Douglas. His knowledge of law and politics was in play as a delegate to the 1861 convention to revise the Illinois state constitution, while his long-sustained journalistic advocacy of a well-equipped common-school system made suitable his appointment to the state board of education for the terms of 1861–64 and 1868–72. His final term in Congress in 1865–67 saw him on the ways and

means committee and among the foremost to urge immediate resumption of specie payments.

Year by year he had acquired lots and land in Chicago and Cook County to an extent that brought him the reputation of holding title to more real estate than any other man in Chicago. A stock farm of about five thousand acres at Summit in Cook County was planned by him as a resource and place of heart's ease for his later years, but this vision was never realized: comment ran that during life "he changed his stopping place as often as he did his shirt"; he had the hotel habit, the noise of the city was melodious to him, and the turmoils of politics and affairs more attractive than farming. When asked for his rules of life he said: "I get up in the morning when I'm ready, sometimes at six, sometimes at eight, and sometimes I don't get up at all. . . . Eat when you're hungry, drink when you're thirsty, sleep when you're sleepy, and get up when you're ready." He was active in behalf of state and local historical societies, read reminiscent addresses before them, wrote a three-volume *Wentworth Genealogy* (1878), and grieved over his loss in the Chicago fire of his most cherished manuscripts and papers, including a diary in which nearly every day during many years he had made entries "somewhat in the style of John Quincy Adams." He presented Dartmouth College with $10,000, and served as president of the Dartmouth Alumni Association in 1883. While his discourses at educational institutions were bland and urbane, he was as a stump speaker sarcastic and "blunt as a meat ax" as often as he was argumentative. His quick replies, positive attitudes, and gruff manners had added support from a deep-chested, three-hundred-pound body, a height of six feet six inches, the nickname of "Long John," and a varied anger and drollery. The anecdote was widely told, published, and believed that once when running for mayor he walked out on the courthouse steps and faced a waiting crowd that let out a tumultuous yell of greeting. He gazed in calm scorn at them, not taking his hat off, and then delivered the shortest and most terrifying stump speech ever heard in Illinois: "You damn fools, . . . you can either vote for me for mayor or you can go to hell." He had personal warmth and forthright utterance, once telling a Congressional colleague, Abraham Lincoln, he "needed somebody to run him" as Senator William H. Seward in New York was managed by Thurlow Weed, Lincoln replying that only events could make a President. John Wentworth was married in Troy, N. Y., Nov. 13, 1844, to Roxanna Marie, daughter of Riley Loomis. She was in failing health for many years and died in 1870. Of their five children, only one survived him. His death called forth a remarkable series of commentaries and reminiscences on a figure that had striven with the generations who found Chicago a swamp mudhole and saw it made into an audacious metropolis.

[A. T. Andreas, *Hist. of Chicago* (3 vols., 1884); *Biog. Sketches of the Leading Men of Chicago* (1868); Joseph Kirkland, *The Story of Chicago* (1892); *Encyc. of Biog. of Ill.* (1892); *Biog. Dir. Am. Cong.* (1928); *Daily Inter Ocean* (Chicago), Oct. 17, 1888; "Scrap Book," Chicago Hist. Soc.; files of Chicago newspapers; conversations with persons who knew Wentworth.]   C. S.

WENTWORTH, PAUL (d. December 1793), spy, is assumed, from Gov. John Wentworth's reference to him as "my near relation" (Wentworth, *post*, p. 13) and from his possession of land in New Hampshire, to be a member of the Wentworth family of that colony, but the connection is not traced. A man of apparent education and talents, he lived before the Revolution in many places, the West Indies, New Hampshire, London, Paris, relying for financial support on his abilities as a stock jobber and on the profits of a Surinam plantation. He had one ambition—to obtain from the British government some office that would give him the political prestige he considered commensurate with his dignity and standing as a gentleman. Governor Wentworth, who seems to have thought highly of him, obtained for him, in 1770, an appointment to the council of New Hampshire; but he did not, apparently, care to forsake his financial activities for a minor colonial office. He did, however, serve the colony as its London agent in the early seventies.

With the outbreak of hostilities he, like his kinsman, supported the British side. His travels in America and his wide acquaintance with Americans, both in the colonies and in London, made him valuable to the government, which gave him immediate employment in its spy service, where he hoped the reward of his endeavors would be a baronetcy, a seat in Parliament, and an administrative post. He became one of the important members of the secret service, appointing and directing spies, digesting and interpreting their reports for the ministry, and making frequent trips to the Continent, where,

under assumed names and various disguises, he himself often performed the more dangerous and delicate missions. Through him Edward Bancroft [*q.v.*] was brought into the service, and to him Bancroft's often very valuable reports were made. Wentworth, hating the ungentlemanly nature of his position, was, nevertheless, hard-working, daring, alert, and completely unscrupulous in his methods of obtaining information. His most noteworthy exploit was his attempt to halt the negotiations between France and the United States, which, in December and January 1777–78, he realized were rapidly approaching their culmination. He made frantic efforts to persuade Silas Deane and Benjamin Franklin to consider British terms of reconciliation, going far beyond his instructions in the offers he dangled before them. Franklin finally promised to talk with any regularly appointed peace commissioner, and Wentworth hastened back to London, only to find that George III could not be persuaded of any immediate danger. As a result, Wentworth's activity only served to hasten the French alliance, since Franklin took good care to inform Vergennes that British overtures of peace were being made. By this time Wentworth was aware that his visits to Paris were being closely scrutinized by the police, and thereafter he remained in London. For his services before the French alliance and for the great danger he had run Lord North believed he deserved special recompense; but George III distrusted Wentworth for his stock gambling; and the only return he received, therefore, aside from his salary and expenses was a seat in Parliament in 1780, which lasted six weeks. He stayed on in London after the war, continuing his business activities and making further futile efforts at a political career. In 1790 he retired to his Surinam plantation, where he died.

[B. F. Stevens' *Facsimiles of MSS. in European Archives Relating to America, 1773–1783* in Lib. of Cong.; *Provincial Papers, Docs. and Records . . . New-Hampshire*, vol. VII (1873); "The Revolutionary Diplomatic Correspondence of the U. S.," 50 Cong., 1 Sess., *House Miscellaneous Doc.*, No. 603 (1889), ed. by Francis Wharton, vol. VI, p. 630; S. F. Bemis, "British Secret Service and the French-American Alliance," *Am. Hist. Review*, April 1924; L. D. Einstein, *Divided Loyalties* (1933); John Wentworth, *The Wentworth Geneal.* (1878), vol. III, pp. 7–13.]
M. E. L.